Christ Our Life

7

Jesus the Way, the Truth, and the Life

Teacher's Guide

Authors

Sisters of Notre Dame
Chardon, Ohio

Reviewers

Sister Mary Judith Bucco, S.N.D.

Sister Ann Mary McLaughlin, S.N.D.

Sister Margaret Mary Friel, S.N.D.

Sister Mary Donnalee Resar, S.N.D.

Sister Mary Jean Hoelke, S.N.D.

Sister Katherine Mary Skrabec, S.N.D.

Sister Mary Cordell Kopec, S.N.D.

Sister Eileen Marie Skutt, S.N.D.

Sister Mary Charlotte Manzo, S.N.D.

Sister Mary Jane Vovk, S.N.D.

LOYOLAPRESS.
A JESUIT MINISTRY
Chicago

Imprimatur

In accordance with c. 827, permission to publish is granted on April 16, 2014, by Most Reverend Francis J. Kane, Vicar General of the Archdiocese of Chicago. Permission to publish is an official declaration of ecclesiastical authority that the material is free from doctrinal and moral error. No legal responsibility is assumed by the grant of this permission.

Christ Our Life **found to be in conformity**

The Subcommittee on the Catechism, United States Conference of Catholic Bishops, has found the doctrinal content of this manual, copyright 2016, to be in conformity with the *Catechism of the Catholic Church*.

Acknowledgments

Excerpts from the *New American Bible with Revised New Testament and Psalms* Copyright © 1991, 1986, 1970 Confraternity of Christian Doctrine, Inc., Washington, DC. All rights reserved. No portion of the *New American Bible* may be reprinted without permission in writing from the copyright holder.

Excerpts from the English translation of *The Roman Missal* © 2010, International Commission on English in the Liturgy, Inc. (ICEL); excerpts from the English translation of *Rite of Penance* © 1974, ICEL; excerpts from the English translation of *Pastoral Care of the Sick* © 1982, ICEL; excerpts from the English translation of *Rite of Christian Initiation of Adults* © 1985, ICEL. All rights reserved.

English translation of *Te Deum* by the International Consultation on English Texts.

Excerpts from *Catechism of the Catholic Church*. English translation of the *Catechism of the Catholic Church* for the United States of America copyright © 1994, United States Catholic Conference, Inc.—Libreria Editrice Vaticana.

Excerpts from the *Compendium of the Catechism of the Catholic Church* © 2005, Libreria Editrice Vaticana. Used with permission. All rights reserved.

Excerpts from the *United States Catholic Catechism for Adults* © 2006 United States Conference of Catholic Bishops (USCCB). Used with permission. All rights reserved.

Excerpts from *Go and Make Disciples: A National Plan and Strategy for Catholic Evangelization in the United States* © 2002 United States Conference of Catholic Bishops (USCCB). Used with permission. All rights reserved.

Excerpts from the *National Directory for Catechesis*. Copyright © 2005 United States Conference of Catholic Bishops, Inc., Washington, DC. No portion of this text may be reproduced by any means without written permission from the copyright holder.

Excerpt from *Statement of the U.S. Bishops: Welcome and Justice for Persons with Disabilities*. Copyright © 1998 United States Conference of Catholic Bishops, Inc., Washington, DC. No portion of this text may be reproduced by any means without written permission from the copyright holder.

Excerpts from Vatican conciliar, postconciliar, and papal documents are from the official translations, Libreria Editrice Vaticana, 00120 Citta del Vaticano. Copyright © Libreria Editrice Vaticana.

Excerpt from *Through Death to Life* by Rev. Joseph M. Champlin. © 1990 by Ave Maria Press, P.O. Box 248, Notre Dame, Indiana 46556. Used with permission of the publisher.

Excerpt from "Time Out" reprinted from *Listenings: Meditations for Everyone* by Andrew Costello with permission from the author. Copyright © 1980 by Andrew Costello. Published by Thomas More, 200 East Bethany Drive, Allen, TX 75002.

Quotation from Rev. Demetrius R. Dumm, O.S.B., used by permission of Rev. Dumm, St. Vincent Archabbey, Latrobe, PA 15650.

Excerpts from *To Know and Follow Jesus: Contemporary Christology* © 1984 by Thomas Hart; *Day by Day with Pope John Paul II* © 1982 edited by Angelo Pisani; Paulist Press, Mahwah, NJ.

"Epistle" from *Good Morning, America* © 1928 and renewed 1956 by Carl Sandburg, reprinted by permission of Harcourt, Inc.

Poem "Footprints in the Sand" is the property of the Estate of Mary Stevenson.

For more information related to the English translation of the *Roman Missal, Third Edition*, see www.loyolapress.com/romanmissal.

Cover art: Lori Lohstoeter
Cover design: Loyola Press, Jill Arena
Interior design: Loyola Press, Think Design Group

Photography: v www.colonialarts.com; vii(t) The Crosiers/Gene Plaisted, OSC; vii(b) The Crosiers/Gene Plaisted, OSC; T498 Bill Wittman; T499(b) Bob Daemmrich/PhotoEdit; T500 Phil Martin Photography

Photos and illustrations not acknowledged above are either owned by Loyola Press or from royalty-free sources including, but not limited to: Agnus, Alamy, Comstock, Corbis, Creatas, Fotosearch, Getty Images, Imagestate, iStock, Jupiter Images, Punchstock, Rubberball, and Veer.

Loyola Press has made every effort to locate the copyright holders for the cited works used in this publication and to make full acknowledgment for their use. In the case of any omissions, the Publisher will be pleased to make suitable acknowledgments in future editions.

Acknowledgments continue on page T553.

© 2016 Loyola Press
and Sisters of Notre Dame, Chardon, Ohio

ISBN-13: 978-0-8294-3973-1

ISBN-10: 0-8294-3973-0

LOYOLAPRESS.
A JESUIT MINISTRY

3441 N. Ashland Avenue
Chicago, Illinois 60657
(800) 621-1008
www.loyolapress.com

Printed in China.

14 15 16 17 18 19 20 21 22 23 RRD/China 10 9 8 7 6 5 4 3 2 1

DEDICATION

THE SISTERS OF NOTRE DAME GRATEFULLY
REMEMBER PERSONS FROM THEIR PAST WHOSE
MINISTRY OF CATECHESIS THEY ARE PRIVILEGED
TO CONTINUE IN THE PRESENT.

Sister Maria Aloysia Wolbring (1828–1889) is the foundress of the Sisters of Notre Dame of Coesfeld, Germany. She and the first sisters of this new community were formed in the spiritual and pedagogical tradition of Reverend Bernard Overberg. The sisters presented God, our loving and provident Father, as not only caring for persons more than anyone else ever could, but also as challenging them to a responsible love for themselves, for all other people, and for creation. One of Sister Aloysia's students recalled: "Her religious instructions meant more to us than the sermons preached in church. She spoke from deepest conviction and tried to direct our hearts to God alone. Best of all, she did not require too much piety of us. 'Children,' she would say, 'always follow the golden middle way—not too little, not too much.'"

Reverend Bernard Overberg (1752–1826) began his life's work of shaping teacher formation and catechesis in 1783 in the diocese of Münster, Germany. Reverend Overberg sought to present the Church's faith and teaching in such a way as to lead children and adults toward a deep, mature relationship with God in Jesus Christ. Faith, experienced through the lens of salvation history and related to everyday life, was to touch both the mind and the heart, calling forth reflection, prayer, and active response. His approach to catechesis was the way the Coesfeld Sisters of Notre Dame were led to know God in their childhoods and how they were later formed as catechists.

Saint Julie Billiart (1751–1816), foundress of the Sisters of Notre Dame de Namur, was the source of the Rule by which the Coesfeld Sisters of Notre Dame were formed. With Christian education designated as the main work of the congregation, the sisters had a framework within which to continue the mission they had begun as lay teachers. As they learned more about Julie, the sisters were inspired by the story of how this simple French woman became a remarkable catechist who helped renew the people's faith after the chaos of the French Revolution. As a young girl, Julie's deep faith and love impelled her to share the Good News with others. During a twelve-year period in which she suffered a crippling illness, Julie devoted herself to catechizing women and children. Julie's confidence in the goodness and provident care of God remained unshaken in the face of misunderstandings on the part of some bishops, priests, and even her own sisters. Always open to the Spirit, she courageously carried out her ministry and taught others to proclaim the Good News. The more the Coesfeld Sisters of Notre Dame came to know about Julie, the more they desired to make known God's goodness: "How good God is." Today they regard her as their spiritual mother.

GRADE 7

Contents

Unit 1

Gather and Go Forth   T313
Student pages follow each chapter.

What Catholics Should Know

T421

Saints and Feast Days

T447

The Catechist's Handbook

T491

Glossary

T527

Index

T542

Scripture Index

T550

Christ Our Life

Welcome to *Christ Our Life*: New Evangelization Edition

Since 1973, *Christ Our Life* has taught students that each of our lives is centered on Jesus. This revised edition responds to the Church's call for a New Evangelization, guiding students to **know, proclaim, witness,** and **share** the Catholic faith. New pages added to each chapter help students feel secure in their faith knowledge and in proclaiming Christ to others. Students learn that sharing Gospel values transforms the world and helps them follow

Jesus' command to "make disciples of all nations." *(Matthew 28:19)*

Based on a spiral curriculum, each lesson integrates Scripture, Catholic doctrine and Tradition, and the Church's social teachings. *Christ Our Life: New Evangelization Edition* empowers teachers and parents to grow in their own faith as they pass on to students the love we find in Jesus.

KNOW · PROCLAIM · WITNESS · SHARE

NEW!

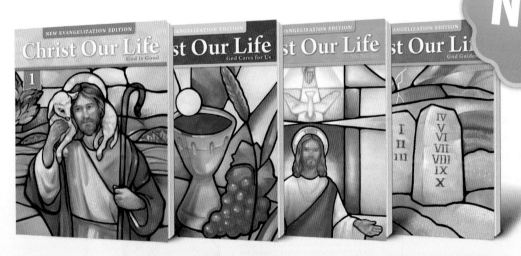

- **Offers Practical Applications** for the goals of the New Evangelization
- **Addresses** and responds to the 2013 NCEA: IFG ACRE Assessment
- **Aligns with** the USCCB document *Go and Make Disciples*, NCEA: IFG ACRE domains, and the Six Tasks of Catechesis

Gather and Go Forth

The *National Directory for Catechesis* encourages all Catholics to respond to the call for a New Evangelization, to help bring about faith and conversion to Christ. This new edition of *Christ Our Life* helps Catholics heed this call. With the new Gather and Go Forth pages at the end of each chapter, teachers, parents, and church communities can help students **know, proclaim, witness,** and **share** the Good News of Jesus Christ while meeting the goals set forth in Church documents, including *Go and Make Disciples: A National Plan and Strategy for Catholic Evangelization in the United States.* For more information about the New Evangelization, go to **www.usccb.org**.

NEW to Christ Our Life!

Explicitly addresses the goals of the New Evangelization

Faith facts recall important ideas from the chapter.

Catholic practices connect to each faith fact, offering ways to live our faith.

An **assessment question** supports the first task of catechesis—Knowledge of the Faith—and helps prepare students to take the NCEA IFG: ACRE test.

Biographies of saints inspire students to imitate lives of holiness.

Witness statements ask students to reflect on their present path of faith.

NEW EVANGELIZATION

Gather and Go Forth

CHAPTER 13

Know and Proclaim

Knowing our Catholic faith helps us love as Jesus did. We proclaim Jesus in what we say and do.

We Know Our Faith	We Proclaim Our Faith
In the Sermon on the Mount, Jesus taught that at the heart of God's Law is the call for us to live with one another in love.	As Catholics, we show our love for our neighbors by advocating for laws and policies that respect and promote human dignity.
The Fifth Commandment is "You shall not kill." Jesus wants us to live and care for both the physical and spiritual life.	As Catholics, we help our neighbors meet their emotional and spiritual needs by participating in the Spiritual Works of Mercy.
To love as Jesus loved means cherishing the gift of life. Every person is a child of God made in God's image.	As Catholics, we demonstrate our love for life by calling for legislation and policies that respect all human life beginning at conception and ending with natural death.

Test Your Catholic Knowledge

Fill in the circle that best completes the sentence.

Jesus revealed that we will be judged by:

○ where we live.

● how well we have loved others.

○ our obedience to the letter of the law.

God breathed into us the breath of life, which fills us with his love. In loving as Jesus loved, we encounter God. Christian love nurtures life at all times.

God created mankind in his image;
in the image of God he created them;
male and female he created them.

Genesis 1:27

Scripture invites students to know and love God's Word.

A Catholic to Know

Saint Julie Billiart (1751–1816) began teaching children about God in her hometown of Picardy, France, at age seven. When she was 14, she vowed herself to chastity and performing works of mercy. Even though a mysterious illness left her paralyzed for over 20 years, Julie still lived a full life dedicated to others. Julie founded the Sisters of Notre Dame to care for orphans, educate girls from families who lived in poverty, and train Christian teachers. Julie had learned during her years of pain and sickness that "God is good." Saint Julie is called the "Smiling Saint" whose motto was "How good the good God is."

Saint Julie Billiart

Witness and Share

These sentences describe what Catholics believe. Listen carefully as they are read. Ask yourself, "How strong are my Catholic beliefs?"

My Way to Faith

- I live according to Jesus' Great Commandment to love God and to love my neighbor as myself.
- I view all human life, beginning with the unborn, as a gift from God to be cherished and protected.
- I avoid saying bad things about other people.
- I make sure that my anger does not hurt others.
- I take a stand against any form of discrimination.

Share Your Faith

How do you demonstrate the value and dignity of human life? Write your ideas on the lines. Invite family members and friends to talk with you about how the choices they make respect life.

_____

_____

_____

_____

_____

112 UNIT 2 *Jesus Christ the Truth*

Students make a **discipleship promise** and then **invite others to faith**.

Gather and Go Forth

The **Gather and Go Forth** pages provide teachers with the background, instructional guidelines, and activities to encourage students to embrace the vision of evangelization as the central mission and identity of the Church. With teacher guidance, students learn the importance of their Catholic faith. The beauty and truth of the Good News urges them, with the help of the Holy Spirit, to share their faith and gain disciples for Christ.

PRACTICAL APPLICATIONS for the Goals of the New Evangelization

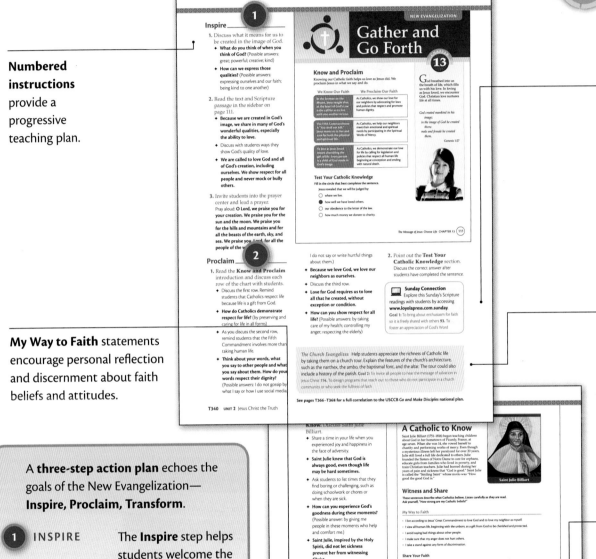

Numbered instructions provide a progressive teaching plan.

My Way to Faith statements encourage personal reflection and discernment about faith beliefs and attitudes.

Online resource boxes suggest ways to utilize technology to enrich faith and align with the goals and objectives of the New Evangelization.

Feature boxes suggest what Catholics might do to accomplish the goals and objectives of the New Evangelization.

Alignment to the USCCB *Go and Make Disciples* document is indicated in each online resource and feature box with a corresponding goal and objective.

A **three-step action plan** echoes the goals of the New Evangelization— **Inspire, Proclaim, Transform.**

1 INSPIRE The **Inspire** step helps students welcome the Holy Spirit and receive God's Word joyfully.

2 PROCLAIM The **Proclaim** step leads students to a deeper understanding of each part of the student pages.

3 TRANSFORM The **Transform** step discusses ways for students to foster Gospel values in our society.

Spiral Curriculum

To ensure consistent progress and development, the *Christ Our Life* series employs the spiral curriculum, originally introduced by Loyola Press in 1973. The program for each grade level builds upon previous ones, following a pattern of continuous growth in depth and scope.

At the heart of the *Christ Our Life* program is a harmonious integration of Scripture, Tradition, and action. In the spiral curriculum, Scripture is centered between the four fundamental themes of the *Catechism of the Catholic Church:* Creed, Sacraments, Morality, and Prayer. In addition, Catholic social teachings are woven into each chapter to encourage active participation in the faith.

To the
Father
through the
Son
in the
Spirit

Christ Our Life

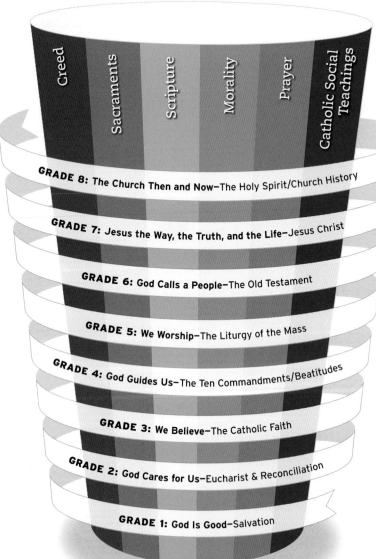

Creed · Sacraments · Scripture · Morality · Prayer · Catholic Social Teachings

GRADE 8: The Church Then and Now—The Holy Spirit/Church History

GRADE 7: Jesus the Way, the Truth, and the Life—Jesus Christ

GRADE 6: God Calls a People—The Old Testament

GRADE 5: We Worship—The Liturgy of the Mass

GRADE 4: God Guides Us—The Ten Commandments/Beatitudes

GRADE 3: We Believe—The Catholic Faith

GRADE 2: God Cares for Us—Eucharist & Reconciliation

GRADE 1: God Is Good—Salvation

Also available:

God Made Me (Pre-K 3)   **God Loves Us** (Kindergarten)

God Made the World (Pre-K 4)   **Confirmed in the Spirit** (Confirmation—also available in a bilingual version)

Program Components

Student Book

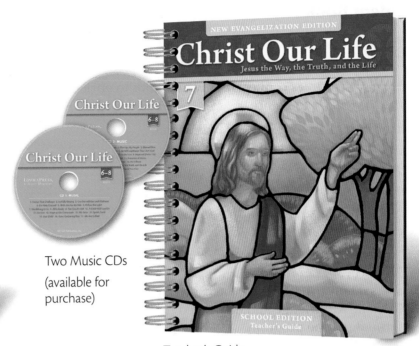

Two Music CDs
(available for
purchase)

Teacher's Guide
(School and Parish editions available)

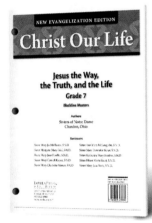

Blackline Masters,
including assessments

Poster

*Catholic Prayer for
Catholic Families*
(available in English and
Bilingual versions)

Online Program Support
www.christourlife.com

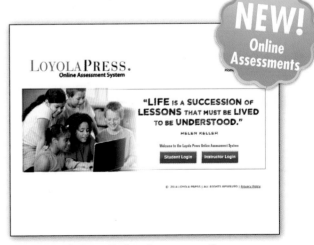

Loyola Press Online Assessment System
(available for purchase)

Student Book

- **Faith content** is developed throughout with Scripture integrated into each lesson.

- **Family resources** connect family and faith to enrich the student's experience.

- **Traditional and familiar prayers** invite personal and communal prayer.

- **A Moment with Jesus** provides specific opportunities for prayer.

- **NEW! Gather and Go Forth** pages at the end of every chapter show students how they can respond to the Church's essential mission to evangelize all people.

- **NEW! Preparation for religious education assessment (ACRE test)** is provided in Test Your Catholic Knowledge and developed in faith content throughout the program.

- **Punchouts and pullouts** bring the content to life in hands-on activities.

- **Parish religious education and Catholic school** needs are met using the same Student Book.

- **Christourlife.com** offers online support, including chapter reviews to test faith knowledge.

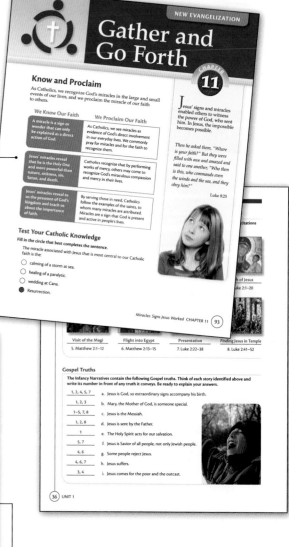

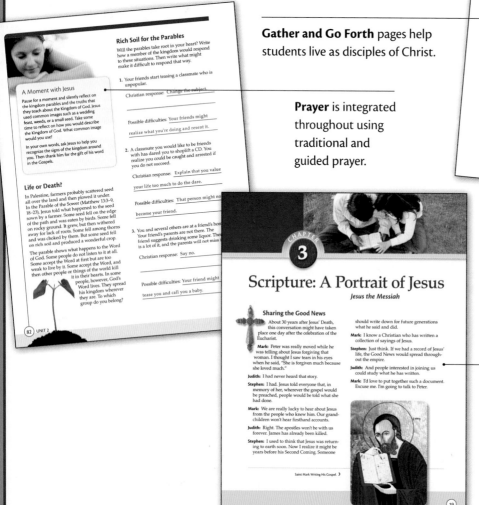

Gather and Go Forth pages help students live as disciples of Christ.

Prayer is integrated throughout using traditional and guided prayer.

Scripture and doctrine help students learn the traditions of the faith and know the Bible as God's Word.

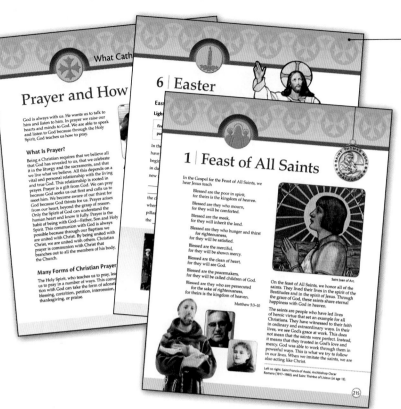

Special Seasons and Lessons and
What Catholics Should Know support
Catholic Tradition and doctrine.

Scripture Booklet

This booklet belongs to

Pullouts in the
back of the book
provide hands-on,
grade-specific
activities.

Family Components

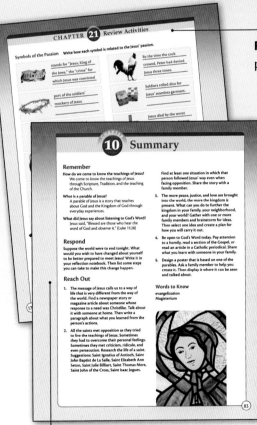

Review of the lesson involves
parents in each chapter.

Family resources
are available online
in English and Spanish.

Family Feature

Deepening Family Faith

Family Feature at the beginning of each
unit offers additional support for parents.

Reach Out activities offer
ideas and activities to reinforce
learning and involve the family.

Catholic Prayer for Catholic Families is
provided for every *Christ Our Life* family.
This guide to prayer contains traditional
prayers plus suggestions for everyday prayer.
(available in English and Bilingual versions)

School Teacher's Guide

- **NEW! A correlation of Grade 7 to the NCEA IFG: ACRE test** assures that students are being prepared in faith knowledge.

- **NEW! Gather and Go Forth** pages help students recognize and respond to the Church's missionary call to make disciples.

- **NEW! A correlation to the USCCB document** *Go and Make Disciples* shows how the new pages respond to the call for Catholic evangelization.

- **Faith Focus** states the aim of each chapter.

- **Preparing for the Faith Experience** offers background resources and support.

- **A four- or five-day teaching plan** breaks lessons into manageable parts.

- **Lesson scripting** offers a flexible teaching option for new or experienced teachers.

- **Special Seasons and Lessons** celebrate the liturgical year and our Catholic way of life.

- **Saints and Feast Days** section tells about honored saints and special days in the Church, calling us to a life of holiness.

- **The Catechist's Handbook** helps teachers pass on the truths of our Catholic faith.

- **Web support and resources** are featured at christourlife.com—register with access code **COL-2016**.

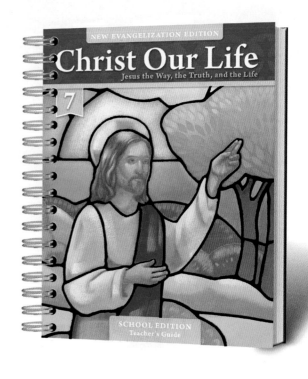

The Catechist's Handbook

The *Christ Our Life* Catechist's Handbook is included in every Teacher's Guide. It provides essential information to help catechists build their programs on a strong foundation.

- **The catechist's important role** in faith formation is featured as central.

- **Background on students' developmental stages** and areas of growth in faith and spirituality supports catechist's effectiveness.

- **Teaching techniques, tools, and methods section** offers ideas for variety and creativity.

- **Music list** provides age-appropriate resource recommendations for each chapter.

- **Catechist tips** provide novice teachers with important information on the basics of teaching.

- **Inclusion strategies** invite full and active participation in religious education.

Posters

Blackline Masters
(includes assessments)

www.christourlife.com

Christourlife.com is a free Web site that offers a wealth of resources. To access protected teacher materials, you will need to register online with **access code COL-2016.**

- **Online Lesson Planning** provides convenience to new and experienced teachers.

- **NEW! Six Tasks of Catechesis** alignment is provided for all grades.

- **Interactive Chapter Reviews** allow students to prepare for upcoming assessments.

- **Activity Finder** offers over 400 activities.

- **Sunday Connection** provides background information and classroom activities to explore the Sunday readings.

- **Blackline Masters** for the entire program are available.

- **Seasonal Resources** feature great ways to connect faith to the liturgical year.

- **Family Resources in English and Spanish** are available online.

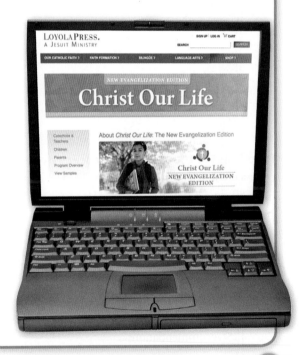

NEW! Online Assessments

Two Music CDs are available for purchase at the following ranges:

Grades 1–3,
Grades 4–5,
Grades 6–8.

Web-based Online Assessment System

- Full-featured test generator

- Printable option

- Complete reporting system

- Secure online testing

Getting Ready for a Lesson

Two teacher-preparation pages introduce the background information and preparation steps for each chapter. The preparation begins with the **Faith Focus,** which provides the theme of the lesson.

Reflecting on the Faith Experience encompasses a consistent three-step preparation process— **Listening, Reflecting, Responding.**

Listening: A Scripture passage related to the Faith Focus invites the catechist to listen to God's Word.

Reflecting: A reflection on the theme provides background information and links the Faith Focus to the catechist's own faith life.

Responding: A prayer starter relates the chapter theme to the catechist's role and invites a personal response to the Faith Focus of the lesson.

Preparing for the Faith Experience provides an overview of the themes for each day of the week, as well as additional information to make lesson preparation easier.

Gather and Go Forth catechist instruction provides support and easy navigation.

Multiple references to Scripture, the *Catechism,* and other resources provide background reading recommendations.

Catholic Social Teaching themes are integrated throughout the program.

Bulletin-board ideas and images are suggested for each chapter.

Three-Step Teaching Method

A three-step teaching method—**Centering, Sharing, Acting**—provides the students with routine and repetition to aid in understanding the content and learning to pray.

Step-by-step directions clearly show the progression of each step in the chapter. These numbered steps guide new and experienced catechists through the chapter.

Learning Outcomes identify clear focus for the chapter.

Words to Know highlights important vocabulary for students.

Icons in each chapter make it easy to locate prayer opportunities and Catholic Social Teaching.

Before You Begin gives helpful teaching tips and additional background information.

Key Terms help the teacher understand important concepts or words in the chapter.

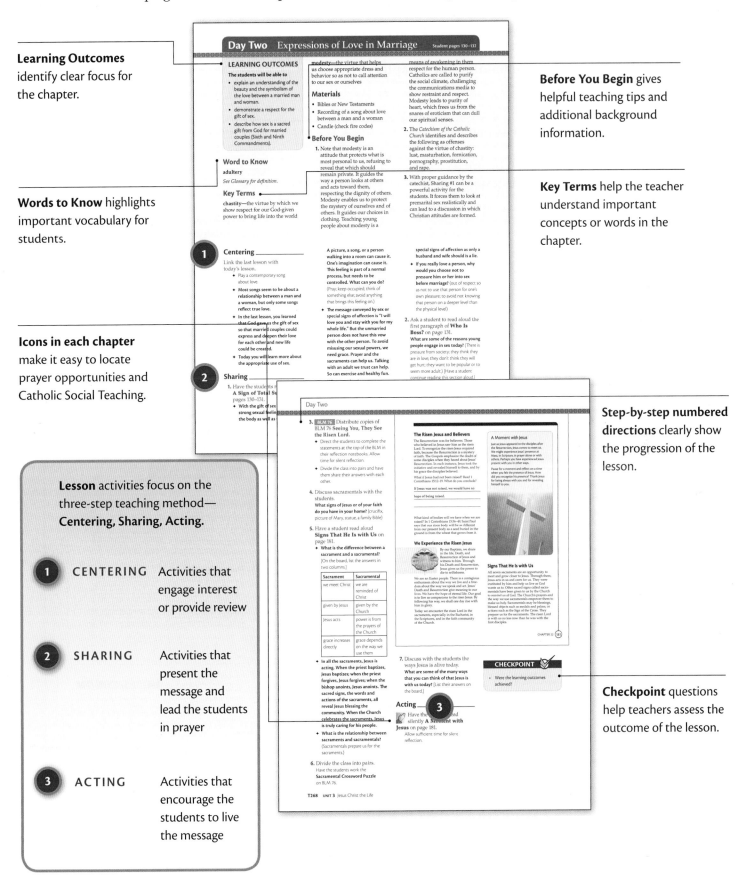

Lesson activities focus on the three-step teaching method—**Centering, Sharing, Acting.**

1 CENTERING Activities that engage interest or provide review

2 SHARING Activities that present the message and lead the students in prayer

3 ACTING Activities that encourage the students to live the message

Step-by-step numbered directions clearly show the progression of the lesson.

Checkpoint questions help teachers assess the outcome of the lesson.

The Program Structure

The *Christ Our Life* series uses a holistic approach to faith formation. A variety of methods and techniques ensure that the Good News is conveyed in ways suited to various learning and teaching styles.

Each chapter is spread over four or five days. Lessons for Days One through Four are designed to be 30–40 minutes long. On Day Five, present the **Gather and Go Forth** pages or choose activities from the **Extending the Chapter** or **Enriching the Faith Experience.**

Because students need structure and delight in predictability, the weekly lessons have a similar pattern:

- experiences leading to a faith message

- faith message, usually from the Bible

- creative activities to internalize the faith message and relate it to everyday life

- age-appropriate variety of prayer experiences

- application of the faith message to everyday life

- lesson closure with the Gather and Go Forth pages

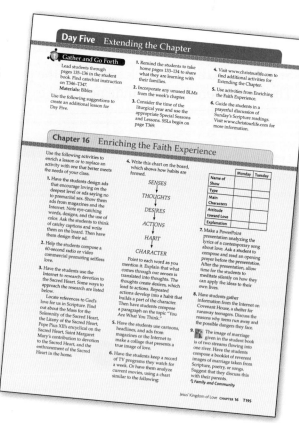

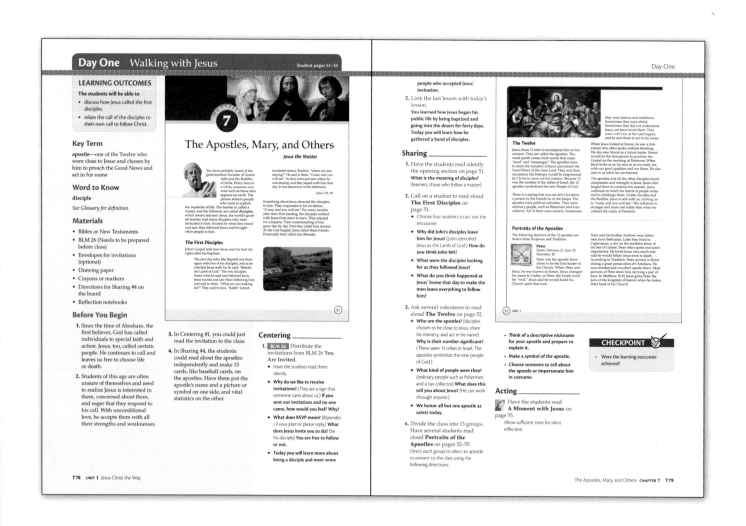

Preparing for the Year

1. Use the **Planning Calendar** on pages OV-16–OV-17 to develop plans based on your school calendar and the year's activities, liturgical seasons, and feasts.

2. In the column on the right, space is provided to note activities that will influence class time and content, such as dates of the movable seasons and days of the Church's liturgical year, holidays, and celebrations in honor of Mary, such as a May crowning.

3. Use the **Table of Contents** and your goals for the year to determine which chapters and special lessons you will teach. Note these on the Planning Calendar.

4. To meet the needs of the students and to adapt to your local circumstances or schedule, you might combine or extend some chapters.

5. Write the **Scripture verses** used in each lesson on note cards and keep them in order in an envelope. When these Scripture verses are read during class, place the appropriate card in the Bible. Reading in this way will reinforce the students' reverence for and understanding of the Bible as God's Word.

6. If you wish, remove the **pullouts** from the back of the Student Books and plan to distribute them when needed.

7. Write the students' names in their books.

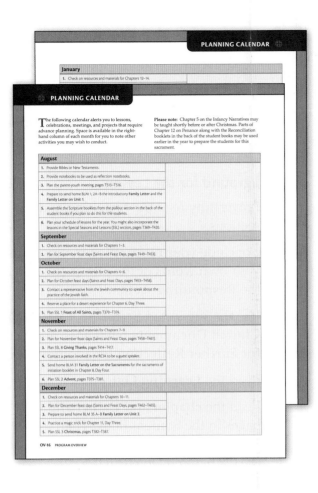

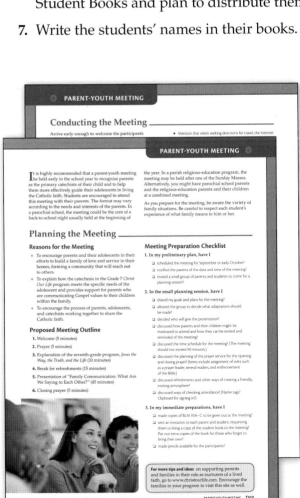

Parent-Youth Meeting

There is no adequate substitute for parental involvement in a child's faith formation. Parents have the privilege and the responsibility to nurture the life of faith that their child received at Baptism. They are the child's first and primary teachers in the ways of the faith.

"Adult catechesis, designed especially for parents, also helps them nourish their own faith, as well as that of their children. Such programs help parents to understand important issues in their own lives and the lives of their children, such as preparation for reception of the sacraments or the question raised by particular moral concerns in the light of the Catholic faith." (*National Directory for Catechesis* #54, 10, C)

The *Christ Our Life* series encourages parents to share with their child their own response to God's Word. A parent-youth meeting held early in the school year helps parents more effectively guide their child in living the Catholic faith as he or she learns about it this year.

See the guidelines for a parent-youth meeting and a sample meeting on pages T513–T516. Keep in mind that the students may come from a variety of family structures or situations. Be careful to respect each student's experience of what family means to him or her.

Preparing for the Week

Each chapter in this guide presents a wealth of ideas, prayer opportunities, teachable moments, and activities. The ideas on these pages can help you understand how each section functions and offer suggestions for how to use the program.

Background for the Lesson

1. Prayerfully read the **Listening** and **Reflecting** sections.

2. Conclude your preparation in prayer, using your own words or the prayer suggested in the **Responding** section.

3. Use the suggested **Scripture**, *Catechism*, **Church Documents** references, and **Scripture for Further Reflection** for additional insights.

4. Read the **Learning Outcomes**.

5. Read the **chapter** and **Gather and Go Forth** pages in the Student Book. Then read the accompanying Teacher's Guide pages behind the Gather and Go Forth tab.

CHAPTER 5

The Early Life of Jesus
JESUS THE SON OF MARY AND JOSEPH

Faith Focus
The Infancy Narratives reveal that Jesus is the Lord, the Son of God who saved us.

Reflecting on the Faith Experience
Take a few moments to reflect prayerfully before preparing the lesson.

Listening

For God so loved the world that he gave his only Son . . .
John 3:16

Reflecting

Certain truths are conveyed most effectively through the symbols of art. The familiar pieces of a nativity set—the figures of Mary, Joseph, the infant, the shepherds and magi, the animals, the star, and the crib—speak eloquently of our faith. They proclaim that God became human for love of us. And because of their religious message, manger scenes are sometimes banned from public places.

The symbols of literature are equally compelling. The evangelists knew this. They presented the birth and infancy of Jesus not as bare historical facts but as moving stories that touch our hearts. Skillfully they shaped their narratives to their themes and their audience. Through them, they shared the significance of Jesus Christ.

In proclaiming Jesus as Lord to the Jewish Christians, the author of Matthew's Gospel makes use of their heritage. He opens by tracing Jesus' lineage from Abraham, the first Jewish person. He weaves references to the Old Testament throughout his narratives. Portraying the Savior as the new Moses, he describes how Jesus, like Moses, came out of Egypt after being persecuted by a king. Jesus relives the Exodus of Israel. From Matthew's version of Jesus' early life, a Jewish Christian would identify Jesus as the Promised One.

The author of Luke apparently writes mainly for Gentile Christians. He traces Jesus' lineage back to Adam. (Luke 3:23–38) But Luke shows how God's promises to Israel are fulfilled in Jesus. The accounts of the birth announcements of Jesus and John and the three canticles he includes (Mary's, Zechariah's, and Simeon's) are based on the Old Testament. In addition, Luke teaches that salvation is extended to all people. He stresses Jesus' ministry to the poor, sinners, and outcasts, like the shepherds to whom an angel declares the birth of a Savior.

Nativity sets and the Infancy Narratives have meaning only for people who believe that Mary's Son accomplished our salvation by dying and rising. It is the Easter people who are addressed in the words of the Christmas carol, "O come, all ye faithful, joyful and triumphant." Those of us who have faith in the Resurrection believe that the baby of Bethlehem, Mary's baby, is divine. We adore him and pray that the Holy Spirit who formed him in Mary's womb will form us into his image.

What does Christmas mean to me?

Responding

Holy Spirit, help my students see the realities mirrored in religious symbols so they may be inspired to bring Jesus forth to the world.

Scripture for Further Reflection

Isaiah 35 God comes to save us and to bring us everlasting joy.

Luke 1:26–38 Mary conceives the Son of the Most High.

Hebrews 1:1–4 God speaks to us through his Son who sustains all things by his mighty Word.

Preparing for the Faith Experience

Day One
The Infancy Narratives

Day Two
Tuned In to God's Messages

Day Three
Delving into the Symbols

Day Four
Infancy Narratives in Art

Day Five
Extending the Chapter

Gather and Go Forth

Scripture in This Chapter

Matthew 1:18—2:23 The birth of Jesus.

Luke 1:5—2:25 Mary says yes to the angel Gabriel. Jesus is born in Bethlehem.

Luke 2:40 Jesus grew with wisdom.

Catholic Social Teaching

The Poor and Vulnerable

Church Documents

Catechism of the Catholic Church. The themes of this chapter correspond to the following paragraphs: 488, 490–499, 525–534.

General Directory for Catechesis #109. The Word of God became man in space and time and rooted in a specific culture. This inculturation of the Word of God is the model of all evangelization by the Church, because the Gospel should touch people at the very center and roots of their culture.

Pastoral Constitution on the Church in the Modern World #22 (Second Vatican Council). Christ, the perfect man, throws light on the riddle of suffering and death. God gives us abundant life.

On the Blessed Virgin Mary in the Life of the Pilgrim Church #8 (Saint John Paul II). The Father chose Mary as Mother of his Son in the Incarnation. Together with the Father, the Son chose her and entrusted her to the Spirit of holiness. Mary is united to Christ and is eternally loved in him.

The Redeemer of Man #8 (Saint John Paul II). Christ the Redeemer penetrated the mystery of human beings and united himself with each person, reforging the link between God and humankind.

Gather and Go Forth

Find catechist instruction for Gather and Go Forth student pages 41–42 on T324–T325.

Enriching the Faith Experience

Use the activities at the end of the chapter to enrich a lesson or to replace an activity with one that better meets the needs of your class.

Bulletin Board

A suggestion for a bulletin-board design for this chapter is pictured. Have the students add symbols from the Infancy Narratives. Suggest that some symbols may be three-dimensional.

Christ Is Born

T52 UNIT 1 Jesus Christ the Way

The Early Life of Jesus CHAPTER 5 T53

Immediate Preparation

1. Read the lesson preparation section including **Before You Begin,** which provides important background information about the content as well as helpful teaching tips. Gather necessary **Materials** for the lesson.

2. Read the **Enriching the Faith Experience** suggestions at the end of the chapter. Activities from this section can substitute for activities found in the lesson or can be used to extend the lesson. Decide which options best meet the needs of the students.

3. Annotate your manual. Make notes that will help the flow of the lesson. Use a highlighter to set off sections you plan to use.

4. Familiarize yourself with the **scripted teacher-talk** in boldface type so that you can present the lesson in your own words as you teach.

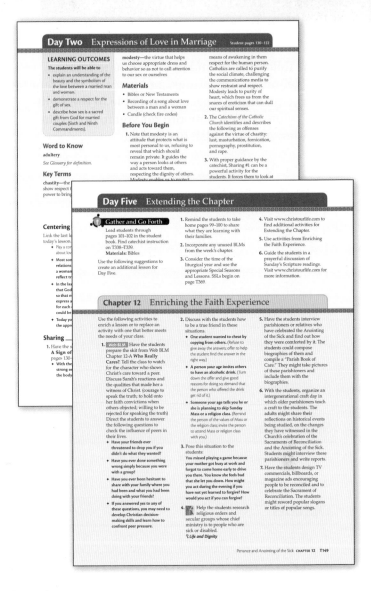

After the Lesson

1. Evaluate your lesson, using the **Checkpoint** at the end of the lesson plan to assess whether the outcomes of the lesson have been met.

2. Write follow-up comments on the lesson plan in your manual. Record ideas for improvement. Consult helpers, parents, and the students who participated in the class to help determine the activities that worked well and those that might be improved.

Online Lesson Planning

In addition to these ideas, you can write and customize your lesson plans at www.christourlife.com. Register online with **access code COL-2016.** Features of christourlife.com include the following:

- **Additional activities,** which are available to integrate into your lesson
- **Customized plans,** which can be saved for future use
- An **e-mail option** that allows you to share your plan with others
- **Personal notes,** which can be added to your lesson plan
- A **complete materials list,** which can assist in class preparation

The following calendar alerts you to lessons, celebrations, meetings, and projects that require advance planning. Space is available in the right-hand column of each month for you to note other activities you may wish to conduct.

Please note: Chapter 5 on the Infancy Narratives may be taught shortly before or after Christmas. Parts of Chapter 12 on Penance along with the Reconciliation booklets in the back of the student books may be used earlier in the year to prepare the students for this sacrament.

August

1. Provide Bibles or New Testaments.

2. Provide notebooks to be used as reflection notebooks.

3. Plan the parent-youth meeting, pages T513–T516.

4. Prepare to send home BLM 1, 2A–B the introductory **Family Letter** and the **Family Letter on Unit 1**.

5. Assemble the Scripture booklets from the pullout section in the back of the student books if you plan to do this for the students.

6. Plan your schedule of lessons for the year. You might also incorporate the lessons in the Special Seasons and Lessons (SSL) section, pages T369–T420.

September

1. Check on resources and materials for Chapters 1–3.

2. Plan for September feast days (Saints and Feast Days, pages T449–T453).

October

1. Check on resources and materials for Chapters 4–6.

2. Plan for October feast days (Saints and Feast Days, pages T453–T458).

3. Contact a representative from the Jewish community to speak about the practice of the Jewish faith.

4. Reserve a place for a desert experience for Chapter 6, Day Three.

5. Plan SSL 1 **Feast of All Saints**, pages T370–T374.

November

1. Check on resources and materials for Chapters 7–9.

2. Plan for November feast days (Saints and Feast Days, pages T458–T461).

3. Plan SSL 8 **Giving Thanks**, pages T414–T417.

4. Contact a person involved in the RCIA to be a guest speaker.

5. Send home BLM 31 **Family Letter on the Sacraments** for the sacraments of initiation booklet in Chapter 8, Day Four.

6. Plan SSL 2 **Advent**, pages T375–T381.

December

1. Check on resources and materials for Chapters 10–11.

2. Plan for December feast days (Saints and Feast Days, pages T462–T465).

3. Prepare to send home BLM 35 A–B **Family Letter on Unit 2**.

4. Practice a magic trick for Chapter 11, Day Three.

5. Plan SSL 3 **Christmas**, pages T382–T387.

January

1. Check on resources and materials for Chapters 12–14.
2. Plan for January feast days (Saints and Feast Days, pages T465–T470).
3. Prepare the Reconciliation booklets in the back of the student books if you plan to do this for the students.
4. Invite a priest to speak to the students about the Sacrament of Penance and Reconciliation.
5. Plan for the Sacrament of Penance and Reconciliation or a non-sacramental celebration of forgiveness.
6. Prepare for the Celebration of Life in Chapter 13.

February

1. Check on resources and materials for Chapters 15–17.
2. Plan for February feast days (Saints and Feast Days, pages T470–T473).
3. Plan SSL 4 **Lent,** pages T388–T397.

March

1. Check on resources and materials for Chapters 18–20.
2. Plan for March feast days (Saints and Feast Days, pages T473–T476).
3. Send home BLM 64 A–B **Family Letter on Unit 3**.
4. Plan for the learning stations in Chapter 18, Day Three.
5. Plan for a class Eucharistic liturgy or a Eucharistic devotion such as Benediction.
6. Plan SSLs 5–6 **Holy Week** and **Easter,** pages T398–T408.

April

1. Check on resources and materials for Chapters 21–22, and SSL 9 **Making Sunday Special,** pages T418–T420.
2. Plan for April feast days (Saints and Feast Days, pages T476–T478).
3. Investigate ways the students can become involved in a project for justice during the study of Chapter 22.
4. Plan SSL 7 **Pentecost,** pages T409–T413.

May

1. Check on resources and materials for Chapters 23–25.
2. Plan for May feast days (Saints and Feast Days, pages T478–T480).
3. Set a date and make plans for the vocation day, Chapter 24, Day Four.
4. Contact people to give talks on vocations.
5. Set a date and time for the celebration of the Eucharist to mark the end of the school year. You might wish to invite parents.
6. Plan with the students a summer spiritual program consisting of prayer, celebration of the sacraments, service to others, and continued use of their reflection notebooks. Also see pages T480–T486 for suggestions on saints and feast days to celebrate in June, July, and August.

SCOPE AND SEQUENCE

The sixth-grade program of the *Christ Our Life* series is devoted to the study of God's saving love as it is revealed in Sacred Scripture, particularly the Old Testament. *God Calls a People* is designed to help the students increase their knowledge of salvation history so that they may respond to God with ever-deepening love and gratitude.

Unit	Chapter	Theme	Scripture	CCC References
1 God Reveals a Plan of Love The students will grow in love for God through a deeper understanding of God's plan of salvation. They will come to appreciate the Old Testament.	1. The Bible Reveals God's Saving Love	We come to know God and Jesus through Scripture.	Isaiah 43:1; Luke 24:13–35; Ephesians 5:8; Mark 16:15	102, 151
	2. Scripture Is God's Saving Word	God, the author of the Bible, speaks to us through it.	Psalm 119:105, 107; Psalm 136:1–7; Luke 11:28	104, 122, 129
	3. Everything God Created Is Good	God created the world and all creatures and made us the stewards of the world.	Genesis 1:1—2:25; Psalm 139:14	280, 283, 288–289, 294, 2415–2418
	4. God Offers Love and Mercy	From the time of the first human beings, sin entered the world and spread, destroying relationships.	Genesis 2:4—3:24; Genesis 4:1–16; Genesis 6—9; Genesis 11:1–9; 1 Peter 1:3	376, 388–390, 404, 410–412
	5. Unit 1 Review	God enters into history and carries out the divine plan to save all people.	Deuteronomy 31:8	53, 287, 421, 759
2 God Forms a Family of Faith The students will understand how God's plan of salvation unfolded in the lives of the patriarchs.	6. Abraham Is Our Father in Faith	Abraham made a covenant of faith with the one true God.	Genesis 12, 15, 17, 22; Psalm 89:1–4, 15–16, 19, 28; James 2:14–24	59–60, 144–146, 166, 762, 1080, 2100
	7. Jacob Is Chosen by God	The covenant promises were passed on through Jacob.	Genesis 25:19–34, 27—32; 1 Peter 2:9; Deuteronomy 14:2	3, 824–825, 2156, 2573
	8. The Israelites Journey to Egypt	God saved the ancient world from famine through Joseph, an upright, forgiving man.	Genesis 37—50; Luke 12:22–32; Psalm 54:6	128, 302–303, 305
	9. Unit 2 Review	God formed the people, gradually revealing himself to them.	Isaiah 26:4	218, 269
3 God Guides the Chosen People The students will view the Exodus as God's greatest act of saving love in the Old Testament. They will come to appreciate the commandments as a gift to deepen their covenant relationship with God.	10. God Rescues the Chosen People from Slavery	God led the Hebrews out of slavery in Egypt.	Exodus 1–15	62, 204–208, 1164, 1328–1330
	11. God Gives Us the Law	God protected the Israelites in the desert, made a covenant with them, and gave them laws.	Exodus 10–17; Exodus 19–26; Exodus 27–34; Deuteronomy 5:1	708, 2056–2063, 2083–2084
	12. We Live the Commandments Today	The Ten Commandments tell us to love God and one another.	Exodus 20:1–17; Mark 12:30–31; Matthew 7:12; John 13:34–35; Psalm 119:47–48	2052–2055, 2069, 2072
	13. Learning God's Way	Like the Israelites, we are called to grow in our ability to make decisions based on faith.	Numbers 13–14; Numbers 20:2–13; Matthew 5:3–12; Romans 12:2	1778–1794, 2070, 2634–2636
	14. God Forgives Us	God forgives us as he did the Israelites in the desert.	Numbers 21:4–9; John 3:14–15; Nehemiah 9:17	1093–1094, 1423–1424, 1440, 1468–1469
	15. God's Chosen People Enter the Promised Land	Joshua led the Israelites into the Promised Land.	Deuteronomy 31–34; Book of Joshua; Matthew 25:32–46	1898–1899, 1930, 2234–2236
	16. Unit 3 Review	The Jewish people remember what God has done for them, and they honor God's Word.	Luke 6:27–28	132, 201
4 God Leads the Chosen People The students will appreciate the roles and contributions of the judges and the first three Israelite kings.	17. The Period of Judges	When the Israelites turned from God and were attacked by enemies, God saved them through the judges.	Judges 4, 5; Judges 6–8; Judges 13–16; The Book of Ruth; Luke 12:28	210, 1432, 2496
	18. The Kings of Israel	Samuel anointed Saul, and later David, as kings of Israel.	1 Samuel 1—4:7; 1 Samuel 8; 1 Samuel 10–16; 2 Samuel 5; Acts of the Apostles 10:38	695, 1293–1296, 2013, 2528
	19. David and Solomon	David, the greatest king, sinned and repented. Solomon, despite his gift of wisdom, turned to idols and caused the division of the kingdom.	1 Samuel 16:1–12; 2 Samuel 5–8, 11–12; 1 Kings 1–3; Psalm 51; Mark 1:14–15	583, 709, 1093, 2579–2580, 2586–2589
	20. Unit 4 Review	Through good leaders and bad, God is faithful to the people.	Isaiah 41:10	128, 205
5 Prophets Prepare the Lord's Way The students will appreciate the messages of God delivered through the prophets. They will desire to work for justice.	21. Elijah and Amos Speak for the Lord	Prophets such as Elijah and Amos spoke for God, calling people to worship God alone and to practice justice.	1 Kings 18, 21; 2 Kings 2; Book of Amos; 1 Thessalonians 5:15	61, 64, 218, 2420–2423, 2581–2584
	22. Isaiah Proclaims the Promised Messiah	Isaiah called the people to be faithful and spoke of a suffering servant to come.	Book of Isaiah; Matthew 7:21–23	208, 711–714
	23. Prophets Proclaim God's Everlasting Love	Jeremiah suffered for calling people to justice, while Ezekiel prophesied during the Exile in Babylon.	2 Kings 22–25; Jeremiah 1, 7; Jeremiah 18, 29—33, 38; Jeremiah 31:31–34; Ezekiel 1, 18; Ezekiel 34, 36–37; Acts of the Apostles 10:43	64, 218–221, 709–710, 1431
	24. The Savior Is Jesus, the Son of God	John the Baptist prepared for the Messiah, Jesus Christ, who fulfilled the Scriptures.	Matthew 3:1–7, 11 1:2–15, 14:3–12; Matthew 14:1–12; Luke 1:5–25, 57–80; Luke 1:26–38, 39–56; Luke 2:1–7, 21	488, 523, 717–720
	25. Unit 5 Review	The prophets renewed the people in their faithfulness to God.	1 Peter 4:10	64, 218, 522

The children should

- come to a deeper appreciation of the person of Christ and of his presence in his Church through the study of salvation history.
- grow in their relationship with God and in giving witness of their faith.

Prayer in this grade
- Psalms
- *Memorare* to the Blessed Virgin

Catholic Social Teaching Themes	Words Learned	Saints and Holy People*
The Poor and Vulnerable	Old Testament	Saint Jerome
God's Creation, Solidarity, Rights and Responsibilities	interpretation, Law, Pentateuch, revelation, Torah, tradition	Saint Luke
God's Creation, Life and Dignity, Rights and Responsibilities, Work and Workers, The Poor and Vulnerable, Solidarity, Family and Community	free will	Saint Anthony of Padua
Family and Community, The Poor and Vulnerable, Rights and Responsibilities	conscience, sin	Adam and Eve, Noah, Saint Maria Goretti
		Saint Thomas Aquinas
Family and Community, Rights and Responsibilities, Life and Dignity	Abraham, covenant, sacrifice	Abraham, Isaac, Saint Dominic
Rights and Responsibilities, Solidarity	Israelites	Jacob, Saint Elizabeth of Hungary
Rights and Responsibilities, Solidarity, Family and Community, God's Creation, Life and Dignity, The Poor and Vulnerable	Divine Providence	Joseph, Saint Joachim and Ann
		Saint Justin
Solidarity, Rights and Responsibilities, The Poor and Vulnerable	Exodus	Moses, Aaron, Saint Anselm
Rights and Responsibilities, God's Creation, Life and Dignity, Work and Workers	Ark of the Covenant, idolatry	Moses, Aaron, Saint Mary Margaret Alacoque
Rights and Responsibilities, Life and Dignity, Solidarity, Work and Workers, Family and Community	blasphemy, blessing, Holy Days of Obligation, natural law, Ordinary Time, perjury, social justice	Saints Fabian and Sebastian
Rights and Responsibilities, Life and Dignity, The Poor and Vulnerable	intercession	Moses, Saint Boniface
Family and Community, Solidarity	grace, mortal sin, venial sin, virtue	Moses, Saint Maximilian Mary Kolbe
Rights and Responsibilities, The Poor and Vulnerable, Family and Community	Confirmation, hell, heaven, purgatory	Moses, Joshua, Saint Leo the Great
		Saint John Chrysostom
Solidarity, Rights and Responsibilities, Life and Dignity, The Poor and Vulnerable, Family and Community	abstain	Deborah, Gideon, Samson, Ruth, Saint Clare
Family and Community, The Poor and Vulnerable, Life and Dignity	anoint, Christ, Messiah	Samuel, Saul, Saint Margaret of Scotland
The Poor and Vulnerable, Life and Dignity	Judaism, Temple	David, Nathan, Solomon, Saint Benedict
		Saint Bernard of Clairvaux
Rights and Responsibilities, The Poor and Vulnerable, Family and Community, God's Creation, Solidarity	prophet, Spiritual Works of Mercy	Elijah, Amos, Archbishop Oscar Romero, Saint Agatha
The Poor and Vulnerable, Solidarity, Rights and Responsibilities, Work and Workers, Life and Dignity	Amen, Holy	Isaiah, Saint Charles Lwanga
The Poor and Vulnerable, Solidarity, Rights and Responsibilities, Family and Community, Work and Workers	Exile, Jews, synagogue	Jeremiah, Ezekiel, Saint Pius X
Family and Community, Life and Dignity, The Poor and Vulnerable	Magnificat	Mary, the Mother of Jesus; John the Baptist; Elizabeth; Zechariah, Saint Angela Merici
		Saint Aloysius Gonzaga

* Information on more saints can be found in Saints and Feast Days, pages T497–T512.

The seventh-grade program of the *Christ Our Life* series is devoted to the study of God's saving love as it is revealed through his Son, Jesus. *Jesus the Way, the Truth, and the Life* is designed to help young adolescents grow in their knowledge of Jesus, that they may love him more ardently and serve him more generously.

Unit	Chapter	Theme	Scripture	CCC References
1 Jesus Christ the Way The students will have a deeper understanding of who Jesus is and will desire to follow Jesus.	1. The Impact of Jesus	Jesus, our Savior, is the Son of God and a human being.	John 10:30; Colossians 1:15; Mark 16:15	464–469
	2. Friendship with Jesus	Jesus is truly human. He invites us to friendship with him.	John 15:12–17; Revelation 3:20; John 15:15	470–478
	3. Scripture: A Portrait of Jesus	Scripture, God's inspired Word—especially the Gospels—helps us to know Jesus.	John 20:30–31; John 21:25; Matthew 11:27	81–82, 124–127
	4. The World Jesus Lived In	Jesus was a Jewish man who lived in first-century Palestine during the Roman occupation.	Deuteronomy 6:4–5; John 1:14,17	122, 423
	5. The Early Life of Jesus	The Infancy Narratives reveal that Jesus is the Lord, the Son of God who saved us.	Matthew 1:18—2:23; Luke 1:5—2:25,40	488, 490–499, 525–534
	6. The Mission of Jesus	Jesus accepted his mission as Messiah at his baptism and was faithful to it during his temptation.	Matthew 3:1–17; Matthew 4:1–11; Hebrews 4:15	535–540
	7. The Apostles, Mary, and Others	Jesus called disciples, in particular Mary and the apostles, to share in his mission.	Luke 8:21; John 1:35–39; Philippians 3:8	494, 551–552, 857–860
	8. Baptism and Confirmation	In the sacraments, we receive and celebrate the life Jesus won for us.	Romans 6:3–4; 1 Peter 2:9	1127–1129, 1212, 1239–1243, 1300–1305
	9. Unit 1 Review	Through Jesus, we find the way to the Father.	Matthew 7:21,24–27; John 1:1–2,10–12; John 14:6	460, 618, 654
2 Jesus Christ the Truth The students will know what it means to follow Jesus in daily life.	10. Parables: Stories Jesus Told	Some truths taught by Jesus and his Church are contained in parables.	Matthew 13:3–9,18–23; Luke 12:16–21; Luke 8:10	543–546
	11. Miracles: Signs Jesus Worked	The power of Jesus over nature, sin and evil, sickness, and death was displayed in his miracles.	Mark 2:1–12; Mark 4:35–41; John 2:1–12; Luke 8:25	547–550, 1503–1504
	12. Penance and Anointing of the Sick	Jesus continues to heal body and spirit in the sacraments.	Luke 15:3–7; Luke 15:8–10; Luke 15:11–32; 2 Corinthians 5:20	1420–1421, 1440, 1448, 1499, 1502, 1511–1513, 1524
	13. The Message of Jesus: Choose Life	Keeping Jesus' Great Commandment of love means to respect life.	Matthew 5:21–48; Matthew 22:36–40; Luke 10:29–37; Genesis 1:27	2268–2287, 2302–2317, 2447–2448
	14. The Challenge of the Beatitudes	In the Beatitudes, Jesus gives us guidelines for a happy life in this world and the next.	Matthew 5:3–10; Mark 10:21; Romans 8:35,37	1716–1719
	15. Jesus' Kingdom of Justice and Truth	Jesus expects us to live in honesty and faith, respecting others and the things of this world.	Mark 1:15; Luke 19:1–10; Matthew 5:37	2393, 2401–2402, 2407–2408, 2467–2470, 2477–2487
	16. Jesus' Kingdom of Love	A follower of Jesus regards sex as a sacred gift used to express deep, life-giving love within marriage.	Genesis 1:27; Ephesians 5:25–33; Romans 12:9–10	478, 2332–2337, 2341–2342, 2347, 2360, 2380–2381, 2522
	17. Unit 2 Review	Jesus teaches us the truth that we can live by.	Psalm 25; Matthew 13:44–46; John 4:24	459, 638
3 Jesus Christ the Life The students will have a greater appreciation of the life Jesus won for us by his death and Resurrection.	18. Living Faith in Jesus	Through faith and virtue, our life of grace grows, and we become more like Jesus.	John 3:1–21; John 4:4–30; 1 Timothy 4:12	1805–1809, 1813–1815, 1817–1818, 1822–1824
	19. Opposition to Jesus	Jesus' suffering led to eternal life and glory for him and for us.	Matthew 17:1–8; John 11:1–53; Hebrews 11:1	554–556, 585–586, 591, 618, 1680–1682
	20. The Eucharist	The Eucharist nourishes us with the Body and Blood of Jesus uniting us with him and one another.	Mark 6:30–44; John 15:4–7; John 6:55–56	610–611, 1324–1326, 1341–1344, 1402–1405
	21. Jesus' Final Hours	Jesus' suffering and death won eternal life for us.	Matthew 26:39; Luke 23:39–43; 1 John 3:16	612, 616–618, 632, 678–682, 1023, 1030, 1033, 1040
	22. The Victory of Jesus	Jesus rose from the dead, ascended to the Father, and is still with us.	Luke 24:1–11; 1 Corinthians 15:54–55; Romans 6:5	648–655, 662–664, 904–905
	23. Alive with the Spirit	The Holy Spirit came to the Church, making the members courageous witnesses and forming a community of love.	Matthew 28:19–20; Acts of the Apostles 2:1–41; Galatians 5:25	685–686, 731–733, 737, 747
	24. Matrimony and Holy Orders	Jesus calls each of us to be holy in a special vocation.	Leviticus 19:18; 1 Thessalonians 4:3; 1 Peter 1:15–16	914–916, 1536, 1548, 1570, 1603, 1618, 1644, 1656–1658
	25. Unit 3 Review	Jesus frees us from sin and leads us to life in God.	John 3:1–5,16; John 4:47–53; John 3:16	505, 520, 521

The students should • grow in knowledge and love of Jesus through prayer and studying the Gospels. • appreciate that the sacraments enable them to respond to the call to follow Jesus, live by his teachings, and proclaim God's kingdom in word, worship, witness, and service.

Prayer in this grade • Prayer to Saint Michael • Morning Offering • Prayer of the Penitent • Act of Faith • Prayer for Christlikeness (John Henry Newman) • Nicene Creed

Catholic Social Teaching Themes	Words Learned	Saints and Holy People*
	eternal life, Incarnation	Saint Lucy
		Saint Martin of Tours
	evangelist, synoptic	Saint Mark
	Gentiles, Pharisees	Saint Mary Magdalene
The Poor and Vulnerable	doctrine, Infancy Narratives, inerrancy, Mother of God	Mary, Saint Bernadette Soubirous; Saint Juan Diego
Rights and Responsibilities		John the Baptist; Saint Peter Claver
Family and Community	disciple	The twelve apostles; Saint Andrew
	mystagogy, Mystical Body of Christ	Saint Paul
		Saint Vincent de Paul
Solidarity	evangelization, Magisterium	Saint Thérèse of Lisieux; Blessed Teresa of Calcutta; Dorothy Day; Saint Stephen
Solidarity	miracle	Saint André Bessette
Life and Dignity		Saint Francis of Assisi
Solidarity, Life and Dignity, Rights and Responsibilities	abortion, racism, suicide, ageism, scandal, euthanasia, sexism	Saint Julie Billiart
Life and Dignity, Solidarity		Saint Anthony Claret
God's Creation, Rights and Responsibilities, The Poor and Vulnerable, Life and Dignity, Work and Workers	Catholic Social Teaching, greed, social sin	Saint: Martin de Porres, Rose Philippine Duchesne, Julie Billiart, Vincent de Paul, Louise de Marillac, Maximilian Kolbe, Margaret of Scotland; Blessed: Teresa of Calcutta, Kateri Tekakwitha, John of Capistrano
Family and Community	adultery	Saint Agnes
		Saint Maria Goretti
	cardinal virtues, prudence, fortitude, temperance, justice, Theological Virtues	Saint John Bosco
		Saint Paul Miki
Solidarity	transubstantiation	Saint Isidore the Farmer
	Last Judgment, particular judgment	Saint Andrew Dung-Lac
Rights and Responsibilities, Solidarity	apostle, Ascension	Saint Thérèse of the Child Jesus
Solidarity, The Poor and Vulnerable	Fruits of the Holy Spirit	Saint Peter
Family and Community		Saint John Leonardi
		Saint John the Evangelist

* Information on more saints can be found in Saints and Feast Days, pages T447–T490.

SCOPE AND SEQUENCE

The eighth-grade program of the *Christ Our Life* series is devoted to the study of God's faithful love as it is revealed in the Church founded by Jesus Christ. *The Church Then and Now* is designed to help young teens grow in their knowledge and love of the Church.

Unit	Chapter	Theme	Scripture	CCC References
1 The Mystery of the Church The students will deepen their understanding and appreciation of the Church.	1. A Community of Disciples	The Church is the community of disciples, the Body of Christ, loved and redeemed by Christ.	Luke 13:20–21; John 10:1–16; John 15:1–8; 1 Corinthians 12:12–31; Mark 16:15	781–798, 829, 963–975
	2. Tracing Our Roots	The Church, which began with God's Chosen People, includes all the living and dead who have responded to God's love.	Acts of the Apostles 2:1–13; Luke 18:16	120–133, 836–848, 2041, 2043, 2180
	3. A Closer Look	The Church—the community of disciples—is a herald of the Good News, a sacrament, an institution, a servant, and a mystical communion.	Acts of the Apostles 1:24–26, 2:38, 2:46–47, 4:32, 5:42, 6:2–3, 11:28–29; Isaiah 42:6	774–776, 787–791
	4. A People of Prayer	The Church deepens its relationship with God through prayer, especially the eucharistic liturgy and the Liturgy of the Hours.	Matthew 5:44; Matthew 6:9; Mark 1:35; Luke 11:9; Psalms 5:2–3	1070–1073, 1174–1178, 1343–1344, 1396, 2607–2616
	5. A People of Service	The love of Christ is shown in the service that Church members give as they live the Beatitudes and perform works of mercy.	Matthew 5:3–10; Matthew 10:8; Matthew 25:31–46; 1 Corinthians 12:4–6; Ephesians 2:19–22	799–801, 876, 951, 1716–1719, 2003
2 The Marks of the Church The students will grow in their understanding of the four marks of the Church—one, holy, catholic, and apostolic.	6. One in the Spirit	The Church is one in faith, worship, governance, and charity.	Acts of the Apostles 4:32; Ephesians 4:1–3; 1 Corinthians 12:12–20; John 17:22	791, 811–822, 834, 864
	7. Made Holy in the Spirit	The Church is holy in Jesus its founder, in its mission, and in its members who are all called to holiness.	Isaiah 11:1–3; Leviticus 19:1–2	737–739, 768, 823–829
	8. A Church That Is Catholic	The Church is catholic, or universal: for all people of all nations and all times.	Luke 14:15–24; Matthew 28:18–20; 1 Corinthians 9:22–23	830–856
	9. An Apostolic Church	The Church is apostolic, carrying on the faith and the mission of the apostles under the apostles' successors.	Acts of the Apostles 1:15–26; Acts of the Apostles 2:42	857–865, 880–892
3 The History of the Church: Part I The students will be able to identify key people and events in the Church's history.	10. The First Years	After the coming of the Holy Spirit on Pentecost, the faith spread from Jerusalem to Rome, from Jews to Gentiles, despite persecution.	Acts of the Apostles 5—10, 15; John 16:23	848–850, 861–862
	11. The Church Grows	Led by the efforts of Peter and Paul, the early Church grows and gives witness to Jesus Christ.	Acts of the Apostles 9:1–22, 22:2–16, 26:9–18; Acts of the Apostles 10; Acts of the Apostles 15; Galatians 1:15–17; Romans 15:21	179, 183, 747, 1486, 1490, 2505–2506
	12. A House Built on Rock	After the persecutions, the Church, faced with heresy, clarified its beliefs through the councils and through the teachings of the Church Fathers.	Psalm 62:2–3; John 15:20	461–478, 770–771, 817, 914–924, 2089
	13. A Light in Darkness: Part I	Strong popes, monks, and holy men and women helped preserve civilization and the faith during invasions from northern tribes.	Matthew 5:14–16; John 8:12	817, 873, 920–921, 925–927, 2089
	14. A Light in Darkness: Part II	The Church often served as a beacon of light during the Middle Ages.	John 17:21; Matthew 5:14–16; Matthew 22:37	866–867, 937, 2133–2134
4 The History of the Church: Part II The students will be able to identify key people and events in the Church's history.	15. The Church Faces Challenges	A worldly Church gave rise to the Protestant Reformation.	Matthew 28:20; Matthew 16:18; John 14:16,26	843–847, 1471–1479
	16. Reforming the Church	The Church undertook its own reform in the Council of Trent.	Luke 21:15; Philemon 20	817–821
	17. In a Changing World	The Church responded to a changing world.	Psalm 139:13–17; Matthew 25:35–37,40	884, 891, 1901–1904, 1938–1942
	18. Signs of the Times	The Church responded to the Industrial Revolution with concern for those who were poor and oppressed.	Luke 10:29–37; James 2:18	1895, 1921, 1925, 1943–44, 1947, 2250, 2451–52, 2254, 2458, 2461
	19. The Church in North America	After difficult beginnings, the Church in North America flourished when freedom of religion was granted.	Luke 9:1–6; Luke 1:26–38; Ephesians 1:22–23	2104–2109
5 The Witness of the Church The students will realize what it means to live a Christian life. They will desire to live by Christ's moral standards.	20. The Way of Holiness	In answering our call to holiness, we are helped by virtue and hindered by vice.	1 John 4:8; John 14:6; John 13:34	1768, 1805–1813, 2013–2014
	21. The Way of Faith	God is to be loved above everyone and everything, and God's name honored. (First and Second Commandments)	Exodus 20:2–7; Matthew 22:37	2083, 2132, 2142–2155
	22. The Way of Worship	Sunday is to be a day for worship and rest.	Exodus 20:8; Psalm 95	2168–2188
	23. The Way of the Family	God commands us to obey lawful authority and to respect human life. (Fourth and Fifth Commandments)	Exodus 20:12–13; Luke 10:29–37; Acts of the Apostles 5:29; 1 Ephesians 3:14,17	2196–2246, 2258–2317
	24. The Way of Human Dignity	Sex is to be respected and used only when it is a sign of the permanent commitment of marriage. (Sixth and Ninth Commandments)	Exodus 20:14,17; Matthew 5:27–28; John 15:12; John 15:13–14; 1 Corinthians 6:19–20	2331–2391, 2514–2527
	25. The Way of Justice and Truth	The human rights to own property and to know the truth are to be respected. (Seventh, Eighth, and Tenth Commandments)	Exodus 20:15–17; Matthew 25:31–40,45; John 14:1–7	2401–2449, 2464–2503, 2534–2550

The students should • come to a deeper understanding of the Church by studying its images, history, and members. • grow in love for Catholic beliefs and ritual and strive to respond to God's love through Christian morality, service, prayer, and witness.

Prayer in this grade • Reflective prayer • The Liturgy of the Hours

Catholic Social Teaching Themes	Words Learned	Saints and Holy People*
Family and Community, Rights and Responsibilities, Life and Dignity	Church, Communion of Saints, mystery, Second Vatican Council, sanctify	Mary, Mother of the Church; Saint Hedwig
Solidarity	Buddhism, Islam (Muslims), Justification, New Testament, Old Testament, Paschal Mystery, purgatory, salvation history, Scripture	Saint: Matthew, Mark, Luke, John; Abraham, King David; Saint Teresa of Avila
Family and Community, The Poor and Vulnerable, Solidarity	canon law, Pentecost	Avery Dulles; Saint Robert Bellarmine
God's Creation, Family and Community, The Poor and Vulnerable, Work and Workers	Liturgy, Liturgy of the Hours, prayer	Mary, Mother of the Church; Saint Thérèse of Lisieux; Saint John Paul II; Saint John Vianney
The Poor and Vulnerable, Rights and Responsibilities, Family and Community, God's Creation	Beatitudes, Corporal Works of Mercy, vocation, witness	John Henry Newman; Saint Lawrence
Solidarity, Life and Dignity, Family and Community	apostolic, catholic, ecumenism, holy, Marks of the Church, one	Saint Clement I
Family and Community, Life and Dignity, Solidarity, Rights and Responsibilities, God's Creation, The Poor and Vulnerable	Counsel, Doctor of the Church, fear of the Lord, fortitude, knowledge, piety, Sacraments at the Service of Communion, Sacraments of Healing, Sacraments of Initiation, understanding, wisdom	Saint: Thomas More, Catherine of Siena, Angela Merici, John Chrysostom, Clare of Assisi, Ambrose; Blessed Miguel Pro; Venerable Barney Casey
Life and Dignity, Solidarity	culture, interreligious dialogue	Saint: Katharine Drexel, Damien, Francis Xavier; Charles de Foucauld, Mother Teresa
Family and Community, Life and Dignity, The Poor and Vulnerable, Work and Workers, Solidarity, Rights and Responsibilities, God's Creation	bishop, collegiality, diocese, infallibility, pope	Saint: Peter, Blessed John XXIII, John Paul II, Catherine of Siena; Leo XIII, Benedict XV, Pius XI, Pius XII, Paul VI, Benedict XVI
Solidarity, Life and Dignity, Family and Community, The Poor and Vulnerable	epistle, deacon, martyr	Saint: Peter, Paul, Stephen, Perpetua
Family and Community, Solidarity, Rights and Responsibilities, The Poor and Vulnerable, Life and Dignity	Council of Jerusalem, ecumenical council	Saint: Peter, Paul, Ignatius of Antioch
Rights and Responsibilities, Solidarity, Life and Dignity, Family and Community, The Poor and Vulnerable	heresy, poverty	Saint: Anthony of Egypt, Pachomius, Ignatius of Antioch, Cyprian, Athanasius, Ambrose, Basil, John Chrystostom, Jerome, Monica, Augustine; Sister Dorothy Kazel
The Poor and Vulnerable, Family and Community, Work and Workers, Rights and Responsibilities, Solidarity, Life and Dignity	virtue	Saint: Pope Gregory the Great, Pope Gregory VII, Benedict, Augustine of Canterbury, Boniface, Margaret of Scotland, Cyril, Methodius, Wenceslaus
Life and Dignity, Family and Community, The Poor and Vulnerable, God's Creation	excommunication, Mendicant Order, schism, spirituality, Summa Theologiae	Saint: Dominick, Francis of Assisi, Gregory the Great
Life and Dignity, The Poor and Vulnerable, Solidarity, Rights and Responsibilities	annulment, indulgences, Protestant Reformation	Saint: Catherine of Siena, Ignatius of Loyola
Solidarity, Life and Dignity, The Poor and Vulnerable	meditation	Saint: Charles Borromeo, Teresa of Ávila, Thomas More, John Fisher, Ignatius of Loyola, Francis Xavier, John of the Cross
The Poor and Vulnerable, Life and Dignity, Rights and Responsibilities, Solidarity	rationalism	Saint: Vincent de Paul, Julie Billiart; Blessed Marie-Rose Durocher
Work and Workers, The Poor and Vulnerable, Rights and Responsibilities, Life and Dignity, Solidarity, Family and Community, God's Creation	encyclical	Saint: Thérèse of Lisieux, Francis de Sales, Joseph the Worker, Jane de Chantal, Margaret Mary Alacoque, John Bosco; John XXIII, John Paul II; Blessed: Leo XIII, Benedict XVI
Solidarity, Work and Workers, The Poor and Vulnerable, Life and Dignity, Rights and Responsibilities, God's Creation	Immaculate Conception	Saint: Juan Diego, Elizabeth Ann Seton, John Neumann, Frances Xavier Cabrini, Rose of Lima; John Carroll, James Gibbons, Dorothy Day
God's Creation, The Poor and Vulnerable, Life and Dignity, Solidarity, Rights and Responsibilities, Family and Community	capital sins	Saint: Augustine, Isidore, Maria de la Cabeza
God's Creation, Life and Dignity, Solidarity	sacrifice, sacrilege, vow	Saint Hilary
Work and Workers, Solidarity, Family and Community	holy day of obligation, liturgical year, Lord's Day, Sabbath	Saint Paul of the Cross
Rights and Responsibilities, Family and Community, Solidarity, Life and Dignity, Work and Workers	obedience	Saint Francis de Sales
Life and Dignity, Family and Community, Rights and Responsibilities	chastity, Matrimony	Saint: Maria Goretti, Thomas More
Work and Workers, Family and Community, God's Creation, The Poor and Vulnerable, Solidarity, Life and Dignity, Rights and Responsibilities	calumny, detraction	Saint Louis of France

*Information on more saints and holy people can be found in Saints and Feast Days, pages T513–T560.

Grade 7 of *Christ Our Life* encourages faith knowledge that helps children articulate their Catholic faith. The Grade 7 curriculum prepares learners to participate in the NCEA IFG: ACRE assessment [National Catholic Educational Association Information for Growth: Assessment of Children/Youth Religious Education] © 2013. **The following correlation chart shows how the Grade 7 program aligns with the objectives of the ACRE assessment.**

Grade 7

Domain 1: Knowledge of the Faith

Student Objective: To know and understand basic Catholic teaching about the Incarnate Word Jesus Christ, the way, the truth, the life	**Student Pages**
1.1 Trinity: A community of Three Persons in one indivisible God and the central mystery of faith	This objective is covered in Chapters: 1–3, 5, 19 v, 31, 43, 45–49, 65, 67, 69, 71, 74–75, 85, 87, 93, 95, 101, 137, 139, 155, 165, 167, 171–173, 176, 181, 183–185, 188–193, 203–205, 209, 217, 221, 223–225, 227–228, 236–238, 241
1.2 Creed: a summary of the faith	151, 182, 220
1.3 God's activity in human history	This objective is covered in the Scripture sidebar on the Gather and Go Forth pages: 9, 17, 25, 33, 41, 49, 59, 67, 75, 85, 93, 101, 111, 119, 127, 135, 143, 153, 161, 169, 177, 185, 193, 201, 209 This objective is covered in Chapters: 3, 4, 10–11, 19–23 v–vi, 4, 6–8, 11, 13–16, 35–36, 39–40, 44–45, 57–58, 74, 96, 99, 104, 110, 113, 117, 125, 138–139, 148, 151–152, 203–205, 209, 217–221, 223–225, 227–228, 236, 240, 247–249
1.4 Church history: central stories, key events, major figures, and saints	This objective is covered in A Catholic to Know on the Gather and Go Forth pages: 10, 18, 26, 34, 42, 50, 60, 68, 76, 86, 94, 102, 112, 120, 128, 136, 144, 154, 162, 170, 178, 186, 194, 202, 210 21, 38, 41, 52–55, 57, 83, 151, 163, 191, 199, 215–216

Domain 2: Liturgical Life

Student Objectives: To know the Paschal Mystery of Jesus: • In the Church's liturgical life—feasts, seasons, symbols, and practices • In the sacraments as signs of instruments and grace	**Student Pages**
2.1 Liturgical year	This objective is covered in Special Seasons and Lessons on pages: 213–228 39, 41, 209, 243
2.2 Liturgical symbols	71, 75, 151, 161, 209, 218, 225
2.3 The Mass: Nature, Liturgy of the Word, and Liturgy of the Eucharist	17, 22, 25, 163–169, 204–205, 243–244
2.4 Roles in liturgy	23, 25, 145–166, 197, 204
2.5 Celebration of sacraments as signs of grace and encounters with Christ	11, 46, 48, 61, 71, 97, 181, 184–185, 204, 217, 242
2.6 Sacraments of Initiation: Baptism, Confirmation, and Eucharist	9, 46, 62–67, 71, 149, 163–166, 189, 192–193, 204–205, 211, 242

The **ACRE assessment** is a source of information used to monitor and evaluate the effectiveness of a religious education program in the following six domains:
- Knowledge of the Faith
- Liturgical Life
- Moral Formation
- Prayer
- Communal Life
- Missionary Spirit

For more information about the NCEA IFG: ACRE edition, please visit www.ncea.org.

	Domain 2: Liturgical Life (continued)
2.7 Sacraments of Healing: Penance and Reconciliation and Anointing of the Sick	95–101, 139, 212, 242
2.8 Sacraments at the Service of Communion: Holy Orders and Matrimony	129–132, 134–135, 196–197, 199–201, 212, 243
2.9 Rite of Christian Initiation of Adults	61–62, 65–67, 71

Domain 3: Moral Formation

Student Objectives: • To be knowledgeable about the teachings of Jesus and the Church as the basis of Christian morality and to understand Catholic Social Teaching • To be aware of the importance of a well–formed conscience for decision-making	**Student Pages**
3.1 God's plan for Christian life	vi, 49, 103–106, 109–111. 113–119, 121, 131–133, 135, 138–140, 142, 145, 222, 239–240, 243, 245
3.2 Nature and aspects of personal and social sin and virtue	11, 46–49, 139, 149, 151–152, 154, 177
3.3 Principles of Catholic Social Teaching: life and dignity of the human person; call to family; community and participation; rights and responsibilities; preferential option for the poor and vulnerable; dignity of work and rights of workers; solidarity; care for God's creation	90–91, 99, 105–107, 109–111, 117, 119, 121–122, 124–125, 127, 135, 139, 142, 145, 203, 249–250
3.4 Conscience, freedom, decision–making, responsibility, the common good, and the courage to act	9, 11, 46–48, 82, 110, 123–124, 126, 134, 137–138, 154, 173, 245–246
3.5 Morality as based on natural and divine law	129–134
3.6 Pursuit of a life of holiness	This objective is covered in My Way to Faith on the Gather and Go Forth pages: 10, 18, 26, 34, 42, 50, 60, 68, 76, 86, 94, 102, 112, 120, 128, 136, 144, 154, 162, 170, 178, 186, 194, 202, 210 13, 17, 33, 49, 69–70, 83, 106, 113–117, 119, 124, 130–131, 137, 145, 149, 151–152, 154–155, 172–173, 191, 203, 216

Domain 4: Prayer

Student Objective: To recognize and learn how to engage in Catholic forms of personal and communal prayer and ways of deepening one's spiritual life	**Student Pages**
4.1 The Lord's Prayer, Hail Mary, Glory Be, meal prayers, Sign of the Cross, Act of Contrition, Apostles' Creed	vi, 7, 9, 17, 49, 119, 154, 193, 233–234
4.2 Sacramentals: Rosary, Stations of the Cross, holy water, etc.	161, 181, 183–185, 234–238
4.3 Devotional practices rooted in different cultures, e.g., novenas, *posadas*, *simbang gabi*, *quinceañeras*	31, 39, 133–135, 233
4.4 Purpose and forms of prayer such as blessing, petition, intercession, thanksgiving, adoration, and praise	15, 59, 75, 85, 109, 154, 172, 177, 199, 231–232

Grade 7

	Domain 4: Prayer (continued)
4.5 Personal prayer and spiritual reflection including vocal prayer, meditation, and contemplative prayer as basic and fruitful practices in the life of the disciple of Jesus	This objective is covered in A Moment with Jesus on pages: 6, 14, 21, 29, 38, 45, 55, 63, 82, 90, 96, 106, 116, 124, 131, 148, 158, 166, 173, 181, 190, 198 This objective is covered in the Respond activity on pages: 7, 15, 23, 31, 39, 47, 57, 65, 83, 91, 99, 109, 117, 125, 133, 151, 159, 167, 135, 183, 191, 199, 14–16, 23, 47, 180, 183
4.6 Shared prayer, including family prayer and prayer with small communities of faith	This objective is covered in Celebrating on pages: 72–73, 108, 140–141, 206–207, 226 57, 183

Domain 5: Communal Life

Student Objectives: • To know the origin, mission, structure, and communal nature of the Church • To know the rights and responsibilities of the Christian faithful	**Student Pages**
5.1 Marks of the Church (one, holy, catholic, and apostolic)	220, 258
5.2 Mary as model of the Church	37–39, 41, 56–57, 59, 74, 161
5.3 Church: People of God, Body of Christ, Communion of Saints	61, 97, 177, 189, 231, 242
5.4 Leadership of the Church: order and charisms	55, 59, 204
5.5 The teaching role of the Magisterium	79, 83–84, 139
5.6 Ecumenism: the pursuit of unity among Christian churches	65, 193
5.7 The mission of the Church, and the rights and responsibilities of the Christian faithful	33, 75, 167, 192, 209, 222
5.8 Church as a communion: universal, diocesan, parish, domestic church (family), Christian communities, and ecclesial movements	This objective is covered in the Family Feature on pages: 2, 78, 146 57, 65, 83, 99, 167, 177, 189–192, 201, 231
5.9 Theological Virtues: God's gifts of faith, hope and love; development of character; Christian habits; cardinal virtues: prudence, fortitude, temperance, and justice	11, 15–17, 132–133, 135, 139, 145, 149–152, 154, 204–205, 241

Domain 6: Missionary Spirit

Student Objectives: • To recognize the centrality of evangelization as the Church's mission and identity, embodied in vocation and service • To be aware of how cultures are transformed by the Gospel	Student Pages
6.1 Evangelization, including the New Evangelization	This objective is covered on the Gather and Go Forth pages: 9–10, 17–18, 25–26, 33–34, 41–42, 49–50, 59–60, 67–68, 75–76, 85–86, 93–94, 101–102, 111–112, 119–120, 127–128, 135–136, 143–144, 153–154, 161–162, 169–170, 177–178, 185–186, 193–194, 201–202, 209–210 7, 23, 56, 79, 167, 175, 182, 191–192
6.2 Commitment to discipleship	This objective is covered on the Gather and Go Forth pages: 9–10, 17–18, 25–26, 33–34, 41–42, 49–50, 59–60, 67–68, 75–76, 85–86, 93–94, 101–102, 111–112, 119–120, 127–128, 135–136, 143–144, 153–154, 161–162, 169–170, 177–178, 185–186, 193–194, 201–202, 209–210 51, 56–57, 75, 85, 127, 137, 183, 185, 189–190, 209
6.3 Baptismal/vocational call as lay, ordained, or religious	This objective is covered on the Gather and Go Forth pages: 9–10, 17–18, 25–26, 33–34, 41–42, 49–50, 59–60, 67–68, 75–76, 85–86, 93–94, 101–102, 111–112, 119–120, 127–128, 135–136, 143–144, 153–154, 161–162, 169–170, 177–178, 185–186, 193–194, 201–202, 209–210 46, 59, 64, 85, 127, 195–201, 209
6.4 Responsibility to those in need, promoting the common good, and working for the transformation of society through personal and social action	This objective is covered on the Gather and Go Forth pages: 9–10, 17–18, 25–26, 33–34, 41–42, 49–50, 59–60, 67–68, 75–76, 85–86, 93–94, 101–102, 111–112, 119–120, 127–128, 135–136, 143–144, 153–154, 161–162, 169–170, 177–178, 185–186, 193–194, 201–202, 209–210 37, 47, 65, 83, 90, 93, 97, 99, 106–107, 109–110, 122–125, 127, 142, 145, 167, 199, 208–209, 241

Welcome

Note to Students

Dear Students,

You are entering the stage of life when you begin to ask some of the hard questions such as: Who am I? How do I know what is right? What is the meaning of life and death? Why do people suffer? These are questions that we can spend our lives trying to answer, especially if we try to do it alone. They are difficult questions, but good questions, because they can help us to arrive at a deeper faith and a deeper understanding of life.

Fortunately, we have Jesus who shows us how to live a life of faith, hope, and love. He is the center of our human existence. Jesus is what he calls himself, the Way, the Truth, and the Life.

Jesus is the Way. Through his words and actions, Jesus shows us what God is like. He shows us that God is always ready to reach out to the lost, to love the forgotten, and to forgive the sinner. Jesus shows us a God of unconditional love. Jesus is the way to his Father, and the way to peace and happiness. He is the way to help us fulfill the purpose of our lives.

Jesus is the Truth. Jesus reveals the Father to us. By his words and actions, he shows us the truth about God. It is a truth that all people seek. By the gift of the Holy Spirit, this truth is continuing to be revealed through the work, teachings, and worship of the Church.

Jesus is the Life. Throughout his life, Jesus promised to those who believe and follow him a share in his divine and eternal life. Jesus gives us this faith and continues to strengthen it through Scripture, prayer, the sacraments, the faith community, and the Church. It is faith that is alive and growing.

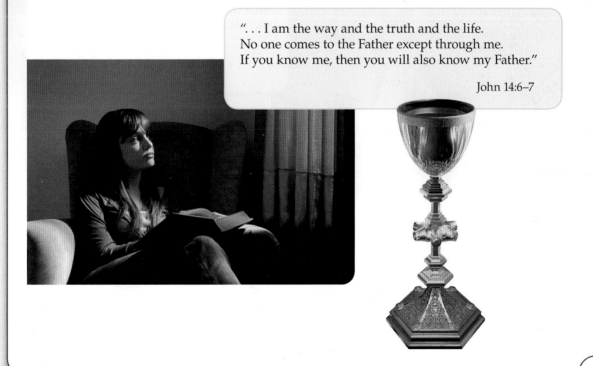

"... I am the way and the truth and the life.
No one comes to the Father except through me.
If you know me, then you will also know my Father."

John 14:6–7

Note to Students

Jesus the Way, the Truth, and the Life is a tool to help you deepen your friendship with Jesus.

This course will help you learn more about how to live and nourish your faith. You will learn about what life was like in Palestine when Jesus lived. By studying the Scriptures, especially the Gospels, you will come to understand how the words and actions of Jesus apply to the lives of believers today. The course will focus on the mystery of our redemption through the death and Resurrection of Jesus. We will examine the Beatitudes as a code of life that can bring us happiness and peace.

An important part of living our faith is taking the time to pray and to celebrate the sacraments. You will learn different ways of praying, such as meditation and the Rosary. The sacraments are sacred moments when we encounter the risen Jesus. Through our participation in them, we are empowered to continue Jesus' mission of love in the world.

Each day may you respond with an open mind and an open heart to Jesus who is *the Way, the Truth, and the Life.*

Erasmus.

Lord Jesus, the Way,
   the Truth,
   and the Life,
we pray,
do not let us stray
      from you,
   the Way,
nor distrust you,
   the Truth,
nor rest in anything else but you,
   the Life.
Teach us by the Holy Spirit
   what to do,
what to believe,
and where to take our rest.

Prayer of Erasmus,
16th-century scholar

UNIT 1

Jesus Christ the Way

GOAL

The students will have a deeper understanding of who Jesus is and will desire to follow Jesus.

1 The Impact of Jesus
JESUS THE SON OF GOD

The students explore their own identity. They are reminded of God's unconditional love for them that calls them to be the best they can be. They consider the impact of Jesus on the world, reviewing the doctrine that Jesus is true God and true man.

2 Friendship with Jesus
JESUS THE SON OF MAN

The students study the basis for our faith in Jesus. They see that Jesus is completely human. They ponder the meaning of true friendship and then are led to realize that Jesus invites them to friendship with him. They are introduced to the reflection notebook as a means of growing in friendship with Christ.

3 Scripture: A Portrait of Jesus
JESUS THE MESSIAH

The students learn how the Gospels came to be written. They study the characteristics of each Gospel and become familiar with the books of Christian Scripture. They recognize the Bible's importance in coming to know Jesus better. They assemble a Scripture booklet to use for Scripture-based prayer.

4 The World Jesus Lived In
JESUS THE NAZARENE

The students study the culture of first-century Palestine when Jesus lived. They learn about the land, the political and religious situations, customs, and family life. They study the Jewish faith and practices.

5 The Early Life of Jesus
JESUS THE SON OF MARY AND JOSEPH

The students read the Infancy Narratives as proclamations that Jesus is the Son of God who saved us. They review Catholic doctrines about Mary, the Mother of God. They are encouraged to listen to the Word of God and act on it as she did.

6 The Mission of Jesus
JESUS THE CHRIST

The students see Jesus as a prophet, priest, and king who accepted his mission to proclaim and make present the Kingdom of God. They learn the significance of his baptism and temptations in the desert. They study temptation and sin and how to resist them.

7 The Apostles, Mary, and Others
JESUS THE MASTER

The students reflect on the impact Jesus had on the first disciples. They come to realize that their own relationship with him can gradually deepen too. They learn what is required of a disciple. They meet each of the twelve apostles and find out why Mary is the first and best disciple.

8 Baptism and Confirmation
JESUS THE SAVIOR

The students learn that Jesus is still with us through the seven sacraments and that we accept his call to discipleship in the Sacraments of Initiation. They learn of their own call to service. The students study the Rite of Christian Initiation of Adults (RCIA).

9 Unit 1 Review

The students review the main concepts of Unit 1. They participate in a celebration that leads them to reflect on what Jesus means to them and to renew their love of him.

The Impact of Jesus
JESUS THE SON OF GOD

Faith Focus

Jesus, our Savior, is the Son of God and a human being.

Reflecting on the Faith Experience

Take a few moments to reflect prayerfully before preparing the lesson.

Listening

> And the Word became flesh
> and made his dwelling among us,
> and we saw his glory,
> the glory as of the Father's
>   only Son,
> full of grace and truth.

John 1:14

Reflecting

No person has affected others as much as Jesus Christ, the Jewish carpenter from Palestine. People either despised him or adored him. To some he was an agent of Satan, to others he was the Son of God, and to everyone he was a mystery.

Christians believe that Jesus is the Way to the Father, to eternal happiness. We believe that he is the second Person of the Trinity, the beloved Son who exists in a community of love with the Father and the Holy Spirit. The Church tries to explain the mystery of the Trinity. It teaches that from all eternity, the Father reflects on his perfections. His infinite thoughts are the Word, a Person. This Person, the Son of the Father, is in his likeness. These two perfect Persons respond to each other with a love so powerful that their love becomes a third Person, the Holy Spirit. These three Persons are eternal and equal. They were all present at creation, and as the One God, they achieve our salvation in history.

The love the Father has for us prompted him to send his Son to become one of us so we could join with them. In loving obedience,

the Son became incarnate in Jesus, a man who taught us the meaning of love and saved us from sin and death. Jesus revealed God to us, and he revealed ourselves and our high calling. By his life, suffering, Death, Resurrection, and ascension, Jesus became our Savior and Lord. Now in his humanity, he is with the Father, while we are able to share in divinity through grace and the power of the Holy Spirit. Once we know who he is, he becomes the alpha and omega, our beginning and end. We walk in his footsteps, doing good. We commit ourselves to living out his life, message, and mission. We live as an Easter people, in a community of faith and love looking forward to resurrection. However, we live Christianity never in certainty, only in hope. Carl Sandburg captures in the following poem the enigma Christ is:

Epistle

Jesus loved the sunsets of Galilee.
Jesus loved the fishing boats forming
   silhouettes against the sunsets
   of Galilee.
Jesus loved the fishermen on the
   fishing boats forming silhouettes
   against the sunsets on Galilee.
Then Jesus said: Good-bye, good-bye,
   I will come again:
Jesus meant that good-bye for the
   sunsets, the fishing boats, the
   fishermen, the silhouettes all and
   any against the sunsets of Galilee.
The good-bye and the promise meant
   all or nothing.

Jesus challenges us to decide who he is. This is the most important decision we ever make. Accepting Jesus as God and Savior is a risk that involves our whole life.

What role does Jesus play in my life?

Responding

Holy Spirit, enlighten me so that I help my students see Jesus more clearly.

Scripture for Further Reflection

John 3:16 God loved the world so much that he gave his only Son, Jesus.

Acts 2:32–36 God has raised Jesus and has made him Lord and Messiah.

Romans 8:28–30 We were chosen by God to be images of his Son and to partake in his glory.

Preparing for the Faith Experience

Scripture in This Chapter

John 10:30 The Father and Jesus are one.

Colossians 1:15 Image of the Invisible God

Mark 1:15 Proclaim the Gospel to every creature.

Church Documents

Catechism of the Catholic Church. The themes of this chapter correspond to the following paragraphs: **464–469.**

National Directory for Catechesis #48. The students should learn to recognize their own dignity and their importance not only for what they will do in the future but for who they are now.

The Redeemer of Man #8 (John Paul II). Jesus is the image of the invisible God. He and the Father are one.

Catechesis in Our Time #5 (John Paul II). The goal of catechesis is to develop communion and intimacy with Jesus.

Gather and Go Forth

Find catechist instruction for Gather and Go Forth student pages 9–10 on T316–T317.

Enriching the Faith Experience

Use the activities at the end of the chapter to enrich a lesson or to replace an activity with one that better meets the needs of your class. Bookmark www.christourlife.com to find Web BLMs for this chapter.

Bulletin Board

A suggestion for a bulletin-board design for this chapter is pictured. See page T501 for further explanation of how to use bulletin boards.

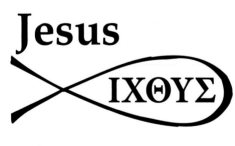

Jesus

ΙΧΘΥΣ

Christ
Son of God
Savior

LEARNING OUTCOMES

The students will be able to

- identify the Bible, the student book, and the class as means to know Jesus.
- assess their knowledge of Jesus.

Materials

- Student book
- Bibles or New Testaments
- BLM 1, BLM 2A–B, BLM 3, BLM 4A–B
- Prism (optional)
- Ceremony items: candles [check fire codes], Bible, table, recorded music [find suggestions for Chapter 1 on page T517]
- Bright-colored paper

Before You Begin

1. **BLM 1, 2A–B** Prepare BLM 1 and 2A–B to be sent home. BLM 1, **Family Letter,** is about the entire course. BLM 2A–B is a **Family Letter on Unit 1.**

2. **BLM 4A–B** Use BLM 4A–B **Pre-Test/Post-Test** to plan your lessons for the year. Save the students' tests to return with the post-tests.

Note to Students

Jesus the Way, the Truth, and the Life is a tool to help you deepen your friendship with Jesus.

This course will help you learn more about how to live and nourish your faith. You will learn about what life was like in Palestine when Jesus lived. By studying the Scriptures, especially the Gospels, you will come to understand how the words and actions of Jesus apply to the lives of believers today. The course will focus on the mystery of our redemption through the death and Resurrection of Jesus. We will examine the Beatitudes as a code of life that can bring us happiness and peace.

An important part of living our faith is taking the time to pray and to celebrate the sacraments. You will learn different ways of praying, such as meditation and the Rosary. The sacraments are sacred moments when we encounter the risen Jesus. Through our participation in them, we are empowered to continue Jesus' mission of love in the world.

Each day may you respond with an open mind and an open heart to Jesus who is *the Way, the Truth, and the Life.*

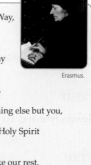

Erasmus.

Lord Jesus, the Way,
the Truth,
and the Life,
we pray,
do not let us stray
from you,
the Way,
nor distrust you,
the Truth,
nor rest in anything else but you,
the Life.
Teach us by the Holy Spirit
what to do,
what to believe,
and where to take our rest.

vi

Note to Students

Dear Students,

You are entering the stage of life when you begin to ask some of the hard questions such as: Who am I? How do I know what is right? What is the meaning of life and death? Why do people suffer? These are questions that we can spend our lives trying to answer, especially if we try to do it alone. They are difficult questions, but good questions, because they can help us to arrive at a deeper faith and a deeper understanding of life.

Fortunately, we have Jesus who shows us how to live a life of faith, hope, and love. He is the center of our human existence. Jesus is what he calls himself, the Way, the Truth, and the Life.

Jesus is the Way. Through his words and actions, Jesus shows us what God is like. He shows us that God is always ready to reach out to the lost, to love the forgotten, and to forgive the sinner. Jesus shows us a

God of unconditional love. Jesus is the way to his Father, and the way to peace and happiness. He is the way to help us fulfill the purpose of our lives.

Jesus is the Truth. Jesus reveals the Father to us. By his words and actions, he shows us the truth about God. It is a truth that all people seek. By the gift of the Holy Spirit, this truth is continuing to be revealed through the work, teachings, and worship of the Church.

Jesus is the Life. Throughout his life, Jesus promised to those who believe and follow him a share in his divine and eternal life. Jesus gives us this faith and continues to strengthen it through Scripture, prayer, the sacraments, the faith community, and the Church. It is faith that is alive and growing.

"... I am the way and the truth and the life. No one comes to the Father except through me. If you know me, then you will also know my Father."

John 14:6-7

Centering _____

1. Introduce yourself to the students.
   - ✦ Tell them why you are glad to be teaching them.
   - ✦ Mention that this year's topic is the most interesting of the whole religion program, Jesus.

2. Use a prism to explain this year's activity.
   - ✦ **What happens to pure, white light when it shines through a prism?** [Demonstrate the prism.] (It is separated into the colors of a rainbow.) **Can someone list all the colors in a column on the board?** (red, orange, yellow, green, blue, indigo, violet)
   - ✦ **Our lives can be compared to white light. If we put them through a prism, we would find they have many aspects, such as our relationships with family members.** [Write *family* after *red*.] **What are some other aspects?** (relationship with God, friends, learning, hobbies, jobs, health, skills, cultural activities) [Have students write each response beside a color.]
   - ✦ **Faith in Christ makes each area of our lives a true, vibrant color. This year as you learn more about Jesus, all aspects of your lives will be enriched. His names reveal ways that he touches our lives.**

3. Hold a contest to list names for Jesus.
   - ✦ Direct the students to find a partner. Give a sheet of paper to each pair.
   - ✦ Explain that they will have two minutes to list names or titles for Jesus.
   - ✦ When time is up, have the longest list read aloud. Let other students add to it.
   - ✦ **You already know a lot about Jesus, but the Bible and your books will extend your knowledge.**

Sharing _____

1. Present the students with their books and Bibles or New Testaments.

✦ **BLM 3** Distribute BLM 3 **Jesus the Way, the Truth, and the Life.**

✦ Lead the students in prayer.

✦ Have the students write their names in their books.

✦ Have them turn to the Contents on page iii to discover titles for Jesus that they had not thought of.

✦ Let them page through their books.

2. Have a student read aloud **Note to Students** on pages v–vi.

Let us pray together the Prayer of Erasmus at the bottom of page vi.

3. **BLM 4A–B** Administer the pre-test on BLM 4A–B.

✦ **This pre-test will tell me what you already know and what to stress in teaching about Jesus.**

✦ **At the end of the year, it will help you see the progress you made.**

4. Ask the students to set goals for their religion class this year.

✦ They might refer to the note on page v for ideas.

✦ Have them work in small groups to create two or three goals. Have each group share their goals aloud.

✦ Write the goals on the board and have each student copy them and refer to them frequently.

Acting _____

Have the students write a prayer.

✦ **Choose a color and decide what part of your life that color represents.**

✦ **After you have chosen a color, write a prayer in which you ask Jesus to help you live fully that part of your life.**

✦ Prayers can be written on bright-colored paper and then posted to form a rainbow.

✦ Example:

Jesus, blue is for my friends. They make me feel strong and happy like a blue sky. They splash laughter over me like a blue lake. Keep us true to one another. May my friends be better people because of me.

Family Feature

Jesus Shows Us the Way

JESUS WAS fully God and fully man. He wasn't play acting when he wept over the death of his friend Lazarus or lost his patience with the money changers in the Temple. Though subject to human trials and temptations, Jesus showed how to remain close to the Father no matter what befell him. Here are some habits that can help us follow Christ's way:

• *Jesus listened.* Time and again, groups of people came up to Jesus with a challenge. He listened calmly and completely before replying, even to those no one else would bother listening to—children, sinners, and enemies. We are called to do the same.

• *Jesus sought time alone.* Jesus often retreated from the crowds and his disciples to be alone. Purpose and patience come from being able to center ourselves, whether it

means taking 10 minutes to meditate at the end of our workday or stepping away for a quick time out whenever our impulse is to rant at someone.

• *Jesus prayed.* Jesus prayed alone and with others, but he prayed often. The prayer he taught us, the Lord's Prayer, is a wonderful prayer to guide us through our day. But Jesus also taught us to pray from the depths of our experience—as he did during his time of agony in the garden of Gethsemane.

• *Jesus had priorities.* Jesus put first things first by taking to heart the words of the ancient prophets: God cares about the poor. He taught us to seek first the Kingdom of God, especially in service to those in most need.

Visit **www.c**

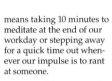

God of Love

God says:
It is I, the strength and
It is I, the wisdom of m
It is I, the light and gra
It is I, the Trinity.
It is I, the unity.
I am the sovereign goo
It is I who teach you to
It is I who teach you to
It is I who am the lastin

ABOVE: Rembrandt van Rijn, *Ecce Homo*, 17th century, oil on canvas, Dutch.

(2) UNIT 1

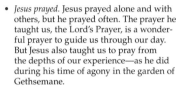

UNIT **1**

Jesus Christ the Way

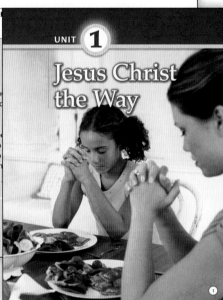

CHECKPOINT

• Were the learning outcomes achieved?

• What word describes the students' attitudes toward religion class?

LEARNING OUTCOMES

The students will be able to

- express God's unconditional love for them.
- discuss how they have value and are worth loving.
- name specific abilities they have as human beings.

Materials

- Bible on table
- BLM 5
- Bookmark or paper star for each student, with his or her name on it
- Questions written on the board:
  1. *How would the world be different if you didn't exist now or in the future?*
  2. *Why do you exist?*

Before You Begin

1. Seventh grade students are going through puberty and tend to have low self-esteem. They need the assurance that it is all right to be who they are and that they are lovable.

2. It is essential for the students to realize that they are responsible for their growth in all areas and that they can take control of their lives.

3. An alternative activity for Acting #1 and #2 is to play soft music as the students reflect prayerfully on a time in their lives when someone showed special love or concern for them. Have them consider these questions:
  1. What did this experience tell me about myself?
  2. What did it tell me about God?
  3. Why do I want to remember this?

The Impact of Jesus

Jesus the Son of God

Who Are You?

You are one of God's special gifts to the world. You are unique! You make the world sparkle as no one else ever will. Like a diamond, you have many facets. You have gifts to discover and develop: skills, talents, and qualities. Like a pebble thrown into a pond, your life creates a ripple. What you do affects those around you. You count!

Who you think you are has a lot to do with who you are now and who you will become. That is why it is important to have a true picture of yourself. There is no better time than the present for discovering the mystery and the miracle of *you*.

Check the characteristics found at each level of creation.

	Things	Plants	Animals	People
Exist	✓	✓	✓	✓
Grow		✓	✓	✓
Eat/Drink		✓	✓	✓
Reproduce		✓	✓	✓
Breathe		✓	✓	✓
Move			✓	✓
Have 5 senses			✓	✓
Think				✓
Choose				✓

How do you differ from plants, animals, and the rest of creation? You have been created body and soul by God. God directly created your soul united to your body within your mother.

What makes you human are the powers of your soul: your God-given gifts of intellect (ability to think) and free will (ability to choose and love). These are divine powers. You are made in God's image. You can share God's truth, goodness, and beauty and can some day share God's glory forever. With your intellect you can make decisions and judgments, and you can laugh. With your free will you can love and sacrifice. Because you have this freedom, you are responsible for your acts.

The whole of the material world has been created for your good. That means you are to see that what God has given you as a gift is to be cared for and to be used wisely.

3

Centering

1. Have several students perform a skit of wrapping a student as a gift.
  ✦ **What is the message of this skit?** (The person is a gift.)
  ✦ **Why could we wrap up any one of you this way?** (All are gifts.)

2. Have the students discuss with a partner the questions on the board.
  ✦ Have a few students share their answers.
  ✦ Lead them to conclude that they are important and that God created them because God loves them.
  ✦ **Scripture calls you God's work of art. In Psalm 139, we pray about ourselves. We say to God:**

  You formed my inmost being;
  you knit me in my mother's womb.
  I praise you, so wonderfully you made me.

  ✦ **In the last lesson, you found out that knowing Jesus enriches all aspects of your life. Before you find out more about who he is, you will learn more about who you are.**

Sharing _____

1. Have the students read silently the first column of **Who Are You?** on page 3.
   + **How are you like a diamond and a pebble?**
   + Help the students fill in the chart.

2. Call on a student to read aloud the second column on page 3.
   + **What two special gifts make us images of God and different from the rest of creation?** (intellect, free will) **What can we do with these powers?** (choose, think, judge, love)
   + **The gifts of intellect and free will enable us to fill our role as caretakers of the rest of creation. They also help us discover who we are and what God has in mind for us.**
   + **All of us are different. Look around. Our differences are to be respected and cherished. Why?**

3. **BLM 5** Distribute copies of BLM 5 **An I-Opener.**
   + Allow students sufficient time to complete the activity.
   + Ask for a show of hands to see how many students belong to each of the four categories. Then divide the class into groups of three or four. (Form groups with students of differing birth orders.)
   + Have the students share their answers to the question.

4. Call on volunteers to give one insight they gained during the lesson.

Acting _____

1. Lead the students in this activity to affirm and respect their gifts and differences.
   + Give each a bookmark or a paper star with his or her name.
   + Have the class pass these around so that each student can write a good trait of the person named on the paper.
   + Have the students return the bookmarks or stars to their owners.

2. Lead the students in a prayer of thanks.
   + **We are going to pray a litany. When your name is mentioned, place your bookmark** (or star) **near the Bible as a sign of your gratitude to God.**
   + [Conclude by praying aloud this prayer naming the students.] **Father, we thank you for loving us so much. You have given us life and more gifts than we realize. Lead us to you and to a true appreciation of our gifts and the gifts of others. Please respond, "We thank you, Father." For the gift of** [Name] **we say: We thank you Father.**

CHECKPOINT

+ Were the learning outcomes achieved?

LEARNING OUTCOMES

The students will be able to

- identify Jesus as Son of God, true God and true Man, and Savior.
- define *eternal life* and *Incarnation*.
- explain some of the implications of the Incarnation.

Words to Know

eternal life   Incarnation

See the Glossary for definitions.

Key Terms

Jesus—the Son of God as a human being; the Savior

Paschal Mystery—the suffering, Death, Resurrection, and ascension of Jesus

Savior—Jesus, who saved us from sin and death

Trinity—the mystery of one God in three Persons: Father, Son, and Holy Spirit

Materials

- Bibles or New Testaments
- Plant
- Three signs: *God the Father, God the Son, God the Holy Spirit*

Before You Begin

1. The doctrines presented in this lesson are the foundation of Christian faith. Most of the students will be familiar with them. To clear up any confusion and to instruct those for whom the material is new, teach this lesson thoroughly.

2. Prepare three students in advance to participate in Sharing #9.

3. You might display pictures of artists' conceptions of Jesus and then discuss aspects of Jesus captured by each picture.

Centering

1. Lead the students in a discussion of mystery.
   - ✦ **Think about someone you love very much. Write down how much you know about that person.** (Allow the students time to write down their answers.)
   - ✦ **Now write down how much you do not know about that person.** (Allow the students time to write down their answers)
   - ✦ **Look over your two lists. What you might notice is that no matter how much you love someone, there will always be a part of him or her that is a mystery to you.**
   - ✦ **You are a mystery in many ways, but that's what makes you exciting.**

2. Link the last lesson with today's lesson.
   - ✦ **Our faith holds many mysteries that God has revealed to us. We will reflect on three central mysteries that the Church has named: the Trinity, the Incarnation, and the Paschal Mystery. These mysteries are related to Jesus.**

   - ✦ **In the last lesson, you found out about yourself and what makes you a unique person. Today you will learn about the person who makes your life worthwhile: Jesus, the most unique person in the world.**

Sharing

1. Have the students read silently **It Is in Your Hands** on page 4.

2. Direct the students to make two columns on paper.
   - ✦ **In the first column, make a list of things you like about your life. In the second column, make a list of the things you do not like about your life.**
   - ✦ **Over which aspects of your life do you have no control?** (heredity, family, weather)
   - ✦ **How can what we have inherited work for us?** (good health) **against us?** (poor health)
   - ✦ **A gift may be both a help and a hindrance. What are the benefits of being athletically gifted? the drawbacks?**
   - ✦ **In what ways are parts of our life out of our control?** (where we live, our families)

   - ✦ **In what ways can we control our personal environment?** (We can choose our friends, entertainment, reading material.)
   - ✦ **What else can we control?** (our reactions, attitudes, habits)
   - ✦ **What are some reasons for a change in attitude?** (We may be influenced by others, our health, our dispositions, and the weather.)

3. Show the students a plant.
   - ✦ **Why must a plant be turned often?** (so that each side gets light)
   - ✦ **What happens if a part of the plant does not get enough light?** (It will wither.)
   - ✦ **Our lives can be compared to a plant. The challenge in life is to keep all sides growing so that growth and beauty emerge.**
   - ✦ **Growth may not always be even, but we are called to keep trying.**

4. Direct the students to underline the six basic areas of growth from the second paragraph in **It Is in Your Hands** on page 4.
   - ✦ Discuss how the students can be growing in each area.

     Mentally—(reaching out for knowledge, reading, observing, asking questions, making mistakes, learning)

Physically—(growing, taking care of your health, exercising, sleeping, balancing your life)

Spiritually—(seeking God's will for you, serving others, growing closer to Christ)

Emotionally—(understanding your feelings, finding healthy ways to express yourself, looking for positive ways to solve problems)

Socially—(learning to live with others, growing in concern for people; respecting differences)

Culturally—(appreciating beauty, keeping a sense of wonder, growing in interests.)

✦ **Describe God's love for you.** (It is free, everlasting, and unconditional.)

✦ **God loves you, flaws and all.** [Write these sentences on the board: *What you are is your gift from God. What you become is your gift to God.*]

5. Have students read aloud **Carpenter with Influence** on page 4.
   How did you answer the question? How would your life be different if Jesus had not lived?

6. Read aloud to the class **Friends of Jesus.**

It Is in Your Hands

God has made you a member of a particular family. From your parents, you received certain traits. That is called heredity. You did not choose your inherited traits, such as curly hair or a quick temper. Psychologists think that even your place in the birth order of your family (first, middle, or last) shapes your personality traits. You also live in a particular area. It is your environment. You cannot control many things in your physical environment. However, you can control your personal environment: the friends you choose, the movies you see, the books you read, and the TV programs you watch. More importantly, you can control your reactions and attitudes. You can decide to develop good habits or bad habits.

You are growing in many ways: mentally, physically, spiritually, emotionally, socially, and culturally. You are responsible for what you do with your life. But Jesus is always with you, supporting you, calling you to further growth, and leading you to himself. The key

(4) UNIT 1

to knowing yourself and becoming the best person you can be is to know Jesus.

Carpenter with Influence

Have you ever heard of Rameses the Great? He was king of the Egyptian empire over 3,000 years ago. During the 67 years of his reign, Rameses was considered a god. He had many large monuments built as tributes to himself. Carved in these monuments were descriptions of his mighty deeds. Now Rameses is just a mummy in a museum and a name in a history book.

Jesus Christ lived about 2,000 years ago in Palestine. He was a Jewish craftsman who spent about the last three years of his life as a traveling preacher. He taught about the Kingdom of God and the laws of love. He healed the sick. To some religious leaders, though, he was a troublemaker. He attracted crowds and associated with everyone, even outcasts. The Romans executed Jesus as a criminal when he was in his early thirties. After his body vanished from his tomb, some of his followers saw him alive, risen from the dead. They began a movement called the Way, now known as Christianity. Today more than a billion people believe that Jesus is God and try to live by his teachings.

Jesus has a powerful and lasting influence because of who he is.

What are the signs of Jesus' influence in the world today?

Answers will vary.

Friends of Jesus

Some people believe so strongly in Jesus that they devote their lives to him. Thérèse Martin lived in France in the 1800s. At age 15 she entered a strict Carmelite convent to lead a life of prayer and sacrifice.

Some people believe so strongly in Jesus that they die for him. For refusing to give up her faith, 13-year-old Lucy was killed by the Romans in the fourth century. Maximilian Kolbe, a priest who tried to live as Jesus did, was in a German prison camp during World War II. When a prisoner escaped, 10 men were chosen to be starved to death as punishment. Maximilian took the place of a man with a family and became a martyr.

✦ **You may know people today who are committed Christians like those in the story. Can you tell about them?**

7. Have volunteers read aloud **Who Is Jesus?** on page 5.
   ✦ **What are the meanings of *eternal life* and *Incarnation*?** (living with God forever; God becoming human)
   ✦ **Have the students explain the following words:**
   Trinity (The mystery of one God in three Persons—Father, Son, and Holy Spirit)
   Abba (Father; Daddy; how Jesus addressed God)

Jesus (the Son of God as a human being the Savior)

Paschal Mystery (the suffering, Death, Resurrection, and ascension of Jesus)

8. Discuss with the students the Greek word for fish, *ichthys,* and Jesus.
   ✦ **What is the connection between a fish and Jesus?** (In Greek, each letter of the word *fish* begins a word in the phrase "Jesus Christ, Son of God, Savior.") [Refer to the bulletin-board]
   ✦ **To help identify another Christian, a believer might draw half a fish in the dirt with a toe. If the person recognized the sign, he or she would complete it.**

The Impact of Jesus **CHAPTER 1** **T9**

9. Ask three volunteers to reenact the Trinity.

✦ Give the volunteers the signs to wear. Have them form a triangle by facing one another with arms outstretched.

✦ **The Father, Son, and Holy Spirit are a community of love. Each person is distinct, yet together they are one God. All are equal in power, and all have no beginning and no end.**

✦ Direct the "Father" to send the "Son" with words such as "Son, go to the people I love and become one of them. Save them from sin and death."

✦ Have the student who is God the Son remove his or her sign, write "Jesus: human" on the other side of it, put it on again, and sit among the class members.

10. Discuss with the students basic concepts about Jesus.

✦ **Why is studying about Jesus the best way to know about God?** (Jesus is the perfect Revelation of God.) **How else has God revealed God's self to us?** (through creation, Scripture, deeds)

✦ **Why did God the Son become a man?** (in obedience to the Father, to save us)

✦ **What did Jesus save us from?** (sin and death)

✦ **When did Jesus come to be?** (when God the Son became one of us)

✦ **Was God pretending to be man?** (No, God really was human.) **What are some human things he did?**

✦ **When do we proclaim the mystery of our faith?** (at the eucharistic celebration or Mass) **What words do we use to proclaim this mystery after the**

consecration? (Any of these:
1. We proclaim your Death, O Lord, and profess your Resurrection until you come again.
2. When we eat this Bread and drink this Cup, we proclaim your Death, O Lord, until you come again.
3. Save us, Savior of the world, for by your Cross and Resurrection you have set us free.)

Who Is Jesus?

A fish holds the answer to this question. During the persecutions of the first Christians, they used the sign of a fish as a secret means of identification. In Greek, each letter of the word *fish (ichthys)* begins a word in the phrase "Jesus Christ, Son of God, Savior."

The Christ

Jesus is the Christ, which means the Messiah, the great leader sent by God. He is the one the prophets foretold and the Jewish people awaited. Jesus, however, was much more than the Israelites expected.

Son of God

With the help of the Holy Spirit, the followers of Jesus came to realize that Jesus was the Son of God. Jesus had often referred to God as "my Father." He even called God *Abba,* a Hebrew word for "Dad."

As Son of God, Jesus was God too. Like the Jewish and Muslim people, Christians believe in one God. What makes us different is our belief in the Trinity. This main Catholic dogma (belief) states there are three Persons in one God: Father, Son, and Holy Spirit. These divine Persons are equal and work together. They have always existed together in a community of love, and they always will.

At a point in time, God the Father sent his only Son to give us **eternal life.** His Son, the Second Person of the Trinity, obeyed the Father and became man, Jesus. Jesus then is a person who has both a divine nature and a human nature. He is completely God and completely human. Jesus is not only Emmanuel, which means "God with us," but he is our brother. The mystery of God becoming human is called the **Incarnation** (*in + carn* = in the flesh). God shared in our humanity so that we could share in divinity.

Since Jesus is God, when we look at Jesus, we know what God is like. God had revealed himself to us before. Creation gives clues about his power and goodness. The Old Testament also tells of God's love through God's words and actions in history. With the Incarnation, God is revealed to us as fully divine and fully human. Jesus said, "The Father and I are one." (John 10:30) We call Jesus the Word from the Father. Despite God's Revelation, God remains a mystery beyond words.

Savior

Jesus is also the Savior. Even his name, Jesus, means "the Lord saves." By his life, especially through the Paschal (Easter) Mystery, Jesus rescued the human race. The Paschal Mystery is the work of salvation accomplished by Jesus Christ through his suffering, Death, Resurrection, and Ascension. By taking our sins upon himself, and dying and rising, Jesus ended the power of sin and death over us. He made it possible for us to have eternal life. At every Eucharist, we, the community of believers, proclaim and celebrate this great mystery of our faith.

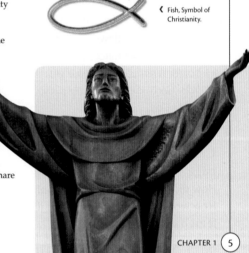

❮ Fish, Symbol of Christianity.

11. Introduce the prologue of John's Gospel.

+ **There are clues to the mystery of Jesus' identity found in a hymn that opens the Gospel of John. It is called the prologue.**

+ Tell the students to listen for the clues as you read aloud John 1:1–4,10–12,14.

+ **What truths does this early Christian hymn contain?** (Jesus is God. The Son of God always was. He participated in the act of creation. Belief in him makes us children of God. He is human like us. He loves us.)

Acting _____

1. 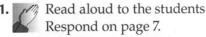 Read aloud to the students Respond on page 7.

+ **An ancient way of praying is by repeating a prayer to Jesus over and over again. This prayer, called the Jesus Prayer, can lead to an experience of his presence.**

+ Have the students quiet themselves, body and mind, by focusing on their breath as they inhale and exhale slowly and deeply.

+ Remind the students that Jesus is with them and suggest that they focus all their attention on him.

+ Guide them to use this prayer by repeating the first two parts as they inhale, "Lord Jesus Christ, Son of God" and the next two parts as they exhale "have mercy on me, a sinner."

+ Give the students two or three minutes to pray the Jesus Prayer silently.

+ Suggest that once they grow familiar with the words, they can close their eyes to avoid distractions.

+ **How was this experience of the Jesus Prayer for you?**

2. At the end of class, have the students tear out page 2. Encourage them to share this Family Feature with their families.

CHECKPOINT

- Were the learning outcomes achieved?

- Do the students' responses to the Jesus Prayer indicate a need for more prayer experiences like this?

LEARNING OUTCOMES

The students will be able to

- discuss who Jesus is for them now.
- spend time in silent prayer with Jesus.
- demonstrate an understanding of the key concepts in this chapter.

Materials

- BLM 6
- BLM 7 Quiz
- Slips of paper, one for each student
- Video camcorder (optional)
- Instrumental music or a song about Jesus
- Half sheets of drawing paper

Before You Begin

1. It is not uncommon in Catholic tradition to speak of Jesus as a friend. Saint Ignatius of Loyola taught his followers that prayer should resemble one friend speaking with another. Pope John Paul II, in his talk at World Youth Day XII, told young people, "Like the first disciples, follow Jesus! Do not be afraid to draw near to Him, to cross the threshold of His dwelling, to speak to Him face to face, as you talk with a friend."

2. Periodically we should ask ourselves, Who is Jesus to me? During this lesson, the students are confronted with this question.

3. For Sharing #3, the students might write and decorate their favorite title of Jesus instead of drawing a fish. Those who finish their art projects early may begin working on the Review Activities on page 8.

4. For Acting #1, make the classroom conducive to prayer. If possible, prepare the three soloists ahead of time for BLM 6 **One Solitary Life**.

5. For a homework assignment, you might have the students write a What If story: What if I had followed Jesus during the years of his public life?

6. When planning today's lesson, keep in mind that Day Four is when the students take the quiz for this chapter. Reserve time at the end of class for this assessment. The quiz can also be administered on Day Five.

A Moment with Jesus

No single image of Jesus contains everything there is to know about him. Pause for a moment and reflect on your favorite image of Jesus. What does that image of Jesus tell you about who God is?

In your own words, ask Jesus to reveal himself to you in a deeper way this year. Then thank Jesus for teaching you about God the Father.

Who Is Jesus for You?

Jesus is your personal Savior. He gives you an *identity*. You are not a "nobody." You are a beloved child of God. Jesus gives you a destiny—eternal happiness. He loved you enough to die a painful death for you. He is always ready to save you again from sin.

Our opinions of people change. For instance, Mark Twain said that when he was 14, he thought his father did not know anything. When he was 21, he was surprised how much his father had learned in 7 years! You will realize who Jesus is, gradually. Sometimes one aspect of him will be spotlighted and sometimes another.

Look at the Contents on page iii. What title of Jesus is your favorite now? Why? How did you first come to know about Jesus? Who helped you to know him? How can you come to know him better?

> He is the image of the invisible God.
> Colossians 1:15

Saint Augustine, retablo (Mexican folk art painting), 19th century.

How Others See Jesus

The Lord has turned all our sunsets into sunrises. (Clement of Alexandria)

We should rather choose to have the whole world against us than to offend Jesus. (Thomas à Kempis)

The Son is the face of the Father, for he who sees the Son sees the Father also. (Saint Ambrose)

Christ is never conquered. (Saint Augustine)

You are the Good Shepherd; look for me, a lamb, and do not overlook me in my wanderings. (Saint Andrew of Crete, eighth century)

6   UNIT 1

Centering

1. Link the last lesson with today's lesson.
   - ✦ The last lesson was demanding because the basic doctrines about Jesus were reviewed: the Trinity, the Incarnation, and the Paschal Mystery.
   - ✦ Today's lesson is more personal. Today you will reflect on the role of Jesus in your own life.

2. Hand out the slips of paper.
   - ✦ On this paper, answer this question: What does Jesus mean to me?
   - ✦ Tell them that their responses will be recorded later if they wish.

3. Direct the students to read **How Others See Jesus** on page 6.

Have the students turn to the person sitting next to them and take turns sharing which of the quotations they like best and why.

Sharing _____

1.  Have the students turn to **A Moment with Jesus** on page 6.

✦ Explain to the students that you are now going to share a few minutes of prayer together.

✦ Lead the students through the prayer, allowing sufficient time for silent reflection.

2. Have the students read the first paragraph of **Who is Jesus for You?** on page 6.

✦ **Circle the answer to the question posed by the title.** (personal Savior)

✦ **In what ways is Jesus our Savior?** (He tells us who we are—beloved children of God. He is our guide for a successful life. He died for us and is always ready to save us again.)

✦ Have the students finish reading this section and answer the questions.

✦ **How did your thoughts about Jesus at age five differ from your thoughts of him now?**

✦ Have the students form groups of three or four and share their answers to the questions.

3. Ask volunteers to record what Jesus means to them while the class works on an art project.

✦ Distribute half sheets of drawing paper and have the students design fish on them.

✦ Direct the students to print the Greek word for fish from the bulletin-board.

✦ Encourage them to be creative with their designs, adding color, descriptive words, or symbols.

✦ Collect and save the drawings so they can be glued in the students' reflection notebooks later.

✦ Have the students use the video camcorder to record their reflections on Jesus in another room or in the hall.

✦ Provide background music as the students work.

4. Choose or let the students choose an activity from Reach Out on page 7.

5. Lead the Students through the Summary and Review Activities on pages 7–8.

6. BLM 7 Distribute and administer BLM 7, **Chapter 1 Quiz.**

Use this opportunity to assess the students' understanding of the main concepts in the chapter. If there is not sufficient time for the students to complete the quiz, consider moving it to Day Five.

Acting _____

1.  Provide a prayer experience using the recording the students made.

✦ BLM 6 Distribute copies of BLM 6 **One Solitary Life.** Divide the class into two groups and choose three students for the solo parts.

✦ Read the words and definitions at the top of the BLM.

✦ Invite the class to be silent and focus on Jesus.

✦ Have the students read aloud **One Solitary Life.**

Summary

CHAPTER **1**

Remember

Who is Jesus?
Jesus is the Son of God and the Savior. He is truly God and truly man.

What is the Trinity?
The Trinity is the mystery of one God in three divine Persons: Father, Son, and Holy Spirit.

What is the Incarnation?
The Incarnation is the mystery of God becoming man.

What does the Paschal Mystery include?
The Paschal Mystery includes the suffering, Death, Resurrection, and Ascension of Jesus.

Respond

"Lord Jesus Christ, Son of God, have mercy on me, a sinner." This is the Jesus Prayer, an ancient prayer popular in the Eastern Church. It is recited repeatedly. Try to pray it often.

Reach Out

1. Ask some friends and relatives what Jesus means to them. Invite them to share with you how knowing Jesus calls them to be the best they can be.

2. Create a poster or a flyer that calls attention to one of Jesus' titles. Put it somewhere in your home where it will cause people to reflect on who Jesus is.

3. Teach someone the Jesus Prayer. Commit yourself to pray it regularly.

4. Write an acrostic prayer to Jesus in which each letter in his name or one of his titles starts a line. Example:

Jesus, my God and Savior,

Each day you call me to love and

Serve others. Help me to

Understand what I must do

So that I might be with you forever.

Words to Know
eternal life
Incarnation

7

+ Watch the tape the students prepared.

+ Allow sufficient time for quiet reflection.

2. At the end of class, have the students tear out and take home pages 7–8.

CHECKPOINT

- Were the learning outcomes achieved?

- How well did the students participate in class activities and discussions?

- What attitude do the majority of your students seem to have toward Jesus?

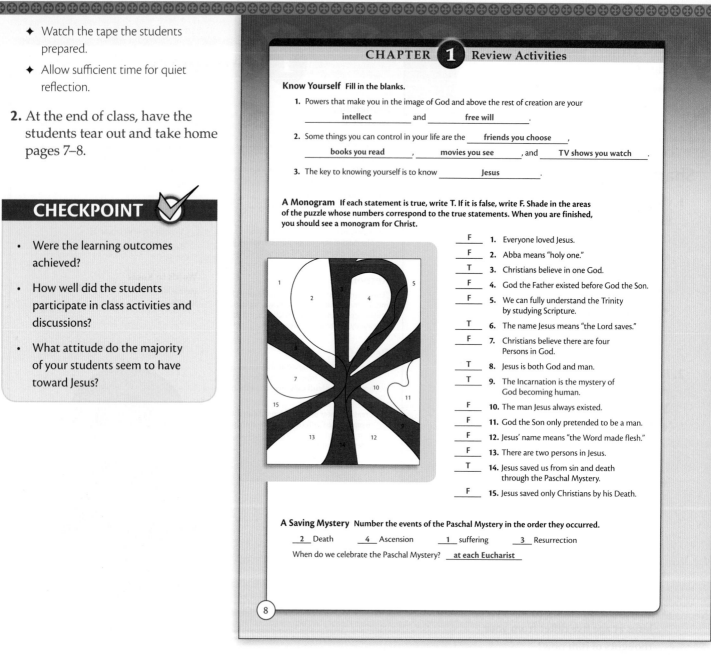

CHAPTER 1 Review Activities

Know Yourself Fill in the blanks.

1. Powers that make you in the image of God and above the rest of creation are your ___intellect___ and ___free will___.

2. Some things you can control in your life are the ___friends you choose___, ___books you read___, ___movies you see___, and ___TV shows you watch___.

3. The key to knowing yourself is to know ___Jesus___.

A Monogram If each statement is true, write T. If it is false, write F. Shade in the areas of the puzzle whose numbers correspond to the true statements. When you are finished, you should see a monogram for Christ.

F	1. Everyone loved Jesus.
F	2. Abba means "holy one."
T	3. Christians believe in one God.
F	4. God the Father existed before God the Son.
F	5. We can fully understand the Trinity by studying Scripture.
T	6. The name Jesus means "the Lord saves."
F	7. Christians believe there are four Persons in God.
T	8. Jesus is both God and man.
T	9. The Incarnation is the mystery of God becoming human.
F	10. The man Jesus always existed.
F	11. God the Son only pretended to be a man.
F	12. Jesus' name means "the Word made flesh."
F	13. There are two persons in Jesus.
T	14. Jesus saved us from sin and death through the Paschal Mystery.
F	15. Jesus saved only Christians by his Death.

A Saving Mystery Number the events of the Paschal Mystery in the order they occurred.

__2__ Death   __4__ Ascension   __1__ suffering   __3__ Resurrection

When do we celebrate the Paschal Mystery? __at each Eucharist__

8

Day Five Extending the Chapter

 Gather and Go Forth

Lead students through pages 9–10 in the student book. Find catechist instruction on T316–T317.

Use the following suggestions to create an additional lesson for Day Five.

1. Remind the students to take home pages 7–8 to share what they are learning with their families.

2. Incorporate any unused BLMs from the week's chapter.

3. Consider the time of the liturgical year and use the appropriate Special Seasons and Lessons. SSLs begin on page T369.

4. Visit www.christourlife.com to find additional activities for Extending the Chapter.

5. Use activities from Enriching the Faith Experience.

6. Guide the students in a prayerful discussion of Sunday's Scripture readings. Visit www.christourlife.com for more information.

Use the following activities to enrich a lesson or to replace an activity with one that better meets the needs of your class.

1. **BLM 8** Use BLM 8 **Temperament Indicator** to help students determine their temperaments.
   + Although we have many sides to our personalities, we have a basic disposition, or attitude. We tend to react in certain ways.
   + In the fourth century B.C., a Greek thinker identified four dispositions. Each of these has its positive and negative sides. Most of us are a combination of these dispositions.
   + Once you know your basic disposition, you can accent your positive points and manage your negative points.
   + Present each temperament with its positive and negative points.

   Sanguine
   - is kind, friendly, generous, fair
   - is pleasant to be with
   - enjoys fun and causes lots of it
   - forgives and forgets easily and quickly
   - likes different kinds of activities
   - puts off duties; wastes time
   - is seldom serious; is very talkative
   - goes too far in joking

   Phlegmatic
   - is patient, forgiving, calm, meek
   - does not worry; works neatly, carefully
   - sticks to a job; does not rush; easygoing
   - is not concerned about trouble
   - does not try to improve
   - tends to be lazy and somewhat selfish

   Melancholic
   - is serious and loyal
   - concentrates well
   - has very strong feelings
   - remembers friends; is grateful for a long time
   - tends to look at the dark side of things
   - can be moody and silent
   - worries too much about everything

   Choleric
   - is courageous; loves a challenge
   - loves to work; is good at organizing
   - has strong feelings; is enthusiastic
   - shows leadership; aims at success
   - has little patience when others fail
   - tends to be bossy; wants to run things
   - finds it hard to forgive
   - often stubborn, hot-tempered

   + Have the students write examples of things they have done that show their temperaments. For the things they have listed that have negative connotations, ask them to think and write about a more positive way they could handle the situation.

2. Assign groups of students one of the following Scripture references that tell what Jesus called himself. Have them read their passage, discuss its meaning, and make a poster for it.
   + **John 6:35** (I am the bread of life.)
   + **John 8:12** (I am the light of the world.)
   + **John 10:7** (I am the gate for the sheep.)
   + **John 10:11** (I am the good shepherd.)
   + **John 11:25** (I am the resurrection and the life.)
   + **John 15:5** (I am the vine, you are the branches.)

3. Have the students write a prayer to Jesus that focuses on one of his titles or have them bring in their favorite prayers to Jesus and analyze the words.

4. Have the students write a letter to you telling what they hope to learn in class this year or have the students write a letter to themselves from Jesus telling what he expects of them.

5. Have the students create a poem or a collage about themselves, their characteristics, and their gifts.

6. Invite the students to make an "I Am" mask out of paper. Ask them to decorate their masks in ways that show who they are. Encourage them to use words, colors, and ribbons. Tell them to be prepared to explain their masks to the class.

7. **Web BLM** Have the students work on Web BLM Chapter 1-A **A VIP: Me** at home.

Friendship with Jesus
JESUS THE SON OF MAN

Faith Focus

Jesus is truly human. He invites us to friendship with him.

Reflecting on the Faith Experience

Take a few moments to reflect prayerfully before preparing the lesson.

Listening

Behold, I stand at the door and knock. If anyone hears my voice and opens the door, [then] I will enter his house and dine with him, and he with me.

Revelation 3:20

Reflecting

Sharing a meal is a universal sign of friendship. The word *companion* even comes from two Latin words that mean "with bread." A companion is someone with whom we break bread. Christ wants to be our companion, our friend. He knocks on the door of our life and waits with gifts of life and love. He does not force us, but leaves us free to choose whether or not we will open our hearts to him.

Friendship with the living God is more than we dare to dream. The distance between God's transcendence and our being creatures would seem to prevent friendship. To make matters worse, human sin widens the gap between the all-holy God and us.

God, however, takes the initiative and bridges the chasm. God establishes a covenant with Abraham and speaks to Moses face to face. Finally, God shows the immensity of his love by becoming human, walking among us, living like us, giving us a sacred meal to celebrate with him, and ultimately, suffering and dying for us. God establishes a new and everlasting covenant. What more proof of our Creator's love for us do we need?

Responding to this infinite love means rooting out all sin and selfishness. It entails living and loving as God did on earth. This task is not impossible because our divine friend is with us to strengthen us in our struggles and heal us when we fail. Through our Baptism, the Holy Spirit, the Spirit of love, dwells in our hearts, ever ready to empower us to love. With God's help, we strive for the essence of friendship, which Emerson says is "entireness, a total magnanimity and trust." As we seek to deepen our friendship with Christ by spending time with him, by listening to his Word, by celebrating Eucharist, and by treasuring his daily gifts, we anticipate our future union in heaven. There at the eternal wedding banquet, we will know the fullness of love.

We pray:

O God, who have commanded
    us
to listen to your beloved Son,
be pleased, we pray,
to nourish us inwardly by your
    word,
that, with spiritual sight made
    pure,
we may rejoice to behold your
    glory.
Through our Lord Jesus
    Christ, your Son,
who lives and reigns with you
    in the unity of the Holy
    Spirit,
one God, for ever and ever.

*Collect Prayer for the
Second Sunday of Lent*

How do I cultivate my friendship with the Lord?

Responding

Spirit of love, help me convince my students that Jesus desires their friendship.

Scripture for Further Reflection

Sirach 6:14–17 A faithful friend is a treasure beyond price.

Isaiah 41:8–16 God speaks to the descendants of Abraham, comforting them by reminding them of his loving care in the past and promising them help in the future.

Preparing for the Faith Experience

Day One
Human Like Us

Day Two
Being Friends

Day Three
Invited by Jesus

Day Four
Cultivating Friendship with Jesus

Day Five
Extending the Chapter

Gather and Go Forth

Scripture in This Chapter

John 15:12–17 I call you friends.

Revelation 3:20 Jesus stands at the door.

Church Documents

Catechism of the Catholic Church. The themes of this chapter correspond to the following paragraphs: **470–478.**

General Directory for Catechesis #41. The Son of God entered human history, assumed human life and death, and brought about a new covenant between God and the human race.

Declaration on Religious Liberty #1, #10–11 (Second Vatican Council). Christ, our Lord and Master who is meek and humble of heart, works patiently, attracting and inviting men and women to follow him in the freedom of true faith.

2004 World Youth Day Message #7 (Saint John Paul II). One way to be an enthusiastic friend of Jesus is to present the Lord to all those who wish to see him, especially those who are farthest away from him. God uses our friendships with others to lead our friends to a knowledge of God's love.

Gather and Go Forth

Find catechist instruction for Gather and Go Forth student pages 17–18 on T318–T319.

Enriching the Faith Experience

Use the activities at the end of the chapter to enrich a lesson or to replace an activity with one that better meets the needs of your class.

Bulletin Board

A suggestion for a bulletin-board design for this chapter is pictured. Papers displaying students' reflections on friendship with Jesus could be displayed.

I call you friends

LEARNING OUTCOMES

The students will be able to

- discuss that Jesus is truly human and like us in all ways except sin.
- explain faith, Tradition, and Scripture.
- describe how the sacraments keep us in touch with Jesus.

Key Terms

faith—believing and trusting when one doesn't understand

Scripture—sacred writings containing God's Revelation; the written testimony of people's beliefs

Tradition—the Revelation of God through truths handed down by the Church from the time of the apostles in teachings, liturgy, writings, and the lives of Christians

Materials

- BLM 9
- Recorded music: Find suggestions for Chapter 2 on page T517.

Before You Begin

1. The more the students realize that Jesus is truly and fully human, the better. As one seventh-grader expressed it, "To know he experienced some of the same things I do gives me great encouragement."

2. The union of the divine and human natures of Jesus is a mystery. We should not forget that Jesus is God, nor should we emphasize his divinity to the point that his humanity is overshadowed.

Centering

1. Link the last lesson with today's lesson.
   - ✦ The last lesson focused on Jesus as God: how he is the Second Person of the Trinity, how through the Incarnation and the Paschal Mystery, he saved us from sin and death.
   - ✦ Today you will learn more about the humanity of Jesus. You will see that he was human as you are, and therefore God knows firsthand some of the same things you experience.

2. **BLM 9** Distribute copies of BLM 9 **How Well Do You Know Your Friend?**
   - ✦ Have the students work in groups of four to supply as much data on Jesus as they can.
   - ✦ Tell them to write in the correct information as you check their answers.

Sharing

1. Ask a volunteer to read aloud the first paragraph of **Jesus, Fully Human** on page 11. **How did you answer the question?** [Write a list of the students' responses on the board.]

2. Have a student finish reading this section.
   - ✦ **Why can we call Jesus our brother?** (He is one of us in the human family. His Father is our Father.)
   - ✦ **What things mentioned were things you never thought about Jesus doing before?**
   - ✦ **If you model your life on Jesus, what kind of things would you be doing?** (loving acts) **Christ shows us what it means to be fully and truly human.**
   - ✦ **Jesus grew the way all people do. He was born naked, hungry, and helpless. He had to learn the same things you did. What did Mary and Joseph have to teach him?** (how to talk, walk, eat; manners, Jewish customs) **Jesus was once your age. He knew what it meant to be a child, a teenager, and an adult.**
   - ✦ **How would you describe Jesus' personality?** [Have volunteers list the words at the board.] (gentle, good-natured, fun-loving, truthful, courageous, determined, compassionate)

3. Have a student read aloud the first two paragraphs of **Someone You Can Trust!** on page 11.
   - ✦ **What is faith?** (believing and trusting when you don't understand; a power; a gift) **What is Tradition? What is Scripture? Underline the definitions in your books.**
   - ✦ **How are Tradition and Scripture alike?** (Faith is built on them; God reveals himself to us in them; they contain beliefs.)

4. Distinguish between tradition and Tradition.
   - ✦ **What do we mean by tradition?** (a way of acting that has been practiced for a long time) **What tradition opens the Olympic games?** (A torch is carried.) **What traditions does your family have for Christmas, birthdays, or other special occasions?**
   - ✦ **The Church has traditions like this too. We take holy water as we enter a church. We celebrate Advent before Christmas. We receive ashes on Ash Wednesday.**
   - ✦ **More important is the type of tradition in religion that is written with a capital T. This Tradition stands for the basic truths we believe that have been handed down from generation to generation.**

- ✦ **These truths are essential to our Catholic faith. Unlike tradition with a lowercase *t*, they do not change.**
- ✦ **What doctrines about Jesus are considered Tradition with a capital *T*?** (He is the Son of God. He is true God and true man. He was born of the Virgin Mary. He suffered, died, and rose. He will come again to judge us.)

5. Provide practice in distinguishing between tradition and Tradition. Ask students to respond to each example below by answering "Capital T" or "lowercase t."

- • **Jesus is true God and true man.** (T)
- • **Most children receive First Holy Communion in the second grade.** (t)
- • **There are three Persons in God.** (T)
- • **The Bible is God's Word.** (T)
- • **Mary is the Mother of God.** (T)
- • **We abstain from meat on Fridays in Lent.** (t)
- • **Jesus is truly present in the Eucharist.** (T)
- • **Men and women religious make three vows.** (t)
- • **There will be a resurrection of the body.** (T)

6. Have the students finish reading silently **Someone You Can Trust!** on page 11.

- ✦ **In what ways is faith strengthened?** (staying in touch with Tradition, Scripture, and faith-filled people; meeting Jesus in the sacraments)
- ✦ **How can you strengthen your faith?** (Study your faith, read the Bible, join in parish activities, celebrate the sacraments, especially Eucharist and Reconciliation.)

7. Have the students use these words in a sentence: *Son of Man, faith, Tradition, Scripture.*

CHAPTER 2

Friendship with Jesus

Jesus the Son of Man

Jesus, Fully Human

Suppose you are a brilliant scientist. In your laboratory, you are trying to design a robot that acts like a human being. What characteristics must your robot have to resemble a real person? (Hint: Think about what makes *you* human.)

Jesus sometimes referred to himself as the Son of Man. In one sense, this title means a human being. Jesus had all the traits in your list. He was like us in all things except sin. He breathed air, ate food, laughed, and got tired. He knew love, sadness, disappointment, and fear. He faced difficult decisions and had to live with the consequences of his choices. Like us, he learned and he suffered and died. He was not just pretending to be human. Amazing as it sounds, God the Son really became a man named Jesus.

Since Jesus is God, there is no evil in him. As a perfect person, Jesus reveals to us what we can be. He is our model for being human. Anyone who wants to lead a rich, full life has only to follow in his footsteps. To be like Jesus is not as impossible as it seems because God calls us to faith in him and empowers us through grace.

Someone You Can Trust!

When you are learning a new language, there are many words you do not recognize at first. You spend a lot of time looking them up in a dictionary until you become more familiar with the language. Faith is somewhat like being able to recognize those words. It is a supernatural power and a *gift*. Not everyone sees Jesus for who he is. Sometimes it requires a little help from others.

That Jesus lived is certain. Some early writings refer to him. That Jesus is God in the flesh, however, is a matter of faith. Faith is believing and trusting when you do not completely understand. Faith in Jesus is based on Scripture and Tradition. Those are two ways that God reveals himself, but they form a single "deposit of faith." Scripture is the Word of God, the written testimony of the faith of the early Church. Tradition is the truths handed down by the Church from generation to generation, from the time of the apostles. It includes teachings, liturgy, writings, and the lives of Christians.

Having faith in Jesus and being committed to him is a lifelong challenge. You can even expect to lose sight of Jesus at times. You can remain strong in the Christian faith by staying in touch with Scripture, Tradition, and faith-filled people. The sacraments are the special means Jesus has given to us to keep in touch. When we celebrate the sacraments, we receive the grace of the Holy Spirit that keeps us in a close relationship with Jesus. You and he will be special friends.

(11)

Acting

 Lead the students in the following reflection.

- ✦ **Think about the great love God has shown for us by sharing our life and even our death . . .** [Pause.] **Thank God in your heart . . .** [Pause.] **Ask God to teach you how to live well . . .** [Pause.] **Ask for the grace to deepen your faith.** [Pause.]
- ✦ **Let's pray together the Act of Faith on the inside back cover of your book.** [See page T446.]

 CHECKPOINT

- • Were the learning outcomes achieved?

LEARNING OUTCOMES

The students will be able to

- describe the privileges and responsibilities that are part of friendship.
- identify some of Jesus' friends in Scripture.

Key Term

friendship—a relationship of love and trust between people

Materials

Paper

Before You Begin

Friends are very important to students at this age. Peer influence is becoming stronger than parental influence. The type of friends the students choose will greatly affect their psychological, social, emotional, and moral growth.

Friends, a Human Need

One of the most important things in your life right now is your friends. People need friends at every point in their lives. Having friends is a wonderful and necessary part of being human. You may have friendly relationships with many people, but have only a few deep and lasting relationships. A true friend is a gift from God.

What Is a Friend?

Read these definitions of a friend. Then write your own definition.

Friend

1. A person whom one knows well and is fond of. (dictionary definition)

2. A friend is someone who knows everything about you and still accepts you. (Saint Augustine)

3. A friend is someone who will always help you and stay with you no matter what happens. (junior high student)

4. A friend Answers will vary.

_____

_____

_____

_____

The Real Thing

In true friendship, people help each other to become the best they can be. If you usually get into trouble when you are with certain people, they are not true friends. Friends do not lead each other to be selfish, unkind, disobedient, or dishonest. Instead they support each other in choosing good and avoiding evil, even when evil "looks like fun" and "everybody else is doing it." Friends help each other overcome temptation and habits of sin.

Friendship is not always easy. Sometimes you or your friends may be selfish or bossy. You or they may reveal a secret or not do a fair share of a job. You can be a bad influence on each other in a way that damages your relationship. When you fail to be real friends, you need to repair the damage in order to keep building your friendship. How?

Jesus' Friends

Jesus had friends. He was popular and attracted many people, young and old. Of

True Blue Friends

Discuss or role-play situations that challenge friendships such as these.

Jean's family has an extra ticket for the world premier of a movie. Jean invited Linda, her best friend. Linda has a gymnastics meet that same night. She has a commitment to her team, but Jean will be disappointed if she says no. What are Linda's options? Which choice do you think is better? How can Jean help Linda make her decision?

Miguel and Sam have been friends since third grade. They have always enjoyed playing tennis together. This year Miguel made the school track team. Whenever Sam wants to play tennis, Miguel is busy. Sam and Miguel still want to be friends. What can they do? Can friends be involved in different activities and still remain close?

(12) UNIT 1

Centering _____

Link the last lesson with today's lesson.

- ✦ **In the last lesson we saw that Jesus was like us in all things except sin.**

- ✦ **Today we will see that because having friends is very human and very important, Jesus, who is truly human, has friends.**

Sharing _____

1. Have the students read **Friends, a Human Need** on page 12.

   - ✦ Allow time for the students to complete the activity **What Is a Friend?**

   - ✦ **Which definition of a friend did you like best? What are some of your personal definitions of a friend?**

2. Ask the students to list six of the most important people in their lives.

   Tell them to indicate which ones fit the various definitions of friend in this section.

3. Discuss with the students what real friendship is.

   - ✦ **Why is it important to have friends? Are these reasons valid throughout life?**

   - ✦ **What are some different needs for friendship at different stages in our lives?**

   - ✦ **What is the difference between having a friendly relationship and having a true and lasting friendship?**

   - ✦ **What qualities must a true friend have?**

4. Have the students read silently **The Real Thing** on page 12.

✦ **What are the two most important ideas in this section?** (Allow a few students to express their opinions.)

✦ **When was a time when you experienced the support of a true friend?**

5. Direct the students to discuss in groups or role-play the situations in **True Blue Friends** on page 12. The students might suggest additional situations.

6. Ask a student to read aloud **Jesus' Friends** on pages 12–13.

✦ Have the class circle the names of Jesus' friends.

✦ **Jesus was human in his need for friends. Who were some of the people Jesus was closest to?** (Peter, James, John, Lazarus, Martha, Mary, Mary Magdalene)

✦ **What are some of the qualities of a friend Jesus possesses?**

Acting

1. Refer the students to their original list of important people.

✦ **The Bible has a proverb on friends: "A faithful friend is a sturdy shelter; he who finds one finds a treasure."** (Sirach 6:14)

✦ Direct the students to draw a simple house that includes a foundation, a roof, and a fireplace.

✦ Have students label how the important people in their lives are like each one.

✦ **Does that person support you?** (Invite students to add other symbolic details to their house.)

2. Invite the students to spend a few moments praying.

✦ Invite the students to pray for the friends in their life, asking Jesus to bless their relationships.

✦ Pray the Lord's Prayer on the inside front cover of the students' book. [See page T445.]

CHECKPOINT ✓

• Were the learning outcomes achieved?

LEARNING OUTCOMES

The students will be able to

- name reasons why Jesus wants their friendship.
- explain why a relationship with Jesus is an essential part of life.

Materials

- BLM 10
- Overhead projector or tape for the back of the puzzle pieces

Before You Begin

1. Students need to know that Jesus loves them no matter what. He wants them to share their questions, anger, disappointments, and loneliness as well as their joys.

2. Your class will have students who already enjoy a relationship with Jesus, those who are ready to meet him on a deeper level, and those who do not know him well and have little desire to know him. Try to motivate all three groups to grow in love for Jesus.

3. You may wish to make several puzzle sets so groups of students can work on them simultaneously.

---

these, several became his closest friends. From the twelve apostles, he singled out Peter, James, and John to share special events with him. He loved Lazarus and his sisters, Martha and Mary. When Lazarus died, Jesus felt so bad that he cried. Mary Magdalene was another friend. She stayed with Jesus through the Crucifixion, and she was the first one he appeared to after the Resurrection.

Invitation to Joy

Look, I am standing at the door, knocking. If one of you hears me calling and opens the door, I will come in to share a meal at that person's side.

Adapted from
Book of Revelation 3:20

Jesus invites you to friendship. He knocks at the door of your life, a door that you alone can open. You are free to open it or not. Jesus loves you and wants you to be happy. He wants you to know the joy that comes to those who walk through life with him. With Jesus at your side, you can be at peace even when you suffer.

You saw that Jesus' title Son of Man can refer to his being human. It can also refer to his Second Coming. In the Book of Daniel, the Son of Man is someone who comes in glory at the end of the world.

Jesus would like you, his friend, to share his glory, to spend an eternity of happiness with him, his Father, and the Holy Spirit. Will you enter into friendship with him? Will you feast with him at the banquet of heaven?

The Ultimate Test

Like all friendships, friendship with Jesus has its responsibilities. Jesus asks a great deal of you. Read John 15:12–17 in which Jesus speaks to you about being friends. Think about his words and complete these statements:

1. Jesus said that the greatest love a person can have for a friend is: <u>to lay down your life.</u>

2. Jesus said we are his friends if we do what he commands, namely, <u>keep his commandments; love one another.</u>

3. When I act as Jesus' friend, I know I can count on his Father's help, for Jesus said <u>whatever we ask the Father in Jesus' name the Father will give us.</u>

4. Add two endings to the following statement. Then rank all of them, using number 1 for the most difficult. **Answers will vary.**

   It is not always easy to carry out Jesus' command. I find it difficult to

   _____ help with work at home.

   _____ listen when adults talk.

   _____ be kind when others do not play well in a game.

   _____ be happy when someone gets what I want.

   _____ _____

   _____ _____

CHAPTER 2 13

Centering

1. **BLM 10** Pass out the pieces from BLM 10 **Jesus at the Center** except for the chi-rho (☧). Have students work the puzzle on the overhead projector or at the board. Present the missing piece last. **What does the chi-rho stand for?** (Christ. The chi [X] is Greek for *CH*, and the rho [P] stands for *R*.) **It has been a monogram for Christ since the early second century. This activity was a parable in action. What lesson does it teach?** (There is a missing piece in our lives without Jesus.)

2. Link the last lesson with today's lesson.
   In the last lesson, you saw that Jesus, like all human beings, had a need to have friends and to be a friend. Today you will see how anxious he is to be your friend too.

Sharing

1. Call on someone to read aloud **Invitation to Joy** on page 13.
   A friend wants only the best for his or her friends. What does Jesus want for us? (peace and joy; an eternity of happiness with him, his Father, and the Holy Spirit; a share in his glory)

2. Ask students to study the picture of Jesus knocking at a door on page 13.
   - This picture illustrates the Scripture quotation.
   - **Jesus does not force the door open. He waits for us to open the door. Jesus cannot come in unless we let him in.**
   - **Before we open our lives to him, we must first hear his knock. How do we do this?** (by being quiet sometimes)
   - **Jesus desires to share a meal with us. What is sharing a meal a sign of?** (friendship) **Jesus does not say he will share a meal only if we are perfect or even very good. He loves and accepts us as we are now and wants to come in now.**

3. Have the students read **The Ultimate Test** on page 13.
   - **Look up John 15:12–17 in your Bibles (or New Testaments). Read the passage and then answer the questions in this section.**
   - Allow time for students to answer the questions. Check the answers to the objective statements.
   - Some students might be willing to share what they wrote for statement #4.

4. Ask the students to turn to page 16 in their books.
   Have them look at the image of Jesus with the children on this page as you read aloud a Letter from a Friend.

5. Have the students spend time reflecting on their friendship with Jesus.
   - Allow sufficient time for silent reflection.
   - **Let us pray together the Doxology on the inside front cover of your book.** [See page T445.]

Letter from a Friend

Dear Friend,

I just wanted to send a note to tell you how much I love you and care about you. I saw you yesterday with your friends. The way you support one another is inspirational. You are fortunate to have friends you can trust and count on. As evening drew near, I gave you a sunset to close your day and a night sky full of stars. Did you see them? The next time you look into the sky, remember to think of me, because I am your friend as well.

I watched you fall asleep last night. I started to reflect on the day and all of the gifts placed before you. Did you notice them? I have so many more to give you. Let's make some time together soon so we can talk about it.

Today I saw you when you felt confused and alone. I understand how you felt. My friends let me down and hurt me sometimes too. I want you to believe that I am with you, even when you feel alone. I really love you. I try to tell you in the blue sky and in the green grass. I whisper it in the leaves on the trees and breathe it in the colors of the flowers. I shout it to you in the mountain streams and sing it in the song of the birds. I clothe you with warm sunshine and perfume the air with nature's scents. My love for you is deeper than the oceans and bigger than the biggest want or need in your heart.

If only you knew how much I long to help you. I want you to meet my Father. He'd like to help you too. My Father is that way, you know. Just call to me, ask me, talk with me. I have so much more to share with you. But, I won't hassle you. I'll wait, because I love you.

Your friend,
Jesus

(Source unknown)

Acting

Discuss with the students one of the ways we make friends.
- **We often make new friends through people we already know. Their friends become our friends.**
- **This is true concerning friendship with Christ. Those who know and love him lead others to him.**
- **Francis Xavier shared a room with Ignatius of Loyola while both were students at the University of Paris. Francis thought Ignatius was rather strange. Ignatius, however, thought very highly of Francis and wanted to introduce him to Christ. This introduction took much time, patience, and prayer. Ignatius finally awakened Francis to realize that the things he did were empty and useless because they did not include Christ. Once Francis opened his life to Christ, he also saw Ignatius in a new light, and they became friends, encouraging each another to follow Christ ever more closely. Ignatius eventually founded the Society of Jesus, and Francis Xavier became one of its great missionaries.**
- **What are some of the ways you can draw your friends closer to Jesus? Can you do this today?**

CHECKPOINT

- Were the learning outcomes achieved?

LEARNING OUTCOMES

The students will be able to

- identify prayer and action as two ways to know Jesus better.
- keep a reflection notebook as a means of spiritual growth.
- demonstrate an understanding of the key concepts in this chapter.

Materials

- Recorded music: Find suggestions for Chapter 2 on page T517.
- Bibles or New Testaments (optional)
- Fish drawings from Chapter 1, Day Four
- Reflection notebooks
- BLM 11 Quiz

Before You Begin

1. The school might provide a reflection notebook for each student. Otherwise, have the students purchase a spiral notebook, a folder with clasps, or a bound book with lined pages. The students could design a cover for it, using a drawing, a favorite picture of Jesus, symbols of their friendship with him, or a favorite quotation or title.

2. If you tell the students that their reflection notebooks are confidential and will not be read, they will be more likely to write honestly. Remind them that they also must respect one another's privacy in regard to reflection notebooks. Speaking from your own experience about the value of keeping a reflection notebook would be a powerful influence.

3. High school and college students can give meaningful witness talks to young people. Adults involved in the Cursillo movement, Marriage Encounter,

RCIA (Rite of Christian Initiation of Adults) and other adult programs are usually comfortable giving witness talks. Invite them to share their faith with your students. Meet beforehand to discuss your aims for the lesson and the content of their talks.

4. When planning today's lesson, keep in mind that Day Four is when the students take the quiz for this chapter. Reserve time at the end of the class for this assessment. The quiz can also be administered on Day Five.

Growing in Friendship

Being Jesus' friend is more than knowing about him. It is knowing him personally. Luke 10:38–42 describes a visit Jesus made to Martha and Mary. While Martha prepared the meal, Mary spent time with Jesus. When Martha complained that Mary was not helping her, Jesus told her that Mary had chosen the better part.

As Jesus' friend, you are not only to serve him, but you are also to spend time with him. This is the only way you will get to know him. Do you see yourself more like Martha or Mary at this time?

> You are my friends if you do what I command you.
> John 15:14

A Moment with Jesus

Have you ever stopped to think what it really means to have Jesus as a friend? Take a moment and silently read the Scripture above. Pause and reflect on ways you can nurture your friendship with Jesus. Thank Jesus for his presence in your life.

Tips for Reflection Notebook Writers

1. Use the time you set aside for writing to do only reflective writing.

2. Be honest with the Lord and with yourself. Write how you really think and feel.

3. Be willing to share anything with the Lord. The Holy Spirit will help you choose what to write.

4. Listen to the Lord. He will speak to you through his Word, through other people, through events of your day, or through your own thoughts.

5. Keep your notebook private. Do not show it to others. Write to God alone. You may not feel totally free if you think someone else might read your reflections.

6. Make your notebook special and keep it neat, but do not worry too much about spelling and punctuation.

7. Reread your notebook every now and then to see how God has spoken to you and has been acting in your life.

(14) UNIT 1

Keeping in Touch: A Reflection Notebook

The time you spend with Jesus is prayer time. A good way to enrich your prayer time is to keep a reflection notebook. It is a book you use to write about yourself and your relationship with the Lord. You can write anything you want to say to God. You can tell God what you think and how you feel. You can share your joys and sorrows. You can thank God for gifts and graces. You can praise God and ask forgiveness. You can ask questions. What you write to God becomes your prayer. Sometimes you might even write a response God might make to you.

Your reflection notebook can be a real treasure. When you reread it, you will come to know yourself better. You will be reminded of God's great love for you and realize how God is working in your life. Best of all, a reflection notebook is a way to deepen your love for your friend Jesus.

Centering _____

1. Begin a discussion by doing one of these activities.

   a. Play a popular song about friendship and discuss what it teaches about friendship.

   b. Ask several students to share a story of a friend who suddenly was no longer a friend. Elicit the students ideas about why the change took place.

2. Link the last lesson with today's lesson.

   In the last lesson, you learned that Jesus calls you to friendship. Today you will learn ways to respond to Jesus' invitation to friendship and keep the relationship growing.

Sharing

1. Ask the students to think about people they know.
What is the difference between knowing someone and knowing about someone?

2. Have the students read **Growing in Friendship** on page 14.

◆ You may want to ask a student to read the story of Martha and Mary from Luke 10:38–42.

◆ Engage the students in a discussion of the question at the end of the section.

◆ **What things are necessary to keep a friendship growing?** (time together, honesty, willingness to share, willingness to sacrifice)

◆ **How do these qualities show themselves in our friendships? How are they shown in our friendship with Jesus?**

3. Have the students turn to **A Moment with Jesus** on page 14.
Lead the students through the prayer experience, allowing sufficient time for silent reflection.

4. Have a volunteer read aloud **Keeping in Touch: A Reflection Notebook** on page 14.
Why do you think a reflection notebook is a useful way to help us grow spiritually?

5. Ask a volunteer to read aloud **Tips for Reflection Notebook Writers** on page 14.
After each tip, ask students why it is good advice.

CHAPTER 2 Summary

Remember

What is faith?
Faith is a gift from God to believe and trust when we do not understand.

How does God reveal himself?
God reveals himself in Scripture and Tradition.

What is Scripture?
Scripture is the Word of God in the Bible. It is the written testimony of faith of the early Church.

What is Tradition?
Tradition is the Revelation of God through beliefs handed down by the Church from the time of the apostles.

What command of Jesus will you follow if you are his friend?
You will follow his command to "love one another as I love you." (John 15:12)

Jesus with Friends Mary and Martha, mosaic, Franciscan Church, Bethany, El-Azariya, Israel.

Respond

Find a blank book or a spiral notebook to use for your reflection notebook. Decorate it if you wish. Decide on a regular time when you will write in your reflection notebook.

Reach Out

1. Thank God for the true friends in your life. Do something special for one of them.

2. Write in your reflection notebook an explanation of why Jesus is a good best friend.

3. List reasons why you are a good friend. You might ask your friends for suggestions.

4. Make a list of five ways to make friends and five ways to lose friends.

5. Use one of the following prayer starters each day this week. Write your conversation in your reflection notebook.

- Tell Jesus about the beautiful things you saw today.
- Tell Jesus how you feel today and why.
- Talk to Jesus about something that you heard or saw today that made you sad.
- Talk to Jesus about gifts God has given you and how you can share them.
- Think about one wonderful person. Thank God for creating that person.
- Did you see a person who was lonely or hurting? Ask Jesus to show you how you could help.

15

6. Share your friendship with Christ in a witness talk. You might include the following.

+ **How you came to know Jesus as a friend**

+ **In what ways is your life different because he is your friend**

+ **How your friendship with Jesus has helped you**

+ **What you do to make your friendship with Christ grow**

+ **Ways you spend time with Christ**

+ **If other people have ever made fun of you for following Christ and how you reacted**

+ **How you try to introduce Jesus to others**

7. Encourage the students to share some thoughts about their friendship with Jesus.

8. Lead the students through the Summary and Review Activities, pages 15–16.

9. BLM 11 Distribute and administer BLM 11 **Chapter 2 Quiz.**

Use this opportunity to assess the students' understanding of the main concepts of the chapter. If there is not sufficient time for the students to complete the quiz, consider moving it to Day Five.

Acting _____

1. Direct the students to put together their reflection notebooks.

+ Ask them to read and carry out Respond on page 15. Return the fish they drew to be pasted into the notebooks.

+ If you do not have reflection notebooks for the students, let them set a deadline for getting their own.

2. Assign or let the students choose an activity for their reflection notebooks from Reach Out on page 15.

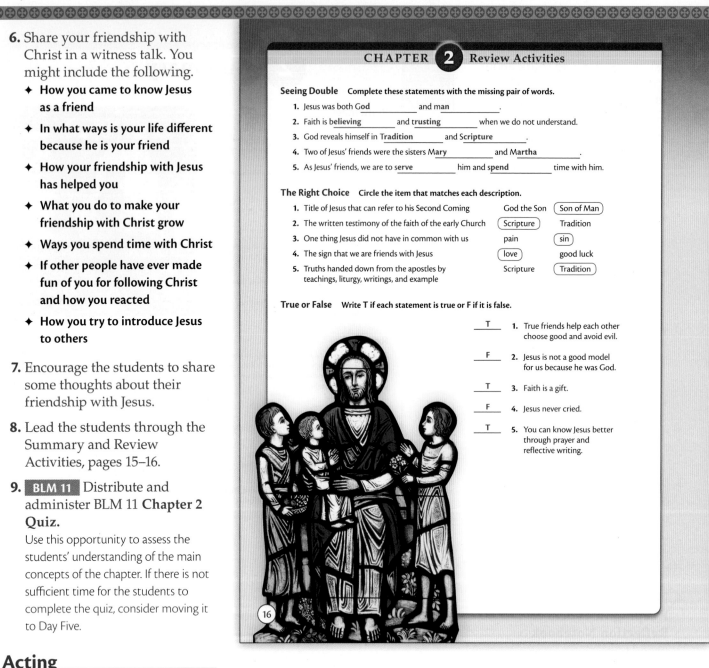

CHAPTER 2 Review Activities

Seeing Double Complete these statements with the missing pair of words.

1. Jesus was both God _____ and man _____.
2. Faith is believing _____ and trusting _____ when we do not understand.
3. God reveals himself in **Tradition** _____ and **Scripture** _____.
4. Two of Jesus' friends were the sisters **Mary** _____ and **Martha** _____.
5. As Jesus' friends, we are to **serve** _____ him and **spend** _____ time with him.

The Right Choice Circle the item that matches each description.

1. Title of Jesus that can refer to his Second Coming — God the Son — (Son of Man)
2. The written testimony of the faith of the early Church — (Scripture) — Tradition
3. One thing Jesus did not have in common with us — pain — (sin)
4. The sign that we are friends with Jesus — (love) — good luck
5. Truths handed down from the apostles by teachings, liturgy, writings, and example — Scripture — (Tradition)

True or False Write T if each statement is true or F if it is false.

T 1. True friends help each other choose good and avoid evil.
F 2. Jesus is not a good model for us because he was God.
T 3. Faith is a gift.
F 4. Jesus never cried.
T 5. You can know Jesus better through prayer and reflective writing.

16

3. Lead the students in prayer.

+ **Friends often have nicknames for one another. What would Jesus call you? It could be one word or a descriptive phrase. [Pause.] Ask Jesus what he would call you. Talk about it with him now.**

+ Allow sufficient time for silent reflection.

4. At the end of class, have the students tear out and take home pages 15–16.

CHECKPOINT ✓

• Were the learning outcomes achieved?

• What do the students' reactions to keeping a reflection notebook reveal?

Day Five   Extending the Chapter

Gather and Go Forth

Lead students through pages 17–18 in the student book. Find catechist instruction on T318–T319.

Use the following suggestions to create an additional lesson for Day Five.

1. Remind the students to take home pages 15–16 to share what they are learning with their families.

2. Incorporate any unused BLMs from the week's chapter.

3. Consider the time of the liturgical year and use the appropriate Special Seasons and Lessons. SSLs begin on page T369.

4. Visit www.christourlife.com to find additional activities for Extending the Chapter.

5. Use activities from Enriching the Faith Experience.

6. Guide the students in a prayerful discussion of Sunday's Scripture readings. Visit www.christourlife.com for more information.

Chapter 2   Enriching the Faith Experience

Use the following activities to enrich a lesson or to replace an activity with one that better meets the needs of your class.

1. Divide the class into groups and have each create a collage or a creative project on friendship.

2. Invite someone to give a witness talk to your class. Provide him or her with suggested topics such as those in #6 on page T26.

3. Reflect with the students on how friends share their lives with one another. Tell the students that if Jesus is our friend, we should go to him with our joys and sorrows. Offer the following situations and ask the students how they would share them with Jesus. Ask how they would address him and what they would say. You may want to divide the students into small groups and assign each group a topic.
   + **You are watching a beautiful sunset on a crisp autumn afternoon.**
   + **Your best friend has just learned that his dad has cancer and will probably die soon.**
   + **All your friends have gone to see an R-rated movie that your parents will not allow you to see. You know that your parents have made this decision because they care, but you feel left out.**
   + **You have won first place in the regional track meet and received a trophy that made your team regional champs.**
   + **Your little brother barely missed being hit by a car when he ran out into the street to get a ball.**

4. Have the students learn about the friendship Jesus had with Peter or John by reading the following Scripture passages. Ask the students to write or to dramatize a conversation that might have taken place the first time Jesus met the apostles after his Resurrection.

Peter	John
Matthew 16:13–23	Matthew 4:21–22
Mark 14:32–42	Mark 10:35–40
John 1:40–42	Luke 22:7–13
John 13:2–11	John 13:21–30
John 13:36–38	John 18:15–16
John 18:10–11	John 19:25–27
John 18:15–27	

5. Have the students create Wanted posters advertising for the perfect friend. Invite them to use markers, colored pencils, and paint to get their message across. Ask them to list clearly the traits and characteristics of a perfect friend. Then have them go through the traits and characteristics point by point to see if Jesus fits the picture. The students can write their thoughts in their reflection notebooks.

Scripture: A Portrait of Jesus
JESUS THE MESSIAH

Faith Focus

Scripture, God's inspired Word—especially the Gospels—helps us to know Jesus.

Reflecting on the Faith Experience

Take a few moments to reflect prayerfully before preparing the lesson.

Listening

Now Jesus did many other signs in the presence of [his] disciples that are not written in this book. But these are written that you may [come to] believe that Jesus is the Messiah, the Son of God, and that through this belief you may have life in his name.

John 20:30–31

Reflecting

There is really only one Gospel: the Good News that Jesus is truly the Messiah, the Redeemer promised by the Father and that his life, Death, and Resurrection reveal the mystery of God's love for us. The early Christians were convinced that Jesus' Death and rising ushered in a new age in which all who accepted him as their Lord and Savior would experience his transforming power. They told about the life of Jesus from their vantage point of the other side of Easter. Decades after the Resurrection, the existing written and oral traditions of the sayings and works of Jesus were compiled into four documents. Under the guidance of the Holy Spirit, each Evangelist shaped the Good News with a unique style and emphasis for a particular group of people. All of the documents conveyed the message that Jesus' life and Resurrection are extremely significant for humankind. For if we follow him, "the one who raised the Lord Jesus will raise us also with Jesus." (2 Corinthians 4:14)

The Gospels are inexhaustible treasures that bring us closer to the Lord of life. In the words of John Henry Cardinal Newman: "When we contemplate Christ as manifested in the Gospels . . . then we shall at length believe in him with a conviction, a confidence, and an entireness, which can no more be annihilated than the belief in our senses." (*Parochial and Plain Sermons,* III) The more we discover who Jesus is, the more fervently we can echo Peter's words, "Master, to whom shall we go? You have the words of eternal life." (John 6:68)

Since the Gospels are the Word of God, they have supernatural power. Louis Evely advises in *That Man Is You,* "We have to read them the way we'd have touched Christ: with the same reverence, the same faith, the same expectancy." Through the Gospels, we find the way to a full human life. Our emphasis in teaching the Christian Scriptures should be on the importance of reading them with prayerful reflection, expecting to encounter the Lord and open to being transformed.

Do I have a regular plan for reading Scripture?

What are my favorite Gospel passages? Why?

Responding

Holy Spirit, may I share my experience with Scripture in such a way that my students are drawn to the Word of God as well.

Scripture for Further Reflection

Matthew 11:27 Jesus is the fullness of God's Revelation about himself; to know Jesus is to know God.

Colossians 3:16 The Word of Christ must dwell in us.

Preparing for the Faith Experience

Scripture in This Chapter

John 20:30–31 Jesus the Messiah

John 21:25 Jesus' Deeds

Matthew 11:27 No one knows the Father except the Son.

Church Documents

Catechism of the Catholic Church. The themes of this chapter correspond to the following paragraphs: **81–82; 124–127.**

National Directory for Catechesis #1. Through the ages, the disciples of Jesus have been enthusiastic in proclaiming to the whole world the Gospel message. Their mission to the world is always related to the person of Jesus Christ.

Dogmatic Constitution on Divine Revelation #17–20 (Second Vatican Council). The writings of the New Testament faithfully hand on what Christ's words and deeds revealed about his Father and himself. The Gospels are the principal source for the life and teaching of Jesus, but the epistles of Saint Paul and the other inspired apostolic writings formulate more precisely Christ's teaching and proclaim his saving power. The authors of the four Gospels selected things that had been passed down to them by word of mouth or in writing and used those things to tell us the truth about Jesus.

Gather and Go Forth

Find catechist instruction for Gather and Go Forth student pages 25–26 on T320–T321.

Enriching the Faith Experience

Use the activities at the end of the chapter to enrich a lesson or to replace an activity with one that better meets the needs of your class.

Bulletin Board

A suggestion for a bulletin-board design for this chapter is pictured. Words may be traced on strips of paper, or any other letter patterns may be used.

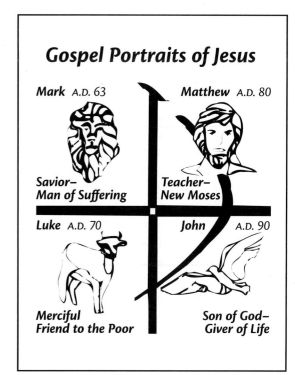

Gospel Portraits of Jesus

Mark A.D. 63
Savior–
Man of Suffering

Matthew A.D. 80
Teacher–
New Moses

Luke A.D. 70
Merciful
Friend to the Poor

John A.D. 90
Son of God–
Giver of Life

LEARNING OUTCOMES

The students will be able to

- describe the purpose of the Gospels and how they came to be written.
- identify the books of Christian Scriptures.
- identify Christian Scriptures as a means to know Jesus better.

Key Term

Christian Scriptures—New Testament; the 27 books of the second part of the Bible

Materials

- Bibles or New Testaments
- Words written on the board: *friends, adult as a child, Abraham Lincoln.*

Before You Begin

1. For many centuries, Bibles were not generally available. They were not printed until about 1456. Beginning with the Protestant Reformation, Catholics were not encouraged to read the Bible. Most contributions to biblical scholarship were made by Protestants. Then in 1943, Pope Pius XII issued the encyclical *Divino Afflante Spiritu*, recommending that Catholic biblical scholars study the Bible and take advantage of new knowledge and discoveries in archaeology and languages. In the Second Vatican Council's *Dogmatic Constitution on Divine Revelation*, biblical scholars are encouraged to continue energetically their work of exploring divine writings.

2. Help students become aware of the insights of modern biblical scholarship. Use your school, parish, or diocesan resource library to choose age-appropriate materials for individual or class research projects.

3. Prepare three students before class to read the conversation in Sharing #1.

Centering _____

1. Refer to the words written on the board: *friends, adult as a child,* and *Abraham Lincoln.*
   - Conduct the following discussion, writing the answers next to the matching terms on the board.
   - **We come to know about people in different ways, depending on how close in time we live to them. What is the best way for you to learn about your friends?** (personal contact)
   - **How could you find out what your mother or father or another adult was like as a small child?** (Ask their parents or others who knew them.)
   - **How could you learn about Abraham Lincoln?** (books)
   - **The Good News of Jesus passed through three stages that can be paired with these three ways of knowing people.** [Read aloud the italicized words which you have added to on the board.]

   - **At first, people knew Jesus from *experience* (personal contact), by seeing him and listening to him. After he ascended, the early Christians knew about him from the *oral stories of eyewitnesses* (adult as a child). After the witnesses died, people came to know Jesus from the *written accounts* (books) of his life.**

2. Link the last lesson with today's lesson.
   - **In the last lesson, you learned that Jesus invites you to friendship. In order to respond, you must first know him.**
   - **Today you will learn about the Gospels, one of the best introductions to Jesus.**

Sharing _____

1. Have three students take the parts in **Sharing the Good News** on page 19.
   - **What reasons for writing the Gospels are given or implied in the conversation?** (The apostles were dying. Details of the stories

would not be forgotten or changed if they were written down. The faith could be spread through writings. Gospels could be used for instructing people who wanted to become Christians.)

   - **Where did the Gospel writers get their information?** (from oral accounts of the apostles, collections of sayings and events from Jesus' life)

   - **When the first Christians met for the breaking of the bread, someone would speak about Jesus and his teachings. In what parts of our Eucharist do we continue this tradition?** (the Gospel reading and the homily)

2. Have a volunteer read aloud **The New Testament** on page 20.

By what year were the books of the New Testament completed? (about A.D. 125) **Why are these books called the New Testament?** (They testify to the life, Death, and Resurrection of Jesus Christ.)

3. Direct the students to use their Bibles or New Testaments to complete the activity.

✦ **How many books are in the first part of the Bible, the Old Testament?** (46)

✦ **It is called the Old Testament because it represents the covenant God made with the Hebrew people before Jesus came. The original parchment scrolls of the books no longer exist. We have copies and translations.**

4. Read aloud to the students the story of Saint Jerome.

Saint Jerome

Saint Jerome is best known for his translation of the Bible. As a young man, Jerome was quite a scholar, familiar with the works of great thinkers such as Cicero. A dream changed Jerome's life. He dreamed that he was before a judge in dazzling light. When he was asked what his religion was, Jerome answered, "I am a Christian." The judge replied, "You lie. You are a Ciceronian, not a Christian. Where your treasure is, there your heart is also."

Jerome then became a hermit and later a priest. He spent most of his adult life reading and writing about the Bible. About A.D. 383, the pope commissioned him to translate the New Testament from Hebrew and Greek into Latin, the language of the people. Jerome also translated the Old Testament from the original Hebrew into Latin. After meeting some opposition, Jerome's Bible became popular and was used for centuries.

CHAPTER 3

Scripture: A Portrait of Jesus

Jesus the Messiah

Sharing the Good News

About 30 years after Jesus' Death, this conversation might have taken place one day after the celebration of the Eucharist.

Mark: Peter was really moved while he was telling about Jesus forgiving that woman. I thought I saw tears in his eyes when he said, "She is forgiven much because she loved much."

Judith: I had never heard that story.

Stephen: I had. Jesus told everyone that, in memory of her, wherever the gospel would be preached, people would be told what she had done.

Mark: We are really lucky to hear about Jesus from the people who knew him. Our grand-children won't hear firsthand accounts.

Judith: Right. The apostles won't be with us forever. James has already been killed.

Stephen: I used to think that Jesus was return-ing to earth soon. Now I realize it might be years before his Second Coming. Someone should write down for future generations what he said and did.

Mark: I know a Christian who has written a collection of sayings of Jesus.

Stephen: Just think. If we had a record of Jesus' life, the Good News would spread through-out the empire.

Judith: And people interested in joining us could study what he has written.

Mark: I'd love to put together such a document. Excuse me. I'm going to talk to Peter.

Saint Mark Writing His Gospel. ❯

(19)

What did Jerome's dream make him realize? (The important thing is to know Jesus.)

5. Review how to locate a Scripture reference.

✦ **References to Scripture passages are like a mailing address.** [On the board write *Mt. 8:23–26* and *23 Oak Street, Chicago, IL.*]

✦ **In an address, you have the house number, city, and state. Scripture passages are like an address. Mt. is the abbreviation for the Gospel of Matthew, just as IL is for Illinois. The 8 is the chapter within the Gospel, like the city in the address, Chicago. The 23–26 are the verses within that** chapter, just as 23 is the street number in the address.

✦ **Using your Bibles (or New Testaments) look up Mt. 8:23–26. Would someone read this passage to the class?**

6. Have the students read silently **Who Is This Jesus?** on page 20.

+ Ask volunteers to share their responses to the question.

+ Assign each student one passage from this section. Have the students find the term in the New Testament and explain it to the class.

7. Explain that several religions have sacred writings.

+ Muslims have the Qur'an, Mormons have the Book of Mormon, and Hindus have the Veda.

+ How would you answer if someone from one of these religions asked what the Bible is about?

Acting

1. Choose or let students choose an activity from Reach Out on page 23.

2. Lead the students in reflective prayer. Have the students close their eyes and be still. Suggest that they tell Jesus they want to know him better.

CHECKPOINT

• Were the learning outcomes achieved?

• Do any students need help locating Scripture references?

The New Testament

All of the books that form the New Testament were written by about A.D. 125. They testify to the life, Death, and Resurrection of Jesus. They tell us that Jesus, the Son of God, is the Messiah, the Savior that the people of the Old Testament longed for. Most exciting, they proclaim that Jesus is our risen Lord and is alive in our lives today.

By the Numbers

Use the list of the books in your Bible to complete this outline of the New Testament. Fill in the name and number of each type of book.

Number	Name
4	Gospels
1	Acts of the Apostles
21	Letters (Epistles)
1	Book of Revelation
TOTAL #: 27	

Gospels: Knowing About Jesus

The word *gospel* means "good news." The Gospels are four accounts of the life and teachings of Jesus. They are documents of faith. According to John 20:31, they were written "that you may [come to] believe that Jesus is the Messiah, the Son of God, and that through this belief you may have life in his name." John's Gospel ends:

> There are also many other things that Jesus did, but if these were to be described individually, I do not think the whole world would contain the books that would be written.
>
> John 21:25

The Gospels were not meant to be biographies. They are more like portraits. Each Gospel writer chose incidents and shaped what he wrote to present what he considered was most important to know about Jesus. In addition, each writer directed his message about the risen Lord to members of his local Christian community. That is why some of the stories in the Gospels are told in a different way. The Gospels all proclaim the same news: *Jesus is the Messiah, the Son of God, who revealed the Father's love for us and saved us.*

Who Is This Jesus?

He said

• I am the way and the truth and the life. (John 14:6)
• I am with you always, . . . (Matthew 28:20)
• I am the bread of life. (John 6:48)
• Follow me. (Luke 5:27)
• [You] hypocrites . . . (Matthew 15:7)
• Young man, I tell you, arise! (Luke 7:14)
• This is my body, . . . (Luke 22:19)
• Whoever has seen me has seen the Father. (John 14:9)

He felt

• grief (John 11:35)
• love (Mark 10:21)
• anger (John 2:13–17)
• gentleness (Luke 19:5)

• sympathy (Matthew 9:18–19)
• affection (Mark 6:30–31)
• frustration (Luke 13:34)
• compassion (Matthew 15:32–38)

He did

• die on a cross (John 10:14–18)
• feed the hungry (Matthew 15:32–38)
• curse a fig tree (Matthew 21:18–22)
• make breakfast (John 21:1–14)
• change water into wine (John 2:1–11)
• go to a wedding (John 2:1–2)
• pray all night (Luke 6:12)
• eat with sinners (Mark 2:13–17)

What kind of person would say, feel, and do such things?

20 UNIT 1

LEARNING OUTCOMES

The students will be able to

- describe the main message of the Gospels.
- identify the features of the four Gospels.
- compare and contrast the four Gospel accounts.

Words to Know

evangelist   synoptic

See the Glossary for definitions.

Key Terms

discourse—a long speech

Gentile—a non-Jewish person

Gospels—the four inspired books that give an account of the life and teachings of Jesus

Materials

- Bibles or New Testaments
- BLM 12A–B
- Several books about Jesus

Before You Begin

1. *The Dogmatic Constitution on Divine Revelation* from the Second Vatican Council discusses the process of writing the Gospels. The writers of the four Gospels selected some things from the many that had been handed down by oral tradition or in writing, reducing some of them to a synthesis, explaining some according to the situation of their churches, and maintaining the form of proclamation, but always in a way that they wrote the honest truth about Jesus. (n. 19)

2. *Gospel* means "good news." The four Gospels present God's saving action in the life, Death, and Resurrection of Jesus Christ. Mark's Gospel was written in Rome by A.D. 70. Matthew and Luke were written in the following decades using Mark's gospel as a basis. The Gospel of John was written in its final form around A.D. 100. Though each Gospel tells the Good News from its own specific perspective, together they present the story of our salvation in Jesus Christ.

3. Many facts about the Gospels are presented in this lesson. The emphasis, however, should be on prayerful study of and reflection on the Bible, especially the Gospels, with openness to its invitation to receive fullness of life from the Lord.

4. You may prefer to carry out the Gospel lab in Sharing #2 and #3 as a whole class activity. In this case, insert the comments from Sharing #3 as you work each section.

Centering _____

1. Give to the students the following oral quiz.
   - ✦ **What is the best-selling book in the world?** (Bible)
   - ✦ **What was the first book run off on Gutenberg's new invention, the printing press, in 1456?** (Bible)
   - ✦ **Which book has been translated into almost 2,000 different languages?** (Bible)
   - ✦ **Why is the Bible so popular?**

2. Link the last lesson with today's lesson.
   - ✦ Hold up books about Jesus, including the New Testament, and comment on each.
   - ✦ **Thousands of books have been written about Jesus. If you could read only one, which one would be best?** (New Testament)

   - ✦ **Why?** (It is written by people who lived near the time of Jesus. It is the Word of God.)
   - ✦ **In the last lesson, you were introduced to the books of the New Testament. What stages did the Gospels go through?** (the experience of Jesus, oral stories of eyewitnesses, written records)
   - ✦ **Today you will take a closer look at the greatest books in the Bible, the Gospels.**

Sharing

1. Have a student read the first two paragraphs of **Gospels: Knowing About Jesus** on page 20.

   ✦ **Why is** *gospel* **a good name for the Gospels?** (It means "good news." Jesus, the subject of the Gospels, is good news.)

   ✦ **What are the Gospels called?** (documents of faith)

   ✦ **How are the Gospels like portraits of Jesus?** (Each writer chose different aspects of Jesus to highlight.)

2. **BLM 12A–B** Distribute BLM 12A–B **Gospel Lab.**

   ✦ Read aloud the directions at the top of the BLM.

   ✦ Have the students work alone or in groups to complete the activity. Allow sufficient time to complete the activity.

3. Discuss the students' answers to the Gospel Lab.

   ✦ [Point #1] **We call the Gospels by the names of Matthew, Mark, Luke, and John, but it may be that other people did the actual writing and editing. For instance, members of John's community might have written his Gospel; a follower of Saint Matthew the apostle might have written his Gospel.** *Q* **is from the German word** *quelle,* **which means "source."**

   ✦ [Point #2] **You can compare what happened to accounts about Jesus to what happens to a joke or a story as it is passed on. Details and sometimes even the punch line are changed.**

   ✦ **How is a Gospel like a family photo album?** (The photos may be taken by different people. They usually are of significant events. They don't tell everything. They aren't necessarily in order. They may be grouped according to topic. Family members may have separate albums with different pictures or some of the same pictures. The

pictures can be arranged differently.)

4. Have several students read aloud the remaining paragraphs of **Gospels: Knowing About Jesus** on page 21.

5. Read aloud with the students the Gospel chart on page 21.

   ✦ Call on students to read the description of each Gospel going across the chart.

   ✦ **What was the first Gospel written?** (Mark) **the last Gospel?** (John)

   ✦ **Where did the symbols for the Evangelists come from?** (the opening of each of their Gospels)

Although we are not certain who wrote the Gospels, Tradition gives the credit to Matthew, Mark, Luke, and John. These men are called the **Evangelists,** which means "proclaimers of the Good News." The Gospel of Mark was probably the first to be written. The writers of the Gospels of Matthew and Luke most likely drew their material from Mark and from another source that biblical scholars call "Q." Because the Gospels of Mark, Matthew, and Luke are so much alike, they are called **synoptic.** *Synoptic* means "same view." John's Gospel, the last to be written, has the style of a deep, religious poem and contains discourses (long speeches) and stories not found in the other Gospels.

The Gospels were written after Jesus sent the Holy Spirit. As Jesus had promised, the Spirit instructed the apostles and reminded them of all Jesus had taught. With the help of the Holy Spirit, the writers of the Gospels understood Jesus better than the people who knew him when he was living on earth. Through the help of the same Holy Spirit, Jesus is alive for us today. The Holy Spirit continues to be with

the Church that Jesus founded, enlightening us so we may know the meaning of Scripture. Did you ever wish that you were alive when Jesus was so you could know him better? Actually, because of the Gospels, we probably understand Jesus more than his friends and neighbors did.

A Moment with Jesus

Each of the Evangelists—Mark, Matthew, Luke, and John—paint a unique portrait of Jesus in a way that their readers will understand him more easily.

Take a moment now to silently read the Portrait of Jesus in the table below. Then pause and think about which descriptions of Jesus are important to highlight for people today. Ask Jesus to help you proclaim the Good News through your words and actions.

	MARK A.D. 63–70	MATTHEW A.D. 80–100	LUKE A.D. 70–90	JOHN A.D. 90–100
Traditional Evangelist	Mark, companion of Peter	Matthew, apostle	Luke, Greek doctor, Gentile, companion of Paul	John, apostle
Symbol from the Opening	Lion (John's voice in the wilderness)	Man (the human ancestry of Christ)	Ox (Zechariah offering sacrifice)	Eagle (the Divine Word, thoughts soaring above Earth)
Main Audience	Persecuted Christians	Jewish converts	Gentile (non-Jewish) Christians	Christians defending their faith
Characteristics	Short, fast-moving	Quotations from Hebrew Scriptures Five sermons	Infancy stories Warm, human portraits	Poetic, symbols Reflective discourses
Portrait of Jesus	Man of action Man of suffering	Teacher New Moses	Savior and friend of all: sinners, the poor, women, Samaritans	Son of God Giver of life

CHAPTER 3 (21)

   ✦ **Who wrote for Jewish converts?** (Matthew) **What features of his Gospel indicate this?** (quotations from Hebrew Scriptures to show that Jesus fulfills them; the five sermons that would remind them of the Pentateuch [the Torah], the five books of the Jewish Law; the portrait of Jesus as the new Moses)

   ✦ **Who wrote for Gentile Christians?** (Luke) **Why do you think he especially wrote for Gentiles?** (He was one himself.) **What picture of Jesus did he give?** (Savior of the whole human race; friend to all sinners, the poor, women, Samaritans)

♦ **What characteristics of John's Gospel make it unique?** (poetic, symbols, reflective, discourses)

♦ **Why are the first three Gospels set in the same color in the chart?** (They are the synoptic Gospels. They are similar.)

♦ **Looking at each Gospel's characteristics and portraits of Jesus, which Gospel would you be most drawn to read? Why?**

Acting

1. Explain to the students how we know Jesus.
Why might we know more about Jesus from the Gospels than people who lived with him? (We have the advantage of the Holy Spirit's guiding the Evangelists as they interpreted Jesus' life and guiding the Church to know the meaning of the Scriptures.)

2. Have the students turn to **A Moment with Jesus** on page 21.
Lead the students through the prayer experience allowing sufficient time for silent reflection.

CHECKPOINT

• Were the learning outcomes achieved?

• What signs are there that the students understand what the Gospels were meant to be?

Day Three   Discovering Jesus

Student pages 22–23

LEARNING OUTCOMES

The students will be able to

• describe what is meant when we say the Bible was inspired.

• identify and describe the books of the Bible.

Key Terms

Acts of the Apostles—book in the New Testament that describes the early days of the Christian community

Book of Revelation—last book in the New Testament which encourages persecuted Christians to accept the Cross and hope for the triumph of God at the end of the world

epistles—letters to the early Christians that are in the New Testament

inspiration—the action of God moving the human authors of the Bible to communicate what he wanted made known

Materials

• BLM 13

• Scripture booklets from the back of the student book

Before You Begin

1. **BLM 13** At the end of this lesson, collect copies of BLM 13 **Who Do You Say I Am?** from those students who would like to have them used in a celebration.

2. You may wish to have the students' Scripture booklets assembled ahead of time.

Centering

1. **Name a famous living person. Ask the students if they know him or her.**
   Distinguish between kno*wing* and *knowing about.*

2. **Link the last lesson with today's lesson.** [Write on the board *Can you know Jesus?*]
   ✦ **Have you ever felt that Jesus was very much with you? Maybe you were in church, or watching a sunset, or even having some kind of trouble.**
   ✦ **In the past lessons, you have seen that the Gospels can help us know about Jesus. Why?** (They originated during his time.) **Today you will see why the Gospels can also bring us to know Jesus personally.**

Sharing

1. **Call on a student to read aloud Gospels: Knowing Jesus on page 22.**
   ✦ Have the students underline the definition of *inspiration.*
   ✦ **How is inspiration for an English assignment different from biblical inspiration?** (Inspiration for an assignment is a natural idea. Biblical inspiration is from God and reveals him to us. God inspired the authors of the Bible to convey what God wanted known by using their own style and background.)
   ✦ **Why can we come to know Jesus personally in the Gospels?** (They are his all-powerful, living Word.)
   ✦ **Reading Scripture, then, is a form of prayer.**
   ✦ Have the students respond to the question at the end of this section.
   ✦ **How did you answer the question about how we honor the Gospels at Mass?**

2. **Ask students to read silently Other Inspired Books on page 22.**
   ✦ **What is the last book in the Bible?** (Book of Revelation)

Gospels: Knowing Jesus

God is the author of the Bible. However, he did not dictate the words to the Evangelists and other Scripture writers. God inspired all the books in the Bible. Inspiration is the action of God that moves people to communicate what God wants made known, using their own background, culture, language, and style. Inspiration makes the Gospels the Word of God. The Gospels, then, do not only help us know about Jesus. They help us know him personally because they are his all-powerful, living Word. Whenever we read Scripture, we meet God, and God speaks to us.

How are the Gospels honored at Mass?

A deacon or priest proclaims the Gospel;

we stand to hear it; the Gospel is sometimes

incensed; after it is read, we respond, "Praise

to you, Lord Jesus Christ;" the deacon or

priest kisses the Gospel book.

Other Inspired Books

In the Acts of the Apostles, Luke tells the story of the early Church. It begins with the

The Evangelists Luke and John.

Ascension of Jesus and continues with the coming of the Holy Spirit on Pentecost. The story tells how the first Christian communities were formed. Peter is the hero in the first part of the Acts of the Apostles. His first sermon results in the conversion of about 3,000 people. Through the intercession of Peter, some of the first miracles are performed. Peter recognizes that the Holy Spirit is calling the Church to move beyond the boundaries of the Jewish people and to proclaim the Gospel to the world.

Saint Paul.

The apostle Paul is introduced as a persecutor of Christians. Through the direct intervention of Jesus, Paul is converted and becomes the greatest missionary in the early Church. While on his missionary journeys, Paul establishes Christian communities throughout the area around the northern Mediterranean Sea. In the final chapter of the Acts of the Apostles, although Paul is a prisoner in the city of Rome, he continues to proclaim the Gospel.

Next in the Bible are the letters, or epistles. Although they appear after the Acts of the Apostles in the New Testament, most of the letters were written before the Gospels. Most of the letters are from Paul, a man who never met Jesus, except as the risen Lord. There are also letters attributed to Peter, James, John, and Jude. Those letters tell us of the issues the early Church had to face as the people explored what it meant to be Christian in the Roman world.

The last book of the Bible is the Book of Revelation. It is a strange and difficult book to understand because the symbols it uses are generally unfamiliar to us. Written during a time of persecution, the Book of Revelation encourages Christians to accept the Cross for God who has already triumphed in Jesus.

22 UNIT 1

✦ **What is Acts of the Apostles about?** (How Peter, Paul, and the other disciples founded the first Christian communities; the progress of Christianity from Jerusalem to Rome)

✦ **Who wrote most of the letters in the New Testament?** (Paul)

✦ **What are these letters about?** (issues about being a Christian in a Roman world)

✦ **What is another name for these letters?** (epistles)

✦ **What book uses symbols?** (Revelation)

3. **BLM 13** Distribute copies of BLM 13 **Who Do You Say I Am?**

◆ **Each piece of the mosaic gives us a part of a picture of Jesus.**

◆ Have a student read the introductory section including Matthew 16:16.

◆ Have the students write Peter's answer.

◆ Read aloud to the students Mark 1:40–41. Complete the activity according to the directions. (The leper knelt and said that he believed Jesus could cure him. He was cured when Jesus touched him and said, "Be cured.")

4.  Assign each student a passage or two in the mosaic.

◆ Invite the students to spend a few moments in silent prayer and talk to Jesus about what they read.

◆ Ask the students to share what they wrote.

Acting

1. Have the students read silently Respond on page 23.

◆ Direct the students to assemble the Scripture booklet from the Lesson Pullouts in the back of the student book.

Scripture Booklet

This booklet belongs to _____

◆ Ask a student to read aloud page 2 of the booklet. Page through the booklet with the students and familiarize them with the contents.

2. Lead the students in prayer.

◆ **Let us pray the psalm verses on page 3 of the Scripture booklet to praise and thank God for giving us his Word in Scripture.**

◆ Separate the class into two sides and have them alternate praying the verses.

CHAPTER 3 Summary

Remember

What is the Gospel?
The Gospel is the Good News that Jesus' life, Death, and Resurrection have freed us from the power of sin and death.

What is inspiration?
Inspiration is the action of God that directs people to write what he wants made known through their own language and style.

What is the New Testament?
The New Testament consists of 27 books, arranged according to the kind of writing (Gospels, Acts of the Apostles, Letters, Book of Revelation).

Respond

Meet Jesus every day through his Word in the Bible. Assemble the Scripture booklet in the back of this book. Use it to know Jesus better.

Reach Out

1. Read Philippians 3:7–9 to find out how Saint Paul describes what Jesus means to him. Then answer these questions to yourself:
   • How much does Jesus mean to me?
   • Do I treasure Jesus' friendship enough to spend time with him every day?
   • How would I rate my own openness to Jesus?
   • What will I do to know Jesus better?

2. Interview three teenagers or adults who seem to have a strong friendship with Jesus. Ask them to share how Jesus reveals himself to them in their daily lives.

3. Inquire about the process of becoming a lector in your parish. Reflect on whether you might be called to be a lector and proclaim the Word of God in your Christian community.

4. Think of something Jesus said or did. Write it in your reflection notebook. That statement is Jesus' message to you. He is telling you something about himself. He wants its meaning to grow in your heart and move you to love him more.

Write about Jesus' message, including some of these ideas:
   • What it means to you
   • How it makes you feel about yourself
   • How you think Jesus would like you to respond
   • Something you will do to respond
   • Your thanks that Jesus has spoken to you.

Words to Know

Evangelist   synoptic

23

CHECKPOINT

• Were the learning outcomes achieved?

• Do the students seem to desire to deepen their relationship with Jesus?

LEARNING OUTCOMES

The students will be able to

- plan a celebration of God's Word.
- demonstrate an understanding of the key concepts in this chapter.

Materials

- BLM 14, BLM 15, BLM 16
- BLM 17 Quiz
- Song for the celebration (optional)

Before You Begin

1. If the Word of God is to be "living and effective" (Hebrews 4:12), filling us with joy and strength, we must take time to listen to and reflect on it. Then we will attain "wisdom for salvation" and become "equipped for every good work." (2 Timothy 3:15–17)

2. Have all materials ready for the celebration so that the students can begin working immediately.

3. **BLM 16** You may wish to give BLM 16 **Quotations from Jesus** to the Scripture Quotation Committee in preparation for the celebration.

4. When planning today's lesson, keep in mind that Day Four is when the students take the quiz for this chapter. Reserve time at the end of the class for this assessment. The quiz can also be taken on Day Five.

Centering _____

1. Link the last lesson with today's lesson.
   - **You have been learning about who Jesus is through the study of the Gospels.**
   - **Today you will put into practice what you have been learning by planning and praying a celebration of Scripture.**

2. Discuss with the students being open to God's Word.
   - **What is the purpose of shades or blinds on windows?** (they let the sun in when open and block the sun when closed.) **Jesus is like the sun. He is always there for us. We can allow his light to influence us or we can block it out.**
   - **In our celebration, we will pray for openness to Jesus in his Word.**

Celebrating _____

1. **BLM 14–15** Distribute copies of BLM 14 **Listening to God's Word** *Planning Guide,* and BLM 15 **Listening to God's Word** *Procession and Bible Enthronement.*
   - List the five groups needed and explain their duties. Select a student to lead each group.
   - Assign work areas and give the leaders a copy of the celebration and the section of the planning guide that applies to their group.
   - Instruct the groups on their responsibilities.
   - Groups that finish early might begin the Review Activities on page 24.

2. Lead the students in the prayer service BLM 15 **Listening to God's Word** *Procession and Bible Enthronement.*

Acting _____

1. Discuss the celebration with the students.
   Did you have any new insights about Jesus during the celebration?

2. Lead the students through the Summary and the Review Activities, pages 23–24.

3. **BLM 17** Distribute and administer BLM 17 **Chapter 3 Quiz.**
   Use this as an opportunity to assess the students' understanding of the main concepts of the chapter. If there is not sufficient time for the students to complete the quiz, consider moving it to Day Five.

4. At the end of class, have the students tear out and take home pages 23–24.

CHECKPOINT

- Were the learning outcomes achieved?

Gather and Go Forth

Lead students through pages 25–26 in the student book. Find catechist instruction on T320–T321.

Use the following suggestions to create an additional lesson for Day Five.

1. Remind the students to take home pages 23–24 to share what they are learning with their families.

2. Incorporate any unused BLMs from the week's chapter.

3. Consider the time of the liturgical year and use the appropriate Special Seasons and Lessons. SSLs begin on page T369.

4. Visit www.christourlife.com to find additional activities for Extending the Chapter.

5. Use activities from Enriching the Faith Experience.

6. Guide the students in a prayerful discussion of Sunday's Scripture readings. Visit www.christourlife.com for more information.

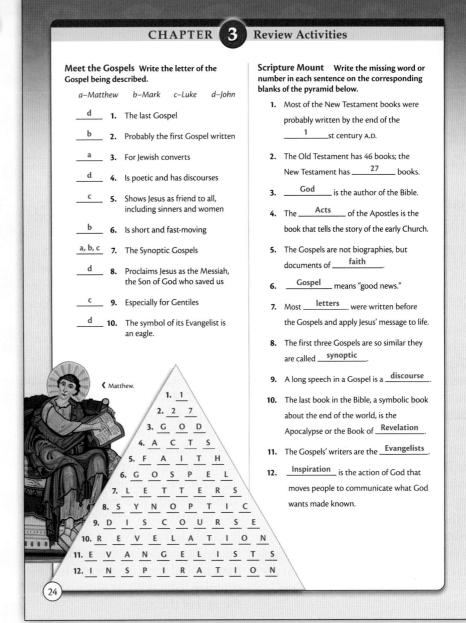

CHAPTER **3** Review Activities

Meet the Gospels Write the letter of the Gospel being described.

a–Matthew   b–Mark   c–Luke   d–John

- **d** 1. The last Gospel
- **b** 2. Probably the first Gospel written
- **a** 3. For Jewish converts
- **d** 4. Is poetic and has discourses
- **c** 5. Shows Jesus as friend to all, including sinners and women
- **b** 6. Is short and fast-moving
- **a, b, c** 7. The Synoptic Gospels
- **d** 8. Proclaims Jesus as the Messiah, the Son of God who saved us
- **c** 9. Especially for Gentiles
- **d** 10. The symbol of its Evangelist is an eagle.

‹ Matthew.

Scripture Mount Write the missing word or number in each sentence on the corresponding blanks of the pyramid below.

1. Most of the New Testament books were probably written by the end of the __1__st century A.D.

2. The Old Testament has 46 books; the New Testament has __27__ books.

3. __God__ is the author of the Bible.

4. The __Acts__ of the Apostles is the book that tells the story of the early Church.

5. The Gospels are not biographies, but documents of __faith__.

6. __Gospel__ means "good news."

7. Most __letters__ were written before the Gospels and apply Jesus' message to life.

8. The first three Gospels are so similar they are called __synoptic__.

9. A long speech in a Gospel is a __discourse__.

10. The last book in the Bible, a symbolic book about the end of the world, is the Apocalypse or the Book of __Revelation__.

11. The Gospels' writers are the __Evangelists__.

12. __Inspiration__ is the action of God that moves people to communicate what God wants made known.

1. 1
2. 2 7
3. G O D
4. A C T S
5. F A I T H
6. G O S P E L
7. L E T T E R S
8. S Y N O P T I C
9. D I S C O U R S E
10. R E V E L A T I O N
11. E V A N G E L I S T S
12. I N S P I R A T I O N

24

Chapter 3   Enriching the Faith Experience

Use the following activities to enrich a lesson or to replace an activity with one that better meets the needs of your class.

1. **BLM 16** Use BLM 16 **Quotations from Jesus** to make a set of Gospel quotations. Cut them apart and put them in a box. Have the students draw one and read it as Jesus' personal message to them. Let them ponder its meaning for them in silence and then respond in their reflection notebook.

2. Allow students time to work on their Scripture booklets.

3. Help the students research one of these topics:
   - the difference between Jewish, Protestant, and Catholic Bibles
   - versions of the Bible
   - the Dead Sea Scrolls

4. Discuss the meaning of the saying "You might be the only Bible some people will ever read."

5. Encourage the students to memorize Scripture. Give them a list of key passages. Hold contests and award prizes.

6. Write on cards the abbreviations of the books of the New Testament. Show them to the students and let them tell the name of the book or one fact about it.

The World Jesus Lived In
JESUS THE NAZARENE

Faith Focus
Jesus was a Jewish man who lived in first-century Palestine during the Roman occupation.

Reflecting on the Faith Experience
Take a few moments to reflect prayerfully before preparing the lesson.

Listening

"Jesus the Nazorean, the King of the Jews."

John 19:19

Reflecting

Thomas Hart in *To Know and Follow Jesus: Contemporary Christology,* offers this alternative version of the Caesarea Philippi incident: "Jesus came with his disciples one day to Caesarea Philippi, and he said to them, 'Who do you say that I am?' And they said to him, 'You are the Revealer. You are the absolute, unsurpassable victory of God's self-bestowal. You are the second person of the Blessed Trinity. You are the unbroken contact with the Ground of Being. You are the man for others. You are the Word Incarnate. You are the proleptic manifestation of the eschaton.'

"And Jesus said, 'What?'"

Before Jesus became the glorified risen Lord, he was a man of flesh and blood who experienced life much as we do. A Jewish man, living in first-century Palestine, Jesus had a family, neighbors, a country, and a religion. The history of his people was his history. The culture of Palestine and the beliefs and practices of the Jewish faith shaped his thinking, his attitudes, and his actions. Political unrest and various social and religious groups were part of his daily life.

The environment in which Jesus lived for about 30 years influenced his teachings and his stories. It explained his actions, people's reaction to him, and what happened

to him. An understanding of the religious, social, and political world at the time of Jesus makes for a better understanding of him and his teachings. It brings the Gospel to life. How much more impact the parable of the Good Samaritan has, for instance, when one is aware of the hatred Jesus' people bore toward the Samaritans.

Jesus' life was limited to a particular time and place. Yet his message is for all people who would ever live on earth. The challenge of Jesus' disciples is to distill his universal truths and values and translate them for the contemporary world. Through study and prayer, we are able to carry out Christ's mandate to teach all nations. We act confidently, knowing that because Jesus is more than mortal man, he keeps his promise to be with us always, until the end of the ages.

Jesus is with us as we teach our students about the circumstances of his human life. As they become familiar with the world Jesus experienced and relate it to their own lives, Jesus becomes more real to them, someone who understands their situations and is keenly interested in them.

If Jesus were in my shoes, how would he act with my family, at my workplace, in my neighborhood?

Responding

Jesus, help me make you more real to my students.

Scripture for Further Reflection

Hebrews 2:17 Jesus had to become like us in every way, so that he might be a merciful high priest and eliminate our sins.

Preparing for the Faith Experience

Scripture in This Chapter

Deuteronomy 6:4–5 The Lord alone is God.

John 1:14 The Word became one of us.

John 1:17 Grace and truth came through Jesus Christ.

Church Documents

Catechism of the Catholic Church. The themes of this chapter correspond to the following paragraphs: **122, 423.**

General Directory for Catechesis #199. Special attention needs to be given to catechesis in relation to the Jewish religion. Religious instruction and catechesis should promote understanding and dialogue. It is especially important that an objective of catechesis be to overcome every form of anti-Semitism.

Dogmatic Constitution on Divine Revelation #12 (Second Vatican Council). To understand Scripture, attention must be given to literary form and the intention of the writer in his particular circumstances of time and culture.

The Jewish People and Their Sacred Scriptures in the Christian Bible #57. The New Testament does not add anything to what the Old Testament says about the Promised Land, but we should never forget that a specific land was promised by God to Israel and received as a heritage.

Notes on the Correct Way to Present the Jews and Judaism #8 (Commission for Religious Relations with the Jews). An exclusively negative picture of the Pharisees is likely to be inaccurate and unjust. If Jesus shows himself severe towards the Pharisees, it is because he is closer to them than to other contemporary Jewish groups.

Gather and Go Forth

Find catechist instruction for Gather and Go Forth student pages 33–34 on T322–T323.

Enriching the Faith Experience

Use the activities at the end of the chapter to enrich a lesson or to replace an activity with one that better meets the needs of your class. Bookmark www.christourlife.com to find Web BLMs for this chapter.

Bulletin Board

A suggestion for a bulletin-board design for this chapter is pictured.

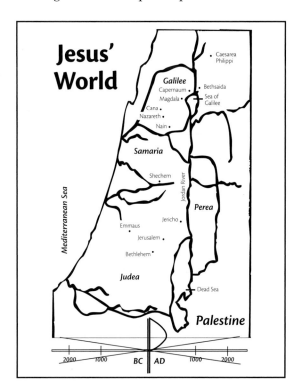

LEARNING OUTCOMES

The students will be able to

- name and locate Palestine's three main regions and its geographical features.
- describe the political situation in Palestine.
- name the various religious groups among the Jewish people.

Words to Know

Gentiles   **Pharisees**

See the Glossary for definitions.

Materials

- Globe or world map
- Map of Palestine from the Lesson Pullouts in the back of the student book [see separate poster with TE] or a simple drawing of Palestine, showing Galilee, Samaria, and Judea

Before You Begin

1. *Shema* is the first word in Hebrew of Deuteronomy 6:4: "Hear, O Israel! The LORD is our God, the LORD alone!" The Shema is recited twice a day, in the morning and in the evening. The first part of it is also written on the scroll inside a mezuzah, and is recited when entering and leaving a home. It is the main expression of the Jewish belief in the oneness of God.

2. Do not make the students responsible for knowing all the facts in this chapter. Most of the information is presented only to set the scene for the life of Jesus and to give the students an idea of his world. The information will make future lessons more meaningful.

3. An alternative plan for Sharing in Day One and Day Two would be to have students present the five main sections of the chapter.

Jerusalem, Israel. ❯

CHAPTER 4

The World Jesus Lived In

Jesus the Nazarene

The Land Jesus Walked

You probably eat with knives, forks, and spoons, and not your fingers. Your parents will not be choosing a husband or wife for you. Some customs that you would find strange are perfectly normal for people in other times and countries. The way you live, your attitudes, and values are largely determined by the country and time in which you live. What else determines what you are like?

When the Son of God became man, he chose to live 2,000 years ago in a country in the Middle East called Palestine. The United States is more than 230 years old, but consider how life has changed since the time of George Washington. Imagine then the difference between the world that shaped Jesus and your world. Knowing about life during his time will help you understand Jesus and the Gospels.

During Jesus' time, Palestine was as large as Vermont and had three main areas: Galilee in the north, Samaria, and Judea in the south. (To remember the order of Galilee, Samaria, and Judea, think "God Sent Jesus.") Nazareth, a town in the hills of Galilee, was the place where Jesus grew up. During his public ministry, his home base was Capernaum, a town near the Sea of Galilee. Jesus' life began in Bethlehem and ended in Jerusalem, both in Judea.

Galilee is mountainous and beautiful. The Sea of Galilee (also called Lake Gennesareth) is to

the east, and Mount Hermon is to the north. Although most of Galilee was rural during Jesus' time, major trade routes passed through its large trading cities. Greek and Roman culture were popular in Galilee. Many Galilean Jews were originally of non-Jewish origin. For this reason, Judeans looked down on Galileans.

Samaria was avoided by Jewish people when they traveled. The Samaritans were considered heretics because they had intermarried with foreigners and worshiped in their own temple on Mount Gerizim instead of at the Temple in Jerusalem.

Judea is a dry, hot land. The Dead Sea is to the east, and wilderness is to the south. Jerusalem was the capital city where Israel's kings had lived. It was also the holy city because the Temple was there. Jerusalem is sacred to Jews, Christians, and Muslims.

To the west of Palestine is the Mediterranean Sea. Within Palestine the Jordan River flows south through the Sea of Galilee and into the Dead Sea.

When Jesus lived, towns in Palestine were surrounded by walls. Food and crafts were sold in markets just outside the walls. Every night the city gates were locked, and guards kept watch.

(27)

Day One: Divide the class into five groups and have each choose a section to present **(The Land Jesus Walked, The Political Scene, Some Religious Groups, Jesus' Religion, Daily Life in Palestine)** on pages 27–30. Encourage creativity. Let them spend 10 minutes reading and planning how to share the material. Have the first group give its presentation.

Day Two: Review the regions and land features of Palestine, and then have the rest of the groups give their presentations.

Centering

Link the last lesson with today's lesson.

✦ **In the last lesson you learned that Scripture helps us know about Jesus.**

✦ **Today you will learn about the time and country he lived in. This will help you to understand Scripture better.**

Sharing

1. Have a student read aloud the first paragraph of **The Land Jesus Walked** on page 27. **Who has met someone from another country? What are some of their customs that are different from ours?** [Lead the students in a discussion of the question.]

2. Have a student read aloud the second paragraph of this section. **What are some of the questions you have about when Jesus lived?**

3. Ask a volunteer to locate Palestine on a globe or map. **What two continents is Palestine a gateway between?** (Europe and Asia)

4. Have several students read aloud the rest of **The Land Jesus Walked** on page 27.

✦ Refer to the Map of Palestine from the Lesson Pullouts in the back of the student book. [See separate poster with TE.]

✦ **Where in Palestine would you prefer to live? Why?**

5. Elaborate to the students about daily life in Palestine. **During the day, the squares and alleys of the town were crowded with people: children playing, merchants selling their wares, beggars looking for food or coins. The people greeted each other with** *shalom* **which means "peace" and kissed instead of shaking hands.**

❮ The Western Wall in Jerusalem.

The Political Scene

When Jesus lived, Palestine was occupied by Rome, which had conquered it in 63 B.C. During Jesus' lifetime, Augustus Caesar and then his stepson, Tiberius Caesar, were the Roman emperors. Herod the Great was king of Palestine until shortly after Jesus' birth. Although he was a great builder and rebuilt the Temple, he is remembered most for his cruelty. He killed many of his family for fear that they would overthrow his rule. After his death, Palestine was divided among his three sons: Archelaus, Herod Antipas, and Philip. Archelaus ruled Judea and Samaria until Augustus replaced him with Roman procurators such as Pontius Pilate, who sentenced Jesus to death. Herod Antipas, whom Jesus called "the fox," ruled Galilee. Philip ruled the region east of Galilee.

In general, Rome respected Jewish religious practices. Jewish men, for instance, did not have to serve in the army because their religion did not permit them to mix with **Gentiles**, or non-Jews. However, the Jewish people resented the presence of Roman troops, Roman laws, and Roman taxes. Jewish men who collected taxes for Rome were the least popular men in town. These tax collectors, also called publicans, were allowed

Augustus Caesar.

to keep any money they collected beyond their quota.

Some Religious Groups

The **Pharisees** were largely middle-class Jews. They were known for their love of the Torah, or the Law, the first five books of the Bible. Some schools of Pharisees interpreted the Law strictly and added 613 regulations. The Pharisees believed in angels and in our resurrection. The Gospels show Jesus scolding some of them for stressing external observances instead of a spirit of love and worship. The Pharisees, however, were sincerely seeking holiness. They preserved the Jewish religion after Jerusalem was destroyed by Rome in A.D. 70. The scholarly teachers among the Pharisees were called scribes.

The Sadducees were wealthy and powerful political leaders. Most were priests. They worked closely with Rome and, unlike the Pharisees, did not believe in resurrection or in adding to the Law. The Sanhedrin was a group of 71 Jewish men in Judea who served as a supreme council. The chief high priest presided over it. He was not only a spiritual leader but almost a king. Caiaphas was the high priest at the end of Jesus' life, assisted by his father-in-law, Annas.

Zealots were freedom fighters who sometimes used violence to overthrow Rome's control of Palestine. The Essenes were men unhappy with the way Jewish faith was lived. Seeking a pure life, many withdrew to the desert. There they lived in communities, doing penance and waiting for the coming of God.

(28) UNIT 1

---

6. Direct the students to read silently **The Political Scene** on page 28. **What were the advantages and disadvantages of the Roman occupation?** (Rome didn't interfere with the practices of the Jewish people and protected them. The Jewish people had to obey Roman laws and pay Roman taxes.)

7. Have the students refer to the poster **Palestine** in the back of their books. Point out the territory governed by the following rulers:

a. Augustus Caesar (All)

b. Tiberius Caesar (All)

c. Herod the Great (Palestine)

d. Herod Antipas (Galilee)

e. Archelaus (Judea and Samaria)

f. Pontius Pilate (Judea and Samaria)

g. Philip (Region east of Galilee)

8. Have the students read **Some Religious Groups** on page 28.

✦ **This section identifies six groups that were important when Jesus lived.**

✦ **For each of these groups, underline a word or phrase that summarizes its identity.** (Pharisees—*Law*; Scribes—*teachers*; Sadducees—*priests*; Sanhedrin—*supreme council*; Zealots—*freedom fighters*; Essenes—*lived in communities*)

9. Write the headings *Pharisees* and *Sadducees* on the board. **In what ways are these groups different from each another?** [Have the students list the differences under the headings.]

Pharisees	Sadducees
laymen	priests
middle class	upper class
added laws to the Torah	were against adding laws to the Torah
believed in resurrection	did not believe in resurrection

10. Have the students take turns being a pilot flying over Palestine.
Have them comment on the view from the plane pointing out geographical features.

11. Have a student describe a group studied in this lesson.
After the description, have another student name the group.

Acting

 Lead the students in the prayer activity Respond on page 31.

CHECKPOINT

- Were the learning outcomes achieved?
- Do the students need more practice describing life in Jesus' time?

Day Two   Religion and Life in Jesus' Day   Student pages 29–31

LEARNING OUTCOMES

The students will be able to

- explain how Jesus practiced his religion.
- identify some of the Jewish feasts.
- describe what daily life was like in Jesus' time.

Key Terms

Hanukkah—an eight-day Jewish festival that recalls the fight for religious freedom against the Syrians and the rededication of the Temple in 165 B.C.

Passover—the Jewish feast at the end of spring that commemorates the Exodus

Pentecost—the Jewish feast of the Ten Commandments and of thanksgiving for the harvest

Rosh Hashana—the Jewish New Year, celebrated with prayer and solemnity; it begins a 10-day period of reflection that ends with Yom Kippur

Sabbath—the Lord's Day; a day of rest; Saturday

Tabernacles (Sukkot)—the fall Jewish feast of seven or eight days to recall the time the Israelites lived in tents (booths) in the desert

Yom Kippur—the Day of Atonement; day of fasting and repentance

Materials

- Flash cards: *Passover, Pentecost, Tabernacles, Rosh Hashana, Yom Kippur, Hanukkah*
- Paper
- Felt-tipped markers or paint

Before You Begin

1. The following information may help answer students questions:
  - *Kosher* means "good and proper." Many Jewish people eat only kosher food as prescribed by the law of Moses.
  - Judaism today has three main branches: Orthodox, Conservative (moderate), and Reform (open to changing tradition).
  - The fringed prayer shawl, or *tallit*, is worn by male worshipers as a reminder to observe God's law and achieve holiness.
  - *Mezuzah* means "doorpost." It is a small box that contains the Shema, from Deuteronomy 6:4–9; 11:13–21 on one side and the word *Shaddai*, The Mighty One, on the other side. The mezuzah is placed on the upper third of the doorway. It is touched when entering or leaving the home and the Shema is recited.
  - Phylacteries are strapped to the head as a symbol of intellectual loyalty, and to the hand as a reminder to serve God with all one's might. They are boxes containing passages from the Old Testament. The straps are wound seven times around the arm, three times around the hand, and three times around the ring finger and middle finger.
  - Yarmulkes, or skullcaps worn by Jewish males, show reverence to God. It became a custom to wear them after the time of Jesus.

2. If student presentations are used to teach this chapter, then Sharing #2 and #3 on Jewish feasts will not be covered. You might teach them in the next class.

3. Matzoh, unleavened Jewish bread, could be offered to the students as part of Sharing #4 or at the end of class.

Centering

1. Discuss with the students the Jewish background of Jesus. **What nationality were Jesus and his parents Mary and Joseph?** (Jewish) **What was their religion?** (Jewish)

2. Link the last lesson with today's lesson. **To understand Jesus, we must understand not only what it meant to live in first-century Palestine, but also what it meant to be Jewish. What do you already know about the Jewish people?**

Sharing

1. Have the students read silently **Jesus' Religion** page 29.

✦ **What customs did Jesus practice?** (praying at home, praying before eating, praying the Shema, touching the mezuzah, putting on a prayer shawl and phylacteries for prayer, going to the Temple for major feasts, resting on the Sabbath, praying at the synagogue) **What are some religious customs that you practice?**

✦ **Like the Jewish people, we pray before meals. We have other similar customs. What are our holy water fonts like?** (mezuzahs) **priests' vestments?** (phylacteries) **the Lord's Prayer?** (the Shema) **our cathedral?** (the Temple) **our parish church?** (the synagogue)

2. Introduce to the students the three major Jewish feasts.

✦ **What are our greatest religious holidays?** (Christmas and Easter) **What do these celebrate?** (Jesus' birth, Jesus' Resurrection) **They are related to the greatest happening of our religious history: the coming of the Redeemer. The three greatest Jewish feasts are related to their greatest happening: the Exodus.** [Post the flash card of each feast as you explain it.]

✦ ***Passover* commemorates the Exodus. A special meal is eaten during which the Exodus is retold.**

Jesus' Religion

Jesus was Jewish. Jewish families prayed many prayers together at home. They prayed before and after eating. Morning and evening they prayed the Shema, the main commandment:

> Hear, O Israel! The LORD is our God, the LORD alone! Therefore, you shall love the LORD, your God, with all your heart, and with all your soul, and with all your strength.
>
> Deuteronomy 6:4–5

A Moment with Jesus

Pause for a moment and silently read the Scripture passage above. Imagine Jesus learning this prayer and praying it each day. Take a moment to reflect on how you express your belief in God each day. Ask Jesus to help you love God with all your heart, soul, and strength.

On entering and leaving a house, Jewish people touched the mezuzah. It was a small case on the right post of a doorway that held a copy of the Shema. At prayer, devout men put a prayer shawl on their heads and strapped small boxes (phylacteries) to their foreheads and arms. These boxes contained the Word of God. People greeted one another by saying *shalom*, which means "peace."

Everyone who was able traveled to the Temple in Jerusalem to observe the three major feasts: Passover, Pentecost, and Tabernacles. The Temple, the symbol of the Jewish faith, was the only place where sacrifices were offered. It was a huge and majestic building. Twenty men were needed to open one of its thirteen gates. Twenty thousand people worked there. During Jesus' time, the Temple was undergoing an expansion ordered by Herod the Great. In

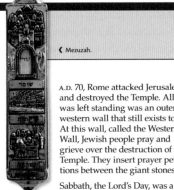

❬ Mezuzah.

A.D. 70, Rome attacked Jerusalem and destroyed the Temple. All that was left standing was an outer western wall that still exists today. At this wall, called the Western Wall, Jewish people pray and grieve over the destruction of the Temple. They insert prayer petitions between the giant stones.

Sabbath, the Lord's Day, was a day of strict rest. Among forbidden activities were tying a rope, putting out a lamp, and walking more than a half mile. Sabbath services were held at local synagogues. These were the centers of prayer, education, and social life in the towns. The scrolls of the Torah were read and preached there.

The Law declared what made a person unclean or unfit for worship. Actions such as touching a sick or dead person and dealing with Gentiles required special prayers, washings, or passage of time before the person became clean.

Maurice Denis, *Jesus Christ, Mary and Joseph*, early 20th century. ❭

CHAPTER 4 (29)

✦ **On *Pentecost*, the Jewish people celebrate the Ten Commandments and give thanks for the harvest. It was on this feast that the Holy Spirit came to the apostles.**

✦ **The feast of *Tabernacles*, or *Sukkot*, in the fall recalls the time the Israelites lived in tents in the desert. Some Jewish people make booths out of branches and live in them during the seven or eight days of the feast.**

✦ **These are the three major Jewish feasts. There are other feasts.**

3. Show the flash cards for *Rosh Hashana, Yom Kippur,* and *Hanukkah.*

✦ ***Rosh Hashana* is the Jewish New Year. It is celebrated by prayer**

and solemnity and begins a 10-day period of reflection.

✦ **The most sacred day in the Jewish faith, except for the Sabbath, is *Yom Kippur*, the Day of Atonement. This is a day of fasting and repentance. What period of our Church year does it remind you of?** (Lent)

✦ ***Hanukkah*, which falls near Christmas, is the "feast of lights." Long ago when the Jewish people were persecuted by the Syrians and their Temple vandalized, they fought for religious freedom and won. The Temple was rededicated. A tradition says that although there was only enough oil to burn in the Temple for one** day, it lasted for eight days. On each of the eight nights of Hanukkah, Jewish people light a candle on the eight-branched menorah.

4. Call on volunteers to read aloud **Daily Life in Palestine** on page 30.

✦ Divide the students into groups of three or four. Have them discuss what they found surprising and what would have been difficult for them and why.

✦ Have one student from each group give a brief report of their discussion.

Acting

1. Lead the students in **A Moment with Jesus** on page 29.

✦ Allow sufficient time for silent reflection.

✦ Mention that we, too, believe in the one God.

2. Distribute paper and have the students print and decorate the Shema.
They can glue the prayer in their reflection notebook or display it at home.

3. Choose or let the students choose an activity from Reach Out on page 31.

CHECKPOINT ✓

• Were the learning outcomes achieved?

• Do any sections need further clarification?

Daily Life in Palestine

Imagine that you lived in Palestine when Jesus did. Your house is made of clay bricks or stones held together with mud and straw. Its one room has a dirt floor. At night, you sleep on a mat on the dirt floor. Your pillow is a piece of wood or a stone. In hot weather, you climb the outside steps up to the roof to sleep. The roof is made of sticks bound by long grass and covered with earth. In your house are a table, a spinning wheel, and a wooden bowl for measuring grain. Since there are no windows, an olive-oil lamp burns all day on a stand. At the far end of your house, a cave shelters your goat and donkey.

You probably belong to a large family. Your father is a farmer, a craftsman, or a fisherman. He has a beard and large brown eyes. He wears a sleeveless gown covered by a long tunic that is fringed at the bottom and tied with a belt. A white cloth on his head is held in place by a cord. A heavy cloak made of camel hair or goat hair serves him as a coat or a blanket. He leads the family prayers. You and your mother are considered his property.

Your mother cooks outside, grinding grain and baking bread. She wears a decorated tunic and sandals, and she never goes out without a veil over her face. She looks forward to her daily walk to the town well. There she meets and chats with other women before carrying home her water jug on her head. Your mother is not allowed to know how to read or write, but she memorizes Scripture from the synagogue service.

If you are a boy, you go to synagogue school. There a rabbi teaches you to read and write by studying Scripture. Your father teaches you his trade. If you are a girl, your mother prepares you to be a good wife. You hope to have many sons. Your parents will arrange a marriage for you. You might not see your husband until your wedding day.

You do not attend public entertainment because the Gentiles are there. Your life revolves around prayer and religious celebrations, especially those that mark stages of life. Weddings can last seven days. For funerals, even poor people hire flute players and mourners for a procession to the stone tombs.

You eat twice a day while sitting cross-legged outside on the ground. Instead of a fork or spoon, you use your hands. Besides bread, your meals include honey, spiced foods, cheese, vegetables, fruit, and fish. You seldom have meat or eggs. Water and wine are the usual drinks.

You probably speak Aramaic, but you also know some Hebrew for prayer and perhaps some Greek, which is the language of the land.

❰ James Tissot, *The Presentation of Christ in the Temple*, 1886–1894, watercolor.

LEARNING OUTCOMES

The students will be able to

- apply knowledge of the world Jesus lived in to passages of the Gospels.
- explain that Jesus lives in us.
- describe how they can be Jesus for the world today.

Materials

- Bibles or New Testaments
- BLM 18
- Recorded music: Find suggestions for Chapter 4 on page T517.

Before You Begin

Christ revealed this mystery: the One God, the God who created heaven and earth, lives in our hearts. This truth adds new dimensions to human relations, the life of the community, and our world sorely in need of peace and justice. With God hidden in us, we have power to transform history.

Centering _____

Link the last lesson with today's lesson.

✦ **Imagine what someone in the year 3000 would think if he or she found a newspaper from our century with the headline "New York Yankees Slaughter San Francisco Giants." If that person of the future didn't know about our baseball teams, what ideas might the person get from the words?**

✦ **Today you will see that the background information you have learned is very useful for reading the Gospels.**

Sharing _____

1. **BLM 18** Have the students work on BLM 18 **Using What You Know** individually or in groups. [Check their answers.]

2. Explain to the students that Jesus could become a man only at one point in time.

   ✦ **Jesus had to live in a particular time and place, but his life and message are for people in every century and every nation. He lives on in his Church, touching people through the sacraments and through you.**

   ✦ **Jesus reaches *all* people through us.**

   ✦ Have a student locate and read aloud John 14:23.

3. Discuss with the students Jewish history and customs. **Why is it important to study Jewish history and customs?** (to understand Jesus and Scripture better)

Acting _____

1. Have the students imagine Jesus in their shoes.

   ✦ Take them through the day, beginning with getting out of bed. Pause so they can reflect on how Jesus would have acted in the situations they met or will meet during the day.

   ✦ Let some students role-play some of these situations or make up skits in which Jesus is a teenager.

2. Invite the students to sing or listen to a song about being like Jesus for the world.

CHECKPOINT

- Were the learning outcomes achieved?

LEARNING OUTCOMES

The students will be able to

- review salvation history.
- trace the history of the Jewish people since the time of Jesus.
- demonstrate an understanding of the key concepts in this chapter.

Key Term

salvation history—the story of how God entered into history and carried out the divine plan to save all people

Materials

- BLM 19
- BLM 20 Quiz
- String or masking tape at least 20 feet long
- Large card with *0* written on it

Before You Begin

1. Salvation history began when God promised redemption, freedom from sin and death, to our first parents in paradise. How God prepared for the fulfillment of this promise is the story of the Old Testament. The New Testament is the story of how Jesus actually accomplished redemption. But salvation history continues in the life of the Church until all life and creation are united in Christ through the Spirit and brought to the Father at the end of time.

2. You might invite a Jewish person to speak on the practice of the Jewish faith.

3. When planning today's lesson, keep in mind that Day Four is when the students take the quiz for this chapter. Reserve time at the end of class for this assessment. The quiz can also be administered on Day Five.

CHAPTER 4 Summary

Remember

Who do we believe Jesus of Nazareth is?
And the Word became flesh
and made his dwelling among us,
and we saw his glory,
the glory as of the Father's only Son,
full of grace and truth.

John 1:14

Respond

Create this scene in your mind. You are sitting with Jesus on a grassy hillside overlooking the Sea of Galilee. Hundreds of brilliant wildflowers surround you. Before you the blue lake sparkles in the sun. You hear the water lapping against the shore. The hills across the lake are also blue. You feel very comfortable and relaxed next to Jesus.

What would Jesus say to you? What would you say to him? Think about it. Then write your conversation in your reflection notebook.

Reach Out

1. Find out what the Holy Land is like today. Write a report that includes geographical, political, religious, and cultural aspects of the Holy Land.

2. Ask a Jewish person to tell you about his or her religious customs and feasts. You might be able to visit a Jewish temple, or synagogue.

3. Make a relief map of Palestine out of dough and paint it.

4. The Gospel of Mark has Aramaic phrases scattered throughout. Find the meaning of these by looking up the references:

   Talitha koum (Mark 5:41)

   Ephphatha! (Mark 7:34)

   Golgotha (Mark 15:22)

   Eloi, Eloi, lema sabachthani? (Mark 15:34)

5. Research how the Christian religion has been adapted to other cultures.

   Visit a Byzantine Catholic church or other Eastern rite church.

   Attend a liturgy in a parish where the dominant culture is different from yours.

   Ask people about Catholic customs in other countries.

6. Write the story of Jesus' life as if it were set in our country. What if Jesus had been born in our country and was living now? Where would he live? What would his life be like? How would he teach people? How would he die?

Words to Know

Gentiles   Pharisees

31

Centering

1. Link the last lesson with today's lesson.
   - ✦ **You have learned about the Gospels that tell us about Jesus. You have learned about the land and customs where Jesus lived.**
   - ✦ **Today you will learn the highlights of the history of Jesus' people, the Jewish people.**

2. Run string or tape along the room for a timeline. Have a student hold a card marked *0* and stand in the middle.
   - ✦ **What do b.c. and a.d. stand for?** (B.C. means "Before Christ," and A.D. stands for *Anno Domini,* which means "in the year of the Lord," or the Christian era.)
   - ✦ **We divide all history by Jesus' coming. There was some error in calculating the birth of Jesus. It is thought that he was actually born around 4 b.c. The years before Christ are from highest to lowest.**
   - ✦ **It took a long time for God to prepare people for the coming of Jesus.** [Write *salvation history* on the board.] **How would you define *salvation history*?** (Salvation history is the story of God's love for people. It tells how God has entered into history and carried out the divine plan to save all people.)

Sharing

1. **BLM 19** Divide the class into groups. Give each student BLM 19 **Salvation History.**
   - ✦ Unscramble the names on the timeline and write your answers on the corresponding blanks.
   - ✦ After you have unscrambled the words, write a summary of the main events of each time period, mentioning the people listed.

2. Check the groups' answers and have the groups read its summaries.

3. Read aloud to the students The Prophets: A Summary. As you read, have a student place other students along the timeline to represent the people in boldface. Have the groups check its summary.

The Prophets: A Summary

God called **Abraham,** the first patriarch, about 1850 B.C. Abraham showed faith in the One God by his willingness to move to Canaan and to sacrifice his only son **Isaac.** Isaac had two sons, **Jacob** and Esau. **Joseph,** one of Jacob's 12 sons, was sold into slavery in Egypt. During a famine, Joseph fed the people, and Jacob (renamed Israel) and his family settled in Egypt. After many years, the Israelites were forced into slavery. They lived in Egypt for about 300 years until **Moses** led them out around 1280 B.C. After wandering for about 40 years, the freed people entered Canaan, the Promised Land, under **Joshua's** leadership.

For about 200 years the Israelites were ruled by judges. Two who led them to victory were Samson and **Samuel.** In 1020, **Samuel** anointed **Saul** as first king of Israel. The greatest king, **David,** ruled from 1000 to 961 B.C.. His son **Solomon** died in 922 B.C. After him, the kingdom was divided. In 722 B.C., the northern kingdom of Israel fell to the Assyrians. In 587 B.C., the southern kingdom of Judah fell to the Babylonians, and the Judeans were exiled to Babylon. Forty years later the Jewish people returned home. The prophets spoke or wrote God's Word. **Amos** called the people to social justice, and **Isaiah** told them of God's holiness and the Messiah. **Jeremiah** spoke of the new covenant. **Ezekiel** urged the people to hope. **John the Baptist,** the last and greatest prophet, preached repentance in immediate preparation for the Messiah.

4. Lead the students through the Summary and the Review Activities, pages 31–32.

5. **BLM 20** Distribute and administer BLM 20 **Chapter 4 Quiz.**
   Use this as an opportunity to assess the students' understanding of the main concepts of the chapter. If there is not sufficient time for the students to complete the quiz, consider moving it to Day Five.

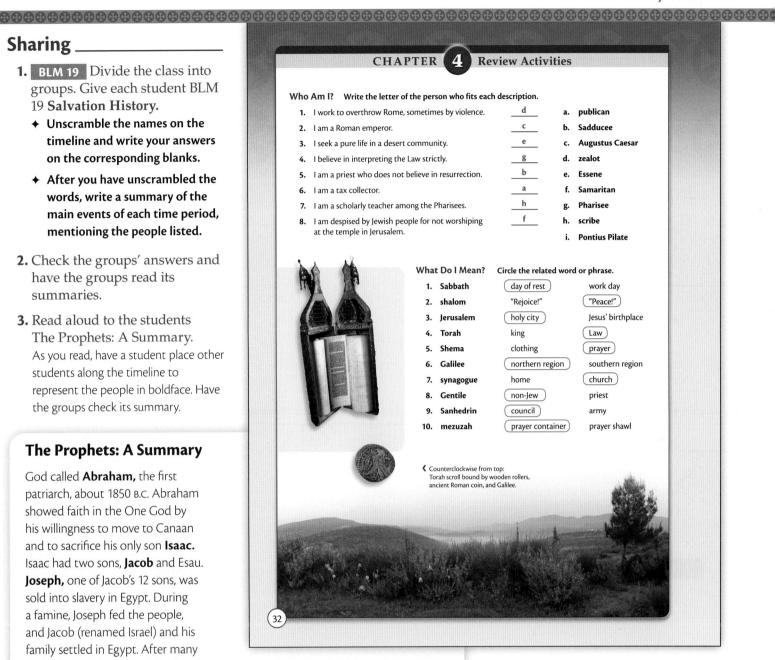

CHAPTER 4 Review Activities

Who Am I? Write the letter of the person who fits each description.

1. I work to overthrow Rome, sometimes by violence. — d
2. I am a Roman emperor. — c
3. I seek a pure life in a desert community. — e
4. I believe in interpreting the Law strictly. — g
5. I am a priest who does not believe in resurrection. — b
6. I am a tax collector. — a
7. I am a scholarly teacher among the Pharisees. — h
8. I am despised by Jewish people for not worshiping at the temple in Jerusalem. — f

a. publican
b. Sadducee
c. Augustus Caesar
d. zealot
e. Essene
f. Samaritan
g. Pharisee
h. scribe
i. Pontius Pilate

What Do I Mean? Circle the related word or phrase.

1. Sabbath — (day of rest) — work day
2. shalom — "Rejoice!" — ("Peace!")
3. Jerusalem — (holy city) — Jesus' birthplace
4. Torah — king — (Law)
5. Shema — clothing — (prayer)
6. Galilee — (northern region) — southern region
7. synagogue — home — (church)
8. Gentile — (non-Jew) — priest
9. Sanhedrin — (council) — army
10. mezuzah — (prayer container) — prayer shawl

❮ Counterclockwise from top: Torah scroll bound by wooden rollers, ancient Roman coin, and Galilee.

32

Acting _____

1. Have the students compose one-line prayers based on something they learned in class.

   Ask for volunteers to share their prayers with the class.

2. Have the students reflect on how God has worked in their lives so far.

   ✦ **Imagine how in the next fifteen years God will continue to bring you close and help you grow into the person you are meant to be.**

   ✦ Volunteers might share their thoughts in groups or with the class. Others might choose to record their thoughts in their reflection notebooks.

   ✦ **Your personal history is extremely important to God and to the entire people of God.**

3. At the end of class, have the students tear out and take home pages 31–32.

CHECKPOINT

- Were the learning outcomes achieved?

Day Five   Extending the Chapter

Gather and Go Forth

Lead students through pages 33–34 in the student book. Find catechist instruction on T322–T323.
Materials: Bibles

Use the following suggestions to create an additional lesson for Day Five.

1. Remind the students to take home pages 31–32 to share what they are learning with their families.

2. Incorporate any unused BLMs from the week's chapter.

3. Consider the time of the liturgical year and use the appropriate Special Seasons and Lessons. SSLs begin on page T369.

4. Visit www.christourlife.com to find additional activities for Extending the Chapter.

5. Use activities from Enriching the Faith Experience.

6. Guide the students in a prayerful discussion of Sunday's Scripture readings. Visit www.christourlife.com for more information.

Chapter 4   Enriching the Faith Experience

Use the following activities to enrich a lesson or to replace an activity with one that better meets the needs of your class.

1. Have the students report on a topic from this chapter that interests them.

2. Put together an imaginary time capsule from first-century Palestine.

3. Have the students make a plaque or poster with the Shema lettered on it.

4. Have the students begin a class "Christian Scriptures Glossary" with illustrations. Give volunteers one page of the glossary to complete.

5. Write terms in squares on a grid and cover them with numbered pieces of paper. Have team members alternate in choosing a pair of squares to uncover. If the words match and the student defines the term, the team gets a point.

6. Have students draw or illustrate a map of the places they learned about in this chapter. Encourage them to decorate it anyway they wish.

7. Have students imagine that they lived in Palestine around the time of Jesus. Ask them to write a few paragraphs describing what their life is like. Have the students refer to what they learned in this chapter.

8. **Web BLM** Have the students review the terms and concepts from the chapter by using Web BLM Chapter 4-A **The Name of the Game.** Divide the students into two teams, Alpha (beginning) and Omega (end). Read a definition from the BLM and have the first student from team Alpha give the answer. If he or she cannot answer, ask the first person from team Omega. If a student gives the correct answer when first asked, the team receives one point. If a member of the opposite team answers the question, that team receives two points. When a correct answer is given, have the student write the answer on the board. The team with the most points wins.

The Early Life of Jesus
JESUS THE SON OF MARY AND JOSEPH

Faith Focus

The Infancy Narratives reveal that Jesus is the Lord, the Son of God who saved us.

Reflecting on the Faith Experience

Take a few moments to reflect prayerfully before preparing the lesson.

Listening

> For God so loved the world
> that he gave his only Son . . .
>
> *John 3:16*

Reflecting

Certain truths are conveyed most effectively through the symbols of art. The familiar pieces of a nativity set—the figures of Mary, Joseph, the infant, the shepherds and magi, the animals, the star, and the crib—speak eloquently of our faith. They proclaim that God became human for love of us. And because of their religious message, manger scenes are sometimes banned from public places.

The symbols of literature are equally compelling. The evangelists knew this. They presented the birth and infancy of Jesus not as bare historical facts but as moving stories that touch our hearts. Skillfully they shaped their narratives to their themes and their audience. Through them, they shared the significance of Jesus Christ.

In proclaiming Jesus as Lord to the Jewish Christians, the author of Matthew's Gospel makes use of their heritage. He opens by tracing Jesus' lineage from Abraham, the first Jewish person. He weaves references to the Old Testament throughout his narratives. Portraying the Savior as the new Moses, he describes how Jesus, like Moses, came out of Egypt after being persecuted by a king. Jesus relives the Exodus of Israel. From Matthew's version of Jesus' early life, a Jewish Christian would identify Jesus as the Promised One.

The author of Luke apparently writes mainly for Gentile Christians. He traces Jesus' lineage back to Adam. (Luke 3:23–38) But Luke shows how God's promises to Israel are fulfilled in Jesus. The accounts of the birth announcements of Jesus and John and the three canticles he includes (Mary's, Zechariah's, and Simeon's) are based on the Old Testament. In addition, Luke teaches that salvation is extended to all people. He stresses Jesus' ministry to the poor, sinners, and outcasts, like the shepherds to whom an angel declares the birth of a Savior.

Nativity sets and the Infancy Narratives have meaning only for people who believe that Mary's Son accomplished our salvation by dying and rising. It is the Easter people who are addressed in the words of the Christmas carol, "O come, all ye faithful, joyful and triumphant." Those of us who have faith in the Resurrection believe that the baby of Bethlehem, Mary's baby, is divine. We adore him and pray that the Holy Spirit who formed him in Mary's womb will form us into his image.

What does Christmas mean to me?

Responding

Holy Spirit, help my students see the realities mirrored in religious symbols so they may be inspired to bring Jesus forth to the world.

Scripture for Further Reflection

Isaiah 35 God comes to save us and to bring us everlasting joy.

Luke 1:26–38 Mary conceives the Son of the Most High.

Hebrews 1:1–4 God speaks to us through his Son who sustains all things by his mighty Word.

Preparing for the Faith Experience

Scripture in This Chapter

Matthew 1:18—2:23 The birth of Jesus.

Luke 1:5—2:25 Mary says yes to the angel Gabriel. Jesus is born in Bethlehem.

Luke 2:40 Jesus grew with wisdom.

Catholic Social Teaching

The Poor and Vulnerable

Church Documents

Catechism of the Catholic Church. The themes of this chapter correspond to the following paragraphs: **488, 490–499, 525–534.**

General Directory for Catechesis #109. The Word of God became man in space and time and rooted in a specific culture. This inculturation of the Word of God is the model of all evangelization by the Church, because the Gospel should touch people at the very center and roots of their culture.

Pastoral Constitution on the Church in the Modern World #22 (Second Vatican Council). Christ, the perfect man, throws light on the riddle of suffering and death. God gives us abundant life.

On the Blessed Virgin Mary in the Life of the Pilgrim Church #8 (Saint John Paul II). The Father chose Mary as Mother of his Son in the Incarnation. Together with the Father, the Son chose her and entrusted her to the Spirit of holiness. Mary is united to Christ and is eternally loved in him.

The Redeemer of Man #8 (Saint John Paul II). Christ the Redeemer penetrated the mystery of human beings and united himself with each person, reforging the link between God and humankind.

Gather and Go Forth

Find catechist instruction for Gather and Go Forth student pages 41–42 on T324–T325.

Enriching the Faith Experience

Use the activities at the end of the chapter to enrich a lesson or to replace an activity with one that better meets the needs of your class.

Bulletin Board

A suggestion for a bulletin-board design for this chapter is pictured. Have the students add symbols from the Infancy Narratives. Suggest that some symbols may be three-dimensional.

Christ Is Born

LEARNING OUTCOMES

The students will be able to

- explain the significance of the Infancy Narratives.

- recall the Gospel stories of Jesus' birth and early life.

Words to Know

inerrancy

Infancy Narratives

See the Glossary for definitions.

Materials

- Bibles or New Testaments
- Recording of Christmas carols

Before You Begin

1. By this time, the students are familiar with the Infancy Narratives. It is not necessary to teach all the details surrounding Jesus' birth and infancy. This lesson focuses on the underlying meaning of the stories; however, it is good to be prepared to answer students' questions. Many books with up-to-date discussions of the Infancy Narratives are available.

2. The Scriptures teach without error the truth that God wanted for the sake of our salvation. This is known as inerrancy. Fundamentalism treats the Bible as a scientific text and demands that every fact in the Bible must be upheld for a person to be a faithful Christian. The Catholic Church rejects this view. Catholics believe that Scripture is the Word of God expressed in human words. In order to understand what God is saying through them, we need to understand the historical and cultural situation in which Scripture was written.

CHAPTER

5

The Early Life of Jesus

Jesus the Son of Mary and Joseph

Stories of an Infant God

What does Christmas mean to you?

If Jesus had not died and risen, we would have nothing to celebrate at Christmas. But Jesus did rise, showing himself to be the Son of God, our Savior. That is why we celebrate his birthday. The first Christians, however, did not. The recent astounding events of his Death and Resurrection were uppermost in their minds. As time went on, Christians wondered about Jesus' origins and early life. Soon stories were circulating.

Stories about Jesus' birth and early life are in the Gospels of Matthew and Luke. They are called **Infancy Narratives.** The evangelists wrote them in a way that shows who Jesus was. They present the mystery of his coming through beautiful and miraculous events:

- The Annunciation—Jesus' conception in Mary by the power of the Holy Spirit

- The Visitation—the recognition of his presence by Elizabeth and John

- The Nativity—Jesus' birth

- The Presentation—the offering of Jesus to God in the Temple

Biblical scholars have theories about the Infancy Narratives. For instance, they discuss who the magi were and whether the story is historical or symbolic. It does not matter if there were three kings or not. The Church teaches that the Scriptures contain the truth that is necessary for us to know for our salvation. This is called **inerrancy.** The all-important truth in the Infancy Narratives is that Jesus came to save us.

At Jesus' birth around 4 B.C., there was no video equipment to capture the events. Maybe Mary told Luke the stories of Jesus' birth. Maybe the evangelists added events and symbols to make a point or to fulfill prophecies. What we do know is that the Infancy Narratives are God's Word. They proclaim the meaning of who Jesus is for us.

Mini-Gospels

The Infancy Narratives are known as the "Gospels in miniature" because they tell the same Good News as the whole Gospels. They show all the aspects of Jesus' love. They reveal Jesus' identity, his mission, the role of the Holy Spirit in his life, Jesus' concern for all, his suffering, and his rejection. The main message of the narratives is the same as the Easter message: *Jesus is Lord, the Son of God who saved us.* That message is proclaimed in many ways. As you review the stories, listen for it and for other messages God may be sending you.

(35)

3. You might write on a large sign "Jesus is Lord, the Son of God who saved us" and post it during Sharing #3. Keep it displayed for the remainder of the year.

Centering _____

1. Have the students write about what Christmas means to them. [Play Christmas carols.] Ask for volunteers to share their answers.

2. Link the last lesson with today's lesson.
   - ✦ **You learned that knowing the culture of the Gospels helps to understand them.**
   - ✦ **Today you will see that knowing the intentions of the Evangelists helps too.**

Sharing

1. Have a student read aloud the first paragraph of **Stories of an Infant God** on page 36.

   ✦ **How did you answer the meaning of Christmas for you?**

   ✦ **Which feast is greater—Christmas or Easter?** (Easter) **Why?** (because Jesus' Resurrection gave meaning to his whole life)

   ✦ Have the students finish reading silently this section.

   ✦ **What do we call the Gospel stories of Jesus' birth?** (Infancy Narratives) **What do they tell us?** (who Jesus was for Christians)

   ✦ **What is the value of studying the Infancy Narratives?** (They are God's Word and hold a message for us.)

2. Ask a student to read aloud **Mini-Gospels** on page 35. **What message is proclaimed in many ways in the Infancy Narratives?** (Jesus is Lord, the Son of God who saved us.)

3. Read aloud to the students the directions for **An Album of Jesus** on page 36.

   ✦ Divide the class into groups. Assign each picture to a group. Have the group read the passage and think of a title for the picture.

   ✦ Ask the students to prepare a "living picture" or tableau of the story. Have the students assume poses depicting the story while a narrator explains who they are and what is happening.

   ✦ Have each group present its story. Tell the students to say the title of the picture and then give the "living picture" summary.

4. Have the students work on the activity **Gospel Truths** on page 36. Check their answers.

An Album of Jesus

Each picture in this album matches a story from the Infancy Narratives. Look up the Scripture citations and read the verses. Then write a title for the picture.

Annunciation
1. Luke 1:26–28

Joseph's Dream
2. Matthew 1:18–25

Visitation
3. Luke 1:36, 39–56

Birth of Jesus
4. Luke 2:1–20

Visit of the Magi
5. Matthew 2:1–12

Flight into Egypt
6. Matthew 2:13–15

Presentation
7. Luke 2:22–38

Finding Jesus in Temple
8. Luke 2:41–52

Gospel Truths

The Infancy Narratives contain the following Gospel truths. Think of each story identified above and write its number in front of any truth it conveys. Be ready to explain your answers.

1, 2, 4, 5, 7	a.	Jesus is God, so extraordinary signs accompany his birth.
1, 2, 3	b.	Mary, the Mother of God, is someone special.
1–5, 7, 8	c.	Jesus is the Messiah.
1, 2, 8	d.	Jesus is sent by the Father.
1	e.	The Holy Spirit acts for our salvation.
5, 7	f.	Jesus is Savior of all people, not only Jewish people.
4, 6	g.	Some people reject Jesus.
4, 6, 7	h.	Jesus suffers.
3, 4	i.	Jesus comes for the poor and the outcast.

36 UNIT 1

---

5. Discuss with the students Mary's journeys.

   ✦ Have the students use the map of Palestine from the Lesson Pullouts in the back of the student book. [See separate poster with TE.]

   ✦ Retrace Mary's journey, recalling the key events of the Infancy Narratives starting at Nazareth, to Judea, back to Nazareth, and from Nazareth to Bethlehem, to Jerusalem, to Egypt, to Nazareth, and to Jerusalem.

   ✦ **What does Mary journey show us?** (all the key events of the Infancy Narratives)

Acting

1. Have the students do Respond on page 39.
   Play music as they work, such as "Magnificat."

2. Choose or let the students choose an activity from Reach Out on page 39.

CHECKPOINT

- Were the learning outcomes achieved?

LEARNING OUTCOMES

The students will be able to

- relate God's calling of Mary to their own unique call.
- describe Mary's role in salvation history and her special graces.
- define the words *doctrine* and *Mother of God*.

Words to Know

doctrine

Mother of God

See the Glossary for definitions.

Key Term

Assumption—the Catholic doctrine that Mary was assumed into heaven body and soul at the end of her life

Immaculate Conception—the Catholic doctrine that since the time of her conception, Mary was preserved from all sin, including Original Sin

Virgin Birth—the Catholic doctrine that Mary conceived and gave birth to Jesus solely through the power of the Holy Spirit

Materials

- Recorded music: Find suggestions for Chapter 5 on page T517.

Before You Begin

1. This would be an appropriate time to review praying the Rosary, on page 237 of the student book. Otherwise you might teach the Rosary in Chapter 7 when Mary is studied. [See page T429.]

2. Christians throughout the centuries developed the idea that the Mother of Jesus was also conceived without Original Sin. This does not mean that, unlike the rest of humanity, Mary did not need to be saved. Rather, the belief in Mary's original sinlessness celebrates God's victory over sin and death in the moment the woman who is to be the Mother of his son comes into existence. Through her Son the sin of Adam and Eve is overturned so it is fitting that in her very beginning, the grace of God's power over sin is seen. The doctrine of the Immaculate Conception is about Mary's conception, not the virginal conception of Jesus. The feast is celebrated on December 8.

Centering _____

1. Link the last lesson with today's lesson.
   - ✦ **In the last class, you saw that the purpose of the Infancy Narratives was to proclaim one important message. What was that message?** (Jesus is Lord, the Son of God who saved us.)
   - ✦ **Today you will meet two people who are models in listening to God's messages.**

2. Have two volunteers talk to the wall for 30 seconds.
   - ✦ **How did you feel?** (foolish, frustrated) **Why?** (The wall cannot hear or speak back.)
   - ✦ **God speaks to us often. How?** (at Mass, in the Bible, through his Son, through events and people)
   - ✦ **Sometimes when God speaks to us it is like speaking to a brick wall. Too often we do not really listen to God's words of love, advice, or commands. Like a brick wall, we do not respond. Those who hear God's words and follow them become holy.**

Sharing

1. Have several students read aloud the first three paragraphs of **Mary, a Listener** on page 37.
   - ✦ Have the students read silently the fourth paragraph, and answer the question.
   - ✦ **What are some of the ways you thought that you, like Mary, could be a Christ-bearer?**

2. Read aloud to the students the last paragraph, calling attention to the word *doctrines.*
   - ✦ **The Immaculate Conception refers to Mary's conception, not Jesus'. From the first moment of her existence, her conception, Mary was always in the state of grace. God was always with her. Sin never separated her from God.**
   - ✦ **Some Protestants think that Mary had other children after Jesus because the Gospels refer to Jesus' brothers. Catholics translate *brothers* to mean "relatives."**
   - ✦ **We believe that Mary was always a virgin and that Jesus' birth was miraculous—through the power of the Holy Spirit.**
   - ✦ **Unlike the rest of us, who have to wait until the end of the world for the resurrection of the body, Mary has already been taken up to heaven body and soul. This is called the Assumption. No one knows if Mary underwent death as we do.**

3. ✝ Have a student read aloud **A Modern Mary** on page 37.
   ✝ *The Poor and Vulnerable*
   How do Rosemary's attitudes resemble Mary's? (She listened, trusted, and acted on God's word.)

Mary, a Listener

The heroine of the Infancy Narratives is Mary, a woman who was always open to God. By her faith, expressed when she answered yes, Mary became the mother of Jesus. Because Jesus is God, Mary is *Theotokos,* or the **Mother of God.** When the Son of God became the Son of Mary, he took the substance of his flesh from her. Jesus bore her features. He lived with her for about 30 years. She made his clothes, cooked his food, and taught him to walk and talk. He took care of her, obeyed her, and loved her. She witnessed his growth, his joys and sorrows, and his prayer. She knew his smile, the touch of his hand, and his thoughts and feelings. Forever he will call her Mother.

Mary listened to God, which led to action. She was prepared to risk all she had for love of God. She responded to Gabriel, "Let it be," *(fiat)* calling herself God's handmaid. She willingly became the Mother of the Redeemer, a dangerous and painful mission. After the Annunciation, Mary did not just sit and think about herself. She went to help Elizabeth. At all times, she cooperated with the work of her Son, even when it meant standing at the foot of the Cross.

Mary's "Let it be" echoed God's "Let it be" that began creation. She made possible the new creation that Christ brought about. As Saint Irenaeus put it, "Mary's obedience helped untie what Eve's disobedience had tied."

Do you *listen* to God speak to you in quiet prayer time? through your parents, teachers, brothers, and sisters? Do you listen to your friends' needs? to calls to share your money or time with the poor? Do you *act?*

It is said that Mary bore Jesus in her heart before she bore him in her womb. How can you be a Christ-bearer today?

Answers will vary.

We believe that because Mary is the Mother of God, she was given special gifts. These privileges of Mary are Catholic **doctrines.**

- The Immaculate Conception—Mary was never in the state of sin, neither Original Sin, nor personal sin.
- The Virgin Birth—Mary conceived Jesus solely through the power of the Holy Spirit. (We believe she was always a virgin.)
- The Assumption—Mary went to heaven body and soul at the end of her life.

A Modern Mary

After raising four children, Rosemary Koenig felt God calling her to serve others. With little money and at the age of 65 she opened the Shelter of God's Love in Chicago. It was a home for eight people with disabilities like Pam, who is blind; Margie, a young girl with cerebral palsy; and Evelyn, a grandmother who has multiple sclerosis. Each evening after dinner, the community prayed for the world. A few years later, Rosemary started another Shelter where senior citizens could live together. Rosemary trusted God for everything. In surprising ways, the Shelters' needs were met: a van, a computer, an assistant director. Like Mary, Rosemary listened to God and then acted. She let God do great things through her. Rosemary died in 2005 at the age of 92.

---

4. Discuss with the students others who hear and follow God's Word.
   Do you know some people like Mary, Jesus' mother, and Rosemary Koenig, the woman in this story who heard the Word of God, said yes, and followed? [You might want to share some examples of people you know.]

5. Have several students read aloud **Honoring Mary** on page 38.

- ✦ **Why does the Church honor Mary?** (She is the new Eve. She obeyed God with her whole heart and soul.)

- ✦ **Why was Mary important to the people of the Middle Ages?** (She was a tender, caring mother who helped them into heaven.)

- ✦ **What are some titles given to Mary?** (Mother of Mercy, Queen of Heaven, Refuge of Sinners)

6. Have a student read aloud **Our Lady of Guadalupe** on page 38.

What else do you know about Our Lady of Guadalupe? (She is the Patroness of the Americas. Her feast is celebrated on December 12.)

7. Have a student read **Our Lady of Lourdes** on page 38.

What other apparitions of Mary do you know? (Fatima, Miraculous Medal)

Acting _____

Lead the students in **A Moment with Jesus** on page 38.

- ✦ Explain that you are now going to share a few minutes of prayer together.

- ✦ Allow sufficient time for silent reflection.

- ✦ Pray together the *Memorare* found on the inside back cover of the student book. [See page T446.]

Honoring Mary

Throughout the centuries, the Church has honored Mary. The early Church saw her as the new Eve. Eve was disobedient to God; Mary obeyed God with her whole heart and soul.

During the centuries of the Middle Ages, from about 900 to 1500, Mary became even more important to Christians. Europe was going through difficult times with wars and sickness. To the people, Mary was seen as a tender and caring Mother of Mercy and refuge of sinners.

The people felt that they had a special friend in Mary. God chose his mother not from the palaces of kings and queens, but from a quiet, small village. Mary was a young girl from a humble family. She was honored with the title of Queen of Heaven and Refuge of Sinners.

Many cathedrals were built in Europe and named after Mary. She was celebrated in poetry, hymns, prayers, and sermons. Mary's Assumption into heaven was especially celebrated. Since Mary is the Mother of Christ, it was only fitting that after her time on earth she would be assumed body and soul into heaven. There are many examples of appearances Mary has made to help people and to encourage them to pray.

Our Lady of Guadalupe

In 1521 Mary appeared to Juan Diego in Mexico. She told him that she wanted a church built in her honor. When Juan Diego brought her request to his bishop, the bishop asked for a sign. In response to the bishop's request, Mary filled Juan Diego's cloak with roses. When Juan Diego opened the cloak for the bishop, they discovered the beautiful image of Our Lady of Guadalupe on the cloak. This image is still on display in Mexico and is visited by thousands of pilgrims every year. Our Lady of Guadalupe is the Patroness of the Americas.

Our Lady of Lourdes

In 1858 Mary appeared to Bernadette Soubirous, a girl from a poor family in France. Bernadette  received 18 messages from Our Lady in the grotto of Lourdes. Mary proclaimed to Bernadette that she was the Immaculate Conception. The teaching of the Church is that Mary was conceived without Original Sin. Obediently following the instructions of Mary, Bernadette discovered a spring that proved to be a source of miraculous healing. Since that time, millions of people have visited Lourdes. Many continue to visit today to honor Mary and to pray for healing.

St. Bernadette of Lourdes.

Under the title of the Immaculate Conception, Mary is also the Patroness of the United States. She continues to intercede for us, her children, today.

Our Lady of Guadalupe.

A Moment with Jesus

God chose Mary, a young girl from a poor family, to be the Mother of God. Pause and think about this for a moment.

Her yes to God is an example for us. Take a moment and ask Jesus to show you how you are being called to say yes to God at this time in your life. Thank Jesus for the gift of Mary to the Church.

38

CHECKPOINT

- Were the learning outcomes achieved?

LEARNING OUTCOMES

The students will be able to

- review the people, places, and things in the Infancy Narratives.
- apply the message of a symbol from the Infancy Narratives to their own lives.
- demonstrate an understanding of Mary's *Magnificat*.

Key Term

canticle—song

Materials

- BLM 21
- Three words in another language printed on the board or on flash cards. (Examples from French: *maison* [may-ZONE]—house; *bouche* [boosh]—mouth; *chat* [shah]—cat)
- Six numbered slips of paper, each with a verse or two of the *Magnificat*: Luke 1:46–47, 48, 49, 50–51, 52–53, 54–55
- Reflection notebooks
- Recorded music: Find suggestions for Chapter 5 on page T517.

Before You Begin

The *Magnificat*, Mary's song of praise, resembles the prayer of Hannah, the mother of Samuel. (See 1 Samuel 2:1–10.) The *Magnificat* may have been a Jewish hymn adapted by the Christian community. Its themes are joy in the Lord, God's favor to the poor, the reversal of fortune, and the fulfillment of Old Testament promises. It is a fitting prayer for Mary. When the *Magnificat* is prayed daily in Evening Prayer, we stand because it is from the Gospel.

Centering _____

Link the last lesson with today's lesson.

- ✦ [Refer to the words in another language.] **These words are symbols for objects.**
- ✦ **How could these word-symbols become meaningful to you?** (through familiarity and usage)
- ✦ **In the same way, biblical symbols and biblical verses take on more meaning as we become familiar with them.**
- ✦ **Today we will review the symbols of the Infancy Narratives we have studied in the last two lessons. Then we will experience applying Scripture to our lives.**

Sharing _____

1. **BLM 21** Distribute copies of BLM 21 **Infancy Narrative Word Search.**
   Have the students do the word search and write the sentences independently or with partners.

2. Have several students read aloud the sentences they composed from the BLM.

3. Explain to the students about the canticles in the Infancy Narratives.
   - ✦ **The Infancy Narratives contain three canticles, or songs. Can you recall any of the people who said hymns of praise in these stories?** (Mary, Zechariah, Simeon)

- ✦ **The canticles of these people have become favorite prayers of the Church. Every day, religious, priests, and some lay people pray the canticles during the Prayer of Christians, the Liturgy of the Hours, which is the official Church prayer. Zechariah's canticle is prayed in the morning, Mary's in the evening, and Simeon's at night.**

- ✦ **Today you will look more closely at Mary's canticle. It is called the *Magnificat*, which is Latin for the opening words "My soul proclaims." You will see what the words of the canticle meant to Mary and what they can mean to you.**

4. Divide the class into six groups.

◆ Give each group a paper containing a verse from the *Magnificat*.

◆ Instruct the groups to read their verse, discuss why Mary said it, and then discuss why they could say it.

5. Have each group read its verse aloud and report the results of its discussion.

Acting

 Lead the students in praying the *Magnificat*. Have the students stand.

Have each group pray its verse aloud when you call its number.

CHECKPOINT ✓

- Were the learning outcomes achieved?

CHAPTER 5 Summary

Remember

What do the Infancy Narratives proclaim?
The Infancy Narratives proclaim the Good News that Jesus is the Son of God and Savior of the world.

What privileges did God give Mary because she was the Mother of God?
Mary's privileges are the Immaculate Conception, the Virgin Birth, and the Assumption.

Why did Jesus come?
Jesus said, "I came so that they might have life and have it more abundantly." (John 10:10)

Respond

What might God be saying to you through a person or symbol in the Infancy Narratives? Spend some time in quiet reflection, then write your thoughts in your reflection notebook. (Ideas: Mary, star, Joseph, angel's song, Elizabeth, Magi, innkeeper, manger, shepherd, Simeon, holy innocents, Anna.)

Reach Out

1. Find out how the celebration of Christmas by your family came to be the way you know it.

2. Research the Christmas customs of another country and culture. Look for information about food, decorations, activities, and music.

3. Share the Good News of the story of Christmas:
   - Tell a child the story.
   - Design a Christmas card based on the Gospel story of Christmas. Give it to someone special.
   - Make a mural of the events surrounding Jesus' birth or a mobile of Christmas symbols. Put your mural or mobile where it can be seen.
   - Prepare a creative presentation to tell the Christmas story.

4. Ask at least 12 people of different ages what Christmas means to them, and write down their responses.

5. Pray Mary's Magnificat in Luke 1:46–55. Notice that Mary praises how God treats the poor and lowly.

6. Use a liturgical calendar or a reference book to find the dates we celebrate the Annunciation; the Visitation; the Nativity; the Presentation; the Epiphany; the Solemnity of Mary, Mother of God; and the feasts of the Holy Innocents and the Holy Family.

Words to Know

doctrine
inerrancy

Infancy Narratives
Mother of God

39

LEARNING OUTCOMES

The students will be able to

- describe the mysteries presented in the Infancy Narratives.
- demonstrate an understanding of the key concepts in this chapter.

Materials

- Picture of the Nativity
- Activity 1:
  Two sheets of manila paper and two sheets black construction paper for each student
  Watercolors
  Paper cutter
  Scissors

Glue
Water

- Activity 2:
  One sheet of white drawing paper and one sheet of black construction paper for each student
  Paint, crayons, or felt-tipped markers
  Glue
  pencils
- BLM 22 Quiz

Before You Begin

1. Choose one of the art activities in Sharing #2 to do with the students.

2. When planning today's lesson, keep in mind that Day Four is

when the students take the quiz for this chapter. Reserve time at the end of class for this assessment. The quiz can also be administered on Day Five.

Centering

1. Show the students a picture of the Nativity.
   The Nativity has been the favorite subject of artists for centuries. Why do you think this is so?

2. Link the last lesson with today's lesson.
   - **In the last few lessons, you have learned the importance of the Infancy Narratives.**
   - **Today you will have an opportunity to express the message of these stories through art.**

Sharing

1. Have the students name each part of the Infancy Narratives found in Matthew and Luke.
   - **What are the parts of the Infancy Narratives?** (the Annunciation, the Visitation, the Nativity, the Presentation)
   - **How would you represent these different parts artistically? Which part is your favorite?**

2. Help the students carry out one of these activities.
   - **Activity 1:** Silhouettes on woven wet washes using two sheets of manila paper and two sheets of black construction paper

     Step 1. Wet the manila papers completely. Then with the paper in a vertical position, use watercolor to paint two-inch bands of color in this order: yellow, orange, red, green, blue, purple. The colors will blend into one another.

     Step 2. While the paint is drying, design and cut silhouettes of one of the stories from one sheet of black paper. The insides of the silhouettes might be cut away. Cut the other black sheet in two on the diagonal.

     Step 3. When the paint is dry, cut the manila sheets in 1/2-inch strips, one sheet long vertical strips, and the other short horizontal strips. Keep the strips in their original order.

Step 4. Weave the strips. Place the ends of the long strips along the first short strip, alternating one over and one under. Glue these ends down.

Then weave the rest of the short strips through the long strips and glue down the ends.

Step 5. Glue the black silhouettes onto the background. Place the two triangles on the back slightly separated so that 1/2 inch of black shows around the picture.

- **Activity 2:** Stained-glass windows

  Step 1. Students may cut the top of the drawing paper so it is dome-shaped.

  Step 2. Direct them to draw a scene with pencil and make thick black dividing lines through it.

  Step 3. Have them color the picture and mount the scenes on black construction paper.

3. Have the students arrange their art in sequence around the room.

4. Lead the students through the Summary and Review Activities, pages 39–40.

5. BLM 22 Distribute and administer BLM 22 **Chapter 5 Quiz.**

Use this opportunity to assess the student's understanding of the main concepts in the chapter. If there is not sufficient time for the students to complete the quiz, consider moving it to Day Five.

Acting _____

1. Invite the students to reflect on the mysteries represented in their art.

Close by praying the Angelus from the inside back cover of the student book.

2. At the end of class, have the students tear out and take home pages 39–40.

CHECKPOINT

- Were the learning outcomes achieved?

- What does the quality of the art and the degree of students cooperation say about the students' attitude toward this lesson?

CHAPTER **5** Review Activities

The Honest Truth   Write Y for yes or N for no in answer to each question.

Y	**1.**	Was Easter more important than Christmas to the early Christians?
N	**2.**	Does the Gospel of John include Infancy Narratives?
N	**3.**	Are all of the details in the Infancy Narratives historically true?
Y	**4.**	Do the Infancy Narratives proclaim that Jesus is Lord, the Son of God, who saved us?
Y	**5.**	Were the writers of the Infancy Narratives inspired by God?
N	**6.**	Was Elizabeth present at the Annunciation?
Y	**7.**	Was Mary always free from sin, even Original Sin?
Y	**8.**	Is the Assumption, Mary's being taken into heaven body and soul, a Catholic doctrine?

A Christmas Crossword   Fill in the puzzle.

Across

2. A Galilean woman who was sinless and full of grace

5. The holy man who was allowed to see the Messiah before he died and who prophesied sorrow for Mary

7. The king who wanted to put the newborn king to death

8. The holy family fled to this place.

11. The messenger at the Annunciation

12. Mary was betrothed to this man.

14. When Mary became pregnant, Joseph intended to take this action allowed by Jewish law.

Down

1. Men who followed a star to Bethlehem

3. A relative of Jesus who was six months older than Jesus

4. Jesus was conceived by this power.

5. The first to hear the good news of Jesus' birth

6. Mary helped this older relative during the woman's pregnancy.

9. When Jesus was lost in Jerusalem, his parents found him here doing his Father's work.

10. When Jesus was born, he was laid in this.

13. Mary's child was his Son.

40

Day Five Extending the Chapter

Gather and Go Forth

Lead students through pages 41–42 in the student book. Find catechist instruction on T324–T325.

Use the following suggestions to create an additional lesson for Day Five.

1. Remind the students to take home pages 39–40 to share what they are learning with their families.

2. Incorporate any unused BLMs from the week's chapter.

3. Consider the time of the liturgical year and use the appropriate Special Seasons and Lessons. SSLs begin on page T369.

4. Visit www.christourlife.com to find additional activities for Extending the Chapter.

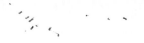

5. Use activities from Enriching the Faith Experience.

6. Guide the students in a prayerful discussion of Sunday's Scripture readings. Visit www.christourlife.com for more information.

Chapter 5 Enriching the Faith Experience

Use the following activities to enrich a lesson or to replace an activity with one that better meets the needs of your class.

1. Have the students pretend to be Saint Joseph and tell the events of the Infancy Narratives from his point of view.

2. Coordinate the making of a booklet called "Guide to the Infancy Narratives from A to Z." Let each student choose a letter and think of words from the stories that begin with it. Then have the students write and design a page for their letter.

3. Have the students research and present how other Christians around the world celebrate Christmas. Encourage them to use books, the Internet, friends, and relatives.

4. Have students make dioramas of a scene from an Infancy Narrative. Tell students to cut out figures and glue to stand in a box on its side.

5. Ask volunteers to lead committees that will gather supplies for people in need. Have each group select an item or theme: canned goods, winter clothes, baby items. Allow time for students to plan, organize and take action. *The Poor and Vulnerable*

6. Have the students read the following passages from the Old Testament and then explain how each was fulfilled according to the Infancy Narratives.

Psalm 2:7–9   Isaiah 11:1–2

Isaiah 7:13–14   Micah 5:1

Isaiah 9:1–2   Malachi 3:1

Isaiah 9:5–6   Hosea 11:1

Isaiah 40:3,9

7. Direct the students to research on the Internet how various cultures display a nativity scene at Christmas. They can present their research as a PowerPoint presentation or by putting together one of the scenes from their research.

The Mission of Jesus
JESUS THE CHRIST

Faith Focus

Jesus accepted his mission as Messiah at his baptism and was faithful to it during his temptation.

Reflecting on the Faith Experience

Take a few moments to reflect prayerfully before preparing the lesson.

Listening

Filled with the holy Spirit,
Jesus returned from the Jordan
and was led by the Spirit into
the desert . . .

Luke 4:1

Reflecting

How often have we said to ourselves "I've got to get away from all this for a while!" or "I need time to think!"? We need distance from daily life in order to reflect and plan, to marshal our resources, and to renew our commitments. John the Baptist felt this need, for he prepared for his mission by living in the desert wilderness to strengthen himself for what was to come. Christ himself, in his humanity, felt the need to go into the desert wilderness to prepare for his mission as Messiah.

Throughout his life, Christ took time to be alone with his Father, whether it was in a quiet place, in Peter's boat, or on a mountain. Aware of our needs, God invites us to share Jesus' desert experience when he says, "Come away by yourselves to a deserted place and rest a while" (Mark 6:31) or "I will lead her into the desert and speak to her heart" (Hosea 2:16). As one spiritual writer states it,

> Everyone must be like Jesus
>   and every once in a while
>   spend a night alone
>   on a mountain in communion
>   with the Father.
> Otherwise, when we find
>   ourselves
>   in the garden of despair

because of rejections,
or cancer,
or sudden death,
we won't know the Father's will
we won't be able to reach for
    His cup
like a runner in the race.

*Time Out,
Andrew Costello, C.Ss.R.*

Desert experiences may range in time from a half hour in a quiet room to an afternoon in a park to a weekend retreat. The important thing is the opportunity to refresh ourselves, to renew our love, to strengthen our relationship with Christ, and to revitalize our determination to follow his way. Just as Jesus was led by the Spirit, so we, too, must let the Spirit lead us. Then we can rest assured of God's loving care in all situations of life, as God promised through the words of the psalmist:

> Whoever clings to me I will
>   deliver;
>   whoever knows my name I
>   will set on high.
> All who call upon me I will
>   answer;
>   I will be with them in distress;
>   I will deliver them and give
>   them honor.
> With length of days I will
>   satisfy them
> and show them my saving
>   power.
>
> *Psalm 91:14–16*

Do I need to plan a desert experience?

How well do I fulfill my mission of catechist?

Responding

Jesus, help my students cope with the temptations that most threaten their relationship with you.

Scripture for Further Reflection

Hosea 2:16 God lures our souls into the wilderness and speaks to our hearts.

Hebrews 4:15; 5:2 Jesus feels our weaknesses and has been tempted as we are.

Preparing for the Faith Experience

Scripture in This Chapter

Matthew 3:1–17 John the Baptist

Matthew 4:1–11 Jesus is tempted.

Hebrews 4:15 Jesus sympathizes with us.

Catholic Social Teaching

Rights and Responsibilities

Church Documents

Catechism of the Catholic Church. The themes of this chapter correspond to the following paragraphs: **535–540.**

National Directory for Catechesis #36. The whole Church is a priestly people. Through Baptism, all the faithful share in the priesthood of Christ, the common priesthood of the faithful.

Pastoral Constitution on the Church in the Modern World #13 (Second Vatican Council). There is taking place within each of us a struggle between good and evil. We would not be able to overcome the power of evil by ourselves, but the Lord himself came to free and strengthen us.

Pastoral Constitution on the Church in the Modern World #13 (Second Vatican Council). Life on earth is a dramatic struggle between good and evil. By ourselves, we are not able to overcome the assaults of evil, but the Lord himself came to free us by overcoming the devil, the "prince of this world."

Declaration on Religious Liberty #14 (Second Vatican Council). The disciple has a crucial obligation to Christ to grow in knowledge of truth, announce it faithfully, and defend it vigorously.

Gather and Go Forth

Find catechist instruction for Gather and Go Forth student pages 49–50 on T326–T327.

Enriching the Faith Experience

Use the activities at the end of the chapter to enrich a lesson or to replace an activity with one that better meets the needs of your class.

Bulletin Board

A suggestion for a bulletin-board design for this chapter is pictured.

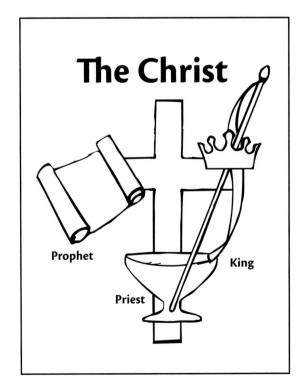

The Christ

Prophet

Priest

King

LEARNING OUTCOMES

The students will be able to

- explain that the mission of Christ was to proclaim and make present the reign of God.
- identify the roles of Jesus as prophet, priest, and king.
- explain the significance of Jesus' baptism.

Key Terms

Christ—the anointed one; Messiah

John the Baptist—relative of Jesus who prepared the way for him by preaching repentance and baptizing

king—one who has the greatest power and authority

priest—one who represents the people in offering sacrifice to God

prophet—one who hears God's Word and proclaims it

Materials

- Bibles or New Testaments
- Quotation written on the board: *"We are each called to do a certain work. No one can do it for us. If we fail to do it, it won't be done."*
- Words written on board or on flash cards: *Christ, Messiah, prophet, priest, king*
- Thick stick for a staff (optional)
- Stole or strip of material that looks like a stole
- Paper rolled like a scroll
- Crown
- Microphone (optional)

Before You Begin

1. Just as the Church has a mission to accomplish, so each individual Christian has a mission in the world. Our mission begins with ourselves and our families, but does not end there. Our Baptism commits us to reach out to others, witnessing to God's love and proclaiming the Good News of Jesus Christ to everyone we meet, to the society of which we are a part, and to the world at large.

2. Have the students rehearse before they present the play in Sharing #7.

3. You might prefer to introduce Jesus' baptism by working out a Gospel harmony with the students. Have them read Matthew 3:13–17; Mark 1:9–11; Luke 3:21–22, and John 1:29–34 and then chart the comparisons listed in the third column.

Account	John's Meeting with Jesus	After the Baptism
Matthew	John doesn't want to baptize Jesus; Jesus insists.	Heavens open. Spirit descends as a dove. A voice speaks to everyone.
Mark	Jesus is baptized by John.	Heavens are torn open. Spirit descends. A voice speaks only to Jesus.
Luke	Jesus is baptized by John.	Heavens open. Spirit descends as a dove. A voice speaks only to Jesus.
John	Jesus is baptized by John.	John describes how he saw the Spirit descend as a dove. John is told that the one the Spirit rests on will baptize with the Holy Spirit.

Centering _____

1. Show a stole, a scroll, and a crown.
   Was Jesus a priest, a prophet, or a king? (He was all three.)

2. Call on a student to read aloud the quotation on the board.
   - ✦ **What does this mean to you?**
   - ✦ **Our special work in life is our mission. The word *mission* comes from the word for "sent." We carry out our mission in the roles we have.**

3. Have a student read aloud the first paragraph of **The Role of Messiah** on page 43.
   Ask them to list their roles. Have volunteers share what they wrote.

4. Link the last lesson to this lesson.
   - ✦ **In the last lesson, you learned that the Infancy Narratives proclaim Jesus to be the Messiah.**
   - ✦ **Today you will see how Jesus began his mission in the world.**

Sharing _____

1. Have the students read silently the rest of **The Role of Messiah** on page 43.
   How are the terms on the board related? (*Christ* and *Messiah* are synonyms. They mean "the anointed one." *Prophet*, *priest*, and *king* are the three roles Jesus had as the Christ.)

2. Explain Christ's roles of priest, prophet, and king.
   Ask a student to name the role and another to tell how Jesus fulfilled it:

- **This stole represents the people in offering sacrifice to God.** (Priest. Jesus stood for us when he offered himself on the Cross. He represents us at Mass.)

- **This scroll speaks for God and calls people to conversion.** (Prophet. Jesus proclaimed the Good News that the Father sent him to reveal. He said, "Repent. The kingdom is at hand.")

- **This crown has the greatest power and authority in a kingdom.** (King. Jesus is Lord of the universe as a result of his Death and Resurrection.)

3. Check the students' knowledge of the Messiah and his kingdom.
   - ✦ **Why wasn't Jesus the kind of Messiah the Israelites expected?** (They expected a king who would make them a superpower. Jesus' kingdom was not of this world.)
   - ✦ **What was Jesus' mission?** (to proclaim and make present the reign of God)
   - ✦ **What is meant by "the reign of God"?** (peace, justice, love)
   - ✦ **The reign of God, or the Kingdom of God, is not a place. It is a state of being. It exists when people live together in love that is like God's unconditional love.**

4. Discuss the role of John the Baptist.
   - ✦ **Whose mission in life was to prepare the people of Palestine for Jesus?** (John the Baptist)
   - ✦ **Because of his special role, the Gospel tells us about the events surrounding his birth.**

5. Have one of the students read aloud Luke 1:57–66, the birth of John the Baptist.
   - ✦ **There are many special events surrounding the birth of John the Baptist. How was his birth announced?** (An angel announced John's coming to his father, Zechariah, and told him to name his son John.)

CHAPTER 6

The Mission of Jesus

Jesus the Christ

The Role of Messiah

All of us have a number of roles in life. Your favorite aunt, for instance, might also be a wife, a mother, a lawyer, and the captain of her bowling team. List some of your roles.

Answers will vary.

_____

_____

In addition to being God's Son, Jesus is the Christ. *Christ* means "anointed one." The Israelites anointed their prophets, priests, and kings with oil. As God's anointed one, Jesus was a prophet, priest, and king.

Christ is another name for *Messiah*. Jesus was not the Messiah many Jewish people expected. In their minds, the Messiah would help them overthrow Rome. Jesus' mission as Messiah, however, was to proclaim and make present the reign of God. He was to bring about the Kingdom of God, in which all people live in peace and love.

God's kingdom is not a place. It is the rule of God over our hearts.

Jesus was the Messiah who preached humility and love of neighbors and enemies. He was the Messiah who suffered and died for us.

Jesus began this mission when he was about 30 years old. The Gospels tell how the Holy Spirit strengthened Jesus for his mission and how he accepted it.

A prophet hears God's Word and proclaims it. Jesus delivered the Good News that the Father wanted made known. He proclaimed, "Repent, the kingdom is at hand." Like many prophets before him, Jesus was killed for proclaiming God's words.

A priest represents people in offering sacrifice to God. Jesus stood for all of us when he offered himself to the Father on the Cross.

A king is a man who rules in God's name. Jesus is Lord of the universe as a result of his incarnation, Death, Resurrection, and Ascension.

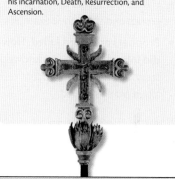

(43)

- ✦ **What happened to Zechariah?** (He expressed doubt that his aged wife Elizabeth and he would have a child. He lost his power to speak.)

- ✦ **How was John named?** (After the baby was born, relatives and neighbors wondered what to name him. Zechariah wrote on a tablet, "His name is John." At that moment, he could talk again.)

- ✦ **What did Zechariah do after John was born?** (He prayed a prayer known as the Canticle of Zechariah. It is a song of praise that priests, religious, and lay people pray in the Liturgy of the Hours, the official prayer of the Church (Luke 1:68–79).

6. Compare the births of Jesus and John the Baptist.
   In Luke's Gospel, how was John's birth similar to Jesus' birth? (It was announced by an angel who gave the baby's name. Both births were miraculous: Mary was a virgin; Elizabeth was old. Mary and Zechariah prayed canticles.)

7. Assign parts in the play **Launching the Mission** on page 44.

(Newscaster, Woman, Man, Boy, John) Have the students act it out.

8. Discuss John the Baptist.

✦ **Why did John baptize people?** (as a sign of repentance for their sins)

✦ **John first refused to baptize Jesus, saying, "I ought to be baptized by you." Why did John say this?** (He recognized that Jesus was the Messiah and without sin.)

9. Ask several students to read aloud Luke 3:10–14.

✦ Ask them to imagine what messages John would have for them related to each role they listed for themselves on page 43. (Examples: Grandchildren, respect your grandparents. Do chores without pay. Students, do your homework well.)

✦ Have the students form small groups and share their examples.

✦ **Prophets are often killed. How did John die?** (If no one knows the story, tell it or have a student read aloud Mark 6:17–29.)

10. Refer to the words *priest*, *prophet*, and *king* on the board or on flash cards.

How do we share these roles of Jesus since we are anointed with oil at Baptism? (We are priests when we unite ourselves to Jesus at Mass and offer ourselves with him to the Father. We are prophets when we spread the teaching of the Gospel, the Good News. We are kings, a royal people, because we are sons and daughters of God and heirs of the Kingdom of Heaven.)

Launching the Mission

In the Gospel of Luke when Mary, pregnant with Jesus, came to help her relative Elizabeth, Elizabeth's baby leaped for joy. The baby grew up to be John the Baptist, the prophet who prepared the way for Jesus. The following is a news report about Jesus' baptism by John.

Newscaster: We are on location at the Jordan River to find out what attracts the people of Judea to John the Baptist. Let's ask them about this strange man from the desert, who lives on nothing but grasshoppers and honey. Pardon me, may I ask you a few questions?

Woman: Certainly.

Newscaster: When did you first hear about John the Baptist?

Woman: The day he started to preach here. When I heard he was here, I just had to come to hear him.

Newscaster: What kinds of things does John say?

Woman: He says to repent for our sins because the Kingdom of God is near.

Newscaster: Do you think John is the Messiah?

Woman: No. He says that the Messiah is greater than he is and that he's not even worthy to untie the Messiah's sandal.

The Jordan River.

❮ John the Baptist.

Newscaster: Thank you. *(turns to a man passing by)* Sir, may I have a word with you?

Man: Only a minute. I want to get down there before John stops baptizing.

Newscaster: Why do you want to be baptized?

Man: To show that I am sorry for my sins and be ready for the Messiah when he comes.

Newscaster: Do you think that will be soon?

Man: I sure do. John says so.

Newscaster: Thank you, sir. *(turns toward the riverbank)* Just one more man is waiting for baptism. He's going to the river. Something seems to be wrong. John is hesitating. *(pause)* I guess it's all right now. They're wading out into the river . . . the man is under the water . . . there, he's up . . . they're back on the riverbank, but look at their faces! *(stops a boy)* Pardon me. Do you know the young man whom John just baptized?

Boy: That's Jesus. He comes from Nazareth.

Newscaster: Thank you. We'll try to find out what happened. Here comes John. Pardon me, sir. What happened? You look as if you've seen something extraordinary.

John: You're right. I just baptized the Messiah.

Newscaster: How do you know?

John: After Jesus was baptized, the heavens opened up. I saw a dove come down and hover over his head. Then I heard a voice saying, "This is my beloved Son, with whom I am well pleased." Don't you see what that means? Jesus is the Messiah. Praised be the God of Israel!

Newscaster: Praised be the God of Israel! What more can be said? No doubt, we'll be hearing more about this Jesus from Nazareth. This is Isaac Jacobs reporting from Judea.

Acting

 Point out that being a Christian is a public act that takes courage.

✝ Rights and Responsibilities

Discuss how John and Jesus were courageous in fulfilling their mission. End with a prayer for courage:

 God grant me the serenity to accept the things I cannot change . . .

courage to change the things I can . . .

and the wisdom to know the difference.

The Serenity Prayer by Reinhold Niebuhr

CHECKPOINT

• Were the learning outcomes achieved?

LEARNING OUTCOMES

The students will be able to

- explain the significance of Jesus' temptation.
- apply Jesus' experience of temptation to their own times of temptation.
- define types of sin and name factors that lessen guilt.

Key Terms

epiphany—revelation or manifestation of God

mortal sin—a serious offense against God that destroys our friendship with him and causes us to lose grace and eternal life

Original Sin—the sin of Adam and Eve that is passed on to their descendants, who are born without grace and vulnerable to evil

sin—choosing to do what is wrong or omit what is good

temptation—person or thing that entices us to do what is wrong or omit what is good

venial sin—an offense that weakens our relationship with God

Materials

- Reflection notebooks
- Flash cards: *venial sin, mortal sin, Original Sin*

Before You Begin

1. Original Sin is not something that we do, but is something we inherit from an act our first parents did. It is not an act that we commit, but a condition into which we are born that causes us to be inclined to commit personal sins. Baptism removes Original Sin, but we struggle with its effects our entire lives.

2. Making good moral choices is difficult because of temptation. Choices that appear to be good, in reality may lead us to sin. When we pray "lead us not into temptation," we are asking God for the help we need before we make our choices. Overcoming temptation is possible only through prayer. Jesus overcame temptation in the desert and in the garden of Gethsemane through prayer.

3. For students at this age, it is important to stress that temptation is not a sin.

4. You might provide an opportunity for the Sacrament of Reconciliation in conjunction with this lesson.

Centering

1. Have the students read silently **Anointed for the Mission** on page 45.

   ✦ **Why was Jesus baptized if he had no sins?** (Jesus' baptism was not a Christian baptism for the forgiveness of sin. Jesus' baptism was a sign that he accepted his mission as Messiah. He took on the sins of the world.)

   ✦ **What is an *epiphany*?** (a revelation or manifestation of God) **What do we celebrate on the feast of the Epiphany?** (the adoration of the Magi) **How was that event an epiphany?** (Jesus was revealed as the Messiah to the Gentiles.)

   ✦ **What was the epiphany at Jesus' baptism?** (The Trinity was revealed: the voice of the Father, the Spirit as a dove, and Jesus, the Son of God.)

   ✦ **How did the Father affirm Jesus in his mission?** (He said, "This is my beloved Son, with whom I am well pleased.")

2. Say "Testing 1,2,3" and ask the students what you are doing. (checking a sound system)

   ✦ **This microphone test makes sure that messages will carry.**

   ✦ **Temptations test us to see if we are strong enough to carry God's messages.**

3. Link this lesson with the last lesson.

   ✦ **You have learned about Jesus' baptism and his anointing for his role as the Christ. Like all of us, Jesus was tested.**

   ✦ **Today you will see that he proved strong enough to be the Messiah, to proclaim the Good News, and make present the reign of God.**

4. Have the students read silently **A Moment with Jesus** on page 45.

   ✦ Explain that you are going to share a few minutes of silent prayer together.

   ✦ Lead the students through the prayer experience, allowing sufficient time for silent reflection.

Sharing

1. Have a student read aloud **The Messiah's Test** on page 45.
   - ✦ **What did Jesus do in the desert?** (pray and fast) **Why?** (to prepare for his mission)
   - ✦ **Why is a desert a good place to do this?** (You can be alone and not distracted.)
   - ✦ **What kind of kingdom was the true Messiah's?** (a spiritual kingdom based on faith and love)
   - ✦ **Satan tested Jesus in the desert. He tempted him to be a different kind of Messiah. Let's look at Jesus' temptation in the desert more closely.**

2. Choose two students to take the parts of Jesus and Satan in **The Temptations** on page 45.
   - ✦ Introduce each temptation by reading the description and the setting. After each temptation, have the class read the conclusion together.
   - ✦ **What kind of kingdom was the Messiah to proclaim?** (a spiritual one based on faith and love)
   - ✦ **What three kinds of messiahs did Satan tempt Jesus to be?** (one with a kingdom based on material goods, one with a kingdom based on magic tricks, and one with a kingdom of military power to overthrow Rome)
   - ✦ **In what three areas of human weakness did Satan tempt Jesus?** (physical pleasure, pride, and power) **These things are good in themselves, but when they are excessive, they can be harmful.**
   - ✦ **How was Jesus able to withstand Satan's attacks?** (He had been praying and fasting. He used Scripture to answer Satan.)
   - ✦ **For what things are people today willing to sell their souls?** (money, sex, success, fame) [List the students' answers on the board.]
   - ✦ **Power and wealth can be abused. For example, power is used wrongly when a father exerts his influence to keep his son out of**

court for drunken driving, or when the captain of a team uses her power to exclude from a game a player she doesn't like.
   - ✦ **Wealth is used wrongly when a person buys friends or when wealthy people fail to help those who are poor and needy. Can you think of other examples?**

3. Discuss with the students the difference between temptations and sins.
   - ✦ **How many of you think that temptations are sins?**
   - ✦ **If a temptation is a sin, what would that make Jesus?** (a sinner, which is impossible)

4. Ask the students to read silently the first paragraph of **Our Test** on page 46.
   - ✦ **What three things tempt us to sin?** (Satan, people and things in the world, and our weak nature) **Think of examples of how each of these can lead you into temptation.**
   - ✦ **What is the difference between temptations and sin?** (Temptations are people or things that entice us to do what is wrong and omit what is good. Sin is choosing to do what is wrong and to omit what is good.) *Entice* **means "to lure or to attract us to desire something."**

Anointed for the Mission

Jesus was sinless. Why then did he go to John for baptism? The baptism of Jesus was a sign that he accepted his mission as Messiah. He was ready to proclaim and make present the Kingdom of God. Also, Jesus took on the sins of the world. Jesus' going into the water symbolized that he was ready to die for us.

The Gospels proclaim the identity of Jesus by describing an epiphany that occurred after his baptism. An epiphany is a revelation or manifestation of God. The Father's voice, the Holy Spirit like a dove descending upon Jesus, and Jesus the Son are a revelation of the Trinity—the three Persons in one God. The Father strengthened Jesus for his mission, and the Spirit anointed him for his work.

A Moment with Jesus

Jesus' baptism marked the beginning of his mission. Take a moment now to reflect silently on the story of Jesus' baptism. What do you imagine it was like for Jesus to begin his mission of proclaiming God's kingdom? Pause for a moment to reflect on how your Baptism calls you to live. Ask the Holy Spirit to help you be a faithful witness of God's love in the world.

The Messiah's Test

After his baptism, Jesus was led by the Spirit into the desert. There, alone, he prayed and fasted for 40 days to prepare for his mission. His ancestors, the Hebrews, had been formed into God's people by 40 years in the desert. Now Jesus would grow into his role in the same way. While the Hebrews, however, often failed their tests, Jesus overcame Satan and refused to compromise with evil. Faithful to his Father, he proved to be the true Messiah whose kingdom was spiritual and based on faith and love. He walked out of the desert stronger and ready to live his role fully.

The temptations according to Matthew are shown below.

The Temptations

Temptation to physical pleasures

Jesus is hungry after fasting.

Satan: *"If you are the Son of God, command that these stones become loaves of bread."*

Jesus: *"One does not live on bread alone, but by every word that comes from the mouth of God."*

The Kingdom of God is not based on material goods.

Temptation to pride

Satan takes Jesus to the tower of the Temple.

Satan: *"If you are the Son of God, throw yourself down. Scripture says that the angels will support you with their hands."*

Jesus: *"Scripture says, 'You shall not put the Lord, your God, to the test.'"*

The Kingdom of God is not based on magic tricks.

Temptation to power

Satan takes Jesus to a high mountain and shows him all the kingdoms of the world.

Satan: *"All these I shall give you if you will prostrate yourself and worship me."*

Jesus: *"Get away, Satan! Scripture says, 'The Lord, your God, shall you worship and him alone shall you serve.'"*

The Kingdom of God is not based on a show of political power.

45

---

5. Ask a student to read aloud the remaining paragraphs of **Our Test** on page 46.

+ [Post the appropriate flash cards.]

+ **What kind of sin do we usually commit?** (venial)

+ **What sin explains the evil and the weakness in us?** (Original Sin)

+ **Why is *mortal* a good name for mortal sins?** (They destroy the divine life in us, and our relationship with God. They are deadly because they prevent us from having eternal life.)

+ **Mortal sin is committed only if we do or omit something serious, we know it is serious, and we willingly and freely do it.**

+ **What are some factors that determine how guilty we are for a sin?** (knowledge, pressure from outside forces, circumstances that weaken our will power, our intentions)

+ **Can you think of examples, real or made-up, that show someone whose guilt is lessened because of circumstances?**

+ **What are our weapons against temptations?** (our friendship with Jesus, fasting, self-control, the sacraments, praying, God's grace)

Acting

1. Ask a student to read aloud the directions for **Resisting Temptation** on page 46. Divide the class into pairs to write their own examples. Ask some of the students to role-play their test cases.

2. Have the students do the Respond activity on page 47. Conclude by praying the Lord's Prayer, in which we ask God to keep us from temptation and evil.

3. Choose or let the students choose an activity from Reach Out on page 47.

Our Test

You will never meet the devil dressed in a red suit and carrying a pitchfork. However, the power of evil is real. Satan, the world around us, and our own weak nature tempt us to sin. Temptations are people, circumstances, and things that entice us to do what is wrong or to omit doing what is good. We can recognize temptations because they are contrary to Jesus' teaching. Of themselves, temptations are not sins. Sin is actually choosing to do what is wrong or to omit what is good.

Sin offends God and hurts our relationships with him and other people. Sins are called venial when they weaken our relationship with God. Sins that are more serious and completely break our relationship with God are called mortal (deadly) sins. The degree of our guilt for sin depends on

• the seriousness of the matter

• our knowledge

• pressure from outside forces

• circumstances that weaken our willpower

• our intentions

Who seems to be guiltier: someone who steals money to provide food for his family or

someone who steals money so she can buy an expensive car?

Because of Original Sin, the consequences of the sin of our first parents, we are left weak, and doing what is right often involves a struggle. Our means for resisting temptation are fasting, self-control, the sacraments, prayer, and friendship with Jesus, who knows what it is like to be tempted. Also, the Trinity dwells in us since our Baptism. We can rely on God's grace to help us meet the challenge of evil. When we overcome temptation, we fulfill our roles in life—especially our role as baptized Christians.

Resisting Temptation

Below is a temptation to keep you from fulfilling your role as a son or daughter. Write a response to the temptation. Then choose a role from the list you made on page 43 and write your own test.

Role: Son or daughter

Tempter: What your mom wants this time is unreasonable. No one else your age would do that. Don't do what your mom wants.

You: Remember to honor your father and

mother.

Role: Answers will vary.

Tempter:

You:

CHECKPOINT

• Were the learning outcomes achieved?

• Do the students understand the distinction between temptation and sin?

LEARNING OUTCOMES

The students will be able to

- participate in a desert experience.
- integrate the themes of this chapter with their own personal prayer.

Materials

- Bibles or New Testaments
- Reflection notebooks
- Recorded music: Find suggestions for Chapter 6 on page T517.
- Background music CD (optional)

Before You Begin

1. After preparing the students and giving them directions for their desert experience, allow them to be on their own, guided by the Spirit. Ideally the experience should be done outdoors. You can also use a large area such as an all-purpose room or an auditorium. Respect the students' privacy by not asking them to share their experiences. Tell them that if they have any problems with the process, they are welcome to discuss it with you. The best preparation for this lesson is to say a prayer for your students that the Spirit may lead them into the desert and speak to their hearts.

2. You may wish to make copies of the process in Sharing #1 for the students.

Centering

1. Explain why people participate in a desert experience.
   - ✦ **People set aside prolonged times for prayer and solitude when seeking new understanding of themselves and of life.**
   - ✦ **John the Baptist went to the desert to better understand his mission and to prepare for it. After his baptism and at other times, Jesus did the same.**
   - ✦ **Richard Byrd, an Arctic explorer, spent over 4 winter months in total darkness alone at the South Pole. He not only recorded weather, but came away with a new understanding of himself and of life.**
   - ✦ **Many indigenous peoples spend time alone in a deserted place, seeking wisdom before making decisions or entering a new phase of life.**

2. Prepare the students for the desert experience.
   - ✦ **Today you will participate in a mini-desert experience.**
   - ✦ **Since Jesus is the Way, you will follow his example of prayer and fasting in the desert.**

Sharing

1. Discuss with the students that a desert experience can take different forms.
   - ✦ **Like Jesus and John the Baptist you will fast, pray, and read Scripture.** [Walk the students through the process.]
   - ✦ **Fast by refraining from talking to others or disturbing them in any way.**
   - ✦ **Pray to the Holy Spirit to enlighten your mind and open your heart to God's love.**
   - ✦ **Read Matthew 6:25–34, in which Jesus tells us to trust in his loving care of us.**
   - ✦ **Think and pray about these questions:**
     - *What is Jesus telling me?* **Summarize his message in your own words.**
     - *How would a Christian respond?*
     - *What can I do in response to Jesus' words?* **Talk with Jesus about this. Tell him what you'd like to do, what difficulties you expect, and how you hope to accomplish what you set out to do.**
     - *How will I get the spiritual strength and courage to do this?* **Christ is always ready and willing to give us the grace we need. How often do I ask him for it?**
   - ✦ **Listen to what Christ is saying to you.**
   - ✦ **Write in your reflection notebook what Christ says to you and what you say to him.**

2. Send the students to the assigned areas.
   - ✦ You might play instrumental music as they pray and then turn up the volume as a signal to come back together.
   - ✦ The desert experience could last between 25–35 minutes.

3. Give the students a moment of silence to thank God for the graces they experienced.

Acting

1. Have the students sing or listen to an appropriate song.
   Suggestions: "Be Not Afraid" or "Spirit of God."

2. Ask the students for their reactions to the desert experience.
   Suggest that they carry out a desert experience on their own sometime.

CHECKPOINT

- Were the learning outcomes achieved?

- Did the desert experience seem meaningful to the students?

CHAPTER 6 Summary

Remember

What are Jesus' three roles as the Christ?
Jesus' three roles as the Christ are prophet, priest, and king.

What was Jesus' mission?
Jesus' mission was to proclaim and make present the reign of God.

What do we learn from Jesus' baptism?
From Jesus' baptism, we learn that there are three Persons in one God—the Father, the Son, and the Holy Spirit.

What is temptation?
Temptation is any person or thing that entices us to do what is evil or to omit doing what is good.

Respond

Author Pearl Buck said, "Youth is the age of temptation." Here are some questions for you to reflect on and respond to in your reflection notebook.

- What is my biggest temptation right now?
- What am I doing to resist it?
- What does Christ expect of me?
- With Christ's help, what more can I do to overcome this temptation?

Reach Out

1. At times, we need to get away from it all, to find a quiet place to pull ourselves together, to think, and to pray. Your "desert place" might be a special place where you can be alone. It might be the early morning, at night before going to bed, or a quiet Sunday afternoon. Plan a visit to your desert place. Decide when you will go there and what you will think about or pray about. Write about your desert experience in your reflection notebook.

2. Read Philippians 1:27–28. What do you think Saint Paul meant by this advice? How does it apply to your life right now? Think about that during a desert experience, then discuss it with members of your family. Ask them how they interpret Saint Paul's advice.

3. Conduct a round-robin discussion with a small group of friends or family members. Write a thought-provoking question on the bottom of a sheet of paper. Then pass the paper around. Each person writes a response at the top of the paper and folds it over before handing it to the next person. After the paper has circulated, unfold it and read aloud the answers, allowing time for comment.
   Sample questions:
   - How would you reply if someone said, "The devil made me do it!"?
   - At times, we all face the temptation to do something to be popular or admired. How do you handle this temptation?

4. Show you belong to God's kingdom by doing something to oppose an injustice. Talk with your family about an issue that affects your community or members of your family. Together, write a letter to the editor, write or e-mail your state senator or representative, or make a phone call to a local official to express your opinion as a disciple of Jesus.

47

Day Four Making Decisions

Student pages 47–48

LEARNING OUTCOMES

The students will be able to

- define a good decision-making process.
- apply the process in their own lives.
- demonstrate an understanding of the key concepts in this chapter.

Materials

- Bibles or New Testaments
- BLM 23, BLM 24
- BLM 25 Quiz
- Reflection notebooks

Before You Begin

1. Jesus said he is the Way to the Father. By reflecting on his love for us, his life, and his teachings, we are better able to cope with the daily choices placed before us. The "way" is not some formula for holiness. We need to use all of our resources and gifts.

2. Approaches presented here may be used throughout the year to answer questions, especially those requiring some type of active response to a situation.

3. When planning today's lesson, keep in mind that Day Four is when the students take the quiz for this chapter. Reserve time at the end of class for this assessment. The quiz can also be administered on Day Five.

Centering

Discuss our roles and how we make decisions.

✦ **No matter what roles we have, we all must make decisions and work out problems. Those of us who follow Christ make decisions in keeping with his values.**

✦ **In this lesson, you will learn some guidelines for making mature Christian decisions.**

Sharing

1. Read and discuss the following situation with the students:

   ✦ **Joshua, Brittany, and José are playing Frisbee. They hear yelling and see two younger boys fighting. Brittany and José want to break it up. Joshua doesn't.**

   ✦ **What is the problem that Brittany, Joshua, and José face?** (whether or not they should break up the fight)

   ✦ **Think of as many possible solutions to this problem as you can.** [Write each solution in a separate column on the board.]

   ✦ **For each solution, think of the pros and cons, the consequences of each.** [Record these on the board, noting the values and standards that are guiding the students.]

   ✦ **Now that we have some idea of what could be done, what do you think *should* be done and *why*?** (Remember that a judgment should not be based simply on the number of pros. It is important to point out that one con may be stronger than all the pros combined.)

2. **BLM 23, 24** Distribute copies of BLM 23 **Solving Problems** and BLM 24 **Two Problems.**

   ✦ Explain the decision-making steps on BLM 23 **Solving Problems.**

   ✦ Divide the class into groups. Have the students discuss the two dilemmas on BLM 24 **Two Problems** using the decision-making steps. (The students may demonstrate various levels of cognitive and moral development.

CHAPTER 6 Review Activities

Identification To what do the following phrases refer?

1. Jesus' mission: <u>to proclaim and make present the reign of God</u>

2. Jesus' anointing for his mission: <u>baptism</u>

3. Jesus' test: <u>temptation by Satan</u>

4. Jesus' type of kingdom: <u>spiritual, one of love for God in our hearts</u>

5. A person who speaks for God: <u>prophet</u>

6. A manifestation of God: <u>epiphany</u>

Temptations In each situation, decide if the person is guilty (G) or only tempted (T). Write the correct letter for each situation.

__G__ 1. Sue Ellen shoplifts a necklace and does not get caught.

__G__ 2. Robert has a bad cold. When his brother picks on him, Robert punches him.

__T__ 3. Jill does not like Patty. She always has the urge to avoid her and to say things to hurt her.

__T__ 4. Jane considers going to a party where she knows there will be beer.

__G__ 5. Mark joins in when boys on the bus make fun of a student in special education classes.

__G__ 6. The Sunday after Ann's family returns from camping, Ann says she is too tired to go to Mass. Her mother tells her to stay home, so she does.

__T__ 7. Frequently during the day, the sexy scenes in a video Carl saw come into his mind without his willing it.

Three of a Kind Write a short description that identifies each set of words.

1. _____ roles of Christ _____
   prophet • priest • king

2. _____ the temptations of Christ, or what a false Messiah's kingdom is built on _____
   material goods • magic tricks • political power

3. _____ what Jesus was tempted with _____
   pleasure • pride • power

4. _____ the three types of sin _____
   mortal • venial • original

5. _____ sources of temptation _____
   Satan • the world • human nature

6. _____ factors that lessen guilt _____
   knowledge • circumstances • intention

7. _____ aids to fight temptation _____
   self-control • sacraments • grace

48

The sharing may expose them to a higher level of thinking and moral growth, creating tension that helps them clarify their ideas and understand the approach of others.) Have the students explain what should be done and why.

3. Direct the students to think of a situation in their own lives that calls for a decision.
   Have them write about it in their reflection notebooks.

4. Lead the students through the Summary and the Review Activities on pages 47–48.

5. **BLM 25** Distribute and administer BLM 25 **Chapter 6 Quiz.**

Use this opportunity to assess the students' understanding of the main concepts in the chapter. If there is not sufficient time for the quiz, consider moving it to Day Five.

Acting

1. Have the students pray Philippians 1:6, 9–11.

2. At the end of class, have the students tear out and take home pages 47–48.

CHECKPOINT ✔

• Were the learning outcomes achieved

Day Five   Extending the Chapter

Gather and Go Forth

Lead students through pages 49–50 in the student book. Find catechist instruction on T326–T327.
Materials: Bibles

Use the following suggestions to create an additional lesson for Day Five.

1. Remind the students to take home pages 47–48 to share what they are learning with their families.

2. Incorporate any unused BLMs from the week's chapter.

3. Consider the time of the liturgical year and use the appropriate Special Seasons and Lessons. SSLs begin on page T369.

4. Visit www.christourlife.com to find additional activities for Extending the Chapter.

5. Use activities from Enriching the Faith Experience.

6. Guide the students in a prayerful discussion of Sunday's Scripture readings. Visit www.christourlife.com for more information.

Chapter 6   Enriching the Faith Experience

Use the following activities to enrich a lesson or to replace an activity with one that better meets the needs of your class.

1. Have volunteers make a video of the life of John the Baptist.

2. In connection with the lesson for Day One, provide practice in handling situations that require courage. Draw these cartoon balloons on the board or on a transparency.

> "Let's have some fun with that old man walking down the street."

> "So you're one of those Catholics, huh?"

> "Aw, come on. Your mom will never find out."

> "What's the matter? Afraid to smoke pot?"

✦ Divide the class into four groups and assign one cartoon to each group. Have the students write a response to fit each of these circumstances in the balloons:

- **The question is asked by someone of whom you think highly.**

- **It is asked by someone who annoys or makes fun of you.**

- **You are listening to your conscience.**

✦ Have the students discuss their answers within the groups and prepare a summary. As the summaries are given, allow interaction with the rest of the class.

✦ Help the students to see that listening to our conscience often requires courage.

✦ Students might draw cartoon balloons for other situations in which courage is needed. Ask the class for solutions.

3. Ask a group of students to write examples of how people their age are likely to face temptation. Have them present these situations to the class for suggestions on how to handle the temptations.

4. Distribute large sheets of drawing paper to the students and have them design posters using prophetic messages they compose. Display these with the caption "Repent, for the kingdom is at hand."

5. Draw on the students' knowledge to list the means that modern-day prophets use to speak to people (protest marches, placards, e-mails, demonstrations, letters to the editor, billboards, magazines, newspapers, blogs, radio and TV spots). Have a discussion about messages the students have heard from modern-day prophets.

6. Have the students compose a prayer to pray in time of temptation.

7. Suggest that students write a "Person of Courage" award for someone in their family, listing things that person does that give evidence of his or her courage.

The Apostles, Mary, and Others
JESUS THE MASTER

Faith Focus

Jesus called disciples, in particular Mary and the apostles, to share in his mission.

Reflecting on the Faith Experience

Take a few moments to reflect prayerfully before preparing the lesson.

Listening

The next day John was there again with two of his disciples, and as he watched Jesus walk by, he said, "Behold, the Lamb of God." The two disciples heard what he said and followed Jesus. Jesus turned and saw them following him and said to them, "What are you looking for?" They said to him, "Rabbi" (which translated means Teacher), "where are you staying?" He said to them, "Come, and you will see." So they went and saw where he was staying, and they stayed with him that day.

John 1:35–39

Reflecting

In creating, sustaining, calling, and supporting, God constantly reveals who he is. In Jesus, we discover how God feels about us, how willing he is to shower unconditional and lasting love on us. The depths of the richness of God can be studied. We study God's attributes, qualities, and Revelation in the events of salvation history. We are familiar with titles and sayings of Christ; the redemption on the Cross, the victory over sin and death, and his Resurrection. Knowledge of God may lead to virtuous living. But to live the Christian life of radical love requires more than knowledge of God. It requires knowing God by meeting God in Jesus.

Millions of people have heard of Jesus and the Revelation of the Father's love, but not all have been transformed. Jesus called twelve apostles impelled by the Spirit to carry his message to the known limits of the world. While some hear and walk away, others are caught in the power and glory of the experience of Jesus. What changes lives is the gift of seeing, of encountering Jesus. Peter saw Jesus from afar. He encountered Jesus in moments of love and forgiveness. Nathaniel heard of Jesus through a friend. He encountered him in a penetrating look that revealed Christ's knowledge of him. Paul knew of Jesus from others, but his life was transformed as he encountered Christ in a vision's blinding light.

God always takes the first step. We don't understand why or how; divine motives and methods are too mysterious for us. But we can comprehend God's language of love: the look that frees, the touch that heals, the call that moves us out of our smallness into the vastness of Christian love. And in return, God seeks only the triumph of love in our midst.

This is how all will know that you are my disciples, if you have love for one another.

John 13:35

What is the story of my encounter with Jesus?

Responding

Lord Jesus, may the experiences I plan for class deepen my students' relationship with you.

Scripture for Further Reflection

Psalm 42–43 We thirst for God who is our shelter and hope; within the depths of our soul we long for God.

Philippians 3:7–16 Those who have come to a deep, interior knowledge of Christ desire only to follow him, in pursuit of the goal, God's calling, in Christ Jesus.

Preparing for the Faith Experience

Day One
Walking with Jesus

Day Two
Those Who Followed Jesus

Day Three
The Best Disciple

Day Four
Witnessing to Jesus

Day Five
Extending the Chapter

† Gather and Go Forth

Scripture in This Chapter

Luke 8:21 Jesus and His Family

John 1:35–39 Come and See

Philippians 3:8 I gain all in Christ.

Catholic Social Teaching

Family and Community

Church Documents

Catechism of the Catholic Church. The themes of this chapter correspond to the following paragraphs: 494, 551–552, 857–860.

General Directory for Catechesis #43. Jesus Christ founded the Church built on the apostles. He gave the apostles the Holy Spirit and sent them to preach the Gospel to the whole world, a task that they faithfully discharged.

Decree on the Pastoral Office of Bishops #2 (Second Vatican Council). Christ commanded the apostles to teach all peoples, to sanctify them in truth, and to give them spiritual nourishment. Bishops have been designated by the Holy Spirit to take the place of the apostles as pastors of souls and to carry on the work of Christ.

Pastoral Constitution on the Church in the Modern World #28 (Second Vatican Council). Because we love Christ, we are impelled to proclaim the truth to all people.

Decree on the Apostolate of Lay People #6 (Second Vatican Council). Every true follower of Jesus diligently uses his or her talents to lead others to Christ or to inspire them to live more fully according to his love.

Gather and Go Forth

Find catechist instruction for Gather and Go Forth student pages 59–60 on T328–T329.

Enriching the Faith Experience

Use the activities at the end of the chapter to enrich a lesson or to replace an activity with one that better meets the needs of your class.

Bulletin Board

A suggestion for a bulletin-board design for this chapter is pictured.

The First Believers

Peter
Andrew
James the Greater
John
Philip
Bartholomew
Matthew
Thomas
James the Less
Jude
Simon
Judas
Matthias

LEARNING OUTCOMES

The students will be able to

- discuss how Jesus called the first disciples.
- relate the call of the disciples to their own call to follow Christ.

Key Term

apostle—one of the Twelve who were close to Jesus and chosen by him to preach the Good News and act in his name

Word to Know

disciple

See Glossary for definition.

Materials

- Bibles or New Testaments
- BLM 26 (Needs to be prepared before class)
- Envelopes for invitations (optional)
- Drawing paper
- Crayons or markers
- Directions for Sharing #4 on the board
- Reflection notebooks

Before You Begin

1. Since the time of Abraham, the first believer, God has called individuals to special faith and action. Jesus, too, called certain people. He continues to call and leaves us free to choose life or death.

2. Students of this age are often unsure of themselves and need to realize Jesus is interested in them, concerned about them, and eager that they respond to his call. With unconditional love, he accepts them with all their strengths and weaknesses.

3. In Centering #1, you could just read the invitation to the class.

4. In Sharing #4, the students could read about the apostles independently and make 13 cards, like baseball cards, on the apostles. Have them put the apostle's name and a picture or symbol on one side, and vital statistics on the other.

CHAPTER 7

The Apostles, Mary, and Others

Jesus the Master

You have probably heard of the great teachers Socrates of Greece (left) and the Buddha of India. Every once in a while, someone very wise such as those men appears on earth. The person attracts people who want to explore the mysteries of life. The teacher is called a master, and the followers are called **disciples**, which means learners. Jesus, the world's greatest teacher, had many disciples who were dedicated to him. Excited by what they heard and saw, they followed Jesus and brought other people to him.

The First Disciples

John's Gospel tells how Jesus met his first disciples after his baptism:

> The next day John [the Baptist] was there again with two of his disciples, and as he watched Jesus walk by, he said, "Behold, the Lamb of God." The two disciples heard what he said and followed Jesus. Jesus turned and saw them following him and said to them, "What are you looking for?" They said to him, "Rabbi" (which translated means Teacher), "where are you staying?" He said to them, "Come, and you will see." So they went and saw where he was staying, and they stayed with him that day. It was about four in the afternoon.

John 1:35–39

Something about Jesus attracted the disciples to him. They responded to his invitation, "Come, and you will see." For many months after their first meeting, the disciples walked with Jesus from town to town. They enjoyed his company. Their understanding of him grew day by day. First they called him teacher. At the Last Supper, Jesus called them friends. Eventually they called him Messiah.

(51)

Centering _____

1. **BLM 26** Distribute the invitations from BLM 26 **You Are Invited.**

   ✦ Have the students read them silently.

   ✦ **Why do we like to receive invitations?** (They are a sign that someone cares about us.) **If you sent out invitations and no one came, how would you feel? Why?**

   ✦ **What does RSVP mean?** (*Répondez s'il vous plait* or please reply.) **What does Jesus invite you to do?** (be his disciple) **You are free to follow or not.**

   ✦ **Today you will learn more about being a disciple and meet some** people who accepted Jesus' invitation.

2. Link the last lesson with today's lesson.

You learned how Jesus began his public life by being baptized and going into the desert for forty days. Today you will learn how he gathered a band of disciples.

Sharing _____

1. Have the students read silently the opening section on page 51.
What is the meaning of *disciples*? (learners, those who follow a master)

2. Call on a student to read aloud **The First Disciples** on page 51.
  ◆ Choose four students to act out the encounter.
  ◆ **Why did John's disciples leave him for Jesus?** (John identified Jesus as the Lamb of God.) **How do you think John felt?**
  ◆ **What were the disciples looking for as they followed Jesus?**
  ◆ **What do you think happened at Jesus' home that day to make the men leave everything to follow him?**

3. Ask several volunteers to read aloud **The Twelve** on page 52.
  ◆ **Who are the apostles?** (disciples chosen to be close to Jesus, share his ministry, and act in his name) **Why is their number significant?** (There were 12 tribes in Israel. The apostles symbolize the new people of God.)
  ◆ **What kind of people were they?** (ordinary people such as fishermen and a tax collector) **What does this tell you about Jesus?** (He can work through anyone.)
  ◆ **We honor all but one apostle as saints today.**

4. Divide the class into 13 groups. Have several students read aloud **Portraits of the Apostles** on pages 52–55. Direct each group to select an apostle to present to the class using the following directions:

they were jealous and ambitious. Sometimes they were afraid. Sometimes they did not understand Jesus, yet Jesus loved them. They were with him at the Last Supper, and he sent them to act in his name.

The Twelve

Jesus chose 12 men to accompany him on his mission. They are called the apostles. The word *apostle* comes from words that mean "send" and "messenger." The apostles were to share the ministry of Jesus and preach the Good News of the risen Lord. They and their successors, the bishops, would be empowered by Christ to carry out his mission. Because 12 was the number of the tribes of Israel, the 12 apostles symbolized the new People of God.

There is a saying that you can tell a lot about a person by the friends he or she keeps. The apostles were political nobodies. They were ordinary people, such as fishermen and a tax collector. All of them were sinners. Sometimes

When Jesus looked at Simon, he saw a fisherman who often spoke without thinking. He also saw Simon as a future leader. Simon would be the first person to proclaim the Gospel on the morning of Pentecost. When Jesus looks at us, he sees us as we really are, with our good qualities and our flaws. He also sees in us what we can become.

The apostles and all the other disciples found compassion and strength in Jesus. Jesus challenged them to continue his mission. Jesus continues to touch the hearts of people today and to challenge them. Unlike Socrates and the Buddha, Jesus is still with us, inviting us to "come, and you will see." His influence is stronger and more real today than when he walked the roads of Palestine.

Portraits of the Apostles

The following sketches of the 12 apostles are drawn from Scripture and Tradition.

 Peter
Feasts: February 22, June 29, November 18
Peter was the apostle Jesus chose to be the first leader of his Church. When Peter met Jesus, he was known as Simon. Jesus changed his name to *Cephas*, or Peter, the Greek word for "rock." Jesus said he would build his Church upon that rock.

Peter and his brother Andrew were fishermen from Bethsaida. Later they lived in Capernaum, a city on the northern shore of the Sea of Galilee. Peter often spoke and acted impulsively. He loved Jesus very much and said he would follow Jesus even to death. According to Tradition, Peter arrived in Rome during a great persecution of Christians. He was arrested and crucified upside down. Most pictures of Peter show him carrying a pair of keys. In Matthew 16:19, Jesus gives Peter the keys of the kingdom of heaven when he makes Peter head of his Church.

 52 UNIT 1

- **Think of a descriptive nickname for your apostle and prepare to explain it.**
- **Make a symbol of the apostle.**
- **Choose someone to tell about the apostle or impersonate him in costume.**

Acting _____

 Have the students read **A Moment with Jesus** on page 55.
Allow sufficient time for silent reflection.

CHECKPOINT

- Were the learning outcomes achieved?

LEARNING OUTCOMES

The students will be able to

- identify the principal characteristics of the apostles.

- explain the role of the pope and bishops as those who carry on the teaching of the apostles.

- discuss how to pray reflectively using a Scripture passage.

Key Term

College of bishops—The organization of Roman Catholic bishops together with all the other Eastern Catholic Church leaders.

Materials

- Bibles or New Testaments

- Recorded music: Find suggestions for Chapter 7 on page T517.

- Name cards for the apostles: *Peter, Andrew, James the Greater, John, Philip, Bartholomew (Nathanael), Matthew, Thomas, James the Less, Jude, Simon, Judas, Matthias*

Before You Begin

1. We use the term *apostolic succession* to describe our belief that the bishops who are guiding the Church today are following the same mandate that was given by Christ to his apostles. Apostolic succession means that today's bishops are teaching the same faith that was handed down from the apostles. They are guided by the Holy Spirit in the same way the apostles were.

2. If students made cards of the apostles in the previous lesson instead of preparing group presentations, direct the questions in Sharing #2 to all the students, letting them refer to their cards.

Andrew
Feast: November 30

Andrew was one of the first men Jesus called to follow him. After Andrew met Jesus, he brought his brother Peter to meet Jesus. Andrew's name means "manly" and "courageous." His symbol is an X-shaped cross, because it is believed that he died on one. Centuries after his death, missionaries taking his relics to Scotland were shipwrecked. They reached shore safely and introduced the Scots to Jesus. Because so many people came to follow Christ, Andrew was named the patron saint of Scotland. He is also the patron saint of Russia.

James the Greater
Feast: July 25

Two apostles were named James. James the Greater was the brother of John. James and John were sons of Zebedee and Salome. With their father, they worked as fishermen and were partners with Peter.

James and John once asked Jesus to give them places of honor in his kingdom. Peter, James, and John were the only apostles chosen to witness the Transfiguration of Jesus and the raising of Jairus's daughter from the dead. They were the only three to be near Jesus during his agony in the garden. James was the first apostle to be martyred for Christ. He was beheaded in Jerusalem at the command of King Herod. His symbols are a traveler's staff and a pilgrim's bell. James is the patron saint of Spain.

John
Feast: December 27

John is sometimes called the teenage apostle. Unlike the other apostles, he was not married. Although at one time Jesus called James and John "sons of thunder," John developed into a gentle, sensitive man, an apostle of love. We think John is the person referred to in John's Gospel as "the disciple Jesus loved." John was the only apostle to stand beneath the Cross, and Jesus

asked him to take care of Mary. The story is told that whenever John was asked to speak in his old age, all he would ever say was "Little children, love one another. Love one another." He was the only apostle to die a natural death. According to Tradition, John was the fourth Evangelist. His symbol is an eagle.

Philip
Feast: May 3

Philip, like Peter and Andrew, came from Bethsaida. He received a direct invitation from Jesus to follow him. Convinced that Jesus was the one Moses and the prophets had written about, Philip told his friend Nathanael to come and see. We learn from writers of the early Church that Philip did great missionary work in Asia Minor, where he is buried. (Asia Minor roughly corresponds to the Asian portion of present-day Turkey.) Philip's symbol is a column or pillar because of the tradition that he died hanging from one of these.

Bartholomew
Feast: August 24

Bartholomew is believed to be Nathanael, the man whom Philip introduced to Jesus. *Bartholomew* may mean "son of Tolomai," in Hebrew, *bar Tolomai*. Jesus, who knows the thoughts of all hearts, spoke of him as an Israelite without guile. That means he was straightforward and honest and did not try to deceive people. Bartholomew traveled east to preach the Gospel. While in Armenia (a country east of present-day Turkey), he was arrested, tortured, and finally put to death. His symbol is a knife, the instrument of his torture.

Matthew
Feast: September 21

Matthew, also called Levi, was a tax collector. He lived in Capernaum, where Jesus did much of his public ministry. Matthew is remembered for his prompt response to Jesus' call. He immediately left

Centering

Play a song about following Jesus.

Sharing

1. Act as a master of ceremonies to introduce the presentations of the apostles or ask a student do it.

   ✦ **The apostles were chosen to share the ministry of Jesus and act in his name.**

   ✦ **They were privileged to live with Jesus for about three years, listening to his teachings and watching what he did. Because the apostles told about their experiences, we now know about Jesus.**

2. Distribute the name cards of the apostles to the students and have them stand in a row.

- ✦ **If the question I ask applies to the apostle whose name card you hold, raise up your card.**

- ✦ **Who were fishermen?** (Peter, James the Greater, John, and Andrew)

- ✦ **Who was a tax collector?** (Matthew)

- ✦ **Who was a Zealot?** (Simon)

- ✦ **Who had charge of the common funds?** (Judas)

- ✦ **Which three apostles did Jesus choose to be with him for special events?** (Peter, James the Greater, John)

- ✦ **Which apostles were married** (all except John)

- ✦ **Which apostles were martyred?** (all of them except John)

- ✦ **Which apostles were brothers?** (Peter and Andrew, James the Greater and John, James the Less and Jude) [Have the pairs stand together.]

- ✦ **Who was appointed the first head of the Church?** (Peter)

- ✦ **Who were the "sons of thunder"?** (James the Greater and John)

- ✦ **Who betrayed Jesus?** (Judas)

- ✦ **Whom did Jesus call "an Israelite without guile"?** (Bartholomew, or Nathanael)

- ✦ **Who was chosen to replace Judas?** (Matthias)

- ✦ **Who didn't believe that the other apostles saw the risen Lord?** (Thomas)

- ✦ **Who brought his brother to Jesus?** (Andrew)

- ✦ **Who brought his friend to Jesus?** (Philip)

- ✦ **Which apostle stayed at the Cross and was given Mary as a mother?** (John)

- ✦ **Which apostles were credited with writing Gospels?** (Matthew and John)

- ✦ **Which apostles have letters in the New Testament that bear their names?** (Peter, John, James, Jude)

- ✦ **Which apostles were crucified, according to tradition?** (Peter, Andrew)

- ✦ **Which apostle did Jesus rename "the rock"?** (Peter)

---

his money booth and followed Jesus. The Gospel according to Matthew was often quoted by the early Christians and is presented as the first of the four Gospels in the New Testament. Tradition tells us that Matthew died a martyr's death, probably in Ethiopia in eastern Africa. His symbol as an Evangelist is the head of a man.

Thomas
Feast: July 3

The apostle Thomas is best remembered as "doubting" Thomas. He was not with the other apostles when Jesus came to them after the Resurrection.

Thomas claimed that he would not believe that Jesus had truly risen unless he could touch his wounds. Once he saw Jesus, however, Thomas immediately fell to his knees and exclaimed, "My Lord and my God!"

Thought to be a house builder by trade, Thomas is usually shown carrying carpenters' tools. He is the patron saint of carpenters, architects, and people who are blind. Thomas is thought to have brought the Good News to India, where he died a martyr and was buried.

James the Less
Feast: May 3

James the Less is the brother of the apostle Jude. He was given the title "the Less" to distinguish him from the other apostle James. Perhaps he was shorter or younger than the other James. His mother was Mary of Clopas, a follower of Jesus and possibly a cousin of the Blessed Virgin Mary.

According to Tradition, James the Less was the first bishop of Jerusalem. Some scholars believe that the letter bearing his name may not have been written by him. James is said to have been beaten to death by Jews who were angry that Paul had escaped death by appealing to Caesar. James's symbol is a cudgel, or club.

Jude
Feast: October 28

A brother of James the Less and perhaps a cousin of Jesus, this apostle is also known as Thaddeus. For reasons unknown, Saint Jude has become popular as the patron of hopeless cases. He preached the Gospel in the region between the Tigris and Euphrates Rivers and Persia (Iran), and one of the letters in the New Testament bears his name. Some pagan magicians are believed to have killed him for exposing how they were fooling the people. His symbol is an ax, the instrument used in his martyrdom.

Simon
Feast: October 28

Simon from Cana was the only apostle who was a Zealot. When Simon chose to follow Jesus, he had to channel his zeal into the peaceful pursuit of the Kingdom of God. He first preached the Gospel in Egypt and then went to Persia with Jude. It was there that he suffered martyrdom when he was beaten with clubs and then sawed into pieces. His symbol is a saw.

Judas

From his name, Judas Iscariot is believed to have come from a town in Judea. He was entrusted with the care of the common funds. He helped himself to some of the money that belonged to all. He also betrayed Jesus for 30 pieces of silver. When he realized what he had done, he did not return to Jesus to receive his loving forgiveness as Peter did. Instead, Judas hanged himself. According to the Acts of the Apostles, Judas fell and died in a field he had bought with his blood money.

(54) UNIT 1

3. Ask a volunteer to read aloud the first three paragraphs of **Successors of the Apostles** on page 55.

✦ **Who carries on the teaching of the apostles today?** (the pope and the bishops)

✦ **What responsibilities are given to the pope?** (He is the Bishop of Rome, the pastor of the whole Church, and has universal power in the care of souls.)

4. Have a student read aloud the rest of this section.

✦ **What role do the bishops play in the Church?** (successors of the apostles, principal pastors of their local churches, source of unity)

✦ **In what ways do the pope and bishops work together?** (keep the faith alive, exercise the authority of Jesus Christ)

Acting

1. Direct the students to do the Respond activity on page 57.

2. Have the students memorize the names of the apostles.

CHECKPOINT

- Were the learning objectives achieved?

- How did the students respond to the presentations on the apostles?

Matthias
Feast: May 14

We learn from the Acts of the Apostles that Matthias was selected to take the place of Judas. Matthias was a follower from the beginning of Jesus' ministry and had been a witness of the resurrected Lord. It is believed that he preached in Palestine and was martyred by crucifixion. His symbol is a lance.

A Moment with Jesus

Each of the sketches above gives a glimpse of the men whom Jesus chose to be his apostles. Pick one of them, reread the sketch of him, and reflect on how he carried out the mission of Jesus. What does his symbol tell you about his relationship with Jesus?

Pause for a few moments and ask Jesus to help you deepen your relationship with him and his Church. Thank Jesus for calling you to follow him.

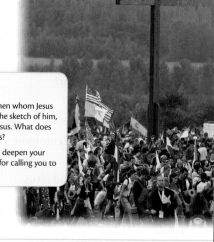

Pilgrims at World Youth Day, Germany, 2005. ❯

Successors of the Apostles

The primary role of the apostles was to witness to the life, Death and Resurrection of Jesus Christ. Our Catholic faith is built on the foundation that the apostles have given to us.

Jesus intended that the faith of the apostles be proclaimed to the end of time. So the teaching of the apostles is carried on by their successors—the pope and the bishops of the Catholic Church.

The pope, the bishop of Rome, is the successor of Peter, who was appointed by Jesus to be the head of the Church. The pope is the pastor of the whole Church and has the universal power in the care of souls.

The bishops of the Catholic Church are successors of the apostles and are the principal pastors of their local churches (dioceses). The bishops are the visible source and foundation of unity in the local Church.

With the pope, the college of bishops exercises the authority of Jesus Christ over the whole Church. They keep alive the faith in Jesus witnessed by the first apostles in their lives and in their deaths.

Pope Francis.

CHAPTER 7 55

LEARNING OUTCOMES

The students will be able to

- explain how Mary is the first and best disciple.
- discuss the role of witness and apply it to Mary and to themselves.

Key Term

witness—one whose life gives testimony to his or her beliefs

Materials

- Bibles or New Testaments
- BLM 27
- Blue ribbon marked "Best Disciple"

- Scripture references from Sharing #3 written on slips of paper or on the board
- Writing paper or drawing paper
- Marian hymn (optional)

Before You Begin

1. There is surprisingly little about Mary in the New Testament. She does not play a major role in Jesus' public ministry, and the Gospels do not mention her in connection with the Resurrection. Yet Mary clearly came to be revered in the early Church because of her role as mother of the Savior and her commitment to him.

2. Mary was called Mother of the Church as early as the 12th century. In 1964, during the Mass at the end of the third session of the Second Vatican Council, Pope Paul VI officially proclaimed Mary as Mother of the Church.

3. The activity in Sharing #2 may be done individually or by the entire class instead of in groups.

4. You may wish to teach the students to pray the Rosary. **The Rosary** is on pages 236–237. (T428–T429)

Centering

Help the class to determine that Mary is the first and best disciple.

- **In the last lesson, you came to know the apostles better. Suppose you were to give an award to the best disciple.** [Show the ribbon.] **What questions would you ask in order to select the winner?** (Who loved Jesus most? Who was most like him in doing the Father's will?)

- **What qualities would you look for?** [List the responses on the board.]

- **Who is the first and best disciple?** (Mary)

Sharing

1. Have the students read silently **The First and Best Disciple** on page 56.

   - Ask them to write the Scripture verse in the space provided.

   - **Why is Mary the first disciple?** (She was the first one to believe and follow Christ. She brought him into the world. She devoted her life to him for thirty years before his public ministry.)

- **What does it mean to be a witness?** (to believe and act on that belief)

- **How was Mary a witness?** (She trusted that Jesus would help at the wedding feast. She stood faithful at the foot of the Cross.)

- **Who does Jesus call the real members of his family?** (those who hear the Word of God and keep it)

2. Divide the class into nine groups.
   Distribute the slips of paper containing the Scripture references from Sharing #3 or assign references from the board. Read the directions.

   - **Look up the passage and read it.**

   - **Prepare an explanation of how it shows Mary as a believer and disciple.**

   - **Think of a practical example of how someone your age can imitate Mary.**

3. Have each group explain its Scripture passage and its example.

   Family and Community

   - (Luke 1:26–38) The Annunciation. Mary was totally open to God in her life. She was ready to be the maidservant of God. Her answer was always yes to God's will.

   - (Luke 1:39,46–56) The Visitation. Mary spread the Good News, praising God and reaching out to help others.

   - (Luke 2:1–7) The Nativity. Despite hardship and inconvenience, Mary was faithful to her call. She was loving and caring, a true life-giver.

   - (Luke 2:15–20) Mary knew how to ponder, to consider how present God was to her, and how he worked in her life. She knew prayer and meditation.

   - (Luke 2:33–35) Mary, like every disciple, had to face difficulties and pain. In choosing to be Christ's mother, she chose to be identified with his ministry and his suffering.

✦ (Luke 8:19–21) Mary is one who heard the Word of God and kept it. Jesus calls those who do so his family.

✦ (John 2:1–12) Mary was obedient and faith-filled, a disciple who saw the needs of others and turned to Jesus for aid.

✦ (John 19:25–27) Mary was faithful even when all others fled. She accepted suffering at the foot of the Cross and is the mother and model of all those who follow Christ.

✦ (Acts 1:14) Mary was present in the upper room, praying and waiting. She was there, open to the Holy Spirit, even as she had been at the Annunciation.

4. Discuss the new qualities of a true disciple that the students found in the Scripture study.

✦ **What are some new qualities of a disciple you found in these various scripture passages?** [Add these to the list on the board.]

✦ **Each of you is called to grow as a disciple in these areas as well.**

5. Refer the students to the Hail Mary on the inside front cover of their books.

✦ **Mary is so close to her Son that we turn to her and ask her to intercede with God on our behalf.**

✦ **The Hail Mary has three parts: the words of the angel Gabriel** (Luke 1:28)**; the words of Elizabeth to Mary** (Luke 1:42)**, which were added in the 11th century; and a prayer of petition to Mary added in the 15th century. This addition also included her title Mother of God, a title proclaimed by the Council of Ephesus in the fifth century.**

6. Have the students compose a prayer to Mary.

✦ Suggest that they follow the structure of the Hail Mary. (the first part a Scripture passage about Mary; the second part a prayer of petition).

The First and Best Disciple

The Acts of the Apostles tells us that on Pentecost when the Spirit came, Mary, the mother of Jesus, was with the disciples. Her presence was fitting because she was the first one to believe and follow Christ. Her faith and obedience made her open to God's will in her life. Mary brought Jesus into the world through the power of the Holy Spirit. She devoted her life to him for 30 years before he began his public ministry. One of her titles is Queen of Apostles.

The highest praise of Mary is that she fits her Son's description in Luke 8:21. Write Jesus' words here:

"My mother and my brothers are _____

those who hear the word of God _____

and act on it."

True disciples, the real members of Christ's family, believe and act on their beliefs. Someone whose life gives testimony to his or her beliefs is called a witness. Mary was a witness. At a wedding feast, she trusted that her Son would help when the wine ran out. She told the servants, "Do whatever he tells you." During the suffering and Death of Jesus, many followers fled in fear. Mary, however, stood faithful at the foot of the Cross. There Jesus called her the mother of John, the beloved disciple. From the moment of the Incarnation, when she became the mother of Jesus, Mary became the mother of all believers. Mary is the mother of Jesus and the Mother of the Church, his mystical body.

Mary is the model for everyone who seeks Jesus Christ. In our struggles to be faithful

◁ Statue of Mary, Cartagena, Colombia.

56

disciples, she not only inspires us, but she also prays for us and loves us.

The Way of the Witness

1. Read the concerns junior high students have about seriously following Jesus. Write a concern of your own. Then rank the concerns from the greatest (8) to the least (1).

_____ They will not have as much fun.

_____ They may lose their friends.

_____ They will have to treat everyone kindly.

_____ They will be made fun of.

_____ Their families will not understand them.

_____ They will have to work too hard.

_____ They will have to give up too many things.

_____ Other: _____

Think about how you would answer each question. For each question, write your answer below.

2. If people your age decided to be real friends of Jesus, what things would they most likely have to change in their lives?

_____

3. If people your age decided not to grow in their love for Jesus, what things would they be giving up?

_____

4. What do you think is the best way for junior high students to witness to one another? to the world?

_____

✦ Have the students illustrate or decorate their prayers.

Acting _____

1.  Distribute copies of BLM 27 **Mary in Our Life.** Allow the students to choose one or two activities for extra credit. You may wish to assign bonus points for their work.

2. Ask several students to pray their prayer to Mary. You may also choose to have the class listen to or sing a Marian hymn.

CHECKPOINT ✓

• Were the learning outcomes achieved?

LEARNING OUTCOMES

The students will be able to

- identify the role other people have had in leading them to deeper faith.
- discuss the powerful impact they have on others.
- demonstrate an understanding of the key concepts in this chapter.

Key Term

missionary—one who is sent to proclaim the Good News and bring others to know and love God

Materials

- Diagram drawn on the board:

- Reflection notebooks
- Large book drawn on the board, or brought in, titled "The Book of Your Life"
- BLM 28 Quiz

Before You Begin

1. We are all called through Baptism to bring Jesus to others, to have missionary hearts. We can be more authentic witnesses to Jesus if we periodically try to discern if our lives truly reflect our beliefs. Young people need to develop habits of reflection if they are to grow in Christ Jesus.

2. This lesson would be more memorable if you were to have a missionary or a lay volunteer come to class and speak of his or her special call and work.

3. Videos and other material on the missions are available from Maryknoll, Catholic Relief Services, the Society for the Propagation of the Faith, the Extension Society, and your diocesan office.

4. When planning today's lesson, keep in mind that Day Four is when the students take the quiz for this chapter. Reserve time at the end of class for this assessment. The quiz can also be administered on Day Five.

CHAPTER 7 Summary

Remember

Who were the apostles?
The apostles were the 12 men chosen by Jesus to share his ministry and preach the Good News of the risen Lord.

What is a disciple of Jesus?
A disciple of Jesus is a follower of Jesus who is dedicated to him.

What is a witness?
A witness is someone whose life gives testimony to his or her beliefs.

Why is Mary a disciple?
Mary is a disciple because she was open to God's will and lived it faithfully.

What did Jesus demand of his disciples?
Jesus said, "Whoever wishes to come after me must deny himself, take up his cross, and follow me." (Matthew 16:24)

Respond

Jesus' invitation to you to become his disciple includes an RSVP. It requires a response. Write a letter in your reflection notebook, responding to Jesus' invitation.

Reach Out

1. Make a flash card for each of the apostles. Write the name on one side and three interesting facts on the other side. Ask someone at home to work with you, then test each other on your knowledge of the apostles. On each apostle's feast day, display the card where your family will see it.

2. Gather with one or more family members and read aloud Luke 8:21. Then together name members of your extended family who exemplify Jesus' message in the Scripture passage.

3. Think of someone in your family or a close family friend whom you think has been a faithful witness to Jesus in his or her life. Spend some time with that person and ask him or her to share with you the joys and difficulties he or she has experienced in following Jesus.

4. Jesus prepared for important events, such as choosing his apostles, by praying. Read Luke 6:12–13, 22:31–32, and 22:39–46. When do you pray? If a friend asked you why you pray, what would you say? Use your own words to ask Mary in prayer to help you be a better disciple.

5. At the end of the day, think of all the good things you have seen and heard during the day. Decide on one specific thing you will do the next day to bring the light of Jesus to others.

Word to Know

disciple

57

Centering _____

1. Show the "Book of Your Life."
   - ✦ **For each of you, your book of life is unfolding.**
   - ✦ **Many characters will walk in and out of your story. Some will be helpful and others will not.**

2. Have the students copy the diagram from the board.
   - ✦ **For each of us, there are certain people who have an important influence on us.**
   - ✦ **On the arrows, write the names of people who have most influenced you.**

3. Give the students time to reflect on the significant people they named.

✦ They might answer these questions in their reflection notebook or on paper:

• **How did these people influence you?**

• **Who has taught you the most about life?**

• **Who has brought you the closest to Jesus? How?**

✦ **You have been learning about apostles, disciples, and witnesses. You also have been influenced, formed, and brought closer to God by Christian witnesses.**

✦ **Today you will think about what kind of witness you are for others. You will reflect on your own missionary heart.**

Sharing _____

1. Explain what is meant by a "missionary heart."

✦ **What comes to your mind when you hear the word** *missionary*?

✦ **What kind of person has a missionary heart?** (one who reaches out to others to share his or her friendship with Jesus)

2. Discuss how the Gospel shows the influence the disciples had on one another.

✦ **Peter was singled out by Jesus for a special role. In Matthew's Gospel, Jesus says ". . . you are Peter and upon this rock I will build my church."** (Matthew 16:18) **How did Peter first find out about Jesus?** (His brother Andrew brought him to Jesus.)

✦ **How can people your age share Jesus with their families?** (share what they've learned in class, encourage their families to celebrate the Eucharist and other sacraments, reach out in love and service)

✦ **How did Bartholomew come to know Jesus?** (His friend Philip brought him to Jesus.)

✦ **How did the first two disciples come to know Jesus?** (John the Baptist pointed Jesus out to them.)

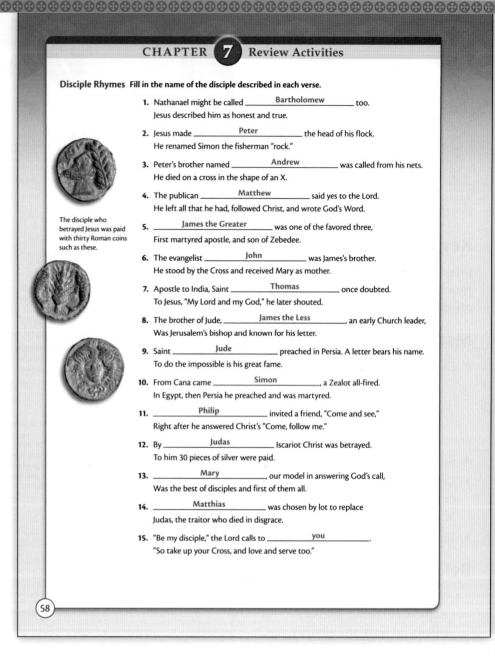

CHAPTER 7 Review Activities

Disciple Rhymes Fill in the name of the disciple described in each verse.

1. Nathanael might be called _____Bartholomew_____ too.
Jesus described him as honest and true.

2. Jesus made _____Peter_____ the head of his flock.
He renamed Simon the fisherman "rock."

3. Peter's brother named _____Andrew_____ was called from his nets.
He died on a cross in the shape of an X.

4. The publican _____Matthew_____ said yes to the Lord.
He left all that he had, followed Christ, and wrote God's Word.

5. _____James the Greater_____ was one of the favored three,
First martyred apostle, and son of Zebedee.

6. The evangelist _____John_____ was James's brother.
He stood by the Cross and received Mary as mother.

7. Apostle to India, Saint _____Thomas_____ once doubted.
To Jesus, "My Lord and my God," he later shouted.

8. The brother of Jude, _____James the Less_____, an early Church leader,
Was Jerusalem's bishop and known for his letter.

9. Saint _____Jude_____ preached in Persia. A letter bears his name.
To do the impossible is his great fame.

10. From Cana came _____Simon_____, a Zealot all-fired.
In Egypt, then Persia he preached and was martyred.

11. _____Philip_____ invited a friend, "Come and see,"
Right after he answered Christ's "Come, follow me."

12. By _____Judas_____ Iscariot Christ was betrayed.
To him 30 pieces of silver were paid.

13. _____Mary_____, our model in answering God's call,
Was the best of disciples and first of them all.

14. _____Matthias_____ was chosen by lot to replace
Judas, the traitor who died in disgrace.

15. "Be my disciple," the Lord calls to _____you_____.
"So take up your Cross, and love and serve too."

The disciple who betrayed Jesus was paid with thirty Roman coins such as these.

58

✦ Share an event in your life in which someone brought you closer to Jesus.

3. Talk with students about their role in other people's lives.

✦ **Each of you has a role in the life stories of many other people. On the diagram, add four more arrows pointing away from the circle.**

✦ **On these arrows, write the names of people you influence with your life.**

4. Discuss the power of being an example.
What are some ways you teach others by your words, actions, and attitudes?

5. Have the students complete **The Way of the Witness** on page 56.
Check the students' answers.

6. Lead the students through the Summary and the Review Activities on pages 57–58.

7. **BLM 28** Distribute and administer BLM 28 **Chapter 7 Quiz.**
Use this opportunity to assess the students' understanding of the main concepts in the chapter. If there is not sufficient time, consider moving it to Day Five.

Acting

1. Choose or let the students choose an activity from Reach Out on page 57.

2. Lead the students in prayer.

   ✦ The students will have a chance during the prayer to insert the names of those who influence them.

   ✦ **Father, thank you for the wonderful people you have put** into our lives. Please bless all those people who have brought us closer to you, especially . . .

   ✦ **Father, please help us be powerful witnesses to Jesus by our words, actions, and attitudes. Please give us the grace to be good influences on . . .**

3. At the end of class, have the students tear out and take home pages 57–58.

CHECKPOINT

- Were the learning outcomes achieved?

- How have the students' responses indicated a growing awareness that they can influence others to come to Christ?

Day Five Extending the Chapter

✝ Gather and Go Forth

Lead students through pages 59–60 in the student book. Find catechist instruction on T328–T329.

Use the following suggestions to create an additional lesson for Day Five.

1. Remind the students to take home pages 57–58 to share what they are learning with their families.

2. Incorporate any unused BLMs from the week's chapter.

3. Consider the time of the liturgical year and use the appropriate Special Seasons and Lessons. SSLs begin on page 369.

4. Visit www.christourlife.com to find additional activities for Extending the Chapter.

5. Use activities from Enriching the Faith Experience.

6. Guide the students in a prayerful discussion of Sunday's Scripture readings. Visit www.christourlife.com for more information.

Chapter 7 Enriching the Faith Experience

Use the following activities to enrich a lesson or to replace an activity with one that better meets the needs of your class.

1. **BLM 29** Use BLM 29 **Christian Witness Award** and each week have the class nominate one student they feel has given witness to Christ and the Gospel. They can write their nominations on a slip of paper. They should also write reasons why that person deserves recognition. The student with the most nominations receives the Christian Witness Award with the slips of paper attached.

2. Read to the students the poem "The Road Not Taken" by Robert Frost. Have them discuss how certain choices they make completely change their lives. Also point out the impossibility of traveling both paths. Choosing one path eliminates the other.

3. Guide the students in an in-depth study of Peter. Use these Scripture references:

Strengths
- Matthew 14:22–29 (courage, faith)
- Mark 8:29–30 (knows Jesus is the Christ)
- Luke 5:4–11 (humble, willing to admit sinfulness)
- Luke 22:61–62 (repents)
- John 6:67–71 (loyal)
- John 13:6–10 (loving, devoted)

Weaknesses
- Matthew 14:28–33 (weak faith)
- Luke 22:34–61 (betrays Jesus)
- John 13:6–8 (stubborn, proud)

4. Suggest that the students read other accounts of the call of Christ to discipleship. They could illustrate the Scripture selections or present them to the class in some dramatic form (skit, puppet show, video).

- The call of Levi (Luke 5:27–28; Mark 2:13–14)
- The call of Matthew (Matthew 9:9)
- The call of the four (Matthew 4:18–22; Mark 1:16–20; Luke 5:1–11)
- The choice of the Twelve (Mark 3:13–19; Luke 6:12–16)
- The mission of the seventy-two (Luke 10:1–20)
- The rich young man (Mark 10:17–22)

5. Ask students the questions in Sharing #2 on page T81.

Baptism and Confirmation
JESUS THE SAVIOR

Faith Focus

In the sacraments, we receive and celebrate the life Jesus won for us.

Reflecting on the Faith Experience

Take a few moments to reflect prayerfully before preparing the lesson.

Listening

"It was not you who chose
me, but I who chose you and
appointed you to go and bear
fruit that will remain . . . "

John 15:16

Reflecting

Before the world was made, we were chosen by the Father. Through the saving acts of Jesus, encountered at Baptism, we became members of the Body of Christ. Since then, we have not been alone in our search for God. In our parish, we have a family of faith and love. Through the sacraments, celebrated with the community, we have been welcomed, empowered to witness, nourished, reconciled, supported in a life of commitment, and strengthened in illness.

Today the Rite of Christian Initiation of Adults (RCIA) is a spiritual journey where a person learns to be a Christian from a faith community. This rite shows the relationship among Baptism, Confirmation, and the Eucharist. Through these sacraments, we enter into a lifelong covenant with God.

Baptism celebrates our decision to accept Christ's teachings and belong to the Church. It is a sharing in the Death and Rising of Christ, by which we die to sin and rise to eternal life. As children of God, enriched with grace and the gifts of the Holy Spirit, cleansed from Original Sin and personal sin, we can "be Christ" and face the world with the Gospel of Jesus. To live our baptismal commitment is to support one another so that we can pray, witness, and exercise charity to the point where it costs.

Confirmation strengthens our baptismal call. We are sealed with the Holy Spirit, permanently marked as God's possessions, and enabled to witness to Christ. We are prophets who possess the vision of the kingdom and preach that vision.

The Eucharist is the culmination of Initiation. When we receive the Body and Blood of Christ, we nourish the gifts we are given from God and deepen our commitment to Christ. The Eucharist is the perfect sign of the unity between God and his people. It is the principal source of charity among us. Each time we receive the Eucharist, we commit ourselves to furthering Christ's kingdom of justice and mercy.

We belong to a Church that gives witness to Christ, worships God, and serves Christ and his people. Gifted for this mission, we carry it out in our parishes, in our careers, in our community, and in our families.

How am I involved in the RCIA program?

How do I evaluate myself as a member of the Catholic Church?

Responding

Holy Spirit, help me instill in my students pride in and gratitude for their Church membership.

Scripture for Further Reflection

John 3:5 No one can enter the Kingdom of God without being born of water and Spirit.

Colossians 3:9–10 Baptism is putting off the old self and putting on the new self in Christ.

1 Peter 2:9 Baptism makes a person a sharer in Christ and, like him, an anointed priest and king.

Preparing for the Faith Experience

Day One
Signs of Salvation

Day Two
RCIA:
A Community Affair

Day Three
Sacraments of Initiation

Day Four
A Christian Initiation Booklet

Day Five
Extending the Chapter

 Gather and Go Forth

Scripture in This Chapter

Romans 6: 3–4 Life in God

1 Peter 2:9 We live in God's light.

Church Documents

Catechism of the Catholic Church. The themes of this chapter correspond to the following paragraphs: **1127–1129, 1212, 1239–1243, 1300–1305.**

National Directory for Catechesis #36. Through the sacraments of Baptism, Confirmation, and the Eucharist, we are incorporated into the Church, strengthened for participation in the Church's mission, and welcomed to partake of the Body and Blood of Jesus Christ.

Everyday Christianity (USCCB). We are all called by our Baptism and Confirmation to live our faith in the world as spouses and parents, adults and children, employers and employees, consumers and investors, citizens and neighbors.

To Teach as Jesus Did #22 (USCCB). The life of the Spirit unites us as a body. One person's problem is everyone's problem, and one person's victory is everyone's victory.

Gather and Go Forth

Find catechist instruction for Gather and Go Forth student pages 67–68 on T330–T331.

Enriching the Faith Experience

Use the activities at the end of the chapter to enrich a lesson or to replace an activity with one that better meets the needs of your class.

Bulletin Board

A suggestion for a bulletin-board design for this chapter is pictured.

New Life in Christ

LEARNING OUTCOMES

The students will be able to

- explain the purpose and value of signs, symbols, and rituals.
- identify sacraments as encounters with Christ through signs and words that give us grace and empower us to share in Christ's mission.
- name the three categories of sacraments and the sacraments that belong to each.

Word to Know

Mystical Body of Christ

See the Glossary for definition.

Key Term

sacrament—an outward sign of an inward grace instituted by Christ

in which we encounter him at key points in our journey of life and grow in grace

Materials

- Bibles or New Testaments
- Cards, candles, bows, and other objects used in celebrating a birthday

Before You Begin

1. Sacraments are part of the liturgy, or the public worship of the Church. They are visible signs that signify invisible, divine things. In the sacraments, natural objects and actions are used to make present or effective the sacred, or the holy. The Eastern Rite Churches call sacraments *mysteries.*

2. When we say that the seven sacraments are instituted by Christ, we mean that they flow from his life and ministry. There is a direct or implicit scriptural basis for all of them. Three councils (Lyons II, 1274; Florence, 1439; Trent, 1547) finally settled the number of sacraments at seven.

3. The sacraments can be a difficult topic to teach. Students at this age can be led to deepen their understanding of the sacraments by relating them to other symbols and rituals in their lives.

4. You may wish to begin or end the class by actually celebrating the birthday or baptismal birthday of a student.

Centering _____

1. Begin a discussion about the relationship between celebrations and sacraments.
   - ✦ **Has anyone recently celebrated someone's birthday?**
   - ✦ **What were some of the things you did to make it special?** (rituals, objects)

2. Present the objects you brought that symbolize a birthday celebration.
   - ✦ **By themselves, these things mean little. But when they are used as part of a birthday celebration, we give them special meaning. They become symbols. What are we celebrating at a birthday party?** (the life of someone we know and love)
   - ✦ **What do the birthday objects and rituals express?** (our joy and gratitude for the person who has a birthday)
   - ✦ **Does a birthday party with all its symbols bring about another year of life for the person?** (no)

3. Introduce the topic of this lesson.
   - ✦ **Today you will learn about powerful celebrations whose symbols make present the Christ you have been studying and that bring about new divine life in us.**
   - ✦ **Do you know what these celebrations are?** (sacraments)

Sharing _____

1. Review with the students what they already know about the sacraments.
   - ✦ Use one of the following activities:
   - ✦ **Activity 1:** Read each statement, directing the students to raise their hand if it is true. Give the correct answer.
     - **Through the sacraments, we come in contact with the saving power of Jesus' Death and Resurrection.** (true)
     - **Through meeting Jesus in the sacraments, we receive grace.** (true)
     - **There are only three sacraments instituted by Christ.** (false)

- **Sacraments do not need visible or outward signs in order to be conferred.** (false)
- **Anointing of the Sick is the name of a sacrament.** (true)
- **How much we benefit from the sacraments depends on our depth of faith and our openness to God.** (true)
- **The whole believing community is strengthened each time a sacrament is celebrated.** (true)
- ✦ **Activity 2:** Ask the students what they know about the sacraments. List their responses on the board.

2. Have the students read silently **The Seven Sacraments** on page 61.
   Why are sacraments important to our relationship with Jesus? (They deepen our relationship with him. In them we encounter Jesus, who strengthens his divine life in us enabling us to carry out our mission as his disciples.)

3. Give an overview of the sacraments.

✦ **Many religions use rituals involving natural things as a way to get in touch with the divine. Christians, too, believe that natural objects, words, and actions can bring us to experience God.**

✦ **Sacraments are saving actions. They bring us out of the power of darkness into light. Unlike birthday parties, which do not give life, sacraments cause life, divine life.**

✦ **We celebrate sacraments as a faith community. Why does this make sense?** (God originally saved a people, the Chosen People. The members of Christ's Church are bound together as members of his Body. Celebrations are usually held with a group of people. Sacraments strengthen us to love and serve others better.)

✦ **Most Protestants accept two sacraments: the ones we call Baptism and Eucharist. Catholics accept seven. They are celebrations for particular needs in life.**

4. Explain the grouping of the sacraments.

✦ **The sacraments can be grouped in three categories according to their purpose: Sacraments of Initiation, Sacraments of Healing, and Sacraments at the Service of Communion.** [Write these on the board for the following activity.]

✦ Divide the class into pairs. Refer the students to the Sacrament Chart on pages 211–212. [See pages T311–T312.]

✦ **Using the Sacrament Chart, place each sacrament under the heading where it belongs.** (Sacraments of Initiation: Baptism, Confirmation, and Eucharist; Sacraments of Healing: Penance and Reconciliation, Anointing of the Sick; Sacraments at the Service of Communion: Matrimony, Holy Orders.)

CHAPTER 8

Baptism and Confirmation

Jesus the Savior

The Seven Sacraments

Friendships are built by signs and words. Signs and words celebrate and seal our relationships. Our friendship with Jesus grows through the signs and words of the seven sacraments that he entrusted to his Church. Sacraments are special encounters with Jesus Christ at key times during our journey of life. We celebrate our relationship as the **Mystical Body of Christ.** Through the sacraments, Christ acts in us to save us; we celebrate his grace, his divine life in us. The sacramental grace we receive through the work of the Holy Spirit enables us to carry out our mission as his disciples.

The sacraments give us the grace that they signify. The grace is always present and does not depend on the worthiness of the minister. However, a sacrament will only accomplish what it intends if the person receiving the sacrament is open to cooperating with God's grace. Baptism, Confirmation, and Holy Orders confer a permanent character or seal, so they are celebrated only once.

Christian Initiation

Adolescents and adults become disciples of Jesus and join the community of believers through a process called the Rite of Christian Initiation of Adults (RCIA). The RCIA takes place in the midst of the parish community. It has three steps: catechumenate, election, and initiation. The last step is the celebration of the Sacraments of Baptism, Confirmation, and the Eucharist. The people preparing for initiation are already part of God's household. They are assured of salvation even if they should die before being baptized. They have the baptism of desire. The following story tells how Joe began participating in the RCIA process.

Chris and Joe, high school juniors, rang the doorbell at St. Jude's rectory.

"Relax, Joe. Father Shea's great," Chris encouraged. Before Joe could reply, the door opened and there was Father Shea.

"Hello, Chris, how are you?"

"Fine," Chris replied. "Father, this is my friend Joe. We'd like to talk with you."

"Sure, come in." Father led them to his office.

Chris spoke first. "Joe wants to become a Catholic, Father, and I would like to sponsor him."

Father Shea smiled at Joe, "What made you decide this, Joe?"

(61)

5. Review the symbols of the sacraments as shown in the Sacrament Chart.

✦ **Symbols are signs or objects that stand for something. They make us respond. What are some symbols in today's world that evoke a response in people?** (pink ribbons, American flag, a swoosh, words such as "thank you")

✦ **The symbols used in the sacraments are simple and basic. Their meaning is clear.** [Read aloud **Essentials of the Rite** on the chart.]

✦ Give examples of these words, actions, or objects that have meaning to us because they are a part of daily life.

6. Explain the connection between the sacraments and Scripture.

✦ **The seven sacraments are rooted in Scripture, in the words and actions of Jesus.**

✦ Have several students look up and read each passage aloud.

✦ **What sacrament is each passage talking about?**

- Matthew 28:19 (Baptism)
- Mark 14:22–25 (Eucharist)
- Acts 8:17 (Confirmation)
- James 5:13–15 (Anointing of the Sick)
- John 20:19–23 (Reconciliation)
- Mark 10:6–9 (Matrimony)
- Luke 22:14–20 (Holy Orders)

Acting

1. Divide the class into groups and have them plan a ritual celebrating an event in life.
   - List events on the board and have each group choose one. (Examples: losing a first tooth, going to school for the first time, making the honor roll, going into the hospital) Have the students plan a short ritual that includes symbolic words, actions, and objects.

✦ What have you learned by planning this celebration?

2. Pray with the students:

Jesus, in your wisdom, you saved us. You are with us in the sacraments. Help us to realize the meaning of these gifts so we can enter more deeply into the celebrations of the sacraments and come to love you better. Amen.

CHECKPOINT

- Were the learning outcomes achieved?
- What signs were there that the students understood the role of symbols in their lives?

Day Two   RCIA: A Community Affair

Student pages 61–63, 66, 211

LEARNING OUTCOMES

The students will be able to

- describe the Rite of Christian Initiation of Adults (RCIA).
- explain the role of the community in the RCIA process.

Word to Know

mystagogy

See the Glossary for definition.

Key Terms

catechumen—a person preparing to become a member of the faith community

elect—those who are formally called to the Sacraments of Initiation during the Rite of Enrollment

exorcism—prayers against the evil spirit that teach us the mystery of sin and how Christ the Redeemer has saved us

Rite of Christian Initiation of Adults (RCIA)—the program through which people become members of the Church

Rite of Enrollment—the ceremony in which catechumens become the elect

scrutinies—petitions and exorcisms that strengthen the catechumens in their decision to live for Christ

sponsor—the person who assists the catechumen in his or her journey of faith

Materials

- Bibles or New Testaments
- BLM 30A–C
- Water, white robe, candle, chrism, bread, wine (If unavailable, list them on the board.)

Before You Begin

1. Modeled on the practice of the early Church, the RCIA is the standard process for incorporating new members into the Church. Prospective Catholics are brought into the Church through the shared experiences of the community. As it initiates new members, the local community is renewed.

2. The seven sacraments are no ordinary signs. They actually effect what they signify. For example, the water of Baptism signifies washing, and the Sacrament of Baptism washes away sin. In each sacrament, there is an encounter with God. The person receiving the sacrament, as well as the entire community, is changed.

3. This lesson may be taught without BLM 30A–C **Christian Initiation** by omitting the questions that refer to this BLM.

For an alternative plan, have the students work independently, reading **Christian Initiation** on pages 61–62 and using the Review on page 66 as a study guide.

4. You might invite someone from your parish's RCIA program to speak to your class about his or her experiences.

5. For Sharing #5 you might read this prayer of exorcism:
   Lord Jesus,
   by raising Lazarus from
      the dead
   you showed that you came
      that we might have life
   and have it more abundantly.

   Free from the grasp of death
   those who await your life-
      giving sacraments
   and deliver them from the
      spirit of corruption.

   Through your Spirit, who
      gives life,
   fill them with faith, hope,
      and charity,
   that they may live with you
      always
   in the glory of your resurrection,
   for you are Lord for ever
      and ever.
   Amen.

   *Rite of Christian Initiation
   of Adults, #175*

6. You may wish to prepare a PowerPoint presentation for Sharing #7 on the symbols used in the sacraments.

Centering

1. Discuss initiation rites with the students:
   + Among some Native American tribes, when it came time for a boy to be recognized as an adult, he was sent alone into the wilderness for an extended time on a vision quest.
   + During this time, the boy fasted and watched for some sign to be revealed to him, such as an animal, a pebble, a feather, or a piece of bark. That symbol reminded him of his period of initiation and the wisdom it revealed to him.
   + Initiation rites are external signs or rituals that a person goes through to belong to a group. What initiation rituals do you know?

2. Explain the initiation rituals of the Catholic Church.
   + For anyone age seven or older who has not been baptized, the initiation rituals of the Catholic Church are called the Rite of Christian Initiation of Adults, or RCIA. [Write this on the board.]
   + This rite, the RCIA, involves three of the sacraments we learned about in the last class. These are Baptism, Confirmation, and the Eucharist.

Sharing

1. Ask a student to read aloud the first paragraph of **Christian Initiation** on page 61.
   + What are the three steps of Initiation? (catechumenate, election, and initiation)
   + Have volunteers continue reading aloud this section.
   + How were Chris and his family witnesses? (The family spirit attracted Joe; Chris answered Joe's questions.) Like Joe, you look at others to see what it means to be a Catholic. Your friends look at you. What have people asked you about your faith?

   + What did Chris mean when he said he wanted to sponsor Joe? (to assist Joe in becoming a Catholic)
   + What process will Joe go through to become a Catholic? (the Rite of Christian Initiation of Adults) What is Joe called now? (an inquirer) Why? (He is inquiring about the faith and studying it.)
   + Read aloud the journal entry for September 8 in **Responding to the Call** on page 62.

2. BLM 30A–C Distribute BLM 30A–C **Christian Initiation.** Have the students work on BLM 30A Part 1. Inquirers: Seeking God. Point out that external signs remind us of deeper mysteries.

3. Call on a volunteer to read aloud the journal entry for October 10 on page 62.
   + What is the first step of the RCIA? (the catechumenate) What do the candidates ask of the Church? (faith) Why? (to have eternal life)
   + How do you think Chris will help Joe as his sponsor? (help him to know Christ and his teachings, show him how to live the Gospel and serve others)
   + Why did Father Shea make a cross on each catechumen? (The cross is the symbol of Christ's victory over sin and death.)
   + Catechumens leave Mass after the homily because they are not initiated into the mysteries of our faith. They learn more about the Scriptures at this time.

4. Have the students complete Part 2. Catechumenate: Learning His Way on BLM 30A.
   + "Yes" answers are signs of a healthy Christian life.
   + Have a student read aloud the journal entry for February 12 on page 62.
   + How is Joe preparing to live the faith? (He is studying the life of Christ, the Church's teachings, praying with the community, and trying to set a good example.)

5. Discuss with the students the second step of the RCIA process.
   + What is the second step in the RCIA process? (election)
   + Lent is the most intense time of preparation during the RCIA process.
   + Call on two students to read aloud the journal entries for March 3 and March 10 on page 62.
   + What rite did Joe celebrate on the first Sunday of Lent? (Rite of Election or Enrollment) Why is he now called one of the *elect*? (He is elected, or chosen, by Christ.)
   + Why are the Sacraments of Initiation Easter sacraments? (Through them we share Christ's Paschal Mystery, his passion, Death, Resurrection and ascension; we die to sin and share new life in Christ.)
   + Why do you think the enrollment book is also called "the book of life"? (Life refers to eternal life, the hope of Christians.) Why was it a risk for the early Christians to have their names in this book? (During persecutions, early Christians could be killed.)
   + In the early Church, the elect were brought before the bishop many times to be questioned about their character and their motives. What forms do these scrutinies take today? (petitions and exorcisms) The exorcisms free the catechumens from the effects of sin and the influence of the devil.
   + Why does Joe receive the Creed and the Lord's Prayer? (These are Christian treasures given as gifts to Joe. The community shares its beliefs and the prayer the Lord gave to it.)

6. Have the students complete Part 3. Purification and Enlightenment: Entering the Mystery on BLM 30B. Direct the students to the Apostles' Creed on the inside front cover of their books. [See page T445.]

7. Ask volunteers to read aloud **Sacraments of Initiation** on pages 62–63.

+ **Why does the faith community have an important role in the RCIA?** (Living the Christian life can be difficult. The community will support the new Christians.)

+ **What do these symbols mean?** [show the symbols. Point to the list or use the PowerPoint presentation.]

  • **Water** (life and death; sharing in the dying and rising of Jesus)

  • **White robe** (clothed with Christ)

  • **Candle** (new life in the risen Jesus)

  • **Chrism** (anointing; christened)

  • **Bread** (the Body of Christ as spiritual food)

  • **Wine** (the Blood of Christ as spiritual drink)

+ **Open your books to the Sacrament Chart on page 211. What are the essential words of each Sacrament of Initiation?** [See page T311.]

+ **What will Joe do during the period of mystagogy?** (live the faith, share in the Eucharist, serve others)

8. Direct the students to BLM 30C Part 4. Sacraments of Initiation: Celebrating Him and Part 5. Mystagogy: Being Led Deeper into the Mystery.

+ Part 4 shows that the sacramental symbols are rooted in Scripture.

+ Part 5 explains what happens to the newly baptized after Easter, relating it to every Christian's life.

Joe began his story. He and Chris had met at basketball. Joe often stayed at Chris's house for supper. He sensed that the spirit he enjoyed so much there was connected with the family's religious beliefs. One day Joe asked Chris about his religion. Chris explained that faith in Christ helped him understand life and gave him a desire to serve others. He told Joe about the Church. Their conversations led to this meeting with Father Shea.

When Joe finished speaking, Father said that Joe could begin the Rite of Christian Initiation. Chris would be his sponsor and assist him.

Responding to the Call

Here is part of the journal Joe kept during the RCIA process.

Thursday, September 8

All of us who want to be Catholics met in the church hall tonight with our sponsors. We prayed and were introduced. The leader told us how he came to the faith, and then he had us tell our own stories. We're called inquirers, ones who are studying the faith. We'll meet once a week.

Saturday, October 10

Tonight we became catechumens. Before Mass we and our sponsors met at the church entrance. Father Shea called our names and asked, "What do you ask of God's Church?" We said, "Faith." He asked, "What does faith offer you?" We answered, "Eternal life." Then he prayed that we would follow the Gospel under Christ's leadership. He asked everyone if they were ready to help us. They answered, "We are." Father Shea made a cross on our foreheads, saying, "By this sign of love, Christ will be your strength. Learn now to know and follow him." We entered the church but stayed only until the end of the homily. After we're baptized, we'll stay for the whole Mass.

Friday, February 12

With school, basketball, and catechumen meetings, the months have really been busy. We catechumens know one another well because we have studied the life of Christ and the Church's teachings together and because we have prayed together. Father Shea told us that as followers of Christ, we should set a good example. I've been trying to play fair and watch my language.

Sunday, March 3

Today is the first Sunday of Lent. We had the Rite of Sending of the Catechumens for Election at Mass. After the Homily, Father Shea called the sponsors and us catechumens to the altar. He asked the sponsors if we were taking our formation seriously and if we were ready to be presented to the bishop for the rite of election. They said we were. That afternoon we stood before the bishop as he asked us similar questions. Then the bishop declared that the Church called us to the Sacraments of Baptism, Confirmation, and Eucharist. We wrote our names in the book of the elect. We are now the elect.

Sunday, March 10

On three Sundays in Lent, we have scrutinies at the 10:00 A.M. Mass. They are petitions and exorcisms. Exorcisms are prayers against the evil spirit. They teach repentance, the mystery of sin, and how Christ the Redeemer saved us. The scrutinies strengthen our decision to live for Christ. After the scrutinies are presentations. Today Father Shea presented us with the Creed. On the last Sunday, he will give us the Lord's Prayer.

Sacraments of Initiation

The night of the Easter Vigil is momentous for Joe, Chris, and the community of St. Jude's. Joe and Chris together with others have walked a journey of faith in response to God's call.

This is a very decisive moment in Joe's life. Following Christ and living his values will be difficult. That is why the faith community is there for support. Joe and the community listen to Saint Paul's words about "dying to sin."

(62) UNIT 1

Acting

1. Explain to the students that Christian Initiation continues in the life of every believer.

+ **Each believer continues throughout his or her life into a deeper initiation into the Christian life. Each one of you is in mystagogy.**

+ **What are three ways you can worship this week and three ways you can serve?**

2. Pray the Lord's Prayer with the students.

Remember those who are considering becoming a Catholic.

CHECKPOINT

• Were the learning outcomes achieved?

LEARNING OUTCOMES

The students will be able to

- explain that we are reborn in Baptism, strengthened in Confirmation, and nourished by the Eucharist.

- discuss how that by Baptism we are made God's sons and daughters, incorporated into Christ's Death and Resurrection, sanctified by the Holy Spirit, and welcomed into the community of believers.

Key Terms

Baptism—the first sacrament which cleanses us of Original Sin and all other sin, makes us sons or daughters of God, fills us with grace, and makes us members of the Church

Confirmation—the Sacrament of Initiation that deepens the gifts of Baptism, seals us with the Holy Spirit, and increases our responsibility to witness to the faith

Eucharist—the sacrament that is the fullness of Christian Initiation; the Body and Blood of Christ offered to the Father and shared with the community of believers

Materials

- 2 inflated balloons
- Cards with statements from Sharing #7
- Reflection notebooks

Before You Begin

A detailed study of the Eucharist is in Chapter 20.

After the Homily, Joe and the other elect go to the baptismal font for a profession of faith. They make their baptismal vows, publicly rejecting Satan and evil and declaring their faith. As the water of Baptism flows over Joe, he remembers that water is a sign of death and life. He is entering into the Death of Jesus and experiencing a new life of grace. He becomes alive in the life of Jesus and shares in the glory of his Resurrection. When Joe's godparents put a white robe over his head, he is being "clothed with Christ." His sins are forgiven, and he has new life in Jesus Christ. His godparents hand him a lighted candle, a symbol of his life in Christ. Joe is now a full-fledged member of the Church. He may stay for the whole liturgy.

Next Joe celebrates Confirmation. He is anointed with a mixture of olive oil and balsam called chrism. He knows that now he is expected to proclaim his faith and that the Holy Spirit will strengthen and guide him.

The Mass continues. During the Liturgy of the Eucharist, Joe recalls that Christ died and rose so that he could live. When he receives the Body and Blood of Jesus, Joe makes an act of faith. He is not afraid. The community of believers will help him grow spiritually. They will help him live his faith during the coming months of **mystagogy**, a time to learn more about his faith and how to live it.

The signs and words of the Sacraments of Initiation express our relationship with Jesus as Savior. In Baptism, Confirmation, and the Eucharist, we receive the new life Jesus won for us. Through each of these sacraments, he becomes our personal Savior, and we commit ourselves to him.

Baptism: Water and Spirit

Jesus said you must be born of water and the Spirit to enter the Kingdom of Heaven. When the priest or deacon pours water over you at Baptism and says "I baptize you," you enter into the dying and rising of Jesus through the Holy Spirit. You are removed from the reign of evil and strengthened against it. You receive divine life, and you are invited to share eternal life with Jesus. You become a new creation. You become a Christian, willing to give witness to Christ, eager to share his teachings with others, prepared to sacrifice all for him. Because Baptism marks you forever as a follower of Jesus, you can be baptized only once.

A Moment with Jesus

No matter how old we are when we are baptized, our responsibilities as members of the Church are the same. Pause for a few moments and reflect silently on these questions: How do I live my baptismal call in my daily life? How can I give witness to Christ in my life at home and school?

Ask the Holy Spirit to help you be aware of how you can follow Jesus more closely today. Then thank Jesus for calling you to be a member of the Church.

A Flood of Gifts

Are you aware of all the tremendous gifts you receive through Baptism?

You become
- a temple of the Trinity and share in God's life (grace)
- a child of God and heir to heaven
- a member of the faith community, the Church.

You
- are forgiven Original Sin and any personal sins
- receive the Holy Spirit and his gifts
- share in the priesthood of Christ
- receive the virtues of faith, hope, and love.

CHAPTER 8 (63)

Centering

1. Choose six students and form them into two teams: a team of five students and a team of one student.
    - ✦ Give each team an inflated balloon. The rules are to keep their left hand behind their back and their left foot stationary.
    - ✦ The team that keeps the balloon in the air the longest wins. Play the game several times.
    - ✦ **If the balloon represents the grace of God, what do you think it means?** (It is better to be part of a community to sustain God's grace in your life.)

2. Explain to the students that all of the sacraments are community actions.
   The Sacraments of Initiation that we are currently studying make us members of the faith community. Today we will look more closely at the meaning these rituals have for the faith community.

Sharing _____

1. Have the students read silently **Baptism: Water and Spirit** and **A Flood of Gifts** on page 63.

   + **In the early days of the Church, Baptism was done by immersion. The whole person went down into the water. There are parishes that celebrate Baptism this way today. Why is immersion a better sign than pouring for baptism?** (Immersion reminds us of death. Baptism is a sharing in the Death and Rising of Jesus.)

   + **What are three ways you show you have become a Christian?** (giving witness to Christ, sharing his teachings, and being prepared to sacrifice all for him)

   + **In the early Church, people were baptized only as adults. At the Easter Vigil, they received the Sacraments of Initiation as Joe did. Why do you think the Church began to welcome children as members?** (Parents wanted their children to share in the gifts of Baptism. They promised to teach them to be Christian.)

   + **If a child dies before being baptized, we trust in God's mercy and pray for the child's salvation.**

   + **Which gift listed under A Flood of Gifts means most to you? Why?**

2. Direct the students to pray **A Moment with Jesus** on page 63.
   Allow sufficient time for silent reflection.

3. Have the students work in pairs on **Signs of Baptism** on page 64.

   + **Why are symbols in religious ceremonies important?** (Through them, the Church speaks in a concrete way about our life of faith and the mysteries of God.)

   + **Have any of you ever witnessed a Baptism?** (Invite them to share their experiences.)

   + You might go through the steps for the Baptism of a child:

Rite of Infant Baptism

I. Reception
   A. Called by name
   B. The Sign of the Cross on the forehead

II. Celebration of God's Word
   A. Scripture reading and homily
   B. Intercessions and Litany of Saints
   C. Exorcism and anointing

III. Celebration of Sacrament
   A. Blessing and invocation of God over baptismal water
   B. Renouncing of sin and professing of faith by parents and godparents
   C. Baptism
   D. Anointing with chrism
   E. Clothing with white garment
   F. Lighted candle
   G. Ephphetha (prayer over ears and mouth)
   H. Lord's Prayer
   I. The blessing of mother, father, assembly

---

4. Have the students read silently **Confirmation: Sealed with the Spirit** on page 64.

   + **What symbolic actions does the bishop perform at Confirmation?** (He lays his hand on you and anoints you with chrism.)

   + **What are the sacramental words the bishop says?** ("[Name], be sealed with the gift of the Holy Spirit.")

   + **What does it mean to be sealed with the Spirit?** (It is a spiritual sign that makes you more like Jesus. It shows that you are God's special possession and renews your call to witness to Christ through service.)

   + **Baptism and Confirmation are sacraments you celebrate only once. By them, you are marked for life as a Christian, one who belongs to Christ.**

   + **How will you show people that you are Christ's follower?** (by constantly growing in your understanding of Christ's message; in your ability to love him and others; being Christ's witness; and showing by your actions his kingdom of justice and mercy.)

   + **Many of you have already received the Holy Spirit at Baptism.**

   + **In Confirmation, you will be strengthened by the Spirit so you can better understand what your baptismal commitment calls you to do.**

5. Have a student read aloud **Eucharist: Made One in the Spirit** on page 64.

   + **Why is the Eucharist the high point of Christian Initiation?** (It strengthens and nourishes God's life in a Christian. When Christians receive the Eucharist, they possess Jesus and he acts in them.)

   + **The three Sacraments of Initiation are interrelated. Baptism enables Christians to have faith in the Eucharist. Confirmation calls Christians to deeper faith and more active service. The Eucharist strengthens faith and enables Christians to serve through strength from Jesus.**

6. Direct the students to the Sacrament Chart on page 211. Have the students read silently about each of the Sacraments of Initiation. [See page T311.]

7. Call on several students to pick a card.

   + **You are to read the statement on the card, say if it is true or false and then explain your answer.**

   + **Baptism completes the process of the Rite of Christian Initiation.** (False. Baptism is the first step in the Initiation process. Confirmation and the Eucharist complete the process. Becoming a Christian takes constant effort and openness to God's grace.)

   + **Other people should be able to tell by our words and actions that**

---

we are baptized Christians who belong to the Church. (True)

✦ **In Confirmation, the Holy Spirit gives us so much strength that we don't have to try anymore.** (False. The Holy Spirit does strengthen us, but only when we are open to him and cooperate. If we stop trying, we become weak, like muscles that haven't been used.)

✦ **The Eucharist nourishes the life of God in a Christian.** (True)

✦ **Baptism is the only time we receive the Holy Spirit and are anointed with chrism.** (False. At Confirmation, we are strengthened by the Spirit and anointed.)

✦ **Through the Sacraments of Initiation, God acts in our lives to help us serve others.** (True)

✦ **We are followers or witnesses of Jesus only if we never do anything wrong.** (False. We are followers or witnesses of Jesus if we try to be like him. Sometimes we fail. That is why we need the Eucharist to keep our faith strong.)

✦ **The Sacraments of Initiation help you to be true followers of Christ. They help you to be courageous witnesses to his message.**

Acting

1. Choose or let the students choose an activity from Reach Out on page 65.

2. Have the students do the Respond activity on page 65.

Signs of Baptism

See how many signs and symbols used at Baptism you understand by matching them with their definitions.

a–oil   b–candle   c–water   d–profession of faith   e–chrism   f–cross   g–white robe   h–godparents

__g__ 1. Symbol of being clothed with Christ and sign of new dignity

__h__ 2. Two people who represent the Christian community and promise to assist the newly baptized to grow in faith

__c__ 3. Symbol that shows that the newly baptized is cleansed of sin, dies with Christ, and is raised up with him to eternal life

__a__ 4. Sign of being strengthened and healed

__d__ 5. Promises the newly baptized makes to reject evil and to believe in the Trinity and the truths of the faith

__b__ 6. Symbol of the light of faith and the call to walk as children of light

__f__ 7. Sign made on the forehead of the newly baptized as a reminder of the saving power of Christ's Death and Resurrection

__e__ 8. Sign used in anointing that shows that the newly baptized has received the Holy Spirit and shares in the priesthood of Christ

Confirmation: Sealed with the Spirit

Confirmation always used to be celebrated with Baptism. Catholics of the Eastern rites still celebrate it that way. In Confirmation your baptismal gifts are deepened and perfected. The Spirit who came to the Church on Pentecost comes to you more fully. The bishop lays his hand on you, anoints you with chrism, and says, "(Name), be sealed with the gift of the Holy Spirit." You respond, "Amen." The anointing renews your call to witness to Christ through service. You are anointed to be priest, prophet, and king with Jesus and to share in his mission. You can be confirmed only once because Confirmation marks you permanently as God's special possession.

Through Baptism and Confirmation, the Holy Spirit empowers you to share your faith with others. You are Christ's follower, constantly growing in your understanding of his message and in your ability to love him and others. You are Christ's witness, showing by your actions his kingdom of justice and mercy.

Eucharist: Made One in the Spirit

The Eucharist completes and fulfills Christian Initiation. Christians gather together to celebrate the Lord's passion, Death, Resurrection, and Ascension and to join him in offering perfect worship to the Father. They become one with Jesus and with one another just as the grains of wheat become one in the bread and the grapes become one in the wine. At the Eucharist, the Christian community is strengthened by Jesus Christ's Body and Blood which it receives in Holy Communion. The members are prepared to carry on his work.

 64 UNIT 1

CHECKPOINT ✓

• Were the learning outcomes achieved?

LEARNING OUTCOMES

The students will be able to

- discuss their reception of the Sacraments of Initiation.
- discuss their gratitude to God for the grace of membership in the Church.
- demonstrate an understanding of the key concepts in this chapter.

Materials

- BLM 31, BLM 32A–B
- BLM 33 Quiz
- Quotation written on board: *As each one has received a gift, use it to serve one another as good stewards of God's varied grace.* (1 Peter 4:10)
- Unlined paper
- Markers, crayons, or colored pencils

- Stapler, yarn, or needle and thread
- Cardboard or construction paper
- Glue
- Perforated adhesive cloth, binding tape, paper clips (optional)
- Instrumental music CD (optional)

Before You Begin

1. **BLM 31** Send BLM 31 **Family Letter on the Sacraments** home early so parents or guardians have time to respond. Adapt the letter for those families who are not Catholic. The Initiation booklet gives non-Catholic students a chance to share their faith tradition.

2. Tell the students in advance to bring to class the information

and photographs they need to make their booklets on the celebration of the Sacraments of Initiation.

3. Because the booklet activity probably requires more than one class, the students might complete it at home. The booklets could be displayed for the school or parish.

4. You may wish to substitute Enriching The Faith Experience #1 for the booklet activity.

5. When planning today's lesson, keep in mind that Day Four is when the students take the quiz for this chapter. Reserve time at the end of class for this assessment. The quiz can also be administered on Day Five.

Centering _____

1. Discuss the Scripture verse on the board with the students.
   - ✦ **Which three sacraments initiate us into the life of grace?** (Baptism, Confirmation, and the Eucharist)
   - ✦ **What people are you called to serve?** (every person God places in our life: family members, friends, schoolmates, neighbors, parishioners)

2. Tell the students about the booklet they will make.
   - ✦ **Today you are going to reflect on the times you celebrated the Sacraments of Initiation. These were important events for you, your families, and your parish.**
   - ✦ **Through the grace of these sacraments, you have been growing and learning what it means to be a member of the Church. You have tried to serve the Kingdom of God through witness, worship, and service.**
   - ✦ **Making this booklet will give you the opportunity to describe your**

experiences of Initiation and of growth in Christian attitudes and actions.

Sharing _____

1. Inform the students about their parents' letters.
   Your parents have written letters to you for your books. [Pass out the letters. Allow time for the students to read them.] **They can be used on page 4 of your books.**

2. **BLM 32A–B** Distribute copies of BLM 32A–B **Directions: Sacraments of Initiation Booklet.**
   - ✦ Have the students follow the directions on the BLM. See that they have the materials they need.
   - ✦ Staple or sew the books together with yarn or doubled thread. You might play instrumental music as the students work. For a more durable book, follow these directions above using paper 8 1/2 inches long by 5 1/2 inches wide:
   - ✦ Construct the booklet with the students using these directions.

- ✦ **Step 1.** Use unlined sheets of paper to copy the final draft of the book. Clip the unlined paper over a sheet of notebook paper so the lines show through as guides. Use the red line at the left as a margin so no words will be sewn into the binding. In addition to this margin, leave at least a 1/2-inch margin.

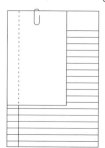

- ✦ **Step 2.** Add a title page, a contents page (optional), and a blank page to the front and to the back. Clip all the pages together. Draw a line 1/4 inch from the left and draw a dot every half inch down the length of the line.

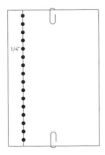

✦ **Step 3.** Sew the pages together: Down through #2, up through #1, and tie a knot in the tail; down through #3, up through #2; down through #4, up through #3. Continue to the bottom and tie off.

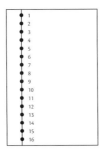

✦ **Step 4.** For the cover, cut two pieces of cardboard 9 by 6 inches (that is, 1/2 inch wider and longer than the pages).

✦ **Step 5.** Use sturdy fabric such as burlap, wallpaper, or contact paper to cover the cardboard. This cover material should be 16 1/2 inches by 13 inches. Decorate the covers with applique, embroidery, liquid embroidery, or other fabric.

✦ **Step 6.** Set the cardboard on the cover material, leaving 2-inch margins on all sides, and 1/2 inch between the pieces of cardboard.

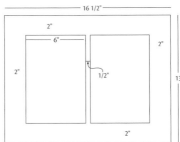

✦ For contact paper, place the cardboard on the sticky surface. Cut on the dotted lines as shown. Fold the remaining paper in over the cardboard. For fabric or wallpaper, draw around the cardboard with pencil or chalk, lift the cardboard and put glue on these rectangles. Place the cardboard on the sticky

---

Remember

What is the Rite of Christian Initiation of Adults (RCIA)?
The Rite of Christian Initiation of Adults is the process through which people become disciples of Jesus and join the Catholic Church.

What are the Sacraments of Initiation?
The Sacraments of Initiation are Baptism, Confirmation, and the Eucharist. In Christian Initiation, a person is reborn in Baptism, strengthened in Confirmation, and nourished by the Eucharist.

Why are the Sacraments of Initiation important?
The Sacraments of Initiation make a person a member of the Church and empower him or her to carry out the mission of Christ in the world.

Respond

The Gifts of the Holy Spirit are wisdom, understanding, counsel (right judgment), knowledge, fortitude (courage), piety (reverence), and fear of the Lord (wonder and awe).

Choose one of the gifts and write a prayer asking the Holy Spirit to strengthen you in practicing that gift. Write your prayer in your reflection notebook.

Reach Out

1. Brainstorm with members of your family ways you can serve
   • one another
   • your parish community
   • other people

   Then write a family pledge that includes how you will do the above and have each member sign it. Place the pledge where everyone can see it.

2. Take a survey of five parish members you know, asking them the following questions:
   • What do you like best about your parish?
   • How does your parish help you?
   • How do you help your parish?

   Use the answers to prepare a report and share your findings in class.

3. Interview someone from another Christian faith tradition about how Baptism is celebrated in his or her church. Discuss with your classmates and teacher the similarities and differences between the two baptismal ceremonies.

Words to Know

mystagogy
Mystical Body of Christ

65

---

surface and cut on the dotted lines. Glue the remaining fabric to the cardboard.

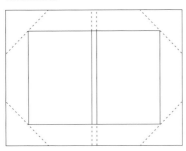

✦ **Step 7.** Glue the book to the cover or use perforated adhesive cloth binding tape (purchased from any library supply company). Cut two pieces the length of the book, one for the front of the book, the other for the back. Place the strips so that

half covers the stitching and the other half adheres to the cardboard.

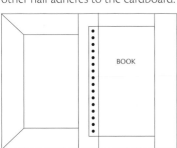

✦ **Step 8.** Glue blank paper to the inside of the front and back of the cover to hide raw edges.

3. Lead the students through the Summary and the Review Activities on pages 65–66.
   At the end of class, have them tear out the pages to take home.

4. **BLM 33** Distribute and administer BLM 33 **Chapter 8 Quiz.**

Use this opportunity to assess the students' understanding of the main concepts in the chapter. If there is not sufficient time for the students to complete the quiz, consider moving it to Day Five.

Acting

1. Have the students reflect on living our Christian commitment.

+ Tell the students to sit quietly with their heads down or eyes closed.

+ **Have you ever . . .**

• **given away something you really wanted to someone else?**

• **volunteered for a job?**

• **freely chosen to finish a job when you did not want to?**

• **paid attention at Mass because you believed that Jesus was present?**

+ **Ask the Holy Spirit to help you live out your baptismal vows.**

2. At the end of class, have the students tear out and take home pages 65–66.

CHECKPOINT

• Were the learning outcomes achieved?

• How could I improve the process of making the Initiation booklets?

CHAPTER 8 Review Activities

Write the Rite Words Identify the major terms of the RCIA defined below.

1. The person who assists a candidate in learning about the Catholic faith:
S P O N S O R

2. The rite involving petitions and exorcisms about repentance, the mystery of sin, and redemption for the "elect" during the third, fourth, and fifth Sundays of Lent:
S C R U T I N I E S

3. The process of becoming a Christian (abbreviation):
R C I A

4. The rite of celebrating the listing of names of catechumens preparing for the Sacraments of Initiation:
E N R O L L M E N T

5. People interested in studying about the Catholic faith:
I N Q U I R E R S

6. A person who has completed the catechumenate and is ready to enter the Lenten period of intense preparation for the Sacraments of Initiation:
E L E C T

7. The Easter season experience when the newly baptized learn more about their faith and how to live it:
M Y S T A G O G Y

8. Prayers that the catechumen be delivered from the power of evil and receive the gifts of the Spirit:
E X O R C I S M S

9. The handing on of the ancient documents of the faith, the Creed, and the Lord's Prayer:
P R E S E N T A T I O N S

10. People selected by the catechumen to help him or her prepare for Baptism and lead a genuine Christian life:
G O D P A R E N T S

11. A person who studies the teachings of the Gospel and the Church and prepares to receive the Sacraments of Initiation:
C A T E C H U M E N

12. Liturgical celebration at which a person celebrates the Sacraments of Initiation:
E A S T E R   V I G I L

Sacrament Match Write the letter of the sacrament that corresponds to each statement: Baptism (B), Confirmation (C), or the Eucharist (E).

_C_ **1.** Laying on of hands by the bishop is a sign.

_B_ **2.** We receive the Holy Spirit and his gifts for the first time.

_C_ **3.** We are anointed with chrism and called to be a witness of Christ.

_E_ **4.** The community offers perfect worship to the Father.

_E_ **5.** The community is nourished by the Body and Blood of Jesus.

_B_ **6.** We become children of God and heirs to heaven.

_E_ **7.** The community celebrates the Paschal Mystery of Jesus and makes it present.

_B_ **8.** Original Sin is forgiven.

66

Day Five   Extending the Chapter

 Gather and Go Forth

Lead students through pages 67–68 in the student book. Find catechist instruction on T330–T331.

Use the following suggestions to create an additional lesson for Day Five.

1. Remind the students to take home pages 65–66 to share what they are learning with their families.

2. Incorporate any unused BLMs from the week's chapter.

3. Consider the time of the liturgical year and use the appropriate Special Seasons and Lessons. SSLs begin on page T369.

4. Visit www.christourlife.com to find additional activities for Extending the Chapter.

5. Use activities from Enriching the Faith Experience.

6. Guide the students in a prayerful discussion of Sunday's Scripture readings. Visit www.christourlife .com for more information.

Use the following activities to enrich a lesson or to replace an activity with one that better meets the needs of your class.

1. Have the students create a crossword puzzle using words associated with Christian Initiation.

2. Guide groups of students in making a baptismal scroll that illustrates each phrase of the Lord's Prayer and the Apostles' Creed.

3. Help the students determine Christian responses to situations. Direct them to fold a sheet of paper into three columns. At the top of each column, they should write a duty that comes from Baptism: *witness, share Christ's teachings, sacrifice.* Read aloud the following situations and have them answer these questions.
   ✦ **If this really happened, how would you give active witness to Christ? Write your answer in column 1.**
   ✦ **How would you share his teachings with others? Write your answer in column 2.**
   ✦ **How would doing this be a sacrifice for you? Write your answer in column 3.**
   ✦ Situations:
      1. **You are in a department store with your friends and all of you are very tired from shopping. A group of older women are walking very slowly in front of you. One of your friends yells a nasty remark to the women and then shoves past them. The rest of your friends laugh.**
      2. **You are having lunch at school and you hear some of your classmates at the table behind you call you a mean name. They say it loud enough for everyone at your table to hear.**
      3. **You are staying after school with several of your friends. The teacher is out of the classroom, and you and your friends start throwing an**
      eraser around the room. When it is your turn to throw it, you knock the teacher's radio off the cabinet and break it.
      4. **Your parents find out you are smoking cigarettes and ground you for two weeks. They forbid you to smoke again.**
      5. **A group is standing in line at the drinking fountain. Someone starts to dunk people's faces in the fountain. When you dunk a girl, she lets out a scream, and you are the only one who gets in trouble with the teacher.**
   ✦ Have the students discuss their responses.
   ✦ **What does it take to give witness to Christ?** (courage, strength of character, great love, and faith)
   ✦ **From your answers, how do you best share the teachings of Christ with others?** (by our own lives)
   ✦ **The gifts and graces of Baptism help us to live out our baptismal commitment to Christ. Can you share with us how they have helped you in a particular situation?** [You might begin by sharing an experience from your own life.]

4. Ask the students to collect rocks or shells. Then have them write on the rocks or shells psalm quotations referring to Baptism. The following verses might be used.

Psalm 27:4	Psalm 51:8–9
Psalm 32:11	Psalm 63:2
Psalm 34:2–3	Psalm 63:3–4
Psalm 34:6–7	Psalm 63:5–6
Psalm 34:8–9	Psalm 66:1–2
Psalm 34:14–15	Psalm 66:8–9
Psalm 34:16–17	Psalm 89:3–4
Psalm 42:2–3	Psalm 89:21–22
Psalm 43:3	

5. Help the students learn more about the symbolism of water by having them look up the following Scripture references and write how each shows that water is a sign of life.
   a. Genesis 1:9–11
   b. Exodus 14:15–31
   c. Exodus 17:1–7
   d. 2 Kings 5:1–14
   e. Mark 1:1–8
   f. John 4:5–42
   CHALLENGE QUESTION:
   g. Revelation 22:1
   Answers:
   a. God created water to bring life to humans, animals, and plants.
   b. Water brought life to the fleeing Israelites.
   c. Water refreshed the thirsty Israelites in the desert.
   d. Water cleansed Naaman of leprosy.
   e. John the Baptist baptized many people in the Jordan River.
   f. The Samaritan woman was promised living water.
   g. John's vision of baptismal water was a river bringing life.

6. Have the students design bookmarks and send them to students who will be confirmed this year. The design could be one of the Gifts of the Holy Spirit found in the student book on page 243 [See page T435]. Suggest that the students also send letters expressing their faith and support. These could be sent when the confirmation students make their retreat.

Faith Focus

Through Jesus, we find the way to the Father.

Reflecting on the Faith Experience

Take a few moments to reflect prayerfully before preparing the lesson.

Listening

Then Jesus said to his disciples, "Whoever wishes to come after me must deny himself, take up his cross, and follow me."

Matthew 16:24

Reflecting

The Scriptures tell us that following the Lord involves suffering. It entails leaving behind one way of living and adopting another. As followers of a crucified Redeemer, we choose to live the mystery of the Cross, aware that accepting hardships strengthens and frees us to grow in God's life and to experience the joy of his resurrection.

The apostles who responded to Jesus' call to follow him were ordinary people. They dreamed of greatness and pursued happiness. Like us, they needed the warmth of acceptance and the joy of accomplishment. They had the assorted shortcomings and failings common to all members of the human family. Yet Jesus invited them. He invited them just as they were. And he invites us just as we are. All he asks is that we come with a generous spirit ready to risk all for the love of him. Membership in his Church is a commitment to follow Jesus in new and ever-changing situations.

Only by accepting Jesus can we know the peace and joy of living like him, spending time with him, and sharing his message of love with others. Then we can truly pray during the Eucharist:

Therefore, as we celebrate the memorial of his Death and Resurrection, we offer you, Lord, the Bread of life and the Chalice of salvation, giving thanks that you have held us worthy to be in your presence and minister to you.

from Eucharistic Prayer #2

What do I find is my greatest hardship as a Christian? my greatest joy?

Responding

Spirit of Christ, help my students feel and express gratitude for their faith and the gifts that come with being a Christian.

Scripture for Further Reflection

John 14:5–7 Jesus is the way to the Father.

Colossians 3:12–17 The Word of God shows us how to live as Christians who are called to be one in Christ.

Preparing for the Faith Experience

Day One
Witness to the Way

Day Two
Review

Day Three
Unit 1 Test

Day Four
Celebrating Jesus Christ the Way

Day Five
Extending the Chapter

 **Gather and Go Forth**

Scripture in This Chapter

Matthew 7:21,24–27 God's Word is our foundation.

John 1:1–2,10–12 Jesus is the Word.

John 14:6 Jesus is the way.

Church Documents

Catechism of the Catholic Church. The themes of this chapter correspond to the following paragraphs: **460, 618, 654.**

General Directory for Catechesis #41. It is the task of catechesis to show who Jesus Christ is, his life and ministry, and to present the Christian faith as the following of the person Jesus.

Jesus Christ, the Bearer of the Water of Life #5 (Pontifical Council for Culture). Those who invite others to meet Jesus Christ, the bearer of the water of life, will more likely be listened to if they have clearly been affected by their own encounter with Jesus.

Gather and Go Forth

Find catechist instruction for Gather and Go Forth student pages 75–76 on T332–333.

Enriching the Faith Experience

Use the activities at the end of the chapter to enrich a lesson or to replace an activity with one that better meets the needs of your class.

LEARNING OUTCOMES

The students will be able to

- explain what it means to be a witness.
- evaluate their own witness.

Materials

- Sentence written on the board, *Human beings influence one another.*
- Reflection notebooks (optional)

Before You Begin

You might tell of the witness of someone with whom the students are familiar to supplement the story of **The Doughnut Priest** on page 70.

Unit 1 Review

Jesus Christ the Way

Looking Back

In Unit 1, you have looked at who Jesus is and who he is in your life. You have reflected on how the Son of God became man to save us from sin and death. You were reminded that Jesus calls you to friendship with him. You respond to that invitation to friendship through prayer, reading Scripture, and celebrating the sacraments. The purpose of this unit is to help you understand more fully how Jesus is the way to the Father, the way to everlasting happiness.

Before you continue with this chapter, ask yourself these questions. Write your answers on the lines below.

1. How have your thoughts changed about Jesus? about yourself? about others?

   _____

   _____

2. How do you know Jesus can fill you with peace even when suffering enters your life?

   _____

   _____

3. What are two things you can do to know Jesus better and follow him?

   _____

   _____

Workshop of Giovanni Bellini, *Christ Carrying the Cross,* 16th Century, oil on panel.

Personal Inventory

Use this inventory as a tool to reflect on how you are following Jesus. Write your answers in your reflection notebook. Choose one area that you would like to improve.

- ○ Do you help your friends become the best people they can be?
- ○ Do you ask forgiveness when you have failed to be a good friend?
- ○ Do you open your heart to Jesus and spend time with him each day?
- ○ Do you listen to Christ's message proclaimed at Sunday Mass?
- ○ Do you follow in Christ's footsteps by sacrificing for others?
- ○ Do you give loving service to others?
- ○ Do you act for peace and justice?

(69)

Centering _____

1. Discuss with the students the sentence on the board.
   - ✦ Call on a student who shows some self-control. Challenge the student to stand before the class and keep a straight face.
   - ✦ Have other students try to make the person smile without touching him or her.
   - ✦ **What are some other ways we influence one another?** (You might begin by pointing out current fads and how they try to influence our thinking.)

2. Link the last lesson with today's lesson.

- ✦ **Jesus counts on us to influence one another in such a way that we become his followers and, therefore, better people.**

- ✦ **In this lesson, you will experience the witness of a man who spent his life carrying out the ministry of Jesus. His story will help you consider how effective you are as a witness.**

Sharing _____

1. Have the students read silently **Looking Back** on page 69. Allow time for the students to answer the three questions. Have the students form groups of three or four and share their answers.

2. Using their reflection notebooks, have students complete the **Personal Inventory** on page 69. **What qualities do you think a witness for Christ needs most?** [List the qualities on the board.]

3. Ask several students to read aloud **The Doughnut Priest** on page 70.
   - ✦ **How did Father Valine live out his baptismal commitment?** (by becoming a priest; by keeping the Church alive in Utah)
   - ✦ **What were some unusual things about the witness of Father Valine?** (He continued his work although he was in his nineties; he

traveled great distances; he used unique fundraising methods.)

✦ **What difficulties must Father Valine have experienced as he carried out his ministry?** (loneliness, poor conditions, bad weather, people who rejected his message)

✦ **What do you admire most about Father Valine?**

✦ **What other people do you know who witness courageously for Jesus?**

4. Discuss with the students that they can inspire others:

   ✦ **We are inspired by others to live as Jesus wants us to.**

   ✦ **On the other hand, we have the power to inspire others. First, though, we must know what Jesus' way means.**

5. Direct the students to work on **Testing Your Strength** on page 70.
   Discuss the students' answers.

Acting _____

1. Explain to the students that Father Valine was a home missionary.

   ✦ **Father Valine was a home missionary because he worked right in his own country. You can also be a home missionary by witnessing to Jesus in your own home.**

   ✦ **What are some ways you can be a home missionary?** (inviting a friend to come to Mass with you; asking your family to pray together at home)

2. With the students, pray a litany for missionaries.

   ✦ Use the prayer. "Jesus, the first missionary, give us _____". Have the students insert a quality mentioned in Sharing #2 each time you pause.

   ✦ Repeat the prayer until you have gone through the list.

UNIT 1 REVIEW

The Doughnut Priest

Following Jesus can lead to surprising roles. For one man, it meant becoming a priest who made doughnuts.

Father Joseph Valine, O.P. (1897–1992), ministered to people in Utah in an area larger than Rhode Island. At the age of 90 he was the pastor of three missions. He traveled only 300 miles a week, down from the 600 miles he used to drive.

Father Valine went to Utah in 1941 at the bishop's request. At that time, Catholics made up only 3 percent of the population of Utah, and they lived far apart. World War II barracks, a library, a trailer, and parishioners' homes all served as churches at different missions until a real church could be built. Father Valine built seven churches with donations and income from his hobbies. For years he catered dinners and farmed more than 200 acres of alfalfa. Then he became a doughnut maker. Every Saturday Father Valine made doughnuts to sell. Farmers and tourists paid whatever they wished for a bag of 10 doughnuts.

In Milford, a town in which 90 percent of the people are Mormon, June 10, 1976, was proclaimed "Father Valine Day." It was a tribute to his love of God and people. In 1988 he received an award from the Catholic Church Extension Society. It was the Lumen Christi (Light of Christ) Award. What can you do to help spread the light of Christ to the world?

Testing Your Strength

How well do you understand what it means to follow Christ? Read each statement. If it is a Christian response, write C on the line. If it shows a selfish, unloving attitude, write S.

S	**1.**	I cannot volunteer for that task. I want to play basketball during noon recess.
S	**2.**	Here comes the principal! She always has a job for everyone she sees. Let's get away from here.
C	**3.**	I will sign up for the cleanup committee. I hate that kind of work, but I do not think anyone will volunteer for it.
S	**4.**	There is a boycott against grapes to support the grape pickers who are treated unjustly. It will not make a difference if I keep eating grapes, my favorite fruit.
C	**5.**	Mother, you look tired! Let me put the baby to bed.
C	**6.**	No, I am not going to take it. That is stealing!
S	**7.**	I do not have any money for the missions. I need this change to buy gum.
C	**8.**	I am good in art. I will volunteer to make the get-well card from our class.
C	**9.**	The yard is a mess after the storm. Maybe I can get it cleaned up before Mom comes home.
S	**10.**	I cannot do what Dad told me. Everyone will laugh at me.

70

CHECKPOINT ✓

- Were the learning outcomes achieved?

- What did the students' reactions to the stories of the witnesses reveal?

LEARNING OUTCOMES

The students will be able to

- recall the significant facts and basic concepts introduced in Unit 1, Jesus Christ the Way.
- identify material that needs more study.

Materials

Reflection notebooks

Before You Begin

You may prefer to have the students work on Reviewing #1 independently or in pairs. If so, the students can write clues on a sheet of paper and the answers can be checked when everyone is finished.

Centering _____

1. Lead the students in prayer.
   - ✦ 🙏 **Look at the picture of Jesus on page 69.**
   - ✦ **We have been studying about Jesus the Way. This is one artist's rendition of Jesus.**
   - ✦ **Take a moment to look carefully at this painting and reflect on what it reveals to you about Jesus.**
   - ✦ **Recall some of the titles of Jesus we have studied in this unit. Jesus is Son of God** [pause]**, Son of Man** [pause]**, Messiah** [pause]**, the Nazarene** [pause]**, son of Mary and Joseph** [pause]**, the Christ** [pause]**, Master** [pause]**, and the Savior** [pause]**. Which one speaks most to you now?**
   - ✦ **Take a moment to speak to Jesus in your heart and listen for what he has to say to you.** [Pause.]

2. Inform the students of today's lesson.
   - ✦ **Today you will review what you have learned about Jesus and the Sacraments of Initiation.**

UNIT 1 REVIEW

Find the Truth Statements

Write an X before any true statements about Jesus.

_____	1.	Jesus is too great to be a real friend.
X	2.	Jesus is the Son of God, the second Person of the Trinity.
_____	3.	Jesus means "the anointed."
_____	4.	Jesus only pretended to be a man.
X	5.	Jesus saved us from sin and death by dying and rising.
X	6.	Jesus showed us how to live.
_____	7.	The Gospels agree on all the details about Jesus.
X	8.	Jesus sent the Holy Spirit to help us understand him.
X	9.	Jesus was Jewish.
_____	10.	Jesus was accepted as the Messiah by everyone who knew him.
X	11.	Jesus was tempted.
X	12.	Jesus associated mostly with common people and those who were poor or outcast.

Sacraments of Initiation

Baptism • Confirmation • Eucharist

Answer these questions in your reflection notebook.

1. How is Jesus present today in these sacraments?
2. How are the three Sacraments of Initiation related?
3. What gifts do we receive in Baptism?

Rite Order

Number the parts of the Rite of Christian Initiation of Adults in order.

4	Enlightenment
1	Time for Inquiry
6	Mystagogy
3	Rite of Election or Enrollment
2	Catechumenate
5	Initiation

Sign Readers

What do these sacramental signs mean?

- water
  It signifies death and life, dying to sin, dying and rising with Christ, and our new life of grace. It also signifies washing, the cleansing from sin.

- chrism
  We are anointed to be priests, prophets, and kings with Jesus and share in his mission.

- "I baptize you."
  We are washed, our sins are forgiven, and the reign of evil no longer rules us.

- laying on of hands
  The Holy Spirit comes to us.

- "Be sealed with the gift of the Spirit."
  We are marked as God's property.

71

Reviewing _____

1. Have the students play **Word Puzzle About Jesus** on page 74.
   - ✦ Divide the students into two teams. Appoint a captain for each team to alternate giving word locations such as 3 Down.
   - ✦ The captain calls on a member of the opposite team whose hand is raised to identify the word.
   - ✦ If someone gives a wrong answer, the other team may answer and get extra points. Give five points for a right answer. Possible answers:

Across

2. **apostles**—the Twelve who followed Jesus and acted in his name
7. **Incarnation**—mystery of God becoming man
10. **Evangelist**—one of the Gospel writers
11. **Gospels**—the accounts of Jesus' life and teachings; documents of faith
13. **John the Baptist**—relative of Jesus who announced his coming; the prophet who called all to repent and be baptized
14. **Infancy Narratives**—Gospel stories about Jesus' birth and infancy; they are the Gospel in miniature

16. **Mary**—the first and best disciple; mother of Jesus; Mother of God

17. **Trinity**—one God in three persons: Father, Son, and Holy Spirit

18. **disciple**—one who learns from a master; a follower of Jesus

Down

1. **witness**—one who acts according to his or her beliefs

3. **Pharisees**—group of religious laymen who stressed keeping the Law

6. **sacraments**—seven outward signs through which Jesus acts in us to give grace

8. **RCIA**—Rite of Christian Initiation of Adults by which persons become members of the Church

5. **Zealots**—Jewish freedom fighters who tried to overthrow Rome

4. **Paschal Mystery**—the passion, Death, Resurrection, and ascension of Jesus by which he redeemed us

9. **Palestine**—Jesus' country

15. **Christ**—the Messiah; anointed one

12. **Shema**—the prayer that Jewish people pray twice daily

2. Play a game of categories with the students:
   + The first student in each row goes to the board.
   + Name a category taken from the unit. (Categories: names of Jesus, New Testament books, apostles, Infancy Narratives, parts of Palestine, religious groups in Palestine, evangelists, sacraments, symbols in the Sacraments of Initiation, effects of Baptism)
   + After a category is given, each student at the board writes something that belongs to it. Each then hands the chalk to the next person in the row.
   + The listing continues until no one can give an answer.
   + A point is given for each correct answer. Continue the game with a new category.

3. In pairs, have the students do **Find the Truth Statements** on page 71. Check their answers.

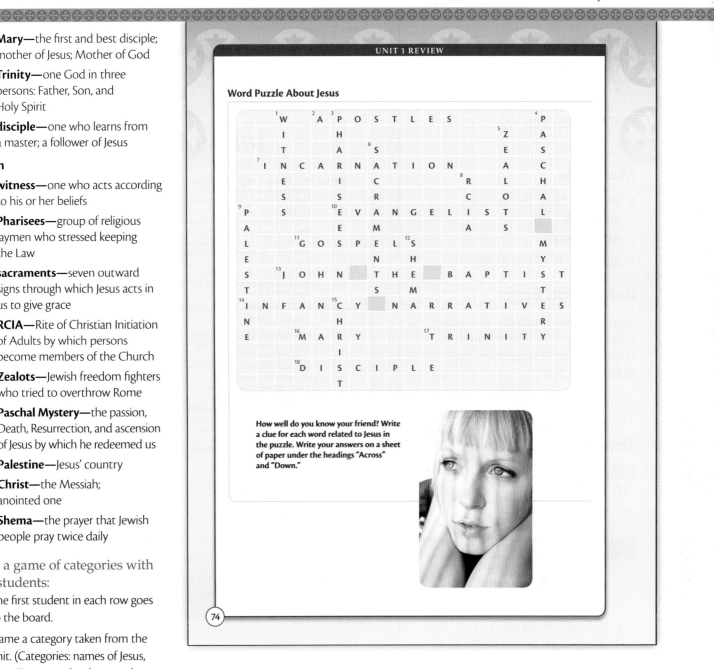

UNIT 1 REVIEW

Word Puzzle About Jesus

How well do you know your friend? Write a clue for each word related to Jesus in the puzzle. Write your answers on a sheet of paper under the headings "Across" and "Down."

74

4. Discuss **Sacraments of Initiation** on page 71.
   + **Question 1:** (Jesus acts in us in the sacraments. Through them, we receive grace and his life that he won for us. By word and sign, he helps us at certain high points of our journey.)
   + **Question 2:** (Baptism gives us the right to the other sacraments. Confirmation confirms what happened at Baptism. At the Eucharist, we celebrate the death and rising that made Baptism possible. We are strengthened to live out the commitment of Baptism and Confirmation.)
   + **Question 3:** [See the list on page 63 of the student book.]

5. Have the students work independently on **Rite Order** and **Sign Readers** on page 71.

Acting

Pray with the students the Prayer to the Holy Spirit found on the inside back cover of the student book. [See page T446.]

CHECKPOINT

• Were the learning outcomes achieved?

LEARNING OUTCOME

The students will be able to

- demonstrate an understanding of the key concepts in Unit 1, Jesus Christ the Way.

Materials

- Bibles or New Testaments (optional)
- BLM 34A–B
- Scripture booklets (optional)

Before You Begin

Students who finish the test early may use their Scripture booklets. Have them read some messages from pages 9–10.

Testing _____

BLM 34A–B Administer BLM 34A–B **Unit 1 Test.**

CHECKPOINT

- Was the learning outcome achieved?
- Judging from the test results, which concepts need clarification?

UNIT 1 REVIEW

Celebrating

Jesus the Way

Leader: Jesus Christ. Everyone who hears about him is faced with a decision. Either Jesus is God or he is not. Either he is our Savior or he is not. Whatever we decide about him involves a risk. Our whole life is at stake. Do you, like millions of others, choose to believe that Jesus is the Son of God? Or do you think he was a liar? a fool? a failure? In the Gospels, the first Christians share their faith in him.

Reader 1: A reading from the Gospel of John. (John 1:1,2,10–12)

In the beginning was the Word,
    and the Word was with God,
    and the Word was God.
He was in the beginning with God.
He was in the world,
    and the world came to be
        through him,
    but the world did not know him.
He came to what was his own,
    but his own people did not
        accept him.
But to those who did accept him
    he gave
    power to become children
        of God.

The gospel of the Lord.

All: Praise to you, Lord Jesus Christ.

Leader: People who knew Jesus reacted to him in different ways.

Side 1: John the Baptist said, "Behold, the Lamb of God, who takes away the sin of the world."

Side 2: The disciples said, "What sort of man is this, whom even the winds and the sea obey?"

Side 1: The Pharisees said, "He drives out demons by the prince of demons."

Side 2: His neighbors said, "Where did this man get such wisdom and mighty deeds?"

Side 1: Some said, "Look, he is a glutton and a drunkard, a friend of tax collectors and sinners."

Side 2: Peter said, "You are the Messiah, the Son of the living God."

Side 1: Nathanael said, "Rabbi, you are the Son of God; you are the King of Israel."

Side 2: The Samaritans said, "We know that this is truly the Savior of the world."

Side 1: The Pharisees said, "Look and see that no prophet arises from Galilee."

72

LEARNING OUTCOMES

The students will be able to

- clarify their attitudes toward Jesus.
- identify through prayer a desire to be a more faithful follower of Jesus.

Materials

Two songs about Jesus to begin and end the prayer celebration, such as "Lord of the Dance" or "Your Love, O Lord."

Before You Begin

1. In his famous autobiography, *Confessions,* Saint Augustine (354–430) tells of his struggle to find God. He was born in North Africa to a Christian mother (Saint Monica) and a pagan father. As a young man, he led a life in search of earthly pleasures. After his conversion, he went on to become a bishop and writer. He is a Doctor of the Church and patron of theologians.

2. Select a leader and two readers ahead of time to prepare parts for the prayer service **Celebrating Jesus the Way** on pages 72–73. Choose or let the students choose two songs about Jesus. The celebration should be held in church or in another appropriate place.

Centering

1. Introduce the story of Saint Augustine's life.

✦ **Some people spend many years trying all kinds of things they think will make them happy.**

✦ **They decide to drink or use drugs to make them feel good. They may try to get a lot of money or friends. But people who seek power, pleasure, or popularity eventually discover that these things alone can never satisfy them.**

✦ **One person who spent years discovering this was Saint Augustine.**

2. Read to the class the story of Saint Augustine.

Saint Augustine Finds the Way

Augustine lived in the fourth century. He is regarded as one of the world's greatest thinkers, but it took him years to discover what life was all about. When he was young, Augustine lived for pleasure instead of becoming a better person.

By the time Augustine was 32, he realized he had searched for happiness in all the wrong places. One day, a Christian named Ponticianus told Augustine and his friend Alypius about the life of Saint Anthony. After Ponticianus left, Augustine turned to his friend and said, "Alypius, if there is happiness in being a friend of God, I will be one."

Not long after that, Augustine prayed to be delivered from his sins. He heard a voice like that of a child chanting "Take up and read. Take up and read." Augustine opened the Bible and read the first verses his eyes fell upon. It was Romans 13:13–14. Reading it, Augustine realized what he must do to be freed from his sinful past.

Never again could anyone or anything keep Augustine from knowing the joy of the Lord. He

converted and was baptized by Saint Ambrose at the Easter Vigil in 389.

Augustine left behind many beautiful writings. In one work, he prayed, "Too late have I loved thee, O beauty ever ancient and ever new."

Celebrating

1. Remind the students that you are finished with **Unit 1: Jesus Christ the Way.**

✦ **You have seen how Jesus is a friend who loves us and continually invites us to know him better. He invites us to go with him to the Father.**

UNIT 1 REVIEW

Side 2: Some Jewish people said, "We are not stoning you for a good work but for blasphemy. You, a man, are making yourself God."

Side 1: Martha said, "I have come to believe that you are the Messiah, the Son of God."

(Personal reflection: I say . . .)

Reader 2: A reading from the Gospel of Matthew. (Matthew 7:21,24–27)

"Not everyone who says to me, 'Lord, Lord,' will enter the kingdom of heaven, but only the one who does the will of my Father in heaven. Everyone who listens to these words of mine and acts on them will be like a wise man who built his house on rock. The rain fell, the floods came, and the winds blew and buffeted the house. But it did not collapse; it had been set solidly on rock. And everyone who listens to these words of mine but does not act on them will be like a fool who built his house on sand. The rain fell, the floods came, and the winds blew and buffeted the house. And it collapsed and was completely ruined."

The gospel of the Lord.

All: Praise to you, Lord Jesus Christ.

Leader: Jesus invites everyone to believe in him. If you believe in Jesus, you will believe in his words and act on them. As a friend and follower of Jesus, you will want to change anything in your life that is against the Father's law of love.

(Personal reflection: One thing that I can change is . . .)

Leader: Jesus is our way to the Father. He proclaimed the coming of the Kingdom of God. Let us pray with the words he taught us.

All: Our Father . . .

Leader: May the grace and peace of Jesus Christ, who is our Way, be with us now and always.

All: Amen.

(73)

✦ **Each of you has heard his invitation repeatedly, and now it's up to you to decide what to do about it.**

✦ **We will join together in prayer to reflect on what Jesus means to each of us.**

2. Begin **Celebrating Jesus the Way** on pages 72–73.

✦ Divide the group into two sides for the choral reading.

✦ Allow sufficient time for periods of personal reflection.

Acting

1. Ask for the students' reactions to the prayer celebration.

2. At the end of class, have the students tear out and take home pages 69–74.

CHECKPOINT

- Was the learning outcome achieved?

- Have the students met the Lord during the study of this unit?

Day Five   Extending the Chapter

 Gather and Go Forth

Lead students through pages 75–76 in the student book. Find catechist instruction on T332–T333.

Use the following suggestions to create an additional lesson for Day Five.

1. Remind the students to take home pages 69–74 to share what they are learning with their families.

2. Incorporate any unused BLMs from the week's chapter.

3. Consider the time of the liturgical year and use the appropriate Special Seasons and Lessons. SSLs begin on page T369.

4. Visit www.christourlife.com to find additional activities for Extending the Chapter.

5. Use activities from Enriching the Faith Experience.

6. Guide the students in a prayerful discussion of Sunday's Scripture readings. Visit www.christourlife.com for more information.

Chapter 9   Enriching the Faith Experience

Use the following activities to enrich a lesson or to replace an activity with one that better meets the needs of your class.

1. Encourage a group of students to prepare a concert of recorded songs about Jesus. An announcer should introduce the category of each song such as: folk, traditional hymn, soul, rock. The announcer should also explain what the lyrics say about the composer's image of Jesus.

2. Have the students make posters that call people to follow Jesus. The slogans may be based on popular commercials.

3. Direct the students to research on the Internet someone who is a Christian witness. They could prepare a written or an oral report on it. They may also present their research as a PowerPoint presentation.

4. Have the students draw five columns and rows on a sheet of paper for a bingo game. Direct them to write terms they have studied in all the blocks except the center "free" space. Play bingo, using a set of cards prepared with the terms from this unit. After each term is read, have someone define it.

5. Play "To Tell the Truth." Three people claim to be a certain person (such as Peter), but only one is telling the truth. A panel directs questions to the three, which may be answered only by yes or no. After 10 questions, the panel or class votes for the one they think is the "real" person.

6. Have the students make a class scrapbook called "The Lord." Place in the scrapbook favorite poems, pictures, stories, and holy cards of Jesus. Additional items may be added throughout the year. Place the scrapbook in a place where the students can read it, such as a prayer corner.

Jesus Christ the Truth

Goal

The students will know what it means to follow Jesus in daily life.

10 Parables: Stories Jesus Told
JESUS THE STORYTELLER

The students learn how the teachings of Jesus have been handed down by the Church. They become familiar with the parables that he told to teach truths about God and God's kingdom. They come to see that the kingdom is here and that they can live the spirit of the kingdom in genuine, self-sacrificing love. Then they analyze their fidelity to Christ's message.

11 Miracles: Signs Jesus Worked
JESUS THE MIRACLE WORKER

The students learn more about Jesus through some of his signs. They witness his power as well as his love and concern for others. They become aware of the importance of faith in those he helped. They consider ways of imitating his compassion by meeting the needs of people in today's world.

12 Penance and Anointing of the Sick
JESUS THE HEALER

The students study the way the Church shares in the healing ministry of Christ through the sacraments of Penance and Reconciliation, and the Anointing of the Sick. They consider the meaning and the importance of reconciliation and how it is accomplished. They also learn Christian attitudes toward the celebration of the Sacrament of Reconciliation or a nonsacramental reconciliation service.

13 The Message of Jesus: Choose Life
JESUS THE TEACHER

The students consider the implications of Christian love. They see that Jesus calls us to go beyond the letter of the law. They reflect deeply on their responsibility to respect, nurture, and protect the gift of life. They study the Fifth Commandment, sins against life, and the works of mercy.

14 The Challenge of the Beatitudes
JESUS THE LIGHT OF THE WORLD

The students learn the new way of life that Jesus lived and taught—the Beatitudes. They study the meanings of each beatitude and practical ways to live them.

15 Jesus' Kingdom of Justice and Truth
JESUS THE KING

The students see how the Seventh and Tenth Commandments protect our right to freedom and to own property. They also study the Eighth Commandment, which protects our right to know the truth and to have a good reputation. They learn how the practice of honesty and truthfulness builds love and trust in the community.

16 Jesus' Kingdom of Love
THE SACRED HEART

The students are presented with the Christian view of the sacredness of sex. They see it in the context of true love, marriage, and family life. They learn that the Sixth and Ninth Commandments require fidelity as a protection of family life. They are taught ways to lead a chaste life.

17 Unit 2 Review

The students review the main concepts of the unit. They participate in a celebration of the teachings of Jesus.

Parables: Stories Jesus Told

JESUS THE STORYTELLER

Faith Focus

Some truths taught by Jesus and his Church are contained in parables.

Reflecting on the Faith Experience

Take a few moments to reflect prayerfully before preparing the lesson.

Listening

"If one walks during the day,
he does not stumble, because
he sees the light of this world.
But if one walks at night, he
stumbles, because the light is
not in him."

John 11:9–10

Reflecting

We can walk in darkness where
Satan blinds us to the saving truth,
or we can walk in the light of divine
truth revealed by Christ. Jesus
promised, "If you remain in my
word . . . you will know the truth,
and the truth will set you free."
(John 8:31–32) Through the life and
message of Jesus, we are able to
possess the complete truth. We are
free to welcome it and act according
to it or to choose to be like some of
Jesus' contemporaries who, though
they had seen many signs, did not
believe in him.

The parables were one way Jesus
revealed truths. Through these
stories about ordinary people and
things, Jesus turned conceptions
of God and God's kingdom upside
down. He taught that God was as
surprising in his mercy as a king
who cancels completely a servant's
enormous debt. He taught that
the kingdom was open to sinners,
outcasts, and foreigners. He taught
that in God's sight a contrite sinner
is better than a righteous Pharisee.
In parables, Jesus instructed us
how to walk in light: to pray with
perseverance, to use our talents, to
share our wealth, and to show love
even to our enemies.

By applying the parables to our
own lives, we will have the light of
life. We will be like the five wise
bridesmaids whose lamps burned
brightly to greet the bridegroom.
We will be as deliriously happy
as the merchant who became
owner of the priceless pearl. But as
disciples of the light, we also have a
responsibility to let our light shine
before all.

When we live by the truth that
the Lord proclaimed, we are on
a journey to the heavenly city—
the city that has no need for the
light of the sun or moon since it
is lit by the radiant glory of God.
(Revelation 21:23) Jesus' life, Death,
and Resurrection assure us of the
triumph of God's kingdom over the
forces of darkness. Our glory is to
share in that triumph and to bring
others to know it.

What is my favorite parable?

*What message does it hold for me at
this particular point in my journey?*

Responding

Spirit of Truth, open the minds and
hearts of my students to a parable
they most need to hear.

Scripture for Further Reflection

John 16:13–15 Only when we
are enlightened by the Holy
Spirit, the Spirit of truth, can
we come to possess the full
truth of Jesus' divinity and its
implications for our lives.

Hebrews 4:1–13 We are invited
to obedient faith in the Good
News, for it teaches us what we
must do to attain eternal life.

Preparing for the Faith Experience

Scripture in This Chapter

Matthew 13:3–9, 18–23 Parable of the Sower

Luke 12:16–21 Parable of the Rich Fool

Luke 8:10 Jesus taught about God's kingdom using parables

Catholic Social Teaching

Solidarity

Church Documents

Catechism of the Catholic Church. The themes of this chapter correspond to the following paragraphs: **543–546.**

General Directory for Catechesis #15. Jesus, in the parable of the sower, proclaims the Good News that the Kingdom of God is near, in spite of the tensions, conflicts, and difficulties of the world. The Gospel seed makes fertile the history of humankind and promises a rich harvest.

National Directory for Catechesis #28. Jesus used his parables to invite his listeners to a new way of living based on faith in God, hope in the kingdom, and love for God and neighbor.

Dogmatic Constitution on Divine Revelation #2 (Second Vatican Council). Revelation is realized by words and deeds. Works of God bear out realities signified by words; words bring to light the mystery in works.

Declaration on Religious Liberty #10 (Second Vatican Council). A person cannot give adherence to God unless, drawn by the Father, he or she submits with a faith that is reasonable and free.

Gather and Go Forth

Find catechist instruction for Gather and Go Forth student pages 85–86 on T334–T335.

Enriching the Faith Experience

Use the activities at the end of the chapter to enrich a lesson or to replace an activity with one that better meets the needs of your class.

Bulletin Board

A suggestion for a bulletin-board design for this chapter is pictured.

Kingdom of Heaven

LEARNING OUTCOMES

The students will be able to

- discuss how we received revealed truth.
- identify parables as stories that convey truths about God, God's kingdom, and how its members should live.

Words to Know

evangelization   **Magisterium**

See the Glossary for definitions.

Key Terms

doctrine—a belief taught by the Church as true

dogma—a truth revealed by God that is officially defined by the Church as an article of faith for Catholics

Magisterium—the teaching authority of the Church

parable—a story of something familiar from life experiences used to teach a truth about God and the kingdom

Materials

- Bibles or New Testaments
- BLM 35A–B
- Candle or flashlight (check fire codes) (optional)
- Chart written on board:
  CHANNELS OF TRUTH

  $$C\underline{}$$
  $$\downarrow$$
  $$C\underline{} \rightarrow (A\underline{} \rightarrow T\underline{} \rightarrow M\underline{})$$
  $$\downarrow$$
  $$S\underline{}$$

- Flash cards: *doctrine, dogma, creed, Magisterium, parable, Scripture, Tradition*

Before You Begin

1. The most predominant image in the preaching of Jesus in the Synoptic Gospels is the Kingdom of God. The emphasis is always on the activity of God ruling, not on a geographical

place. When God rules, those who are poor are vindicated, those who are oppressed are liberated, and justice and peace are experienced by all. God's kingdom is like a hopeful sower who harvests far more than he imagined. It is like a banquet you are invited to by surprise. God's rule will be fulfilled in the future. We also discover God's kingdom in our lives in surprising ways, calling for a response from us.

2. **BLM 35A–B** Prepare BLM 35A–B **Family Letter on Unit 2** to be sent home.

3. Make sure the students understand that the truths taught by Jesus and the Church do not change. Through the centuries, the Holy Spirit leads us to new insights into their full meaning.

4. Have the students compile a list of parables. Direct them to divide a page into two columns and title one column "Parable" and the other "A Message." Have them record the name of each parable and a message as they learn them in later lessons.

Family Feature

"The Little Way" Leads to Big Results

SAINT THÉRÈSE OF LISIEUX had none of the power that comes from controlling wealth or armies. Yet this humble young French saint has influenced Catholicism as few others have. After she died of tuberculosis at the age of 24 in the late 1890s, her meditations were published. She's most famous for outlining a spiritual path she called the "Little Way." It's the practice of doing small things with great love, finding spiritual sustenance and patience to make it through the day.

- As Thérèse once explained to novices at the convent, "You know well enough that Our Lord does not look so much at the greatness of our actions, nor even at their difficulty, but at the love with which we do them."

- Dorothy Day, a cofounder of the Catholic Worker Movement, was deeply devoted to Saint Thérèse. "No act, however apparently

insignificant, is without meaning when done within the awareness of God's loving presence," she wrote. "Whatever our situation in life—a mother with children at home or a mother working, a store clerk, a scholar, a nursing home assistant, a suburbanite, an assembly line worker—all of us, in the ordinary and required activity of daily life, have available to us in the Little Way a means to holiness, to love as God loves us."

- Blessed Mother Teresa had more in common with Thérèse than her name. Like Dorothy Day, she dedicated herself to loving care of the world's poor. She wrote, "We can do no great things; only small things with great love." She also said, "Sometimes it is harder for us to smile at those who live with us, the immed... is to sm... us. Let...

Visit **www.c...**

Left to right: Saint Thérèse, Dorothy Day, Mother Teresa.

Love Anyway

People are often unreasonable, irrational, and self-centered. Forgive them anyway.

If you are kind, people may accuse you of selfish, ulterior motives. Be kind anyway.

If you are honest and sincere people may deceive you. Be honest and sincere anyway.

What you spend years creating, others could destroy overnight. Create anyway.

If you find... jealous. Be...

The good y... good anyw...

Give the b... Give your...

—F...

Dr...

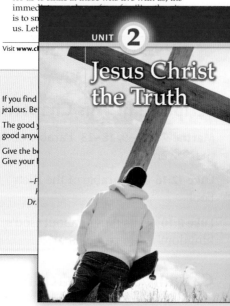

UNIT **2**

Jesus Christ the Truth

Centering

1. Choose one of the following activities, depending on your class and circumstances:

   a. Have the students experience light in darkness. Gather the class in a dark place, or make the classroom as dark as possible. Conduct a short discussion on darkness, our fear of it, and how it can be harmful. Then light a candle or turn on a flashlight and let the students discuss their observations.

   b. Lead the students in a discussion of darkness and light.

   ✦ **Do you remember a time when you were afraid of the dark?** [Let the students tell about their experiences.]

   ✦ **What advantages come from placing a light in the darkness?**

2. Help the students relate the unit theme of Jesus the Truth with the theme of light.

   ✦ Read or have a student read from Ephesians 5:8–9: For you were once darkness, but now you are light in the Lord. Live as children of light, for light produces every kind of goodness and righteousness and truth.

   ✦ **What is the keyword in this passage?** (light)

   ✦ **How is light related to truth?** (Light helps us see what is true and real.)

   ✦ **Today we will consider how we receive the light of truth from Jesus the Son of God.**

Sharing

1. Have the students read silently **Living in the Light** on page 79 and answer the questions.

   ✦ **What is truth?** (what is real)

   ✦ **How do you feel when you find out someone lied to you?** (angry, hurt, disappointed, foolish)

   ✦ **We all appreciate knowing the truth. Can you think of a time when someone told you something and later you both discovered it wasn't the truth?**

CHAPTER 10

Parables: Stories Jesus Told

Jesus the Storyteller

Living in the Light

What is it like to walk in the dark without being able to see well? What might happen?

It is difficult and frightening. You bump

into things, stumble, fall, or lose your way.

Jesus calls himself the Light of the World. He shows us the right path in life and helps us see where we are going. Jesus, the Son of God, is the source of all truth. All his life was a teaching. His teachings are the truth that light our way to the Father. They give us knowledge of how to be a better person in the light of God's commandments. Jesus revealed the love of God and God's plan for us. He proclaimed the message of salvation.

If we follow Jesus' teachings, we will know the happiness of his friendship. Walking with Jesus is the sure way of following God's will and eventually entering the kingdom. Walking with him, we live well on earth and arrive safely at the kingdom. What God has revealed, especially through Jesus, is the foundation of our faith.

Teachings of Twenty Centuries

Jesus commissioned his apostles to teach the Good News to all nations. Through their ministry of **evangelization,** the apostles handed on Jesus' message through the words they taught and the good example they gave to others. They shared Jesus' mission in stories, customs, prayers, and creeds, or professions of faith that we find based in the New Testament.

Bishops, the successors of the apostles, also have the right and duty to teach everything Jesus has revealed. The teaching authority of the Church is called the **Magisterium.** It is at work primarily in the pope and in the bishops teaching together and in union with the pope. The Magisterium is present in liturgy and in the practice of the faith—whenever doctrines contained in Scripture and Tradition are taught. A doctrine is a belief the Church holds and teaches. A doctrine that is officially defined by the Church as a truth revealed by God, an article of faith for Catholics, is a dogma. Some doctrines are more important than others. It is Church doctrine that Jesus is God and that Mary was sinless.

For 2,000 years the Church has preserved the doctrines Jesus taught and has gained new insights. Truth does not change, but the Holy Spirit continually leads the Church to a deeper understanding. On our journey of life, we can look to the Church for truths to guide us—the truths that Jesus taught.

 (79)

✦ **Why can we trust Jesus to tell us the absolute truth?** (He is God. He is Truth. He cannot lie or be mistaken.)

✦ **What kind of truths did Jesus reveal?** (knowledge of human life and of divine things, the love of God and God's plan for us)

2. Ask a student to read aloud **Teachings of Twenty Centuries** on page 79.

   ✦ Call on volunteers to fill in the chart on the board. As the chart is being filled in, clarify the concepts, using the questions that follow.

✦ Chart

Christ
↓
Church → (Apostles → Tradition → Magisterium)
↓
Scripture

✦ **What is Scripture?** (the Bible; the Word of God) **Tradition?** (the message of Jesus that was handed on through the spoken words and example of the apostles and through the Catholic Church) [Refer students to page 11 of their book.]

✦ **Which came first: Scripture or Tradition?** (Tradition)

✦ **What is a dogma?** (a truth revealed by God that is officially defined by the Church as an article of faith for Catholics)

✦ **Are all doctrines dogmas?** (No. They are not all officially defined as articles of faith for Catholics.)

✦ **What dogmas have you studied this year?** (the Trinity, the Incarnation, the Immaculate Conception, the Virgin Birth, the Assumption)

✦ **What is the Magisterium?** (the teaching authority of the Church) **The word is derived from a Latin word for "teacher." The official pastors of the Church have the right and duty to teach the truths of Scripture and Tradition.**

✦ **Who is primarily responsible for official Catholic teachings in the Church?** (the pope and bishops)

✦ **Why is our understanding of some truths Jesus taught different from that of the early Christians?** (The Holy Spirit has guided us to a deeper understanding of truths.)

3. Explain to the students how we grow in our understanding of Jesus' message.

✦ **The ideas, customs, and values of people living at a particular time and place affect greatly the growth of the human race. With each new century, we come to a better understanding of many things. We learn from what we have seen and experienced.**

✦ **The Church also grows in understanding the message of Jesus. The mysteries he taught us are so deep that there is always more to understand. Jesus did not give us detailed directions for handling every problem that might arise. Rather, he gave us principles that enable us to find the best response to a problem.**

✦ **Slavery is an example. The principles of Jesus imply that slavery is evil, but only gradually did people realize it. The Church always preached the rights of all people but did not always understand what these teachings meant or how they applied to problems. In early Christian times, Christians were urged to**

Stories That Teach

Jesus was a master teacher. He used stories about the stuff of his everyday life: sowers and seeds, fishermen and nets, shepherds, thieves, and yeast. He spoke of ordinary happenings: looking for a lost object, getting paid for work, and asking a friend for help. The stories Jesus told about God and his kingdom are called parables. In a parable, a comparison is made between something familiar and the truth Jesus wants to bring to our attention.

A parable usually has an unexpected twist that shows the Kingdom of God in images we use in everyday life. It encourages us t o see things differently.

After hearing a parable, we make a judgment about the events in the story and then apply it to ourselves. Often we find that our way of thinking and acting is being challenged by God. The discovery challenges us to change our lives for the better.

How a Short Story Works

Read the Parable of the Rich Fool and then answer the questions on a sheet of paper.

> "There was a rich man whose land produced a bountiful harvest. He asked himself, 'What shall I do, for I do not have space to store my harvest?' And he said, "This is what I shall do: I shall tear down my barns and build larger ones. There I shall store all my grain and other goods and I shall say to myself, "Now as for you, you have so many good things stored up for many years, rest, eat, drink, be merry!"' But God said to him, 'You fool, this night your life will be demanded of you; and the things you have prepared, to whom will they belong?' Thus will it be for the one who stores up treasure for himself but is not rich in what matters to God."
>
> Luke 12:16–21

The Rich Fool, Jesus Mafa Collection, France.

1. **A story has a main character and other characters.** Who are the characters in this parable?
2. **A story has a setting.** Where does this story take place?
3. **A story has a plot, the action.** What happens in this story?
4. **The action centers around a struggle.** What problem does the main character face?
5. **A story's main character might have a flaw.** What is the rich man's flaw?
6. **Conversation in a story tells us what a character is like.** How do you know what the rich man is like?
7. **Some stories have surprise endings.** What happened to the rich man that he did not expect?
8. **Stories mirror real life.** Are there people like the rich man? Have you ever been like the rich man? Do you know of anyone who had an experience like the rich man's?
9. **Stories draw us into them and make us think.** How do you think the rich man felt when God spoke? Why was he a fool? What do you think happened after he died?
10. **Stories have a theme, a message.** What meaning do you find in this parable? What questions does the story make you ask yourself?

A parable has layers, like an onion. To reveal its meanings, ask questions like those above.

 80 UNIT 2

be kind to their slaves, but slavery was not condemned. It took many centuries before people understood that slavery is a grave offense against human dignity.

4. Have the students read silently **Stories That Teach** on page 80.

✦ **As you read, underline words that help explain what a parable is.**

✦ **What did you underline?.** (ordinary happenings, stories, comparison, kingdom, judgment)

5. Discuss the elements of a story with the students.

✦ [Write the students' answers on the board.]

✦ **What are the elements of a story?** (characters, plot, conflict, setting, dialogue, theme)

6. Call on a student to read aloud the Parable of the Rich Fool under **How a Short Story Works** on page 80.

Discuss the questions that follow the parable.

1. The characters are a rich man and God.

2. The setting is a large farm.

3. The man's harvest is great. He decides to build larger barns to hold all his harvest and to relax and enjoy life. God tells him he will die that night.

4. The man doesn't know what to do with his great harvest.

5. The man is greedy. He plans to hoard his wealth. He spends time gathering earthly wealth instead of treasure for heaven.

6. As the man talks to himself, we learn that he plans to live an easy, selfish life.

7. Death puts an end to everything.

8. Many people today devote all their energy to making money and do not consider the next life.

9. The man probably felt shock, despair, and regret. He was foolish for living as if this life were everything. His belongings went to someone else. He might be spending eternity in purgatory or hell.

10. Answers will vary.

7. Divide the class into four groups.

+ Assign each group a parable in **Probing the Parables** on page 81 to read and match with a truth it teaches.

+ Have someone from each group tell the story and a truth it reveals.

8. Place the flash cards face-down.

+ Call on students to draw a card and define the word.

+ Have another student read the definition in the Glossary as a check.

9. Ask the students to explain these statements:

+ **Our faith is founded on divine, not human, teachings.** (Jesus is the Son of God, and therefore his teachings are divine Revelation.)

+ **Some of the teachings of the Church are not found in the Scriptures.** (Teachings have also been handed down in Tradition. Some truths the Church teaches are based on Tradition and are not recorded in Scripture.)

+ **The Church grows in understanding of the meaning of Jesus' teachings.** (The more the Church prays and studies the message of Jesus, the more the Spirit leads us to understanding.)

Probing the Parables

Read each parable and match it with a truth.

a. The Pharisee and the Tax Collector (Luke 18:9–14), *image at right*
b. The Lost Sheep (Luke 15:4–7)
c. The Workers in the Vineyard (Matthew 20:1–16)
d. The persistent friend (Luke 11:5–8)

_b_	1.	God loves sinners and is glad when they return to a good life.
_c_	2.	Sinners who truly repent even at the last minute will have the fullness of joy in heaven.
_a_	3.	Beware of being proud of your goodness and judging others.
_d_	4.	Keep praying to God, and your prayers will be answered.

Kingdom Parables

Jesus proclaimed the Kingdom of God, which is already here but not yet fully. In this kingdom, God and God's people live together in peace, justice, and love. The parables listed in the table below give insights into the kingdom. Read them and fill in the blanks in each statement. Notice which Gospel contains all of these kingdom parables.

THE PARABLE	A TRUTH IT TEACHES
The Mustard Seed Matthew 13:31–32 **The Yeast** Matthew 13:33	1. From a small beginning the kingdom <u>grew and spread throughout the world</u>
The Net Matthew 13:47–50 **The Weeds** Matthew 13:24–30	2. On earth <u>the good</u> and <u>the bad</u> live together until <u>the end of the world</u>.
The Pearl of Great Price Matthew 13:45–46 **The Hidden Treasure** Matthew 13:44	3. The person who finds the kingdom feels <u>very happy</u> To possess it, he or she is willing to <u>sell everything</u>.
The Wedding Feast Matthew 22:2–14	4. The kingdom is open to <u>all people</u> We are free to <u>enter or not</u>.

Acting

1. Lead the students in a time of prayer.

+ Have a student read aloud John 8:12–15.

+ Allow time for silent reflection.

+ Close by praying together the Act of Faith on the inside back cover of the student book. [See page T446.]

2. At the end of the class, have the students tear out page 78. Encourage them to share this Family Feature with their families.

CHECKPOINT

• Were the learning outcomes achieved?

• Do any students have difficulty understanding the concepts regarding the truth the Church teaches?

LEARNING OUTCOMES

The students will be able to

- explore the meaning of the parables of the kingdom.
- discuss that the kingdom is worth any sacrifice.

Materials

- Bibles or New Testaments
- Flour, yeast, pan, cup of warm water (optional)
- Box (optional)
- BLM 36
- Song about the kingdom
- Reflection notebooks

Before You Begin

1. Parables are stories that use images from everyday life in order to make a point. Jesus' parables were usually about the Kingdom of God. Because parables are so down-to-earth, Jesus seemed to use them in order to make his message easier for his listeners to understand. Parables, however, often contain some element that is unexpected or unusual. The meaning of a parable is never too obvious. The purpose of a parable is not to settle issues but to challenge us to think more deeply about how God works in our lives.

2. Jesus brought God's kingdom to earth. He showed us that to live in the spirit of the kingdom requires self-sacrificing love. Jesus invites us to accept the reign of God, to allow him to free us from sin and lift us up into his own life.

3. Appoint students ahead of time to prepare to read the parables for Sharing #1.

4. Draw on the students' previous knowledge for this lesson. Instead of reading the parables in Sharing #1 and #3, ask them to tell the stories.

Centering

Choose one of these activities.

a. Ask two volunteers to illustrate the effect of yeast in dough. Have them mix the flour, yeast, and water according to the directions on the yeast package and then knead the mixture. Place the dough in a pan and set it in a warm spot.

b. Show a box and tell the students that what they want more than anything else in the world is in it. (Let each student imagine something.) Explain to the students that you are going to auction off the box, and they may bid money and possessions. Hold the auction.

✦ **What you just experienced is something Jesus used in his parables about the kingdom.**

✦ **Today we will study the parables of the kingdom.**

Sharing

1. Have the students read aloud **Kingdom Parables** on page 81.

✦ **What are some words found in the parable just read that complete the statement of a truth it teaches?**

✦ **In the parable you experienced earlier today, how did the yeast** work in the dough? or **How did you feel as you were bidding in the auction?**

2. Discuss with the students what we are to do as members of the kingdom.
🕆 **Solidarity**

✦ **BLM 36** Distribute BLM 36 **The Price of Admission.**

✦ Have the students complete the BLM independently. Discuss their answers.

3. Write the word *crisis* on the board.

✦ **What comes to mind when you hear the word crisis?** (A crisis is a turning point. People respond in different ways. After a crisis, people can be bitter or better.)

✦ **The crisis parables warn us not to postpone things. They help us think about what we should do while we still have time. They call us to repent. The parable of the ten bridesmaids is a crisis parable.**

✦ **Why is the parable of the ten bridesmaids a crisis parable?** (It tells us to be prepared for the end of the world.)

4. Ask the students to tell one thing they should remember about the parables of the kingdom.

Acting

1. Choose or let the students choose an activity from Reach Out on page 83.

2. Direct the students to carry out the Respond activity on page 83 in their reflection notebook.

CHECKPOINT

- Were the learning outcomes achieved?
- How familiar are the students with the parables?

LEARNING OUTCOMES

The students will be able to

- compare how their lives measure up to the teachings of Jesus contained in the parables.

- choose to change an attitude or a behavior in response to a parable.

Materials

- BLM 37
- How-to book or ad for self-improvement
- Words written on the board: *God, kingdom, members*

Before You Begin

1. Not everyone who hears the Good News accepts it. Some are hard of heart and actively work against it. Others turn away when they realize that Jesus' message places demands upon them that present a risk to some of their social or physical comforts. True disciples accept the Gospel message and invite God to act in their lives.

2. Encourage the students to pray, using page 8 of their Scripture booklets.

A Moment with Jesus

Pause for a moment and silently reflect on the kingdom parables and the truths that they teach about the Kingdom of God. Jesus used common images such as a wedding feast, weeds, or a small seed. Take some time to reflect on how you would describe the Kingdom of God. What common image would you use?

In your own words, ask Jesus to help you recognize the signs of the kingdom around you. Then thank him for the gift of his word in the Gospels.

Life or Death?

In Palestine, farmers probably scattered seed all over the land and then plowed it under. In the Parable of the Sower (Matthew 13:3–9, 18–23), Jesus told what happened to the seed sown by a farmer. Some seed fell on the edge of the path and was eaten by birds. Some fell on rocky ground. It grew, but then withered away for lack of roots. Some fell among thorns and was choked by them. But some seed fell on rich soil and produced a wonderful crop.

The parable shows what happens to the Word of God. Some people do not listen to it at all. Some accept the Word at first but are too weak to live by it. Some accept the Word, and then other people or things of the world kill it in their hearts. In some people, however, God's Word lives. They spread his kingdom wherever they are. To which group do you belong?

82 UNIT 2

Rich Soil for the Parables

Will the parables take root in your heart? Write how a member of the kingdom would respond to these situations. Then write what might make it difficult to respond that way.

1. Your friends start teasing a classmate who is unpopular.

   Christian response: Change the subject.

   _____

   Possible difficulties: Your friends might realize what you're doing and resent it.

2. A classmate you would like to be friends with has dared you to shoplift a CD. You realize you could be caught and arrested if you do not succeed.

   Christian response: Explain that you value your life too much to do the dare.

   Possible difficulties: That person might not become your friend.

3. You and several others are at a friend's home. Your friend's parents are not there. The friend suggests drinking some liquor. There is a lot of it, and the parents will not miss it.

   Christian response: Say no.

   _____

   Possible difficulties: Your friend might tease you and call you a baby.

Centering

Link the last lesson with today's lesson.

✦ Show the how-to book or the ad for self-improvement.

✦ **We are often interested in becoming better people: learning new skills, improving our looks, and becoming healthier. It's one thing to hear about ways to improve, but another to apply them.**

✦ **Jesus wanted to help people change for the better, but he knew that some people who listened to him had fixed ideas. So Jesus simply said what he had to say and left it up to us to take it or leave it.**

✦ **You have learned about the advice Jesus gave in parables. Today you will study possible reactions to this advice.**

Sharing

1. Call on students to read aloud **Life or Death?** on page 82.

   ✦ As the first paragraph is read, list these words on the board: *path, rocky ground, thorns, rich soil.*

   ✦ **Which situation stands for someone . . .**

   - **who accepts Christ but then gets in with a bad crowd that leads him or her into doing wrong?** (thorns)

   - who refuses to go to church or follow the teachings of Christ? (path)

   - who reads Scripture, prays, and tries to love as Jesus did? (rich soil)

   - who grew up Catholic and went to Catholic school but when hardships came, gave up the faith? (rocky ground)

2. Read aloud the opening paragraph of **Rich Soil for the Parables** on page 82.

   ✦ Have the students form small groups. Assign one of the three situations to each group for discussion.

✦ Have each group report its conclusions, perhaps in the form of a skit.

✦ Use these questions to evoke more thought:

- **Why do you think it is a Christian response?**

- **Do you think most people or only a few would react that way?**

- **Do you think the reaction is just?**

- **How could a person handle that kind of response?**

3. **BLM 37** Distribute copies of BLM 37 **Parable Parallels.** Have the students work independently or in pairs. Check their answers.

4. Have the students name a parable and what heading it belongs under.
Under which heading does this parable belong—*God, kingdom,* or *members*? Why?

Acting _____

 Lead the students in praying **A Moment with Jesus** on page 82.
Allow sufficient time for silent reflection.

CHECKPOINT ✓

- Were the learning outcomes achieved?

CHAPTER 10 Summary

Remember

How do we come to know the teachings of Jesus?
We come to know the teachings of Jesus through Scripture, Tradition, and the teaching of the Church.

What is a parable of Jesus?
A parable of Jesus is a story that teaches about God and the Kingdom of God through everyday experiences.

What did Jesus say about listening to God's Word?
Jesus said, "Blessed are those who hear the word of God and observe it." (Luke 11:28)

Respond

Suppose the world were to end tonight. What would you wish to have changed about yourself to be better prepared to meet Jesus? Write it in your reflection notebook. Then list some steps you can take to make this change happen.

Reach Out

1. The message of Jesus calls us to a way of life that is very different from the way of the world. Find a newspaper story or magazine article about someone whose response to a need was Christlike. Talk about it with someone at home. Then write a paragraph about what you learned from the person's actions.

2. All the saints met opposition as they tried to live the teachings of Jesus. Sometimes they had to overcome their personal feelings. Sometimes they met criticism, ridicule, and even persecution. Research the life of a saint. Suggestions: Saint Ignatius of Antioch, Saint John Baptist de La Salle, Saint Elizabeth Ann Seton, Saint Julie Billiart, Saint Thomas More, Saint John of the Cross, Saint Isaac Jogues.

Find at least one situation in which that person followed Jesus' way even when facing opposition. Share the story with a family member.

3. The more peace, justice, and love are brought into the world, the more the kingdom is present. What can you do to further the kingdom in your family, your neighborhood, and your world? Gather with one or more family members and brainstorm for ideas. Then select one idea and create a plan for how you will carry it out.

4. Be open to God's Word today. Pay attention to a homily, read a section of the Gospel, or read an article in a Catholic periodical. Share what you learn with someone in your family.

5. Design a poster that is based on one of the parables. Ask a family member to help you create it. Then display it where it can be seen and talked about.

Words to Know
evangelization
Magisterium

83

LEARNING OUTCOMES

The students will be able to

- demonstrate an understanding of the meaning and purpose of the parables of Jesus.
- translate a parable into the language and culture of today.
- demonstrate an understanding of the key concepts in this chapter.

Materials

- Bibles or New Testaments
- Paper
- Quotation written on the board: *"Ask not what your country can do for you; ask what you can do for your country."*
- Materials for Acting #1
- BLM 38 Quiz

Before You Begin

1. Have students make up their own parables rather than translate one of Jesus'. Tell them to think of something that happened or they observed that had a message about life imbedded in it. Have them write an account of it.

2. Plan ways to share the students' parable projects with the rest of the school and with the parish.

3. When planning today's lesson, keep in mind that Day Four is when the students take the quiz for this chapter. Reserve time at the end of class for this assessment. The quiz can also be administered on Day Five.

CHAPTER 10 Review Activities

Parables in Art Choose a parable about God. Write its title and message. Then draw a picture to represent it. Do the same for the Kingdom of God and for the members of the kingdom.

Title: _____

God: _____

Title: _____
The Kingdom of God: _____

Title: _____
Members of the Kingdom: _____

True or False Write T if the statement is true or F if it is false.

___F___ **1.** Scripture was written before Tradition began.
___T___ **2.** The Magisterium is the teaching authority of the Church.
___F___ **3.** The Church can change dogmas.
___T___ **4.** The Holy Spirit leads us to new understandings of Christ's teachings.
___F___ **5.** Parables are stories meant only for the people in Jesus' time.
___T___ **6.** The Kingdom of God is already here.
___T___ **7.** The parables urge us to listen to God's Word and to serve the kingdom.

84

Centering

1. Discuss the quotation on the board.
   + **Do you know who used this saying?** (John F. Kennedy)
   + **President Kennedy was known for his powerful speeches. After he died, Theodore C. Sorenson, who had been his personal advisor and speech writer for 11 years, had a difficult time finding another job. His style of writing was so recognizable that other people would not hire him to write for them.**

2. Prepare the students to write their own parables.
   Imagine that Jesus has asked you to write a parable for him. He wants you to convey his message using people, objects, and problems of today. For example, the story of the Good Samaritan could be retold as a story of a person whose car breaks down on a highway.

Sharing

1. Discuss some of the elements of Jesus' parables.
   + **What are some of the items, occupations, or circumstances in the parables that were characteristic of Jesus' time but are not common today?**

✦ **What changes might Jesus make if he were telling the parable today?** [Record the students ideas on the board.]

2. Divide the class into groups of three.
   Tell each group to select a parable and rewrite the story in a modern setting.

3. Have a student from each group read aloud the group's parable.
   What is the purpose of your parable?

4. Lead the students through the Summary and Review Activities on pages 83–84.

5. **BLM 38** Distribute and administer BLM 38 **Chapter 10 Quiz.**
   Use this opportunity to assess the students' understanding of the main concepts in the chapter. If there is not sufficient time for the students to complete the quiz, consider moving it to Day Five.

Acting

1. Have the groups present their parables in various ways.
   They can be presented as a cartoon strip, a video, a DVD, music, a skit, or art.

2. Lead the students in prayer.
   Lord Jesus, your parables are so familiar that we often do not really listen to them. Help us see how your Word calls us to change our ideas. Thank you for showing us what your Father is like. Help us to accept your truth and to love others, all others, with the same love you have for us.

3. At the end of class, have the students tear out and take home pages 83–84.

CHECKPOINT

- Were the learning outcomes achieved?

- Did the parables the students wrote indicate that they understand what Jesus tells us about life and God?

Day Five Extending the Chapter

Gather and Go Forth

Lead students through pages 85–86 in the student book. Find catechist instruction on T334–T335.
Materials: Bibles

Use the following suggestions to create an additional lesson for Day Five.

1. Remind the students to take home pages 83–84 to share what they are learning with their families.

2. Incorporate any unused BLMs from the week's chapter.

3. Consider the time of the liturgical year and use the appropriate Special Seasons and Lessons. SSLs begin on page T369.

4. Visit www.christourlife.com to find additional activities for Extending the Chapter.

5. Use activities from Enriching the Faith Experience.

6. Guide the students in a prayerful discussion of Sunday's Scripture readings. Visit www.christourlife.com for more information.

Chapter 10 Enriching the Faith Experience

Use the following activities to enrich a lesson or to replace an activity with one that better meets the needs of your class.

1. Have the students present a few of the parables as plays. Ready-made scripts can be found in *Acting Out the Miracles and Parables* by Mary Kathleen Glavich, S.N.D. (Twenty-Third Publications). You might have students play charades by acting out a parable and letting the class guess which one they think it is.

2. Post pictures of the parables. Put a quotation from each parable on a card. Challenge the students to match each card with a picture and name the parable. If pictures are not available, the students could simply name the parable.

3. Have the class set up a display of objects and pictures of objects that Jesus used in the parables: seeds, a piece of net, weeds, a wrapper from a package of yeast, pictures of fishermen, shepherds, a banquet. The students can list the parable in which the item is used on a poster or banner as part of the display.

4. Have the students set a parable to music.

5. Help the students make a Parable Quilt. List symbols for different parables. Let students sign up for the one they wish to work on. Have them design their parable on sheets of paper. Glue the parables on a large sheet of paper with a border and connecting pattern to form a quilt. If you have the necessary resources, you may be able to create a quilt out of fabric.

6. Ask the students to list five sayings of Jesus they know by heart. Make a tally to find out which sayings are listed most often.

7. Direct the students to write a parable in storybook form, complete with illustrations.

8. Challenge the students to make a rebus that states a parable's message. Have them exchange papers and try to figure out each other's message and the parable that conveys it.
Example:
Keep praying for what you need—
The Persistent Friend
(Luke 11:5–8)

🔑 +P ✋ +ing 4 👁 u 🦵 +d

9. Have the students design a book jacket for one of the parables. Post the book jackets.

10. Have the students make a booklet or a story strip of the parable on the book jacket, using pictures from magazines and the Internet.

11. Tell the students to write a New Year's resolution for a character from a parable.

12. Have the students rewrite a parable in an expanded form, adding description, detail, and events that came before and after.

13. Direct the students to summarize a parable in a couplet, as in the following example:
From a tiny mustard seed
The Church grew very large indeed.

14. Have the students tell or write a parable from the point of view of one of the characters.

Miracles: Signs Jesus Worked
JESUS THE MIRACLE WORKER

Faith Focus

The power of Jesus over nature, sin and evil, sickness, and death was displayed in his miracles.

Reflecting on the Faith Experience

Take a few moments to reflect prayerfully before preparing the lesson.

Listening

He went about doing good and healing all those oppressed by the devil, for God was with him.

Acts 10:38

Reflecting

The more God is present, the more normal miracles are. In Jesus, the Son of God, the impossible becomes possible. The miracles of Jesus as recorded in Scripture fit the pattern of his entire life. They are essential parts of his mission and his ministry. He proclaims the kingdom in which God breaks through all barriers. He preaches the future in the present by describing a kingdom that is already here but not yet fully. Jesus tells parables that turn thinking upside down. He speaks and lives paradoxes. In the area of morality, he calls us to go beyond. The miracles are signs of a kingdom in which God overturns the present reality.

The wondrous deeds of Jesus reveal the power of God working through him. He is master over nature, life, and death. He conquers Satan and all forms of evil. The miracles manifest the goodness, compassion, and mercy of Jesus. He not only preached the coming of the kingdom and the way to salvation, he lived his message by being healer, teacher, and Savior in his miracles. People were healed physically, mentally, and spiritually by the power of his love. All the miracles culminate in the miracle of Jesus' Death and Resurrection, his ultimate and complete triumph over evil.

An integral component of Jesus' miracles was faith. The faith of people in need or of their friends and relatives was often the catalyst for Jesus' acts of power. He demanded faith, praised it where he found it, and chided those whose faith was weak. His miracles led people to greater faith. Today these miracles still invite us to trust in Jesus and accept salvation.

How often we stand in need of healing! To us, as to the people of his time, Jesus poses the question "Do you believe I can do this?" Our faith response should be such that he will then say "Go your way; your faith has saved you." (Mark 10:52)

Do I realize that the universe is more mysterious than I can imagine?

Do I have the faith that expects miracles?

Responding

Spirit of power and might, increase my students' faith that they, too, may conquer evil and move mountains.

Scripture for Further Reflection

Jeremiah 33:6–9 In speaking of the restoration of Jerusalem, Jeremiah tells of God's plan to cure his people and to forgive every sin.

Luke 7:22–23 Jesus tells the disciples of John the Baptist that the blind see, the lame walk, lepers are cleansed, the deaf hear, the dead are raised to life, and the Good News is proclaimed to all.

Preparing for the Faith Experience

Scripture in This Chapter

Mark 2:1–12 The Healing of a Paralytic

Mark 4:35–41 The Calming of a Storm at Sea

John 2:1–12 The Wedding at Cana

Luke 8:25 Jesus calms the winds and sea.

Catholic Social Teaching

Solidarity

Church Documents

Catechism of the Catholic Church. The themes of this chapter correspond to the following paragraphs: **547–550; 1503–1504.**

Dogmatic Constitution on Divine Revelation #4 (Second Vatican Council). Jesus completed and perfected Revelation by his presence. He did this by manifesting himself in words and works, especially by his Death, Resurrection, and sending of the Spirit to deliver us from sin and death and raise us to eternal life.

Decree on the Apostolate of Lay People #31c (Second Vatican Council). Works of charity and mercy are a striking testimony to the Christian life. From childhood, the faithful must be taught to be compassionate and generous to those in need.

Instruction on Prayers for Healing #I, 1 (Congregation for the Doctrine of the Faith). Jesus' healings were signs of his Messianic mission, manifestations of the victory of the Kingdom of God over every kind of evil, and symbols of the restoration to health of the whole human person, body and soul.

In All Things Charity #III (USCCB). By healing those who were sick and disabled, Jesus returned them to good health, to their families and to their communities. He embodied the compassion of God and set relationships right within the community.

Gather and Go Forth

Find catechist instruction for Gather and Go Forth student pages 93–94 on T336–T337.

Enriching the Faith Experience

Use the activities at the end of the chapter to enrich a lesson or to replace an activity with one that better meets the needs of your class.

Bulletin Board

A suggestion for a bulletin-board design for this chapter is pictured.

Jesus

LEARNING OUTCOMES

The students will be able to

- explain what a miracle is.
- discuss how miracles reveal the identity and mission of Jesus.
- identify the truths that the miracle stories reveal.

Word to Know

miracle

See Glossary for definition.

Materials

- Bibles or New Testaments
- Empty box or can with a lid
- Paper, crayons, markers (optional)
- Recorded music: Find suggestions for Chapter 11 on page T518.

Before You Begin

1. Of themselves, miracles do not prove that Jesus was God. Other people in Jesus' time were able to work miracles too. In fact, Jesus' foes accused him of working miracles through Satan's power. Also, what we call miracles, others might be able to explain scientifically.

2. In miracles, Jesus teaches through deeds. He shows he is more powerful than Satan or anything that is a sign of Satan's strength.

3. On Day One, the students prepare presentations of three miracles that they will give on Day Two. Instead of group presentations of the miracles in Sharing #4, you may prefer to read and discuss each miracle with the class.

4. For Day Three, you will need some treats to give to the class.

Centering

1. Show the class the empty container. Put the lid on the container.

   ✦ **What would you think if when you opened the container, it was filled with cookies or candy?** [Leave the container closed.]

   ✦ **Why would you be surprised if all of a sudden the container was filled?**

   ✦ **We do not know all there is to know about the natural laws of the universe. We are continually making new discoveries. Can you name some recent discoveries?** (the world connected by the Internet, a new planet, a new species of animal)

2. Discuss with the students miracles that happen today.

   ✦ You may have a miracle story of your own to share with the students.

   ✦ **Does anyone have a miracle story they would like to share?** (The story may be one that they witnessed or one they heard about.)

3. Link the last lesson to today's lesson.

   ✦ **In the last lesson, you learned how Jesus taught by words.**

   ✦ **In this lesson, you will learn how he taught by deeds.**

Sharing _____

1. Have the students read silently **Beyond Explanation** on page 87.
   Have the students answer the questions either individually or in small groups.

2. Ask a student to read aloud **Miracles Make Sense** on page 87.
   ✦ **What are some natural phenomena that you would consider miracles?**
   ✦ **Why would you expect Jesus to work miracles?** (He is the Son of God.)
   ✦ **What are other names for miracles?** (acts of power, signs)
   ✦ **What was Jesus' mission?** (to proclaim the Kingdom of God and make it present)
   ✦ **How were Jesus' miracles related to his mission?** (They were signs of the kingdom.)

3. Direct the students to read silently **Acts That Teach** on pages 87–88.
   ✦ Have the students find the Scripture verse mentioned in the second paragraph.
   ✦ **What do Jesus' miracles reveal about him?** (He is the Holy One. He is goodness, mercy, and life. He has power over nature, sin, sickness, Satan, and death.)
   ✦ **The Jewish people believed that suffering was the result of a person's sin or the sin of his or her parents or grandparents. How did Jesus react to this belief?** ("Neither he nor his parents sinned; it is so that the works of God might be made visible through him." John 9:3)
   ✦ **We believe that because of Christ, in the end, death will be destroyed and we will have eternal life.**

CHAPTER **11**

Miracles: Signs Jesus Worked
Jesus the Miracle Worker

Beyond Explanation

- The pastor of a poor parish can't pay his electric bill. He prays to the Sacred Heart. The next day's mail brings a check from an anonymous donor for the exact amount of the bill.
- As Ruth picked up the newspaper, she realized she locked herself out of the house. She said a prayer asking God to help her find a solution. Just then her sister drove up to return the spare key she used when watering the plants while Ruth was on vacation.
- According to the Gospels, Jesus worked fantastic cures:

  The crowds were amazed when they saw the mute speaking, the deformed made whole, the lame walking, and the blind able to see, and they glorified the God of Israel.

  Matthew 15:31

Do you believe in miracles? Why or why not?

Answers will vary.

Miracles Make Sense

The universe is filled with marvelous events and mysteries. Natural wonders, such as a spectacular sunset or a newborn baby, make us aware of God's presence. In miracles, God's presence is seen in our world even more

dramatically. A **miracle** is a phenomenon that seems to have no natural cause and can be explained only as a direct intervention of God. The Gospels contain many examples of miracles performed by Jesus as signs of God's love and concern for the people.

The Synoptic Gospels call miracles acts of power, but John's Gospel calls them signs. Jesus' extraordinary acts were signs that the kingdom he proclaimed is among us. Miracles were one way that Jesus taught truths about himself, the kingdom, and its members.

Acts That Teach

Jesus' miracles reveal that he is the Holy One. He is goodness, mercy, and life. The miracles show him to be Lord over nature, sin, sickness, Satan, and death.

Some people believed that suffering and death were the result of personal sin. Read John 9:1–3. How did Jesus react to this belief?

Pain, weakness, suffering, and death are the result of Original Sin. Except Jesus and Mary, each person throughout history bears its weight and suffers its effects. People longed for the Messiah who would free them from bondage to sin. The disciples of John the Baptist asked Jesus, "'Are you the one who is to come, or should we look for another?'"

✦ **We may never fully understand the mystery of evil or of suffering. We can let suffering destroy us, or we can turn it into something beneficial. We can unite our sufferings, great and small, with Christ's sufferings.**

✦ **The disciples of John the Baptist knew that the Messiah would be recognized by the signs foretold by the prophets. When they asked Jesus if he was the one to come, Jesus referred to these prophecies. What were the disciples to understand from Jesus' reply?** (Because he performed such works, he must be the one they were looking for.)

✦ **What truths does Jesus teach through his miracles?** (The law of love surpasses all human laws. The kingdom is open to everyone. God is compassionate and loving. Faith is important.)

4. Have a student read aloud the first paragraph of **Miracle Stories** on page 88.

✦ Divide the class into three groups. Have each group choose one of the stories to present to the class.

✦ Pictures can be prepared and shown during the reading. The truths from the stories can be pointed out by the group or from the class.

✦ Presentations should include a reading of the story from the book and a discussion of its truths.

5. Clarify for the students the differences between miracles and parables.

✦ **How is a miracle different from a parable?** (Miracles are acts; parables are words.)

✦ **How are they the same?** (Jesus taught by using both miracles and parables.)

Acting

Have the students listen to or sing an appropriate song.

Some suggestions are "I Will Never Leave You" or "Too Many Walls."

CHECKPOINT

• Were the learning outcomes achieved?

• Do the students demonstrate an understanding of Christ's power over all things, as shown by his miracles?

(Matthew 11:3) He replied, "'Go and tell John what you hear and see: the blind regain their sight, the lame walk, lepers are cleansed, the deaf hear, the dead are raised, and the poor have the good news proclaimed to them.'" (Matthew 11:4–5) Jesus' healing of physical evils is a sign of his victory over all evil. Jesus is truly the Savior of the world.

The miracles teach lessons just as the parables do. When Jesus healed on the Sabbath and touched unclean people, he showed that God's law of love surpasses all human laws. When he worked miracles for outcasts, sinners, and Gentiles, he showed that God's kingdom is open to all. When he worked wonders for people in need, he showed God's compassion and love. The miracles also teach the importance of faith. Jesus often praised the faith of the people who came to him for help. Where there was no faith, he worked no miracles.

Miracle Stories

Many people became disciples of Jesus because they saw his miracles. They watched him heal the sick and bring the dead back to life. They saw him break Satan's hold over people. They

Julius Schnorr von Carolsfeld, *The Marriage at Cana*, 1819.

realized that in Jesus, God was with them. The following Gospel stories about miracles are rewritten as eyewitness accounts. As you read them, be open to their teachings. After each one, list the truths that it reveals to you.

Wine Overflowing
as told by Mary (John 2:1–12)

I remember the first miracle Jesus worked. My son, some of his new friends, and I were at a wedding in Cana. Everyone was having a good time, but the wine was getting low. If it ran out, the newlywed couple and their families would be deeply embarrassed. Thinking my son could help somehow, I merely said to him, "They have no wine." Jesus answered, "Woman, how does your concern affect me? My hour has not yet come." I wasn't sure what he meant, but I knew I could depend on him. I told the servants, "Do whatever he tells you."

Sure enough, Jesus ordered the servants to fill six stone jars with water. These jars, used for ritual washings, each held about 20 to 30 gallons. When they were filled to the brim with water, Jesus told the servants to take some to the headwaiter. I watched the headwaiter sip the wine. He went to the bridegroom and said, "Everyone serves good wine first and keeps the cheaper wine until people have had plenty to drink, but you have kept the best wine until now." Jesus' new friends were also astounded. They remembered that providing in abundance for people is a sign that God was present to his people in a special way. Many of his friends came to believe in him that day.

Truths: Jesus has power over nature. Jesus proclaims the kingdom is here by his actions. Jesus' compassion shows God's compassion. Mary is an intercessor. Marriage is a blessed institution. Providing in abundance is a sign of God's presence in a special way.

88 UNIT 2

LEARNING OUTCOMES

The students will be able to

- discuss Jesus' power over nature, sin and evil, sickness, and death.
- explain that they can turn to Jesus in times of need.

Materials

- Bibles or New Testaments
- Pictures for presentations (optional)
- Paper
- Reflection notebooks

Before You Begin

You might assign the chart in Sharing #2 as homework.

Centering _____

Link the last lesson with today's lesson.

- ✦ Have the students open their books to **Acts That Teach** on pages 87–88.
- ✦ **In this reading from yesterday, underline the teachings within each miracle.**
- ✦ **What did you underline?**
- ✦ **Today you will look at some miracles for the truths they teach.**

Sharing _____

1. Have each group give its presentation on the miracles. Direct the students to write the truths in their books as each presentation is being done. Below is additional information on each miracle.

Wine Overflowing

- The amount of 120 to 180 gallons is a lot of wine. Abundant wine was a sign of the kingdom. Amos prophesies that in the time of restoration, "The juice of grapes shall drip down the mountains, and the hills shall run with it." (Amos 9:13)

Rising from Paralysis and Sin
as told by a friend (Mark 2:1–12)

When we heard that Jesus the healer was home again in Capernaum, four of us decided to take our paralyzed friend to him. With great hope we carried our friend on his mat to the house where Jesus was preaching. To our dismay, people packed the house and crowded around the door. We couldn't even get near Jesus. Then we had a brilliant idea. We hoisted our friend up the side steps to the roof. We broke through the thatched roof right above Jesus and carefully lowered the mat holding our friend through the opening. You should have seen the look on the people's faces! The crowd made room for our friend.

Jesus said to him, "Child, your sins are forgiven." We knew that the religious leaders sitting there were probably horrified since only God can forgive sins. Jesus seemed to read their minds. He asked, "Which is easier to say to the paralyzed man, 'Your sins are forgiven' or 'Rise, pick up your mat and walk'? So that you may know that I have authority to forgive sins,"—then he said to our friend, "Rise, pick up your mat, and go home." With that, our friend, who hadn't even been able to move his little finger, stood and picked up his mat. He passed through the crowd of people and out the door a free man.

Truths: Jesus has power over <u>sickness and sin.</u>

Like God, Jesus has power to forgive sins.

Friends can bring healing by their faith and

concern. Jesus was a popular speaker.

Stilling a Storm
as told by Peter (Mark 4:35–41)

One evening after a hard day of teaching, Jesus said, "Let's cross the lake." Leaving the crowd

on the shore, we got in our boat and sailed off. Jesus was so exhausted that before long he was sound asleep on a cushion. Suddenly a violent storm blew up. Huge waves crashed over us, filling our boat with water. We woke Jesus, shouting, "Teacher, don't you care that we are perishing?" First, he commanded the wind to stop. Then he said to the sea, "Quiet. Be still." At his word the wind ceased and everything became very calm. With disappointment written on his face, he asked us why we were terrified. He asked, "Don't you have faith yet?" All we could do was marvel at what we had seen and wonder who he was. Never in all our years of sailing have we met someone whom the wind and sea obeyed.

Truths: Jesus has power over <u>nature. Jesus</u>

became tired as all humans do. He has divine

power. We can have faith during the storms

of life when it appears that Jesus is sleeping.

Laura James, *Jesus Calms the Storm*, 1995. ❯

CHAPTER 11 ⑧⑨

- A wedding feast was a popular symbol of God's kingdom. In his parables, Jesus compared heaven to a wedding feast.
- Jewish wedding celebrations lasted several days.
- Jesus' words to Mary point to his crucifixion when he again addressed her as "Woman." The "hour" refers to his Death and Resurrection.
- Jesus used the jars set aside for the many washings that the Pharisees required during meals. Jesus brought new wine from these jars just as he replaced rigid human-made rules with a new way of life.
- The last words attributed to Mary in Scripture are "Do whatever he tells you." (John 2:5)

Rising from Paralysis and Sin

- The roofs of Jewish houses were a mixture of clay and twigs.
- Healing the man's physical infirmity, a visible miracle, made Jesus' healing of the man's wound of sin, an invisible miracle, more believable.

Stilling a Storm

- The Sea of Galilee is known for its sudden storms.
- The sea was a symbol of chaos and destruction. In Genesis, God brings forth creation from the watery chaos by a word. Only God has power over the sea.

2. Direct the students to work on **A Burst of Miracles** on page 90.

- ✦ Have the students make the chart with the headings listed. After they finish the assignment, correct the chart.

  (Luke 5:1–11: nature, helped his friends fish, Simon Peter and apostles

  Mark 10:46–52: sickness, healed the blind man, Bartimaeus

  Luke 7:1–10: sickness, healed a Gentile's slave at a distance, centurion

  Mark 9:14–29: Satan, cast a devil out of a boy, the boy's father

  Luke 7:11–17: death, brought a widow's son back to life, people)

- ✦ Review each miracle story with the students by asking these questions.
- ✦ **What alternatives did Jesus have?**
- ✦ **What decision did he make?**
- ✦ **How did his decision affect the people?**
- ✦ **Why do you think he made this decision?**
- ✦ **What would have been the result if Jesus had made an alternative decision?**

Acting

1. Have the students do the Respond activity on page 91.

2. Pray the following prayer with the students.

Jesus, we come to you for help. At times, we are blind to your truth. Sometimes we are deaf to your words. Our hands and feet can be slow to do your will. We struggle with temptation, but we believe you are Lord and God. We have faith in your love for us. Heal us by the power of your grace. Amen.

A Burst of Miracles

Learn more about Jesus by reading the miracle stories listed below. Summarize the stories using a chart with three columns labeled "Power Over . . . ," "How Jesus Showed Compassion," and "Who Showed Faith?"

- Luke 5:1–11 — Great catch of fish
- Mark 10:46–52 — Blind Bartimaeus
- Luke 7:1–10 — Centurion's slave
- Mark 9:14–29 — Possessed boy
- Luke 7:11–17 — Widow's son

A Man for Others

Compassion is sympathy for people who are suffering and a desire to reduce or relieve their pain—even to suffer in their place. It is being one with them in their suffering. Jesus showed limitless compassion for people who were poor, sick, sinners—for anyone who was suffering. His desire to help people often moved him to work miracles. Jesus has the same compassion for us today. He wants us to turn to him with faith when we are suffering. Sometimes he helps us through one another.

As followers and friends of Christ, we respond to others as he did. We reach out with compassion to people who are suffering, and we work the "miracle" of kindness. Our miracles will not be as spectacular as those of Jesus. However, with the help of his grace, we can perform miracles of love such as:

- healing someone with kind words;
- encouraging sinners by showing them forgiveness;
- going out of our way to help someone;
- doing a hidden act that brightens someone's day;
- helping a friend overcome temptation and make the right decision;
- bringing an outsider into the circle of friendship;
- persuading our family to sponsor a child in another country who is poor.

What miracles can you work today?

Answers will vary.

How would these miracles be wonders?

They are reminders of God's love and concern for people.

What would these miracles be signs of?

our faith and commitment to Christ

A Moment with Jesus

The practice of compassion is needed in our world. Reflect for a moment on how Jesus showed compassion for people who suffered. Then silently think about the people you see every day—family, friends, strangers. Who might need a compassionate word or deed? Decide how you will respond to that person. Then thank Jesus for the opportunity to make his compassion known in the world.

CHECKPOINT ✓

- Were the learning outcomes achieved?

LEARNING OUTCOMES

The students will be able to

- explain how Jesus was motivated by compassion to work miracles.
- perform "miracles" of kindness by imitating the compassion of Christ.

Materials

- Bibles or New Testaments
- BLM 39
- A mug or cup with a handle, and coins for a magic trick
- Container from Day One filled with treats

Before You Begin

Through the power of Jesus, his followers are enabled to do marvelous things. They can not only dream of what can be, but can work to make it come true. Students can be led to see that they can right wrongs, heal hurts, and confront evil in order to make a better world.

Centering

1. Perform a magic trick for the students. [Select a student to be your assistant.]
   - ✦ Ask a student to give your assistant a penny, nickel, dime, or quarter. Have your assistant place the coin under a mug or a cup with a handle, while your back is turned. When you turn around, tell what coin is hidden.
   - ✦ Trick: Instruct your assistant ahead of time to indicate the coin by setting the handle of the cup to an hour on the clock. (The place at which your assistant stands is six o'clock. A penny is three o'clock, a nickel is six o'clock, a dime is nine o'clock, and a quarter is twelve o'clock.)

2. Discuss the difference between the purpose of magic tricks and Jesus' miracles.
   What do you think the difference is between the purpose of a magician's tricks and the purpose of Jesus' miracles? (The magician intends to entertain. Jesus' miracles were in response to needs.)

3. Link the last lesson with today's lesson.
   - ✦ **You have seen how Jesus' miracles reveal his identity, confirm his divine mission, and demonstrate his power over nature, sin, Satan, sickness, and death.**
   - ✦ **Today you will reflect on what prompted his miracles and how we can imitate him.**

Sharing

1. Have a student read aloud the first two paragraphs of **A Man for Others** on page 90.
   - ✦ Direct the students to underline the definition of *compassion*.
   - ✦ **Have you ever experienced someone's compassion for you?**
   - ✦ **Someone once defined compassion as "your pain in my heart."**

2. Discuss with the students how the followers of Jesus performed miracles.
   - ✦ **Jesus told his followers that they would do even greater wonders than he did.**

- ✦ **Throughout the centuries, Christians have been working "miracles" of compassion. Do you know examples of saints and people today who have done things to help those in need?** [List the students' answers on the board.]

- ✦ You may want to include some of the following people:
  - Saint Peter Claver—African slaves in Latin America
  - Saint Vincent de Paul—the sick, poor, and orphans in France
  - Saint Frances Cabrini—the poor and suffering Italians in the United States
  - Saint Damien—the lepers on the island of Molokai in Hawaii
  - Dorothy Day—the working poor and suffering in the United States
  - Mother Teresa (Blessed)—the poor and abandoned around the world, the dying, rejected babies, AIDS victims

3. Have the students answer the questions from **A Man for Others** on page 90.

✝ *Solidarity*

The miracles the students work might be wonders because they are rare in today's world. They would be signs of faith and commitment to Christ.

4. **BLM 39** Pass out copies of BLM 39 **Christlike Compassion.** Have the students work in pairs to complete the chart. Ask them to share their ideas.

Acting

1. Lead the students in **A Moment with Jesus** on page 90.

Allow sufficient time for silent reflection.

2. Work your own miracle for the students.

✦ **I am going to do a small miracle for you, the miracle of kindness.**

✦ Take out the filled container and pass around the treats you brought for the students.

CHECKPOINT ✓

- Were the learning outcomes achieved?

- How do the students give evidence of imitating or desiring to imitate Christ's love and compassion for people?

CHAPTER 11 Summary

Remember

What do Jesus' miracles show him having power over?

Miracles show Jesus having power over nature, sin, sickness, Satan, and death.

What can we do if we have faith?

Jesus said, "If you have faith the size of a mustard seed, you will say to this mountain, 'Move from here to there,' and it will move. Nothing will be impossible for you."

Matthew 17:20

Word to Know

miracle

Respond

Jesus often praised the faith of the person who had asked for his help. How strong is your faith? Choose three of the questions below and answer them in your reflection notebook.

- Which actions of yours show that you believe in God?
- What do you do to strengthen your faith?
- When have you turned to Jesus for help?
- How have you given witness to your faith when it was tested by what others said and did?
- How do you thank God for the gift of faith?
- How have you tried to share your faith with others?

Reach Out

1. Jesus and Mary were welcome guests at the wedding feast of Cana. Would they have been welcome at the last party you attended? Why or why not? Do you think they would have been happy to be there, or might they have been uncomfortable? With a group of friends or with your family, set some ground rules for parties. How can you create a party environment in which Jesus and Mary would feel comfortable?

2. Reflect on these questions about miracles:
- Why do you think that faith is important for a miracle?
- What miracles can you pray for today?

3. Plan and present a trilogy of miracle plays. Invite another class, your family, or members of your parish. You might record your plays to show to people who cannot attend.

4. Find out about miracles that have occurred in recent times. Look for stories about miracles in magazines, newspapers, or online. Prepare a report to share with your class.

5. Friends tend to imitate each other. They often like the same music, clothes, books, movies, or sports. Sometimes they even think alike. In what ways are you like your friend Jesus? How can you be more like him? Think about those questions and write your thoughts in your reflection notebook. Begin by listing qualities or virtues of Jesus. Do you have any of those qualities? Select one quality that you would like to improve. Plan actions you will take to accomplish that.

6. Think of ways to imitate the compassion of Jesus and bring healing to others. Here are some things you might consider doing.

- Send a card or note to someone who is ill or living alone.
- Offer to read to an elderly person, or write letters for him or her.
- Do something to give someone who cares for you extra rest, especially when he or she seems very tired or is not feeling well.
- Plan to visit a nursing home. Call to find out times and rules for visiting. Ask an adult to be your advisor and to help you decide what you will do on your visit.
- Be considerate and quiet around the house when someone is ill or has a headache.
- Send a donation to an organization that helps people who are suffering from a war.

(91)

LEARNING OUTCOMES

The students will be able to

- name more of Jesus' miracles.
- express their faith in Jesus' miracles through drama.
- demonstrate an understanding of the key concepts in this chapter.

Materials

- Bibles or New Testaments
- Props for plays (optional)
- BLM 40 Quiz

Before You Begin

1. For the students' plays, you might use prepared scripts such as those in *Acting Out the Miracles and Parables* by Sister M. Kathleen Glavich, S.N.D. (Twenty-Third Publications, 1988).

2. When planning today's lesson, keep in mind that Day Four is when the students take the quiz for this chapter. Reserve time at the end of class for this assessment. The quiz can also be administered on Day Five.

CHAPTER 11 Review Activities

What Do You Think?   Use what you learned to answer these questions.

1. Before a person is canonized (declared a saint), usually two miracles worked through the person's prayers must occur. Why are miracles a good test for sainthood?
   Miracles are a sign of God's presence.

2. When two people witness an extraordinary event, one might respond "It's a miracle," and the other, "It's just a coincidence." What makes the difference in their responses?
   Miracles are a matter of faith. The person who has the eyes of faith sees the miracle.

3. How are miracles like parables?
   Miracles, like parables, are means Jesus used to teach about God, the kingdom, and its members.

Miracle Mix   Unscramble the letters of the words under the lines to complete the sentences.

1. A ___miracle___ is an act of power, a wonder through which God gives us a sign.
   crliema

2. The miracles of Jesus were a sign of the presence of the ___kingdom___.
   gdimkon

3. Pain, suffering, and death are the result of ___Original Sin___.
   ilogarin ins

4. Jesus' miracles show his power over all ___evil___.
   live

5. Miracles are closely linked with ___faith___.
   tifha

6. Jesus' first miracle was in response to ___Mary___.
   ayrM

7. When Jesus healed the paralyzed man, he also ___forgave___ him his sins.
   voefgar

8. Jesus' calming the storm showed his power over ___nature___.
   etanur

9. Jesus healed the centurion's ___slave___ who was ill and about to die.
   vleas

10. Jesus raised to life the son of a ___widow___.
    wwoid

11. Jesus worked miracles because he had ___compassion___.
    mssoopcnai

12. We are like Jesus when we are ___kind___.
    dikn

92

Centering

Link the last lesson with today's lesson.

- ✦ **There are almost 40 miracle stories in the Gospels.**
- ✦ **Today you will study some of them by acting them out.**

Sharing

1. Divide the class into six groups. Assign a miracle to each group from the following list.
   Have the group read the miracle, plan a skit, choose parts, and practice.
   - Matthew 20:29–34 The Blind Men at Jericho
   - Mark 1:23–28 The Demoniac

- Mark 6:45–52 Jesus Walks on Water
- Mark 7:31–37 The Deaf Man
- Luke 17:11–19 The Ten Lepers
- John 4:46–54 The Royal Official's Son
- John 5:1–9 The Sick Man at the Sheep Pool

2. Have each group present its play. When the groups are finished, discuss their work.
   - ✦ **Which aspect of Jesus' miracle does your play show?**
   - ✦ **Which miracle story did you like the most? Why?**

3. Lead the students through the Summary and Review Activities on pages 91–92.

4. **BLM 40** Distribute and administer BLM 40 **Chapter 11 Quiz.**
   Use this opportunity to assess the students' understanding of the main concepts in the chapter. If there is not sufficient time for the students to complete the quiz, consider moving it to Day Five.

Acting

1. Choose or let the students choose an activity from Reach Out on page 91.

2.  Prepare the students for a moment of quiet prayer. Ask them to reflect on the "miracles" in their lives.

   ✦ Begin the prayer with a simple phrase such as "Jesus, giver of all that is good and holy, I thank you for the miracle of . . ."

   ✦ Go around the room and let each student add one word or phrase to the prayer.

3. At the end of class, have the students tear out and take home pages 91–92.

CHECKPOINT

- Were the learning outcomes achieved?

Day Five   Extending the Chapter

Gather and Go Forth

Lead students through pages 93–94 in the student book. Find catechist instruction on T336–T337.

Use the following suggestions to create an additional lesson for Day Five.

1. Remind the students to take home pages 91–92 to share what they are learning with their families.

2. Incorporate any unused BLMs from the week's chapter.

3. Consider the time of the liturgical year and use the appropriate Special Seasons and Lessons. SSLs begin on page T369.

4. Visit www.christourlife.com to find additional activities for Extending the Chapter.

5. Use activities from Enriching the Faith Experience.

6. Guide the students in a prayerful discussion of Sunday's Scripture readings. Visit www.christourlife.com for more information.

Chapter 11   Enriching the Faith Experience

Use the following activities to enrich a lesson or to replace an activity with one that better meets the needs of your class

1. Help the students research saints or people today who have shown kindness to those who were poor, ill, or disabled. Have the students write a report and present it to the class.

2. Have the students write a paragraph on the topic "A Healing Presence." Ask them to address ways they can bring healing and joy to their families, their school, or their neighborhoods.

3. Have the students write on cards scriptural messages from the miracle stories. Tell the students to exchange the cards with one another and tell which miracle it refers to. Have them memorize their own scriptural message and the one they receive.

"Your son will live."	John 4:53
"It is I. Do not be afraid."	John 6:20
"[Y]our faith has saved you."	Luke 17:19
"Quiet! Be still!"	Mark 4:39
"Take courage, it is I, do not be afraid!"	Mark 6:50
"Be opened!"	Mark 7:34
"Courage, child, your sins are forgiven."	Matthew 9:2
"Lord, Son of David, have pity on us!"	Matthew 20:31

4. Read the following story to the students. You might conclude by playing a song such as "I Surrender/St. Theresa's Prayer."

> After World War II, some American soldiers visited a church that had been bombed. They found a broken crucifix with parts missing from the body of Christ. These words were posted below it:
>
> "I have no feet but yours; I have no hands but yours. Yours are the eyes through which I look out over the world. Yours is the voice that speaks my Word. Yours is the heart that must bring my love to all."

✦ **Why do you think this crucifix was not repaired?**

✦ **Would it have been better to have had it repaired? Why or why not?**

✦ **What belief of ours does this story illustrate?**

5. Have the students bring in pictures or articles from newspapers or magazines that show the need today for miracles of love and healing. Let the students work in groups to make collages of these pictures.

6. Let the students design pennants or banners, using these Scripture texts:

John 4:53	Mark 7:35
John 6:20	Matthew 9:2
Luke 17:19	Matthew 9:22
Mark 4:39	Matthew 20:32
Mark 6:51	

7. ✝ Lead the students in a discussion of how your parish or school has shared with those in need. Then have them consider things they might do to help. Decide on one thing and plan to carry it out.

✝ *Solidarity*

- Plan a service project to help younger students in the school.
- With a priest in the parish, prepare and attend a liturgy for those in a nursing home.
- Visit a hospital or assisted living facility.
- Send homemade gifts or cards for the holidays to homes for elderly people or children who are disabled.
- Collect food, clothing, or toys for those who are poor.

8. Let the students choose people in need from a group of pictures that you have gathered from magazines or newspapers. Have each student glue the picture at the top of a sheet of paper and write a paragraph below telling why the needy people are special to God and how they can be helped.

Penance and Anointing of the Sick
JESUS THE HEALER

Faith Focus
Jesus continues to heal body and spirit in the sacraments.

Reflecting on the Faith Experience
Take a few moments to reflect prayerfully before preparing the lesson.

Listening

Strengthen the hands that
    are feeble,
  make firm the knees that
    are weak,
Say to those whose hearts are
    frightened:
  Be strong, fear not!
Here is your God . . .
  he comes to save you.

Isaiah 35:3–4

At sunset, all who had people
sick with various diseases
brought them to him. He laid
his hands on each of them and
cured them.

Luke 4:40

Reflecting

In days of pain, when joy is only
a memory and there is wave
upon wave of suffering. In days
of weakness, when time has
robbed life of easy movement
and independence. In days of
darkness when loneliness is the
only companion of silent nights and
days. In days of guilt, when courage
and innocence seem impossible,
and all of life wears the smudge
of human selfishness and neglect,
the human heart and spirit yearn.
There is a voice in the midst of
the suffering, the loneliness, and
the discouragement that calls,
"Seek me."

Once, in Palestine, people who
were sick, lonely, aged, and guilt-
burdened sought and found what
they were seeking. Their sadness
became joy and peace. This
transformation was brought about
by a look, a word, a smear of mud,
a splash of water, and an outpouring
of the love of a Savior who came
for the afflicted and sinners. Jesus
came to free sin-bound hearts and
disease-ridden bodies. With every
healing, God's love and mercy burst
through the world's darkness. Evil
and death lost their power. God's
kingdom was manifested.

The treasure and power of this
kingdom have been handed on
to the Church. The priest heals
in Jesus' name, using signs and
symbols that Jesus used: the touch
of a hand, the pouring of oil, the
granting of absolution, the depth
of faith and the power of words—
healing, freeing, and transforming.

Our own hands have power to
heal by a handshake of peace,
a reassuring pat, a gentle
caress. Our words can heal by
expressing forgiveness, acceptance,
encouragement, enthusiasm,
understanding, and advice. We can
be oil for others: soothing, healing,
and strengthening. The world is
waiting for healers who follow in
Christ's footsteps. It is straining
for the bright burst of his power,
a power called love. When the
kingdom comes in its fullness and
we stand in our wholeness, we shall
recognize that those who healed
were those who loved.

*How can I participate more actively in
healing, which is the very heart of the
work of redemption?*

Responding

Life-giving Spirit, motivate my
students to heal and to be healed.

Scripture for Further Reflection

Luke 5:30–32 Jesus tells the
Pharisees he has come to call
sinners.

John 20:22–23 Jesus tells his
apostles to receive the Holy
Spirit giving them the ability to
forgive sins.

2 Corinthians 5:18–21 Through
Christ, we were reconciled to
God making us ambassadors
of reconciliation.

Preparing for the Faith Experience

Day One
Reconciliation Heals the Spirit

Day Two
Sin and Forgiveness

Day Three
Healing for Body and Spirit

Day Four
A Reconciliation Celebration

Day Five
Extending the Chapter

Gather and Go Forth

Scripture in This Chapter

Luke 15:3–7 The Lost Sheep

Luke 15:8–10 The Lost Coin

Luke 15:11–32 The Lost Son

2 Corinthians 5:20 Ambassadors for Christ

Catholic Social Teaching

Life and Dignity

Church Documents

Catechism of the Catholic Church. The themes of this chapter correspond to the following paragraphs: 1420–1421; 1440; 1448; 1499; 1502; 1511–1513; 1524.

General Directory for Catechesis #163. Jesus showed himself to be interested in the needs of every person, both body and soul. He heals and forgives, corrects and encourages with words and deeds.

National Directory for Catechesis #36. The Anointing of the Sick unites the sick person to the passion of Christ. This sacrament strengthens the person to endure, in a Christian manner, the sufferings of illness or old age.

Constitution on the Sacred Liturgy #73–75 (Second Vatican Council). The Anointing of the Sick, once known as Extreme Unction, is not only for those at the point of death. It is for all the faithful who are sick and in need of healing grace.

Rite of Penance #6 (Congregation for Divine Worship). The follower of Christ who is moved by the Holy Spirit to come to the Sacrament of Reconciliation is experiencing a conversion of heart. This conversion is marked by sorrow for sin and the intent to lead a new life. It is expressed by the confession of sins to a priest, due satisfaction, and amendment of life. God grants pardon for sin through the Church, working through the ministry of priests.

Gather and Go Forth

Find catechist instruction for Gather and Go Forth student pages 101–102 on T338–T339.

Enriching the Faith Experience

Use the activities at the end of the chapter to enrich a lesson or to replace an activity with one that better meets the needs of your class. Bookmark www.christourlife.com to find web BLMs for this chapter.

Bulletin Board

A suggestion for a bulletin-board design for this chapter is pictured.

RECONCILIATION
May God give you pardon and peace.

The Lord save you and raise you up.
ANOINTING OF THE SICK

LEARNING OUTCOMES

The students will be able to

- describe how the Sacrament of Penance and Reconciliation continues Christ's ministry of healing.
- identify the three rites for the Sacrament of Reconciliation.
- demonstrate an understanding of God's forgiveness and our call to forgive.

Key Terms

absolution—pardon for sin

confession—telling sins to a priest

contrition—sorrow for failing to love; promise of conversion

penance—a prayer, an act of self-denial, or a work of charity that makes up for damage or pain caused by sins and helps to overcome sin

Sacrament of Penance and Reconciliation—the sacrament in which Christ offers forgiveness and reconciliation to those who have turned away from God and the community

Materials

- BLM 41
- Bibles or New Testaments
- Reconciliation booklets from the back of the student books
- Box containing slips of paper with sins written on them
- Long-reach stapler
- Paper

Before You Begin

1. The Sacrament of Penance and Reconciliation is referred to in many ways. It is called the sacrament of conversion because we take the first step in returning to God from whom we have strayed. It is called the sacrament of confession because we disclose our sins to a priest and acknowledge God's holiness and his mercy toward us. It is called the sacrament of forgiveness because through the priest's absolution, we receive God's pardon and peace. It is called the sacrament of reconciliation because through it we experience the love of God who constantly calls us back to him.

2. You might have a priest speak about the sacrament and answer any questions. The students might tour the parish reconciliation rooms and make banners for them.

3. For Sharing #3, present the parables by using a PowerPoint presentation or other visual aid. You could have students act out the parables, or write reflections on them and present them in a penitential celebration.

Centering _____

1. Discuss with the students how we reach out to others at various times in our lives.
   - ✦ As I read the following situations, make a list of the people you would go to for help.
   - ✦ If you were having problems in school? [Pause.]
   - ✦ If your eyesight is starting to blur? [Pause.]
   - ✦ If you were feeling down and needed to talk? [Pause.]
   - ✦ If your dad or mom lost his or her job? [Pause.]
   - ✦ If you lied about someone in class and then felt sorry about it? [Pause.]
   - ✦ If your grandmother just died? [Pause.]
   - ✦ Why did you choose the people on your list? [Pause.]

   - ✦ What do you expect these people to do for you? [Write *healers* on the board.]
   - ✦ What comes to mind when you hear or see this word?
   - ✦ Would you consider the people on your list healers? Why?

2. Link the last lesson with today's lesson.
   - ✦ You have seen how Jesus worked miracles to heal people.
   - ✦ Today you will learn about Jesus' ministry of healing and how each of you is called to heal.

Sharing _____

1. Have the students read silently the opening section on page 95.
   - ✦ **How was Jesus a healer?** (He healed the world of sin, and he heals us, body and soul. Jesus healed through miracles.)
   - ✦ **How does Jesus heal today?** (in the Sacraments of Reconciliation and the Anointing of the Sick, other sacraments, acts of charity, and the prayer of the community)

2. Call on volunteers to read aloud **Healing of Spirit** on page 95.
   - ✦ Have the students form small groups of three or four to share their responses to the questions.
   - ✦ Choose someone from each group to share the group's answers.

3. Ask a student to read aloud **Healing of Forgiveness** on page 96.
   - ✦ Where parables are cited, you may choose to read or tell them in your own words.
   - ✦ **How do we know that God wants to forgive us?** (Jesus instituted a sacrament for the forgiveness of sins. He told his disciples to forgive in his name. His parables show his forgiveness.)
   - ✦ **What part of the parable of the lost son do you like the best?**

- ✦ **How does the Sacrament of Reconciliation help sinners?** (Their sins are forgiven. They receive the grace to change their lives and follow Christ more closely. They also receive a sign that the Christian community also forgives them.)

- ✦ **How would you define reconciliation?** (Reconciliation is a process. It is not only asking for forgiveness and receiving it. It is also rebuilding trust, showing how you feel about the wrong you have done, healing hurts, strengthening friendships, and turning your whole life over to God as you turn away from sin.)

4. Explain to the students the three rites used to celebrate the Sacrament of Penance and Reconciliation.

   - ✦ **There are three rites or ways that we celebrate the Sacrament of Penance and Reconciliation: Individual Reception; the Rite for Several Penitents with Individual Confession and Absolution; the Rite for Several Penitents with General Confession and Absolution.**

   - ✦ **All three rites have the same elements that are the basis of the Sacrament of Reconciliation.**

5. Have the students read silently **Receiving God's Forgiveness** on page 96.

   - ✦ **As you read, circle the keywords that define the common elements of the Sacrament of Penance and Reconciliation.** (contrition—true sorrow; confession—telling your sins; penance—prayer, act of self-denial, or a work of charity; absolution—pardon)

6. Explain to the students additional information about the Sacrament of Reconciliation.

   - ✦ **We need to be sorry for our sins so that we can be forgiven.**

   - ✦ **Every sin is an offense against God and injures the human family.**

CHAPTER 12

Penance and Anointing of the Sick

Jesus the Healer

When was the last time you needed healing? All people need healing in some way. It may be the healing of a sick and weakened body, or it may be the healing of a spirit wounded by sin and guilt. Jesus came to heal the world of sin and to heal us—body and soul. While on earth he healed people by word and by touch, showing God's love and mercy. Nearly one-fifth of the Gospels deals with healings. Christ's healing ministry continues today especially in the Sacraments of Penance and Reconciliation and the Anointing of the Sick. His ministry is also carried on in other sacraments, in works of charity, and in the prayer of the community. Being Christian means both being healed and healing.

Healing of Spirit

Every time Steve walked into math class, he saw the boarded-up window. The principal was still trying to find out who had broken it the night of the basketball tournament.

Every day Steve waited to get caught. He was quieter at home. The few remarks he did make to his brothers and sisters were harsh. How they all annoyed him lately! Steve and his friends found themselves tense and quick to argue. The daily reminder of the boarded-up window unnerved them.

Steve was working on his bike when his father walked up to him. Steve had always found it easy to talk to him, but now he did not even want to look at his father.

"It's a good day for fishing, Steve."

"I'm kind of busy today. Maybe some other time."

Steve's father was patient, but insistent. Soon they were at the lake. Far away from school, the broken window, and the other guys, Steve found it easier to talk. Before long the whole story poured out. Steve's father listened carefully, looking intently at his son.

Yes, it was an accident but he had been foolish to run away from it. Yes, in some way he wanted to make up for it.

Already Steve felt the relief of a burden being lifted. Together, he and his father spoke to the principal. Every day after classes, Steve would work in the school until he could pay for a new window.

What kind of healing did Steve need?

Who helped Steve become healed? How?

What were some of the effects of Steve's guilt, and who felt them?

If you had been with Steve the night the window was broken, what would you have done?

95

- ✦ **The priest represents Christ and the community of believers.**

- ✦ **The priest is bound to secrecy.**

- ✦ **All mortal sins must be confessed.**

7. **BLM 41** Distribute BLM 41 **The Three Rites of Reconciliation.**

   - ✦ Divide the class into three groups.

   - ✦ Assign each group a rite to read. When the groups are finished, call on someone from each group to explain the rite.

8. Discuss the three rites for the Sacrament of Reconciliation. **At what times in your life would you think you might use the various rites?** (*Individual Reception*—when they need to talk with the priest about a problem. *The Rite for Several Penitents with Individual Confession and Absolution*—when a group has been working, praying, or preparing for another sacrament; during Advent or Lent when everyone tries to follow Christ more closely. *The Rite for Several Penitents with General Confession and Absolution*—when there are not enough priests for a large group of people who do not have another opportunity for the sacrament.)

9. Have the students turn to the Sacrament Chart on page 212.
Direct them to read silently the summary for the Sacrament of Penance and Reconciliation. [See page T312.]

Acting

1. Have the students assemble the Reconciliation booklet from the back of the student book.

✦ Begin by pointing out the features of the booklet. Then have the students assemble the booklets.

Reconciliation Booklet
Have mercy on me, God, in your goodness; in your abundant compassion blot out my offense.
PSALM 51:3

This booklet belongs to

✦ **Fold the page back and forth on the perforation several times and then tear it out.**

✦ **Cut the page in half on the dotted line.**

✦ **Put the upper half [4–5] on top of the lower half [2–7].**

✦ **Fold the pages in half and check that they are in the correct order.**

✦ **Staple the pages at the fold and write your name on the cover.**

✦ **You can use your booklet when we celebrate the Sacrament of Reconciliation.**

2. Direct the students to role-play going to confession.

Greek icon depicting the parable of the prodigal son.

Healing of Forgiveness

Sin cripples and wounds us. Jesus showed God's mercy and love for sinners. He gave his disciples the authority to forgive others in his name. Today, in the Sacrament of Reconciliation, sins we have committed after Baptism are forgiven through Jesus' priests. We are reconciled to God and others. We are healed. Individual confession of serious sins followed by absolution is the ordinary way of celebrating the Sacrament of Reconciliation.

Jesus told three parables to show how anxious God is to forgive us after we have sinned: The Lost Sheep (Luke 15:3–7), The Lost Coin (Luke 15:8–10), and The Lost Son (Luke 15:11–32), better named The Forgiving Father. Read those parables, realizing how good it is to be forgiven, to be welcomed home with love and acceptance.

In the Sacrament of Reconciliation, sinners who are sorry for their sins and intend not to sin again can be certain of God's forgiveness. They receive the grace to change their lives and follow Christ more closely. The sacrament is also a sign that the Christian community, which has been harmed by their sin, forgives them too.

Receiving God's Forgiveness

Four elements must be present whenever the Sacrament of Reconciliation is celebrated:

Contrition

This is true sorrow for failing to love. You intend not to sin again and are ready to model your life on the life of Jesus. Conversion, turning away from sin and turning toward God, is at the heart of the sacrament.

96 UNIT 2

Confession

When you tell your sins to the priest, discussing them is more helpful than just listing them. Talk about things in school, at home, and at recreation places that keep you from being the kind of person Jesus expects you to be. Ask questions.

Penance

Conversion of heart is shown by an act of penance or satisfaction. It may be a prayer, an act of self-denial, or a work of charity that makes up for damage or pain your sins have caused. It can help you begin again and live more completely for Christ.

Absolution

God, through the ministry of the Church and its priest, gives you pardon for your sins with these words:

"God the Father of mercies,
through the death and resurrection
of his Son
has reconciled the world to himself
and sent the Holy Spirit among us
for the forgiveness of sins;
through the ministry of the Church
may God give you pardon and peace,
and I absolve you from your sins
in the name of the Father, and of the Son,
and of the Holy Spirit."

A Moment with Jesus

In the Gospels, Jesus teaches us that God the Father is always ready to forgive us. Choose one of the three parables mentioned above and reread it. Then pause for a moment to think about the ending.

Recall a time that you were in need of forgiveness and found love and acceptance in return. Ask Jesus for the grace to forgive others just as you have been forgiven. Then thank him for showing you the Father's mercy and love.

✦ Ask several volunteers to play the penitent and the priest. Set up several pairs.

✦ Penitents can draw sins from the box that was prepared earlier.

3.  Have the students read silently **A Moment with Jesus** on page 96.
Allow sufficient time for silent reflection.

CHECKPOINT

• Were the learning outcomes achieved?

LEARNING OUTCOMES

The students will be able to

- discuss their understanding of the need for reconciliation.
- review their own attitudes toward reconciliation.

Materials

- BLM 42A–B, BLM 43A–B
- Paper

- Clear glass bowl filled with water
- Red and blue food coloring
- Overhead projector (optional)

Before You Begin

1. The peace that the world and individuals need and long for will be brought about through reconciliation. In this lesson, the students learn the importance of reconciliation and study how it can be achieved.

2. Link the last lesson with today's lesson.
   - ✦ **Just as the good in each person encourages and strengthens the Body of Christ, so the sins of each person hurt and weaken the Body of Christ.**
   - ✦ **That is why, after we have sinned, we need to be reconciled, not only with God, but with the entire community. Reconciliation also affects everyone.**
   - ✦ **Today we will take a closer look at sin and reconciliation.**

2. You might have the questions in Sharing #5 discussed in groups.

3. Consider having the students compose a family reconciliation service.

Centering _____

1. Set a bowl of water in front of the class. Ask for two volunteers.
   - ✦ **You will try to color one-half of the water blue and one-half red.**
   - ✦ Direct one student to put a drop of blue food coloring in one side of the bowl and the other student to put a drop of red in the other side.
   - ✦ **What happened to the colors?** (They mixed together.)
   - ✦ **How does this demonstration symbolize the effects of the actions of individuals?** (Whatever we do has an effect on others.)
   - ✦ **Just as it was impossible to keep one color from mixing with the other, so it is impossible for us not to affect and to be affected by the actions of one another in the community.**
   - ✦ **Sin changes us. Because it alters our relationships of love, and because of our membership in the Body of Christ, there is no such thing as private sin.**

Sharing _____

1. Have the students read silently **Mending Relationships** on page 97.
   - ✦ **Some people today try to resolve a problem by seeking revenge or filing a lawsuit. What example of forgiveness do we have?** (Christ, who forgave freely, completely, and lovingly) **We need to reach out to others who need reconciliation and peace. It is an important part of belonging to a faith community.**
   - ✦ **At times, complete reconciliation with others is not possible. There needs to be openness and readiness on both sides. If one person is not willing to forgive, the other person cannot do much about it.**
   - ✦ **How can we respond in a situation like this?** (by being patient and concerned; by praying for the other person; by always keeping the door open for reconciliation)
   - ✦ **We sometimes say we forgive when our actions and attitudes show that we do not. Then we need to pray for God's help.**

2. **BLM 42A–B** Distribute copies of BLM 42A–B **Learning to Reconcile and to Be Reconciled.**
   - ✦ Direct the students to read the story silently.
   - ✦ **What did Mike do that was actually wrong?** (Mike was not wrong because he got caught. He was wrong in taking the beer, drinking it, and breaking school and home rules.) **His offense changed some relationships in his life. It calls for reconciliation.**
   - ✦ **What could Mike have done after he found out what was planned for the party?** [Discuss the pros and cons of the options the students propose.]
   - ✦ **How do you think Mike felt by the end of the story? How do you think he would have felt if he had not been caught?**

- ✦ **At the end of the story, there is the statement "It was going to be a very long day." Why?** (Mike would have to face his friends, the principal and coach, and his team members. The day would be difficult because of the guilt he felt and because he has the responsibility of evaluating his actions and their consequences.)

3. **Draw a circle on the board and label it** *Mike.*
   Have several students draw circles around it with the names of the other characters.

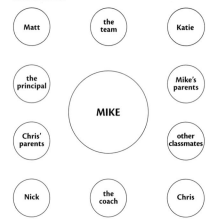

- ✦ **For each person or group listed, describe what the relationship was like before the party and what it was like at the end of the story.** [As you discuss each relationship, draw a line connecting the circles. If the relationship has been disrupted by the events of the party, place an X on the connecting line.]

4. **Point out Mike's roles in this situation.**
   - ✦ **Mike has two roles in this situation: he has sinned and he is a member of a community in which others sin.** (the Church and the school) **He must deal with his failings, and the failings of others.**
   - ✦ **Who will Mike find hardest to forgive?** (Nick and Chris) **Why?** (They were the friends who were involved in planning the party, and they encouraged him to become involved. They were not punished nor were they loyal to Mike in his time of need.)

5. Direct the students to answer the questions at the end of BLM 42B.
   Allow sufficient time for the students to answer the questions.
   1. **How can Mike be reconciled to God?** (by prayer; through the Sacraments of Reconciliation and the Eucharist; by good works, acts of charity, fasting, almsgiving; through the penitential rite at Mass [a non-sacramental penitential prayer])
   2. **How can Mike be reconciled with his parents?** (by apologizing; by discussing with them how he feels about his conduct; by asking their advice)
   3. **How can Mike be reconciled with his coach? his principal?** (by apologizing; by not holding grudges or pouting; by accepting his punishment as the necessary consequence of his actions; by being kind and honest in the future)
   4. **How can Mike be reconciled with his friends who were at the party?** (by not holding grudges because they were not punished; by turning down any invitations to parties where similar activities are planned; by being honest about how he feels because of what happened; by forgiving them)
   5. **How can he be reconciled with Chris, who was not thrown off the team?** (Students may question why Mike should seek reconciliation since Chris appears to be most responsible for the situation. Point out that Christian reconciliation is the obligation of all, not just the one who is at fault. Mike's attempt to reconcile may include approaching Chris on friendly terms. Mike may be able to point out to Chris a more responsible way of acting. He could tell Chris to be honest and open about his actions at the party and accept the consequences. Reconciliation for the two friends may also mean talking over the situation, forgiving each another, and promising to support each another in the future.)

6. **How can Mike be reconciled, at peace, within himself?** (through prayer and meditation on God's great love for him; by realizing his weakness and dependence on the grace of God; by forgiving himself and concentrating more on the future than on the past; by planning some means of improvement) **As Mike becomes reconciled with God and with the other people involved, he will experience the fruit of reconciliation, which is peace.**

7. **Who should be the first to forgive and begin the process of reconciliation? Why?** (All have the obligation to seek reconciliation.)

8. **What should Mike's friends, parents, coach, principal, and other people in his life do to help Mike experience reconciliation?** (Reach out to him in forgiveness and acceptance; affirm his goodness; ask him to take on responsibilities that will give him the opportunity to express and establish that he can be trusted; be willing to forget the incident and show that it has been forgotten.)

Acting

1. **BLM 43A–B** Distribute BLM 43A **Response-Ability: Reconciliation.**
   Have the students answer the personal questions. Assign the Scripture activity on BLM 43B as homework.

2. Pray the Act of Contrition with the students from their Reconciliation booklets.

Mending Relationships

The father in the parable of the lost son had two sons. The older son, who refused to forgive his repentant brother, was refusing to love. He too was a sinner and in need of reconciliation.

When were you last called to forgive someone? Did you tell the person he or she was forgiven? Was your relationship restored? When were you last forgiven? How did you know you were forgiven? How did you feel?

Christ challenges us and gives us the grace to forgive as he forgave—freely, completely, and lovingly. God's greatest desire is that we ask forgiveness for our sins and forgive others as we have been forgiven.

Healing of Body

On a spring day, Lisa came home with a headache and a 103° fever. Her mom took her to the doctor. A physical exam and blood test showed Lisa had mononucleosis. She would need to stay home to rest for at least two weeks and not participate in school activities.

Family and friends called and wrote. They visited, brought cards and flowers, and shared news. Everyone listened as Lisa talked about her experiences and what she had learned. Day by day, Lisa became the lively girl they had known before. With loving care and rest, she would continue her summer activities and be ready for school in the fall.

Who helped Lisa regain health? How?

See previous two paragraphs for the ways

people showed interest in and concern for Lisa.

A Gift for the Suffering

The book *Old Age Isn't for Sissies* suggests the difficulty of being weakened by age. Old age and illness often bring frustration, discouragement, and even bitterness. Those who are sick may feel lonely, and wonder why God permits them to suffer. They may envy the energy

and health of others. Some elderly people fear losing their independence. People who are elderly and sick may be impatient and feel unappreciated. There can be many temptations for them at a time when they feel very weak.

Christ understands suffering. He knows the pain, the stress, and the emptiness that we endure. Through the celebration of the Sacrament of the Anointing of the Sick, he strengthens and comforts the seriously ill, grants them forgiveness, and restores their health if it is God's plan for them.

Check the attitudes that apply to you.

What is your attitude toward sickness? Do you
○ refuse to think about it until it happens to you personally?
○ complain when you are ill?
○ think it is a punishment from God?
○ pray when you are sick?
○ thank God for your health?

What is your attitude toward people who are sick and elderly? Do you
○ pray for them?
○ feel sorry for them, but find it difficult to be around them?
○ find joy in visiting them?

People who are sick and elderly can unite their sufferings with Christ and offer them for the Church. What other gifts can they bring to the community?

Because elderly people have much life experi-

ence, they also have wisdom. They have time

to listen to others. They sometimes recognize

the gifts of youth and encourage them when

no one else does. Those who suffer with cour-

age and patience inspire and teach us.

CHAPTER 12 97

CHECKPOINT

- Were the learning outcomes achieved?

LEARNING OUTCOMES

The students will be able to

- explain how the Sacrament of the Anointing of the Sick continues Christ's ministry of healing.
- explain the rite of the Anointing of the Sick.
- show concern for the spiritual and physical needs of others.

Key Term

viaticum—the rite in which a dying person receives Holy Communion

Materials

- Sample of oil
- Reflection notebook

Before You Begin

Until the 1970s, the Sacrament of the Anointing of the Sick was known as Extreme Unction. In popular language, it was referred to as the "last rites", and it was considered to be reserved for people about to die. The sacrament was usually celebrated in private because of the gravity of the person's situation and because the person's confession was heard. Since the Second Vatican Council, this sacrament has recaptured its focus as one of the Sacraments of Healing, as it was practiced in the early Church. Its communal nature is encouraged, calling all God's people to pray for and celebrate the healing power of Jesus.

Students bring various backgrounds to the topic of healing. Their frames of reference may include fake faith healers and painful experiences of praying for cures that never happened. Students with particular difficulties should be directed to caring and competent people who can help them.

Centering

1. Discuss with the students what it is like when they are sick.
   - ✦ **Remember a time when you were sick. What was it like for you?**
   - ✦ Have them share their experience with a partner, telling how they felt and their thoughts as they suffered.

2. Link the last lesson with today's lesson.
   - ✦ **As you learned in our study of the Sacrament of Reconciliation, community support is important in our healing when we sin. The community is also important in the healing of physical illness.**
   - ✦ **Today we will see how Christ reaches out to heal us in the Sacrament of the Anointing of the Sick.**

Sharing

1. Direct the students to read silently **Healing of Body** on page 97.
   - ✦ Have the students answer the questions.
   - ✦ **Do you think the love and concern shown by others helped Lisa recover more quickly?** (Science has acknowledged the importance of positive mental attitudes, faith, and love for regaining health.)

2. Have the students read **A Gift for the Suffering** on page 97.
   - ✦ Have the students complete the activity at the end of the reading.
   - ✦ **What are some of your attitudes towards sickness? toward people who are sick and elderly?**
   - ✦ **Why is oil a good sign for this sacrament?** [Show the students a sample of oil.] (Oil is used for healing, strengthening, and soothing.)

- ✦ **How is the Sacrament of the Anointing of the Sick a gift?** (It strengthens and comforts people who are seriously ill, grants them forgiveness, and may restore them to health.)

- ✦ **How does the book's description of people who are sick or elderly compare with your experiences?**

- ✦ **What are some needs of those who are sick or elderly?** [Have the students write these on the board.]

- ✦ **The Rite of Anointing and Pastoral Care of the Sick stresses caring for the sick as a means of witnessing to Christ and being Christian healers.**

- ✦ **In caring for others, we often receive much more than we give. What are some of the answers you gave about the gifts that those who are sick or elderly bring to us?**

3. Have the students read silently **The Anointing of the Sick** on page 98.

◆ In the past, the Sacrament of the Anointing of the Sick was called *Extreme Unction*, which means "last anointing." People thought it was only for those who were actually dying. Now we celebrate it as the early Christians did, as a sacrament for those who are sick or aged. It is meant to strengthen them spiritually and physically if it is God's will.

◆ Whenever people are seriously ill, they may receive the Anointing of the Sick and continue to do so as their illness progresses.

◆ At Masses in which the Anointing of the Sick is celebrated, many people are anointed.

◆ What is the special rite for those who are dying? (viaticum) **How does it help these people?** (Jesus comes to them in Holy Communion and accompanies them on the last stage of their journey.)

◆ For those who are near death, the Church offers forgiveness and strength through the Sacraments of Reconciliation, followed by the Anointing of the Sick and viaticum. Listen to one of the prayers in the rite that expresses the care and concern of the whole Church.

Prayer After Anointing

Father in heaven,
through this holy anointing
grant N. comfort in his/her suffering.

When he/she is afraid, give him/her
courage,
when afflicted, give him/her
patience,
when dejected, afford him/her hope,
and when alone, assure him/her of
the support of your holy people.

We ask this through Christ our Lord.
R̸. Amen.

The Anointing of the Sick

The Sacrament of the Anointing of the Sick may be celebrated anywhere. At times a parish anointing service is held for all those in need of the sacrament. Usually the Church is represented by at least the priest, family, and friends who have gathered to pray for the sick person.

The priest sprinkles the sick person with holy water, recalling Baptism when he or she was given new life through Christ's passion and Resurrection. Then everyone participates in the penitential rite. The sick person may celebrate the Sacrament of Reconciliation in private at this time. Then God's Word is proclaimed, offering comfort and hope to all.

Next, just as Jesus often healed by touching, the priest lays his hands on the head of the sick person. This act signifies invoking the Holy Spirit to come upon the sick person. It also signifies the blessing and prayers of the Church and its union with the sick person. Then the priest anoints the person with oil on the forehead and hands, saying,

"Through this holy anointing may the Lord in his love and mercy help you with the grace of the Holy Spirit. May the Lord who frees you from sin save you and raise you up."

The ancient practice of anointing with oil means healing, soothing, and strengthening. It is a sign of the presence of the Holy Spirit.

After the anointing, everyone prays for the physical and spiritual health of the one anointed. The sacrament concludes with praying the Lord's Prayer, receiving Holy Communion, and a blessing.

Food for the Journey
A person who is dying may receive Holy Communion in a special rite called *viaticum*. The word means "with you on the way." In viaticum, Jesus accompanies us through the struggles at the end of life and into the banquet of the heavenly kingdom. The rite includes a renewal of the baptismal profession of faith and may end with everyone giving the dying person the sign of peace.

Do you know someone who is seriously ill or elderly? What can you do to help that person?

The Gift of Healing

Today Christ's healing ministry is very much alive. Not only does Christ bring healing to us through the Sacraments of Penance and Reconciliation and the Anointing of the Sick but through certain people. At times, God gives people a special gift of healing for the good of others and the Church. Working through them, Jesus responds to the faith and prayers of sick people and their friends. He continues to cure people with many kinds of illnesses—physical, mental, and spiritual. Often the greatest healing is spiritual.

Each one of us, though, is called to be a healer through our words and actions, our prayers and sacrifices.

When have you been healed?

Answers will vary.

How have you helped heal someone else?

Answers will vary.

 UNIT 2

---

4. Direct the students to read silently **Food for the Journey** on page 98.

◆ Ask volunteers to answer the questions at the end of the section.

◆ Answers should include encouraging a sick person to request the Anointing of the Sick, and suggesting that some parishes hold a communal celebration of this sacrament periodically.

5. Ask a student to read aloud **The Gift of Healing** on page 98.

◆ Share your own stories of healing. Ask the students to share their stories of healing.

◆ Have the students discuss the questions at the end of the reading.

6. Refer the students to the Sacrament Chart on page 212. Have them read the summary for the Sacrament of the Anointing of the Sick. [See page T312.]

Acting _____

1. Discuss with the students ways they can show Christ's loving and healing.

How can you show Christ's loving and healing to your classmates who are having problems? (Some problems may be drugs and alcohol, tension with divorced or separated parents, disobedience, temptations to run away, shoplifting, bad language, viewing pornography.)

2. Have the students do the Respond activity on page 99.

3. Choose or let the students choose an activity from Reach Out on page 99.

4. Pray with the students a prayer for those who are sick.

✦ **Think of someone you know who is sick and in need of prayer. As we pray this litany adapted from the Sacrament of the Anointing of the Sick, think of that person.**

✦ **As we pray, you will repeat the response "Lord, have mercy" after me.**

✦ **Bless those we pray for today.** [Pause.] **Fill them with new hope and strength. Lord, have mercy.** [Response]

✦ **Relieve their pain and free them from harm. Lord, have mercy.** [Response]

✦ **Free them from sin and do not let them give way to temptation. Lord, have mercy.** [Response]

✦ **Sustain all the sick with your power. Lord, have mercy.** [Response]

✦ **Assist all who care for those who are sick. Lord, have mercy.** [Response]

✦ **Give life and health to our brothers and sisters, your friends who are sick. Lord, have mercy.** [Response]

CHECKPOINT

- Were the learning outcomes achieved?

- What signs are there that the students grew in their understanding and compassion for those who are sick?

LEARNING OUTCOMES

The students will be able to

- plan and participate in a celebration of the Sacrament of Penance and Reconciliation.
- demonstrate a deeper understanding of the Sacrament of Penance and Reconciliation.
- demonstrate an understanding of the key concepts in this chapter.

Materials

- Bibles or New Testaments
- BLM 44A–B
  Song books
  Reconciliation booklets
- BLM 45A–B
- BLM 46 (optional)
- BLM 47 Quiz

Before You Begin

1. Contact your parish priest to arrange a time for the celebration of the Sacrament of Penance and Reconciliation. Give him a copy of your plan. Request that several priests be present for individual confession.

2. **BLM 46** You may wish to hold a non-sacramental celebration of forgiveness using BLM 46 **Celebration of Reconciliation**. Make it clear that this penitential service is not the sacrament, but a preparation for celebrating the sacrament.

3. Include a ritual in the communal reconciliation ceremony. Have the students suggest rituals or choose from these: give a sign of peace; sprinkle water; burn incense to symbolize their prayers rising to God.

   The students can write one of their faults on paper and put them in an urn before the altar. The papers can be burned and the ashes used to make crosses

on their foreheads—symbols of repentance.

   Dramatize a parable of forgiveness or an account of Christ forgiving sin.

   Have the students bring in gifts for those who are poor.

4. The students might make banners or other decorations for the church to reinforce the theme to be used in the ritual.

5. When planning today's lesson, keep in mind that Day Four is when the students take the quiz for this chapter. Reserve time at the end of class for this assessment. The quiz can also be administered on Day Five.

CHAPTER 12 Summary

Remember

How do the Sacraments of Healing heal us?
In the Sacrament of Reconciliation, Christ offers forgiveness and reconciliation to those who have turned away from God and the community. In the Sacrament of the Anointing of the Sick, Christ offers forgiveness, healing, and strength to those who are weakened by age or sickness.

What are the four elements of the Sacrament of Reconciliation?
The four elements of the Sacrament of Reconciliation are contrition, confession, penance, and absolution.

What is viaticum?
Viaticum is the rite in which a dying person receives Holy Communion.

How can we bring healing to others?
We can bring healing to others by
- being willing to forgive and to ask for forgiveness;
- visiting, supporting, and caring for people who are sick or elderly;
- praying for people who suffer physically, mentally, or spiritually.

Respond

Suffering is a part of everyone's life. Recall one of your own experiences of suffering. Then read 2 Corinthians 4:7–18. In your reflection notebook, write your reflections on suffering: its mystery, its value, and what it has done for you. Include who or what gave you hope during this time.

Reach Out

1. Reconciliation begins at home. Try to recognize one good quality of every member of your family. Write a short note to each one, thanking him or her for sharing that gift with the family. Plan to celebrate with your family the Sacrament of Reconciliation or a reconciliation ceremony.

2. Read how Jesus deals with two women who were sinful: The Pardon of the Sinful Woman (Luke 7:36–50) and A Woman Caught in Adultery (John 7:53–8:11). Write a paragraph about how Jesus related to sinners.

3. Speak with people who care for people who are sick or elderly and ask them to share their experiences with you. They could be ministers of care in your parish or workers in a hospital or home for elderly people. Write your reactions and present them to the class.

4. Adopt a person in your parish who is a shut-in. Write to the person, make cards or small gifts, and do things for him or her throughout the year.

5. Make banners, design remembrances, and prepare refreshments for your parish celebration of the Anointing of the Sick.

6. Find examples in the news recently of nations, churches, companies, or individuals that have asked forgiveness. Write a paragraph about the value of forgiveness for the good of society.

Jan Sanders van Hemessen, detail from *Christ and the Woman Taken in Adultery*, 16th Century. Jesus points to an inscription that defends a persecuted woman.

(99)

Centering

1. Have the students read Luke 15:17–20 about the lost son's preparation for his return to his father.

   Life and Dignity
   - The father loved his son even though he squandered his inheritance. His son's life was more important than the money.

   - There are two types of preparation for the Sacrament of Reconciliation: preparation of the liturgy and preparation of the heart. In this section of the parable, we read of the son's preparation of the heart for returning to his father.

2. Inform the students of the date and time for their celebration of the Sacrament of Reconciliation.

+ **Today we will plan and prepare for our celebration of the Sacrament of Reconciliation.**

+ **We will also plan a welcome-home celebration for one another.**

Sharing _____

1. Decide on a theme for the celebration of the Sacrament of Reconciliation.
You may suggest a theme based on the parable of the Lost Son: forgiveness, the bountiful mercy of God, the forgiveness of one another. [Write the themes on the board.]

2. **BLM 44A–B** Distribute BLM 44A–B **Celebration of Reconciliation** *Planning Guide.*

+ List the six groups needed and refer to the planning guide for explanations of their duties. Choose a volunteer to lead each group.

+ Divide the class into the groups and assign work areas.

3. **BLM 45A–B** Give each group a copy of BLM 45A–B **Celebration of Reconciliation** *Planning Sheet*

+ **In your groups, prepare your section of the celebration.**

+ **Be sure your choices follow the theme we have chosen.**

+ **Group leaders, make sure your group's choices are put on the planning sheet in the correct section.**

4. Have the group leaders report on their group's decisions.

+ Make a master copy of the celebration and post it.

+ Give copies of the master to the readers and the priest who will preside at the celebration.

+ Remind students to bring their Reconciliation booklets to the celebration.

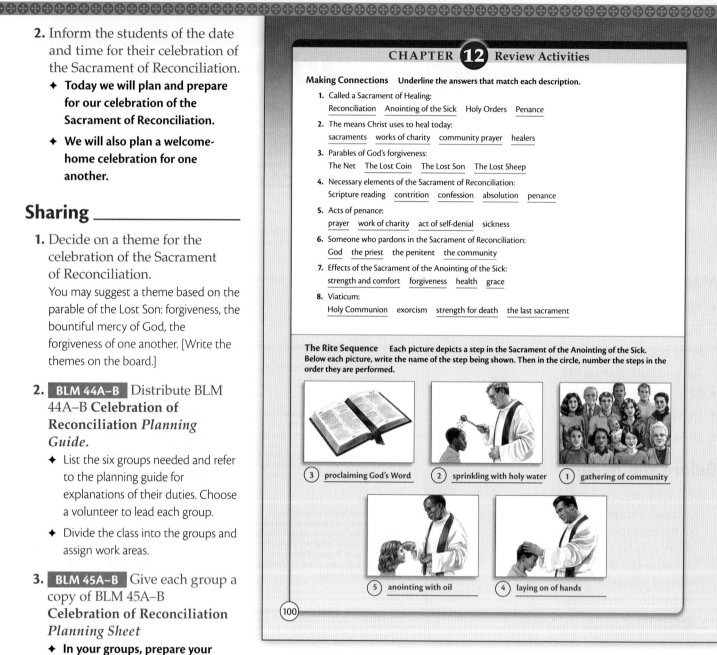

CHAPTER **12** Review Activities

Making Connections   Underline the answers that match each description.

1. Called a Sacrament of Healing:
Reconciliation   Anointing of the Sick   Holy Orders   Penance

2. The means Christ uses to heal today:
sacraments   works of charity   community prayer   healers

3. Parables of God's forgiveness:
The Net   The Lost Coin   The Lost Son   The Lost Sheep

4. Necessary elements of the Sacrament of Reconciliation:
Scripture reading   contrition   confession   absolution   penance

5. Acts of penance:
prayer   work of charity   act of self-denial   sickness

6. Someone who pardons in the Sacrament of Reconciliation:
God   the priest   the penitent   the community

7. Effects of the Sacrament of the Anointing of the Sick:
strength and comfort   forgiveness   health   grace

8. Viaticum:
Holy Communion   exorcism   strength for death   the last sacrament

The Rite Sequence   Each picture depicts a step in the Sacrament of the Anointing of the Sick. Below each picture, write the name of the step being shown. Then in the circle, number the steps in the order they are performed.

③ proclaiming God's Word   ② sprinkling with holy water   ① gathering of community

⑤ anointing with oil   ④ laying on of hands

(100)

5. Lead the students through the Summary and Review activities on pages 99–100.

6. **BLM 47** Distribute and administer BLM 47 **Chapter 12 Quiz.**
Use this opportunity to assess the students' understanding of the main concepts in the chapter. If there is not sufficient time for the students to complete the quiz, consider moving it to Day Five.

Acting _____

1. Sing a song chosen for the celebration of the Sacrament of Reconciliation.

2. At the end of class, have the students tear out and take home pages 99–100.

CHECKPOINT

• Were the learning outcomes achieved?

• How did the students show interest in planning their celebration of the Sacrament of Reconciliation?

• Do the students show a willingness to forgive others as God forgives them?

Day Five   Extending the Chapter

Gather and Go Forth

Lead students through pages 101–102 in the student book. Find catechist instruction on T338–T339.
Materials: Bibles

Use the following suggestions to create an additional lesson for Day Five.

1. Remind the students to take home pages 99–100 to share what they are learning with their families.

2. Incorporate any unused BLMs from the week's chapter.

3. Consider the time of the liturgical year and use the appropriate Special Seasons and Lessons. SSLs begin on page T369.

4. Visit www.christourlife.com to find additional activities for Extending the Chapter.

5. Use activities from Enriching the Faith Experience.

6. Guide the students in a prayerful discussion of Sunday's Scripture readings. Visit www.christourlife.com for more information.

Chapter 12   Enriching the Faith Experience

Use the following activities to enrich a lesson or to replace an activity with one that better meets the needs of your class.

1. **Web BLM** Have the students prepare the skit from Web BLM Chapter 12-A **Who Really Cares?**. Tell the class to watch for the character who shows Christ's care toward a peer. Discuss Sarah's reactions and the qualities that made her a witness of Christ. (courage to speak the truth; to hold onto her faith convictions when others objected; willing to be rejected for speaking the truth) Direct the students to answer the following questions to check the influence of peers in their lives.
   + **Have your friends ever threatened to drop you if you didn't do what they wanted?**
   + **Have you ever done something wrong simply because you were with a group?**
   + **Have you ever been hesitant to share with your family where you had been and what you had been doing with your friends?**
   + **If you answered yes to any of these questions, you may need to develop Christian decision-making skills and learn how to confront peer pressure.**

2. Discuss with the students how to be a true friend in these situations.
   + **One student wanted to cheat by copying from others.** (Refuse to give away the answers; offer to help the student find the answer in the right way.)
   + **A person your age invites others to have an alcoholic drink.** (Turn down the offer and give good reasons for doing so; demand that the person who offered the drink get rid of it.)
   + **Someone your age tells you he or she is planning to skip Sunday Mass or a religion class.** (Remind the person of the values of Mass or the religion class; invite the person to attend Mass or religion class with you.)

3. Pose this situation to the students:
   You missed playing a game because your mother got busy at work and forgot to come home early to drive you there. You know she feels bad that she let you down. How might you act during the evening if you have not yet learned to forgive? How would you act if you can forgive?

4. Help the students research religious orders and secular groups whose chief ministry is to people who are sick or disabled.
   ✝ *Life and Dignity*

5. Have the students interview parishioners or relatives who have celebrated the Anointing of the Sick and find out how they were comforted by it. The students could compose biographies of them and compile a "Parish Book of Care." They might take pictures of these parishioners and include them with the biographies.

6. With the students, organize an intergenerational craft day in which older parishioners teach a craft to the students. The adults might share their reflections on historical events being studied, on the changes they have witnessed in the Church's celebration of the Sacraments of Reconciliation and the Anointing of the Sick. Students might interview these parishioners and write reports.

7. Have the students design TV commercials, billboards, or magazine ads encouraging people to be reconciled and to celebrate the Sacrament of Reconciliation. The students might reword popular slogans or titles of popular songs.

The Message of Jesus: Choose Life

JESUS THE TEACHER

Faith Focus

Keeping Jesus' Great Commandment of love means to respect life.

Reflecting on the Faith Experience

Take a few moments to reflect prayerfully before preparing the lesson.

Listening

Owe nothing to anyone, except to love one another; for the one who loves another has fulfilled the law. The commandments, "You shall not commit adultery; you shall not kill; you shall not steal; you shall not covet," and whatever other commandment there may be, are summed up in this saying, [namely] "You shall love your neighbor as yourself." Love does no evil to the neighbor; hence, love is the fulfillment of the law.

Romans 13:8–10

Reflecting

Jesus Christ has given us a new law of love: to love as he loves. This law of love corresponds to the deepest longing of all human beings. Love is the answer to all our needs as individuals and as a society. There is no real joy without it. Yet we are slow to risk all for the sake of this love. We look for a lighter yoke, an easier task, a less challenging relationship with God and with others. Without the total commitment to loving as Jesus loves, our lives remain hollow and our morality remains a sham.

Christian morality is not merely a list of what is permitted and what is not. Rather, it is an invitation to respond to the love of the one who has called us into being, and, through Jesus, to become all that we are called to be. If our lives are to have any meaning at all, it will be through the law of love.

Love is life-giving. The love of Jesus raised dead bodies to life and filled empty hearts with fire. His love was poured out for all people of all times and places. And it is this love that he has made law. The implications of love and the demands of love have been pushed to their limits in Jesus. By our creation and by our Baptism, we have been drawn into and washed over by this love. We are enabled to love after the example of Jesus. In loving as Jesus loves, we encounter the mystery of God who is love.

Caryll Houselander writes "The ultimate miracle of Divine Love is this, that the life of the Risen Christ is given us to give to one another . . . through the daily bread of our human love." Christian love overflows into actions, service, and caring. It is a risk and a challenge, leaving us open to pain and misunderstandings, as well as to joys and triumphs.

Christian love nurtures life at all times. It protects the unborn and those who are aged; it heals the wounds of hasty words; it hopes all things and engenders that hope in sin-weary humanity. Who has the right to demand such love of us and to challenge us to love our enemies and do good to those who hate and hurt us? Who can see the potential for such love in us—and ask us to see such potential in others? Only God can, who has always known us, always given us the grace, the way, the God who has already spilled into our lives an extravagant love.

How do I promote the Christian view of life?

Responding

Come, Holy Spirit, fill the hearts of your faithful and kindle in them the fire of your love.

Scripture for Further Reflection

Genesis 1:26–27; 2:5–23 God created us in his own image. God breathed into humans the breath of life.

Matthew 5 Jesus presents the spirit of the kingdom in his Sermon on the Mount.

Preparing the Faith Experience

Scripture in This Chapter

Matthew 5:21–48 Teachings of Jesus

Matthew 22:36–40 The Greatest Commandment

Luke 10:29–37 The Good Samaritan

Genesis 1:27 God created mankind in his image.

Catholic Social Teaching

- Solidarity
- Life and Dignity
- Rights and Responsibilities

Church Documents

Catechism of the Catholic Church. The themes of this chapter correspond to the following paragraphs: **2268–2287; 2302–2317; 2447–2448.**

National Directory for Catechesis #45. Obedience to the Fifth Commandment is based on respect for human life, understanding the sacredness of human life, and recognizing the difficulties involved in addressing issues of life and death.

The Redeemer of Man (Saint John Paul II). Part of the Church's mission is the guarding of human rights, not only in the letter of the law, but also in its spirit.

Of Human Life (Paul VI). Every marriage act must remain open to the giving of life. Such conjugal love requires an awareness of responsible parenthood and the appreciation of the value of life.

Declaration on Euthanasia (Congregation for the Doctrine of the Faith). To cause one's own death is as wrong as murder, for only God has dominion over life and death. There are many values to be found in the Christian approach to suffering and death.

Brothers and Sisters to Us (USCCB). Racism is a sin that violates fundamental human dignity. In Christ, there is to be no distinction of persons.

Living the Gospel of Life #23 (USCCB). The Catholic Church adopts a consistent ethic of life and defends the lives of the unborn, sick and elderly, the criminal, and those suffering from poverty, war, and injustice.

Gather and Go Forth

Find catechist instruction for Gather and Go Forth student pages 111–112 on T340–T341.

Enriching the Faith Experience

Use the activities at the end of the chapter to enrich a lesson or to replace an activity with one that better meets the needs of your class.

Bulletin Board

A suggestion for a bulletin-board design for this chapter is pictured. Around the cross, post pictures depicting respect for life—those who are sick or elderly, the unborn, and so on.

LEARNING OUTCOMES

The students will be able to

- discuss their understanding of law and the importance of living by the spirit of the law.
- explain some implications of Jesus' Sermon on the Mount for their own lives.
- describe how Jesus accepts us as we are, but challenges us to grow.

Words to Know

abortion

scandal

See Glossary for definitions.

Materials

- Bibles or New Testaments
- BLM 48 (needs to be prepared ahead of time)
- Word poem written on the board:

```
        L
      I
      F
    L O V E
      I
      F
    L O V E
```

- Acrostic written on the board:

Before You Begin

1. The Sermon on the Mount is a collection of teachings and sayings of Christ. In these teachings, we find the spirit of the Kingdom of God. Jesus fulfills the old Law by returning to its original dynamic meaning. He then transcends it with the call to go beyond any limitations to love. He attempts to do away with a static approach to our relationship with the Father. The Christian always will be called to do more, and to live creatively and responsibly.

2. You might have a group act out the parable of the Good Samaritan as it is read in Sharing #3.

CHAPTER **13**

The Sermon on the Mount, 16th Century, Dutch.

The Message of Jesus: Choose Life

Jesus the Teacher

Fullness of Life

Complete these statements.

My favorite activity is

Answers will vary.

A place in the world I especially like is

Answers will vary.

A person I like to be with is

Answers will vary.

I enjoy eating

Answers will vary.

Life is a precious gift. It enables us to enjoy all those wonderful things and more. Out of millions of possibilities, the Father called you into being and made you the unique person you are. On top of that, Jesus gave his life that you might live forever. He taught us the secret to fullness of life: love. Read his two great commandments in Matthew 22:36–40.

To love as Jesus did means cherishing the gift of life—our own and others. It means reverencing all human beings and avoiding anything that harms them. We look on every child of God made in God's image as "another self." If we truly love, we will enjoy life, and we will enable others to enjoy it. The following stories show Christlike love in action.

A Modern Love Story

During the Vietnam War, a village orphanage was bombed. Several missionaries and children were killed. One eight-year-old girl was badly injured. Without a quick blood transfusion, she would die. An American doctor who came to help asked in halting language and sign language if anyone would be willing to donate blood. After a long silence, one boy, Heng, volunteered.

As Heng lay on a pallet with a needle in his vein, he began to sob. When the doctor asked if it hurt, Heng replied, "No," and tried to hide his crying. But something was wrong. Finally, a Vietnamese nurse arrived who was able to talk to Heng. She explained to the American, "Heng thought he was dying. He thought you had asked him to give all his blood so that the little girl would live."

"Why would you be willing to do that?" the doctor asked Heng.

"She's my friend," Heng said.

(103)

Centering _____

1. Have the students open their books to the **Fullness of Life** on page 103.
   Direct them to complete the statements and share their answers with a classmate.

2. Link the last lesson with today's lesson.
   Healing is part of Jesus' mission to bring us life. In today's lesson, you will learn how the law of the kingdom promotes life.

Sharing

1. Have a student read aloud the rest of this section on page 103 including Matthew 22:36–40.

   ✦ **How is life a gift?** (The Father made us out of millions of possibilities. Jesus gave his life that we might live forever.)

   ✦ **What truth that Jesus taught is conveyed by the word poem on the board?** (Love and life are related. Love leads to fullness of life. Love is shown by cherishing life.)

   ✦ **What is the relationship between the two Great Commandments and the Ten Commandments?** (The Ten Commandments spell out ways of following the two Great Commandments.)

   ✦ **Which commandments tell us how to love God?** (one through three) **Which tell us how to love our neighbor?** (four through ten)

   ✦ **Jesus quotes the Golden Rule, a standard for judging how to love our neighbor. What is it?** (Do to others whatever you would have them do to you. (Matthew 7:12))

2. Have the students read aloud **A Modern Love Story** on page 103.
   How does the boy Heng resemble Christ? (He was willing to die for his friend.)

3. ✝ Direct the students to read silently **An Old Love Story** on page 104. ✝ *Solidarity*

   ✦ Have them include Luke 10:29–37 the parable of the Good Samaritan.

   ✦ **Why do you think the priest and the Levite did not stop to help the man?** (They were in a hurry. They would become unclean by touching him.)

   ✦ **What did the Samaritan's act of mercy cost him?** (supplies, money, and a night's sleep)

   ✦ **What reason might Jesus have for making a Samaritan the hero of the story?** (He wanted to stress loving one's enemies. He was trying to break down prejudice against

---

An Old Love Story

Jesus gave us a model for Christian love in the parable of the Good Samaritan. Read Luke 10:29–37, remembering that the Samaritans and the Jewish people were enemies.

Based on these two love stories, what words would you use to describe Christian love?

selfless, total, unconditional, sacrificial,

forgiving

Go for It!

Christian love is not easy. It is a challenge. Jesus demands an entirely new way of thinking and acting. He admits, "How narrow the gate and constricted the road that leads to life. And those who find it are few." (Matthew 7:14) How are you at accepting challenges? How do you react when

• a group invites you to join them in an activity that would endanger your life?

• a family member, a teacher, or a classmate needs help?

• a friend experiments with cigarettes, alcohol, or drugs?

(104) UNIT 2

A New Understanding

Daily choices are important. They are a reflection of your attitudes and beliefs. Because human acts are done in freedom, you are responsible for your actions. You must live with the consequences of your choices. They shape both your present and future life. You can improve your ability to make good choices by reading and reflecting on Scripture, personal prayer, and the celebration of the Eucharist and the Sacrament of Reconciliation.

The Sermon on the Mount (Matthew 5–7) contains some teachings of Jesus that guide our decisions. Just as Moses climbed Mount Sinai and received the Law, Jesus climbed a hillside and gave us a new understanding of the Law. Jesus teaches us that at the heart of the Law is God's call for us to live with one another in love. With his help and the help of the Holy Spirit, we can become witnesses to God's love for the world.

Find an example in Matthew 5:21–48 of how Jesus teaches us a new understanding of the Law.

Do not be angry, look at a woman lustfully,

divorce, swear, or seek revenge. Love your

enemies.

Letter or Spirit?

Good laws

• protect the freedom, values, and rights that people hold as important;

• protect the common good;

• help all people reach goals and live with dignity.

Jesus said he did not come to destroy the law, but to fulfill it. We are to live not so much by the letter of the law as by the spirit. To live by the spirit of the law is to live the value that the law promotes. It is to live by what the law calls us to do and be. The motives of our hearts that are behind our actions are important.

---

outcasts. He was teaching a new way of thinking.)

✦ Have the students answer the question at the end of this section.

✦ **What words for Christian love did you write?** [Have the students list the words on the board.]

4. Ask a student to read aloud **Go for It!** on page 104.
   Discuss with the students the questions at the end of this section.

5. Call on a volunteer to read aloud **A New Understanding** on page 104.

   ✦ Have the students complete the activity from the Gospel of Matthew.

✦ **Why are daily choices important?** (They tell us much about attitudes and beliefs. You must live with the consequences of your choices. They shape your life, both the present and the future.)

✦ **How can you develop your ability to make good decisions?** (through Scripture, personal prayer, the celebration of the Eucharist and the Sacrament of Reconciliation)

✦ **How did Matthew portray Jesus as Moses in his Gospel?** (Jesus climbs a hillside and gives us a new understanding of the Law, just as Moses once climbed Sinai to receive the Law, the Ten Commandments.)

6. Compare the old understanding of the Law to the new understanding from Jesus. ✞ *Life and Dignity*

✦ Have the students open their books to Matthew 5:21–48 from the previous activity.

✦ Divide the class in half. Have one side represent the old understanding and the other side represent the new understanding of the Law.

✦ **Who can give me an old understanding of the Law from Matthew's Gospel? Who can give me a new understanding of the Law that Jesus gave?**

✦ Introduce each answer by saying "You have learned how it was said . . ." or "But I say . . ."

(**Matthew 5:21–26** *old:* You must not kill. *new:* You must not be angry or call your brother a fool.

Matthew 5:27–30 *old:* You must not commit adultery. *new:* You must not look at a woman lustfully; to do so is to commit adultery in your hearts.

Matthew 5:31–32 *old:* Divorce was permitted. *new:* Divorce is not permitted.

Matthew 5:33–37 *old:* You must not break an oath. *new:* Do not swear at all.

Matthew 5:38–42 *old:* An eye for an eye, a tooth for a tooth. *new:* Do not seek revenge.

Matthew 5:43–48 *old:* Hate your enemy. *new:* Love your enemies; pray for those who persecute you.)

7. Call on several students to read aloud **Letter or Spirit?** on pages 104–105.

✦ **What are some examples of good laws and bad laws?**

✦ **What is meant by the letter of the law as opposed to the spirit of the law?** (The outward observance of the law is the letter of the law. The spirit is its deeper meaning.)

✦ **There is much more to doing the Father's will than keeping the letter of the law. For instance, the law says that killing is wrong. But rarely does a person kill unless something evil has happened inside first. Anger, hatred, or jealousy begins long before the act of violence.**

✦ **On the other hand, some people never harm others physically but are not loving, caring people. They follow the letter of the law but are far from its spirit.**

8. Discuss with the students the values behind the rules we follow.

✦ Ask several students to write on the board a home rule and a school rule.

✦ **What are the values behind these laws?** (respect for life; loving our neighbor)

✦ **The rules that express these values may change, but the values they express will never change.**

✦ **The natural law is unchangeable and permanent. Rules that express it are valid. Both moral laws and civil laws are founded on the natural law.**

9. Guide the students in finding the values that the Ten Commandments protect.

✦ **When we understand the values behind school and home rules, it helps us to live by them more completely and freely.**

✦ **When we understand the values behind the Ten Commandments, we can live by them more completely and freely.**

✦ Have the students turn to the Ten Commandments on page 242 and state the value each one promotes. [See page T434.] (1—love of God; 2—reverence for God; 3—worship of God; 4—authority; 5—life; 6 and 9—sexuality, love, marriage; 7 and 10—right of ownership; 8—honesty and truthfulness)

The Ten Commandments

1. I, the Lord, am your God. You shall not have other gods besides me.
2. You shall not take the name of the Lord, your God, in vain.
3. Remember to keep holy the Sabbath day.
4. Honor your father and your mother.
5. You shall not kill.
6. You shall not commit adultery.
7. You shall not steal.
8. You shall not bear false witness against your neighbor.
9. You shall not covet your neighbor's wife.
10. You shall not covet anything that belongs to your neighbor.

---

10. Have the students work the acrostic on the board.

1. **The deeper meaning of a law that tells you what motive or attitude you should have in doing what is commanded** (SPIRIT)

2. **Something that is held as a good** (VALUE)

3. **The strict, exact meaning of a law** (LETTER)

4. **The person Matthew portrays Jesus as** (MOSES)

5. **The basic law that leads to fullness of life** (LOVE)

6. **God's laws that protect and promote what we value** (COMMANDMENTS)

Acting _____

BLM 48 Present each student with a personalized bookmark from BLM 48 **A Message from Christ.**

Appropriate music may be played as the students reflect on the quotation. Suggest that they use the bookmark in their Bibles or books, or take it home and put it in a special place.

CHECKPOINT

- Were the learning outcomes achieved?

LEARNING OUTCOMES

The students will be able to

- discuss the gift of life and ways to protect and nurture it (Fifth Commandment).
- define certain sins against life and explain why they are wrong.

Words to Know

ageism   sexism

euthanasia   suicide

racism

See Glossary for definitions.

Key Term

prejudice—unreasonable dislike of a particular group of people

Materials

- Bibles or New Testaments
- BLM 49
- Reflection notebooks

Before You Begin

1. To be a pro-life advocate is to be consistent in one's approach to all life issues, from the cradle to the grave. To have a consistent ethic of life is to be someone who, while struggling with a particular life issue, is sensitive to, and not opposed to, other life issues. To have a consistent ethic of life is to affirm that all life issues are linked by a common thread, namely, our belief that all life is sacred.

2. The depth to which the life issues presented in this lesson are developed will depend on the needs and abilities of your students. You may wish to devote more time to this lesson. Make applications to local situations and current concerns whenever possible. Help the students to see the importance of pro-life activities that are truly inspired by love and not by anger, violence, or some other motive.

3. It is essential that catechesis on pro-life issues be clear and according to the insights and teaching of the Church. For more information on life issues, contact the Department of Life Issues of the United States Conference of Catholic Bishops, 3211 Fourth St., N. E., Washington, D.C. 20017, www.usccb.org, or your diocesan, parish, or local organizations.

Read the Ten Commandments on page 242. They express the moral or natural law written in our hearts as a result of our being made in God's image and sharing God's wisdom and goodness. The Law is unchangeable and permanent and is the foundation of moral and civil law. Each of the Ten Commandments asks us to reverence and promote a particular value. If we live according to the truth and the spirit, we grow into the people we were meant to be. When we fail to love, that is, when we sin, we stunt our growth.

Lovers of Life

The Fifth Commandment is "You shall not kill." (Exodus 20:13) Jesus wants us to love and care for all life—physical life and the life of the spirit. We are first of all responsible for our own life.

How can you take care of your health?

proper eating and sleeping habits; exercise;

avoiding junk food, drugs, alcohol, and tobacco

How can you care for your spiritual life?

prayer, the sacraments, living according to

God's will

The following topics are matters of life and death. Some of these issues are debated a great deal. For each topic, the teaching of Jesus and of his Church upholds the supreme value of life.

Anger

Argue. Yell. Hit. Hurt someone's feelings. Get even. These are ways we express anger. Anger is an emotion that can work for good or evil. It can supply the energy you need to change things that are wrong. Jesus was angry with the money changers in the Temple (John 2:13–17), but his anger was motivated by love.

It is necessary to channel anger properly. When out of control, anger can lead to sin. Angry words to a friend can destroy a relationship. Letting anger build up inside can lead you to hurt others in a desire to get even.

What advice would you give a friend who has trouble controlling his or her anger?

Talk it out with someone. Seek help from a

counselor.

Scandal

It is easy to see how fights and unkind words hurt people. **Scandal**, or bad example, can harm people just as much. We are influenced, for better or worse, by what others do. Good example encourages and inspires, but bad example damages. Younger children usually try to imitate their older brothers and sisters and friends. Not fully understanding right from wrong, they may simply follow and learn to do what is wrong. Read Matthew 18:6–7 to find out how serious an offense Jesus considers bad example.

Abortion

Abortion is the killing of an embryo or a fetus, a developing baby, before birth. A baby has the right to life, the right to know, love, and serve God as a human being in the world. A baby can't defend himself or herself. We must protect his or her right to life.

Centering _____

Link the last lesson with today's lesson.

✦ As you learned in the last lesson, there is a value behind every law.

✦ In today's lesson, you will learn about a commandment protecting a value that is very much challenged in our world today.

Sharing _____

1. Call on a student to read aloud the first paragraph of **Lovers of Life** on page 105.

Give the students time to answer the questions and then discuss their ideas.

2. Have a student read aloud the last paragraph of this section.

- ◆ Divide the students into six groups with a leader in each group.

- ◆ Assign each group a life-related issue: 1—anger, 2—scandal, 3—abortion, 4—suicide, 5—euthanasia, 6—violence and war.

3. BLM 49 Give each leader the discussion card that applies to his or her topic from BLM 49 **Discussion Cards.**

- ◆ Go over the ground rules for group discussions on page T499.

- ◆ **First, read silently your topic's section in the book on pages 105–107. As a group, answer the questions on the card.**

- ◆ **Prepare practical examples related to the issue, perhaps in the form of a skit. Be ready to present your group's findings to the class.**

4. Have each group give its report. The following material is additional catechesis. ✝ *Life and Dignity*

- ◆ **Anger** Guide the students to an understanding of the differences between immediate feelings of anger and anger that has been consented to and nurtured in the heart. The students should also be made aware of a "justified anger" that sees evil and takes action, but does not do so at the expense of respect for individuals or their property.

- ◆ **Scandal** If there is love and respect for the other person, then there will be real concern about him or her. We live in a community and are very much affected by what we see and hear.

- ◆ **Abortion** The general guideline is that abortion, a direct and deliberate attack on life in the womb is forbidden. Point out that a *miscarriage* (a natural termination of a pregnancy) is not abortion. Under certain circumstances, for example cancer of the uterus, when the treatment of a medical condition of the pregnant woman

---

Are you less important if you have poor eyesight or get poor grades? Are you more important if you are wealthy or popular? The importance of life does not depend on such things. Human life is valuable in and of itself. Some people believe that babies who are developmentally disabled and babies whose parents can't care for them properly are better off not being born. They think that such children should be killed in an abortion. The Catholic Church rejects that belief. We must work and pray that people will see the value of all human life. Each infant deserves a chance to live despite all odds.

In some countries, abortion is legal under certain conditions. A law may make it legal, but it cannot make it right. People who abort a baby are subject to excommunication; that is, to being cut off from the Church and the sacraments.

Suicide

Life sometimes seems unbearable. Some people see **suicide** as a way to end their problems. Suicide is the deliberate taking of one's own life. It is seriously wrong. Suicide not only contradicts our natural inclination to be alive, but it also breaks the ties that bind the person to family, nation, and human society in general. The responsibility for suicide may be diminished because of psychological problems, anguish, or fear. Even though a person who commits suicide has done an act contrary to moral law, the Church recognizes that God can provide that person with an opportunity for repentance. The Church prays for people who have taken their own lives. People who speak or act in a way that encourages suicide are committing a serious moral wrong.

What would you say to a boy who wants to die because the girl he likes just ignores him?

Answers will vary.

A Moment with Jesus

Loving ourselves and others as Jesus taught us is not as easy as it might sound. It calls us to care for the life of the body and the spirit.

Take a moment to think about what that means for you at this time in your life. What challenges to living out the Fifth Commandment in its fullest sense do you face now? Ask the Holy Spirit to inspire and strengthen you. Then thank Jesus for the gift of life in all its forms.

Getting Through a Crisis

When you or someone close to you is going through a time of crisis, it is good to know some actions that can help. What makes each of these actions a wise choice?

- Recall a problem that you solved. Remember how painful it was, but how you handled it eventually. Things change with time. Give yourself time.
- Talk with someone who cares about what you are going through and can help, such as a parent, a teacher, or a counselor.
- Try to become involved in activities, sports, or hobbies. Be with people who can support you.
- Reach out to others who may be experiencing pain. It may take the weight off of your problem.
- Bring your concerns to God and ask for help and guidance. Trust that God's love for you is greater than you can ever imagine.

(106) UNIT 2

---

cannot be safely postponed until the unborn child is viable, it is permitted to treat the condition even if it indirectly results in the death of the unborn child.

- ◆ **Suicide** The statistics on suicide are alarming. Young people may know of others who have attempted or committed suicide. They may even be considering it themselves. Suicide as such is morally wrong. In most suicides, however, there is a question of mental stability. In such a case, guilt may be reduced or even absent. But if the suicide is fully deliberate, it is seriously sinful. Again, we cannot judge the interior state of the person and must turn trustingly to the Father. The students should be told healthy ways to handle depression, failure, and feelings of worthlessness, such as going to a counselor or priest for help.

- ◆ **Euthanasia** It might be necessary to emphasize the difference between mercy killing and the use of only ordinary means to preserve life. The means of *due proportion* required by the Church to treat the sick implies ordinary or reasonable means. Deciding if a treatment is of due proportion can be difficult. It must take into account the cost and burden of the medical care, the pain, the wishes of the sick person, the results, and others' needs. "Ordinary means" differs from country to country depending on what is standard treatment. Each case must be handled individually.

The family must discuss the situation with experts and pray for guidance in making its decision.

✦ **Violence and War** Over the centuries, the Catholic Church has developed criteria for addressing the possibility of war. The Just War Theory begins with the belief that all citizens and governments are obligated to work for the avoidance of war. But the Church recognizes that it is sometimes necessary to use force to obtain justice. Force should only be used after all peaceful means have failed. These are the conditions that must be met before force is used: 1. the damage inflicted by the aggressor must be lasting, grave and certain; 2. all other means must have been shown to be impractical or ineffective; 3. there must be serious prospects of success; 4. the use of arms must not produce evils or disorders graver than the evil to be eliminated.

5. Have a student read aloud **Capital Punishment** on page 107.

✦ You might have the class debate the issue of capital punishment.

✦ **Many European nations have abolished capital punishment, or use it only for military or national security offenses. In the United States, 32 states use it, but executions are infrequent. Death can be administered by hanging, electrocution, gas chamber, firing squad, or lethal injection.**

✦ **Arguments for the death penalty: The death penalty deters crime. If an individual has the right to kill in self-defense, society has the right to kill those who threaten it. In bargaining, it can motivate criminals to admit their guilt in order to receive a lesser punishment.**

✦ **Arguments against the death penalty: The murder rate in the states without the death penalty is the same as in those that have it. Innocent people may be killed. The death penalty is practiced unfairly: nonwhites are executed**

Euthanasia

Euthanasia, or mercy killing, is direct intervention to end life for the purpose of ending human suffering. It causes a person to die before he or she would die naturally. Although people defend it as a kind way to treat those who suffer, it is wrong. It is contrary to the respect due to a person and his or her Creator.

Consider illness and aging from a Christian point of view. First, God alone creates. He alone has the right over life and death. Second, illness and aging may help the individual and the community in many ways. Pain may call forth love and courage. Third, illness can prepare us for eternal life and help us realize that God is the important one in life. Finally, sickness and aging are part of God's plan. Many things that happen are a mystery, but we trust that God who has gifted us with life uses all things for our good.

Allowing a person to die without artificial support is not wrong if continuing such treatment is overly burdensome in prolonging the life of a dying person. The Church teaches that extraordinary means that only prolong a person's life need not be used. The decision whether or not to use life-support systems should take into consideration the sick person, the doctor's advice, and the hope of results. Under any circumstance, ordinary care should be given. Any action to kill a seriously ill person is morally wrong.

Violence and War

Followers of Christ, the Prince of Peace, work against things that destroy peace. The violence in our communities—the drive-by shootings, gang fights, muggings, and murders—is evil, creates fear, and disturbs the peace.

Peace cannot be attained without free communication between people and respect for the dignity of every human person. Peace is the work of justice. Peace is not just the absence of war nor just a balance of powers. War results in death, suffering, and destruction. It is to be avoided unless it is necessary to protect people and their rights. Over the centuries the Church

has identified strict conditions that countries must meet before they enter into war.

Capital Punishment

For the common good, a government has the right to punish criminals. In 2005 the American Catholic bishops began a campaign to end the death penalty in the United States. In the document, *A Culture of Life and the Penalty of Death,* the bishops wrote, "We renew our common conviction that it is time for our nation to abandon the illusion that we can protect life by taking life. Ending the use of the death penalty would be one important step away from a culture of death toward building a culture of life."

Life-Threatening "Isms"

Prejudice, the unreasonable dislike of a particular group of people, is wrong. It is an attitude that causes harm to people and denies them their rights. Draw a line connecting each "ism" with its description.

racism — Prejudice against older people

ageism — Regarding a race as inferior

sexism — Treating members of a certain sex unfairly

Works of Mercy

In Matthew 25:31–46, Jesus reveals that we will be judged by how we have loved others at the end of the world. We who have loved him by cherishing the lives of our brothers and sisters will be rewarded. We can foster their physical life by the Corporal Works of Mercy. We can promote their spiritual life by the Spiritual Works of Mercy. The works of mercy are listed on page 243. Which one can you practice today?

---

disproportionately; people who are poor don't have the same access to legal defense. The Lord says, "Do not kill."

6. Direct the students to read silently **Life-Threatening "Isms"** on page 107.
   ✝ *Rights and Responsibilities* **What other offenses against life are in this reading? What is the meaning of prejudice?**

Acting

1. Have a student read aloud **Getting Through a Crisis** on page 106.

2. Lead the students through the prayer experience **A Moment with Jesus** on page 106.
   Allow sufficient time for silent reflection.

3. Choose or let the students choose an activity from Reach Out on page 109.

CHECKPOINT

• Were the learning outcomes achieved?

• Are the students aware of current life issues that present a problem?

LEARNING OUTCOME

The students will be able to

- identify the Spiritual and Corporal Works of Mercy and ways to carry them out.

Materials

- Bibles or New Testaments
- BLM 50
- Large sheets of paper for lists
- Glue or tape
- Scissors
- Magazines with small pictures

Before You Begin

As the students grow in awareness of the call to love as Christ loves, they will need to realize that love must be expressed in practical ways. Our obligation to love our neighbors is a matter of justice and charity. Even more, it is a matter of mercy, which means loving to the point of giving our lives for others, even when it's difficult. How to do this is spelled out in the works of mercy.

Centering

Link the last lesson with today's lesson.

✦ **Think of a number from 1 to 10. How many thought of the number seven? Why?** (It is a lucky number.)

✦ **To the Jewish people, the number 7 stood for perfection. Today you will learn about two sets of seven things that help us follow Jesus in perfect love: the Corporal and Spiritual Works of Mercy.**

Sharing

1. Have several students read aloud Matthew 25:31–46. ✗ *Solidarity*

   ✦ **What are the actions the king expects of those called to the kingdom?** [Write them on the board.] (Feed the hungry; give drink to the thirsty; welcome the stranger; clothe the naked; visit the sick; visit those in prison.)

   ✦ **These works, along with burying the dead, are the Corporal Works of Mercy. They are corporal because they refer to the body.** *Corporal* **means "of the body."**

2. Direct the students to read silently **Works of Mercy** on page 107.

   Have the students turn to page 243 to find the Corporal and Spiritual Works of Mercy. [See page T435.]

   Corporal Works of Mercy: Feed the hungry, give drink to the thirsty, clothe the naked, shelter the homeless, visit the sick, visit the imprisoned, bury the dead.

   Spiritual Works of Mercy: Counsel the doubtful, instruct the ignorant, admonish the sinner, comfort the afflicted, forgive offenses, bear wrongs patiently, and pray for the living and the dead.

3. Divide the class into pairs Assign each pair a work of mercy.

   In the next five minutes, list realistic ways you can perform your work of mercy. [Have the students write their lists on the board.]

4. Lead the class in designing a symbol for one of the works of mercy.

   Choose one work of mercy you feel especially called to practice. Today you are going to make a symbol of it.

5. BLM 50 Distribute the patterns from BLM 50 **Display for Works of Mercy.**

   ✦ **Cut out the pattern.**

   ✦ **Fold it on the lines and shape it into a cube. Note which way to write and glue pictures so they turn out right side up.**

   ✦ **On one side, write your work of mercy and one or two ways you intend to practice it.**

   ✦ **On the other sides, put pictures and words from magazines that illustrate it.**

   ✦ **Put your name on the box. Glue it together.** (Collect the boxes for use in the celebration in the next lesson.)

Acting

 Have the students do the Respond activity on page 109.

✦ Allow sufficient time for silent reflection.

✦ Pray aloud with the students: **Lord, we need to love as you do to bring life to others. Make our love real. It will not always be perfect. When it is difficult to love and serve others, help us to see you in them and give us the patience to go on. Amen.**

CHECKPOINT ✓

- Was the learning outcome achieved?

LEARNING OUTCOMES

The students will be able to

- demonstrate prayerfully their appreciation of life through ritual.
- name their intention to promote life through loving service.
- demonstrate an understanding of the key concepts in this chapter.

Materials

- Bibles or New Testaments
- Recorded music: Find suggestions for Chapter 13 on page T518.
- Two candles, matches (check fire codes)
- Works of mercy boxes from Day Three
- Table with a stand for the Bible and space for the candles and boxes
- Large sheets of drawing paper
- Crayons or markers
- BLM 51 Quiz

Before You Begin

1. Group prayer celebrated properly can nourish the faith life of the students and lead them to fuller participation in parish communal liturgies. It is important to set the right mood. A sense that something significant is taking place should be part of the preparation and the celebration.

2. Consider adapting the celebration by including a slide or PowerPoint meditation on an aspect of life or by inviting a young adult or a senior citizen to give a witness talk on the meaning of life. You may also collect food or clothing for those in need.

3. If your class did not make works of mercy boxes, they can draw their symbols or make symbols of life out of craft materials.

4. If possible, have the celebration in church or in a special prayer room. Otherwise, prepare the classroom appropriately. The students may leave their works of mercy boxes on the table after the celebration as a reminder of the prayer.

5. When planning today's lesson, keep in mind that Day Four is when the students take the quiz for this chapter. Reserve time at the end of class for this assessment. The quiz can also be administered on Day Five.

Celebrating

Celebrating Life

Leader: The Lord our God has gifted us with life. We are called to care for that precious gift of life in ourselves and others. Let us celebrate life!

Song and Procession with Bible

Leader: God has given us life by creating us. Jesus has given us life by redeeming us. The Holy Spirit leads us to the fullness of life in the Father and the Son. Let us listen to God now as he calls us to choose life.

Reader 1: A reading from the Book of Deuteronomy 30:15–20. *(Passage is read from Bible.)*

Leader: Let us pray.

All: Let us choose life today and always. We know that those who follow you, Lord, will have the light of life.

Song or Alleluia

Leader: We know we have love for God if we show love to others. Let us listen to the Word of God calling us to show our love in practical ways.

Reader 2: A reading from the Gospel of Luke 6:27–38. *(Passage is read from Bible.)*

Leader: Let us pray.

All: We are your people, Lord, called to love as you love.

Presentation of Symbols

Leader: Let us thank the Lord for his gift of life. Our response is, "Thank you, Jesus, for life."

Reader 1: For the power I have to walk down the street, run through a park, dance, and laugh, I say . . .

For the times I've enjoyed watching a sunset, swimming at the beach, and sitting by a fire, I say . . .

For the experiences of sharing in the Eucharist, being part of a family, and gathering with friends, I say . . .

Individual prayers may be added.

Leader: Let us show gratitude for life by living with love. Our response is, "Jesus, make me fully alive."

Reader 2: Whenever I can lend a hand to help the aged or reach out to help a child . . .

Whenever I can forgive someone who hurt me . . .

Whenever I have a chance to make a friend, to say a kind word, or to think of others first . . .

Individual prayers may be added.

Leader: For all the people in our life, for all who love us and for all who do not, let us pray . . .

All: Our Father . . .

Closing Song

108

Centering

1. Explain to the students the flow of the celebration on page 108. Explain any rituals involved: where the students will stand, sit, and walk.

2. Have the students volunteer for the various parts. [Reader 1, Reader 2, and two candle bearers] Give the readers time to practice. Reader 1 could process in with the Bible and place it on the stand. The leader could be the catechist or a student. A student can also be in charge of the music.

Celebrating

Conduct the celebration **Celebrating Life** on page 108.

Sharing

1. Lead the students through the Summary and Review activities pages 109–110.

2. **BLM 51** Distribute and administer BLM 51, **Chapter 13 Quiz.**

   Use this opportunity to assess the students' understanding of the main concepts in the chapter. If there is not sufficient time for the students to complete the quiz, consider moving it to Day Five.

Acting

1. Discuss with the students the meaning of the symbols and readings in the celebration. **What was the meaning of the symbols in the celebration? the readings?**

2. Have the students design respect-for-life posters.

3. At the end of class, have the students tear out and take home pages 109–110.

CHECKPOINT

- Were the learning outcomes achieved?

---

13 Summary

Remember

What did Jesus teach us in the Sermon on the Mount?
In the Sermon on the Mount, Jesus taught us the way to the Father and called us to live a life of love and holiness.

Why must life be preserved and respected?
All life is a gift from God to be loved, preserved, and respected for God's honor and glory. Human life is a special gift because we are created in God's likeness, redeemed, and destined to live forever in God's kingdom.

What are Jesus' two great commandments?
He said to him, "You shall love the Lord, your God, with all your heart, with all your soul, and with all your mind. This is the greatest and the first commandment. The second is like it: You shall love your neighbor as yourself." (Matthew 22:37–39)

Respond

God calls us to love as he loves, which is quite a challenge. Read 1 Corinthians 13:4–7. In your reflection notebook, rewrite the passage, replacing the word *love* with your own name. List one way in which you will try to live what you have written. Ask Jesus to help you grow in love.

Reach Out

1. What is meant by the statement "It is not enough to be anti-abortion; you must also be pro-life"? Write your response. Then ask a parent, a grandparent, and an older teenager to comment on the same statement.

2. Read Psalm 136 or Psalm 148. Illustrate either psalm or compose your own litany of thanksgiving or song of praise patterned after those psalms.

3. **Charity begins at home!** Try one of these.
   - Go to bed on time for a week.
   - Pray an original prayer at home before a meal.
   - Use your allowance in some way for your family instead of for yourself.
   - Offer to do two extra jobs at home to replace the ordinary turn of someone else in your family.

4. **Find out what a national or local pro-life group is doing to fulfill Jesus' commandment of love. Write a report. Get involved in the group's activities.**

5. **Write a story or play about someone you know who protects and nurtures life.**

Words to Know

abortion	racism	suicide
ageism	scandal	
euthanasia	sexism	

Jesus as the peacemaker, stained glass, St. Jerome Parish, Maplewood, Minnesota. ❯

109

Day Five Extending the Chapter

Gather and Go Forth

Lead students through pages 111–112 in the student book. Find catechist instruction on T340–T341.

Use the following suggestions to create an additional lesson for Day Five.

1. Remind the students to take home pages 109–110 to share what they are learning with their families.

2. Incorporate any unused BLMs from the week's chapter.

3. Consider the time of the liturgical year and use the appropriate Special Seasons and Lessons. SSLs begin on page T369.

4. Visit www.christourlife.com to find additional activities for Extending the Chapter.

5. Use activities from Enriching the Faith Experience.

6. Guide the students in a prayerful discussion of Sunday's Scripture readings. Visit www.christourlife.com for more information.

Chapter 13   Enriching the Faith Experience

Use the following activities to enrich a lesson or to replace an activity with one that better meets the needs of your class.

1. ✝ Have the students act out the parable of the Good Samaritan (Luke 10:29–37) or write scripts for modern parallels of it and for the works of mercy. ✝ *Solidarity*

2. Conduct a courtesy campaign. The students might compose courtesy rules and prepare announcements and make posters.

3. ✝ Have the students mount on paper a newspaper article related to life issues. They should then write a letter to the editor or a person in the article as Jesus would have written it. ✝ *Life and Dignity*

4. Give the students a paper with a cross or chi-rho (☧) and the quotation "They'll know I am Christian because . . ." Have them complete the phrase and decorate the page.

5. Have the students create banners. Direct the students to draw and cut out the letters *L-I-F-E*, using large sheets of paper. On the letters, have them glue or draw pictures representing ways to respect. Post the banners in the classroom.

6. Encourage the students to bring in a family photo for sharing. You could secretly ask the parents to send in baby pictures of their children. Post the pictures with a caption about life. Let the students guess who the babies are.

7. Have the students look up the following references and match them with their summaries after you scramble the order of the words. They may create Scripture matches, word searches, and other puzzles on life and love.

- Luke 17:4 Love forgives over and over again.
- John 15:13 The offering of Christ's life was a sign of his great love.
- Romans 13:10 Love does not hurt others, and it fulfills all the commandments.
- Colossians 3:12–14 You should be clothed with love, kindness, and patience.
- James 2:14–16 Love should be practical. Good works are signs of faith and love.

CHAPTER 13 Review Activities

Scripture Search In chapters 6 and 7 of Matthew, Jesus gives advice to people who would follow him. Read the passages and complete the summary sentences.

1. (6:1–4) Do good deeds in ____secret____.
2. (6:19–21) Work for ____heavenly____ treasures that alone give real security.
3. (6:24) Serve ____God____, not ____mammon (wealth)____. You cannot serve them both.
4. (6:25–34) Trust in ____the Father____ for what you need.
5. (7:1–5) Avoid ____judging____ so that you yourself receive a merciful judgment.
6. (7:6) Treat holy things with ____care____.
7. (7:11) Pray to the heavenly ____Father____.
8. (7:12) Treat others ____as you want to be treated____. This is called the ____golden____ rule.

Sentence Sense Use each of the following terms in a sentence that reveals what you have learned.

1. choices ____Answers will vary.____
2. challenge of Christ ____
3. good laws ____
4. spirit of the law ____
5. works of mercy ____

Fifth Commandment Issues Write the letter of the term for each definition.

d	1. Direct intervention to end life	a. prejudice
f	2. Regarding a particular race as inferior	b. scandal
b	3. Bad example	c. ageism
a	4. Unreasonable dislike of a particular group of people	d. euthanasia
g	5. The killing of an embryo or a fetus before birth	e. suicide
e	6. The deliberate taking of one's life	f. racism
c	7. Prejudice against older people	g. abortion

110

The Challenge of the Beatitudes
JESUS THE LIGHT OF THE WORLD

Faith Focus

In the Beatitudes, Jesus gives us guidelines for a happy life in this world and the next.

Reflecting on the Faith Experience

Take a few moments to reflect prayerfully before preparing the lesson.

Listening

When he saw the crowds, he went up the mountain, and after he had sat down, his disciples came to him. He began to teach them . . .

Matthew 5:1–2

Reflecting

The Beatitudes are at the center of the mystery of the Kingdom of God. Through them, God breaks into our world with a new power, a new message, and new consolations, enabling us to live with a new hope. Christian living means living the Beatitudes.

Blessed are the poor in spirit. Those people are happy who are poor, who avoid the arrogance and aggressiveness of the wealthy. The poor in spirit do not cling to the world's goods as if they were everything. Nor are they worried because, as God's children, they depend entirely on God. They have a new vision. Their joy is in the one treasure, Jesus.

Blessed are they who mourn. The mourning that is called blessed was experienced by Jesus in the hard-heartedness, betrayal, and disbelief of his disciples and the crowds. He dealt with it by praying. The consolation given those who follow his example inspires them to give all and suffer all for the kingdom.

Blessed are the meek. Instead of apathy, distrust, or hostility, the gentle show calmness and compassion. They have strength from Jesus and his love.

Blessed are they who hunger and thirst for righteousness. These people strive to be faithful to their covenant with God. They do what is right. They are open to God's Word and respond like Jesus, who gave himself to doing the Father's will.

Blessed are the merciful. Here is love poured out and overflowing. Our forgiving love of those who offend us and our love for our needy brothers and sisters obtain God's forgiveness of our offenses.

Blessed are the clean of heart. The clean of heart focus on God and God's will. They see God in everything and at every moment. They witness to Jesus that others may live.

Blessed are the peacemakers. The peacemaker builds up, encourages, and strengthens the community through forgiveness, acceptance, and endurance.

Blessed are they who are persecuted for the sake of righteousness. To be persecuted for right is to stand at the side of Jesus. His love gives us the strength to suffer with him. From persecution, the kingdom comes to life in us and in the Church.

Jesus demands loving even unto death. His Beatitudes call us to radical self-giving. They run counter to the values of our times. Yet they are the source of true happiness here and in the hereafter. We need to be touched by God's Spirit to translate the Beatitudes into our lives and the lives of others. Then we can pray with sincerity the words that Jesus taught us: "Your will be done. Your kingdom come."

Who is a living example of the Beatitudes for me?

Responding

Jesus, Lord of Life, help me convince my students that your Beatitudes bring happiness.

Scripture for Further Reflection

John 15:18–20 We are called to be identified with Jesus which means being persecuted for him and being his witnesses to the world.

Romans 8:35,37 No troubles, worries, lack of food or clothes, or even persecution can keep us from Christ.

Preparing for the Faith Experience

Scripture in This Chapter

Matthew 5:3–10 The Beatitudes

Mark 10:21 The Rich Young Man

Romans 8:35,37 Jesus conquers all.

Catholic Social Teaching

- Life and Dignity
- Solidarity

Church Documents

Catechism of the Catholic Church.
The themes of this chapter correspond to the following paragraphs: **1716–1719.**

General Directory for Catechesis #115.
The love of God and neighbor sum up the Ten Commandments, which are lived in the spirit of the Beatitudes and constitute the foundation of the Christian life proclaimed by Jesus in the Sermon on the Mount.

National Directory for Catechesis #44.
Students should be taught the Ten Commandments and the Beatitudes, and they should also be given an understanding of how the spirit of the Beatitudes permeates the Ten Commandments.

On the Hundredth Anniversary of Rerum Novarum #57 (John Paul II). The social teaching of the Gospel is not a theory. It is the basis and motivation for action. This action is the source for the Church's preferential option for the poor.

Gather and Go Forth

Find catechist instruction for Gather and Go Forth student pages 119–120 on T342–T343.

Enriching the Faith Experience

Use the activities at the end of the chapter to enrich a lesson or to replace an activity with one that better meets the needs of your class.

Bulletin Board

A suggestion for a bulletin-board design for this chapter is pictured. Shade marks indicate areas to be used for a collage of contemporary illustrations of the Beatitudes, contributed by the students.

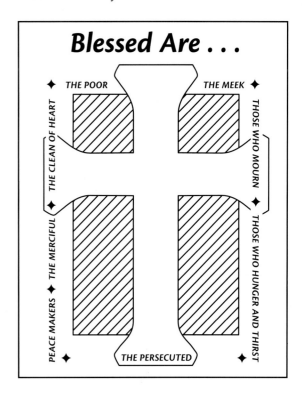

Blessed Are . . .

THE POOR THE MEEK

THE CLEAN OF HEART THOSE WHO MOURN

THE MERCIFUL THOSE WHO HUNGER AND THIRST

PEACE MAKERS THE PERSECUTED

LEARNING OUTCOMES

The students will be able to

- identify the Beatitudes as guidelines for Christlike living, which can lead to happiness now and in the hereafter.
- explain each beatitude.

Key Terms

Beatitudes—a set of guidelines for Christlike living that will make us happy and lead us to eternal life

meek—gentle and humble

Materials

- Bibles or New Testaments
- Recorded music: Find suggestions for Chapter 14 on page T518.

Before You Begin

1. The Beatitudes presented here are from Matthew 5:1–12. The Beatitudes in Luke 6:20–26 are strongly social and coupled with woes. Jesus' Beatitudes announced the in-breaking of the kingdom to those who are poor, outsiders, or rejected. To live the Beatitudes is to participate in the mystery of the kingdom, but they are not easy to live. It takes faith, conviction, and courage to find the happiness they promise.

2. The concepts in this lesson may be difficult for the students to grasp. The activities of the following days will help to clarify these concepts.

CHAPTER **14**

Charles Rolt, *The Sermon on the Mount*, 1861.

The Challenge of the Beatitudes

Jesus the Light of the World

We are programmed to seek eternity. We long to live forever. People such as Spanish explorer Ponce de León have searched for a legendary fountain of youth that gave people health and eternal life.

A rich young man who obeyed the commandments asked Jesus for the secret of eternal life. Jesus did not tell him to cross an ocean, climb a high mountain, or destroy a monster in order to win eternal life. He set before the young man an even greater challenge. He looked at him, loved him, and said to him, "'Go, sell what you have, and give to [the] poor and you will have treasure in heaven; then come, follow me.'" (Mark 10:21) The man walked away sad. He had many possessions.

How to Be Happy

In Matthew's Gospel, Jesus began the Sermon on the Mount by spelling out how to follow him. He gave us the Beatitudes, guidelines for Christlike living that will make us happy and lead us to eternal life. If we live those guidelines, our lives will be blessed. Each beatitude pairs a value with a promise. People who live in the light of those values journey safely and surely. Someday they will reach the Kingdom of Heaven where they will not "need light

from lamp or sun, for the Lord God shall give them light, and they shall reign forever and ever." (Revelation 22:5)

Called to Be Happy

Read the Beatitudes in Matthew 5:3–10. List below the people who will be blessed. They are the people whose way of life will bring them happiness.

1. the poor in spirit _____
2. they who mourn _____
3. the meek _____
4. they who hunger and thirst for righteousness
5. the merciful _____
6. the clean of heart _____
7. the peacemakers _____
8. they who are persecuted for

the sake of righteousness

113

Centering _____

1. Direct the students to read silently the first two paragraphs on page 113.
   - ✦ **What do all people strongly desire?** (to live forever)
   - ✦ **What did Jesus tell the rich young man to do in order to have eternal life?** (to do more than follow the commandments; to sell all, give all to the poor, and to follow him) **Notice that Jesus loved the young man, but did not force him to follow him.**

2. Link the last lesson with today's lesson.
   - ✦ **What are some rules for having a happy life?** [List the students' ideas on the board.]
   - ✦ **In this lesson, you will discover the secret of happiness that Jesus revealed. It will enrich the life you learned to protect and nourish in the last lesson.**

Sharing _____

1. Ask a volunteer to read aloud **How to Be Happy** on page 113.
   - ✦ **What did Jesus give us so that we know what it means to follow him?** (the Beatitudes)

◆ **What are the Beatitudes?** (a set of guidelines for Christlike living that will make us happy and lead us to eternal life)

◆ **The Beatitudes are attitudes that help us to be what we are meant to be.**

◆ Have the students complete the activity **Called to Be Happy** on page 113. Go over the students' responses.

2. Direct the students to **The Be-Attitudes** on page 114.
   ◆ **What do you think this heading means?** (The Beatitudes are Christian attitudes that help us be what we are called to be.)
   ◆ Have a student read aloud the first paragraph of this section.
   ◆ **In today's lesson you will study each beatitude, see how Jesus lived it, and reflect on ways you can live it.**

3. Guide the students through the sections on each of the Beatitudes pages 114–116. Have the students read aloud about the Beatitude and complete the activity in each the section.

   First beatitude: poor in spirit
   ◆ **How can wealthy people still be poor in spirit?** (They can have the attitudes of those who are poor: dependence on others, gratitude, and willingness to share. They can remember that everything we have comes from God. They can turn to God in their needs and avoid spending their lives collecting wealth.) *Life and Dignity*

   ◆ **How does being poor in spirit help you love God and others?** (People who are poor in spirit are detached from the things of this world. They look to God for help and support. They trust and love God. They are willing to share with others.)

   ◆ **Later in the Sermon on the Mount, Jesus explains how the poor in spirit regard the goods of the earth.** [Read aloud Matthew 6:25–33.] **How are people who are poor in spirit freer than those**

The Be-Attitudes

Jesus was poor in fact and in spirit. People who are poor are dependent on others in ways that people with money are not. People who are economically poor can be rich in other ways, such as in happiness, gratitude, and a generous spirit. Although we may not be poor financially, we can still be poor in spirit. That means having the attitudes of the poor. We remember that everything we have comes from our Creator, and so we depend on and turn to God for our needs. Rather than spending our lives collecting as much wealth as we can, we are willing to give up the things we have.

> Blessed are the poor in spirit,
> for theirs is the kingdom of heaven.
>
> Matthew 5:3

Check your response to each question.

	Yes	No
Do I let other people help me?	○	○
Do I let God help me?	○	○
Do I share with others?	○	○
Do I thank God for what I have?	○	○
Do I regard people as more important than things?	○	○

> Blessed are they who mourn,
> for they will be comforted.
>
> Matthew 5:4

Jesus felt sad when people suffered. He was filled with sorrow for those hurt by sin. He wept when his friend Lazarus died, and he wept for Jerusalem because it would be destroyed. When we truly love others, their failings and their sorrows make us feel sad.

Why do you confide in other people when something gives you sorrow?

They offer comfort and strength.

When do you take hurts and sorrows to Jesus?

Answers will vary.

> Blessed are the meek,
> for they will inherit the land.
>
> Matthew 5:5

A meek person is gentle and humble. Jesus was a gentle person. Cardinal Newman wrote that a gentleman is someone who never gives pain to another. A gentle person is not a wimp. On the contrary, being gentle takes great strength and courage. It is easier to be pushy, bossy, inconsiderate, stubborn, and mean. A gentle person is polite, kind, patient, and strong enough to love everyone as Jesus did.

What else do gentle people do?

They do not take offense.

(114) UNIT 2

---

who are not? (They do not have the worry and tension of those whose lives depend on possessions.)

Second beatitude: mourning
◆ **When people share their pain with you, what should you try to do?** (Listen; respect their feelings; cheer them up; give advice.) **What won't you do if you respect them?** (Ignore them; treat their feelings lightly; break confidence, unless getting help is essential.)

◆ **Why do people go to Jesus when they have problems?** (He understands us perfectly. He is wise, powerful, and loving.)

◆ **When did Jesus experience sorrow?** (when his disciples did not understand him; when Lazarus died;

when people didn't accept his message; when Judas betrayed him)

◆ **When we experience sorrow from our sins or make mistakes, we need to turn to others and to Jesus for help and comfort. At what other times might we feel sorrow?**

◆ **When others cause us sorrow, how can we be like Christ?** (We can forgive them and keep on loving them.)

Third beatitude: meekness

✦ **What does *meek* mean?** (gentle, kind, mild, humble) **The Gospel records only one time when Jesus told us to imitate a quality of his. He said, "Learn from me, for I am meek and humble of heart."** (Matthew 11:29)

✦ **Why must you be strong in order to be gentle?** (It's easy to be bossy, inconsiderate, stubborn, and mean. The gentle suffer for love of others.)

✦ **What do gentle people do in dealing with others?** (They listen, care, forgive, and speak the truth.)

✦ **Gentleness is the strength to control selfish feelings. Gentle people approach each person as someone to be loved, someone who is fragile, and someone who is loved by the Father. They try not to cause another pain.**

Fourth beatitude: hungering and thirsting for righteousness

✦ **Think of a time when you were very hungry or very thirsty. The craving you felt is the craving we need to have for what is right. How can you tell if you hunger and thirst for what is right?** (You are bothered by injustice. You act to right wrongs. You strive to live right even when others do not accept you because of it.)

✦ **A person who lives by this beatitude will pay any price to do God's will and to grow in friendship with God. There is no holding back, no hiding behind excuses. He or she is open to God and responds "yes."**

Fifth beatitude: mercy

✦ **How did Jesus show mercy?** (He forgave those who killed him. He was a friend to sinners. He healed the sick.) **How can we be merciful like Jesus?**

✦ **Mercy prompts us to go out of our way to forgive others and not wait until they apologize. Mercy leads us to be the first to show love, the first to be of service.**

> Blessed are they who hunger and thirst
> for righteousness,
> for they will be satisfied.
>
> Matthew 5:6

When you are hungry or thirsty, you do something about it. People who hunger and thirst for what is right act to make the kingdom come in this world. They try to live by the values Jesus taught and to help others live Jesus' way. They desire to keep their friendship with God.

> Blessed are the merciful,
> for they will be shown mercy.
>
> Matthew 5:7

Jesus is a friend of the poor, of outcasts, of sinners. He forgave sinners and people who hurt him. Jesus asked his Father to forgive his executioners. He forgives us. As imitators of Jesus, we must have a heart for others and be willing to forgive them.

> Blessed are the clean of heart,
> for they will see God.
>
> Matthew 5:8

Think of a bicycle wheel. Every spoke is attached to the hub. Jesus' life is like a wheel. He did many things: curing, preaching, and praying. The center of all his activity was the Father's will. Being pure in heart means having God at the hub of your life. All your days, thoughts, actions, and decisions are centered on and flow from God. Your gifts are used as God wishes—for the good of all.

What can we foolishly put at the center of our life in place of God?

money, fame, power, pleasure, another person

> Blessed are the peacemakers,
> for they will be called children of God.
>
> Matthew 5:9

Jesus brought peace wherever he went. He reconciled us with God. Jesus brought God's love so that we could share it with everyone for the good of everyone. To be a peacemaker, we must first be at peace ourselves. Then we can spread peace to the community.

Check the statements that express true peace.

○ Peace means having everything go the way you want.

☑ Peace means coming to grips with yourself— your strengths and your weaknesses.

○ Peace means going along with the crowd when there is trouble and praying you do not get caught.

☑ Peace means forgiving those people who hurt you.

☑ Peace can mean conflict—that you will have to stand up for what is right.

☑ Peace means knowing that God made you and that you are valuable to God and others.

○ Peace means not getting involved.

(115)

Sixth beatitude: cleanness of heart

✦ [Draw on the board a wheel with spokes.]

✦ **Why is Jesus' life like a wheel?** (Every spoke is connected to the hub.) **Everything Jesus did was centered on the Father's will.)**

✦ **What does it mean to be clean of heart?** (to center all your days, thoughts, actions, and decisions on God; to use your gifts as God wishes) **What can we put at the center of our life in place of God?** (others, money, possessions, ourselves) **This does not lead to happiness.**

✦ **Being clean of heart requires right motivations and self-control in doing the things of** God. **It means putting on the mind and heart of Christ. It helps to ask ourselves:** *Am I doing this for selfish reasons or because it is what God wants?*

Seventh beatitude: peace

✦ **What is peace?** (the right order of things; the absence of evil and unrest)

✦ **What does it mean to be at peace with ourselves?** (to accept our strengths and weaknesses; to realize that God loves us as we are) **Why is this difficult?** (We like to think we are perfect.) **Why is it easier to help others when you have peace inside?**

✦ **Which definitions of true peace did you check?**

✦ **Does peace mean to avoid conflict and not get involved?** (Sometimes peace requires confrontation and action.)

✦ **What is the meaning of the saying "If you want peace, work for justice"?** (Peace is brought about by people who strive to make the world just.) **What are some examples?**

Eighth beatitude: being persecuted for the sake of righteousness

✦ **How can a person your age be persecuted for doing what is right and be happy even though you are suffering?** (peace and joy of knowing you did the right thing)

✦ **This beatitude calls us to suffer for and with Jesus. Someday you will have the joy of eternal life. Moreover, you will lead others to follow the Gospel.**

Acting

Choose or let the students choose an activity from Reach Out on page 117.

CHECKPOINT ✓

• Were the learning objectives achieved?

> Blessed are they who are persecuted for the sake of righteousness, for theirs is the kingdom of heaven.
>
> Matthew 5:10

Persecution is the outcome for many people who live the Gospel seriously. People will hurt you by their words and actions. Because Jesus lived and spoke the truth, he was crucified. As his disciples, we are called to face the challenge of what it means to be Christian. We do it with joy when we have a personal love for Jesus.

Let Your Light Shine

The teaching of Jesus was revolutionary. It made people see themselves, others, and the world differently. Today Christian values still sometimes conflict with the world's values. When you live by the Beatitudes, you dare to be different. It will be hard, but as Jesus promised, you will be happy.

Although Jesus is "The true light, which enlightens everyone" (John 1:9), some people prefer to live in darkness. Will you turn away from Jesus like the rich young man, or will you grasp Jesus' hand and follow him?

Check the statements below that reflect Christlike thinking.

○ Get even.

☑ Forgive in order to become a stronger person.

○ Be number one no matter what.

☑ Welcome people who are different from you.

○ Take the easy way out.

○ Make as much money as you can.

○ Lie or cheat as long as you do not get caught.

☑ Give away some of your possessions to help people who are poor.

☑ Stand up for people who are homeless, imprisoned, or outcast.

○ Mind your own business.

○ Do whatever makes you feel good.

When we live like Christ, his light shines forth in us. Read Matthew 5:14–16 and fill in the missing words in the following sentence.

Jesus wants us to be

like a city on a _____mountain_____

and a lamp on a _____lampstand_____ .

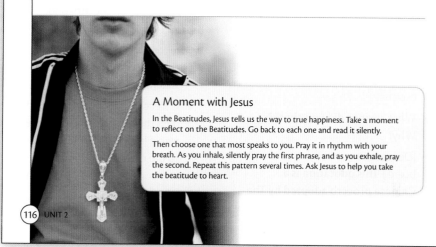

A Moment with Jesus

In the Beatitudes, Jesus tells us the way to true happiness. Take a moment to reflect on the Beatitudes. Go back to each one and read it silently.

Then choose one that most speaks to you. Pray it in rhythm with your breath. As you inhale, silently pray the first phrase, and as you exhale, pray the second. Repeat this pattern several times. Ask Jesus to help you take the beatitude to heart.

 116 UNIT 2

Day Two The Mind and Heart of Christ

LEARNING OUTCOMES

The students will be able to

• explain how Jesus lived the Beatitudes and how he expects his disciples to do so.

• name ways to live the spirit of the Beatitudes.

Materials

• BLM 52A–B, BLM 53

• Quotation written on the board: *It is better to light one candle than to curse the darkness.*

• One large sheet of drawing paper for each student

• Scissors

• Glue

• Crayons or felt-tipped pens

• Stapler or yarn

• Magazines that can be cut for pictures

Before You Begin

The Beatitudes give us a clear idea of who Jesus is. Each one shows a different facet of his spirit. His way of life is to be followed by every disciple.

Father James Keller, M.M. (1900–1977) founded The Christophers in 1945. He believed that every person had something to offer the world. At the end of World War II, he began the formation of The Christophers, taken from the Greek words for *Christbearer*. Through newsletters, and radio and television programs, he focused attention on taking personal responsibility for sharing one's talents and making the world a better place.

Centering

Explain the relationship between Jesus and the Beatitudes.

+ **Jesus does not ask anything of us he did not do or experience himself. Each beatitude shows us an aspect of his spirit.**

+ **You will learn more about Jesus today by looking closely at his life and the lives of his friends. You will come to understand the Beatitudes better as you see them lived out.**

Sharing

1. **BLM 52A–B** Distribute copies of BLM 52A–B **The Beatitudes in Other Words** to the students. Read the directions aloud. Have the students complete the sheet independently. Check their answers.

2. Have a student read aloud **Let Your Light Shine** on page 116.
   + Direct the students to complete the exercise.
   + **What sayings did you check? Why?**
   + [Discuss the quotation on the board.] **This quotation is a Chinese proverb adopted by The Christophers. What do you think it means?**
   + **What are some examples of individuals who have made a difference in the world?**

3. **BLM 53** Distribute copies of BLM 53 **Two Beatitude People.**
   + Ask several students to read the stories aloud to see how one man and one woman lived the Beatitudes.
   + **Which offense against life did Martin Luther King fight against?** (prejudice and racism)
   + **Which Beatitudes in particular did he live?** (four and eight: hunger and thirst for righteousness, persecuted for the sake of righteousness)
   + **In the United States, Martin Luther King Day is celebrated on the third Monday of January.**

+ **Do you think that Dorothy Day was happy in this life? Why or why not?**

+ **What beatitudes in particular did she live?** (one and four: poor in spirit, meek)

+ **Some people regard Dorothy Day as a saint. Why?**

4. Guide the students in making a Beatitude book.
   + This book is similar to the *Happiness Is . . .* books by Charles Schulz, creator of *Peanuts*.
   + Distribute a sheet of drawing paper to each student. Have them design their page the same way, either horizontal or vertical.
   + Direct them to write the statement *Happiness is . . .* on one side and pictures drawn by them or cut from magazines on the other side.
   + The happiness statement should be related to a beatitude, and the illustration should match the statement.
   + Collect the students' pages and bind them together with staples or yarn. Have someone read the book to the class.

Acting

Lead the students through the prayer experience **A Moment with Jesus** on page 116.

+ Allow sufficient time for silent reflection.

+ Conclude with the following prayer:
   O God, who show the light of your truth
   to those who go astray,
   so that they may return to the right path,
   give all who for the faith they profess
   are accounted Christians
   the grace to reject whatever is contrary to the name of Christ
   and to strive after all that does it honor.
   Through our Lord Jesus Christ, your Son,
   who lives and reigns with you in the unity of the Holy Spirit,
   one God, for ever and ever.

   Collect Prayer for the Fifteenth Sunday in Ordinary Time

CHECKPOINT ✓

+ Were the learning outcomes achieved?

LEARNING OUTCOMES

The students will be able to

- describe how great is the call to serve.
- discuss solutions to problem situations that are in line with the Beatitudes.

Materials

- BLM 54A–B
- Sponge
- Paper towel
- Facial tissue
- Three paper cups with a little water in them
- Small notepaper
- Box
- Recorded music: Find suggestions for Chapter 14 on page T518.

Before You Begin

In the Beatitudes, we find ways to respond to the love Jesus showed us in surrendering his life for us.

Centering

Link the last lesson with today's lesson.

- ✦ Conduct an experiment to find out which absorbs water better—a sponge, a paper towel, or a facial tissue.
- ✦ Ask for three volunteers. Give each a small cup of water and the sponge, paper towel, or facial tissue.
- ✦ **When I say go, you will spill the water out of your cup and then wipe it up with what you were given. Go!**
- ✦ **What absorbs the water best?** (the sponge)
- ✦ **Things more dangerous than water spill into our lives: people's anger, their resentment, hurtful actions, and unkind words.**
- ✦ **How is the life of a Christian like that of a sponge?** (When we meet anger, resentment, and so on, we absorb it with calmness and strength. It does not spread. If we are like the paper towel or facial tissue, we are only partly effective.)
- ✦ **We are good absorbers when we live the Beatitudes. Today we will discuss and act out ways of living the Beatitudes in specific situations.**

Sharing

1. **BLM 54A–B** Divide the class into eight groups. Give each group a card from BLM 54A–B **Living the Beatitudes.**
   - ✦ Have each group read the card, discuss the situation, and think of a response based on the Beatitudes.
   - ✦ Direct them to write a skit to illustrate their answers. Each member of the group should participate in the skit.

2. Have each group perform its skit for the class.
   - ✦ After each skit is performed, discuss the following questions:
   - ✦ **What beatitude was acted out in this skit?**
   - ✦ **Was the response showing a Gospel standard of responding? Why or why not?**

3. Discuss with the students the connection between their lives and the Beatitudes.
   What is the relationship between your life and the Beatitudes?

Acting

1. Ask the students to reflect on which beatitude is most needed in their lives now.
   - ✦ **On a sheet of paper, write a sentence or two telling what beatitude you need in your life.**
   - ✦ **It may take the form of a prayer. *Lord, help me to practice the beatitude "Blessed are they who are persecuted for the sake of righteousness." I need courage to make decisions and stick by my choices.***
   - ✦ **It may be in the form of a resolution by completing the statement *I will let my light shine by working for peace in the world.***
   - ✦ **Do not put your name on the paper. Fold your paper in half and place it in this box.**
   - ✦ **We are going to use them in our prayer.**

2. Lead the students in praying the Beatitudes in their lives.
   - ✦ **Let us pray that each of us has the strength to live his or her beatitude.**
   - ✦ Play a song quietly while the box is passed around. Have each student select a paper and read it aloud.

CHECKPOINT

- Were the learning outcomes achieved?
- Were the students' solutions to the problems Christian and realistic?

LEARNING OUTCOMES

The students will be able to

- discuss what life would be like if they lived according to the Beatitudes.
- identify ways to live the Beatitudes in their lives.
- demonstrate an understanding of the key concepts in this chapter.

Materials

- Bibles or New Testaments
- BLM 55A–B
- BLM 56 Quiz
- Titles written on the board: *Cinderella, Robin Hood, King Arthur, Sleeping Beauty*
- Reflection notebooks

Before You Begin

1. The Beatitudes make the kingdom more real as we live the radical demands of the Gospel.

2. This lesson is a good time to incorporate mission activities.

3. After the students complete their Kingdom Calendars from Sharing #4, remind them to review what they have written for each day next week.

4. When planning today's lesson, keep in mind that Day Four is when the students take the quiz for this chapter. Reserve time at the end of class for this assessment. The quiz can also be administered on Day Five.

CHAPTER 14 Summary

Remember

What are the Beatitudes?
The Beatitudes are guidelines for Christlike living that will make us happy and lead us to eternal life.

What did Jesus say we are to do to have eternal life?
Jesus said, "Go, sell what you have, and give to [the] poor and you will have treasure in heaven; then come, follow me." (Mark 10:21)

Respond

If you want world peace, then promote world forgiveness. Forgive people who hurt you. Saint Paul tells us the power of words in Ephesians 4:32. Look up this verse. Think it over. In your reflection notebook, write about a time you spoke words of forgiveness. Tell how your words helped you and the other person.

Reach Out

1. The Beatitudes give us ways to help others. Think about how you can help at home. Decide on one new thing you can do. You might talk to your parents about it, or you may wish to make it a "hidden caring." Write it in your reflection notebook and check every day to see if you are keeping it.

2. Read chapters 5 and 6 in the Gospel of Matthew. Pick out a favorite verse. Write it on paper, decorate it, and display it in your room. It will be a reminder to share as Jesus did.

3. Kind words heal. They promote peace and show mercy. Write a letter to an older relative or someone who is sick. Share good news with them.

4. The poor in spirit and those who hunger and thirst for justice share things with each other. Ask your parents if you can give clothes you do not need to those who need them and cannot afford them. Talk with your parents or teacher about where you can take the clothes.

5. Cut out newspaper articles about people living the Beatitudes. Glue them on paper and write a summary of each article. Share them with your class or your family.

Stained glass window depicting Jesus and the rich young man, St. Columba's Church, Ottawa, Illinois. ❯

117

Centering

1. Discuss with the students fictional kingdoms.
   - ✦ **What do the four stories on the board have in common?** (They are fairy tales or legends.) **What makes them unrealistic?** (Everything works out, and the people always live "happily ever after.")
   - ✦ **What is the hero like?**
   - ✦ **What kind of adventure happens?**
   - ✦ **Who always wins?**

2. Compare fictional kingdoms to God's kingdom.
   - ✦ **People have always told stories about an ideal kingdom where everything goes right.**
   - ✦ **Jesus spoke of a kingdom too. But his kingdom is not a fairy tale or legend. It is real and has begun already. It began as Jesus entered into history and saved the world.**
   - ✦ **He taught us all we need to know to make the kingdom real and alive. He described it with words such as *openness, peace, courage, generosity, mercy,* and *everlasting happiness.***

Sharing

1. Read aloud the story A Kingdom Day.
   - ✦ **You will have a chance to see how real the kingdom can be right now. As I read this story, picture in your mind what this kingdom looks like.**

A Kingdom Day

I come into the room and the whole class smiles. The students greet me and talk with me. Everyone in the room feels happy because each person knows we all like one another. No one is yelling, hurting people's feelings, or complaining about homework. In fact, all the homework is done. It is done so well that there will be no homework assigned today. During class, everyone pays attention to me and to one another. When someone has an idea, everyone listens. Members of the class are volunteering to help, to participate, and even to clean the room. Everyone speaks pleasantly in a normal tone of voice. There is no arguing. The desks are clean, and no one tries to get out of work. You and others compliment one another several times.

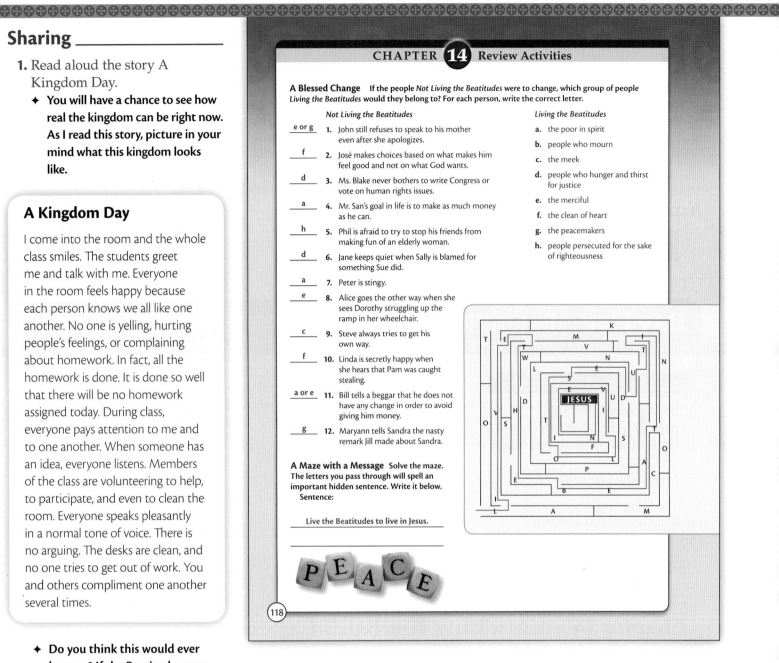

CHAPTER **14** Review Activities

A Blessed Change   If the people *Not Living the Beatitudes* were to change, which group of people *Living the Beatitudes* would they belong to? For each person, write the correct letter.

Not Living the Beatitudes

e or g   **1.** John still refuses to speak to his mother even after she apologizes.

f   **2.** José makes choices based on what makes him feel good and not on what God wants.

d   **3.** Ms. Blake never bothers to write Congress or vote on human rights issues.

a   **4.** Mr. San's goal in life is to make as much money as he can.

h   **5.** Phil is afraid to try to stop his friends from making fun of an elderly woman.

d   **6.** Jane keeps quiet when Sally is blamed for something Sue did.

a   **7.** Peter is stingy.

e   **8.** Alice goes the other way when she sees Dorothy struggling up the ramp in her wheelchair.

c   **9.** Steve always tries to get his own way.

f   **10.** Linda is secretly happy when she hears that Pam was caught stealing.

a or e   **11.** Bill tells a beggar that he does not have any change in order to avoid giving him money.

g   **12.** Maryann tells Sandra the nasty remark Jill made about Sandra.

Living the Beatitudes

a. the poor in spirit

b. people who mourn

c. the meek

d. people who hunger and thirst for justice

e. the merciful

f. the clean of heart

g. the peacemakers

h. people persecuted for the sake of righteousness

A Maze with a Message Solve the maze. The letters you pass through will spell an important hidden sentence. Write it below.
Sentence:

   Live the Beatitudes to live in Jesus.

118

- ✦ **Do you think this would ever happen? If the Beatitudes were practiced, this would be the case.**
- ✦ **You will have a chance to imagine what a day would be like if everyone lived the Beatitudes.**

2. **BLM 55A** Distribute copies of BLM 55A **A Day in the Kingdom.**
   - ✦ Read aloud the first two sentences. Have the students underline *positive, practical* and make sure they know what that means.
   - ✦ Divide the students into groups of four or five to work the top of the BLM.

3. Have the groups share their answers.
   Remember that these are values in the Beatitudes that are expressed in a modern way. [List on the board the

words the students suggested for living a day in the kingdom.]

4. **BLM 55B** Distribute copies of BLM 55B **Kingdom Calendar.**
   - ✦ Read aloud the sentences under Kingdom Calendar.
   - ✦ Have the students fill in the Kingdom Calendar according to these instructions:
   - ✦ **Sunday: Write a beatitude to work on in the coming week.**
   - ✦ **Monday: Write something Jesus did to make the kingdom come.**
   - ✦ **Tuesday: Write a service or an action you could do for the kingdom.**

- ✦ **Wednesday: Write a petition you will pray that day for the coming of the kingdom.**
- ✦ **Thursday: Write the name of someone you can make happy now in the kingdom.**
- ✦ **Friday: Write a sacrifice you could make for the kingdom.**
- ✦ **Saturday: Glue a picture or draw a symbol of the kingdom.**
- ✦ Encourage the students to fill in the rest of the calendar on their own.

5. Lead the students through the Summary and Review Activities on pages 117–118.

6. **BLM 56** Distribute and administer BLM 56, **Chapter 14 Quiz**.

Use this opportunity to assess the students' understanding of the main concepts in the chapter. If there is not sufficient time for the students to complete the quiz, consider moving it to Day Five.

Acting

1. Lead the students in the following reflection:

By saving us, Jesus gave us a story that has all the makings of a happy life. Every time we think more of others than of ourselves, we help make the kingdom come. Let's think of times when we can do this. [Pause.] **Every time we do an action in the name of Jesus, we are working for the kingdom. Every time we do what he did, we show that we are his disciples.** [Pause. Invite the students to offer spontaneous petitions.]

2. Have the students do the Respond activity on page 117.

3. At the end of class, have the students tear out and take home pages 117–118.

CHECKPOINT

- Were the learning outcomes achieved?

- What evidence is there that the students understand that the kingdom is among us?

Day Five   Extending the Chapter

✝ Gather and Go Forth

Lead students through pages 119–120 in the student book. Find catechist instruction on T342–T343.
Materials: Flameless candle

Use the following suggestions to create an additional lesson for Day Five.

1. Remind the students to take home pages 117–118 to share what they are learning with their families.

2. Incorporate any unused BLMs from the week's chapter.

3. Consider the time of the liturgical year and use the appropriate Special Seasons and Lessons. SSLs begin on page T369.

4. Visit www.christourlife.com to find additional activities for Extending the Chapter.

5. Use activities from Enriching the Faith Experience.

6. Guide the students in a prayerful discussion of Sunday's Scripture readings. Visit www.christourlife.com for more information.

Chapter 14   Enriching the Faith Experience

Use the following activities to enrich a lesson or to replace an activity with one that better meets the needs of your class.

1. Tell the students to make two columns on a sheet of paper, one titled *News* and the other *Beatitudes.* Using this chart, tell them to watch the news and in the first column, list all the items about suffering they hear. Next to each item they should put the beatitude that would best bring healing to the situation.

2. Run a BIONIC (Believe It Or Not I Care) Week in the classroom. Make beatitude pennants. Every morning pick and announce a different beatitude to work on. Every time you see someone practicing that Beatitude, give the student a pennant. At the end of the week, present each student with a BIONIC award. This can be a badge covered with clear contact paper.

3. Direct the students to write out the Beatitudes, inserting a picture in place of the subject of each. The picture should show justice and charity in action. Examples:
- ✦ **Blessed are the** (picture of peacemakers)**, for they will be called children of God.**
- ✦ **Blessed are the** (picture of those showing mercy)**, for they will be shown mercy.**

4. Have the students watch the movie *Entertaining Angels: The Dorothy Day Story* (1996) as an example of someone living out the Beatitudes in her life. They can prepare a report on her life and legacy. More information is available at the Catholic Worker Web site.

5. Have each student poll six people from among his or her family members and neighbors. Tell them to ask the people what they think is the biggest issue that needs to be solved in the world. Make a three-column chart with the headings: **Important Issues   Who Says   Why**

   ✦ Use this to stimulate thought and discussion by the students. They may not be able to solve world problems, but they can mention one of these issues during spontaneous petitions in school or at Mass.

   ✦ Have the students examine their own lives to see if they are causing unnecessary conflict or wasting things. Encourage the students to resolve to improve the world by improving their own attitudes and actions first.

   ✦ Direct the students to keep up-to-date on issues so they can make informed comments to others and show they are trying to promote justice.

6. Help the students become mission minded. Plan a way the students can extend their love, such as having a day of prayer and sacrifice, sponsoring an auction, or putting out a box for donations to the missions. Ideas and materials for mission activities may be obtained from the following societies at The Catholic World Mission Web site.

   • Society for the Propagation of the Faith
   • Pontifical Mission Societies
   • The Society of St. Peter Apostle

   • Holy Childhood Association
   • Missionary Union of Priests and Religious

7. Suggest that the students write to a mission pen pal. In this way, they can show concern for someone overseas and become his or her friend.

8. Sponsor a mission month. Every week do something special to make the class or school more aware of serving and caring for others. Plan the details with your class and try to involve as many members of the school as possible. Here are some suggestions.

   ✝ *Solidarity*

   • Each week have a short PA announcement for the school. It could be a prayer or a reading from Scripture. Chapters 5, 6, and 10 of the Gospel of Matthew include appropriate readings.

   • Design a bulletin-board display with a Beatitudes caption. Leave room in one corner to post the week's announcement as a reminder for the school of what they are to be working on.

   • Invite a mission coordinator of your diocese or someone from your town or parish council to speak about what they do and why it is important to serve.

   • Sponsor a campaign to collect food, clothes, or toys to give to those who are poor.

   • Design posters on the Beatitudes to remind the school of the reason for service to others.

   • Find a symbol and make it into buttons that the students can wear as a reminder of their participation in mission awareness month.

   • Ask the students to find ways to give service and show courtesy everywhere in the school.

9. Have the students pick a member of their family and decide which beatitude that person best exemplifies. They should write an explanation of how the person lives this beatitude and add a picture of the person if they wish.

10. Help the students design a banner for each beatitude, incorporating a symbol for it. Hang the banners in the school hallways as reminders of the life Jesus challenges us to live.

11. Introduce the students to The Christopher Movement. *Christopher* means "Christbearer." The purpose of The Christophers is to encourage everyone to show personal responsibility and initiative in raising the standards of all phases of human endeavor. Their popular News Notes leaflets are free to students. Write to:
    The Christophers
    12 East 48th Street
    New York, NY 10017
    or visit www.christophers.org.

Jesus' Kingdom of Justice and Truth
JESUS THE KING

Faith Focus

Jesus expects us to live in honesty and faith, respecting others and the things of this world.

Reflecting on the Faith Experience

Take a few moments to reflect prayerfully before preparing the lesson.

Listening

You have been told, O man,
   what is good,
   and what the LORD requires
   of you:
Only to do the right and to
   love goodness,
   and to walk humbly with
   your God.

Micah 6:8

Reflecting

We are of infinite value and dignity because we are created us in God's divine image and likeness. The Son of God died for love of us. God's vision for us is that we "live happily ever after" with God. But we were created free—free to choose to belong to God's kingdom or not. We can walk in the way of justice, loving tenderly as members of the kingdom of peace, or we can set ourselves outside the kingdom by living selfishly in dishonesty and deceit.

The Seventh, Eighth, and Tenth Commandments guide us to show love and respect for others by living in justice and truth. They forbid stealing, cheating, lying, envy, and greed. But they set no limits on what we can do for one another through justice and love.

Real love and honest respect free us to walk in another person's shoes. We are able to look for opportunities to give to another the most comfortable place, the best food, our time, and the best deal. More fundamentally, if we are people of the kingdom, we are zealous to see that our brothers and sisters all over the world enjoy the

rights God bestowed on them. We confront attitudes and actions that institutionalize injustice. We secure conditions that enable all people to freely and actively contribute to society. We seek justice even to the point of renouncing some of our rights so as to place goods and materials more generously at the service of others. These actions call for a shift in attitude, from independence to interdependence.

The supreme test is to be respectful of others' rights and generous in sharing when there is no visible response. Then we imitate Jesus, the King who announced the Kingdom of God on earth. He was entirely a man for others whose love and availability brought them to his Father. The closer we grow in friendship with Christ, the more sensitive we will be in responding to his call to share his goodness, and the more we will bring the kingdom to completion.

How can I live more simply so that others may simply live?

What project for justice can my class undertake?

Responding

Spirit of justice and truth, let the experiences of this lesson touch the hearts of my students, particularly in those areas of justice and truthfulness where they need further formation.

Scripture for Further Reflection

Jeremiah 22:15–16 Integrity of life is proof that one knows God.

Matthew 5:37 What you speak, speak truthfully.

Romans 8:1–11 We are of the Spirit and not of the flesh because the Spirit of Christ dwells in us.

Preparing for the Faith Experience

Day One
A Fair Deal

Day Two
The Power of Words

Day Three
Truth and Justice Trials

Day Four
Witnesses to Righteousness

Day Five
Extending the Chapter

Gather and Go Forth

Scripture in This Chapter

Mark 1:15 The kingdom is at hand.

Luke 19:1–10 Zacchaeus

Matthew 5:37 Let your "yes" mean "yes."

Catholic Social Teaching

- God's Creation
- Rights and Responsibilities
- The Poor and Vulnerable
- Life and Dignity
- Work and Workers

Church Documents

Catechism of the Catholic Church.
The themes of this chapter correspond to the following paragraphs: **2393, 2401–2402, 2407–2408, 2467–2470, 2477–2487.**

The Splendor of Truth #34 (John Paul II). Each of us has an obligation to seek the truth and to adhere to it once it is known, and we have a right to be respected in our journey in search of the truth.

Sharing Catholic Social Teaching (USCCB). As Christians, we pray for God's kingdom of justice and peace. We work to break down the barriers that get in the way of serving God's kingdom of justice and peace.

Economic Justice for All #24–25 (USCCB). Decisions must be judged in light of those who are poor. Human dignity, realized in community and with the whole of God's creation, is the norm against which every social institution must be measured.

Gather and Go Forth

Find catechist instruction for Gather and Go Forth student pages 127–128 on T344–T345.

Enriching the Faith Experience

Use the activities at the end of the chapter to enrich a lesson or to replace an activity with one that better meets the needs of your class.

Bulletin Board

A suggestion for a bulletin-board design for this chapter is pictured. Display newspaper and magazine articles related to truth and justice, backed by torn tissue paper.

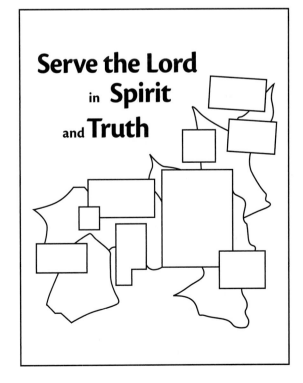

LEARNING OUTCOMES

The students will be able to

- list reasons to respect ownership and the property of others.
- identify ways to be people of justice.
- make decisions based on honesty.

Words to Know

Catholic Social Teaching

greed

social sin

See Glossary for definitions.

Key Terms

covet—to desire what belongs to another

envy—feeling deprived or sad over another person's material possessions or success

justice—fairness; giving all people what they deserve; respecting the rights of others

restitution—returning or paying for a stolen item or repairing or paying for a damaged item

Materials

- Bibles or New Testaments
- Paper cut and marked as $50 bills, one per student
- Reflection notebooks

Before You Begin

1. The social doctrine of the Church was developed in the 19th century when the Church encountered modern industrial society with structures for the production of goods and new forms of labor and ownership. The Church's social teaching provides criteria and guidelines for judgment.

2. "What profit is there for one to gain the whole world yet lose or forfeit himself?" (Luke 9:25) In this lesson, the students will learn reasons for living honestly. In addition, it is hoped the students will clarify their values in the light of eternity.

3. This lesson is an excellent time to heighten students' consciousness of problem areas around the world that cry out for justice. Incorporate current issues in the discussion whenever appropriate.

4. You might be able to involve the class in working for a particular cause related to justice. This would help them make a connection between their faith and how they live their lives.

5. Instead of Centering #1, the students may simply rank items in this list from 1 to 5 based on each item's importance to them. Tell the students to let 1 stand for the most important item.

____ Money

____ Other people

____ Grades

____ Service to family and friends

____ Things you own (MP3 player, clothes, video games and so on)

6. You might want to prepare to tell the story of Zacchaeus for Sharing #3.

CHAPTER 15

Jesus' Kingdom of Justice and Truth

Jesus the King

One day on the front page of a newspaper there was a story about John Shultz. He was a dog warden who had received a $2,500 raise. Although he had five children and did not own his home, Mr. Shultz decided to split his raise with four assistants because he thought they too deserved more pay. Why was that front-page news? What if everyone acted like Mr. Shultz?

Jesus announced, "The kingdom of God is at hand. Repent, and believe in the gospel." (Mark 1:15) It is the proclamation of God's merciful love reaching out to include everyone, especially people who are poor, rejected, and sinners. God's kingdom is a kingdom of love and peace where everyone lives in justice and truth.

All members of the Church are called to serve God's kingdom and create a just world. The Church challenges us to act on behalf of justice and serve the Kingdom of God. The Church's body of teaching on social justice issues is called **Catholic Social Teaching.** People such as Mr. Shultz serve the kingdom.

A Crucial Decision

Are you putting too much value on things that do not matter? The kingdom calls us to be sure that our values are in line with Jesus' values. Serving God's kingdom is up to us.

A sinner named Zacchaeus decided to change his life when Jesus, out of love, called up to him. Zacchaeus's decision gained him the kingdom. Read his story in Luke 19:1–10.

What actions showed that Zacchaeus was ready to serve the values of the kingdom?

People First

For Christians, people are more important than things. The dignity of the human person is valued over material goods. If you love others, you will respect their right to own property. You will not steal from them or cheat them. You will support and strengthen them by participation in all that promotes their well-being. Possessions are good. They can help you grow in your friendship with God and others. Possessions, however, are to be respected as gifts from God. We care for our world and use all things as God intended.

The Seventh and Tenth Commandments help you to act on those beliefs. The Seventh Commandment, *You shall not steal*, tells you to be honest. You protect your property and the property of others. You work honestly to earn things. The dignity of work is an important way in which we participate in God's creation. Work united to Christ's actions can help redeem the world. You share what you have—not only material goods but also spiritual goods—to

(121)

Centering

1. Distribute the $50 bills to the students.

♦ Divide the class into pairs.

♦ **You are to decide how you would spend this money.**

♦ **Divide the bill into three proportional sections. Write in your expenses.**

♦ **When you are finished, tell your partner how you decided to spend your $50.**

2. Link the last lesson with today's lesson.

♦ **Your decisions were determined by the values you hold. Followers of Jesus share his values.**

♦ **In this class, you will take a closer look at two values that are woven through the Beatitudes studied in the last lesson, which are justice and truth.**

Sharing

1. Direct the students to read silently the first paragraph on page 121.

Have the students answer the questions.

2. Have the students read silently the rest of the opening section.

♦ **What keywords describe the Kingdom of God?** (God's love includes all people; it is love, peace, justice, and truth.)

♦ **Our values give direction to our lives. We form them according to the teachings of Jesus Christ. What did you learn about your values from the way you spent your $50?**

♦ **How do we acquire our values?** (No one can force the standards of Christ on another; they must be freely chosen. We can influence others by the power of example.)

3. Ask a student to read aloud **A Crucial**

Quentin Metsys, *The Moneylender and His Wife* (detail), 1514.

contribute toward the common good. The Tenth Commandment, *You shall not covet your neighbor's goods,* tells you to be honest even in your attitudes toward others and their things. An honest person avoids envy and greed.

Envy Kills

Envy is feeling deprived or sad because of another's belongings, talents, or success. When you are envious, you cannot appreciate people. An unhealthy competition grows. Sometimes competition is good because it motivates you to achieve. In unhealthy competition you look for the faults of others, compare their talents to yours, and put them down. When you see signs of envy in yourself, remember that God loves you for who you are. Thank God for the gifts given to

others. Practice good will, humility, and trust in God's providence.

Greed Destroys

Greed is the desire to possess and control things. It is the root of most wars. Greedy people want more than their neighbor and may be willing to get it unfairly. People who steal and cheat do not respect the fundamental rights and responsibilities of others. They break down trust in the community.

To be forgiven for stealing and for damaging property, it is essential to pay restitution. This means that stolen property must be returned or paid for, and damaged items must be repaired or paid for. This may be done anonymously. If direct restitution is not possible, restitution can be made by contributing to a charity.

A Sinful World

Social sin is a term for situations and institutions that harm people and are opposed to the will of Christ. When a person or group of people is deprived of food, clothing, shelter,

Priorities

1. Is cheating on a test as wrong as stealing from a store? Explain.

Yes, stealing answers on a test is taking ideas and work from another person.

2. How does not wasting food or material things help other people?

Waste, neglect, or vandalism reduces material goods to uselessness. When we save food or money, we can share them with others. Food and other material goods should be used creatively to serve the needs of everyone.

3. If someone drops a $20 bill and does not notice it, why should you return it?

The lost money still belongs to that person. Taking it is stealing.

122 UNIT 2

Decision on page 121.

✝ *The Poor and Vulnerable*

♦ Read or tell the story of Zacchaeus from Luke 19:1–10. Allow time for the students to answer the question.

♦ **What would be a good title for this story?**

♦ **Why did Zacchaeus give up his money?**

♦ **What did the people think when they saw Jesus invite himself to supper at Zacchaeus's house?**

♦ **What are some lessons we can learn from the story of Zacchaeus?** (Jesus helps us to be honest with God and others. We are obliged to pay back to others what we have taken. God forgives.)

♦ **There are several requirements for making good moral decisions. We need to make them out of love for God and for people. We must be free to make them. We must look for creative ways to handle moral problems. Finally, it is important to do what is right whether anyone sees us or not.**

4. Have the students silently read **People First** on pages 121–122.

✝ *Life and Dignity God's Creation*

♦ **Why are people more important than things?** (God created people in his divine image and likeness with the right to possess property.)

- **People are valuable. We need to be actively concerned for one another. We should never treat people like things.**

- **Can you give an example of how one of your possessions helps you to become a better person?**

- **When we respect a person's property, we respect the person. What do the Seventh and Tenth Commandments forbid?** (The Seventh Commandment tells us not to steal. The Tenth Commandment tells us not to covet anything that belongs to our neighbor.) ***Covet* means "to desire very much what belongs to another."**

- **How do we show respect for things and people?** (by protecting property, working honestly, sharing, and being satisfied with what we have)

- **What efforts are you making to protect our environment?**

5. Ask several students to read aloud **Envy Kills** and **Greed Destroys** on page 122.

   ⚔ *Rights and Responsibilities*

- **Why do people feel envy?** (They compare themselves with others. They are not satisfied with their own gifts. They want to be first or better than others.) **What would teenagers want that could lead them to envy someone?**

- **How does envy cause us to harm ourselves and others?** (It wastes energy. It can lead to sins that cause others to get hurt or suffer.)

- **Greedy people sin because possessions have become more important to them than God or others. They may go to any extreme to get what they want.**

- **How can restitution be made?** (by returning or paying for stolen items; by repairing or paying for damaged items; by contributing to a charity)

- **What can you do to make another person feel important?**

6. Have a student read aloud **A Sinful World** on pages 122–123.

---

and security, there is an injustice. The goods of the earth belong to everyone.

As followers of Christ, we are responsible for resisting those situations and promoting justice and respect. We are called to change unjust systems and organizations. The first step is to change our own attitudes.

The Power of Words

In the Letter of James, the tongue is compared to the rudder that controls a ship. It is small but mighty. The letter also says, "Consider how small a fire can set a huge forest ablaze. The tongue is also a fire." (James 3:5–6) Followers of Christ value truth. They speak the truth to one another and about one another. When they hurt another person by untruths, half-truths, or gossip, followers of Christ repair the damage they have done.

Truth builds relationships. We depend on one another to tell the truth. Lying is saying what is not true with the intention of deceiving. It breaks down trust, causes confusion, and prevents people from knowing what is real. God gave us minds to know the truth and hearts to go to others in love. The Eighth Commandment is *You shall not bear false witness against your neighbor.* It forbids untrue words and acts and anything that damages another's good name.

Why Do People Lie?

Fear is the number one reason people lie. Some people are afraid others will not like them, so they cover up truth and exaggerate. Lying about yourself and your achievements is much easier than being real. People who lie do not have to say I'm wrong, I'm sorry, or I don't know.

To be "on top" is another reason people lie. Some people want to impress others and get their attention. They may lie to win, to be popular, to get good grades, or to get out of work or trouble. But a lie only works for the moment. In the end a person loses friends, peace, and, worst of all, friendship with God.

Kayla's Campaign

"Look who's running for student council!" remarked Jena sarcastically as she looked across the room. There stood Kayla Adams handing out campaign buttons.

"Looks decent," said Zach to Jena as he looked up from doing his homework.

"Shows what you know," answered Jena. "She really thinks she's something."

"Well, she was class treasurer last year," Alexis reminded the group around Jena. "She was captain of the cheerleaders."

"Kids like her," claimed Tyrone.

"The teachers like her!" corrected Jena. "She's so sweet to their faces. The kids don't know about her, or they wouldn't vote for her. That's for sure."

"The kids don't know what?" asked Alexis.

Jena lowered her voice, "Well, I'm only going to tell you. I heard that she took money from the class treasury last year and that she lifts stuff from stores."

"I've never heard that," said Zach.

"I don't believe it," snapped Tyrone.

"You vote for her if you want, but I'm not," said Jena firmly.

Alexis frowned and muttered, "I didn't know she was *that* kind of person."

⚔ *Rights and Responsibilities*
Work and Workers

- **How would you explain social sin in your own words? Can you give some examples?** (slavery, gender discrimination, unfair employment practices, extreme poverty in wealthy nations)

- **How do people work against social sin?** (nonviolent methods such as boycotts, protests, positive propaganda, introducing and supporting better laws)

7. Direct the students to work on the questions in **Priorities** on page 122.
   Go over the students' answers.

Acting

Have the students write a prayer in their reflection notebooks, using these starters.

- *Honesty is important to me because . . .*

- *I am most honest with . . .*

- *I trust Jesus will help me to be honest when . . .*

CHECKPOINT

- Were the learning outcomes achieved?

- In what ways have the students grown in understanding honesty?

LEARNING OUTCOMES

The students will be able to

- explain how truthfulness is necessary for building relationships (Eighth Commandment).
- identify ways to become a people of truth.

Materials

- Bibles or New Testaments
- Two glasses of a drink with the contents covered and labeled incorrectly

Before You Begin

1. When we speak truth, we encounter Jesus who referred to himself as "the way and the truth and the life" (John 14:6). The Eighth Commandment calls us to live in truth and to live in Christ by not misrepresenting ourselves to others. Our obligation to live in truth flows from our baptismal vocation to live as God's people, bearing witness to God who is the truth. We are called to live in truth in both deeds and words respecting the reputation of others, avoiding deception, and making reparations for the times we are untruthful.

2. The more we love our neighbors, the more impossible it becomes to lie. Behind truth is all that is real. Our life is real when we know who we are in a loving relationship with the Father.

3. You may wish to prepare students to act out the story in **Kayla's Campaign** on page 123 for Sharing #3.

Centering

1. Have two volunteers select a glass to drink. Hand them the glasses labeled incorrectly.
   - **Take a sip of the drink. Does the drink taste the way it is supposed to?** (No. The drinks are not labeled correctly.)
   - **Do you think what I did is a lie?**
   - **Lies are not equally serious, but all are wrong because they deceive people.**

2. Direct the students to read silently **The Power of Words** on page 123.
   - **Why is telling the truth important?** (It builds relationships. When people tell the truth, they can love and trust each other.)
   - **What does the Eighth Commandment forbid?** (untrue words and acts; anything that hurts the good name of another)

Sharing

1. Recall with the students the spending exercise from the last lesson.
   - **Do you think your decisions on how to spend the $50 in the last lesson were honest?**
   - **Why do you think people lie?**

2. Have a student read aloud **Why Do People Lie?** on page 123.
   - **Why does lying lead to a lack of peace?** (fear of being caught; telling more lies to cover up) **For example, if you lie to your parents, you are always afraid that they will find out. You might tell more lies to cover up the first one.**
   - **When might you be tempted to lie?** (playing sports, doing homework, getting grades, making friends, doing jobs, when asked about some wrongdoing)
   - **Is exaggeration lying?** (yes if it stretches the truth; no if it is clearly meant as a joke)
   - **Why is it good to admit I'm wrong, I'm sorry, and I don't know?** (When people admit their mistakes, they help us realize that we all make mistakes and need one another's support.)
   - **Speaking the truth is right because people base their thoughts and actions on what others tell them. Exaggerations, gossip, and rumors can ruin reputations and destroy people's lives.**

3. Assign students the parts of Jena, Zach, Tyrone, Alexis, and the narrator in **Kayla's Campaign** on page 123.

Direct the students to write the answers to the three questions on page 124 and then discuss them.

4. Call on a student to read aloud **Keeping Confidences and Promises** on page 124.
   - **Why is silence necessary?** (to stop gossip; to guard family confidences)
   - **Why do people share secrets with one another?** (as a sign of trust and confidence in the other person; they want to share a part of their lives with someone else) **If we hear a secret, what are we obliged to do?** (not tell it to others)
   - **What questions should we ask before we tell truths that may hurt others?** (Is it necessary? Is it kind?)
   - **When may we read others' letters, diaries, or journals?** (only when they offer to share them with us)
   - **When can silence be a lie?** (when we do not say something is untrue; when telling the truth would clear someone's name; when we do wrong and don't admit it)

5. Have the students read silently **Living in Truth** on page 124.
   - **What are the benefits of telling the truth?** (confidence, courage; responsibility for your actions; gain trust and respect of others; further God's kingdom)

◆ **What are some of the ways we learn to be truthful?** (the good example of others and by our practice of truthfulness)

◆ **What are some of the ways you have learned from others to tell the truth?**

◆ **What are some examples of ways you have told the truth?**

6. Direct the students to read silently **Having Problems Being Truthful?** on page 124. **Do you think any of these steps would be helpful in telling the truth? Why or why not?**

Acting

1. Have the students do the Respond activity on page 125.

2. Lead the students through the prayer experience **A Moment with Jesus** on page 124.
Allow sufficient time for silent reflection.

CHECKPOINT

- Were the learning outcomes achieved?

- How have the students indicated a growing awareness of the value of truthfulness?

---

1. What did Tyrone and Alexis first think of Kayla?
They seem to respect Kayla because of her leadership roles and popularity.

2. How has Jena hurt Kayla?
By passing on a rumor of Kayla's stealing, Jena is ruining Kayla's reputation. The students will be less likely to vote for her.

3. Do you think Jena lied? Explain.
We don't know if Kayla stole or not. Even if what Jena said was true, she should not have spread it around. She should have confronted Kayla herself. What Jena did was unkind and unfair.

Keeping Confidences and Promises

Confidences are intended to be kept private, so they are not repeated. Silence is necessary when you are tempted to spread gossip. Keep family confidences within the family and guard other promises. Priests, doctors, lawyers, secretaries, and other professional people are bound to keep information about their work private. Before revealing information that may hurt others, we should ask if it is necessary and if it is kind.

Having Troubles Being Truthful?
Use these steps to help you change.

Pray   Tell Christ you desire to be truthful. Ask him to help you. Do this every morning.

Think   Look at your real self. Christ loves you. He died so that you could share eternal life with him.

Reflect   Catch yourself exaggerating? Lying? Spreading rumors? Decide why you do this and stop it.

(124) UNIT 2

When someone tells you something in confidence, it is a way of saying: I trust you, I like you, I respect you. Sharing that confidence with others would be wrong. Reading another person's private letters or journal would also be wrong.

In some circumstances, however, if you have information about a person's intent to harm oneself or others, you have the responsibility to speak to someone in legitimate authority.

Keeping promises is being true to your word. It lets others know they can rely on you.

Silence is not always good, however. When can silence be a lie?

A Moment with Jesus

Truth is a powerful thing. It builds relationships and strengthens trust and respect.

Stop for a moment now and quietly reflect on what you've read so far in this chapter. What one aspect of justice and truth stands out as most important for you right now? In your own words, share it with Jesus. Ask him to help you live the values of the Kingdom of God as Jesus did. Thank Jesus for calling you to be his disciple.

Living in Truth

Being a truthful person goes hand in hand with your strength of character. You have confidence and courage. You take responsibility and cope with consequences. You gain the trust and respect of others. Honesty also builds a better society. By being truthful, you show Christ's unselfish love and spread his peace all around you. You further God's kingdom.

Day Three   Truth and Justice Trials

LEARNING OUTCOMES

The students will be able to

- review ways we practice truth and justice and ways we do not.

- explain how reverence for people determines how we make moral choices.

Materials

- BLM 57

- List of terms on the board or written on slips of paper: *envy, greed, cheating, stealing, vandalism, polluting, lying, telling a secret, breaking a promise, ruining a reputation*

- Candle (check fire codes) (optional)

- Markers (optional)

Before You Begin

Jesus left no formula for making correct decisions, but he praised the decisions people made out of faith and love. He expects us to use our natural talents to make decisions and use the guidelines he gave us in the commandments and the Gospel.

Centering

Link the last lesson with today's lesson.

✦ **Why do you think we have such great interest and concern in the hearings or the trials that involve the behavior or ethics of government officials?** (We demand honesty and truth from our leaders.)

✦ **In this lesson, you will hold mock trials of people who have not been honest or truthful. It will help you understand the values in the Seventh, Eighth, and Tenth Commandments.**

Sharing

1. Divide the students into 10 groups.

✦ Let each group either choose a term from the board or draw a slip of paper. Be sure all the words are used.

✦ **Plan a trial for a person who has failed God and the community by committing the offense assigned to your group.**

✦ **Decide what the person did. Give the culprit a name related to the crime, such as Sally Shoplifter.**

✦ **Write one or two sentences that the judge can say to get the person to repent and avoid the crime in the future.**

✦ **Think of a punishment that is the opposite of the harm the culprit did.** For instance, remember that after stealing, Zacchaeus gave money to the poor.

✦ **Choose a prosecutor, a judge, and a culprit to enact the last day of the trial. The prosecutor will explain the crime, and the judge will give the talk and impose the sentence.**

2. Have each group enact its trial.

3. **BLM 57** Distribute BLM 57 **Value E-mail.**

✦ **Write an e-mail of 15 words or less summarizing how to live the Seventh, Eighth, and Tenth Commandments.**

✦ The students can use markers to design the e-mail. Invite volunteers to share their work.

✦ Example:

> **From:** Ralph <ralph@email.com>
> **To:** Ray <ray@email.com>
> **Subject: Value E-mail**
>
> Ray,
> Speak honestly. Give generously.
> Love others sincerely.
> -Ralph

Acting

 Lead the students in shared prayer. You might have the students form a circle.

✦ **In our prayer, we will ask God for the grace to be just and truthful members of the kingdom.** [Pause.]

✦ **Lord, we want to act honestly so people will trust us. We want to be truthful. We want to live your words, Jesus, but we need your grace to give us courage and strengthen our character. Thank you for our families, friends, and others who have led us to know the values of your kingdom.**

✦ After your prayer, have students share a prayer, using their Value E-mails.

✦ A lighted candle could be passed to the student praying.

CHECKPOINT ✓

• Were the learning outcomes achieved?

• What did the judges' statements reveal about the students' understanding of honesty and truthfulness?

Day Four Witnesses to Righteousness

Student pages 125–126

LEARNING OUTCOMES

The students will be able to

• describe the lives of people who lived the ideal of Christian love.

• demonstrate an understanding of the key concepts in this chapter.

Materials

• BLM 58A–C
• Mask
• World map or globe
• BLM 59 Quiz

Before You Begin

1. Students need real heroes to imitate. They need to see that holiness is not to be the exception but the normal expression of our love. When people allow Christ to work in them, they live lives of generosity and service. They become heroes in the true sense of the word. Those who love Christ give without counting the cost and show courage in hardship and in daily life. They are fully human and live with a balance of common sense and heroic charity.

2. When planning today's lesson, keep in mind that Day Four is when the students take the quiz for this chapter. Reserve time at the end of class for this assessment. The quiz can also be administered on Day Five.

Centering

Show the students a mask.

+ **What is the purpose of a mask?**
  (to hide one's identity)

+ **When do you wear masks?**
  (Halloween, at parties)

+ **Sometimes people hide behind such things as power, pleasure, status, money, or popularity. They use these as masks to hide from becoming the people God intends them to become.**

+ **Jesus teaches us to be ourselves and let his love and grace shine in us. We are called to be people who are real and don't hide behind masks.**

+ **Today we will explore the lives of a few people who lived the Gospels heroically and became the best they could be. Some of these people the Church has recognized as saints. All of them teach us how to have the attitudes of Christ.**

+ **How would you describe those who have the attitudes of Christ?**

Sharing

1. **BLM 58A–C** Distribute copies of BLM 58A–C **Christian Witnesses.**

   + **Read silently the life stories of the eight great men and women and then answer the questions.** (Allow time to complete the activity.)

   + **How did you answer the question for each life story?**

   + **Do you know of any other stories about the lives of these people?**

   + Point out on a map or a globe the places where these people have lived and worked.

   + **What do all these people have in common?**

2. Lead the students through the Summary and Review Activities pages 125–126.

3. **BLM 59** Distribute and administer BLM 59 **Chapter 15 Quiz.**

CHAPTER 15 Summary

Remember

What do the Seventh and Tenth Commandments tell us?
The Seventh and Tenth Commandments tell us to be honest and to respect others' property.

What does the Eighth Commandment tell us?
The Eighth Commandment tells us to be truthful in our words.

What is Catholic Social Teaching?
Catholic Social Teaching is the Church's body of teaching on social justice issues.

Respond

Read John 14:23–27. The peace Jesus gives is not free from troubles or difficulties. It is a deep, inner peace that comes from being true to God, yourself, and others.

In your reflection notebook, write about an experience you had trying to be truthful. Was it hard? Did you ask Jesus or anyone else to help you? How did you handle it? Would you act differently in the future? Why or why not?

Reach Out

1. Jesus often spoke about riches and the kingdom. Read his parable about the rich man and Lazarus (Luke 16:19–31) and decide what the rich man's crime was. Then read these passages: Luke 12:15–21, Matthew 6:19–21, Matthew 6:24, and Matthew 19:23–24. Prepare a one-minute talk encouraging people to use the wealth of this world justly.

2. Compliment members of your family, classmates, or other people you meet whenever you can during a day. Do this for three days, keeping a tally. Share your results with the class.

3. Make up a short play about someone who stole something and how he or she made restitution.

4. Remember that everything we use is property to be respected. Take care of the things you have and use. Try cleaning your room and keeping it neat for one week.

5. Write an article for your school newspaper or bulletin on the value of honesty as opposed to stealing or cheating. Tell how honesty makes the whole school better.

Words to Know
Catholic Social Teaching
greed   social sin

"What does love look like? It has feet to go to the poor and needy. It has eyes to see misery and want. It has ears to hear the sighs and sorrows of others."

–Saint Augustine

Saint Augustine. ❯

(125)

Use this opportunity to assess the students' understanding of the main concepts in the chapter. If there is not sufficient time for the students to complete the quiz, consider moving it to Day Five.

Acting

1. Ask students to choose a saint they admire. Invite them to spend time in silent prayer.

   + **Spend a few moments sharing with this saint about your life and the qualities you admire in him or her. Ask the saint to pray for you.**

+ Pray together the Doxology on the inside front cover of the student book.

2. At the end of class, have the students tear out and take home pages 125–126.

CHECKPOINT ✓

• Were the learning outcomes achieved?

Day Five Extending the Chapter

Gather and Go Forth

Lead students through pages 127–128 in the student book. Find catechist instruction on T344–T345.

Use the following suggestions to create an additional lesson for Day Five.

1. Remind the students to take home pages 125–126 to share what they are learning with their families.

2. Incorporate any unused BLMs from the week's chapter.

3. Consider the time of the liturgical year and use the appropriate Special Seasons and Lessons. SSLs begin on page T369.

4. Visit www.christourlife.com to find additional activities for Extending the Chapter.

5. Use activities from Enriching the Faith Experience.

6. Guide the students in a prayerful discussion of Sunday's Scripture readings. Visit www.christourlife.com for more information.

CHAPTER 15 Review Activities

Seven, Eight, or Ten? Check *Yes* if the person's values are in line with Jesus' values. Check *No* if the person's values are not. Record the number of the commandment (7, 8, or 10) related to the action.

	Yes	No	Number
1. Mike uses someone else's ID to buy beer.		✓	8
2. Susan copies from Tyler's test.		✓	7, 8
3. Jerry admits he made a mistake.	✓		8
4. Eddie accepts change for $20 when he gave the cashier $10.		✓	7
5. Nita cannot eat all of her lunch. She saves it instead of throwing it away.	✓		7
6. Sam was involved in drinking after the roller-skating party. When his parents ask if he was drinking, he says, "Some of the guys were," implying that he was not.		✓	8
7. Carol says that when her sister uses her things, she takes one of her things to pay her back.		✓	7
8. Patsy says nice things to a teacher to get what she wants.		✓	8
9. Rosa knows Jean is hurting herself by taking drugs but does not say anything for fear of losing her friendship.		✓	8
10. Ken resents that Carlos has many expensive things.		✓	10
11. David broke Pete's CD by accident and offers to pay for it.	✓		7
12. Maria changes the subject when Joe starts criticizing Ann.	✓		8
13. Megan promised to be home by 10:00, but she stays out until 11:00.		✓	8
14. Abby copies her history report from the encyclopedia.		✓	7, 8
15. Nancy reads her sister's journal.		✓	8
16. Julie refuses to tell a secret although many people are mad at her.	✓		8
17. Dan feels happy when other people win. He tries hard not to compare himself to others.	✓		10
18. George does not want to spend his allowance money on school supplies, so he always borrows supplies from others.		✓	7
19. Jeff discovers his brother got into trouble for vandalism. He keeps this knowledge within the family.	✓		8
20. John scratches words into desks and marks up walls.		✓	7
21. Mark knows Alex shoplifts but does not tell their classmates.	✓		8

Seventh Commandment	**Eighth Commandment**	**Tenth Commandment**
You shall not steal.	You shall not bear false witness against your neighbor.	You shall not covet your neighbor's goods.

126

Chapter 15 Enriching the Faith Experience

Use the following activities to enrich a lesson or to replace an activity with one that better meets the needs of your class.

1. Explain that for centuries people have made up short sayings or proverbs to help remember a law or good advice. Read the following modern proverbs and discuss their meaning. Then have the students make up original proverbs about the Seventh, Eighth, and Tenth Commandments, using modern comparisons. Direct them to write their proverbs on 6-by-8-inch cards and decorate them.

✦ **The generous man is like a tree of good fruit: there is no poison in him.**

✦ **The one who cheats is like a decayed tooth: white on top, rotten inside.**

✦ **The honest person is like a well-running car: you can depend on him or her in any season.**

2. Divide the class into groups to investigate how your school is using its resources to protect the environment. You might have groups such as recycling, heating and cooling, and use of electricity and water. The students can report the groups' findings to the class. The groups could then develop plans to help the school better use its resources.
✝ *God's Creation*

3. Direct the students to find quotations on honesty and truthfulness. Have them print them on poster board and display the posters around the classroom.

Jesus' Kingdom of Love
JESUS THE SACRED HEART

Faith Focus

A follower of Jesus regards sex as a sacred gift used to express deep,
life-giving love within marriage.

Reflecting on the Faith Experience

Take a few moments to reflect prayerfully before preparing the lesson.

Listening

Let love be sincere; . . .
anticipate one another in
showing honor.

Romans 12:9–10

Reflecting

We were made by love for love. Our
deepest longing is to love and to be
loved. The presence of sin makes
selfless love difficult. We do not
always recognize real love but go
after cheap imitations that leave
us still thirsting. Often what we
perceive as loving others is merely a
form of self-love.

God is love. Jesus then is Love
Incarnate. The beauty, the greatness,
and the mystery of the Father's self-
giving love is played out in his life.
Jesus gives the ultimate lesson in
love: he dies for love of us. The love
in his Sacred Heart is more precious
than life to him.

God shines in true love because
it is a reflection of himself. The
love between a man and woman
permanently committed to each
other in marriage is a sign of Jesus'
love for the Church. The love of
a married couple entails total
surrender and complete openness.
It culminates in a union touched
with ecstasy and gifted with life-
giving power. Sex has been called
the liturgy of love. Married love
is sacred, fruitful, and a gift to
the world.

Selfless, faithful love is difficult;
some might say impossible. It
is especially challenging in an
age of increased life expectancy
and in a society in which many
people have difficulty living the
Christian ideal. We try to love
like Jesus, but we do not always
succeed. In our weakness, we turn
to God to prepare us for this love
and to sustain us in it. Saint John
of the Cross wrote that in the end
we will be judged on love. We all
desire to be united with God one
day in heaven. With a love beyond
imagining, God speaks to us:

Because you are precious in
my eyes
and glorious, and because
I love you . . .
Fear not, for I am with you; . . .

Isaiah 43:4–5

*How can I counteract the forces that
demean the Christian ideal of totally
committed love?*

Responding

Spirit of love, make my students
open to the Christian attitude
toward sex.

Scripture for Further Reflection

Genesis 2:5–7,18–25 From
the beginning, God saw the
creation of man and woman as
good. Their union is according
to the divine plan.

Ephesians 5:21–33 Marriage is
a reflection of the love of Christ
for his Church. Husbands and
wives should respect and love
each other.

Preparing for the Faith Experience

✝ **Gather and Go Forth**

Scripture in This Chapter

Genesis 1:27 We are created in
God's image.

Ephesians 5:25–33
Wives and Husbands

Romans 12:9–10 Love one another.

Catholic Social Teaching

Family and Community

Church Documents

Catechism of the Catholic Church.
The themes of this chapter
correspond to the following
paragraphs: **478, 2332–2337,
2341–2342, 2347, 2360, 2380–2381,
2522.**

National Directory for Catechesis #45.
The followers of Christ reject the
values and practices of a sexually
permissive society. They practice
chastity through modest behavior,
dress, and speech, resisting
lustful desires and temptations,
pornography, and indecent
entertainment.

Of Human Life #8–13 (Paul VI).
In marriage, conjugal love is
described as fully human, total,
faithful, and exclusive until death.
It is given by God for the dual
purpose of union and procreation.
Responsible parenthood is viewed
as a mission given by God.
Educators and those who are
responsible for the common good
are called to "create an atmosphere
favorable to education in chastity."

***Human Sexuality from God's
Perspective*** (USCCB). Marriage is
a vocation, a path to union with
God. The love of the married
partners is sacramental because
of its ability to mirror God's love,
which is total and permanent.

Gather and Go Forth

Find catechist instruction for
Gather and Go Forth student
pages 135–136 on T346–T347.

Enriching the Faith Experience

Use the activities at the end of
the chapter to enrich a lesson or
to replace an activity with one
that better meets the needs of
your class.

Bulletin Board

A suggestion for a bulletin-board
design for this chapter is pictured.
Down the sides, you might put
the words of a song the students
think expresses Jesus' love, or a
list of qualities they most admire
in friends.

The Sacred Heart

Jesus' Kingdom of Love

LEARNING OUTCOMES

The students will be able to

- describe how love builds on friendship.
- demonstrate an understanding of the commitment and responsibilities of marriage.
- explain that sex is a gift from God to be used in marriage to express love and to create new life.

Key Terms

sex—the God-given gift by which a married man and woman express and deepen their love and cooperate with God in bringing forth new life

sexuality—maleness or femaleness

Materials

- Bibles or New Testaments
- Building blocks
- Chart written on the board:

Five Levels of Friendship

Casual	
Friend	
Close Friend	
Best Friend	
Intimacy	

Before You Begin

1. Because the gift of sexuality comes from God, men and women possess personal dignity. They are equals to one another. Our sexuality affects all aspects of the human person in the unity of our body and soul. The expression of sexual love in a married relationship between a man and a woman is to be both unitive and procreative. The unitive dimension of marriage can be understood as the mutual and total self-giving of spouses to each other. The procreative dimension is the participation of the spouses in the creation of new life. The expression of sexual love between spouses is therefore cooperation with the creative act of God.

2. Respect for the gift of sex and for the sacredness of marriage and family life is a Christian value that must be presented in the best way possible. In adapting this lesson to your students' needs, decide which topics need emphasis. Questions about issues such as homosexuality, pornography, HIV, and masturbation may arise. Prepare by reading current information, checking what is being taught in sex-education programs, reading Church teachings, and consulting a priest and a doctor.

3. Many influences exert power on the moral values of young adolescents. Positive influences include the models of loving, caring parents and teachers. Negative influences include attractive and exploitative TV programs, songs, movies, Web sites, and books.

4. For many adults, sexuality is a delicate and anxiety-filled topic. This is equally true of young adolescents. They may express their anxiety by giggling, by silence, or by ridicule that mimics the media. One reason for this reaction may be the developmental stages of the students. They will be at different levels of sexual maturity. Be aware that some may feel guilty because of past experiences. The first and best way to meet the needs of different students is to direct them to ask their parents to answer their questions about sex.

5. You may wish to plan educational programs for parents. A priest, deacon, or other person knowledgeable about moral theology may be invited to speak to parents, to students, or to both on sexual morality, and to answer their questions. Topics that might surface are homosexuality, premarital sex, unmarried couples living together, the pressure of society and the media, and sexual and nonsexual signs of affection. It would be good to have parents and students write questions and give them to the speaker in advance.

Centering _____

1. Place the building blocks in the center of the room.
   - Invite the students to come forward one at a time to begin building a structure. Each student might add a few pieces to the structure. Be sure to stress that the students should not let the structure collapse.
   - **This structure is like our friendships. They need to build on a strong foundation so they do not collapse. The same is true of the gift of our sexuality. It must be treated with great care; otherwise it can be damaged.**
   - **The Church gives us rules about sex so that we will have a strong foundation on which to build our sexuality.**
   - **There are some people who see a structure like this and want to run in and knock it down. In the same way, some people rush in to sexual relationships, not realizing the damage they can do.**

2. Link the last lesson with today's lesson.
   - **What does the word** *pretense* **mean?** (a false show)
   - **How can love be a pretense?** (Someone could be pretending to

love in order to reach a goal or to satisfy his or her own needs.)

+ **Real love is at the heart of everything you have studied so far: the Incarnation, the sacraments, the commandments, and the Beatitudes.**

+ **In this lesson, you will learn about real love. Real love is the foundation upon which we build our friendships and our sexuality.**

Sharing

1. Discuss the five levels of friendship with the students, using the chart on the board.
   + **There are at least five levels of friendship:** *casual*, *friend*, *close friend*, *best friend*, **and** *intimacy*.
   + **Each of these levels has different degrees of what we reveal about ourselves, what our commitment is, and what is appropriate touch.**
   + **Sometimes people can confuse the need for intimacy with sexual feelings. Intimacy is a total self-giving of who we are to another person. In marriage, that also means sexual giving.**

2. Have the students read silently the opening paragraph on page 129.
   + Direct the students to complete the exercise.
   + **What are some of the qualities of friendship you listed?**
   + Ask the students to read silently the rest of the section.
   + **Why is a heart the symbol of total love?** (It stands for our whole being, our life. When it stops beating, we die.) **How did Jesus show us total love in reality and in symbol?** (He gave his life for us; his heart was pierced by a lance.)

CHAPTER 16

Jesus' Kingdom of Love

Jesus the Sacred Heart

Do you know a couple who have celebrated their 50th wedding anniversary? They are probably best friends. Name some qualities of friendship that would help a man and woman stay happily married.

sharing time, trust, respecting differences,

helping, valuing each other, honesty

Friendship is one of the greatest gifts you can give to another person. In sharing your time, your affection, your thoughts and feelings, you are sharing yourself.

Sometimes you see the initials of two lovers inside a heart. A heart stands for a person's whole being. Jesus' love is greater than friendship. He gave his life so that we would be happy. When Jesus died on the Cross, his heart was pierced by a lance. His sacred heart has symbolized his great love ever since.

People who serve God's kingdom try to imitate Jesus' totally selfless love. In doing so, they find meaning for life and great joy. Such selfless love exists in a special way between a man and woman who are married.

Marriage: Made in Heaven

"God created man in his image; . . . male and female he created them." (Genesis 1:27) Our maleness or femaleness is our sexuality. Every cell in a man's body is marked as male, and every cell in a woman's body is marked as female. Our sexuality colors everything we do: the way we think, the way we react, the way we move, the way we talk.

God has placed within men and women an attraction for each other. They need and enjoy each other. God wanted them to grow in friendship. But more than friendship, God wanted

a man and a woman
to join in a love so complete, so selfless,
that their two lives would blend into one
like two streams blending into one river.

Their union sealed by a marriage vow would last as long as they both live.

Read Ephesians 5:25–33 and complete the following comparison:

The love of marriage is like the love of

Christ for his Church .

When God calls a Catholic man and woman to make a lifelong commitment in marriage, God blesses their union through the Sacrament of Matrimony. Throughout their lives together, the couple will rely on the strengthening grace of the sacrament. Not all people have an ideal marriage. It is something to strive for.

129

3. Direct the students to read silently the section **Marriage: Made in Heaven** on pages 129–130.
   + Have the students work on the Scripture activity.
   + **What is sexuality?** (maleness or femaleness) **Who created sex?** (God)
   + [Explain to the students the image for marriage the book presents.] **Marriage is like two streams uniting in a river. The man and woman unite their lives completely.**

+ **To what does Scripture compare marriage?** (the love of Christ for his Church)

+ **How does the Sacrament of Matrimony help a married couple?** (God blesses the marriage. The grace of the sacrament strengthens the couple throughout their lives.)

+ **What aspect of married love do you think would be most difficult?**

4. Have several students read aloud **Prepare Now!** on page 130.

+ **Was Carla experiencing love?** (No, not real love. She was probably just in the first stage of love, a physical and emotional attraction.)

+ **If you weren't able to check anything in the list yet, don't worry. Every person grows according to a different time schedule. You will change and grow at your own rate.**

+ **How can group dating help a marriage later?** (It makes it easier to find the right marriage partner. It gives you knowledge and skills needed for forming a lifelong relationship and for dealing with other people.) **How does group dating make it easier to find the right marriage partner?** (You learn that there are many types of people in the world and so you are better prepared to make a good choice.) **Boys and girls who cling to the first person they meet limit their growth. What knowledge and skills does group dating teach?** (You learn and practice social skills such as communication, forgiveness, and courtesy.)

+ **How else can you prepare for marriage?** (Practice love by helping your neighbor, giving time to family members, and forgiving those who hurt you.)

5. Discuss with the students the activity on moral qualities.
What are some of the moral qualities you chose? Why?

6. Call on a student to read aloud **Sex: A Gift from God** on page 130.
✝ Family and Community

+ **Why is the gift of sex holy?** (It is a power to create new persons. It is a share in God's power to create.)

+ **How does God protect this gift?** (by the unbreakable bond of marriage)

+ **What are the purposes of the sacred gift of sex?** (to help married couples express and deepen their

---

Married love includes

- sharing all things
- treasuring the other person as he or she is
- meeting the joy and pain of daily life together
- cherishing the children God sends
- being faithful until death.

Married couples use their good qualities to grow in love and to build a good marriage.

Prepare Now!

Carla is talking with her friends by the drinking fountain at school. Ted passes by and says, "Hi." Suddenly Carla's heart begins to beat rapidly. Her face turns red. She feels clumsy, and she cannot say anything to say. Why do you think she is or is not in love?

If you ever feel like Carla, congratulations. It is a sign of a change going on within you. Here are other signs of change. Check the ones you notice in yourself:

○ I seek more privacy.
○ I change moods quickly.
○ I daydream often.
○ I am easily embarrassed.

These signs point to a special awakening within you. Just as there are stages in our physical, intellectual, and emotional growth, mature love requires that we pass through stages. It may be a slow process.

You can prepare yourself now for the lifetime commitment of marriage by meeting as many people as possible. At your age, it is important to learn about people and how to get along with them. Group dating will make it easier for you to find the right marriage partner if God is calling you to marriage. It will also give you knowledge and skills needed for forming a lifelong relationship and for dealing with other people.

Another way you can prepare for marriage is by practicing love in various situations. How gener-

---

ous are you in helping your neighbors? How loyal are you to your friends? Do you sacrifice yourself and your time for family members? Can you forgive easily? If you learn how to love now, you have a better chance of experiencing deep, lasting love in your marriage.

Check the moral qualities you most admire in people of the opposite sex who are your own age.

○ kindness   ○ honesty
○ prayerfulness   ○ truthfulness
○ gentleness   ○ self-control
○ justice   ○ friendliness
○ prudence   ○ forgiveness
○ courage   ○ unselfishness
○ respect   ○ compassion

Sex: A Gift from God

God has given each of us special gifts that are holy. Among these gifts is sex, an ability to show and deepen love and to create new persons. In this gift, God invites married men and women to share in his own power to create life. The ability to share our deepest selves with another is so sacred that God intended it to be protected by the unbreakable bond of marriage, which is the union of one man and one woman. For people who are called to marriage, sex is a joy that God has given along with the responsibilities of raising a family.

Having sex before we are ready is asking for trouble. We are not ready until we are free to take on the responsibilities of loving someone for life and being a parent. Each person born needs to belong to a loving family and learn about love from a loving mother and father.

Priests, sisters, brothers, and single people sacrifice this joy in living their vocation. Their love is focused on Christ and all his people.

A Sign of Total Surrender

Would you wash a car with motor oil? Of course not. Harm comes from not using

---

love for each other, to create life, and to form a family) [Have the students underline these purposes.]

+ **Why do you think God made the gift of sex so attractive?** (to help married couples express their love and to guarantee that the human race would continue)

7. Discuss with the students depictions of a happy marriage.
Think of a happy marriage from a real-life situation, from TV, or from a book. What do you think makes a happy marriage?

Acting
 Have the students reflect on the building blocks.

+ **Let us pray for help to understand God's values and to make decisions according to them so that we might come to love with a true, selfless love that is built on a strong foundation.**

+ Allow time for silent reflection.

CHECKPOINT

- Were the learning outcomes achieved?

- What attitudes toward sex did the students manifest during this lesson?

LEARNING OUTCOMES

The students will be able to

- explain an understanding of the beauty and the symbolism of the love between a married man and woman.
- demonstrate a respect for the gift of sex.
- describe how sex is a sacred gift from God for married couples (Sixth and Ninth Commandments).

Word to Know

adultery

See Glossary for definition.

Key Terms

chastity—the virtue by which we show respect for our God-given power to bring life into the world

modesty—the virtue that helps us choose appropriate dress and behavior so as not to call attention to our sex or ourselves

Materials

- Bibles or New Testaments
- Recording of a song about love between a man and a woman
- Candle (check fire codes)

Before You Begin

1. Note that modesty is an attitude that protects what is most personal to us, refusing to reveal that which should remain private. It guides the way a person looks at others and acts toward them, respecting the dignity of others. Modesty enables us to protect the mystery of ourselves and of others. It guides our choices in clothing. Teaching young people about modesty is a means of awakening in them respect for the human person. Catholics are called to purify the social climate, challenging the communications media to show restraint and respect. Modesty leads to purity of heart, which frees us from the snares of eroticism that can dull our spiritual senses.

2. The *Catechism of the Catholic Church* identifies and describes the following as offenses against the virtue of chastity: lust, masturbation, fornication, pornography, prostitution, and rape.

3. With proper guidance by the catechist, Sharing #1 can be a powerful activity for the students. It forces them to look at premarital sex realistically and can lead to a discussion in which Christian attitudes are formed.

Centering _____

Link the last lesson with today's lesson.

- ✦ Play a contemporary song about love.
- ✦ **Most songs seem to be about a relationship between a man and a woman, but only some songs reflect true love.**
- ✦ **In the last lesson, you learned that God gave us the gift of sex so that married couples could express and deepen their love for each other and new life could be created.**
- ✦ **Today you will learn more about the appropriate use of sex.**

Sharing _____

1. Have the students read silently **A Sign of Total Surrender** on pages 130–131.
   - ✦ **With the gift of sex comes a strong sexual feeling that affects the body as well as the emotions.**

A picture, a song, or a person walking into a room can cause it. One's imagination can cause it. This feeling is part of a normal process, but needs to be controlled. What can you do? (Pray; keep occupied; think of something else; avoid anything that brings this feeling on.)

- ✦ **The message conveyed by sex or special signs of affection is "I will love you and stay with you for my whole life." But the unmarried person does not have this vow with the other person. To avoid misusing our sexual powers, we need grace. Prayer and the sacraments can help us. Talking with an adult we trust can help. So can exercise and healthy fun.**
- ✦ **When people who are not married try to cause sexual feelings in themselves or in another person, that action is wrong. For unmarried people to willfully enjoy sexual pleasure is wrong. For them to use sex or**

special signs of affection as only a husband and wife should is a lie.

- ✦ **If you really love a person, why would you choose not to pressure him or her into sex before marriage?** (out of respect so as not to use that person for one's own pleasure; to avoid not knowing that person on a deeper level than the physical level)

2. Ask a student to read aloud the first paragraph of **Who Is Boss?** on page 131.
   What are some of the reasons young people engage in sex today? (There is pressure from society; they think they are in love; they don't think they will get hurt; they want to be popular or to seem more adult.) [Have a student continue reading this section aloud.]

3. Have the students read silently **A Double Safeguard** on page 131.
   - ✦ Direct the students to answer the question. You might want to clarify these sins:

fornication—sex between persons who are unmarried

homosexual acts—sex between persons of the same sex

masturbation—causing sexual pleasure in one's own body to the point of orgasm

rape—forcing someone to have sex

✦ **What is the Sixth Commandment?** (You shall not commit adultery.)

✦ **What does *adultery* mean?** (the act of being sexually unfaithful to one's husband or wife) **Adultery and any other act contrary to God's plan for the use of sex is forbidden by this commandment, whether the act is performed alone or with another person.**

✦ **What is the Ninth Commandment?** (You shall not covet your neighbor's wife.) **What does this mean?** (God wants us to respect the gift of sex in our thoughts and desires.)

✦ **Often on TV and in movies, premarital sex, which is sex before marriage, and sex outside of marriage don't seem to hurt anyone. Why is this portrayal unrealistic?**

✦ **Research shows that if a person has premarital sex, that person is more likely to break up with his or her partner before marriage, get a divorce, commit adultery, or be less satisfied with a married sex life.**

4. Lead the students in prayer, using **A Moment with Jesus** on page 131. Allow sufficient time for silent reflection.

5. Ask a student to read aloud **Perfect Love** on page 132.

✦ **Jesus taught us by his words and example to be chaste, to become the best we can become. What is the virtue of chastity?** (a habit by which we show respect for our God-given power to bring life into the world)

✦ **When does God intend sex to be used?** (in the married state by wife and husband)

---

things for the purpose for which they were intended.

The same principle applies to the use of our sexual power. The gift of sex comes with instructions, but many people ignore them. Those people learn the hard way that our happiness in this life and in the life to come depends on using God's gifts correctly.

The gift of sex, the gift of self, is far more precious than any material object. It is a gift that must be treasured and saved for marriage. The only love that this gift can honestly express is the total surrender of a man and woman who are united together in marriage and committed to support each other, no matter what. Sex expresses the complete self-lessness and oneness of married couples. It signifies a deep, faithful love. To use it in any other way cheapens it.

Who Is Boss?

The sexual drive is very powerful. Using sex for purposes for which it was not intended is like playing with dynamite. People who have sex outside of marriage risk contracting sexually transmitted diseases. They may suffer psychological damage that marks them for life and harms their marriage. Many young people who have sex wish they had not. Why do you think young people engage in sex today?

Each person faces the challenge of learning to control his or her sexual drive. Otherwise that drive will begin to control the person. What does that mean? It is like riding a bike down a steep hill in the city and discovering that the brakes do not work. The bike is taking you right into heavy traffic! You want to be in control of your thoughts, words, and actions—your human powers. God teaches you what to do and gives you the grace to do it. Jesus was once an adolescent too. He understands the changes you are going through and sees you learning to deal with the ups and downs of life.

One way to keep your sexual drive in control is to participate in good activities such as sports, hobbies, or service. Some other ways to protect your intimate center are modesty, patience, decency, and good judgment.

A Moment with Jesus

Sex is a precious gift of love from God. Like any gift, it is a reflection of the giver. Pause and reflect for a moment on the faithful love of God for you.

Then think of the married couples you know. As you imagine each one, ask God to bless them and help them to grow in love of him and of each other.

A Double Safeguard

God gave us two commandments to safeguard the sacred gift of sex: the Sixth Commandment, *You shall not commit adultery,* and the Ninth Commandment, *You shall not covet your neighbor's wife.*

In the Sixth Commandment, God forbids any sexual act that is contrary to the sacredness of marriage. That includes **adultery**, the act of being sexually unfaithful to one's husband or wife, as well as artificial means of birth control and same-sex unions. Any violation of God's plan for the use of sex, either alone or with someone else, is wrong.

God wants us to respect sex, not only in our words and actions but also in our thoughts and desires. God tells us that in the Ninth Commandment. As all God's laws do, these two commandments protect us from hurting ourselves and others. What problems and heartaches result from not following them?

Commitments are broken; people are betrayed,

hurt, and angered; families are destroyed;

children are harmed; the community is

weakened; people lose self-respect; sexual

diseases are transmitted.

✦ **Who must practice chastity?** (all people whether married or not) **How do married people practice chastity?** (by being faithful to their marriage partners) **How do unmarried people practice chastity?** (They abstain from sex completely.)

✦ **Sometimes people have engaged in sexual behavior before they knew it was wrong. If they didn't realize it was wrong at the time, it was not a sin.**

6. Discuss with the students Scripture's teaching on chastity.

✦ Have a volunteer read aloud Matthew 5:27–28 to find Jesus' teaching about adultery.

✦ **What does Jesus teach about adultery in Matthew's Gospel?** (If we look at another person with lust, we have committed adultery in our heart.)

✦ Have a volunteer read 1 Corinthians 6:19–20 to hear Saint Paul's teaching on why we are chaste.

✦ **What reasons does Saint Paul give for being chaste?** (Our bodies are the temples of the Holy Spirit. We are not our own property but have been purchased for God.)

✦ **When did we become the temples of the Holy Spirit?** (at Baptism) **Why are we not our own property?** (God created us. Adam and Eve sinned. Jesus redeemed us by his sufferings and Death on the Cross.)

Acting

 Lead the students in prayer. [Light the candle.]

✦ Direct the students to let the flame help them focus their attention.

✦ **Father, you have created us, giving us life through our parents, and you have watched over us all these years. You see us growing and changing according to your plan. Help us to accept and love ourselves and your plan for us. Help us to reverence the life-giving mystery of our sexual power. We ask this in Jesus' name. Amen.**

✦ Allow time for silent reflection.

CHECKPOINT

• Were the learning outcomes achieved?

Perfect Love

The Sixth and Ninth Commandments call us to practice the virtue of chastity. Chastity helps us to integrate our sexuality with our spiritual nature. It helps us to be completely human, able to give to others our whole life and love. A chaste person recognizes that our power to bring new life into the world should be used only by husband and wife and according to the divine plan. All people are called to practice chastity. For married people, chastity is being faithful to their partner. For unmarried people, it means forgoing the use of the power of sex completely.

Christ challenges us to become perfect as our heavenly Father is perfect. To mirror God's perfect love, we must be pure in our thoughts, words, and actions. We must be like Christ, our model of chastity.

If you really believed that God is within you, would you have sex outside of marriage?

Breaking Through Illusions

Which line segment is longer?

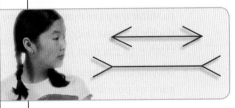

The line segments are equal. Were you fooled by this optical illusion? A design can appear to be something it is not. Illusions are not only found in designs, but also in ideas and opinions. Whenever an idea appears appealing but is contrary to God's plan, it offers only an illusion of goodness. It is a trap.

Do Not Be Fooled

Many TV shows, videos, Web sites and maybe even the lifestyle of some of your friends and neighbors show that many people do not recognize the true value of the gift of sex. They act on illusions such as the following:

• Using sexual powers can prove love and popularity.

• Sex may be used for entertainment.

• Using language that makes fun of sex is adult behavior.

Why are these ideas based on illusions?

Planning for Real Love

Here is a plan to help Christians of all ages break through illusions about the gift of sex. Use the word box to complete the plan.

chaste	loved by God	modesty
	self-control	values

1. Decide to reverence yourself and all you have been given by God. You are valuable and very precious because you are ___loved by God___.

2. Discipline yourself. Do not always choose the easy way. Strong, unselfish people show ___self-control___.

3. Use common sense. Reading books, watching movies and TV programs and visiting Web sites that have a respectful attitude toward sex will help you to be ___chaste___.

4. By dressing, speaking, and acting in a way that shows you respect yourself and others, you will be practicing ___modesty___.

5. Develop healthy friendships with people who agree with your ___values___.

Day Three Attitudes Toward Love and Sex Student pages 132–133

LEARNING OUTCOME

The students will be able to

• identify and use aids such as prayer, the sacraments, and self-discipline to live a chaste life.

Materials

• Ruler
• BLM 60
• Reflection notebooks

Before You Begin

For Sharing #2, you might add situations that are particularly relevant to your class.

Centering

1. Direct the students to look at the line segments on page 132. **Which line is longer?** (They are the same length.)

2. Have a student read aloud **Breaking Through Illusions** on page 132.

   ✦ **What is an optical illusion?** (something that looks different from what it really is)

   ✦ **How can an idea be an illusion?** (It can appear appealing but not be according to God's plan.)

✦ Today you will see how some people act based on illusions about sex and how you can avoid being tricked.

Sharing _____

1. Call on a student to read aloud **Do Not Be Fooled** on page 132.

   Ask volunteers to explain each illusion.

   1. **Use of sex doesn't prove love. In marriage, sex expresses a permanent commitment of love that is already there. Pressuring someone to sin shows a lack of real love. Someone who is thought of as sexy is not necessarily more popular. Physical appearance is only a very small part of the total person.**

   2. **To think it is all right to use sex for entertainment is false. The gift of sex and its accompanying feelings are good within marriage. Just as rain is good until it causes a flood and destroys people and property, so sex, if not used according to God's plan, will gradually destroy a person.**

   3. **Using language that makes fun of sex is not adult behavior. Mature Christians respect the gift of sex too much to do anything like this. Why would some boys or girls use this kind of language?** (to get attention, to show off, to gain friends)

2. Read and discuss the following situations with the students.

   ✦ **Here are some situations where sexuality is used incorrectly.**

   ✦ **Jenny went to a party with her friends. Josh tried to persuade her to sit next to him. Jenny knew that when Josh sat next to girls, he spent his time hugging and kissing them. So Jenny would not join him.**

   ✦ **Why would this take courage for Jenny?**

   ✦ **Why do you think Josh treats girls this way?** (He is seeking his own pleasure and does not respect girls.)

✦ **One day Justin brings pornographic pictures from the Internet into the cafeteria. Suddenly he is quite popular with the boys in his class. Now he wants to bring in pornographic pictures more often.**

✦ **Why are pornographic pictures, Web sites, and magazines harmful?** (They use sex for entertainment and cause sexual feelings. Pornography treats people as objects.)

✦ **What helpful advice would you give Justin?** (Tell him it is wrong to make fun of sex and there are better ways to make friends.)

✦ **Lauren and Stephanie want their youth group to accept them and to think they are mature, so they decide to wear sexy, revealing clothes to the next meeting.**

✦ **Do you think these girls have a good or poor image of themselves?** (poor image because they lack confidence; otherwise they would not try to be something they are not)

✦ **What probably influenced them to wear sexy, revealing clothes?** (TV, music, fashion magazines, other girls, their desire to be accepted and to appear mature)

✦ **How could they grow in respect for themselves and become really mature?** (by thinking positively about themselves, by wearing modest clothes even when others do not)

✦ **What does it mean to dress modestly?** (to dress in a way that does not draw attention to oneself or one's sex)

3. Discuss with the students chastity and ways to practice it. [Write *chastity* on the board.]

   ✦ **Through Baptism, Christians are given the courage and self-control to lead lives modeled on Jesus. You need to practice soccer to become a good player. You also need to practice courage and self-control to live a chaste life.**

✦ **Chastity helps a person grow in all areas of love. People who are not controlled in matters of sex will never be able to love on the deepest level. Sex is only one part of love. A person who sees it as the only part cannot mature in all the other areas of love. His or her approach to others is "I need you for sex. I don't care about you as a person."**

✦ **Unselfish love wants the best for the one we love. Therefore, we reverence the one we love and encourage him or her to stay chaste. This love also increases reverence for ourselves. Each chaste act shapes us as strong, honest, caring individuals. Chastity increases our ability to love.**

4. Have the students complete the activity **Planning for Real Love** on page 132.

5. Choose or let the students choose an activity from Reach Out on page 133.

Acting _____

1. **BLM 60** Distribute BLM 60 **Knowing How to Say No.**

   Have the students work on the BLM individually and then discuss their responses.

2. Direct the students to do the Respond activity on page 133.

   Allow time for silent reflection.

CHECKPOINT

- Was the learning outcome achieved?

- Have the students shown that they can distinguish between Christian values and societal values of sex?

- Is there a topic in this lesson that needs more guidance? If so, how can you provide it?

LEARNING OUTCOMES

The students will be able to

- review the decision-making process.
- use the decision-making process to make moral decisions related to sex.
- demonstrate an understanding of the key concepts in this chapter.

Materials

- BLM 61
- BLM 62 Quiz
- Paper

Before You Begin

1. Adolescence is an age of extremes in moods, behavior, and goals. Many of the troubled situations in which the students find themselves are caused by their moods and their inability to distinguish between what they feel like doing and what they should do. While catechists can sympathize with the struggles and the confusion, they must also provide guidelines for helping the students make decisions.

2. When planning today's lesson, keep in mind that Day Four is when the students take the quiz for this chapter. Reserve time at the end of class for this assessment. The quiz can also be administered on Day Five.

CHAPTER 16   Summary

Remember

What is the purpose of the Sixth and Ninth Commandments?
The purpose of the Sixth and Ninth Commandments is to protect marriage, the family, and the sacred gift of sex.

In God's plan, when is the gift of sex to be used?
In God's plan, the gift of sex is reserved for use in marriage.

What does the virtue of chastity help us to do?
The virtue of chastity helps us to integrate our sexuality with our spiritual nature. All people are called to practice chastity.

Respond

Choose a point in the plan on page 132. In your reflection notebook, list specific actions and practical ways that you will carry out the point. Then write a note to Jesus, asking him to help you, particularly if there is a situation or a person bothering you.

Reach Out

1. Get together with one of your friends and share some ways you can support each other in practicing chastity. After your conversation, write in your reflection notebook. Make two columns. In one column, list the ways you asked your friend to support you. In the other column, list the ways your friend asked you for support.

2. Choose a popular song that you think expresses the values of Christian love. Reflect on why it shows Jesus' view of love and how living this song can make you a better person.

3. Research devotions to the Sacred Heart of Jesus. Use prayer books, Catholic encyclopedias, or the Internet to find information about where and when the devotion began, artwork associated with the Sacred Heart, religious orders dedicated to the Sacred Heart, and novenas, litanies, and other prayers to the Sacred Heart.

Word to Know
adultery

The Sacred Heart of Jesus. ❯

(133)

Centering

1. Present Jesus as a model in making decisions.
   - ✦ Jesus really enjoyed nature, people, and parties, but he wanted to make decisions that pleased his Father. He never went to extremes with pleasure.
   - ✦ Like Jesus, we need to make decisions that allow us to enjoy life, but that also please God, our Father. We will then keep a balance that will lead to inner peace and happiness.

2. Discuss making decisions with the students.
   - ✦ What are some decisions you had to make today?
   - ✦ Sometimes in our lives we have to make tough decisions.
   - ✦ Today you will review a decision-making process and see how it can help you make good decisions regarding sex.

Sharing

1. **BLM 61** Distribute copies of BLM 61 **Decisions Needed.**

- ✦ This decision-making process is designed to help you make mature Christian decisions. The various parts of the process give guidelines to help you make decisions in your lives.

- ✦ We will work through the first problem together. [Have a student read aloud the problem.]

- ✦ **What is the problem that Justin faces?** (whether to attend the X-rated movie or not) [Write the problem on the board.]

- ✦ **Think of as many solutions or options to this problem as you can.** [Point out the section marked *Options*. Write three options on the board. Then have the students choose the one that appears best.]

- ✦ Let's consider the pros and cons involved with this choice by answering the various questions under the section that is labeled *Consequences*.

- ✦ Our final step will be to consider the option based on our *Values* and answer the two questions. We will assume that Justin sincerely tries to follow Jesus.

    1. Will this option express Justin's values?

    2. Will Justin be proud of himself if he makes this decision?

- ✦ Having considered all the consequences, do you think Justin should choose this option? Why or why not?

2. Divide the students into groups of four or five.

    - ✦ Have the students work out the other problem in their groups using the decision-making process.

    - ✦ Choose one student from each group to write down the group's decisions, explaining what should be done and why. Have the groups present their findings.

3. Lead the students through the Summary and Review Activities, pages 133–134.
At the end of class, have the students tear out the pages to take home.

CHAPTER **16** Review Activities

What Is Dangerous? When are sexually tempting situations dangerous? Rate each of the following situations. Color the traffic light RED if the situation is so dangerous you should stop it. Color it YELLOW if it is somewhat dangerous and you should proceed with caution. Color it GREEN if it is safe to go ahead without being sexually tempted.

Situation	Rating
1. Using drugs	R
2. Attending a party without adult supervision	Y
3. Going on a group date	G
4. Being alone with a person of the opposite sex at your house when nobody else is home	R
5. Being alone with a person of the opposite sex in a movie theater	Y
6. Going to a supervised party	G
7. Attending a school dance with friends	G
8. Going to a basketball game with a person of the opposite sex	G
9. Walking home after school with a person of the opposite sex	G
10. Meeting a person of the opposite sex at the park late at night	R
11. Meeting a person of the opposite sex at a restaurant	G
12. Drinking alcohol	R

Reprinted by permission from Junior High Ministry Magazine, copyright 1987, Group Publishing, Box 481, Loveland, CO 80539.

True or False Write T if the statement is true or F if it is false.

- T **1.** Sexuality is our maleness or femaleness.
- F **2.** If a marriage does not work out, a Catholic couple may divorce and remarry.
- T **3.** Sex is sacred.
- T **4.** Sex outside of marriage is wrong and harmful.
- F **5.** Some people do not have to practice chastity.
- T **6.** Through sex, men and women cooperate with God in the act of creation.
- T **7.** The love between a married man and woman is a symbol of the love of Christ for us.

(134)

4. **BLM 62** Distribute and administer BLM 62 **Chapter 16 Quiz.**
Use this opportunity to assess the students' understanding of the main concepts in the chapter. If there is not sufficient time for the students to complete the quiz, consider moving it to Day Five.

Acting

1. Apply the decision-making process to the students' lives.
    - ✦ **Think of a situation in your own life that calls for a decision. Use this decision-making process to help you make that decision.**
    - ✦ **Remember, God does not force you to do the right thing. God**

trusts you to use your mind and heart to make the right decisions and carry them out.

2. Pray together the Prayer to the Holy Spirit on the inside back cover of the student book. [See page T446.]

CHECKPOINT ✓

- Were the learning outcomes achieved?

- Were the students able to arrive at decisions that reflected Christian values?

- Did the students interact in a respectful manner?

Gather and Go Forth

Lead students through pages 135–136 in the student book. Find catechist instruction on T346–T347.
Materials: Bibles

Use the following suggestions to create an additional lesson for Day Five.

1. Remind the students to take home pages 133–134 to share what they are learning with their families.

2. Incorporate any unused BLMs from the week's chapter.

3. Consider the time of the liturgical year and use the appropriate Special Seasons and Lessons. SSLs begin on page T369.

4. Visit www.christourlife.com to find additional activities for Extending the Chapter.

5. Use activities from Enriching the Faith Experience.

6. Guide the students in a prayerful discussion of Sunday's Scripture readings. Visit www.christourlife.com for more information.

Chapter 16   Enriching the Faith Experience

Use the following activities to enrich a lesson or to replace an activity with one that better meets the needs of your class.

1. Have the students design ads that encourage loving on the deepest level or ads saying no to premarital sex. Show them ads from magazines and the Internet. Note eye-catching words, designs, and the use of color. Ask the students to think of catchy captions and write them on the board. Then have them design their ad.

2. Help the students compose a 60-second radio or video commercial promoting selfless love.

3. Have the students use the Internet to research devotion to the Sacred Heart. Some ways to approach the research are listed below.

   Locate references to God's love for us in Scripture. Find out about the Mass for the Solemnity of the Sacred Heart, the Litany of the Sacred Heart, Pope Pius XII's encyclical on the Sacred Heart, Saint Margaret Mary's contribution to devotion to the Sacred Heart, and the enthronement of the Sacred Heart in the home.

4. Write this chart on the board, which shows how habits are formed.

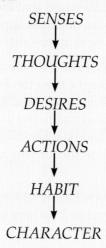

SENSES

↓

THOUGHTS

↓

DESIRES

↓

ACTIONS

↓

HABIT

↓

CHARACTER

Point to each word as you mention it. Explain that what comes through our senses is translated into thoughts. The thoughts create desires, which lead to actions. Repeated actions develop into a habit that builds a part of the character. Then have students compose a paragraph on the topic "You Are What You Think."

5. Have the students use cartoons, headlines, and ads from magazines or the Internet to make a collage that presents a true image of love.

6. Have the students keep a record of TV programs they watch for a week. Or have them analyze current movies, using a chart similar to the following:

	Monday	Tuesday
Name of Show		
Type		
Main Characters		
Attitude toward Love		
Explanation		

7. Make a PowerPoint presentation analyzing the lyrics of a contemporary song about love. Ask a student to compose and read an opening prayer before the presentation. After the presentation, allow time for the students to meditate silently on how they can apply the ideas to their own lives.

8. Have students gather information from the Internet on Covenant House, a shelter for runaway teenagers. Discuss the reasons why teens run away and the possible dangers they face.

9. The image of marriage given in the student book is of two streams flowing into one river. Have the students compose a booklet of reverent images of marriage taken from Scripture, poetry, or songs. Suggest that they discuss this with their parents.
✝ *Family and Community*

Unit 2 Review

Faith Focus
Jesus teaches us the truth that we can live by.

Reflecting on the Faith Experience

Take a few moments to reflect prayerfully before preparing the lesson.

Listening

No one patches an old cloak with a piece of unshrunken cloth, for its fullness pulls away from the cloak and the tear gets worse. People do not put new wine into old wineskins. Otherwise the skins burst, the wine spills out, and the skins are ruined. Rather, they pour new wine into fresh wineskins, and both are preserved.

Matthew 9:16–17

Reflecting

Jesus' words in Matthew describe his own teaching of the truth. New life could not be given to the old order merely by patching; that would only weaken it. Jesus raised the whole law to a new plane. He did not destroy the old wineskin, but he brought the new wineskin, the new order of living, that preserved all that was good, universal, and life-giving. His was a radical morality demanding that those who claim to belong to the Father demonstrate it by their mercy and their love. His was the radical morality of the new spirit of the Kingdom of God.

Unit 2, Jesus Christ the Truth, presented the law of love that prevails in this kingdom. In a world that depends so much on reasonableness, the path of Christ appears to be folly. Love is unreasonable. In a world that depends so much on narrow views of justice, the demands of Christ appear immoderate. Love is merciful. In a world that idolizes self, the ways of Christ appear insane. Love is other-centered.

Following Christ the Way demands that we accept Christ the Truth. Living the truth will lead to suffering and death. But in Christ, suffering and death lead to life— eternal life in the kingdom.

How open am I to the new and perhaps surprising ways Jesus may be asking me to show love?

Do I take time to evaluate the direction my life is taking based on my daily actions?

Responding

Spirit of Truth, deepen my students' understanding of the truths of our faith.

Scripture for Further Reflection

Luke 12:32 The Father has given the kingdom to the followers of Christ.

John 14:14–21 The Father and the Son make their home with those who love God and keep God's Word.

Preparing for the Faith Experience

Scripture in This Chapter

Psalm 25 Prayer for Forgiveness and Guidance

Matthew 13:44–46
The Buried Treasure

John 4:24 God is Spirit.

Church Documents

Catechism of the Catholic Church.
The themes of this chapter correspond to the following paragraphs: **459, 638.**

Dogmatic Constitution on the Church #3–6 (Second Vatican Council). The coming of the kingdom, prepared for in the Old Testament by signs and symbols, was fulfilled in the coming of Christ. Those who follow Christ and believe "have truly received the kingdom."

Dogmatic Constitution on the Church #8 (Second Vatican Council). The Church is a community of faith, hope, and love, but it is also a visible organization through which Christ communicates truth and grace to everyone.

Dogmatic Constitution on the Church #30–36 (Second Vatican Council). The faithful must support one another in the journey to greater holiness and further the plan of all creation to the praise of God. They are called to bring the values of the kingdom to the world today.

In All Things Charity (USCCB). The Kingdom of God belongs to those who are poor and lowly and to everyone who stands with them, shows mercy to them, and hungers and thirsts for justice.

Gather and Go Forth

Find catechist instruction for Gather and Go Forth student pages 143–144 on T348–T349.

Enriching the Faith Experience

Use the activities at the end of the chapter to enrich a lesson or to replace an activity with one that better meets the needs of your class.

LEARNING OUTCOMES

The students will be able to

- explain what it means to live in truth.

- evaluate how they live the message of Jesus.

- review important concepts from the unit.

Materials

- Seven 2-by-9-inch strips of stiff paper for each student (The strips should be of various colors light enough to write on.)

- Crayons or felt-tipped pens

- Reflective background music for Acting (optional)

Before You Begin

You might have the students make a tower (see Sharing #3) for Unit 1, Jesus Christ the Way, and for Unit 3, Jesus Christ the Life. It will serve as a summary of the entire course on Jesus.

Centering

Link the topics of Unit 2 Jesus Christ the Way to today's lesson.

- **In Unit 2, you learned what it means to be a disciple. You learned how a disciple serves the kingdom from what Jesus told us in the parables.**

- **You learned the Beatitudes which teach us about how we are to be in the world as Christ's disciples.**

- **You learned that our faith calls us to respect life, people, and property and to cherish the gift of sex.**

- **In essence, you learned the foundation for living a Christian life.**

- **Today you will build a tower on that foundation helping you to understand what it means to be a disciple of Jesus Christ the Truth.**

Sharing

1. Ask the students to read silently **Looking Back** on page 137. Allow time for the students to answer the questions. Divide the students into groups of three or four to share their answers.

2. Have the students complete the **Personal Inventory** activity on page 137.
   - Discuss with the students how Jesus' principles are influencing their lives.
   - **How are the truths of Jesus influencing your decisions and actions?**

3. Direct the students in constructing a Words to Live By tower.
   - Give each student seven strips of paper. These correspond to the seven chapters in the unit.
   - Read aloud the following directions:
   - **Fold over one end of each strip half an inch. Cut off the corners of this end to make a flap. Fold**

   each strip of paper into three even pieces up to the flap.
   - **While the paper is folded, cut a rectangle about 1 ½-by-¼ inches from the top and bottom, leaving room for writing.**

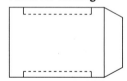

   - **Open the strips. Using a strip for each chapter, write in the center of a section (1) a summary sentence; (2) something special you recall from the chapter, perhaps from your reflection notebook; and (3) a resolution or prayer that refers to the chapter.**
   - **Decorate the sections.**

- **Glue the flap of each section and stack the sections to form a tower.**

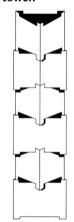

Acting

Invite the students to read silently Ephesians 4:15 on page 137.

- Using their answers to the Personal Inventory, have the students reflect on how they are growing in every way into him who is the head, Christ.

- Allow sufficient time for silent reflection.

CHECKPOINT

- Were the learning outcomes achieved?

LEARNING OUTCOMES

The students will be able to

- recall the significant facts and basic concepts introduced in Unit 2, Jesus Christ the Truth.
- list behaviors that show an appreciation of the values of the Kingdom of God.

Materials

- Bibles or New Testaments
- Paper
- Drawing paper
- Crayons or markers
- Examples of mandalas (optional)

Before You Begin

You may wish to assign the activities in the student book as homework and then in class use some of the livelier review activities listed under Enriching the Faith Experience.

Centering _____

Call on a student to read Ephesians 4:15 from page 137.

- ✦ In this unit, you have learned about the truths of Christ so that you can live by them.
- ✦ Today you will continue reviewing the main ideas of the unit.

CHAPTER 17   Unit 2 Review

Jesus Christ the Truth

Looking Back

In Unit 2, you have looked at some of the values and demands of Christian living. You have learned that Jesus calls you to live in his truth. He has called you to serve the kingdom. Your attitudes, thoughts, and actions should show that you know what it means to serve the kingdom. Jesus asks you to base your decisions on God's law and on his example. He challenges you to respect life, to respect people and property, to live honestly, and to cherish the gift of sex.

Ask yourself these questions. Write your answers in your reflection notebook.

1. How has this unit helped me understand what Jesus asks of those who follow him?

2. What do I need to remember when I am tempted or when others make it difficult for me to do the right thing?

3. What practical steps can I take to live the life of a disciple?

> Rather, living the truth in love, we should grow in every way into him who is the head, Christ.
>
> Ephesians 4:15

Personal Inventory

How well do you let the principles Jesus taught guide your judgments and direct your actions? Circle **u** (usually), **o** (often), or **s** (seldom).

1. Do you think of what Jesus would want you to do or say in situations?
   u   o   s

2. Do you go to people you respect for advice?
   u   o   s

3. Do you see that little things in life (at home, at school) are opportunities to show respect for others and for property?
   u   o   s

4. Do you go out of your way to serve others?
   u   o   s

(137)

Reviewing

1. Have the students complete the activities **Parable Truths** and **Change Your Attitude!** on page 138.
What are some of the ways you are living the Beatitudes now?

2. Direct the students in the following word game:
   + **Now you will see where living the Beatitudes leads.** [Read aloud the directions.]
   + **Write the word *Beatitudes* on a sheet of paper.**
   + **Take off the first two letters and double the last.**
   + **Reverse the *IT* and change the *T*s to *P*s.**
   + **Remove the *U*.**
   + **Add the eighth letter of the alphabet to the beginning.**
   + **Change the *D* to *N*.**
   (The letters should spell *happiness*.)

3. Divide the class into groups. Assign a problem in **Help Wanted** on page 138 to each group.
   + Have the groups discuss the situations and present their solutions to the class, perhaps in the form of a skit.
   + After each group has presented, give the students time to write their answers to the personal questions.

4. Divide the class into pairs. Have them complete **Puzzling Possibilities** on page 139.

Acting

 Guide the students to pray using a mandala.
   + **A mandala is a geometric design in a circle that is used in Buddhism and Hinduism as an aid to meditation.** [Show examples if possible.]
   + **Think of a teaching of Jesus that you studied in this unit.**

UNIT 2 REVIEW

Parable Truths

Which parable do the type of people listed need to hear? Write the letter of the parable on the line.

___b___ 1. Envious or greedy   a. The Rich Man and Lazarus (Luke 16:19–31)

___d___ 2. Careless about using gifts   b. The Workers in the Vineyard (Matthew 20:1–16)

___a___ 3. Selfish, uncaring   c. The Unforgiving Servant (Matthew 18:21–35)

___c___ 4. Holds grudges   d. The Talents (Matthew 25:14–30)

Change Your Attitude!

Fill in the blanks with a key word from a beatitude.

PEACEMAKERS

THIRST FOR RIGHT

CHRISTLIKE

MERCIFUL

CLEAN OF HEART

MOURN

PERSECUTED

MEEK

POOR IN SPIRIT

How can you live a beatitude in your present situation?

Answers will vary.

Help Wanted

How would you respond to the following letters? Write your answers on a sheet of paper.

Help! I was with a group of friends at the mall yesterday, and before I left I stole a calculator.

Help! My mom and I argue constantly. She never really understands and won't let me do anything.

Help! My friends and I had been sneaking beer from our parents. I decided to stop and told my parents what I had done. They have called the parents of all my friends and told them about it.

Help! I am in junior high and I have been going to many parties with Pat. I know we are getting too serious and I am really worried about this.

Now switch. Imagine yourself in one of the situations. What would you do in each situation? How do you wish you could handle such situations?

(138)

+ **Draw a large circle on drawing paper and in it, draw something that stands for that teaching.**
+ **As you look at your mandala, talk to Jesus about how you will try to live by that teaching.**

 CHECKPOINT

- Were the learning outcomes achieved?
- Do the students seem prepared to take the unit test?

LEARNING OUTCOME

The students will be able to

- demonstrate an understanding of the key concepts in Unit 2, Jesus Christ the Truth.

Materials

- BLM 63A–B
- Reflection notebooks or Scripture booklets (optional)

Before You Begin

Students who finish the test early may review their reflection notebooks or read some citations from pages 9–10 of their Scripture booklets.

Testing _____

BLM 63A–B Administer BLM 63A–B **Unit 2 Test**.

CHECKPOINT

- Was the learning outcome achieved?
- Judging from the test results, which concepts need clarification?

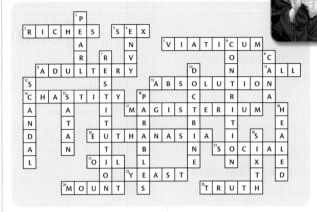

Puzzling Possibilities

Fill in the puzzle.

Across

2. What the young man had that Jesus said makes it difficult to get into heaven

3. Gift from God to create life

5. Communion for a dying person

9. Sexual unfaithfulness to a spouse

11. Who the kingdom is open to

13. The pardon of our sins in the Sacrament of Reconciliation

14. Virtue by which we respect our sexual power

17. Teaching authority of the Church

19. Mercy-killing

21. Kind of sin that is an evil in an institution or a situation and that everyone in society is responsible for changing

22. Used in the Anointing of the Sick

23. Subject of a parable that tells of the growth of the kingdom

24. Site of the Beatitudes, according to Matthew

25. What Jesus is the source of as a guide for us in life

Down

1. Subject of a parable about the kingdom's value

4. Feeling deprived or sad because of something another person has or has achieved

6. True sorrow for sin

7. Repairing or paying for property stolen or damaged

8. Place of the first miracle

10. Belief taught by the Church as true

12. Bad example

15. The evil one that Jesus overcame

16. Stories Jesus told about God and the kingdom

18. What Jesus did for people out of compassion

20. Commandment that protects marriage and the family

(139)

LEARNING OUTCOMES

The students will be able to

- demonstrate a deeper appreciation of the truths Jesus has revealed.
- express a Gospel teaching in art.
- participate in the experience of communal prayer.

Materials

- One 7-by-12-inch sheet of aluminum foil for each student
- Two songs and reflective music for the celebration
- Table or bulletin-board to display artwork the from prayer activity
- Reflection notebooks

Before You Begin

Take time before the celebration to prepare the students for the prayer activity. Have the aluminum foil available. Point out the part of the celebration where they will do the art activity. Remind the students that it is part of the prayer and it will be done in silence. Show the students where to place their artwork when they finish.

UNIT 2 REVIEW

Celebrating

Jesus Christ the Truth

Opening Song

Leader: Let us praise God, who guides us through life.

All: Amen.

Leader: Each of us is on a journey. As we follow Jesus Christ, the Way, we discover what it means for us to live in truth. Jesus Christ, the Truth, is our model. Let us pause and reflect on how we witness to his truth.

Reader 1: A reading from the holy Gospel according to Matthew. (Matthew 13:44–46)

The kingdom of heaven is like a treasure buried in a field, which a person finds and hides again, and out of joy goes and sells all that he has and buys that field. Again, the kingdom of heaven is like a merchant searching for fine pearls. When he finds a pearl of great price, he goes and sells all that he has and buys it.

The gospel of the Lord.

All: Praise to you, Lord Jesus Christ.

Leader: Let us pause for a moment of silence and reflect on what we just heard.

What are you willing to do in order to make following Jesus a priority in your life?

Time for personal reflection

Leader: Christ Jesus, you are the Truth. You have enlightened our minds and touched our hearts.

Side 1: Thank you for the truth and mysteries you have revealed to us.

Side 2: May we grow in understanding your teachings, the teachings of the Church.

Side 1: Thank you for your parables.

Side 2: May we take their lessons to heart and serve your kingdom.

Side 1: Thank you for your miracles.

Side 2: May we always look to you for healing in our lives.

(140)

Centering

Discuss with the students their favorite Gospel teaching.

- ✦ **What is your favorite Gospel teaching?** (could be a parable or a miracle story) **Why is this your favorite?**
- ✦ **What does this Gospel teaching tell you about the teachings of Jesus?**

Celebrating

1. Prepare the students for the prayer celebration.
   - ✦ **Today you will have an opportunity to express your gratitude to God for revealing his truths through Jesus.**

- ✦ **The celebration, Jesus Christ the Truth, is on pages 140–141 of your book. During the course of the celebration, you will focus on one teaching and speak to Jesus about it.**

- ✦ Choose one student to be the Reader. Divide the students into two groups: Side 1 and Side 2. Practice the songs that will be sung.

2. Hold the celebration. Remind students that this is prayer.

3. Ask the students for their reactions to the celebration.

Acting

1. Have several students read aloud **A Junior High Student**

Puts Faith into Action on page 142.
How is Maggie living out the truths Jesus taught? [Explore with the students opportunities for service in your area.]

2. Divide the class into two groups to work on **A Treasure for the Daring** on page 142. Hold a contest to see who can be the first group to decipher the passage.

CHECKPOINT ✓

- Was the learning outcome achieved?

Day Five   Extending the Chapter

Gather and Go Forth

Lead students through pages 143–144 in the student book. Find catechist instruction on T348–T349.

Use the following suggestions to create an additional lesson for Day Five.

1. Remind the students to take home pages 138–142 to share what they are learning with their families.

2. Incorporate any unused BLMs from the week's chapter.

3. Consider the time of the liturgical year and use the appropriate Special Seasons and Lessons. SSLs begin on page T369.

4. Visit www.christourlife.com to find additional activities for Extending the Chapter.

5. Use activities from Enriching the Faith Experience.

6. Guide the students in a prayerful discussion of Sunday's Scripture readings. Visit www.christourlife.com for more information.

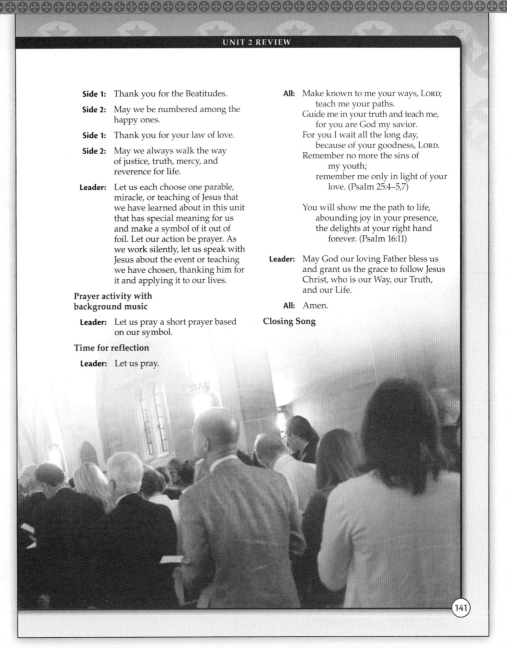

Side 1: Thank you for the Beatitudes.

Side 2: May we be numbered among the happy ones.

Side 1: Thank you for your law of love.

Side 2: May we always walk the way of justice, truth, mercy, and reverence for life.

Leader: Let us each choose one parable, miracle, or teaching of Jesus that we have learned about in this unit that has special meaning for us and make a symbol of it out of foil. Let our action be prayer. As we work silently, let us speak with Jesus about the event or teaching we have chosen, thanking him for it and applying it to our lives.

Prayer activity with background music

Leader: Let us pray a short prayer based on our symbol.

Time for reflection

Leader: Let us pray.

All: Make known to me your ways, LORD; teach me your paths.
Guide me in your truth and teach me, for you are God my savior.
For you I wait all the long day, because of your goodness, LORD.
Remember no more the sins of my youth;
remember me only in light of your love. (Psalm 25:4–5,7)

You will show me the path to life, abounding joy in your presence, the delights at your right hand forever. (Psalm 16:11)

Leader: May God our loving Father bless us and grant us the grace to follow Jesus Christ, who is our Way, our Truth, and our Life.

All: Amen.

Closing Song

(141)

Chapter 17   Enriching the Faith Experience

Use the following activities to enrich a lesson or to replace an activity with one that better meets the needs of your class.

1. Review vocabulary by playing Beat the Clock. Allow five minutes for students to review words in this unit. Tell them they will try to beat the clock as they match words with definitions. Have them close their books. Then recite a series of definitions at a steady pace for a set time (30 seconds or a minute). Do not repeat any definitions. As students hear a definition, they should write the word being defined. Check their responses. Continue until all important words are reviewed.

2. Have the students create a video, computer slide show, play, puppet show, or PowerPoint presentation of any of the topics covered in this unit. The Sermon on the Mount contains many possibilities for creative interpretation.

3. Play It's Academic to review the unit. Prepare, or have students prepare, questions with one- or two-word answers for each chapter. Put these in envelopes with the chapters clearly marked. Divide the class into three teams. Appoint a timekeeper and a scorekeeper. Choose three students from each team to form a panel. Have each panel choose a captain who sits in the middle. Explain that you make the final decisions on answers and procedures, and that a team that doesn't follow directions may lose five or ten points.

Chapter Enrichment

Panels may choose categories for each other. Categories should not be repeated until all have been presented.

✦ **Round 1:** Four one-minute questions are asked of a team. These may be discussed among the members, but the captain gives the final answer. The panel may pass if it does not know an answer. At the end of the round, the other teams may answer passed questions. Each correct answer earns five points. The other two teams also play for a minute.

✦ **Round 2:** This is the same as Round 1, but five points are deducted for incorrect answers. Repeat rounds with new panels.

✦ **Round 3:** Ten questions from any category may be answered by any team. The first captain to ring a bell will have the chance to answer. Correct answers are worth ten points. For incorrect answers, ten points are deducted. After an incorrect answer, the next team to ring the bell may try to answer.

4. Ask the students to consider popular songs and to explain how their message either supports or denies the teachings and values of Christ and Christian morality.

5. Let the students prepare a montage, a combined use of sound, silence, and pictures, to create a unified impression of the teachings of Jesus.

6. Tell the students to interview their parents, pastor, or others on the topic "What does it mean to be a Christian?" Have the students record the interviews on tape or video. Play a few interviews at the beginning of some classes.

A Junior High Student Puts Faith into Action

How does a young person live the message of Jesus today? For Margaret Blazunas, the 14-year-old shown here with her pastor, Father John White, S.J., following Jesus' way of love is not only fulfilling but fun.

Maggie has been volunteering at McGregor Home, a retirement community, since she was in the fifth grade. She helps the residents with crafts, takes out their curlers in the beauty shop, scoops out ice cream at the ice-cream parlor, and reads letters from their children. Maggie says that she benefits from doing these works of mercy and enjoys listening to the stories the people tell. Her life is also enriched by new friends, such as Mrs. Cooley, one of the residents.

After Maggie volunteered last summer, the director of volunteers wrote a letter to Maggie's principal. In it she expressed appreciation for the 67 hours of service that Maggie gave. She commented, "Maggie is always willing to try something new. Our residents enjoyed her enthusiastic manner. She was a joy to have here." Maggie has also worked after school at St. Patrick's Hunger Center, preparing and serving meals for people who are homeless in Cleveland, Ohio.

As the president of Student Council at Gesu School, Maggie leads the student body in service activities. The students in her school assist with doughnut Sundays at the parish and promote Red Ribbon week (a "students against drugs" program) in the school.

Why does this busy teenager make time to help others? Maggie traces her spirit of faith-in-action to her father, who is a member of the Knights of Columbus, an organization at the service of the Church. Maggie's personal convictions motivate her. She believes serving is really important. She does not see it as something she has to do in order to get service points for Confirmation. To Maggie, reaching out to others is something God wants her to do. Maggie believes that being a Catholic requires more than going to Mass. She says we have to take our faith out of the religion class and act on what we hear in the Gospels. For her, "Being a Catholic is doing what Jesus would do."

Maggie encourages other students to try volunteering now so that volunteering will become a habit they will have as adults. Besides, speaking from experience, Maggie says that when you help people in need, you feel great.

A Treasure for the Daring

Jesus promises a treasure to those who live by his truth. To discover what it is, fill in the blanks by unscrambling the letters below them. To check your answer, search John 14.

Whoever ___loves___ me will keep my ___word___ and my ___Father___ will love him,
     seovl   rdwo   reahFt

and we will ___come___ to him and ___make___ our ___dwelling___ with him.
      meco   keam   gliednlw

142

UNIT 3

Jesus Christ the Life

Goal
The students will have a greater appreciation of the life Jesus won for us by his Death and Resurrection.

18 Living Faith in Jesus
JESUS THE PROPHET
The students are made more conscious of the spiritual life and the importance of spiritual growth through two Gospel stories. They come to understand grace as a free gift of God, as friendship with him. They also reflect on the Theological Virtues of faith, hope, and love, and the cardinal virtues of prudence, justice, temperance, and fortitude.

19 Opposition to Jesus
JESUS THE SUFFERING SERVANT
The students study the mystery of the Transfiguration. They witness Jesus' power over life and death in his raising Lazarus from the dead. They consider the opposition that grew against him. They consider the Christian view of death in relation to Jesus, themselves, and those they love.

20 The Eucharist
JESUS THE BREAD OF LIFE
The students learn how Jesus continues to be present with us, drawing us deeper into the mystery of his life through the Eucharist. They reflect on the power of the Eucharist to transform us into a united people who live, serve, hope, and share as followers of Christ. The students study the parts of the Mass preparing and celebrating a Eucharistic liturgy.

21 Jesus' Final Hours
JESUS THE LAMB OF GOD
The students see in Jesus' suffering a model for their own response to suffering. They enter into a reflective prayer experience based on the agony of Jesus in the garden. They view the Cross in the light of the great love Jesus showed for his Father and

for all of us when he chose to sacrifice his life. They learn about the last things: the particular judgment, the Last Judgment, heaven, purgatory, and hell.

22 The Victory of Jesus
JESUS THE RISEN LORD
The students study the Resurrection stories and what they mean for us. They consider how we experience the risen Lord in the sacraments, Scripture, and the faith community. They learn the role of sacramentals in the Church. They come to understand the Ascension as a call to witness.

23 Alive with the Spirit
JESUS THE HEAD OF THE CHURCH
The students study the transforming power of the Holy Spirit in the life of the Church and in their own lives. They study the characteristics of the Christian community. They are encouraged to turn to the Spirit of Christ for guidance and strength as they spread the Good News and form Christian communities today.

24 Matrimony and Holy Orders
JESUS EMMANUEL
The students consider their personal call to holiness and various vocations through which Christians can become holy: the single life, the married life, the priesthood and diaconate, and the religious life. They explore how Christians in each of these vocations can share in the mission of Christ.

25 Unit 3 Review
The students review the concepts of this unit. They participate in a celebration on the journey of life as a Christian.

Living Faith in Jesus
JESUS THE PROPHET

Faith Focus
Through faith and virtue, our life of grace grows, and we become more like Jesus.

Reflecting on the Faith Experience

Take a few moments to reflect prayerfully before preparing the lesson.

Listening

For those who live according to the flesh are concerned with the things of the flesh, but those who live according to the spirit with the things of the spirit. The concern of the flesh is death, but the concern of the spirit is life and peace. For the concern of the flesh is hostility toward God; it does not submit to the law of God, nor can it; and those who are in the flesh cannot please God. But you are not in the flesh; on the contrary, you are in the spirit, if only the Spirit of God dwells in you. Whoever does not have the Spirit of Christ does not belong to him.

Romans 8:5–9

Reflecting

Imagine you are walking alone through the crowded streets of a city. People are everywhere. Some smile; some do not. You journey from one side of town to the other. At the end, you might feel a sense of loneliness, isolation, or emptiness. Imagine taking that same walk with one person you love. Then, even if the streets are deserted, there is a joy, a sharing, and a delight. Those feelings have little to do with spatial closeness to other human beings, but everything to do with a personal relationship.

And so it is in the spiritual life. God is ever with us, for he created us. Our being is totally dependent on him. But by grace, by the coming of God in love, his presence within us changes. God no longer simply exists within a person by creation; God *dwells* there, the divine indwelling. We are bonded to him by a new life. He is near, and his call of love awakens in us a love that answers. This is grace. This gift cannot be measured, just as any relationship defies measurement. But it can be deepened and strengthened. It can transform us. Yet it can also be rejected. Although God always takes the initiative, we, by that unfathomable gift of freedom, can be open to God or close our hearts.

With so much at stake, with so many invitations to divine love, our greatest journey in life becomes the journey of the spirit. What matters in life is not the petty pacing between success and failure or the empty racing toward recognition. It is not the accumulation of wealth or friends, nor the securing of all the good things in life. Love alone matters. Love is the continual turning to catch the gaze of divine love, the continual yearning to be so fired with God's love that our whole being will be sparked with his Spirit and will enkindle that same love and life in everyone we meet.

How aware am I of the Spirit dwelling in me?

Do I devote as much time and care to my spiritual life as I do to my physical life?

Responding

Holy Spirit, guide my students to a mature spiritual life.

Scripture for Further Reflection

John 10:10 It is through Christ that we experience abundant life.

2 Corinthians 3:18 Our growth and our transformation in Christ is progressive and the work of the Lord in the Spirit.

Preparing for the Faith Experience

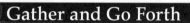
Scripture in This Chapter

John 3:1–21 Nicodemus

John 4:4–30 The Samaritan Woman

I Timothy 4:12 Set an example

Church Documents

Catechism of the Catholic Church. The themes of this chapter correspond to the following paragraphs: **1805–1809, 1813–1815, 1817–1818, 1822–1824.**

General Directory for Catechesis #88. Faith is moved by divine grace and cultivated by the action of the Church. It matures throughout our lives, and catechesis is at the service of this growth.

Decree on the Apostolate of Lay People #4 (Second Vatican Council). Lay people are called to a living union with Christ, nourished by participation in the liturgy and lived out in the ordinary tasks of daily life. Their exercise of faith, hope, and love, animated by the Spirit within, is a powerful witness in the Church.

The Splendor of Truth #64 (Saint John Paul II). We need to know God's law, but more importantly, we must find our true good in those virtuous attitudes expressed in prudence and the other cardinal virtues, as well as the Theological Virtues of faith, hope and charity.

Gather and Go Forth

Find catechist instruction for Gather and Go Forth student pages 153–154 on T350–T351.

Enriching the Faith Experience

Use the activities at the end of the chapter to enrich a lesson or to replace an activity with one that better meets the needs of your class. Bookmark www.christourlife.com to find Web BLMs for this chapter.

Bulletin Board

A suggestion for a bulletin-board design for this chapter is pictured.

LEARNING OUTCOMES

The students will be able to

- explain that God initiates all life and grace, but that they are free to accept or reject it.
- discuss their responsibility to respond to God's invitation to grow spiritually.

Key Terms

grace—the free gift of God's life in us; friendship with God that strengthens us and makes us holy; the prompting of the Spirit to do good

sanctifying grace—God dwelling within us

Sanhedrin—the Supreme Council of the Jews

spiritual life—friendship with God

Materials

- Bibles or New Testaments
- Reflection notebooks
- BLM 64A–B
- Art drawn on board:

GROW

Before You Begin

1. **BLM 64A–B** Prepare BLM 64A–B **Family Letter on Unit 3** to be sent home.

2. Young people are especially involved in the search for the meaning of their lives. As they reach out to others in service, they must also reach inward to their relationship with God.

3. You may wish to supplement this lesson with personal testimonies of faith and other activities of witnessing.

4. For Centering #1, you might present a PowerPoint presentation of the stages of life. Ask the students for the needs people have at each stage. Point out the need for God at every level.

Family Feature

Deepening Family Faith

FAITH IS NOT AN ABSTRACT IDEA. It is a reality that is rooted in a relationship with God. Like any other important relationship, our relationship with God deserves our attention. We are called to nurture our family's faith at home, in the parish, and in the world.

Home is a natural place to introduce our children to traditional Catholic practices, such as prayer, seasonal celebrations, and acts of kindness, forgiveness, and the other virtues. In the context of the family, faith is caught as well as taught. Children observe not only what we as parents say, but especially what we do. They learn their faith each time they see us welcome people into our home, share our faith around the kitchen table, or turn to God in prayer. They learn by the religious art we choose to put on our walls as well as by how we make room for the needy at our family table and in our family budget.

We are also members of a parish family. The heart of parish life is the weekly celebration of the Eucharist. Parishes offer a number of other ways for members to grow in their relationship with God. Many offer Bible study and adult faith formation sessions on a variety of topics. During Advent and Lent, parishes offer times of prayer and reflection with opportunities to participate in the Sacrament of Penance and Reconciliation. Your parish may offer events where the whole family can learn about your faith and about service opportunities to help those in need.

Lay people in the Church have the mission of bearing witness to Christ. This mission extends beyond our neighborhood to our city, our country, and our world. We have the responsibility to act in ways that promote justice, di... dignity o... informed... paper, go... or subscr... newspape...

Because y... child's de... at home, i... are callin... your who... fun. Our...

Visit **www.c**

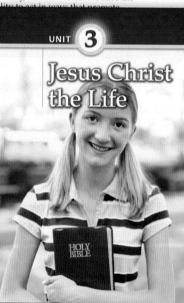

UNIT 3

Jesus Christ the Life

(146) UNIT 3

Centering _____

1. Discuss with students the process of growth.

   ✦ **How do you know you are growing? What are some characteristics of growth?**

   ✦ *Growth is usually gradual.* **People go through growth spurts. But most growth can't be seen right away. You may wear size 8 shoes for years and only gradually work your way into 8 ½ or 9.**

   ✦ *Growth can be painful.* **You might hear "Don't worry—it's only growing pains."**

- ✦ *Growth can be frustrating.* Some parts of your bodies seem to grow without notifying the rest of you. You look in the mirror and your nose seems too big or your ears seem too large, or you are all legs.

- ✦ *Growth can be confusing.* Things you liked doing a month ago no longer interest you. One moment you think you have the best family in the world, and the next minute you wish you were stranded on an island.

2. Discuss growth in friendship with Jesus.

- ✦ **How does friendship show characteristics of growth?** (It grows gradually; it may be more intense at times; it can be painful and confusing.)

- ✦ **Friendship with Jesus can influence everything in your life: how you speak; what you do and think; how you act; how you evaluate the things you see and hear. We refer to friendship with Jesus as our spiritual life. Like any other friendship, it can grow in spurts, gradually, or even painfully.**

- ✦ **What would happen to you if you stopped eating, exercising, and sleeping? How long would it be before you noticed that something was wrong with you?**

- ✦ **What would happen if you ignored your friendship with Jesus, your spiritual life? Why wouldn't you notice it quickly?** (The spiritual life is deep and internal.)

- ✦ **In this lesson, you will find out more about taking care of your friendship with Jesus so that he is for you not only the way and the truth, but also the life.**

Sharing _____

1. Call on volunteers to read aloud **An Incredible Life** on page 147.

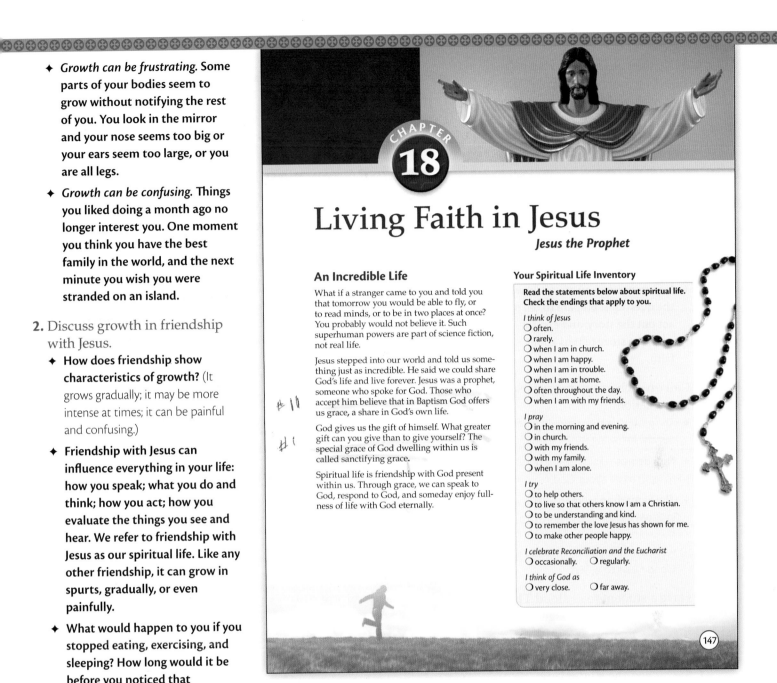

CHAPTER 18

Living Faith in Jesus
Jesus the Prophet

An Incredible Life

What if a stranger came to you and told you that tomorrow you would be able to fly, or to read minds, or to be in two places at once? You probably would not believe it. Such superhuman powers are part of science fiction, not real life.

Jesus stepped into our world and told us something just as incredible. He said we could share God's life and live forever. Jesus was a prophet, someone who spoke for God. Those who accept him believe that in Baptism God offers us grace, a share in God's own life.

God gives us the gift of himself. What greater gift can you give than to give yourself? The special grace of God dwelling within us is called sanctifying grace.

Spiritual life is friendship with God present within us. Through grace, we can speak to God, respond to God, and someday enjoy fullness of life with God eternally.

Your Spiritual Life Inventory

Read the statements below about spiritual life. Check the endings that apply to you.

I think of Jesus
- ○ often.
- ○ rarely.
- ○ when I am in church.
- ○ when I am happy.
- ○ when I am in trouble.
- ○ when I am at home.
- ○ often throughout the day.
- ○ when I am with my friends.

I pray
- ○ in the morning and evening.
- ○ in church.
- ○ with my friends.
- ○ with my family.
- ○ when I am alone.

I try
- ○ to help others.
- ○ to live so that others know I am a Christian.
- ○ to be understanding and kind.
- ○ to remember the love Jesus has shown for me.
- ○ to make other people happy.

I celebrate Reconciliation and the Eucharist
- ○ occasionally. ○ regularly.

I think of God as
- ○ very close. ○ far away.

(147)

- ✦ **How would you describe a spiritual life to someone who has never heard of it?**

- ✦ Direct the students to underline the definitions of *grace, sanctifying grace,* and *spiritual life.*

2. Introduce to the students **Your Spiritual Life Inventory** on page 147.

- ✦ **How do you know whether you are physically healthy and spiritually healthy?** (You are energetic, focused, and have no pain; you pray and receive the sacraments.)

- ✦ **This inventory is a way for you to check the health of your spiritual life.**

- ✦ Have the students complete the activity.

3. Have the students evaluate their spiritual life.

- ✦ **Draw a straight line across the top of page 147, divide it into 10 equal segments, and number them from 1 to 10.**

- ✦ **Look over your responses to the inventory and rate yourself on the line chart. Let 10 represent a strong spiritual life and 1 represent a weak spiritual life.**

1 ┼─┼─┼─┼─┼─┼─┼─┼─┼ 10
Ugh!   Great!

- ✦ **In this lesson, you will discover ways to grow in faith.**

4. Have the students read silently **Life Is a Journey** on page 148. **How is life a journey?** [Point out the smaller journeys along the way: from selfishness to love, from greed to generosity, from self to others.]

5. Divide the class into two groups.

✦ Assign each group one of the following sections to present: **Nicodemus: Night Class** or **The Woman at the Well** on page 148.

✦ **In your group, you are to answer the questions, prepare to tell or act out the story, and explain what the story tells us about faith.**

6. Call on each group to give its presentation.

✦ The groups' answers should point out the following truths about faith:

✦ **Nicodemus**—Faith means seeking to learn more about God.

✦ **The Samaritan woman**—Jesus initiated the process of growth in the woman. He led her to faith. She was open to it and then spread the Good News to others.

7. Have a student read aloud **The Faithful Friend** on page 148.

Acting

1. Lead the students in prayer, using **A Moment with Jesus** on page 148. Allow sufficient time for silent reflection.

2. Have the students complete the Respond activity on page 151.

3. Choose or let the students choose an activity from Reach Out on page 151.

4. At the end of class, have the students tear out page 146. Encourage them to share this Family Feature with their families.

Life Is a Journey

Life is a journey from birth through death to eternal life. For the believer, life is the journey to the Father, through the Son, in the Spirit. Jesus came that we may have eternal life. He invites us to believe in him and to share his friendship and love. Throughout the Gospels, people respond to his invitation. The following two stories of encounters with Jesus tell us about faith.

Nicodemus: Night Class

Nicodemus, a Pharisee and probably a member of the Sanhedrin, wanted to know more about Jesus.

Read John 3:1–21.

Why do you think Nicodemus came at night?

Nicodemus probably came at night so that

the other Pharisees would not see him.

Nicodemus needed faith to see that Jesus was more than a teacher or a miracle worker.

What did Jesus tell Nicodemus we must do to enter the Kingdom of God? (John 3:5)

To enter the Kingdom of God, Jesus said we

must be born of water and the spirit.

What must happen to Jesus so we may have eternal life? (John 3:14)

So that we may have eternal life, Jesus must be

lifted up. That means he must be lifted up on

the Cross for our sins.

After Jesus died, Nicodemus brought spices for his body and helped to bury it. His encounter with Jesus transformed Nicodemus into a true believer.

The Woman at the Well

The Jewish people did not associate with Samaritans. (See page 27.) Nor did they speak to women in public. So when Jesus spoke to the Samaritan woman, she was surprised. The Samaritan woman, who had had five husbands, accepted Jesus' invitation to a life of faith. After she came to believe in Jesus, she spread the news to her entire town. At first, people believed in Jesus because of what the woman told them. Then, when they met him and heard him personally, their faith deepened.

Read John 4:4–30.

What did Jesus tell the Samaritan woman he could offer? (John 4:14)

Jesus said whoever drinks the water he offers

will never thirst again. The water is a spring

welling up to eternal life. It is grace, God's life.

The Faithful Friend

To both of these people—Nicodemus and the Samaritan woman—and to many others, Jesus reached out to offer life. The same is true in your spiritual life: Jesus begins the relationship. Then he is always there, inviting, forgiving, helping, caring, loving.

A Moment with Jesus

Jesus does not wait for us to look for him. He comes to meet us where we are. Pause for a moment to reflect on the stories of Nicodemus and the Samaritan woman. Jesus invited each of them to a deeper relationship with him. Then ask Jesus to help you recognize his invitation to greater friendship with him. Thank him for walking with you on your spiritual journey.

CHECKPOINT

• Were the learning outcomes achieved?

• In what ways have the students demonstrated increased interest in or awareness of the spiritual life?

LEARNING OUTCOMES

The students will be able to

- explain grace as a free gift of God, a share in divine life, and friendship with God.
- express a desire to grow in the life of faith on the journey to the Father.
- name and explain the Theological Virtues and the cardinal virtues.

Words to Know

cardinal virtues

fortitude

justice

prudence

temperance

Theological Virtues

See Glossary for definitions.

Materials

Terms written on the board: *faith, hope, charity, prudence, justice, fortitude, temperance*

Before You Begin

1. If we were baptized as infants, grace transformed us without any cooperation on our part. However, once we reach the age of reason, we are to cooperate with the grace we received. We can grow in the love and friendship of God. Love that is given and received transforms us.

2. It is important to speak of grace in terms of relationship and friendship and not as something poured into our souls.

Centering _____

1. Have the students divide a sheet of paper into three columns.

   ✦ Label the first column *Alone,* the second column with the name of your best friend, and the third column *My Parents or Guardian or Respected Adult.*

   ✦ I will read two situations to you and ask questions about each one. [Choose two from the following six situations to read aloud.]

   Situations:

   a. At a shopping mall, some friends approach you and offer you a cigarette.

   b. Your younger brother or sister asks you to help with his or her homework.

   c. You see an elderly man carrying a shopping bag and having difficulty opening a door.

   d. You find a $10 bill on the sidewalk.

   e. You are offered a ride with a group of high school kids who have been drinking.

   f. You are asked to join a group that plans to do volunteer work during vacation at a home for senior citizens.

   ✦ What would you do if this happened while you were alone? Write your answer in the first column.

   ✦ What would you do if you were with your best friend? Write your answer in the second column.

   ✦ What would you do if you were with your parents? Write your answer in the third column.

   (You could also have the students role-play a situation three times, each time with one of the three different circumstances.)

2. Direct the students to look over their responses.

   ✦ Did your behavior change from column to column? What do you think that means? (Other people affect our behavior.)

   ✦ Just as other people influence how we act, your friendship with Jesus also influences the way you act.

3. Link the last lesson with today's lesson.

   ✦ In the last lesson, you learned how faith brings us to a relationship with Jesus, our spiritual life.

   ✦ Today you will learn more about grace and the powers that come with this spiritual life, powers that influence our actions.

Sharing _____

1. Direct the students to read silently **Dan's Difficult Day** on page 149.

   ✦ Ask them to think over what their response would have been and write it on the line.

   ✦ Have you ever wanted to explode in anger or give up, but something inside of you gave you the courage to respond differently? Would someone tell us about it?

   ✦ Have you ever felt called to do some good deed without being asked or even without having anyone know you did it? Would someone tell us about it?

   ✦ These are ways your friendship with God can affect your lives. Good friends bring out the very best in each other. If you are close to God, then this will show in everything you do, not just at Mass or in religion class. This is how grace works.

2. Have several students read aloud **Grace—It Is Free!** on page 149.

   ✦ What are some of the words or phrases that describe grace? [List them on the board.] (friendship, God's invitation, presence, life, inspirations, desire, Christian life, strengthens, more like Jesus)

◆ **What do we do to deserve grace?**
(We do nothing. Grace is a free gift.)

3. Have the students read silently **Hints from God** on page 149 and write their responses.
You might point out incidents in your own life or situations you observed among the students that have shown an openness to God's grace.

4. Direct the students to read silently **Super Strength for the Journey** on page 149. **God has gifted us with special powers to deepen our friendship with God. These powers are called virtues. What does *virtue* mean?** (Virtue is a power or habit for doing good.)

5. Ask several students to read aloud **Theological Virtues** on page 150.
◆ **What are the definitions of *faith*, *hope* and *charity*?** (Faith is belief in God and all that is revealed in the Catholic Church; Hope is trust that God will give us eternal life; Charity, or love, is our love for God and putting him first in our lives.)
◆ **On the inside back cover of your book, there are prayers about the Theological Virtues called Acts of Faith, Hope, and Love. I encourage you to pray and memorize them.**

6. Direct the students to read silently **Cardinal Virtues** on page 150.
What is the difference between the Theological Virtues and the cardinal virtues? (Theological Virtues are gifts from God centered on God. Cardinal virtues are fundamental to leading a moral life.)

7. Play a virtues matching game with the students.
◆ Divide the class into two teams and have them stand in two lines. Let pairs of students compete in answering the questions.
◆ The student who first answers correctly remains standing. The students may refer to the list of virtues on the board.

Dan's Difficult Day

For Dan, it had been a hard day at school. There had been a surprise quiz in history, he had forgotten his English homework, basketball practice had been canceled, he got in trouble for talking in class, and he had an argument with his friend. By the time he got home, he had had it! Dan's mother also had a difficult day. Her work at the office had brought her problems. She had already done the laundry at home and was in the midst of preparing dinner.

When Dan walked into the house, his mother greeted him with a list of jobs to do, reminded him to watch his younger brother, told him to clean his room, and not to play the radio so loud. As Dan heard all this, he felt like arguing. Instead, he thought about how his mother felt and what would be the right thing to do.

What decision would you have made if you had been in Dan's place?

Answers will vary.

Grace—It Is Free!

Original Sin left us with a tendency to do wrong. Dan's urge to do what is right was from the Holy Spirit. It is something that you often experience: God's invitation to deeper friendship—or grace. Grace has many meanings. You have already seen it as God's life. God's presence in you (sanctifying grace) brings about changes in your life. It prompts you to do what is good.

Grace is a free gift. You must be open to it, however, to share in God's life. Actual grace gives you the desire to lead a Christian life.

Actual grace strengthens you to make decisions and act according to the Father's will. Through actual grace, you can believe Jesus' message, choose to do good, and turn more and more to Christ.

Grace works like human friendship. When you become friends with someone, you often grow

alike. You begin to see things the same way. The more you accept Christ's offer of friendship, the more influenced you are by him. You begin to see things and make decisions as he would. You avoid sin to imitate his obedience to God. You become more like Jesus.

Hints from God

God inspired Dan to do what was good. By choosing to do the right thing, he grows closer to God. However, Dan could reject God's friendship and help. If he did, he would be turning away from God and from all that could make him happy. Even then, God would call to him to think about what he had done and start anew.

Think of any way you have experienced God's grace today. It may have been a good thought. It may have been something you saw or heard that made you think of God, God's love for you, or all God has done for you. Write it below.

Answers will vary.

Super Strength for the Journey

You can respond to God and deepen your friendship through virtues poured into your heart at Baptism. A virtue is an attitude or a way of living that enables you to do good. Virtues grow and develop through graces received through prayer, good works, and the sacraments, especially the Eucharist. You have received Theological Virtues and cardinal virtues. You might think of them as the vitamins of your spiritual life.

CHAPTER 18 (149)

◆ **What virtue is related to . . .**

courage? (fortitude)

despair? (hope)

control? (temperance)

fairness? (justice)

belief? (faith)

overeating? (temperance)

prayer? (love, faith, or hope)

others' rights? (justice)

deciding what's right? (prudence)

presumption? (hope)

trust in God? (faith)

meeting difficulties? (fortitude)

Sunday worship? (love or faith)

asking advice? (prudence)

counting on eternal life? (hope)

helping needy brothers and sisters? (charity)

carrying out one's duties? (justice)

drinking too much? (temperance)

helping those who are poor? (charity or justice)

praying every day? (faith, love)

8. Discuss with the students how they have lived the virtues today.
◆ **There are many ways we live one or more of the virtues every day. Take a few moments to think of how you have lived the virtues today.** [Pause.]
◆ **What are some of the ways you have lived the virtues today?**

Acting

1. Direct the students to read silently **Life Means Growth** on page 150.

   Allow time for the students to reflect on the questions.

2. Lead the students in prayer.

   ◆ **God speaks to us through the happenings of our everyday lives. God speaks through people, experiences, and events to shape our spiritual lives. God speaks through music.**

   ◆ **Think of a hymn or a popular song. Is there a line in it that seems to have a message from God for you? Pray about this line.**

   ◆ Allow time for silent reflection.

CHECKPOINT ✓

- Were the learning outcomes achieved?

- How have the students shown an understanding that friendship with God influences every part of their lives?

Theological Virtues

Theos means "God." The **Theological Virtues**—faith, hope and charity—are gifts given by God and centered on God. They lead us to know, love, and trust God. With their help, we are capable of acting as God's children and reaching our journey's end: eternal life with God.

Faith is the virtue by which we believe God completely and accept as true all that God has revealed and teaches through the Catholic Church. Faith helps us grow in our understanding of God's goodness. We often use a creed to express the truths we believe. We are united in what we believe and in whom we believe.

We believe because we trust a person. When we really trust, we are willing to stake our life on what we believe.

Read the Act of Faith on the inside back cover of your book. What words tell why you can believe God?

who can neither deceive nor be deceived

The virtue of hope is the trust and confidence that God will give us eternal life and all the help necessary along the way. Two sins against hope are despair and presumption. Despair is to believe God cannot or will not help and so to give up even trying to be saved. Presumption is to expect God automatically to give all you hope for even though you do not cooperate with God's grace or make any efforts to live a Christian life. You presume on the goodness of God. Also, presumption is to think you can find eternal life without God.

Charity (love) is that virtue that helps us to love God and to give God first place in our lives. Our model is the love shown in the life and Death of Jesus. Saint Paul wrote about the various gifts given by God. Read 1 Corinthians 13:1–13.

What is the most important gift? _____love_____
Why? (See verse 8.)

Faith.

Cardinal Virtues

The **cardinal virtues** are fundamental to leading a moral life. They are habits that allow us to do good acts and to give the best of ourselves. The cardinal virtues order our feelings and actions according to human reason and faith. The word *cardinal* means "hinge." Our spiritual life hinges on the cardinal virtues.

Prudence is the virtue that directs us to decide what is good. Prudent people ask responsible people for advice. They think through their beliefs and choices and reflect before they act.

Justice is the virtue that guides us to respect the rights of others. It gives us the determination to protect those rights and to fulfill our responsibilities to people and to God.

Fortitude is the virtue that gives us the courage to do what is right even when it is very difficult. It may mean having patience, being generous, enduring ridicule, or not responding to peer pressure.

Temperance is the virtue that helps us to control our desire for pleasure. Temperance keeps us from overdoing it in eating, drinking, sex, money, and the way we dress, act, and speak.

Life Means Growth

You can easily see how you have grown and changed physically and intellectually over the years. How about spiritually? How much more do you know about God and your faith now than you did before? How much has your life become a reflection of your Christian values and ideals? Growing closer to Jesus is vital and takes energy and time—a lifetime. Remember that life in Christ and prayer are inseparable.

(150) UNIT 3

LEARNING OUTCOMES

The students will be able to

- describe how their relationship with Christ has permeated their lives.
- describe a growing understanding of the spiritual life.

Materials

- BLM 65A–F
- Materials for each station:

  Station 1

  Copies of BLM 65A

  Bibles or New Testaments

  Pens or pencils, crayons, felt-tipped pens, or colored pencils

  Poster for prayer intentions with Matthew 7:7 written on it: "Ask and it will be given to you; seek and you will find; knock and the door will be opened to you."

  Station 2

  Copies of BLM 65B

  Bibles or New Testaments (optional)

  Pens and pencils

  Copy of Prayer To Know Myself on the board or on a card

  Station 3

  Copies of BLM 65C

  Bibles or New Testaments

  Paper and pens or pencils

  Station 4

  Copies of BLM 65D

  Pens or pencils

  Stationery and envelopes

  Station 5

  Copies of BLM 65E

  Bibles or New Testaments

  Paper and pens or pencils

  Magazines and newspapers

  Scissors

  Tape or glue

  Station 6

  Copies of BLM 65F

  Bibles or New Testaments

  Pens or pencils

Before You Begin

1. This lesson is like an in-class retreat. It may require several days, so you may want to drop the activities of Day Four. If you prefer not to carry out the learning stations, you might have the students complete any part of BLM 65A–F intended for the learning stations.

2. Be sure that you are familiar with the contents of each station before beginning this activity. Have all the materials and directions prepared beforehand.

3. To set up the stations, you might:
   - Arrange desks into clusters, with one desk in each cluster holding the directions and source materials.
   - Post directions for the stations on the wall or on the board. Directions for each station are on page T215 under Sharing #1.
   - Set the materials on a general supply table.
   - Set up tables around the room or use cardboard boxes as room dividers for the sections.
   - Make individual packets of materials for the students to eliminate some of the walking in the room.
   - Move to another room that has tables.

4. Only a few students at a time should work at a station. Students may visit the stations in any order. They may do the reflective sections of the BLM at their desks.

5. Discussion time at the end of the learning stations activity is vital.

Centering _____

1. Discuss with the students spiritual growth.
   - ✦ Imagine a how-to book on spiritual growth with two sections: *Good Advice* and *Bad Advice.*
   - ✦ What are some of the things you would list under each of these? [Write the students' answers on the board under the headings. Save for the Acting prayer activity on page T215.]

2. Prepare the students for today's activity.
   Today you will have an opportunity to work on your own spiritual growth by using several faith learning stations. It will be like going on a retreat in class.

Sharing

1. Go to each station and point out the directions and materials to the students.

Station 1: Directions

1. Quietly and prayerfully read and follow the directions on BLM 65A **Growing in Love Means Looking Inward: Prayer.**

2. Write a prayer intention on the poster with a colored marker.

Station 2: Directions

1. **Read and follow the directions on BLM 65B Growing in Love Means Looking Inward: Personal Characteristics.**

2. **Read the Prayer to Know Myself and write your own prayer.**

Prayer to Know Myself

Lord, teach me to know myself; teach me to know you. Help me to see how everything that happens in my life can bring me closer to you. Let me see within myself all the gifts and talents you have given me. Let me be grateful for them and use them to grow in love by serving others. Teach me to pray. Teach me to listen. Teach me to see—to see you in my life, in others, in every way you show yourself to me. Teach me to take the time to turn my life around and follow you. Where I am strong, support me, guide me, direct my life. Where I am weak, strengthen me, protect me, help me depend on you. My life is so new, so fresh. So much lies ahead, but I need you with me every day. So I ask: teach me to know myself; teach me to know you. Amen.

Station 3: Directions

1. **Read and answer the questions on BLM 65C Growing in Love Means Looking at Jesus.**

2. **Write the answer to #3 on a separate sheet of paper and answer these questions:**

   a. **In general, what kind of people did Jesus have as friends?**

   b. **Read John 15:14. What do you think Jesus meant? List four reasons why Jesus would call *you* his friend.**

Station 4: Directions

Read and follow the directions on BLM 65D Growing in Love Means Reaching Outward.

Station 5: Directions

1. **Read and follow the directions on BLM 65E Growing in Love Means Reaching Out Even More.**

2. **Find an article about someone giving service or someone needing our help. Cut it out, mount it on paper, and write how service is being given or how we could help the person in need.**

Station 6: Directions

Read and answer the questions on BLM 65F Growing in Love Means Planning for More Growth.

2. Divide the students into six groups.
Assign each group one of the six stations to begin. Be available to help the students.

3. Discuss the students' findings.
   ✦ **Station 1: As you grow in your spiritual life, you will discover more meaning in simple religious activities. Scripture reading will become more and more a reflective activity. Remember, prayer is real conversation with the Lord.**

   ✦ **Station 2:** (Some answers to the second activity on BLM 65B depend on the students' explanations.)

   ✦ **Station 3: Jesus loves everyone and calls every person to his friendship. Even though all the people in the Scripture passages were sinners, and some turned away from him, Jesus remained faithful and loving.**

   ✦ **Station 4: Sometimes we reach out to those who are poor or to others who are far away, but we fail to see the needs of those close to us. Gratitude is an important Christian virtue.**

   ✦ **Stations 5 and 6:** [See the Answer Key at the back of the packet of BLMs.]

Acting

 Pray with the students for God's help on the spiritual journey.
Use the Good Advice list from the beginning of the lesson. Examples:

• **Lord, teach us to spend time with you in conversation every day.** [Response: Lord, hear our prayer.]

• **Lord, help us to be aware of the feelings and needs of others.** [Lord, hear our prayer.]

• **Lord, help us learn of you by reading the Scriptures daily.** [Lord, hear our prayer.]

CHECKPOINT

• Were the learning outcomes achieved?

• How would I change the procedure for the faith learning stations next time?

LEARNING OUTCOMES

The students will be able to

- discuss the demands of Christian love.
- describe the cost of Christian love.
- demonstrate an understanding of the key concepts in this chapter.

Materials

- Bibles or New Testaments
- Reflection notebooks
- Paper
- BLM 66 Quiz
- Drawing paper and felt-tipped pens (optional)

Before You Begin

Christ has given us the means to love. Christian love means loving even those who hate us or do evil to us. It means caring sincerely about others and being willing to take risks to help them. Empowered by God's grace and the Theological Virtues, we need not find authentic Christian charity impossible.

CHAPTER 18 Summary

Remember

What is grace?
Grace is a free gift of God's life in us. It is friendship with God that strengthens us and makes us holy.

What are the Theological Virtues?
The Theological Virtues are powers given by God at Baptism and centered on God: faith, hope, and charity.

What are the cardinal virtues?
The cardinal virtues—prudence, justice, fortitude, and temperance—are fundamental to leading a moral life. They are habits that allow us to order our feelings and actions according to human reason and faith.

Respond

What matters in life is how you respond to Christ. Responding with love and longing will bring you eternal life. If you respond with indifference or hostility, you risk separation from God. Read Luke 9:18–21. If Jesus were to ask you the same two questions, what would you say? Write your responses in your reflection notebook.

Reach Out

1. Look at the Apostles' Creed or Nicene Creed on the inside front cover of your book. On paper, design a series of church windows based on it. Or write a creed in your own words. To get ideas, read these expressions of faith found in Scripture:
   - Mark 8:29
   - Romans 1:3–5 or 8:34
   - 1 Corinthians 15:3–8
   - 2 Timothy 2:8
   - 1 John 2:22

2. Jesus offered the Samaritan woman living water. Water has many uses. It can destroy life or save it. It can nourish, cleanse, and refresh. Find examples in the Bible and in everyday life where water is used in any of the ways mentioned above. How is it used in John 13? How did John the Baptist use it?

3. Write an autobiography of your faith life. Begin with your Baptism and name the people and events that have helped you grow in faith. Include your favorite prayers and Scripture stories. List the parishes you have been a member of and saints who have inspired you. Share your story with someone.

4. Tape three cardboard boxes end-to-end to make a kiosk, a pillar that serves as a bulletin board. On your kiosk, put pictures and captions encouraging people to live their faith, especially by helping people who are poor. Display your kiosk in your parish.

Words to Know

cardinal virtues	prudence
fortitude	temperance
justice	Theological Virtues

Joachim Patinir, *The Baptism of Christ*, 16th century, Dutch.

151

Centering

Link the last lesson with today's lesson.

- ✦ You have learned much about growing in the spiritual life. You have also learned that love is the essence of the spiritual life.
- ✦ Today you will find out more about what love really demands of us.

Sharing

1. Have the students read silently the following Scripture verses.

Luke 6:27–35	Luke 6:45
Luke 6:36–38	Luke 9:23–26

- ✦ **What do these passages tell us about the demands of Christian love?**

- ✦ **In Luke 6:27–36 two kinds of love are presented: that of sinners and that of the followers of Christ.**

- ✦ **Whom do sinners love?** (those who love them; those who do good things for them; Luke 6:31–33)

- ✦ **To whom do sinners lend?** (to those from whom they expect to receive something; Luke 6:34)

- ✦ **How is our love as followers of Christ supposed to be different?** (We are to love our enemies, do good, and lend without any hope of return.)

- ✦ **Our love should have three qualities.** [Write these on the board as you explain them.]

Sincerity—We should do good to others out of our love for God and for our neighbor.

Unselfishness—We should love others and do good to them without demanding or expecting any kind of reward.

Universality—We should show love and do good for anyone, regardless of nationality, race, faith, social position, physical or mental condition, popularity, or any other quality that might keep us from being kind to a person.

2. Discuss with the students how their school is living the qualities of Christian love and service.

   ✦ **How do you think our school shows or does not show these qualities of Christian love and service?**

   ✦ **Are there particular areas where it seems these qualities are missing?** (the cafeteria, the playground, on the bus, in the hall)

   ✦ Divide the class into pairs. Assign to the students the areas where students felt these qualities were missing.

   ✦ **With your partner, write two or three announcements that encourage students and teachers to show Christian love and service sincerely, unselfishly, and universally in the area you are assigned.**

   ✦ **The announcements should be about 30 seconds long and written to be read over the public address system. Refer to the Scripture passages in Luke for ideas of what to include.**

   ✦ If possible, arrange to use the announcements on the public address system throughout the year.

3. Lead the students through the Summary and Review activities, pages 151–152.

4. **BLM 66** Distribute and administer BLM 66 **Chapter 18 Quiz.**

   Use this opportunity to assess the students' understanding of the main concepts in the chapter. If there is not sufficient time for the students to complete the quiz, consider moving it to Day Five.

Acting

1. Lead the students in a prayerful reflection.

   ✦ **As I read the following questions to you, write your thoughts, prayers, and concerns in your reflection notebooks:**

   • **Is my love sincere because it comes from my heart?** [Pause.]

CHAPTER **18** Review Activities

Hendrik Siemiradzki, *Christ and the Woman of Samaria*, 1890, oil on canvas, Poland.

Words of Life   Use each word in a sentence that reveals its meaning.

1. grace
   Grace is our share in God's divine life.

2. sanctifying grace
   Sanctifying grace is the special grace of God's dwelling within us.

3. virtue
   A virtue is a way of living or habit for doing good.

4. cardinal virtue
   A cardinal virtue is a virtue that orders our feelings and actions according to human reason and faith.

People of Faith   Write yes or no in answer to each question.

Yes   1. Did Nicodemus have more faith at the end of Jesus' life?

Yes   2. Did Jesus tell Nicodemus that we would have eternal life because Jesus would be lifted up?

No   3. Would Jesus be following a Jewish practice by speaking with a Samaritan woman?

Yes   4. Did Jesus lead the Samaritan woman to believe in him?

Yes   5. Did the Samaritan woman bring other people to Jesus?

No   6. Did Jesus tell Nicodemus that there is nothing we can do to enter the Kingdom of God?

152

• **Is my love unselfish because I expect no return for favors done?** [Pause.]

• **Is my love universal because I show love to everyone without exception?** [Pause.]

• **What do I find hardest about loving as I read Luke, chapter 6?** [Pause.]

✦ Read aloud Matthew 6:25–34 to encourage the students to place their trust in God, who will support them always.

✦ Conclude by praying the Lord's Prayer.

2. At the end of class, have the students tear out and take home pages 151–152.

CHECKPOINT

• Were the learning outcomes achieved?

• Were the students able to understand the challenge of Christian love?

• Did the students make the connection between their relationship with God and the various activities of their lives?

Gather and Go Forth

Lead students through pages 153–154 in the student book. Find catechist instruction on T350–T351.
Materials: Bibles

Use the following suggestions to create an additional lesson for Day Five.

1. Remind the students to take home pages 151–152 to share what they are learning with their families.

2. Incorporate any unused BLMs from the week's chapter.

3. Consider the time of the liturgical year and use the appropriate Special Seasons and Lessons. SSLs begin on page T369.

4. Visit www.christourlife.com to find additional activities for Extending the Chapter.

5. Use activities from Enriching the Faith Experience.

6. Guide the students in a prayerful discussion of Sunday's Scripture readings. Visit www.christourlife.com for more information.

Chapter 18 Enriching the Faith Experience

Use the following activities to enrich a lesson or to replace an activity with one that better meets the needs of your class.

1. **Web BLM** Use Web BLM Chapter 18-A **How Others See It** to provide the students with suggestions for growing closer to God.

2. **Web BLM** Use Web BLM Chapter 18-B **Moral Virtues in Action** to lead the students to a better understanding of the cardinal virtues.

3. Have the students design posters on some phase of the spiritual life such as the Theological Virtues and the cardinal virtues, using pictures from magazines, cards, the Internet, or their own drawings.

4. Read or have a student read aloud Ephesians 3:14–21 as a prayer. You might distribute copies of it to the students to keep as reminders of God's love for them.

5. The students could make a collage of their lives. Cut out cardboard in the shape of a circle to make a clock face. Have the students glue pictures on the clock depicting their activities at that point in the day. Have them write phrases expressing their thoughts throughout the day. Be sure the students include the spiritual. Have them look at their collages to determine if they are taking enough time and care to nourish growth in all aspects of their lives. You might suggest that they make a collage of their celebration of Sunday or another Church feast.

6. Have the students list what they find hardest about prayer and what they find easiest.

7. Have the students write original acts of faith, hope, and love. Tell them to refer to the prayers Acts of Faith, Hope and Love on the inside back cover of their books. [See page T446] These may be used as closing prayers, or they may be duplicated and bound as a set of class prayers for use throughout the year.

8. Have the students design posters on the theme of the spiritual life, using pictures, cards, or their own illustrations.

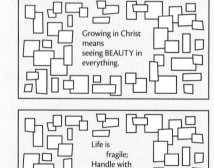

9. The stories of Nicodemus and the Samaritan woman involve water, a powerful Christian symbol. Have the students learn more about the meaning of water.

   ✦ Have the class make a collage using pictures of water to illustrate the many ideas associated with it.

   ✦ Suggest that the students make their own computer slide show or PowerPoint presentation using pictures from nature and actual life to bring out the idea of living waters and new birth.

   ✦ Let the students renew their baptismal promises. Take them to the parish baptismal font for this. Have them notice any symbols that appear on the font.

   ✦ Water is a dominant theme in Scripture. Have the students research the following Scripture passages and identify water as washing, purifying, destroying, expressive of evil and death, powerful, refreshing, or life-giving.

Genesis 1:2	Psalm 93:3–4
Genesis 6:5–9:28	Psalm 105:41
Exodus 14:21–22	Psalm 114:3
Exodus 15:25,27	Matthew 14:22–23
Exodus 17:1–7	Matthew 27:24
Jonah 2:1–11	Mark 1:5
Joshua 3:14–17	Mark 4:35–41
Psalm 18:16–17	Mark 6:45–52
Psalm 26:6	John 6:16–21
Psalm 51:4–9	Romans 6:3–11
Psalm 69:2–3	Colossians 2:12
Psalm 78:11–1	1 Peter 3:21

◆ Discuss the different forms of water such as rain, a spring, a fountain, or storms. Ask the students to write poems expressing the characteristics of each kind of water. Ask which kind they would most identify with Christ, with Baptism, and with the Spirit?

10. Tell the students to collect medium-sized flat rocks. Have them use markers and black felt tipped pens to write the different truths listed in the Nicene or Apostles' Creed. These rocks can then be stacked as a "firm foundation of the faith." Leave them assembled in the prayer corner of the room. This may also be done with Scripture quotations on life, grace, friendship, faith, hope, and love.

11. Have the students make a mobile displaying the cardinal virtues. Provide each student with a 11-by-17-inch light-colored sheet of construction paper. The students should fold their papers in fourths and punch a small hole in the top of each section for the string. They can illustrate each of the cardinal virtues or write quotations related to them.

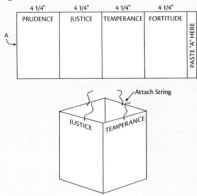

Opposition to Jesus
JESUS THE SUFFERING SERVANT

Faith Focus

Jesus' suffering led to eternal life and glory for him and for us.

Reflecting on the Faith Experience

Take a few moments to reflect prayerfully before preparing the lesson.

Listening

> Faith is the realization
> of what is hoped for and
> evidence of things not seen.
>
> *Hebrews 11:1*

Reflecting

Faith is a deep, personal, radical trusting in Jesus, who saves because he is always faithful. It is what the Hebrews termed "to know God," to believe in one's heart in another. Faith fortifies the believer with the strength and courage to carry on in pain and suffering when there seem to be no answers. It helps the person to trust in the face of risk, insecurity, and uncertainty. This faith is a total, unconditional surrender to God, where the believer walks into the unpredictable future with courage and joyful expectancy.

Faith is evident in attitudes, in the way we receive and relate to life. It helps us look at the unknown, the ambiguity of life, the mystery of the future, and see beyond to the great, incomprehensible God, who is incredibly gentle, forgiving, generous, and strengthening. It helps us come to know who Jesus is and discover how we can be one with the Father through him and in the Holy Spirit. We pray, "Lord, increase our faith."

Without an understanding of who Jesus is and the faith to believe that his Resurrection heralds our own, death can look like the final end, the ultimate terror. But Jesus changed the nature of death when he accepted his own Death in obedience to the Father.

The Death of Jesus was anticipated by his raising Lazarus from the dead. Jesus returned physical life to his friend, but Lazarus would die again. However, in this sign, an even greater restoration was foreshadowed. According to the Gospel of John, this miracle resulted in the Sanhedrin's decision that one man should die to save the Jewish nation from Roman destruction. When Jesus accepted his suffering and surrendered to death, the Father accepted his gift and raised him from the dead. Death was transformed into a final act of love and submission. For the Christian, death is coming home to the Father. The loss of loved ones is still painful. Death is still feared. But through Jesus' promises, we receive the strength to hope for an eternal life in glory where every tear will be wiped away.

Do I take advantage of Jesus' presence and his love for me by turning to him in time of trial and suffering?

Do I approach the future with anticipation or with worry?

Responding

Jesus, help my students to develop a Christian attitude toward suffering.

Scripture for Further Reflection

John 5:24–28 Jesus is the source of eternal life. Anyone who listens and believes in him will pass from death to eternal life.

2 Corinthians 4:16–18 What we see will pass away. But what we cannot see will last forever.

Preparing for the Faith Experience

 Gather and Go Forth

Scripture in This Chapter

Matthew 17: 1–8 The Transfiguration of Jesus

John 11:1–53 The Raising of Lazarus

Hebrews 11:1 Faith

Church Documents

Catechism of the Catholic Church. The themes of this chapter correspond to the following paragraphs: **554–556, 585–586, 591, 618, 1680–1682.**

Pastoral Constitution on the Church in the Modern World #18 (Second Vatican Council). Our Christian faith tells us that our bodily death will be vanquished when we are restored to wholeness by an almighty and merciful Savior.

Pastoral Constitution on the Church in the Modern World #22 (Second Vatican Council). Through faith, we Christians also believe that we can be united even now to our loved ones who have already died.

The Dignity of Older People and Their Mission in the Church and in the World #11 (Pontifical Council for the Laity). Jesus reversed the significance of death, which is no longer a condemnation but a moment of hope of coming face-to-face with the Lord.

Gather and Go Forth

Find catechist instruction for Gather and Go Forth student pages 161–162 on T352–T353.

Enriching the Faith Experience

Use the activities at the end of the chapter to enrich a lesson or to replace an activity with one that better meets the needs of your class.

Bulletin Board

A suggestion for a bulletin-board design for this chapter is pictured. Have the students list deceased relatives or friends for whom they pray.

Through his suffering, my servant shall justify many, and their guilt he shall bear.

Isaiah 53:11

LEARNING OUTCOMES

The students will be able to

- explain how the Transfiguration prepared the apostles for Jesus' Death and Resurrection.

- apply a deeper faith in Jesus in their lives.

- describe how both joys and sorrows can work for our good through faith.

Key Term

Transfiguration—the glorified appearance of Jesus witnessed by Peter, James, and John

Materials

- Bibles or New Testaments
- Cardboard cross and tape
- Small pieces of paper
- Box with situations for Centering #1

- Recorded music: Find suggestions for Chapter 19 on page T519.
- Reflection notebook

Before You Begin

In the Transfiguration, Jesus shows the apostles Peter, James, and John who he is and tells them that he will endure. This prophetic event lets these disciples know about the passion and Death that will lead to his glorification. The disciples, too, will have to participate in the mystery of the Cross so as to be transfigured, to be like Christ.

Centering _____

1. Discuss with the students how different situations can cause different feelings.
   - ✦ **Every day of our lives, we are given different situations that cause us to feel a certain way.**
   - ✦ **In this box, I have written down some of these situations. We are going to play a game of charades where one of you will act out the situation and the rest of you will guess what the feeling is.**
   - ✦ Ask two students to pick the situations out of the box and silently act them out.
     - *falling asleep during class and being called on*
     - *collecting money door-to-door for a fund-raiser*
     - *congratulating a student who won a class election*
     - *impatiently anticipating the arrival of a good friend who has been away for a long time*
     - *cheering for a winning touchdown*
     - *tasting a dish a friend has made for you that isn't very good, but wanting to be kind*
     - *getting caught chewing gum in class*
   - ✦ **Each of these situations shows us that life is full of joys, sadness, and excitement.**

2. Have the students read silently the introductory paragraph on page 155.
   How does faith help you in times of joy and sorrow? (In joy, we become aware of God's power and goodness. In sorrow, faith helps us believe that God is with us to bring good out of our sorrow.)

3. Link the last lesson with today's lesson.
   - ✦ **The life of grace you learned about in the last lesson is given to us because of the sufferings of Jesus.**
   - ✦ **Today you will learn about the sufferings Jesus went through for all of us.**

Sharing _____

1. Have a student read aloud the first paragraph of **Glory Through Suffering** on page 155.
   - ✦ **What does Isaiah indicate will be the results of Jesus' suffering?** (He will have glory, and many will be redeemed.)
   - ✦ **The Gospels record that Jesus predicted his suffering and death three times. When Peter responds, "God forbid," Jesus says, "Get behind me, Satan. You are an obstacle to me." Why do you think Jesus scolds Peter?** (Peter is suggesting that the plan of

the Father not be fulfilled. This could be a temptation for Jesus.)
   - ✦ **How did Jesus strengthen the apostles' faith in him?** (He let Peter, James, and John see him transfigured.)

2. Ask the students to read silently the account of the Transfiguration in Matthew 17:1–8.
   - ✦ **What happened to Jesus?** (v.2) (Jesus was transfigured. His face shone like the sun, and his clothes became white as light.)
   - ✦ **What did Peter want to do to prolong the moment?** (v.4) (Peter wanted to build three tents.)
   - ✦ **What did the voice from the cloud say?** (v.5) (The voice said, "This is my beloved Son, in whom I am well pleased; listen to him.")
   - ✦ **How did the event confirm the disciples' faith?** (It showed them the glory of Jesus. They heard the Father's words of approval. The presence of Moses and Elijah discussing the passion indicated that it had to be so. Moses represented the Law and Elijah the prophets.)

3. Have a student read aloud the rest of this section.
   - ✦ **Why would it be hard for the apostles to understand that Jesus would suffer on the Cross?** (They followed him as the Messiah. They

had seen his miracles. Crowds flocked to hear him. He was innocent.)

- ✦ **What does the mystery of the Transfiguration teach?** (that glory comes from the Cross)
- ✦ **How was the Cross a part of Jesus' glory?** (Through his Death, he would rise. The Cross was the means of our redemption. Through it, Jesus showed love for the Father and us.)
- ✦ **How can suffering bring about good?** (Accepted with faith, suffering can make you strong, open, and loving. It can lead to a share in the glory of Christ.)

4. Have the students read silently **Faith Builders** page 155 and complete the activity.

- ✦ **Why should you be able to experience the presence of Jesus in good times as well as in difficult times?** (Jesus never abandons us. He uses all events to bring us closer to him.)
- ✦ **How can faith help you come closer to Jesus in one of these situations?**

5. Read aloud the modern parable Footprints to the students. **What does this modern parable tell us about suffering?**

CHAPTER 19

Opposition to Jesus

Jesus the Suffering Servant

In moments of joy, faith helps you become aware of God's presence, his power and his goodness. Faith can fill your heart with gratitude to God. But you also have times of sorrow and disappointment. In those moments, your faith can help you to believe that God is with you and will bring good out of the sorrows. Faith can help you accept them with trust. Through sorrows, you can become the person God has called you to be.

Glory Through Suffering

Suffering was part of Jesus' life. Words from the prophet Isaiah apply to him:

> Because of his affliction
> he shall see the light in fullness of days;
> Through his suffering, my servant shall justify many,
> and their guilt he shall bear.
>
> Isaiah 53:11

For Jesus the road to glory was through suffering. This was difficult for the apostles to understand until the Spirit came at Pentecost. When Jesus first predicted what he must undergo as the suffering servant, Peter would not hear of it. The apostles needed stronger faith for the trials to come. So Jesus took Peter,

James, and John to a mountain (possibly Mount Tabor) where they saw him transfigured.

Jesus willingly endured suffering and death for the sake of our salvation. His choice shows his love for the Father and us. The **Transfiguration** teaches us that glory comes through the Cross. Just as the Israelites passed from death to life in the Exodus, Jesus passed from death to Resurrection. Because Jesus knew suffering, he is a willing companion on our road through suffering. He wants to share in our lives as we walk with him on the road to glory.

Faith Builders

The Father tells us how to meet joys and sorrows. He says, "Listen to my Son." Jesus speaks to us and strengthens our faith especially in Scripture, in prayer, and in the sacraments. We believe that Jesus is with us in all the events of life.

Check the events in which you have experienced the presence or guidance of Jesus.

- ○ being misunderstood by parents
- ○ taking a test
- ○ participating in the Sunday Eucharist
- ○ losing a friend
- ○ making a decision

How could faith help you to come closer to Jesus in one of those situations?

(155)

Footprints

One night a man had a dream in which he was walking along the beach with the Lord. Across the sky flashed scenes from his life. In each scene, he noticed two sets of footprints in the sand; one belonging to him, and the other to the Lord.

When the last scene of his life flashed before him, he looked back at the footprints in the sand. He noticed that many times along the path of his life there was only one set of footprints. He also noticed that it happened at the very lowest and saddest times in his life.

This really bothered him, and he questioned the Lord about it. "Lord, you said that once I decided to follow you, you'd walk with me all the way. But I have noticed that during the most troublesome times in my life, there is only one set of footprints. I don't understand why, when I needed you the most, you would leave me."

The Lord replied, "My precious, precious child, I love you and I would never leave you. During your times of trial and suffering, when you see only one set of footprints, it was then that I carried you."

6. Discuss with the students human responses to suffering.

- ✦ **Jesus does not promise that we will not suffer. He makes it very clear that those who follow him will experience the Cross. But he promises us that he will be with us, strengthening our faith and giving meaning to our pain.**
- ✦ **People who accept suffering in a spirit of faith can be a source of inspiration and encouragement to others, helping them to see the meaning of the Cross.**
- ✦ **Can you give examples of people who grew stronger through suffering?**

7. Have the students act out the Transfiguration.

◆ Assign students to be Jesus, Moses, Elijah, Peter, James, John, and the voice of the Father.

◆ **The Transfiguration of Jesus strengthened the apostles' faith. They were able to accept his suffering and later their own suffering.**

Acting _____

1. Have the students look up the following Scripture verses.

◆ **What do these Scripture verses tell us about faith?**

◆ **Mark 9:23** (For one who has faith, anything is possible.)

◆ **John 6:47** (Those who believe have eternal life.)

◆ **Ephesians 2:8** (Faith is a free gift from God. We are saved by the grace of God.)

2. Lead the students in a prayer experience on faith.

◆ In the front of the room, place the paper or cardboard cross and tape.

◆ **On the small piece of paper, write a situation in your life that you want Jesus to help you with. Fold the paper in half.** (Allow time for silent reflection.)

◆ [Play a song about faith.] **As the music plays, I will call you forward to place your paper on the cross.** (Call the students forward by rows.)

◆ Finish by praying a litany of faith, using the checklist on page 155 of the student book. Example:

Lord, help us accept in faith the times when we are misunderstood by our parents. [Pause.]

We pray to the Lord.

[Response: Lord, by your Cross, you have helped us.]

Lord, help us accept in faith the stress and difficulties of taking a test. [Pause.]

We pray to the Lord.

[Response: Lord, by your Cross, you have helped us.]

A Wall of Opposition

Jesus faced difficulties throughout his public life. Sometimes people did not understand him or accept him. From the beginning, the religious leaders watched his every move with suspicion. They did not like his popularity and his criticism of their rigid view of the law. Instead of being open and changing their narrow-minded attitudes, they gradually built a wall of opposition.

For each stone, look up the Scripture passage and write the form of opposition that Jesus faced. Choose the form from the Opposition Box below.

Luke 4:16–30
attempted to
throw him off a cliff

Luke 8:34–37
asked him to leave town

Mark 11:15–19
looked for a way to
put him to death

John 10:31–33
accused him
of blasphemy

Matthew 12:22–24
said he had power
from the devil

John 8:54–59
picked up stones
to throw at him

OPPOSITION BOX
- picked up stones to throw at him
- asked him to leave town
- said he had power from the devil
- accused him of blasphemy
- attempted to throw him off a cliff
- looked for a way to put him to death

In the face of such opposition, Jesus remained true to his goal—to do the will of the Father and to proclaim the kingdom. The raising of his friend Lazarus from the dead united the forces of opposition and was the immediate cause of Jesus' Death. In the account of Jesus' suffering, Death, and glory, life and death are intertwined.

CHECKPOINT

- Were the learning outcomes achieved?

LEARNING OUTCOMES

The students will be able to

- explain Jesus' courage in the face of opposition.
- describe a Christian attitude toward death.

Materials

- Bibles or New Testament
- Recorded music: Find suggestions for Chapter 19 on page T519.
- Reflection notebooks

Before You Begin

Be sensitive to students who have experienced a death of or separation from a significant person in their lives. It is also important to communicate your Catholic beliefs regarding eternal life. Students may have difficulty discussing death. Before the lesson, you might discuss the serious nature of the material and your confidence in the students' ability to handle the topic.

Man Dead Four Days Lives!

BETHANY—A man dead for four days was restored to life yesterday by the Galilean preacher and wonder-worker, Jesus of Nazareth.

Lazarus, a distinguished citizen of Bethany, died Monday after a brief illness. Prescribed Jewish burial rituals were performed, and the body was laid in the family tomb outside the city.

Miracle Reported

Yesterday Jesus, a close friend of the family, arrived and requested that the tomb be opened. The deceased man's sister Martha objected, for she knew what the body would be like after four days.

Tomb of Lazarus in Bethany, Israel.

Nevertheless, at Jesus' insistence, the stone was removed. Observers said that Jesus commanded Lazarus to come out. Seconds later the corpse appeared in its burial clothes at the entrance of the tomb. At the order of the Galilean, the sisters of Lazarus unwound the burial linens and found themselves face-to-face with their brother, alive and well!

Excitement runs high today as people discuss proclaiming Jesus as the Messiah. The Sanhedrin is expected to convene to address the issue and determine the action it will take. A reliable source has disclosed that the members fear Jesus' power to draw crowds will attract Rome's attention.

From Death to Life

Behind a front-page news article, there is an inside story. To find out the inside story about the raising of Lazarus, read John 11:1–53. Then answer the following questions:

1. Why didn't the apostles want Jesus to go to Lazarus?
2. What encouraging message did Jesus give Martha?
3. What were Jesus' emotions at the tomb?
4. How did Jesus show that he was following his Father's will?
5. What attitude toward death did Jesus have? Mary and Martha?

You can imagine how people flocked to Jesus after he raised Lazarus from the dead. According to the Gospels, when Jesus rode into Jerusalem on a colt near the feast of Passover, a great crowd greeted him. They waved palm branches, a sign of welcome for a conqueror. They shouted, "Hosanna! Blessed is he who comes in the name of the Lord, the king of Israel." The Pharisees were helpless to stop the demonstration. They cried, "Look, the whole world has gone after him."

Pachomian Brotherhood, detail of Lazarus from modern Byzantine-style icon, Mount Athos, Greece.

CHAPTER 19 157

(handwritten) Jesus told Martha, "I am the Resurrection and the life."

Centering

1. Have the students complete these sentences on paper.
   - When I hear the word *death*, I think . . . [Pause.]
   - People fear death because . . . [Pause.]
   - Considering my own death, I . . . [Pause.]
   - The connection between death and Jesus is . . . [Pause.]
   - The Church tells us that death is . . . [Pause.]
   - Ask the students to share their answers.

2. Link the last lesson with today's lesson.

   - You have learned about what the Transfiguration meant for Jesus and the disciples.
   - Today you will study events that led to the suffering and Death of Jesus as foretold in the Transfiguration.

Sharing

1. Explain the position of Jesus' opponents.
   Some religious leaders felt threatened by Jesus' criticism of their hypocrisy and by his conviction that he was sent by God. They were upset because he healed people on the Sabbath. They were afraid that if Jesus became too powerful, Rome would crush the Jewish people. Closed to Jesus' message, they tried to get others to reject him.

2. Have a student read aloud the first paragraph of **A Wall of Opposition** on page 156.
   Work on the exercise with the students reading aloud each Scripture reference.

3. Have a student read aloud the last paragraph of this section.
   What role did the raising of Lazarus play in Jesus' struggle? (Uniting the opposition, it caused Jesus' Death.)

4. Have a student read aloud **Man Dead Four Days Lives!** on page 157.
   Ask the student to read the article as a news announcer would.

5. Have a student read aloud the first paragraph of **From Death to Life** on page 157.

✦ After completing the reading on Lazarus (John 11:1–53), have the students answer the questions.

✦ The following answers contain additional background information.

1. The disciples were afraid that the religious leaders would kill Jesus. (John 11:8) They remembered that they had tried to arrest Jesus for identifying himself with God. (John 10:36–39)

2. "Your brother will rise." (John 11:23) "I am the resurrection and the life; whoever believes in me, even if he dies, will live, and everyone who lives and believes in me will never die." (John 11:25–26)

3. Jesus was deeply moved. (John 11:35, 38) Explanations include sorrow for the loss of a friend and fear and anguish at the thought of his own death.

4. He prayed aloud, thanking his Father for hearing him. (John 11:41–42) He also worked a miracle, which showed that he is one with the Father. Some people recalled that Jesus had opened the eyes of a blind man. (John 9:30–34) This was a sign of God's power and of Jesus as the Messiah sent by God. (Luke 4:18) Mentioning this in the Lazarus story stresses that Jesus brings people from the blindness and death of sin to eternal light and life.

5. Jesus said, "I am the resurrection." (John 11:25) For us, death is a mystery. But Jesus has power over death. Through his Death and Resurrection, Jesus has become the source of eternal life for anyone who believes in him. For Mary and Martha, death is final; once someone is dead, nothing can be done. Martha expresses belief in a "last day" when there will be a general resurrection.

6. Call on a student to read aloud the last paragraph of this section.
How does the Church remember Jesus' triumphant entry into

A Dead End?

If you took a poll asking "How do you view death?" you might find answers like these:

- Death is beautiful. It is coming home to God.
- Death is cruel and meaningless. It is a total end of life.
- Death is frightening. I do not want to think about it.
- Death is a mystery. I cannot understand it.
- Death means goodbye. I do not want to lose what I have.
- Death is confusing. There must be life after death, but I am not sure what kind.

Raising Lazarus was a sign that Jesus could give eternal life to those who believe in him. Not long after that miracle, Jesus freely and obediently offered his life to the Father in order to free us from our sins and give us eternal life. By offering his life, he changed death into a doorway leading to happiness with God.

The Christian Views Death

Through Baptism, you share in the life won by Jesus' Death and Resurrection. God has called you to live in friendship with him that is beyond death and lasts forever. Death can be your final yes to God. You can accept it and offer your life to the Father as Jesus did. Here are four positive ways of looking at death for a Christian:

- You are united with God in the kingdom of love forever.

- You are freed from evil's power forever.
- You deepen your relationship with all those who have already died and are united with Christ.
- You have a new relationship in love with those who have not yet died.

If death means all these good things, why are we afraid? Death, the result of sin, brings pain and suffering. It leads us into the unknown, away from all that is familiar and loved.

Even Jesus dreaded death. The night before he died, he went to the garden of Gethsemane. There he faced his coming death and was overwhelmed with fear. As he prayed, he was strengthened to accept death. Jesus willingly gave his life to the Father. Like him, we are called to accept our fear and give ourselves with trust into the hands of our Father. Our faith and our hope in eternal life strengthen us to do this.

When Someone You Love Dies

Imagine how empty and lonely life would be if your best friend moved away. A similar experience on a deeper level is the loss through death of someone you love. The emptiness and loneliness are great. At such times, remember that through your union with Christ, you remain united to the one you love and that suffering will lead to a life of glory together.

A Moment with Jesus

It takes faith to believe in eternal life. With eyes of faith, we can see beyond today and believe in God's promise of life after death.

Pause for a moment and think about your own belief in eternal life. How has it been a comfort to you in times of loss? Reflect on the gift that faith is. Then thank Jesus for your faith and for the promise of eternal life.

(158) UNIT 3

Jerusalem? (We celebrate Passion or Palm Sunday a week before Easter. A ritual of blessing palms and a procession may precede the Mass. We receive the palms, which are a sacramental.)

7. Have the students read silently **A Dead End?** on page 158.

✦ **Circle the view of death that is similar to your own.**

✦ **What did the miracle of the raising of Lazarus show?** (Jesus had power over physical life and death. He also proclaimed that he was the source of eternal life.)

✦ **How did Jesus change death?** (He died willingly and obediently. He

changed death into a doorway leading to happiness with God.)

8. Direct the students to read silently **The Christian Views Death** on page 158.

✦ **What is the relationship between your Baptism and Christ's Death and Resurrection?** (Through Baptism, we share in the life won by Christ's Death and Resurrection.)

✦ **As we grow in hope, we rely on God for strength to face difficulties. As we grow in love, we become less selfish.**

✦ **Through death, we offer our final act of giving and enter the kingdom of total love.**

- **What is a Christian response to death?** (final yes to God, offering our lives as Jesus did, willingly and obediently)

- **Before he was forced to drink poison, the philosopher Socrates wrote reasons why he could look forward to death. For instance, he thought death might mean sleeping forever—a pleasant thought for some! Which of the four positive ways of looking at death for a Christian appeals to you most?**

- **Why are people afraid of death?** (It can bring pain and suffering. We fear the unknown and leaving all that is familiar and loved.)

- **A Christian has many helps for facing death. The Eucharist puts us in touch with Jesus' Death and**

Resurrection, our hope for resurrection. Through prayer, we unite our desires with God's will, an attitude that prepares us to accept death. The New Testament nourishes our faith with references to eternal life.

- **How can we handle our fear of death as Jesus did?** (We can accept our fear and give ourselves with trust into the hands of our Father. We are strengthened by our faith and our hope for eternal life.)

9. Have a student read aloud **When Someone You Love Dies** on page 158.
   As a Christian, what hope can you cling to when a loved one dies? (Someday you will be together again in glory.)

Acting

1. Have the students read John 11:25–26.
   Ask the students to reflect prayerfully on the question Jesus asks Martha. Direct them to write their responses in their reflection notebooks. Pray together the Hail Mary found on the inside back cover of the student book.

2. Choose or let the students choose an activity from Reach Out on page 159.

CHECKPOINT

- Were the learning outcomes achieved?

Day Three   Our Journey Through Life

LEARNING OUTCOMES

The students will be able to

- list events in Christ's life on a timeline.
- plan events in their spiritual journey.

Materials

- Bibles or New Testaments
- Picture of a busy city street
- Map of Palestine

- Timeline drawn on the board:

  •—•—•—•—•—•—•—•

- One 3-by-25 ½-inch strip of paper for each student
- Rulers
- Crayons or felt-tipped pens
- Instrumental music (optional)

Before You Begin

1. Jesus' entire life can be seen as a journey back to the Father. John's Gospel reflects this image: "Jesus knew that his hour had come to pass from this world to the Father." (John 13:1) Each person's life can be seen as a journey or pilgrimage. All God's people travel together toward the fullness of the kingdom. The Rite of Christian Initiation of Adults (RCIA) emphasizes recognizing and sharing our spiritual journeys.

2. The faith perspective with which we view the events of life and make daily decisions leads to our goal of eternal life.

Centering

1. Discuss with the students how we journey through life.
   - Show the picture of a busy city street or ask the students to imagine it.
   - **Imagine that you are watching people on a busy street. You might see some people who wander aimlessly. They don't seem to know where they are going. What other traveling styles**

might you observe? (a person who moves deliberately, one who stops and chats, one who is confused)

- **Life has been compared to a journey. People on their life journeys also have different traveling styles.**

- **The aimless wanderers go from day to day, allowing events to happen to them and meeting people who happen to come along. These people might**

complain that nothing good ever happens to them, but they never try to make their lives different.

- **What other traveling styles can there be in life?** (People can know why they're living, have a goal, and strive for it. Confused people may try to stop living or go the wrong way, making poor choices. Half-hearted people may get distracted in moving toward their goal.)

2. Link the last lesson with today's lesson.

You have been studying the end of Jesus' life. Today you will look at the course of his life and your life.

Sharing _____

1. Discuss with the students important journeys in the Bible.
What are some examples of important journeys in the Bible? (Abraham was called by God from Haran to Canaan. Moses and the Israelites were called out of Egypt to the Promised Land of Canaan. Jesus journeyed from Galilee, where he grew up, to Judea, where he was killed.)

2. Refer to the map of Palestine from the Lesson Pullouts in the back of student book. [See separate poster with TE.]
Ask a student to trace the journey of Jesus on the map.

3. Have a student read aloud John 16:28.
By listening to Jesus' Journey, we can see that his life can be looked at as a spiritual journey back to the Father. [Read aloud to the students Jesus' Journey.]

Jesus' Journey

The Father sent Jesus into the world to save everyone from sin and death. While on Earth, Jesus announced his Father's kingdom and called people to change their lives and live for God. He healed people, forgave sins, entered into debates, and challenged the religious leaders who weren't really bringing God's ways to the people. His works brought him closer to his Death because they angered the leaders. Jesus relaxed with friends, enjoyed children, the beauties of nature, and sharing meals. He worshiped in the Temple and the synagogues, and he prayed alone. These events, both joys and sorrows, were important parts of his journey. Finally, he died on the Cross and entered into eternal glory at his Resurrection. He had reached his goal.

4. Have the students chart the events of Jesus' life on a timeline.

✦ Use the timeline on the board. Each segment represents five years in the life of Jesus. [Show a ruler.]

✦ **A timeline is like a ruler. It is divided into equal spaces. While a ruler marks inches, a timeline marks years.**

✦ **What are the main events in Jesus' life?** (born in a village; childhood; worked in a carpenter shop; traveled as a preacher; trial and death; buried in a grave; rose from the dead; ascended)

5. Explain to the students about their spiritual journey.

✦ **Each of us is on a journey. No two journeys are exactly alike. Think about your life from its beginning up to this minute.** [Pause.]

✦ **At one point in time, you were created. You were born into a certain family. Then you were baptized and became a member of God's family, the Church. You started your spiritual journey.**

✦ **What is the goal of our spiritual journey?** (to live eternally with God, our Father; to contribute to the building of God's kingdom; to do the Father's will) **Is your goal any different from Jesus' goal?**

6. Give a strip of paper to each student.

✦ Recall the timeline discussion from earlier in the lesson.

✦ **Divide the paper into blocks, one for each year of your life.**

✦ **Put the date of your birth at the top of the first block.**

✦ **In the second block, put 1 for your first year. Fill in your ages in the rest of the blocks, leaving room for writing.**

✦ **Let us pray for help in remembering our journey so far: "Come, Holy Spirit, bring to our memories the important people and events that helped us on our journey."**

✦ **In each block, put people and events for a given year. Include those that have helped you know God better and times that people encouraged you and cared about you. These are experiences that helped you to believe that God loves you.**

✦ **You might add instances when you chose to follow Christ's teachings and moved forward on your journey.**

✦ **Try to design a symbol for each year and put it in the box.**

7. Lead the students to think about their future.

✦ **Your timeline goes only up to today. Think about your journey into the future. In the Bible, Job saw his journey continuing on through death. He said, "For my years are numbered now, and I am on a journey from which I shall not return."** (Job 16:22)

✦ **Knowing that eventually everyone has to die can make us more aware of how valuable each day of life is and how we need to live it wisely.**

✦ **How will you spend your years? Do you plan to graduate from high school? go to college? get married and have a family? be a priest, deacon, or religious? live a single life? what goal will guide your decisions?**

✦ **List your ideas for the future on the back of your timeline.**

8. Discuss with the students their timeline and Jesus' timeline.
How is your journey like the journey of Jesus?

Acting _____

Have the students read silently **A Moment with Jesus** on page 158. [Play soft music.]

✦ Allow sufficient time for silent reflection.

◆ Pray with the students the following prayer adapted from Psalm 139.

◆ **Lord, you know me through and through. You know all my actions. Even from far away you can read my mind. I have always been in your loving care, even when I was hidden within my mother before I was born. Your strong hand kept me safe even** before I knew you were there. As the future unfolds, Lord, I know you will guide me through all the ups and downs of my life. I know that you who created me will guide me safely home to you.

CHECKPOINT

- Were the learning outcomes achieved?

- How do the students show they understand that Jesus' goal and mission should be their own goal and mission?

Day Four From Death into Life

LEARNING OUTCOMES

The students will be able to

- discuss the normal reactions to death.

- name and describe the three parts of the Catholic funeral rite.

- explain how the Catholic funeral rite celebrates the Christian view of death.

- demonstrate an understanding of the key concepts in this chapter.

Materials

- Bibles or New Testaments
- BLM 67
- BLM 68 Quiz
- The three Catholic funeral rites written on flash cards: *Vigil, Funeral Liturgy, Rite of Committal*
- Song about the Resurrection
- Candle (check fire codes)

- Slips of paper with a Scripture reference, one for each student:

Job 19:26	*1 Corinthians 15:57*
Wisdom 3:1	*2 Corinthians 5:7*
Isaiah 55:12	*Ephesians 2:4–6*
Psalm 116:15	*Philippians 3:21*
John 6:39	*Colossians 3:3–4*
John 6:68	*1 Thessalonians 4:14*
John 11:25–27	*1 Thessalonians 4:17*
Romans 8:18	*2 Timothy 1:10*
Romans 8:38–39	*2 Timothy 2:11*
Romans 14:8	*Hebrews 13:14*
1 Corinthians 2:9	*1 Peter 1:8–9*
1 Corinthians 6:14	*1 Peter 5:10–11*
1 Corinthians 13:12	*2 Peter 1:11*
1 Corinthians 15:22	*Jude 1:20–21*
1 Corinthians 15:49	*1 John 3:2*
1 Corinthians 15:55	

Before You Begin

1. The death of a loved one is an experience of intense loss. It is frightening and mysterious.

Christians, however, find bright rays of hope in the midst of these many tears. We believe that death is not an end, but a beginning; that a beloved has passed through death from this present, temporary life to a perfect, permanent one; that he or she who saw God in faith on earth now sees the Lord face to face in heaven; that while death separates us now, it is but for a time only. Soon we will be reunited as God tells us in the Bible with those we love . . .

Rev. Joseph M. Champlin
Through Death to Life

2. If questions about cremation arise, explain that while cremation is permissible, the Church prefers that the dead be buried to show respect for the human body, which will share in the resurrection.

3. When planning today's lesson, keep in mind that Day Four is when the students take the quiz for this chapter. Reserve time at the end of class for this assessment. The quiz can also be administered on Day Five.

Centering _____

1. Discuss loss and how people respond to it.
   - ◆ **What are some recent losses that you have experienced in your life?** [Write the students' responses on the board.] (a failing grade; losing a pet, a game, a friend, or money)

- ◆ **Which of these is the most important loss, and which is the least important?**

- ◆ **What are some of the ways people respond to loss?** (Some refuse to admit it; some become angry; some accept it peacefully.)

2. Link the last lesson with today's lesson.
   - ◆ **You have learned that Jesus, who is fully God and fully human, died for us.**
   - ◆ **Today you will learn the great mystery of death that Jesus shared with us as a human being.**

Sharing

1. Read the story My Friend Steve to the students.

My Friend Steve

Hi! My name is Manny and I just turned 12 and I've got to talk to someone. Two days ago my best friend Steve, who lives across the street, and I discovered a half-covered cave in the woods and claimed it. We waded through the stream on our way home, instead of using the bridge as we usually do. We had a lot of fun.

Then that night Steve rode his bike to the drugstore to buy some batteries and was hit by a car. I heard the ambulance down the street, but it wasn't until later that the neighbors told my mom that the ambulance had come for Steve. Then my mom told me that Steve had died. Now I wonder, what is it like to die?

You know, Steve and I both liked chocolate fudge ice cream and played on the same basketball team. In the winter, we went sledding down the big hill by the hospital. I want him back. I don't want Steve to be gone. I would do anything to get him back. We shared so much together, and he was my best friend. Why did Steve have to die?

Yesterday all the kids were playing outside, and I said to my mom, "How can they do that when Steve's dead? Have they forgotten already? Don't they understand?" I couldn't eat. I haven't eaten anything since Steve left. How could I?

I went with my parents to the funeral home. I didn't want to, but at the last minute I changed my mind. I wanted Steve to know that I cared and that I hadn't forgotten him. Does Steve know that I still remember him and really miss him? His mom and uncle were right in front of the coffin. His mom was crying softly. There were many people standing around, talking about Steve, telling stories of things he said and did. Some were praying quietly. I said a prayer for Steve too. Some people told Steve's mom that they were sorry this happened and that they cared. I looked right at Steve. He looked like he was fooling around—pretending to sleep. But I knew he wasn't fooling. It was then that I truly began to realize that Steve wasn't coming back. He was really gone. And I found an empty room where I just stood and cried.

In the car on the way home, my mom put her arm around me like I was a little kid. I couldn't tell her, but it felt good. I hate to think that Steve is gone forever, that I'll never see him again. Will I see him again?

CHAPTER 19 — Summary

Remember

What is the Christian view of death?
For a Christian, death is a final chance to accept God's will and offer oneself freely to God, following the example of Jesus.

What is Jesus' promise of eternal life?
Jesus said, "I am the resurrection and the life; whoever believes in me, even if he dies, will live." (John 11:25)

What is the Transfiguration?
The Transfiguration is the glorified appearance of Jesus that was witnessed by the apostles Peter, James, and John.

Respond

The apostle Thomas had a special meeting with Jesus. Read John 20:19–29. What did Thomas say to Jesus when he met him? What did Jesus say to Thomas? Did you ever have to believe without seeing? What did you feel like? What helped you to have faith in Jesus? Answer these questions in your reflection journal.

Reach Out

1. Read Luke 7:11–17, Luke 8:49–56, and John 11:1–44. Create a front-page news story for one of the passages from Luke. Or, with a small group, make up a skit for one of the three passages.

2. Make a photo album of the main events in Jesus' life. Draw the photos and add captions. Include the times of opposition Jesus faced. Share your photo album with younger family members. Use it to teach them about Jesus.

3. When have you faced opposition for acting as a Christian? How did you respond? Reflect on the incident in your reflection notebook. Write a prayer asking to meet opposition courageously.

4. Imagine that a close relative of your friend has died. Write a sympathy note, sharing the Christian view of death. Decorate the note with Resurrection symbols.

5. Participate in the funeral for someone in your parish. Pray for him or her as a representative of the faith community. Report on what you observed that strengthened your faith.

Thomas's special meeting with Jesus, stained glass, St. Mary's Church, Killarney, Ireland. ❯

(159)

---

2. Discuss the story with the students.

✦ **What are Manny's feelings in this story?** (sad, confused, lost, lonely, in need of assurance)

✦ **What actions did he take?** (talked to someone, asked questions, went to the funeral home, prayed for Steve, cried, accepted comfort from his mother)

✦ **How did the other people in the story react?** (Manny's mom told him about Steve's death and took him to the funeral home. Steve's mother cried softly. The visitors told stories about Steve, prayed for Steve, said they were sorry and that they cared. The kids in the neighborhood played outside as usual.)

- **If Manny were your friend, what would you say to him about Steve's death? How would you answer his questions?**

- **If you were Steve's friend, how could you help the family at this painful time?** (Attend the wake and funeral; write a sympathy note; pray for Steve and for his family; offer to baby-sit for younger children in Steve's family; look for ways to help his family, such as emptying the garbage and running errands. In the future, continue to visit his family, to be of service, to visit Steve's grave, and to pray for him.)

3. Explain the Christian view of death, using student's comments and covering these points:

   - **On earth, we know God through faith; in heaven, we see him face-to-face.**

   - **We are only temporarily separated from our loved ones by death. They are with God, which we, too, will be someday.**

   - **At wakes, people share the sorrow of the family and friends, support them, and pray for the deceased person.**

4. Explain the various parts of the Catholic funeral rite.

   - **At funerals, the Church celebrates the Paschal Mystery of Jesus. What are some reasons for a funeral?** (to honor and pray for the dead, to comfort and support the family and friends, to express and strengthen our faith and hope in eternal life)

   - **There are three parts to Catholic funerals.** [Post flash cards as you explain the parts.]

   Vigil **The wake service takes place wherever the body is placed during the time before the funeral. It may include songs, prayer, Scripture, homily, intercessions, a litany, the Lord's Prayer, and a blessing.**

   Funeral Liturgy **The body is received at the church door. The Mass before burial is the heart of**

CHAPTER 19 Review Activities

Sorting Events If the statement refers to the Transfiguration, write T. If it refers to the raising of Lazarus, write L.

T	1.	Moses and Elijah spoke with Jesus.
L	2.	Jesus proclaimed that he was the resurrection and the life.
T	3.	Peter wanted to stay on the mountain with Jesus.
T	4.	The apostles learned that glory comes from the Cross.
L	5.	The Pharisees were determined to kill Jesus.
T	6.	The apostles' faith was confirmed.
T	7.	The Father told us to listen to his Son Jesus.
T	8.	Jesus appeared in glory.
L	9.	People in Jerusalem greeted Jesus as the king of Israel.
L	10.	Jesus showed his humanness.

Not Wanted Give examples of how Jesus was rejected.

His own people of Nazareth tried to throw him off a cliff. He was asked to leave town.

Crowds picked up stones to throw at him. He was accused of blasphemy. He was said to have power

from the devil. Plans were made to kill him.

Riddles Answer these questions.

1. Why is death a comma, not a period?

   Death is a doorway to eternal life; it is not a dead end.

2. Why can we say Jesus "loved us to death"?

   Jesus loved us so intensely that he died for us.

3. Why is life after life better than life?

   In heaven we will be united with God in his kingdom of love forever. We will be freed from the power

   of evil. We will deepen our relationship with all those who are already united with Christ. We will have

   a new relationship in love with those who have not yet died.

4. How do you turn death into a yes?

   We accept death and offer our lives to the Father as Jesus did.

160

---

the funeral rite. It ends with a final commendation and farewell.

Rite of Committal The burial includes a Scripture verse, prayer over the grave, intercessions, the Lord's Prayer, concluding prayer, and prayer over the people.

- **Can anyone add information about one of these from personal experience?**

5. **BLM 67** Distribute copies of BLM 67 **Through Death to Life.** Have the students read the directions and complete the exercise about the funeral Mass.

1. **White vestments are normally used to stress the Resurrection,**

but violet or black vestments may be used.

2. **Resurrection songs are appropriate for funerals.**

3. **Water and a white garment are used at Baptism when we first share in the Resurrection of the Lord.**

4. **The paschal candle is lit on Holy Saturday at the Easter Vigil.**

5. **These readings are the Word of God.**

6. **Jesus promised, "Whoever eats my flesh and drinks my blood has eternal life, and I will raise him on the last day."** (John 6:54)

7. **Incensing the body may take place during the rite. It shows**

that the body of the person is important because it was the temple of the Holy Spirit. The rising smoke represents our prayers for the deceased rising up to God.

6. Discuss with the students the importance of the community at the time of death.
How do members of the faith community help one another at the time of someone's death? (by praying, by being present, by witnessing to their faith in eternal life, by expressing sympathy)

7. Lead the students through the Summary and Review Activities, pages 159–160.

8. **BLM 68** Distribute and administer BLM 68 **Chapter 19 Quiz.**
Use this opportunity to assess the students' understanding of the main concepts in the chapter. The quiz can also be taken on Day Five.

Acting _____

1. Give each student a slip of paper with a Scripture reference.
Look up the passage on your piece of paper. You will read your passages during our prayer service.

2. Lead the students in a time of prayer.
✦ **Each of you will read your passage. We will do this by rows. You will read your passage and pause so that the passage can be reflected on. Then the next person in the row will read his or her passage.** [Light the candle and pray the opening prayer.]

✦ **Lord Jesus, thank you for dying that we might live forever. Strengthen my faith in eternal life as we listen to your Word.**

✦ Have the students read their passages. End the service with a song.

3. At the end of class, have the students tear out and take home pages 159–160.

CHECKPOINT

• Were the learning outcomes achieved?

• What evidence is there that the students share the Christian view of death?

Day Five   Extending the Chapter

Gather and Go Forth

Lead students through pages 161–162 in the student book. Find catechist instruction on T352–T353.
Materials: Bibles

Use the following suggestions to create an additional lesson for Day Five.

1. Remind the students to take home pages 159–160 to share what they are learning with their families.

2. Incorporate any unused BLMs from the week's chapter.

3. Consider the time of the liturgical year and use the appropriate Special Seasons and Lessons. SSLs begin on page T369.

4. Visit www.christourlife.com to find additional activities for Extending the Chapter.

5. Use activities from Enriching the Faith Experience.

6. Guide the students in a prayerful discussion of Sunday's Scripture readings. Visit www.christourlife.com for more information.

Use the following activities to enrich a lesson or to replace an activity with one that better meets the needs of your class.

1. Have the students create a *Wall of Opposition* mural, showing times when Jesus courageously kept proclaiming the kingdom even when people refused to accept his message. They could refer to Chapters 5–10 in John's Gospel.

2. Help the students design a banner that captures the essence of the Christian view of death. Donate it to the parish to be used for funerals.

I have come that they may have LIFE!

3. Direct the students to write an essay on the topic: "The best way to prepare for a Christian death is to lead a good Christian life."

4. Have the students research funeral traditions in various countries, in different parts of our country, or in various ethnic groups such as the Latino, African-American or Korean-American communities. Tell them to write a report on one custom, adding a sketch or picture to illustrate it. The students could present their research as a PowerPoint presentation.

5. Ask the students to write a conversation that Mary, Martha, or one of the bystanders might have had with Lazarus after he was raised from the dead.

6. Let the students read silently 1 Corinthians 15:40–55 and 2 Corinthians 5:1–10, and list the things each quotation says about eternal life.

7. The bishop consecrates every Catholic cemetery where the bodies of believing Christians are buried. Take the students to a cemetery and allow them to do rubbings of gravestones, using paper and pencil or crayon. Or have them fix up a grave by weeding, picking up trash, or placing flowers on it.

8. Invite a speaker to witness to the class on suffering and the growth that comes from it. Choose the person carefully and meet with him or her beforehand. Discuss the purpose of the class. After the speaker shares the values of suffering in his or her life, relate it to Jesus in his passion, and explain that we join our suffering to his.

9. Invite a local Catholic funeral director to speak to the class about various aspects of the funeral process. Some funeral homes have prepared presentations.

10. Direct the students to consider a situation in which they faced opposition for speaking or acting as a follower of Jesus. Ask them what their response was. Encourage them to pray, asking for help in facing future opposition as courageously as Jesus did in his life. Allow time for prayer.

The Eucharist
JESUS THE BREAD OF LIFE

Faith Focus

The Eucharist nourishes us with the Body and Blood of Jesus uniting us with him and one another.

Reflecting on the Faith Experience

Take a few moments to reflect prayerfully before preparing the lesson.

Listening

For I received from the Lord what I also handed on to you, that the Lord Jesus, on the night he was handed over, took bread, and after he had given thanks, broke it and said, "This is my body that is for you. Do this in remembrance of me." In the same way also the cup, after supper, saying, "This cup is the new covenant in my blood. Do this, as often as you drink it, in remembrance of me." For as often as you eat this bread and drink the cup, you proclaim the death of the Lord until he comes.

1 Corinthians 11:23–26

Reflecting

God constantly calls us into deeper union. The Eucharist, the heart of Christian life, expresses and strengthens our union with God and with one another. In the Mass, as a community, we worship the Father with Christ in one act of thanks and praise. In the Eucharist, the risen Lord is sacramentally present as God and man. He makes present his sacrifice on the Cross and the victory of his Resurrection. We join our lives with his in an offering to the Father. In faith and love, we approach the table of the Lord to be nourished by the Body and Blood of Christ. In communicating all that he has and is, Jesus unites all who partake of his Body and Blood, forming them in a mysterious way into one body; for the Eucharist is both the sign and source of our unity in Christ.

In the Eucharist, Jesus does things for us as he did for his followers in Palestine. But his influence on our lives depends on our faith and generosity. He worked miracles for those who believed in him, for those who gave themselves to him. What he asks is faith and love: faith that will move mountains and love that is willing even to die for others, as Christ has died for us.

We go forth from the Eucharist in peace to love and serve the Father and one another with the mind and heart of Jesus Christ. Imbued with Christ's presence, we can meet the situations of life with greater vitality. Nourished by the Eucharist, we can be like "the Son of Man [who] did not come to be served but to serve. . . . " (Matthew 20:28) Christ will never fail us. If we cooperate with his grace, we will recognize him in our brothers and sisters. Let us pray:

Grant us, O Lord, we pray,
that the course of our world
may be directed by your
   peaceful rule
and that your Church may
   rejoice,
untroubled in her devotion.

Collect Prayer
Eighth Sunday in Ordinary Time

How can I make the Mass more meaningful?

Responding

Holy Spirit, instill in my students a desire to participate wholeheartedly in Mass.

Scripture for Further Reflection

John 6:56–57 Jesus' flesh and blood are real food to strengthen us in our spiritual journey.

Hebrews 12:18–29 The new covenant that Jesus entered into with us brings forgiveness of sins and a new relationship with God, but it also demands our generous response.

Preparing for the Faith Experience

Scripture in This Chapter

Mark 6:30–44 Jesus Feeds the Five Thousand

John 15:4–7 The Vine and the Branches

John 6:55–56 Jesus' flesh is true flesh.

Catholic Social Teaching

Solidarity

Church Documents

Catechism of the Catholic Church. The themes of this chapter correspond to the following paragraphs: **610–611, 1324–1326, 1341–1344, 1402–1405.**

General Directory for Catechesis #115. The Holy Eucharist occupies a unique place to which all of the other sacraments are ordained. Catechists should present the Eucharist as the "sacrament of sacraments."

The Constitution on the Sacred Liturgy #10 (Second Vatican Council). All aspects and activities of the Christian life and the Church lead to the liturgy or flow from it.

The Eucharist in Its Relationship to the Church #9 (Saint John Paul II). The Eucharist is Christ's saving presence in the community of the faithful and its spiritual food. It is therefore the most precious possession that the Church can have in its journey through history.

Gather and Go Forth

Find catechist instruction for Gather and Go Forth student pages 169–170 on T354–T355.

Enriching the Faith Experience

Use the activities at the end of the chapter to enrich a lesson or to replace an activity with one that better meets the needs of your class. Bookmark www.christourlife.com to find Web BLMs for this chapter.

Bulletin Board

A suggestion for a bulletin-board design for this chapter is pictured.

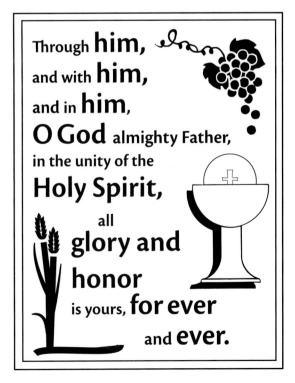

Through **him,** and with **him,** and in **him,** **O God** almighty Father, in the unity of the **Holy Spirit,** all **glory and honor** is yours, **for ever and ever.**

LEARNING OUTCOMES

The students will be able to

- explain that the Eucharist is a memorial meal in which Christ's Death and Resurrection are made present.

- express an awareness of Jesus' love evident in his presence and action in the Mass.

- explain that Jesus nourishes and strengthens individuals and the community through the Eucharist, the center of Christian life.

Key Terms

covenant—an agreement between God and human beings

Eucharist—a sacrament in which the Paschal Mystery of Jesus is both called to mind and made present under the appearance of bread and wine. We offer Jesus with ourselves to the Father, and are united through eucharistic communion with Jesus, the Father, and the Holy Spirit, and with one another.

Passover—the Jewish feast commemorating with a meal God's saving action of leading the Israelites from slavery in Egypt to the Promised Land

Materials

- Bibles or New Testaments
- Souvenir
- crayons or felt-tipped pens
- Diagram written on the board:

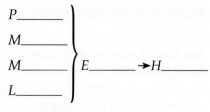

SACRED MEALS

P_____
M_____
M_____ } E_____ →H_____
L_____

- Reflection notebooks

Before You Begin

1. As the students at this age become more independent, they tend to rebel against structures they have grown up with, including participating in Mass. They may complain that the Mass is boring and that they get nothing out of it. The challenge to the catechist is to lead the students to realize what is happening during the Eucharist. Our goal is to make the Eucharist so attractive and necessary that the students feel encouraged to participate.

2. If possible, the students should plan to celebrate a Eucharist together.

Centering _____

1. Show a souvenir to the students.
   - ✦ **Why do we enjoy souvenirs?** (They help us relive an experience or remember a person who is no longer with us.)
   - ✦ **Jesus wanted to leave more than a remembrance, more than a souvenir for us. He wanted to remain with us. How did he do this?** (He gave us the Sacrament of the Eucharist.)

2. Link the last lesson with today's lesson.
   - ✦ **In the last lesson, you learned that Jesus won eternal life for us by his suffering.**
   - ✦ **Today you will learn how we participate in his saving actions.**

Sharing _____

1. Have a student read aloud **The Way We Celebrate** on page 163.
   - ✦ Divide the class in pairs to discuss their answers to the questions.
   - ✦ **Does anyone have a particularly striking experience of celebrating Mass to share with the class?**

2. Direct the students to read silently **More Than a Memory** on page 163.
   - ✦ **Why is the Eucharist a tremendous gift?** (It is a way Jesus remains with us. He teaches us. He offers his life for us, and he nourishes us. He unites us with himself and with one another. It is a sign of his permanent love for us.)
   - ✦ **Why is the Eucharist the greatest of all sacraments?** (All other sacraments exist because of the dying and rising of Christ that is celebrated in the Eucharist.)

- ✦ **Why is the Eucharist the heart of the Christian life?** (Jesus offers his life for us, nourishes us, and makes us one.)

- ✦ **What does it mean to call Jesus Mediator?** (A mediator is a go-between who settles conflicts for two opposing parties. Jesus goes between us and the Father. Through him, we are reconciled with the Father.)

3. Ask a student to read aloud the first two paragraphs of **Meals That Made History** on page 163.

- ✦ **How is the Passover meal like the Eucharist?** (It commemorates God's saving action. It is an act of worship and builds the community.)

- ✦ **How is it different?** (At the Passover meal, God is not sacramentally present in the food consumed. The rescue of the Jewish people from Egypt does not continue to take place. In the Eucharist, Christ is present whole and entire, body, blood, soul, and divinity under the appearance of bread and wine. His once-and-for-all sacrifice that saves us from sin becomes sacramentally present.)

- ✦ **Protestants celebrate the Lord's Supper as one of their two sacraments. Their other sacrament is Baptism.**

- ✦ **Most Protestants do not believe that Jesus is actually present under the signs of bread and wine. The meal is only a remembrance of him.**

- ✦ **What difference does this understanding of the Eucharist make in our worship? Our reception of Holy Communion? our churches?**

4. Direct the students to complete the activity in this section.

- ✦ [Read aloud Mark 6:30–44.] Have the students answer the question.

- ✦ **What are some of the ways you thought the miracle in Mark is like the Eucharist?**

- ✦ Call on a student to read aloud the last paragraph of the section on page 164.

- ✦ **Why did many of the disciples leave Jesus?** (What he said sounded outrageous. It sounded like cannibalism.)

CHAPTER
20

The Eucharist

Jesus the Bread of Life

The Way We Celebrate

- During Pope John Paul II's visit to the United States in 1995, a eucharistic celebration was held outdoors. Thousands of people in Baltimore, Maryland, participated.
- In Uganda, Father Dan, a missionary, parks his truck where Catholics gather for Mass. He sets up an altar alongside the road, and the people celebrate the Eucharist.
- Mr. and Mrs. Fields celebrated their sixtieth wedding anniversary with a Mass. Friends and relatives gathered around the altar to break bread together.

Which celebration of Mass most impressed you? Why?

Answers will vary.

More Than a Memory

All Masses are special. Before Jesus died, he gave us a precious gift—a way he could remain with us. He gave us the Eucharist. In this sacrament, he is present with us under the appearances of bread and wine. Jesus acts in every eucharistic celebration. He continues to teach us by his word and example. He is our one and only Mediator making the offering of his life present to us. Jesus Christ nourishes us with his Body and Blood, and he unites us with himself and with one another in the Catholic community. The Eucharist is a sign of Jesus' permanent love for us. It is the perfect act of worship and the heart of Christian life.

Meals That Made History

God prepared humankind for the gift of the Eucharist. Long ago, God rescued the Israelites from slavery in Egypt and brought them to freedom. To commemorate that great saving event, Jewish people celebrate a special Passover meal. Another hint of the Eucharist occurs in the story of the Israelites' journey to the Promised Land. God fed them in the desert with manna, a breadlike substance.

Preparation for the Eucharist continued when Jesus fed great crowds with bread and fish.

Read Mark 6:30–44. How is this miracle like the Eucharist?

God feeds his people. Jesus takes the bread,

says a blessing, and breaks the bread.

The apostles give the food to

the people. The food

miraculously

multiplies.

(163)

5. Ask a student to read aloud **The Last Supper** on page 164.

✦ **Jesus was a good teacher. He used actions to teach. To impress the lesson of love on our minds, what did he do?** (He washed the feet of the apostles. He offered himself under appearances of bread and wine.)

✦ **During the Passover meal, blessings were said, wine was drunk, and bread was eaten. What startling declaration did Jesus make when it came to these parts of the meal?** (He said the bread was his Body and the wine was his Blood. He said his Body and Blood would be given for many.)

✦ **What do the sacrifice on Calvary and the Eucharistic Liturgy have in common?** (The same sacrifice that Christ offered on Calvary is sacramentally made present and offered for us and with us at each Eucharist.)

6. Have the students read silently **A New Covenant** on page 164.

✦ [Write the headings *Hebrew Covenant* and *New Covenant* on the board. Under *Hebrew Covenant*, list *commandments* and *blood of animals*.]

✦ **What is a covenant?** (an agreement between God and humanity)

✦ **What in the new covenant corresponds to the words under *Hebrew Covenant*?** (Law of Love, Blood of Jesus) [Have the students write these answers under *New Covenant*.]

✦ **At the sacrifice of the Eucharist, Jesus is both priest and victim. As the priest, he is the one doing the offering. As the victim, he is the one who is offered. As a priestly people, we join in his offering of himself to the Father, and we offer ourselves as victims with him.**

7. Ask a student to read aloud **A Thanksgiving Meal** on page 164.
Have the students answer the question.

8. Ask the students to figure out what words belong in the diagram at the board.

SACRED MEALS

Passover
Manna
Multiplication of loaves
Last Supper
} *Eucharist* → *Heaven*

9. Direct the students to the Sacrament Chart on page 211. Have the students read the summary of the Eucharist. [See page T311.]

Acting

 Have the students do the Respond activity on page 167. Allow time for silent reflection.

CHECKPOINT

- Were the learning outcomes achieved?

- What evidence is there that the students are growing in appreciation for the great mystery we celebrate in the Eucharist?

Day Two Nourished to Serve

Student pages 164–167

LEARNING OUTCOMES

The students will be able to

- explain the structure and prayers of the Eucharist.

- discuss how in receiving the Eucharist, they become one with Christ and others.

Word To Know

transubstantiation

See Glossary for definition.

Key Terms

Liturgy of the Eucharist—the second part of the Eucharist, in which we offer Jesus and ourselves to the Father, the bread and wine are transformed into the Body and Blood of Jesus Christ, and we receive him in Holy Communion

Liturgy of the Word—the first part of the Eucharist, in which we hear and respond to the Word of God

Roman Missal—the official book of prayers and directives for the celebration of the Eucharist

Materials

- Bibles or New Testaments

- Candle and light bulb

- Readings from the upcoming Sunday's Liturgy of the Word

- Missalettes for each student

- Roman Missal (optional)

- Chart written on the board.

- Pictures on cards:

Before You Begin

After the Resurrection, the disciples gathered again and again to celebrate the Eucharist. They were convinced that the risen Jesus Christ was present when they gathered in his name. There was joy in being together as a Church. There was rejoicing because, through the Eucharist, Jesus Christ was with them, and together they looked forward to loving and serving him for the sake of the kingdom.

Centering

1. Show the candle and light bulb to the students.

✦ **Where does the candle get its power?** (from itself; from the wax, which is its fuel)

✦ **Where does the light bulb get its power?** (from outside of itself; from an electrical current through an outlet)

✦ **In your spiritual life, are you more like a candle or a light bulb?** (light bulb, because our source of power is Christ)

✦ **Our greatest source of power is the Eucharist.**

2. Link the last lesson with today's lesson.

✦ **In the last class, you learned that the Eucharist was the means Christ chose to stay with us.**

✦ **Today you will learn about the prayers and actions of the Eucharist, which empower us to live Christ's life.**

Sharing

1. Call on a student to read aloud **The Liturgy of the Word** on page 164.

✦ List the parts of the Liturgy of the Word on the board and comment using the readings from the coming Sunday as examples.

✦ *Reading(s)* There is one reading on weekdays and two on Sunday. These readings may be taken from the Old Testament such as Genesis or Isaiah or the New Testament such as Acts, Epistles, or Revelation.

✦ *Responsorial psalm* This is related to the first reading. We join in on the response, which is usually sung.

✦ *Alleluia verse* This introduces and heralds the Gospel. During Lent, there is a substitute for the alleluia. This is usually sung.

✦ *Gospel* God proclaims the Good News. Christ is present in the Gospels Matthew, Mark, Luke or

In Chapter 6 of John's Gospel, after that miracle, Jesus promised the Bread of Life. Many people could not accept it when he said, "Whoever eats my flesh and drinks my blood has eternal life." Those people no longer followed him.

The Last Supper

Jesus' last meal with the apostles was probably a Passover meal. At that meal, Jesus put a towel around his waist and washed the feet of the apostles like a servant. He told them that if he, the master and teacher, washed their feet, they ought to wash one another's feet. Then Jesus showed a greater proof of his love. He took bread, blessed it, broke it, and gave it to the apostles, saying, "This is my body which will be given for you; do this in memory of me." Then he took a cup, passed it to the apostles and said, "This is my blood of the covenant, which will be shed for many." The next day Jesus would die on the Cross for us. The sacrifice offered at the Last Supper was the sacrifice of Calvary.

Jesus now offers that same sacrifice to the Father for us and with us in the Eucharist. Each time we celebrate the Eucharist, we come in contact with the dying and rising of Jesus. Only validly ordained priests can preside at the Mass and pray the prayer of consecration over the bread and wine.

A New Covenant

Sacrifices and covenants were familiar to the Jewish people. They considered the Covenant, or agreement, God made with them at Sinai

164 UNIT 3

as their birthday as God's people. There God revealed the divine name to the Jewish people and gave them the Law. They agreed to live by the Law. The Covenant was sealed by a ritual in which the blood of sacrifices was sprinkled on the altar and on the people. At the Last Supper, Jesus gave us a new commandment. He said, "Love one another. As I have loved you so you also should love one another." Humankind entered a new covenant with God sealed by the blood of Jesus. All who die and rise with Christ at Baptism share in the celebration of this covenant. They offer Christ's sacrifice and grow in love.

A Thanksgiving Meal

Eucharist means "thanksgiving." This sacrament is the greatest act of praise and thanksgiving we can offer God. We are obliged to participate in the Eucharist on the Lord's Day and on every holy day of obligation. Some people celebrate Mass on other days and benefit from the grace it offers. Any time something wonderful happens and your heart is full of joy and gratitude to God, consider celebrating Mass to give God thanks.

What days might you make special by participating in the Eucharist?

birthday, baptismal day, patron or favorite

saint's feast day, a national holiday

The celebration of the Eucharist has two main parts: the Liturgy of the Word and the Liturgy of the Eucharist.

The Liturgy of the Word

During the Liturgy of the Word, God speaks to us in the readings. In the Gospel, we are assured of God's love for us. We hear Jesus teach us what the Father wants us to know and what he wants us to do to lead a new life. The homily gives us insight into what God's words mean for us. Then we ask God's help in the Prayer of the Faithful. Nourished and strengthened by God's Word, we are fed with the Bread of Life in the Liturgy of the Eucharist.

John. At times, lighted candles, a procession, and incense are used.

✦ *Profession of faith* The people of God pray together the Nicene Creed, a profession of Baptism.

✦ *General intercessions* We pray for the needs of the Church, public authorities, the salvation of the world, those in need, and the local community.

2. Ask a student read aloud **The Liturgy of the Eucharist** on page 165.

- ✦ Show the students the pictures of wheat and grapes.

- ✦ **How do these pictures symbolize oneness?** (Many grains of wheat become one bread; many grapes become one wine.)

- ✦ **What unity takes place at the Eucharist?** (Sharing the Body and Blood of Jesus Christ, we become one body, the Body of Christ.)

3. Have the students look up John 15:4–7, The Vine and the Branches.
Why is this a good symbol? (Apart from Jesus, we have no life, just as a branch separated from the vine dies.)

4. Distribute to the students the missalettes.

- ✦ Have the students open to the page where the prayers for the Mass begin.

- ✦ Divide the students into pairs to work on the sections **He Takes Bread, He Gives Thanks, He Offers Himself,** and **Jesus Gives Himself to Us** on pages 165–166. Have the students use the missalettes as they read and work.

- ✦ If you have a Roman Missal, show it to the students as part of this activity.

- ✦ **Which prayers and actions of the Communion Rite express the unity of the community with Christ and with one another?** (*Our Father*—We pray together; the words *Our Father* show unity. *Sign of Peace*—We show that we accept and are reconciled with one another; we give to others the peace that Jesus gives us. *Breaking of Bread*—The priest shows that we will share in the one Body of Jesus. *Lamb of God*—Together we ask for mercy and peace.)

- ✦ **Why wouldn't it be right for people who are not baptized, not Catholic, or in the state of mortal sin to receive Holy Communion?** (They are not one with the community in faith. The unity that

---

The Liturgy of the Eucharist

Jesus' words and actions of the Last Supper are repeated at every Eucharist. By them we not only call to mind the Paschal Mystery, but Jesus makes it actually present. We offer Jesus to the Father and ourselves with him. Then we receive Christ's Body and Blood under the appearances of bread and wine. By sharing this meal, we form the Church. Just as many grains of wheat make one bread and many grapes make one wine, so we are made one in Christ. Together we become more like him. Together we are sent to bring his love to the world.

Read John 15:4–7. What symbol did Jesus use to describe our relationship with him?

vine and branches

Use these answers for the questions in the next sections on the Liturgy of the Eucharist:

- Amen.
- Lord, I am not worthy that you should enter under my roof, but only say the word and my soul shall be healed.
- Blessed be God for ever.
- Holy, holy, holy Lord God of hosts.
- We proclaim your Death, O Lord, and profess your Resurrection until you come again.

He Takes Bread

The Liturgy of the Eucharist begins with the Presentation and Preparation of the Gifts. We take bread and wine to the priest. He says a prayer over each gift. These prayers remind us that the bread and wine symbolize the gifts of God and the work of our hands. They symbolize each one of us and our offering with Jesus. What do we respond to each of these prayers?

Blessed be God for ever.

He Gives Thanks

Then the priest says a prayer of thanks called the Preface. With him, we offer thanks and praise through Jesus to the Father. We thank the Father for his Son Jesus who became man and redeemed us through his Cross and Resurrection. Then we join the angels and saints in a song of praise. What is its first line?

Holy, holy, holy Lord God of hosts.

He Offers Himself

The Preface is at the beginning of the Eucharistic Prayer, the high point of our act of worship. The priest stretches his hands over the gifts and calls on the Holy Spirit to make them holy. Then he prays the words of the Institution Narrative at the Last Supper, and Jesus Christ's Body and Blood become present on the altar under the appearances of bread and wine. This change in substance is called **transubstantiation.** Jesus Christ is present, living and glorious, soul and divinity.

The Eucharistic Prayers are found in the *Roman Missal*, the official book of prayers and directions for Mass. Here are the words of the Institution Narrative.

Over the bread the priest says,

Take this, all of you, and eat of it,
for this is my Body,
which will be given up for you.

Over the wine he says,

Take this, all of you, and drink from it,
for this is the chalice of my Blood,
the Blood of the new and eternal covenant,
which will be poured out for you and for many
for the forgiveness of sins.

Do this in memory of me.

The priest then invites us to proclaim the Mystery of Faith that we celebrate. What is one of the memorial acclamations?

We proclaim your Death, O Lord, and profess
your Resurrection until you come again.

CHAPTER 20 (165)

---

the Eucharist symbolizes is not there.)

- ✦ **How do we prepare for the Eucharist even before coming to the liturgy?** (For one hour prior to reception, we fast from food and liquid except water and medicine. We live every day as a follower of Jesus in charity.)

- ✦ **How do we prepare for receiving Jesus during the eucharistic celebration?** (praying and singing wholeheartedly, listening to the readings)

- ✦ **Why shouldn't we talk or chew gum while going up to receive Holy Communion?** (It shows a lack of respect and a lack of faith in Christ's presence.)

5. Direct the students to read silently **He Sends Us to Announce the Gospel** and **A Feast Without End** on page 166.

- ✦ Refer to the chart on the board.

- ✦ Starting with "You," point to the respective circles as you ask the following questions. Write the responses on the board.

- ✦ **How do YOU respond in prayer after receiving Jesus?** (Praise him, thank him, tell him our needs, trust him, permit him to act.)

- ✦ **What does JESUS CHRIST do at Communion?** (shares his life with us, strengthens us, changes us)

- ✦ **What happens to members of the COMMUNITY during reception**

of Communion? (We are drawn close to one another, and become one with Christ and with all others.)

✦ **How do we live out the eucharistic celebration after we have been sent like the apostles at the dismissal of the Mass?** (We are more aware of needs, more able to serve. We bring the Good News to all.)

✦ **Where will the greatest feast be?** (in heaven) **Heaven was often spoken of as a banquet or wedding feast.**

✦ **In the Presentation and Preparation of the Gifts, what gifts do we offer that symbolize God's gifts to us and our own work?** (bread and wine; gifts for the Church and for those who are poor)

✦ **What do we respond to the prayer that ends "It will become our spiritual drink"?** (Blessed be God forever.)

✦ **What is our response to "Through him, and with him, and in him, O God, almighty Father, in the unity of the Holy Spirit, all glory and honor is yours, for ever and ever"?** (Amen.)

✦ **What prayer of praise and thanks follows the Preface?** (Holy, Holy, Holy/Preface Acclamation)

✦ **For whom do we pray during the Eucharistic Prayer?** (the Church on earth, those who have died, and everyone)

As the priest continues the Eucharistic Prayer, united with Jesus we give praise to the Father. We pray for the Church on earth, for those who have died, and we remember Mary and the saints. The priest concludes this prayer with a hymn of praise (a doxology):

Through him, and with him, and in him,
O God, almighty Father,
in the unity of the Holy Spirit,
all glory and honor is yours,
for ever and ever.

What is our response to voice our agreement with all that is taking place?

Amen.

Jesus Gives Himself to Us

In the Communion Rite of the Mass, Jesus gives us himself as food and drink. We prepare to receive him by praying together the prayer Jesus taught us, the Lord's Prayer. We are called to reconciliation and to unity in faith and love, so we exchange a sign of Christ's peace. While the priest breaks the bread, we pray that Jesus, the Lamb of God, will have mercy on us and grant us his peace. Before receiving Jesus Christ in Holy Communion, we pray together a prayer that expresses both our weakness and our trust in God. What is it?

Lord, I am not worthy that you should enter under my roof, but only say the word and my soul shall be healed.

The Church encourages us to receive Holy Communion at every Mass. When we receive Jesus, we praise and thank and love him. We tell him of our needs, confident that he will help us. All who share the Body and Blood of Jesus Christ are drawn into union with the Father and the Holy Spirit and with one another. Here is a mystery. As we accept Christ in Holy Communion, we also agree to accept and support one another in the Christian community and others in the world. If we

(166) UNIT 3

permit him, Jesus will gradually change us into the people he calls us to be.

A Moment with Jesus

In the Eucharist, Jesus gives himself to us as real food. We are fed and nourished by the Body and Blood of Christ.

Pause for a moment and imagine yourself at Mass preparing to receive Communion. Reflect on what this means for you as a follower of Christ. In your own words, share with Jesus your hopes about growing into the person he wants you to be. Then thank Jesus for the gift of himself to you in the Eucharist.

He Sends Us to Announce the Gospel

Having been reminded of and renewed by Jesus' love, we are more aware of others' needs and more able to serve them. With Jesus, we go forth to announce the Gospel to all.

A Feast Without End

In the Eucharist, we share in the communion of saints. We are united with all the members of the Church in heaven and on earth. We can pray for those in purgatory. At Mass, we carry out the same liturgy or praise of God's glory that echoes through heaven. Our thanks and praise are preparation for the time when we will give God glory forever. The Eucharist is a sign and pledge of the banquet of God's kingdom. There people who have been faithful to the covenant will share life with God forever.

Acting

1. Choose or let the students choose an activity from Reach Out on page 167.

2. Lead the students in prayer, using **A Moment with Jesus** on page 166.
   ✦ Allow sufficient time for silent reflection.
   ✦ Conclude by praying the Take, Lord, and Receive prayer of Saint Ignatius Loyola on the inside back cover of the student book. [See page T446.]

CHECKPOINT

- Were the learning outcomes achieved?
- Do the students need more instruction on the various parts of the Mass?

LEARNING OUTCOMES

The students will be able to
- work together to plan a liturgy.
- explain the parts of the Mass.

Materials

- Bibles or New Testaments
- BLM 69A–B, BLM 70
- Lectionary
- Sacramentary
- Song books
- Art supplies (optional)
- Missalette for each student

Before You Begin

1. Experience with a eucharistic celebration can bring the students into personal contact with Christ and his saving work and deepen their relationship with him.

2. In this lesson, the students work in small groups to plan a Mass. The planning, however, could be done with the entire class working together. The ideal arrangement would be to work with the priest who will celebrate the liturgy.

3. A copy of the liturgy planning sheet should be sent in advance to the priest who will be celebrating the Mass.

4. You might wish to set aside an extra class or an art period for making banners or other decorations that reinforce the theme of the Mass.

5. Consult other liturgy resources such as *Weekday Liturgies for Children* by Mary Kathleen Glavich, S.N.D. (Twenty-Third Publications) for ideas to make the Mass being planned more memorable and meaningful to the students.

Centering

1. Connect the students' lives with the eucharistic celebration.
   - **Reflect for a moment on what is going on in your life.** [Pause.]
   - **What is your relationship with Jesus like?** [Pause.]
   - **The Eucharist you will plan and celebrate will help you in your life and strengthen your friendship with Jesus. It will give you the desire to follow him more closely.**
   - Announce the time and place when the Mass will be celebrated.

2. Link the last lesson with today's lesson.
   - **You have been studying the truths about why Jesus came and what he did for us.**
   - **Today you will plan a eucharistic celebration, the culmination of all that you have learned.**

Sharing

1. Have several students read aloud the readings for the day of the Mass from the Lectionary.
   - **What common themes are there in these readings?**
   - **Which theme is the best one for our celebration?**

2. Divide the students into five groups to plan the Mass.
   - Instruct the students to move into their groups for planning.
   - Explain the tasks of the various groups.

   Group 1: Write an introduction welcoming everyone and explaining the theme of the Mass. Plan the entrance procession and suggest a Eucharistic Prayer.

   Group 2: Prepare the first reading, responsorial psalm, Alleluia, and the general intercessions.

   Group 3: Prepare the church or chapel for the celebration and plan the presentation of the gifts.

   Group 4: Plan the praise and thanksgiving after Holy Communion, allowing some time for silent reflection. Plan some simple reminder of the theme to give each person who celebrates the liturgy with the class.

   Group 5: Select songs for the various parts of the Mass.
   (Students may be able to accompany the songs on instruments or lead the singing.)

3. **BLM 69A–B** Appoint a leader for each group. Give each leader a copy of BLM 69A–B **Liturgy Planning Sheet.**
   - Let the students know how much time they have for planning.
   - Instruct the students to write their plans on the planning sheet.

4. Visit each group and give assistance when necessary.

5. **BLM 70** Have the groups report their planning.
   - Write down the groups' planning on BLM 70 **Notes on the Liturgy.**
   - Make one copy for the priest and one to post in the classroom.
   - Collect the planning sheets.

Acting

1. Pray with the students in preparation for the Mass.
   - Have the students sing one of the songs they selected for the Mass.
   - Provide a few moments of quiet so that the students can ask Jesus to help them praise the Father with him through their celebration.

2. The class may want to invite parents, relatives, and other members of the school to the Mass.

   ✦ You might form a welcome committee to write invitations.

   ✦ The committee might also greet the guests as they arrive and pass out the song sheets.

3. Remind the students who will be readers or leaders to practice their parts at home. Tell them when they will be able to practice in church.

CHECKPOINT

- Were the learning outcomes achieved?

- How well did the students enter into the planning of the Mass?

CHAPTER 20 Summary

Remember

What is the Eucharist?
The Eucharist is the sacrament in which the Paschal Mystery of Jesus is both called to mind and made present under the appearances of bread and wine. We offer Jesus with ourselves to the Father, and we are united through eucharistic communion with Jesus, the Father, and the Holy Spirit, and with one another.

What is the new commandment of Jesus?
I give you a new commandment: love one another. As I have loved you, so you also should love one another. This is how all will know that you are my disciples, if you have love for one another.

John 13:34–35

What are the two main parts of the eucharistic celebration?
The two main parts of the eucharistic celebration are the Liturgy of the Word and the Liturgy of the Eucharist.

What is transubstantiation?
Transubstantiation is the change of the substances of bread and wine into the Body and Blood of Christ.

Respond

Think of a symbol that represents you. Maybe it is an eagle to show your interest in the environment, or a football, or a computer. Draw your symbol in your reflection notebook and write a prayer offering yourself to the Father.

Reach Out

1. Make next Sunday a day to share a meal— spiritual and physical. Invite a relative or friend to celebrate the Eucharist with you. Then eat together afterwards, either at home or in a restaurant. Discuss thoughts or feelings that occurred to you during the liturgy.

2. Think of someone you can offer loving service to this week. Write three things you will do for that person and then do them. Afterward, spend some time reflecting on your experience. How did your acts of loving service affect the person? How did they affect you?

3. Participate in the Eucharist at an Eastern Catholic Church or at another parish. Write a short paragraph about the similarities and differences you noticed.

4. Pay close attention to the readings and homilies of the next eucharistic celebration you attend. Write a paragraph explaining what God was saying to you that day. Then share your reflections with someone in your family.

5. Compile quotations about the Eucharist from John 6 and 1 Corinthians 10 and 11. Use one quotation to design a card for someone celebrating his or her First Holy Communion.

Word to Know
transubstantiation

167

Day Four Celebrating the Eucharist

Student pages 167–168

LEARNING OUTCOMES

The students will be able to

- participate in the Eucharist.
- discuss their awareness of the love and friendship Jesus offers us.
- demonstrate an understanding of the key concepts in this chapter.

Materials

- Liturgy planning sheet
- Song sheets
- Gifts on the offertory table
- Respective parts for readers and leaders
- BLM 71 Quiz

Before You Begin

1. When we celebrate the Eucharist, Jesus Christ is present in the believers gathered together, in the priest, in the Word of God proclaimed, and especially under the appearances of bread and wine. In faith, we recognize him and respond with love. In faith, we join our offering to his in praise of the Father.

2. If possible, have parents and other adults present for the liturgy. Young people are conscious of and affected by the faith and worship of adults around them.

3. When planning today's lesson, keep in mind that Day Four is when the students take the quiz for this chapter. Reserve time at the end of the class for this assessment. The quiz can also be administered on Day Five.

Centering

1. Have the students practice the entrance song and any new songs.

2. Remind the students of their active participation in the celebration.

◆ **You are invited to be actively involved in the Mass. Remember that you are to join the priest in offering Jesus' sacrifice to the Father.**

◆ **Your wholehearted responses to the priest's prayers are a sign of your faith.** [Practice a few responses.]

◆ **What are some of the ways you can make your reception of the Eucharist meaningful?**

Celebrating

 Participate in the eucharistic celebration.

Sharing

1. Lead the students through the Summary and Review activities, pages 167–168.

2. **BLM 71** Distribute and administer BLM 71 **Chapter 20 Quiz.**

◆ Use this opportunity to assess the students' understanding of the main concepts in this chapter.

◆ If there is not sufficient time for the students to complete the quiz, consider moving it to Day Five.

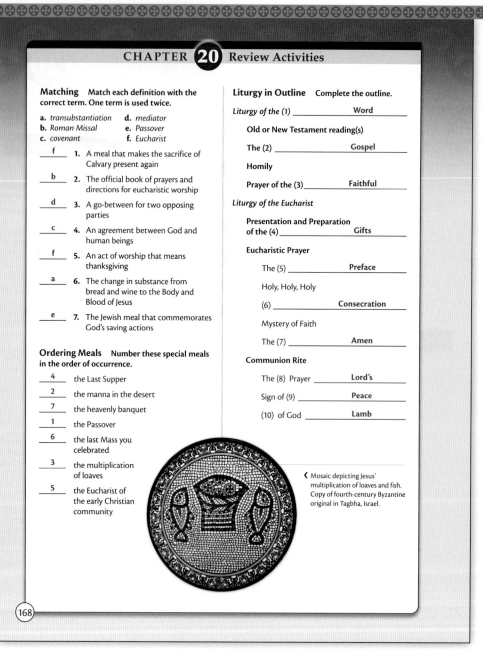

CHAPTER 20 Review Activities

Matching Match each definition with the correct term. One term is used twice.

a. transubstantiation   d. mediator
b. Roman Missal   e. Passover
c. covenant   f. Eucharist

___f___ **1.** A meal that makes the sacrifice of Calvary present again

___b___ **2.** The official book of prayers and directions for eucharistic worship

___d___ **3.** A go-between for two opposing parties

___c___ **4.** An agreement between God and human beings

___f___ **5.** An act of worship that means thanksgiving

___a___ **6.** The change in substance from bread and wine to the Body and Blood of Jesus

___e___ **7.** The Jewish meal that commemorates God's saving actions

Ordering Meals Number these special meals in the order of occurrence.

___4___ the Last Supper
___2___ the manna in the desert
___7___ the heavenly banquet
___1___ the Passover
___6___ the last Mass you celebrated
___3___ the multiplication of loaves
___5___ the Eucharist of the early Christian community

Liturgy in Outline Complete the outline.

Liturgy of the (1) ____Word____

Old or New Testament reading(s)

The (2) ____Gospel____

Homily

Prayer of the (3)____Faithful____

Liturgy of the Eucharist

Presentation and Preparation of the (4) ____Gifts____

Eucharistic Prayer

The (5) ____Preface____

Holy, Holy, Holy

(6) ____Consecration____

Mystery of Faith

The (7) ____Amen____

Communion Rite

The (8) Prayer ____Lord's____

Sign of (9) ____Peace____

(10) of God ____Lamb____

❮ Mosaic depicting Jesus' multiplication of loaves and fish. Copy of fourth-century Byzantine original in Tagbha, Israel.

168

Acting

1. Guide the students to evaluate their worship.

◆ **How have we celebrated God's love for us?**

◆ **Did our singing and praying show our love for Jesus and the Father?**

◆ **What message did God give us in the readings and the homily?**

2. At the end of class, have the students tear out and take home pages 167–168.

CHECKPOINT

• Were the learning outcomes achieved?

• Did the students' participation in the Mass demonstrate a deeper understanding of the Eucharist?

Gather and Go Forth

Lead students through pages 169–170 in the student book. Find catechist instruction on T354–T355.

Use the following suggestions to create an additional lesson for Day Five.

1. Remind the students to take home pages 167–168 to share what they are learning with their families.

2. Incorporate any unused BLMs from the week's chapter.

3. Consider the time of the liturgical year and use the appropriate Special Seasons and Lessons. SSLs begin on page T369.

4. Visit www.christourlife.com to find additional activities for Extending the Chapter.

5. Use activities from Enriching the Faith Experience.

6. Guide the students in a prayerful discussion of Sunday's Scripture readings. Visit www.christourlife.com for more information.

Chapter 20 Enriching the Faith Experience

Use the following activities to enrich a lesson or to replace an activity with one that better meets the needs of your class.

1. **Web BLM** Use Web BLM Chapter 20-A **Eucharistic Devotions** to teach the students about devotions to the Eucharist.

2. Have the parts of the Mass written on slips of paper in a paper bag. Let each student draw a slip and write a letter to a friend describing the part of the Mass and explaining its purpose.

3. Direct the students to write a paragraph or two on the topic "The world would be different if all Catholics lived what they celebrate at Mass."

4. Conduct group work on the four Eucharistic Prayers, using the following guide.

   • Thanksgiving—Underline phrases that deal with thanksgiving or praise.

   • Epiclesis—Put a circle around the part in which the celebrant calls down the Holy Spirit to make the gifts holy.

   • Institution Narrative—Put a box around the Gospel account of Jesus at the Last Supper.

   • Offering—Put a star next to the part in which the priest offers the sacrifice of Jesus back to the Father.

   • Intercessions—Put a check next to any petitions that the Church makes to the Father.

5. Have the students engage in service projects, such as collecting food or money for those who are poor, writing cards for shut-ins or those who are sick or visiting nursing homes. *Solidarity*

6. Ask the students to read Matthew 5:23–24 and Matthew 6:12. Discuss the relationship between forgiving others and celebrating Mass. Invite the students to think of someone whom they find hard to forgive and pray for help.

7. Urge the students to encourage their parents to subscribe to Catholic periodicals that explain doctrine, the sacraments, and prayer, and include reflections on the Sunday readings. Show samples and indicate how they can be obtained.

8. Give groups of students large poster paper. Have them fold it into three parts so it can stand, label them *GO IN PEACE, GLORIFYING THE LORD, BY YOUR LIFE*, and then illustrate each section.

Faith Focus
Jesus' suffering and Death won eternal life for us.

Reflecting on the Faith Experience

Take a few moments to reflect prayerfully before preparing the lesson.

Listening

The way we came to know love was that he laid down his life for us; so we ought to lay down our lives for our brothers.

1 John 3:16

Reflecting

Suffering leads to growth; death leads to life. Nature reflects this pattern in the planted seed becoming a flower and the cocooned caterpillar being transformed into a butterfly. Human experience reflects this pattern in the common sufferings and separations and the small deaths that come into every human life, such as moving to an unfamiliar city or losing a job. This pattern shines through the mystery of the Cross, the mystery of God's love transforming evil, hatred, and pain into goodness, love, and joy.

Jesus did not need to suffer as we do in order to be rid of selfishness and to grow in authentic love. He did not need to endure the consequences of sin. Driven by limitless love for his Father and for us, he accepted his passion and death freely, obediently, trustingly, and humbly. Through such obedience he stood directly opposed to the evil of sin and humanity's desire to be self-absorbed. In his person, Jesus reconciled all of us to God.

Jesus also showed how God responds to hatred and suffering. His response is not blind revenge or almighty power. Our God's response is one of healing. If our God responds in this way, can our response be any different? As God's people we learn acceptance in love,

acting freely, obediently, trustingly, and humbly. In the risen Jesus, we see the result of following in his footsteps where death leads to eternal life.

For Christians, all suffering is in relation to Jesus, in him, and through him. We expect to be transformed with Jesus in redemptive love by the mystery of his Cross, the mystery of his suffering, and the mystery of his Resurrection.

Saint John Paul II summarizes the Christian view of suffering:

Suffering is not sterile; it is not wailing lost in the desert wind, nor some blind and inexplicable cruelty. Indeed, the Gospel explains and interprets it: pain constitutes the direct participation in Christ's redemptive sacrifice and, as such, it has a precious function in the life of the Church.

It is a mysterious but real treasure for all the faithful— by means of that circulation of grace which Christ the head spreads throughout his mystical body, and which the members of the body exchange with one another.

Day by Day, *Saint John Paul II*

In recent suffering, how did I show faith and hope?

Responding

Spirit of Jesus, help my students feel and express gratitude to Jesus for offering his life for them.

Scripture for Further Reflection

Isaiah 53:2–7 The suffering servant of Yahweh, Jesus, humbly accepted punishment for the people's sins. Isaiah's prophecy describes the role of Jesus in God's plan of salvation.

John 12:24–26 The pattern of dying and growing is reflected in the image of a grain of wheat producing an abundant harvest. The same is true of those who follow Jesus.

Preparing for the Faith Experience

Gather and Go Forth

Scripture in This Chapter

Matthew 26:39 Jesus asks to have this cup pass from him.

Luke 23:39–43 Jesus on the Cross

1 John 3:16 Jesus laid down his life for us.

Church Documents

Catechism of the Catholic Church. The themes of this chapter correspond to the following paragraphs: **612, 616–618, 632, 678–682, 1023, 1030, 1033, 1040.**

National Directory for Catechesis #1. Christ himself is the Good News, proclaiming the Kingdom of God and bringing about our salvation by his suffering, Death, and Resurrection.

Directory on Popular Piety and the Liturgy, #128 (Congregation for Divine Worship). Christians see the Cross as an expression of the triumph of Christ over the powers of darkness. They adorn the cross with precious stones and use it as a sign of blessing on one's self, on others, and on objects.

Gather and Go Forth

Find catechist instruction for Gather and Go Forth student pages 177–178 on T356–T357.

Enriching the Faith Experience

Use the activities at the end of the chapter to enrich a lesson or to replace an activity with one that better meets the needs of your class.

Bulletin Board

A suggestion for a bulletin-board design for this chapter is pictured. The sign INRI could be on a sheet of rolled paper. A picture of Jesus could be posted over the heart.

LEARNING OUTCOMES

The students will be able to

- describe the physical and mental suffering that Christ endured to redeem us.
- discuss how to respond to suffering after the example of Jesus.

Key Term

passion—the events from the Last Supper to Jesus' Death on the Cross; suffering

Materials

- Bibles or New Testaments
- Seed
- Plant
- Word written on the board: *evil*
- Picture of Christ in the garden of Gethsemane (optional)

Before You Begin

1. The mystery of the Cross is the mystery of love. Jesus' love was stronger than human weakness, which retreats from pain and suffering. His love was stronger than the hate that nailed him to the Cross. For the Christian, the Cross is a universal sign of hope. It is a symbol

   - showing the cost of discipleship;
   - revealing the conflict we may feel between our will and the will of our Father in heaven;
   - proclaiming that even apparently senseless suffering can be redemptive if accepted in faith, trust, and love.

2. The students need times to encounter God in prayer, but no one can be forced to pray. In class, some students may not even attempt prayer. As long as these students don't interfere with anyone else, they can be left alone. By patience and by the expression of your own convictions, you may provide the inspiration these students need.

Centering _____

1. Show the students a seed and a plant.
   How do these two objects reflect a pattern of death to new life found in nature? (The seed is buried in the ground and appears to be dead, but then it germinates, breaks through the ground, and grows into a plant.)

2. Link the last lesson with today's lesson.
   - ✦ You have learned how Jesus provided the Eucharist as a means for us to participate in his Paschal Mystery.
   - ✦ Today you will reflect on the first two aspects of this mystery: his suffering and Death.

Sharing _____

1. Have the students read silently **The Good in Goodbye** on page 171.
   Divide the class into pairs to share their answers to the questions.

2. Compare Jesus' suffering with our suffering.
   - ✦ Jesus' suffering was different from our suffering. He did not have to suffer for his own sins, and he did not suffer in order to be rid of his own selfishness. Jesus freely chose to suffer.
   - ✦ Some people may ask "If Jesus was God, how could he suffer?" His suffering was like ours because of the Incarnation, Jesus' human birth. He suffered in his humanity, not in his divinity. He experienced our weakness and shared our pain.

- ✦ **Why did Jesus sacrifice his comfort, his life, and his reputation?** (He loved his Father and us. In choosing to suffer, he fulfilled God's plan that all people be saved.)

3. Have a student read aloud the Scripture passage John 12:24 and **Jesus' Passion** on page 171.

✦ **What are some of the effects of Jesus' suffering?** (He entered into glory. He brought all people back to God. He won for us forgiveness, salvation, and eternal life.)

✦ **What death-to-life image did Jesus use to explain his suffering and that of his faithful followers?** (a grain of wheat falling into the ground, dying, and growing)

✦ **Why is Jesus called the Lamb of God?** (He offered himself to the Father. He was the perfect sacrifice.)

✦ **What are some of the events included in Jesus' passion?** (Last Supper, plot of leaders, Judas's treason, arrest of Jesus, the trials, Crucifixion, Death)

✦ **These events were part of a basic Gospel message that the apostles preached before the Gospels were written.**

4. Discuss with the students their response to suffering.

✦ **What are some of the ways you respond to pain and suffering?** [Write their responses on the board.] (crying, fighting, throwing a temper tantrum, giving up, taking medicine)

✦ **How did Jesus respond to his suffering?** (He was overwhelmed, but he accepted it.)

✦ **What motivated Jesus to respond to suffering in this way?** (He wanted to obey his Father in heaven and promote the coming of his kingdom.)

✦ **Do you think that letting people harm him was a weak response? Why or why not?** (No, because Jesus accepted it out of love. This response demanded strength, truthfulness, and constancy.)

✦ **We can respond firmly to people and stand up for our rights without violence, like Jesus who spoke the truth and did not act like a coward. It is harder to respond in this way than to** ignore the situation, to get revenge, or to give up.

✦ **Can someone think of an example of a person who responded as Jesus did?**

CHAPTER **21**

Michelangelo da Merisi Caravaggio, *The Taking of Christ*, 1602.

Jesus' Final Hours

Jesus the Lamb of God

The Good in Goodbye

Emma covered her face with her hands and sobbed. "I can't move again. I just can't! Not another town and school! Just when I find friends! Just when I make the team! We always move just when I finally *belong*!"

Moving can be painful. Being separated from familiar places and people can seem like dying. Every person meets "little deaths," as a part of life. Through these "deaths" a person gains new opportunities for life.

Write one good thing that may come from moving.

new friends, new experiences
_____

What "little death" have you suffered that resulted in something good?

Answers will vary.
_____

What good result came from it?

Answers will vary.
_____

[U]nless a grain of wheat falls to the ground and dies, it remains just a grain of wheat; but if it dies, it produces much fruit.

John 12:24

Jesus' Passion

Like the grain of wheat, Jesus had to suffer and die in order to enter into his glory. He died as a result of sin. By his obedience and love, he brought all humankind back to God. He won for us forgiveness, salvation, and eternal life. The Jewish people sacrificed animals and the first fruits of their crops to God. Jesus offered himself to the Father for us. Like other sacrifices, his was to make up for sins and to gain benefits. Jesus was the Lamb of God—the perfect sacrifice. The events from the Last Supper to Jesus' Death on the cross are called his passion. The word *passion* means "a powerful emotion such as love, joy, hatred, or anger." We use the word *passion* to express how Jesus showed his love for us.

(171)

5. Have the students read silently **His Source of Strength** and **Our Response** on page 172.

✦ **Where did Jesus find the strength to keep going and giving?** (in prayer, in union with his Father)

✦ **How can we find meaning in our suffering?** (realizing that we share in the Father's saving plan; that our suffering is united with that of Jesus for the redemption of the world)

✦ **What response should we have toward suffering?** (We should eliminate it if we can, comfort those who are suffering, and unite our suffering to that of Jesus.) **Can you give an example of how you or someone you know has responded in these ways?**

6. Have a student read aloud **Obituary** on page 172.

✦ **Crucifixion was a disgraceful form of punishment used mainly for slaves and foreigners. Roman citizens were beheaded, which was considered a more humane execution.**

✦ **Crucified people died of asphyxiation. On the Cross, they had to push up with their legs to breathe. Eventually they became too weak to push themselves up, and they suffocated.**

✦ **What was Jesus' crime?** (The Jewish leaders accused him of blasphemy because he claimed to be the Son of God. The Romans sentenced him to death for declaring himself a king.)

✦ **Why do you think Pilate ordered Jesus crucified even though Pilate thought Jesus was innocent?** (Pilate feared displeasing the Roman rulers, losing his job, and causing a riot.)

✦ **In the Gospel of Matthew, Pilate washes his hands and declares he is innocent of Jesus' blood.**

✦ **How do you think Mary felt at the foot of the Cross? John?**

7. Write the word *evil* on the board. Ask a student to reverse the letters.

His Source of Strength

Under the pressure of exhaustion, rejection, loneliness, and evil, where did Jesus find the strength to go on? How could he keep loving and forgiving?

The answer lies in his union with his Father. Jesus knew the depth of his Father's love. Through prayer, he received strength to suffer and die for us. He prayed,

> "My Father, if it is possible, let this cup pass from me; yet, not as I will, but as you will."
>
> Matthew 26:39

Our Response

Suffering will always be a mystery, something we cannot fully understand. Only when we, like Jesus, trust in the Father's love and accept the suffering he permits does suffering have any meaning. As Jesus' followers, we can

- work to eliminate the evil around us
- try to relieve the pain of others
- unite our suffering with his in love
- accept suffering without self-pity or anger
- offer our sufferings for other people
- gain strength as Jesus did, through prayer and union with our Father.

Obituary

JESUS OF NAZARETH died about 3:00 P.M. Friday as a result of crucifixion at the hands of Roman soldiers.

Jesus, a former carpenter, was a controversial Jewish figure. He was popular in Galilee and Judea for his teachings and his healings.

On Thursday, Judas Iscariot, one of Jesus' followers, led soldiers to him. They arrested him in a garden and brought him to the Jewish leaders. The Sanhedrin accused him of blasphemy because he claimed to be the Son of God. The high priest Caiaphas sent him to Pontius Pilate for execution.

Finding him innocent, Pilate offered to release him, but most of the people demanded that Barabbas, a revolutionary, be freed instead. After having Jesus scourged, Pilate ordered him crucified on the charge that he had declared himself a king.

At Jesus' Death, his mother, Mary, a disciple named John, and some women were present.

Burial was immediate since the next day was the Sabbath. Soldiers guarded the tomb because Jesus had predicted he would be raised in three days.

✦ **What does *evil* spell backwards?** (*live*)

✦ **How does spelling *evil* backwards summarize what Jesus did?** (By undergoing *evil*, his suffering, and Death, Jesus turned evil into life so that we might *live*.)

8. Explain to the students the method of meditation they will experience.

✦ **One way to learn about the passion of Jesus is to enter into the mystery of it through prayer.**

✦ **The type of prayer we will pray today may be new to you. In it, we use our breathing and our concentration. We use our thoughts, imagination, and emotions. This method helps us**

relax, heightens our awareness of God, and increases our openness to God. It is called meditation.

✦ **In part one, we will make our breathing even. You can feel when your breathing is deep and in steady rhythm. We will then focus our attention on the picture and try to let go of all other thoughts, worries, and plans.**

✦ **In part two, we will use our imagination to reflect on Jesus and his apostles going to the garden of Gethsemane after the Last Supper. We will think about what happened there and try to enter into Jesus' feelings.**

9. Read aloud the prayer meditation In the Garden. [You may want to highlight the pauses to remind yourself.]

 Invite the students to look at the picture you brought in, or to close their eyes and imagine the scene. Keep your voice calm and evenly paced.

In the Garden

Begin to relax, breathing deeply and evenly. [Pause.] Focus your attention on the picture of Jesus in the garden of olive trees. Notice the details. Concentrate on the picture and let go of all other thoughts. [Pause.]

Close your eyes and see the garden in your mind. Imagine yourself just outside the garden. You are alone, and it is dark and quiet. You can smell the fresh, clear, night air and feel a gentle breeze. You hear a cricket. The full moon is casting shadows of the trees. You can see objects rather clearly. Look around and notice what is in the garden. [Pause.] Gradually you hear voices. You see Jesus coming. His apostles are following him, looking happy, though somewhat confused, and talking loudly about the evening. [Pause.] *They came to a small estate called Gethsemane, and Jesus said to his disciples, "Stay here while I pray." Then he took Peter and James and John with him.* You recognize them. They were the ones Jesus took with him for the Transfiguration, when his glory was revealed. Now he wants them near again. Look! He's inviting you to come, too, to be close to him in his prayer. You decide to go with them. [Pause.] Notice in the moonlight a change in Jesus' face and in the way he is standing. *And a sudden fear came over him and great distress. And he said to them, "My soul is sorrowful to the point of death."* Try to understand how Jesus feels and why. Try to be with him in his sorrow. [Pause.] Hear Jesus say, *"Wait here and keep awake."* And going on a little farther he threw himself on the ground and prayed that, if it were possible, this hour might pass him by. In the moonlight, you watch Jesus. Try to hear his prayer. Try to feel what he feels. [Pause.]

"Abba (Father)!" he said. "Everything is possible for you. Take this cup away from me." Realize that the cup Jesus speaks about is the cup of suffering. It is the pain of his passion and his Death. Try to understand a little of what Jesus will face when he leaves the garden. [Pause.] And he said, *"But let it be as you, not I, would have it."* Imagine what it costs Jesus to surrender to his Father's way of doing things. Reflect on the love that Jesus must have for his Father and the love he must have for us, because he will suffer and die for us, for our sins. [Pause.] *He came back and found them sleeping.* But you are not sleeping. You are awake and aware of him. You go over to be with him. He asks you to share this time with him, and you are willing. Take time now to be near him, to comfort him the best that you can. [Pause.]

Take a moment to tell Jesus your suffering. Let him comfort you. Feel his eyes looking at you with understanding. Feel his support and encouragement. Speak to him now. [Pause. Be sensitive to how long the students can maintain the dialogue.]

When Jesus left the garden, the situation had not changed. He had been betrayed by one of his own apostles. He was going to face his passion: the awful pain, the embarrassment, loneliness, disappointment, and ridicule, the cruelty of the people he had tried to help, the people to whom he offered love. In his prayer, he was strengthened to meet this suffering courageously and willingly out of love for his Father and for us. Like Jesus, you, too, can find strength to face difficulties through prayer.

Acting

Conclude the prayer with the Sign of the Cross.

The Sign of the Cross represents God's great love for us. It is the sign by which we have been saved.

CHECKPOINT

- Were the learning outcomes achieved?

- Did the students' response to the prayer experience indicate growth in prayer?

LEARNING OUTCOMES

The students will be able to

- explain how Jesus understands our pain because he experienced it.
- assess their pain in relationship to Jesus and unite it with his suffering.
- discuss how it takes courage to handle suffering.

Materials

- Bibles or New Testaments
- BLM 72A–D
- Stapler or paper punch
- Yarn or string for binding the booklets in Sharing #2
- Felt-tipped pens
- Background music for Sharing #4
- Reflection notebooks

Before You Begin

1. To help develop the devotional life of the students and provide an opportunity for them to enter more deeply into the passion of Jesus, this lesson is centered on the Stations of the Cross. In this prayer, which is steeped in Catholic tradition, the students journey with Jesus from Pilate's court to Jesus' redeeming Death on the Cross and his burial.

2. The traditional Stations of the Cross is composed of 14 stations. Each represents a moment of suffering in the passion of Jesus. Stations 1, 2, 5, 8, and 10 through 14 are based on Scripture. Stations 3, 4, 6, 7, and 9 are based on popular tradition. A person moves from station to station, meditating on the suffering of Jesus at each one. The passion of Jesus has meaning only in relation to the Resurrection. In many churches today, a 15th station on the Resurrection is often added.

3. You might provide an opportunity for the students to go to church or to the prayer room and read the passion account or pray the Stations of the Cross silently.

Centering _____

1. Discuss with the students the dimensions of human suffering.
   - ✦ **Can you think of someone who does not suffer, who is free from pain?**
   - ✦ **Suffering is part of everyone's life. What types of human suffering are there?** [List the students' answers on the board.] (physical pain, injustice and persecution, emotional pain)
   - ✦ **Can you think of people who are sincerely following Christ and who experience a great deal of suffering?** (The students might mention saints or people they know.)
   - ✦ **Some people think that if they pray, celebrate Mass on Sunday, and obey the laws of the Church, they should not have any problems or suffering. They may even blame God for the pain they experience. What would you say to these people?** (Jesus was the person closest to God the Father, and Jesus suffered. Mary, his mother,

is known as the Mother of Sorrows. She watched her son, Jesus, die on the Cross. Jesus promised that his followers would suffer persecution [John 16:1–4]. God has given people the freedom to choose to do good or evil.)

2. Ask a student to read aloud Matthew 25:41–45.
   What do you think Jesus is telling us in this passage? (When we refuse to help someone, we are refusing to help Jesus who suffers with us.)

3. Link the last lesson with today's lesson.
   - ✦ **In the last lesson, you learned about Jesus' suffering and Crucifixion.**
   - ✦ **Today you will learn a prayer, the Stations of the Cross, that will help you enter into Jesus' suffering.**

Sharing_____

1. Have the students turn to pages 239–240. Explain the Stations of the Cross to the students. [See pages T431–T432.]
   - ✦ **How many of you have prayed the Stations of the Cross? Can someone explain it?** (The 14 stations represent moments of suffering in the story of Jesus' passion. A person walks from station to station, while praying and thinking about Jesus' passion. Each station may be represented by a wooden cross alone or together with a picture or statue. The closing prayer, sometimes included as a 15th station, reflects on the Resurrection of Jesus.)
   - ✦ **What might we realize from praying the Stations of the Cross?** (how much Jesus has suffered for love of us; how evil sin is because it leads to so much pain and suffering; how we can unite our suffering with Jesus'; how much he shares our pain, having been lonely and ridiculed himself)

2. **BLM 72A–D** Distribute copies of BLM 72A–D **The Stations of the Cross** to the students.
   - Read aloud the directions.
   - **Cut along the dotted line at the top and the bottom of the sheets. Be sure to keep them in order: A, B, C, and D.**
   - **Fold sheet 72A in half so the top and bottom of the page meet. Put it on your desk with stations 1 and 14 facing up.**
   - **Fold sheet 72B the same way. Put it on top of the first sheet with stations 3 and 12 facing up.**
   - **Fold sheet 72C and put it on top of the other sheets with stations 5 and 10 facing up.**
   - **Fold sheet 72D and put it on top of the other sheets with stations 7 and 8 facing up.**
   - **Fold the pages to form the booklet and bind it with staples, yarn, or string.**

3. Explain to the students that each station follows the same format.
   Each of the 15 stations follows the same pattern: the title, an appropriate Scripture passage, a brief explanation of the moment, and a place for you to apply the event to what is happening in today's world or to your personal lives.

4. Have the students complete the Stations of the Cross booklets to appropriate background music. Encourage the students to use their Bibles or New Testaments for additional information.

5. Divide the class into small groups and assign one station to each group.
   Have the students read the explanation in the booklet for their station and complete one of the following activities:

   a. Design a symbol or picture of the station on drawing paper. These symbols may be used to make a Stations of the Cross in the school hallway or on the classroom wall. If you wish, the symbols may be drawn on overhead transparencies.

   b. Create a meditation for their station with dialogue and music.

   c. Create a collage showing how the suffering of the station, such as loneliness, persecution, and pain, is still experienced today.

   d. Create a tableau with costumes and props. These may be photographed and used for prayer.

6. Have each group name its station and share the results of its activity with the class.

7. Choose a date to pray the Stations of the Cross with the students.
   - Tell the students when they will pray the Stations of the Cross as a class.
   - Collect the booklets until it is time to use them.

Acting

1. Invite the students to a moment of quiet prayer.
   - **Think of a difficult situation you are facing now.** [Pause.]
   - **Remember that Jesus is here to support you, to help you grow, to help you change what must be changed, or to help you accept things as they are.** [Pause.]
   - Allow sufficient time for silent reflection.
   - **Let's pray together the Act of Hope that is on the inside back cover of your book.** [See page T446.]

2. Have the students complete the Respond activity on page 175.

CHECKPOINT

- Were the learning outcomes achieved?
- How well do the students understand the Stations of the Cross and apply it to their own lives and the world?

LEARNING OUTCOMES

The students will be able to

- explain how to return Christ's love by showing love to others.
- describe death, judgment, heaven, and hell in the light of Christian teachings and hope.
- define *Last Judgment* and *particular judgment*.

Words to Know

Last Judgment

particular judgment

See the Glossary for definitions.

Key Terms

Parousia—the Second Coming of Christ in glory when God's plan of salvation will be revealed

purgatory—the purification after death that transforms people not yet perfect in love for heaven

Materials

- Bibles or New Testaments
- List written on the board:

  WAYS SOMEONE SHOWS LOVE

  Gives you gifts

  Changes plans to make you happy

  Compliments you

  Chooses to go with you to activities

  Follows your advice

  Defends you when others criticize you for doing what is right

- Flash cards: *particular judgment, purgatory, hell, heaven, Parousia, Last Judgment*
- Background music

Before You Begin

1. In this lesson, the students consider how they can return in their daily lives the love represented by the Cross.

2. Encourage the students to use page 12 of their Scripture booklets.

3. At death, we will learn how much we have become like Jesus, how well we learned to love unselfishly, and where we belong: in heaven, purgatory, or hell.

   The particular judgment is realizing one's eternal destiny. At death, a person sees himself or herself in the way that God does.

   The three alternatives at death are heaven for those who have become totally like Jesus; purgatory for those who are like Jesus, but still need to be purified; and hell for those who refuse to live by God's command to love, and die in the state of mortal sin, having turned away from God. Heaven is the state of happiness for those who have died in Christ and are totally purified from obstacles to perfect union with God. It is an eternal community of love, existing in endless joy.

Hell is without joy, without love, because it is without God. Hell is a choice for a life of selfishness and sin. Purgatory is a state of purification for those who have died in Christ. They experience great love and peace because eventually they will be in heaven and see God. But they also must grow in spiritual maturity so they can be in God's presence. After the Last Judgment, purgatory will no longer exist.

The Parousia is the Second Coming of Christ. Its purpose is to reveal God's entire plan of salvation. This event can come at any time. When it does, time will end, and the resurrection of the dead will occur. Christ, the risen Lord, who has been with his Church throughout the ages, will appear in glory. The Kingdom of God begun on earth will be manifested in its fullness. Christ will present it to his Father.

The Last Judgment is the general judgment of the human race at the final resurrection of the dead. This will be a social judgment, because it will manifest to the world God's justice in condemning sinners and God's mercy toward those who are saved. It will also be a total judgment, weighing the moral conduct of people according to the blessings or injuries that resulted from their actions.

Centering _____

1. Discuss with the students ways someone shows love from the list on the board.

   ✦ **What are some other ways that someone shows love?**

   ✦ **What is the way that shows the most love?** [Take a hand vote and mark the number of responses next to each item.]

2. 🙏 Have the students read silently **A Moment with Jesus** on page 173.

   ✦ Allow sufficient time for silent reflection.

   ✦ **It is often in moments of great difficulty or suffering that we come to know the depth of our trust and love in God. Jesus experienced this as well. His unwavering trust of the Father is**

   an example for us. [Read aloud John 15:13.]

3. Link the last lesson with today's lesson.

   ✦ **Jesus tells us and shows us the measure and depth of his love. He has loved each of us so much that he gave his life for us.**

   ✦ **Today we will think about our response to Jesus' love.**

Sharing _____

1. Call on a student to read aloud **Free to Love** on page 173.

   ✦ Allow time for the students to answer the question and read the Scripture passage.

   ✦ **How can you tell your love for God is real?** (if you show love to other people)

2. Discuss with the students Jesus' love for the Father and for others.

   ✦ **Jesus lived a life of love for the Father and for others. Jesus' followers must also learn to live their lives in this way. To do this is a lifetime project.**

   ✦ Have a volunteer read aloud **A Lifetime Project** on page 173.

   ✦ **How do the decisions you make affect your future?** (Each decision you make forms you into a certain type of person, either more like Christ or less like Christ. Each time you make a decision, it is easier to make the same choice in the future.)

   ✦ **How does God help you with every decision and yet leave you free to choose?** (God gives you guidance and grace for each decision but never forces you to do what is right.)

3. Begin a discussion about life after death.

   Life after death is a mystery. It is beyond our experience. We use words such as *Parousia* and *heaven* in an attempt to explain it, but we can't answer all our questions.

4. Have the students read silently **After Death, Then What?** on page 173 and **The End of the World** on page 174.

A Moment with Jesus

No one likes to suffer. Even Jesus prayed that his final moment of suffering would pass him by. Take a moment and look carefully at the picture that accompanies the obituary. Then silently read the Scripture verse from Matthew on page 172.

Reflect on the experience of Jesus and how his trust and love in his Father helped him through his time of suffering. Then thank Jesus for his obedience to the Father and for showing us how great is God's love for us.

Free to Love

Jesus wants you to share his glory, his joy. The best response you can give is to love him freely—not because you are afraid, or because you have to, or because others do, but because he is so good and you really *want* to love him.

How can you tell if you really love God?

Answers will vary.

Read 1 John 4:20–21. Compare your answer to that passage.

A Lifetime Project

> . . . that he may grant you in accord with the riches of his glory to be strengthened with power through his Spirit in the inner self, . . .
>
> Ephesians 3:16

On your journey to the Father, you have many chances to love him and others. Your choices make you who you are. How does that happen? Each time you choose to be honest, it is easier to be honest in the future. You are becoming a more honest person. On the other hand, each time you choose to be unkind, you make it easier to be unkind again. Gradually you could become a cruel person.

The change is so gradual that you and others may not be aware of it. With every decision, however, you grow stronger or weaker in the Lord. As you respond to God's grace or reject it, you set a pattern for your life.

After Death, Then What?

At the moment of death, you will see your hidden self and realize how much you have become like Jesus. Then, based on that likeness, you will realize before God how you fit or do not fit into the kingdom of love. That moment is called the **particular judgment.**

After death, there are three possibilities:

- People who have become like Jesus by loving perfectly can enter God's presence, see God face to face, and know a boundless joy. This is called heaven.

- People may need to be purified of remaining selfishness, because only those totally transformed by love can enter the kingdom. This purification is called purgatory.

- People who have freely refused in serious ways to follow God's command to love are in the state of mortal sin. Anyone in this state cannot enter heaven but will be outside of it forever. This eternal separation from God for whom we long is called hell.

(173)

5. Divide the class into pairs. Have the students answer the questions from **The Last Things** on page 174.

Go over the students' answers. [See Before You Begin #3. The paragraphs correspond to the questions in this section.]

6. Direct the students to read silently **A Thief Enters Heaven** on page 174.

✦ Have the students complete the exercise.

✦ **Jesus offers forgiveness up to the moment of a person's death.**

7. Turn the flash cards face-down. Call on students to choose a card and then define the word on it. Continue this process until all the words have been defined.

Acting

1. Choose or let the students choose an activity from Reach Out on page 175.

2. Conclude the lesson by praying together the Hail Mary.

Mary made the decision to follow Jesus with all her mind, body, and soul. Together let us pray the Hail Mary, asking God to give us the same grace he gave Mary.

CHECKPOINT

- Were the learning outcomes achieved?

- Do the students seem to realize that their eternal future depends on their response to God's love?

The End of the World

At the end of time, Jesus will return in glory to judge the living and the dead. At that Second Coming, or Parousia, the resurrection from the dead will take place. God will reveal the plan of salvation in all its glory. The eternal destiny of the human race and of every person will be revealed in the **Last Judgment.** The souls of the just will be reunited with their glorified bodies. The universe will be transformed, and God will be "all in all." Christians long for the Parousia when God "will wipe every tear from their eyes." (Revelation 21:4) We pray, "Come, Lord Jesus!" (Revelation 22:20) If you knew Christ would return next week, how would you live differently?

The Last Things

Can you answer these questions?

1. What will you learn about yourself from God at the moment of your death?
2. What is the moment called when a person finds out about his or her eternal destiny?
3. Describe the three alternatives for a person at the moment of death.
4. What is the Parousia and its purpose?
5. What is the Last Judgment?

A Thief Enters Heaven

Read Luke 23:39–43.

How did the penitent thief show his faith in Jesus?

He defended Jesus from criticism and

respected his claim to be king.

Write Jesus' response to the penitent thief.

"Amen, I say to you, today you will be with

me in paradise."

No matter what the penitent thief had done in the past, Jesus welcomed him into the kingdom because the thief reached out in love. The same Jesus is always ready to forgive you and offer you his love, even to the moment of death.

LEARNING OUTCOMES

The students will be able to

- review events of Christ's passion.
- analyze decisions to see whether they reach out to others or satisfy personal desires.
- evaluate the groups they belong to and how they influence their following of Christ.
- demonstrate an understanding of the key concepts in this chapter.

Materials

- Bibles or New Testaments
- BLM 73, BLM 74
- BLM 75 Quiz
- Tape
- Flash cards numbered from 1 to 8 on one side and the letters below with the question on the reverse side.
  1. E *What happens at the moment of death?*
  2. N *On what will a person be evaluated at the moment of death?*
  3. I *What two things does a person learn at the particular judgment?*
  4. S *What type of people will enter heaven at death?*
  5. I *What sort of people will need purgatory?*
  6. C *What kind of people will be in hell?*
  7. O *How can we live in order to anticipate death with joy?*
  8. D *What is the relationship between a decision we make today and the particular judgment?*

Before You Begin

1. At the end of our lives, we shall be judged on love. This realization should affect our daily decisions. Often decisions that reflect the challenge of Gospel living are difficult to carry out. At these times, a Christian group that offers support, encouragement, and understanding can be vital.

2. Saint John Paul II taught that we can only begin to understand the meaning of suffering when we look to the Cross of Christ. "In the Cross of Christ not only is the Redemption accomplished through suffering, but *also human suffering itself has been redeemed.*" Saint John Paul II explains that suffering "is *supernatural* because it is rooted in the divine mystery of the Redemption of the world, and it is likewise deeply *human,* because in it the person discovers himself, his own humanity, his own dignity, his own mission." Human suffering has been redeemed in the Death and Resurrection of Jesus. As Jesus told us in the parable of the Last Judgment in Matthew 25:31–46, whatever we do for those who suffer, we do for Jesus. (*On the Christian Meaning of Human Suffering,* 19 and 31)

3. When planning today's lesson, keep in mind that Day Four is when the students take the quiz for this chapter. Reserve time at the end of class for this assessment. The quiz can also be administered on Day Five.

Centering _____

1. Tape the flash cards on the board with the number side up.
   - ✦ On the back of each numbered card are a letter and a question. When you are called on, turn the card over and read the question. Then call on a classmate to answer the question.
   - ✦ After the question is answered, tape the card to the board with the letter side facing up. [Begin with card #1.]

   Answers:
   1. E A person experiences the particular judgment.
   2. N on the ability to love as Jesus loves; on how he or she showed love to others
   3. I A person learns how much he or she has become like Jesus and if he or she fits into heaven.
   4. S those who have been totally transformed into Christ by love
   5. I those who have selfishness still within them
   6. C those who refused to love and don't fit into God's kingdom
   7. O Live each day in love. Consistently make decisions that show love for God and others.
   8. D Each decision to do good, to love God and others, makes us more like Jesus. The decision I make today will also make it easier to make the same kind of decision in the future. Gradually I will become a loving person.
   - ✦ **What do these scrambled letters spell?** (*decision*)

2. Link the last lesson with today's lesson.
   In the last lesson, you learned how the decisions you make in life have consequences for the afterlife. Today you will examine decision making and the influence others have on us.

Sharing _____

1. Discuss with the students two of the motives for making decisions.

   ✦ **We all want to be mature and act grown-up. A sign of a mature person is the ability to think of God and others rather than only of oneself. The Great Commandment that Jesus gave us tells us the same thing. What are they?** (You shall love the Lord, your God, with all your heart, with all your soul, and with all your mind. You shall love your neighbor as yourself. [Matthew 22:37,39])

   ✦ **To follow these commandments, we sometimes have to decide to reach out to others even though it may mean suffering, pain, or misunderstanding.** [Write *Willing to Reach Out* on the board.] **It might seem easier or safer not to get involved.** [Write *Wanting to Be Safe* on the board.]

   ✦ **There are questions people ask themselves before making a decision, such as, Do I have to do it? or What can I get out of it?**

   ✦ **What question do you think a Christian who is striving for maturity in Christ would ask before making a decision?** (How can I make a decision like Jesus? How can I bring Jesus' love into this situation?)

   ✦ **Remember that besides considering the reasons for making a decision, we must also consider the consequences. Accepting responsibility for what happens as a result of our decision is a sign of maturity.**

2. Discuss with the students the following two situations:

   ✦ Have the students determine what type of decision was made, using the phrases on the board.

   ✦ **A woman was stabbed to death late one night. Dozens of her neighbors and others heard her screams and saw what happened. No one came to her rescue. No one called the police. What type of**

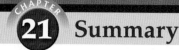

CHAPTER 21 Summary

Remember

What is the supreme act of God's love for all people?

The supreme act of God's love for all people is Jesus' Death on the cross. In obedience to the Father, Jesus offered his life for our sins so that all could have eternal life.

How does the Gospel explain this act of love?

For God so loved the world that he gave his only Son, so that everyone who believes in him might not perish but might have eternal life.

John 3:16

Respond

Imagine that you are standing on Calvary while Jesus is dying. Experience the sights and sounds around you. Now focus your attention on Jesus in his suffering. Realize that your sins are part of the burden he is carrying. Be with him now, supporting him with your love, knowing that your love can ease his burden. Record your thoughts and feelings in your reflection notebook.

Reach Out

1. Find the traditional "Seven Last Words of Christ" in Scripture. See Mark 15:34; Luke 23:34,43,46; and John 19:26,28,30. Make a mobile to display the words, or compose a prayer based on the meaning of Jesus' words for today.

2. The mystery of Jesus passing through death to glory is the core of Christian belief. Using a missalette, list references to the Death and Resurrection of Christ in each of the four Eucharistic prayers.

3. Take a survey of five people of various ages. Ask each one to complete these statements:
   • When I was younger, I thought heaven was like . . .
   • Now I think heaven is . . .
   • I look forward to heaven because . . .

4. Read about the Last Judgment in Matthew 25:31–46. Imagine you are one of the sheep or the goats. How would you feel?

Words to Know

Last Judgment   particular judgment

Fra Angelico, *Last Judgment*, 15th century. Detail showing the separation of the saved (left) and the damned (right). ❯

(175)

---

decision was made by the observers? (*Wanting to Be Safe*) **What were the consequences?** (The woman died. Possibly other crimes were committed in that area because the criminals felt no one would stop them. The people involved had to live with the fear and guilt that accompanied their decision.)

   ✦ **A group of people were having lunch at an outdoor café. Across the street they saw two thieves run up to an elderly woman, knock her down and grab her purse. As the thieves ran down the street, several people from the café jumped up. Some helped the woman and some ran after the thieves. As the thieves tried to escape, over 25 people**

surrounded them so they could not run. The thieves dropped the purse and fell to the ground. They were afraid of what the people surrounding them might do. **What decision was made by the bystanders?** (*Willing to Reach Out*) **What were the consequences?** (The thieves were captured. The bystanders' action might have been in the news giving other people the courage to fight crime.)

3. **BLM 73** Distribute BLM 73 **Decisions in the Passion** to the students.

   ✦ Read aloud the directions to Part 1.

   ✦ Have the students complete the chart, using their Bibles or New Testaments. Check the students' answers.

4. Share with the students a decision you had to make recently and its consequences. Direct the students to complete Part 2 of BLM 73. Ask volunteers to share their responses.

5. Discuss with the students situations in which not getting involved is the Christian decision.

✦ **Decision making is a complex process. The solution to a dilemma may be good in one situation and not in another. As Christians, we need to study the Gospels, the Church teachings, and pray for guidance.**

✦ **Individuals are often influenced in their decisions by a group to which they belong. To what groups do you belong?** (family, class, team, parish, club, friends)

✦ **What are some of the positive ways a group can influence?** (Groups can encourage us to stand up for truth, to be respectful of other's feelings, and to be responsible for what we say and do.)

✦ **What are some of the negative ways a group can influence us?** (Groups can urge us to do the opposite of what we know is best. They might pressure us to give up our sense of honesty and of doing the right thing in order to belong.)

6. Refer the students back to BLM 73 **Decisions in the Passion.**

✦ **Place a check next to the name of anyone who was influenced in a negative way by a group.** [Pause.] (Judas, Peter, Pilate)

✦ **Place a star next to the groups and individuals who influenced others.** [Pause.] (apostles, Sanhedrin, crowd, soldier)

✦ **Put a cross next to those who reached out to others instead of playing it safe with the group.** [Pause.] (Jesus, Mary, good thief, Joseph of Arimathea)

7. Discuss with the students the powerful influence a group can have on an individual.

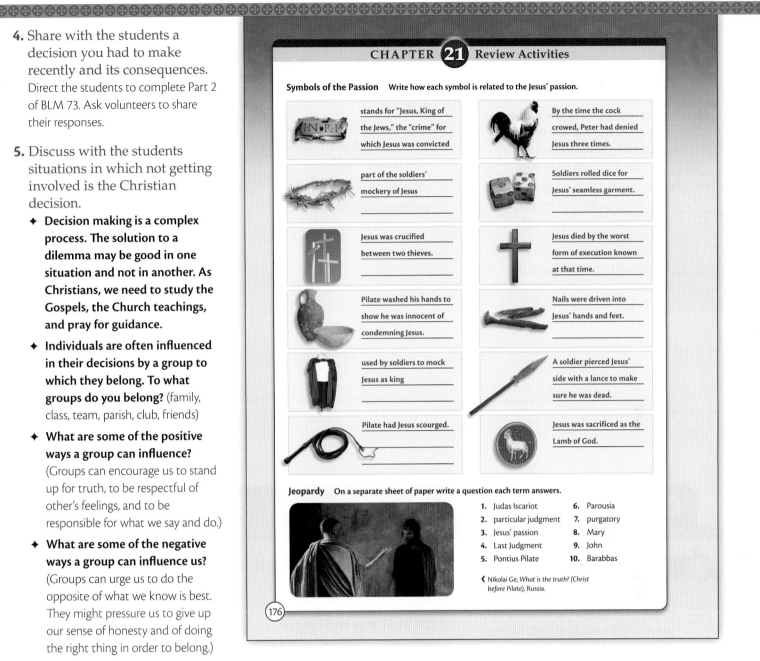

CHAPTER 21 Review Activities

Symbols of the Passion Write how each symbol is related to the Jesus' passion.

stands for "Jesus, King of the Jews," the "crime" for which Jesus was convicted

By the time the cock crowed, Peter had denied Jesus three times.

part of the soldiers' mockery of Jesus

Soldiers rolled dice for Jesus' seamless garment.

Jesus was crucified between two thieves.

Jesus died by the worst form of execution known at that time.

Pilate washed his hands to show he was innocent of condemning Jesus.

Nails were driven into Jesus' hands and feet.

used by soldiers to mock Jesus as king

A soldier pierced Jesus' side with a lance to make sure he was dead.

Pilate had Jesus scourged.

Jesus was sacrificed as the Lamb of God.

Jeopardy On a separate sheet of paper write a question each term answers.

1. Judas Iscariot
2. particular judgment
3. Jesus' passion
4. Last Judgment
5. Pontius Pilate
6. Parousia
7. purgatory
8. Mary
9. John
10. Barabbas

❮ Nikolai Ge, *What is the truth? (Christ before Pilate)*, Russia.

176

✦ **A person who wants to be accepted and to belong to a group will be influenced to some degree by the group.**

✦ **People who believe in their own ability to make good decisions and who know who they are may be able to stand up to the group.**

✦ **How is Jesus the model for us in decision making?** (He reached out to others even when it meant pain, suffering, rejection, loneliness, ridicule, and death. Sometimes Jesus' decisions were not the same as the apostles' decisions.)

8. **BLM 74** Distribute to the students copies of BLM 74 **We Need Support.**

Have the students complete the activity.

9. Lead the students through the Summary and Review Activities, pages 175–176.

10. **BLM 75** Distribute and administer BLM 75 **Chapter 21 Quiz.**

Use this opportunity to assess the students' understanding of the main concepts in the chapter. If there is not sufficient time for the students to complete the quiz, consider moving it to Day Five.

Acting

1. Invite the students to pray for the groups to which they belong.

   ✦ **Let us ask God to give us the courage and the love to be Christian influences on the groups to which we belong.**

   ✦ Pray the Prayer for Christlikeness with the students on the inside back cover of the student book. [See page T446.]

2. At the end of class, have the students tear out and take home pages 175–176.

CHECKPOINT ✓

- Were the learning outcomes achieved?

- How have the students shown that Gospel values are influencing their decision making?

- Were the students' attitudes toward group influence altered or reinforced?

Day Five   Extending the Chapter

Gather and Go Forth

Lead students through pages 177–178 in the student book. Find catechist instruction on T356–T357.
Materials: Bibles

Use the following suggestions to create an additional lesson for Day Five.

1. Remind the students to take home pages 175–176 to share what they are learning with their families.

2. Incorporate any unused BLMs from the week's chapter.

3. Consider the time of the liturgical year and use the appropriate Special Seasons and Lessons. SSLs begin on page T369.

4. Visit www.christourlife.com to find additional activities for Extending the Chapter.

5. Use activities from Enriching the Faith Experience.

6. Guide the students in a prayerful discussion of Sunday's Scripture readings. Visit www.christourlife.com for more information.

Use the following activities to enrich a lesson or to replace an activity with one that better meets the needs of your class.

1. Help the students design stained-glass windows, using black construction paper for the frames and tissue paper or paper painted with watercolors for the glass. Suggest that they include in the design symbols of the passion: whip, nails, crown of thorns, cross, inscription from the cross (*INRI*), sponge on a thin reed.

2. Direct the students to make a Holy Week diary in which they pretend to be an apostle who records what took place from Passion Sunday until Christ's Resurrection. The students should record the part the apostle played in the various episodes, his reactions, and his feelings.

3. Have the students make up three modern-day situations: one in which a person decides to reach out in spite of the group's opinion; one in which a person plays it safe because of the group's opinion; and one in which a person reaches out and the group is supportive. Call on a volunteer to read aloud a situation. Have that student call on another student to describe the decision that was made and to explain how the involved person reacted to the influence of the group.

4. Suggest that the students write in their reflection notebooks about a group to which they belong. Then make two columns on the board, one labeled *Willing to Reach Out* and one *Wanting to Be Safe*. Have the students list decisions they made that were influenced by their group and the consequences of the decision.

5. Make flash cards to review terms in this lesson. Divide the class into two teams and appoint a scorekeeper. Spread the flash cards face-down on a desk. Alternate teams, having volunteers pick a card, read the term, and explain it. Each correct answer receives a point. If a student is unable to explain a term, the other team has a chance to answer and receive two points.

6. Ask the students to research the following topics and present a report to the class.
   • The history and nature of crucifixion
   • Gethsemane and Calvary today
   • Roman trial procedures and Sanhedrin trial procedures
   • Famous paintings of the passion
   • The history of the Stations of the Cross

7. Have the students read one of Isaiah's servant songs, Isaiah 42:1–4; 49:1–6; 50:4–9; 52:13–16; or 53:1–12. Tell the students to copy phrases they feel could be applied to Jesus. Have them write these phrases on paper and decorate the paper with appropriate symbols.

8. Have the students study the prayers of Jesus at the Last Supper, in the garden of Gethsemane, and on the Cross. Have them write in their reflection notebooks what they have learned about Jesus from these prayers.

9. Help the students make a relief map of Jerusalem and the surrounding area as it was in the time of Jesus. They could add buildings and people to create the scene of Holy Week.

10. Let the students discuss what might have happened if Jesus had been given a fair trial with honest witnesses. Then have each student choose a person from Jesus' life and write two questions the lawyer might ask that person if he or she were on the witness stand at Jesus' trial. Each student should then answer the questions as the character would. Finally, stage a fair trial for Jesus, with one of the students as prosecutor. He or she can use the class questions to interrogate the witnesses. You may wish to put on the trial for an audience of parents or other students.

11. Have the students create mobiles that describe the Kingdom of Heaven. Tell them to use Scripture references with symbols or sketches. They might hang the mobiles from the ceiling of the classroom, in the windows, or at home. Possible references include the following:
   • Matthew 22:1–14
   • Matthew 25:1–13
   • John 14:2–3
   • Romans 8:38–39
   • 1 Corinthians 2:9–10
   • Philippians 3: 20–21
   • Colossians 3:3–4
   • Revelation 21–22

The Victory of Jesus
JESUS THE RISEN LORD

Faith Focus

Jesus rose from the dead, ascended to the Father, and is still with us.

Reflecting on the Faith Experience

Take a few moments to reflect prayerfully before preparing the lesson.

Listening

. . . to know him and the power of his resurrection and [the] sharing of his sufferings by being conformed to his death, if somehow I may attain the resurrection from the dead.

Philippians 3:10–11

Reflecting

The Resurrection is God's guarantee that those who trust the Father and follow his plan through the mystery to the end as Jesus did will have victory. In the upper room, Jesus appears and shows his wounds. He says, "My friends, look what they tried to do to keep me away from you. But they could not do it. Because love is stronger than death. Here I am. Let us rejoice!" They did just that. Filled with joy, they went out and preached "Don't be afraid of life as mystery. Don't be afraid of life that doesn't seem to be success. Don't be afraid of dying. It is all more than worthwhile. We have seen the risen Lord. We have seen what God can do with human weakness where there is trust, love, care and service." (Rev. Demetrius Dumm, O.S.B.)

A band of frightened disciples had an experience of the risen Christ that radically changed them. Christ had broken the power of death. They could share his power; through Baptism, they would share eternal life with him. The deepest of all desires is the desire for life, and Jesus fulfills this desire forever.

The early Christians realized that dying and rising were happening every day, especially in the Eucharist. Christ had opened their eyes to what life was about. He had given them a mission and dared them to love in a way that was costly. Today Jesus is the companion of every Christian. He gives each one courage for his or her mission. The Church is a saved and saving community. Jesus teaches and enables Christians to risk their lives, jobs, and reputations for his kingdom of peace and justice. Whenever a Christian stands up for truth, fights an unjust status quo, or speaks up for a neighbor despite opposition, he or she is joined by others who proclaim the Gospel of the risen Christ.

Today Christians practice their faith where it is forbidden. Christians bring the Gospel to those who have nothing. Contemplatives embrace a life of prayer and penance that makes no sense to this world, but that brings strength and hope to many. Christians everywhere make the risen Christ visible. They endure suffering patiently, give themselves to thankless tasks, and speak the truth in love. They are a sign of hope. Through their witness, others see how powerful Jesus is and entrust their lives to him.

How do I communicate my belief in the Resurrection?

Responding

Spirit of the risen Lord, let the hope of the Resurrection sustain my students all their lives.

Scripture for Further Reflection

Romans 6:3–11 Jesus rose to a new life. Through Baptism, we die and rise with him. When we rise, it will be to a new and different life from our mortal life.

1 Corinthians 15:12–34 If Christ had not been raised from the dead, our faith in Baptism and eternal life would be in vain. At the end of time, everything in Creation will be ruled by Christ, and he will give everything to his Father.

Preparing for the Faith Experience

Day One
Jesus Lives!

Day Two
I Am Still with You

Day Three
Sent to Be Christian

Day Four
Building a New World

Day Five
Extending the Chapter

Gather and Go Forth

Scripture in This Chapter

Luke 24:1–11 The Resurrection of Jesus

1 Corinthians 15:54–55 Christ is victorious over death.

Romans 6:5 United with Christ

Catholic Social Teaching

- Rights and Responsibilities
- Solidarity

Church Documents

Catechism of the Catholic Church. The themes of this chapter correspond to the following paragraphs: **648–655, 662–664, 904–905.**

General Directory for Catechesis #16. All of reality is marked by the dynamism that bursts forth from the Resurrection of Christ, the seed that renews believers in the hope of a definitive fulfillment.

Dogmatic Constitution on the Church #48 (Second Vatican Council). The promised restoration has already begun in Christ. We calculate the sufferings of the present not worthy to be compared to the glory to come.

Redeemer of Man #18 (John Paul II). The Church must always be aware of the dignity of divine adoption of Christ through the Holy Spirit and of our destiny of grace and glory.

Sharing Catholic Social Teaching (USCCB). Our commitment to social justice is at the heart of who we are and what we believe. If Catholic education and formation fail to communicate our social tradition, they are not fully Catholic.

Gather and Go Forth

Find catechist instruction for Gather and Go Forth student pages 185–186 on T358–T359.

Enriching the Faith Experience

Use the activities at the end of the chapter to enrich a lesson or to replace an activity with one that better meets the needs of your class. Bookmark www.christourlife.com to find Web BLMs for this chapter.

Bulletin Board

A suggestion for a bulletin-board design for this chapter is pictured.

risen **Jesus** *alive in...*

Eucharist

Scripture

Faith community

LEARNING OUTCOME

The students will be able to

- describe the significance of the Resurrection and the appearances of the risen Lord.

Word to Know

apostle

See Glossary for definition.

Materials

- Bibles or New Testaments
- Drawing paper
- Crayons or felt-tipped pens
- Recorded music: Find suggestions for Chapter 22 on page T520.
- Reflection notebooks

Before You Begin

The basis for all early Christian catechesis, preaching, hymns, and prayers was the Resurrection. It is the central mystery of our faith. No one witnessed the Resurrection, but it changed the course of history. In the Gospels, Easter morning has the atmosphere of total surprise. The appearance of Jesus makes an unforgettable impression on the witnesses. They realize the authenticity of his teachings and the importance of the mission he gave them.

Centering _____

1. Guide the students in imagining what heaven might be like for them.

   ✦ **Why do you think people have always been fascinated by life after death?**

   ✦ **No one has given us a description of heaven. Saint Paul once wrote "What eye has not seen, and ear has not heard, and what has not entered the human heart, what God has prepared for those who love him, . . ."** (1 Corinthians 2:9)

   ✦ **We are going to use our imagination to picture what is ahead for us in eternal life. Sit comfortably. Close your eyes and imagine that you are in heaven. What does it look like?** [Pause.] **sound like?** [Pause.] **What is going on around you?** [Pause.]

   ✦ **Now imagine that you have a chance to return to earth and visit.** [Pause.] **Open your eyes and write down what you would tell your parents, your best friend, or a stranger about heaven.** [Ask volunteers to share their responses.]

2. Have the students complete the activity **I Believe** on page 179. **Why is the fifth item false?** (because we believe that God created each of us to be one unique person for all eternity)

3. Link the last lesson with today's lesson.

   ✦ **In the last lesson, you saw that Jesus died, as we all must die.**

   ✦ **Today you will learn the events that followed Jesus' Death and how they changed our lives forever. You will study the basis for our belief in eternal life: the Resurrection.**

Sharing _____

1. Call on a student to read aloud the first two paragraphs of **He Is Risen** on page 179.

   ✦ **Who witnessed the Resurrection?** (no one)

   ✦ **What basic facts do we know about the Resurrection?** (Jesus' tomb was open and empty. Christian believers had the experience of seeing Jesus risen.)

   ✦ **Why do you think the Gospel versions of the Resurrection do not agree?** (They were written some time after Jesus' Death and Resurrection and were based on oral tradition. They were not written as proofs, but to proclaim that Jesus had risen. They were not historical documents but faith documents.)

2. Discuss with the students what Jerusalem might have been like during the Death and Resurrection of Jesus.

   ✦ **If you were in Jerusalem right after Jesus' Death, how would you describe the mood of the people?** (They were discouraged and disappointed because they had believed Jesus was the Messiah. The apostles were defeated and sad over the loss of their friend and leader.)

   ✦ **How do you think the news that Jesus had risen from the dead changed the mood of different groups of people?** (The soldiers were afraid; the women disciples were excited; the apostles were amazed and thrilled.)

3. Have a student read aloud the directions for the activity in **He Is Risen** on pages 179–180.

   ✦ Assign one of the three Scripture references to each student. After they have looked up their reference and written an answer, call on several students to tell the story they read.

   ✦ You may wish to call on several students with each Scripture reference to get different perspectives.

   ✦ The Easter stories include the following:

   • **Guards and women** (Matthew 28:1–10) Women went to view the tomb; a violent earthquake occurred; a white-robed angel came from heaven and rolled away the stone; the guards were like "dead men"; the angel gave news of the Resurrection; women were to inform the disciples; on their way, they met Jesus who said, "Do not be afraid."

   • **Mary of Magdala, Peter, John** (John 20:1–18) Mary found the stone rolled away and told Peter and John that the Lord was taken away; John got to the tomb first and saw the wrappings on the ground; Peter went in and saw that the cloth for the head was rolled up separately; Mary stayed weeping at the tomb and looked inside; two angels were in the tomb and asked why she was crying; Mary saw Jesus and thought he was the gardener until he said her name; Jesus told Mary not to cling to him but to tell the disciples that he was returning to his Father.

CHAPTER 22

The Victory of Jesus

Jesus the Risen Lord

I Believe

What do you believe about eternal life? Circle *T* if you believe the statement is true or *F* if you believe it is false.

For everyone who believes in Jesus and listens to his words, eternal life has already begun. ⓣ F

You must have faith to believe in the Resurrection. ⓣ F

Christ's Resurrection is a promise of our future glory. ⓣ F

No one saw the Resurrection take place. ⓣ F

After we die, we come back to earth as other persons (reincarnated). T ⓕ

The Resurrection was the greatest event in human history. ⓣ F

He Is Risen

Jesus lives! The **apostles**, those who accompanied Jesus in his ministry, were stunned to hear those words. Jesus of Nazareth, who died by crucifixion and was buried in a borrowed tomb, now was alive. He was still with them, appearing to his friends. Jesus was in Galilee. He was in Judea. He was eating fish. He was in the upper room. He was hiking to Emmaus.

No one saw the Resurrection happen. The Gospel accounts of it vary. However, they agree on two facts: there was an open, empty tomb, and the disciples had the experience of seeing Jesus risen! In the Gospel Easter stories, the early Christians convey something that is beyond human experience.

As you read the following Scripture passages, imagine you are a reporter in Jerusalem at the time of the Resurrection. Write one thing you learn from these witnesses:

Guards and women (Matthew 28:1–10)

Answers will vary.

Mary of Magdala, Peter, John (John 20:1–18)

Answers will vary.

Thomas (John 20:24–29)

Answers will vary.

(179)

• **Thomas** (John 20:24–29) Thomas had not seen Jesus with the other apostles; he would not believe until he actually touched the wounds and the side of the Lord; eight days after Easter Sunday, the disciples and Thomas were in the upper room and Jesus came among them; Jesus invited Thomas not to doubt, but to touch his side; Thomas professed his faith; Jesus commended those people who have not seen, yet still believe.

4. Direct the students to read silently **Jesus Glorified** on page 180 and Luke 24:36–43.

✦ **Did Jesus look and act like a ghost?** (He looked the same, but glorified. He did the same things, but he was full of power, mystery, and glory.) **To Jesus' followers, eating proved that he was a person and not a ghost.**

✦ **What unusual things did Jesus do after he rose?** (passed through locked doors, appeared and disappeared) **Was Jesus a different person?** (He was the same person but changed.)

✦ **How was Jesus' Resurrection different from the raising of Lazarus?** (Jesus would not die again. Lazarus was not raised by his own power, but by the power of Jesus. Jesus had a glorified body.)

✦ **What did Jesus give us by his Death and Resurrection?** (a share in his eternal life)

✦ **When would the disciples understand fully who Jesus is?** (at Pentecost)

5. Have a student read aloud Luke 24:1–11.
What do you imagine the women felt when they heard the angel's words and returned from the tomb?

6. Ask a student to read aloud the first paragraph of **The Risen Jesus** on page 180.

✦ **What do you imagine the women felt when they told the apostles what they saw and heard at the tomb?**

✦ Have a student read aloud the rest of the section.

✦ **Who else did the risen Jesus appear to?** (two disciples on the road to Emmaus) **How did they finally recognize Jesus?** (when he broke the bread)

Now pretend you are a follower of Jesus at the time of the Resurrection. What meaning would one of these stories have for you?

Answers will vary.

_____

Jesus Glorified

After Jesus died, his human soul united to his divine person went to the realm of the dead and opened the gates of heaven for the holy ones there. Then he appeared on earth with his risen, glorious body. Jesus' appearances astounded the disciples and changed them forever. He had lived among them and had died. Now they saw him glorified. Death had no more power over him. As Saint Paul wrote:

> "Death is swallowed up in victory.
> Where, O death, is your victory?
> Where, O death, is your sting?"
>
> 1 Corinthians 15:54–55

Jesus was doing the same things he did before: teaching, forgiving, consoling, eating, and talking with his disciples. However, now they

saw him full of power, mystery, and glory. Jesus was the risen Lord who had passed beyond death. Unlike Lazarus, he would not die again. His words and his teachings were the authentic Word of God and would never pass away. Jesus had brought a totally new way of living—a way to share in eternal life, God's life. Looking at the risen Jesus, the disciples began to realize that they, too, would live as he did! Not until Pentecost, though, would they really understand who Jesus was and be empowered for their mission.

The Risen Jesus

Read Luke 24:1–11. In first-century Jewish society, women could not serve as public witnesses. Luke writes that "their story seemed like nonsense and they did not believe them." Imagine what it must have been like to be one of these women.

What led the disciples to believe that Jesus had been raised from the dead? The angels at the tomb told them so: "Why do you seek the living one among the dead? He is not here, but he has been raised." (Luke 24:5–6) The angels also reminded the women that Jesus had predicted that he would be put to death by sinners and rise on the third day.

Then Jesus appeared to his disciples. Luke tells us about Jesus' appearance to two disciples on the road to Emmaus, a village near Jerusalem. The two disciples talked with someone they believed to be a stranger. As they talked, the stranger explained and interpreted for them all that Scripture predicted about Jesus. Finally, while together at a meal, Jesus took bread, said the blessing, broke it, and gave it to them. With the breaking of the bread, the disciples recognized the stranger as Jesus.

Amazed, the two disciples returned to share the news with the other disciples. However, they arrived in Jerusalem to hear the reports from the disciples there: "The Lord has truly been raised and has appeared to Simon!" (Luke 24:34)

❮ Jesus and disciples on the way to Emmaus.

Acting

1. Have the students write a news story on one of the Resurrection events.

✦ **You are reporters for the *Jerusalem Daily* newspaper. Take an event from the Resurrection and write an article about it.** (Examples: women at the tomb, eyewitness account of one of the tomb guards, interview the apostle Thomas)

✦ **Be sure to include a headline and a drawing.**

2. Have the students do the activity Respond on page 183.

CHECKPOINT

• Was the learning outcome achieved?

LEARNING OUTCOMES

The students will be able to

- identify ways the risen Jesus is present.
- explain what it means to live as a person of faith.
- describe what sacramentals are.

Key Term

sacramentals—objects, words, and actions that are sacred signs

given by the Church and which can make us holy by the prayers of the Church and by the way we use them

Materials

- BLM 76
- Blindfold
- Card with directions for Centering #1
- Samples of sacramentals
- Reflection notebooks

Before You Begin

The effectiveness of Church-instituted sacramentals depends on the faith of those who use them and the prayer of the Church. Superstition must be avoided in their use; they must not be thought of as magical.

Centering

1. Have two students volunteer for a trust walk.
   - Have one student blindfolded. The other student leads the blindfolded student around the room.
   - Give the leader a card with directions, such as walk down two aisles, pick up a certain book, put it on a certain shelf, or get a coat.
   - The class should remain quiet, even if the blindfolded student has difficulty.

2. Discuss the trust walk experience with the students.
   - **What was hardest about being blindfolded?**
   - **On whom did the blindfolded volunteer depend?** (the student giving directions) **What feelings did the blindfolded student need to have toward the helper?** (absolute trust and confidence)
   - **Why is faith like this situation?** (It is confidence in Jesus to lead us through life. It is depending on God the way the blindfolded student depended on the helper.)

3. Link the last lesson with today's lesson.
   - **You have learned that after the Resurrection, Jesus still lives.**
   - **Today you will study the ways Jesus is with us, guiding us in our faith.**

Sharing

1. Call on a student to read aloud **The Risen Jesus and Believers** on page 181.
   - **People who met the risen Jesus had these convictions: Jesus was the Son of God; they must tell the world about him; by living out his teachings, all people could see what Jesus was like; his followers will have eternal life.**
   - **What quality did all of the people who saw Jesus have in common?** (faith)
   - **Name someone who saw the risen Jesus and tell how he or she recognized him.** (*Mary of Magdala* [John 20:16] Jesus called her by name; *Disciples on the road to Emmaus* [Luke 24:30–35] Jesus broke bread with them; *Thomas* [John 20:26–28] He was invited to put his hand in Jesus' wounds; *Disciples fishing* [John 21:4–7] They caught so many fish.) **In each case, Jesus took the first step and opened the eyes of his disciples to recognize him.**
   - **What insights into the Resurrection are in Paul's letter to the Corinthians?** (Our whole faith depends on the Resurrection. Our risen bodies will be totally different.)

2. Have the students read silently **We Experience the Risen Jesus** on page 181.
   - **How do all Christians share Christ's Death and Resurrection?** (through Baptism)
   - **In what three ways do we encounter the risen Lord?** (in the Eucharist, Scripture, and the faith community) **Jesus was always present in the first Christians' minds and hearts in these three ways as well. This changed them, and they began to act more like Jesus.**
   - **How does participating in the Eucharist increase our faith?** (Jesus is really present in the Eucharist. We are strengthened by the faith of the other believers celebrating with us.)
   - **In what way does reading Scripture help our faith?** (Scripture is God speaking to us. The more we reflect on it, the more our attitudes and actions become like Christ's through the Holy Spirit.)
   - **In the faith community, we share our faith and are Christ for one another. When we see people who act like Jesus, we are led to a deeper love of him. Hearing about other people's faith experiences encourages us in our own faith. We have a duty to strengthen one another in faith and help build a community of faith.**

3. **BLM 76** Distribute copies of BLM 76 **Seeing You, They See the Risen Lord.**

✦ Direct the students to complete the statements at the top of the BLM in their reflection notebooks. Allow time for silent reflection.

✦ Divide the class into pairs and have them share their answers with each other.

4. Discuss sacramentals with the students.

What signs of Jesus or of your faith do you have in your home? (crucifix, picture of Mary, statue, a family Bible)

5. Have a student read aloud **Signs That He Is with Us** on page 181.

✦ **What is the difference between a sacrament and a sacramental?** [On the board, list the answers in two columns.]

Sacrament	Sacramental
we meet Christ	we are reminded of Christ
given by Jesus	given by the Church
Jesus acts	power is from the prayers of the Church
grace increases directly	grace depends on the way we use them

✦ **In all the sacraments, Jesus is acting. When the priest baptizes, Jesus baptizes; when the priest forgives, Jesus forgives; when the bishop anoints, Jesus anoints. The sacred signs, the words and actions of the sacraments, all reveal Jesus blessing the community. When the Church celebrates the sacraments, Jesus is truly caring for his people.**

✦ **What is the relationship between sacraments and sacramentals?** (Sacramentals prepare us for the sacraments.)

6. Divide the class into pairs. Have the students work the **Sacramental Crossword Puzzle** on BLM 76.

The Risen Jesus and Believers

The Resurrection was for believers. Those who believed in Jesus saw him as the risen Lord. To recognize the risen Jesus required faith, because the Resurrection is a mystery of faith. The Gospels emphasize the doubt of some disciples when they heard about Jesus' Resurrection. In each instance, Jesus took the initiative and revealed himself to them, and by his grace the disciples believed.

What if Jesus had not been raised? Read 1 Corinthians 15:12–19. What do you conclude?

If Jesus was not raised, we would have no

hope of being raised.

_____

What kind of bodies will we have when we are raised? In 1 Corinthians 15:36–49, Saint Paul says that our risen body will be as different from our present body as a seed buried in the ground is from the wheat that grows from it.

We Experience the Risen Jesus

By our Baptism, we share in the life, Death, and Resurrection of Jesus and witness to him. Through his Death and Resurrection, Jesus gives us the power to die to selfishness.

We are an Easter people. There is a contagious enthusiasm about the way we live and a freedom about the way we speak and act. Jesus' Death and Resurrection give meaning to our lives. We have the hope of eternal life. Our goal is to live as companions to the risen Jesus. By following his way, we shall one day rise with him in glory.

Today we encounter the risen Lord in the sacraments, especially in the Eucharist, in the Scriptures, and in the faith community of the Church.

A Moment with Jesus

Just as Jesus appeared to the disciples after the Resurrection, Jesus comes to meet us. We might experience Jesus' presence at Mass, in Scripture, in prayer alone or with others. Perhaps you have experienced Jesus present with you in other ways.

Pause for a moment and reflect on a time when you felt the presence of Jesus. How did you recognize his presence? Thank Jesus for being always with you and for revealing himself to you.

Signs That He Is with Us

All seven sacraments are an opportunity to meet and grow closer to Jesus. Through them, Jesus acts in us and cares for us. They were instituted by him and help us live as God wants us to. Other sacred signs called sacramentals have been given to us by the Church to remind us of God. The Church's prayers and the way we use sacramentals empower them to make us holy. Sacramentals may be blessings, blessed objects such as medals and palms, or actions such as the Sign of the Cross. They prepare us for the sacraments. The risen Lord is with us no less now than he was with the first disciples.

CHAPTER 22 (181)

---

7. Discuss with the students the ways Jesus is alive today.

What are some of the many ways that you can think of that Jesus is with us today? [List their answers on the board.]

Acting _____

 Have the students read silently **A Moment with Jesus** on page 181.

Allow sufficient time for silent reflection.

CHECKPOINT

• Were the learning outcomes achieved?

LEARNING OUTCOMES

The students will be able to

- explain the significance of the Ascension.
- discuss Christ's call to be a witness to the world.

Word to Know

Ascension

See Glossary for definition.

Materials

- Bibles or New Testaments
- BLM 77, BLM 78
- BLM 79
  Reproduced on stiff paper with students' names
- Five large sheets of white paper
- Black markers
- Reflective music for Acting #5

Before You Begin

1. The Ascension proclaims that Jesus is Lord equal to the Father and the Holy Spirit in power and majesty. It calls all to the Kingdom of God, a kingdom of justice and love, that Jesus proclaimed by dying on the Cross. We work to see that Jesus is recognized and honored by all people on earth. His Ascension is our call to witness, to act, to bring justice and peace to all.

2. For Acting #4, you might print the statements on separate slips of paper and distribute them to the students to pray.

Centering _____

1. Compare graduations to the Ascension.

   ✦ **Soon it will be time for graduations from college, high school, grade school, and kindergarten. What mixed emotions do graduates experience on their day of graduation?** (excitement about starting a new phase of life; reluctance to leave the school and their friends)

   ✦ **As part of the graduation ceremony, a guest speaker usually addresses the graduating class. What challenges might he or she propose to the graduates?** (Be the best person you can be, accept responsibility, have courage, become active in your community.)

   ✦ **This type of sending-off speech is like the missioning talk Jesus gave to his disciples at the end of his time with them. For about 3 years, and then for 40 days after the Resurrection, Jesus had taught his followers his Way. At the Ascension, he sent them out to carry on his work.**

2. Link the last lesson with today's lesson.
   In the last lesson, you reflected on the ways the risen Lord is still with us, supporting us in his work. Today you will take a closer look at what Jesus sends us to do.

Sharing _____

1. Have the students read silently the first paragraph of **Ascension: Jesus Is Lord** on page 182.

   ✦ After they have answered the question, ask a few students to share their responses.

   ✦ Have the students read silently the rest of the section and complete the activity.

   ✦ **What do you think is meant by "the right hand of the Father"?** (The biblical interpretation is a special place of God's goodness and power.)

   ✦ **When we say "Jesus is Lord," what do we mean?** (We believe he is God and reigns over the heavens and the earth, the living and the dead. We see all things as subject to him, including ourselves.)

2. Call on a student to read aloud **Missioned to Make a Difference!** on page 182.

   ✦ Allow time for the students to look up and copy the Scripture verse. Ask a student to read aloud the verse.

   ✦ **What was going to happen to the apostles when they received the Holy Spirit?** (They would become "other Christs" in the world.)

   ✦ **No matter what our age, our talents, or our circumstances, we, too, are to be witnesses. What** does it mean to say "actions speak louder than words"? (Actions show visibly what we believe. They show that the words we speak are true.)

   ✦ **Why is it hard to be a real witness?** (Not everyone will like what you do, and you could be criticized or left out.)

   ✦ **Imagine you are with students who start to tease an unpopular student. In what ways can you act like another Christ?** (Be silent and not join in. Point out the student's good qualities. Speak up for the student. Invite him or her to join you in an activity. Be kind to the student.)

   ✦ **This is how Christ wants us to act. He wants us to love our friends and those who are not our friends. Sometimes by being kind to difficult people, we can help them become loving and caring people.**

Acting _____

1. Choose or let the students choose an activity from Reach Out on page 183.

2. **BLM 77–78** Distribute copies of BLM 77 **Be a Friend to All** and BLM 78 **Lend a Hand—Share Yourself.**

   ✦ Divide the class into five groups

   ✦ Read aloud the directions:

- ✦ **Discuss and write suggestions for the situations helping people understand Christian justice on BLM 77 Be a Friend to All.**

- ✦ When the students have finished with BLM 77, assign one story from BLM 78 to each group and give each group a large sheet of paper. Read aloud the directions:

- ✦ **Divide the sheet of paper into three columns labeling them** *People's Needs, Ways to Meet Them,* **and** *Ways the People Can Help Themselves.* [Write these on the board.] **Read the assigned story from BLM 78 Lend a Hand—Share Yourself. Discuss the story, writing your responses to the headings under each column.**

3. Have the groups share their solutions for BLM 77 and the story from BLM 78.

    Rights and Responsibilities Solidarity

   - ✦ Remember that on topics of justice and peace, students' attitudes often reflect their parents' attitudes.

   - ✦ Encourage the students to express themselves openly. Lead them to see the wisdom of the Church's teaching.

4. Pray a litany on discipleship with the students.

   - ✦ **These statements are based on the words of Saint John Paul II. After each statement, please respond "Here I am, Lord. Send me."**

   - ✦ **We need disciples who can give their lives freely, with firm faith and mature conviction, with utter generosity and without regret. We pray,** [Response]

   - ✦ **We need disciples who want Jesus as their friend and who will put all their confidence in him. We pray,** [Response]

   - ✦ **We need disciples who can reach out to embrace the world, who will serve, heal, and reconcile. We pray,** [Response]

   - ✦ **We need disciples who will take risks, who are not afraid to**

Ascension: Jesus Is Lord

Goodbyes can be sad. People who love each other find it hard to be separated. When have you experienced such a goodbye?

Answers will vary.

The **Ascension** is Jesus' return to his Father. In the person of Jesus, humanity is already with God. The early Christians believed that Jesus would come again soon in glory. As time went on, however, they realized that the Second Coming might be in the far distant future. While they waited, Jesus' invisible but very real presence remained with them.

Read Acts of the Apostles 1:6–11. Name two unusual things that happened at Christ's leave-taking.

Jesus was lifted up, and a cloud took him

from their sight. Two men in white told the

disciples that Jesus was taken up into heaven

and would return the same way.

In the Nicene Creed, we pray, "He ascended into heaven and is seated at the right hand of the Father." The Ascension was more than just a goodbye. It completed the glorification of Jesus. Being seated at the right hand of the Father showed he was Lord of the universe. Before, Jesus had limited his activity to

Palestine. Now his influence extends to the ends of the universe. When we say Jesus is Lord, we say we believe he reigns over heaven and earth, the living and the dead. We see all things as subject to him—including ourselves. We believe his teachings are God's words.

Missioned to Make a Difference!

Jesus, filled with the Holy Spirit, promised that Spirit to his disciples. His Spirit would make them "other Christs." What did Jesus predict about them? See Acts of the Apostles 1:8.

You will be my witnesses in Jerusalem,

throughout Judea and Samaria and to the

ends of the earth.

We, too, witness to Christ Jesus and make the world aware of his justice and love. Our call to be his witnesses is a call to action! We are "givers" in a world of "takers." We are responsible for our acts and selfless in serving. We are not afraid to take risks for love of Jesus and to do the right things. We wait for Jesus to return and to change our bodies "to correspond in form to his glorified body." (adapted from Philippians 3:21)

witness to Christ by their words, acts, and attitudes. We pray, [Response]

- ✦ **We need disciples who won't hold grudges, and who will support the community by caring for those who are poor, sick, and unloved. We pray,** [Response]

5. **BLM 79** Distribute the mission statement cards made from BLM 79 **Mission Statement.**

   - ✦ You might play appropriate reflective music.

   - ✦ Give the students sufficient time to reflect on their mission message.

- ✦ **Keep your mission card in a place where you will be reminded of your mission every day.**

CHECKPOINT

- • Were the learning outcomes achieved?

- • In what ways have the students shown insights into the call to service that will help build a community of peace and justice?

LEARNING OUTCOMES

The students will be able to

- discuss their responsibility as Jesus' followers to care for those who are poor and to be of service to others.
- describe ways to help those who are poor.
- demonstrate an understanding of the key concepts in this chapter.

Materials

- Bibles or New Testaments
- 70 cards listing things the students value such as no homework passes, coupons for candy, or more computer time
- Markers
- Paper cut in the shape of a loaf of bread, one for each student
- Basket
- Table
- BLM 80 Quiz
- Recorded music: Find suggestions for Chapter 22 on page T520.

Before You Begin

1. Salvation is not a private matter. Our baptismal call challenges us to embrace and respond to God's invitation and to extend it to all others. God desires that all people be saved. When Jesus commanded his apostles to go forth and proclaim the Good News, he told them to bring that message to every nation. (Matthew 28:19) Under the guidance of the Holy Spirit, the Church strives to carry out the mission of Jesus, a mission that compels us to proclaim the Gospel to those who do not yet believe in Christ, to strive for Christian unity, and to maintain a respectful dialogue with those who do not yet accept the Gospel.

---

22 Summary

Remember

Why is the Resurrection of Jesus significant?
The Resurrection of Jesus is significant because it shows that Jesus is the Son of God and that we will rise someday.

What does the Ascension tell us?
The Ascension tells us that, by returning to his Father in heaven, Jesus is Lord of the universe.

How do we encounter the risen Lord today?
We encounter the risen Lord today in the sacraments, especially in the Eucharist, in the Scriptures, and in the faith community.

Respond

How exciting it must have been for the disciples on the road to Emmaus to learn from Jesus himself the meaning of his passion, Death, and Resurrection. Their hearts were "burning within them" at his words. He gave them more than words. With the breaking of the bread, he was made known to them and their hearts were opened.

Write in your reflection notebook what you would have said to Jesus if you had been on the Emmaus journey (Luke 24:13–35). Then write a prayer telling how and where you will be a witness.

Reach Out

1. Read 1 Corinthians 15:1–58. This letter of Saint Paul contains the earliest written statement about the Resurrection. It was probably written sometime between A.D. 54 and 56. Some Christians in Corinth had weakened in the faith, and Paul wanted them to know that the Resurrection was our greatest hope.

   With your family and friends, discuss how the Corinthians may have reacted to Paul's letter. Imagine that you are a member of their community and write a response to Paul expressing your belief.

2. Pray to become a peaceful person who brings the joy of the risen Jesus to others.

3. Jesus is life. Find Scripture verses from the Gospel of Saint John and make holy cards to give away. Write a cheerful message on the back of each card.

   Here are some verses you could use.

John 1:3–4	John 5:26	John 6:51
John 3:16	John 6:27	John 6:58
John 3:36	John 6:35	John 6:63
John 4:14	John 6:40	John 8:12
John 5:21	John 6:47	John 10:17–18
John 5:24	John 6:48	

4. Bring to class a newspaper article that reports a need in the world. Give the article to your teacher for posting, and then remember these needs in prayer.

5. Make a booklet of drawings and explanations of sacramentals. You could divide it into three sections: in the home, in church, and in your own life; or sacred objects, sacred actions, and sacred words.

Words to Know

apostle   Ascension

(183)

---

2. Our faith requires concrete actions on behalf of less fortunate people. We have a responsibility to use our gifts and talents to serve others. We believe that God is the God both of the Exodus and of the Resurrection, always ahead of us, calling us on.

3. The facts in this lesson should not be presented in a way that students feel guilty or defensive about what they have. This lesson is not a call to pity, but a call to justice and mercy. It is a call to find new and resourceful ways of serving, praying for, and loving those who are poor.

4. You might supplement this lesson with activities and materials provided by mission societies, such as Catholic Relief Services, Maryknoll, or the Catholic Campaign for Human Development.

5. When planning today's lesson, keep in mind that Day Four is when the students take the quiz for this chapter. Reserve time at the end of class for this assessment. The quiz can also be administered on Day Five.

Centering

1. Distribute unequally the 70 cards representing things the students value.

◆ Example, for a class of 20:

- give 4 students 13 rewards each,
- give 6 students 2 rewards each,
- give 6 students 1 reward each,
- give 4 students nothing.

◆ **How do you feel about how the cards were distributed?**

◆ **How do you feel about the number of cards you received?**

◆ **If every person is equal, should every person get an equal amount of money?** (No, some do more work or work that requires more skill. But everyone should have enough money to live a full human life.)

◆ **Are people in the world poor because there isn't enough money for everyone to live a decent life?** (No, some people have more money than they need. It's not distributed fairly.)

2. Link the last lesson with today's lesson.

◆ **In the last lesson, you learned about your mission to the world as a Christian.**

◆ **Today you will look at specific ways you can carry out your mission to build a better world.**

Sharing

1. Have the students read silently the parable of the rich man and Lazarus (Luke 16:19–31).

🌿 *Rights and Responsibilities*

◆ **What is there in the parable that makes you angry?** (the injustice Lazarus experienced)

◆ **Who are people that are like Lazarus today?** (people who have nothing; homeless people)

◆ **What are the challenges that face people who are poor?** (homelessness, poor education, lack of food, insufficient health care)

CHAPTER 22 Review Activities

Who Am I?   Answer these riddles.

1. I am the first person Jesus appeared to according to the Gospel of John.

Mary of Magdala

2. I explained Scripture to two disciples on the road to Emmaus.

Jesus

3. I was invited to touch Jesus' wounds when I did not believe the apostles had seen him.

Thomas

4. I was the first disciple to recognize that the stranger who helped us fish was Jesus.

John

5. I was the first apostle to go into the tomb.

Peter

6. I am the Lord of the universe.

Jesus

Which apostle touched Jesus' wounds?

(184)

What Am I?   Answer these riddles.

1. I am what Jesus ate to prove he was alive.

fish

2. When Jesus broke me, the disciples recognized him.

bread

3. I am what you need to believe in the Resurrection.

faith

4. I was Jesus' first words to his apostles.

Peace be with you.

5. I am Jesus' return to the Father in glory.

Ascension

6. I was conquered by Jesus.

death

7. I am the great miracle that made all Jesus' words believable.

Resurrection

8. I am a blessed object or action that has power to make you holy by the prayers of the Church.

sacramental

Meeting Jesus   Name four ways that we can encounter the risen Lord today.

1. the sacraments

2. the Eucharist

3. Scripture

4. the faith community

◆ **Why do they lack these basic needs?**

◆ **In the parable of the rich man and Lazarus, what was their fate in eternity?** (Lazarus went to heaven, and the rich man suffered.)

◆ **Was the rich man punished because he was rich?** (No, he was punished because he ignored Lazarus. He refused to realize his responsibility for others.)

◆ **God won't send someone we know back from the dead to tell us to share. How do we know we must share?** (through the teachings of Jesus and his Church)

◆ **Christian responsibility is something we need to learn and to practice.**

2. Have the students take the Christian Responsibility Quiz.

◆ The quiz can be dictated.

◆ **You are to answer the following questions with how you would respond: S for seldom, O for often, and U for usually.**

1. When you see jobs around the house that need to be done, do you do them without being asked?

2. When you are upset, do you take time to calm down and to think before you act?

3. When you hear about floods, famines, wars, or injustice in the world, do you remember to pray for the people who are suffering?

4. Do you volunteer to work for your family or for others without being paid?

5. Do you think about your future and the service you can give?

6. Do you give some of your personal money to help others?

7. Do you watch the news, read blogs, or see documentaries or other shows that keep you informed about the needs of the world and how you can help?

8. Do you try not to ask your parents to buy you new things just because your friends have them?

✦ **If you answered "usually" for most statements, you have a good understanding of Christian responsibility. If not, you can begin today to grow in your understanding.**

✦ **The more you act with responsibility in your immediate surroundings, the more conscious you will be of the needs throughout the world.**

3. Lead the students through the Summary and Review Activities, pages 183–184.

4. **BLM 80** Distribute and administer BLM 80 **Chapter 22 Quiz.**

Use this opportunity to assess the students' understanding of the main concepts in the chapter. If there is not sufficient time for the students to complete the quiz, consider moving it to Day Five.

Acting _____

1. Give each student a piece of paper shaped like a loaf of bread.

Direct them to compose a prayer for peace and justice and write it on the loaf.

2. Conclude the lesson with a prayer service for peace and justice.

Step 1: Put a basket on a table.

Step 2: Select a leader.

Step 3: Pray the Lord's Prayer.

Step 4: Have the students bring their loaves of bread to the table and place them in the basket.

Step 5: The leader prays:

Jesus speaks to you. Listen and respond to him. "I have no feet but yours. I have no hands but yours. Yours are the eyes through which I look out over the world. Yours is the voice that speaks my word. Yours is the heart that must bring my love to all." [Allow sufficient time for silent reflection.]

Step 6: Play a song about justice.

3. At the end of class, have the students tear out and take home pages 183–184.

CHECKPOINT ✓

- Were the learning outcomes achieved?

- What evidence is there that the students are enthusiastic about being involved in some action to promote social justice?

Gather and Go Forth

Lead students through pages 185–186 in the student book. Find catechist instruction on T358–T359.

Use the following suggestions to create an additional lesson for Day Five.

1. Remind the students to take home pages 183–184 to share what they are learning with their families.

2. Incorporate any unused BLMs from the week's chapter.

3. Consider the time of the liturgical year and use the appropriate Special Seasons and Lessons. SSLs begin on page T369.

4. Visit www.christourlife.com to find additional activities for Extending the Chapter.

5. Use activities from Enriching the Faith Experience.

6. Guide the students in a prayerful discussion of Sunday's Scripture readings. Visit www.christourlife.com for more information.

Chapter 22   Enriching the Faith Experience

Use the following activities to enrich a lesson or to replace an activity with one that better meets the needs of your class.

1. **Web BLM** Use Web BLM Chapter 22-A **Caring for One Another** to have the students ponder real problems in the world today. Have them discuss the questions at home or in groups and write suggestions for the situations. Here is some additional information:

   1. ✝ Help educate those who are poor so that they can help themselves. Refer to *The Pastoral Constitution on the Church in the Modern World #69,* (Second Vatican Council) or *Living the Gospel of Life: A Challenge to American Catholics* (USCCB).
      ✣ **Solidarity**

   2. Refer to *A Call to Action* (Pope Paul VI) or *Peace on Earth* (Pope John XXIII).

   3. Refer to *The Pastoral Constitution on the Church in the Modern World* #81 (Second Vatican Council).

   4. Refer to the *Rite of the Anointing of the Sick* or the *Declaration of Euthanasia* (The Congregation for the Doctrine of the Faith).

   5. Refer to *Rich in Mercy* (Pope John Paul II).

   6. Provide education on responsible parenthood and the Church's guidelines on natural family planning. Promote a positive attitude toward life by supporting pro-life issues, writing to legislators, voting for candidates who respect life, and supporting education on the primacy of the family and the importance of developing religious values. Refer to *Of Human Life* (Paul VI), *The Gospel of Life* (Pope John Paul II), and the *Declaration on Christian Education* (Second Vatican Council).

2. **Web BLM** Hold the celebration on Web BLM Chapter 22-B **Celebrating the Journey** about the Resurrection and our call to witness.

3. Read aloud the prayer of Easter Sunday morning. Ask what graces we request in it.

   God our Father, creator of all, today is the day of Easter joy. This is the morning on which the Lord appeared to men who had begun to lose hope and opened their eyes to what the scriptures foretold: that first he must die, and then he would rise and ascend into his Father's glorious presence. May the risen Lord breathe on our minds and open our eyes that we may know him in the breaking of bread, and follow him in his risen life. Amen.

   Daytime Prayer
   The Liturgy of the Hours

4. Have the students act out a Resurrection account for a younger class from these passages:

John 20:1–10	John 21:15–23
John 20:11–18	Luke 24:13–35
John 20:24–29	Luke 24:36–43
John 21:1–14	Acts 1:3–9

5. Have the students compose letters to their parish. Put this outline on the board.
   Dear Friends of _____ Parish,
   To me, being Christian means

   _____.
   Qualities I see in a strong
   Christian are _____.
   My parish has shown me how to
   live like a
   Christian by _____. Some ways
   I show what it
   means to be a Christian are
   _____. You can
   support me in living my Christian
   life by _____.

   Sincerely,

   _____

6. Encourage the students to find out about the lives of the following Christians. Two students might prepare an interview, with one of them being the heroic person and the other a reporter. Or several students could be famous Christians and the class could ask questions of them.

- Mother Teresa
- Vincent de Paul
- Maximilian Kolbe
- Martin de Porres
- Ambrose
- Father Damian
- Mother Cabrini
- Cardinal Ngugen Van Thuan
- Rose Hawthorne Lathrop
- Edith Stein
- John Paul II
- Elizabeth Ann Seton

7. Have the students adopt a homebound person from the parish. They can offer their services, such as carrying out the trash, washing windows, weeding, visiting, playing cards, and running errands.

8. Have the students find out if their parish provides babysitting during Mass. If not, encourage the students to form a baby-sitting club. If it does, they could offer their services.

9. Have the class write and sign a one-page meditation on peace and justice. Check to see if it could be published in the Sunday bulletin.

10. Invite the students to a hunger day. Have them meet on a Saturday at the parish center, skipping lunch and donating the money saved to those who are poor. The schedule could be as follows:

- Scripture reading of Matthew 25, followed by making mission boxes on the works of mercy
- Service on the parish grounds
- Video on hunger or those who are poor
- Group discussion of ways to live poverty
- Craft activity to make something for children's homes, hospitals, or nursing homes
- Prayer service or liturgy
- Soup supper

11. Suggest donating time spent watching TV to volunteer at a hospital, work at the church, or help a neighbor. This service might mean visiting those who are sick, cutting a lawn, cleaning the parish hall, coaching children's teams, or running errands for an elderly person.

12. The students could donate baby clothes, toys, or other items to an organization such as Birthright.

13. Have the students make a dictionary of words associated with the sacraments. Each entry should include the word, its pronunciation, its definition, and any relevant illustrations.

Alive with the Spirit
JESUS THE HEAD OF THE CHURCH

Faith Focus

The Holy Spirit came to the Church, making the members courageous witnesses and forming a community of love.

Reflecting on the Faith Experience

Take a few moments to reflect prayerfully before preparing the lesson.

Listening

Rather, living the truth in love, we should grow in every way into him who is the head, Christ, from whom the whole body, joined and held together by every supporting ligament, with the proper functioning of each part, brings about the body's growth and builds itself up in love.

Ephesians 4:15–16

Reflecting

When the Spirit came at Pentecost, accompanied by wind and fire, a new era began. The power of love and faith was liberated, bathing the world in a hope that neither trial nor persecution could dim. In the outpouring of that Spirit, the Church as the community of believers was born, and its mission was launched. The disciples were empowered to proclaim Christ to the world. This mission would bind them together with a common vision and a common dedication to one another. The Spirit brought life and grace to a world that needed to be whole again. We, the Church, hunger to be one body: one visible community in the Lord, witnessing together. We devote all we are to our one Lord. In one faith, we anchor our trust in him. By one Baptism, we are plunged into a new life in him. And we become one family, bonded together forever, children of one God.

As Christians, we each carry a responsibility to be open to the Spirit. We also carry a responsibility for one another. Christ sent his Spirit so that a community of love would grow in his name. We cannot walk away from this community, this family, without injury to the whole body and to ourselves. This is the meaning of community: we are united in Christ, on a journey to Christ, needing, sharing, giving, and caring—each member affecting the whole.

Pentecost is a continuing event. The Spirit still empowers us for mission and binds us to one another. Just as our hearts have been transformed in the light of grace, so must we transform the earth.

Accepting Pentecost means taking risks, without which there can be no sharing in common, no deep faithfulness to the tradition of the apostles, no lasting community, or no breaking of bread. For these marks of the early Christian community identify only those who take the risk of serving the kingdom. The Christian must reshape life according to the priorities of the kingdom. Together in the unity and peace that are the gifts of the Spirit, we live as one Body of Christ. Making up for one another's weaknesses, we struggle on until we have been built up in love, growing in all ways into Christ and his kingdom.

How closely do I identify with the Church?

How important is the Spirit in my life?

Responding

Spirit of power and might, help me to generate in my students enthusiasm for the faith.

Scripture for Further Reflection

Acts 2:1–47 The Holy Spirit came to Mary and the apostles on Pentecost, giving gifts that enabled them to preach the Good News to people of all nations. The apostles baptized thousands, giving birth to the Church.

Galatians 5:22–26 The Spirit brings gifts to counter our sinfulness. The Spirit is our life.

Preparing for the Faith Experience

Day One
A Spirit-Filled Community

Day Two
A Community of Love

Day Three
The Power of the Spirit

Day Four
A Journey Pageant

Day Five
Extending the Chapter

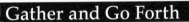

Gather and Go Forth

Scripture in This Chapter

Matthew 28:19–20 Make disciples of all people.

Acts of the Apostles 2:1–41 The Coming of the Spirit

Galatians 5:25 Follow the Spirit

Catholic Social Teaching

- Solidarity
- The Poor and Vulnerable

Church Documents

Catechism of the Catholic Church. The themes of this chapter correspond to the following paragraphs: **685–686, 731–733, 737, 747.**

General Directory for Catechesis #43. The Holy Spirit increases the Church's understanding of the Gospel and helps the Church proclaim the Gospel throughout the world.

Dogmatic Constitution on the Church #4 (Second Vatican Council). The Holy Spirit was sent to the Church on Pentecost to sanctify it, to guide it in the works of ministry, to bestow on it various charismatic gifts, and to adorn it with his fruits.

Gather and Go Forth

Find catechist instruction for Gather and Go Forth student pages 193–194 on T360–T361.

Enriching the Faith Experience

Use the activities at the end of the chapter to enrich a lesson or to replace an activity with one that better meets the needs of your class.

Bulletin Board

A suggestion for a bulletin-board design for this chapter is pictured. You might post student examples of ways to put Scripture verses into action, words or pictures from Reach Out #3 on page 191 in the student book.

Know that I am with you always; yes, to the end of time.

Matthew 28:20

LEARNING OUTCOMES

The students will be able to

- describe the account of Pentecost in Scripture.
- explain that with the coming of the Spirit at Pentecost, the disciples were strengthened for mission and the Christian community was formed.

Key Term

Pentecost—the coming of the Holy Spirit upon Mary, the apostles, and the disciples, empowering them to proclaim the Good News as courageous witnesses and to form a community of love, the Church

Materials

- Bibles or New Testaments
- Reflection notebooks

Before You Begin

1. Whatever happened in the room at Pentecost was dramatic and visible. It completely transformed the early Christian community. The outpouring of the Spirit is grace, a free gift of God, which awakens in all those who are open to it a spiritual power that can transform individuals and, through them, the whole world.

2. Students might prepare to dramatize Pentecost for Sharing #4.

3. Pentecost was the second great annual pilgrim feast for the Jewish people. It was an agricultural feast celebrated after the wheat and grain harvest in Palestine. It is also referred to as the Feast of Weeks, because the harvest was celebrated seven weeks (or the 50th day) after the Passover, marking the beginning of the grain harvest. Pentecost references in the scriptures include the following: Exodus 23:14–17; Exodus 34:22 (Feast of Weeks, feast at the fruit harvest); Leviticus 23:15–21; Numbers 28:26–31; Deuteronomy 16:9–12.

   Later, Pentecost became a celebration of God's Covenant with Moses and the People of God on Mount Sinai. At that occurrence, wind and fire indicated the presence and activity of God.

4. In liturgical prayers and art, we use symbols with biblical backgrounds to represent the Holy Spirit. The fire that appeared on Pentecost recalls the burning bush on Mount Sinai through which God spoke to Moses. Fire symbolizes the strength and force of the Spirit. The wind recalls the wind that blew over the waters at the beginning of Creation. The wind symbolizes the Holy Spirit breathing life into the Church. Water represents the cleansing and life-giving action of the Holy Spirit at Baptism.

5. The Acts of the Apostles was written in Greek by Luke around A.D. 63 and can best be understood as a sequel to his Gospel. It can be called the "Gospel of the Church" for it shows how the Church continued announcing the Kingdom of God, the Good News of Christ. The topic of Acts is the work of the Holy Spirit in the Church and in the disciples.

Centering

1. Discuss with the students what it means to stand up for what you believe.

   What are some events in your life that gave you the courage and strength to stand up for what you believe? (standing up to defend someone or something you believe in; refusing to share your homework or test answers; sacrificing your free time to help a person in need; making a very important decision on your own)

2. Link the last lesson with today's lesson

   ✦ **In the last lesson, you learned that the Resurrection changed life completely for Jesus and for his followers. Can you think of some event in your life that changed you?** (learning to read; traveling to another country; learning to ride a bike; playing an instrument; meeting a challenge in sports or in school)

   ✦ **Today you will learn about an event, Pentecost, that changed Jesus' disciples from being afraid of sharing Jesus with others to being courageous witnesses of his life, Death, and Resurrection.**

Sharing

1. Direct a student to read aloud the first two paragraphs of **Turning Points** on page 187.

   ✦ **How did Helen Keller feel after she came to know that the letters referred to water?**

   ✦ **How do you think her life changed?**

   ✦ **Helen spoke of a "strange new sight." What do you think she meant by that?** (She felt new understanding; she was able to "see" with her mind.)

2. Ask a student to read aloud the remainder of this section.

- ✦ Have the students answer the question. Ask volunteers to share their answers.

- ✦ **A deep religious experience can be a turning point in a person's life. Do you recall any saints or people in the Bible who were changed after an encounter with God or another experience?** (Moses, the prophets, Paul, Ignatius, and Bernadette) [Refer to Saints and Feast Days on pages T447–T490.]

3. Explain to the students the turning point of salvation history.

- ✦ **The Death of Christ, his Resurrection and ascension, and the sending of the Spirit on Pentecost form the greatest turning point in all of salvation history.**

- ✦ **With the coming of the Holy Spirit, a whole new era was begun. The apostles and disciples were now able to understand more deeply all that Jesus had revealed and were empowered to proclaim this message of salvation to all the world.**

4. Have the students read silently **Pentecost: Touched by the Spirit** on page 187.

- ✦ **Why do you think the disciples needed help in preaching about Jesus?** (They were afraid they would be put to death too.)

- ✦ Direct several students to read aloud the story of Pentecost from Acts 2:1–24 or 2:1–41.

- ✦ You may want to have a group of students dramatize the passage.

5. Direct the students to read silently **Spirit Alive** on page 188.

Discuss the students' answers. [Write as column headings on the board *Fire*, *Wind* and *Holy Spirit*.] Possible answers:

Fire	Holy Spirit
produces heat and warmth	produces the warmth of love, the fire of enthusiasm

Alive with the Spirit

Jesus the Head of the Church

Turning Points

Many people have experienced turning points: events that changed them and turned their lives around. Helen Keller was one of these people. An illness as an infant left her blind and deaf. By the time she was seven, she had become uncontrollable. Helen's family hired Anne Sullivan to teach her sign language, to reach somehow into the darkness of her life. It seemed an impossible task, until one day Anne held one of Helen's hands under a pump and spelled "w-a-t-e-r" into her other hand. As Helen explained later:

Helen Keller.

Write about a turning point in your life or in the life of someone you know about.

Answers will vary.

_____

> Somehow the mystery of language was revealed to me. I knew then that "w-a-t-e-r" meant the wonderful cool something that was flowing over my hand. That living word awakened my soul, gave it light, hope, joy, set it free! . . . Everything had a name, and each name gave birth to a new thought. As we returned to the house every object which I touched seemed to quiver with life. That was because I saw everything with the strange, new sight that had come to me.
>
> from *The Story of My Life* by Helen Keller

That was Helen's turning point. Although she would continue to struggle as she learned to cope in the world, her whole life had changed. She had been transformed.

Pentecost: Touched by the Spirit

A turning point occurred for all humanity the day the Holy Spirit came to the Church. It was the harvest feast of Pentecost in Jerusalem, a time for pilgrims to gather in the holy city and praise God for fields of grain. Mary and the disciples were all gathered in the upper room of a house. They were waiting. They had been commissioned by Christ to go and baptize, to bring the good news of salvation and love to all people. They knew what they were to do, but they needed help. They needed confidence and guidance. They needed Christ. So they put all their trust in Christ and waited, praying. Suddenly there was a tremendous sound— as if a powerful wind was filling the house. Something like tongues of fire appeared and rested on each person. The disciples were filled with the Holy Spirit. The Spirit of God touched and transformed them.

Fire	Holy Spirit
provides light	provides the light of knowledge and understanding
is powerful	is powerful in our lives
melts objects so that they can be recast and molded	melts our hardened hearts, unites us to one another and to Christ, and helps us take on the image of Christ
totally transforms materials	can help us totally transform our lives and attitudes
purifies, sterilizes, and cleanses	helps us purify our intentions and cleanse our hearts of sin
provides a welcoming atmosphere	helps establish an atmosphere of love and acceptance

Wind	Holy Spirit
can be felt, but is not seen	We can experience the Spirit's power, but we cannot see the Holy Spirit. We can see only the results.
can be gentle and refreshing	refreshes and inspires us, gently urging us toward Christ
cannot be controlled; is free	is free and ever-present, alive and working where we may least expect divine activity
[air] is essential for life	is essential for our life in Christ
can produce more power	can inspire people whose example may inspire others

6. Have a student read aloud the first paragraph of **Out of Hiding** on page 188.

- ✦ Assign each Scripture reference to a student to locate and read aloud.
- ✦ After each passage is read, have the students record their answers.

7. Discuss with the students what the disciples were like before and after Pentecost.

- ✦ On the board, draw two columns for a chart. Label one *Before* and the other *After.* Fill in the chart with the students' answers.
- ✦ **How did the apostles feel before the coming of the Spirit?** (afraid) **How were they after the Spirit came?** (courageous, bold)
- ✦ **How much did they understand Jesus' teachings before the Spirit came?** (very little) **How were they different after the Spirit came?** (They understood more fully.)
- ✦ **How were the disciples and apostles preparing? What was their attitude?** (They were praying, waiting, and hoping for guidance.) **How were they after the Spirit came?** (excited, enthusiastic)
- ✦ **Before the Spirit came, they were a closed group, united only with one another. How were they after the Spirit came?** (They were open to all people and longed to preach to all people.)

The completed chart:

Before	After
afraid	courageous, bold
understanding very little	understanding more fully
praying, waiting, hoping	excited, enthusiastic
closed group	open to all

8. Have the students read silently the rest of the section **Out of Hiding** on page 188.

Acting _____

1. Have a student read aloud **Fearless Followers** on page 189.

Spirit Alive

What the disciples experienced on Pentecost was beyond description. However, the two elements associated with the coming of the Spirit can help us understand how the Spirit changed their lives. In Scripture, wind and fire are signs of God's presence.

Name a characteristic of wind.

Answers will vary.

How is the Holy Spirit's activity like wind?

Answers will vary.

Name a characteristic of fire.

Answers will vary.

How is the Holy Spirit's activity like fire?

Answers will vary.

Out of Hiding

How did the coming of the Spirit affect the disciples in the upper room? Read the verses listed. Then write what happened through the power of the Holy Spirit.

Acts of the Apostles 2:4,11
The apostles were able to speak foreign languages and be understood.

Acts of the Apostles 2:14
Peter was empowered to address the crowd.

Acts of the Apostles 2:41
About three thousand accepted Peter's message and were baptized that day.

Acts of the Apostles 2:43
The apostles were able to work many wonders and signs.

Acts of the Apostles 2:44–45
They formed a community. They lived together, shared all things, and helped those in need.

The Holy Spirit was present at the baptism of Jesus when he was anointed for his mission. The same Spirit empowered the disciples to fulfill their mission. Here is the mission Christ gave to the disciples and to us.

"Go, therefore, and make disciples of all nations, baptizing them in the name of the Father, and of the Son, and of the holy Spirit, teaching them to observe all that I have commanded you."

Matthew 28:19–20

The most important change the disciples experienced was deep within their hearts. With the continuing presence of the Spirit, they became enthusiastic, courageous witnesses to Christ.

 188 UNIT 3

- ✦ Draw two columns on the board. Label one *NO!* and the other *YES!*
- ✦ **What are five things it takes real courage to refuse?** [List these under *NO!*]
- ✦ **What are five things that we as real Christians need the courage to uphold?** [List these under *YES!*]

2. Discuss with the students their experiences of courage.
What are some experiences in your life when you had the courage to refuse something that was wrong or to stand up for something you believed in? [You might give examples from your own life as a way of witnessing to the students.]

3. Have the students do Respond on page 191.
Allow sufficient time for silent reflection.

CHECKPOINT

- Were the learning outcomes achieved?
- In what ways did the students show an ability to discover the workings of the Holy Spirit in their lives?

LEARNING OUTCOMES

The students will be able to

- describe the characteristics of the early Christian community.
- discuss how to be open to the transforming power of the Spirit in their own lives.

Word to Know

Fruits of the Holy Spirit

See Glossary for definition.

Materials

- Bibles or New Testaments
- Old telephone book
- 6-by-9-inch red construction paper, one piece for each student
- White drawing paper, smaller than the red, two pieces for each student
- Scissors
- Glue
- Hole punch, string, hangers
- Copies of *Te Deum* prayer for Acting

Before You Begin

1. The Fruits of the Holy Spirit are indications of the Spirit's work in us. The tradition of the Church lists 12 Fruits of the Holy Spirit. (See page 243 in the student book and page T435) The last four fruits—faithfulness, modesty, self-control, and chastity—are directly connected to the Sixth Commandment.

2. Encourage the students to work page 11 of their Scripture booklets.

Fearless Followers

The Holy Spirit's power is not limited to the early Christians or to great saints and leaders. Through Baptism, you and all the faithful are gifted with the Spirit. Our encounter with the Spirit usually does not involve drastic changes, roaring winds, and tongues of fire. Instead, we grow a little each day through struggles and moments of love and understanding. In time, we become true followers of Jesus, living the way he taught us to live.

One of the most effective ways to spread the Good News is to live caring lives. People are attracted to Christ when they see Christians living his message. That kind of living, however, takes courage: courage to say no to the evil spirit, courage to say yes to the Spirit of Christ. When have you shown Christian courage?

Community of Love: The Church

At Pentecost, the Church was born with the Spirit as its strength and guiding force. All that had been foretold by the prophets was accomplished, and a new era in salvation history was begun.

After the Spirit had come upon the disciples, they did not just walk off to the farthest limits of the earth, preaching the Good News. Their first response was to form a community of believers. The community was a gift of God. In many ways, it was also a miracle because persecution and hardships surrounded the disciples.

The Christians had a common vision—a deep devotion to Jesus Christ, his way of life, and the Kingdom of God. As they sought to love Christ more, they showed a real concern for people who were poor and needy, and a thirst to spread the Good News. They also loved one another in Christ. They were bonded to one another more closely than a club or a team. They were the family of believers, the Mystical Body of Christ. In Christ, the head of the Church, they were a new people reconciled to God. They shared his ministry. They celebrated his saving mysteries.

The unity among Christians echoes the unity among the Persons of the Trinity. Four actions that bonded the community together are named in Acts of the Apostles 2:42. They are

- devotion to the teaching of the apostles
- communal life
- the breaking of bread
- prayers.

Church Bonds

Read about these bonds and the growth of the early Christian community in Acts of the Apostles 2:42–47; 4:32–35; and 5:12–16. With those passages in mind, check possible endings to the following statement.

The description of the early Church in the Acts of the Apostles

○ seems impossible.
○ is something I would like to experience.
○ makes me want to try to be a better member of the community of believers.
○ could never happen again.

Check the ways the people in the early Christian community were like people in your parish.

○ The Eucharist was the center of the community's life.
○ Not everyone agreed on what the Church and its practices should be.

○ The people prayed together often.
○ They showed concern for those in need and went out of their way to help them.
○ They gathered in one another's homes for meals and sharing.
○ They willingly gave money and possessions to others in the community.
○ They spoke openly about their love for Christ and the Church.
○ They attracted more and more people to their community.
○ Some members seriously failed to live up to the ideals of Christian life.

CHAPTER 23   (189)

Centering

Link the last lesson with today's lesson. Write C_____ W_____ on the board.

- ✦ **Do you remember from the last lesson how the event of Pentecost changed the followers of Christ?** (They became *Courageous Witnesses* to Jesus.)

- ✦ **Another effect the coming of the Holy Spirit had on the followers of Christ was transforming them into a community of believers we refer to as the Church.**

Sharing

1. Discuss with the students the power of community.

   - ✦ Give a student a sheet of paper and ask him or her to tear it in half. **Why was that so easy?** (It is a thin piece of paper.) [Hand the student an old telephone book.]

   - ✦ **Now try to tear this in half. Why is this paper harder to tear?** (Although the book is only paper, when so much paper is bound together, it is difficult to tear.)

   - ✦ **In a similar way, the support system of a community, where there is mutual sharing, makes us strong.**

2. ✝ Direct the students to read silently **Community of Love: The Church** on page 189.

☗ *Solidarity*
The Poor and Vulnerable

◆ Have a student read aloud the qualities of a church community in the third paragraph.

◆ Direct the students to underline the qualities.

- a common vision—a deep devotion to Jesus Christ, his way of life, and the Kingdom of God
- concern for people who were poor and needy
- a thirst to spread the Good News
- loved one another in Christ.

3. Have three students read aloud the Scripture passages from **Church Bonds** on page 189.

◆ After reading the passages, direct the students to complete the exercise.

◆ **What did you think about the description of the early Christian community?**

◆ **How did your parish compare to these qualities?**

◆ **What if we changed** *parish* **to** *family*? **How would your family compare?**

4. Ask a student to read aloud **You and the Community of Believers** on page 190.
There are signs by which others can see that the Spirit is alive and active in a person. These are called the Fruits of the Holy Spirit.

5. Have the students read silently **Fruits of the Holy Spirit** on page 190.
Direct the students to complete the activity. Go over their answers.

Acting

1. Distribute to the students the red construction paper and the white drawing paper.

◆ **Draw a flame on the red paper and cut it out. Make two flames from the white paper, large**

You and the Community of Believers

You are a part of the community, the Church that was born on Pentecost. Like the apostles, you have a mission from Christ. You are to be a courageous witness to the Good News for the whole world and a loving, enthusiastic member of the community of believers, the Church.

Your role as a witness and disciple may not extend to all the world, but you are important and vital wherever you are. The Holy Spirit is at work in you this very moment. Remember, however, it may take a lifetime to be totally open to the transforming power of the Spirit.

Fruits of the Holy Spirit

How can you tell you are open to the Spirit? What will your life be like? Galatians 5:22–23 contains a list of the qualities that we call the **Fruits of the Holy Spirit** found in the life of a true disciple: love, joy, peace, patience, kindness, generosity, faithfulness, gentleness, and self-control. Church tradition has added three more: modesty, goodness, and chastity.

Choose three Fruits of the Holy Spirit. Describe how they show the presence of the Spirit in your life.

Answers will vary.
_____
_____
_____
_____
_____
_____

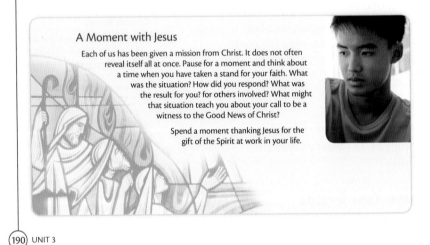

A Moment with Jesus

Each of us has been given a mission from Christ. It does not often reveal itself all at once. Pause for a moment and think about a time when you have taken a stand for your faith. What was the situation? How did you respond? What was the result for you? for others involved? What might that situation teach you about your call to be a witness to the Good News of Christ?

Spend a moment thanking Jesus for the gift of the Spirit at work in your life.

(190) UNIT 3

---

enough to write on, but small enough to fit on the red flame.

◆ **Write a prayer for courage on one white flame and a prayer for community on the other.**

◆ **Glue the white flames on either side of the red flame. Now punch a hole in the top, thread string through it, and tie the flames on a hanger.**

Prayer for Community

Front

Prayer for Courage

Back

2. Have the students do activity #3 from Reach Out on page 191. [Refer to bulletin-board.]

3. 🙏 Have the students read silently **A Moment with Jesus** on page 190. Allow sufficient time for silent reflection.
Let's pray together the Prayer to the Holy Spirit on the inside back cover of your book. [See page T446]

CHECKPOINT

- Were the learning outcomes achieved?

- How do the students' prayers reveal a trust in the Holy Spirit?

LEARNING OUTCOMES

The students will be able to

- describe the role of the Spirit in the Church.
- evaluate their commitment and response to their local Christian community.

Materials

- Bibles or New Testaments
- BLM 81

- Recorded music: Find suggestions for Chapter 23 on page T520.
- Reflection notebooks

Before You Begin

Young people understand what spirit is all about. They know when there is plenty of spirit at school events, and they know when there is no spirit at all. They will have no difficulty relating to the effect of the Holy Spirit on the lives of people. Certainly God can work quietly and gently in our lives, but our young people might best understand the Spirit as someone who is an energizer, a source of enthusiasm. When we say that we are Spirit-filled, we mean that God has filled us with an enthusiasm for following Jesus Christ and for spreading the Good News.

Centering

1. Read aloud the Tower of Babel from Genesis 11:1–9
    - ✦ **The events of the tower of Babel and Pentecost are worth comparing.** [Draw two columns on the board. Label one *Babel* and the other *Pentecost*.]
    - ✦ **What are some of the ways these two events compare with each other?**
    - ✦ *Babel:* division and confusion caused by sin; common language was gone; people were no longer able to understand one another; people scattered to all parts of the world.
    - ✦ *Pentecost:* Spirit united the people; through the gift of tongues, they had a common understanding; Spirit began a new age of love; all divisions were overcome; the apostles scattered to the ends of the earth to proclaim the Good News.)

2. Link the last lesson with today's lesson.
    - ✦ **You have learned how the Spirit transformed the disciples and formed the Church.**
    - ✦ **Today you will learn more about the working of the Spirit within the Church and within you.**

Sharing

1. **BLM 81** Distribute copies of BLM 81 **The Activity of the Spirit.**
    - ✦ Divide the class into pairs to complete the BLM. Go over the students' answers.
    - ✦ Ask volunteers to share their responses to the last question.

2. Discuss with the students the two activities of the Spirit at Pentecost.
    - ✦ **The Spirit's activities are the empowering of witnesses and the building of a community.**
    - ✦ **In what ways do you witness to Christ?**
    - ✦ **In what part of your life do you need courage the most?**
    - ✦ **How often do you pause and call upon the Spirit for help? for guidance? for strength?**
    - ✦ **What kind of community member are you? in your parish? in your family? among your friends?**
    - ✦ **How do you show that you understand your responsibility to serve others?**
    - ✦ **How aware are you of the needs of others in your parish? in your family? among your friends? throughout the world?**
    - ✦ **How often do you call upon the Holy Spirit to show you how you can be a more active and mature member of your community?**
    - ✦ **If someone watched you for a day, how could he or she tell that you were a disciple of Christ?**
    - ✦ Allow time for quiet reflection.

3. Play a song about the Holy Spirit.
    Have the students reflect on the words to see what they tell about the Spirit and the action of the Spirit.

Acting

 Direct the students to compose a prayer to the Holy Spirit.
    - ✦ **In your reflection notebooks, compose a one-sentence prayer to the Holy Spirit. Ask for the grace to become a mature, loving member of the faith community.**
    - ✦ **You may want to pick one particular area to pray for: your response to the Spirit in the parish, in your family, or among your friends.**
    - ✦ Allow time for silent reflection.

CHECKPOINT

- Were the learning outcomes achieved?

LEARNING OUTCOMES

The students will be able to

- review salvation history.
- identify more strongly with our common journey to the Father.
- demonstrate an understanding of the key concepts in this chapter.

Materials

- Bibles or New Testaments
- BLM 82A–D
- BLM 83 Quiz

Before You Begin

1. Pentecost inaugurated a new age. Now is a fitting time to recap the faith journey. Our heritage and our stories are a vital part of who we are today as a Church. Their retelling, the passing on of the faith, is the responsibility of every Christian.

2. The Journey Pageant may require more than one lesson. The material might also have to be adapted to your local situation.

3. If the pageant is staged in a large room, the characters for different scenes may all be in position and then come to life when a spotlight is shone on them.

4. Scenery, backdrops, props, costumes and multimedia effects enhance the production.

5. When planning today's lesson, keep in mind that Day Four is when the students take the quiz for this chapter. Reserve time at the end of class for this assessment. The quiz can also be administered on Day Five.

Centering

1. Discuss with the students the power of a play.
   - ✦ Have any of you ever been to a play?
   - ✦ How is seeing a play different from reading a book? from a story on TV?
   - ✦ Do you think people remember a story better when it is told to them, when they see it acted out, or when they themselves act it out? Why?

2. Read aloud Church Drama.

3. Explain to the students that they will perform their own pageant.
   In this lesson, you will perform your own pageant tracing the faith journey of the Church from Creation to Pentecost. It is the journey of faith to a richer and fuller life.

Church Drama

The Church uses the arts to pass on our beliefs. Stained-glass windows depict scenes from Scripture and from our faith. Songs contain the truths of our faith. In the early Middle Ages, priests wrote and performed plays in churches for their congregations. The earliest of these plays—a simple dialogue involving the angel at the tomb, Mary of Magdala, and the apostles after the Resurrection—was added to the Easter service around the 10th century. Later, plays were written for other important feasts.

Eventually plays moved outside the churches. Some plays grew so long that they took three or four days to perform and had as many as 5,000 people in them. Those plays based on Scripture stories were called mystery plays. Those based on the lives of the saints were called miracle plays. By the late Middle Ages, these plays were performed on pageants.

A pageant was a wagon-or float-like structure used as a stage. Each float represented an episode or a scene of the story, such as Noah and the ark or the sentencing of Jesus to death. A series of these wagons would pass through a town, stopping at spots where seats were set up for viewing the scenes. By the 14th century, pageants were common, especially during festivals such as Corpus Christi. These pageants would portray all of Scripture, from Creation to the final judgment.

Sometimes pageants formed a circle on the outskirts of town. People would stand or sit in the middle. There a presenter would direct their attention to the scenes and explain what was going on.

Sharing

1. Describe the flow of the pageant and roles needed for each scene.
   - ✦ Write the scene and roles needed on the board. Each group should have a presenter who introduces the play. Have the students choose what role they would like to perform. [The narrator reads the non-speaking parts in the Bible.]

- **Creation**—Three or four readers can divide the section.
- **The Fall**—Adam, Eve, God, the serpent, narrator
- **Cain and Abel**—Cain, Abel, God, narrator
- **The Covenant with Noah**—God, Noah
- **The Call of Abraham**—God, Abram, Lot, Sarai, narrator

- **Abraham and Isaac**—God, Abraham, Isaac, narrator
- **The Exodus**—Narrators, groups of Israelites and soldiers
- **The Ten Commandments**—God, Moses, narrators
- **The Death Of Moses**—narrators
- **The Prophecy of Nathan**—Nathan, David, God, narrator

- **Birth of Jesus**—Mary, Joseph, angels, shepherds
- **John the Baptist**—John the Baptist, tax collector, soldier, followers, narrator
- **Sermon on the Mount**—Jesus, followers
- **Crucifixion**—Jesus, women, soldiers, narrator
- **Resurrection**—(*The Empty Tomb:* Mary of Magdala, Peter, John, Jesus, narrator or *The Road to Emmaus*—Two disciples, Jesus, narrator)
- **Pentecost**—Peter, the apostles, Mary, crowd, narrator

✦ The narration may be read, but the dialogue for each scene from Scripture should be memorized.

2. **BLM 82A–D** Distribute BLM 82A–D **The Journey Pageant** to the students.

   Have the students choose their roles and memorize their parts. Meet briefly with each group to answer any questions.

3. Rehearse the pageant by scenes and then as a whole.

   Invitations may be written to parents, other classes, or parishioners.

4. Have the students perform the pageant.

5. Lead the students through the Summary and Review activities, pages 191–192.

   At the end of class, have the students tear out the pages to take home.

6. **BLM 83** Distribute and administer BLM 83 **Chapter 23 Quiz.**

   Use this opportunity to assess the students' understanding of the main concepts in the chapter. If there is not sufficient time, consider moving it to Day Five.

Acting

 Lead the students in the *Te Deum* (You Are God).

Some medieval mystery plays ended with the praying or singing of this prayer:

CHAPTER 23 Summary

Remember

What is the significance of Pentecost?
At Pentecost, the Holy Spirit was poured out upon Mary, the apostles, and other believers, empowering them to proclaim the Good News as courageous witnesses and to form a community of love, the Church. At Pentecost, the Church was born, and a new era of salvation history began.

How is the Church a community?
As a community, we are bonded by love for Christ and for one another, and by service to the world with the guidance and strength of the Holy Spirit. Like the early Christian community, we share in the teaching of the apostles (expressed in the Apostles' Creed and the Nicene Creed), community life, the breaking of the bread, and prayers (especially the sacraments).

What are the Fruits of the Holy Spirit as listed in Galatians 5:22–23?
The Fruits of the Holy Spirit are love, joy, peace, patience, kindness, generosity, faithfulness, gentleness, and self-control.

Respond

The Holy Spirit empowers you to be a courageous witness to the Good News of Christ. There are times when you are called to stand up for what is right. Think of a time when you did what you knew to be right, even when it was difficult. Record the incident in your reflection notebook. Include how you felt before, during, and after making your decision. Then compose your own prayer to the Holy Spirit to use at times in the future when you will need strength and support.

Reach Out

1. Read a biography of Saint Paul, Saint Ignatius of Loyola, Saint Bernadette Soubirous, or one of your favorite saints. Find out about the turning points in his or her life and report your findings to the class.

2. The Spirit, the gift and power of God, directs the growth of the Christian community and enables its members to carry out the ministry of Christ through various gifts. Read 1 Corinthians, Chapters 12, 13, and 14, which list many of the gifts and tell how they can be used for the Church. Then think of your own community—your parish. How evident are these gifts in the parish? Be ready to explain.

3. There is much you can do right now as a member of the family of believers. Read these Scripture passages. Write a summary of each and two or three ways you can put Christ's message into action today.

   Romans 12:9–13   Colossians 3:16–17

   1 Corinthians 10:31   1 Peter 4:10–11

Word to Know

Fruits of the Holy Spirit

Saint Bernadette Soubirous. ❯

(191)

You are God: we praise you;
You are God: we acclaim you;
You are the eternal Father:
All creation worships you.
To you all angels, all the powers
   of heaven,
Cherubim and Seraphim, sing in
   endless praise:
Holy, holy, holy, Lord, God of power
   and might,
Heaven and earth are full
   of your glory.

The glorious company of apostles
   praise you.
The noble fellowship of prophets
   praise you.
The white-robed army of martyrs
   praise you.
Throughout the world the holy

Church acclaims you:
Father, of majesty unbounded,
Your true and only Son, worthy
   of all worship,
And the Holy Spirit, advocate
   and guide.
You, Christ, are the king of glory,
The eternal Son of the Father.

When you became man to set
   us free
You did not spurn the Virgin's
   womb.
You overcame the sting of death,
And opened the kingdom of heaven
   to all believers.
You are seated at God's right hand
   in glory.
We believe that you will come, and
   be our judge.

Come then, Lord, and help your
people,
Bought with the price of your
own blood,
And bring us with your saints
To glory everlasting.

*English translation
by Compendium of
the Catechism of the
Catholic Church*

CHECKPOINT

- Were the learning outcomes
achieved?

CHAPTER 23 Review Activities

Pentecost Acrostic   Use these clues to solve the puzzle.

1. They were in the upper room with Mary when the Holy Spirit came.
2. A visible sign of the Spirit's power to enlighten
3. A sign of the Spirit's invisible action
4. What the apostles spoke in after the Spirit came
5. The city where Pentecost took place
6. The community the followers became on Pentecost
7. What the Spirit gave the apostles
8. Qualities that are signs of the Spirit's presence in us
9. How many thousands of people were baptized on Pentecost

1.   A P O S T L E S
2.   F I R E
3.   W I N D
4.   T O N G U E S
5.   J E R U S A L E M
6.   C H U R C H
7.   C O U R A G E
8.   F R U I T S
9.   T H R E E

The Church: Ever Ancient, Ever New   Match each action you might do with a characteristic of the early Church.

a. devotion to the apostles' instruction
b. communal life
c. the breaking of bread
d. prayers

  c 1. Celebrate the Eucharist.
  b 2. Donate to Catholic Charities.
  a 3. Attend religion classes.
  d 4. Participate in parish liturgies and devotions.

Your Mission   How can you follow Christ's command to baptize all nations and teach the Good News?

Answers may include inviting a friend to church,

talking about Jesus, supporting the missions,

teaching by drawing people to Jesus through

good example.

PHOTO: Young Catholic pilgrims from Pennsylvania attend Mass at World Youth Day, Germany, 2005.

192

Day Five   Extending the Chapter

Gather and Go Forth

Lead students through
pages 193–194 in the student
book. Find catechist instruction
on T360–T361.
Materials: Bibles, flameless
candles

Use the following suggestions to
create an additional lesson for
Day Five.

1. Remind the students to take
home pages 191–192 to share
what they are learning with
their families.

2. Incorporate any unused BLMs
from the week's chapter.

3. Consider the time of the
liturgical year and use the
appropriate Special Seasons
and Lessons. SSLs begin on
page T369.

4. Visit www.christourlife.com to
find additional activities for
Extending the Chapter.

5. Use activities from Enriching
the Faith Experience.

6. Guide the students in a
prayerful discussion of
Sunday's Scripture readings.
Visit www.christourlife.com for
more information.

Use the following activities to enrich a lesson or to replace an activity with one that better meets the needs of your class.

1. Have the students research agencies in their neighborhood that offer services to those who are poor, such as a food pantry or a soup kitchen. Several students could organize a day when the class volunteers to help. Or the students could organize a food or clothing drive in the school to donate to the local groups.
   ✝ *The Poor and Vulnerable Solidarity*

2. Direct the students to illustrate a Scripture reference about the Spirit or the Christian life on a watercolor wash. Directions:
   ◆ **Choose a quotation from Scripture or from a song. Wet a 9-by-12-inch sheet of paper and then brush on paint—bright colors for joy, darker colors for a more subdued effect.**
   ◆ **While the paper is drying, find a picture that matches the mood or theme, or draw one on an unlined index card or paper.**
   ◆ **Place the picture on the dry paper, leaving room for the quotation.**
   ◆ **Very lightly draw lines a half inch apart, and then using a fine-point marker or lettering pen, write the quotation, filling the entire sheet as much as possible.**
   ◆ **Make a frame from larger paper, leaving a one-inch margin on the top and sides and an inch and a half at the bottom.**

   Possible Scripture references:
   • The love of God has been poured out into our hearts through the holy Spirit that has been given to us. (Romans 5:5)
   • For those who are led by the Spirit of God are children of God. (Romans 8:14)
   • Do you not know that you are the temple of God, and that the Spirit of God dwells in you? (1 Corinthians 3:16)

   • Whatever you do, do everything for the glory of God. (adapted from 1 Corinthians 10:31)
   • Where the Spirit of the Lord is, there is freedom. (2 Corinthians 3:17)
   • Let us not grow tired of doing good . . . (Galatians 6:9)

3. Have the students evaluate their various communities by asking the following questions.
   ◆ **What does *community of believers* mean to you? Do you think it is important to be involved in your parish community? Describe your participation in your parish community. How active and involved are you? Would you like to be more involved?**
   ◆ **Share an experience in which you really felt a part of a group. What helped you experience such a sense of belonging?**
   ◆ **Would you agree or disagree with these statements: If God were to come into your life now in a visible way . . .**
     • **you would pray to God more.**
     • **you would always be happy.**
     • **you would love your family more.**
     • **you would not be afraid of anyone anymore.**

4. Have the students evaluate their ideas of courage.
   ◆ **How can you show courage in your family? in school? with your friends? on teams? with younger children?**
   ◆ **How do you think the following people would define courage: Saint Francis of Assisi? Pope Francis? Saint Maximilian Kolbe? Blessed Teresa of Calcutta?**
   ◆ **How have these people shown courage: your parents? a teacher? your best friend? the Catholic Church? missionaries?**
   ◆ **When in your own life have you shown courage?**
   ◆ **How did Jesus show courage?**

   ◆ **What characteristics would you look for in a courageous witness for Christ?**

5. Have the students pair off or form groups. Distribute a large sheet of paper to each pair or group. Tell the students to consider the various types of community groups they belong to: class, school, parish, team, neighborhood, city, country. Assign or have the students choose one of these groups. They should illustrate some aspect of the community they have chosen. On the top of the paper, have the students write the following:

   _____:
   We are a family when we . . .
   or

   _____:
   We are building community because we . . .

   The students should complete the phrase and illustrate it. Then distribute three or four smaller sheets of paper. On these sheets, the students should write other ways the group they have chosen can serve others. These smaller sheets can then be attached to the larger sheet.

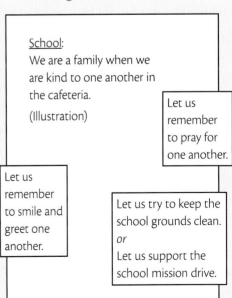

School:
We are a family when we are kind to one another in the cafeteria.
(Illustration)

Let us remember to pray for one another.

Let us remember to smile and greet one another.

Let us try to keep the school grounds clean.
or
Let us support the school mission drive.

Matrimony and Holy Orders
JESUS EMMANUEL

Faith Focus

Jesus calls each of us to be holy in a special vocation.

Reflecting on the Faith Experience

Take a few moments to reflect prayerfully before preparing the lesson.

Listening

. . . as he who called you is holy, be holy yourselves in every aspect of your conduct, for it is written, "Be holy, because I [am] holy."

1 Peter 1:15–16

Reflecting

The universal call to holiness is heard from the beginning of salvation history: ". . . it is I, the LORD, who make you holy." (Exodus 31:13). The words *holy* and *holiness* have an awesome ring. Holiness is the all-encompassing attribute of God: ". . . O holy One, LORD of all holiness . . . " (2 Maccabees 14:36); ". . . holy is God!" (Psalm 99:5).

What does it mean for us to be holy? In the Old Testament, holiness or sanctity is often equated with keeping God's laws. Throughout his life, Jesus taught by word and example that love is the way.

I give you a new commandment: love one another. As I have loved you, so you also should love one another.

John 13:34

The challenge of Jesus rings in the ears of every one of us. We are responsible for opening our hearts and lives to that grace that empowers us to move on to newer heights of love. The summons to holiness is an invitation to each person to be his or her best self. Each individual has the potential to develop into a person rich in the fully realized virtues (powers) of body, mind, and soul through a love

for God that motivates everything in life. Enlightened, supported, and sustained by grace, each one of us can walk with assurance and peace on the journey through life into eternal blessedness. The only real failure in life is not to be a saint. Each of us must be holy. The path we take may be different from that of our friends, but the goal is the same.

It is important for each person to discover his or her vocation toward which God's graces and gifts have been directed. All of us must pray to find the path the Lord has chosen for us so that we can love God most completely. God gently leads us to the state where we can best fulfill our call to holiness—where each of us can become his or her best self and live a life of love.

How seriously do I take my call to holiness?

How can I use the opportunities of my current state of life to become holier?

Responding

Eternal Father, help my students to recognize their vocation and to enter into it wholeheartedly.

Scripture for Further Reflection

Matthew 19:3–6 Questioned about the lawfulness of divorce, Jesus quotes Genesis 1:27–28 and asserts that no one may divide what God has joined.

1 Corinthians 4:1 Those called to the ordained ministry are servants and teachers of the mysteries of God.

1 Peter This entire letter explains how people in various states of life are to be holy in all they do.

- ✦ Read aloud the Scripture passage.
- ✦ **How would you know if a person is holy?**
- ✦ **Who is the holiest person who ever lived?** (Jesus)

2. Direct the students to finish reading this section silently.

- ✦ **How can you respond to God's call right now?** (develop my talents so I can serve others better; witness to God's love in my family and with my friends)

- ✦ **What might you become in response to God's call?** (a member of the laity who is single or married; a member of a secular institute; a sister or brother, deacon, or priest)

- ✦ **Which way of life is best?** (All are ways to holiness. The one that is best for you is the one to which God calls you.)

- ✦ **Each way of life has its joy and pain. Each challenges a person to discover and develop his or her talents. Each offers opportunities to grow in holiness and to bring people to the kingdom through loving service.**

- ✦ **The work of bishops, priests, deacons, and religious is easily recognized as the work of Christ. Their lifestyle is a public witness, and the work they do is related to the Church.**

- ✦ **Lay Christians also share in Christ's mission at work, at home, or with friends. Their work is like yeast, which can't be seen but which reaches all parts of the dough and makes it grow.**

- ✦ **How can the laity carry on the mission of Christ?** (They can make decisions using Gospel values; reach out to people who are needy; work for laws that uphold God's laws; hold Church roles such as eucharistic minister, lector, and catechist.)

- ✦ **How can a lay Catholic sometimes influence others more than an ordained person or a religious?** (A lay Catholic can bring Christ's values to places where ordained people and religious are

CHAPTER **24**

Matrimony and Holy Orders

Jesus Emmanuel

What Do I Do?

The activities of your everyday life are a part of God's plan for you at this time. Your life is like a puzzle, but God will help you to put all the pieces together. He calls you through the ordinary events of your life to become like his Son, Jesus. God calls you to a particular vocation in life and is preparing you for it now.

Your Life Call

You and every Christian have received one universal call from God at Baptism. You can find it in 1 Thessalonians 4:3.

Your call to holiness is a call to develop your talents so you can serve God and others better. It is a call to witness to God's love within your family and parish, among your friends and classmates. In the future, God may call you to remain a member of the laity as a single or married person. God may call you to be a member of a secular institute, a sister or brother in a religious order, a deacon, a religious or diocesan priest, or a bishop. God may even call you to several vocations.

In all of these lifestyles, Jesus accompanies us on our journey. He is Emmanuel—God with us. He supports us with his grace. Every vocation is meant to lead us to be holy and to share

in Jesus' mission. The best way of life for you is the one to which God calls you.

Call to Single Life

God calls some people to the single life. Unmarried people can be involved in a wide range of activities and can spend their lives in service to others. They become signs of God's love. They may make private vows. Some single people choose to live a vowed life as members of secular institutes. They live consecrated lives of prayer and service, while keeping their jobs in the world.

Think of an unmarried person you admire. How does he or she serve others?

Answers will vary.

What qualities make him or her like Christ?

Answers will vary.

Why can an unmarried person serve in a way that others cannot serve?

Answers will vary.

(195)

not present. Lay people may have more influence over their peers.)

- ✦ **Should a normal young person who has faults and gets into trouble consider becoming a priest, a deacon, or a religious?** (yes) **Why?** (Priests, deacons and religious are human. They are sinners like everyone else and desire to serve God.)

3. Have the students read silently **Call to Single Life** on page 195 and complete the activity.

- ✦ Divide the class into pairs to share their answers.

- ✦ **What are some of the characteristics of the single life?** [Write the students' answers on the

large sheet of paper under *Single Person*.]

4. Discuss with the students aspects of the single life.

- ✦ **Some people choose the single life. Others are single because they are not yet married, are widowed, are separated from their spouse, or because they have family responsibilities.**

- ✦ **The media sometimes presents the single life as an escape from responsibility and commitment. However, the single life is a call from God, a call with a mission.**

- ✦ **Single people can sometimes have more flexibility in giving time for service.**

* Secular institutes are composed of lay men and women who have consecrated themselves to God by private vows or promises. They retain their careers and social activities, live with others or alone, and work to improve the human condition. They are unlike religious, who take public vows and live in community.

Single Person

* remains unmarried (may take private vows)
* is involved in a wide range of activities
* is a sign of God's never-failing love.

If in a secular institute,
* makes vows
* lives a consecrated life of prayer and service
* keeps job in the world.

5. 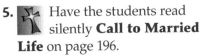 Have the students read silently **Call to Married Life** on page 196.

   ✝ *Family & Community*
   * Direct the students to answer the question.
   * **What are some of the characteristics of married life?** [Write the students' answers on the large sheet of paper under *Married Person*.]

Married Person

* joins one man with one woman as husband or wife
* makes a lifelong commitment
* accepts the children God wants to give them through the marriage and leads them to holiness
* reflects God's eternal love
* encourages the other to grow in holiness
* reaches out to parish, country, and world
* upholds the dignity and rights of all people

6. Read aloud the first two paragraphs of **A Covenant of Love** on page 196.
   * **What do you remember about covenants?** (God made covenants

---

Call to Married Life

God calls most people to a lifelong commitment as husband or wife in marriage. By their generous love for each other and for the children God sends them, husbands and wives support and encourage each other to grow in holiness and to lead their children to holiness.

How can a couple help each other to be holy?

They can help each other grow in love for God

and others, encourage each other to pray,

give good example, forgive each other, and

trust in God.

A Covenant of Love

When 6:30 P.M. rolls around, Mrs. Rufo expects Kim to come over and babysit for her. Kim promised that she would come, and Mrs. Rufo trusts that Kim will be faithful to her promise.

To make a promise to someone can be a sign of love. If you love a person deeply, you might make a covenant. A covenant is a binding and solemn promise, a vow.

On their wedding day, Catholic couples make a covenant of love with each other before God. Jesus raised the natural reality of marriage to the level of a sacrament, the Sacrament of Matrimony. The Church celebrates marriage as something holy. The priest represents Jesus as he witnesses the couple's vows in the presence of the believing community. The man and woman act as ministers of the sacrament to each other. They bestow and receive the sacrament in the essential part of the ceremony: the exchange of vows. These vows bind them in a lifelong partnership. In the following version of the marriage vows, underline what Robert and Ann promise to do.

I, Robert (Ann), take you, Ann (Robert), to be my wife (husband). I promise to be true to you in good times and in bad, in sickness and in health. I will love you and honor you all the days of my life.

Covenant Fidelity

The love of Robert and Ann is a sign of Jesus' love for and union with the Church. Through the Sacrament of Matrimony, Jesus enables married couples to remain faithful to their wedding promises. Their faithfulness, or fidelity, is symbolized by the rings they give each other. Christian marriage is founded on the sacredness of human life and the family. Children are the supreme gift God offers married people—a sign of their love.

Before marrying, a person has to ask:
* Am I ready to share my life with another person for life?
* Am I aware what living with another person day after day really means?
* Do I really want to have children—with all that raising children involves?

196 UNIT 3

---

with Abraham, Noah, Moses, and the Israelites. Jesus instituted the New Covenant in his blood.)

* **What is the first part of the definition of *Matrimony* from the Glossary in the back of your book?** [Write the definition on the board.] (Matrimony is a solemn agreement between one woman and one man to be partners for life both for their own good and for bringing up children.)

* Finish reading aloud this section. [Call the students' attention to the marriage vow at the end of the section.]

* **What is the rest of the definition of *Matrimony* in the Glossary?** (Marriage is a sacrament when the

agreement is properly made between baptized Christians.)

* **As Christ is faithful to his Church, so are husbands and wives called to be faithful to their marriage partners.**

* **A husband and wife can help each other grow in love for God and others, encourage each other to pray, give good example, forgive each other, and trust in God.**

7. Direct the students to read silently **Covenant Fidelity** on page 196.
   * **What is Christian marriage founded on?** (the sacredness of human life and the family)

◆ Have a student read aloud the questions in **Before marrying, a person has to ask** on page 196.

◆ **What does it mean to be ready for marriage?** (You realize what marriage means. You've asked yourself questions about it. You can assume the responsibilities of it.)

8. Explain the diagram of the Trinity.

   ◆ **From the time of Creation, God planned that husbands and wives should find happiness, love, and security in each other and share this with their children. In this way, the family mirrors the life of the Trinity.**

   ◆ **The love that binds a family is so powerful that a communion of people is formed: a unity of deep and intimate sharing.** [Draw on the board the new diagram of the family.]

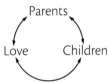

Parents

Love   Children

9. Show the yarn and the completed knitted article.

   ◆ **How did the yarn become the article?** (It took many stitches, maybe many types of stitches, and some ripping out and starting over.)

   ◆ **How is a family like this knitted article?** (It is made up of individuals whose lives are knitted together. Tensions can pull them apart, but many stitches of love keep them joined. Together they form a different unit from what they are separately. The knitted article is meant to be used or worn. So, too, Christian families are meant to serve beyond themselves. Their mission is the mission of Christ and his Church, to carry on the roles of Christ as king, priest, and prophet.)

10. Direct the students to read silently Matrimony under Sacraments at the Service of Communion on the Sacrament Chart page 212. [See page T312.]

Acting

1. Have the students read silently **Mission to Love** on page 197. **How can the family live out its mission of** *Serving,* *Worshiping* **and** *Evangelizing?* [Write these words on the board.]

Serving

- Visit, write, or phone those who are sick and elderly.
- Show love and support for one another.
- Volunteer to help one another at home.
- Volunteer time and material goods to the parish and others in need.
- Forgive one another.
- Obey parents and respect one another.
- Help neighbors in need.

Worshiping

- Celebrate the Eucharist on Sundays and holy days.
- Show love and reverence for the values of Christ.
- Pray for the pope, bishops, priests, and religious.
- Have religious objects visible in the home.
- Say grace before meals.
- Engage in family prayer celebrations.
- Celebrate sacraments together.

Evangelizing

- Proclaim the Gospel to one another and to others.
- Reach out to the neighborhood and world, supporting Christian values in government and society.
- Volunteer as catechists.
- Respect and obey the rules of the Church.
- Accept, respect, and appreciate others.
- Talk about others' religion.
- Listen to the problems of others and give Christian advice.

2. Lead the students in prayer.

   ◆ **Lord, in the Bible you tell us, Whatever you do, do for God's glory.** (adapted from 1 Corinthians 10:31) **Give us the grace to be holy and give you glory in the state of life we choose to follow.**

   ◆ **Now let us pray together the Vocation Prayer from the inside front cover of your book.**

3. Have the students do Respond on page 199.

CHECKPOINT

- Were the learning outcomes achieved?

LEARNING OUTCOMES

The students will be able to

- identify the mission of bishops, priests, and deacons as being leaders in word, sacrament, and service.

- discuss their appreciation for those who serve us as ordained ministers.

Materials

- BLM 84 (optional)

- Diagram drawn on the board, a chart, or a transparency:

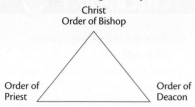

Christ
Order of Bishop

Order of Priest   Order of Deacon

Religious and Christian faithful through Baptism, which makes them like Christ

- Large sheet of paper labeled *Ordained Minister*

- Markers

- Two sets of three flash cards *Word, Sacrament, Service*

- Materials for Acting #1

Before You Begin

1. Matthew Chapter 10 records the choosing of the apostles as ones sent to proclaim the Gospel. These men are reminded of the fearlessness they are to have in facing opposition and of the personal cost of discipleship. They lead the faith community at worship and act in the name of Christ and the Church.

2. The Sacrament of Holy Orders begins with the bishop, who stands in apostolic succession. Through him, the sacrament is shared in part with the priests (presbyters) and deacons. All priests gain their pastoral authority from union with the bishop.

3. If any students show an interest in becoming a priest, be sure to encourage and support them.

Mission to Love

Throughout their married life, a husband and wife experience the effects of the sacrament. Jesus unites them and their children in a community of life and love. The family participates in the life and mission of Jesus by being king, priest, and prophet. The family builds up the Church and upholds the rights of all.

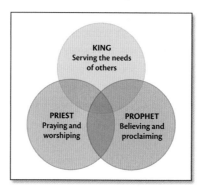

KING
Serving the needs of others

PRIEST
Praying and worshiping

PROPHET
Believing and proclaiming

Call to Priesthood and Diaconate

God calls some men through the Church to an ordained ministry of service for the life and growth of the community. Through the Sacrament of Holy Orders, they become deacons, priests, or bishops forever.

A deacon assists the bishops and priests in teaching, preaching, celebrating the liturgy, and caring for those in need. Every priest is first a deacon. Some men are called to be permanent deacons. They must be at least 35 years old, and many of them are married.

A priest works with the bishop to bring Jesus to the world through word, sacrament, and service. His life is deeply rooted in the Christian community. He is committed to being a leader, a mediator, and a servant in God's family.

A bishop is ordained by another bishop with the laying on of hands. As successor to the apostles, he has the fullness of the priesthood. With his brother bishops, he is responsible for the People of God. In addition to exercising his priestly duties, he shepherds the people in a diocese, teaching, sanctifying, and governing them.

A Leader in Proclaiming God's Word

A main role of the priest is to preach and teach the Gospel. He helps us understand the teachings of Jesus and the Church. To do this well, a priest reflects on the Word of God and studies what the Church teaches. He tries to proclaim the Word by his life as well as by his words.

A Mediator Through Sacraments

Jesus was the perfect priest because he was the perfect mediator between God and all people. By Baptism, all Christians share in his priesthood (the universal or common priesthood). We participate in the Eucharist and in other sacraments, but bishops and priests have a special share in Christ's priesthood (the ministerial priesthood). The greatest responsibility of a priest is to preside at the Eucharist when we offer Jesus and ourselves to the Father. The priest also calls us to be reconciled to God and to others, forgives sins, and administers other sacraments.

A Servant of the Church

Jesus ministered to sinners and to people who were sick, troubled, and poor. He offered his life on the cross out of love. Ordained men have different gifts for different works, but they all minister to us as Jesus did. Some priests are diocesan priests who serve in a diocese under the local bishop. Together these priests and the bishop are responsible for the pastoral care of a diocese. Other priests, such as the Jesuits, the Dominicans, and the Franciscans, belong to religious orders. They may serve in a diocese or in the special activities of their order.

Centering

1. Discuss with the students the qualities of a priest.
   - ✦ **What are some of the positive qualities people look for in a priest?**
   - ✦ **How do you think a priest spends a typical day?**

2. Link the last lesson with today's lesson.
   In the last lesson, you studied the call to be single or married. Today you will find out about the call and role of ordained ministers.

Sharing

1. Explain to the students the diagram of Holy Orders.
   This diagram illustrates how we all share in the priesthood of Christ.

2. Direct the students to read silently **Call to Priesthood and Diaconate** on page 197.
   What are some of the characteristics of an ordained minister? [Have a student write the responses on the sheet labeled *Ordained Minister*.]

Ordained Minister

Deacon
- ordained
- assists priests and bishops
- helps by teaching, preaching, baptizing, witnessing weddings, caring for those in need

Priest
- ordained
- empowered in Christ's name
- proclaims the Gospel
- presides at the celebration of the Eucharist and the sacraments
- serves the faith community in leadership
- cares for those in need

3. Refer to the diagram on the board.
   - **An order is a grade or type of ordained ministry in the Church. What orders are included in the Sacrament of Holy Orders?** (deacons, priests, bishops)
   - **What does each do?** (Deacons assist the bishops and priests in teaching, preaching, celebrating the liturgy, and caring for those in need. They can baptize and preside at weddings. Bishops exercise priestly powers; shepherd the people in a diocese; teach, sanctify, and govern them. Priests work with the bishop to bring Jesus to the world through word, sacrament, and service. All are connected through Baptism.)
   - **Who is the bishop of our diocese? Who is our parish priest?**
   - **What two types of deacons are there?** (men preparing for priesthood, permanent deacons)
   - **How do we share in Christ's priesthood?** (By Baptism, we participate in the Eucharist and in other sacraments.)

4. Discuss the roles of priests.
   - **What two types of priests are there?** (diocesan and religious) **Diocesan priests serve in a particular diocese under the local bishop. Religious priests belong to a community. They make vows and live by the rules of the community. They may serve in a** diocese or in the special works of their community.
   - **What are the three roles of a priest?** (a leader in proclaiming God's Word, a mediator in the sacraments, a servant of the Church)
   - **What must priests do in order to teach the Word of God?** (reflect on the Word in prayer, study what the Church teaches)
   - **In what two ways does the priest proclaim the Gospel?** (by his life and words)
   - **What is the greatest responsibility of a priest?** (to preside at the Eucharist)
   - **What other spiritual works does the priest do?** (forgives sins, celebrates the other sacraments, counsels, blesses, leads prayer services and retreats)
   - **Why do you think the priest is given the title Father?** (He is a spiritual "father" because he brings the life of grace through teaching God's Word and through the sacraments, especially the Eucharist.)

5. Have the students read silently about Holy Orders under Sacraments at the Service of Communion on the Sacrament Chart on page 212. [See page T312.]

6. Divide the students into two teams.
   - Give one member of each team a set of the flash cards *Word*, *Sacrament*, and *Service*.
   - **I will read a sentence about the role of a priest. You are to hold up the flash card that role is fulfilling. The one who answers first receives a point. Then pass the cards to the next team member.**
   - **He preaches the homily at the eighth-grade graduation.** (Word)
   - **He teaches fifth-grade religion.** (Word)
   - **He celebrates Mass.** (Sacrament)
   - **He helps the Smith family work out family difficulties.** (Service)
   - **He visits Joe, who broke his leg.** (Service)
   - **He baptizes the Martinez baby.** (Sacrament)
   - **He helps with the teen club dance.** (Service)
   - **He coordinates the food drive.** (Service)
   - **He trains lectors for liturgies.** (Word)
   - **He hears confessions.** (Sacrament)
   - **He makes sure there is good lighting and ventilation in the church.** (Service)
   - **He witnesses the marriage of John Sims and Mary Hastings.** (Sacrament)
   - **He holds a retreat for men.** (Word)

Acting

1. Choose a way to support your parish priest.
   a. On half sheets of paper, let the students write a date and two ways they will support him that day. Have the students add designs, assemble the pages, and present the book.
   b. **BLM 84** Give each student a circle from BLM 84 **Jesus Leads His Priests in Worship and Service** and paper ½ inch wide and 4½ inches long. Have them fill in the circle and then accordion-pleat the piece of paper and glue it to the back. Attach the "springs" to a poster so the circles stand out. Add the caption "Jesus Leads His Priests in Worship and Service." Display the poster in church or present it to the priest.

2. Close with a litany of gratitude for priests. Invite the students to mention one thing priests do for which they are grateful. Have everyone join in the response: *We thank you, Lord.*

CHECKPOINT ✓

- Were the learning outcomes achieved?

LEARNING OUTCOMES

The students will be able to

- identify how religious serve the Church.
- describe the vows of chastity, poverty, and obedience.
- discuss their vocation.

Key Terms

chastity—vow of religious to be unmarried and chaste for the sake of the kingdom

obedience—vow of religious to listen to God particularly as he speaks through superiors

poverty—vow of religious to live a simple lifestyle and to give up control of material possessions

Materials

- Bibles or New Testaments
- Large sheet of paper labeled *Man or Woman Religious*
- Scripture references for Sharing #2 written on the board
- Instrumental music (optional)

Before You Begin

1. Religious life is the response to a call, a gift, and a mystery. God calls an individual to live totally for the kingdom. The person's response of total surrender becomes concrete in his or her everyday routine. In the daily sacrifices of their lives, religious live their baptismal commitment, centering their lives solely on God.

2. Religious try to express publicly by their lives what every Christian life should be—a reflection of Christ present in the world. By their vows, they witness to the kingdom of the Father, where total dependence on him is the norm, where love of him is the greatest joy, and where his will is the most important factor in all their decisions.

3. Religious belong to a particular community that has been established so that a certain gift, or charism of the Spirit, can be shared with the whole Church. Sent by the Church, religious bring the love, truth, compassion, and healing of Jesus to others.

Centering _____

1. Discuss with the students men and women religious.
   What do you know about sisters, brothers, and priests who belong to religious communities?

2. Link the last lesson with today's lesson.
   You have already studied the single, married, and ordained states of life. Today you will find out more about men and women religious.

Sharing _____

1. Have the students read silently **Call to Religious Life** on page 198.
   - ✦ **What are religious called to be?** (signs of Christ's love and his kingdom) **What are some of the characteristics of those who live in religious life?** [Write the students' responses on the sheet labeled *Man or Woman Religious*.]

Man or Woman Religious

- dedicates life to God's service
- follows teachings and example of Christ
- makes public vows or promises
- joins in a common work
- may be a priest, deacon, brother, or sister
- shares in mission of Christ and his Church
- belongs to a community

- ✦ **What do all religious have in common?** (prayer, community life, vows)

- ✦ **Why do religious pray every day?** (Jesus often prayed. Prayer helps religious deepen their friendship with God, giving them strength and courage.)

- ✦ **Some men and women religious are called contemplatives. Their main responsibilities are to offer their lives to God in silence, prayer, and sacrifice.**

- ✦ **These religious live most of the day in silence as they work and pray. Some examples of contemplative orders are the Poor Clares, Carmelites,** Trappists, Carthusians, and Cistercians.

- ✦ **When an individual answers God's call to enter religious life, he or she joins a particular community. The members pray together, share meals together, and build friendships with one another. They encourage one another to live according to the Gospel and to serve the needs of the Church.**

- ✦ **How does the Glossary define *vow*?** (A deliberate and free promise made to God by people who want especially to dedicate their lives to God. The vows give witness now to the kingdom that is to come.)

- ✦ **By the vows of chastity, poverty, and obedience, religious dedicate their whole lives to God and living as Jesus lived.**

2. Have the students match the following Scripture verses with the vows that religious make.
   - ✦ Assign students to read aloud each verse.
   - ✦ **Does this Scripture passage refer to poverty, chastity, or obedience?**

- **Matthew 8:20** (poverty)
- **Matthew 19:21** (poverty)
- **Mark 14:35–36** (obedience)
- **John 4: 33–34** (obedience)
- **John 8:28–29** (obedience)
- **1 Corinthians 7:32–34** (chastity)

3. Discuss with the students the vows religious make.

+ **Can you show that Jesus lived the vows?** (He was poor, and he taught his followers to seek the kingdom and trust their heavenly Father for what they needed. He loved his Father and every person, even to the extent of giving up his life. Jesus never married, but he saw others as his family—with God as Father. He obeyed his Father in all things. He used his gifts according to his Father's plan.)

+ **How does living the vows of chastity, poverty, and obedience help religious serve others?** (Chastity allows religious to love God with undivided hearts and to tend to the needs of all people. Poverty permits them to live simply and to share their talents. By being at God's disposal and by obeying authority as to how and where to work, the members of a religious community combine their talents to serve God and others to the fullest.)

4. Refer the students to the works of mercy on page 243 in the student book. [See page T435]

+ **Religious serve Christ through the works of mercy. After I read each example, raise your hand if you know what work of mercy is being done.**

+ **Sister Jean writes and lectures. Her views on peace and justice are sometimes criticized.** (Instruct the ignorant, bear wrongs patiently, forgive all injuries.)

+ **Brother Roberto teaches science. On weekends, he helps youth groups with retreats and service projects.** (Instruct the ignorant, counsel the doubtful, warn the sinner.)

Call to Religious Life

God calls some people to dedicate their lives to his service as members of religious communities. Religious come from a variety of backgrounds and can be found serving in many different ways and in all parts of the world. There are certain things that all religious have in common. All are called to be signs of Christ's love and his kingdom in a special way. Their life of prayer, which unites them to Christ, enables them to follow him more closely. Their life in community provides them with the love and support of other religious. Their vows free them to love and serve God and others and to belong more completely to him. They share in a particular way in the mission of the Church.

Religious usually make three vows:

- chastity—being unmarried and chaste for the sake of the kingdom

- poverty—living a simple lifestyle and giving up control of material possessions

- obedience—listening to God particularly as he speaks through superiors.

Listen

You probably will not receive a text message from God telling you your vocation. The process of figuring out your vocation is slow but can be exciting. To hear God's call, develop the skill of listening.

LISTEN to God.
Pray in quiet. Gradually you will hear God's gentle but persistent call.

LISTEN to yourself.
Find out your likes and dislikes, strengths and weaknesses, hopes and fears.

LISTEN to others.
Talk over your plans for the future with a counselor, coach, parent, priest, or teacher.

LISTEN to the needs of the world.
Choose a need that you want to help fill. Do something now to help fill it.

A Moment with Jesus

Figuring out our call in life takes time. It requires that we pay attention to what goes on around us and how we respond to it. Pause now and silently pray the Prayer to Discern My Life Call.

Lord Jesus,
Help me to become a good listener.
Show me your plan for my life.
Bind me so close to you in friendship
    that I will be filled with your love.
Then I will bring your love to those
    who are struggling, confused, or lonely.
Show me the way I can best use my life
    to serve people in your name.
        Amen.

Take some time to share with Jesus, in your own words, any thoughts you have about your calling in life. Then spend a moment in silence, and listen to what Jesus wants to share with you. Thank him for his friendship and his help.

(198) UNIT 3

+ **In prayer, Carmelite Sister Anne places the needs of individuals and of the world before God. She also writes to people in the state prison.** (Pray for the living and the dead, visit the imprisoned.)

+ **Brother Paul runs a soup kitchen, collects clothing, and helps people find jobs.** (Feed the hungry, clothe the naked.)

+ **The elderly residents at St. Anthony Home look forward to Sister Natalie's visits. She helps them accept the loss of their loved ones and their own deaths.** (Visit the sick, comfort the sorrowing, bury the dead.)

+ **Father Roger often works late housing, feeding, and counseling**

runaway teens. Twice a week he talks with teens at a detention home. (Feed the hungry, shelter the homeless, counsel the doubtful, comfort the sorrowing, visit the imprisoned.)

Acting

1. Have the students read silently **Listen** on page 198.

+ Guide them in imagining their future.

+ Imagine that you are viewing your life. Visualize yourself in the next few years . . . shouting for your college team at a sports rally . . . at graduation in cap and gown, receiving your diploma. Now what will you do?

✦ Will you go on for further education, start your career, settle down and get married, or move toward Holy Orders or religious life? [Pause.]

✦ Picture yourself as an adult Christian. Where are you? What are you doing? To what vocation do you imagine God has called you? [Pause.] **Speak to God now about the plans God has for you.**

2. Choose or let the students choose an activity from Reach Out on page 199.

CHECKPOINT

- Were the learning outcomes achieved?

Day Four   A Vocation Day

Student pages 198–200

LEARNING OUTCOMES

The students will be able to

- describe such faith concerns as commitment, response to God, and service in the Church.

- discuss Christ's call in their own lives.

- demonstrate an understanding of the key concepts in this chapter.

Materials

- Bibles or New Testaments
- BLM 85, BLM 86
- BLM 87 Quiz
- Construction paper

- Poster board
- Drawing paper
- Felt-tipped markers, scissors, and glue
- Songs for the prayer service
- Vocation fliers (optional)

Before You Begin

1. In this lesson, the students will prepare for a vocation day that can be used in a regular class or as part of a larger school vocation program. Activities can be added from Enriching the Faith Experience.

2. On the day of the program, write the order of the program on the board. Begin with the Scripture passage "There are different kinds of spiritual gifts but the same Spirit; there are different forms of service but the same Lord; there are different workings but the same God who produces all of them in everyone." (1 Corinthians 12:4–6) Have the groups present the skits and end with the prayer service.

3. When planning today's lesson, keep in mind that Day Four is when the students take the quiz for this chapter. Reserve time at the end of class for this assessment. The quiz can also be administered on Day Five.

Centering _____

Discuss with the students days that are dedicated to special people.

✦ **What are some days dedicated to special people?** (Mother's Day, Father's Day, Grandparents' Day, Columbus Day, Secretary's Day)

✦ **In today's class, we are going to prepare to dedicate a day to vocations, a Vocation Day.**

Sharing _____

1. **BLM 85** Divide the class into six groups. Write on the board the six groups.
   - *Group 1: Skit: "Come and See"*
   - *Group 2: Skit: "Disappointed"*
   - *Group 3: Skit: "Under the Fig Tree"*
   - *Group 4: Skit: "Beyond Torn Nets"*
   - *Group 5: Prayer Service*
   - *Group 6: Vocation Posters*
   - ✦ Distribute the appropriate card from BLM 85 **Called to Follow** *Cards for Group Work* to each group.

✦ Select a student to lead each group. Have the leader read the directions on the card to their group.

✦ Inform the students where the materials are for their group.

2. **BLM 86** Distribute copies of BLM 86 **Celebrating Our Discipleship** to the leader of Group 5 for the prayer service.

3. Move from group to group to help and encourage the students.
   Show the leaders where to store their completed projects until the Vocation Day.

4. Lead the students through the Summary and Review activities, pages 199–200.

5. **BLM 87** Distribute and administer BLM 87 **Chapter 24 Quiz.**

   Use this opportunity to assess the students' understanding of the main concepts in the chapter. If there is not sufficient time for the students to complete the quiz, consider moving it to Day Five.

6. Practice the songs for the prayer service.

Acting

1. Lead the students in prayer, using **A Moment with Jesus** on page 198. Allow sufficient time for silent reflection.

2. At the end of class, have the students tear out and take home pages 199–200.

CHECKPOINT ✔

- Were the learning outcomes achieved?

CHAPTER 24 Summary

Remember

What is the universal call that all Christians receive from God?
All Christians receive the universal call to holiness.

What is meant by a vocation?
A vocation is a call from God to a particular way of life in which a person can share Christ's mission and reach holiness.

What is the love between a married couple a sign of?
The love between a married couple is a sign of Christ's love for his Church and his union with it.

What is the mission of bishops, priests, and deacons?
The mission of bishops, priests, and deacons is to give Jesus Christ to the world through word, sacrament, and service.

What are the three vows that most religious make?
Religious usually make vows of chastity, poverty, and obedience.

Respond

The basis for every vocation is the call to be holy, the call to love. In your reflection notebook, write the important events of yesterday. Do any of them show that you are aware of your call to be holy and to love others? Were there specific times when you blocked this call by refusing to show God's love to your parents? to your brothers and sisters? to your friends? to others? Read John 13:34 and evaluate how you responded to this message today.

Reach Out

1. Pray daily that you will recognize the special life call that God has for you. Pray for your friends too.

2. Write a newspaper article about the service given by lay Christians, religious, or priests in your parish. Give specific examples to show how they bring Christ to others.

3. List ways that people can be involved in your parish and diocese. Ask your parents to add to the list.

4. Read the life of a founder of a religious order. Find out what led him or her to start a religious community. Share your research with the class.

5. With a partner, create a colorful, appealing poster inviting young people to consider entering religious life or becoming a priest.

6. Interview a priest. Ask him to share how he experienced God's call to the priesthood and what it has meant to him.

Pope Francis. ❯

(199)

Day Five   Extending the Chapter

Gather and Go Forth

Lead students through pages 201–202 in the student book. Find catechist instruction on T362–T363.

Use the following suggestions to create an additional lesson for Day Five.

1. Remind the students to take home pages 199–200 to share what they are learning with their families.

2. Incorporate any unused BLMs from the week's chapter.

3. Consider the time of the liturgical year and use the appropriate Special Seasons and Lessons. SSLs begin on page T369.

4. Visit www.christourlife.com to find additional activities for Extending the Chapter.

5. Use activities from Enriching the Faith Experience.

6. Guide the students in a prayerful discussion of Sunday's Scripture readings. Visit www.christourlife.com for more information.

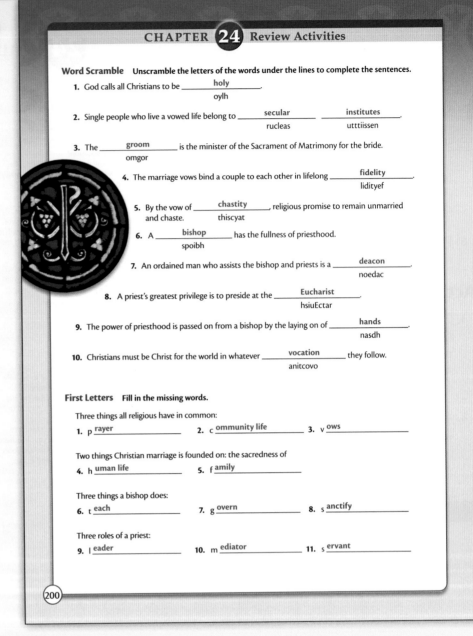

CHAPTER **24** Review Activities

Word Scramble   Unscramble the letters of the words under the lines to complete the sentences.

1. God calls all Christians to be ___holy___.
   oylh

2. Single people who live a vowed life belong to ___secular___ ___institutes___.
   rucleas   utttiissen

3. The ___groom___ is the minister of the Sacrament of Matrimony for the bride.
   omgor

4. The marriage vows bind a couple to each other in lifelong ___fidelity___.
   lidityef

5. By the vow of ___chastity___, religious promise to remain unmarried and chaste.   thiscyat

6. A ___bishop___ has the fullness of priesthood.
   spoibh

7. An ordained man who assists the bishop and priests is a ___deacon___.
   noedac

8. A priest's greatest privilege is to preside at the ___Eucharist___.
   hsiuEctar

9. The power of priesthood is passed on from a bishop by the laying on of ___hands___.
   nasdh

10. Christians must be Christ for the world in whatever ___vocation___ they follow.
    anitcovo

First Letters   Fill in the missing words.

Three things all religious have in common:

1. p ___rayer___   2. c ___ommunity life___   3. v ___ows___

Two things Christian marriage is founded on: the sacredness of

4. h ___uman life___   5. f ___amily___

Three things a bishop does:

6. t ___each___   7. g ___overn___   8. s ___anctify___

Three roles of a priest:

9. l ___eader___   10. m ___ediator___   11. s ___ervant___

200

Chapter 24   Enriching the Faith Experience

Use the following activities to enrich a lesson or to replace an activity with one that better meets the needs of your class.

1. **Web BLM** Use copies of Web BLM Chapter 24-A **How Does Television Look at the Family?** to evaluate how TV presents the family. Point out ways TV influences the way we think. The sheets may be worked in groups, individually, or by the class as a whole.

2. **Web BLM** Introduce the students to famous priests through Web BLM Chapter 24-B **Priests You Would Like to Meet.** After each skit, have the students list virtues they noted in the priest, such as love of Jesus, generous service, charity, goodness, love of those who are poor, prayerfulness, patience, compassion, sense of humor, and courage.

3. **Web BLM** Use copies of Web BLM Chapter 24-C **What Do Bishops Do?** to deepen the students' understanding of the bishop and his role in the Church. Discuss the students' answers. Have the students find out about the symbols connected with the bishop (miter, crosier, bishop's chain, bishop's ring, cathedral) and make a poster or PowerPoint presentation explaining them.

4. Have the students write notes of appreciation to people who serve in the parish. Encourage them to express the importance of the person's contributions to the parish community and the gifts he or she is sharing.

5. Suggest that the students interview a layperson who is involved in parish service: lector, choir director, acolyte, person in charge of hospitality, religious education coordinator, or leader of a parish group. Questions might deal with the following:
   + the need in the parish for people willing to serve;
   + reasons why this person is involved in serving the parish;
   + results of the work in terms of personal satisfaction.

6. Encourage the students to design brochures containing pictures and information about the different vocations in life and various careers. Display these brochures.

7. Arrange a Shadow Day in which students spend time with a priest, deacon, or religious, finding out about the person's ministry and working with him or her. Let the students report on their experiences.

8. Lead the students to a deeper appreciation of their own families by having them construct family shields. Tell them that in heraldry, a shield is supposed to reflect the qualities of the person or family it represents. Have the students each draw a shield on construction paper and cut it out. Then have them design their family name vertically, horizontally, or diagonally on the shield. Have them decorate the rest of the shield with photos or symbols of their family's actions in living out the values of being an evangelizing, praying, and serving community.

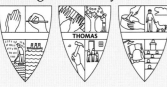

9. Invite a married couple to speak to the class about how they share in the mission of Christ and his Church. Choose a couple who is involved with the youth group, projects in the parish, or ministry to other families. Help them prepare their talk by giving them the following set of questions to answer.
   + How did you two first meet? How did you decide to get married?
   + What special things do you remember about your marriage ceremony?
   + How does Jesus fit into your lives as a married couple?
   + How have your ideas of marriage changed since you have been married?
   + How do you, as a married couple, serve the Church now?

   Use similar questions for a deacon and his wife.

10. Have the students compose a litany of thanksgiving for various aspects of their family lives. Tell them to post it at home for the other members to read.

11. Have the students look up Saint Paul's instructions to the early bishops and list the qualities he expected of them.
   + **1 Timothy 4:12–15** (a teacher of the Gospel; an example in love, faith, and purity; a preacher of truth)
   + **2 Timothy 1:6–13** (called to be holy, self-controlled, know sound teaching, spirit of faith, able to bear hardships for the sake of the Good News, trust in God, love)
   + **Titus 1:7–9** (hospitable, sensible, understand tradition, moral and devout, teach sound doctrine, not quick-tempered)

12. Allow the students to ask a retired priest to become a pen pal. Each month, have them write to their priest pen pal about his home, school, or parish. Call the diocesan office for information on retired priests.

13. Have the students look up the following Scripture passages that tell us how to be holy. Ask them for examples from Jesus' life that match each passage.
   + **Matthew 5:16** (Give good example.) Jesus lived what he taught. He chose to obey his Father even when it wasn't convenient.
   + **Matthew 6:14–15** (Forgive others.) Jesus forgave sinners. On the Cross he forgave his enemies.
   + **Matthew 6:25–26** (Trust God.) Jesus had no home or material possessions. He didn't spend his time worrying about his food or his clothes.
   + **Luke 10:27** (Love God.) Jesus lived on earth because his Father desired it. He drove the money-changers out of his Father's house. He often spent time praying to his Father.
   + **John 13:34** (Love others.) Jesus counseled, healed, defended, and taught people. He reached out to people when he was tired and thirsty (Samaritan woman) or when he was surrounded by a crowd.
   + **1 Corinthians 10:31** (Do all for God's glory.) Jesus said that he always did the things that pleased his Father.

14. Contact your diocesan office for information and materials on vocations. Additional resources such as a catalog of information and lesson plans are available from:
   National Coalition for Church Vocations
   5420 S. Cornell Ave., #105
   Chicago, IL 60615
   1-800-671-6228
   or www.nccv-vocations.org

Faith Focus
Jesus frees us from sin and leads us to life in God.

Reflecting on the Faith Experience

Take a few moments to reflect prayerfully before preparing the lesson.

Listening

"And behold, I am with
you always, until the end
of the age."

Matthew 28:20

Reflecting

As the Gospel writers reflected
on the life, Death, Resurrection,
and Ascension of Jesus, they saw
that his life and ministry were
intimately connected with the
Holy Spirit. In Matthew's Gospel,
we read "But if it is by the Spirit
of God that I drive out demons,
then the kingdom of God has come
upon you." (Matthew 12:28) At his
baptism and the beginning of his
ministry, Jesus is shown as God's
Son, overshadowed by the Holy
Spirit. Then Luke reminds us "Jesus
returned to Galilee in the power of
the Spirit,. . . " (Luke 4:14) And at
Nazareth, Jesus opens the Scriptures
and proclaims "The Spirit of the
Lord is upon me,. . . " (Luke 4:18)
If Jesus acts, the Spirit acts. If Jesus
sanctifies, the Spirit sanctifies. That
is why two councils in the fourth
century affirmed our belief in the
Holy Spirit, the Lord and life-giver.

Those who believe in Jesus receive
this life-giving Spirit and become
children of God. They allow their
lives to be strengthened and guided
by the gifts of this Advocate. They
put their gifts at the service of
others. Like the early apostles,
they must go out and bear witness,
bringing all to know the richness of
eternal life.

The Holy Spirit is the Giver of Life.
The dynamic power of the Spirit
transforms the lives of Christians
and ministers of the Church,
enabling them to use their charisms
and ministries for the building up of
the Church. The Spirit unites us and
creates community in the Church
so that we may love and serve one
another generously. The Spirit frees
us to seek unity until all form one
body, the Church. In the Spirit, Jesus
keeps his promise to be with us
until the end of the world. The Spirit
brings us new life so we can lift our
voices in prayer and praise to God,
praying:

> Father of light, from whom
>   every good gift comes,
> send your Spirit into our lives
> with the power of a mighty
>   wind,
> and by the flame of your
>   wisdom
> open the horizons of our
>   minds.
> Loosen our tongues to sing
>   your praise
> in words beyond the power
>   of speech,
> for without your Spirit
> man could never raise his
>   voice in words of peace
> or announce the truth that
>   Jesus is Lord,
> who lives and reigns with you
>   and the Holy Spirit,
> one God, for ever and ever.
> Amen.

> *Pentecost, Liturgy of the Hours*

How do I let Jesus be Lord of my life?

Responding

Holy Spirit, teach my students to
tap your power in order to live their
lives to the fullest.

Scripture for Further Reflection

John 3:5 Every person receives
life through water and the
Spirit.

Colossians 2:12–13 Through
Baptism, we have been buried
and raised to new life with
Christ.

Preparing for the Faith Experience

Day One
Review

Day Two
Unit 3 Test

Day Three
Celebrating Our Journey in Life

Day Four
End-of-the-Year Test

Day Five
Extending the Chapter

✝ Gather and Go Forth

Scripture in This Chapter

John 3:1–5,16 We are born of water and Spirit. In Jesus, we are given eternal life.

John 4:47–53 Jesus heals the official's son.

Church Documents

Catechism of the Catholic Church. The themes of this chapter correspond to the following paragraphs: **505, 520, 521.**

General Directory for Catechesis #53. Our faith in Jesus leads us to make a commitment to think like him, to judge like him, and to live as he lived, and in doing so, we unite ourselves to the Church, the community of disciples.

Pastoral Constitution on the Modern World #22 (Second Vatican Council). Christians feel the need and the duty to battle against evil through many trials and even to suffer death. But following the dying Christ, they hasten forward to resurrection in the strength that comes from hope.

Gather and Go Forth

Find catechist instruction for Gather and Go Forth student pages 209–210 on T364–T365.

Enriching the Faith Experience

Use the activities at the end of the chapter to enrich a lesson or to replace an activity with one that better meets the needs of your class. Bookmark www.christourlife.com to find web BLMs for this chapter.

LEARNING OUTCOMES

The students will be able to

- recall the significant facts and basic concepts introduced in Unit 3, Jesus Christ the Life.
- describe the new life through the Spirit that Jesus shares with us.

Materials

- Coins or bingo markers
- Ingredients for Acting #2:
  4 cups unsifted flour
  1 cup salt
  1½ cups water
  acrylic paints, varnish or shellac
  8½-by-11 inch card-stock paper, or aluminum foil
- Reflection notebooks
- Background music for Reviewing #1 and Acting #2

Before You Begin

You may want to refer back to Chapter 17 Unit 2 Review. In that chapter, the students built a Words to Live By tower that outlined the major themes in Unit 2. It was suggested that the students also build a tower for the reviews of Unit 1 and Unit 3. The tower can be a helpful way to have students recall the major concepts of the unit. The outline and materials needed for the building of the tower can be found on page T198.

CHAPTER 25 Unit 3 Review

Jesus Christ the Life

Looking Back

In Unit 3, you studied the life, Death, and Resurrection of our Lord. You know that before he ascended into heaven, he commanded you to witness to his teachings and to follow the example of his life. He sent the Holy Spirit to strengthen and guide you to love one another and form a community.

Not only have you learned about Jesus' life, but you understand your own life better. You know that Jesus offers you eternal life. Your spiritual life grows through daily prayer, frequent prayerful celebration of the sacraments (especially the Eucharist), reflection on the Scriptures, and the love and support of the faith community, the Church. As a disciple, you reach out to serve your family, school, parish, and even the world. You prepare to use your gifts in the vocation to which God calls you. Following Jesus' way and living his truth will bring you his life!

As you complete this book, ask yourself these questions:

1. **How has learning about Jesus Christ, the Life, helped me become more loving and supportive in my family community, school community, and parish community?**

2. **How is my life like the life of Jesus in prayer, in helping people who are poor, and in forgiving others?**

3. **What practical steps can I take to deepen my friendship with Jesus?**

Personal Inventory

Take a close look at your spiritual life. Put a check by the statements that indicate where you have grown.

My Life and God: Do I

- ○ pay more attention at Sunday Mass?
- ○ celebrate the Sacrament of Reconciliation more frequently?
- ○ think of Jesus at times during the day?
- ○ have greater self-respect because I believe God loves me?

My Life and Other People: Do I

- ○ keep calm when my parents and I disagree?
- ○ talk kindly to people I dislike?
- ○ have the courage to decide as Jesus would want me to and stick to my decision?
- ○ forgive others when they hurt me?

My Life and Situations: Do I

- ○ try harder in my schoolwork?
- ○ remain content with what I have?
- ○ volunteer to help where there is a need?
- ○ take care of my health by eating nutritious foods, exercising, and getting enough sleep?
- ○ admit I make mistakes?
- ○ take good care of the earth?

203

Centering

1. Discuss with the students the word *journey*.
   What does the word *journey* mean? (to travel from one place to another; to pass from one state or experience to another)

2. Link Unit 3, Jesus Christ the Life, with today's lesson.
   - ✦ **Throughout Unit 3 Jesus Christ the Life, you have studied Jesus' journey, his passing through death to glory. You have come to understand that you, too, have a spiritual journey to make.**
   - ✦ **Today you will review Jesus' journey and your own.**

Reviewing

1. Have the students read silently **Looking Back** on page 203.
   - ✦ **Use your reflection notebooks to answer the three questions.**
   - ✦ Allow sufficient time for silent reflection.
   - ✦ Have the students form groups of three or four to share their answers. You may want to set a reflective tone by playing instrumental music.

2. Direct the students to complete the **Personal Inventory** on page 203.

✦ The Personal Inventory gives you the opportunity to reflect on how you have grown during this class. It has you look at different areas of your life: your relationship with God, with other people, and with situations in your life.

✦ After you choose your answers, use your reflection notebook to write a paragraph about the area where you have grown the most and why.

3. Have the students play **Coin Flick** on page 204.

✦ Divide the students into pairs or larger groups to play the game.

✦ Provide each group with a coin or bingo marker. Read aloud the directions.

✦ As the students play the game, walk among them to make sure they are giving satisfactory answers.

4. Direct the students to complete the exercise **Find the Misfit** on page 205.
Go over the correct answers with the students.

5. Direct the students to **Life Savers** on page 208.

✦ In this activity, you will practice giving advice to people who have hurt their communities.

✦ Divide the students into groups of three or four. Have each group discuss the situations and give possible solutions. (The exercise could also be done individually.)

✦ Discuss with the students their answers to the situations.

1. A class project, such as a play, is a community project. Peggy has hurt the community effort and inconvenienced the members. She needs to be more responsible. She should show up early the next time or meet with the other actors and rehearse her lines during her free time to make up what she missed. She should also be honest with the director and apologize.

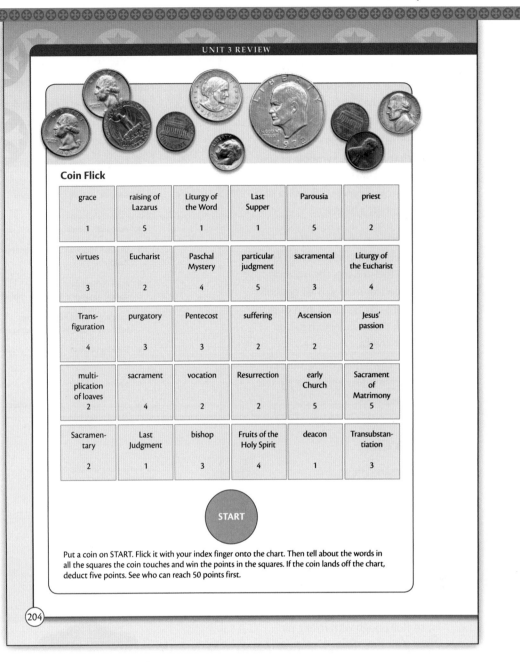

UNIT 3 REVIEW

Coin Flick

grace	raising of Lazarus	Liturgy of the Word	Last Supper	Parousia	priest
1	5	1	1	5	2
virtues	Eucharist	Paschal Mystery	particular judgment	sacramental	Liturgy of the Eucharist
3	2	4	5	3	4
Trans-figuration	purgatory	Pentecost	suffering	Ascension	Jesus' passion
4	3	3	2	2	2
multi-plication of loaves	sacrament	vocation	Resurrection	early Church	Sacrament of Matrimony
2	4	2	2	5	5
Sacramen-tary	Last Judgment	bishop	Fruits of the Holy Spirit	deacon	Transubstan-tiation
2	1	3	4	1	3

START

Put a coin on START. Flick it with your index finger onto the chart. Then tell about the words in all the squares the coin touches and win the points in the squares. If the coin lands off the chart, deduct five points. See who can reach 50 points first.

204

2. Rick upset the whole family. He should apologize, explain that he was crabby, and not try to excuse himself.

3. The students are glad to loan Tom money, but justice requires that he return the amount as soon as possible.

4. Ellen broke a piece of equipment the students share and need to complete their work. She should be honest with the teacher and admit that she was chiefly responsible for the accident. Since the other students who were with Ellen when the accident occurred probably share some of the responsibility, they should join her in offering to repair the broken piece of equipment or to replace it.

5. A community cannot remain intact if members of the group hate or hurt one another. Jessica and her friends should include rather than exclude the girl. They should apologize and show by genuinely charitable actions that they are including her.

6. Miguel's parents and classmates must tell him that all are to have a fair chance at the test. Miguel is not learning responsibility when his parents cover up for him or when other students tell him what has been included on the test. To prepare adequately, Miguel could ask members of the class to review with him several days before the test.

Acting

1. Discuss with the students symbols of the spiritual life.

✦ **Why is the Cross a symbol of Jesus?** (Through the Cross, Jesus won eternal life for us.)

✦ **What are some symbols of your spiritual life?** (a vessel, a butterfly, an arrow, a candle, a flower, a jar, a mountain, a heart)

2. Have the students make symbols of their spiritual lives.

✦ Give the students the materials needed for making their symbols: baker's clay, 8½-by-11 inch card-stock paper, aluminum foil, or other media.

✦ Have them draw the symbol on paper first. Play appropriate music as they work.

Baker's Clay

4 cups unsifted flour

1 cup salt

1½ cups water

• Place flour and salt in a bowl. Add water gradually, mixing with fingers until smooth. If clay is too stiff, add more water. Knead for about five minutes. Clay may be kept in a plastic bag until time to use. Roll dough with rolling pin and cut out or form shapes with wet knife or fingers. To join pieces, add a dab of water and press them together.

• Preheat oven to 350°. Bake clay on foil or cookie sheet until hard. Large pieces may take an hour. Allow to cool on a rack. DO NOT EAT!

✦ If using baker's clay, have the students paint symbols made from the clay, using acrylic paints. Masking tape can be used for making stripes and patterns. Spray the finished symbols with a protective coating of varnish or shellac.

Find the Misfit

Put an X on the word in each group that does not match the rest. Write how the remaining words are alike.

All are . . .

1. prudence   ho̶pe   justice   fortitude — cardinal virtues

2. Eucharist   Jesus' Death   Last Supper   Transfi̶guration — forms of Jesus' sacrifice

3. Bap̶tism   Death   Resurrection   Ascension — events in the Paschal Mystery

4. memorial   meal   voc̶ation   sacrifice — what the Eucharist is

5. heaven   Parousia   Last Judgment   Pas̶sover — things at the end of time

6. Mary of Magdala   apostle   disciples on way to Emmaus   Ju̶das — witnesses to the Resurrection

7. suf̶fering   speaking in tongues   baptisms   birth of Church community — events connected with Pentecost

8. breaking of bread   ca̶reers   prayer   possessions in common — characteristics of the early Church

9. poverty   chastity   fid̶elity   obedience — religious vows

10. teach   sanctify   govern   wr̶ite — duties of a bishop

Giovanni Girolamo Savoldo, *St. Mary Magdalene Approaching the Sepulchre*, 16th century. ❭

---

3. Have a student read aloud the quotation from Saint Basil on page 208.

✦ Invite the class to pray silently, asking Jesus to help them be generous and just.

✦ Allow sufficient time for silent reflection.

CHECKPOINT ✓

• Were the learning outcomes achieved?

• Are the students prepared for the unit test?

LEARNING OUTCOME

The students will be able to

- be evaluated on how well they have learned the concepts in Unit 3, Jesus Christ the Life.

Materials

- BLM 88A–B
- Reflection notebooks or Scripture booklets

Before You Begin

Those students who finish the test early might read over their reflection notebooks or use their Scripture booklets, especially pages 6–7.

Testing

1. Discuss with the students the taking of the test.

   Today you will take a test to assess what you have learned in Unit 3, Jesus Christ the Life. The real test for all of us will be whether or not we put the teachings of Jesus into practice.

2. **BLM 88A–B** Administer BLM 88 A–B **Unit 3 Test.**

CHECKPOINT ✓

- Was the learning outcome achieved?

- Judging from the test results, which concepts need clarification?

Life Savers

Tell how each of these situations has hurt the community and what can be done to rebuild it.

1. Peggy missed play rehearsal because she was too tired to go.

2. Rick was grouchy, so he started an argument during dinner.

3. Tom keeps borrowing money from different members of the class, but never gets around to paying it back.

4. Ellen was playing in the classroom with others and accidentally broke the pencil sharpener. The teacher does not know who did it.

5. Jessica and her friends wrote a note to one of the girls in the room, telling her she was weird and they hated her.

6. When Miguel does not have enough time to study, his parents write a note to the teacher so he will be excused from tests. Then Miguel asks other students what was on the test so he knows what to study.

Words to Ponder

The bread you do not use is the bread of the hungry;

the garment hanging in your wardrobe is the garment of him who is naked;

the shoes that you do not wear are the shoes of one who is barefoot;

the money that you keep locked away is the money of the poor;

the acts of charity that you do not perform are so many injustices that you commit.

—*Saint Basil*

208

LEARNING OUTCOMES

The students will be able to

- respond with praise and thanks to God for the gift of his risen life and for the Holy Spirit.
- assess their spiritual growth and plan for the future.

Key Term

pilgrim—one who makes a journey for a holy purpose

Materials

- Bibles or New Testaments
- Candles and matches (check fire codes)
- Table
- Symbols made in the Day One lesson Acting #2
- Songs for the celebration

Before You Begin

Students with roles in the celebration need time to prepare before it takes place. The three readings may be arranged as a tableau or memorized and acted out.

UNIT 3 REVIEW

Celebrating

Our Journey in Life

Leader: The Father calls to us with love. The glory of the Son shines on us. The love of the Spirit fills us with life. Let us celebrate our journey of life by signing ourselves with the Sign of the Cross.

All: In the name of the Father and of the Son and of the Holy Spirit. Amen.

Leader: Come, faithful pilgrims, and celebrate life.

Song

Leader: Jesus has told us "I am the Way, and the Truth, and the Life. I have come that you may have life and life to the full." Jesus taught people how to make the pilgrimage to eternal life.

Reader 1: A reading from the Gospel of John. (adapted from John 3:1–5,16)

All: Glory to you, Lord.

Reader 1: A Pharisee named Nicodemus, a leading Jew, came to Jesus at night and said,

Nicodemus: Rabbi, we know that you are a teacher who has come from God; for no one can do these signs that you are doing unless God is with him.

Jesus: Amen, Amen, I say to you no one can see the kingdom of God without being born from above.

Nicodemus: How can a person once grown old be born again?

Jesus: Amen, I say to you, no one can enter the kingdom of God without being born of water and Spirit. . . . God so loved the world that he gave his only Son, so that everyone who believes in him might not perish but might have eternal life.

All: You will show me the path of life and guide me to joy forever.

Reader 2: A reading from the Gospel of John. (adapted from John 4:47–53)

All: Glory to you, Lord.

Reader 2: Now there was a royal official whose son was ill at Capernaum. Hearing that Jesus had arrived in Galilee from Judea, he went and asked him to come and cure his son who was near death.

Nobleman: Sir, come down before my child dies.

Jesus: You may go; your son will live.

Reader 2: The man believed what Jesus had said and left. While he was on his way back, his servants met him and told him that his boy would live.

Nobleman: When did my son begin to recover?

Servants: The fever left him yesterday about one in the afternoon.

(206)

Centering _____

1. Write the words *pilgrim* and *pilgrimage* on the board.

- ✦ **What does the word *pilgrim* mean?** (one who makes a journey for a holy purpose)
- ✦ **Why do people make pilgrimages?** (to ask God for something or to thank God)
- ✦ **In the early days of the Church, there were pilgrimages only to the Holy Land. Later, the shrines of saints became places of pilgrimage for many people.**
- ✦ **Before going on a pilgrimage, the pilgrims often asked their bishops for written permission and received a special blessing.**

Pilgrims could be identified by their costumes: a large hat, simple clothing, a pouch, and a walking stick.

- ✦ **During their stay at the shrine, the pilgrims celebrated the sacraments and sometimes devoted themselves to works of mercy in the nearby towns. Before leaving the shrine, the pilgrim left an offering and took some remembrance of the graces received.**
- ✦ **There are pilgrimages today. The cross used at World Youth Day (WYD) is carried in pilgrimage from one site to another. In 2013, WYD was held in Rio de Janeiro,** Brazil. The cross was then carried in pilgrimage to the next site for WYD.

2. Discuss with the students the celebration based on a pilgrimage theme.

- ✦ **We are going to hold a celebration based on a pilgrimage. We will come to the celebration with the spirit of a pilgrim, seeking God's blessing.**
- ✦ Tell the students the order of the celebration and practice the songs. Be sure they know when and where to place their symbol.

Celebrating

Carry out the celebration **Our Journey in Life** on pages 206–207.

Acting

Discuss with the students a pilgrimage to the Holy Land.

✦ **Some people are privileged to make a pilgrimage to the land where Jesus lived. In your book are several pictures of Palestine today. Where are they?** (page 27, Jerusalem; page 28, the Western Wall in Jerusalem; page 32, Galilee; page 44, the Jordan River; page 157, Tomb of Lazarus in Bethany, Israel)

✦ You might get books, slides, or computer images about the Holy Land to show the students.

CHECKPOINT

- Were the learning outcomes achieved?

UNIT 3 REVIEW

Nobleman: That was the same time Jesus told me "Your son will live."

All: You will show me the path of life and guide me to joy forever.

Prayer

Leader: Jesus is with us on our journey. In each sacrament, he acts to bring us to fullness of life.

Side 1: In you we have been baptized. We have put on Christ.

All: We are your people, Lord. Make us holy.

Side 2: We have been given the gift of the Spirit. We are to witness to you by lives of faith and love.

All: May we live the Gospel with courage, eager to proclaim the Good News to all.

Side 1: We have been nourished by the one bread and one cup and have been made one in you.

All: We are strengthened in love and promise to serve you, Lord, in one another.

Side 2: You have given us forgiveness and peace.

All: We are ready to change our lives by acts of charity, good example, and prayer.

Side 1: You have healed us. You conquered death and opened for us the way to eternal life.

All: Help us to imitate you, who went about doing good, healing and serving the sick.

Side 2: You have shown us the value of love and faithfulness by blessing marriage.

All: We will try to support our families by generous love and service.

Side 1: You have given us bishops, priests, and deacons to witness to the Gospel and celebrate the sacraments.

All: We pray that they draw close to you. Give many others the grace to devote themselves to your service.

Leader: As a sign of Christ's presence among us, let us offer one another a sign of peace.

Sign of Peace

Come, faithful pilgrims, let us continue to travel the path of the Gospel that Jesus has shown. Let us go now to love and serve the Lord.

All: Thanks be to God.

Closing Song

(207)

Day Four End-of-the-Year Test

LEARNING OUTCOMES

The students will be able to

- evaluate their growth in knowledge and understanding of our faith.
- review the main concepts learned about Jesus in the program *Jesus Christ the Way, the Truth, and the Life.*

Materials

- BLM 4A–B Post-Test
- Reflection notebook (optional)

Before You Begin

1. Compare the scores of the students on this post-test with their scores on the pre-test to measure their growth in knowing and understanding the faith.

2. Suggest that students who finish the test early summarize in their reflection notebooks how the year's study of Jesus has influenced them. You might wish to ask them to evaluate the course as well.

Testing

BLM 4A–B Administer the post-test from BLM 4A–B **Pre-Test/Post-Test.** This was also the pre-test given at the beginning of the year.

CHECKPOINT

- Were the learning outcomes achieved?
- What do the post-tests reveal about the students' mastery of the year's material?

Gather and Go Forth

Lead students through pages 209–210 in the student book. Find catechist instruction on T364–T365.
Materials: Bibles

Use the following suggestions to create an additional lesson for Day Five.

1. Remind the students to take home pages 203–208 to share what they are learning with their families.

2. Incorporate any unused BLMs from the week's chapter.

3. Consider the time of the liturgical year and use the appropriate Special Seasons and Lessons. SSLs begin on page T369.

4. Visit www.christourlife.com to find additional activities for Extending the Chapter.

5. Use activities from Enriching the Faith Experience.

6. Guide the students in a prayerful discussion of Sunday's Scripture readings. Visit www.christourlife.com for more information.

Chapter 25   Enriching the Faith Experience

Use the following activities to enrich a lesson or to replace an activity with one that better meets the needs of your class.

1. **Web BLM** Use Web BLM Chapter 25-A **Sacrament Search** to review the sacraments.

2. Play a game of Pilgrim's Progress. Give the students five minutes to review the words from this unit, using the Remember sections from each chapter or the Glossary. Use the definitions from the Glossary for your questions. Begin on one side of the room. Have one student stand next to the student seated at the first desk. Give a definition to these two students. Whoever answers correctly first moves to stand next to the person at the second desk. The other student remains seated at the first desk. Rotate around the room as many times as necessary.

3. Have the students compile a *Who's Who* book of people who played a role in the life of Jesus. Ask them to list the people they studied. Each student can choose a different person and prepare a one-page biography with a picture representing him or her. Compile the pages into a book.

4. Have the students use the Map of Palestine from the Lesson Pullouts in the back of the student book to trace the life journey of Jesus. [See separate poster with TE.] List the Scripture references below on the board. Have the students look them up, label the events and their locations, and then number the events in chronological order. Several events can be interchanged, since we do not know the exact order. Students should have a general idea of the sequence of events. On the map, have them locate the places referred to in order of their occurrence. Do not put the sequence numbers or the title on the board with the Scripture references.

13. *Acts 2:1–13* Pentecost—Jerusalem
5. *John 4:4–30* Samaritan Woman—Sychar
12. *Acts 1:6–12* Ascension—Jerusalem
7. *John 11:1–44* Raising Lazarus—Bethany
6. *Luke 9:28–36* Transfiguration—Mount Tabor
10. *John 20:1–10* Resurrection—Jerusalem
8. *Luke 22:39–46* Agony in the Garden—Mount of Olives
9. *Mark 15:22–27* Crucifixion—Jerusalem
4. *Luke 18:35–43* Blind Man—Jericho
3. *Luke 4:16–19* Teaching in Synagogue—Nazareth
1. *Luke 2:4–7* Birth—Bethlehem

11. *John 21:1–14* Apparition to Apostles—Sea of Galilee
2. *John 2:1–11* Wedding Feast—Cana

5. Conduct a game of Resurrection Bingo. Ask the students to fold a sheet of paper into thirds vertically and horizontally. In the middle block, have them draw a small tombstone marked *Free!* Then tell them to choose eight Glossary terms and fill in the remaining blocks with these words in any order they wish. Example:

Transfiguration	Hope	Agony in the Garden
Ascension	FREE!	Creed
Parousia	Spiritual Life	Pentecost

Use the definitions from the Glossary to call bingo clues. Let the students place a small *x* in pencil in the corner of the block with the correct answer. The winner is the first one to get a row of *x*'s (vertically, horizontally, or diagonally). Other bingo rules can be applied to the game if you wish.

Sacrament Chart

SACRAMENTS OF INITIATION

	Baptism	Confirmation	Eucharist
Minister	Priest Deacon (in emergency, anyone)	Bishop Abbot (by delegation) Priest (by delegation)	*For consecration:* Bishop or priest *For distributing:* Bishop, priest, deacon, acolyte and, in need, extraordinary minister of Holy Communion
Recipient	*In general:* Any unbaptized person *In particular:* • Infants or persons not yet at the age of reason • Adults and those of the age of reason who desire Baptism	Roman rite: Baptized persons not yet confirmed who are of the age of reason and wish to be confirmed	Baptized persons in the state of grace who are of the age of reason, believe in the real presence, and are properly disposed
Essentials of the Rite	Pouring of water or immersion into water with the words "(Name), I baptize you in the name of the Father, and of the Son, and of the Holy Spirit."	Laying on of hands and anointing with chrism on the forehead with the words "(Name), be sealed with the gift of the Holy Spirit."	Celebration of the Eucharistic Liturgy with its two main parts: the Liturgy of the Word (Scripture readings, homily, and Prayer of the Faithful) and the Liturgy of the Eucharist (thanksgiving, consecration of bread and wine, and communion)
Effects	• cleanses the soul of sin: original and personal • brings about new birth in the Holy Spirit • incorporates one into the Body of Christ (Church) • bestows the Gifts of the Holy Spirit • gives a share in God's life (sanctifying grace), in faith, hope, and love • indelibly marks the person • admits one into Christ's roles of priest, prophet, and king	• increases and deepens baptismal grace through the outpouring of the Holy Spirit • indelibly marks the person • unites one more firmly with Christ • empowers one to witness to Christ courageously • increases the Gifts of the Holy Spirit	• nourishes the life of grace • deepens our union with Christ and his Church • commits us to those who are poor • obtains forgiveness of venial sin and preserves us from grave sin • strengthens the bonds of charity
Some Responsibilities	• respond to the vocation to holiness • reject Satan and sin • follow the teachings of Christ and his Church • participate in the liturgical and the sacramental life of the Church • serve others by sharing the faith and witnessing to it	• grow in faith and witness courageously to the Gospel • develop the ability to lead others to Christ • be willing to suffer for Christ and his Church • participate wholeheartedly in spreading God's kingdom	• celebrate the Eucharist for every Sunday and holy day of obligation • receive Holy Communion at each Mass • show devotion to Jesus in the Eucharist • grow in love for Christ and one another • sacrifice self in service to God and to others

SACRAMENT CHART (211)

	SACRAMENTS OF HEALING		SACRAMENTS AT THE SERVICE OF COMMUNION	
	Penance and Reconciliation	**Anointing of the Sick**	**Matrimony**	**Holy Orders**
Minister	Bishop Priest	Bishop Priest	Bride and groom (A priest or deacon is a witness in the name of the Church.)	Bishop
Recipient	Baptized persons who have committed sin and are sincerely sorry for having offended God	Baptized persons whose health is seriously impaired by sickness or old age	Any baptized man and woman who are free to marry and are willing to enter into a lifelong marriage agreement	Mature males who have completed Christian initiation who knowingly and willingly wish to be ordained, and who have been accepted as candidates by the authority
Essentials of the Rite	Contrition, confession, act of penance, and the words of absolution prayed by the priest	Anointing of the forehead and hands with the oil of the sick and the prayer of anointing prayed by the priest	The marriage covenant of the bride and groom consenting to give themselves permanently to each other in the presence of the priest or deacon and the Church community	Laying on of hands and the words of ordination prayed by the bishop
Effects	• forgives sin • reconciles one with God and the Church • increases grace and the virtue of charity • increases self-knowledge and strengthens the will	• strengthens one to overcome the difficulties of physical illness • through the grace of the Holy Spirit, encourages trust in God • unites one with the sufferings of Christ • brings spiritual and sometimes physical healing	• entitles the married man and woman to special graces that enable them to fulfill their duties • unites husband and wife indissolubly with each other and in Christ • makes the couple a sign of God's love for his people	• configures the recipient to Christ • confers the special graces of the order received: the diaconate, the priesthood, or the episcopate (bishop) • indelibly marks the recipient • enables the recipient to lead, teach, and sanctify the people
Some Responsibilities	• celebrate the Sacrament of Reconciliation regularly • be a reconciler in the faith community • strive for greater holiness by conversion of life	• accept suffering with patience and trust in union with Christ • look toward eternity with hope in God's mercy • offer suffering for the Church on earth and for the souls in purgatory	• grow in love, care, and willingness to endure hardships for each other • share a common life • grow in faith and practice the works of mercy • provide for the physical, emotional, and spiritual needs of their children • give an example of unselfish love	• Deacon: baptize, distribute Communion, bless marriages, conduct funeral services, minister to those who are needy, preach • Priest: preach, be a spiritual leader, celebrate the Eucharist, forgive sins, celebrate other sacraments • Bishop: provide pastoral teaching, fulfill priestly duties, ordain priests, lead diocese

The New Evangelization
The Essential Mission of the Church

Entrusted by Jesus

Jesus' Commission In the Gospel of Matthew, after his Resurrection, Jesus gives this mandate to the apostles: "Go, therefore, and make disciples of all nations, baptizing them in the name of the Father, and of the Son, and of the holy Spirit, teaching them to observe all that I have commanded you. And behold, I am with you always, until the end of the age." (Matthew 28:19–20) The Acts of the Apostles tells us that the apostles and disciples were at first afraid. But their fear disappeared with the coming of the Holy Spirit and the birth of the Church (Acts of the Apostles 2:1–41). Peter went out and boldly proclaimed the Gospel to the gathering crowd.

The mission of the Church to know, proclaim, witness, and share the Word did not end with the early Church. Jesus Christ is with us and continues to send the Holy Spirit to inspire us and give us the courage to proclaim the Gospel. Every generation is called to share the Good News of God's love with the world. Catholic parents are especially called to recognize their vocation as the first catechists for their children to see that they learn the fundamentals of the faith. The children will then be prepared to enter the world with the knowledge they need to become evangelizers for their generation.

The Holy Fathers Speak The popes since the Second Vatican Council have called the Church to realize how central the mission of evangelization is to our identity as Catholics. The call for the Church to be an evangelizing community began in modern times with the Second Vatican Council. This was seen especially in the *Pastoral Constitution on the Church in the Modern World* (1965) and *The Decree on the Missionary Activity of the Church* (1965). This was followed up in 1975 with Pope Paul VI's Apostolic Exhortation, *On Evangelization in the Modern World*. Building on the initiative of Pope Paul VI, Pope John Paul II stressed the need for a New Evangelization in his Apostolic Exhortation *Ecclesia in America*. There Pope John Paul II wrote, "The program of a new evangelization . . . cannot be restricted to revitalizing the faith of regular believers, but must strive as well to proclaim Christ where he is not known."

Pope Emeritus Benedict XVI made New Evangelization the theme of the 2012 Synod of Bishops. Following up the synod, the bishops of the United States published a new document, *Disciples Called to Witness: The New Evangelization*. Pope Francis has made evangelization a

> *"I have come to set the earth on fire, and how I wish it were already blazing!"*
>
> (Luke 12:49)

primary focus of his Apostolic Exhortation, *The Joy of the Gospel*. In that Exhortation, Pope Francis encourages all the Christian faithful ". . . to embark upon a new chapter of evangelization marked by this joy, while pointing out new paths for the Church's journey in years to come." The primary language Pope Francis asks Christians to use is ". . . the language of mercy, which is more about gestures and attitudes than words."

Catechesis and the New Evangelization The *National Directory for Catechesis* affirms that catechesis leads believers to a deeper knowledge and love of Christ and his Church. With the New Evangelization, catechesis is given a missionary dynamic to evangelize the culture, affirming what aligns with Jesus' teaching and challenging what does not. (*NDC* 17.D)

Among its pastoral directives, the *NDC* encourages dioceses and parishes to adopt and implement the goals of *Go and Make Disciples: A National Plan and Strategy for Catholic Evangelization in the United States*. A summary of some fundamental objectives follows: (*NDC* 17.E)

- for every believer to experience a personal conversion to Jesus Christ that leads to renewal and participation in the life of the Church
- to encourage knowledge of Holy Scripture and Tradition of the Church
- for believers to work toward renewing every parish, especially through implementation of the Rite of Christian Initiation of Adults
- for believers to rededicate themselves to the Word of God and the sacraments, especially the Eucharist, and to commit to celebrating the Eucharist every Sunday
- to make evangelical and social justice connections to the Sunday Eucharist
- to call believers to daily prayer, in particular, to pray the psalms and the Liturgy of the Hours, to contemplate Christ's life in the Mysteries of the Rosary, and to revere the Eucharist through adoration of the Blessed Sacrament

- to make all parishes and Catholic institutions welcoming and accessible to all

The New Gather and Go Forth Pages in *Christ Our Life*

The addition of the Gather and Go Forth pages to the *Christ Our Life* program is a response to the Church's call for a New Evangelization including that of Pope John Paul II, who asked each Catholic to evangelize in a way that is "new in its ardor, in its methods, in its expressions."

We become members of the Church through the Sacraments of Initiation: Baptism, Confirmation, and the Eucharist. We celebrate the Eucharist, the source and summit of Christian life, every Sunday. There we hear the Word of God that helps to prepare us to evangelize. As Pope Francis tells us, "God's Word, listened to and celebrated, above all in the Eucharist, nourishes and inwardly strengthens Christians, enabling them to offer an authentic witness to the Gospel in daily life" (*The Joy of the Gospel,* 2013).

The Gather and Go Forth pages in the Student Book show children ways to know, proclaim, witness, and share their faith. In the Catechist's Edition, the three-step teaching plan (Inspire, Proclaim, Transform) guides catechists to help children become more aware and active in their personal relationship with God, the Church, and their call to invite others to the faith.

Beginning on page T316, you can find catechist instruction that accompanies all 25 chapters of the Gather and Go Forth pages in the Student Book. You will also find a full correlation of Grade 7 that shows how these pages align with the goals and objectives expressed by the U. S. bishops in *Go and Make Disciples: A National Plan and Strategy for Catholic Evangelization in the United States.*

If not me, then who will proclaim the Gospel?

If not now, then when will the Gospel be proclaimed?

If not the truth of the Gospel, then what shall I proclaim?

—excerpt from *Prayer for the New Evangelization* (United States Conference of Catholic Bishops)

In the document *Go and Make Disciples,* the U. S. bishops' vision of the New Evangelization is centered around three goals:

- **Goal 1**—to bring about in all Catholics such an enthusiasm for their faith that, in living their faith in Jesus, they freely share it with others;
- **Goal 2**—to invite all people in the United States, whatever their social or cultural background, to hear the message of salvation in Jesus Christ so they may come to join us in the fullness of the Catholic faith;
- **Goal 3**—to foster gospel values in our society, promoting the dignity of the human person, the importance of the family, and the common good of our society, so that our nation may continue to be transformed by the saving power of Jesus Christ.

Jesus' Vision Is Our Own

Being Jesus' witness requires energy, renewed conviction, personal conversion, and enthusiasm from every baptized Catholic.

For Whom Is the New Evangelization Intended? Jesus' commission to the apostles is at the heart of our call to know and share our faith with others. Every member of the Church plays a part in the New Evangelization.

The United States Conference of Catholic Bishops identifies various relationships that people may have to Jesus and his Church. The bishops tell us that each type of relationship has a role in the New Evangelization:

"Evangelization, then, has different implications depending on our relationship to Jesus and his Church. For those of us who practice and live our Catholic faith, it is a call to ongoing growth and renewed conversion. For those who have accepted it only in name, it is a call to re-evangelization. For those who have stopped practicing their faith, it is a call to reconciliation. For children, it is a call to be formed into disciples through the family's faith life and religious education. For other Christians, it is an invitation to know the fullness of our message. For those who have no faith, it is a call to conversion to know Christ Jesus and thus experience a change to new life with Christ and his Church." (*Go and Make Disciples: A National Plan and Strategy for Catholic Evangelization in the United States:* #27)

Roles of Life in the Church Catholics share a common vision to express faith according to their chosen role and state of life. To proclaim Christ is not solely for foreign missionaries, parish priests, bishops, or the pope. Young and old, ordained clergy, professed religious, and the laity share in knowing, proclaiming, and sharing God's Word in ways suitable to their lives.

> *"'[E]veryone who calls on the name of the Lord will be saved.' But how can they call on him in whom they have not believed? And how can they believe in him of whom they have not heard? And how can they hear without someone to preach? And how can people preach unless they are sent?"*
>
> (Romans 10:13–15)

Gifts of Service Each member of the Church uses the Gifts from the Holy Spirit to evangelize. A young person might witness to Christ among friends, playing sports, volunteering, or at school. A parent may express faith in his or her workplace, demonstrating acts of kindness and charity, or championing Catholic Social Teaching in the neighborhood. A priest might share in the Church's mission by leading Scripture study groups, celebrating the Mass on Sunday, or providing counseling to parishioners. A religious sister might share faith by teaching, volunteering in the community, or offering prayers and devotions for the living and the dead. In these and similar ways, Catholics reflect and spread Christ's light and attract others to him.

Embracing the Challenge Catholics who are brimming with joy for God's Word might meet resistance in a culture and society whose values are often on a collision course with Jesus' teaching. Indeed, Catholics are challenged to be "in the world" but not "of the world." Saint Paul reminds us: "Do not conform yourselves to this age but be transformed by the renewal of your mind, that you may discern what is the will of God, what is good and pleasing and perfect." (Romans 12:2) The world is a good place that God created out of his love for us. He sent his Son to live among us and save us from sin. Our Catholic challenge is to live the values of the Kingdom of God as Jesus taught us.

As the Church, the People of God, we pray for ourselves and for one another. We ask the Holy Spirit to help us to know, proclaim, witness, and share the Good News courageously, even in difficult situations. We ask for the saints' intercession, praying that the example of our lives, lived faithfully and authentically, welcomes others to the Church and invites them to know the Father.

Additional Resources

Second Vatican Council Documents on Evangelization
www.vatican.va

- *Dogmatic Constitution on the Church (Lumen Gentium)*
- *On the Mission Activity of the Church (Ad Gentes)*

Vatican Documents on Evangelization www.vatican.va

- *Address to the Plenary Assembly of the Pontifical Council for the Family*
- *Lineamenta for the 2012 Synod: New Evangelization for the Transmission of the Christian Faith*
- *Message for the 2012 World Day of Migrants and Refugees*
- *On Evangelization in the Modern World (Evangelii Nuntiandi)*
- *The Door of Faith*

United States Conference of Catholic Bishops Documents on Evangelization www.usccb.org

- *Go and Make Disciples: A National Plan and Strategy for Catholic Evangelization in the United States*
- *Sons and Daughters of the Light: A Pastoral Plan for Young Adult Ministry*
- *Teaching the Spirit of Mission Ad Gentes: Continuing Pentecost Today*
- *The Hispanic Presence in the New Evangelization in the United States*

Diocesan Evangelization Resources www.usccb.org/about/bishops-and-dioceses/all-dioceses.cfm

Inspire

1. Discuss the meaning of the word *impact* by comparing a gentle snowfall to a blizzard.

   ✦ **How would you describe the difference between these weather events?** (They vary by the degree of power or effect.)

   ✦ **People, things, or events can have power or influence that impacts our lives. What most impacts your life?** (parents; friends; social media; advertising; school)

2. Read aloud the Scripture and text in the sidebar on page 9.

   ✦ Share with students at least one way in which Jesus has impacted your life in a profound way.

   ✦ Invite students to meditate on Jesus. **Think about the impact Jesus has on your life.** [Allow students a few moments of silent reflection.]

   ✦ **How can you proclaim Jesus' impact on your life to others?** [Allow for responses.]

Proclaim

1. Read and discuss the **Know and Proclaim** chart.

   ✦ [Discuss the first row of the chart with students.] **Jesus is true God and true man. All human beings are made in God's image. What does this mean for us?** (Possible answers: we have a soul; we are loving; we are forgiving)

   ✦ **How do we learn more about living as Jesus did?** (Possible answers: celebrating the Eucharist; reading Scripture; praying)

   ✦ After reading the second row, help students appreciate Jesus' unique relationship with God the Father and the Holy Spirit.

   ✦ **Who gave Jesus the message to share with the world?** (God the Father)

   ✦ After reading the third row, ask students to brainstorm ways they can proclaim and celebrate the Paschal Mystery.

Gather and Go Forth

CHAPTER 1

Know and Proclaim

As Catholics we believe that Jesus, the Son of God, became incarnate of the Virgin Mary and assumed a human nature while never losing his divine nature. As such he perfectly expresses what it means for us to love God the Father and one another.

We Know Our Faith	We Proclaim Our Faith
God created us in his image in that he gave us a soul. The soul gives us the ability to think and choose and love.	Because everyone is made in God's image, Catholics strive to help people feel welcome and at home (individually and through the ministry of hospitality).
God the Father, Jesus, and the Holy Spirit form the Three Persons of the Trinity. They exist in a community of love.	When Catholics make the Sign of the Cross, they bless themselves in the name of the Father, and the Son, and the Holy Spirit. The Sign of the Cross is a prayer to the Holy Trinity.
Through the Paschal Mystery—the suffering, Death, Resurrection, and Ascension of Christ—Jesus made it possible for us to have eternal life.	When Catholics celebrate the Eucharist, they proclaim and celebrate the great mystery of faith: the suffering, Death, Resurrection, and Ascension of Jesus.

Test Your Catholic Knowledge

Fill in the circle that best completes the sentence.

The Three Persons in one God are:

○ Jesus, Mary, and Joseph.

○ priest, prophet, and king.

● Father, Son, and Holy Spirit.

○ saints, angels, and apostles.

As Catholics we gather to celebrate the sacraments and listen to God's Word in the Scriptures.

"Go into the whole world and proclaim the gospel to every creature."

Mark 16:15

The Impact of Jesus CHAPTER 1 ⑨

---

2. Discuss with students their practice of praying the **Sign of the Cross**.

   ✦ Lead students in praying the Sign of the Cross in a thoughtful and reverent way.

   ✦ **Do you think of the Sign of the Cross as a prayer or as an introduction to prayer?** [Allow for responses.]

   ✦ **The Sign of the Cross is a beautiful prayer that describes the loving relationship among the Three Persons of the Holy Trinity. Slow down, take the words to heart, and accept the love that the Trinity offers to you.**

3. Point out the **Test Your Catholic Knowledge** section. Allow students time to fill in the circle of their choice before discussing the correct answer.

   🖥 **3-Minute Retreat** Invite deeper reflection on God's Word by accessing **www.loyolapress.com/retreat**. **Goal 1:** To bring about enthusiasm for faith so it is freely shared with others **97**. To foster a deeper sense of prayer

---

See pages T366–T368 for a full correlation to the USCCB *Go and Make Disciples* national plan.

4. Discuss Saint Lucy in the section **A Catholic to Know.**
   - ✦ **The Church gives us role models of faith like Saint Lucy. They show us how to follow Jesus. We are called to be witnesses for Jesus too.**
   - ✦ Tell students about people you consider witnesses for Christ.
   - ✦ **Name some people you know who are witnesses for Jesus.** (Possible answers: parents, friends, relatives, priests)

5. Read the **Witness and Share** introductory text.
   - ✦ Emphasize that each person's relationship with Jesus is unique and develops over a lifetime.
   - ✦ **Look at the faith statements. As you grow in your relationship with Jesus, think about what you need to do to proclaim your faith more confidently.**
   - ✦ [Read aloud the first faith statement.] **Think about where you are in your understanding of your faith today. Hold each statement in your heart and consider what it means to you.** [Allow time for reflection.]
   - ✦ Read aloud the other statements, pausing long enough for reflection.
   - ✦ Remind students that we are always called to a deeper understanding of our faith.
   - ✦ Ask students to choose one faith statement to discuss with their parents, pastor, teacher, or another adult they trust.
   - ✦ Encourage students to grow in this area and then come back to this page later in the year to reflect on the statements again.

6. Read aloud the directions for the **Share Your Faith** activity.
   - ✦ Let students work alone or with a partner and write their ideas.
   - ✦ Remind students that, like any relationship, you only get to know someone by spending time with him or her.

A Catholic to Know

Saint Lucy

The name *Lucy* means "light" and, as such, Saint Lucy is the patron saint of those who are blind or visually impaired. Despite her name, Lucy lived during the dark days of Christian persecution in the Roman Empire in the 300s. Few facts are known about Saint Lucy, except that she lived in Syracuse, a city on the eastern coast of the Italian island of Sicily. She vowed her life in service to Christ, and she lost it in defense of her faith. The fact that she is still mentioned in prayers during the Mass indicates the great respect the Church has for her. Saint Lucy is remembered each year on December 13 for shining a light of courage and inspiration for countless others to follow.

Witness and Share

These sentences describe what Catholics believe. Listen carefully as they are read. Ask yourself, "How strong are my Catholic beliefs?"

My Way to Faith

- I reflect God's image by respecting myself and others.
- I proclaim the mystery of faith reverently during the Mass.
- I pray the Sign of the Cross frequently as a prayer to the Holy Trinity.
- I believe Jesus is my personal Savior.
- I see the world as a gift from God, and I need to care for it and use it wisely.
- I believe that Jesus, the Son of God, assumed a human nature while never losing his divine nature. As a Divine Person, he is true God and true man.

Share Your Faith

Think about what you know about Jesus. What more would you like to know about him? Who is he? What does he mean to you? Write your ideas in your own words on the lines. Invite a trusted adult—relative, teacher, or priest—to talk with you more about his or her relationship with Jesus.

_____

_____

_____

_____

10 | UNIT 1 *Jesus Christ the Way*

Transform

1. Ask students to consider the impact of the media on their thinking and attitudes.
   What are some powerful influences in our society? (Possible answers: advertising, film, videos, TV, social networking) **How can each of these influences be used to witness to faith in Jesus?** [Discuss ideas.]

2. Challenge students to work for peace and social justice.

Tell a partner how mainstream influences could be used to help bring about the Kingdom of God.

3. Lead students in prayer, asking for wisdom and courage to live our Catholic faith in the face of influences that may draw us in other directions.
   Come, Holy Spirit! Fill us with the fire of your love so that we may have the wisdom and strength to live and do your holy will without fear. Amen.

The Church Evangelizes The Holy Spirit gives us the courage to forgive and ask forgiveness, so that we may be reconciled with Christ and one another. Encourage students to celebrate the Sacrament of Reconciliation. Provide students with the examination of conscience on page 248 of the student book to help them prepare for this sacrament. **Goal 1:** To bring about enthusiasm for faith so it is freely shared with others **95.** To foster an appreciation of the presence of Christ in the Eucharist and of all the sacraments

Inspire

1. Read aloud the Scripture in the sidebar on page 17. Discuss with students the value of friends.
   - ✦ **How much value do you place on friendship? What aspects of friendship are most valuable to you?** [Allow time for discussion]
   - ✦ **Friendships usually develop over time. How do you get to know someone as a friend?** (talk, spend time, do things together, find out more about the person)

2. Discuss what friendship with Jesus could mean.
   - ✦ **How do you show that you place great value on friendship with Jesus? How is Jesus a faithful friend?** [Allow time for students to respond to the question and to one another.]
   - ✦ **Jesus is always inviting us into friendship with him. How do you respond?** (Possible answers: open our hearts to Jesus; say yes to Jesus) **How do you get to know Jesus as a friend?** (Possible answers: pray; go to Mass; read the Bible) **As Catholics, we have been invited into friendship with the living God.**

Proclaim

1. Ask students to consider the statements on the left side of the **Know and Proclaim** chart.
   - ✦ Help students compare the ways in which God reveals himself with getting to know more about a friend.
   - ✦ **How do the gifts of faith, Scripture, and Tradition help us know Jesus better?** [Allow time for discussion.]

2. Ask students to consider the statements on the right side of the **Know and Proclaim** chart.
   - ✦ **What do Catholics do to deepen their relationship with Jesus?** (Possible answers: pray; go to Mass; read the Bible) **How do we show others that we are Jesus' friends?** (Possible answers: by how we treat other people; by wearing a cross or a medal; by sharing our faith)
   - ✦ **Why do you need to know about Scripture and Tradition to be a faithful friend to Jesus?** (This is how God reveals himself to us.)

3. Direct students' attention to the **Test Your Catholic Knowledge** question at the bottom of the page. Read aloud the directions. Allow students time to fill in the circle of their choice before discussing the correct answer.

> 🖥 **Daily Inspiration** Find insightful meditations on Scripture at **www.loyolapress.com/daily. Goal 1:** To bring about enthusiasm for faith so it is freely shared with others **93.** To foster an appreciation of God's Word

---

Gather and Go Forth

CHAPTER 2

Know and Proclaim

As Catholics, we believe that Jesus reveals to us the fullness of God's love at work in our world.

We Know Our Faith	We Proclaim Our Faith
Faith in Jesus is a gift from God. It is faith that allows us to believe that Jesus is God in the flesh.	As Catholics, we deepen our relationship with God by going to Mass on Sundays and going on retreats.
Scripture is the Word of God, the written testimony of the faith of the early Church.	Many Catholics read the Bible every day. The Church in the liturgy provides daily Scripture readings for Catholics to read and pray.
Tradition holds the truths of the Church that have been handed down from generation to generation, beginning with the apostles.	Catholics treasure many traditional prayers, such as the Lord's Prayer and the Hail Mary. Traditional prayers help unite the Church with a common way of talking to God.

Test Your Catholic Knowledge

Fill in the circle that best answers the question.

What two things form the single "deposit of faith" on which our faith in Jesus is built?

- ◯ the Crucifixion and Resurrection
- ◯ the sacraments and grace
- ● Scripture and Tradition
- ◯ prayer and liturgy

We are invited into friendship with the living God. As Jesus' disciples, he shares with us everything God the Father told him. With Jesus, we walk toward God.

"I have called you friends, because I have told you everything I have heard from my Father."

John 15:15

Friendship with Jesus CHAPTER 2 ⟨17⟩

The Church Evangelizes At the close of Mass, we are told to "Go in peace, glorifying the Lord by your life." Encourage students to recognize the presence of Jesus in others as well as in the Eucharist by reaching out in friendship to someone who is lonely or feeling left out this week. **Goal 1:** To bring about enthusiasm for faith so it is freely shared with others **94.** To make the evangelizing dimension of Sunday Eucharist more explicit

See pages T366–T368 for a full correlation to the USCCB *Go and Make Disciples* national plan.

4. Read with students about **A Catholic to Know.** Discuss Saint Martin of Tours.

 ✦ Tell students that the saints are role models for how to befriend Jesus. They show us how to deepen our relationship with him.

 ✦ **Saint Martin, inspired by the Holy Spirit, was Jesus' friend. We are invited to be friends with Jesus too.** [Invite students to discuss how Martin acted as a peacemaker and was willing to share.]

 ✦ Share with students examples of people throughout history who have acted as peacemakers.

 ✦ **What can you do to help promote peace around you?** [Let students discuss ideas.]

5. Read the **Witness and Share** introductory text.

 ✦ Explain that friendships develop over time. Our friendship with Jesus will develop throughout our lives.

 ✦ Read aloud the first faith statement. Ask students to think about where they are in getting to know Jesus and where they would like to be.

 ✦ Read aloud the other statements, pausing to allow time for reflection.

 ✦ Ask students to choose one faith statement to discuss with a trusted adult at home or in their parish. Encourage them to record this statement in their journal and look back at it from time to time to see how they've grown in their faith.

 ✦ **When you look at this page in the future, reflect on how your faith life has changed.**

6. Read aloud the directions for the **Share Your Faith** activity.

 ✦ Let students work with a partner or in small groups and write their ideas. **How does thinking of Jesus as a friend help you grow closer to him?**

 ✦ **How does sharing your faith with others strengthen your own faith?**

A Catholic to Know

Saint Martin of Tours

Martin was a peacemaker as a boy, a soldier, and a bishop in the 300s. At age 15, he refused to fight in the Roman army and was taken away in chains. As a soldier, he cut his cloak to give half to a beggar suffering in the cold. That same night he dreamed of Jesus dressed in the beggar's portion of the cloak and, by the next morning, he chose to be baptized. Being both a Christian and a soldier did not appeal to Martin. He refused to fight and was thrown in prison but was soon released. Martin was free to give his life to follow Christ and in 372 he became bishop of Tours, France. As bishop, Martin opposed violence against heretics, despite being beaten for speaking the truth. We remember Saint Martin of Tours as a peacemaker for Christ on November 11.

Witness and Share

These sentences describe what Catholics believe. Listen carefully as they are read. Ask yourself, "How strong are my Catholic beliefs?"

My Way to Faith

• I believe that God gives me the grace to be like Jesus.

• I support my friends by helping them make good choices.

• I pray using traditional Catholic prayers.

• I spend time alone with Jesus.

• I honor sacramental objects in my home, such as sacred statues, candles, medals, and rosaries.

Share Your Faith

Jesus asks you to be his disciple. How do you respond? What do you do that shows you are a disciple? Write your ideas in your own words on the lines. Invite a trusted family member or a friend to tell you about how he or she responds to Jesus' call to discipleship.

_____

_____

_____

_____

(18) UNIT 1 *Jesus Christ the Way*

Transform _____

1. Ask students to think about the value that friendship adds to the lives of people.

 ✦ **What would it be like to have no friends at all?** [Allow time to respond.] **How can the power of your friendship make a difference?** [Discuss ideas.]

2. Challenge students to extend friendship to a classmate, neighbor, or parishioner who is alone.

 ✦ Encourage students to befriend someone who is frequently excluded, ignored, or not usually included in their group of friends.

 ✦ **Look again at what you wrote in Share Your Faith. Tell a partner how being a friend to others is a response to Jesus' invitation of friendship.**

3. Ask students to write a prayer that responds to Jesus' invitation, using their own words.

DRE Connect Share ideas with an online community for faith formation leaders by accessing **dreconnect.loyolapress.com.**

Goal 1: To bring about enthusiasm for faith so it is freely shared with others **98.** To foster a renewed understanding of the faith among Catholics

Inspire

1. Help students appreciate the gift of Scripture.

✦ **We believe that God reveals himself to us in the Person of Jesus Christ and through his holy Word as recorded in the Bible.**

✦ [Hold up a Bible that is wrapped with four layers of wrapping paper.] **The Bible is a gift that keeps on giving. It holds the gift of God's Word.** [Invite a student to tear off the first layer of paper.] **The Bible is a gift that educates God's people.** [Invite a student to tear off the second layer of paper.] **The Bible demonstrates God's love.** [Invite a student to tear off the third layer of paper.] **The Bible celebrates God's presence within us and among us.** [Invite a student to tear off the last layer of paper.]

✦ Hold the Bible for students to see. **We go to the Bible, especially the four Gospels, to learn more about Jesus—his life, his teachings, and his relationship with God the Father.**

2. Read aloud the Scripture on page 25.

✦ Close with a prayer of thanksgiving.

✦ **O God, thank you for sending us your Son. May the example of his life and teachings bring us closer to you and your love. Amen.**

Proclaim

1. Allow students time to read the **Know and Proclaim** introduction and chart.

✦ [Discuss the first row.] **Why are the Gospels considered a special part of the Bible?** (They tell about the life and teachings of Jesus.)

✦ [Discuss the second row.] **The Gospels are at the center of our understanding of who Jesus is.**

✦ Have the class read a Gospel passage such as Mark 2:1–17 or Luke 4:16–21.

✦ **What do these verses tell you about Jesus?** (Possible answers: He is inviting; he is helpful; he is kind and loving.)

Gather and Go Forth

CHAPTER 3

Know and Proclaim

As Catholics, we learn the Good News of the Gospels and share it with the world.

We Know Our Faith	We Proclaim Our Faith
The Gospels tell us about the life, Death, Resurrection, and teachings of Jesus.	Catholics honor the Gospels by standing at Mass while the Gospel is proclaimed by a priest or deacon and by saying "Praise to you, Lord Jesus Christ" after it is read.
The Gospels were written by four Evangelists—Matthew, Mark, Luke, and John—under the inspiration of the Holy Spirit.	Catholics read, study, and pray with the Gospels to come to know and love Jesus more. Many parishes offer Bible studies to help Catholics know Jesus and understand his message.
The New Testament consists of the Gospels, the Acts of the Apostles, Letters, and the Book of Revelation.	Catholics read the Word of God. Some serve as lectors at Mass, proclaiming the Word of God to the assembly. Many Catholics pray and meditate on the Scriptures.

Test Your Catholic Knowledge

Fill in the circle that best completes the sentence.

The Gospels of Matthew, Mark, and Luke are called Synoptic Gospels because:

○ they were written by Jesus' friends.

● they present similar stories of Jesus' life.

○ they present different stories of Jesus' life.

○ they were all written while Jesus was still alive.

J esus came to reveal the mystery of God's saving love. The Gospels reveal the Good News of Jesus. As Catholics, we are inspired by his love to share the Good News with others.

"No one knows the Son except the Father, and no one knows the Father except the Son and anyone to whom the Son wishes to reveal him."

Matthew 11:27

Scripture: A Portrait of Jesus CHAPTER 3 **25**

---

2. Explore with students ways they can share the Word of God.

✦ As you discuss the third row, remind students that "knowing" should be followed by "proclaiming."

✦ **Why do we refer to the Gospels as "the Good News"?** (because Jesus was the Good News whom God sent into the world to save us)

✦ **What do we want to do when we hear good news?** (tell others, celebrate it)

3. Ask students to complete the **Test Your Catholic Knowledge** section at the bottom of the page. Allow students time to fill in the circle of their choice before discussing the correct answer.

 Sunday Connection
Explore this Sunday's Scripture readings with students by accessing **www.loyolapress.com/sunday**.

Goal 1: To bring about enthusiasm for faith so it is freely shared with others **93.** To foster an appreciation of God's Word

---

See pages T366–T368 for a full correlation to the USCCB *Go and Make Disciples* national plan.

4. Read aloud **A Catholic to Know** with students. Discuss how Saint Mark chose to witness to Jesus and why he is a model for us.
How did Saint Mark choose to share his faith? (through writing) **Why?** (to proclaim Jesus) **To whom did he address his Gospel?** (persecuted Christians) **How can we follow his example?** (by finding ways to share the Good News of Jesus through our lives)

5. Read the **Witness and Share** introductory text.
- ✦ Explain that people can choose from a variety of ways to learn about Jesus. We continue to learn throughout our lives.
- ✦ [Read aloud the first faith statement.] **Think about the courage or confidence you receive from hearing the Good News of Jesus. Resolve to learn more about Jesus to boost your confidence in this area.**
- ✦ Read aloud the other statements, pausing to allow time for reflection.
- ✦ Ask students to choose one faith statement to discuss with a trusted adult at home or in their parish. Encourage them to turn the statement into a goal and reassess it at a later date.

6. Read aloud the directions for the **Share Your Faith** activity. Recall early discussions about using gifts in service to God. Let students work together to share and write their ideas.

Transform _____

1. Ask students to find a favorite Gospel story to read.
- ✦ **Why is this your favorite passage?** [Allow time for responses.] **How does it inspire you? What is the "Good News" that it contains?** [Allow time for students to respond and discuss their responses.]

2. Challenge students to put their favorite Gospel story into concrete action.

A Catholic to Know

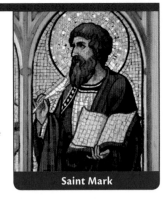
Saint Mark

Saint Mark's Gospel is the shortest and oldest of the Gospels. Mark tells the story of Jesus to proclaim Jesus' message of love to the world. Mark wrote to early Christians to give them hope in the face of persecution for their faith. In Mark's view, Jesus was a man of action, and Mark's Gospel calls us to action. According to Mark, it is not enough to profess to believe in Christ without a willingness to live as he did. Mark's Gospel challenged the early Christians to follow Jesus' path to the Cross and to share in his Resurrection. Saint Mark, the earliest Gospel writer, offers the same challenge to Christians today.

Witness and Share

These sentences describe what Catholics believe. Listen carefully as they are read. Ask yourself, "How strong are my Catholic beliefs?"

My Way to Faith

- I share the Good News through my words and actions.
- I often hear God speak to me whenever I read or hear Scripture.
- I think about how Jesus lived and what he taught when I'm facing difficult decisions in my own life.
- I would like to learn more about Jesus by participating in a Bible study in my school or parish.
- I believe that Jesus is truly present in the Eucharist.

Share Your Faith

Think about a favorite Gospel story that inspires you to follow Jesus. What does Jesus say or do? What effect do his actions have on those present? Use the story to write your own prayer on the lines below or on a separate piece of paper. Then invite a family member or a friend to share his or her favorite Gospel story.

_____

_____

_____

_____

26 UNIT 1 *Jesus Christ the Way*

Which parish ministry or service activity reflects values described in your favorite Gospel story? [Suggest appropriate ministries such as serving at Mass or working in a food pantry.]

3. Encourage students to use their talents to share the Gospel.
If possible, bring in examples of paintings by contemporary artists that proclaim the Gospel. Challenge students who have artistic talent to portray their favorite Gospel story.

Arts & Faith Celebrate how faith is expressed and deepened through art at **www.loyolapress.com/arts-faith**.
Goal 3: To foster gospel values, promoting the dignity of the human person, the importance of the family, and the common good **124.** To encourage Catholic witness in the arts and in the American intellectual community

The Church Evangelizes Encourage families to share the Gospel. Send a reminder to parents suggesting that after Mass, they spend time as a family discussing the readings and the priest's homily. Offer points for discussion and questions for reflection.
Goal 2: To invite all people to hear the message of salvation in Jesus Christ **108.** To develop within families the capacity to share the Gospel

Inspire

1. Have a student read aloud the text in the sidebar on page 33.

✦ Discuss how Jesus' culture and era influenced his message.

✦ **Because Jesus lived thousands of years ago, he delivered his message differently than he might today— he walked from town to town, he referred to his Jewish faith, and he spoke a different language. Because of technology, how would he deliver his message today?** [Allow students to respond.]

✦ **Jesus made the old law of Moses new by proclaiming God's love in the time and place in which he lived. He calls us to do the same today.** Lead students in the following prayer: **Lord, help us proclaim your love and truth, not just with words, but with our entire lives.**

2. Read aloud the Scripture passage on page 33. Discuss how Jesus fulfilled the law of Moses.

✦ **How does something old become new again?** (Possible answers: add improvements; reintroduce it in a new way) **How did Jesus make the law new?** (emphasized God's love; gave new reasons to follow it; made it his own)

✦ **Jesus' life tells the truth of God's love. He calls us to live God's law with grace and new understanding.**

Proclaim

1. Direct students to read the **Know and Proclaim** introduction and chart.

✦ After reading the first row, discuss connections between the facts and practices of our faith.

✦ **Why do Catholics respect Judaism?** (Possible answers: Jesus was Jewish; we share history and common heritage.)

✦ **As Catholics, we respect the Jewish faith because Christianity originated in Judaism. We learn about Jesus and Jewish faith traditions to know and proclaim him.**

NEW EVANGELIZATION

Gather and Go Forth

CHAPTER 4

Know and Proclaim

Catholics share a common heritage with the Jewish people.

We Know Our Faith	We Proclaim Our Faith
Jesus was born into a Jewish family in the town of Bethlehem, part of the kingdom of Judea, which was controlled by the Roman Empire.	Catholics have profound respect for Judaism and seek to learn more about its traditions, many of which influence Catholic practice today.
Jesus practiced Jewish religious customs. He went to the Temple in Jerusalem for major feasts.	Catholics go on pilgrimages to holy sites such as cathedrals. This practice echoes Jewish pilgrimages to the Jerusalem Temple in Jesus' day.
The Sabbath is a day of strict rest observed by Jews.	The Sabbath is a day of strict rest observed by Jews. Since Christ rose from the dead on Sunday, the Catholic celebration of the Lord's Day replaces the Sabbath. Catholics keep the Lord's Day holy by going to Mass on Sunday and holy days of obligation and by being mindful of God throughout the day.

Test Your Catholic Knowledge

Fill in the circle that best answers the question.

Who was most upset that Jesus taught that a spirit of love and worship was more important than external observations of the Law?

○ the Samaritans
● the Pharisees
○ the Romans
○ the Essenes

The World Jesus Lived In CHAPTER 4 (33)

Jesus lived in a particular time and place in the history of God's Chosen People. He was a Jewish man and lived according to Jewish laws and customs. His message is, however, for all times, all places, and all people.

While the law was given through Moses, grace and truth came through Jesus Christ.
John 1:17

✦ [Discuss the second row.] **Jesus prayed the Shema daily, a prayer central to the Jewish faith from the Torah.**

✦ Have students look up the Shema in the Bible (Deuteronomy 6:4–9, 11:13–21, and Numbers 15:37–41). Explain that the Shema can be their prayer too.

2. Encourage students to keep the Sabbath holy.

✦ [Discuss the third row.] **How do you keep Sunday holy?** (Possible answers: I celebrate the Lord's Day by going to Mass with my family; I visit with relatives; I participate in youth ministry events.)

✦ **How do you keep God in your life throughout the day?** (Possible

answers: I say brief prayers; I read Scripture)

3. Ask students to read and answer the **Test Your Catholic Knowledge** question at the bottom of the page.

Allow students time to answer the question before discussing the correct answer.

Español Invite Spanish-language speakers to access **www.loyolapress.com/espanol**.

Goal 2: To invite all people to hear the message of salvation in Jesus Christ **115.** To foster cultural diversity within the unity of the Church

---

See pages T366–T368 for a full correlation to the USCCB *Go and Make Disciples* national plan.

4. Read aloud **A Catholic to Know.** Help students appreciate the significance of Saint Mary Magdalene in our faith history.

   ✦ Invite students to consider her role as a witness. **Without Saint Mary Magdalene, we may not have heard the Good News of Jesus. She bore witness to Jesus even when the others were afraid.**

   ✦ **How do you bear witness to Jesus?** (Possible answers: I go to Mass; I listen to my parents; I help my friends with their homework.)

   ✦ Encourage students to celebrate Saint Mary Magdalene's feast day on July 22.

5. Read the **Witness and Share** introductory text.

   ✦ Explain that being Jesus' disciple is a process that lasts a lifetime.

   ✦ **Look at the faith statements. Think about your life as a disciple today.**

   ✦ **Consider your ability to share what you believe. As Catholic Christians, our words and actions provide witness to Jesus in our time and place in history.**

   ✦ Read aloud each faith statement, pausing to allow time for reflection.

   ✦ Remind students that Jesus' first disciples were, at times, afraid to share their faith for fear of imprisonment and death. Encourage students to overcome their fear of appearing different from others to grow as witnesses of their faith.

   ✦ Ask students to choose one faith statement to discuss with a trusted adult at home or in their parish. Encourage them to come back to this page later in the year to reflect on the statements again.

6. Read aloud the directions for the **Share Your Faith** activity. Let students work individually or in small groups to share and write their ideas. **What impact can your faith have on the world?**

A Catholic to Know

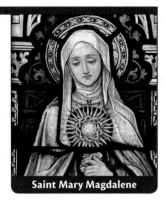

Saint Mary Magdalene

Mary Magdalene has been called the "Apostle to the Apostles." Mary of Magdala, as she was also known, was one of Jesus' first disciples in Galilee. She was present at Jesus' Crucifixion, and when the male disciples fled in fear following Jesus' Death, Mary Magdalene was among the women standing before the empty tomb. She was the first person to witness the risen Christ and the one who proclaimed the Good News of the Resurrection to the twelve apostles. Each year we honor Saint Mary Magdalene's faithful witness to the Paschal Mystery on her feast day, July 22.

Witness and Share

These sentences describe what Catholics believe. Listen carefully as they are read. Ask yourself, "How strong are my Catholic beliefs?"

My Way to Faith

- I respect people of other faiths in my thoughts or actions.
- I find that offering my day to God each morning helps me to live my faith.
- I keep the Lord's Day holy by attending Mass every Sunday and by being mindful of God.
- I believe it is important to have an awareness of Jewish history and customs so that I can understand Scripture better.
- I value sacred spaces in my home, parish, and larger Catholic community.

Share Your Faith

Think about the world in which you live. What events have affected your life? How do those events affect your faith? Write your ideas in your own words on the lines. Invite a family member or a friend to share how the values and attitudes of today's culture impact his or her life.

_____

_____

_____

_____

34 UNIT 1 *Jesus Christ the Way*

Transform _____

1. Ask students to learn more about the lives of young people in modern-day Israel.

   ✦ Share news stories about Israel and discuss some of the challenges faced by the people who live there.

   ✦ Display a map of modern-day Israel to help students understand the news stories.

   ✦ **How are their experiences like or unlike yours?** [Allow time for responses.]

2. Discuss the importance of Jerusalem.
   Jerusalem is sacred to Jews, Christians, and Muslims. How can Jerusalem be a symbol of unity? (Possible answers: It is a sign that we all share Abraham as a father in faith; it is a sign of God's presence.)

3. Pray for peace in Israel.
   Pray aloud: **God of hope and Father of mercy, inspire people to choose peace over violence and to seek reconciliation with enemies. Amen.**

The Church Evangelizes Ask students to invite friends or neighbors of different denominations to attend a Mass or prayer service with you in a Catholic Church. Reciprocate by attending a service with them at their church. **Goal 2:** To invite all people to hear the message of salvation in Jesus Christ. **116.** To deepen ecumenical involvement

Inspire

1. Read aloud the text above the Scripture on page 41.
   - ✦ **What does *authentically* mean?** (Possible answers: credibly; believably; genuinely) **Who do you know that authentically proclaims Christ?** (Possible answers: priest; parents; friends; teachers)
   - ✦ **How are we like the child Jesus?** (God loves us. Our relationship with him grows as we do. Our abilities to proclaim develop over time.)

2. Pray the Scripture on page 41. Help students understand that as Jesus grew, so did his ability to share his faith. **Who is the child?** (Jesus) **Why did he need to grow in strength and wisdom?** (to understand what God asked of him and to do it) **What does "God's favor was upon him" suggest?** (that God loved him and gave him grace)

3. Place a crucifix or flameless candle on a table and lead the students in prayer.
   [Have students focus their attention on the crucifix or candle. Then pray the following:] **Lord, send us your Spirit so that we may do your will and be Christ to one another. Amen.**

Proclaim

1. Ask students to read the **Know and Proclaim** introduction and chart.
   - ✦ [Discuss the first row.] **What do Nativity scenes represent?** (belief that God sent his own Son to save the world) **Where in the Bible can we find the story of Jesus' birth?** (in Matthew's and Luke's Gospels) **We tell the story over and over and celebrate it at Christmas. The belief that Jesus is fully human and fully divine is central to our faith.**
   - ✦ [Discuss the second row.] **What role does Mary play in the Infancy Narratives?** (She is the mother of Jesus. She said yes to God; through Mary, Jesus came into the world.)

Gather and Go Forth

CHAPTER 5

Know and Proclaim

Catholics bring the Good News of the Gospel to life in the way they live out the teachings of the faith.

We Know Our Faith	We Proclaim Our Faith
The Infancy Narratives tell us the stories of Jesus' birth and early life. They can be found in the Gospels of Matthew and Luke.	Catholics display scenes of the Nativity at Christmas. These displays remind people that Jesus came to save the whole world.
Mary listened to God, which led her to bring Jesus into the world.	As Catholics, we seek to bring the Good News to the world through our words and interactions with others.
Mary is the Mother of God because she is the mother of Jesus. Mary has a privileged place in the Church.	Catholics honor Mary with special celebrations, such as the May Crowning, when a statue of the Blessed Virgin Mary is crowned with a wreath of flowers.

Test Your Catholic Knowledge

Fill in the circle that best completes the sentence.

When Mary said yes to the angel Gabriel, she agreed to:

- ○ marry Joseph.
- ● become the Mother of God.
- ○ be written about in the Gospels.
- ○ be the mother of John the Baptist.

From the time of his birth, Jesus grew in God's love so that he could proclaim it to all humankind. As Catholics, we understand that we are also called to grow in our faith so that we can authentically proclaim Christ.

The child grew and became strong, filled with wisdom; and the favor of God was upon him.
Luke 2:40

The Early Life of Jesus CHAPTER 5 41

- ✦ [Discuss the third row.] **Why do we call Mary the Mother of God?** (We believe Jesus is God.) **How do we honor Mary's life?** (by saying yes to God; with feasts; by praying the Rosary and other devotions)

2. Remind students that the power of the Holy Spirit enables us to know and proclaim God's love authentically. **Mary said yes to God with her life. We ask the Holy Spirit for the grace and wisdom to say yes with our lives. How do you say yes to God?** [Allow time for discussion.]

3. Point out the **Test Your Catholic Knowledge** section. Allow students time to complete the sentence before discussing the correct answer.

Español Invite Spanish-language speakers to access **www.loyolapress.com/espanol**.

Goal 1: To bring about enthusiasm for faith so it is freely shared with others **103**. To foster greater appreciation of cultural and ethnic spirituality

See pages T366–T368 for a full correlation to the USCCB *Go and Make Disciples* national plan.

4. Read aloud **A Catholic to Know.** Help students understand that Juan Diego did not seek the Mother of God—she sought him.

✦ Invite students to consider how we are often called upon to do the unexpected or something we believe is beyond our capabilities. **Describe a time when you had to do something that you thought you couldn't do.** [Allow time to respond.] **How did you respond?**

✦ Juan Diego did not believe he was worthy to meet the Mother of God. When called, however, he responded. Discuss with students someone in your community who responds to God's call like Saint Juan Diego did.

5. Read the **Witness and Share** introductory text.
✦ Explain that our understanding of faith develops throughout our lives.

✦ **Look at the faith statements. Think about the development of your faith life until today and the ways you are growing in God's love.**

✦ [Read aloud the first faith statement.] **Think about how to develop and share what you believe. Pray to the Holy Spirit for help and guidance.**

✦ Read aloud the other statements, pausing to allow time for reflection.

✦ Remind students that we can make choices to grow in our relationship with God and in our ability to proclaim him with confidence. Encourage them to ask God for the grace to grow in wisdom and grace as disciples of Jesus.

✦ Ask children to choose one faith statement to discuss with a parent or trusted adult. Encourage students to return to this page later in the year and reconsider each faith statement.

6. Read aloud the directions for the **Share Your Faith** activity. Let students work individually or with partners to share and write their ideas.

A Catholic to Know

Saint Juan Diego

Juan Diego (1474–1548) was a reluctant saint. When the Blessed Virgin Mary appeared to him at Tepeyac in Mexico, he asked her to find someone more worthy to take her message to the bishop. She appeared three times, always with the dark skin of the native people, adorned with native and Christian symbols, and speaking Juan's own Nahuatl language. Juan convinced the bishop when an image of Mary miraculously appeared on the inside of his cloak. Because Juan Diego said yes, Our Lady of Guadalupe remains a sign of hope and compassion for the Mexican people and for millions of believers around the world.

Witness and Share

These sentences describe what Catholics believe. Listen carefully as they are read. Ask yourself, "How strong are my Catholic beliefs?"

My Way to Faith

- I am familiar with the Scripture stories of Jesus' birth.
- I believe that Mary is the Mother of God.
- I pray prayers like the Hail Mary and other prayers that honor Mary.
- I share the message of Christmas throughout the year through my words and interactions with others.
- I welcome Jesus into my own life.

Share Your Faith

Think about how you can make Jesus' presence more evident for yourself and those around you. Where do you see Jesus acting in your life? Write your ideas in your own words on the lines. Invite a family member or a friend to share how Jesus is present in his or her life.

_____

_____

_____

_____

Transform _____

1. Ask students to think about the relationship between mothers and their children. **What kind of mother was Mary?** (Possible answers: loving; caring) **What kind of help did she need to raise Jesus?** [Allow time to respond.] **How can you make a difference in the lives of mothers?** (Possible answers: I can obey my parents; I can offer to babysit for friends and relatives; I can say thank you to my mother.)

2. Challenge students to find ways they can offer support for children in need through a social service agency. [Read Matthew 19:13–14.] **Through our service to others, we bring Jesus' love into the world.**

3. Lead students in praying the Hail Mary for the care and protection of children and mothers everywhere.

The Church Evangelizes Under the guidance of their pastors, many Catholic parishes support food pantries that help fight local hunger. Encourage students to bring in nonperishable food items that can be delivered to a local food pantry. **Goal 3:** To foster gospel values, promoting dignity of the human person, the importance of the family, and the common good. **125.** To involve every Catholic in areas of public policy

Inspire

1. Ask students to consider the life of Jesus.

   What are some ways your lives are like Jesus' life? How are your lives different? [Allow time for student responses. Same: Jesus experienced fear and joy; different: Jesus always did the will of his Father.] **How might knowing that Jesus was like you in so many ways help you trust him?** (Possible answers: He understands me; he knows what I am going through.)

2. Read aloud the text and Scripture in the sidebar on page 49. Discuss Jesus' presence in the sacraments.

   Where do you feel God's presence the most? How does that give you strength? [Allow time for discussion.] **The Holy Spirit works through the sacraments to gives us the gifts of strength and courage to face our challenges.**

3. Display a crucifix.
   - ✦ Ask students to reflect on the challenges you face as you reread the Scripture passage in the sidebar on page 49.
   - ✦ **Jesus knows our weaknesses and our challenges. He shares our struggles. Knowing that, we can trust him. What would you like to share with him?** [Allow time for personal reflection.]
   - ✦ Close with the following prayer: **Jesus, we trust in you. Amen.**

Proclaim

1. Read the **Know and Proclaim** introduction and chart with students.
   - ✦ As you discuss the first row, ask a student to read aloud Matthew 5:9. Discuss ways students can be peacemakers. Suggest that students can be peacemakers by protecting those who are poor and vulnerable.
   - ✦ [As you discuss the second row, ask a student to read aloud Matthew 3:13–17.] **What does this verse describe?** (the baptism of Jesus) **What did the Holy Spirit appear as?** (as a dove) **What did**

Gather and Go Forth

CHAPTER **6**

Know and Proclaim

We grow strong in the knowledge of our faith to proclaim Jesus as Messiah with courage and conviction.

We Know Our Faith	We Proclaim Our Faith
Jesus' mission was to proclaim and make present the Kingdom of God, in which all people live in peace and love.	Responding to the beatitude "Blessed are the peacemakers," Catholics pray for peace in the world during the Prayer of the Faithful.
Jesus' baptism revealed the Trinity. The Father, the Son, and the Holy Spirit are three Persons in one God.	Catholics pray the Glory Be to the Father (Doxology) to give praise to the Trinity. Catholics also praise the Trinity whenever they pray the Sign of the Cross.
Sin offends God and hurts our relationship with him. Sin also hurts our relationships among people.	Fasting is a practice many Catholics use to try to resist the temptation to sin. One common form of fasting is to abstain from eating meat on Fridays, especially during Lent. Catholics also fast by giving up things they enjoy as a sacrifice to God.

Test Your Catholic Knowledge

Fill in the circle that best completes the sentence.

As Catholics, we believe sin:
- ● is a conscious choice to do what is wrong.
- ○ makes God stop loving us.
- ○ can never be forgiven.
- ○ is always mortal.

J esus understands the tests we face. Catholics rely on God's grace, which is present in the sacraments, to meet the challenge of evil.

For we do not have a high priest who is unable to sympathize with our weaknesses, but one who has similarly been tested in every way, yet without sin.

Hebrews 4:15

The Mission of Jesus CHAPTER 6 (49)

God the Father declare about Jesus? (Jesus was his son with whom he was pleased.) **What are some actions you can take today to please God?** (Possible answers: give him praise and thanks; help people in need)

- ✦ Ask a student to read about Jesus' temptations in the desert (Matthew 4:1–11) before discussing the third row.
- ✦ **How was Jesus tested?** (He was tempted to turn stones into bread; offered the kingdom of the earth; and tempted to jump off the walls of the holy city and be saved by angels.)
- ✦ **Jesus faced temptations just as we do. Where did he find strength to resist temptation?** (Prayer to God) **How can you develop your strength of faith in**

God? [Allow time for discussion.] **As your faith gets stronger, so will your desire to proclaim it.**

2. Point out the **Test Your Catholic Knowledge** section. Allow students time to complete the sentence before discussing the correct answer.

> 🖥 **Sunday Connection**
> Explore this Sunday's Scripture readings with students by accessing **www.loyolapress.com/sunday**.
> **Goal 1:** To bring about enthusiasm for faith so it is freely shared with others **96.** To foster a greater appreciation of the power of God's Word in our worship

---

See pages T366–T368 for a full correlation to the USCCB *Go and Make Disciples* national plan.

3. Read aloud **A Catholic to Know.** Discuss how Saint Peter Claver's life and work demonstrated the dignity of human life.

✦ **What risks did Peter Claver take to be a witness to Christ? What did he have to give up?** [Allow time for discussion.]

✦ **What does Saint Peter Claver's example of Christian living tell us about how people should be treated?** (Possible answers: with dignity; compassion) **Peter Claver treated each person as a child of God. His witness is a model for us to follow.**

✦ Discuss with students someone in your community who treats others with dignity like Saint Peter Claver did.

4. Read the **Witness and Share** introductory text.

✦ Explain that our faith journey lasts a lifetime, but that Jesus accompanies us on that journey, helping us make good choices.

✦ **Think about where you are on your faith journey. Remember that you are a child of God.**

✦ Read aloud each faith statement, pausing to allow time for reflection.

✦ Encourage students to ask God for the courage to make peace and avoid sin.

✦ Ask students to choose one faith statement to discuss with a trusted adult. Encourage them to write it in their journal and look back at it from time to time to see how they've grown in their faith.

5. Read aloud the directions for the **Share Your Faith** activity.
Suggest that prayer, service, and study are ways to exercise and gain strength in their faith. Have students complete the activity.

Transform _____

1. Ask students to read Micah 6:8.
✦ **What does God require of you?** (Possible answers: to do justice; to love goodness)

A Catholic to Know

Peter Claver (1581–1654) ministered to the African slaves in South America for more than 40 years. These slaves suffered incredible cruelty. They were crowded together in the lower holds of ships for the long voyage to what is now Colombia, during which approximately one-third would die from mistreatment. Peter Claver treated their wounds and supplied fresh food and drink upon their arrival. Despite their miserable travel, living, and work conditions, Peter Claver wanted to help restore their dignity and let them know they were children of God and precious in God's sight. We honor Saint Peter Claver's tireless ministry to African slaves on September 9.

Saint Peter Claver

Witness and Share

These sentences describe what Catholics believe. Listen carefully as they are read. Ask yourself, "How strong are my Catholic beliefs?"

My Way to Faith

• I believe that God loves me even when I sin.

• I act as a peacemaker between my friends when they argue.

• I believe that I am called to share in Jesus' mission to build the Kingdom of God among people today.

• I pray to God for the grace to avoid temptation and sin.

• I seek to correct injustice when I see it.

• I work to restore human dignity when I see it being denied.

Share Your Faith

Think about ways in which you can take a more active role in your parish community—through prayer, service, or study with others. Write your ideas on the lines and plan to implement at least one of them in the next month. Invite a friend or family member to participate with you.

_____

_____

_____

_____

50 UNIT 1 *Jesus Christ the Way*

✦ Point out the Gifts of the Holy Spirit on page 241 of the students' books.

✦ **What gifts would help you the most in promoting justice?** [Let students respond.]

2. Ask students to consider injustices they encounter.

✦ **Where do you see a need for justice in your world?** [Let students respond.]

✦ **How can you make a difference for someone else?** (Discuss ideas.)

3. Challenge students to work for peace and correct injustice where they can.

✦ **What can you do if you know someone who is often teased or bullied?** [Let students respond.]

✦ **How does making a positive difference in someone's life proclaim your faith?** (Possible answers: it shows you care; it's what Jesus did.)

The Church Evangelizes Ask students to lead their families in prayer during a meal, encouraging them to make family members more aware of God's presence among them. Ask them to encourage their families to live the Gospel message from the upcoming Sunday Mass. **Goal 1:** To bring about enthusiasm for faith so it is freely shared with others. **94.** To make the evangelizing mission of Sunday Eucharist more explicit

Inspire

1. Read the text and Scripture passage in the sidebar on page 59 with students.
   ✦ **What is rubbish?** (Possible answers: stuff you can throw away; things of little relative value)
   ✦ **Saint Paul is willing to lose all things he considers rubbish to gain Christ. What things could he have had in mind?** (Possible answers: wealth, power, popularity)
   ✦ **How did Saint Paul indicate the value he placed on Christ?** (He said he doesn't need anything else.)

2. Discuss distractions that students have.
   What "rubbish" keeps you from Christ? How can giving up those things bring you closer to him? [Allow time for discussion.]

3. Invite students to gather in the prayer center.
   ✦ Pray the following prayer: **My God and my all, how I long to love you, with all my heart and all my soul.**
   ✦ Repeat the prayer two or three times. Invite the students to reflect quietly on these words before praying the Sign of the Cross.

Proclaim

1. Read the **Know and Proclaim** introduction and chart with students.
   ✦ Before discussing the first row, reread the description of the apostles on pages 53–55. Ask students if they have a favorite apostle.
   ✦ **Think about your favorite apostle. What does he tell you about following Jesus?** [Let students respond.]
   ✦ After reading the second row, discuss Pope Francis and his concern for the poor. If time allows, bring in copies of a recent homily by Pope Francis to discuss with students.
   ✦ [Discuss the third row.] **Mary was the first and best disciple. How do you honor Mary?** (I pray the

Hail Mary and other prayers to Mary.)
   ✦ **As disciples, we are called to know and proclaim the Gospel.**

2. Direct students' attention to the **Test Your Catholic Knowledge** question at the bottom of the page. Read the directions aloud. Allow students time to complete the sentence before discussing the correct answer.

NEW EVANGELIZATION

Gather and Go Forth

CHAPTER 7

Know and Proclaim

Knowing the teachings of the Church enables us to proclaim the truth of Christ.

We Know Our Faith	We Proclaim Our Faith
The apostles shared in the ministry of Jesus and preached the Good News of the Resurrection.	Many Catholics share in the ministry of Jesus by teaching religious education classes in their parish. They help pass on the truth of the Church to another generation of Catholics.
The pope is the Bishop of Rome. He is the successor of Peter, who was chosen by Jesus to be the head of the early Church.	Catholics pray for the pope and bishops during the Eucharistic Prayer at Mass. Many Catholics have a picture of the current pope in their home.
Mary is the model for discipleship. She is the mother of Jesus, the Mother of the Church, and the mother of all believers.	Catholics may show their devotion to Mary by placing a statue of her in a flower garden or by planting a Mary garden. They may wear a medal as a sign of devotion to Mary.

Test Your Catholic Knowledge

Fill in the circle that best completes the sentence.

The bishops of the Roman Catholic Church:

○ are elected by representatives of parish churches.

○ can choose any diocese they wish to serve.

● are the principal pastors of their dioceses.

○ have universal power in the care of souls.

As disciples, Catholics desire only to follow Christ, share in his mission, and live with him forever. This desire leads us to know and proclaim him with our lives.

For his sake I have accepted the loss of all things and I consider them so much rubbish, that I may gain Christ.

Philippians 3:8

The Apostles, Mary, and Others CHAPTER 7 59

 Daily Inspiration Find insightful meditation on Scripture at **www.loyolapress.com/daily**. **Goal 1:** To bring about enthusiasm for faith so it is freely shared with others **93.** To foster an appreciation of God's Word

---

The Church Evangelizes Offer students ideas to help them prayerfully prepare for celebrating the sacraments. For example, suggest that they read Matthew 5:23–26 before celebrating the Sacrament of Penance and Reconciliation and then attending Mass. **Goal 1:** To bring about enthusiasm for faith so it is freely shared with others **95.** To foster an appreciation of the presence of Christ in the Eucharist and of all the sacraments

See pages T366–T368 for a full correlation to the USCCB *Go and Make Disciples* **national plan.**

3. Read aloud **A Catholic to Know.** Help students understand the work of disciples.
   - ✦ Invite students to connect the goals of a fisherman with the goals of fishers for men and women. **What does it mean to "catch" people?** (to gather more disciples for Jesus) **How do disciples "catch" people?** (by sharing the faith with them)
   - ✦ **Saint Andrew went from catching fish to being a disciple of Christ. He shared his faith in a way that caused others to believe and to follow Jesus Christ.**

4. Read the **Witness and Share** introductory text.
   - ✦ Explain that the way we live our lives demonstrates our commitment to Jesus and whether or not we are effective messengers of the faith.
   - ✦ **Think how you honor your call to grow as a witness to faith in Jesus.**
   - ✦ Read aloud each faith statement. Pause to allow time for reflection after each one.
   - ✦ Recommend that students choose one faith statement to discuss with a parent or teacher. Encourage them to turn the statement into a goal for spiritual growth this year. Have them reassess their progress later in the year.

5. Read aloud the directions for the **Share Your Faith** activity.
   The call to discipleship is for everyone, but how we proclaim our faith is unique. [Have students complete the activity.]

Transform _____

1. Ask students to consider the costs of discipleship in our current society.
   What responsibilities do you have as a disciple that others may not? (Possible answers: focusing on Christ; learning about my faith; sharing it with others) **How does discipleship make you stand out from others?** [Discuss ideas.]

A Catholic to Know

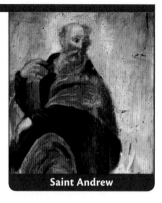
Saint Andrew

Andrew and his brother, Simon Peter, were fishermen when Jesus promised to make them "fishers of men." Andrew was originally a follower of John the Baptist but, at Jesus' baptism, he recognized the truth of John's proclamation—that Jesus was truly the Lamb of God. Following the Ascension of our Lord, Andrew traveled to Greece, where he preached the Good News of Jesus' Resurrection. Around the year A.D. 70, Andrew was crucified and tied to an X-shaped cross for two days, proclaiming Christ to the crowds as he died. The X-shaped cross remains Saint Andrew's symbol, along with fish and a fisherman's net.

Witness and Share

These sentences describe what Catholics believe. Listen carefully as they are read. Ask yourself, "How strong are my Catholic beliefs?"

My Way to Faith

- I answer the call to live as a disciple of Jesus Christ.
- I honor Mary by praying Marian prayers such as the Hail Mary and the Rosary.
- I look to the pope, the Church, and its leaders to help me deepen my relationship with Jesus.
- I follow Jesus, even though some friends do not believe.
- I share my experiences of faith in Jesus with my friends and family.

Share Your Faith

Do you know a friend or family member who does not go to church very often? Think of one way you might invite that person back to Jesus. Write your ideas on the lines and then invite that person to attend Mass with you.

_____

_____

_____

_____

_____

---

2. Help students understand that discipleship means making choices they think Jesus would make.
   When you are faced with a difficult decision, ask yourself "What would Jesus do?" The answer to that question can help you make good choices.

3. Direct students to read Psalm 106:3–4 and discuss how these verses describe discipleship.

Explain that disciples work for justice. Finish by praying aloud: **Come to us Lord, and help us as we pray for _____ .** Ask students to complete the prayer with their own intentions for the world.

The Church Evangelizes Encourage students to become involved in a faith formation ministry, such as Bible study, that helps families apply their faith in everyday situations and brings them closer together. **Goal 2:** To invite all people to hear the message of salvation in Jesus Christ **108.** To develop within families the capacity to share the Gospel

Inspire

1. Read aloud the text in the sidebar on page 67 and discuss how we praise God through the sacraments.
   What are sacraments? (outward signs of God's grace) **We receive God's grace in the sacraments of the Church.**

2. Read the Scripture passage on page 67 with students.
   ✦ **What does "called out of darkness into his wonderful light" refer to?** (God has called us from sin to eternal life in him.) **How does this make us a people of his own?** (God wants us to have eternal life in him.)

   ✦ **Why do we offer praise to God?** (It is our loving response to a loving God.) **How do we offer praise?** (Possible answers: by going to Mass; by praying; by thanking God)

3. Invite students into a brief period of silence.
   Pray aloud the following prayer:
   O God, may your gift of the sacraments to your Church bring us into your wonderful light. Amen.

Proclaim

1. Have a student read the **Know and Proclaim** chart.
   ✦ As you discuss the first row, review students' understanding of the Sacraments of Initiation.

   ✦ **How do we participate in the Church's mission?** (Possible answers: through the works of mercy; by proclaiming Jesus in all we say and do) **How do the Sacraments of Initiation prepare us for our role as disciples?** (They make us members of the Church and empower us with the Holy Spirit to become Christ for others.)

   ✦ As you discuss the second row, remind students that the sacraments also support us as disciples.

   ✦ **How do you show others that you are a disciple of Jesus'?** (Possible answers: by sharing my faith; by respecting myself and others; by participating in the Mass and

sacraments) **Who gives us the strength and guidance to share our beliefs?** (the Holy Spirit)

   ✦ [Discuss the third row.] **How can you help in the formation of new Catholics?** (Possible answers: by setting a good example in the way I pray and serve others.)

2. Point out the **Test Your Catholic Knowledge** section. Allow students time to fill in the circle of their choice before discussing the correct answer.

Gather and Go Forth

CHAPTER **8**

Know and Proclaim

Knowledge of our Catholic faith supports us as we proclaim our beliefs in what we say and do.

We Know Our Faith	We Proclaim Our Faith
The Sacraments of Initiation make a person a member of the Church, sharing in the mission of Christ.	Catholics rely on the Gifts of the Holy Spirit to carry out the mission of Christ. These gifts help Catholics live a moral life.
The Sacraments of Initiation are the foundation for life in the Catholic Church.	Newly baptized Catholics put on a white garment to show that they are a new creation in Christ, are anointed with chrism and sealed with the Holy Spirit at Confirmation, and nourished by the Body of Christ in the Eucharist.
The Rite of Christian Initiation of Adults (RCIA) is the process through which some people become full members of the Catholic Church.	Catholics participate as catechists and sponsors for the RCIA and pray for those entering the Church through the Sacraments of Initiation. The entire community participates in the formation of new Catholics.

Test Your Catholic Knowledge

Fill in the circle that best completes the sentence.

Baptism, Eucharist, and Confirmation are called the Sacraments of:

○ Penance and Reconciliation.

○ the Holy Spirit.

○ Holy Orders.

● Initiation.

Baptism and Confirmation CHAPTER 8 ⟨67⟩

Catholics encounter Christ in the sacraments. Through them, we praise God as his chosen people.

But you are "a chosen race, a royal priesthood, a holy nation, a people of his own, so that you may announce the praises" of him who called you out of darkness into his wonderful light.

1 Peter 2:9

🖥 **Special Needs** Explore ways to invite students with special needs to know God better at **www.loyolapress.com/special-needs**. **Goal 2:** To invite all people to hear the message of salvation in Jesus Christ **106.** To make every Catholic institution more welcoming

---

The Church Evangelizes Invite a member of a local chapter of the Knights of Columbus to explain to the class how he extends the presence of the Catholic Church in the community. **Goal 2:** To invite all people to hear the message of salvation in Jesus Christ **114.** To design programs that reach out to those who do not participate in a church community or who seek the fullness of faith

See pages T366–T368 for a full correlation to the USCCB *Go and Make Disciples* national plan.

3. Read aloud **A Catholic to Know.** Discuss the conversion of Saint Paul.

   ✦ Tell students that Saint Paul was a man of great faith, but he didn't always believe in Christ. His incredible story of conversion is an example of the power of the Holy Spirit at work.

   ✦ Invite students to read about Paul's conversion in Chapter 9 of the Acts of the Apostles.

   ✦ **Saint Paul, inspired by the Holy Spirit, acted as a witness for Christ as he wrote his epistles. He invites us to be witnesses too.**

   ✦ Share a conversion story about yourself or someone you know.

4. Read the **Witness and Share** introductory text.

   ✦ Explain that our way to faith lasts a lifetime. **Look at the faith statements and think about how you are growing in your understanding of yourself as a child of God.**

   ✦ Read aloud the faith statements. Allow time for reflection after each one.

   ✦ Ask students to share a faith statement with a trusted adult and discuss how they can grow in their faith. Encourage them to revisit this statement later in the year.

5. As students complete the **Share Your Faith** activity, remind them that God is present in both the ordinary and extraordinary events of our lives.
   Provide time for students to write their ideas. Invite them to share their encounters.

Transform _____

1. Ask students to think about how the sacraments influence the way they view the world.

   ✦ **What do the sacraments teach you about God's presence?** (Possible answers: God is very close; God cares for us and the world.)

A Catholic to Know

Saint Paul

Paul was a Jew who at first thought it was necessary to persecute Christians. On his way to Damascus, a blinding flash of light knocked him to the ground. Jesus spoke to him in an experience so powerful that Paul became one of Christ's most devoted disciples in an instant. As a convert, Paul became the "Apostle to the Gentiles," and he proved to be the right man to build a bridge between the Jews and Gentiles. Paul proclaimed Christ with a zealousness that profoundly influenced the first-century Church's understanding of discipleship in ways that continue to the present day. About half the epistles in the New Testament were written by Paul or attributed to him.

Witness and Share

These sentences describe what Catholics believe. Listen carefully as they are read. Ask yourself, "How strong are my Catholic beliefs?"

My Way to Faith _____

• I believe that Christ is present today in the sacraments.

• I receive support from the faith community as I follow Christ.

• I give thanks for being a member of the Church.

• I live as a child of God and an heir to heaven living the Ten Commandments.

• I give witness to Christ by being merciful and forgiving toward others.

• I read Saint Paul's letters to help me understand how to live a Christian life.

Share Your Faith

The sacraments of the Church are signs of God's presence, but there are many other ways to recognize God's presence. Think of everyday people, things, or events that reveal God's presence and write them on the lines. Invite a family member or friend to share the times when he or she has encountered God.

_____

_____

_____

_____

68 UNIT 1 *Jesus Christ the Way*

✦ **How are sacraments models for the way we should treat one another?** (Possible answers: I can be forgiving; I can help people heal; I can be thankful.)

2. Pray for strength to be a sacramental people.
   Pray aloud a prayer of Saint Teresa of Ávila: **"Christ has no body now but yours. No hands, no feet on earth but yours. . . . You are his Body."**

💻 **DRE Connect** Share ideas with an online community for faith formation leaders by accessing **dreconnect.loyolapress.com.**
Goal 2: To invite all people to hear the message of salvation in Jesus Christ **111.** To cultivate an active core of the baptized to serve as ministers of evangelization

The Church Evangelizes Ask students to share ways their families celebrate the sacraments together. Suggest that the class write an article for the parish bulletin about the importance of family faith sharing. **Goal 3:** To foster gospel values, promoting dignity of the human person, the importance of the family, and the common good **122.** To foster the importance of family

Inspire

1. Direct students' attention to the text in the sidebar on page 75.
   - ✦ Read the account of the Transfiguration of Jesus, Mark 9:2–8. **What does God ask of us?** (to listen to Jesus) **What does Jesus ask us to do?** (love God; love neighbor; pick up your cross) **What did Jesus come to proclaim?** (God's love)

2. Lead students in a guided reflection.
   - ✦ Begin with the following prayer: **Most glorious Lord, open our hearts to your Word.**
   - ✦ **Imagine you are sitting around a table with Jesus and the disciples, sharing a meal.** [Allow a moment or two for students to imagine themselves in the scene.]
   - ✦ **One of the disciples asks, "Master, where are you going? How can we know the way?"** [Allow a moment for students to reflect on these questions.]
   - ✦ Read the Scripture verse on page 75.
   - ✦ **Jesus is the way. Where does he take you?** [Pause for reflection.] **Jesus is the truth. Do you listen?** [Pause for reflection.] **Jesus is the life. How does he live in you?** [Pause for reflection.]
   - ✦ Pray aloud: **Lord Jesus Christ, you are our life. Amen.**

Proclaim

1. Ask a student to read aloud the **Know and Proclaim** chart.
   - ✦ [Discuss the first row.] **How do the saints you have learned about so far inspire you?** [Let students respond.] **The lives of the saints show us how we too can live our lives for Christ.**
   - ✦ [Discuss the second row.] **What are some ways we meditate on the mysteries of faith?** (Possible answers: the Rosary, reflecting on Scripture). **These are ways to respond to Jesus' friendship. What are some other ways you can respond to Jesus' friendship?** (doing chores; visiting the elderly; including others in activities)
   - ✦ [Discuss the third row.] **How does light symbolize the work of disciples?** (Possible answers: Jesus leads us from the darkness of sin into God's light. Disciples follow his example and lead others to God.)
   - ✦ **How do you bring light into the world?** [Let students respond.]

2. Remind students that the mission of the Church is their mission too.
   By the grace of Baptism, you are also part of the Body of Christ, and share in his mission to lead people to the Father.

3. Have students answer the **Test Your Catholic Knowledge** question at the bottom of the page.

Allow students time to fill in the circle of their choice before discussing the correct answer.

> **Arts & Faith** Celebrate how faith is expressed and deepened through art at **www.loyolapress.com/arts-faith**.
> **Goal 3:** To foster gospel values, promoting the dignity of the human person, the importance of the family, and the common good **124**. To encourage Catholic witness in the arts and in the American intellectual community

---

Gather and Go Forth

CHAPTER 9

Know and Proclaim

We seek to know and proclaim Jesus by knowing and understanding our Catholic faith.

We Know Our Faith	We Proclaim Our Faith
Jesus is the Son of God who became man to save us from sin and death.	Catholics celebrate the lives of saints who set an example for how to participate in the mission of Christ and his Church. Saints' feast days are celebrated during the Mass and the Liturgy of the Hours.
Catholics respond to Jesus' friendship through prayer, celebrating the sacraments, and reading Scripture.	*Lectio divina* ("sacred reading") is a way Catholics pray using Scripture. In *lectio divina*, Catholics meditate on the Word of God and the mysteries of Christ.
God became man in the Person of Jesus to invite ordinary people to share in his divinity.	As sharers in Christ's divinity, Catholics are called to bring light to the world. Catholics hold lighted taper candles at the Easter Vigil on Holy Saturday to symbolize our call to carry the light of Christ to the world.

Test Your Catholic Knowledge

Fill in the circle that best completes the sentence.

The Word became flesh in the event called the:

- ○ Passover.
- ● Incarnation.
- ○ Assumption.
- ○ Resurrection.

To know God, we must know and follow Jesus. As Catholics, we know Jesus through Sacred Scripture and Sacred Tradition. We meet Jesus in the sacraments and in one another.

Jesus said to him, "I am the way and the truth and the life. No one comes to the Father except through me."

John 14:6

Unit 1 Review CHAPTER 9 75

See pages T366–T368 for a full correlation to the USCCB *Go and Make Disciples* national plan.

4. Read aloud **A Catholic to Know** and discuss Saint Vincent de Paul.
   - ✦ Review with students the Spiritual and Corporal Works of Mercy on page 243.
   - ✦ **What works of mercy do you think Saint Vincent de Paul performed?** (Possible answers: feed the hungry; visit the sick)
   - ✦ **How does Saint Vincent de Paul inspire you to be more like Jesus?** (Allow time for discussion.)
   - ✦ Have students discuss a modern-day hero who helps those in need like Saint Vincent de Paul.

5. Read the **Witness and Share** introductory text.
   - ✦ Explain that, like Saint Vincent de Paul, one's faith journey often takes some unexpected twists and turns.
   - ✦ **Think about your understanding of discipleship today and consider how well you respond to Jesus' call of discipleship.**
   - ✦ Read aloud the faith statements. Allow time for reflection after each one.
   - ✦ Encourage students to select a faith statement to discuss further with a trusted adult. Encourage them to return to this statement later and see how they have grown in this area as disciples.

6. Read aloud the directions for the **Share Your Faith** activity. Remind students that witness takes many forms. **Actions often speak louder than words.** [Have students complete the activity.]

Transform _____

1. Ask students about charitable organizations in their community.
   - ✦ Point out that people often bring food to church for people in need.
   - ✦ **How can your support of charities like the Society of St. Vincent de Paul help people in need?** [Let students respond.]

2. Help students distinguish between charity and justice.
   - ✦ Clarify that charity deals with immediate needs, while justice attempts to address the root causes of a problem.
   - ✦ **As Catholics, we understand that charity is not enough; we need to work for justice.**

3. Lead students in a prayer inspired by the Society of St. Vincent de Paul:
   Lord Jesus, you who willed to become poor, give us eyes and a heart directed toward those who are poor; help us to recognize you in them—in their thirst, their hunger, their loneliness, and their misfortune. Amen.

A Catholic to Know

Vincent de Paul was born in 1580 in France. Vincent was appointed the court chaplain to Queen Margaret of Valois. For years, he lived a life of wealth and comfort. However, when he heard the confession of a dying servant, Vincent opened his eyes to the fact that the spiritual needs of the French peasantry were not being met. He devoted the remainder of his life to caring for those who were poor. He established societies and charities to perform the Spiritual and Corporal Works of Mercy by establishing hospitals, orphanages, and homes for those who were mentally ill. Saint Vincent de Paul is the patron of all charitable societies. Many parishes have a St. Vincent de Paul Society that serves those who are poor and in need.

Saint Vincent de Paul

Witness and Share

These sentences describe what Catholics believe. Listen carefully as they are read. Ask yourself, "How strong are my Catholic beliefs?"

My Way to Faith

- • I believe that Jesus brings me peace even when I am hurting.
- • I volunteer for tasks when I think I can be helpful.
- • I share my gifts with people who are in need.
- • I follow Jesus as my role model.
- • I admire people who follow in Christ's footsteps by sacrificing for others.

Share Your Faith

We follow in Christ's footsteps by proclaiming his message with our deeds. Consider the things you do. How do they proclaim your faith? Write about one deed on the lines. Invite others to share their faith with you.

_____

_____

_____

_____

76 UNIT 1 *Jesus Christ the Way*

💻 **Español** Invite Spanish-language speakers to access **www.loyolapress.com/espanol**. Goal 2: To invite all people to hear the message of salvation in Jesus Christ 115. To foster cultural diversity within the unity of the Church

---

The Church Evangelizes Send home a newsletter with suggestions, prayers, or activities that encourage meaningful reception of the Eucharist. If possible, include witness statements from people in the parish. **Goal 1:** To bring about enthusiasm for faith so it is freely shared with others 95. To foster an appreciation of the presence of Christ in the Eucharist and all the sacraments

Inspire

1. Read the text in the sidebar on page 85 with students.
   - ✦ **How does Jesus reveal God to us?** (by word and example) **How does Jesus use stories to teach the disciples?** (He speaks in a way people understand.)
   - ✦ **Jesus' parables help us understand the mysteries of God.**

2. Read the Scripture passage on page 85 with students and explore how God reveals the mysteries of faith.
   - ✦ **What is a mystery?** (Possible answer: something that cannot be explained or completely understood)
   - ✦ Explain that the mysteries of faith are things that cannot be fully understood but are revealed through the revelation of God's love.
   - ✦ **What are some mysteries of our faith?** (Possible answers: the Incarnation; the Resurrection, the Ascension)
   - ✦ **While words cannot fully explain the mystery of God, we do know God in the Person of Jesus Christ.**

3. Write a prayer on the board for students to read.
   - ✦ *Most high, glorious God, enlighten the darkness of my heart and give me true faith, certain hope and perfect charity, sense and knowledge, Lord, that I may carry out your holy and true command. Amen.*
   - ✦ Invite students to pray this prayer together. Begin and end the prayer with the Sign of the Cross. Explain that this was the prayer of Saint Francis of Assisi before the crucifix in the chapel of San Damiano.

Proclaim

1. Read and discuss the **Know and Proclaim** chart with students.
   - ✦ As you discuss the first row, remind student that learning the truth of Jesus Christ is a lifelong journey.
   - ✦ **How can we learn about Jesus?** (Possible answers: from Scripture,

---

Gather and Go Forth

CHAPTER 10

Know and Proclaim

Knowing our Catholic faith helps us know God's truth. We proclaim God's truth in what we say and do.

We Know Our Faith	We Proclaim Our Faith
Jesus is the Light of the World. His teachings are the truth that lights the way to God.	Catholic young people participate in youth leadership conferences and youth ministry events to better understand how God is calling them.
Jesus taught using parables. His teachings used familiar things to teach the truths about God.	Catholics pray with and meditate on sacred art that often depicts the parables of Jesus. Catholics apply the lessons of the parables to everyday life.
Jesus' teaching are known through Scripture, Tradition, and the teachings of the Church.	Catholics participate in Scripture study, whether in person or online, to come to know the teachings of Christ.

Test Your Catholic Knowledge

Fill in the circle that best answers the question.

What are all baptized Catholics responsible to do?

- ◯ pray the Rosary each Saturday
- ◯ attend daily Mass
- ◯ pray after meals
- ● evangelize others

Parables: Stories Jesus Told CHAPTER 10 **85**

Jesus revealed truths about God through parables. By applying Jesus' parables to our own lives, we will bring light to the world.

"Knowledge of the mysteries of the kingdom of God has been granted to you; but to the rest, they are made known through parables, so that 'they may look but not see, and hear but not understand.'"

Luke 8:10

Tradition; prayer; meditation) **What is the truth that Jesus taught us?** (Possible answers: God loves us and wants to be with us.)

- ✦ As you discuss the second row, remind students that as disciples, we proclaim Jesus' truth to the world.
- ✦ Remind students about the parable of the Good Shepherd and the Sower and the Seed.
- ✦ **What is your favorite parable? What do these parables teach you about God?** [Allow time for discussion.]
- ✦ Discuss the third row. Remind students that studying Scripture helps us know God better and understand what he wants for us.

2. Direct students' attention to the **Test Your Catholic Knowledge** question at the bottom of the page. Read the directions. Allow students time to fill in the circle of their choice before discussing the correct answer.

> 💻 **3-Minute Retreat** Invite deeper reflection on God's Word by accessing **www.loyolapress .com/retreat. Goal 1:** To bring about enthusiasm for faith so it is freely shared with others **97.** To foster a deeper sense of prayer

See pages T366–T368 for a full correlation to the USCCB *Go and Make Disciples* national plan.

3. Read aloud **A Catholic to Know.** Discuss what it means to be a martyr for faith.

- ✦ Tell students that some people have given their lives to follow Jesus.

- ✦ **Following Christ requires sacrifices. What sacrifices have you witnessed others make to follow Christ? What sacrifices have you had to make?** [Allow time for discussion.]

- ✦ Invite students to learn more about Saint Stephen by reading Acts of the Apostles 6:1—8:1.

- ✦ **Saint Stephen was a witness for Christ in the early Christian community and inspires our faithful witness.**

4. Read the **Witness and Share** introductory text.

- ✦ Explain that the Christian journey requires us to know Jesus and spend time with him.

- ✦ **Think about your life as a witness and truth seeker today.**

- ✦ Read aloud the faith statements, pausing to allow time for reflection.

- ✦ Ask students to choose one faith statement to discuss with a trusted adult.

- ✦ Ask students to record the faith statement they chose in a journal and look back at it from time to time to see how they've grown in their faith.

5. Have students complete the **Share Your Faith** activity. Ask volunteers to share their parables with the class.

Transform

1. Ask students to look on the inside front cover of their books and examine the Apostles' Creed for statements of faith. **How do you live the Apostles' Creed?** [Let students respond.] **What can you do to grow stronger in faith?** [Discuss ideas.]

2. Challenge students to think about the values of society.

- ✦ **If society had a creed, what would it be?** (Possible answers: the Bill of Rights; survival of the fittest;

life, liberty, and the pursuit of happiness)

- ✦ Have students point out the differences between society's creed and the Apostles' Creed.

- ✦ **What part of this "social creed" needs to be changed to help bring about God's kingdom?** (Possible answer: It has to put others first.)

3. Lead students in praying the Apostles' Creed.

A Catholic to Know

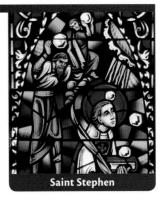

Saint Stephen

The story of Saint Stephen, deacon and martyr, is recounted in the Acts of the Apostles. (Acts 6:1—8:1) Chosen by the apostles as a man filled with faith and the Holy Spirit, Stephen became a deacon and assisted the Twelve. Stephen became known for working great wonders and signs among the people, prompting false accusations of blasphemy. During interrogation by the high priests, he proclaimed Christ and challenged their piety. Angered, they drove him from the city and stoned him to death. Saint Stephen died speaking words of forgiveness for his executioners. We honor his witness to Christ on December 26.

Witness and Share

These sentences describe what Catholics believe. Listen carefully as they are read. Ask yourself, "How strong are my Catholic beliefs?"

My Way to Faith

- I read the Gospels to learn more about Jesus' teachings.
- I look to the Church to learn the truth about Jesus.
- I believe that the invitation to the Kingdom of God is given to all people.
- I encourage my friends to do the right thing if they are tempted to act in ways contrary to the example of Jesus.
- I read about the lives of the saints to better understand what it means to be a disciple.

Share Your Faith

Think about Jesus' parables. Write your own parable on the lines below and continue it on a separate sheet of paper. What truth about God are you trying to share? What lesson are you trying to teach? Invite others to listen to your parable.

_____

_____

_____

_____

_____

86) UNIT 2 *Jesus Christ the Truth*

🖥️ **Sunday Connection**
Explore this Sunday's Scripture readings with students by accessing **www.loyolapress.com/sunday**.
Goal 1: To bring about an enthusiasm for faith so it is freely shared with others **96.** To foster an appreciation of the power of God's Word in our worship

The Church Evangelizes Show the class religious art in a variety of media. Help students understand the artist's message regarding his or her experience of God. Encourage students to express their faith in art using the medium of their choice.
Goal 3: To foster gospel values, promoting dignity of the human person, the importance of the family, and the common good **124.** To encourage Catholic witness in the arts and in the American intellectual community

Inspire

1. Read the text in the sidebar on page 93.
   - ◆ Ask students to describe some of Jesus' miracles.
   - ◆ **What do these miracles tell you about God's goodness?** [Allow time for discussion.]
   - ◆ Share your experiences of miracles with students. Ask them share their stories of miracles.
   - ◆ **As Catholics, we recognize God's presence and power in signs and miracles. We stand in wonder and awe at God's love.**

2. Invite students into the prayer center and lead a guided reflection.
   - ◆ Ask students to quiet their minds and bodies and put themselves in God's presence. Read the Scripture verse in the sidebar on page 93.
   - ◆ **Imagine you are in a small boat on a large lake, caught in the middle of a storm. The boat is about to sink.** [Pause for a moment. Then reread the Scripture verse.]
   - ◆ **In the storms of our lives, when we feel like we are being tossed among the waves, we trust that Jesus will calm the storm.** [Allow a few moments for reflection.]
   - ◆ Pray aloud: **O God, thank you for showing us your love through your many miracles. May we always trust in you. Amen.**

Proclaim

1. Read the **Know and Proclaim** introduction and discuss each row of the chart with students.
   - ◆ Discuss the first row and help students understand the role of faith in recognizing miracles.
   - ◆ **What are some natural wonders that remind you of God's presence?** [Let students respond.]
   - ◆ **What makes something a miracle?** (It can only be explained as a direct action of God.) **What does God reveal through his miracles?** (that he is the Lord)
   - ◆ [Discuss the second row.] **How does God work through us?** (By

sharing his love, compassion, and mercy.) **How can you reveal God through your actions?** (by performing works of mercy)

   - ◆ As you discuss the third row, remind students that we also learn about God's compassion and love from the miracles he worked through the saints.
   - ◆ **Awareness of God and faith in his power allow us to recognize God's miracles.**

2. Discuss Jesus' miracles.
   - ◆ **List five things Jesus had power over.** (nature, sin, sickness, Satan, death)
   - ◆ **In which miracle did Jesus show that he had power over nature?** (the calming of the sea) **Sin?** (healing the paralyzed man)

Sickness? (healing the centurion's slave) **Satan?** (casting out demons) **Death?** (raising Lazarus from the dead)

3. Point out the **Test Your Catholic Knowledge** section. Allow students time to complete the sentence before discussing the correct answer.

> 🖥 **3-Minute Retreat** Invite deeper reflection on God's Word by accessing **www.loyolapress .com/retreat. Goal 1:** To bring about enthusiasm for faith so it is freely shared with others **97.** To foster a deeper sense of prayer

---

Gather and Go Forth

CHAPTER **11**

Know and Proclaim

As Catholics, we recognize God's miracles in the large and small events of our lives, and we proclaim the miracle of our faith to others.

We Know Our Faith	We Proclaim Our Faith
A miracle is a sign or wonder that can only be explained as a direct action of God.	As Catholics, we see miracles as evidence of God's direct involvement in our everyday lives. We commonly pray for miracles and for the faith to recognize them.
Jesus' miracles reveal that he is the Holy One and more powerful than nature, sickness, sin, Satan, and death.	Catholics recognize that by performing works of mercy, others may come to recognize God's miraculous compassion and mercy in their lives.
Jesus' miracles reveal to us the presence of God's kingdom and teach us about the importance of faith.	By serving those in need, Catholics follow the examples of the saints, to whom many miracles are attributed. Miracles are a sign that God is present and active in people's lives.

Test Your Catholic Knowledge

Fill in the circle that best completes the sentence.

The miracle associated with Jesus that is most central to our Catholic faith is the:

- ○ calming of a storm at sea.
- ○ healing of a paralytic.
- ○ wedding at Cana.
- ● Resurrection.

Jesus' signs and miracles enabled others to witness the power of God, who sent him. In Jesus, the impossible becomes possible.

Then he asked them, "Where is your faith?" But they were filled with awe and amazed and said to one another, "Who then is this, who commands even the winds and the sea, and they obey him?"

Luke 8:25

Miracles: Signs Jesus Worked CHAPTER 11 ⓽③

See pages T366–T368 for a full correlation to the USCCB *Go and Make Disciples* national plan.

4. Read aloud **A Catholic to Know.** Discuss Saint André Bessette.

- ✦ Remind students that they can encourage people they know who are seriously or chronically ill to celebrate the Sacrament of the Anointing of the Sick.

- ✦ **The Church offers God's healing through the Sacrament of the Anointing of the Sick.**

- ✦ **How can you imitate Saint André's concern for those who are sick?** (Possible answers: I can pray for them; I can make get-well cards; I can encourage and visit them.)

- ✦ Remind students that God is the source of all miracles; we cannot take credit for them.

- ✦ **Although André Bessette was acclaimed widely as a worker of miracles, he humbly credited God and the intervention of Saint Joseph for the miraculous healings that were reported.**

5. Read the **Witness and Share** introductory text.

- ✦ Explain that our way to faith and witness requires that we constantly seek God's presence.

- ✦ **Think about how God is at work in your life and in the lives of those around you.**

- ✦ Read aloud each faith statement. Allow time for reflection.

- ✦ Remind students that we are always called to greater awareness of God's presence. Encourage them to ask God for the eyes to see him and people in need along their journey.

- ✦ Ask students to choose one faith statement to discuss with their parents, pastor, teacher, or another trusted adult. Encourage them to revisit this statement later in the year.

6. Read aloud the directions for the **Share Your Faith** activity.

- ✦ **How can you be a sign of God's presence in the lives of people you know?** (Possible answers: I can be kind; I can work for peace.)

- ✦ Have students complete the activity.

A Catholic to Know

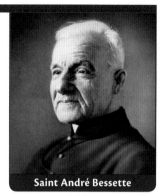

Saint André Bessette

"I am sending you a saint," read the message from André Bessette's pastor to the Holy Cross brothers in Montreal, Canada. They were not convinced that the illiterate young man in fragile health was suitable for their teaching order, and they asked him to leave. André appealed, however, and was assigned work as a porter in a school. Brother André became known for his unwavering devotion to Saint Joseph. He spent many hours praying for people who were sick, and they reported miraculous healings. Taking no credit for these cures, Brother André gave gratitude to Saint Joseph's intervention. Brother André died on January 6, 1937.

Witness and Share

These sentences describe what Catholics believe. Listen carefully as they are read. Ask yourself, "How strong are my Catholic beliefs?"

My Way to Faith

- I look for signs of God's active presence in my life.
- I spread Jesus' miraculous love to others by performing works of mercy.
- I honor the saints of the Catholic Church and imitate their witness.
- I help my friends overcome temptations and make good decisions.
- I can name some of Jesus' miracles, such as Jesus healing a blind man.
- I recognize Jesus' miracles as signs that he is the Son of God.

Share Your Faith

Consider how the Holy Spirit may be working miracles in your life. Write your ideas on the lines. Resolve to increase your awareness of God's presence, and invite a friend or family member to share with you the miracles of God in his or her life.

_____

_____

_____

_____

94 UNIT 2 *Jesus Christ the Truth*

Transform _____

1. Ask students to collect one story about individuals who experienced a miracle.

- ✦ Invite students to share the stories they collected.

- ✦ **What do these stories tell you about God's love?** [Allow time for discussion.]

2. Encourage students to help others recognize God's miracles by sharing God's love with others.

- ✦ Discuss places where people may not be aware of God's presence.

- ✦ **How can you bring awareness of God to those places?** [Allow time for discussion.]

3. Ask students to write a prayer of thanksgiving for the miracles in their lives.

The Church Evangelizes Send a letter home with students, encouraging their families to invite a relative or neighbor who may feel distanced from their Catholic faith to come to Mass or to an event at your Catholic school or parish. Recommend faith-sharing activities that they can all do, such as discussing the readings or explaining the liturgy. **Goal 2:** To invite all people to hear the message of salvation in Jesus Christ **113.** To design programs of outreach for those who have ceased being active in the Church

Inspire

1. Read the text and Scripture passage in the sidebar on page 101.

   ✦ **What is an ambassador?** (Possible answers: a representative; a messenger) **What does an ambassador do?** (represents one government, organization, or group to another) **What are the responsibilities of an ambassador?** (to build relationships between people or nations)

   ✦ **How would you describe what an ambassador for Christ is?** (one who represents Jesus) **What does an ambassador for Christ do?** (Possible answers: invites others to hear his message; build relationships between others and God) **When do we become ambassadors for Christ?** (at our Baptism)

2. Discuss how students can be ambassadors for Christ.

   ✦ **As an ambassador for Christ, you are called to help people build their relationships with Jesus and one another.**

   ✦ **How can you invite someone to hear the message of Jesus?** (Possible answers: by example; by following Jesus faithfully; by talking about him)

3. Invite students to gather in the prayer center.
   Pray aloud: **Lord, through our actions and words, may we be representatives of you and your Church. Amen.**

Proclaim

1. Read the **Know and Proclaim** introduction and chart with students.

   ✦ As you discuss the first row, emphasize that healing and reconciliation are necessary for our relationships with God and with one another.

   ✦ **From what kinds of illnesses do people require healing?** (physical, mental, spiritual) **What are examples of spiritual healing?** (Possible answers: giving comfort;

offering advice; offering and receiving forgiveness)

   ✦ [Discuss the second row.] **How does the Sacrament of Reconciliation heal us?** (It mends our broken relationship with God, with the Church, and with one another.)

   ✦ [Discuss the third row.] **How can you bring healing to others?** (Possible answers: by praying for people who are suffering; by visiting those who are sick or elderly; sending cards; by supporting people and organizations that provide care)

2. Review the works of mercy on page 243 of the student book.

   ✦ Remind students that performing the works of mercy is one way to be an ambassador for Christ.

   ✦ **Visiting those who are sick is a Corporal Work of Mercy. Comforting and consoling one another are examples of the Spiritual Works of Mercy.**

3. Point out the **Test Your Catholic Knowledge** section. Allow students time to select an answer choice before discussing the correct answer.

   🖥 **DRE Connect** Share ideas with an online community for faith formation leaders by accessing **dreconnect.loyolapress.com**.

   Goal 2: To invite all people to hear the message of salvation in Jesus Christ **109.** To equip active Catholic members to exercise their baptismal call to evangelize

---

Gather and Go Forth

CHAPTER 12

Know and Proclaim

God's compassion and mercy are present in our Catholic faith. We proclaim our faith by healing and comforting others.

We Know Our Faith	We Proclaim Our Faith
Christ's healing ministry continues today, especially in the Sacraments of Healing.	Catholics continue Jesus' healing ministry by operating hospitals. Catholic health care providers act in ways that respect and protect human dignity and serve the common good.
Contrition, confession, penance, and absolution must be present during the Sacrament of Reconciliation.	As Catholics, we admit our sorrow for having sinned when we pray the Act of Contrition during the Sacrament of Reconciliation. Then the priest offers absolution.
Through the Sacrament of the Anointing of the Sick, Jesus comforts and strengthens people who are seriously ill.	All Catholics are responsible for the care of those who are sick. Catholics who suffer from serious illness or the elderly in poor health celebrate the Sacrament of the Anointing of the Sick.

Test Your Catholic Knowledge

Fill in the circle that best completes the sentence.

The Anointing of the Sick is a Sacrament of Healing for those:

○ with any physical ailments.

● who are elderly or experiencing serious illness.

○ who don't attend Mass regularly.

○ who have celebrated the Sacrament of Reconciliation.

As ambassadors for Christ, Catholics unite themselves in friendship with God and with one another. We can follow Christ and be healers, too, by using kind words of forgiveness and understanding.

So we are ambassadors for Christ, as if God were appealing through us. We implore you on behalf of Christ, be reconciled to God.

2 Corinthians 5:20

Penance and Anointing of the Sick CHAPTER 12 **101**

See pages T366–T368 for a full correlation to the USCCB *Go and Make Disciples* national plan.

4. Read aloud **A Catholic to Know.** Discuss Saint Francis of Assisi.

♦ Read Matthew 25:31–46 aloud.

♦ **Think about this passage. How can you show that you follow this teaching of Jesus'?** (I practice the works of mercy.)

♦ **Saint Francis of Assisi was inspired by the Holy Spirit to witness for Christ. His example continues to inspire others to follow Jesus.** [Have students discuss a modern-day hero who inspires people to follow Christ like Saint Francis of Assisi.]

5. Read the **Witness and Share** introductory text.

♦ Explain that the saints accompany us on our lifelong journey of faith.

♦ **Look at each faith statement. Think about those areas where you require God's forgiveness and mercy.**

♦ Read aloud each faith statement. Pause after each one for reflection.

♦ **We always need healing and reconciliation—with God and with one another.**

♦ Encourage students to ask God for the grace to forgive and be forgiven.

♦ Ask students to choose a faith statement to discuss with a trusted adult. Encourage them to return to these statements later in the year to see how they have grown in faith.

6. Read aloud the directions for the **Share Your Faith** activity. Have students complete the activity and share their ideas.

Transform _____

1. Ask students to consider individuals in their community with physical disabilities.

♦ Share and discuss a newspaper article about a person with a disability who overcame an obstacle.

♦ **Imagine if you were in a similar situation. How would you want to be treated?** (Possible answers: with respect; with assistance) **How might you respond if you were in**

a **similar situation?** [Let students respond.]

♦ **Saint Francis said, "For what a man is before God, that he is and nothing more." What do you think this means?** (Possible answers: people are not defined by their disability; all people are loved by God.)

2. Ask students to write a prayer asking God for the grace to use their abilities to serve as an ambassador for Christ.

A Catholic to Know

Saint Francis of Assisi

Francis of Assisi (1182–1226) dreamed of becoming a knight. However, when he had a chance to become a soldier, he realized that his dreams of glory were not what he had expected. After experiencing hatred, fighting, and a yearlong imprisonment, he began to look for more meaning in life. One day, while praying in an old church, Francis heard a voice say, "Francis, go and repair my house which, as you can see, is falling into ruin." Francis gave up everything he had and went about rebuilding the church by hand. Eventually, Francis saw that he was not called to rebuild church buildings but the Church itself. He modeled his life after Jesus, and he spread the message of God's loving care to all creatures.

Witness and Share

These sentences describe what Catholics believe. Listen carefully as they are read. Ask yourself, "How strong are my Catholic beliefs?"

My Way to Faith

- I pray for people who are sick and suffering.
- I visit those who are sick and elderly, such as my grandparents.
- I thank God for my health and the health of others.
- I express sorrow for my sins when I pray the Act of Contrition.
- I recognize that my sins affect the whole community.
- I offer words of comfort to people who are hurting and suffering.

Share Your Faith

Consider how you are sorry for anyone you have hurt. On the lines below, write down some ways you can make up for those hurts. Invite family members or friends to discuss how they forgive others and seek forgiveness for themselves.

_____

_____

_____

_____

Special Needs Explore ways to invite students with special needs to know God better at **www.loyolapress.com/special-needs. Goal 2:** To invite all people to hear the message of salvation in Jesus Christ **106.** To make every Catholic institution more welcoming

---

The Church Evangelizes Invite someone who was a sponsor for a catechumen to speak to the class about the importance of sharing faith. Have the guest explain how serving as a sponsor helped him or her grow in faith. **Goal 1:** To bring about enthusiasm for faith so it is freely shared with others **92.** To foster an experience of conversion and renewal in every parish

Inspire

1. Discuss what it means for us to be created in the image of God.

   ✦ **What do you think of when you think of God?** (Possible answers: great; powerful; creative; kind)

   ✦ **How can we express those qualities?** (Possible answers: expressing ourselves and our faith; being kind to one another)

2. Read the text and Scripture passage in the sidebar on page 111.

   ✦ **Because we are created in God's image, we share in many of God's wonderful qualities, especially the ability to love.**

   ✦ Discuss with students ways they show God's quality of love.

   ✦ **We are called to love God and all of God's creation, including ourselves. We show respect for all people and never mock or bully others.**

3. Invite students into the prayer center and lead a prayer.
   Pray aloud: **O Lord, we praise you for your creation. We praise you for the sun and the moon. We praise you for the hills and mountains and for all the beasts of the earth, sky, and sea. We praise you, Lord, for all the people of the world. Amen.**

Proclaim

1. Read the **Know and Proclaim** introduction and discuss each row of the chart with students.

   ✦ Discuss the first row. Remind students that Catholics respect life because life is a gift from God.

   ✦ **How do Catholics demonstrate respect for life?** (by preserving and caring for life in all forms)

   ✦ As you discuss the second row, remind students that the Fifth Commandment involves more than taking human life.

   ✦ **Think about your words, what you say to other people and what you say about them. How do your words respect their dignity?** (Possible answers: I do not gossip by what I say or how I use social media;

I do not say or write hurtful things about them.)

   ✦ **Because we love God, we love our neighbors as ourselves.**

   ✦ Discuss the third row.

   ✦ **Love for God requires us to love all that he created, without exception or condition.**

   ✦ **How can you show respect for all life?** (Possible answers: by taking care of my health; controlling my anger; respecting the elderly)

2. Point out the **Test Your Catholic Knowledge** section. Discuss the correct answer after students have completed the sentence.

🖥 Sunday Connection
Explore this Sunday's Scripture readings with students by accessing **www.loyolapress.com.sunday**. **Goal 1:** To bring about enthusiasm for faith so it is freely shared with others **93.** To foster an appreciation of God's Word

---

The Church Evangelizes Help students appreciate the richness of Catholic life by taking them on a church tour. Explain the features of the church's architecture, such as the narthex, the ambo, the baptismal font, and the altar. The tour could also include a history of the parish. **Goal 2:** To invite all people to hear the message of salvation in Jesus Christ **114.** To design programs that reach out to those who do not participate in a church community or who seek the fullness of faith

See pages T366–T368 for a full correlation to the USCCB *Go and Make Disciples* national plan.

NEW EVANGELIZATION

Gather and Go Forth

CHAPTER **13**

Know and Proclaim

Knowing our Catholic faith helps us love as Jesus did. We proclaim Jesus in what we say and do.

We Know Our Faith	We Proclaim Our Faith
In the Sermon on the Mount, Jesus taught that at the heart of God's Law is the call for us to live with one another in love.	As Catholics, we show our love for our neighbors by advocating for laws and policies that respect and promote human dignity.
The Fifth Commandment is "You shall not kill." Jesus wants us to live and care for both the physical and spiritual life.	As Catholics, we help our neighbors meet their emotional and spiritual needs by participating in the Spiritual Works of Mercy.
To love as Jesus loved means cherishing the gift of life. Every person is a child of God made in God's image.	As Catholics, we demonstrate our love for life by calling for legislation and policies that respect all human life beginning at conception and ending with natural death.

Test Your Catholic Knowledge

Fill in the circle that best completes the sentence.

Jesus revealed that we will be judged by:

○ where we live.

● how well we have loved others.

○ our obedience to the letter of the law.

○ how much money we donate to charity.

God breathed into us the breath of life, which fills us with his love. In loving as Jesus loved, we encounter God. Christian love nurtures life at all times.

God created mankind in his image;
in the image of God he created them;
male and female he created them.

Genesis 1:27

The Message of Jesus: Choose Life CHAPTER 13 (111)

3. Read aloud **A Catholic to Know.** Discuss Saint Julie Billiart.
- ✦ Share a time in your life when you experienced joy and happiness in the face of adversity.
- ✦ **Saint Julie knew that God is always good, even though life may be hard sometimes.**
- ✦ Ask students to list times that they find boring or challenging, such as doing schoolwork or chores or when they are sick.
- ✦ **How can you experience God's goodness during these moments?** (Possible answer: by giving me people in these moments who help and comfort me.)
- ✦ **Saint Julie, inspired by the Holy Spirit, did not let sickness prevent her from witnessing Christ.**

4. Read the **Witness and Share** introductory text.
- ✦ Explain that the paths we take in life depend on the choices we make. Our choices must respect life.
- ✦ **Look at the faith statements. You proclaim Jesus by what you say and do.**
- ✦ Read aloud each faith statement. Allow time for reflection after each one.
- ✦ Ask students to choose one faith statement to discuss with a trusted adult. Encourage them to write it in their journal and look back at it from time to time to see how they have grown in their faith.

5. Read aloud the directions for the **Share Your Faith** activity. Let students work in small groups to complete the activity. Invite each group to share its ideas.

Transform _____

1. Ask students to consider how prejudices are incompatible with respect for life.
How can you treat people with respect, regardless of age, race, or gender? [Discuss ideas.]

A Catholic to Know

Saint Julie Billiart (1751–1816) began teaching children about God in her hometown of Picardy, France, at age seven. When she was 14, she vowed herself to chastity and performing works of mercy. Even though a mysterious illness left her paralyzed for over 20 years, Julie still lived a full life dedicated to others. Julie founded the Sisters of Notre Dame to care for orphans, educate girls from families who lived in poverty, and train Christian teachers. Julie had learned during her years of pain and sickness that "God is good." Saint Julie is called the "Smiling Saint" whose motto was "How good the good God is."

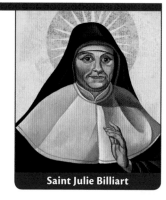

Saint Julie Billiart

Witness and Share

These sentences describe what Catholics believe. Listen carefully as they are read. Ask yourself, "How strong are my Catholic beliefs?"

My Way to Faith

- I live according to Jesus' Great Commandment to love God and to love my neighbor as myself.
- I view all human life, beginning with the unborn, as a gift from God to be cherished and protected.
- I avoid saying bad things about other people.
- I make sure that my anger does not hurt others.
- I take a stand against any form of discrimination.

Share Your Faith

How do you demonstrate the value and dignity of human life? Write your ideas on the lines. Invite family members and friends to talk with you about how the choices they make respect life.

_____

_____

_____

_____

(112) UNIT 2 *Jesus Christ the Truth*

---

2. Challenge students to identify laws, policies, and customs that respect life.
- ✦ **What can you do to help others respect life?** [Let students respond.]
- ✦ **How does respecting all life help bring about God's kingdom here on earth?** [Let students respond.]

3. Lead students in a prayer for life.
Pray aloud: **Father in heaven, take root in our land so that we all may** **embrace your infinite love and light. Amen.**

Arts & Faith Celebrate how faith is expressed and deepened through art at **www.loyolapress.com/arts-faith**. **Goal 3:** To foster gospel values, promoting the dignity of the human person, the importance of the family, and the common good **124.** To encourage Catholic witness in the arts and in the American intellectual community

The Church Evangelizes Teach the themes of Catholic Social Teaching by hosting a "write for rights" event in class. Have students write letters to local, state, and national leaders, encouraging work for social justice. **Goal 3:** To foster gospel values, promoting dignity of the human person, the importance of the family, and the common good **125.** To involve every Catholic in areas of public policy

Inspire

1. Ask students to identify the challenges they face.
   - ✦ **What are some of the challenges in your life?** (Possible answers: relationships with family; a class at school; sports) **How do you overcome them?** (Possible answers: I discuss issues with my family; I ask for help from a teacher or coach.) **What might it cost to overcome these challenges?** (Possible answer: To do well in school, I may have to spend less time with my friends.)
   - ✦ Sometimes we face challenges in being disciples of Jesus'. But we can count on God's love to overcome them.

2. Read aloud the text and Scripture in the sidebar on page 119.
   - ✦ **What does it mean to be persecuted?** (to be harassed, bullied, or mistreated) **In what ways was Jesus persecuted?** (He was taunted, arrested, and crucified.)
   - ✦ Jesus experienced many of the challenges we do and more. His love and understanding gives us strength.

3. Have students gather around a flameless candle in the prayer center.
   Pray aloud: **Lord, in times of darkness, your light always leads me down a path of hope. Jesus, forever be my light. Amen.**

Proclaim

1. Read and discuss the **Know and Proclaim** chart.
   - ✦ [Discuss the first row.] **We proclaim the Gospel by living the Beatitudes. Centering our lives on God is what disciples are called to do.**
   - ✦ **Think about things you have that are important to you. When can holding on to those things hurt you or others?** [Allow time for student to respond.]
   - ✦ Discuss the second row. Remind students that practicing charity

makes us more like Christ who always thought of the poor.
   - ✦ Discuss the third row. Encourage students to pray the Morning Offering (this prayer can be found on page T445.)

2. Read Matthew 5:3 on page 114 and explain what it means to be "poor in spirit."
   People who are poor in spirit depend totally on God and turn to God for their needs. Why do the poor in spirit inherit the kingdom of heaven? (By depending on and turning

to God, they make his kingdom present in the world.)

3. Have students answer the **Test Your Catholic Knowledge** question.

> 💻 **3-Minute Retreat** Invite deeper reflection on God's Word by accessing **www.loyolapress.com/retreat**. **Goal 1:** To bring about enthusiasm for faith so it is freely shared with others **93**. To foster an appreciation of God's Word

> *The Church Evangelizes* Invite a guest to speak to the class about ways he or she lives the Catholic faith in the workplace. Encourage students to discuss practical ways of living the faith in the workplace with adults in their family. **Goal 1:** To bring about enthusiasm for faith so it is freely shared with others **102**. To promote and develop a spirituality for the workplace

See pages T366–T368 for a full correlation to the USCCB *Go and Make Disciples* national plan.

Gather and Go Forth

CHAPTER 14

Know and Proclaim

We live the truths of our Catholic faith, and we proclaim that faith in the way we love one another.

We Know Our Faith	We Proclaim Our Faith
The Beatitudes are guidelines for discipleship that bring happiness and lead to eternal life.	As Catholics, we are called to be poor in spirit. We are not ruled by a desire for material goods and depend totally on God.
Jesus, as the Son of God, teaches us all we need to know about the Father's will for us. Through Christ, in the Holy Spirit, we approach the Father with all our needs.	Catholics practice solidarity with those who are poor by seeking justice and practicing charity.
Being pure of heart means having God as the center of your life. To be pure of heart, all your thoughts, actions, and decisions are centered on God.	Catholics pray the Morning Offering to center their lives in God. This prayer of self-giving reflects an openness to God's love and offers the day to God.

Test Your Catholic Knowledge

Fill in the circle that best answers the question.

In the Sermon on the Mount, Jesus taught about the meaning of true happiness. What are these teachings called?

- ○ the Ten Commandments
- ○ the Golden Rule
- ● the Beatitudes
- ○ the New Law

The Challenge of the Beatitudes CHAPTER 14   (119)

Following Jesus can sometimes be a great challenge and may come at a cost, but Jesus promises us his constant presence.

What will separate us from the love of Christ? Will anguish, or distress, or persecution, or famine, or nakedness, or peril, or the sword? No, in all these things we conquer overwhelmingly through him who loved us.

Romans 8:35,37

4. Read aloud **A Catholic to Know.** Discuss Saint Anthony Claret.

+ **Anthony Claret dreamed of being a missionary. He founded a congregation called the Missionary Sons of the Immaculate Heart of Mary, or the Claretians.**

+ Distribute copies of a prayer to the Immaculate Heart of Mary.

+ **What does this prayer tell you about being a disciple? What desires does it express? What are some things the prayer asks for?** [Allow time for discussion.]

+ Explain that Anthony founded a religious publishing house. Discuss ways of spreading Catholic literature.

5. Read the **Witness and Share** introductory text.

+ Explain that as people grow and change, the paths they take in faith will twist and turn, but God makes those paths straight.

+ **Look at the faith statements. Examine how your daily habits and practices put God at the center of your life.**

+ Read aloud the faith statements, pausing after each one to allow time for reflection.

+ Ask students to choose one faith statement and discuss it with a trusted adult.

+ Encourage students to write this statement in their journal and return to it from time to time to see how they've grown in their faith.

6. Read aloud the directions for the **Share Your Faith** activity. Allow time for students to complete the activity.

Transform _____

1. Ask students to share the Beatitudes.

+ **How can you share the message of the Beatitudes among your friends, your school, and your neighborhood?** [Let students respond.]

A Catholic to Know

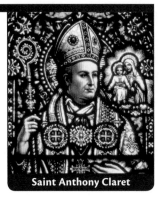

Born in Catalonia, Spain, in 1807, Anthony was the 5th of 11 children. He became a priest, eventually becoming archbishop of Santiago, Cuba, in 1850. At the time, the political climate in Cuba was unstable. It had not had an archbishop for 14 years. Being bishop of Santiago did not provide ideal conditions for preaching the Cross of Christ. Anthony tried to renew the priests in their vocations. He gave them an example by preaching in all the churches and spending hours hearing confessions. He made political enemies by working for updated farm methods and educating slaves. Once he was stabbed, yet when his attacker was sentenced to death, Anthony pleaded for him and obtained a prison sentence instead.

Saint Anthony Claret

Witness and Share

These sentences describe what Catholics believe. Listen carefully as they are read. Ask yourself, "How strong are my Catholic beliefs?"

My Way to Faith

• I follow Jesus' teachings in the Beatitudes.

• I am moved to action when I see other people suffering.

• I place God at the center of my life.

• I live a just life.

• I use self-control and respectful behavior when people try to insult me.

• I depend on and turn to God for all my needs.

Share Your Faith

What do the Beatitudes mean to you? Choose one and rewrite it using your own words, saying how you can live it. Invite family members and friends to share their ideas on what the Beatitudes mean to them.

_____

_____

_____

_____

120 UNIT 2 *Jesus Christ the Truth*

+ Encourage students to explore the use of technology as a means to share the Gospel message.

2. Challenge students to live the Beatitudes by practicing acts of kindness.

+ **How might helping others help you grow in your relationship with God?** (Possible answer: I gain compassion.)

+ **How can the example of your life make a difference?** [Discuss ideas.]

3. Lead a prayer to the Holy Spirit. Pray aloud: **Lord, may your Holy Spirit be a lamp to our feet. By your light may we journey safely and surely to the Kingdom of Heaven. Amen.**

Español Invite Spanish-language speakers to access **www.loyolapress.com/espanol**. Goal 2: To invite all people to hear the message of salvation in Jesus Christ **106**. To make every Catholic institution more welcoming

The Church Evangelizes Ask students to find information about service groups in the parish or local community and the work they do. Send home a class newsletter and recommend that students and their families consider participating in a service event with one of these groups. **Goal 3:** To foster gospel values, promoting dignity of the human person, the importance of the family, and the common good **121**. To involve parishes and local service groups in the needs of their neighborhood

Inspire

1. Discuss the importance of honesty.
   - ✦ **Why is honesty important in relationships? How can dishonesty damage a relationship?** [Discuss ideas.]
   - ✦ Remind students that honesty in our relationship with God is extremely important.
   - ✦ **Is it possible to be dishonest with God? Why or why not?** [Let students respond.] **God knows everything about us. He knows our thoughts, our fears, our hopes, and our dreams. We cannot be dishonest with God, but we can be dishonest with ourselves in God's presence.**

2. Read aloud the text and Scripture in the sidebar on page 127.
   - ✦ Explain that God expects us to live in justice and truth.
   - ✦ **Jesus Christ is the Way, the Truth, and the Life. When we act in truth and with justice, we will know God's love.**

3. Invite students into the prayer center and ask them to examine their day prayerfully.
   - ✦ **Invite the Holy Spirit to lead you as you review the events of your day. Were there times when you strayed from the truth? Were there times when you needed God's strength to live in his truth?**
   - ✦ Allow a few moments for silent prayer. Conclude by praying the Sign of the Cross.

Proclaim

1. Read and discuss the **Know and Proclaim** chart.
   - ✦ Discuss the first row. Remind students that social justice comes from the dignity all people have by being created in God's image. All people have equal rights.
   - ✦ [Discuss the second row.] **Why does work have dignity?** (Possible answers: It imitates God's work in creation; it allows people to pay for

---

Gather and Go Forth

CHAPTER 15

Know and Proclaim

Catholics are people of integrity. We live in truth and justice and act to share our faith and the truth it proclaims.

We Know Our Faith	We Proclaim Our Faith
All members of the Church are called to serve God's kingdom, build a just world, and act on the behalf of justice.	As Catholics, we consider working for social justice to be an important part of our baptismal call. We work to make sure all people have a just share of the earth's resources.
Followers of Christ are called to transform situations and institutions that harm people and are opposed to God's will.	Catholics support efforts to respect the right of workers to a fair wage and safe and humane working conditions. To support workers, Catholics encourage employers to treat their employees with respect and justice.
The Eighth Commandment calls us to live in truth.	Catholic media seeks to report the news in truth and without bias.

Test Your Catholic Knowledge

Fill in the circle that best answers the question.

What is Catholic Social Teaching?

- ○ the Church's laws that govern how parishes operate
- ● the Church's body of teaching on social-justice issues
- ○ the Church's body of teaching on faith and morals
- ○ the Church's laws that govern religious orders

As disciples, we show our love and respect for one another by living in justice and truth. We choose to walk in the way of justice as members of God's kingdom of peace.

"Let your 'Yes' mean 'Yes,' and your 'No' mean 'No.' Anything more is from the evil one."

Matthew 5:37

Jesus' Kingdom of Justice and Truth CHAPTER 15 (127)

---

the things they need to live.) **How can you support the dignity of work and workers?** (Possible answer: I can thank people for their work; I can be polite to workers.)

- ✦ [Discuss the third row.] **How does speaking honestly help us in proclaiming our faith?** (Possible answer: If we are honest, people can trust that the message we share is true.)

2. Clarify that justice is a virtue.
   - ✦ **What do you think of when you think of justice?** (Possible answers: fairness; impartiality; laws)
   - ✦ **Justice is a virtue. When we act with justice, we give God and people what is rightfully theirs**
   - ✦ **How do you show justice to God?** (by obeying his commandments)

How do you show justice to other people? (Possible answers: by respecting their dignity; by promoting the common good)

3. Read the directions to the **Test Your Catholic Knowledge** question.
   Allow students enough time to answer the question.

> 💻 **DRE Connect** Share ideas with an online community for faith formation leaders by accessing **dreconnect.loyolapress.com**.
> **Goal 1:** To bring about enthusiasm for faith so it is freely shared with others **98.** To foster a renewed understanding of the faith among Catholics

---

See pages T366–T368 for a full correlation to the USCCB *Go and Make Disciples* national plan.

4. Read aloud **A Catholic to Know.** Discuss Saint John of Capistrano.

- ✦ **John did not let his advanced years in age or his illness stop him from helping others.**

- ✦ Explain to students that as governor, John ended political corruption and fought crime.

- ✦ **John of Capistrano sought justice both as an attorney and as a priest. We witness for Jesus when we seek justice.**

- ✦ Have students recommend a service project they could do in their school or neighborhood that would show they are trying to build a Christlike spirit like Saint John of Capistrano.

5. Read the **Witness and Share** introductory text.

- ✦ Encourage students to think about their witness to truth.

- ✦ Read aloud each faith statement, allowing time for reflection.

- ✦ Remind students that we are always called to seek justice. Encourage them to ask God for the grace to grow as witnesses to Jesus Christ the Truth.

- ✦ Ask students to choose a faith statement as an area for personal and spiritual growth. Encourage them to discuss it further with a trusted adult.

- ✦ Remind students to return to this page later in the year and reflect on the faith statements again.

6. Read aloud the directions for the **Share Your Faith** activity.

- ✦ Remind students that dishonesty is incompatible with their lives as young Christian men and women.

- ✦ Have students complete the activity.

Transform _____

1. Ask students to consider careers that involve working for justice in society.

- ✦ **What careers exist in the justice system?** (Possible answers: police officer; lawyer; judge) **Is it necessary to work in the justice system to work for justice?** [Allow time for discussion.]

A Catholic to Know

Saint John of Capistrano

Saint John of Capistrano (1386–1456) was called the "soldier saint." He began his adult life as an attorney in Naples, Italy, when the king appointed him governor of Perugia. During a war between Perugia and a neighboring town, he was betrayed and imprisoned. During his stay in prison, John realized he could serve God more directly. He became a priest and established Franciscan communities of renewal throughout Europe with the zeal that helped him drive out crime as a governor. At age 70, Pope Pius II asked John to help lead the resistance against the invading Ottoman Empire. Aided by John's preaching and enthusiasm, the Hungarian general John Hunyadi led 70,000 soldiers in defeating the Turkish attack.

Witness and Share

These sentences describe what Catholics believe. Listen carefully as they are read. Ask yourself, "How strong are my Catholic beliefs?"

My Way to Faith

- I help build a more just world by respecting the property of others.
- I support the rights of workers and the dignity of work.
- I thank people for their work.
- I tell the truth, even if it will get me or my friends in trouble.
- I can be trusted with things that people tell me in confidence.
- I am happy for other people when good things happen to them.

Share Your Faith

Consider ways in which you can practice honesty in your relationships with God and with others. Write your ideas on the lines. Invite a friend or family member to discuss the value of honesty in his or her family and community.

_____

_____

_____

_____

(128) UNIT 2 *Jesus Christ the Truth*

- ✦ Write the following quote from Pope Paul VI on the board: "If you want peace, work for justice." Ask students how peace and justice are related.

- ✦ **How can seeking justice for all people bring about peace?** [Discuss ideas.]

2. Challenge students to find role models who work for peace and social justice.

- ✦ Ask students to share their research.

- ✦ **How does their witness inspire you to work for justice?**

3. Ask students to write prayers for people who suffer from injustice and violence.

> 💻 **Daily Inspiration** Find insightful meditations on Scripture at **www.loyolapress.com/ daily**. **Goal 1:** To bring about enthusiasm for faith so it is freely shared with others **93.** To foster an appreciation of God's Word

The Church Evangelizes Explain the Church's teaching on the dignity of work and the rights of workers. Share with students recent news articles that highlight how Catholics work to protect the dignity of work and the rights of workers. Include a discussion of Saint Joseph, the patron saint of workers. **Goal 3:** To foster gospel values, promoting dignity of the human person, the importance of the family, and the common good **123.** To develop groups to explore issues of the workplace and lay spirituality

Inspire

1. Discuss with students how they show love.

   ✦ **Think about someone you love. How does that person make you feel?** (Possible answers: safe; important; happy) **How do we show someone we love him or her?** (Possible answers: by showing respect; putting him or her first; sharing with him or her)

   ✦ **What does the word *sincere* mean?** (honest, genuine, true) **Why is it important for love to be sincere?** (Love has to be honest to have lasting meaning.)

   ✦ **How do the Sixth and Ninth Commandments safeguard the gift of love?** (They help us protect love by safeguarding the gift of sex.)

2. Read aloud the text and Scripture in the sidebar on page 135.
   We need to live our lives in ways that honor God. [Explain that, as Catholics, we want God to be the center of our lives.]

3. Invite students into the prayer center and read 1 Corinthians 13:4–7.

   ✦ Read the passage slowly. Allow time for students to reflect on the passage.

   ✦ **Pick a word or phrase that has meaning for you. What is God trying to tell you?** [Allow time for reflection.]

   ✦ Pray aloud: **O Lord, your love never fails. Give us the grace to love you and our neighbors as ourselves. Amen.**

Proclaim

1. Read aloud the **Know and Proclaim** introduction. Have volunteers read the chart.

   ✦ [Discuss the first row.] **How do your acts of love for your family, friends, and neighbors communicate Jesus' love?** (By loving one another, we show our love for Jesus and he shares in our love.)

   ✦ [Discuss the second row.] **What are signs of healthy relationships?** (Possible answers: trust; respect; concern for one another; mutual sharing) **What are signs of unhealthy relationships?** (Possible answers: lack of trust or respect; tension; isolation)

   ✦ [Discuss the third row.] **By acting in a way that shows that you respect yourself, you show respect to others.** [Encourage students to practice modesty and restraint.]

2. Remind students that the Sacrament of Matrimony is a sacred sign of God's love.
   Respecting yourself, developing healthy relationships, and growing in relationship with God will prepare men and women to be loving and committed marriage partners in the future.

3. Direct student's attention to the **Test Your Catholic Knowledge** question.
   Allow students time to fill in the circle of their choice before discussing the correct answer.

   🖥 **Arts & Faith** Celebrate how faith is expressed and deepened through art at **www.loyolapress.com/arts-faith**.
   Goal 3: To foster gospel values, promoting dignity of the human person, the importance of family, and the common good **124.** To encourage Catholic witness in the arts and in the American intellectual community

---

Gather and Go Forth

CHAPTER 16

Know and Proclaim

Knowing the truths of our Catholic faith enables us to proclaim our beliefs in loving relationships.

We Know Our Faith	We Proclaim Our Faith
Marriage is the lifelong commitment between a man and a woman. God blesses their union through the Sacrament of Matrimony.	Going to Mass helps married Catholics imitate Jesus' selfless love.
Sex is a gift from God that allows a husband and wife to deepen their love for each other and to participate in God's creation of life.	Young Catholics prepare for marriage by developing healthy relationships and by practicing acts of love, such as helping their neighbors, spending time with their families, and forgiving others.
The Sixth and Ninth Commandments help people safeguard the sacred gift of sex.	Catholics practice modesty by enjoying entertainment that shows restraint and respect for the dignity of other people.

Test Your Catholic Knowledge

Fill in the circle that best answers the question.

Which virtue grows out of following the Sixth and Ninth Commandments?

○ prudence
○ courage
● chastity
○ justice

God is love. We are made to love one another and to love God. To love perfectly as God loves, we must be pure in our words, thoughts, and actions.

Let love be sincere; hate what is evil, hold on to what is good; love one another with mutual affection; anticipate one another in showing honor.
Romans 12:9–10

Jesus' Kingdom of Love CHAPTER 16 (135)

See pages T366–T368 for a full correlation to the USCCB *Go and Make Disciples* national plan.

4. Read aloud **A Catholic to Know.** Discuss Saint Agnes.

- ✦ Discuss the picture of Saint Agnes that accompanies the text.

- ✦ **Saint Agnes is often pictured with a lamb sitting at her feet. What does this tell you about her?** (Possible answers: She was like Christ in suffering death for her faith; she was a faithful member of the flock.)

- ✦ Discuss pictures of other saints of other saints and what they mean. For example, Saint Francis of Assisi is often pictured with animals because he preached the Word of God to every creature.

- ✦ **Saint Agnes, inspired by the Holy Spirit, chose Christ. Whatever our circumstances, we can choose Jesus too.**

5. Read the **Witness and Share** introductory text.

- ✦ Explain that the Holy Spirit guides us on our faith journey.

- ✦ Read aloud each faith statement. Allow time for reflection after each one.

- ✦ Ask students to choose a faith statement to discuss with a trusted adult. Encourage them to ask questions about relationships and marriage as they grow in understanding of God's plan for their lives.

- ✦ **Come back to this page later in the year and reflect on these statements again.**

6. Have students complete the **Share Your Faith** activity. Help students understand that their entertainment choices impact their understanding of healthy relationships.

Transform _____

1. Discuss the responsibilities of loving one person for life. **What are some of the things married love includes?** (Possible answers: sharing; treasuring another person as he or she is; being faithful; trust; forgiveness; unselfishness; honesty; compassion; understanding)

A Catholic to Know

Saint Agnes

Agnes was a beautiful child who lived in Rome in the 200s. She lived during the reign of Emperor Diocletian, and his widespread persecution of Christians put everyone at risk. At only 12 years old, Agnes already had a deep faith in God. When her persecutors attempted to force her to worship at the pagan altars, she fearlessly refused. Since she had dedicated her life to God, she resisted offers to marry. Agnes showed unusual valor and inner strength. She prayed as she was threatened with punishment and cruel treatment. Finally, her persecutors ran out of patience and executed Agnes. Because the power of her faith was greater than the cruelty she suffered, Saint Ambrose, the bishop of Milan, honored her death as "a new kind of martyrdom."

Witness and Share

These sentences describe what Catholics believe. Listen carefully as they are read. Ask yourself, "How strong are my Catholic beliefs?"

My Way to Faith

- I believe that Christ raised Matrimony to the dignity of a sacrament in which a baptized man and a baptized woman make a lifelong commitment of love to one another.

- I will reserve sex for marriage because it is a gift from God.

- I look to Christ as a model for living a chaste life.

- I sacrifice my time to help others in need.

- I limit my enjoyment of entertainment to those forms that are respectful of other people.

Share Your Faith

Consider what you read, the music you listen to, and what you watch on TV. Do these forms of entertainment respect others and reflect healthy relationships? Write examples of entertainment that respect God's plan. Invite a friend to share ideas for your list.

_____

_____

_____

_____

---

2. Remind students about the importance of chastity.

- ✦ **How can you develop the virtue of chastity?** (by being pure in thoughts, words, and actions.)

- ✦ **Chastity places us in right relationship with God and one another.** [Discuss ways students can live a chaste life by dressing modestly, exercising self-control, and being kind.]

3. Pray for guidance and strength to live the Catholic faith.

Pray aloud: **Lord, may your light help us value what is right and good in your sight. Amen.**

Special Needs Explore ways to invite students with special needs to know God better at **www.loyolapress.com/special-needs**. Goal 3: To foster gospel values, promoting dignity of the human person, the importance of the family, and the common good **126.** To involve the Catholic Church in the media

The Church Evangelizes Invite a married couple to talk to the class about how they bear witness to Christ's love in their marriage. **Goal 3:** To foster gospel values, promoting dignity of the human person, the importance of family, and the common good **122.** To foster the importance of the family

Inspire

1. Discuss with students their understanding of truth.

- ✦ **What is truth?** (Possible answers: that which is real or genuine; fact or reality; accuracy; fidelity) **Why is truth important?** (Possible answers: to distinguish from fantasy or lies; to know whom or what to trust; to build honest relationships)

- ✦ Discuss the value students place on honesty.

- ✦ **What can be a consequence of dishonesty within a family?** (Possible answers: Family members don't help one another; they fight a lot.) **In society?** (Possible answers: People fight; they do not resolve their differences; injustice occurs; they don't know who to trust.)

- ✦ **Jesus calls us to be seekers of truth and to conduct all our relationships with honesty and integrity.**

2. Read the text and Scripture in the sidebar on page 143.

- ✦ **We believe that Jesus is the Way, the Truth, and the Life. To be faithful to Jesus, we have to be true to what the Church teaches about him.**

- ✦ Discuss ways students can develop an honest relationship with Jesus through prayer and study.

- ✦ **In Jesus there are no lies or falsehoods. A relationship with Jesus is real, genuine, and honest. He is faithful to us and asks for our fidelity in return.**

3. Lead students in a prayerful review of their day.
Ask student to reflect on their actions and words throughout the day. Have them say a silent prayer asking for the strength and wisdom to grow closer to Christ.

Proclaim

1. Ask students to read the **Know and Proclaim** introduction and chart.

- ✦ After reading the first row, discuss the role of the saints in the lives of Catholics.

Gather and Go Forth

CHAPTER 17

Know and Proclaim

We seek to know the truths of our Catholic faith. Then we proclaim our beliefs in truth and with respect for others.

We Know Our Faith	We Proclaim Our Faith
Jesus calls his disciples to live in his truth and to base their decisions on God's law and his own example.	Catholics imitate the lives of the saints to help them understand how to live by God's command and Jesus' example.
Jesus challenges his disciples to respect life, people, and property; to live honestly; and to cherish the gift of sex.	Catholics believe that civic virtue is a moral obligation. They exercise their civic duties by working toward legislation that promotes the life and dignity of all people.
The Fifth, Sixth, and Ninth Commandments are God's gift to his people to help them respect the dignity of themselves and others.	With the help of the Holy Spirit, Catholics develop the virtues of prudence and temperance to channel and control their desires in order to respect others.

Test Your Catholic Knowledge

Fill in the circle that best completes the sentence.

The Church works to strengthen society by:

○ punishing sinners.

● respecting all stages of life from conception to natural death.

○ making everyone happy.

○ ignoring the challenges society faces.

As disciples, we are people of truth because our faith rests in Jesus. Following Christ the Way demands that we follow Christ the Truth.

"God is Spirit, and those who worship him must worship in Spirit and truth."

John 4:24

- ✦ **Which saints inspire you? Why?** [Let students respond.]

- ✦ [Discuss the second row.] **Why do we demonstrate respect for all life?** (because life is created by God and what God created is good) **How can we share this truth with others?** [Allow time for discussion.]

- ✦ After reading the third row, remind students that prudence and temperance are virtues that lead us to do good.

- ✦ **How does thinking before acting lead you to do good?** (Possible answer: it helps me avoid unintended consequences that may hurt others.)

2. Remind students that a just society is one that respects life.

- ✦ **In what ways does our society disrespect life?** (through actions like capital punishment; legalized abortion; euthanasia; pollution)

- ✦ **How can we show respect for life** (Possible answers: protecting the unborn; ending the death penalty; caring for the elderly)

3. Point out the **Test Your Catholic Knowledge** section. Allow students time to fill in the circle of their choice before discussing the correct answer.

 Daily Inspiration Find insightful meditations on Scripture at **www.loyolapress.com/daily**. **Goal 1:** To bring about enthusiasm for faith so it is freely shared with others **93.** To foster an appreciation of God's Word

See pages T366–T368 for a full correlation to the USCCB *Go and Make Disciples* national plan.

4. Read aloud **A Catholic to Know.** Discuss how Saint Maria Goretti witnessed to her faith.

✦ Explain to students that Maria was brought up in a family that had strong faith in God's love.

✦ **While in prison, Alessandro was bitter and angry, and at first refused to repent for his crime. But after his dream, he spent the remainder of his 27-year sentence trying to make up for his crime.**

✦ **What are some things you can do to make up for hurts you cause others?** (Possible answers: I can repair the harm I caused; I can do works of service; I can ask for forgiveness.)

✦ **Maria's story is one of forgiveness. Who do you need to forgive? Who do you need to ask for forgiveness?** [Allow time for students to reflect.]

✦ Explain to students that Maria Goretti is a model of purity. Encourage them to pray three Hail Mary's daily for that intention.

✦ Discuss with students someone in your community who is as forgiving as Saint Maria Goretti.

5. Read the **Witness and Share** introductory text and **My Way to Faith** statements.

✦ Allow students time to reflect after each statement.

✦ Remind students that their faith journey lasts a lifetime. Their faith will grow and develop with them.

✦ **Ask God for the grace to grow in your ability to recognize the truth and make moral choices.** [Remind students that we are always called to live according to God's truth.]

✦ Ask students to choose a faith statement to discuss with a trusted adult. Encourage them to reflect on this statement later in the year to see how they have grown spiritually.

6. Have students complete the **Share Your Faith** activity. **As disciples, we must follow Jesus' teachings in word and deed.**

A Catholic to Know

Saint Maria Goretti

Maria Goretti, the modern patron of youth, showed a deep love of God, respect for her body, and Christlike forgiveness. Maria was born in 1890 in Italy. When she was twelve, Maria was attacked by a man named Alessandro. Maria resisted, and Alessandro stabbed her 14 times. Before Maria died from her wounds, she forgave Alessandro and prayed for God to have mercy on him. While in prison, Alessandro had a dream that Maria forgave him. After his release, Alessandro begged forgiveness of Maria's mother. She forgave him, and the two attended Mass together the following day. When Maria Goretti was canonized in 1950, her mother, brothers, sisters, and Alessandro were all present.

Witness and Share

These sentences describe what Catholics believe. Listen carefully as they are read. Ask yourself, "How strong are my Catholic beliefs?"

My Way to Faith

• I base my decisions on Jesus' examples.

• I respect the property of other people.

• I get advice from people who are virtuous.

• I read the Gospels to help guide my decisions.

• I obey the Ninth Commandment by respecting myself and others.

• I practice chastity by respecting my sexuality.

Share Your Faith

Consider the ways in which you let Jesus' truth guide what you say and do. How do you decide between right and wrong? Write your ideas on the lines, and invite a family member to discuss how Jesus helps him or her decide between right and wrong.

_____

_____

_____

_____

_____

(144) UNIT 2 *Jesus Christ the Truth*

Transform _____

1. Ask students to investigate the purpose and function of a truth and reconciliation commission.

✦ Explain that truth and reconciliation commissions are established in regions of the world that have suffered violence. These commissions help people come to terms with the past and foster reconciliation.

Truth and reconciliation commissions help people express regret and demonstrate a commitment to reconciliation.

✦ **How can a commitment to truth and reconciliation bring about an end to a conflict?** (Possible answers: It will help us forgive one another; it gets rid of the desire for revenge; it helps build trust and dialogue.)

2. Encourage students to celebrate the Sacrament of Reconciliation. Remind student that this sacrament brings peace to our personal conflicts.

The Church Evangelizes If the parish's youth ministry uses social media to communicate with young people, encourage students to use social media to keep informed about events at the parish. **Goal 2:** To invite all people to hear the message of salvation in Jesus Christ **112.** To effectively invite people to our Church

Inspire

1. Ask students to explain the concept of a role model.

✦ **What is a role model?** (a person who serves as an example, whose behavior is emulated by others) **Whose example do you follow? Why?** [Allow students to respond.]

✦ Discuss how each of us looks to others for inspiration. Share with students people you look to for inspiration.

✦ Ask students to list qualities they look for in a role model, such as passion, ability to inspire, values, commitment, and overcoming obstacles. Record the qualities on the board.

2. Read aloud the text and Scripture in the sidebar on page 153.

✦ Discuss how Jesus is a role model.

✦ **Of the qualities listed on the board, which ones do you see in Jesus? Why?** [Let students respond.] **How could you benefit from imitating Jesus?** (I will inherit eternal life.)

✦ **Jesus is our example of a life lived in union with God. He has called us to be examples for others so they will also come to know God.**

3. Lead students in a prayer to be like Christ.
Invite students to join you in the Prayer for Christlikeness by John Henry Cardinal Newman, which is on the inside back cover of the student book.

Proclaim

1. Read the **Know and Proclaim** introduction and chart with students.

✦ [Discuss the first row.] **Developing a spiritual life requires more than only going to Mass. A healthy spirituality puts us into a living relationship with God. What are some ways you develop your spiritual life?** (Possible answers: I read about saints; I perform works of charity; I think about Scripture.)

Gather and Go Forth

CHAPTER **18**

Know and Proclaim

We seek to grow in our love of the Catholic faith and proclaim our love by following the example of Jesus' life.

We Know Our Faith	We Proclaim Our Faith
Grace is a free gift from God. Sanctifying grace sustains us and compels us to preserve our relationship with God.	Catholics develop their spiritual life by praying such prayers as the Rosary and by doing penance such as fasting and giving alms.
Faith, hope, and charity are the Theological Virtues. These virtues are given by God and focus on God.	At the beginning of the Rosary, Catholics pray three Hail Marys, one for each of the Theological Virtues. These virtues help bring them closer to God.
The cardinal virtues of prudence, justice, fortitude, and temperance lead us to a moral life and allow people to do good acts.	Catholics develop the cardinal virtues by thinking before they act, considering the needs of others, being strong when facing opposition, and practicing restraint.

Test Your Catholic Knowledge

Fill in the circle that best answers the question.

What do we call our growing, loving relationship with God?

◯ tradition

● spirituality

◯ sanctifying grace

◯ particular judgment

O ur greatest journey in life is the journey of the spirit. We grow in our faith as we grow in our ability to be more like Jesus in what we say and do.

Let no one have contempt for your youth, but set an example for those who believe, in speech, conduct, love, faith, and purity.
1 Timothy 4:12

Living Faith in Jesus CHAPTER 18 (153)

✦ As you discuss the last two rows of the chart, explain the difference between the Theological Virtues and the cardinal virtues.

✦ **How do we get the Theological Virtues?** (They are gifts from God.) **How about the cardinal virtues?** (through training and practice)

2. Remind students that grace is a gift from God.

✦ **What is grace?** (the Holy Spirit alive in us) **Why do we need grace?** (to help us live as God wants us to live)

✦ **Increased awareness of grace helps us live as God wants, developing habits and attitudes of virtue. Grace and virtue together enable us to live our Christian vocation.**

3. Direct student's attention to the **Test Your Catholic Knowledge** question at the bottom of the page.
Read the directions and allow students time to fill in the circle of their choice before discussing the correct answer.

The Church Evangelizes Ask students to interview family members about how they express Christian values in the workplace and find support for their spiritual lives. Invite students to share what they learned with the class. **Goal 1:** To bring about enthusiasm for faith so it is freely shared with others **102.** To promote and develop a spirituality for the workplace

See pages T366–T368 for a full correlation to the USCCB *Go and Make Disciples* national plan.

4. Read aloud **A Catholic to Know.** Discuss Saint John Bosco.

  ✦ Explain that like Saint John Bosco, we are called to share our faith and teach others that Jesus loves them.

  ✦ **We can use our words and actions to teach people about Jesus' love.** [Brainstorm a list of words students can use and actions they can perform that show others that Jesus loves them.]

  ✦ Have students discuss a modern-day hero who teaches people about Jesus' love like Saint John Bosco.

5. Read the **Witness and Share** introductory text.

  ✦ Explain that people on a journey choose a path. Our way to faith and witness lasts a lifetime.

  ✦ **Think about your spirituality. Are you growing in the habits and practices that will lead you to a deeper relationship with Jesus?**

  ✦ Read aloud each faith statement, pausing after each one to allow students time for reflection.

  ✦ Remind students that we are always called to conversion. Encourage them to ask God for the grace to develop their spiritual gifts.

  ✦ Ask students to choose one faith statement to discuss with a trusted adult. Encourage them write this statement in their journal and return to it from time to time to see how they have grown in their faith.

6. Have students complete the **Share Your Faith** activity. Share with students ways in which you develop and nurture your spiritual life.

Transform _____

1. Work with students to compile a list of virtues.

  ✦ Remind students that virtues are good habits. Ask students how their list helps them draw closer to God and others.

  ✦ Brainstorm ways to develop those virtues.

2. Challenge students to grow in virtue.

A Catholic to Know

Saint John Bosco

John was the youngest son of a peasant family. His father died when John was two, and the family became very poor. As a youngster, John taught religion to other boys and got them to go to church. Encouraged by a priest, John entered the seminary. John started gathering boys together on Sunday for a day in the country. They would begin with Mass, followed by breakfast and games. The afternoon would include a picnic, a catechism lesson, and evening prayers. John Bosco gave a father's care to rowdy, neglected boys. He opened workshops to train boys to be shoemakers and tailors. In 1859 John began a religious community of priests which is still active today, caring for boys who have been neglected.

Witness and Share

These sentences describe what Catholics believe. Listen carefully as they are read. Ask yourself, "How strong are my Catholic beliefs?"

My Way to Faith

- I rely on the virtues of faith, hope, and love to bring me closer to God.
- I devote time and energy to developing my spiritual life.
- I think before I act, consider the needs of others, show strength in the face of opposition, and show self-control.
- I let others know that I am a Christian by the way I live.
- I do good to others without expecting anything in return.

Share Your Faith

Consider ways in which you can take a more active role in developing your spirituality by exploring different forms of prayer and service. Write your ideas on the lines, and invite a family member or friend to join your exploration of faith.

_____

_____

_____

_____

154 UNIT 3 *Jesus Christ the Life*

The virtues help us live according to God's Law and bring about God's kingdom. [Lead a discussion on how living and developing the cardinal virtues—prudence, justice, fortitude, and temperance—will help build a better world.]

3. Ask students to write a prayer to the Holy Spirit for the guidance and strength necessary to live a virtuous life.

3-Minute Retreat Invite deeper reflection on God's Word by accessing **www.loyolapress .com/retreat. Goal 1:** To bring about enthusiasm for faith so it is freely shared with others **97.** To foster a deeper sense of prayer

The Church Evangelizes Have students research the Catholic Worker Movement founded by Dorothy Day to learn about its mission, services, and impact on Catholic values in the workplace. Encourage students to think of Dorothy Day as a role model who worked for peace and justice. **Goal 3:** To foster gospel values, promoting dignity of the human person, the importance of the family, and the common good **123.** To develop groups to explore issues of the workplace and lay spirituality

Inspire

1. Discuss faith.
   - ✦ **What does the word *faith* mean to you?** (Possible answers: belief; trust; loyalty) **Why is faith important?** (Possible answers: It gives me strength; it gives me confidence.)
   - ✦ **Have you ever heard the expression, "actions speak louder than words"? What are some actions you can do to proclaim your faith?** (Possible answers: praying Scripture; practicing Catholic devotions; performing the Corporal and Spiritual Works of Mercy)

2. Read aloud the text and Scripture in the sidebar on page 161.
   - ✦ **Faith is a deep, personal, radical trusting in Jesus. Our faith is evident in the way we receive both good things and bad things in life.**
   - ✦ Remind students that our faith is evident in the way we treat others.
   - ✦ **We do good works to demonstrate our faith to others and to bring about the Kingdom of God on earth. Through the eyes of faith, we find evidence of God everywhere.**

3. Pray together the Act of Faith.

Proclaim

1. Have volunteers read the **Know and Proclaim** introduction and chart.
   - ✦ [Discuss the first row.] **Think of a difficult time. Where did you find comfort?** (Possible answers: with friends; with family; with Jesus.)
   - ✦ [Discuss the second row.] **Jesus suffered too. He understands the difficulties we face, and he knows our sufferings.** [Explain that sadness and tragedy are realities of life, but we have hope in Christ.]
   - ✦ **Jesus gives us the strength to get through difficult times.**
   - ✦ [Discuss the third row.] **What does the Paschal Mystery teach us?** (Suffering can lead to salvation.)

Gather and Go Forth

CHAPTER 19

Know and Proclaim

We proclaim the truths of our Catholic faith in times of joy and sorrow.

We Know Our Faith	We Proclaim Our Faith
Faith helps us believe that God is with us even in times of sorrow. Faith can help us accept sorrow with trust.	Because Mary was a mother who lost her son, many Catholics pray to her under the title "Our Lady of Sorrows." The Seven Sorrows of Mary recall the challenges that Mary had as a disciple of Christ.
Jesus willingly endured suffering and death for the sake of our salvation. The Transfiguration teaches us that salvation comes through the Cross.	Catholics commemorate the suffering and Death of Jesus when they walk the Stations of the Cross. Pictures or statues depict Jesus carrying the Cross, stumbling as he walks, his crucifixion, and Death.
By offering his life to the Father, Jesus changed death into a doorway that leads to happiness with God.	The paschal candle is lit during Catholic funerals. It is also lit during Baptisms, on the Easter Vigil, and during the Easter season, connecting death with life.

Test Your Catholic Knowledge

Fill in the circle that best completes the sentence.

In his Transfiguration, Jesus teaches that:

- ○ Mary is his mother.
- ○ all sins will be forgiven.
- ● glory comes through the Cross.
- ○ the Father, Son, and the Holy Spirit are one.

Opposition to Jesus CHAPTER 19 (161)

Our faith allows us to trust in God with courage and confidence even in times of pain and suffering. Through Jesus, we receive the strength to hope for an eternal life in glory.

Faith is the realization of what is hoped for and evidence of things not seen.

Hebrews 11:1

Through his Death and Resurrection, Jesus teaches us that suffering is temporary, while life with God is forever.

2. Read Phillipians 2:5–11.
   - ✦ Explain that through his humility, Jesus was exalted.
   - ✦ **Jesus chose to suffer with us because he loves us. Through his suffering, he brought God's love to us all.**
   - ✦ Ask students how they can proclaim their faith in eternal life with Jesus.

3. Point out the **Test Your Catholic Knowledge** section. Read the directions. Allow students time to fill in the circle of their choice before discussing the correct answer.

 Español Invite Spanish-language speakers to access **www.loyolapress.com/espanol.** **Goal 2:** To invite all people to hear the message of salvation in Jesus Christ **106.** To make every Catholic institution more welcoming

---

The Church Evangelizes Encourage students to help the RCIA team during the Easter Vigil. Students can assist in handing out candles, carrying dry clothes for the catechumens, and welcoming the newly baptized. **Goal 1:** To bring about enthusiasm for faith so it is freely shared with others **92.** To foster an experience of conversion and renewal in every parish

See pages T366–T368 for a full correlation to the USCCB *Go and Make Disciples* national plan.

4. Read aloud **A Catholic to Know.** Discuss the role of missionaries in spreading the faith.

✦ Explain that Paul Miki and his companions had to walk 300 miles through the snow and freezing rain. Paul Miki and his companions preached the Good News of Christ along the way.

✦ **Think about Saint Paul Miki. How did he witness to Christ in the way he suffered?** (Possible answers: He preached the Gospel up until his death; he sang hymns of joy and praise.)

✦ **The Cross and the passion of Jesus are powerful symbols of our faith.** [Invite students to make their own crosses to display in the classroom.]

✦ Remind students that they do not have to go to faraway places to be missionaries. They can spread their faith in their own communities.

5. Read the **Witness and Share** introductory text.

✦ Explain that the journey of faith is not always easy, but we never travel alone.

✦ **Jesus is with us always, especially during times of difficulty and trouble.**

✦ Read aloud each faith statement. Allow time for reflection. Encourage students to ask God for the grace to grow as witnesses to their faith.

✦ Ask students to choose one faith statement as an area for personal and spiritual growth. Encourage them to discuss it with a trusted adult. Have students reflect on this statement later in the year.

6. Read aloud the directions for the **Share Your Faith** activity.
Have students complete the activity and share their experiences.

Transform _____

1. Ask students to think about what it means to be a missionary.
How do you welcome people who witness the Gospel into your life?

A Catholic to Know

On February 5, 1597, 26 men were crucified in Nagasaki, Japan. Among these men was a Jesuit brother named Paul Miki. When Japan first allowed foreign visitors to enter the country in 1549, Saint Francis Xavier was among the first missionaries to share the Good News of Christ with the Japanese people. Paul Miki was one of a small but committed group of Christian converts. Christianity spread rapidly until 1587, when Emperor Hideyoshi expelled all foreign missionaries, beginning an era of Christian persecution. Paul Miki and his companions met their death singing psalms of praise and joy. Their witness to the faith continues to give Christians the strength to profess their faith.

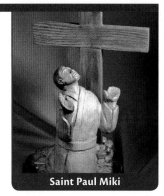
Saint Paul Miki

Witness and Share

These sentences describe what Catholics believe. Listen carefully as they are read. Ask yourself, "How strong are my Catholic beliefs?"

My Way to Faith

• I turn to Jesus when things are hard.

• I am comforted by God's presence during times of sorrow.

• I remain true to Jesus even in the face of opposition.

• I believe that as a good Christian, when I die, I will be with God in his kingdom forever.

• I thank God for the gift of eternal life.

Share Your Faith

Think about the times your faith has given comfort to you and your family during experiences of suffering and sorrow. Write your experiences on the lines. Invite a family member to share how his or her faith provided comfort in times of sorrow and distress.

_____

_____

_____

_____

_____

_____

(Possible answers: I listen to them; I follow their example.)

2. Encourage students to be missionaries by making works of art that proclaim their faith. Invite students to share their artwork with the class. Remind students to show respect to religious objects and articles.

3. Lead students in a reflection on defending the faith as Saint Paul Miki did.

Pray aloud: **O God, grant that, by the intercession of Paul Miki and his companions, we may hold on to the faith we profess with courage. Amen.**

Arts & Faith Celebrate how faith is expressed and deepened through art at **www .loyolapress.com/arts-faith.** Goal 3: To foster gospel values, promoting the dignity of the human person, the importance of the family, and the common good **124.** To encourage Catholic witness in the arts and in the American intellectual community

The Church Evangelizes Prepare the students to lead the Way of the Cross for their families and for the parish during Holy Week. Have them use some of their own prayers to demonstrate the modern-day connections students have made with this traditional form of prayer. Goal 2: To invite all people to hear the message of salvation in Jesus Christ **110.** To use special times in parish and family life to invite people to faith

Inspire

1. Read the text in the sidebar on page 169.
   - ✦ **Why is eating important?** (Possible answer: food gives us energy)
   - ✦ **What kinds of things do you do when you gather together to eat a meal?** (Possible answers: we tell stories; we say a prayer thanking God for food, friends, and family.)
   - ✦ **When we celebrate the Eucharist, we gather around the altar as a family of faith.**

2. Pray aloud the Scripture on page 169.
   As Catholics, we understand the need to nourish our soul frequently with the real food of Jesus' Body and Blood in the Eucharist. [Remind students to fast for an hour before attending Mass as a reminder that the Eucharist is true food.]

3. Lead the students in a silent reflection.
   Invite students to reflect on the Eucharist and the sacrifice Jesus made of himself. After a few moments, have students silently pray the Sign of the Cross.

Proclaim

1. Read the **Know and Proclaim** introduction and chart.
   - ✦ Discuss the first row of the chart. Remind students that the greatest act of praise and thanksgiving we can offer God is the Eucharist.
   - ✦ **The Eucharist is the source of who we are as Catholics and the summit of all we hope to be.**
   - ✦ [Discuss the second row of the chart.] **During the Liturgy of the Word, we hear Jesus teach us what the Father wants us to know.** [Invite students to share a favorite reading or Homily.]
   - ✦ [Discuss the third row of the chart.] **As a eucharistic people, how do we look through the eyes of faith to see Jesus in the faces of those we meet?** (I see the image of God in other people.)

2. Discuss transubstantiation.
   - ✦ Reinforce that Jesus is truly present in the Eucharist.
   - ✦ **We witness the miracle of transubstantiation through the eyes of faith.**

3. Point out the **Test Your Catholic Knowledge** section. Allow students time to complete the question before discussing the correct answer.

Gather and Go Forth

CHAPTER 20

Know and Proclaim

As Catholics, we are people of the Eucharist. We proclaim our belief in Jesus' Body and Blood in all that we say and do.

We Know Our Faith	We Proclaim Our Faith
At the Last Supper, Jesus gave his disciples a new commandment to love one another.	Catholics consider the Eucharist to be the most appropriate way to express joy and gratitude for God's blessings.
During the Liturgy of the Word, we are nourished and strengthened by God's Word revealed to us in Scripture.	During the Liturgy of the Word, the priest or deacon gives a homily in which he explains how the Scripture readings relate to the lives of Catholics.
During the Liturgy of the Eucharist, we offer Jesus and ourselves to the Father and then receive Christ's Body and Blood.	Catholics proclaim the Mystery of Faith during the Liturgy of the Eucharist. In the Mystery of Faith, Catholics proclaim Jesus' Death and Resurrection until he comes again.

Test Your Catholic Knowledge

Fill in the circle that best answers the question.

What do we call the change in substance from bread and wine to the Body and Blood of Christ in the Eucharist?

- ● transubstantiation
- ○ metamorphosis
- ○ transfiguration
- ○ reformation

The Eucharist is spiritual food that nourishes us on our journey of faith. We go forth from the Eucharist in peace to love and serve the Father and one another.

"For my flesh is true food, and my blood is true drink. Whoever eats my flesh and drinks my blood remains in me and I in him."

John 6:55–56

The Eucharist CHAPTER 20 **169**

Sunday Connection
Explore this Sunday's Scripture readings with students by accessing **www.loyolapress.com/sunday**.
Goal 1: To bring about enthusiasm for faith so it is freely shared with others **96.** To foster a greater appreciation of the power of God's Word in our worship

The Church Evangelizes Encourage students to meet with other young people after Mass. They can discuss the readings and the Homily from the Liturgy of the Word. **Goal 1:** To bring about enthusiasm for faith so it is freely shared with others **94.** To make the evangelizing mission of Sunday Eucharist more explicit

See pages T366–T368 for a full correlation to the USCCB *Go and Make Disciples* national plan.

4. Read aloud **A Catholic to Know.**

+ Discuss the simplicity in the way Saint Isidore lived his faith.

+ **We too are called to live simple lives. In what ways is your life similar to Saint Isidore's?** [Allow time for discussion.]

+ Invite students to pray for farmers today so that they may reap a generous harvest for all the world to share. Ask students to pray aloud their petitions.

+ **May our witness also reap a bountiful harvest for Christ.**

5. Read the **Witness and Share** introductory text.

+ Explain that the Eucharist nourishes us on our spiritual journey.

+ **Look at the faith statements. Think about how the Eucharist nourishes you.**

+ Read aloud each faith statement. Allow time for reflection.

+ **We are always called to share in Christ's Body and Blood.** [Encourage students to ask God for the grace to grow in appreciation of the gift of the Eucharist.]

+ Encourage students to discuss a statement with a trusted adult. Invite them to return to and reflect on these statements later in the year.

6. Read aloud the directions for the **Share Your Faith** activity. If possible, take students to the eucharistic chapel and give them time to pray their prayer of thanksgiving before the Blessed Sacrament.

Transform _____

1. Ask students to consider the problem of hunger in their community. **Why is hunger a problem in our community and around the world?** (Possible answers: damage to the environment; lack of resources; poverty; war) **How can you make a difference in getting food to hungry people?** (Possible answers: I can volunteer at a food pantry; I can participate in a food drive.)

A Catholic to Know

Isidore had three great loves in his life: God, his family, and the soil he farmed. Isidore was born in Spain more than 900 years ago. As soon as he was old enough, he began to work as a farmer. He worked all his life for a wealthy landowner named John de Vargas. Isidore prayed continuously as he worked the fields. He and his wife, Maria, were well-known for their generosity to people who were poorer than themselves. Isidore was gifted with miracles. More than once he fed hungry people with food that multiplied in response to those in need. Isidore died in 1130 following a peaceful life of manual labor. He and his wife prove that poverty, hard work, and sorrow (their only child died as a little boy) cannot destroy human happiness.

Saint Isidore the Farmer

Witness and Share

These sentences describe what Catholics believe. Listen carefully as they are read. Ask yourself, "How strong are my Catholic beliefs?"

My Way to Faith

• I receive strength and nourishment in the Eucharist.

• I believe that the Body and Blood of Jesus is truly present under the forms of bread and wine.

• I offer acts of loving kindness to others.

• I thank Jesus for the gift of the Eucharist.

• I receive guidance from God when I listen to the Scripture readings at Mass.

Share Your Faith

Consider ways in which you can thank God for the Eucharist. Write a prayer of thanks on the lines, and invite a friend or family member to attend eucharistic adoration with you. Pray a prayer of thanksgiving for the gift of the Eucharist before you go to bed tonight.

_____

_____

_____

_____

(170) UNIT 3 *Jesus Christ the Life*

---

2. Challenge students to help feed those who are hungry. **How does feeding those who are hungry show that you are a disciple of Christ?** (Possible answers: by showing love for our neighbors; it's what Jesus would do; it's a Corporal Work of Mercy)

3. Ask students to pray the prayers Grace Before Meals and Grace After Meals with every meal.

Remind students that praying before and after meals is a way to express gratitude to God.

> **DRE Connect** Share ideas with an online community for faith formation leaders by accessing **dreconnect.loyolapress.com**. **Goal 2:** To invite all people to hear the message of salvation in Jesus Christ 111. To cultivate an active core of the baptized to serve as ministers of evangelization

The Church Evangelizes Send home a class newsletter and encourage students and their families to read a Scripture passage at every meal. During the meal, the family can share their reflections on the Scripture. Readings for every day of the year can be found at www.usccb.org/bible/readings. **Goal 2:** To invite all people to hear the message of salvation in Jesus Christ **108.** To develop within families the capacity to share the Gospel

Inspire

1. Ask students to consider the value of life.

✦ **What are some ways you help your friends and family members when they face hard times?** (Possible answers: comfort and console them; give them advice; help them meet their physical needs)

✦ **Why do you help them?** (Possible answers: I care about them; they would do the same for me.)

✦ **Jesus knows that because of sin we face many challenges and difficulties. What did he do to save us from sin?** (He sacrificed his own life for us.)

2. Invite students to the prayer center.

✦ Invite them to rest in God's presence.

✦ Read aloud the Scripture and text in the sidebar on page 177.

✦ **How do we know Jesus loves us?** (He gave up his life for us; he gave us the Holy Spirit.) **What does this say about our value to Jesus?** (He loves us beyond compare.)

✦ **What does Jesus ask from us in return?** (to love one another)

3. Lead students in a silent reflection.

✦ Allow students a few moments to reflect on the love Jesus showed by his sacrifice and how they can imitate his love.

✦ Pray aloud: **Jesus, thank you for offering your life for us. With the help of the Holy Spirit, may we love one another as you love us.**

Proclaim

1. Read the **Know and Proclaim** introduction and chart aloud.

✦ [Discuss the first row of the chart.] **What does it mean to be reconciled?** (to make a relationship whole again) **Why is reconciliation important?** (Possible answers: to heal; to make peace)

✦ As you discuss the second row of the chart, remind students that just

as we pray for others, the saints can pray for us. Encourage students to ask the saints to pray for them.

✦ As you discuss the third row of the chart, ask students to take turns reading Matthew 13.

✦ **Jesus' parables tells us about the Kingdom of Heaven. He began his earthly ministry by preaching that the Kingdom of Heaven is at hand.**

2. Point out the **Test Your Catholic Knowledge** section.

> 🖥 **3-Minute Retreat** Invite deeper reflection on God's Word by accessing **www.loyolapress.com/retreat**. **Goal 1:** To bring about enthusiasm for faith so it is freely shared with others **93.** To foster an appreciation of God's Word

---

NEW EVANGELIZATION

Gather and Go Forth

CHAPTER **21**

Know and Proclaim

As we seek to know our Catholic faith, our hearts burn with the desire to proclaim our beliefs in what we say and do.

We Know Our Faith	We Proclaim Our Faith
Jesus died for our sins. By his obedience and love, he reconciled us with God.	Catholics place crucifixes in their homes and places of gathering to recall Jesus' passion, Death, and Resurrection.
After death, only people who have loved like Jesus can enter God's presence. Those in need of purification experience purgatory. The eternal separation from God is called hell.	Catholics are united with the saints when they celebrate the Eucharist, and they ask the saints to intercede on their behalf and for the whole world.
Jesus will return to reveal the eternal destiny of every person in the Last Judgment.	Catholics learn about the Kingdom of Heaven by reading the Gospels.

Test Your Catholic Knowledge

Fill in the circle that best answers the question.

What is the Last Judgment?

○ the eternal separation from God

○ the period of purification of the soul of any remaining selfishness

● the revelation of the destiny of the human race and of every person

○ the moment where you realize before God how you fit into the kingdom of love

Jesus' Final Hours CHAPTER 21 (177)

J esus transformed death through his Resurrection. As Catholics, we expect to be transformed with him by the mystery of his Cross and Resurrection. We walk the way of Jesus to eternal life with him.

The way we came to know love was that he laid down his life for us; so we ought to lay down our lives for our brothers.

1 John 3:16

The Church Evangelizes Include occasional activities in class such as viewing movies about the lives of saints and other holy people to nurture faith, fellowship, and community. **Goal 1:** To bring about enthusiasm for faith so it is freely shared with others **91.** To foster an experience of conversion and renewal in the heart of every believer, leading to a more active living of Catholic life

See pages T366–T368 for a full correlation to the USCCB *Go and Make Disciples* national plan.

3. Read aloud **A Catholic to Know.** Discuss Saint Andrew Dung-Lac's witness in the face of persecution.

◆ Explain to students that the persecutions in Vietnam did not end in the 19th century. During the Vietnam War, Catholics suffered persecution under the Communists of North Vietnam and were forced to abandon their homes and flee south.

◆ **Despite the centuries of persecution, the Catholic Church in Vietnam is alive today because of people like Saint Andrew Dung-Lac.**

◆ Invite students to discuss reasons why the Church remained strong. Possible answers may include the Gifts of the Holy Spirit, the love the people had for their faith, and the examples of the saints.

◆ Have a student read aloud Luke 10:29–37, the Parable of the Good Samaritan.

◆ **What does Jesus tell us about how we should treat people who have been mistreated?** (We should be kind and help them.)

4. Read the **Witness and Share** introductory text.

◆ Explain that people on a journey choose paths and those paths may be challenging at times.

◆ **Look at the faith statements. Think about how you respond to suffering.**

◆ Read aloud each faith statement, Allowing time for reflection.

◆ Remind students that pain is part of life. Encourage them to ask God for the grace to find strength in Jesus.

◆ Ask students to choose one faith statement to discuss with a trusted adult. Encourage them to reflect on this statement throughout the year.

5. Read aloud the directions for the **Share Your Faith** activity.
Share with students ways that Jesus comforts you in your trials. Then have them complete the activity.

A Catholic to Know

The Catholic faith came to Vietnam in 1615 when the Jesuits opened the first mission in Da Nang. Eventually, foreign missionaries were banned and persecution began. Catholics went into hiding. Many people opened their homes and offered a place to hide. Persecutions continued. Between 1820 and 1862, a total of 117 Vietnamese martyrs died. Among them was Andrew Dung-Lac, a parish priest. In 1988, Pope John Paul II canonized Saint Andrew and the others—brave bishops, priests, and lay Catholics. Today the Church in Vietnam is strong. Catholics honor Saint Andrew's witness for Christ on November 24.

Saint Andrew Dung-Lac

Witness and Share

These sentences describe what Catholics believe. Listen carefully as they are read. Ask yourself, "How strong are my Catholic beliefs?"

My Way to Faith

- I recall Jesus' passion and Death by reflecting on the crucifix.
- I believe that I will be reunited with God after my death.
- I pray for the souls in purgatory, that they may be united with God.
- I find strength in prayer during times of suffering.
- I do not inflict pain and suffering upon others.

Share Your Faith

Consider how you respond to difficult times. Write how Jesus comforts and helps you in your trials. Invite a trusted adult to discuss how faith comforts him or her at difficult times in life.

_____

_____

_____

_____

178 UNIT 3 *Jesus Christ the Life*

Transform _____

1. Remind students to demonstrate their faith.

◆ Ask students to make a list of things they do because of their faith, such as listening to their parents, being kind to all people, and paying attention during the Mass.

◆ **How do these actions proclaim your faith to others?** [Let students respond.]

2. Encourage students to demonstrate their faith by celebrating the Sacrament of Reconciliation.
Reconciliation helps bring about God's kingdom of peace.

💻 **Español** Invite Spanish-language speakers to access **www.loyolapress.com/espanol.**
Goal 2: To invite all people to hear the message of salvation in Jesus Christ **106.** To make every Catholic institution more welcoming

---

The Church Evangelizes Send home a newsletter to encourage students and their families to make their homes a friendly and inviting place where the faith is celebrated. **Goal 2:** To invite all people to hear the message of salvation in Jesus Christ **114.** To design programs that reach out to those who do not participate in a church community or who seek the fullness of faith

Inspire

1. Read aloud the text and Scripture in the sidebar on page 185.

   ✦ **Think about victories you've had. Maybe it was a goal you scored in a soccer game, a good grade you received on a test, or a good performance in band or drama. What memories do you have about that experience?** [Let students respond.]

   ✦ **How did that victory become possible?** (Possible answers: I had to practice; I had to study; I had to have courage.) **What made that victory special for you?** (Possible answers: I had to work hard; I made my parents proud.)

   ✦ Discuss with students the magnitude of victory represented by the Resurrection.

   ✦ **Jesus persisted in his mission of bringing people to the Father in spite of obstacles. Following Jesus is not easy, but for disciples of Christ, victory is assured.**

2. Join the class in the prayer center.
   Pray aloud: **Lord Jesus Christ, in your Resurrection, you give us hope. Give us the grace to share in your victory of all victories! Make us deserving of the prize you have won for us. Amen.**

Proclaim

1. Read the **Know and Proclaim** introduction and chart with students.

   ✦ [Discuss the first row of the chart.] **We find evidence of Jesus' Resurrection in Scripture, in the sacraments, in the lives of the saints, and even in one another.**

   ✦ After reading the second row of the chart, remind students that sacramentals are meant to remind us of the hope we have in Christ's promises. Share with students any sacramentals you pray with, such as a Rosary or medal.

   ✦ **One sacramental is the brown scapular that represents a special devotion to Our Lady of Mount**

Carmel. The brown scapular reminds us of Mary's promise to help us receive God's grace.

   ✦ [Discuss the third row of the chart.] **Which gifts do you think is the most helpful for you?** [Let students respond.]

2. Point out the **Test Your Catholic Knowledge** section. Allow students time to fill in the circle of their choice before discussing the correct answer.

See pages T366–T368 for a full correlation to the USCCB *Go and Make Disciples* national plan.

NEW EVANGELIZATION

Gather and Go Forth

CHAPTER 22

Know and Proclaim

We learn the truths of our Catholic faith to proclaim our belief in the risen Lord.

We Know Our Faith	We Proclaim Our Faith
The Resurrection is a mystery of faith. To recognize the risen Lord requires faith.	Catholics encounter the risen Lord in the sacraments, especially the Eucharist. Catholics also encounter the risen Lord in the Scriptures and in the Church.
The Ascension is Jesus' return to his Father. It completed the glorification of Jesus.	As Catholics, we use sacramentals, such as medals, or prayers, such as the Sign of the Cross, to remind us of the presence of the risen Christ, to prepare us for the sacraments, and to help us grow in holiness.
Jesus promised to send the Holy Spirit to his disciples. His Spirit would enable them to bear witness to him.	Catholics rely on the Gifts of the Holy Spirit to act with justice and love in the world.

Test Your Catholic Knowledge

Fill in the circle that best completes the sentence.

Grace enters our lives in the celebration of the sacraments by the power of the:

● Holy Spirit.

○ Magisterium.

○ Acts of the Apostles.

○ Communion of Saints.

As Catholics, we share in the suffering of Jesus Christ, knowing we will share in his glory. We direct our hope toward Christ's Resurrection.

For if we have grown into union with him through a death like this, we shall also be united with him in the resurrection.

Romans 6:5

The Victory of Jesus CHAPTER 22 (185)

💻 **DRE Connect** Share ideas with an online community for faith formation leaders by accessing **dreconnect.loyolapress.com.**
Goal 2: To invite all people to hear the message of salvation in Jesus Christ. **109.** To equip active Catholic members to exercise their baptismal call to evangelize

---

The Church Evangelizes Discuss poverty as a class. Help the students identify people in their community who are poor and discuss ways to help provide for their basic needs. **Goal 3:** To foster gospel values, promoting dignity of the human person, the importance of the family, and the common good **127.** To involve Catholics in the questions of economic systems

3. Read aloud **A Catholic to Know.** Discuss Saint Thérèse of Lisieux.

✦ **Thérèse always wanted to be a missionary, but her health was strained by caring for those in her convent who were sick. Since she could not go on missions, she offered up her sufferings for missionaries.**

✦ Encourage students to think of ways they help the missions by making personal sacrifices, such as offering donations and prayers.

✦ The book *The Story of a Soul* is a memoir of Saint Thérèse's spiritual journey. Have students write a sentence that tells one thing they want to do for Christ to show their love for him.

✦ Invite students to pray Saint Thérèse's last words: **My God, I love you.**

4. Read the **Witness and Share** introductory text and **My Way to Faith** statements.

✦ Allow time for reflection.

✦ Ask students to choose one faith statement to discuss with a trusted adult.

✦ Encourage students to return to faith statements from earlier chapters and reflect on how they have grown.

✦ Remind students that even though the journey of faith is long, we can be confident that we will arrive at our final destination: union with God!

5. Read aloud the directions for the **Share Your Faith** activity.

Let students work with a partner and write their ideas.

Transform _____

1. Encourage students to use their gifts to serve God.

✦ Remind students that Saint Thérèse praised God as she served the sisters in her convent who were sick.

✦ **How can you use your gifts and talents to praise God?** (Possible answers: singing in the choir; comforting those who suffer.)

A Catholic to Know

Thérèse was born into a middle-class family in France in 1873. She thought seriously about God and prayed that her love of God would grow. Thérèse entered a Carmelite convent at Lisieux at age 15. She prayed often and did the most ordinary tasks in the convent: scrubbing floors, washing dishes, setting the tables, sewing, dusting, and cooking. Thérèse proved that we can become saints by doing ordinary things extraordinarily well. She explained it in her biography: "I want to seek a way to heaven, a new way, very short, very straight—the way of trust and self-surrender . . . I am a very little soul, who can offer only little things to Our Lord." Thérèse called her path to holiness "The Little Way." Like Thérèse, we can do every act, even small things, for the love of God.

Saint Thérèse of Lisieux

Witness and Share

These sentences describe what Catholics believe. Listen carefully as they are read. Ask yourself, "How strong are my Catholic beliefs?"

My Way to Faith

• I will live as a disciple so I can share in the glory of Christ's Resurrection.

• I am aware that the risen Christ dwells in me when I pray the Sign of the Cross.

• I recognize the true presence of Christ in the Eucharist.

• I bear witness to the risen Lord in my words and deeds.

• I use sacramentals to help me live a life of holiness.

Share Your Faith

Consider how you can practice the "Little Way." What are some little actions you do every day, and how can you do them for the love of God? Write your ideas on the lines and invite a friend to practice the "Little Way" too.

_____

_____

_____

_____

---

2. Challenge students to share their gifts with others.

✦ Explain that inclusiveness proclaims the risen Christ. Have students discuss ideas for including people who may feel neglected or alone.

✦ **Jesus told his disciples to proclaim the Gospel to every creature; he did not want to neglect anyone.**

3. Pray with students Take, Lord, and Receive found on the inside back cover of their books.

Special Needs Explore ways to invite students with special needs to know God better at **www.loyolapress.com/special-needs**. **Goal 3:** To foster gospel values, promoting dignity of the human person, the importance of the family, and the common good **126.** To involve the Catholic Church in the media

---

The Church Evangelizes Invite the families of students to gather for a social event after class, such as having a meal or playing games. **Goal 2:** To invite all people to hear the message of salvation in Jesus Christ **110.** To use special times in parish and family life to invite people to faith

Inspire

1. Lead students in a discussion of spirit.

   ✦ **Have you ever been to a pep rally? What did it inspire in you?** (Possible answers: pride in my school; good feelings)

   ✦ **How does the Mass inspire you?** [Let students respond.]

   ✦ **At Pentecost, the apostles were filled with the Holy Spirit and energized to proclaim the Gospel to the world!**

2. Read aloud the text and Scripture on page 193.

   ✦ **When we can love what is true and good, we live in the Holy Spirit and follow the Spirit.**

   ✦ Remind students that they live spiritual lives. Encourage students to participate in the spiritual life of the Church.

   ✦ **The apostles formed communities to support one another. How does the Church support you?** (Possible answer: by praying for me and with me.)

3. Invite students into the prayer center and gather around a flameless candle.

   ✦ Explain that fire is a symbol of the Holy Spirit.

   ✦ Ask students to imagine the Holy Spirit burning like the candle in their hearts.

   ✦ Ask students to offer petitions aloud. After each one, pray aloud: **Come, Holy Spirit!**

Proclaim

1. Read the **Know and Proclaim** introduction and chart together.

   ✦ [Read the first row in the chart.] **How do we keep the Spirit alive in our hearts?** (Possible answers: by going to Mass; by praying)

   ✦ [Read the second row.] **How can you develop relationships with non-Catholic Christians?** (Possible answers: by being friends with them; by talking about God)

Gather and Go Forth

CHAPTER **23**

Know and Proclaim

As Catholics, we see the Church as a sign of God's grace. The Holy Spirit inspires us to proclaim our Church to the world.

We Know Our Faith	We Proclaim Our Faith
On the feast of Pentecost, the disciples were filled with the Holy Spirit. The Spirit empowered them to fulfill Jesus' mission.	Many Catholics pray the Prayer to the Holy Spirit, which begins with the words "Come, Holy Spirit, fill the hearts of your faithful."
The Church was born on Pentecost with the Holy Spirit as its strength and guiding force.	Catholics believe that the unity of all Christians reflects the unity of the Trinity. Catholics work with other Christians on social justice projects.
Through Baptism, all the faithful are gifted with the Holy Spirit. Through Confirmation, the faithful are sealed with the Spirit.	Catholics recognize seven gifts of the Holy Spirit: wisdom, understanding, counsel, piety, knowledge, and fear of the Lord. Catholics refer to the Holy Spirit as the "Spirit of Truth."

Test Your Catholic Knowledge

Fill in the circle that best answers the question.

In which of the following books of the Bible can we learn the most about the role of the Holy Spirit in guiding the Church?

○ the Song of Songs

○ the Gospel of John

○ the Book of Wisdom

● the Acts of the Apostles

Christ sent his Spirit so that a community of love would grow in his name. As Catholics, we recognize the Holy Spirit at work in the Church, which is a sacrament of unity and salvation for the world.

If we live in the Spirit, let us also follow the Spirit.
Galatians 5:25

Alive with the Spirit CHAPTER 23 (193)

✦ [Read the third row.] **When do you use each Gift of the Holy Spirit?** [Let students respond.]

✦ Ask students to write an acrostic with one of the Gifts of the Holy Spirit.

2. Read the directions to the **Test Your Catholic Knowledge** question. Allow students time to fill in the circle of their choice before discussing the correct answer.

 Daily Inspiration Find insightful meditations on Scripture at **www.loyolapress.com/daily**. **Goal 1:** To bring about enthusiasm for faith so it is freely shared with others **93.** To foster an appreciation of God's Word

The Church Evangelizes Invite someone who participated in a Christ Renews His Parish retreat to speak to the class about promoting Catholic faith in action for parishioners and their families. **Goal 1:** To bring about enthusiasm for faith so it is freely shared with others **91.** To foster an experience of conversion and renewal in the heart of every believer, leading to a more active living of Catholic life

See pages T366–T368 for a full correlation to the USCCB *Go and Make Disciples* national plan.

3. Read aloud **A Catholic to Know.** Discuss Saint Peter.

✦ **Two letters in the New Testament are said to have been written by Peter. These letters encourage Christians to remain faithful to Christ in both faith and conduct, even in the face of persecution.** [Encourage students to read excerpts from the Letters of Peter, such as 1 Peter 3:9 or 2 Peter 1:5–7. Discuss how they can apply his instructions.]

✦ **Peter was said to have been crucified in Rome in what is now St. Peter's Square in Vatican City.** [Explain that Saint Peter was executed during the persecutions under the Roman Emperor Nero.]

✦ Have students write a sample "text message" to a friend that encourages him or her to remain faithful to Christ despite teasing or peer pressure. Have students read aloud and discuss the messages with partners.

4. Read the **Witness and Share** introductory text.

✦ Explain that the path of our faith journey may take us to unexpected places.

✦ **Silently read the faith statements. Think about where the Holy Spirit is guiding you today.**

✦ Allow time for reflection.

✦ Ask students to choose one faith statement to discuss with a trusted adult. Encourage them to write this statement in the journal and look back at it from time to time to see how they have grown in their faith.

5. Read aloud the directions for the **Share Your Faith** activity.
Let students discuss with a partner and write their ideas.

Transform _____

1. Invite students to grow in the Spirit.

✦ **What are some barriers that prevent you from sharing your faith?** (Possible answers: fear of ridicule; not knowing all the facts of my faith; not praying)

A Catholic to Know

"And so I say to you, you are Peter, and upon this rock I will build my church . . . " (Matthew 16:18) From the time he was introduced to Jesus by his brother Andrew, Peter was a leader and spokesperson among the apostles. When Jesus asked his disciples, "Who do you say I am?" Peter replied, "You are the Christ, the Son of the living God." When Jesus said he was going to suffer and die, it was Peter who objected. When Jesus was arrested, it was Peter who drew his sword to protect him. Peter was the first to preach at Pentecost, and he arranged for the election of Matthias to replace Judas. He worked the first public miracle: curing the lame man at the Temple gate. By his example, Saint Peter reminds us what it means to be a disciple.

Saint Peter

Witness and Share

These sentences describe what Catholics believe. Listen carefully as they are read. Ask yourself, "How strong are my Catholic beliefs?"

My Way to Faith
_____

• I recognize the Holy Spirit at work in my life and the lives of others.

• I participate in events organized by the community of faithful, including Christians of other churches.

• I pray for the Gifts of the Holy Spirit to guide me and help me make decisions.

• I rely on the Holy Spirit to help me understand and proclaim the Gospel.

• I experience a sense of community in my parish.

Share Your Faith

Consider ways in which you can be more enthusiastic or Spirit-filled in sharing your faith with others. Write your ideas on the lines, and invite a family member or friend to participate in a faith-sharing experience with you.

_____

_____

_____

_____

(194) UNIT 3 *Jesus Christ the Life*

✦ **How can you overcome this?** (Possible answers: trusting in God; learning more about my faith; praying to the Holy Spirit for courage)

2. Ask students to compose a prayer to the Holy Spirit that asks for renewal and guidance. Invite students to share their prayers with the class. Encourage students to say their prayer every day.

 **Español** Invite Spanish-language speakers to access **www.loyolapress.com/espanol**.
Goal 2: To invite all people to hear the message of salvation in Jesus Christ **115**. To foster cultural diversity within the unity of the Church

---

The Church Evangelizes Encourage students to read, pray, and examine Scripture with Christians from other denominations. Offer opportunities to have a speaker from another Christian denomination discuss his or her faith with the class. **Goal 2:** To invite all people to hear the message of salvation in Jesus Christ **116**. To deepen ecumenical involvement

Inspire _____

1. Review holiness with students.
   - ✦ **What does *holy* mean?** (dedicated or consecrated to God) **Who is called to holiness?** (everyone) **How does your life reflect holiness?** [Allow time for discussion.]
   - ✦ Emphasize that the call to be holy includes every aspect of our lives.
   - ✦ **As disciples, why must we be holy in all parts of our lives, and not just in one part?** (We are called to love God in body, soul, and spirit.)
   - ✦ **By virtue of our Baptism, we are called to holiness in all that we are and do. Our desire to be closer to God motivates us to strive toward being holy without exception.**

2. Invite students into the prayer center.
   - ✦ Read and discuss the text and Scripture on page 201.
   - ✦ Explain to students that the Sacrament of Matrimony and the Sacrament of Holy Orders are the two Sacraments at the Service of Communion.
   - ✦ **These sacraments ask people to put God at the center of their lives. What do God-centered lives look like?** (Possible answers: prayerful; joyful; helpful; peaceful)
   - ✦ Pray aloud: **Lord, make us holy as you are holy. Amen.**

Proclaim _____

1. Read the **Know and Proclaim** introduction and chart to students.
   - ✦ Discuss the first row of the chart. Remind students that we are signs of God's love to others.
   - ✦ **God is always with us. Sometimes we have to slow down, quiet ourselves, and be still to recognize God's presence.**
   - ✦ Discuss the second row of the chart. Invite students to share ways their families are like a small version of the Church.
   - ✦ **What kind of traditions does your family have? What purpose do they serve?** [Allow time for

students to share.] **The Catholic family takes responsibility for nurturing all types of vocations.**
   - ✦ Remind students that the Sacrament of Matrimony serves the community.
   - ✦ **How do married couples serve the community?** (They make families and provide stability.)
   - ✦ Read the third row of the chart. Remind students that the Sacrament of Holy Orders serves the Church community.

   - ✦ **How do deacons, priests, and bishops serve the Church?** (Possible answers: They administer the sacraments and teach the truths of the faith.)

2. Point out the **Test Your Catholic Knowledge** question. Allow students time to fill in the circle of their choice before discussing the correct answer.

Gather and Go Forth

CHAPTER **24**

Know and Proclaim

We learn the truths of our Catholic faith, and we proclaim them through our vocations in life.

We Know Our Faith	We Proclaim Our Faith
God calls us to a particular vocation through the ordinary events of our lives.	Many Catholics reflect on their day by thinking about God's presence and movement in ordinary events.
God calls some people to be a sign of Christ's love for his Church through the vocation of marriage.	The Catholic family is the domestic church, or a Church in miniature. Catholics consider it their social responsibility to care for and protect the institution of the family.
Matrimony and Holy Orders are the two Sacraments at the Service of Communion.	Catholics pray for an increase in vocations to the priesthood and religious life.

Test Your Catholic Knowledge

Fill in the circle that best answers the question.

Which of the following are the Sacraments at the Service of Communion?

- ● Matrimony and Holy Orders
- ○ Rite of Christian Initiation of Adults
- ○ Baptism, Eucharist, and Confirmation
- ○ Reconciliation and Anointing of the Sick

Through the Sacraments of Matrimony and Holy Orders, Catholics proclaim Christ's holiness with lives of service to others.

As he who called you is holy, be holy yourselves in every aspect of your conduct, for it is written, "Be holy, because I [am] holy."

1 Peter 1:15–16

Matrimony and Holy Orders CHAPTER 24 (201)

The Church Evangelizes Send home a newsletter to families with suggestion for a family art project. Such projects can illustrate how the family lives a faith-filled life.
Goal 1: To bring about enthusiasm for faith so it is freely shared with others **101.** To foster a sense of the domestic church

See pages T366–T368 for a full correlation to the USCCB *Go and Make Disciples* national plan.

3. Read aloud **A Catholic to Know.** Discuss Saint John Leonardi.

✦ John Leonardi's other works included helping establish a seminary for the Propagation of the Faith.

✦ Explain that the Society for the Propagation of the Faith seeks prayer, sacrifice, and support from high school and college students for missions around the world.

✦ **October is World Mission Month. What can you do during the month of October to support the Church's missionary activity?** (Possible answers: I can pray; make donations; learn about missions.)

✦ **Saint John Leonardi's story tells us that one well-lived life can make a difference to God and to others.**

4. Read the **Witness and Share** introductory text.

✦ Explain that people on a journey choose paths. Our way to faith and witness lasts a lifetime.

✦ Read aloud each statement. Allow time for reflection after each one.

✦ Ask students to choose one faith statement to discuss with a parent, priest, or another trusted adult. Encourage them to reflect on statements from earlier in the year to see how they have grown.

5. Read aloud the directions for the **Share Your Faith** activity. Suggest ideas such as reading Scripture as a family or going on an annual pilgrimage to a nearby shrine.

Transform _____

1. Ask students to consider a vocation as a priest or a religious brother or sister.

✦ **Where is your call to holiness leading you?** [Have students reflect silently. Encourage them to record their responses in their journals.]

✦ Remind students that they should not worry if they are unsure. The call to a vocation can come at any time. The important thing is to remain open.

A Catholic to Know

Born in Italy in 1541, John studied pharmacy. He used his knowledge while working in hospitals and prisons. But when he realized that God was calling him to serve his people, John became a priest. John entered the priesthood at a very confusing time. Many people were insecure about what to believe. Despite facing many hardships and opposition, John worked hard to strengthen people's faith through religious education and other pastoral works. John began to train lay leaders and lay catechists. In 1573, John founded a religious order of men. He later published a summary of Christian doctrine. John Leonardi proved by his life that with God, even one person can make many good things happen.

Saint John Leonardi

Witness and Share

These sentences describe what Catholics believe. Listen carefully as they are read. Ask yourself, "How strong are my Catholic beliefs?".

My Way to Faith

· I recognize Jesus' presence with me during the ordinary events of my life.

· I answer the call to be holy and to love others.

· I give witness to God's love in my family, in my school, in my parish, and among my friends.

· I open myself to the calling of the priesthood or religious life.

· I pray with my family regularly.

Share Your Faith

Consider ways in which you can contribute to the prayer life of your family. Write your ideas on the lines, and invite your family to pray with you often.

_____

_____

_____

_____

202 UNIT 3 *Jesus Christ the Life*

✦ Invite a priest to share his call to the priesthood with the class.

2. Write the following prayer on the board and pray together. **O God, your Son Jesus told us the harvest is ready, but the laborers are few. May your Holy Spirit inspire men and women to continue his mission. May this same Spirit make known your will for my life.**

Sunday Connection Explore this Sunday's Scripture readings with students by accessing **www.loyolapress.com/sunday**.
Goal 1: To bring about enthusiasm for faith so it is freely shared with others 93. To foster an appreciation of God's Word

The Church Evangelizes Ask students to interview adult family members about their call to holiness. Have students report their findings to the class. **Goal 3:** To foster gospel values, promoting dignity of the human person, the importance of the family, and the common good 122. To foster the importance of family

Inspire

1. Gather the class in the prayer center.
   - ✦ Ask students to reflect on their faith journey.
   - ✦ **Take a moment and think about the path of faith you have travelled this year.** [Allow a few minutes of silent reflection.]
   - ✦ **Now reflect on what you learned about Jesus, what you learned about yourself, and what you learned about your faith.** [Allow time for reflection.]

2. Read aloud the text and Scripture in the sidebar on page 209.
   - ✦ Remind students that this verse is the central message of the Gospels.
   - ✦ **Why did God send his Son?** (because he loved us) **What is our response to God's love?** (to love him in return and love others)

3. Invite students to pray the Scriptures.
   - ✦ Read John 3:16–21 slowly and prayerfully. Explain that Jesus calls us into the light of God's love.
   - ✦ **How do Jesus' words make you feel?** [Allow a moment for students to reflect quietly on these questions.]
   - ✦ **What difference do Jesus' words make to you?** [Allow students time to reflect quietly before asking them to praise God privately.]

Proclaim

1. Read the **Know and Proclaim** introduction and chart with students.
   - ✦ [Discuss the first row.] **Jesus wants his disciples to live in his truth and to learn and follow his teachings. How have you grown as a disciple?** [Let students respond.]
   - ✦ As you discuss the second row, remind students that they are always at the beginning of their faith journey.
   - ✦ **Just as death is the beginning of eternal life, your faith journey is always beginning anew. What are some ways you can help your faith grow?** (Possible answers: learn more about the saints; serve others)
   - ✦ [Discuss the third row.] **Think of ways you can offer yourself in service to others and to the parish.** [Ask students to share their ideas.]

2. Point out the **Test Your Catholic Knowledge** section. Discuss the correct answer.

Gather and Go Forth

CHAPTER 25

Know and Proclaim

Jesus came to bring light into the world. As we proclaim our Catholic faith, we reflect Jesus' light when we act with love toward one another.

We Know Our Faith	We Proclaim Our Faith
Jesus commanded his followers to give witness to his teachings and to follow the example of his life.	Catholics celebrate the Ascension of Jesus 40 days after Easter or on the following Sunday that follows, depending on their local diocese.
Through Christ, we are offered eternal life. Following his way and living his truth will bring us life everlasting.	Catholics believe that death is not the end but the beginning of eternal life. At a Catholic funeral, the baptismal candle is lit to represent our birth into eternal life through Baptism.
Disciples of Jesus reach out to serve their families, schools, parishes, and the world.	Many Catholics support their parishes and local communities by offering their time, talent, and treasure in service to others.

Test Your Catholic Knowledge

Fill in the circle that best completes the sentence.

By serving the needs of others, we participate in Christ's ministry of:

○ prophet.

○ priest.

● king.

○ laity.

We have received the gifts of Jesus and the call to discipleship from God who loves us. Our response is to follow Jesus Christ to eternal life with God.

"For God so loved the world that he gave his only Son, so that everyone who believes in him might not perish but might have eternal life."

John 3:16

Unit 3 Review CHAPTER 25 **209**

 3-Minute Retreat Invite deeper reflection on God's Word by accessing **www.loyolapress.com/retreat**. **Goal 1:** To bring about enthusiasm for faith so it is freely shared with others **93.** To foster an appreciation of God's Word in the lives of all Catholics

---

The Church Evangelizes Encourage students to attend parish missions by asking them to share what they heard and learned. Spend some time discussing the message of the mission and how they can apply it to their lives. **Goal 2:** To invite all people to hear the message of salvation in Jesus Christ **113.** To design programs of outreach for those who have ceased being active in the Church

---

See pages T366–T368 for a full correlation to the USCCB *Go and Make Disciples* **national plan.**

3. Read aloud **A Catholic to Know.**

- ✦ Explain that three letters in the New Testament and the Book of Revelation are attributed to John.

- ✦ **John is known as the "beloved disciple."** [Have a volunteer read John 21:20–25.]

- ✦ Ask students to find and share verses from the Gospel of John, the Letters of John, or the Book of Revelation, such as John 3:15–16; 14:18–21; 1 John 2:7–11; 3:11–18; 4:7 –11; and Revelation 21:1–4. Share your quote with the class.

4. Read the **Witness and Share** introductory text and **My Way to Faith** statements.

- ✦ **The journey of faith follows the path blazed by love.** Think about how you show your love for God and for others.

- ✦ Encourage students to ask God for the courage to love.

- ✦ Ask students to choose a faith statement for discussion with a trusted adult. Encourage them to continue on their path of spiritual growth in this area.

5. Read aloud the directions for the **Share Your Faith** activity.
Share with students the way you continue to develop your relationship with Jesus. Have students complete the activity.

Transform _____

1. Ask students to show love for neighbor by working for justice.

- ✦ Write the following quote on the board: *Justice is what love looks like in public.*

- ✦ **How is working for social justice an act of love?** (Possible answer: I show that I care about their lives; that I want people to reach their potential)

- ✦ Invite students to share social justice projects they may have worked on throughout the year.

A Catholic to Know

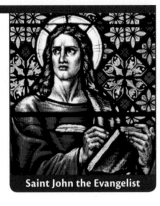

Saint John the Evangelist

John and his brother James, both fishermen, left everything to follow Jesus. John was with Jesus at critical times. Jesus permitted John to watch the miracle of bringing Jairus's daughter back to life, and he witnessed Jesus' Transfiguration. John was the "beloved disciple" and stayed with Jesus throughout his Passion. There is a story that when Saint John was very old, the people had to carry him to where the Christians assembled to worship. Each time he preached, his homily contained the same message: "Little children, love one another." He said that if they really did this, they would be doing what Jesus taught. John's Gospel continues to teach Christians how to love as Jesus loved.

Witness and Share

These sentences describe what Catholics believe. Listen carefully as they are read. Ask yourself, "How strong are my Catholic beliefs?"

My Way to Faith

- I believe that following Jesus Christ faithfully holds the promise of eternal life.
- I pray for the courage to make the decisions that Jesus would want me to make.
- I use my gifts to serve the needs of my parish.
- I seek ways to develop and deepen my relationship with Jesus.
- I respect myself and others because I believe all human beings are made in God's image.

Share Your Faith

Consider ways in which you can seek to develop and deepen your relationship with Jesus. Write your ideas on the lines, and invite a family member or friend to talk with you about his or her own relationship with Jesus.

_____

_____

_____

_____

210 UNIT 3 *Jesus Christ the Life*

---

2. Challenge students to show love for God by keeping God in the center of their lives.

- ✦ Remind students that we need to always grow in our relationship with Jesus.

- ✦ **How can you keep God at the center of your life?** (Possible answers: by praying the Morning Offering; by practicing the "Little Way" of Saint Thérèse of Lisieux; by examining my conscience daily)

3. Have the class pray the Act of Love on the inside back cover of their books.

Arts & Faith Celebrate how faith is expressed and deepened through art at **www .loyolapress.com/arts-faith**.

Goal 3: To foster gospel values, promoting the dignity of the human person, the importance of the family, and the common good **124.** To encourage Catholic witness in the arts and in the American intellectual community

The Church Evangelizes Organize the class to prepare sack lunches that can be handed out to people who are homeless. If enough adult volunteers can be recruited, the class could hand out the meals personally. **Goal 3:** To foster gospel values, promoting dignity of the human person, the importance of the family, and the common good **121.** To involve parishes and local service groups in the needs of their neighborhood

CORRELATION TO *GO AND MAKE DISCIPLES*
A National Plan and Strategy for Catholic Evangelization in the United States

The following chart provides **correlations between concepts taught in Grade 7 and goals of the New Evangelization**, specifically those set by the USCCB in its document *Go and Make Disciples: A National Plan for Catholic Evangelization in the United States*. For a copy of the plan and for further information about the New Evangelization, go to **www.usccb.org**.

Goal I

89. To bring about in all Catholics such an enthusiasm for their faith that, in living their faith in Jesus, they freely share it with others This goal calls Catholics to continue to hear the Good News at ever-deeper levels. The call to holiness, given to every Catholic through Baptism, consecrates each one to God and to the service of the kingdom. This deepening of faith, in holiness, fosters a desire to involve others in that faith, until God will be "all in all" in a transformed world.

STRATEGY	Student Pages	Catechist Pages
90. The strategy of this goal is to so deepen the sense of Scripture and sacrament that Catholics will pray more fully and, with a greater understanding of Christ's call, live as disciples at home, at work, and in today's many cultural settings. This goal also seeks a greater openness to physical, mental, and cultural diversity among Catholics.	**Gather and Go Forth:** 9–10, 17–18, 25–26, 33–34, 41–42, 49–50, 59–60, 67–68, 75–76, 85–86, 93–94, 101–102, 111–112, 119–120, 127–128, 135–136, 143–144, 153–154, 161–162, 169–170, 177–178, 185–186, 193–194, 201–202, 209–210	**Gather and Go Forth:** T316–T317, T318–T319, T320–T321, T322–T323, T324–T325, T326–T327, T328–T329, T330–T331, T332–T333, T334–T335, T336–T337, T338–T339, T340–T341, T342–T343, T344–T345, T346–T347, T348–T349, T350–T351, T352–T353, T354–T355, T356–T357, T358–T359, T360–T361, T362–T363, T364–T365

OBJECTIVES	Student Pages	Catechist Pages
91. To foster an experience of conversion and renewal in the heart of every believer, leading to a more active living of Catholic life	**Gather and Go Forth:** 9–10, 17–18, 25–26, 33–34, 41–42, 49–50, 59–60, 67–68, 75–76, 85–86, 93–94, 101–102, 111–112, 119–120, 127–128, 135–136, 143–144, 153–154, 161–162, 169–170, 177–178, 185–186, 193–194, 201–202, 209–210	**Gather and Go Forth:** T316–T317, T318–T319, T320–T321, T322–T323, T324–T325, T326–T327, T328–T329, T330–T331, T332–T333, T334–T335, T336–T337, T338–T339, T340–T341, T342–T343, T344–T345, T346–T347, T348–T349, T350–T351, T352–T353, T354–T355, T356–T357, T358–T359, T360–T361, T362–T363, T364–T365 **The Church Evangelizes:** T356, T360
92. To foster an experience of conversion and renewal in every parish		**The Church Evangelizes:** T339, T352
93. To foster an appreciation of God's Word in the lives of all Catholics	**Scripture sidebar:** 9, 17, 25, 33, 41, 49, 59, 67, 75, 85, 93, 101, 111, 119, 127, 135, 143, 153, 161, 169, 177, 185, 193, 201, 209	**Inspire step:** T316, T318, T320, T322, T324, T326, T328, T330, T332, T334, T336, T338, T340, T342, T344, T346, T348, T350, T352, T354, T356, T358, T360, T362, T364 **Daily Inspiration:** T318, T328, T345, T348, T360 **Sunday Connection:** T320, T340, T363 **3-Minute Retreat:** T342, T356, T364
94. To make the evangelizing dimension of Sunday Eucharist more explicit		**The Church Evangelizes:** T318, T327, T354
95. To foster an appreciation of the presence of Christ in the Eucharist and of all the sacraments, the sacred signs of our Catholic life		**The Church Evangelizes:** T317, T328, T333
96. To foster a greater appreciation of the power of God's Word in our worship		**Sunday Connection:** T326, T335, T354
97. To foster an even deeper sense of prayer among our Catholic people		**3-Minute Retreat:** T316, T334, T336, T351
98. To foster a renewed understanding of the faith among Catholics	**Gather and Go Forth:** 9–10, 17–18, 25–26, 33–34, 41–42, 49–50, 59–60, 67–68, 75–76, 85–86, 93–94, 101–102, 111–112, 119–120, 127–128, 135–136, 143–144, 153–154, 161–162, 169–170, 177–178, 185–186, 193–194, 201–202, 209–210	**Gather and Go Forth:** T316–T317, T318–T319, T320–T321, T322–T323, T324–T325, T326–T327, T328–T329, T330–T331, T332–T333, T334–T335, T336–T337, T338–T339, T340–T341, T342–T343, T344–T345, T346–T347, T348–T349, T350–T351, T352–T353, T354–T355, T356–T357, T358–T359, T360–T361, T362–T363, T364–T365 **DRE Connect:** T319, T344
99. To foster a sense of discipleship among Catholic adults and children	**Gather and Go Forth:** 9–10, 17–18, 25–26, 33–34, 41–42, 49–50, 59–60, 67–68, 75–76, 85–86, 93–94, 101–102, 111–112, 119–120, 127–128, 135–136, 143–144, 153–154, 161–162, 169–170, 177–178, 185–186, 193–194, 201–202, 209–210	**Gather and Go Forth:** T316–T317, T318–T319, T320–T321, T322–T323, T324–T325, T326–T327, T328–T329, T330–T331, T332–T333, T334–T335, T336–T337, T338–T339, T340–T341, T342–T343, T344–T345, T346–T347, T348–T349, T350–T351, T352–T353, T354–T355, T356–T357, T358–T359, T360–T361, T362–T363, T364–T365
100. To foster active and personal religious experience through participation in small-group and other communal experiences in which the Good News is shared, experienced, and applied to daily life		**Inspire step:** T316, T318, T320, T322, T324, T326, T328, T330, T332, T334, T336, T338, T340, T342, T344, T346, T348, T350, T352, T354, T356, T358, T360, T362, T364
101. To foster a sense of the domestic church within households in which families, individuals, and groups reside		**My Way to Faith:** T317, T329, T337, T363 **The Church Evangelizes:** T362
102. To promote and develop a spirituality for the workplace		**The Church Evangelizes:** T342, T350
103. To foster greater appreciation of cultural and ethnic spirituality		**Español:** T324

The **Gather and Go Forth** pages, Student Book and Catechist's Edition, help students recognize that the Church's mission is also their mission: to tell the Good News of Jesus to the whole world through words and deeds and to reflect the Church's mission to know, proclaim, witness, share, and transform.

Goal II

104. To invite all people in the United States, whatever their social or cultural background, to hear the message of salvation in Jesus Christ so they may come to join us in the fullness of the Catholic faith   This goal means that we are to invite effectively every person to come to know the Good News of Jesus proclaimed by the Catholic Church. This goal goes along with the first one, for, as that goal is sought, Catholics will develop an inviting attitude as a general part of our everyday spirituality. This goal means not only that people are invited but also that an essential welcoming spirit is present in Catholic homes and in all our Catholic institutions: parishes, organizations, hospitals, schools, chanceries, and centers of neighborhood service. This goal also has ecumenical implications.

STRATEGY		Student Pages	Catechist Pages
105. The strategy behind this goal is to create a more welcoming attitude toward others in our parishes so that people feel at home; next, to create an attitude of sharing faith and to develop greater skills to do this; then, to undertake activities to invite others to know the Catholic people better.		**Gather and Go Forth:** 9–10, 17–18, 25–26, 33–34, 41–42, 49–50, 59–60, 67–68, 75–76, 85–86, 93–94, 101–102, 111–112, 119–120, 127–128, 135–136, 143–144, 153–154, 161–162, 169–170, 177–178, 185–186, 193–194, 201–202, 209–210	**Gather and Go Forth:** T316–T317, T318–T319, T320–T321, T322–T323, T324–T325, T326–T327, T328–T329, T330–T331, T332–T333, T334–T335, T336–T337, T338–T339, T340–T341, T342–T343, T344–T345, T346–T347, T348–T349, T350–T351, T352–T353, T354–T355, T356–T357, T358–T359, T360–T361, T362–T363, T364–T365

OBJECTIVES		Student Pages	Catechist Pages
106. To make every Catholic institution, especially our parishes, more welcoming			**Special Needs:** T330, T339 **Español:** T343, T352, T357
107. To help every Catholic feel comfortable about sharing his or her faith and inviting people to discover Christ in our Catholic family of believers		**Gather and Go Forth:** 9–10, 17–18, 25–26, 33–34, 41–42, 49–50, 59–60, 67–68, 75–76, 85–86, 93–94, 101–102, 111–112, 119–120, 127–128, 135–136, 143–144, 153–154, 161–162, 169–170, 177–178, 185–186, 193–194, 201–202, 209–210	**Gather and Go Forth:** T316–T317, T318–T319, T320–T321, T322–T323, T324–T325, T326–T327, T328–T329, T330–T331, T332–T333, T334–T335, T336–T337, T338–T339, T340–T341, T342–T343, T344–T345, T346–T347, T348–T349, T350–T351, T352–T353, T354–T355, T356–T357, T358–T359, T360–T361, T362–T363, T364–T365
108. To develop within families and households the capacity to share the Gospel			**The Church Evangelizes:** T321, T329, T355
109. To equip and empower our active Catholic members to exercise their baptismal call to evangelize		**Gather and Go Forth:** 9–10, 17–18, 25–26, 33–34, 41–42, 49–50, 59–60, 67–68, 75–76, 85–86, 93–94, 101–102, 111–112, 119–120, 127–128, 135–136, 143–144, 153–154, 161–162, 169–170, 177–178, 185–186, 193–194, 201–202, 209–210	**Gather and Go Forth:** T316–T317, T318–T319, T320–T321, T322–T323, T324–T325, T326–T327, T328–T329, T330–T331, T332–T333, T334–T335, T336–T337, T338–T339, T340–T341, T342–T343, T344–T345, T346–T347, T348–T349, T350–T351, T352–T353, T354–T355, T356–T357, T358–T359, T360–T361, T362–T363, T364–T365 **DRE Connect:** T338, T358
110. To use special times in parish and family life to invite people to faith			**The Church Evangelizes:** T353, T359
111. To cultivate an active core of the baptized to serve as ministers of evangelization in their parishes, dioceses, neighborhoods, workplaces, and homes		**Gather and Go Forth:** 9–10, 17–18, 25–26, 33–34, 41–42, 49–50, 59–60, 67–68, 75–76, 85–86, 93–94, 101–102, 111–112, 119–120, 127–128, 135–136, 143–144, 153–154, 161–162, 169–170, 177–178, 185–186, 193–194, 201–202, 209–210	**Gather and Go Forth:** T316–T317, T318–T319, T320–T321, T322–T323, T324–T325, T326–T327, T328–T329, T330–T331, T332–T333, T334–T335, T336–T337, T338–T339, T340–T341, T342–T343, T344–T345, T346–T347, T348–T349, T350–T351, T352–T353, T354–T355, T356–T357, T358–T359, T360–T361, T362–T363, T364–T365 **DRE Connect:** T331, T355
112. To effectively invite people to our Church			**The Church Evangelizes:** T349
113. To design programs of outreach for those who have ceased being active in the Church			**The Church Evangelizes:** T337, T364
114. To design programs that reach out in particular ways to those who do not participate in a church community or who seek the fullness of faith			**The Church Evangelizes:** T330, T340, T357
115. To foster cultural diversity within the unity of the Church			**Español:** T322, T333, T361
116. To deepen ecumenical involvement			**The Church Evangelizes:** T323, T361

Continued from page T367.

Goal III

117. To foster gospel values in our society, promoting the dignity of the human person, the importance of the family, and the common good of our society, so that our nation may continue to be transformed by the saving power of Jesus Christ This goal follows upon the other two: the appreciation of our faith and its spread should lead to the transformation of our society. The pursuit of this goal, however, must accompany the pursuit of the other two because evangelization is not possible without powerful signs of justice and peace, as the Gospel shapes the framework of our lives. The Catholic Church has developed a strong social doctrine concerning the common good—a tradition based on the proper ordering of society and supporting the inalienable dignity of every person. In the United States, this tradition has been cultivated in the advocacy of religious liberty; the pursuit of social justice, especially for those left out of today's society; just economic policies; a consistent ethic of human life; and striving for peace in a nuclear world.

STRATEGIES	Student Pages	Catechist Pages
118. This goal means supporting those cultural elements in our land that reflect Catholic values and challenging those that reject it. Catholics, who today are involved in every level of modern life in the United States, have to address our society as a system and also in particular situations.		**Arts & Faith:** T321, T332, T341, T346, T353, T365 **Shaping the World:** T335, T358
119. The transformation of our society in Christ particularly calls for the involvement and skills of lay men and women who carry the values of the Gospel into their homes.	**Share Your Faith:** 10, 18, 26, 34, 42, 50, 60, 68, 76, 86, 94, 102, 112, 120, 128, 136, 144, 154, 162, 170, 178, 186, 194, 202, 210	**Transform step:** T317, T319, T321, T323, T325, T327, T329, T331, T333, T335, T337, T339, T341, T343, T345, T347, T349, T351, T353, T355, T357, T359, T361, T363, T365 **The Church Evangelizes:** T331, T343, T345, T347, T351, T363
120. This goal requires the strategy of strengthening our everyday involvement with those in need.		**The Church Evangelizes:** T325, T341, T343, T347, T359, T365

OBJECTIVES	Student Pages	Catechist Pages
121. To involve parishes and local service groups in the needs of their neighborhood		**The Church Evangelizes:** T343, T365
122. To foster the importance of the family		**The Church Evangelizes:** T331, T347, T363
123. To develop groups to explore issues of the workplace and lay spirituality		**The Church Evangelizes:** T345, T351
124. To encourage Catholic witness in the arts and in the American intellectual community		**Arts & Faith:** T321, T332, T341, T346, T353, T365 **The Church Evangelizes:** T335
125. To involve every Catholic, on different levels, in areas of public policy		**The Church Evangelizes:** T325, T341
126. To involve the Catholic Church, on every level, in the media		**Special Needs:** T347, T359
127. To involve Catholics, at every level, in questions of economic systems		**The Church Evangelizes:** T358

Special Seasons and Lessons

Liturgical Calendar

The liturgical calendar represents the celebration of the mystery of Christ—from the anticipation of his birth; to his Incarnation; to his Death, Resurrection, and Ascension; to the expectation of his return. The Church marks the passage of time with a cycle of seasons and feast days that invites us to deepen our commitment to Jesus year after year. By inviting the students into these celebrations, you help them grow in the Catholic way of life.

Explaining the Liturgical Calendar

Use or adapt the following script to introduce the students to a basic understanding of the liturgical calendar. Repeat the discussion occasionally throughout the year.

✦ **What do you think the diagram on this page represents?** (Accept reasonable answers.) **It is a liturgical calendar. We normally keep a calendar to mark special days such as birthdays, anniversaries, and holidays. In the same way, the Church keeps a calendar to mark special times in Jesus' life, such as his Death, Resurrection, and return to his Father.**

✦ **In our calendar year, we have seasons—winter, spring, summer, and fall. The liturgical calendar has seasons too. What seasons are shown on this calendar?** (Advent, Christmas, Lent, Easter, Ordinary Time) **Let's find the season we are going to learn about today.**

✦ **Just as our regular calendar has holidays that commemorate the birthdays of important people or recall important events, the liturgical calendar has feast days and holidays. What feast days are shown on this calendar?**

✦ Invite volunteers to name some feast days.

The Year in Our Church

Holy Week
 - Palm Sunday
 - Holy Thursday
 - Good Friday
 - Holy Saturday
 - Easter Sunday

Lent
 - Ash Wednesday

Ordinary Time

Christmas
 - Epiphany
 - Christmas

Advent
 - First Sunday of Advent

Easter
 - Ascension
 - Pentecost

All Souls Day
All Saints Day

Ordinary Time

Winter · Spring · Fall · Summer

Liturgical Calendar

The liturgical calendar highlights the seasons of the Church year. Various colors symbolize the different seasons.

Special Seasons and Lessons

213

1 Feast of All Saints

Faith Focus

In the lives of the saints, we find examples of ways to imitate Christ.

Reflecting on the Faith Experience

Take a few moments to reflect prayerfully before preparing the lesson.

Listening

. . . [R]emembering you in my prayers, that the God of our Lord Jesus Christ, the Father of glory, may give you a spirit of wisdom and revelation resulting in knowledge of him. May the eyes of [your] hearts be enlightened, that you may know what is the hope that belongs to his call, what are the riches of glory in his inheritance among the holy ones, and what is the surpassing greatness of his power for us who believe, in accord with the exercise of his great might, . . .

Ephesians 1:16–19

Reflecting

The rich variety of colors we see when sunlight shines through a prism delights and fascinates us. In much the same way, people through whom the light of Christ shines display to the world the many facets of God's great love. Those people who have allowed the Lord's light to shine out in their words and actions and who have reached the heavenly kingdom are called saints.

Each individual's relationship with God prompts a unique response that reflects his or her understanding of divine love. These personal expressions are varied, but they all reveal divine goodness. Divine light is diffused through the saints as they stand before the Lord, totally open to his love.

The entrance antiphon that we pray in the Common of Holy Men and Women sums up the lives of the saints who intercede for us.

> May all your works thank you,
> O Lord,
> and all your Holy ones bless
> you.
> They shall speak of the glory
> of your reign,
> and declare your mighty
> deeds.

As we honor the saints, we pray in the words of the Collect Prayer of the same Common of Holy Men and Women to follow their example.

> Almighty and eternal God,
> who by glorifying the Saints,
> bestow on us fresh proofs of
> your love,
> graciously grant
> that, commended by their
> intercession and spurred
> on by their example,
> we may be faithful in imitating
> your Only Begotten Son.

In what ways can I allow the light of Christ to shine through me?

Responding

Spirit of Wisdom, enlighten the eyes of my students to see the glory of God that shines through the saints.

Scripture for Further Reflection

Matthew 5:1–12 Jesus teaches us the way to eternal joy.

1 John 3:1–3 We are God's children now.

Preparing for the Faith Experience

One-Day Lesson
Feast of All Saints

Scripture in This Lesson

Matthew 5:3–10 The Beatitudes

Church Documents

Catechism of the Catholic Church. The themes of this lesson correspond to the following paragraphs: **946–959, 1717, 2030, 2156.**

Music in This Lesson

For a list of all the music suggested in this program, see page T517.

Enriching the Faith Experience

Use the activities at the end of the lesson to enrich the lesson or to replace an activity with one that better meets the needs of your class.

Feast of All Saints
Student pages 215–216

LEARNING OUTCOMES

The students will be able to

- describe how the saints lived the spirit of the Beatitudes.
- explain why the feast of All Saints is a day to honor all of the saints.
- identify ways to emulate the saints today.

Key Terms

saint—a person who loved God on earth and now lives with God in heaven.

All Saints Day—a holy day celebrated on November 1 on which we honor all those who now live with God in heaven.

Materials

- Paper
- Markers
- Several copies of books containing the lives of the saints

Before You Begin

1. This lesson focuses on how the Beatitudes are related to our understanding of the saints and holiness. The Beatitudes are taught more completely in Chapter 14, The Challenge of the Beatitudes. You may wish to read Reflecting from this chapter on page T162 in preparation for teaching this lesson.

2. On special occasions, such as the Easter Vigil and Ordination Masses, the Church calls upon the saints for help by praying a Litany of the Saints. When we pray a Litany of the Saints, we say "Saint _____ , pray for us." In this lesson, the students will be invited to pray a modified form of the Litany of the Saints.

Centering _____

Introduce the students to the feast of All Saints.

✦ **November 1 is a Holy Day of Obligation called the feast of All Saints. Each year on this feast, the same Gospel reading is read at Mass. Let's read it together now.**

✦ Have the students turn to **Feast of All Saints** on page 215. Ask a student to read aloud Matthew 5:3–10.

✦ Have a student read aloud the first paragraph on page 215.

✦ **What is a saint?** (a person who is with God in heaven) **Do we know all of the saints?** (no)

✦ **When a person who has lived a holy life dies, people sometimes call that person a saint. If many people think that this person was a great example of how to imitate Jesus, they may want to honor him or her in a special way. They do this by requesting to begin the process where the Church officially declares that person a saint. This process is called canonization.**

✦ **During this process, the Church carefully examines the life of the person being considered for sainthood. If the study shows that the person's life was truly a great example of holiness for other Christians to follow, the person may be canonized.** [Write *canonized* on the board.]

✦ **If a person is canonized by the Church, we can believe that he or she is now with God in heaven. Canonized saints have a special feast day and may be honored in public ways, such as at a Mass. There are also many saints in heaven who are not canonized. We honor these saints on All Saints Day as well.**

Sharing _____

1. Discuss with the students what they may already know about the Beatitudes.

1 | Feast of All Saints

In the Gospel for the Feast of All Saints, we hear Jesus teach

> Blessed are the poor in spirit,
> for theirs is the kingdom of heaven.
>
> Blessed are they who mourn,
> for they will be comforted.
>
> Blessed are the meek,
> for they will inherit the land.
>
> Blessed are they who hunger and thirst
> for righteousness,
> for they will be satisfied.
>
> Blessed are the merciful,
> for they will be shown mercy.
>
> Blessed are the clean of heart,
> for they will see God.
>
> Blessed are the peacemakers,
> for they will be called children of God.
>
> Blessed are they who are persecuted
> for the sake of righteousness,
> for theirs is the kingdom of heaven.
>
> Matthew 5:3–10

Saint Joan of Arc.

On the feast of All Saints, we honor all of the saints. They lived their lives in the spirit of the Beatitudes and in the spirit of Jesus. Through the grace of God, these saints share eternal happiness with God in heaven.

The saints are people who have led lives of heroic virtue that set an example for all Christians. They have witnessed to their faith in ordinary and extraordinary ways. In their lives, we see God's grace at work. This does not mean that the saints were perfect. Instead, it means that they trusted in God's love and mercy. God was able to work through them in powerful ways. This is what we try to follow in our lives. When we imitate the saints, we are also acting like Christ.

Left to right: Saint Francis of Assisi, Archbishop Oscar Romero (1917–1980), and Saint Thérèse of Lisieux (at age 13).

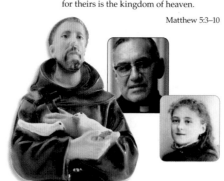

(215)

✦ **What do you think Jesus is teaching us in the Beatitudes?** (Answers will vary.)

✦ **Since the Gospel reading for the feast of All Saints is Jesus' teaching of the Beatitudes, we know that these words have something to do with saints and holiness. Perhaps one way to think about the Beatitudes is to think of them as a job description for a saint. Having read the Beatitudes, what qualities would you look for in a saint?** (Answers will vary.)

2. Have the students work in pairs to write a want ad for a saint. Suggest that the want ad begin in the following way:

✦ [Write this on the board.]
Seeking saints for the Kingdom of God.
Applicants should be . . .

✦ Distribute paper and allow time for the students to complete this activity. Ask several students to share their want ads.

3. Have a student read aloud the last paragraph on page 215.

✦ **If the saints were not perfect, what was it that made them so heroic?** (their trust in God)

✦ **When we imitate the saints, who else are we imitating?** (Christ)

4. Discuss with the students the diversity of witness and example in the lives of the saints, as well as their common features.

✦ **While we see Christ working in the lives of the saints, there is a wide variety of ways that this happens. Let's consider some examples.** [Read these examples to the students.]

• **Saint Martin de Porres was born in Peru in 1579. He is known for the compassion he showed for people who were poor and for people who were sick. He founded an orphanage and a hospital. He also ministered to the people brought from Africa to be slaves. He served all with generosity and compassion, just as Jesus did.**

• **Saint Julie Billiart was born in France in 1751. She is known for teaching and promoting the faith even when such activities had been forbidden by the state authorities during the French Revolution. She taught children about God and protected priests who said Mass for the faithful. She founded a community of religious sisters, the Sisters of Notre Dame de Namur. She did all these things despite her own physical challenge of being paralyzed as a teenager. She followed Jesus by facing difficulties cheerfully and bravely.**

• **Saint Maximillan Mary Kolbe lived in Poland during World War II. He was a prisoner at the Nazi prison camp at Auschwitz. He stepped forward to take the place of another man who was about to be executed. He followed Jesus by laying down his life for another.**

✦ **We could give many more examples of the unique witness each saint offers. And yet, within the diversity of the many saints, we see important qualities that they hold in common.**

5. Have a student read aloud the first three paragraphs of

Saint Rose of Lima.

Qualities of the Saints

• **Saints Are Big Dreamers.** They make the impossible seem possible. They do not let their weaknesses or those of others hold them back from doing good. They believe that with God's grace, nothing can stop them.

• **Saints Are Go-Getters.** They believe that what is written in the Gospel is to be lived every day: turning the other cheek, loving God above all, feeding the hungry, clothing the naked, and following Jesus. When it comes to doing what is right and good, they don't wait for someone else to act first. They jump right in.

• **Saints Are Love-Bringers.** They try to see Christ in every person and in every situation. They continue to show love to us through their intercession with God on our behalf. Saint Thérèse of Lisieux spoke this belief when she said, "I will spend my heaven doing good on earth."

Saint Martin de Porres.

(216) FEAST OF ALL SAINTS

Today we celebrate all the saints together—the ones we know and the ones we don't know. These are the people who help us believe that love is the most important thing in the world. Their lives tell us that what matters most in life is not what we earn or own, not our status or our popularity. What really matters is how much we love God, others, and ourselves and how well we show that love.

Perhaps you know someone who is a big dreamer, a go-getter, and a love-bringer. Perhaps you are one of those special people who want to make this world a better place. Perhaps you are someone following the Good News with joy. Remember, holiness begins with little things: a smile, a helping hand, or a prayer. This is the road to sainthood. The world is waiting for St. You!

Following Their Example

The Collect Prayer of the Common of Holy Men and Women says well what we believe:

Almighty and eternal God,
who by glorifying the Saints,
bestow on us fresh proofs of your love,
graciously grant
that, commended by their intercession and
   spurred on by their example,
we may be faithful in imitating your Only
   Begotten Son.

What are examples of simple things you can do every day to imitate the holiness of the saints?

_____

_____

_____

_____

Qualities of the Saints on page 216.

✦ **What are some examples of saints who were big dreamers, go-getters, and love-bringers?** (Answers will vary.)

✦ Distribute copies of books that contain the lives of the saints. In groups of two or three, have the students choose a saint and identify specific examples of how this saint lived these three qualities.

✦ When the groups have completed the activity, have them present their findings to the class.

6. Discuss with the students the universal call to holiness.

✦ **The feast of All Saints is our feast day as well. At our Baptism, we** were made part of the family of God, which includes all of the saints in heaven. When we emulate the saints, when we live the Beatitudes, we show ourselves to be on our way to sainthood and life with God in heaven.

✦ Ask a volunteer to read aloud the last two paragraphs of **Qualities of the Saints** on page 216.

✦ **What really matters on the road to sainthood?** (how much we love God)

✦ **What are some simple ways we can show holiness?** (with a smile, by helping someone, and by praying)

7. Allow sufficient time for the students to complete the **Following Their Example** activity on page 216. Have some of the students share their answers.

Acting

 Lead the students in praying a Litany of the Saints.

  ✦ Prepare by asking the students to use the information found in Sharing #5 to write petitions. The petitions should take the following form:

Saint Francis, who brought Christ's love to all of God's creatures...

  ✦ To lead this prayer, invite each student to read aloud his or her petition. The response to each petition is "Pray for us." You might conclude the prayer by praying, "All holy men and women..."

  • Were the learning outcomes achieved?

Enriching the Faith Experience

Use the following activities to enrich the lesson or to replace an activity with one that better meets the needs of your class.

1. Have the students research their patron saint or the patron saint of the school or parish. Direct them to write their report as if it were the front page of a newspaper. Read aloud or distribute copies of the following directions:

  a. **Read several books or articles on your saint and take notes as you read. Put page number references in your notes in case you need to check the information.**

  b. **Choose one event from the saint's life for your headline story. Write your headline and list other events and customs from the time your saint lived. Use these shorter stories on the front page.**

  c. **Prepare a rough layout of your page. Articles should be written in columns like a newspaper. You might include pictures or artwork from the time period.**

2. You may wish to adapt this lesson to prepare the students for the All Saints Day liturgy that will be celebrated in the parish. For more information, visit www.christourlife.com.

3. The students might design banners representing particular saints, including significant symbols pertaining to that saint. The banners could be displayed at the parish liturgy for All Saints Day.

4. Encourage the students to research on the Internet the canonization process. The report might include (a) how a person is nominated for canonization, (b) the process of becoming acclaimed as a saint, and (c) what it means to be proclaimed a saint by the Church.

5. As a school project, have each class select a saint as their patron. The students could decorate the door to the classroom in honor of their saint. Or have the students draw their patron saints on cardboard, cut them out, and put them on a long sheet of paper or large bulletin board, creating a mural of saints.

6. November 2 is the celebration of All Souls. On this day, we recall our deceased relatives, friends, and all the faithful departed who may yet be waiting for the full joy of heaven. Christians have always prayed for those who have died. In the 11th century, Saint Odilo, who was an abbot at Cluny, France, required that the members of his monasteries pray for all the dead on the day after All Saints. Soon this custom spread throughout the Church. Invite the students to pray for loved ones and all who have died. You might choose to use this prayer and have the students insert the name of the person they are praying for.

  Eternal rest grant unto [insert *name*], O Lord.

  And let perpetual light shine upon [*him* or *her*].

  May [*his* or *her*] soul and the souls of all the faithful departed,

  through the mercy of God, rest in peace. Amen.

7. To help inform the students about the lives of the saints, use the *Loyola Kids Book of Saints*, *Loyola Kids Book of Heroes*, *My Life with the Saints*, or *Mystics and Miracles* (Loyola Press).

2 Advent

Faith Focus

In Advent, we remember the coming of Jesus in history, and we prepare with hope for his comings in mystery and in majesty.

Reflecting on the Faith Experience

Take a few moments to reflect prayerfully before preparing the lesson.

Listening

And the Word became flesh
and made his dwelling
  among us,
and we saw his glory,
the glory as of the Father's
  only Son,
full of grace and truth.

John 1:14

[W]e await the blessed hope,
the appearance of the glory
of the great God and of our
savior Jesus Christ, . . .

Titus 2:13

Reflecting

Bombarded by the media to prepare for Christmas by shopping and entertaining, how can we keep things in perspective and rediscover the message of peace and love that underlies the season? The Church offers the season of Advent, the four weeks preceding Christmas. Advent not only prepares us for Christmas but also for the ways that Christ comes to us in our lives.

During Advent, our attention focuses on the total mystery of Christ who is the same yesterday, today, and forever. During Advent, we remember his historical coming. As proclaimed in the Gospel of Luke, we recall the fulfillment of God's promise in the birth of his Son, Jesus. We experience the grace of his personal coming into our lives and our world on Christmas Day. We remember and celebrate his coming to us every day in the Eucharist, the sacraments, prayer,

people, and events. We long for Christ's final coming in glory:

But our citizenship is in heaven, and from it we also await a savior, the Lord Jesus Christ. He will change our lowly body to conform with his glorified body . . .

Philippians 3:20–21

The three comings of Christ—in history, in mystery, and in majesty—are one great manifestation of God-with-us. The Advent Scripture readings bring to mind the prophecies of God's promised Savior, the sayings and stories of Jesus, and the early Christian experience in the New Testament letters. Hearing the Word of God, we rediscover our roots, gain a fresh awareness of the demands of Christian life, and welcome with hope the future. In the quiet of Advent, we see the brokenness that still exists in our world and in ourselves. We seek conversion, a change of heart that will open us to the healing power of Christ, who can make us like himself and better prepared for his coming in glory.

The Church calls us to prepare for Christ's coming all year-round. We are called to be ready for his daily comings and for his Second Coming. This prayer from Revelation 22:20 is appropriate every day of the year: "Amen! Come, Lord Jesus!"

In what ways can I practice living in joyful hope?

Responding

Lord Jesus, help us to be welcoming to you as you come to us daily.

Scripture for Further Reflection

John 9:5 Jesus is the light of the world.

Revelation 1:5–6 Jesus is the ruler of the kings of the earth.

Preparing for the Faith Experience

Day One
The Coming of Jesus

Day Two
Symbols of Christ

Day Three
Mary, Our Model for Advent

Scripture in This Lesson

Matthew 25:31–46 When the Son of Man comes in glory, he will judge the nations.

Mark 14:62 Jesus prophecies the Day of Judgment.

Church Documents

Catechism of the Catholic Church.
The themes of this lesson correspond to the following paragraphs: **524, 1095.**

Music in the Lesson

For a list of all the music suggested in this program, see page T517.

Enriching the Faith Experience

Use the activities at the end of the lesson to enrich the lesson or to replace an activity with one that better meets the needs of your class.

Day One   The Coming of Jesus

Student page 217

LEARNING OUTCOMES

The students will be able to

- explain the significance of the three comings of Christ.
- identify and explain the three themes of Advent: remember, prepare, and wait in hope.

Key Terms

Advent—the liturgical season in which the Church remembers Christ's coming in history, prepares for his daily coming in mystery, and waits in hope for his coming in majesty

Parousia— (pah-ROO-see-uh) the second, or final, coming of Christ in glory

Materials

- Bibles or New Testaments
- Prepare three signs: on the first sign, write on one side *remember* and on the other side, write *history*; on the second sign, write on one side *prepare* and on the other side, write *mystery*; on the third sign, write on one side *wait in hope* and on the other side, write *majesty*.

Before You Begin

1. The season of Advent is the beginning of the Church's liturgical year. Advent includes the four Sundays before Christmas. These lessons are best taught during the first week of Advent.

2. The entire Old Testament is an Advent period of waiting and preparing for the Messiah. The history of the Church is an Advent period of waiting for the Lord Jesus to come again in glory and power. While we wait in hope, the Lord comes to us in everyday events.

Centering

1. Discuss with the students the three themes of Advent. [Place the three signs in the classroom, showing the *remember*, *prepare*, and *wait in hope* side.]

- ✦ **What are some experiences you have that require remembering, preparing, and waiting in hope?**

- ✦ **These are also the themes that describe Advent, the season in the Church year we are studying today.**

2. Have the students silently read the opening paragraph on page 217.

- ✦ Direct them to answer the question.

- ✦ **What are some of the ways you answered the question?**

Sharing

1. Have a student read aloud **The Coming of Jesus** on page 217.

2. Discuss with the students the coming of Christ in history.

- ✦ **During Advent, we remember Christ's first coming in history.** [Turn over sign *remember*.] **When did it take place?** (When Mary agreed to be the Mother of God, Jesus was conceived in her womb. He was born in Bethlehem on the first Christmas.)

- ✦ **The people of the Old Testament waited for the coming of Christ in history. From the time of Adam and Eve, God's promise to send a Redeemer was passed down through many generations.**

- ✦ **God chose the Jewish people to keep his promise alive. Finally, God the Father, through his Spirit, sent his Son to be born among us as a man.**

- ✦ **How long did the people wait for their Messiah?** (thousands of years) **What did they do to prepare for his coming?** (They lived according to the Covenant, hoping that God's promise would come true. They handed down the stories and promises of God. They prayed for

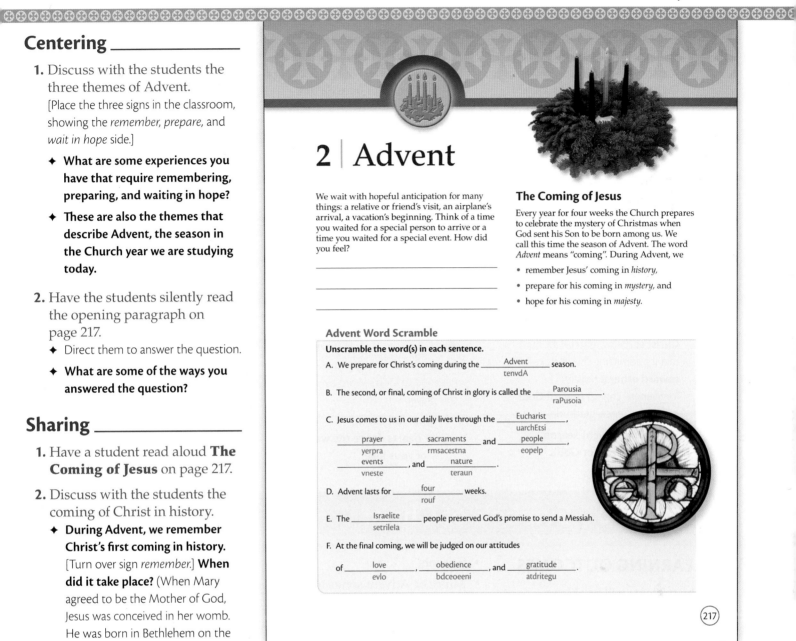

2 | Advent

We wait with hopeful anticipation for many things: a relative or friend's visit, an airplane's arrival, a vacation's beginning. Think of a time you waited for a special person to arrive or a time you waited for a special event. How did you feel?

_____

_____

_____

The Coming of Jesus

Every year for four weeks the Church prepares to celebrate the mystery of Christmas when God sent his Son to be born among us. We call this time the season of Advent. The word *Advent* means "coming". During Advent, we

- remember Jesus' coming in *history,*
- prepare for his coming in *mystery,* and
- hope for his coming in *majesty.*

Advent Word Scramble

Unscramble the word(s) in each sentence.

A. We prepare for Christ's coming during the _____Advent_____ season.
tenvdA

B. The second, or final, coming of Christ in glory is called the _____Parousia_____.
raPusoia

C. Jesus comes to us in our daily lives through the _____Eucharist_____,
uarchEtsi

_____prayer_____, _____sacraments_____ and _____people_____,
yerpra   rmsacestna   eopelp

_____events_____, and _____nature_____.
vneste   teraun

D. Advent lasts for _____four_____ weeks.
rouf

E. The _____Israelite_____ people preserved God's promise to send a Messiah.
setrilela

F. At the final coming, we will be judged on our attitudes

of _____love_____, _____obedience_____, and _____gratitude_____.
evlo   bdceoeeni   atdritegu

(217)

---

the coming of the Messiah, proclaiming that he would come.)

3. Explain to the students how Christ comes to us in our daily lives.

- ✦ **Advent is not just a time to remember the first coming of Christ, his birth in Bethlehem. We also remember that Christ comes to us in our daily lives. In Baptism, we are reborn into the life of Christ. We share in God's life of grace, and Christ comes to us every day. He comes in mystery.** [Turn over sign *prepare*.]

- ✦ **What are some of the ways that Jesus comes to us in mystery during our everyday lives?** (in the

Eucharist; in prayer and sacraments; through people, events, and nature)

4. Ask volunteers to read aloud Matthew 25:31–46 and Mark 14:62.

- ✦ Explain to the students that these two passages refer to the final coming of Christ in majesty.

- ✦ **When Christ comes again at the end of time, he will come in power and glory. We will recognize him as the King over all. He will come in majesty.** [Turn over sign *wait in hope*.]

- ✦ **We refer to this manifestation of God's power and glory as the Parousia. This is also called Christ's Second Coming.**

- ✦ **What will happen at this last coming of Christ, according to Matthew 25:31–46?** (All people will be judged.) **By what standard will Christ judge all people?** (by how they have lived a life of love)

- ✦ **What will happen to all who have tried to do this?** (They will enter body and soul into the Kingdom of God forever.)

- ✦ **As faithful followers of Christ, we want to prepare ourselves for his coming and this final judgment. One way to do this is to examine our attitudes.**

- ✦ **What attitudes toward ourselves would be fitting for a follower of Christ's?** (being grateful for our talents, admitting our mistakes) **toward others?** (loyalty, forgiveness, caring) **toward God?** (love, obedience, gratitude)

- ✦ **During the Advent season, Christians pray for God's** guidance to change selfish attitudes so that we live more Christlike lives. The grace of our Baptism helps us to do this.

Acting

1. Have the students complete the **Advent Puzzle Board** on page 217. Go over their answers and have the students fill in the correct answers.

2. Allow the students time to reflect on and respond to **Preparing for Jesus** on page 218.

3. Lead the students in prayer. Ask a student to read aloud Philippians 4:4–7. Respond to God's Word by praying this prayer.

> **Father in heaven,**
> **our hearts desire the warmth**
> **of your love**
> and our minds are searching for the light of your Word.
>
> **Increase our longing for Christ our Savior**
> and give us the strength to grow in love,
> that the dawn of his coming
> may find us rejoicing in his presence
> and welcoming the light of his truth.
>
> **We ask this in the name of Jesus the Lord.**

First Sunday of Advent
Alternative Opening Prayer

CHECKPOINT ✓

- Were the learning outcomes achieved?

Day Two Symbols of Christ

Student page 218

LEARNING OUTCOMES

The students will be able to

- identify symbols that represent the ways Jesus comes to us in history, in mystery, and in majesty.

- describe how we prepare for Christ through prayer and the practice of Christian attitudes.

Materials

- Bibles or New Testaments
- BLM 90
- Three signs from Day One: *remember/history; prepare/mystery; wait in hope/majesty*
- Drawing paper, half-sheets or precut circles, squares, and triangles
- Felt-tipped markers, crayons, or paints
- Pencils
- Scissors
- Music or Advent songs for Acting #1
- Large candle, matches (check fire codes)
- Cord, yarn, ribbon, or wire
- Place to hang the ornaments from Sharing #3 on one of the following:

  Real or artificial evergreen tree (check local regulations for real tree)

  Tree branches, natural or painted, anchored in a pail of sand

  Paper or cardboard tree on the bulletin board where ornaments can be pinned

  Tree drawn on the board where ornaments can be taped

  Tree mobile or window frame where ornaments can be hung at different lengths.

Before You Begin

In preparation for this lesson, determine which kind of ornament will work best for a Chrismon Tree (a tree with homemade ornaments of Christian symbols) that you have prepared. You can also adapt this activity as best meets the abilities of your students. The ornaments can be as simple as cutting out the symbols shown in the student book or more elaborate, by using these symbols as models.

Centering

Link the last lesson with today's lesson.

✦ **In the last lesson, we discussed three ways that Christ comes to us.** [Show the *remember* sign.] **We remember that Christ came to us in history.** [Turn the sign over to show the word *history.*]

✦ [Show the *prepare* sign.] **We prepare for the ways that Christ comes to us in mystery.** [Turn the sign over to show the word *mystery.*]

✦ [Show the *wait in hope* sign.] **We wait in hope for Christ's coming to us in majesty.** [Turn the sign over to show the word *majesty.* Post these signs on the board with the words *history, mystery,* and *majesty* showing.]

Sharing

1. Have a student read aloud **Symbols of Christ** on page 218.

    ✦ Discuss with the students the symbols for Christ that are shown on this page.

    ✦ **Many Christians use symbols to identify themselves and to express their faith. Let's examine some of these symbols:**

    ✦ **The anchor is a symbol of Christian hope found in the religious art of early Christian communities. It symbolizes Christ who is our hope.**

    ✦ **The fish *Ichthys,* Greek for *fish,* is taken from the first letters of the Greek phrase *Jesus Christ, Son of God, Savior.***

    ✦ **The Chi-Rho is formed with the initial letters of the Greek term for Christ: X (*Ch*), P (*r*).**

    ✦ **The Tau-Rho is a Chrismon, or monogram for the name of Christ.**

2. Have several students locate in their Bibles or New Testaments each of the Scripture passages on page 218.

Preparing for Jesus

How will you prepare for Jesus during the season of Advent? Write about one practice that you will do during the Advent season to strengthen your Christian attitude.

_____

_____

Symbols of Christ

Christians use many different symbols to represent our faith. On the left are four common symbols for Christ.

anchor Chi-Rho

fish Tau-Rho

Other symbols remind us of the ways that Christ comes to us. Look up the Scripture references in the first and third columns and write the names of the symbols on the lines. Discuss the meaning of the symbols listed in the second column, which identify ways that Christ comes to us today.

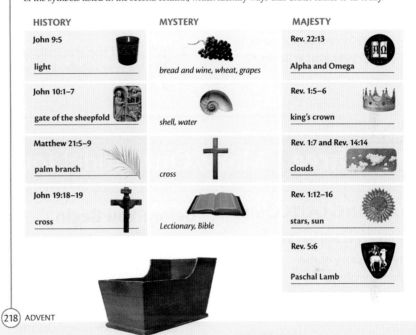

HISTORY

John 9:5 — light

John 10:1–7 — gate of the sheepfold

Matthew 21:5–9 — palm branch

John 19:18–19 — cross

MYSTERY

bread and wine, wheat, grapes

shell, water

cross

Lectionary, Bible

MAJESTY

Rev. 22:13 — Alpha and Omega

Rev. 1:5–6 — king's crown

Rev. 1:7 and Rev. 14:14 — clouds

Rev. 1:12–16 — stars, sun

Rev. 5:6 — Paschal Lamb

218 ADVENT

Have them read the passage aloud. Write the symbols on the board under the correct sign.

History

• light (Jesus called himself the light of the world.)

• gate of the sheepfold (Jesus called himself the gate of the sheepfold.)

• palm branch (It represents Christ's kingship.)

• cross and its inscription (It represents his saving work.)

Mystery

• bread and wine, wheat, grapes (symbols of Christ in the Eucharist)

• shell, water (symbols of Christ's coming in Baptism)

• cross (symbol of Christ's saving work)

• Bible (reminds us that Christ is the Word of God)

Majesty

• Alpha and Omega (the beginning and end of the Greek alphabet; Jesus is the first and the last, the beginning and the end.)

• king's crown (Jesus is King of Kings who will reign in the Kingdom of God.)

• clouds (sign that Jesus will come again in glory)

• stars, sunrise (symbolize Jesus in glory)

• Paschal Lamb (Jesus is the Lamb of God.)

3. Have the students make ornaments for a Chrismon tree based on the symbols discussed.

✦ Distribute paper, pencils, drawing materials, and scissors. Instruct each student to design an ornament based on a symbol found on page 218.

✦ Have the students draw on one side of the paper the symbol chosen and then write on the other side a one-sentence explanation of how it represents Christ. If these ornaments are to hang on the tree, distribute yarn and give instructions for preparing them.

✦ Save the ornaments for use in the prayer celebration in Acting #2.

Acting

1. **BLM 90** Distribute to the students copies of BLM 90 **The Lord Is Coming!**

✦ Assign students the various parts: five leaders, two readers, and four readers of the petitions.

✦ Allow time for the students to practice their reading.

✦ Select opening and closing songs for the prayer service.

✦ Preview the prayer service with the students. Tell them that they will present their symbols with their explanation and then hang them on the tree.

2. Lead the students in the prayer celebration on BLM 90.

3. At the end of the season of Advent, allow the students to take home the ornaments they made.

Encourage them to include these among the decorations on their family Christmas tree.

CHECKPOINT

• Were the learning outcomes achieved?

• Can the students explain the three ways Christ comes to us?

• Are the students able to identify ways they can prepare for Christ during Advent?

Day Three Mary, Our Model for Advent

LEARNING OUTCOMES

The students will be able to

• tell the story of the Annunciation.

• describe how we honor Mary as the mother of Jesus.

• identify ways to imitate Mary's openness to God.

Materials

• Bibles or New Testaments

• Advent music for Acting # 1 (optional)

Before You Begin

1. The scriptural account of the Annunciation in Luke's Gospel is evidence of a divine Revelation to Mary regarding the birth of Jesus. It substantiates Jesus' divine origin from the first moment of his existence on earth. He is both the Son of God and the Son of Mary.

2. Mary's response to the angel at the Annunciation showed how she would respond to God throughout her life. With her yes, she accepted God's plan for her. She was the perfect follower of Jesus. She listened to God's Word and lived it out in the ordinary events of her life. Her yes to God made Mary the Mother of God and of the Church. She is our model of discipleship.

Centering

1. Discuss with the students the various ways to say yes.

✦ **What are the different ways we say yes?** (*sure, okay, yeah, you bet, absolutely*) [Write their answers on the board.]

✦ **What are some of the ways people say yes in other languages?** (*si, oui, ya*) [Write their answers on the board.]

2. Introduce the topic for today's lesson.

Jesus was born because a special woman said yes when God asked her to be the mother of the Savior. Today we will look at the Scripture passage that tells the account of Mary's yes to God.

Sharing

1. Have volunteers do a dramatic reading of the Annunciation from the Gospel of Luke 1:26–38. You will need a narrator, the angel Gabriel, and Mary.

✦ **What was the message the angel came to give Mary?** (The angel told Mary she would have a child who would be called the Son of God.)

✦ **How did Mary react?** (with surprise and puzzlement) **What words did Mary use to say yes?** ("Behold, I am the handmaid of the Lord. May it be done to me according to your word." Luke 1:38)

✦ **Whom did the angel Gabriel promise Mary would come to her?** (the Holy Spirit)

2. Discuss with the students some of the ways Mary prepared for Jesus' coming.

✦ **What are some things Mary may have done to prepare for Jesus' birth?** (Answers will vary.)

✦ **Scripture tells us one way that Mary prepared. What did she do?** (She went to help her cousin Elizabeth and bring to her the news of Jesus' birth.)

✦ **How did Elizabeth help prepare the way for Jesus?** (She was the mother of John the Baptist.)

3. Relate this Scripture to Jesus' coming in history, in mystery, and in majesty.

✦ **When God comes to us, we are asked to respond in faith. Who were some people who responded to God so that Christ could be born among us?** (Mary, Joseph, Elizabeth, and Zechariah)

✦ **How do we respond when Christ comes to us in mystery?** (We pray. We welcome Christ into our hearts.) **How might we respond in faith as we wait for Christ's coming in majesty?** (look for signs of the Kingdom of God, wait in hope and prayer)

✦ **During Advent, we remember the various ways that Christ comes to us. We seek to respond in faith to Christ's presence among us. We strive to make Christ's love present in our world.**

Acting

1. Have the students write the word *Yes* on a piece of paper. Have them compose an Advent prayer based on what they have learned. You might play some Advent songs as they work.

2. Lead the students in praying the *Magnificat* (Luke 1:46–55).

✦ Have several students read aloud their Advent prayers.

✦ Conclude by praying the Hail Mary on the inside front cover of the student book. [See page T445.]

CHECKPOINT ✓

• Were the learning outcomes achieved?

• Can the students identify ways to welcome Christ into their lives during Advent?

Enriching the Faith Experience

Use the following activities to enrich a lesson or to replace an activity with one that better meets the needs of your class.

1. Have the class look up Scripture passages from the Advent liturgies and make a decorative Advent calendar, writing a Scripture quote for each day.

2. **BLM 89** Distribute copies of BLM 89 **The Advent Wreath.** Read aloud the explanation of the Advent wreath. Have the students take the BLM home and suggest that their families use an Advent wreath.

3. To each of the following statements, have the students write on a sheet of paper *true, false,* or *not given,* according to whether the statement can be found in Scripture.

1. **An angel appeared to Joseph and told him that Jesus would be born.** (true; Matthew 1:20–21)

2. **Joseph and Mary both rode donkeys from Nazareth to Bethlehem.** (not given)

3. **The innkeeper said to Joseph and Mary, "There is no room for you in my inn. You may use the stable in the back."** (not given)

4. **Jesus was born in a cave used as a stable.** (not given)

5. **While there may have been other animals, a donkey and a sheep were definitely present at Jesus' birth.** (not given)

6. **The angels told the shepherds to follow the star to Bethlehem.** (false)

7. **The shepherds told Mary the message of the angels.** (true; Luke 2:17)

8. **The angels proclaimed glory to God and peace on earth.** (true; Luke 2:10–14)

4. Have the students paint or draw a large mural showing how Christ came to us in history, how Christ comes to us now in mystery and how Christ will come in glory at the end of time.

5. Let the students make a banner or wall hanging, writing a message from one of the Sunday readings for Advent.

6. Have the students make ornaments for the Chrismon tree decorated on Day Two, based on symbols such as the "O" Antiphons, a shepherd's crook, a scroll (Word of God), or symbols of the sacraments.

3 Christmas

Faith Focus

During the Christmas season, we celebrate the Incarnation, God's love made visible in Jesus.

Reflecting on the Faith Experience

Take a few moments to reflect prayerfully before preparing the lesson.

Listening

"Behold, the virgin shall be
with child and bear a son,
and they shall name him
Emmanuel,"
which means "God is with us."

Matthew 1:23

Reflecting

We all know the story of the first Christmas—of Mary and Joseph searching for a place to stay in Bethlehem, of Jesus being born and laid in a manger, of his birth being announced by angels and indicated by a special star. His love shows itself in his becoming one like us in all our human weakness and limitations, except sin. The real depth of his love, though, was manifested in the mission he came to accomplish by suffering and dying for our sins so that we might be free.

It is God's great love that the Church celebrates with lights, color, and song during this season. This love leads people all over the world to forgive, to give and receive gifts, to rejoice at being home with their families, and to sing Christmas carols. People who understand this feast want to make God's love more visible in their lives. They want to be more caring about family and friends, more welcoming to strangers, and more forgiving of past hurts.

The Collect Prayer for the Mass on Christmas day speaks well of our hope.

Grant, we pray, almighty God,
that, as we are bathed in
the new radiance of your
incarnate Word,
the light of faith, which
illumines our minds,
may also shine through in our
deeds.

Collect Prayer,
Christmas Mass at Dawn

As Catholics, we seek to carry this spirit throughout the year. Sometimes we succeed; sometimes we fail. Through the Sacrament of Reconciliation, we can receive the grace of forgiveness and conversion. The seasons of the liturgical year also provide opportunity for continuing renewal and recommitment to the life of discipleship. Through the mystery of the Incarnation, we participate in making God's love visible in our world, imperfectly, but seen. As we live our days, may Christ always find us making God's love visible.

How can I make God's love visible through my words and actions?

Responding

Lord, allow the mystery of the Incarnation to transform me that your love is made visible in my words and actions.

Scripture for Further Reflection

Luke 2:1–7 Jesus is born.

John 1:9–18 John the Evangelist unfolds the mystery of the Incarnation.

Titus 2:11–14 The birth of Jesus transforms us.

of Jesus is good news to be shared.

- Mary reflected on these things in her heart. We continue to ponder and reflect on the meaning of the Incarnation.

  d. Christmas Mass During the Day: *John 1:1–5,9–14*
  - The Word was with God from the time of Creation and brought light and life to the world.
  - John the Baptist testified to the light that was coming into the world.
  - Through our belief in Jesus, we become children of God.
  - "[T]he Word became flesh and made his dwelling among us . . ." (John 1:14)

  ✦ After each reading is discussed, have the students complete the activity by writing what each Gospel tells us about the Incarnation.

4. Review with the students the parts of the Nicene Creed that state what we believe about the Incarnation.

   ✦ **In the course of Christian history, what is proclaimed in Scripture was also written down in summary form as statements of belief called creeds. We pray one of these creeds, the Nicene Creed, each Sunday at Mass.**

   ✦ **Let's look at one part of the Nicene Creed and identify which words and phrases of this creed summarize our beliefs about the Incarnation.**

   ✦ Have the students turn to the inside front cover of their books to the Nicene Creed. [See page T445.]

   ✦ **What part of the Creed includes statements about our beliefs in Jesus' birth?** (the second stanza)

5. Have a student read aloud the first paragraph of **The Nicene Creed and the Incarnation** on page 220.

   ✦ Direct the students to complete the activity.

   ✦ **What are some of the words or phrases you highlighted in this section of the Creed and what**

Gospel for Christmas Mass During the Day:
John 1:1–5, 9–14 (longer form: John 1:1–18)

_____

_____

_____

After discussing the summaries with your group, identify what these Gospel readings teach us about the Incarnation.

_____

_____

_____

The Nicene Creed and the Incarnation

Each of the Gospels proclaimed at the Masses on Christmas Day contributes to our understanding of the mystery of the Incarnation. We profess our belief in the Incarnation when we pray the Nicene Creed at Mass. The second stanza of the Creed focuses on our beliefs about Jesus. Highlight any words or phrases that remind you of the Gospels that you have read during this lesson.

I believe in one Lord Jesus Christ,
the Only Begotten Son of God,
born of the Father before all ages.
God from God, Light from Light,
true God from true God,
begotten, not made, consubstantial with
   the Father;
through him all things were made.
For us men and for our salvation
he came down from heaven,
and by the Holy Spirit was incarnate of
   the Virgin Mary,
and became man.

Reflection on Emmanuel

The Gospel of Matthew describes Jesus as *Emmanuel,* God-with-us. When do you recognize God's presence in your life?

_____

_____

_____

Leo Cartwright, detail of the nativity, St. Paul Episcopal Cathedral, Detroit, Michigan.

(220) CHRISTMAS

Christmas Gospel does it reflect? ("begotten, not made, consubstantial with the Father"; "incarnate of the Virgin Mary and became man" John's Gospel; "for us men and our salvation, he came down from heaven" Matthew's Gospel; "born of the Virgin Mary and became man" Luke's Gospel)

6. Explain to the students why we bow or genuflect at a part of the Nicene Creed.

   ✦ **When we pray the Nicene Creed at Mass, we bow when saying the words, ". . . by the Holy Spirit . . . and became man" as a sign of our respect for the Incarnation.**

   ✦ **At Christmas, and at the feast of the Annunciation, we genuflect when praying these words.**

Acting

1. Discuss with the students the importance of Christmas.

   ✦ **For many people, the celebration of Christmas is one of the highlights of the year. What makes Christmas so special?** (the focus on family and friends, the gift-giving traditions)

   ✦ **In what ways does the mystery of the Incarnation touch people in a profound way?** (affirms the dignity of human life; shows us the promise of eternal life; helps us seek signs of God's presence in our world and in our lives)

✦ **What are some actions that might flow from our celebration of Christmas and our belief in the Incarnation?** (seeing and serving Christ in others; outreach to those who are poor and marginalized; support for the dignity of human life)

2. Have the students complete the **Reflection on Emmanuel** activity on page 220.

3. Lead the students in prayer.

✦ Sing a Christmas hymn and offer prayers of petition.

✦ **Let us pray that the mystery of the Incarnation continue to empower Christians to see God's presence in our world and one another. After each prayer, respond, "God be with us."**

✦ Have the students offer their petitions. Conclude with a moment of silent prayer.

CHECKPOINT

- Were the learning outcomes achieved?

- Are the students able to discuss the meaning of the Incarnation as proclaimed through the Gospel readings for Christmas?

- Are the students able to identify the significance of the Incarnation to us as Catholics?

Enriching the Faith Experience

Use the following activities to enrich the lesson or to replace an activity with one that better meets the needs of your class.

1. Have the students study the lyrics of popular, religious Christmas carols and compare them with the Gospel accounts of the first Christmas. Direct them to make a list of carols and Scripture references that match.

2. Let each student prepare a scrapbook to use during the Christmas holidays. Titles for pages may include: *Advent Events, Christmas Preparations, Family Favorites* (which include favorite cards, cookies, carols, ornaments, and gift ideas for each member of the family), *Christmas Day, What Christmas Means to Me,* and *How Jesus Comes Through Others.* Allow room on the pages for writings, photos, Christmas cards, and drawings.

3. Hold a Bible storytelling festival for the younger students. Have the students memorize a Bible story related to the coming of Jesus. You might suggest the following directions to the students:

✦ **Absorb the story's message until it is part of you.**

✦ **Tell it over and over, pausing in the right places.**

✦ **Use a conversational voice and look at your audience.**

✦ **Have a good opener and a clinching final sentence.**

Luke 1:5–25,57–80 (Zechariah)

Luke 1:26–38 (Mary and the angel)

Luke 1:39–56 (Mary's visit to Elizabeth)

Matthew 1:18–24 (Joseph and the angel)

Luke 1:57–80 (birth of John the Baptist)

Luke 2:1–20 (birth of Jesus)

Matthew 2:1–12 (visit of the Magi)

Luke 2:22–40 (presentation of Jesus)

Matthew 2:13–15 (flight into Egypt)

4. Have the students reenact the Mexican custom of *Las Posadas,* which means "inn," that portrays Joseph's attempt to find a place to stay in Bethlehem.

✦ Students portraying Joseph and Mary knock on a door. Students on the other side refuse them lodging. Joseph and Mary go away.

✦ After a period of silent prayer, offer intercessions, asking God's forgiveness for lack of hospitality. Sing a verse from a song such as "O Little Town of Bethlehem."

✦ Joseph and Mary return, again knocking. Another group of students sends them away. After a period of silence, offer intercessions for forgiveness for lack of concern for the needs of the poor. Sing another verse from a song.

✦ A third time, Joseph and Mary knock. Joseph begs for a place to stay, explaining that Mary is about to have a child. The third group of students welcomes them joyfully. Another period of silence can be followed by prayers of praise and thanksgiving for God's gift of Jesus.

✦ Conclude by singing the second verse of the song followed by a party.

5. Divide the students into small groups. Assign each group one of the passages from the Old Testament listed below. Have the groups read their passage and then discuss how it is fulfilled by the Infancy Narratives. Give each group time to present its work.
Psalm 2:7–9
Isaiah 7:13–14
Isaiah 9:1–2
Isaiah 9:5–6
Isaiah 40:3,9
Isaiah 11:1–2
Micah 5:1
Malachi 3:1
Hosea 11:1

6. Have the students research the Christmas customs of various cultures. They could present their research to the class through plays, posters, computer graphics, or PowerPoint presentations.

7. Direct the students to present the good news of the story of Christmas by one of the following:
- Tell a child the story.
- Design a Christmas card based on the Gospel story of Christmas and send to someone.
- Make a mural of the events surrounding Jesus' birth or a mobile of Christmas symbols. Put the mural or mobile where it can be seen.
- Put together a computer DVD presentation telling the story of Christmas with images and music.
- Plan a Christmas program using carols about the real meaning of Christmas. Invite students from the lower grades to attend.

8. Lead the students in praying Mary's song of praise, the *Magnificat*. (Luke 1:46–55)
Point out those parts of the prayer where Mary prays for the poor and lowly. Have the students pray for those who are poor or suffering at this time of year.

9. Have the students consult the liturgical calendar or a reference book to identify other feasts of the Christmas season. Direct them to find out what the feast celebrates and why it is part of the Christmas season. Have the students present their research to the class.
- December 26: Saint Stephen
- December 27: Saint John the Evangelist
- December 28: the Holy Innocents
- Sunday between Christmas and New Year's Day: the Holy Family
- January 1: Solemnity of Mary, Mother of God
- Sunday between January 2 and January 8: Epiphany of the Lord
- Sunday after Epiphany: Baptism of the Lord

4 Lent

Faith Focus

Lent is a time for spiritual renewal through prayer, fasting, and almsgiving.

Reflecting on the Faith Experience

Take a few moments to reflect prayerfully before preparing the lesson.

Listening

> Have mercy on me, God, in
>   your goodness;
>   in your abundant compassion
>   blot out my offense.
> Wash away all my guilt;
>   from my sin cleanse me . . .
> Restore my joy in your salvation;
>   sustain in me a willing spirit.
> I will teach the wicked your ways,
>   that sinners may return to you.

Psalm 51:3–4,14–15

Reflecting

Life is frequently compared to a long journey with a definite starting point, constant movement, and a well-defined goal. Like a long journey, life has many shorter journeys along the way. The season of Lent can be looked upon as one of these shorter journeys. It is God's annual invitation to the Christian to leave behind the exile of sin and move more steadily through prayer and penance with Christ to the promised land of Easter. It is during this Lenten journey that we experience in a special way God's love poured out for us.

> [Jesus], though he was in
>   the form of God,
>   did not regard equality with God
>   something to be grasped.
> Rather, he emptied himself,
>   taking the form of a slave, . . .
> he humbled himself,
>   becoming obedient to death,
>   even death on a cross.

Philippians 2:6–8

Are we of the same mind as Christ? Do we try to return love for love? Lent, with its discipline of prayer, fasting, and almsgiving, is an excellent opportunity to do so. By daily meditation, we draw closer to Christ as he moves inevitably toward Calvary. With him, we fast and pray; through him, we find strength to give of ourselves and our goods to those in need; and in him, we rise triumphantly renewed on Easter Sunday with a pledge of our final glorious resurrection at the end of life's journey.

> We adore you, O Christ, and
>   we bless you,
> because by your holy Cross you
>   have redeemed the world.

What Lenten plans do I have to help me better follow Jesus?

Responding

Holy Spirit, guide my students to make good Lenten resolutions and give them the grace to keep them.

Scripture for Further Reflection

Matthew 6:1–18 Jesus teaches his disciples about almsgiving, prayer, and fasting.

Preparing for the Faith Experience

Day One
Ash Wednesday

Day Two
The Season of Lent

Day Three
Celebrating Reconciliation

Scripture in This Lesson

Matthew 6:1–6, 16–18 Jesus teaches us about almsgiving, prayer, and fasting.

Church Documents

Catechism of the Catholic Church. The themes of this lesson correspond to the following paragraphs: **613–617, 1067–1068, 1168–1171, 1434–1438.**

Music in This Lesson

For a list of all the music suggested in this program, see page T517.

Enriching the Faith Experience

Use the activities at the end of the lesson to enrich the lesson or to replace an activity with one that better meets the needs of your class.

Day One Ash Wednesday

LEARNING OUTCOMES

The students will be able to

- identify Ash Wednesday as the beginning of the spiritual journey we call Lent.
- explain the significance of the distribution of ashes on Ash Wednesday.

Materials

- Palm branches
- Ashes
- Bibles or New Testaments
- BLM 91 (needs to be prepared ahead of time)

  cardstock paper or small pieces of poster board

  glue

  decorated box

- Reflective music for Acting #2 (optional)

Before You Begin

1. For centuries, the Church has placed ashes on the foreheads of believers on Ash Wednesday. Since the priest blesses these ashes, they are considered one of the sacramentals of the Church. The Sign of the Cross made with ashes on the forehead is a reminder of the good news of salvation and of God's love manifested to us through Jesus. It expresses the great love Jesus has for his Father and for us. It reminds us to return his love through prayer, penance, almsgiving, and good deeds during the season of Lent.

2. **BLM 91** Before the lesson, prepare the bookmarks from BLM 91 **Bookmarks for Lent.** Use cardstock paper, or glue copies onto small pieces of poster board. Cut the bookmarks and place them in a decorated box.

Centering _____

Discuss with the students the celebration of Ash Wednesday.

- Show the students a piece of palm and some ashes.

- **We will soon begin a new season in the Church year. It is the season in which we prepare for Easter. What is this season of the Church year called?** (Lent) **What is the name given to the first day of Lent?** (Ash Wednesday) **Why is it called Ash Wednesday?** (We begin Lent by having a priest or designated minister make the Sign of the Cross on our foreheads with the blessed ashes.)

- **The ashes we will use on Ash Wednesday come from burning palm branches.** [Show the palm.] **Palm branches, like this one, are blessed and given out in church every year on the Sunday before Easter. What is this Sunday called?** (Palm, or Passion, Sunday) **The leftover palm branches are burned, and the ashes are used** for the blessing on Ash Wednesday.

✦ **Why is the form of a cross used?** (Jesus redeemed us on a cross; he told us we must carry our cross after him.) **The ashes are a sign that during the 40 days of Lent, we will try to die to sin and live in God's love. Today we will prepare to begin our observance of the season of Lent that begins on Ash Wednesday.**

Sharing

1. Discuss with the students the meaning of the two prayer options used when we receive the ashes.

   ✦ Have a student read aloud Genesis 3:19.

   ✦ **To whom does God say this and when?** (to Adam after he had eaten from the tree in the garden) **Adam and Eve disobeyed God, but still God loved them. God sent Adam from the Garden of Eden. God promised to send a Savior who would overcome sin and death. This prayer on Ash Wednesday reminds us of our dependence on God and our need for God's mercy.** *Remember, man, you are dust and to dust you will return.*

   ✦ Have a student read aloud Mark 1:15.

   ✦ **Why does Jesus call for repentance?** (It is the time of fulfillment. The Kingdom of God is at hand.) **This prayer reminds us that Jesus is the one sent by God to forgive sins and restore us to life.** *Turn away from sin and be faithful to the gospel.*

2. Explain to the students that Ash Wednesday is the beginning of a spiritual journey that returns us to God.

   ✦ **Think about a time when you had to admit that you had done something wrong. Maybe you broke something that belonged to someone else and needed to accept responsibility. Or perhaps there was a time when a brother or a sister was getting into**

trouble for something that you had done. How did you feel as you prepared to admit what you had done wrong and take responsibility for your actions? (Answers will vary.)

   ✦ **During the season of Lent, we consider the things that need to be changed in our lives. We take responsibility for the things that we do that are wrong and displeasing to God. This is difficult work.**

3. Discuss with the students the first reading for Ash Wednesday, Joel 2:12–18.

   ✦ **At Mass on Ash Wednesday, we will hear a reading from the prophet Joel. This reading gives us hope as we think about how we might return to the Lord during the season of Lent.**

   ✦ Have a student read aloud Joel 2:12–18.

   ✦ **How will God know that we are returning to him?** (We will give our whole heart to God; we will change more than just our appearances; we will change our hearts.)

   ✦ **In this reading, whom does God want to return to him?** (all of the people; the elders, the students, even the infants) **How will God respond to those who return to him?** (God will show mercy and kindness. God will not be angry and will not punish.)

4. Discuss with the students the Gospel proclaimed on Ash Wednesday, Matthew 6:1–6, 16–18.

   ✦ **At Mass on Ash Wednesday, we hear Matthew 6:1–6,16–18 proclaimed. Let's listen carefully to this Gospel reading.**

   ✦ Have a student read aloud Matthew 6:1–6,16–18.

   ✦ **What are the three practices that Jesus teaches about in this Gospel?** (almsgiving, prayer, fasting) **We already know about prayer. What is fasting?** (giving up food for a period of time) **What is**

almsgiving? (sharing money and possessions with people in need)

   ✦ **The reading from Matthew's Gospel helps us to think about how we will turn away from sin. Our prayer, fasting, and almsgiving during Lent are signs of our change of heart as we return to the Lord. We will learn more about these three Lenten practices in the next lesson.**

Acting

1. Lead the students in prayer.

   ✦ Have a student read aloud Matthew 6:19–21. After the Scripture has been proclaimed, have the students reflect on the treasures in heaven that we prepare for during Lent: forgiveness from sin and eternal life.

   ✦ Allow sufficient time for silent reflection.

   ✦ **We commit ourselves to use this season of Lent to return to the Lord. As a sign of our commitment, let us pray the Lord's Prayer together.**

2. Have each student come to the front of the room to select a bookmark from the box.

   ✦ Have them read the Scripture quotation. The students can design the rest of the bookmark, using a Lenten theme.

   ✦ Suggest that they keep the bookmarks in their Bibles or books. [Play reflective music as the students work on the bookmarks.]

CHECKPOINT

- Were the learning outcomes achieved?

LEARNING OUTCOMES

The students will be able to

- describe Lent as a spiritual journey that calls us to new life in Christ.
- explain that Lent is an annual reminder of our Baptism and a time to pray for catechumens (individuals preparing for Christian initiation at the Easter Vigil).
- list ways for spiritual renewal through Scripture reading, prayer, fasting, and almsgiving.

Key Terms

Lent—the 40 days before Easter during which we prepare, through prayer, fasting, and almsgiving, to change our lives and to live the Gospel more completely

almsgiving—giving aid to those who are poor

fasting—limiting the amount we eat for a period of time to express sorrow for sin and to make ourselves more aware of God's action in our lives

abstinence—denying oneself food, drink, or other pleasures during Lent; Catholics over age 14 abstain from eating meat on Ash Wednesday and Fridays.

Materials

- Hymnals or Lenten missalettes
- Bibles or New Testaments
- Dates for the weeks of Lent, such as *Sunday, February 25 to Saturday, March 3* written on the board
- Reflection notebooks
- Reflective music for Acting #1 (optional)

Before You Begin

1. The Church knows that we are constantly in need of conversion. The days of Lent are a call to conversion, a chance to begin anew to live the Christian life more fully. Lent is also a time to remember the great love manifested in Christ's Death and Resurrection that prompted us to become Christians in the first place.

2. The sequence of Sunday readings in the liturgical calendar are arranged in a three-year cycle: years A, B, and C. After three years, the Church has heard the most important readings from Scripture. Again and again in these readings, we recall God's plan of salvation and his tremendous love for us. The three-year cycle for Lent is laid out under **My Lenten Journey** on page 222. This will be referenced for Acting #1.

Centering

1. Discuss with the students what is needed to take a long road trip or journey.

   ✦ **What is the longest road trip or journey that you have ever taken?** (Answers will vary.)

   ✦ **What are some of the steps you need to do when going on a trip?** (discuss the trip; make preparations; take the journey) [Write on the board: *discussion, preparation, journey*.]

   ✦ **What are some of the details you might discuss when planning for a trip?** (destination, length, route or plan, side trips, stopovers) [Write these answers under *discussion*.]

   ✦ **How do you prepare beforehand for the trip?** (pack lightly, get car checked) [Write these answers under *preparation*.]

   ✦ **On the journey, what must be done to arrive safely?** (observe speed limits, obey traffic signs and signals, follow a map) [Write these answers under *journey*.]

2. Explain to the students that Lent is a yearly journey in the life of every Christian.

   The season of Lent is a time in the Church year when each Christian is asked to set out on a journey. It is a journey that helps us look at our relationship with God. It gives us the time and the equipment we need to make that relationship better.

3. Link the last lesson with today's lesson.

   We saw in the last lesson that Ash Wednesday is the starting point for our Lenten journey. In this lesson, you will learn more about the three aspects of our Lenten journey: prayer, fasting, and almsgiving.

Sharing

1. Have a student read aloud the opening paragraph of **Our Lenten Journey** on page 221.

   ✦ **Many Christians look for opportunities to renew and refresh themselves spiritually, especially during Lent. It is a season where many parishes offer opportunities for spiritual renewal. What are some of the opportunities parishes might offer?** (parish or personal retreats, Bible-study courses, prayer groups, penance services, service projects)

   ✦ **Lent can be like an annual retreat for Catholics. When Lent is completed, we renew our baptismal promises and celebrate Christ's Resurrection on Easter.**

2. Work with the students as they fill in the chart on page 221.

- ✦ **Just as a family discusses a family journey, Christians discuss their Lenten journey.**

- ✦ Have a student read aloud Matthew 6:5–6.

- ✦ **How do we discuss our Lenten journey?** (by praying to God) [Write *praying to God* after *discussion* on the board.] **As we move through our Lenten journey, we talk with God in prayer.**

- ✦ **Lent is a time to renew our love and commitment to Christ. It is a time to pray for ourselves and others, especially for catechumens who are preparing to be received into the Church at the Easter Vigil. What are the Sacraments of Initiation?** (Baptism, Confirmation, and the Eucharist)

- ✦ **Lent is also a good time to pray that those who have been away from the Church may return.**

- ✦ **What is the goal, or destination, of Lent?** (spiritual renewal in Christ) [Have the students write *spiritual renewal in Christ* on the chart.]

- ✦ **A family excursion isn't always the same length, but our Lenten journey is. How long is Lent?** (40 days) [Have the students write *40 days of Lent* on the chart.]

- ✦ **When does Lent begin?** (Ash Wednesday, when Christians are signed with blessed ashes in the form of a cross) **During Lent, Christians spend more time with Christ in prayer, meditation, and the Eucharist in order to draw closer to him.**

- ✦ **After a family decides on a place to visit, how do they find the way?** (They use a map and plan a route. They contact friends, a travel agent, or the Internet for advice.)

- ✦ **For our Lenten journey, we also need a plan, a spiritual plan, if we are to renew ourselves in Christ. We ask those people who know us best to help us. We may ask parents, teachers, and friends to suggest Lenten practices for us. Above all, we turn to Christ in prayer and ask his assistance.**

4 | Lent

Our Lenten Journey

Jesus' journey led to his passion and Death in Jerusalem before he tasted the victory of the Resurrection. Each year we recall his journey during the season of Lent. In Lent, we are on a journey as well, moving closer toward our final destination: eternal life with God.

Our Lenten journey has much in common with a family trip. Complete the chart below, using the Scripture references to help you.

A FAMILY EXCURSION	OUR LENTEN JOURNEY
Discussion with family	*Discussion (Matthew 6:5–6)*
• destination or goal	• spiritual renewal in Christ
• length of trip	• 40 days of Lent
• route or plan	• our spiritual plan
• side trips and stopovers	• prayer and rest on Sunday
Preparation	*Preparation (Matthew 6:1–4)*
• light packing	• giving alms to those in need
• car checkup	• examination of conscience and penance
Journey	*Journey (Matthew 6:16–18)*
• observing speed limits	• fasting
• obeying traffic signs and signals	• abstaining
• following a map	• following a plan for prayer, penance, and almsgiving

(221)

[Have the students write *our spiritual plan* on the chart.]

- ✦ **A family may also discuss side trips and places to stay overnight. Why are these important?** (Drivers and passengers need breaks for rest and refreshment for the trip to be safe and enjoyable.)

- ✦ **During Lent, Christians must also have breaks to regain spiritual energy. When are these breaks in Lent?** (on Sunday) **Sundays are not counted in the 40 days of Lent because each Sunday is a commemoration of Jesus' Resurrection. It is a day to be spent in extra prayer and relaxation instead of work.** [Have

the students write *prayer and rest on Sunday* on the chart.]

3. Explain to the students that Lent is a time of almsgiving.

- ✦ **The next step in a family journey is preparation. Most travelers are advised to pack lightly. During Lent, Christians are asked to pack lightly for the journey**

- ✦ Have a student read aloud Matthew 6:1–4.

- ✦ **What does Matthew's Gospel tell us about how we might pack lightly for our Lenten journey?** (almsgiving) **What is almsgiving?** (giving to those who are in need)

- ✦ **The Church wants us to be particularly mindful of people** who are in need at all times, but more so during Lent. **What kinds of needs might we address during Lent?** (economic, spiritual, physical and emotional needs) **Who might be people in need in your life?** (Answers will vary.)

✦ **How can we help people who are in need, or practice almsgiving?** (by giving money to the missions, service to elderly people, and time to those who are lonely; by showing kindness to family members and others; by praying for victims of violence) [Have students write *giving alms to those in need* on the chart.]

✦ **Periodically during Lent, we give ourselves a spiritual checkup. What are some of the ways we do this?** (examination of conscience, penance) [Have the students write *examination of conscience and penance* on the chart.]

✦ **During Lent, we are encouraged to celebrate the Sacrament of Reconciliation.** [You might offer information here about the parish's opportunities for the Sacrament of Reconciliation during Lent. Note that the Day Three lesson is about the Sacrament of Reconciliation and includes a model for a Reconciliation Service for the season of Lent.]

4. Explain to the students that Lent is a season of penance.

✦ **Drivers and passengers must exercise discipline and self-control on a long trip. If we are to have a good Lenten journey, we too must practice discipline and self-control. We call this penance.** [Read aloud Matthew 6:16–18.]

✦ **What Lenten practice is described in this passage?** (fasting) **What advice does Jesus give us about fasting?** (do not look gloomy; fast in secret in order to get a heavenly reward.) **Jesus fasted in the desert for 40 days before he began his public life.**

✦ **Church law requires fasting and abstaining from meat on certain days during Lent. Fasting means we eat only one full meal a day, with small amounts of food at the other two meals, and no eating in between meals. During Lent, Catholics age 18 and older are bound to fast on Ash Wednesday and Good Friday.**

✦ **What does it mean to abstain?** (to refrain from an action or a practice) **When Catholics speak of abstaining, they usually mean refraining from eating meat, especially during the Fridays of Lent and on Ash Wednesday. This law of abstinence applies to those who are 14 years of age or older.** [Have the students write *fasting* and *abstaining* on the chart.]

✦ **What are other ways to fast and abstain besides from food?** (avoiding angry and unkind words, not watching as much TV or playing video games, or anything that leads to sin) [Have the students write *following a plan for prayer, penance, and almsgiving* on the chart.]

5. Have the students complete the activity **Pillars of the Spiritual Life** on page 222. Ask several students to share their answers.

Acting

1. Have the students look at **My Lenten Journey** on page 222. and take out their reflection notebooks.

   ✦ **During Lent, many people keep a notebook or a journal to write their reflections on the Lenten readings and to chart the progress of their Lenten journey. This year you will use your reflection notebook to reflect upon your Lenten journey.**

   ✦ **First, let's look at the Gospels for the coming Sundays of Lent. Look at My Lenten Journey on page 222. In the column marked** *Sunday,* **you will see three Gospel readings listed with the letter** *A, B,* **or** *C* **before them. All of the Sunday readings we hear at Mass are on a three-year cycle called cycle** *A, B,* **or** *C.* **In that three-year cycle, we hear the most important readings in the Bible.**

   ✦ **Today we will highlight the Gospel readings for this year's Sundays of Lent. There are six Sundays including Palm, or Passion, Sunday during Lent.** [Guide the students in highlighting the Sunday Gospels for this year's Lent. Find the cycle and year near the bottom of page 222.]

   ✦ **Reading and reflecting on the Sunday Gospels helps us to better understand the meaning of Lent. The readings also help us to focus on the themes of Lent such as repentance, forgiveness, and sacrifice.**

   ✦ **Each Friday during Lent, you will spend some time reflecting on the Sunday Gospel and writing your thoughts in your reflection notebooks.** [For additional resources on the Sunday Gospels for Lent, visit www.christourlife.com.]

   ✦ **Also during Lent, many people make resolutions. The resolutions can be giving something up or deciding to do something for others.** [There are five suggested resolutions on the calendar on page 222.] **Each morning you will**

Pillars of the Spiritual Life

Write examples of things you could do during Lent to practice the disciplines of prayer, fasting, and almsgiving.

prayer: _____

fasting: _____

almsgiving: _____

My Lenten Journey

Each Friday in Lent, I will read and reflect on the upcoming Sunday Gospel, writing my thoughts in my reflection notebook. Each morning, I will write a resolution for that day (see examples below). At the end of each week, in my reflection notebook, I will evaluate how well I accomplished my resolutions for that week.

SUNDAY	MONDAY	TUESDAY	WEDNESDAY	THURSDAY	FRIDAY	SATURDAY
1 A. Matthew 4:1–11 B. Mark 1:12–15 C. Luke 4:1–13				I'll try to be kind to someone who isn't a close friend.		
2 A. Matthew 17:1–9 B. Mark 9:2–9 C. Luke 9:28–36						I'll do an extra chore at home.
3 A. John 4:5–42 B. John 2:13–25 C. Luke 13:1–9						
4 A. John 9:1–41 B. John 3:14–21 C. Luke 15:1–3,11–32		I'll avoid wasting food.				
5 A. John 11:1–45 B. John 12:20–33 C. John 8:1–11				I'll limit the amount of time I watch TV or play video games.		
6 A. Matthew 21:1–11 B. Mark 11:1–10 C. Luke 19:29–40						I'll send a note to someone who is sick.

CYCLE A: 2014, 2017, 2020 • CYCLE B: 2015, 2018, 2021 • CYCLE C: 2016, 2019, 2022

❮ Operation Rice Bowl, a Lenten program of Catholic Relief Services, includes praying, fasting, and almsgiving. The program provides aid to people in over 40 countries.

(222)

write a new resolution for that day on your plan.

   ✦ **On Fridays, after you have reflected on the Sunday's Gospel, you will write in your reflection notebook how well you accomplished your resolutions for that week and how to improve.**

   ✦ **At the end of Lent, you will have in your reflection notebook and on My Lenten Journey an account of your Lenten journey.**

   ✦ **Now let's spend some time thinking about some of the resolutions you would like to make for Lent. As a guide, you might want to look at some of the practices for prayer,**

almsgiving, and penance, that you listed under **Pillars of the Spiritual Life** on page 222.

   ✦ **In your reflection notebook and on My Lenten Journey, copy from the board the dates for the weeks of Lent this year. Then write your resolutions for the first week of Lent. Do this for all the weeks of Lent listed on the board.** [Play some reflective music.]

   ✦ Allow sufficient time for quiet reflection.

2. ✍ Lead the students in prayer.
Together let us ask God to be with us and inspire us on our Lenten journey by praying the prayer Take, Lord, Receive by Saint Ignatius of Loyola from the inside back cover of your book. [See page T446.]

CHECKPOINT ✓

- Were the learning outcomes achieved?

- Did the groups' suggested practices indicate they understood prayer, fasting, and almsgiving?

- What signs are there that they intend to use their reflection notebooks?

Day Three Celebrating Reconciliation

LEARNING OUTCOMES

The students will be able to

- identify the Sacrament of Reconciliation as a means to a deeper relationship with Christ.

- prepare for the Sacrament of Reconciliation through a prayer service.

Materials

- Bibles or New Testaments
- Reconciliation booklet from the back of the student book
- BLM 44A–B, 45A–B
- BLM 46 (optional)
- Hymnals
- Student book page 96 (optional)

Before You Begin

1. Jesus never rejects us for our failure to live up to our baptismal commitment. He has provided the Sacrament of Reconciliation to forgive us. This forgiveness helps us to enter more deeply into Christ's life and love after we have sinned.

2. In this lesson, the students prepare for the Sacrament of Reconciliation through a prayer service. You may be able to hold the service in church and offer this as an opportunity for individual confession. If this is not possible, encourage the students to celebrate the sacrament with their families during Lent.

Centering _____

Link the last lesson with today's lesson.

✦ **We have been thinking about the season of Lent as a spiritual journey. What is the destination for this journey?** (spiritual renewal in Christ)

✦ **What are the three parts of the plan for our spiritual journey during Lent?** (almsgiving, prayer, and fasting) **To do these things well, we need discipline and self-control. We also said that during Lent, we check in to see how we are doing in our life with Christ. What did we say helped us in this spiritual checkup?** (examination of conscience and the Sacrament of Reconciliation)

✦ **Today we will talk about the Sacrament of Reconciliation and prepare to celebrate this sacrament during Lent.**

Sharing

1. Discuss with the students the importance of participating in the Sacrament of Reconciliation during Lent.

   ✦ Have a student read aloud 2 Corinthians 5:20—6:2. [This was the Second Reading on Ash Wednesday.]

   ✦ **Why does Paul say that we should be reconciled to God?** (because Jesus, who was without sin, died to save us from sin) **When should this be done?** (now)

   ✦ **There is urgency in Paul's message. Christ has already reconciled us to God through his Death and Resurrection. He wants us to accept the gift of forgiveness that God offers to us. When we consider our lives, we know that we need God's gift of forgiveness and peace. We know that we have sinned.**

   ✦ **During Lent, we make it a priority to examine our lives and to ask God to forgive us for our sins. In most parishes, there are opportunities to celebrate the Sacrament of Reconciliation individually or with others in our parish community throughout the year, but especially during Lent.**

2. Review the Sacrament of Reconciliation that was taught in Chapter 12, page 96.

   ✦ Have the students use their Reconciliation booklets as part of the review.

   ✦ **What are the four parts of the Sacrament of Reconciliation?** (contrition, confession, penance, and absolution)

3. **BLM 44A–B, 45A–B** Have the students plan a Reconciliation service for the season of Lent.

   ✦ Distribute copies of BLM 44A–B **Celebration of Reconciliation Planning Guide** and BLM 45A–B **Celebration of Reconciliation Planning Sheet.** [The students may be familiar with these, as they were used in Chapter 12.]

   ✦ Identify a theme for the service. You may wish to suggest a theme from 2 Corinthians 5:20—6:2, such as *Now is the time to be reconciled to God.*

   ✦ The planning guides on BLM 44A–B will help the students organize their planning. BLM 45A–B identifies the various tasks for the groups.

   ✦ Have the students use hymns and Scripture readings that reflect the season of Lent. They may wish to consider the Sunday readings when choosing Scripture. [Note that the Alleluia verse before the Gospel is omitted during the season of Lent.]

   ✦ Assist the students with their planning. After the groups have finished their tasks, work together to complete a plan for the prayer service using, BLM 45A–B as a guide.

4. **BLM 46** Determine a date and time to celebrate the Reconciliation service that the students have planned.

   ✦ If possible, arrange for the service to be led by a parish priest and include the opportunity for individual confession. Depending on the size of the class, several priests may be needed.

   ✦ If a priest is not available, consider using BLM 46 **Celebration of Reconciliation,** a nonsacramental celebration of Reconciliation.

5. Distribute copies of the Reconciliation service to the students and to the priest. Ask volunteers to serve as readers. Help the students review their parts. Point out the parts that you will take and the parts that everyone will say.

Acting

Celebrate the Reconciliation service with the students.

   ✦ If you are not able to arrange for individual confessions during this prayer service, encourage the students to celebrate the Sacrament of Reconciliation during Lent.

   ✦ Suggest they attend a Reconciliation service at their parish with their families. Give times for scheduled Lenten Reconciliation services, as well as the times for confessions at your parish.

CHECKPOINT

• Were the learning outcomes achieved?

• Do the students seem ready to celebrate the Sacrament of Reconciliation?

Enriching the Faith Experience

Use the following activities to enrich a lesson or to replace an activity with one that better meets the needs of your class.

1. Plan a Lenten liturgy with the class by using one of the Eucharistic Prayers for Reconciliation from the *Roman Missal*. (Remember, there is no *Gloria* or *Alleluia* during Lent.) Invite each student to take an active part in some phase of the project. Invite parents and other classes to attend the Mass.

2. Have the students organize a mission drive involving the entire school or just the upper grades. Encourage the students to donate their personal spending money, perform acts of service, and pray for the missions.

3. Form groups and give the students the following directions for making mobile crosses:
   + **Make a cross from purple paper** (9 by 14 inches).
   + **Make a pink or rose-colored cross and glue it to one side of the purple cross.**
   + **Read the Scripture readings from one Sunday of Lent.** (Assign one to each group.) **Decide what the Gospel message is and write it neatly on one side of the cross.**
   + **On the other side of the cross, place pictures from magazines or the Internet that reflect the message.**
   + **Attach yarn to the tops of the crosses and then hang them as mobiles.**

4. Direct the class to organize a Stations of the Cross for the school. Assign a station to each grade. The class may present the respective station in the form of a play, collage, song, poem, liturgical gesture, or spoken meditation. At the prayer service, have a student read an opening prayer. Between the presentations of the stations, have the students sing the chorus of a song. Finally, have a student read a closing prayer.

5. Read aloud the following quiz questions. Have the students write their answers on a sheet of paper and then check their answers.
   1. **How long does Lent last?** (40 days)
   2. **When does it start?** (Ash Wednesday)
   3. **To what great feast does it lead?** (Easter)
   4. **What is its goal?** (spiritual renewal in Christ)
   5. **For whom does the Church pray especially during Lent?** (catechumens and people who have left the Church)
   6. **Which day of the week is not counted in the 40 days of Lent?** (Sunday)
   7. **Which word means "giving to those in need"?** (*almsgiving*)
   8. **How many full meals may be eaten on a fast day?** (one)
   9. **Name a fast day in Lent.** (Ash Wednesday or Good Friday)
   10. **What must Catholics 14 years of age and older do on Fridays during Lent?** (abstain from eating meat)

5 Holy Week

Faith Focus

During the Easter Triduum, we commemorate our redemption in Christ.

Reflecting on the Faith Experience

Take a few moments to reflect prayerfully before preparing the lesson.

Listening

"I am the resurrection and the life; whoever believes in me, even if he dies, will live, and everyone who lives and believes in me will never die."

John 11:25–26

Reflecting

The focal point of the Church's liturgical year is the Easter Triduum. Its rituals call forth a faith response from us as we contemplate the saving power of Jesus. Each ritual reveals Christ in his hour of glory, which is the hour of our deliverance. Our openness to the mysteries revealed can lead us closer to the risen Christ.

The Easter Triduum is a reminder of the journey we are making, which will carry us through death to glory in Jesus. For those who are willing to look, there are reminders all around us that we are on a journey and that we are passing through this world. The seasons flow through a calm, steady cycle of death and birth, barrenness and abundance. The days themselves bear the same message. The Church lives this cycle in the yearly dying and rising as the Church prepares to celebrate Easter. The rituals used during the Easter Triduum are permeated with signs and symbols of the Paschal Mystery. When we approach these signs and symbols with faith, they are powerful and can move us deeply.

If there is ever a time when we are faced with our solidarity in sin, our shallowness, and our emptiness, it is during the Easter Triduum. If there is ever a time when we are surrounded with love unimaginable, caught up in the ecstasy of our unity with the Suffering Servant, and awed with the sign of our immortality, it is during the Easter Triduum. We are ransomed. We are loved. We contemplate not only Christ's Death and Resurrection, but also the wonder of our own share in it.

How will I prepare myself to celebrate the Paschal Mystery at the Easter Triduum?

Responding

Holy Spirit, lead my students to participate more actively in the Easter Triduum services this year.

Scripture for Further Reflection

Matthew 21:1–11 Jesus enters the city of Jerusalem.

John 13:1–15 Jesus washes the feet of the disciples.

1 Peter 2:20–25 Christ patiently accepted suffering to free us from sin.

Preparing for the Faith Experience

Day One
Palm, or Passion, Sunday

Day Two
The Easter Triduum

Scripture in This Lesson

Mark 14:1—15:47 The passion and Death of Jesus according to Mark

John 18:1—19:42 The passion and Death of Jesus according to John

Church Documents

Catechism of the Catholic Church. The themes of this chapter correspond to the following paragraphs: **1067–1068, 1168–1171.**

Music in This Lesson

For a list of all the music used in this program, see page T519.

Enriching the Faith Experience

Use the activities at the end of the lesson to enrich a lesson or to replace an activity with one that better meets the needs of your class.

Day One   Palm, or Passion, Sunday

LEARNING OUTCOMES

The students will be able to

- explain the celebration of Palm, or Passion, Sunday.
- describe the account of Jesus' passion and Death in the Gospel of Mark.

Materials

- Palm branch
- Bible open to the passion from Mark's Gospel (see Sharing #3)
- List written on the board for Sharing #3

Mark 14:1–11	*Mark 14:53–65*
Mark 14:12–16	*Mark 14:66–72*
Mark 14:17–26	*Mark 15:1–15*
Mark 14:27–42	*Mark 15:16–32*
Mark 14:43–52	*Mark 15:33–47*

- Bibles or New Testaments
- Cross or crucifix
- Reflective music for Sharing #4 (optional)

Before You Begin

When Jesus entered Jerusalem, the crowds welcomed him with shouts of praise and hailed him as a king. We begin Holy Week by remembering this event. We welcome Jesus as our Savior and king. Yet, we know, as the crowds did not, that Jesus' love for us would be shown through his suffering and Death on the Cross. As we celebrate Palm, or Passion, Sunday, we know that Jesus' crown is a crown of thorns. During Holy Week, we follow Jesus, our king, on his way of the Cross. We pray that we will choose to follow him wherever his way of the Cross leads us.

Centering _____

Link the lesson from SSL 4 **Lent** (T388–T397) with today's lesson.

- ✦ We are at that point in our Lenten journey when we might begin to ask "Are we there yet?" The answer is "not yet."

- ✦ We are about to begin the final stages of our journey, the final week of Lent called Holy Week.

- ✦ During Holy Week, our preparations for Easter take on an even greater importance and urgency. Holy Week is an intense journey within the longer journey of Lent.

- ✦ Holy Week begins on the last Sunday of Lent. It continues until the night before Easter. During Holy Week, we remember the most important events in the life of Jesus. We remember his triumphant entry into Jerusalem, the Last Supper with his disciples, and his passion and Death on the Cross.

- ✦ As we have observed Lent as a spiritual journey, during Holy Week, we journey with Jesus on his way of the Cross.

Sharing

1. Discuss with the students Palm, or Passion, Sunday.

- ✦ Show a palm branch that will be blessed on Palm Sunday.

- ✦ **Our Holy Week journey with Jesus on his way of the Cross begins on Palm, or Passion, Sunday. Two special things happen at Mass on Palm Sunday. What are these two things?** (We bless and process with palms; we proclaim the Gospel of Jesus' passion and Death.)

2. Explain to the students the two Gospel readings proclaimed on Passion Sunday.

- ✦ **On Palm Sunday, there are two Gospel readings. A first Gospel reading is proclaimed at the doors of the church before the procession with the palm branches. This Gospel reading tells how Jesus entered Jerusalem to shouts of welcome and praise.**

- ✦ **We know the events that will follow after Jesus enters Jerusalem. The shouts of praise will become cries for Jesus' Death on the Cross. That is why Palm Sunday is also called Passion Sunday. In the second Gospel for this day, we proclaim the Gospel of Jesus' passion and Death.** (The Gospel of Jesus' passion and Death will be proclaimed again on Good Friday.)

- ✦ **In this Gospel, we hear about the many people who encountered Jesus on his way of the Cross. Today you will be invited to think about these people and their responses to Jesus. In these people, we might find traces of our own response to Jesus.**

3. Have the students reflect on the passion of Jesus through a dramatic reading of the passion according to the Gospel of Mark.

- ✦ Assign students to read aloud the Scripture passages written on the board. [Allow time for the students to review their reading.]

- ✦ **Listen carefully as the passion according to Mark's Gospel is proclaimed. Pay attention to the names of the people who are mentioned. Imagine how they felt as they witnessed Jesus making his way to his Death on the Cross.**

4. Have the students choose one of the characters in the passion narrative who caught their attention.

- ✦ Be sure to include the following:

  - Woman who anointed Jesus at Bethany or Simon the leper (Mark 14:1–11)

  - The two disciples sent to prepare for the Passover (Mark 14:12–16)

  - One of the Twelve at the Last Supper (Mark 14:17–26)

  - Peter, James, or John (Mark 14:27–42)

  - A member of the crowd who came to arrest Jesus (Mark 14:43–52)

  - The high priest (Mark 14:53–65)

  - Peter or one of the bystanders in the courtyard (Mark 14:66–72)

  - Pontius Pilate (Mark 15:1–15)

  - A soldier or Simon of Cyrene (Mark 15:16–32)

  - A bystander or one of the women at the Cross or Joseph of Arimathea (Mark 15:33–47)

- ✦ **Choose one of the characters you just heard about in Mark's Gospel. If you cannot think of someone, I can make several suggestions.**

- ✦ **Read the part of the Gospel that pertains to this person. Imagine that you are that person.**

- ✦ **After you spend some quiet time reflecting on what that person experienced, write a one-paragraph monologue as if you were that person telling a friend what you experienced. These monologues will be part of our closing prayer.**

- ✦ Allow sufficient time for the students to complete the activity. [You might play reflective music as the students write.]

Acting

 Lead the students in prayer. Display a cross or crucifix.

- ✦ Invite the students to reflect on the events of Jesus' passion, using the monologues they wrote. [Remind the students that this is prayer.]

- ✦ Have volunteers tell which character they chose and read aloud the monologue they wrote. [You might arrange the order beforehand to reflect the order of the events in Mark's Gospel.]

- ✦ Conclude by praying this prayer.

  Father,
  look with love upon your people,
  the love which our Lord Jesus
  Christ showed us
  when he delivered himself
  to evil men
  and suffered the agony of
  the cross,
  for he lives and reigns with you
  and the Holy Spirit,
  one God for ever and ever.

  Prayer from Good Friday
  Liturgy of the Hours

CHECKPOINT ✓

- Were the learning outcomes achieved?

LEARNING OUTCOMES

The students will be able to

- explain that the Easter Triduum is the commemoration of our redemption in Christ.
- name the rituals of the Easter Triduum and explain their meaning.

Key Terms

Easter Triduum—the liturgical time during which we celebrate the Paschal Mystery; the three days that begin with the Mass of the Lord's Supper on Holy Thursday and end on Easter Sunday evening

elect—former catechumens who were called by the bishop at the Rite of Election to prepare for the Easter sacraments of Baptism, Confirmation, and Eucharist.

ritual—words and actions that help us remember and express our faith

Materials

- Bibles or New Testaments
- BLM 92

  Basin, pitcher of water, towel, apron

  Crucifix
- Candle (check fire codes)
- Paper
- Holy Week or Easter Triduum missalettes
- Large sheets of poster board or paper
- Scissors
- Markers or crayons

Before You Begin

1. Rituals highlight the deeper realities of the liturgical celebrations, but there is always a danger of viewing them as mere formalities. Since they are external in form, rituals can become words and acts devoid of meaning. By taking the time to ponder the significance of the ancient rituals of Catholic worship, we hope to avoid this risk.

2. Although an understanding of these rituals can come through study, a full appreciation of their meaning and beauty comes through by experiencing them. Encourage the students to participate in the Easter Triduum services offered at their parish.

5 | Holy Week

The Easter Triduum—Holy Thursday, Good Friday and Holy Saturday (Easter)—is the high point of the Church year. It is our great three-day celebration that begins on the evening of Holy Thursday and ends on the evening of Easter Sunday. The word *Triduum* means "three days." On these three days, counted from sundown to sundown, we journey with Christ from his Last Supper, through his Death on the cross, to his Resurrection on Easter.

Rituals of the Easter Triduum

Read the Gospel for each liturgy of the Easter Triduum. First, identify the key events from the life of Jesus that are commemorated at each liturgy. Then work with your classmates to identify the liturgical rituals specific to each night of the Easter Triduum.

Holy Thursday
Gospel: John 13:1–15

Events:

- Jesus eats the Last Supper with his disciples.
- Jesus washes the feet of his disciples.
- Jesus transforms bread and wine into his Body and Blood and gives himself as food and drink to his disciples.

Ritual:

- washing of feet
- procession and adoration of the Blessed Sacrament

Good Friday
Gospel: John 18:1—19:42 (John 18:1–40 and John 19:1–42)

Events:

- Jesus is condemned to Death.
- Jesus is crowned with thorns and scourged.
- Jesus carries the cross to Calvary.
- Jesus is crucified.
- Jesus is buried.

Ritual:

- proclamation of the passion
- veneration of the cross

Holy Saturday: the Easter Vigil
Gospel: Matthew 28:1–10 or Mark 16:1–8 or Luke 24:1–12 (choose one)

Events:

- Jesus is raised from the dead.
- Mary Magdalene and the other women find Jesus' tomb empty.

Ritual:

- procession with the paschal candle
- Sacraments of Initiation: Baptism, Confirmation, and the Eucharist

(223)

Centering _____

1. Discuss with the students how we remember special occasions.

   ✦ **How do you remember special occasions?** (write about it in a journal; save mementos; take pictures; have a celebration; make a scrapbook)

   ✦ **Just as we use special words and actions to remember special occasions in our lives, we sometimes use certain words and actions that help us remember the special events in the life of Jesus. We call these words and actions rituals.** [Write *rituals* on the board.] **The rituals during the Easter Triduum help us remember and appreciate the**

Paschal Mystery: Jesus' passion, Death, Resurrection, and Ascension.

✦ **The Easter Triduum begins with the Mass of the Lord's Supper on Holy Thursday and ends on Easter Sunday evening. It is three 24-hour periods or three days long.**

Sharing _____

1. Have a student read aloud the first paragraph on page 223.

2. Read aloud the directions for **Rituals of the Easter Triduum** on page 223.

   ✦ Divide the class into three or four groups. [The Good Friday reading is longer than the others. You might divide the reading into two parts, John 18:1–40 and John 19:1–42, thus creating a fourth group].

   ✦ Assign each group one of the days of the Easter Triduum. Direct each group to read the Gospel for its assigned day and prepare a list of the key events from Jesus' life that are remembered that day.

   ✦ When finished, have each group report the group's list of events to the class. [Direct the students to fill in the answers on page 223.]

   1. Holy Thursday (Jesus eats the Last Supper with his disciples. Jesus washes the feet of his disciples. Jesus changes bread and wine into his Body and Blood and gives himself as food and drink to his disciples.)

   2. Good Friday (Jesus is condemned to Death. Jesus is crowned with thorns and scourged. Jesus carries the Cross to Calvary. Jesus is crucified. Jesus is buried.)

   3. Holy Saturday: the Easter Vigil (Jesus rises from the dead. Mary Magdalene and the other women find Jesus' tomb empty.)

3. Explain to the students the rituals for each day of the Easter Triduum using a missalette as your guide.

The Easter Triduum

Fill in the blanks.

Resurrection	cross
alleluia	Baptism
Holy Thursday	Easter Sunday
salvation	Good Friday
service	

At his Last Supper, Jesus washed the feet of his disciples to give us an example of loving _____service_____. We remember this event on _____Holy Thursday_____.

Because it is the day of our redemption, the day of Christ's Death is called _____Good Friday_____.

When we venerate the cross on Good Friday, we adore Christ and thank him for our _____salvation_____.

The sign of Christ's victory over sin and death is the _____Cross_____.

Holy Saturday is spent waiting for the feast of the _____Resurrection_____.

The elect, former catechumens, pray and, as far as possible, fast on Holy Saturday to prepare for their _____Baptism_____.

We celebrate Christ's Resurrection with prayers of praise and joy on _____Easter Sunday_____.

The Easter word is _____alleluia_____.

224 HOLY WEEK

Be sure to include the following aspects of each night's service. [Have the students fill in the answers on page 223.]

1. Holy Thursday (the washing of feet; procession and adoration of the Blessed Sacrament)

2. Good Friday (proclamation of the passion; veneration of the Cross)

3. Holy Saturday: the Easter Vigil (procession with the paschal candle; Sacraments of Initiation: Baptism, Confirmation, and the Eucharist.)

4. BLM 92 In their small groups, have the students study the rituals used during the Easter Triduum. Assign each group one of the following rituals:

✦ The washing of the feet (Holy Thursday); the veneration of the Cross (Good Friday), or the procession with the paschal candle (Easter Vigil)

✦ Give each group a Holy Week missalette and BLM 92 **Remembering in Ritual** as a guide for the groups's discussion and in preparation for the demonstration of the ritual.

✦ Allow time for each group to give a report on the ritual studied and a demonstration of it. Encourage the students who have participated in the Easter Triduum rituals in their parish to share their experiences.

5. Provide the students with large sheets of poster board or paper.

◆ Have them cut out large crosses. At the top of the cross, have the students draw a symbol for Christ such as the Chi-Rho, the Alpha and Omega, or a lamb.

◆ On each extension of the cross, have them write the name of each day of the Easter Triduum, design a symbol of the day's events, and write a prayer or appropriate Scripture verse.

6. Have the students complete the exercise **The Easter Triduum** on page 224. Check their answers.

Acting

 Lead the students in prayer. Read aloud Philippians 2:5–11. Invite the students to respond to the reading by praying together Take, Lord, Receive from the inside back cover of the student book. [See page T446.]

CHECKPOINT

- Were the learning outcomes achieved?
- How do the students show interest in the rituals of the Triduum?

Enriching the Faith Experience

Use the following activities to enrich a lesson or to replace an activity with one that better meets the needs of your class.

1. Post the times of the Easter Triduum services in the parish. You might wish to make yourself available after the services to answer students questions or share some thoughts.

2. Have the students make crosses for their homes out of sticks of wood tied with twine or cording.

3. Have the students listen to a recording of Handel's *Messiah*. Provide the students with a copy of the basic lyrics. Discuss with them how these words fit into what we remember and celebrate in the life of Jesus during the Easter Triduum.

4. Invite members of your parish liturgy committee to explain to the students how the parish will celebrate the Easter Triduum services.

5. Invite someone from the RCIA who is to receive the Sacraments of Initiation at the Easter Vigil. They could talk about their Lenten journey and what the upcoming rituals of the Easter Triduum mean to them. You may have the person's sponsor attend the class as well to offer his or her perspective.

6. Lead the children in a prayerful discussion of the Scripture readings for Passion Sunday. Visit www.christourlife.com for more information.

7. Dictate the following quiz. Have the students write *yes* if the statement is true and *no* if it is false.

1. **The night before he died, Jesus gave us the Eucharist.** (yes)
2. **Christians venerate the Cross on Holy Saturday.** (no)
3. **The Easter Triduum is the three days from Holy Thursday evening to Easter Sunday evening.** (yes)
4. **Catechumens are baptized on Easter Sunday morning.** (no)
5. **After the Last Supper, Jesus experienced the agony in the garden.** (yes)
6. **On Good Friday, we remember Jesus' Death that redeemed us.** (yes)
7. **The Easter candle, a symbol of death, is lighted on Good Friday.** (no)
8. **Evening Prayer is part of the Liturgy of the Hours.** (yes)
9. **Jesus washed the disciples' feet on Holy Saturday.** (no)
10. **Every Sunday is like celebrating a little Easter.** (yes)

6 Easter

Faith Focus
During the Easter season, we celebrate Jesus' Resurrection and our hope for eternal life.

Reflecting on the Faith Experience
Take a few moments to reflect prayerfully before preparing the lesson.

Listening

[T]he one who raised the Lord Jesus will raise us also with Jesus and place us with you in his presence.

2 Corinthians 4:14

Reflecting

Life is a series of beginnings. We finish one thing and move on to another. Each birthday marks the completion of one year of life and the beginning of the next. Commencement from school ends one phase of life and inaugurates a new phase of life. Even nature renews itself regularly. Each dawn heralds a new day, and every spring brings new life.

Renewal and re-creation are part of the spiritual life as well. Christ summons us to new life in Baptism. He nurtures and restores that life through his sacraments. It is this call to newness of spirit that we celebrate at Easter with joyful solemnity.

By his Death and Resurrection, Jesus proved himself once and for all master over sin and death:

We proclaim your Death, O Lord, and profess your Resurrection until you come again.

Memorial Acclamation 2
The Roman Missal

Because of our Baptism, we too share in Christ's paschal victory and witness to his triumph. The symbols of Easter speak to us of our victory in Christ. We adorn our sanctuaries with Easter lilies, which are reminders of his radiant, risen body. We decorate eggs, tombs from which new life bursts forth. Some Christians wear new clothes on Easter Sunday, a sign that they have laid aside sin and have put on the Lord Jesus. "For all of you who were baptized into Christ have clothed yourselves with Christ." (Galatians 3:27) Christians bake bread or cake in the shape of a lamb or a cross, symbols of Christ's Paschal Mystery. Easter is a triumphant celebration of glorious new life made possible only in Christ Jesus. With the exultant Church, we pray:

O God, who on this day,
through your Only Begotten
Son,
have conquered death
and unlocked for us the path
to eternity,
grant, we pray, that we who
keep
the solemnity of the Lord's
Resurrection
may, through the renewal
brought by your Spirit,
rise up in the light of life.

Collect Prayer
Mass for Easter Sunday

How do I show appreciation for my Baptism, which enables me to share Christ's paschal victory?

Responding

Lord, give my students the grace to realize what your Resurrection means to them.

Scripture for Further Reflection

Luke 24:1–8 The women found the tomb empty on the third day after Jesus died.

1 Corinthians 15:55–56 Death has been conquered by Christ Jesus.

Preparing for the Faith Experience

One-Day Lesson
Easter

Scripture in This Lesson

Hebrews 10:12–24 Jesus offered one sacrifice for sins.

Church Documents

Catechism of the Catholic Church. The themes of this lesson correspond to the following paragraphs: **1067–1068, 1168–1171.**

Music in this Lesson

For a list of all the music suggested in this program, see page T517.

Enriching the Faith Experience

Use the activities at the end of the lesson to enrich the lesson or to replace an activity with one that better meets the needs of your class.

Easter

Student pages 225–226

LEARNING OUTCOMES

The students will be able to

- list the primary liturgical symbols of Easter.
- explain how Easter symbols are present in the liturgy throughout the Easter season.

Key Terms

Liturgy of the Hours—the public prayer of the Church to praise God and to sanctify the day. It includes an Office of Readings before sunrise, Morning Prayer at dawn, Evening Prayer at sunset, and prayer before going to bed. The chanting of psalms makes up the major portion of each of these services.

Materials

- Drawing paper
- Markers or crayons

Before You Begin

1. The Easter Triduum ends with Evening Prayer on Easter Sunday. Evening Prayer is part of the public prayer of the Church called the Liturgy of the Hours, or the Divine Office. This prayer has long been part of the prayer of the Church. Its roots are taken from the prayer life of the Jewish synagogue community. The Liturgy of the Hours includes hymns, psalms, Scripture readings, petitions, the Lord's Prayer, and times of reflective silence. There are seven hours, or times of the day, that are part of this prayer:

   - Matins (readings)
   - Lauds (Morning Prayer)
   - Terce, Sext, and None (Daytime Prayers)
   - Vespers (Evening Prayer)
   - Compline (Night Prayer)

   All Christians are invited to share in this traditional prayer of the Church.

2. We often use symbols to represent the deep mysteries of our faith because symbols can show us what is hard to explain in words. In our liturgical celebrations, symbols convey the depth of the reality we celebrate. This is most evident in our celebration of Easter.

3. The theme of this Easter seasonal corresponds to the lesson taught in Chapter 22, The Victory of Jesus. You may wish to consult this chapter as you prepare for this lesson.

Centering

Discuss with the students the symbols of Easter.

- ✦ **What liturgical season are we beginning?** (Easter)

- ✦ **During the Easter season, there are changes at Mass. Who knows what some of the these changes are?** (The color of the priest's vestments and church decorations have changed from purple to white. The paschal candle is present. we pray the word *Alleluia* again.)

- ✦ **Our celebration of Easter begins at the Easter Vigil. What are some parts of the Easter Vigil?** (Help the students to recall the SSL 5 **Holy Week** lesson on the rituals of the Easter Vigil, including the procession with the paschal candle, the extended Liturgy of the Word, and the Sacraments of Initiation.)

- ✦ **The symbols introduced into the liturgy at the Easter Vigil continue to be displayed and celebrated throughout the Easter season.**

- ✦ **Today we will discuss these symbols to better appreciate what they communicate to us about our life in Christ.**

Sharing

1. Have the students open their books to **Easter Symbols** on page 225.
   What are the three symbols of Easter? (light, word, and water)

2. Discuss with the students the first symbol, light.
   - ✦ **Were you ever home at night when the lights went out because of a storm? What was this like?** [Allow volunteers to share their experiences.]
   - ✦ **The celebration of the Easter Vigil begins in darkness and moves into light. What do you think the symbol of light tells us about our salvation in Christ?** (Christ leads us to eternal life; Christ dispels the darkness of sin and death.) [Help the students read and

6 | Easter

Easter Symbols

Light

fire	Promised Land
paschal candle	Christ

In the history of our faith, fire and light have been symbols of God's presence. At the beginning of the Easter Vigil, the church is in darkness. The priest lights and blesses a new fire. A large candle symbolizing _____ Christ _____ called the _____ paschal candle _____ is carried into the church. It reminds us of the Exodus when the Chosen People were led by a pillar of _____ fire _____ into the _____ Promised Land _____ .

Dirck Bouts, detail from *Altarpiece of the Last Supper,* 15th century. Israelites collecting manna in the desert during the Exodus.

Word

love	Scriptures
Exodus	nine

The stories of our Christian roots are in the _____ Scriptures _____ . The _____ nine _____ readings of the Easter Vigil remind us of God's powerful and faithful _____ love _____ . The story of the _____ Exodus _____ is always read at this Mass.

Water

promises	life
Baptism	Resurrection

In the Easter Vigil, water is a sign of our _____ Baptism _____ . By this sacrament, we share in the Death and _____ Resurrection _____ of Jesus. Baptism is the "new Passover" from death to _____ life _____ . That is why Catholics renew their baptismal _____ promises _____ at the Easter Vigil.

(225)

complete the sentences in the first section, *Light,* on page 225.]

3. Discuss with the students the second symbol, word.
   - ✦ **Why are words so important?** (Words help us to describe and interpret our world and reality.) **What do the words of Scripture help us to do?** (understand God's presence in history; describe how we are saved because of the life, Death, and Resurrection of Jesus)
   - ✦ **The words of Scripture, especially the New Testament, help us to describe and interpret our salvation in Christ. At the Easter Vigil, we recall the action of God in salvation history by proclaiming the words of**

Scripture. [Help the students read and complete the sentences in the second section, *Word,* on page 225.]

4. Discuss with the students the third symbol, water.
   - ✦ **What are some of the ways you use water every day?** (drinking, bathing, cleaning, brushing teeth)
   - ✦ **All of these aspects are included when we experience water as a liturgical symbol at the Easter Vigil.** [Help the students read and complete the sentences in the third section, *Water,* on page 225.]

5. Explain to the students the ways these liturgical symbols continue to be important in the liturgies of the Easter season.

◆ **What was the symbol of Christ our Light that was part of the Easter Vigil?** (paschal candle) Throughout the Easter season, the paschal candle continues to be lighted during Mass. It reminds us of Christ and the Paschal Mystery. It also reminds us that we are sent to bring the Light of Christ to others.

◆ **Throughout the Easter season, we hear the Word of God proclaimed to us in Scripture. We respond with our Easter praise when we sing and pray Alleluia!**

◆ **Throughout the Easter season, we renew the promises of our Baptism at Mass. Often the priest blesses us with holy water at the beginning of Mass to remind us of our Baptism. Sometimes the baptismal font is decorated with flowers and banners during the Easter season to remind us of the importance of our Baptism.**

6. Discuss how these Easter symbols remind us of Baptism. **These Easter symbols of light, word and water remind us of our Baptism. At our Baptism, our parents and godparents were given a candle lighted from the paschal candle. Our Baptism prepared us to follow the Word of God, and we were baptized with water.**

7. Recall the celebration of the Easter Triduum from the SSL 5 **Holy Week** (T401–T403).

◆ Introduce to the students the Liturgy of the Hours.

◆ **The Easter Triduum concludes with Evening Prayer on Easter Sunday. Evening Prayer is part of the public prayer of the Church called the Liturgy of the Hours, or the Divine Office.**

◆ **The Liturgy of the Hours includes hymns, psalms, Scripture readings, petitions, the Lord's Prayer, and times of reflective silence. There are seven hours, or times, that are part of this prayer: Matins (readings), Lauds (Morning Prayer), Terce, Sext, and None (Daytime Prayer),**

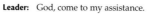

Celebrating

Prayer for Easter

Leader: God, come to my assistance.

All: Lord, make haste to help me.

Leader: Glory to the Father, and to the Son, and to the Holy Spirit:

All: As it was in the beginning, is now, and will be forever. Amen. Alleluia.

Canticle

Leader: Jesus said: Do not be afraid. Go and tell my brothers to set out for Galilee. There they will see me. Alleluia.

(Alleluias may be sung.)

Side 1: Alleluia. Sing praise to our God, all you his servants, all who worship him reverently, great and small.

Side 2: Alleluia. The Lord our all-powerful God is King; let us rejoice, sing praise, and give him glory.

Side 1: Glory to the Father, and to the Son, and to the Holy Spirit:

Side 2: As it was in the beginning, is now, and will be forever. Amen.

Reader: A reading from Hebrews 10:12–14. *(Passage is read aloud.)*

All: This is the day the Lord has made; let us rejoice and be glad, alleluia.

Canticle of Mary (Luke 1:46–55)

Intercessions

Leader: With joy in our hearts, let us call upon Christ the Lord, who died and rose again, and lives always to intercede for us:

All: Victorious King, hear our prayer.

Leader: Light and salvation of all peoples, send into our hearts the fire of your Spirit, as we proclaim your Resurrection.

All: Victorious King, hear our prayer.

Leader: You have triumphed over death, your enemy; destroy in us the power of death, that we may live only for you, victorious and immortal Lord.

All: Victorious King, hear our prayer.

Leader: We pattern our prayer on the prayer of Christ our Lord and say:

All: Our Father . . .

Concluding Prayer

Leader: God our Father, by raising Christ your Son you conquered the power of death and opened for us the way to eternal life. Let our celebration today raise us up and renew our lives by the Spirit that is within us. Grant this through our Lord Jesus Christ, your Son, who lives and reigns with you and the Holy Spirit, one God, for ever and ever.

Liturgy of the Hours: Easter Sunday Evening Prayer

All: Amen.

Dismissal

Leader: Go in peace. Alleluia, alleluia.

All: Thanks be to God. Alleluia, alleluia.

Closing Song

226

Vespers (Evening Prayer), and Compline (Night Prayer).

◆ **All Christians are invited to share in this prayer of the Church. Even if they are not able to pray all seven hours, many people choose to pray Morning and Evening Prayer.**

Acting

1. Have the students turn to **Celebrating Prayer for Easter** on page 226.

◆ **We will conclude our lesson today by praying the Evening Prayer that concludes the Easter Triduum. Let us look at the various parts of the prayer.** [Go over the parts of the prayer with the students.] (introductory verse, canticle, Scripture reading, Canticle of Mary, intercessions, concluding prayer, dismissal, and closing song)

◆ Select and practice an Easter song to end the prayer.

◆ Identify leaders and readers, and allow them time to prepare.

2. Lead the class in praying **Celebrating Prayer for Easter** on page 226.

CHECKPOINT ✓

• Were the learning outcomes achieved?

Enriching the Faith Experience

Use the following activities to enrich the lesson or to replace an activity with one that better meets the needs of your class.

1. Have the students design eggshell mosaics of the Easter symbols studied in this lesson. Have them draw a symbol on heavy paper and then use glue to place crushed and dyed eggshells onto the sections of the picture.

2. Have the students create a headline for a news story reporting an event from one of the following Scripture passages. [Write these Scripture citations on the board.]
   Matthew 28:1–15
   Mark 16:1–8,9–13
   Luke 24:1–12,13–35,36–43
   John 20:1–10,11–18,19–23,24–29
   Have the students write the headline on a 2-by-12-inch strip of paper. Ask the students to read their passage and share their headline with the class.

3. Divide the class into five groups. Assign each group one of the Glorious Mysteries of the Rosary from page 238. [See page T430.] Have the students explain why the mystery is considered glorious and why it fits into the Easter season.

4. With the students, analyze the words of Easter songs in missalettes or hymnals. The students could make a DVD or PowerPoint presentation of the Easter themes and symbols in the songs, using images from today.

5. Direct the students to write imaginary interviews with the people in the Gospels to whom the risen Jesus appeared. Collect the interviews and prepare an "eyewitness" booklet to be displayed. The students could interview such eyewitnesses as Simon Peter, John, Mary, Mary Magdalene, Thomas, the disciples on the road to Emmaus, the apostles, the soldiers at the tomb, Pontius Pilate, or the chief priests.

6. Have the students design stained-glass windows, using black construction paper for the frames and tissue paper or paper painted with watercolor for the glass. Suggest that the design include symbols of Easter such as the paschal candle, an Easter lily, or a lamb.

7. Explain to the students that during the Easter season the prayer *Regina Caeli*, (Queen of Heaven), is recited in place of the *Angelus*. Refer the students to this prayer on the inside back cover of their books. Have them read the prayer and explain why it is said during the Easter season.

8. Lead the students in a prayerful discussion of the Scripture readings for Easter Sunday, for each Sunday of the Easter season, and for the feast of the Ascension. For more information, visit www.christourlife.com.

9. **Web BLM** Lead the students in the celebration from Web BLM Chapter 22-B **Celebrating the Journey.** The celebration uses some of the Easter symbols from this lesson.

10. Let the students act out a Resurrection account for a younger class, using one of the Scripture passages listed below:
    John 20:1–10
    John 20:11–18
    John 20:24–29
    John 21:1–14
    John 21:15–23
    Luke 24:13–35
    Luke 24:36–43
    Acts of the Apostles 1:3–9

11. Have the students make cards for those who were baptized at the Easter Vigil or for the families bringing children for Baptism during the Easter season. Tell the students to write messages explaining the meaning of the Easter symbols they have learned.

7 Pentecost

Faith Focus

On Pentecost, we celebrate the fulfillment of Jesus' promise to send us the Holy Spirit.

Reflecting on the Faith Experience

Take a few moments to reflect prayerfully before preparing the lesson.

Listening

"When the Advocate comes whom I will send you from the Father, the Spirit of truth that proceeds from the Father, he will testify to me. And you also testify, because you have been with me from the beginning."

John 15:26–27

Reflecting

In *Catechesis in Our Time*, Pope John Paul II writes that the Holy Spirit is the principal source of inspiration for all catechetical work and for all catechists. It is the spirit of the Father and of the Son joined together that is the Holy Spirit.

When Pope John Paul II wrote about the Holy Spirit, he made three important affirmations about the role of the Spirit in the Church. First, the Spirit is our teacher within the Church, who acts in our minds and hearts to make us understand and love the depths of God's love. Second, the Spirit transforms us into people who are willing to proclaim the Lord Jesus, even giving up our lives for him. Third, the Gifts of the Spirit enlighten and strengthen us so that we can bear witness to Christ within our daily activities. These gifts help us to build up the Church.

Although there are a variety of gifts, each springs from the Spirit and complements the others. We are all gifted in some way, and we have been given these gifts so that we may help further Christ's kingdom in the world.

On the feast of Pentecost, we celebrate the gift of the Holy Spirit and its importance in our lives. We pray with the Church that the Holy Spirit will direct our use of every gift and that our lives may bring Christ to others.

O God, who by the mystery of
today's great feast
sanctify your whole Church in
every people and nation,
pour out, we pray, the gifts of
the Holy Spirit
across the face of the earth
and, with the divine grace that
was at work
when the Gospel was first
proclaimed,
fill now once more the hearts
of believers.

Collect Prayer
Pentecost

Do I remember to ask the Holy Spirit to work through me so that I may bring Christ to others, especially to the students I teach?

Responding

Holy Spirit, empower my students to live out their faith.

Scripture for Further Reflection

Acts 2:1–4 The disciples receive Jesus' promised gift of the Holy Spirit.

Romans 8:14–17 Those who are led by the spirit of God are children of God.

Preparing for the Faith Experience

Scripture in This Lesson

John 14:15–21 The Spirit of truth remains in us.

John 15:26–27 The Advocate comes from the Father.

John 16:12–15 The Spirit guides us in all truth.

Church Documents

Catechism of the Catholic Church. The themes of this lesson correspond to the following paragraphs: **691–693, 727–741, 1076.**

Music in This Lesson

For a list of all the music used in this program, see page T517.

Enriching the Faith Experience

Use the activities at the end of the lesson to enrich a lesson or to replace an activity with one that better meets the needs of your class.

Pentecost

Student pages 227–228

LEARNING OUTCOMES

The students will be able to

- explain that the feast of Pentecost is our celebration of the outpouring of the Holy Spirit.
- define the meaning of the names Jesus gave to the Holy Spirit: Advocate and Spirit of truth.
- explain how the Holy Spirit helps us in our lives.

Key Terms

Advocate—Jesus' name for the Holy Spirit who comforts us, speaks for us in difficult times, and makes Jesus present to us.

Holy Spirit—the Third Person of the Trinity, who is sent to us as our helper and, through Baptism and Confirmation, fills us with God's life. Together with the Father and the Son, the Holy Spirit brings the divine plan of salvation to completion.

Pentecost—the 50th day after Passover, the Jewish festival Shavuot, the Festival of the Weeks,

commemorating the time when the first fruits were harvested and brought to the Temple. Pentecost also commemorated the giving of the Torah on Mount Sinai. Christians celebrate Pentecost 50 days after Jesus' passover from death to life. On this day, the Holy Spirit was sent from heaven, and the Church was born.

Materials

- Bibles or New Testaments
- Lectionary
- Small poster board or writing paper
- Markers or crayons
- Information from the following Web sites for Sharing #5: Catholic Campaign for Human Development (www.usccb.org/cchd), United States Conference of Catholic Bishops (www.usccb.org), and Catholic Relief Services (www.crs.org).

Before You Begin

1. The Holy Spirit, the Third Person of the Trinity, is known by many names. Jesus called the Holy Spirit the Advocate

and the Spirit of truth. *Advocate,* the Latin translation of the Greek word *Paraclete,* is also translated as "strength" or "comforter." In the New Testament, we also hear the following names for the Holy Spirit: Spirit of God, Spirit of Christ, Spirit of the Lord, the Spirit of Adoption, and Spirit of the Promise. These names speak of the importance and the multifaceted roles of the Holy Spirit in the spiritual life of Christians.

2. Jesus sent the Holy Spirit from the Father to his people to guard and guide as the Church continues his work in this world. The Holy Spirit does this by dwelling within the hearts of individuals. Our life of prayer makes us attentive to the Holy Spirit who acts in and through us. As we respond to the inspirations of the Spirit, we are continuing the life and work of Jesus on earth.

Centering

Discuss with the students the people involved in a courtroom trial.

- ✦ **Many of us have seen TV shows or movies that depict scenes from a courtroom. Perhaps some of us know people who work in the legal profession. Who are some of the people or roles that one expects to find in a courtroom?** (judge, jury, witnesses, defendants, lawyers)

- ✦ **The role of a lawyer is someone who is an advocate for others. The legal system can be very complicated, so people hire lawyers to help them with legal matters.**

- ✦ **When Jesus promised his disciples the gift of the Holy Spirit, he used the word** *advocate*, **which we associate with our judicial system.**

- ✦ **Today we will learn more about the meaning of this word and what it tells us about the work of the Holy Spirit in our lives. What is the name of the day on which the Church celebrates the Holy Spirit in a special way?** (Pentecost)

Sharing

1. Have a student read aloud the first paragraph of **Sending of the Advocate** on page 227.
   - ✦ **When and where did the disciples receive Jesus' promised gift of the Holy Spirit?** (after Jesus ascended to heaven; in the upper room in Jerusalem) **When do we celebrate Pentecost?** (50 days after Easter)
   - ✦ The account of Pentecost is taught in Chapter 23, Alive with the Spirit. If you have already taught this chapter, you might wish to use the Pentecost acrostic on page 192 to review the details.
   - ✦ **Jesus fulfilled his promise to send his disciples a helper, the Holy Spirit. Let's learn more about what Jesus said about the gift he sent.**

7 | Pentecost

Sending of the Advocate

Jesus promised to send the Holy Spirit to his disciples. This promise was fulfilled on the Jewish feast of Pentecost when the Spirit descended upon the disciples gathered in the room in Jerusalem. On the feast of Pentecost, 50 days after Easter, we offer praise and thanksgiving to God for the gift of the Holy Spirit given to the first disciples and given to us as well.

Read each of the Scripture passages from the Gospel of John and answer the questions that follow. In each passage, Jesus is speaking about the Holy Spirit that he will send to his disciples.

"If you love me, you will keep my commandments. And I will ask the Father, and he will give you another Advocate to be with you always, the Spirit of truth, which the world cannot accept, because it neither sees nor knows it. But you know it, because it remains with you, and will be in you. I will not leave you orphans; I will come to you. In a little while the world will no longer see me, but you will see me, because I live and you will live. On that day you will realize that I am in my Father and you are in me and I in you."

John 14:15–20

Saint John the Evangelist

"When the Advocate comes whom I will send you from the Father, the Spirit of truth that proceeds from the Father, he will testify to me. And you also testify, because you have been with me from the beginning."

John 15:26–27

"I have much more to tell you, but you cannot bear it now. But when he comes, the Spirit of truth, he will guide you to all truth. He will not speak on his own, but he will speak what he hears, and will declare to you the things that are coming."

John 16:12–13

What names did Jesus use when he spoke of the Holy Spirit?

Advocate, Spirit of truth

List at least three ways that Jesus says the Holy Spirit will help the disciples.

The Holy Spirit will help the disciples to testify, or bear witness, to Jesus; the Holy Spirit will guide the disciples to truth; the Holy Spirit will live in them and help them to love one another.

227

2. Work with the students on the Scripture passages from the Gospel of John on page 227.
   - ✦ Read aloud the second paragraph on page 227.
   - ✦ Have several students read aloud the Scripture passages.
   - ✦ After all the passages have been read, allow time for the students to answer the questions.

3. Discuss with the students the meaning of the words *advocate* and *advocacy*.
   - ✦ **What are the two names that Jesus called the gift that he would send to his disciples?** (Advocate, Spirit of truth)

- ✦ **As we discussed earlier, a lawyer is considered an advocate in our judicial system. An advocate speaks for another person or works on his or her behalf. How is a lawyer an advocate for his or her client?** (The lawyer speaks for the client and presents his or her case in court.)

- ✦ **People can advocate in other ways as well. To speak on behalf of an issue or a cause is called advocacy. We all have advocates who speak for us in different ways. Parents are advocates for their children for example, when they speak up for their children's needs at school or with doctors.**

- **We sometimes act as advocates for our friends. Can you think of an example?** (When a friend is introduced to a group or a club we belong to, we might speak for him or her to persuade others to include that person in the group; we might advocate for a friend or sibling whom we know has been mistakenly accused by another person.)

- **What are some of the qualities of a good advocate?** (knowledge of the client or the issue; familiarity with the system; authority with those to whom one is making a case; empathy, confidence)

- **Jesus sent us the Holy Spirit to be an Advocate for his disciples and for us. According to the Scripture passages we read, how did Jesus say the Holy Spirit would help his disciples?** (testify on behalf of Jesus; guide the disciples in truth; help the disciples keep Jesus' commandment to love)

- **The action of the Holy Spirit in the lives of the disciples helped them to be advocates for Jesus in the world. They were given the courage to announce the good news of salvation and to act as Jesus did to serve the Kingdom of God. This is what the Holy Spirit can do for us as well.**

4. Have a student read aloud the first paragraph of **The Holy Spirit** on page 228.
    - Have the students read silently each of the descriptions of the help we receive from the Holy Spirit.
    - Allow time for the students to respond to the questions.

5. Explain to the students the ways the Holy Spirit leads us to be advocates for Jesus and the Kingdom of God.
    - **Under the guidance of the Holy Spirit, the Church advocates on behalf of many issues that affect people throughout our world. Some of these issues are poverty and hunger, human dignity and life issues, environmental concerns, and the peaceful resolution of conflicts.**

    - Distribute the information that you've gathered from the Web sites for the Catholic Campaign for Human Development, the United States Conference of Catholic Bishops, and Catholic Relief Services. Direct the students to choose an issue to work on.

    - **After you have chosen your issue, design a small poster or write a paragraph that explains the issue and the change advocated for by the Church.** [Allow time for the students to share their posters or paragraphs. Display the students' work in the school.]

Pentecost mural, St. Louis Cathedral, St. Louis, Missouri.

The Holy Spirit

As our Advocate, the Holy Spirit helps us and prepares us to be Christ's disciples today. The action of the Holy Spirit in our lives prepares us to be advocates for Christ and the Kingdom of God in our world. In a letter to the Church titled *Catechesis in Our Time*, Pope John Paul II summarized how the Holy Spirit helps each of us, and all members of the Church, today. Read these summaries and then answer the questions that follow.

The Holy Spirit is our teacher, helping us to grasp more fully all that Jesus taught. What would you like to understand better about Jesus?

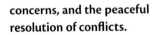

The Holy Spirit is a transforming presence, strengthening us to give witness to Jesus. How can the Holy Spirit help you to become a better witness to Jesus?

The Holy Spirit is a gift-giver. The Gifts of the Holy Spirit build up the community of the Church. They enable us to participate in the work of building the Kingdom of God. What gifts have you been given by the Holy Spirit? What gifts would you ask for?

The Holy Spirit also helps us to pray. Saint Paul wrote in the Letter to the Romans:

> . . . the Spirit too comes to the aid of our weakness; for we do not know how to pray as we ought, but the Spirit itself intercedes with inexpressible groanings. And the one who searches hearts knows what is the intention of the Spirit, because it intercedes for the holy ones according to God's will.
>
> Romans 8:26–27

We pray on Pentecost and every day:

Lord, send out your Spirit, and renew the face of the earth.

Responsorial Psalm Pentecost
Psalm 104:30

228 PENTECOST

Acting

Lead the students in a prayer to the Holy Spirit.

✦ Ask a volunteer to read aloud the text from Romans at the bottom of page 228.

✦ **With the Spirit's help, we can better advocate for the issues you identified in your posters and paragraphs. As we remember these issues, we will pray Psalm 104, which is used on the feast of Pentecost. At the end of each verse, respond with the refrain at the bottom of page 228.** [Read Psalm 104 from the Lectionary for Pentecost Sunday on pages 134–135, [64].]

CHECKPOINT

• Were the learning outcomes achieved?

Enriching the Faith Experience

Use the following activities to enrich the lesson or to replace an activity with one that better meets the needs of your class.

1. Direct the students to read the Pentecost Sequence, a prayer said before the Gospel on the feast of Pentecost. It is found in the Lectionary on pages 134–135 [64]. The students may prepare this as a choral reading and illustrate it with appropriate slides or musical background. This could be presented at the parish Mass on Pentecost.

2. Have small groups make collages illustrating one of the titles given to the Holy Spirit by using pictures and words from magazines or the Internet. A collage about comfort for example, would include pictures of people who need comfort as well as those who are happy because they have been comforted. For examples of titles given to the Holy Spirit, have the students search the Internet for the Litany to the Holy Spirit.

3. **BLM 81** Have the students choose their favorite image of the Spirit from Scripture. Using part of the quotation and the image of the Spirit, have the students design a poster. You may wish to use as a resource the Scripture verses listed on BLM 81 **The Activity of the Spirit** used in Chapter 23.

4. Direct the students to examine the Nicene Creed from the inside front cover of the student book to identify the words that describe our beliefs about the Holy Spirit. [See page T445.]

5. A small group of students could present on-the-spot news broadcasts about Pentecost. The students could interview some of the people who are listening to Peter's speech in their own language from Acts of the Apostles 2:14–36.

6. Have the students illustrate how the Spirit leads us to holiness through the sacraments. Have them draw a large flame on poster board. Inside the flame, have them glue quotations from Scripture or pictures that relate to the sacraments and some of their own written comments on the sacraments. If they wish to use quotations, the following examples would be appropriate:
   Matthew 19:5–6
   Matthew 28:16–20
   John 3:4–5
   John 6:54
   John 20:19–23
   Acts 8:14–17
   James 5:15–16

7. For more information on the Scripture readings for the feast of Pentecost, visit www.christourlife.com.

8 Giving Thanks

Faith Focus

We express thanks to God by prayer, by the Eucharist, and by using our gifts in loving service.

Reflecting on the Faith Experience

Take a few moments to reflect prayerfully before preparing the lesson.

Listening

In all circumstances give thanks, for this is the will of God for you in Christ Jesus.

1 Thessalonians 5:18

Reflecting

What marvelous things God has done for us. Out of sheer goodness and love, God brought us into being and spread at our feet the universe with all its wonders. Then, when we failed to respond to his love, God became one of us and died so that we might live forever. Even now, every day we are surrounded by signs of God's favor and love. Our natural response is to give thanks. How insufficient that seems in view of the gifts and the giver—a mere "thank you" to someone who has saved our life. It almost seems better to stand speechless and overwhelmed with awe. And yet, God desires our expressions of gratitude. So we say thank-you in our prayers, and we show our appreciation by the way we use our gifts.

In his great goodness, God has provided us with a beautiful way to thank him for everything he has given us: the Eucharist. In our celebration of the Paschal Mystery, as we offer Jesus and ourselves to the Father, we are able to give perfect thanks. Gathered with the faith community for the Eucharist, we live the psalmist's words:

I will praise the LORD with
  all my heart
 in the assembled congregation
  of the upright.

Psalm 111:1

When do I thank God for his goodness to me?

Responding

Holy Spirit, help my students to recognize your gifts and give you thanks.

Scripture for Further Reflection

Ezra 3:11 The Israelites thanked God for his enduring kindness.

Colossians 1:9–12 We thank God because we share in the inheritance of the saints.

Preparing for the Faith Experience

The following lesson appears only in the Teacher's Guide.

One-Day Lesson

Giving Thanks

Scripture in This Lesson

Psalm 136 God's love endures forever.

Luke 17:11–19 The 10 lepers

Church Documents

Catechism of the Catholic Church. The themes of this lesson correspond to the following paragraph: 2637.

Enriching the Faith Experience

Use the activities as the end of the lesson to enrich the lesson or to replace an activity with one that better meets the needs of your class.

Giving Thanks

LEARNING OUTCOMES

The students will be able to

- explain that God deserves and desires their gratitude.
- describe how to show gratitude to God.
- express appreciation to God for his gifts to them.

Materials

- Bibles or New Testaments
- Drawing paper
- Crayons or felt-tipped markers
- Pins or tape
- Large piece of cardboard (optional)
- Song of thanksgiving for Acting #1 and #3 (optional)

Before You Begin

1. A group of students might prepare the play in Sharing #1 ahead of time.

2. You might wish to make copies of the poem found in Sharing #5 for the students.

3. Instead of having the students draw pictures in Acting #1, you might provide magazines for the students to cut out pictures.

Centering _____

1. Lead the students in a prayer of gratitude.
   - **Stand and face north and thank God for cold things.**

     Face south and thank God for warm things.

     Face west and thank God for old things.

     Face east and thank God for new things.
   - Pray together the Doxology from the inside front cover of the student book. [See page T445.]

2. Have the students name gifts that are important to them, but that they might take for granted.
   Write their answers on the board. (air, family, freedom, friends, hearing, sight, school, food)

3. Direct the students to choose one of the things mentioned in Centering #1.
   Have them write a paragraph describing what their life would be like if that thing were missing.

4. Have students exchange papers.
   Have the students pass the papers around the room so that each student reads several papers. If the students are in rows, for example, they can pass their papers to the person behind them. The last student in each row can take his or her paper to the person in the first seat.

5. Write the words *think* and *thank* on the board.
   - **The word *thank* comes from the word *think*. That means that to thank someone is to be thinking of them.**
   - **We don't always think about the gifts that surround us. That means we don't always thank God for them.**

Sharing _____

1. Have the students act out the cleansing of the 10 lepers in Luke 17:11–19.
   Have a student read aloud Luke 17:11–19. Then choose volunteers to be Jesus, the Samaritan, and the other nine lepers.

2. Discuss the passage with the students.
   - **What did Jesus do for the 10 lepers?** (He healed them.)
   - **Why was this such a wonderful thing?** (Lepers were cut off from society. The disease made them look awful. They were not able to live fully. Jesus gave them life.)
   - **How do you know that Jesus likes to be thanked?** (He made a point

of asking where the others who were healed were.)

✦ **Why do you think the others hadn't returned to thank Jesus?** (They were excited at being healed and didn't think of it.)

✦ **How do you think Jesus felt?** (hurt, disappointed)

✦ **Did you ever experience having someone forget to thank you? How did you feel?**

✦ **Imagine if when those who were healed returned to their homes and their jobs and one used his legs to steal, one used his tongue to lie, one used his arms to vandalize, one used his fists to beat up others, and one was unfaithful to his wife. Why wouldn't they be showing gratitude to God?** (They would be using their healthy, healed bodies to do things that God forbids. They wouldn't be using God's gifts in the right way.)

✦ **One of the best ways to thank God for the gifts he has given us is to use them as God wishes.**

✦ **How do you think we might thank God for everything?** (tell him in words by praying, and celebrating the Eucharist)

3. Discuss with the students what Eucharist means.

✦ Write *Eucharist* on the board.

✦ **What does the word *Eucharist* mean?** (thanksgiving)

✦ **By ourselves, it is impossible for us to thank God enough for what he's done for us. But God has given us a beautiful way to give thanks by celebrating the Eucharist.**

✦ **How does the Eucharist show gratitude to God?** (In the Eucharist, we offer Jesus and ourselves to the Father. We come as a community to praise and thank God. It takes our time and attention to participate.)

✦ **In the United States, Thanksgiving Day is a national holiday set aside to think about God's gifts and to give thanks. Many people celebrate the Eucharist on this day in order to give perfect thanks to God.**

4. Read aloud and discuss with the students the Collect Prayer from the Thanksgiving Day Mass.

✦ **Father all-powerful,**
your gifts of love are countless
and your goodness infinite;
as we come before you on Thanksgiving Day
with gratitude for your kindness,
open our hearts to have concern
for every man, woman, and child,
so that we may share your gifts in loving service.
Through our Lord.

✦ **What do we thank God for in this prayer?** (God's kindness)

✦ **What do we ask for God to give us?** (to have concern for all people so that we may share God's gifts in loving service)

5. Read the poem "Thanksgiving" to the students.

Thanksgiving

The art of THANKSGIVING
    is THANKSLIVING.
It is thanking God for the gift of life
    by living it triumphantly.
It is thanking God for your talents
    by using them for the common good.
It is thanking God for all that men and women have done for you
    by doing good things for others.
It is thanking God for opportunities by accepting them
    as a challenge to achievement.
It is thanking God for happiness by striving to make others happy.
It is thanking God for beauty by helping to make the world more beautiful.
It is thanking God for inspiration by trying to be an inspiration to others.
It is thanking God for the creative ideas that enrich life
    by contributing to human progress yourself.
It is thanking God for each new day by living it to the fullest.
It is thanking God by giving hands, arms, legs, voice, and heart
    to your thankful spirit.

Source Unknown

Acting

1. Have the students draw something they would like to thank God for and compose a line about it to complete the sentence "Give thanks to the Lord who . . ."
Distribute pins or tape so the students can display their drawings. You might play a song of thanksgiving as they work.

2. Give the students directions for a prayer service of thanksgiving.

✦ **We will pray an adaptation of Psalm 136. It is a litany that has the response "For his mercy endures forever." I will pray the opening verses. Then each of you will post your drawing in the display area.** [This area may be a bulletin board, a chalkboard, or a large piece of cardboard.] **You will then continue the psalm by reading what you wrote in response to "Give thanks to the Lord who . . ." Then all of us will respond, "For his mercy endures forever."**

3. Hold the prayer service of thanksgiving. Begin with the first verses adapted from Psalm 136.

   ✦ **Give thanks to the Lord, for he is good,**

   [Response: For his mercy endures forever.]

   Give thanks to the God of gods,
   [Response]

   Give thanks to the Lord of lords,
   [Response]

   Who alone does great wonders.
   [Response]

   ✦ Have the students continue the prayer as they post their pictures. Conclude with a song of thanksgiving.

4. Plan a class activity in which the students will share their gifts with others.

   ✦ This can be a program or treat for another class or a collection of money or goods for those who are poor.

   ✦ If this lesson is taught near Thanksgiving Day, the students might participate in a school or parish project for that holiday.

5. Dictate to the students the following quiz:

   [1–3] Name three ways we can show gratitude to God. (pray, celebrate the Eucharist, use our gifts in the right ways)

   [4] What is the perfect way to give thanks to God? (celebrate the Eucharist)

   [5] What Gospel event shows that Jesus wants us to express gratitude? (the cleansing of 10 ten lepers)

   [6] What does the word *Eucharist* mean? (thanksgiving)

   [7–8] What do we offer God at the Eucharist in return for all he has done for us? (Jesus and ourselves)

   [9] During this lesson, what is one thing you realized that you should thank God for? (Answers will vary.)

   [10] Name one gift that God has given you and tell how you can use it in a way that shows your gratitude. (Answers will vary.)

CHECKPOINT ✓

- Were the learning outcomes achieved?

- How did the students show their gratefulness to God?

Enriching the Faith Experience

Use the following activities to enrich the lesson or to replace an activity that better meets the needs of your class.

1. Have small groups discuss practical ways to carry out the advice offered in each line of the poem in Sharing #5.

2. Suggest that the students prepare a thanksgiving reflection using a form of media such as a slideshow presentation, digital pictures, or recorded DVD. The prayer could be used for the Communion reflection at a school or parish Mass.

3. Have the students look through the Book of Psalms for expressions of thankfulness. Direct them to note why the psalmist is giving thanks in each case.

4. Allow the students to write thank-you notes to God. Post these in the room and use them in a prayer service.

5. Have the students form a circle. Toss a beanbag to any student. The student who catches the beanbag says a prayer of thanks such as "Thank you, Lord, for your gift of friendship." He or she then tosses the bag to another student who says another the prayer of thanks.

6. Divide the class into groups of three or four. Have each group cut pictures and captions from magazines to make a collage of things for which they give thanks. Tell the students to entitle each collage using cut-out letters or thick black markers, for example: Thank you, Lord, for _____ ; We are grateful _____ ; or Thanks for your gift of _____ .

9 Making Sunday Special

Faith Focus
Sunday, the day of the Resurrection, is a day for worship, rest, and family activities.

Reflecting on the Faith Experience
Take a few moments to reflect prayerfully before preparing the lesson.

Listening

So God blessed the seventh day and made it holy, because on it he rested from all the work he had done in creation.

Genesis 2:3

Reflecting

In the Old Testament, the Sabbath was the day honoring God's creative love. This day was set aside to rejoice, praise, and bless the Creator for the beauty of the land, the vastness of the sea, and God's goodness in all creation. On this day, the Jewish people honored God by having a special meal, reading the Scriptures, praying together, and offering special blessings. After the passion, Death, and Resurrection of Jesus and after Pentecost, Sunday became the day to honor God's new creation. On Sunday, Christians remember that

Jesus is risen and that he sent the gift of his Holy Spirit to the Church. They give thanks and praise to God by celebrating the Eucharist and by remembering his presence in the Christian community and, in a special way, in their families. Like the Jewish people, we begin our holy day the evening before, sometimes celebrating the Eucharist on Saturday evening.

In this hectic, busy time we live in, we need more than ever to keep Sunday as a time for spiritual celebration, for physical and mental rest, and for our families. Sunday is a day to acknowledge Jesus as the Lord of our lives and Lord of our families. When we keep Sunday according to God's plan, we and our families are renewed in the Lord.

How do I make Sunday special?

Responding

Jesus, give my students the grace to prepare to celebrate the Sunday Eucharist.

Scripture for Further Reflection

Isaiah 58:13 Keep the Sabbath as the Lord's holy day.

Matthew 11:28 Come to me and rest.

Preparing for the Faith Experience

One-Day Lesson
Making Sunday Special

Scripture in This Lesson

Exodus 20:8–11 Remember to keep holy the Sabbath day.

John 20:1–20 The empty tomb and the appearance of Jesus to Mary of Magdala and to the disciples

Church Documents

Catechism of the Catholic Church. The themes of this lesson correspond to the following paragraphs: **1166–1167, 2174.**

Enriching the Faith Experience

Use the activities at the end of the lesson to enrich the lesson or to replace an activity with one that better meets the needs of your class.

Making Sunday Special

LEARNING OUTCOMES

The students will be able to

- explain that Sunday is a celebration of the Lord's Resurrection.
- describe Sunday as a day to celebrate the Eucharist and to strengthen family unity.
- identify ways of making Sunday a day of prayer, rest, and family activities.

Materials

- Bibles or New Testaments
- Pullout **Making Sunday Special** from the back of the student book
- Small family pictures the students bring from home (needs to be planned ahead of time)

Before You Begin

1. Students need know to bring in small family pictures for this lesson. Remind them ahead of time to do this.

2. Be careful to respect each student's experience of what family means to them when preparing this lesson.

Centering

1. Discuss with the students the planning of a celebration for a family member.
   Have you ever planned a celebration for a member of your family? What did you do to make that day special? (eat a festive meal with the person; engage in activities the person likes; give gifts and cards to the person; perform kind acts for the person; spend time with the person)

2. Introduce to the students the topic of today's lesson.
   God has given us a particular day of the week, Sunday, to celebrate in a special way. In today's lesson, we will recall the meaning of Sunday and plan ways to make it unique.

Sharing

1. Have a student read aloud Exodus 20:8–11.
   - **What did God say about keeping the Sabbath?** (God said that the Sabbath, or seventh day, is for the Lord and that no work may be done on that day.)
   - **Let's read Genesis 2:1–3 to see the example God gives us.** (God rested on the seventh day.) **By this example, God teaches us to trust. God reminds us not to value too highly the work we do or the things of our daily lives. When we put aside our work, we have time to think, to pray, to be with our family, and to trust in God.**

   - ✦ The Jewish people remembered God's wonderful act of creation on the Sabbath and gave praise. They celebrated by reading the Scriptures, praying, serving a meal, and offering special blessings.
   - ✦ Many types of work were forbidden on the Sabbath. For example, the Jewish people were not to bake or boil anything, not to light a fire in their homes, and not to sew or untie a knot.

2. Have several students read aloud John 20:1–20.
   - ✦ **On which day of the week did Jesus rise from the dead?** (Sunday)
   - ✦ **Because Jesus rose from the dead on Sunday, and his Spirit came on Sunday at Pentecost, the early Christians decided to celebrate Sunday in a special way. Sunday became the day set aside to worship God through Christ in the greatest act of worship, the Eucharist.**
   - ✦ **The early Christians joined together in prayer as a community and as a family. They renewed themselves in the worshiping community and in their family life by sharing meals and activities. They grew in love for God and for one another.**
   - ✦ **How do we Christians celebrate Sunday?** (We celebrate the Eucharist, dress up for church, try to avoid work, and strengthen our community and family lives.)

   - ✦ **Why should Christians worship God by celebrating the Eucharist on Sunday?** (to thank and praise God for all he has done for us through the Death and Resurrection of Jesus; to acknowledge that Jesus is the Lord of our lives; to show our love for God and to do his will; to receive the graces of the Eucharist, which gives us strength)
   - ✦ **How do you think avoiding work and resting on Sunday would help the members of your family?** (They would pray together. Their mental and physical energy would be renewed, which can help them work better during the coming week.)
   - ✦ **What are some things we can do on Sunday to honor God?** (We can celebrate Mass together, discuss the Sunday readings and the homily, and pray together as a family.)
   - ✦ **What are some other things members of your family do together on Sunday?**

3. Have the students carefully remove **Making Sunday Special** from the pullout section in the back of the student books and complete the activities.

Instruct them to encourage the members of their families to add their own promises. Remind the students to fold the paper on the lines and to set it up in a prominent place in their homes.

4. Have volunteers share their prayers for their families and the ways they will make Sunday special for their families.

5. Have the students draw up an agenda for a specific Sunday as described in this lesson.

Acting

1. Encourage the students to do something about family members or friends who do not participate in Sunday Mass.
   + Suggest that they pray for these people or invite them to join the students at Sunday Mass.

✦ **What else could we do to encourage family members or friends to attend Sunday Mass?**

2. Lead the students in prayer. Have them spend a few moments praying for their families.
   Allow sufficient time for silent reflection. Conclude by praying the Lord's Prayer.

3. Dictate to the students the following quiz:
   [1] **When did God rest?** (after Creation)
   [2] **For which people is Saturday the Sabbath?** (the Jewish people)
   [3–4] **What two events occurred on Sunday that influenced Christians to celebrate on Sunday instead of Saturday?** (Jesus rose from the dead

on Sunday, and his Spirit came on Sunday at Pentecost.)
   [5] **What is the greatest act of worship we participate in every Sunday?** (the Eucharist)
   [6–10] **Name five ways to celebrate Sunday as God wishes.** (celebrate the Eucharist, spend extra time in prayer, avoid work, read Scripture, pray together as a family, have fun together with family members, and son on)

CHECKPOINT ✓

- Were the learning outcomes achieved?

- What indication is there that the students intend to improve their celebration of Sunday?

Enriching the Faith Experience

Use the following activities to enrich the lesson or to replace an activity with one that better meets the needs of your class.

1. Encourage the students to plan the celebration of a birthday, an anniversary, or a feast day for someone in their family. The celebration might include a special meal that they prepare and participation at Mass as a family.

2. To help make Sunday a day honoring God's creative love, suggest that the students put flowers or other seasonal symbols on their kitchen or dining room table. Suggest that they change the symbol once a week.

3. Have the students make a documentary of their typical family Sunday or an ideal family Sunday.

4. Let the students exchange family names and have each family pray for the family whose name they chose.

5. Have the students plan a Sunday liturgy. The students can take part in writing the introduction, the petitions, and a reflective prayer for after Holy Communion. They can help select the songs and take part in the preparation of the gifts procession. Preparations can be made to include other environmental expressions for the church.

6. Have the students make chalices out of clay and write the names of their family members on the bases. Tell them to use the chalices as centerpieces at home to remind their families of the importance of the Eucharist as the center of family love.

7. Ask the students to find out how the Church makes special the celebration of important feasts and holy days. The students could research areas such as vestments; styles of liturgy; music; sacred vessels; and the use of incense, holy water, and flowers.

8. Have the students make a family monthly calendar for their homes. Direct them to decorate it with family pictures, stickers, sketches of family activities, appointments, and celebrations. Tell them to post the calendar in an area where the family can see it. Suggest that they keep all the monthly calendars until the end of the year and take time to look over the good times the family members have shared.

9. Suggest that the students take out their family photo album and spend time sharing their family history with other family members.

What Catholics Should Know

(continued on next page)

(continued from previous page)

(230)

Prayer and How We Pray

God is always with us. He wants us to talk to him and listen to him. In prayer we raise our hearts and minds to God. We are able to speak and listen to God because through the Holy Spirit, God teaches us how to pray.

What Is Prayer?

Being a Christian requires that we believe all that God has revealed to us, that we celebrate it in the liturgy and the sacraments, and that we live what we believe. All this depends on a vital and personal relationship with the living and true God. This relationship is rooted in prayer. Prayer is a gift from God. We can pray because God seeks us out first and calls us to meet him. We become aware of our thirst for God because God thirsts for us. Prayer arises from our heart, beyond the grasp of reason. Only the Spirit of God can understand the human heart and know it fully. Prayer is the habit of being with God—Father, Son and Holy Spirit. This communion with God is always possible because through our Baptism we are united with Christ. By being united with Christ, we are united with others. Christian prayer is communion with Christ that branches out to all the members of his body, the Church.

Many Forms of Christian Prayer

The Holy Spirit, who teaches us to pray, leads us to pray in a number of ways. This conversation with God can take the form of adoration, blessing, contrition, petition, intercession, thanksgiving, or praise.

Adoration

In a prayer of adoration, we acknowledge God as Creator and Savior. In adoration we recognize how little we are in respect to God's greatness. Like Mary in the *Magnificat*, we confess with gratitude that God has done great things and holy is his name.

Blessing

To bless someone is to acknowledge the goodness of that person. The prayer of blessing is our response to God's goodness because of all the gifts he has given us. In the prayer of blessing, God's gifts and our acceptance of them come together.

Contrition

Contrition is the prayer of sorrow for sin along with a resolution not to sin again. If contrition is motivated by love of God alone, it is called perfect contrition. If contrition is motivated by fear of just punishment, it is called imperfect contrition.

(231)

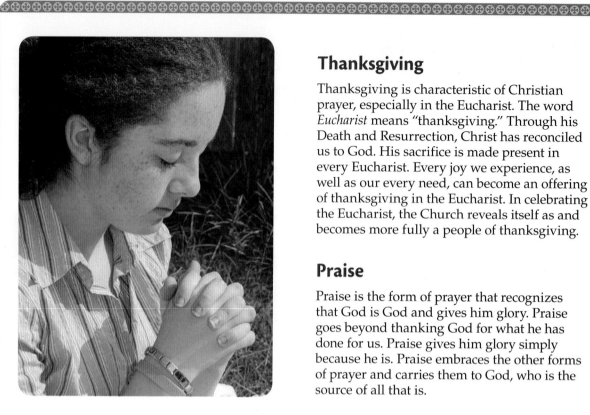

Petition

Petition is much more than asking God for things we want or need. By prayers of petition, we express our relationship with God as our Creator. We depend on him, and we ask him for something for ourselves. Sometimes we sin and turn away from God. The first step in the prayer of petition is turning back toward him and asking for forgiveness. We can then ask God for what we need, confident that he knows what we need before we ask.

Intercession

In prayers of intercession, we ask something on behalf of another. As a prayer form, intercession is a prayer of petition that leads us to pray as Jesus did. Throughout his life on earth, Jesus interceded with the Father on behalf of all people. To pray in this way means that our hearts are turned outward, focused on the needs around us.

Thanksgiving

Thanksgiving is characteristic of Christian prayer, especially in the Eucharist. The word *Eucharist* means "thanksgiving." Through his Death and Resurrection, Christ has reconciled us to God. His sacrifice is made present in every Eucharist. Every joy we experience, as well as our every need, can become an offering of thanksgiving in the Eucharist. In celebrating the Eucharist, the Church reveals itself as and becomes more fully a people of thanksgiving.

Praise

Praise is the form of prayer that recognizes that God is God and gives him glory. Praise goes beyond thanking God for what he has done for us. Praise gives him glory simply because he is. Praise embraces the other forms of prayer and carries them to God, who is the source of all that is.

We Meditate and Contemplate

To meditate is to think about God. We keep our attention and focus on God, using Scripture, prayer books, or religious images to help us concentrate and spark our imagination. To contemplate means that we rest quietly in God's presence.

We Get Ready to Pray

We can get ready for meditation by resting our bodies in a comfortable position, sitting with our backs straight and both feet on the floor. We can close our eyes, fold our hands in front of us, take a deep breath, and then slowly let it out. We can establish a rhythm by slowly counting to three while breathing in and slowly counting to three while breathing out. Concentrating on our breathing helps us quiet our thoughts.

Prayers We Pray as Catholics

We can pray with any words that come to mind. Sometimes when we find that choosing our own words is difficult, we can use traditional prayers. Memorizing traditional prayers such as the following can be very helpful. When we memorize prayers, we take them to heart, meaning that we not only learn the words but also try to understand and live them. See the inside front and back covers of your book for the most frequently used prayers.

Act of Contrition

O my God, I am heartily sorry for having offended Thee, and I detest all my sins because of thy just punishments, but most of all because they offend Thee, my God, who art all good and deserving of all my love. I firmly resolve with the help of Thy grace to sin no more and to avoid the near occasion of sin.
Amen.

Act of Contrition (Prayer of the Penitent)

My God,
I am sorry for my sins with all my heart.
In choosing to do wrong
and failing to do good,
I have sinned against you
whom I should love above all things.
I firmly intend, with your help,
to do penance,
to sin no more,
and to avoid whatever leads me to sin.
Our Savior Jesus Christ
suffered and died for us.
In his name, my God, have mercy.
Amen.

Jesus Prayer

Lord Jesus Christ, Son of God, have mercy on us sinners.

Prayer for Generosity

Eternal Word, only begotten Son of God,
Teach me true generosity.
Teach me to serve you as you deserve,
To give without counting the cost,
To fight heedless of wounds,
To labor without seeking rest,
To sacrifice myself without thought of any reward
Save the knowledge that I have done your will.
Amen.

Peace Prayer of Saint Francis

Lord, make me an instrument of your peace.
Where there is hatred, let me sow love; where
    there is injury, pardon;
where there is doubt, faith; where there is
    despair, hope;
where there is darkness, light; and where there
    is sadness, joy.
Grant that I may not so much seek to be
    consoled as to console,
to be understood as to understand, to be
    loved as to love;
for it is in giving that we receive, it is in
    pardoning that we are pardoned,
And it is in dying that we are born to eternal
    life.

Memorare

Remember, O most gracious Virgin Mary,
that never was it known
that anyone who fled to thy protection,
Implored thy help,
or sought thy intercession,
was left unaided.
Inspired by this confidence
I fly unto thee,
O Virgin of virgins, my Mother.
To thee do I come,
before thee I stand,
sinful and sorrowful.
O Mother of the Word Incarnate,
despise not my petitions,
But in thy mercy hear and answer me.
Amen.

Nicene Creed

I believe in one God,
the Father almighty,
maker of heaven and earth,
of all things visible and invisible.

I believe in one Lord Jesus Christ,
the Only Begotten Son of God,
born of the Father before all ages.
God from God, Light from Light,
true God from true God,
begotten, not made, consubstantial with
    the Father;
through him all things were made.
For us men and for our salvation
he came down from heaven,
and by the Holy Spirit was incarnate of the
    Virgin Mary,
and became man.

For our sake he was crucified under Pontius
    Pilate,
he suffered death and was buried,
and rose again on the third day
in accordance with the Scriptures.
He ascended into heaven
and is seated at the right hand of the Father.
He will come again in glory
to judge the living and the dead
and his kingdom will have no end.

I believe in the Holy Spirit, the Lord, the giver
    of life,
who proceeds from the Father and the Son,
who with the Father and the Son is adored
    and glorified,
who has spoken through the prophets.

I believe in one, holy, catholic and apostolic
    Church.
I confess one Baptism for the forgiveness
    of sins
and I look forward to the resurrection of
    the dead
and the life of the world to come.
Amen.

An Ancient Language of Prayer

From the beginning of the Church until the Second Vatican Council in the 1960s, the Church in the West used Latin as its common language. The Latin language was used in prayer, worship, documents, administration, and all areas of Church life. We have a rich and long tradition of hymns and prayers in Latin.

Even today there are parts of the Mass such as the Holy, Holy, Holy (*Sanctus*) and the Lamb of God (*Agnus Dei*) that are occasionally sung in Latin. Certain prayers that are shared by the universal Church can be learned in Latin and prayed as a sign of the universal nature of the Church.

Signum Crucis (Sign of the Cross)

In nomine Patris
et Filii
et Spiritus Sancti.
Amen.

Gloria Patri* (Glory Be to the Father)

Gloria Patri
et Filio
et Spiritui Sancto.
Sicut erat in principio,
et nunc et semper
et in sae cula saeculorum.
Amen.

Pater Noster* (Our Father)

Pater noster, qui es in caelis:
sanctificetur Nomen Tuum;
adveniat Regnum Tuum;
fiat voluntas Tua,
sicut in caelo et in terra.
Panem nostrum
cotidianum da nobis hodie;
et dimitte nobis debita nostra,
sicut et nos dimittimus
debitoribus nostris;
et ne nos inducas in tentationem;
sed libera nos a Malo.
Amen.

Ave, Maria* (Hail Mary)

Ave, Maria, gratia plena,
Dominus tecum.
Benedicta tu in mulieribus,
et benedictus fructus ventris tui, Iesus.
Sancta Maria, Mater Dei,
ora pro nobis peccatoribus,
nunc et in hora mortis nostrae.
Amen.

Agnus Dei (Lamb of God)

Agnus Dei, qui tollis peccáta mundi:
miserére nobis. (Lamb of God, you take away the sins of the world: have mercy on us.)

Agnus Dei, qui tollis peccáta mundi:
miserére nobis. (Lamb of God, you take away the sins of the world: have mercy on us.)

Agnus Dei, qui tollis peccáta mundi:
dona nobis pacem. (Lamb of God, you take away the sins of the world: Grant us peace.)

Sanctus (Holy, Holy, Holy)

Sanctus, Sanctus, Sanctus, Dóminus Deus Sábaoth. (Holy, Holy, Holy Lord, God of hosts.)

Pleni sunt caeli et terra glória tua. (Heaven and earth are full of your glory.)

Hósanna in excélsis. (Hosanna in the highest.)

Benedíctus qui venit in nómine Dómini. (Blessed is he who comes in the name of the Lord.)

Hosánna in excélsis. (Hosanna in the highest.)

*The English versions of these prayers are found on the inside front cover of this book.

PRAYERS WE PRAY AS CATHOLICS (235)

The Rosary

The Rosary helps us pray to Jesus through Mary. When we pray the Rosary, we think about the special events, or mysteries, in the lives of Jesus and Mary.

The Rosary is made up of a string of beads and a crucifix. We hold the crucifix in our hands as we pray the Sign of the Cross. Then we pray the Apostles' Creed. Next to the crucifix, there is a single bead, followed by a set of three beads and another single bead. We pray the Lord's Prayer as we hold the first single bead and a Hail Mary at each bead in the set of three that follows. Then we pray the Glory Be to the Father. On the next single bead, we think about the first mystery and pray the Lord's Prayer.

There are five sets of 10 beads; each set is called a decade. We pray a Hail Mary on each bead of a decade as we reflect on a particular mystery in the lives of Jesus and Mary. The Glory Be to the Father is prayed at the end of each set. Between sets is a single bead on which we think about one of the mysteries and pray the Lord's Prayer.

In his apostolic letter *Rosary of the Virgin Mary,* Pope John Paul II wrote that the Rosary could take on a variety of legitimate forms as it adapts to different spiritual traditions and different Christian communities. "What is really important," he said, "is that the Rosary should always be seen and experienced as a path of contemplation." It is traditional in some places to pray the Hail, Holy Queen after the last decade.

We end by holding the crucifix in our hands as we pray the Sign of the Cross.

Hail Holy Queen (*Salve Regina*)

Hail, Holy Queen, Mother of Mercy,
our life, our sweetness, and our hope.
To you do we cry,
poor children of Eve.
To you do we send up our sighs,
mourning and weeping in this valley of tears.
Turn, then, most gracious advocate,
your eyes of mercy toward us,
and after this exile
show unto us the blessed fruit of thy womb,
Jesus.
O clement, O loving,
O sweet Virgin Mary.

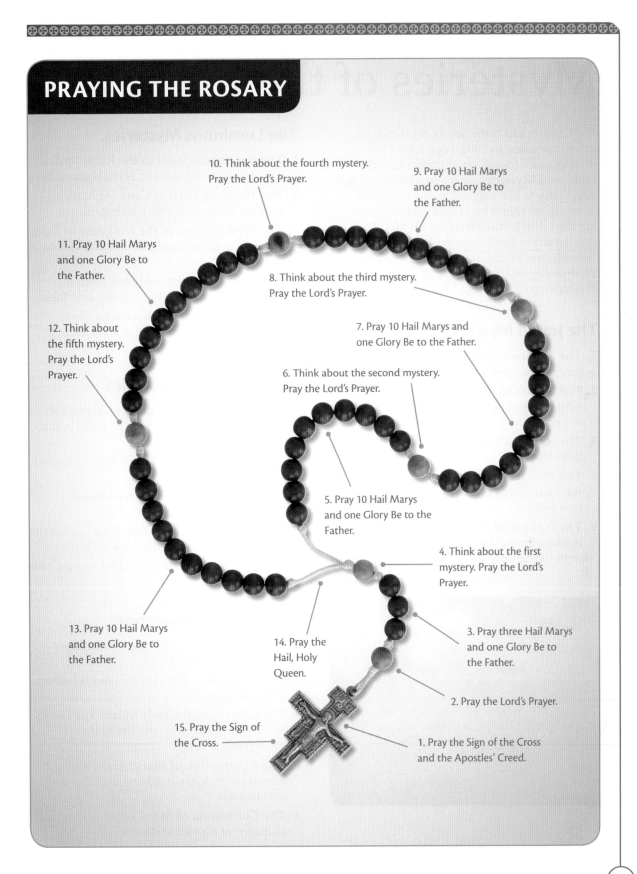

10. Think about the fourth mystery. Pray the Lord's Prayer.

9. Pray 10 Hail Marys and one Glory Be to the Father.

11. Pray 10 Hail Marys and one Glory Be to the Father.

8. Think about the third mystery. Pray the Lord's Prayer.

12. Think about the fifth mystery. Pray the Lord's Prayer.

7. Pray 10 Hail Marys and one Glory Be to the Father.

6. Think about the second mystery. Pray the Lord's Prayer.

5. Pray 10 Hail Marys and one Glory Be to the Father.

4. Think about the first mystery. Pray the Lord's Prayer.

13. Pray 10 Hail Marys and one Glory Be to the Father.

14. Pray the Hail, Holy Queen.

3. Pray three Hail Marys and one Glory Be to the Father.

2. Pray the Lord's Prayer.

15. Pray the Sign of the Cross.

1. Pray the Sign of the Cross and the Apostles' Creed.

Mysteries of the Rosary

The Church had three sets of mysteries for many centuries. In 2002, Pope John Paul II proposed a fourth set of mysteries—the Luminous Mysteries, or the Mysteries of Light. According to his suggestion, the four sets of mysteries might be prayed on the following days: the Joyful Mysteries on Monday and Saturday, the Sorrowful Mysteries on Tuesday and Friday, the Glorious Mysteries on Wednesday and Sunday, and the Luminous Mysteries on Thursday.

The Joyful Mysteries

1. **The Annunciation.** Mary learns that she has been chosen to be the mother of Jesus.
2. **The Visitation.** Mary visits Elizabeth, who tells her that she will always be remembered.
3. **The Nativity.** Jesus is born in a stable in Bethlehem.
4. **The Presentation.** Mary and Joseph take the infant Jesus to the Temple to present him to God.
5. **The Finding of Jesus in the Temple.** Jesus is found in the Temple, discussing his faith with the teachers.

The Luminous Mysteries

1. **The Baptism of Jesus in the River Jordan.** God proclaims that Jesus is his beloved Son.
2. **The Wedding Feast at Cana.** At Mary's request, Jesus performs his first miracle.
3. **The Proclamation of the Kingdom of God.** Jesus calls all to conversion and service to the kingdom.
4. **The Transfiguration of Jesus.** Jesus is revealed in glory to Peter, James, and John.
5. **The Institution of the Eucharist.** Jesus offers his Body and Blood at the Last Supper.

The Sorrowful Mysteries

1. **The Agony in the Garden.** Jesus prays in the garden of Gethsemane the night before he dies.
2. **The Scourging at the Pillar.** Jesus is lashed with whips.
3. **The Crowning with Thorns.** Jesus is mocked and crowned with thorns.
4. **The Carrying of the Cross.** Jesus carries the Cross that will be used to crucify him.
5. **The Crucifixion.** Jesus is nailed to the Cross and dies.

The Glorious Mysteries

1. **The Resurrection.** God the Father raises Jesus from the dead.
2. **The Ascension.** Jesus returns to his Father in heaven.
3. **The Coming of the Holy Spirit.** The Holy Spirit comes to bring new life to the disciples.
4. **The Assumption of Mary.** At the end of her life on earth, Mary is taken body and soul into heaven.
5. **The Coronation of Mary.** Mary is crowned as queen of heaven and earth.

Stations of the Cross

The 14 Stations of the Cross represent events from Jesus' passion and Death. Even before the Gospels were written down, the followers of Jesus told the story of his passion, Death, and Resurrection. When people went on pilgrimage to Jerusalem, they were anxious to see the sites where Jesus lived and died. Eventually, following in the footsteps of the Lord on the way to his Death became an important part of the pilgrimage.

The stations as we know them today came about when it was no longer easy or even possible to visit the holy sites in Palestine. In the 1500s, villages all over Europe started creating replicas of the way of the Cross, with small shrines commemorating the places along the route in Jerusalem. Eventually, these shrines became the set of 14 stations we now know.

The important point to remember about the stations is that they are a prayer. They are not an exercise in remembering events from the past. They are an invitation to make present the final hours of Jesus' life and to experience who Jesus is. It becomes a prayer when we open our hearts to be touched, and it leads us to express our response in prayer. Jesus wants to use any means available to move our hearts so that we know his love for us.

At each station we use our senses and our imagination to reflect prayerfully upon Jesus' suffering, Death, and Resurrection. The stations can allow us to visualize the meaning of his passion and Death and lead us to gratitude. They can also lead us to a sense of solidarity with all our brothers and sisters, especially those who suffer, who are unjustly accused or victimized, who are on death row, who carry difficult burdens, or who face terminal illnesses.

1. Jesus Is Condemned to Death.
Pontius Pilate condemns Jesus to Death.

2. Jesus Takes Up His Cross.
Jesus willingly accepts and patiently bears his Cross.

3. Jesus Falls the First Time.
Weakened by torments and loss of blood, Jesus falls beneath his Cross.

4. Jesus Meets His Sorrowful Mother.
Jesus meets his mother, Mary, who is filled with grief.

5. Simon of Cyrene Helps Jesus Carry the Cross.
Soldiers force Simon of Cyrene to carry the Cross.

6. Veronica Wipes the Face of Jesus.
Veronica steps through the crowd to wipe the face of Jesus.

7. Jesus Falls a Second Time.
Jesus falls beneath the weight of the Cross a second time.

8. Jesus Meets the Women of Jerusalem.
Jesus tells the women to weep not for him, but for themselves and for their children.

9. Jesus Falls the Third Time.
Weakened almost to the point of death, Jesus falls a third time.

10. Jesus Is Stripped of His Garments.
The soldiers strip Jesus of his garments, treating him as a common criminal.

11. Jesus Is Nailed to the Cross.
Jesus' hands and feet are nailed to the Cross.

12. Jesus Dies on the Cross.
After suffering greatly on the Cross, Jesus bows his head and dies.

13. Jesus Is Taken Down from the Cross.
The lifeless body of Jesus is tenderly placed in the arms of Mary, his mother.

14. Jesus Is Laid in the Tomb.
Jesus' disciples place his body in the tomb.

The closing prayer—sometimes included as a 15th station—reflects on the Resurrection of Jesus.

Formulas of Catholic Doctrine

The following formulas present the basic teachings of the Catholic Church. These are core teachings every Catholic should know.

The Great Commandment

The Ten Commandments are fulfilled in Jesus' Great Commandment: "You shall love God with all your heart, with all your soul, with all your mind, and with all your strength. You shall love your neighbor as yourself." (adapted from Mark 12:30–31)

The New Commandment

Before his Death on the Cross, Jesus gave his disciples a new commandment: "I give you a new commandment: love one another. As I have loved you, so you also should love one another." (John 13:34)

The Golden Rule

"Do to others whatever you would have them do to you." (Matthew 7:12)

The Beatitudes

The Beatitudes are the teachings of Jesus in the Sermon on the Mount. They can be found in Matthew 5:1–10. Jesus teaches us that if we live according to the Beatitudes, we will live a happy Christian life. The Beatitudes fulfill God's promises made to Abraham and to his descendants and describe the rewards that will be ours as loyal followers of Christ.

Blessed are the poor in spirit,
for theirs is the kingdom of heaven.
Blessed are they who mourn,
for they will be comforted.
Blessed are the meek,
for they will inherit the land.
Blessed are they who hunger and thirst
for righteousness,
for they will be satisfied.
Blessed are the merciful,
for they will be shown mercy.
Blessed are the clean in heart,
for they will see God.
Blessed are the peacemakers,
for they will be called children of God.
Blessed are they who are persecuted
for the sake of righteousness,
for theirs is the kingdom of heaven.

Moses with the Ten Commandments.

The Ten Commandments

As believers in Jesus Christ, we are called to a new life and are asked to make moral choices that keep us united with God. With the help and grace of the Holy Spirit, we can choose ways to act that keep us close to God, help other people, and be witnesses to Jesus.

The Ten Commandments guide us in making choices that help us live as God wants us to live. The first three commandments tell us how to love God; the other seven tell us how to love our neighbor.

1. I am the Lord your God: you shall not have strange gods before me.
2. You shall not take the name of the Lord your God in vain.
3. Remember to keep holy the Lord's Day.
4. Honor your father and your mother.
5. You shall not kill.
6. You shall not commit adultery.
7. You shall not steal.
8. You shall not bear false witness against your neighbor.
9. You shall not covet your neighbor's wife.
10. You shall not covet your neighbor's goods.

Precepts of the Church

The precepts of the Church describe the minimum effort we must make in prayer and in living a moral life. All Catholics are called to move beyond the minimum by growing in love of God and love of neighbor. The precepts are as follows:

1. To keep holy the day of the Lord's Resurrection. To worship God by participating in Mass every Sunday and every Holy Day of Obligation. To avoid those activities (like needless work) that would hinder worship, joy, or relaxation.
2. To confess one's sins once a year so as to prepare to receive the Eucharist and to continue a life of conversion.
3. To lead a sacramental life. To receive Holy Communion at least once during the Easter season.
4. To do penance, including abstaining from meat and fasting from food on the appointed days.
5. To strengthen and support the Church—assist with the material needs of the Church according to one's ability.

The Four Last Things

There are four things that describe the end of all human life.

death   judgment   heaven   hell

First is the death of the individual. Then immediately after death is the judgment by Christ. The result of this judgment is either heaven (perhaps with a time in purgatory) or hell.

Virtues

Virtues are gifts from God that lead us to live in a close relationship with him. Virtues are like habits. They need to be practiced; they can be lost if they are neglected.

Theological Virtues

The three most important virtues are called *Theological Virtues* because they come from God and lead to God.

faith   hope   charity

Cardinal Virtues

The cardinal virtues are human virtues, acquired by education and good actions. *Cardinal* comes from *cardo,* the Latin word for "hinge," meaning "that on which other things depend."

prudence   justice   fortitude   temperance

Gifts and Fruits of the Holy Spirit

The Holy Spirit makes it possible for us to do what God asks by giving us these gifts.

wisdom   understanding   counsel   piety

fortitude   knowledge   fear of the Lord

The Fruits of the Holy Spirit are signs of the Holy Spirit's action in our lives.

love	kindness	faithfulness
joy	goodness	modesty
peace	generosity	self-control
patience	gentleness	chastity
self-control	modesty	

Works of Mercy

The Corporal and Spiritual Works of Mercy are actions we can perform that extend God's compassion and mercy to those in need.

Corporal Works of Mercy

The Corporal Works of Mercy are the kind acts by which we help our neighbors with their material and physical needs:

- Feed the hungry.
- Give drink to the thirsty.
- Clothe the naked.
- Shelter the homeless.
- Visit the sick.
- Visit the imprisoned.
- Bury the dead.

Spiritual Works of Mercy

The Spiritual Works of Mercy are acts of compassion by which we help our neighbors with their emotional and spiritual needs:

- Counsel the doubtful.
- Instruct the ignorant.
- Admonish the sinner.
- Comfort the afflicted.
- Forgive offenses.
- Bear wrongs patiently.
- Pray for the living and the dead.

When we help others, we are performing works of mercy.

Celebrating and Living Our Catholic Faith

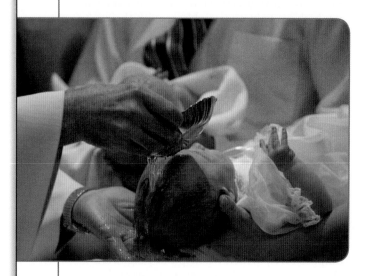

The Mystery of Faith Made Present

The Church was revealed to the world with the coming of the Spirit on Pentecost. This gift of the Spirit ushered in a new era in the history of salvation. This era is the age of the Church in which Christ makes present and communicates his work of salvation through the liturgy. The Church, as Christ's Body, is the first sacrament, the sign and instrument through which the Holy Spirit dispenses the mystery of salvation. In this age of the Church, Christ lives and acts through the sacraments.

The Seven Sacraments

Jesus touches our lives through the sacraments. In the sacraments, physical objects such as water, bread and wine, and oil are the signs of Jesus' presence.

Sacraments of Initiation

These sacraments lay the foundation of Christian life.

Baptism

In Baptism, we are born into new life in Christ. Baptism takes away Original Sin and makes us members of the Church. Its sign is the pouring of water.

Confirmation

Confirmation seals our life of faith in Jesus. The signs of Confirmation are the laying on of hands and the anointing with oil on a person's head, most often done by a bishop. Confirmation and Baptism are received only once.

Eucharist

The Eucharist nourishes our life of faith. We receive the Body and Blood of Christ under the appearances of bread and wine.

Sacraments of Healing

These sacraments celebrate the healing power of Jesus.

Reconciliation

Through Reconciliation we receive God's forgiveness. Forgiveness requires being sorry for our sins. In Reconciliation we receive Jesus' healing grace through absolution by the priest. The signs of this sacrament are the confession of sins, repentance and satisfaction, and the words of absolution.

Anointing of the Sick

This sacrament unites a sick person's sufferings with those of Jesus. Oil, a symbol of strength, is the sign of this sacrament. A person is anointed with the oil of the sick and receives the laying on of hands by a priest.

Sacraments at the Service of Communion

These sacraments help members serve the community.

Matrimony

In Matrimony a baptized man and woman are united with each other as a sign of the unity between Jesus and his Church. Matrimony requires the consent of the husband and the wife as expressed in the marriage promises. The husband and wife and their wedding rings are signs of this sacrament.

Holy Orders

In Holy Orders, men are ordained priests to serve as leaders of the community or as deacons to be reminders of our baptismal call to serve others. The signs of this sacrament are the laying on of hands and the prayer by the bishop asking God for the outpouring of the Holy Spirit.

Holy Days of Obligation

The holy days of obligation are the days other than Sundays on which we celebrate the great things God has done for us through Jesus and the saints. On holy days of obligation, Catholics attend Mass.

Six holy days of obligation are celebrated in the United States.

January 1—Mary, Mother of God

40 days after Easter—Ascension (in many U.S. dioceses the Seventh Sunday of Easter)

August 15—Assumption of the Blessed Virgin Mary

November 1—All Saints

December 8—Immaculate Conception

December 25—Nativity of Our Lord Jesus Christ

The Order of Mass

The Sabbath, the day on which God rested after creating the world, represents the completion of creation. Saturday has been replaced by Sunday as the Sabbath for Christians because it recalls the beginning of the new creation through the Resurrection of Christ. Since it is the day of the Resurrection, Sunday is called the Lord's Day. The Sunday celebration of the Lord's Day is at the heart of the Church's life. That is why we are required to participate in the Mass on Sundays and other holy days of obligation. We also rest from work, take time to enjoy our families, enrich our cultural and social lives, and perform works of mercy. On Sunday, people from all over the world gather at God's eucharistic table.

The Mass is the high point of Christian life, and it follows a set order.

Introductory Rites

We prepare to celebrate the Eucharist.

Entrance Chant

We gather as a community, praising God in song.

Greeting

We pray the Sign of the Cross, recognizing the presence of Christ in the community.

Penitential Act

We remember our sins and ask God for mercy.

Gloria

We praise God in song.

Collect Prayer

We pray for the grace to celebrate this Mass.

Liturgy of the Word

We hear the story of God's plan for salvation.

First Reading
We listen to God's Word, usually from the Old Testament.

Responsorial Psalm
We respond to God's Word in song.

Second Reading
We listen to God's Word from the New Testament.

Gospel Acclamation
We sing "Alleluia!" to praise God for the Good News. During Lent, we sing an alternate acclamation.

Gospel Reading
We stand to acclaim Christ present in the Gospel.

Homily
The priest or deacon explains God's Word.

Profession of Faith
We proclaim our faith through the Creed.

Prayer of the Faithful
We pray for our needs and the needs of others.

Liturgy of the Eucharist

We celebrate the meal Jesus instituted at the Last Supper and remember the sacrifice he made for us.

Presentation and Preparation of the Gifts
We bring gifts of bread and wine to the altar.

Prayer over the Offerings
The priest prays that God will accept our sacrifice.

Eucharistic Prayer
This prayer of thanksgiving is the center and high point of the entire celebration.

- *Preface Dialogue*—We give thanks and praise to God.

- *Holy, Holy, Holy (Preface Acclamation)*—We sing an acclamation of praise.

- *Institution Narrative*—The prayer over the bread and wine whereby, through the power of the Holy Spirit and the ministry of the priest, the bread and wine are transformed into the Body and Blood of Jesus Christ.

- *The Mystery of Faith*—We proclaim Jesus' Death and Resurrection.

- *Amen*—We affirm the words and actions of the Eucharistic prayer.

Communion Rite

We prepare to receive the Body and Blood of Jesus.

- *The Lord's Prayer*—We pray the Lord's Prayer.

- *Sign of Peace*—We offer one another Christ's peace.

- *Lamb of God*—We pray for forgiveness, mercy, and peace.

- *Communion*—We receive the Body and Blood of Jesus Christ.

- *Prayer after Communion*—We pray that the Eucharist will strengthen us to live as Jesus did.

Concluding Rites

We go forth to serve the Lord and one another.

Final Blessing
We receive God's blessing.

Dismissal
We go forth in peace to glorify the Lord by our lives.

Making Good Choices

Our conscience is the inner voice that helps us know the law God has placed in our hearts. Our conscience helps us judge the moral qualities of our actions. It guides us to do good and avoid evil.

The Holy Spirit can help us form our conscience. We form our conscience by studying the teachings of the Church and following the guidance of our parents and pastoral leaders.

God has given every human being freedom of choice. This does not mean that we have the right to do whatever we please. We can live in true freedom if we cooperate with the Holy Spirit, who gives us the virtue of prudence. This virtue helps us recognize what is good in every situation and make the correct choice. The Holy Spirit gives us the gifts of wisdom and understanding to help us make the right choices in life in relationship to God and others. The gift of counsel helps us reflect on making correct choices in life.

The Ten Commandments, the Beatitudes, and the two Great Commandments help us make moral choices. We also have the grace of the sacraments, the teachings of the Church, and the good example of saints and fellow Christians.

Making moral choices involves the following steps:

1. Ask the Holy Spirit for help.

2. Think about God's law and the teachings of the Church.

3. Think about what will happen as a result of your choice. Ask yourself, will the consequences be pleasing to God? Will my choice hurt someone else?

4. Seek advice from someone you respect, and remember that Jesus is with you.

5. Ask yourself how your choice will affect your relationships with God and others.

In making moral choices, we must take into consideration the object of the choice, our intention in making the choice, and the circumstances in which the choice is made. It is never right to make an evil choice in the hope of gaining something good.

The Morality of Human Acts

Human beings are able to act morally only because we are free. If we were not free to decide what to do, our acts could not be good or evil. Human acts that are freely chosen after a judgment of conscience can be morally evaluated. They are either good or evil.

The morality of human acts depends on

- the object chosen;

- the end in view or the intention;

- the circumstances of the action.

For an act to be good, what you choose to do must be good in itself. If the choice is not good, the intention or the circumstances cannot make it good. You cannot steal a digital camera because it is your father's birthday and it would make him happy to have one. But a good act done with a bad intention is not necessarily good either. Participating in a hunger walk, not out of concern for the poor but to impress a teacher from whom you want a good grade, is not necessarily a good act. Circumstances can affect the morality of an

MAKING GOOD CHOICES (247)

A priest performs a blessing following confession.

act. They can increase or lessen the goodness of an act. Acting out of fear of harm lessens a person's responsibility for an act.

An Examination of Conscience

An examination of conscience is the act of looking prayerfully into our hearts to ask how we have hurt our relationships with God and with other people through our thoughts, words, and actions. We reflect on the Ten Commandments and the teachings of the Church.

My Relationship with God

- What steps am I taking to help me grow closer to God and to others? Do I turn to God often during the day, especially when I am tempted?

- Do I participate at Mass with attention and devotion on Sundays and holy days? Do I pray often and read the Bible?

- Do I use God's name and the names of Jesus, Mary, and the saints with love and reverence?

My Relationships with Family, Friends, and Neighbors

- Have I set a bad example through my words or actions? Do I treat others fairly? Do I spread stories that hurt other people?

- Am I loving toward those in my family? Am I respectful of my neighbors, my friends, and those in authority?

- Do I value human life? Do I do what I can to promote peace and to end violence? Do I avoid talking about others in ways that could harm them?

- Do I show respect for my body and for the bodies of others? Do I keep away from forms of entertainment that do not respect God's gift of sexuality?

- Have I taken or damaged anything that did not belong to me? Do I show concern for the poor and offer assistance to them in the ways I am able? Do I show concern for the environment and care for it as God has asked?

- Have I cheated or copied homework? Have I told the truth even when it was difficult?

- Do I quarrel with others just so I can get my own way? Do I insult others to try to make them think they are less than I am? Do I hold grudges and try to hurt people who I think have hurt me?

How to Make a Good Confession

An examination of conscience is an important part of preparing for the Sacrament of Reconciliation. The Sacrament of Reconciliation includes the following steps:

- The priest greets us, and we pray the Sign of the Cross. He invites us to trust in God. He may read God's Word with us.

- We confess our sins. The priest may help and counsel us.

- The priest gives us a penance to perform. Penance is an act of kindness, prayers to pray, or both.

- The priest asks us to express our sorrow, usually by reciting the Act of Contrition.

- We receive absolution. The priest says, "I absolve you from your sins in the name of the Father, and of the Son, and of the Holy Spirit." We respond, "Amen."

- The priest dismisses us by saying, "Go in peace." We go forth to perform the act of penance he has given us.

The Bible

God speaks to us in many ways. One way God speaks to us is through the Bible. The Bible is the most important book in Christian life because it is God's message, or Revelation. The Bible is the story of God's promise to care for us, especially through his Son, Jesus. At Mass, we hear stories from the Bible. We can also read the Bible on our own.

The Bible is not just one book; it is a collection of many books. The writings in the Bible were inspired by the Holy Spirit and written by different authors using different styles.

The Bible is made up of two parts: the Old Testament and the New Testament. The Old Testament contains 46 books that tell stories about the Jewish people and their faith in God before Jesus was born.

The first five books of the Old Testament—Genesis, Exodus, Leviticus, Numbers, and Deuteronomy—are referred to as the *Torah,* meaning "instruction" or "law." The central story in the Torah is the Exodus, the liberation of the Hebrew slaves as Moses led them out of Egypt and to the Promised Land. During the journey, God gave the Ten Commandments to Moses and the people.

A beautiful part of the Old Testament is the Book of Psalms. A psalm is a prayer in the form of a poem. Each psalm expresses an aspect or feature of the depth of human emotion. Over several centuries, 150 psalms were gathered to form the Book of Psalms. They were once sung at the Temple in Jerusalem, and they have been used in the public worship of the Church since its beginning. Catholics also pray the psalms as part of their private prayer and reflection.

The prophets were called by God to speak for him and to urge the Jewish people to be faithful to the Covenant. A large part of the Old Testament (18 books) presents the messages and actions of the prophets.

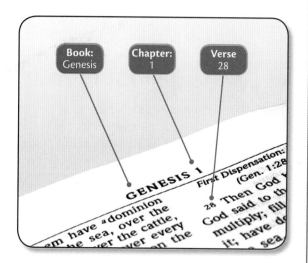

The New Testament contains 27 books that tell the story of Jesus' life, Death, and Resurrection, and the experience of the early Christians. For Christians, the most important books of the New Testament are the four Gospels—Matthew, Mark, Luke, and John. Many of the 27 books are letters written by leaders such as Paul.

How can you find a passage in the Bible? Bible passages are identified by book, chapter, and verse—for example, Genesis 1:28. The name of the book comes first. Sometimes it is abbreviated. Your Bible's table of contents will help you determine what the abbreviation means. For example, *Gn* stands for *Genesis.* After the name of the book, there are two numbers. The first one identifies the chapter, which in our example is chapter 1; it is followed by a colon. The second number identifies the verse or verses. Our example shows verse 28.

How the Old Testament and the New Testament Were Put Together

The Old and New Testaments developed in oral cultures, and much of the material was passed on by word of mouth before ever being written down. Stories from the prehistory of Israel were probably the first part of the Old Testament to be written down. These can be

King David.

found in parts of the 2nd through 11th chapters of Genesis. They would have been written by the court historian of King David around 1000 B.C. This writer always referred to God as Yahweh and spoke of God in human terms. It was this writer who wrote the story of God walking in the garden with Adam and Eve. Other stories developed in the northern kingdom of Israel and favor the religious sites of that region, such as Bethel.

The Old Testament as we know it today did not begin to take shape until the Babylonian Exile (587–537 B.C.). There members of the priestly class took many of the oral and written accounts of God's saving work and put them together in what we know as the Torah, the first five books of the bible—Genesis, Exodus, Leviticus, Numbers, and Deuteronomy.

The writers in Babylon also wrote the opening chapter of Genesis that tells of God's orderly creation of the world in six days and his rest on the seventh day.

The historical books were put together from the court accounts of various kings of Israel and Judah. The psalms were gathered from collections of prayers, and new psalms were written for the temple that was rebuilt after 537 B.C. Other Wisdom Literature was also gathered. Finally, the writings of the prophets were gathered together and collected by

their followers. They included prophets who preached and wrote from 150 years before the exile, such as the first Isaiah and Amos, to the second part of the book of Zechariah, which was probably written after 330 B.C. In the middle of the third century B.C., these books were translated from Hebrew into Greek in Alexandria, Egypt. In time a number of other books, such as First and Second Maccabees, were added to the Bible in Greek. By the end of the first century A.D., religious leaders in Israel decided which books would be in their Bible. They included only the Old Testament books written in Hebrew.

In about year 50, Paul wrote his first letter to the Thessalonians, followed by a second one later that year. This was more than 20 years after the Death and Resurrection of Jesus. Over the next 13 years, Paul wrote letters to other Christian communities as well as to the Christians of Rome, a city he hoped to visit. Meanwhile, Christians were passing on stories about Jesus—his message, his miracles, and others things he did. Probably the first stories to come together centered on his final days— his passion, Death, and Resurrection. This is why all four Gospels tell similar stories about Jesus' last days.

Mark.

The first Gospel to be written was the Gospel of Mark. It was written in Rome during and after Nero's persecution in the second half of the 60s. In the 80s, the authors of the Gospels of Matthew and Luke, using Mark's Gospel as a starting point, wrote their own Gospels for their specific Christian communities. Matthew, Mark, and Luke, though writing about Jesus in different ways, tell stories that are similar enough to be read side by side. Because of their similarities, we call them the *Synoptic Gospels*. They also made use of a collection of Jesus' sayings. The Gospel of John was written in the mid-to-late 90s. It is very different in tone and theology. The last book of the New Testament to be written was Second Peter, shortly after the year 100.

Showing Our Love for the World

The Catholic Church has developed a large body of teaching on social justice issues, because action on behalf of justice and work to create a more just world are essential parts of preaching the Gospel. In the story of the Good Samaritan (Luke 10:29–37), Jesus makes clear our responsibility to care for those in need.

The major development of the social doctrine of the Church began in the 19th century, when the Gospel encountered the modern industrial society. There were new structures for the production of consumer goods, new concepts of society, new types of states and authorities, and new forms of labor and ownership.

Since that time the Church has been making judgments about economic and social matters that relate to the basic rights of individuals and communities. The Church's social teaching is a rich treasure of wisdom about how to build a just society and how to live holy lives amid the challenges of the modern world.

All human life is sacred, and all people must be respected and valued over material goods. We are called to ask whether our actions as a society respect or threaten the life and dignity of the human person. The Catholic Church teaches this responsibility in the following themes of Catholic Social Teaching.

Call to Family, Community, and Participation

Participation in family and community is central to our faith and to a healthy society. Families must be supported so that people can participate in society, build a community spirit, and promote the well-being of all, especially the poor and vulnerable.

Volunteers distribute free bottled water to survivors of Hurricane Jeanne, Florida.

Rights and Responsibilities

Every person has a right to life as well as a right to those things required for human decency. As Catholics, we have a responsibility to protect these basic human rights in order to achieve a healthy society.

Option for the Poor and Vulnerable

In our world, many people are rich while others are poor. As Catholics, we are called to pay special attention to the needs of the poor by defending and promoting their dignity and meeting their immediate material needs.

The Dignity of Work and the Rights of Workers

The basic rights of workers must be respected: the right to productive work, fair wages, and private property; the right to organize, join unions, and pursue economic opportunity. Catholics believe that the economy is meant to serve people and that work is not merely a way to make a living, but an important way in which we participate in God's creation.

Solidarity

Because God is our Father, we are all brothers and sisters with the responsibility to care for one another. Solidarity is the attitude that leads Christians to share spiritual and material goods. Solidarity unites rich and poor, weak and strong, and helps create a society that recognizes that we depend on one another.

Care for God's Creation

God is the Creator of all people and all things, and he wants us to enjoy his creation. The responsibility to care for everything God has made is a requirement of our faith.

A teen weeds a native habitat restoration site, California.

Prayers to Know

Lord's Prayer (Our Father)

Our Father, who art in heaven,
hallowed be thy name;
thy kingdom come,
thy will be done
on earth as it is in heaven.
Give us this day our daily bread,
and forgive us our trespasses,
as we forgive those who trespass against us;
and lead us not into temptation,
but deliver us from evil.
Amen.

Hail Mary

Hail, Mary, full of grace,
the Lord is with thee.
Blessed art thou among women
and blessed is the fruit of thy womb, Jesus.
Holy Mary, Mother of God,
pray for us sinners,
now and at the hour of our death.
Amen.

Glory Be to the Father
(Doxology)

Glory be to the Father
and to the Son
and to the Holy Spirit,
as it was in the beginning
is now, and ever shall be
world without end.
Amen.

Morning Offering

O Jesus, through the Immaculate Heart of Mary,
I offer you my prayers, works, joys and sufferings of this day
for all the intentions of your Sacred Heart,
in union with the Holy Sacrifice of the Mass throughout the world,
for the salvation of souls, the reparation for sins, the reunion
    of all Christians,
and in particular for the intentions of the Holy Father this month.
Amen.

Grace Before Meals

Bless us, O Lord, and these thy gifts,
which we are about to receive from thy bounty,
through Christ our Lord.
Amen.

Grace After Meals

We give thee thanks, for all thy benefits, Almighty God, who live
    and reign for ever.
And may the souls of the faithful departed, through the mercy
    of God, rest in peace.
Amen.

Act of Contrition

O my God, I am heartily sorry for having offended Thee, and I detest
all my sins because of thy just punishments, but most of all because
they offend Thee, my God, who art all good and deserving of all my
love. I firmly resolve with the help of Thy grace to sin no more and to
avoid the near occasion of sin.
Amen.

This book belongs to:

The Apostles' Creed

I believe in God,
the Father almighty,
Creator of heaven and earth,
and in Jesus Christ, his only Son, our Lord,
who was conceived by the Holy Spirit,
born of the Virgin Mary,
suffered under Pontius Pilate,
was crucified, died and was buried;
he descended into hell;
on the third day he rose again from the dead;
he ascended into heaven,
and is seated at the right hand of God the Father almighty;
from there he will come to judge the living and the dead.

I believe in the Holy Spirit,
the holy catholic Church,
the communion of saints,
the forgiveness of sins,
the resurrection of the body,
and life everlasting.
Amen.

Nicene Creed

I believe in one God,
the Father almighty,
maker of heaven and earth,
of all things visible and invisible.

I believe in one Lord Jesus Christ,
the Only Begotten Son of God,
born of the Father before all ages.
God from God, Light from Light,
true God from true God,
begotten, not made, consubstantial with the Father;
through him all things were made.
For us men and for our salvation
he came down from heaven,
and by the Holy Spirit was incarnate of the Virgin Mary,
and became man.

For our sake he was crucified under Pontius Pilate,
he suffered death and was buried,
and rose again on the third day
in accordance with the Scriptures.
He ascended into heaven
and is seated at the right hand of the Father.
He will come again in glory
to judge the living and the dead
and his kingdom will have no end.

I believe in the Holy Spirit, the Lord, the giver of life,
who proceeds from the Father and the Son,
who with the Father and the Son is adored and glorified,
who has spoken through the prophets.

I believe in one, holy, catholic and apostolic Church.
I confess one Baptism for the forgiveness of sins
and I look forward to the resurrection of the dead
and the life of the world to come.
Amen.

Vocation Prayer

Lord, let me know clearly
the work which you are calling me to do in life.
And grant me every grace I need to answer your call
with courage and love and lasting dedication to your will.
Amen.

Prayers to Know

Act of Faith

O my God, I firmly believe
that you are one God in three divine Persons,
Father, Son, and Holy Spirit.
I believe that your divine Son became man
and died for our sins and that he will come
to judge the living and the dead.
I believe these and all the truths
which the Holy Catholic Church teaches
because you have revealed them
who are eternal truth and wisdom,
who can neither deceive nor be deceived.
In this faith I intend to live and die.
Amen.

Act of Hope

O Lord God,
I hope by your grace for the pardon
of all my sins
and after life here to gain eternal happiness
because you have promised it
who are infinitely powerful, faithful, kind, and merciful.
In this hope I intend to live and die.
Amen.

Act of Love

O Lord God, I love you above all things
and I love my neighbor for your sake
because you are the highest, infinite and perfect good, worthy
    of all my love.
In this love I intend to live and die.
Amen.

Prayer to the Holy Spirit

Verse. Come, Holy Spirit, fill the hearts of your faithful.
Response. And kindle in them the fire of your love.
Verse. Send forth your Spirit and they shall be created.
Response. And you shall renew the face of the earth.

Let us pray:
Oh God, by the light of the Holy Spirit you have taught the hearts of your faithful. In the same Spirit, help us to know what is truly right and always to rejoice in your consolation. We ask this through Christ, Our Lord. Amen.

Regina Caeli

Queen of heaven, rejoice, alleluia.
The Son whom you merited to bear, alleluia,
has risen as he said, alleluia.
Rejoice and be glad, O Virgin Mary, alleluia!
For the Lord has truly risen, alleluia.

Let us pray;
O God, who through the resurrection of your Son, our Lord Jesus Christ, did vouchsafe to give joy to the world; grant, we beseech you, that through his Mother, the Virgin Mary, we may obtain the joys of everlasting life. Through the same Christ our Lord. Amen.

Prayer for Christlikeness

Dear Jesus, help me to spread your fragrance everywhere I go;
Flood my soul with your spirit and life:
Penetrate and possess my whole being so completely
That all my life may be only a radiance of yours;
Shine through me and be so in me
That everyone with whom I come into contact
May feel your presence within me.
Let them look up and see no longer me—but only Jesus.
Amen.

John Henry Cardinal Newman

Angelus

Verse. The Angel of the Lord declared unto Mary.
Response. And she conceived of the Holy Spirit.

Hail, Mary, full of grace, the Lord is with thee.
Blessed art thou among women,
and blessed is the fruit of thy womb, Jesus.
Holy Mary, Mother of God,
pray for us sinners,
now and at the hour of our death.
Amen.

Verse. Behold the handmaid of the Lord.
Response. Be it done unto me according to thy word.
Hail Mary.

Verse. And the Word was made flesh.
Response. And dwelt among us.
Hail Mary.

Verse. Pray for us, O holy Mother of God.
Response. That we may be made worthy of the promises of Christ.

Let us pray;
Pour forth, we beseech thee, O Lord, thy grace into our hearts; that we, to whom the Incarnation of Christ, thy Son, was made known by the message of an angel, may by his Passion and Cross be brought to the glory of his Resurrection. Through the same Christ, our Lord. Amen.

Memorare

Remember, O most gracious Virgin Mary,
that never was it known
that anyone who fled to thy protection,
implored thy help,
or sought thy intercession,
was left unaided.
Inspired by this confidence
I fly unto thee,
O Virgin of virgins, my Mother.
To thee do I come,
before thee I stand,
sinful and sorrowful.
O Mother of the Word Incarnate,
despise not my petitions,
but in thy mercy hear and answer me.
Amen.

Prayer to Saint Michael the Archangel

St. Michael the Archangel, defend us in battle,
be our protection against the wickedness and snares of the Devil.
May God rebuke him, we humble pray.
And do thou, O Prince of the Heavenly Host, by the Power of God,
thrust into hell Satan and all evil spirits who wander the earth seeking
    the ruin of souls.
Amen.

Take, Lord, and Receive
(*Suscipe*)

Take, Lord, and receive all my liberty,
my memory, my understanding,
and my entire will,
all I have and call my own.

You have given all to me.
To you, Lord, I return it.

Everything is yours; do with it what you will.
Give me only your love and your grace,
that is enough for me.

St. Ignatius of Loyola

Saints and Feast Days

Calendar of Saints and Feast Days

September

- *3 Gregory the Great
- 8 Birth of Mary
- 9 Peter Claver
- *13 John Chrysostom
- 14 Triumph of the Cross
- 15 Our Lady of Sorrows
- *16 Cornelius and Cyprian
- *17 Robert Bellarmine
- *19 Januarius
- 20 Andrew Kim Taegon, Paul Chong Hasang, and Their Companions
- 21 Matthew
- 26 Cosmas and Damian
- 27 Vincent de Paul
- *28 Wenceslaus
- *28 Lawrence Ruiz and His Companions
- 29 Michael, Gabriel, and Raphael, Archangels
- *30 Jerome

October

- 1 Thérèse of the Child Jesus
- 2 Guardian Angels
- 4 Francis of Assisi
- *6 Bruno
- *6 Bl. Marie-Rose Durocher
- 7 Our Lady of the Rosary
- *9 Denis
- 9 John Leonardi
- *14 Callistus I
- *15 Teresa of Avila
- *16 Hedwig
- 16 Margaret Mary Alacoque
- *17 Ignatius of Antioch
- 18 Luke
- *19 Isaac Jogues, John de Brébeuf, and Their Companions
- *20 Paul of the Cross
- 23 John of Capistrano
- 24 Anthony Claret
- 28 Simon and Jude

November

- 3 Martin de Porres
- *4 Charles Borromeo
- *9 Dedication of Saint John Lateran
- *10 Leo the Great
- 11 Martin of Tours
- *12 Josaphat
- 15 Albert the Great
- *16 Margaret of Scotland
- 16 Gertrude the Great
- *17 Elizabeth of Hungary
- 18 Dedication of the Churches of Peter and Paul
- 18 Rose Philippine Duchesne
- 21 Presentation of Mary
- 22 Cecilia
- *23 Clement I
- *23 Columban
- *23 Bl. Miguel Agustín Pro
- 24 Andrew Dung-Lac and His Companions
- 30 Andrew
- ✝ Christ the King (Last Sunday of the Church Year)

December

- *3 Francis Xavier
- *4 John Damascene
- 6 Nicholas
- *7 Ambrose
- 8 Immaculate Conception
- 9 Juan Diego
- *11 Damasus I
- *12 Our Lady of Guadalupe
- 13 Lucy
- *14 John of the Cross
- 21 Peter Canisius
- *22 Frances Xavier Cabrini
- *23 John of Kanty
- 26 Stephen
- 27 John the Evangelist
- 28 Holy Innocents
- *29 Thomas Becket
- *31 Sylvester I
- ✝ Holy Family (Sunday After Christmas)

January

- 1 Solemnity of Mary, Mother of God
- *2 Basil the Great and Gregory Nazianzen
- *4 Elizabeth Ann Seton
- *5 John Neumann
- ✝ Epiphany (Sunday Between January 2 and January 8)
- 6 André Bessette
- ✝ Baptism of the Lord (Sunday After Epiphany)
- 7 Raymond of Peñafort
- *13 Hilary
- *17 Anthony
- *20 Fabian
- *20 Sebastian
- 21 Agnes
- *22 Vincent
- *24 Francis de Sales
- 25 Conversion of Paul
- 26 Timothy and Titus
- 27 Angela Merici
- *28 Thomas Aquinas
- 31 John Bosco

February

- 2 Presentation of the Lord
- *3 Blaise
- 3 Ansgar
- *5 Agatha
- 6 Paul Miki and His Companions
- *8 Jerome Emiliani
- 10 Scholastica
- 11 Our Lady of Lourdes
- *14 Cyril and Methodius
- 17 Seven Founders of the Order of Servites
- *21 Peter Damian
- *22 Chair of Peter
- 23 Polycarp

✝ Dates vary.
* Material for dates with an asterisk is found in the Grade 8 teacher's guide.

March

3 Katharine Drexel
4 Casimir
*7 Perpetua and Felicity
*8 John of God
9 Frances of Rome
17 Patrick
*18 Cyril of Jerusalem
19 Joseph, Husband of Mary
*23 Turibius de Mongrovejo
*25 Annunciation of the Lord

April

*2 Francis of Paola
4 Isidore of Seville
*5 Vincent Ferrer
*7 John Baptist de la Salle
8 Julie Billiart
*11 Stanislaus
*13 Martin I
*21 Anselm
23 George
*24 Fidelis of Sigmaringen
25 Mark
28 Peter Chanel
*29 Catherine of Siena
*30 Pius V

May

*1 Joseph the Worker
*2 Athanasius
3 Philip and James
*10 Damien
*12 Nereus and Achilleus
*12 Pancras
14 Matthias
15 Isidore the Farmer
*18 John I
20 Bernardine of Siena
*25 Bede the Venerable
*25 Gregory VII
25 Mary Magdalene de Pazzi
26 Philip Neri
*27 Augustine of Canterbury
31 The Visitation

June

*1 Justin
*2 Marcellinus and Peter
3 Charles Lwanga and His Companions
*5 Boniface
6 Norbert
*9 Ephrem
11 Barnabas
13 Anthony of Padua
*19 Romuald
21 Aloysius Gonzaga
*22 Paulinus of Nola
*22 John Fisher and Thomas More
24 Birth of John the Baptist
*27 Cyril of Alexandria
*28 Irenaeus
29 Peter and Paul
*30 First Martyrs of the Church of Rome

July

*1 Bl. Junipero Serra
3 Thomas
*4 Elizabeth of Portugal
*5 Anthony Zaccaria
6 Maria Goretti
*11 Benedict
13 Henry
14 Kateri Tekakwitha
*14 Camillus of Lellis
*15 Bonaventure
16 Our Lady of Mount Carmel
*21 Lawrence of Brindisi
22 Mary Magdalene
*23 Bridget of Sweden
25 James
26 Joachim and Ann
29 Martha
*30 Peter Chrysologus
*31 Ignatius of Loyola

August

1 Alphonsus Liguori
*2 Eusebius of Vercelli
*4 John Vianney
5 Dedication of St. Mary Major
6 Transfiguration
*7 Sixtus II and His Companions
*7 Cajetan
*8 Dominic
*10 Lawrence
11 Clare
*13 Pontian and Hippolytus
*14 Maximilian Mary Kolbe
15 Assumption of Mary
16 Stephen of Hungary
*18 Jane Frances de Chantal
*19 John Eudes
*20 Bernard of Clairvaux
*21 Pius X
22 Queenship of Mary
*23 Rose of Lima
24 Bartholomew
*25 Louis of France
*25 Joseph of Calasanz
27 Monica
*28 Augustine
29 Martyrdom of John the Baptist

✢ Dates vary.
* Material for dates with an asterisk is found in the Grade 8 Teacher's Guide.

Introduction

The Church calendar in the West, the Roman calendar, revolves around Easter. The Church year is divided into Easter and the Easter cycle of feasts, Christmas and the Christmas cycle, and Ordinary Time.

Traditionally, the Church has celebrated the way certain men and women have lived the Paschal Mystery and honored them as saints. Their lives praise Christ, give hope to his followers, and offer an example for people to imitate.

Suggested Activities

◆ At the beginning of class, read or have a student read the sketch in the supplement. In the case of summer saints, have the students named after these saints present the sketches on their birthdays, baptismal anniversaries, or at another suitable time.

◆ You may make copies of the Saints and Feast Days pages and distribute them to the students for their personal use at home.

◆ Encourage the students to do additional research on the saints, especially their patrons, and share their findings with the class. These could eventually be assembled into a class booklet.

◆ On the feast days, use the opening prayer from the Mass for the saint for the class prayer.

◆ Post a calendar that contains the name days of the students as well as their birthdays and baptismal anniversaries.

◆ After presentations of the lives of the saints, relate their lives to the present day.

◆ Encourage the students and their families to celebrate the feast days of patron saints in various ways, such as the following:

• Prepare for the celebrations by observing vigils the night before, during which the students should read about their patrons, read from Scripture, pray the Rosary, or use their own form of prayer.

• Attend Mass on the feast day of their patron.

• Light a baptismal candle or Christ candle in honor of the saint.

◆ Have the students write prayers to the saints.

◆ Keep a saint mural. As each saint is studied, he or she may be added to the mural.

◆ Have the students imagine that they are the saints presented. What would they have done?

The Second Vatican Council made it very clear that all men and women are called to holiness. The saints are our companions. We thank God for the example of their lives that makes Christ more present to us, and we ask for their intercession. By suffering and dying, the saints bore witness to the faith, and their witness encouraged others to remain faithful.

Saints and Feast Days, a book adapted from the *Christ Our Life* series, is available from Loyola Press. It provides stories about hundreds of saints along with suggestions for activities related to each saint. Other useful resources from Loyola Press include *My Best Teachers Were Saints: What Every Educator Can Learn from the Heroes of the Church, My Life with the Saints,* and *Mystics and Miracles: True Stories of Lives Touched by God.*

September

Sept. 8 Birth of Mary

God chose Mary to be the mother of Jesus. So open was she to God's action in her life that she was chosen to bring Christ to the waiting world. The Gospels do not mention Mary's birth, but because of the part she was to play in Christ's life, we know it was special.

We cannot be certain about what the future holds for any newborn infant, but we do know that each life has meaning and purpose. We know that we are gifted and loved by God and that he has given us a part to play in life that cannot be duplicated by any other person. We honor Christ by celebrating his mother's birth and by showing respect and concern for one another. God loves us and has called each of us to do something special in life.

Suggestions

◆ Encourage the students to pray to Mary during the day. They could pray the *Memorare,* the *Regina Caeli,* the *Angelus,* or the Hail Mary, which are found on the inside front and back covers of their books.

◆ The date of the feast of the Birth of Mary was used to fix the date of the feast of the Immaculate Conception. All the Marian feasts are closely related to the mysteries in Christ's life. Have the students explain how these feasts point to Christ as the center of Mary's life.

◆ This feast is believed to have originated in Jerusalem and was celebrated in the Eastern Church before it came to be observed in the Western Church, around the eighth century. Have the students research devotions to Mary celebrated in the Eastern Catholic communities such as the Akathistos prayer to the Virgin Mary. The students could present national customs honoring Mary, including displays, samples of music, and food.

Sept. 9 Saint Peter Claver

Peter Claver, born in Spain in 1581, was trained by the Jesuits. In 1602, he entered the Jesuit novitiate. As a young man, he met Alphonsus Rodriguez, who urged him to follow the call to be a missionary. In 1610, Peter was sent as a missionary to Cartagena in what is now Colombia, South America. There he continued his studies, ministered to the people, and was ordained a priest in 1616. Cartagena's economic success came from being the principal market for the slave trade in the New World. Slaves were brought there, herded into warehouses, and auctioned off to the highest bidder. These slaves had been captured in Africa, chained together in groups of six, crowded into the lower holds of ships, and mistreated during the long journey to Colombia. Ships designed to hold 100–200 people carried 600–800. An estimated one-third of the slaves died during the journey. Whenever a ship arrived in a port, Peter would hurry down with water, medicine, fruits, vegetables, bread, and clothing. His first concern was to tend to their human needs and then to help restore their sense of dignity. He nursed many back to health and, while they were in warehouses awaiting their sale, he would teach and administer the sacraments to them.

There was little Peter could do to change the social structure. People refused to see the evil of slavery. Peter and Father Alphonsus Sandoval tried to be visible signs that these slaves were human beings and children of God. During his 40 years in Colombia, Peter Claver baptized nearly 300,000 Africans.

A man of deep prayer, unbounded energy, and steady devotion, Peter Claver realized that it was his relationship with Christ that nourished his spirit. In 1650, worn out from his work, Peter became ill. He was bedridden for four years. On September 8, 1654, he died. The city that had opposed so many of his efforts honored him greatly after his death. In 1888, he was canonized by Pope Leo XIII.

It takes courage and love to reach out to others when evil seems so strong in a society. But Peter Claver had that kind of courage and love. He saw the suffering Jesus in the slaves he served. And he heard in their cry: "What you do to others, you do to me."

Suggestions

◆ Review with the students the Spiritual and Corporal Works of Mercy found on page 191 (T377). Have them draw pictures of Peter's ministry and how they relate to the works of mercy.

◆ Peter Claver was canonized by Pope Leo XIII. Pope Leo encouraged missionary activity, the rights of workers, and the abolition of slavery. Have the students find out more about this pope and his writings.

◆ On his solemn profession, Peter Claver signed himself "slave of the blacks forever." Discuss the problems of racial tensions, prejudice, and equality. Refer to the document *Brothers and Sisters to Us*, the 1979 U.S. bishops pastoral letter on racism.

◆ Have the students compose a prayer to Peter Claver, asking for his intercession. Ask how they can be modern Peter Clavers.

Sept. 14 Triumph of the Cross

This feast traces its beginning to Jerusalem and the dedication of the church built on the site of Mount Calvary in A.D. 335. But the meaning of the Cross is deeper than any city, celebration, or building. The Cross is a sign of suffering. It is a sign of human cruelty at its worst. But by Christ's love, it has become the sign of triumph and victory. It is a sign of God's love.

Believers have always looked to the Cross in times of suffering. Some people in concentration camps, in prisons, and in hospitals have been known to look to the Cross for comfort. The Cross does not explain our suffering, but it helps us to see our lives united with Christ's suffering.

We often make the Sign of the Cross before and after prayer. In trials and temptations, the Cross is a sign of strength and protection. The Cross is the sign of the fullness of life that is ours. At Baptism, the priest, parents, and godparents make the sign on the forehead of the child. By the Sign of the Cross in Baptism, Jesus takes us as his own in a unique way, and we are welcomed into the community of believers. Today let us look to the Cross often. Let us make the Sign of the Cross and realize we bring our whole selves to God— our minds, souls, bodies, wills, thoughts, hearts. We bring everything we are and will become.

> O cross, you are the glorious sign of our victory. Through your power may we share in the triumph of Christ Jesus.
> *Liturgy of the Hours*

Suggestions

◆ Have the students construct crosses of their own using wood, cardboard, foil, stones, clay, or any other material available.

◆ Take the students to the church or prayer room for a short prayer or meditation on the Cross. Provide Scripture references for meditation such as John 19; Mark 15—16; 2 Timothy 2:10–12; or an appropriate song about the Cross.

◆ Pray the Stations of the Cross with the students or have them compose their own meditations and drawings for the stations.

◆ Encourage the students to do research on Saint Helena and the true Cross. Or have them research her son, the emperor Constantine.

+ Teach the students A Prayer to Christ Crucified.

A Prayer to Christ Crucified

My good and dear Jesus, I kneel before you, asking you most earnestly to engrave upon my heart a deep and lively faith, hope, and charity, with true repentance for my sins, and a firm resolve to make amends. As I reflect upon your five wounds, and dwell upon them with deep compassion and grief, I recall, good Jesus, the words of the prophet David spoke long ago concerning yourself: "they have pierced my hands and my feet, they have numbered my bones!"

Sept. 15 Our Lady of Sorrows

When you love people very much, you share in all their joys and sorrows. That's how it was for Mary, the mother of Jesus. When people accepted Jesus, Mary was filled with joy. But when she saw her Son rejected and hurt, she experienced that pain very deeply. Today we remember Our Lady's share in the sufferings of her Son, and we call upon her as Our Lady of Sorrows. Mary loved Jesus so much that she suffered along with him without complaining or feeling sorry for herself. She carried these sufferings in silence, always knowing that God understood and cared.

Mary is our mother too. That means she rejoices when we draw closer to God. It means she understands our daily pains and sufferings. We may not always understand the mystery of the Cross in our lives, but we do know we need never carry our Cross by ourselves. We are brothers and sisters of Jesus and children of Mary, Our Lady of Sorrows. Today let us turn to Mary. She is near to us and will pray for us. Mary, Our Lady of Sorrows, pray for us.

Suggestions

+ Traditionally, the major sorrows of Mary are listed as seven. Direct the students to research these incidents in Scripture. Have them illustrate the events or design banners for each.

1. The prophecy of Simeon: Luke 2:33–35

2. The flight into Egypt: Matthew 2:13–18

3. The child Jesus lost in the Temple: Luke 2:41–50

4. Mary meets Jesus carrying the Cross: Luke 23:27–29

5. Mary at the foot of the Cross: John 19:25–30

6. Mary receives the body of Jesus: Luke 23:47–56

7. The burial of Jesus: Matthew 27:57–61

(Note that several of the references are not explicit in the Scriptures, but rather come from the traditional understanding of Mary's role in the passion and Death of her Son.)

+ Teach or review with the students several Marian prayers or devotions.

+ Show the students either a picture or replica of Michelangelo's *Pietà*. Display it in the room.

Sept. 20 Saint Andrew Kim Taegon, Saint Paul Chong Hasang, and Their Companions

One hundred thirteen Korean martyrs were canonized together in 1984. Among them were Andrew, a priest; Paul, a 45-year-old seminarian; Columba Kim, a 26-year-old single woman; and a 13-year-old boy. Approximately, 10,000 Catholics were martyred for their faith before religious freedom came to Korea in 1883.

During a Japanese invasion in 1592, some Koreans were baptized. Soon after, Korea cut itself off from the rest of the world. Then, around 1777, Catholic books came into the country, and a small Church began. When a Chinese priest secretly arrived about 12 years later, he found 4,000 Catholics who had never seen a priest. Korea's first Christian community was made up entirely of laypeople. Between 1839 and 1867, there were fierce persecutions. One hundred and three members of this community were martyred along with three bishops and seven priests from the Paris Foreign Mission Society.

Andrew Kim Taegon was the first native Korean priest. He was the son of converts. His father, a farmer, was martyred. Andrew was baptized when he was 15. He then attended the seminary in Macao, China, 1,300 miles away from home. After six years, Andrew returned to Korea and assumed the job of bringing missionaries into the country secretly. He was arrested, tortured, and beheaded.

Suggestions

+ Help the students report on the beginnings of the Church in Korea.

+ Have the students write a composition explaining how laypeople contribute to your parish community.

Sept. 21 Saint Matthew

Matthew, the apostle, is the patron of bankers. He is also known as Levi and was a tax collector in Capernaum. Most tax collectors were hated by the Jewish people because they worked for the Romans, who had conquered their land. A tax collector could use his position honestly or dishonestly.

Matthew was one of those special people chosen by Christ to follow him. So powerful was the call from Jesus that Matthew left his work as a tax collector. He invited Jesus to a special dinner where other tax collectors and sinners were gathered. The Pharisees said to the disciples: "Why does your teacher eat with tax collectors and sinners?" He heard them and said, "Those who are well do not need a physician, but the sick do. Go and learn the meaning of the words, 'I desire mercy, not sacrifice.' I did not come to call the righteous but sinners." (Matthew 9:11–13) Matthew preached the Good News of Christ in various places. His community was probably in Syria. His shrine is in Salerno, Italy.

We can learn much from Matthew. He was a man who knew the power of money. Let us pray today that through the intercession of Saint Matthew, we may not be fooled into thinking money can provide us with the most important things in life. Let us also recall that Christ will provide us with all we need to grow in what really matters. Saint Matthew, pray for us.

Suggestion

Have the students share with those who are poor by collecting money for the missions or sponsoring a food or clothing drive.

Sept. 26 Saints Cosmas and Damian

Little is known about Cosmas and Damian except that they suffered martyrdom for their faith in Syria sometime during the persecutions of Emperor Diocletian, around A.D. 303.

According to legend, Cosmas and Damian were twin brothers born in Arabia who went to Syria to study and practice medicine. They brought their belief in Christ to their patients. They also served people without charging any fees. Lysias, the governor of Celicia, summoned them before him. When Cosmas and Damian proclaimed they were Christians, Lysias had them tortured and beheaded. Their bodies were taken to the city of Cyr (Cyrrhus) in southern Syria. Devotion to these two doctors grew, and many cures were said to have been worked through their intercession. Later, a church in their honor was constructed over the site of their burial. When the Emperor Justinian was sick, he prayed to Saints Cosmas and Damian for a cure. Out of gratitude for receiving this favor, he enlarged the city of Cyr and the church there. Numerous other churches were erected for them at Constantinople and Rome. Their names are included in the First Eucharistic Prayer called the Roman Canon.

Suggestions

+ Along with Saint Luke, Saints Cosmas and Damian are the patrons of doctors, surgeons, and pharmacists. Lead the students in prayer for all those in the medical profession.

+ Ask the students to read the Eucharistic Prayer I and note the saints listed. Have them do research on the martyrologies of the various saints.

Sept. 27 Saint Vincent de Paul

Vincent de Paul was born in Gascony, France, in 1580. He was the son of peasant farmers. As a young boy, he was educated by the Franciscans at Dax and then went on to study at the University of Toulouse. When he was nearly 20, Vincent was ordained a priest. After his ordination, Vincent was on a ship and seized by pirates who sold him into slavery in Tunis, North Africa. Eventually, he escaped and made his way back to Rome. From Rome, he went to France, and there he was appointed court chaplain to Queen Margaret of Valois. He seemed well on the way to a life of wealth and comfort. But at the same time, he came to know Pierre de Berulle. Berulle helped Vincent understand more deeply what it meant to be a true Christian. Vincent came face-to-face with himself and his empty goals.

Vincent changed his life. He worked for a year in a small parish in a peasant area and saw how destitute the people were. So he organized charitable confraternities, which are groups of people who would provide food and clothing for those who were poor. But Vincent saw another kind of poverty, a spiritual poverty. Many of the people had no real understanding of their faith. So Vincent organized priests who would go out to the poor sections and preach to the people. This group of priests became the Congregation of the Mission, or the Vincentian fathers. He also founded the Congregation of the Daughters of Charity with Saint Louise de Marillac.

At night, Vincent would search the city for abandoned babies and find homes for them. He cared for the prisoners who had been made slaves. He remained good friends with many of the rich and influential people and involved them in his work with those who were poor or needy. He did so much for so many that after his death in 1660, he was canonized a saint by Pope Clement XII in 1737. He was named the patron of all charitable societies. Vincent made every day a giving day. Let us make today a giving day.

Suggestions

+ It is said that Vincent de Paul wrote more than 3,000 letters. Discuss with the students how much good can be done through letter and card writing. Have the students write letters to those who need encouragement and care.

+ Vincent de Paul founded two congregations: the Congregation of the Missions, or Vincentians, and the Daughters of Charity. Have the students research the history of these communities and their present apostolate. Also have the students research the St. Vincent de Paul Society, founded in 1833 by Frederic Ozanam. Some students may wish to organize their efforts in support of this group.

+ Vincent was a great supporter of life. Find the organizations in your diocese that support life issues. Invite someone to speak to your class about these organizations. Discuss ways for the students to become involved.

Sept. 29 Feast of Saints Michael, Gabriel, and Raphael, Archangels

God has sent angels to intervene in people's lives when they need protection on their way to heaven. The archangels Michael, Gabriel, and Raphael are three such messengers.

In art, Saint Michael is usually pictured as youthful, strong, clothed in armor, and wearing sandals. Biblical accounts of Michael present him as a mighty leader bringing justice and strength. The Book of Daniel describes him as a heavenly prince who stands guard over God's people, helping the Israelites return from their Persian captivity. Michael, whose name means "Who is like God?," is the principal fighter in the battle against Lucifer, or Satan, written in the Book of Revelation. The early Christians of the second century took courage from these accounts. They believed that Michael's intercession was powerful in rescuing souls from hell.

Art depicting the angel Gabriel most often shows him as communicating God's message. Biblically, he is portrayed as a messenger in three events. The first is to explain to Daniel a vision he had concerning the Messiah. Another time he comes to Zechariah, who is burning incense in the Temple, and tells him that John the Baptist will be born. But most people associate Gabriel with his message to Mary of the birth of Jesus. Gabriel's name means "Strength of God."

Raphael appears in the Book of Tobit. The blind Tobit wants to send his son Tobias on a journey to collect a debt. He finds Raphael and invites him to be a companion and guide. After an adventure-filled journey, Tobias collects the debt, finds a bride, and restores Tobit's sight with a fish's gall. Tobit's family credits the success of the journey and the healing to Raphael. When they offer Raphael a reward, he announces "I am Raphael, one of the seven angels who enter and serve before the Glory of the Lord." (Tobit 12:15) Raphael's name means "God's healing" or "God has healed."

Because of the archangels' closeness to God, the Church urges people to pray to them. In times of temptation, people pray to Michael; in trying to do God's will, people pray to Gabriel; and in sickness, people pray to Raphael.

Suggestions

◆ Have the students learn the Prayer to St. Michael found on the inside back cover of the student book. It is a good prayer to know in times of temptation.

◆ Gabriel is the patron of television and radio workers, broadcasters, and post offices. Have the students read the accounts in Scripture that record Gabriel's messages and write a statement telling what they were.

Daniel 8:15–26; 9:20–27

Luke 1:10–20

Luke 1:26–38

October

Oct. 1 Saint Thérèse of the Child Jesus

Twenty-eight years after Saint Thérèse's death, her autobiography, *The Story of a Soul*, was translated into 35 languages. Thirty-five years after her death, 800,000 copies of the book were sold and two and a half million of the abridged version. Why all of this popularity? Thérèse proved we can become saints by doing ordinary things extraordinarily well. She explained it in her autobiography: "I want to seek a way to heaven, a new way, very short, very straight—the way of trust and self-surrender . . . I am a very little soul, who can offer only little things to Our Lord."

Thérèse was born into a middle-class family in France in 1873. Her father was a watchmaker, and her mother died when Thérèse was five. There were nine children in the family, but only five girls lived. These five girls all entered religious life. Since Thérèse was the youngest, her father had a special place for her in his

heart. He called her "my little queen." She thought seriously about God and prayed to love God deeply.

When her two sisters entered the Carmelite convent at Lisieux, Thérèse wanted to be a nun, and she did not want to wait. However, Thérèse's family and the bishop told her she was too young at 14 to make a commitment for the rest of her life. On a pilgrimage to Rome, Thérèse's family met with Pope Leo XIII, at which time Thérèse asked: "Holy Father, in honor of your jubilee, let me enter Carmel at age 15. If you say yes, everyone would be willing." The pope assured her: "You will, if it is God's will." Thérèse was disappointed. Finally, the bishop sent his approval, and she entered Carmel at age 15.

Thérèse prayed often and did the most ordinary tasks at the convent: scrubbing floors, washing dishes, setting the tables, sewing, dusting, and cooking. Later, she helped the novice mistress, who is a sister in charge of the younger sisters' formation. A flu epidemic spread through the convent killing three sisters. Thérèse's health was strained in caring for those who are sick. She contracted tuberculosis and died at the age of 24.

It was through *The Story of a Soul* that people learned about her path to becoming a saint. She called it the "Little Way." Thérèse decided to do every act, even that of picking up a pin, for love of God. Because of her health, Thérèse could not go to the missions as she desired. Instead, she offered up her sufferings for missionaries. She has been named Patroness of the Missions because she offered her life in a quiet way for the salvation of souls. Her last words were "My God, I love you."

Suggestions

+ Ask the students to think of ways they can make sacrifices for the missions today.

+ Thérèse had a great interest in praying for priests. Encourage the students to pray for their parish priests and to make a point of talking with them after Sunday Mass.

+ The book *The Story of a Soul* is the story of Saint Thérèse's spiritual journey. Have the students write in their reflection notebooks what they want to do for Christ to show their love for him.

Oct. 2 Guardian Angels

Saint Jerome wrote that the human soul is so valuable in heaven that every human person has a guardian angel from the moment the person comes into being. These pure spirits, which we can neither see nor feel, play an important role in our lives.

Angels are messengers from God. In Greek, *angel* means "messenger." In a real but unseen way, these powerful spirits point out to us the ways of God. Guardian angels assist us in study or in our work. In times of temptation, they direct us to do good.

Perhaps the guardian angels are best known for protecting us from physical danger, but their main role is to care for the salvation of our souls. God loves, protects, and is always with us through the care of angels. The angels also offer prayers to God for us. Because angels always see and hear God, they can intercede for us. We should love our guardian angels, respect them, and pray to them.

In early Christianity, there was only a feast for the archangels. But in the 15th and 16th centuries, the feast of the Guardian Angels was unofficially celebrated in Austria, Spain, and Portugal. In 1608, Pope Paul V made it a universal feast. In doing so, he helped to make us aware of the guardian angels, not just one day in October, but every day.

Suggestions

+ Have the students compose their own prayers or poems to the guardian angels. Display these in the classroom. Select one to pray on the feast of the Guardian Angels.

+ Angels have been pictured as chubby cherubs, stately winged guardians, or curly-haired beings playing harps. Have the students design and display symbols that represent angels. They may wish to write scriptural passages under their symbols or use Scripture to find ideas for their symbols. Suggested references are Psalm 103:20; Matthew 4:11; Matthew 18:10; Luke 9:26; Luke 15:10; and Hebrews 13:2.

+ Recommend that the students ask their families to tell them about a time when God took special care of their families. Have each student write out his or her story. Make a scrapbook of these stories for the students to read.

Oct. 4 Saint Francis of Assisi

The son of a wealthy Italian cloth merchant and a devout, loving mother, Francis learned to enjoy life. His fun-loving ways made him popular. Francis dreamed of becoming a knight who would do fantastic deeds. Finally, when Assisi and Perugia were at war, Francis had his chance to be a soldier. But the hatred, fighting, and yearlong imprisonment he experienced were not what he had expected. After his imprisonment and a serious illness, he began to look for more meaning in life.

One day while he was praying in an old church, Francis heard a voice say "Francis, go repair my house which, as you can see, is falling into ruin." Impulsively, Francis rushed home, grabbed bales of cloth, sold them, and took the money to the priest of the church. But the priest refused the money, and Francis's father was very angry. Francis returned the money, gave up his fancy clothes, and decided that he would rely on his heavenly Father.

For the next few years, Francis could be seen in his patched robe tied with a piece of rope, barefoot, and rebuilding the church by hand. One day at Mass, he heard the Gospel reading Matthew 10:7–13. From this, he realized that his life must be based on the Gospel. He believed that he was called to do three things: to be one with his heavenly Father, to work for the Church, and to become as much like Jesus as possible. Because he believed that God was his Father, Francis felt a relationship to all people and to all created things. He considered all as his brothers and sisters. He composed "The Canticle of the Sun," acknowledging the good that creation accomplishes and calling all of God's creation to praise and thank him.

Francis saw that he was to rebuild not churches, but the Church. Alone he started traveling, sleeping on the ground, begging for food, preaching about the Father's loving care and the need for everyone to repent. He tried to convince those who were rich to live a simpler lifestyle and to create better conditions for those who were poor. He offered a sense of dignity to those who were poor. Francis persuaded people to rely on God and to care for one another. Francis met with Pope Innocent III to assure the pope that all of his followers would respect and obey Church authorities. He also received papal approval for his group. Francis wanted more than anything else to become like Jesus. He tried to be humble and compassionate. One day he received the stigmata, the wounds of Christ in his body. When he was dying, Francis asked to be laid on the ground so that he might keep the closest possible touch with creation because through it he had always encountered his Creator.

Suggestions

✦ Francis made a life-size scene of the Christmas crib, using real people and real animals. Let the students do research to answer these questions:

1. What is the story connected with Francis's starting the Christmas crib?

2. How did the people respond to his new idea? How do people respond to the crèche, or Christmas crib scene, today?

3. How have different countries in the world adapted Francis's idea during the Christmas season?

✦ The students may research a Franciscan order and write a one-page report on its history, its present work, its customs, and how it follows the spirit of Saint Francis. A Franciscan might speak to the class on the spirit of Saint Francis.

✦ Have the students find artwork, books, poetry, and legends related to Saint Francis. They might make a display or share their findings with the class.

Oct. 7 Our Lady of the Rosary

In praying to Mary, we are praying to Christ. To the question "Why honor Mary?," Pope Paul VI told us that Mary was to be honored and imitated because in her own life she fully accepted the will of God and did it. Mary placed her whole self at the service of God. Her yes to God was a perfect act of faith. We pray to her because of this yes. She helps us pray that God's will be done and that we can accept his will for us.

The story of the feast of Our Lady of the Rosary involves a struggle between the Ottoman Turks and Christianity. A naval expedition was established, bringing Spain, Venice, and the States of the Church to do battle with the Turks. The day of the battle at Lepanto, 1571, the Rosary Confraternity of Rome was meeting at the Dominican headquarters. The group recited the Rosary for the special intention of the Christians at battle. The Turks were defeated. People believed it was the intercessory power of the Blessed

Virgin that won the victory. Pope Pius V dedicated the day as one of thanksgiving to Our Lady. Pope Gregory XIII changed the name of the feast to Our Lady of the Rosary.

The story renews our love of Mary. When a person is in pain, discouraged, or having trouble accepting God's will, he or she can go to Mary. She will pray to her Son for anyone who calls on her.

Suggestions

✦ Review the Joyful, Sorrowful, Luminous, and Glorious Mysteries of the Rosary on page 186. [See page T372.] Divide the students into pairs and have each pair draw a picture of one of the Mysteries of the Rosary. Display them and have the students explain the mysteries they have drawn.

✦ Rosaries can be obtained from most religious goods stores and at a minimal cost. Try to make sure each student has a rosary. The Apostolate of Fatima/Blue Army also offers rosaries. Visit its Web site for more information.

Oct. 9 Saint John Leonardi

Born in Italy in 1541, John studied pharmacy. He used his knowledge while working in hospitals and prisons. But when he realized that God was calling him to serve his people, he became a priest.

The situation in the Church at the time was very confusing. In 1517, Martin Luther had denied some of the teachings of the Catholic Church. Many people were insecure about what to believe. After his ordination, John Leonardi began to train lay leaders and lay catechists. In 1579, he founded the Confraternity of Christian Doctrine, which is the Church's official association for those engaged in Catholic religious education. He also published a summary of Christian doctrine. In 1573, he founded a religious order of men called the Clerks Regular of the Mother of God, who would strengthen the faith of the people through religious education and other pastoral works. John had to pay a price for teaching the truth. His new order drew opposition, and eventually he was forced to leave his hometown in exile. His friend and spiritual guide, Saint Philip Neri, found him a place to stay.

John's other works included helping to establish a seminary for the Propagation of the Faith, to reform several religious orders, and to start several new orders. While taking care of plague victims, he died in Rome in 1609. John Leonardi proved by his life that God and one person can make many good things happen.

Suggestions

✦ Have the students research the history and the present status of the Society for the Propagation of the Faith. Then have them find out how their parish or school is involved with this group.

♦ Have the students find out about some of the Catholic catechisms. Let them look through a copy of the latest catechism, *Catechism of the Catholic Church*.

Oct. 16 Saint Margaret Mary Alacoque

Born in 1647 into the refined, well-known Alacoque family, Margaret Mary had a rather unhappy childhood. Her father died when she was eight years old. After his death, her mother tried unsuccessfully to collect money that people owed her husband. This proved difficult, so she was forced to share the family farm with her husband's greedy relatives. Margaret Mary was sent to a boarding school but two years later returned home because of illness. At the age of 14, she was cured after praying to Our Lady. However, she and her mother continued to be treated badly.

In 1671, Margaret Mary became a Visitation nun at the convent of Paray-le-Monial in France. Taking care of those who were sick, she received much criticism for being slow, clumsy, and impractical. But she also was known to be humble, honest, patient, and kind. Between 1673 and 1675, Margaret Mary received private revelations from Jesus. His message was "See this Heart which has loved so much and received so little love in return. Tell everyone that I really love them and I want to be loved in return. If you love me, pray and sacrifice for those who do not believe in my love or do not care about my love."

Margaret Mary worked hard to spread devotion to the Sacred Heart of Jesus, the heart that was a symbol of his abundant and forgiving love. This was difficult because the false teaching of Jansenism was very popular. According to this teaching, Jesus did not die for all human beings, but only for those predestined to be saved. Margaret Mary met with opposition from all sides. Even her own sisters at the convent became hostile and made life difficult for her. Finally, she met Father Claude la Colombiere, who believed her and gave her encouragement and spiritual guidance. Gradually, Margaret Mary won the confidence of those around her. The devotion to the Sacred Heart was approved in 1765 by the pope for liturgical observance, 75 years after Margaret Mary's death at the age of 43.

Suggestions

♦ Enthrone the Sacred Heart in the classroom. Explain to the students that this practice shows that Jesus is really Lord, the One that all follow. It also shows that they believe in God's merciful, abundant love for them. Materials on the enthronement for schools and homes may be obtained by writing to The National Enthronement Center or visiting its Web site.

♦ Send for information from the Apostleship of Prayer or visit its Web site.

♦ Devotion to the Sacred Heart leads Christians to help those who are in spiritual or material need. Have the class research Catholic Relief Services for a list of projects in which they could become involved.

Oct. 18 Saint Luke

Luke was one of the evangelists. His Gospel tells of the compassionate, forgiving Christ. In the Acts of the Apostles, also attributed to Luke, he gives us a detailed account of Paul's journeys. We have little information on Luke himself. Since Luke's Gospel is written in Greek, it is thought that Greek was his native tongue. His is a Gospel of human interest and human sympathy. Luke puts stress on the gentleness of Christ as he heals the widow of Nain, speaks to the penitent woman washing his feet, and comforts the weeping woman on his Way to the Cross. It is Luke who includes the parables of mercy: the Good Samaritan and the Lost Son. The repentant thief at the crucifixion is also Luke's addition. His non-Christian origins probably gave him an openness to all people. Samaritans, lepers, publicans, soldiers, sinners, shepherds, and those who were poor all find a special place in his Gospel. Some people call his Gospel the "Gospel of the Poor." Luke writes about Jesus as a master of prayer. Often Jesus is portrayed going alone to speak to his Father or helping his disciples to pray. Luke's Gospel is a Gospel of joy as well as a Gospel of total abandonment. Luke presents the disciples as happy to give all, leave all, and suffer all for Jesus.

Christian tradition recognizes Luke as the "beloved physician" (Colossians 4:14), as Paul calls him. His account of the Acts of the Apostles gives valuable data for describing the post-Resurrection Church.

Suggestions

♦ Luke is the evangelist who wrote the most about Mary. Have the students find the Scripture sources of the Joyful Mysteries of the Rosary, page 186 [See page T372.] in the first chapters of Luke. Let them make a list of these passages from Scripture.

♦ Have the students adapt a story from the Acts of the Apostles for a classroom play. Props and costumes could be prepared.

♦ Luke is considered the Christmas Evangelist. Let the class make a set of Christmas cards by drawing or gluing appropriate pictures on construction paper and writing quotes from Luke's Gospel beneath them.

Oct. 23 Saint John of Capistrano

John of Capistrano's one goal was to serve Jesus Christ. As a young man, John was a successful lawyer and governor in 14th-century Italy. He rid the locality of political corruption. When John was sent as ambassador to another province at age 26, he was imprisoned. During a long stay in prison, John realized that he could serve God more directly. A story is told that Saint Francis of Assisi appeared in a dream and asked him to become a Franciscan.

Once released from prison, John entered the Franciscan order. He worked as a humble novice. After his ordination, he studied under and worked with Bernardino of Siena. While Bernardino preached, John heard confessions. With the zeal that helped him drive out crime as a governor, John worked for the salvation of souls. The world needed a man like him at this time. Schism had split the Church, and several men were claiming to be pope. Thirty percent of the population had been killed by the plague. Many people were losing their faith. John traveled through Italy, Germany, Bohemia, Austria, Hungary, Poland, and Russia, preaching penance and prayer. He helped to reorganize and settle problems within the Franciscan order.

Pope Pius II asked for John's help against the Turkish invasion of Hungary. With the preaching and enthusiasm of John and the skill of the Hungarian general John Hunyadi, 70,000 Christians stopped the Turkish attack. At 70, John was physically ill, but he was still strong in spirit. He died of a disease caught in battle. He is the patron of judges.

Suggestions

✦ An organization in Brussels that takes its name from Saint John of Capistrano uses the motto "Initiative, Organization, Activity." Write these three words on the board while teaching about Saint John of Capistrano. Suggest that the students think of three words that describe their spirit in serving Christ and his Church.

✦ Have the students recommend a service project they could do in their school or neighborhood that would show they are trying to build a strong Christlike spirit.

✦ John struggled to know what he was to become in life. Have the students write in their reflection notebooks a prayer to know their own vocations.

Oct. 24 Saint Anthony Claret

The Spanish priest Anthony Claret was the fifth of eleven children. His family was poor but hard-working and religious. Weaving was a family trade. By age 21, Anthony was educated and in demand as a weaver. At one time, he suffered because of poor health. During his days of recovery, he imagined himself as a Carthusian monk. To get advice about this, Anthony went to the bishop. The bishop suggested that he go to the diocesan seminary and then, if he wished, leave and become a monk. Anthony entered the seminary and was ordained to the priesthood, but his poor health prevented him from being a monk or a Jesuit missionary. He was sent to a small mountain village where he studied medicine and helped those who were

sick. There he discovered more of his gifts. Anthony possessed a wonderful ability for understanding people.

Anthony began preaching throughout Spain. His conviction and courage in spreading devotion to the Immaculate Heart of Mary and to reviving devotion to the Eucharist made him popular. Anthony also began to publish. His book *The Catechism Explained* drew interest from a friend, the bishop of the Canary Islands. The bishop invited him to preach for a year on the islands. Anthony was delighted to go, for he had dreamed of becoming a missionary. When Anthony returned to Spain, he founded a congregation called the Missionary Sons of the Immaculate Heart of Mary, or Claretians. Here was where he wanted to concentrate his efforts, but God had other plans. Anthony was assigned as Archbishop of Cuba, a turbulent island that had not had an archbishop for 14 years. Being bishop of Santiago, Cuba, did not provide ideal conditions for planting the Cross of Christ. Anthony tried to renew the priests in their vocations. He gave them an example by preaching in all of the churches and spending hours hearing confessions.

He challenged the political system of Cuba by working for updated farm methods and credit unions. Anthony wanted the people to own their own farms. He knew that stable material conditions would lead to good family life. He made political enemies by giving instructions to black slaves. On 15 occasions people tried to assassinate him. Once he was stabbed, yet when his attacker was given a death sentence, Anthony pleaded for him and obtained a prison sentence for the attacker instead.

After eight years, he was brought back to Spain to be Queen Isabella II's confessor. He and the queen agreed that he would not live at the palace and would come only to hear her confession and instruct the children. He opened a religious publishing house and wrote over 200 books and pamphlets during this time. In 1886, a revolution took place and all those associated with the court were being accused of treason. Anthony fled to Rome, where the First Vatican Council was in session. Here he defended the infallibility of the pope. Then he returned to a Cistercian monastery in Spain and stayed there in solitude until his death.

Suggestions

✦ With the class set up a library in the back of the room for Catholic papers and magazines, as well as books on saints and the spiritual life. Discuss with the students ways of spreading Catholic literature.

✦ The main issue of First Vatican Council was papal infallibility. Explain the definition of infallibility and discuss how the pope makes infallible statements.

Oct. 28 Saints Simon and Jude

After praying, Jesus decided to choose 12 men who would be his apostles. They would proclaim the Kingdom of God to all people. Simon, the Zealot, was one who was called. The Zealots were a Jewish group who believed that the promise of the Messiah meant a free and independent Jewish nation where they would never have to pay taxes to the Romans again. Some Zealots were also very concerned that the spiritual ideals of their religion be kept, but others in the group acted to overthrow Roman rule.

At the time he called Simon, Jesus also called Jude Thaddeus, brother of James, supposedly a fisherman. Along with 10 other men, these two followed Jesus, lived with him, fled when he underwent his passion, and rejoiced when he rose from the dead. At Pentecost, the apostles were filled with the Spirit and a burning desire to spread the Good News to all people.

Jude traveled to Mesopotamia to preach, and Simon went to Egypt. Eventually, they both ended up in Persia, where they worked together evangelizing the people until they were both martyred. These two unlikely candidates for being apostles witnessed to the risen Lord with their lives. Saint Jude is known as the patron saint of hopeless causes.

Suggestion

Jude has been pictured with a club, which was the instrument of his death, and with a flame over his head to show the Spirit's influence upon him at Pentecost. Simon is pictured with a fish, the symbol of the early Christian's identification with Christ. The Greek initials for *Jesus Christ, God's Son, Savior* spell *fish*. Both saints also have shields. Jude's shield is red with a sailboat that has a cross on it. Simon has a red shield bearing two oars and a hatchet. Have the students design symbols for the two apostles and post them around the room.

November

Nov. 3 Saint Martin de Porres

Martin de Porres was born in Lima, Peru, in 1579. His father was a Spanish nobleman, and his mother was a freed black slave from Panama. Martin's father did not stay with them or support them except for a short time. Martin, his mother, and his sister made a living for themselves. But even in the midst of his own poverty, Martin cared for the needs of other poor people. He often gave away his money or his goods.

When he was 12, Martin became an apprentice to a barber and surgeon. When he was 15, Martin entered the Dominicans, the Order of Preachers, as a lay brother. He did not enter as a religious or to become a priest because he did not feel worthy of it. Nine years later, the community asked that he make his full religious profession. All his life Martin chose to do only the lowliest tasks. He was known to pray long hours, and when he was not praying, he was taking care of the needs of those around him. Martin's care for others also extended outside the walls of his residence. He cared for many of those throughout Peru who were sick. He handled the community's distribution of goods to those who were poor. He founded an orphanage and a hospital, and he also ministered to the slaves who were brought from Africa. Martin was known for his humility, kindness, and gentle manner. He spent most of his days as the head of the infirmary caring for those who were sick at his residence. It was there that he died in 1639. He was canonized in 1962 by Pope John XXIII and was named the patron of interracial justice. He deserved to be called the name the people gave him: "Martin of Charity."

Suggestions

+ While Martin was working in Peru, Peter Claver was ministering in Colombia, and Vincent de Paul labored for those who were poor in France. At the same time, the Reformation was well underway in Europe. Have the students keep a time line of the saints. Include significant historical events so that the students can integrate their religious tradition with historical events.

+ Discuss how racial prejudice is built on ignorance and fear. Have the students find ways to become more alert to prejudice of any kind and how they can be more hospitable to others.

+ Martin was especially devoted to the Holy Eucharist. Remind the students to make visits to the Blessed Sacrament when they are able.

Nov. 11 Saint Martin of Tours

Martin of Tours was born around the year 316 in what is today known as Hungary. He was raised and educated in Italy. His parents were non-Christian. His father was an officer in the army. Martin joined the army when he was 15. At the same time, he was drawn to Jesus and his teachings and became a catechumen, studying and preparing to become a Christian.

A famous story is told about Martin. When he was 18 and stationed in Amiens, France, he was making his rounds one cold winter evening. As he entered the city gates, he saw a poor, naked beggar. Having nothing else to give, Martin cut his own cloak in two and wrapped one half of it around the frozen beggar. That night in a dream Martin saw it was Christ whom he had clothed. He was baptized soon after that.

Being both a Christian and a soldier did not appeal to Martin. He could no longer fight in a war. When he was 23, he refused to arm himself for battle. This came to the attention of the emperor. Martin was accused of being a coward and was thrown in prison. He was soon released, since the enemy had sent a messenger seeking peace. Now Martin was free to give his life to following Christ. He went to study under Hilary, the bishop of Poitiers. Martin's mother eventually became a Christian, although his father did not. In his travels, Martin came across heresy in different towns. Martin preached the truth but was beaten and driven out of town. He never gave up.

Eventually, he returned to Gaul (France) and founded a monastery, probably the first one there. He lived there for 10 years. When the bishop of Tours died, the people would not be satisfied until Martin was made their bishop. Reluctantly, he was ordained bishop in 371. He traveled widely to meet and help the people, teaching and curing them. Martin founded another monastery where he trained priests who would take the Gospel to those who were poor.

When Martin died in 397, he was honored immediately as a saint. He is one of the first people who was not a martyr to be so honored. His shrine at Tours is one of the most-visited places of pilgrimage in Europe. He is known as the Apostle of Gaul, a patron saint of France, the patron of soldiers, and a patron of peace.

Suggestions

+ Much of what we know about Martin of Tours comes from a biography written by his friend Sulpicius Severus. Ask the students to write an event in the life of one of their friends that shows the best characteristic of that friend. Share these stories.

+ Symbols associated with Martin of Tours are a tree, armor, a cloak, a beggar, and a goose. Have the students research these symbols and their meanings.

+ Some biographies mention that Martin was the first to conceive of organizing Church settlements into parishes. Find out how much the students know about their parish: its founding, parish priests, pastoral team, population, active organizations, parish councils, and bordering parishes.

Nov. 15 Saint Albert the Great

Albert the Great is the only saint who was also a leading scientist of his day. So devoted to God and such a seeker of truth was he that he saw the whole created world waiting to be discovered, recorded, and taught. Albert the Great is the patron of scientists, philosophers, and students.

Born in 1206 in Swabia, Germany, Albert came from a noble military family. He studied at the University of Padua in Italy, where he became acquainted with the Dominican order. After some hesitation, Albert became a Dominican, even though his family was against it. He went on to become a teacher. One of his most famous pupils was Thomas Aquinas. Albert studied many subjects such as biology, chemistry, physics, astronomy, geography, economics, politics, logic, and mathematics, in addition to theology, Scripture, and philosophy. For Albert, all these different areas displayed the wonderful plan and providence of God.

Albert was named the provincial superior of the Dominican order in 1254. Three years later, he resigned his post to devote more time to study. He was then appointed Bishop of Regensburg in 1260. After two years as bishop, he was able to go back to writing and teaching until his death in 1280. For Albert, life was filled with wonders to discover. If creation is so wonderful, how much more wonderful is the Creator!

Suggestions

+ If your school sponsors a science fair, have it renamed in Saint Albert's honor, for example, Albert the Great Science Expo.

+ Have the class organize ways to care for the natural environment around the school.

Nov. 16 Saint Gertrude the Great

The most important thing we know about Saint Gertrude, who lived from 1256 to 1301, is that she loved God and was very aware of God's love for her. When she was five, Gertrude was placed in the care of nuns at Helfta, Germany. Later, she became a nun there. When she was 26, she began having mystical experiences, which she later wrote down in a book. Her life from that point on revolved around the study of Scripture, prayer, spiritual reading, and the liturgy of the Church. Gertrude carried her love for Christ to others through the prayers that she wrote and through the journal of her mystical experiences. One of Gertrude's deepest experiences was the love of the Sacred Heart. The heart and seven rings are symbols of her union with Christ.

Suggestions

+ In the Bible, the heart has been understood as the center of the whole life of a man or a woman. Have the students read John 15:9 and John 13:34 and reflect on them in their reflection notebooks.

+ Have several students research what mysticism is and present their findings to the class.

Nov. 18 Dedication of the Churches of Peter and Paul

The Basilica of St. Peter in Rome was built over his tomb, and the Basilica of St. Paul honors the place in Rome where Paul was martyred. These saints give the people of God a sense of what Christianity is all about. Peter and Paul gave their lives to spread the good news that God has redeemed his people. Century after century, saints and sinners alike have found peace and joy in the Church and in her sacraments. Today, as we celebrate the Eucharist in our parish churches, we are united with the community of believers all over the world. There is but one Lord, one faith, one Baptism. We rejoice that we are one People of God.

Suggestions

+ The largest basilica in Christendom today is St. Peter's. Select a few volunteers to research the history of the building of St. Peter's. They could present their research with pictures, paintings, and graphics or with a PowerPoint presentation.

+ Invite the pastor or an associate pastor to present the history of the parish church. Many parishes keep photos or parish annuals available for such presentations.

Nov. 18 Saint Rose Philippine Duchesne

Rose Philippine Duchesne was born in France in 1769 and named for Saint Rose of Lima, the first saint of the New World. Rose attended a school taught by the Visitation sisters. When she was 17 and her family was looking for a husband for her, Rose told them she wanted to become a Visitation sister. Her family objected, but Rose joined the community. When the French Revolution forced religious to leave their convents, Rose returned home. She cared for those who were sick, visited prisoners, and taught.

All that time, Madeline Sophie Barat was starting a community of sisters called the Society of the Sacred Heart. At the age of 33, Rose joined them. She expressed a wish to go to America as a missionary. It wasn't until she was 49 that she and four other sisters were sent at the request of the bishop of St. Louis, Missouri.

Rose was dismayed to discover that there was no work with Native Americans in St. Louis. In fact, the sisters were not expected, so the bishop sent them to a log cabin on the frontier. There they opened the first free school for girls west of the Mississippi. Rose founded six convents from New Orleans to St. Louis. She and the other sisters educated children who were poor.

When Mother Duchesne was 71, she was allowed to resign as the American superior of the order. Father Pierre-Jean De Smet was asking the sisters to open a school for Native Americans in Kansas. Mother Duchesne asked to go. Although she could not speak the language or teach, she could pray. In Kansas, every day she spent four hours in the morning and four hours in the evening praying in the chapel. The Native Americans called her "Woman Who Always Prays." There is a story that one day a Native American child placed kernels of corn on the skirt of her habit. He came back hours later and found them unmoved.

When her health failed, Mother Duchesne returned to Missouri. There she lived a life of prayer and penance until her death on November 18, 1852. She was canonized in 1988.

Suggestion

Have the students find out more about the Catholic firsts in the United States: the first bishop, the first church, the first saint, and the first Catholic school.

Nov. 21 Presentation of Mary

This feast of the presentation of Mary dates back to the sixth century in the East and the 15th century in the West. It is based on an ancient tradition that says Mary was taken to the Temple in Jerusalem when she was three years old and dedicated to God. What we spiritually celebrate on this day is the fact that God chose to dwell in Mary in a very special way. We too become temples of the Holy Spirit at Baptism. We too are invited to be as open to God, as dedicated to God, as Mary was. Let us turn to her often and ask that she help us remain close to God all our lives.

Suggestions

+ Encourage the students to place the needs of others before their own, to listen to what others have to say, and to give others first place in line in imitation of Mary.

+ Today sing a Marian hymn with the class, or honor her with a prayer.

Nov. 22 Saint Cecilia

We know very little about Saint Cecilia, although stories abound. She lived in the second century during the time of great persecutions. In one story dating back to the fifth or sixth century, we are told that as a young girl, Cecilia wanted to give her life to God. Her parents forced her to marry a nobleman named Valerian. In time, she converted him and his brother Tiburtius. All three of them died as martyrs. Cecilia is often pictured with a musical instrument such as a small organ, a harp, or a viola. An account of her wedding says that while the musicians played, Cecilia sang to the Lord in her heart. In the later Middle Ages, she was pictured playing the organ and singing. It is a reminder that the Church has always recognized the value of music and song.

Suggestions

+ Sing one of the psalms or a hymn.

+ Have the students look up information on the catacombs where Saint Cecilia's remains were found. Her remains were taken to Rome, where a basilica was built in her honor.

Nov. 24 Saint Andrew Dung-Lac and His Companions

Vietnam's history includes several persecutions of Catholics. Pope John Paul II canonized 117 Vietnamese martyrs in 1988. Andrew, a parish priest, was one of them.

Of the 117 who died between 1820 and 1862, 96 were Vietnamese, 11 were Spanish, and 10 were French. The group included 8 bishops, 50 priests, and 59 lay Catholics.

The Portuguese brought the faith to Vietnam. In 1615, Jesuits opened the first permanent mission in Da Nang to minister to Japanese Catholics who had been driven out of Japan. The king of one of the three kingdoms of Vietnam banned all foreign missionaries. Priests went into hiding.

Later in the 19th century, three more persecutions occurred. One was caused by the emperor's thinking the Christians were in favor of his son, who was rebelling against him. Foreign missionaries too were martyred. The last to be martyred were 17 laypersons, one only 9 years old. In that year (1862), a treaty with France gave religious freedom to Catholics. Persecutions continued, however.

During the last century, Catholics in Northern Vietnam fled to the South in great numbers. Now the Church in Vietnam is strong.

Suggestions

+ Help the students research Vietnamese Catholics and their customs in the United States.

+ Direct the students to research the distribution of Catholics in the world today.

+ Remind the students that faith is shown not only by dying for it but also by living for it. Have them make a list of the difficult things they do as a result of their faith.

+ Pray the Act of Faith together from the inside back cover of the student book. [See page T388.]

Nov. 30 Saint Andrew

Andrew was the brother of Simon Peter, and they were both fishermen from Bethsaida in Galilee. Andrew had been a follower of John the Baptist. He was one of the first to follow Jesus. Andrew seemed to take a special delight in bringing others to Jesus. It was Andrew who noticed a boy in the crowd with five loaves of bread and two fish, which was the beginning of a meal that fed more than 5,000. It was Philip and Andrew that the Greeks approached when they wanted to see Jesus. Although we do not know much more about Andrew from Scripture, these few events indicate he was a man who was easy to approach, a man faith-filled and loyal, and the kind of man you could trust. Tradition tells us that later, Andrew preached in northern Greece, Epirus, and Scythia, which is now the southern part of Russia. Around the year A.D. 70, he was probably crucified at Patras in Greece. Andrew is the patron saint of Russia and Scotland. An X-shaped cross on which tradition says he was martyred has become his symbol. The fish and the fisherman's net are other symbols of Andrew.

Suggestion

Have the students write and act out scenes from Scripture in which Andrew is mentioned: Mark 1:16–18; Matthew 4:18–20; John 1:35–45; Mark 1:29; John 6:1–15; John 12:20–33; Mark 13:1–4.

Last Sunday of the Church Year Christ the King

Can you imagine a wheel without a center? A center is necessary in a wheel for balance and smooth running. Some people, however, try to live without a center. The feast of Christ the King reminds us that Jesus is our center. He is the beginning and the end. This feast comes on the last Sunday of the Church year, right before Advent. We celebrate Christ not only as King of the world and nations, but as King of our families and of our hearts. The kingdom of Christ is within each of us. Every time we try to make something else the center of our lives, we are thrown off balance. Jesus, the Shepherd-King, loves us and guides us. The feast of Christ the King was established by Pope Pius XI in 1925 to worship Christ's lordship over all the universe.

Suggestions

+ Have the students draw a crown of thorns and a kingly crown and use them as part of a prayer service in honor of Christ the King.

+ The feast of Christ the King somewhat duplicates the feast of the Ascension, where Christ is crowned in glory and honor. Have the students pray the second Glorious Mystery of the Rosary in preparation for this feast.

Dec. 6 Saint Nicholas

Greece, Sicily, and Russia claim Saint Nicholas as their patron. About 400 churches in England alone are named for him. He is one of the most popular saints in the Church.

Nicholas was a fourth-century bishop in Lycia, which was southeast of Turkey. The many stories that are told about Nicholas usually have him helping those who were poor. In one story, he frees three unjustly imprisoned officers, and in another, saves three innocent boys from death. One of the best-known stories concerns a man who was poor and unable to provide dowries for his three daughters. Knowing his daughters might be forced into prostitution, Nicholas devised a plan. One night he took a bag of gold and threw it through an open window into the room where the man was sleeping. Then he hurried away so that no one would know who had given the gold. Twice more Nicholas tried his secret trick, but on the last night that he threw a bag of gold through the window, the father caught him and thanked him.

In the Netherlands, Germany, and Switzerland, children put out their empty shoes on the eve of Saint Nicholas's feast in hopes that they will receive presents from Saint Nicholas. In America and England, the legend of Saint Nicholas has been adapted to that of the modern-day Santa Claus.

Suggestions

◆ Ask the students to make a list of acts of kindness that could be done in secret either at school or at home. Have them try to do one hidden act of kindness each day for a week in imitation of Saint Nicholas.

◆ Suggest that the students make a card or bring in a treat for younger students in the school.

Dec. 8 Immaculate Conception

The people of the United States in 1846, through their bishops, asked Mary to watch over them and their country as their patroness. They chose the title and feast of Mary's Immaculate Conception. This title emphasizes her privilege of coming into the world free from sin. Through the power of Jesus' Death and Resurrection, every human being can be freed from sin at Baptism. Mary was free of sin from the moment of her conception. She never turned from God to do anything that God would not want. Remembering this special privilege given to Mary, people in the United States celebrate Mass on December 8. At the liturgy, they thank God for all the blessings given to the people of their country.

Suggestions

◆ Have the students research on the Internet the National Shrine of the Immaculate Conception in Washington, D.C.

◆ Ask the students to look up these Scripture readings for the feast: Genesis 3:9–15,20; Ephesians 1:3–6,11–12; Luke 1:26–38. Have them discuss why these particular readings were chosen.

Dec. 9 Saint Juan Diego

Juan Diego, an Aztec Indian who lived near Mexico City, was born in 1474. He and his wife, Maria Lucia, walked 14 miles to Mass and religious instruction every Saturday and Sunday. When Juan was 57 and a widower, his life changed.

On December 9, 1531, as Juan was walking to Mass, a beautiful lady dressed as an Aztec maiden surrounded by light appeared to him. She told Juan she was the Immaculate Virgin Mary, the Mother of the true God. She expressed her desire to have a shrine built there at Tepeyac Hill so that she could show her love for the people. She asked Juan to tell the bishop.

When the bishop didn't believe Juan, he returned to the lady and suggested she send someone who could talk better to the bishop. Mary told Juan that he was the one she had chosen and that she would bless him for helping her. Juan visited the bishop again. This time the bishop told him to ask "his Lady" for a sign that she was the Mother of God.

When Juan asked Mary for a sign, she told him to return on Monday for it.

In the meantime, Juan's uncle became very ill, and he stayed home to care for him. By Tuesday, his uncle was dying, so Juan went to get a priest. On the way, he met the Holy Virgin. He apologized for not meeting her the day before. Mary replied, "Do not let anything bother you, and do not be afraid of any illness, pain, or accident. Am I not here, your mother? Are you not under my shadow and protection? What more could you want? Don't worry about your uncle. He is well already."

Mary then told Juan to go to the hilltop and gather flowers. Juan knew that nothing grew on that rocky hill, yet he climbed it. There he found gorgeous roses! He picked them and brought them to Mary, who arranged them in his cloak. Mary told Juan to take them to the bishop.

When the bishop saw Juan, he asked what he had in his tilma, or cloak. Juan opened it, letting the roses fall to the floor. There on Juan's tilma, a life-size image of the Lady began to appear, beautifully painted!

The bishop cried out, "The Immaculate!" The bishop called her Our Lady of Guadalupe, after a shrine in Spain. The picture of Our Lady of Guadalupe depicts Mary as a pregnant, native woman. She spoke to Juan in the native language. Its main message is that Mary loves us and wants to help us. After almost 500 years, the picture on the cloak remains fresh. It can be seen above the main altar in the Basilica of Our Lady of Guadalupe in Mexico. The Church celebrates her feast on December 12.

Juan Diego spent the rest of his life, 17 years, traveling throughout Mexico, telling of his experience and bringing others to the faith. He remained poor, simple, and humble and had a great devotion to the Eucharist. It is said that through his efforts, eight million Aztec Indians were converted to Catholicism. Juan Diego died on May 30, 1548, and was canonized in 2002.

Suggestions

+ Suggest the students make a habit of praying three Hail Marys each night before going to bed.

+ Encourage the students to tell at least one other person the story of Our Lady of Guadalupe.

Dec. 13 Saint Lucy

Lucy, whose name means "light," kept the light of her faith burning and is now enjoying the eternal wedding banquet. She was martyred for being a Christian in A.D. 304 during the persecution of Diocletian. The fact that she is still mentioned in the Eucharistic Prayer I indicates the great respect that the Church has for her.

One story about her portrays Lucy as a young Christian struggling against the non-Christian influences of her friends and of society. Because of her deep longing for Jesus, Lucy vowed to remain unmarried. When her fiancé found out, he reported her to the government for the crime of being a Christian. She proved her faithfulness to Christ by giving her life for him.

Lucy's feast comes during Advent, when we wait for the coming of Christ our Light. Customs have developed around her feast. In Scandinavian countries, young girls dress in white dresses with red sashes that symbolize martyrdom. They carry palms and wear crowns of candles on their heads. In Sweden, the girls dressed as Lucy carry rolls and cookies in procession as songs are sung. A Hungarian custom is to plant a few grains of wheat in a small pot on Saint Lucy's feast. By Christmas, there are little green sprouts, which are signs of life coming from death. It symbolizes the fact that, like Lucy, we enter new life when we die.

Suggestions

+ Have the students research Advent customs from around the world and report on them.

+ Let the students prepare and celebrate a short Advent light service. Use Scripture readings, prayers, and songs on light and let each student light a candle (check fire codes).

Dec. 21 Saint Peter Canisius

Peter Canisius was born in the Netherlands in 1521. Peter's father intended him to marry well and follow a legal career. But after making a retreat under the direction of Peter Faber, one of the first Jesuits, Peter Canisius decided that God was calling him to serve as a Jesuit. Peter entered the order and began his studies for the priesthood. His gifts of preaching were soon recognized, and his first appointment was rector of a college. He was often seen visiting prisoners and those who were sick in his free time. Peter was sent to Germany, where his work won him the name "the Second Apostle of Germany" after Boniface. Peter worked tirelessly, teaching, diplomatically handling the problems of the Church, and bringing back fallen-away Catholics. He cared for those who were sick during the great plague. People loved him so much that he was offered the position of archbishop. Peter refused but administered the diocese for one year.

Peter did much writing to defend the faith. He became the advisor to Pope Pius IV, Pius V, and Gregory XIII. He attended two sessions of the Council of Trent. But one of his greatest concerns was that the middle class and those who were poor understand the Gospel and the teachings of the Church. For this reason, he wrote a catechism that was translated into 15 languages. Peter valued Catholic education and the Catholic press as important means for spreading the faith. His enthusiasm for the apostolic work of the Jesuits drew many vocations. He worked hard so that the clergy received a better education and were carefully selected. Some of his letters to Catholic leaders who showed little interest in the Church were stern yet positive. Peter lived in an age of confusion within the Church, yet he never despaired or became discouraged because he was united with Christ. After he suffered a seizure that left him paralyzed, Peter continued to write religious books for six more years with the aid of a secretary. For his contribution to catechesis, he was made a Doctor of the Church.

Suggestions

+ Have the students make bookmarks for their religion books and design them with religious symbols or Scripture quotes.

+ Saint Peter Canisius loyally supported the Holy Father throughout his life. Have the class include a special prayer for the Holy Father before one of the classes.

Dec. 26 Saint Stephen

After Pentecost, there were two groups of Christian converts from Judaism. In one group, there were Palestinian Jews. In the other group, there were the Greek-speaking Jews, called Hellenists. In the daily distribution of funds or food, the Hellenist widows felt that they were being treated unfairly. The apostles didn't have time to take care of this problem because they had been commissioned to preach the Gospel.

To solve the problem, they called the disciples to a meeting and had them choose men to be in charge of this daily distribution. The apostles prayed over these men and laid hands on them, making them the first deacons. At this point, one of these deacons named Stephen, a man described as filled with the Holy Spirit, began to attract attention. Besides his job as administrator serving those who were poor, he also worked miracles and preached. As a Christian Hellenist, he worshiped in the same synagogue with the Jewish Hellenists. This group resented Stephen's preaching about salvation through Jesus, yet they always seemed to lose any argument they had with him. The situation became so tense that they found witnesses to falsely testify that Stephen had committed blasphemy.

Stephen was arrested and brought before the Sanhedrin. As he spoke, those who were listening were blinded by an anger so strong that they did not even wait for the normal court proceedings. They rushed toward him, sent him out of town, and stoned him. His last words were to ask God to forgive those who were killing him.

Stephen was the first person to be killed for Christ. After his death, a bitter persecution started, and many Christians fled from Jerusalem. Saul, who had approved of Stephen's death, became very active in persecuting Christians. Perhaps it was the courageous example of Stephen that enabled Saul, who became Paul, to find the strength to turn to Christ.

Suggestions

+ The name *Stephen* means "crown." Stephen won the crown of martyrdom. As he died, he forgave his enemies, following Jesus' example. Have a Forgiveness Day with the students. Here are possible activities for the students:

  • Decide to say a kind word or to do a kind deed for someone who has hurt them.

  • Consider if there is anyone in their lives from whom they need to ask forgiveness. Encourage them to work for reconciliation.

  • Pray that they may become channels of forgiveness like Jesus and Stephen.

+ Using chapters 6 and 7 from the Acts of the Apostles, have the students write a skit about Stephen's life and death.

Dec. 27 Saint John the Evangelist

According to Matthew's Gospel, John was sitting in a boat, mending nets with his older brother James and his father Zebedee, when Jesus came by and called them to follow him. John and his brother James said yes to the call. Much of what we know of John's life comes to us through the Gospels. John and his brother James were called Sons of Thunder, possibly because of their fiery tempers. One example of this came when the people in a Samaritan town would not accept Jesus. The brothers wanted to call down fire from heaven to destroy the town. Jesus had to correct their thinking. At another time, the two brothers secretly asked Jesus for a favor. They wanted to have the highest rank in his kingdom. Jesus explained that real greatness comes to those who serve others, not to those who put themselves above others.

John was with Jesus at critical times. With Peter and James, John was permitted to watch the miracle of Jairus's daughter coming back to life, and he witnessed Jesus' Transfiguration on the mountain. Jesus also invited these three to be with him during his agony in the garden.

After Jesus had sent the Holy Spirit upon the apostles, we read in the Acts of the Apostles how John continued to respond to the challenge of Jesus' call. One day he and Peter cured a lame beggar in the name of Jesus and were arrested and kept in jail overnight. The next day the religious leaders listened to their message about Jesus' Resurrection and were amazed that these uneducated fishermen could speak so convincingly. When the leader warned them never to teach in the name of Jesus, both Peter and John said, "Whether it is right in the sight of God for us to obey you rather than God, you be the judges. It is impossible for us not to speak about what we have seen and heard." (Acts of the Apostles 4:19–20) There is a story that when Saint John was very old, the people had to carry him to where the Christians assembled to worship. Each time he preached, he gave the same homily: "Little children, love one another." The people grew tired of hearing the same thing each time and they asked him if he could talk on a different topic. But he said that this is the Lord's Word, and if they really did this, they would do enough.

Suggestions

+ Have the students think about their relationship with Jesus. Ask them to write a letter to him in their reflection notebooks, sharing recent experiences they've had and their feelings about them.

+ Lead the students in praying the Prologue from John's Gospel. (John 1:1–15) Open and close the service with a few verses of an appropriate song.

+ Have the students find quotes about love from the writings of John. Instruct them to copy one quote on drawing paper, decorate the edges, and use it as a banner.

Dec. 28 Holy Innocents

According to the Gospel of Matthew (2:16–18), when the Magi told King Herod of the birth of the new king and how they planned to pay him homage, he was anxious to eliminate his rival king. He ordered all the male children in Bethlehem who were two years old or younger to be killed. The child Jesus was not found because an angel had warned Joseph in a dream to take the child and his mother, Mary, to Egypt. Part of Matthew's intention in telling this story was to parallel the birth of Jesus with that of Moses. Pharaoh's persecution of Hebrew children is the blueprint for Herod's action. Matthew takes pains throughout his Gospel to depict Jesus as the New Moses, the giver of a New Law.

The children who were killed were called Holy Innocents. This feast has been celebrated since the fourth century. The Church traditionally holds that these children were martyrs, not because they died professing Christ, but because they died instead of Christ. This feast can be a consolation to any parent who has lost a child in death. It can remind them that their child shares in the glory of Jesus.

Suggestion

Some children suffer because their lives are in danger from sickness. Have the students make get-well cards for children in nearby hospitals.

Sunday After Christmas
Feast of the Holy Family

On the feast of the Holy Family, we celebrate the family life of Jesus, Mary, and Joseph. These three lived for God and loved and supported one another. The Holy Family is a model for all Christian families.

Each year, one of the following three Gospels is read on this feast. The Gospel of Matthew shows the obedience of Joseph to the angel's command to leave for Egypt and Mary's trust of her husband. Just as these two parents showed fidelity to each other, so all Christian parents need to live in fidelity and mutual support. The Gospel of Luke shows Joseph and Mary bringing Jesus to the Temple to present him to the Lord. There Simeon prophesies that Jesus came for both Israel and the Gentiles. Just as Joseph and Mary showed Jesus to the world, so Christian families give witness to Christ in their lives. A third reading, also from the Gospel of Luke, tells of Jesus coming with his parents to the Temple, but not returning with them. When his parents finally find him, he returns to Nazareth with them and lives obedient to them. In a Christian family, all family members need to cooperate in a loving way.

On this feast, it is fitting for each person to take a new look at his or her own family. It is a look of appreciation for its strengths and a look of understanding for its weaknesses. Let us pray on this feast for the grace to be a loving, trusting, and forgiving member of our family.

Suggestions

◆ Suggest that during the next week, the students try to spend some time with each member of their families to get to know each one better.

◆ Have the students reflect on the statements below, thanking God for what they are doing well and asking God for the grace in the areas they need to improve.

1. I pray that the members of my family will grow in love for one another.
2. I do my share of the work at home.
3. I speak respectfully to family members.
4. I thank the members of my family for the things they do for me.
5. I praise the members of my family for their talents.

January

Jan. 1 Solemnity of Mary, Mother of God

When the bishops met at the Council of Ephesus in 431, Cyril of Alexandria conducted the assembly. Its purpose was to correct the Church's way of understanding how Jesus was both God and man. Controversy existed among teachers of the Church concerning Mary's role. Cyril and the bishops debated the issue. They declared two things. Since Mary is really the mother of Jesus, and Jesus is really God, it must be said that Mary is the Mother of God. The Solemnity of Mary, Mother of God, celebrates her faith and trust in God alone. This feast honors her because she was the faithful, believing daughter of the Kingdom of God.

Elizabeth called Mary "Mother of my Lord" and proclaimed Mary's great faith. No one heard the Word of God and believed it more than Mary. For centuries Mary has been praised because she believed so completely. She is the Mother of God because of her faith in God. The Church wants us to call on Mary and ask her to help strengthen our faith. The Church wants us to imitate her faith. As we honor Mary at today's Mass, we rely on her to help us grow in faith and trust in her divine Son, Jesus.

Suggestions

- ◆ One of the earliest prayers to Mary, the *Memorare*, is from the fourth century. Lead the students in praying this prayer found on the inside back cover of their books. (T446)

- ◆ Muslims have always honored Mary as the mother of a great prophet. She is mentioned more in the Qur'an than in the New Testament. Have the class pray today to Mary, Mother of God, that she may help bring understanding between Christians and Muslims.

- ◆ Have each student bring in a picture of Mary. Display these on a table. Ask the students to discuss the variety of ways people have visualized the Mother of God.

Sunday Between Jan. 2 and 8 Epiphany

The Epiphany of the Lord was celebrated as far back as the second century in the Eastern Church. In the East, the feast meant the adoration of the Magi, the baptism of Christ, and the miracle at Cana. At each of these events, there was some manifestation of Christ's divinity. *Epiphany* means "manifestation" or "revelation." In the West, the feast came to mean the visit of the Magi. Here it refers to God being made known in the person of Jesus to the Magi, who represent all the nations. It is recorded in the Gospel of Matthew. Some astrologers, who were advisors to Eastern kings, traveled to Jerusalem from the East. They followed a star that they believed would lead them to an infant who would be the King of the Jews. When they found the child with his mother, they fell on their knees and offered him gifts of gold, frankincense, and myrrh. The Fathers of the Church later interpreted these gifts as the symbols of Christ's royalty (gold), divinity (incense), and passion (myrrh).

The readings for the feast emphasize the universality of God's power, love, and presence to all people. Jesus is the light to all nations. He has come for all because there are no limits to his love. Jesus will bring all people to his Father.

Suggestions

- ◆ Have the students look up Epiphany customs practiced around the world and share the information they find

- ◆ Let the students read each of these accounts: the Visit of the Magi (Matthew 2:1–12), the Baptism of Jesus (Mark 1:9–11), and the Wedding at Cana (John 2:1–12).

Sunday After Epiphany
Baptism of the Lord

One day Jesus was standing in a crowd listening to John the Baptist. John always challenged his listeners to turn their backs on their sinful way of life and turn to God by public baptism. This was a sign that a person wanted to live according to God's way. After all the people had come forward that day to be baptized,

Jesus came forward. This was confusing to John the Baptist. He knew that Jesus did not need to change the way he was living. But the Gospels record that when Jesus was baptized, a very important thing happened: the presence of a dove and the voice of God affirming that Jesus was his Son showed that the Father and the Spirit were in intimate connection with Jesus.

Jesus, who did the work of the Father, was always one with the power of the Father and the Holy Spirit. After his rising from the dead, Jesus sent the Holy Spirit upon his disciples at Pentecost. Jesus' baptism by John was the beginning of his mission to save all people from their sins. This mission would result in Jesus' passion, Death, and Resurrection. The Gospel records that on his way to Jerusalem, he spoke about his passion and Death as a baptism. "There is a baptism with which I must be baptized, and how great is my anguish until it is accomplished!" (Luke 12:50) Through the power of the Holy Spirit, we have been baptized into Christ's Death and have become the Father's adopted children. As members of the Christian community, we also have a mission, namely to spread the Good News of Jesus by the way we speak and act. When we celebrate the feast of Jesus' baptism, we can also celebrate our own Baptism.

Suggestions

- ◆ Have the students write "eyewitness" accounts of Jesus' baptism, using one of these Gospel accounts as a basis: Matthew 3:13–17; Mark 1:9–11; Luke 3:21–22. Have them choose to be a particular person at the event such as John, a sinner, a passerby, or a newly baptized person.

- ◆ Ask the students to discover as much as they can about their own baptismal day. Have them design a poster or collage that illustrates the important facts and the interesting details. Have them bring in pictures and other remembrances.

- ◆ Have the students list the symbols used in the rite of Baptism: signing on the forehead, candle, water, oil (catechumen and chrism), and white robe. Discuss with them the significance of the symbols.

Jan. 6 Saint André Bessette

André, the eighth of 12 children, was born in 1845 in Montreal and baptized Alfred. His parents, who were French-Canadians, died early. André was adopted when he was 12 and became a farmhand. Later, he tried being a shoemaker, a baker, and a blacksmith, but was unsuccessful.

André decided to join the Congregation of the Holy Cross, but at the end of a year, he was told to leave because of his poor health. A wise bishop convinced the community to allow André to remain. He became a brother and worked as the doorkeeper at the College of Notre Dame for 40 years.

André had a statue of Saint Joseph on the windowsill in his room. He spent many hours praying to Saint Joseph during the night. André began to pray with those who were sick, anoint them with oil, and they would be cured. Before long, hundreds of people were coming to him for healing and spiritual direction. André would say, "It is Saint Joseph who cures. I am just his little dog." André ministered to people 8 to 10 hours a day. He needed 4 secretaries to handle the 80,000 letters he received each year.

The Holy Cross community bought land. André raised money to build first a small chapel, and then a church on the land. For years, he cut students' hair for five cents and saved the money. At the church, he received many visitors. Those who were cured left behind their crutches and canes. It took 50 years to build Saint Joseph's Oratory, which is probably the world's main shrine to Saint Joseph.

Brother André became known as "the Miracle Man of Montreal." He died on January 6, 1937, beatified in 1982, and canonized in 2010.

Suggestions

+ Have the students visit or send a get-well card to someone who is ill.
+ Direct the students to research the gift of healing in the Church today. They might attend an Anointing of the Sick service at your parish.

Jan. 7 Saint Raymond of Peñafort

Born in Spain in 1175, Raymond entered the Dominican order at 47. He already had been a successful lawyer, university teacher, and vicar of a diocese. This brilliant man, who had given example to priests with his zeal and charity to those who were poor, became a novice in the Dominican order. The Dominicans asked him to compile a thorough examination of the correct administration of the Sacrament of Reconciliation. His writing covered sins committed against God and neighbor, and it gave examples of how to handle questions of conscience. This book became a valuable resource book for priests.

Raymond longed to do more for God. Pope Gregory IX noticed his abilities and called him to Rome to be his confessor. He also asked Raymond to collect all the decrees of popes and councils from the past 80 years to put together into one volume. This book was called decretals, which contained material similar to canon law. The pope was so pleased that he told Raymond that he was going to be made an archbishop. Raymond pleaded with the pope to let him return to Spain as an ordinary priest to study, pray, and preach. The pope agreed, and Raymond returned to his Dominican friary.

Three years later, he was elected the master-general of the order. This time he had to obey. While in office, Raymond revised the rule of the Dominicans. He also visited all the houses where the Dominicans lived.

After two years, he asked to resign. He was able to spend the next 35 years in an apostolate to the Muslims and Jews living near him. He lived to be nearly 100 years old.

Suggestions

+ Ask the students to find out if there are any Dominican priests in their area. Have them invite a priest to speak on Saint Raymond to the class.
+ Have the students research what canon law is and how it developed in the Church.

Jan. 21 Saint Agnes

Love is stronger than death. Agnes, a 13-year-old girl living in Rome, gave her life willingly for Christ in the third century. She preferred death so that she could remain a bride of Christ.

The traditional story of Agnes assures us that holiness does not depend on age. Agnes was beautiful, and many men wanted to marry her. She refused each one because she had decided to remain a virgin. One of her suitors was so angry he reported to the governor that she was a Christian. The governor summoned Agnes to the palace. He threatened her with punishment and showed her the tortures that would be used on her body. Agnes looked at the instruments of torture with heroic calmness. The governor had her sent to a house of prostitution to be tempted. All of the men who saw her courage were afraid to touch her. One who looked at her lustfully was struck blind, but Agnes prayed for him, and he regained his sight. The governor, seeing that she could not be persuaded, had her condemned and executed. Saint Ambrose wrote that she went to the place of execution more cheerfully than others go to their wedding.

Suggestions

+ Saint Agnes is often pictured with a lamb at her feet. Ask the students to find out what symbols their patron saint is pictured with. Have them enlarge these symbols and display them in the classroom or at home.
+ Saint Agnes has her name in the Eucharistic Prayer I. Six other women are listed with her. Have the students look in the missalettes to find the names of the other saints. Encourage them to research these women to find out why they are honored as saints.

Jan. 25 Conversion of Saint Paul

Paul, who was also called Saul, had two names because he belonged to two societies. As a Roman citizen, he was given the name Paul. He lived in Tarsus, which was a bustling city and a center for Greek culture. As a Jew of the tribe of Benjamin, he was called Saul. He learned the strict traditions of the Pharisees. He also learned the work of tent-making.

Saul viewed Christianity as an evil force and the enemy of Judaism. After he watched Saint Stephen martyred for his faith, Saul became a leader in the movement to stamp out Christianity. He went into homes and dragged Christians to prison.

One day, he set out from Jerusalem, armed with letters to harass Christians in the Damascus community, a strange thing happened. A great flash of light appeared and he was stunned. "He fell to the ground and heard a voice saying to him, 'Saul, Saul, why are you persecuting me?' He said, 'Who are you, sir?' The reply came, 'I am Jesus, whom you are persecuting.'" (Acts of the Apostles 9:4–5) At this moment, the Resurrection of Jesus overwhelmed him, and he believed that Jesus was alive! Saul entered Damascus, led by the hand of one of his companions because he had been blinded. He followed the Lord's orders to find Ananias, a man who would arrange for his Baptism and cure him of his blindness.

For three years, Paul lived in the Arabian desert. Intellectually and emotionally, the process of conversion continued, and his knowledge of the mystery of Christ deepened. From Arabia, Paul returned to Damascus to preach that Jesus was the Son of God. The Jewish community was confused because they knew Paul's reputation. They had expected his help in destroying Christianity. Seeing that he was a traitor, they plotted to kill him. Discovering the plot, Paul had the disciples lower him in a basket over the city wall so that he could escape.

Paul went to Jerusalem to meet the apostles. At first, the apostles thought he might be playing a trick on them to find out about the Christians to persecute them. Barnabas bravely welcomed Paul and introduced him to Peter and the other apostles. They decided to trust him, and Paul stayed in Jerusalem, preaching fearlessly in the name of Jesus.

From the Acts of the Apostles and Paul's letters, we can gain an idea of the scope of his journeys, the extent of his writings, the intensity of his suffering and his joy. Paul lived up to the words that the Lord said about him at the time of his conversion, ". . . this man is a chosen instrument of mine to carry my name before Gentiles, kings, and Israelites, . . . " (Acts of the Apostles 9:15)

Suggestions

✦ Let the students rewrite the story of Paul's conversion in the Acts of the Apostles, putting the story in a modern setting. Or they may write the story of the conversion of someone they know or someone they have read about.

✦ Have the students think about any times in their own lives when they received a new insight into God or themselves, a kind of conversion. Suggest they write about the experience in their reflection notebooks.

Jan. 26 Saints Timothy and Titus

Saints Timothy and Titus lived in the early Church around the time when the apostles were dying and the Gentile Christians were beginning to take roles of active leadership. Both Timothy and Titus knew Paul and were his traveling companions at times. They were bishops of newly formed Christian communities, but the role of bishops was not clearly defined. They were not attached to just one community but administered a large area and traveled in and out of the Christian communities.

Timothy's father was a Gentile, and his mother was Jewish. Timothy had studied the Scriptures as a young man and was converted by Paul, who was on a missionary journey to Lystra in Asia Minor. Timothy was willing to help Paul and did important work for him. He was ordained to the ministry and sent as a representative of Paul's to the Thessalonians, Corinthians, and Ephesians. He sometimes met with trouble in the communities. However, Timothy proved himself capable enough for Paul to make him leader of the Church in Ephesus. It is in the First and Second Letters to Timothy that some description of a bishop's role is given. Timothy was told that as a bishop, he was to correct innovators and teachers of false doctrine. He was the one to appoint bishops and deacons.

Timothy opposed non-Christian festivals and was killed with stones and clubs. A mention of Titus is found in one of Paul's letters to the Corinthians. He writes that he had gone to Troas and was worried because he did not find Titus there. He then went to Macedonia, where there was trouble among the Christians. Paul writes, "But God, who encourages the downcast, encouraged us by the arrival of Titus . . ." (2 Corinthians 7:6) There was a friendship and bond of preaching the Gospel that Paul had with this Gentile Christian, Titus. Paul's trust in Titus's competence as a peacemaker and administrator was evident. Titus restored obedience and solved difficulties between the Corinthians and Paul. He organized the Church in Crete as its first bishop. He corrected abuses and appointed bishops. Titus carried out his work for the Church in an energetic, efficient, and decisive manner. He died in Crete when he was 33.

Suggestions

✦ Let the students look up the following descriptions Paul gives of his traveling companion, Timothy: 1 Corinthians 4:17; Philippians 2:19–20; and Romans 16:21.

◆ Have the students read the letters to Timothy and Titus. Ask them to list the characteristics of a good bishop.

◆ Have the students write an imaginary chapter of the adventures of Saint Paul, which include Timothy and Titus. Note that this feast is fittingly the day after Paul's.

Jan. 27 Saint Angela Merici

Angela Merici, born in what is now northern Italy in the late 15th century, believed that women held a key role in the formation of Christian living. Her goal was to help the Church and society by restoring strong Christian family life through good education of women and children.

Angela did not have a perfect family life herself. Orphaned early in life, she lived for some years with her uncle's family. Angela grew into a simple, charming woman of good looks and capable leadership abilities. Her faith led her to become a member of a Third Order, dedicating herself to good works and to prayer. Angela received a vision in which it was revealed "Before your death, you will found a society of virgins of Brescia." For 10 years Angela waited patiently for God to help her know what to do. A sign came when Isabetta Patengola invited her to Brescia to keep her company after the death of her husband. After she lived in Brescia for a short time, her eyes were opened to the needs of the city. Deprived girls were unable to get an education. An education was for wealthy people and nuns. Angela began to teach the girls who were poor.

At 57, she formed a religious group of 28 women who thought as she did. Angela decided to call her group the Company of Saint Ursula. Saint Ursula was the patron of universities, and Angela had great devotion to this leader of women. Men's communities already were actively engaged in such charitable works, but women's orders were not. Angela's dream was to use education as a means for building up the faith and for social reform.

Angela's sisters received permission from Rome to live in their own homes and devote themselves to every type of work of mercy, with emphasis on education. They would teach young girls to read and write, and prepare them for what they needed to know about Christian family life. Her sisters wore lay clothes and met once a month for a day of prayer and discussion on their ministries. About 40 years later, Charles Borromeo asked the sisters to become a religious community and to live together in a convent rather than in their own houses. Gradually, they began to wear distinctive habits and were known as the Ursulines. Angela was the first to form a religious order of women that served God outside the cloister.

Suggestions

◆ Today there are many communities of women who actively minister in the Church. Have the students list the names of the communities they know and the ministries in which they engage. They might find out if there are any women religious in their area and invite them to talk to the class.

◆ Let the students research a Third Order and the requirements for membership.

◆ Saint Angela's goal was to revive Christian family life. Have the students check the Sunday bulletin to see what their parish does to strengthen family life.

Jan. 31 Saint John Bosco

John was the youngest son of an Italian peasant family. His father died when he was two, so he was brought up by his mother. The family lived in extreme poverty. There was no possibility for higher education. Once when the family went to hear special sermons for the Holy Year, a priest, Joseph Cafasso, noticed John's intent face as he listened to the homily. The priest questioned John and discovered he had a remarkable memory. When he heard that John wished to be a priest, he encouraged him to enter the seminary. With shoes and clothes provided by charity, John arrived at the major seminary in Turin.

Joseph Cafasso and one of his friends saw John's talent for working with youth. They encouraged him to use his gifts to keep the young people out of trouble. John felt that the boys who were poor needed contact with God's creation. He would gather a group of young boys together on Sunday and take them into the country. The day would start with Mass and was followed by breakfast and outdoor games. The afternoon would include a picnic, a catechism lesson, and closing evening prayers. The groups grew very large. John respected every boy as a person and used gentle, effective discipline. He felt faith should be the framework in which they studied, worked, and prayed.

In 1850, John was able to get a house for himself and 40 boys. His mother was the housekeeper. John Bosco opened workshops to train the boys to be shoemakers and tailors. By 1856, there were 150 boys in residence. At John's oratories, places where the boys lived, John made sure every boy received a religious education. He taught them to play musical instruments, to perform in plays, and to engage in sports. Often when John would go into the villages to preach and celebrate the Sacraments of Reconciliation and the Eucharist, he would take along boys to provide entertainment in the evening. His reputation as a preacher became well-known. He wrote and printed books on Christian faith, using his own press.

In 1859, John started a religious congregation that would serve the Church by helping boys who were poor. John Bosco admired Francis de Sales so much that he named the group the Salesians. They followed the spirituality of Saint Francis de Sales. By the time of his death, this congregation had grown to more than 1,000 members in Italy, France, England, Argentina, Uruguay, and Brazil. When John Bosco died, 40,000 people came to his wake.

Suggestions

◆ Have the students research the Salesians of Don Bosco and the Salesian sisters. They could find out about the ministry they do, where they are located, and how many members they have.

◆ When John Bosco was in the seminary, he started a club called the Cheerful Club. No one was allowed to say or speak in an unkind way. Each one had to do his studies and be cheerful. Try John Bosco's club in the classroom for one week.

February

Feb. 2 Presentation of the Lord

According to the law of Moses, for 40 days after the birth of her son, a woman was excluded from public worship. Then on the 40th day, she would bring an offering of a pigeon or a turtledove to the Temple. It was also customary to bring an offering of thanksgiving and praise to God for the safe birth of the child. In the Gospel of Luke, we read that when Mary and Joseph went to the Temple for the purification, they took the child Jesus to be consecrated to God. They offered a pair of turtledoves or two young pigeons, which was the offering of those who were poor. They were careful to observe all that the law required.

In Luke, we read that there was a man named Simeon in the Temple of Jerusalem at that time, a man ". . . righteous and devout . . . It had been revealed to him by the holy Spirit that he should not see death before he had seen the Messiah of the Lord." (Luke 2:25–26) When Simeon saw the child Jesus, he took the child into his arms and prayed, "'Now, Master, you may let your servant go in peace, according to your word, for my eyes have seen your salvation, which you prepared in sight of all the peoples, a light for revelation to the Gentiles, and glory for your people Israel.'" (Luke 2:29–32) Another name for this feast is Candlemas day. Candles are blessed on this day, and the liturgy suggests that after the blessing, there is a candlelight procession. Today's feast celebrates Jesus' offering of himself to his Father as the Savior of all people.

Suggestions

◆ Have the students participate in the blessing of the candles and in the procession in the parish.

◆ Remind the students that this feast is also recalled in the fourth Joyful Mystery of the Rosary. Pray it together with the class. The Joyful Mysteries are on page 186 in the student book. [See page T372.]

◆ Have the students read and act out the Presentation from Luke 2:22–40.

◆ Sing songs about Christ the Light and about being light for others.

Feb. 3 Saint Ansgar

Ansgar, called the Apostle of the North, was born in France around 801. He entered the Benedictine order and became a powerful preacher and teacher. He was sent as a missionary to Denmark, where for three years he worked and ministered, but with little success. When Sweden asked for missionaries, Ansgar again set out, this time with another monk. On the way, the missionaries were captured by pirates and suffered many hardships before they reached Sweden. Less than two years later, Ansgar was brought back and made bishop of Hamburg.

For 13 years, Ansgar worked and prayed in Hamburg. He was known for his excellent preaching, his great love of those who were poor or sick, and his humble, prayerful life. But in 845, Hamburg was invaded and burned to the ground, and its citizens returned to non-Christian religions.

Ansgar was appointed archbishop of Bremen in 848. He began new missionary work in Sweden and Denmark in 854. He desired to show his love through martyrdom, but he died peacefully at Bremen in 865.

Suggestions

◆ Ask the students to recall a time in their lives when they seemed to be unsuccessful at something they had worked at very hard. What did they learn from the experience? Refer the students to the Glossary to review the meaning of *Divine Providence*, God's loving concern for us that brings good out of all that happens.

◆ Have the students reflect on those things that really matter in life by reading Matthew 25:31–40.

Feb. 6 Saint Paul Miki and His Companions

Nagasaki, Japan, is the city in Japan that has the largest Catholic population. It is also the city on which the second atomic bomb was dropped. But over three centuries ago, it was the scene of another kind of tragedy. On the top of a windy hill, 26 men were crucified for being Christians. These martyrs are Paul Miki and his companions.

By the 1500s, the Church had been well-established in Europe. But the Far East had remained mission territory. Japan had closed its doors to foreigners, and it was not until 1549 that missionaries, such as Francis Xavier, were able to bring the Good News of Christ to these people. Many people became Christians, including the shoguns, the commanders or lords of the various areas. When the first missionaries arrived in Japan, they were welcomed. But when the leader of Nobunaga died, Hideyoshi took command of the region. He sensed a spirit of unity among the Christians and feared they would try to take control of his government.

Hideyoshi issued a decree on July 25, 1587, banishing all missionaries. Some went into hiding so they could continue to minister to the Christians. On December 8, 1596, Hideyoshi arrested and condemned the friars of Miako. Among them were 3 Japanese Jesuits, 6 Franciscans (4 of them Spanish), and 17 Japanese laymen. They were condemned to death by crucifixion. The charge was attempting to harm the government. But the real reason was the fact that they were Christians. Among these Christians were very young men: Louis, age 10; Anthony, age 13; Thomas, age 16; and Gabriel, age 19. The best-known of these martyrs is Paul Miki, who was from a Japanese aristocratic family, a Jesuit brother, and a brilliant preacher.

The 26 men were tortured and forced to walk more than 300 miles from Miako to Nagasaki through the snow and freezing streams. Along the way, they preached to the people who had come out to see them. They sang psalms of praise and joy. They prayed the Rosary and told the people that such a martyrdom was an occasion of rejoicing. Finally, on February 5, they reached Nagasaki where 26 crosses awaited them. It is said that they ran to their crosses, singing. They were bound to the crosses with iron bands at their wrists, ankles, and throats. Then they were stabbed with two lances. Many people came to watch the cruel deaths. Hideyoshi and his soldiers had hoped the example would frighten other Christians. Instead, it gave them the courage to profess their faith as well.

Hideyoshi died in 1598, and for a few years, the persecutions stopped. But by 1612, they had begun again. There are some 3,135 known martyrs from these years of persecution. It is believed there were thousands of others. By the middle of the 17th century, Japan closed its doors to all foreigners again. But in 1858, after France and Japan had signed a treaty, which in part permitted Christianity in Japan, the returning missionaries found thousands of Christians still in Japan, especially around Nagasaki. For 200 years, they carried on the faith in secret.

Suggestions

- ✦ Suggest that the students research the individual martyrs of Nagasaki.

- ✦ One way to identify Christians during the persecutions was the tread picture. These pictures were plates depicting the Crucifixion of Jesus, the Nativity, or other moments from Jesus' life. Suspected Christians were ordered to walk on or tread on the pictures. Those who refused to show such disrespect for the articles were condemned. Remind the students of the respect to be shown to religious articles.

- ✦ For the Japanese Christian, the cross and the passion of Jesus were powerful symbols and meditations for their faith. Display the cross prominently in the classroom. Have the students make crosses out of twigs and wire or yarn. Have them exchange their crosses with other students as reminders that we are all to share in the Cross of Christ.

Feb. 10 Saint Scholastica

From Pope Gregory the Great's book about Saint Benedict, we learn of an event in the lives of Saint Benedict and Scholastica, Benedict's twin sister. In the early sixth century, Benedict had studied in Rome, but decided to devote all his life to the search for God. He established a very important monastery at Monte Cassino. Scholastica founded a community of religious women about five miles south of it. Benedict directed the progress of these women, so Scholastica must have been the abbess there.

Scholastica and Benedict visited together only once a year. They would go to a small house near their monasteries, for no women were permitted at Monte Cassino. On one occasion, Benedict, with several monks, met Scholastica at the house. They spent the day praying and speaking of God and the spiritual life. After they had eaten, they continued their conversation late into the night. When Benedict said he had to return to his monastery, Scholastica begged him to stay and talk a while longer. Benedict refused, saying that his rule required that the monks be in the monastery at night. Heartbroken, Scholastica folded her hands, put her head on the table, and quietly wept and prayed. While she was praying, a terrible storm began. "God forgive you! What have you done?" Benedict exclaimed to his sister. She explained that since he had refused the favor she asked, she had turned to Almighty God instead, and God had granted it. They continued their conversation and prayer until morning. Three days later, Scholastica died. Benedict told the monks that he saw her soul, like a dove, ascend toward heaven. He buried her in the tomb he had built for himself.

Suggestions

✦ Scholastica was united to God by praying short prayers often. Have the students find the following short prayers in Scripture and pray them often. Recommend that they write some of these prayers in their reflection notebooks.

Matthew 8:8	Luke 22:42
Matthew 9:27	John 6:68
Matthew 14:33 or 16:16	John 11:27
Matthew 15:25	John 20:28
Mark 9:24	John 21:17
Luke 1:38	

✦ Direct the students to make a calendar for the upcoming month. Have them write the name of a family member in each day block. On that day, the students can offer special prayers for that relative and send him or her a greeting. Parents, brothers, and sisters can be included often.

Feb. 11 Our Lady of Lourdes

Each year more than 2 million people go to Lourdes, France. They wash in the baths and recall the Lady dressed in white, with a blue sash and yellow roses at her feet. It was a cold day on February 11, 1858. Bernadette Soubirous, 14 years old, her sister, and a friend had gone out to collect firewood. Being weak and sickly, Bernadette fell behind. She came to a stream and was preparing to cross it when she heard a strong wind. As she looked around, she saw a young woman, not much taller than herself, dressed in white, carrying a Rosary on her arm. The smile and gentle manner of the Lady assured her there was nothing to fear. Bernadette began to pray the Rosary, and the Lady joined her in the Doxology. When the Rosary ended, Bernadette told her sister and friend what she had seen. At home, Bernadette's parents were upset by the story, but she was permitted to return to the spot. The Lady appeared to her 18 times from February 11 through July 16.

News of the vision spread, and crowds began to form whenever Bernadette returned to the place where she saw the Lady. At one time, nearly 20,000 people were present. Yet no one saw or heard the Lady but Bernadette. The Lady told Bernadette that she would find happiness in heaven. She told her to do penance and pray for sinners. She instructed Bernadette to tell the priests that a chapel was to be built at the site and processions held. When Bernadette asked who she was, the Lady replied, "I am the Immaculate Conception." This dogma had been defined by the Church four years earlier.

On February 25, 1858, the Lady told Bernadette to dig in the dirt and drink of the stream. Bernadette began to dig with her hands and, after several attempts, she was able to find the stream. It continued to flow until it was producing more than 32,000 gallons of water a day, which it still does. A week later a blind man was cured in those waters. There have been more than 7,000 cures recorded, some of which have been declared miraculous by the Church after a review by doctors, some of whom are not even Christian.

Seeking to get away from the fame, Bernadette entered the Sisters of Charity and Christian Instruction. She was misunderstood and at times harshly treated. After suffering with tuberculosis, she died on April 16, 1879, at the age of 35.

The greatest blessings of Lourdes happen not to the body, but to the soul, the spirit, the very heart of the people who go there.

Suggestions

✦ The song "Immaculate Mary," known also as the Lourdes hymn, is used in procession at the shrine. Have the students sing this song.

✦ Bernadette was canonized by Pope Pius XI on December 8, 1933. One message to her from the Virgin Mary was to pray the rosary. Review the Rosary with the students. Then pray with the class the Glorious Mysteries on page 238. [See page T430.]

✦ Bernadette said that the Lady looked nothing like the images and statues she had seen. The Lady was so much more beautiful and natural. Have the students bring in their favorite pictures, drawings, holy cards, statues, and medals of Our Lady. If they have background information on any of their items, ask them to display those as well.

Feb. 17 Seven Founders of the Order of Servites

Some people fight evils in society in a quiet way by living lives of witness to eternal values. There were seven such men in Florence, Italy, in the mid-13th century. They were wealthy, well-known merchants. But they found themselves in a society in which many people disregarded God's law. Riches and the easy life meant more to these men than concern for those who were poor. But they chose to turn their lives totally over to God and to give witness to all that is good and true. So these seven men withdrew from the city to lead lives of prayer and penance. At first, so many people came to see them on the outskirts of the city that it was necessary for some of them to move to the quieter slopes of Monte Senario.

This group of men had special devotion to the Blessed Virgin, particularly in her seven sorrows. They came to call themselves the Servants of Mary, or Servites. Although they began as monks living apart from the world and devoted to a contemplative lifestyle, they gradually became more like friars and more involved with helping other people in an active apostolate. The order was recognized in 1259, and approved by Pope Benedict XI in 1304. Only one of the founders, Alexis Falconieri, lived to see this approval. In 1888, the seven founders were canonized by Pope Leo XIII.

Suggestions

◆ Discuss with the students the importance of leaders in society who live according to moral principles and values. Have the students list current leaders and indicate what their values appear to be from the type of lifestyle they lead. Discuss the power of good example to inspire others.

◆ Before founding the order of Servites, all seven men had been members of confraternities. Ask the students to find out which confraternities exist in their diocese and in their parish. Invite representatives of various confraternities to speak to the class about the purpose of their groups.

Feb. 23 Saint Polycarp

Around the year A.D. 60, Polycarp was born. He was a disciple of Saint John the Apostle. While still quite young, he became the bishop of Smyrna, which is now in Turkey. Polycarp was one of the most respected leaders in the first half of the second century. Ignatius of Antioch and Irenaeus spoke highly of him, and the people loved him. Polycarp was a Christian leader in a non-Christian world. He was fearless in his love for and defense of Christ, even though persecutions raged. Even as Polycarp prepared for martyrdom, his joy and trust were evident to all.

Polycarp was seized for being a Christian. He was threatened and pressured in many ways, yet he explained to his captors that he had followed Christ for 86 years. Persecution and death would not tear him away from Jesus now. So Polycarp was led into the stadium of Smyrna. The crowd demanded that he be left to the lions, but instead he was sentenced to death by fire. He was finally killed by the sword on February 2, 155, and then his body was burned. A group of Christians took his remains and buried them.

The community of believers celebrated the anniversary of his death with great joy, for in Polycarp they had seen an outstanding example of love and patience. Polycarp, along with Ignatius of Antioch, Clement of Rome, and a few others, is remembered as an Apostolic Father, which is one who was a disciple of the apostles, and bridges the gap between those who lived with Jesus and those who would believe in Jesus by faith.

Suggestions

◆ Today we have a letter that Polycarp wrote the people of Philippi. In the letter, he stressed patience; the following of the Gospels; almsgiving; and prayer for kings, rulers, enemies, and persecutors. Have the students write petitions related to these areas. Encourage them to make a special effort to pray for their enemies and for those who ignore or hurt them in any way.

◆ Have the students research the ancient city of Smyrna. They could report on its cultural, historical, and religious significance.

March

Mar. 3 Saint Katharine Drexel

In 1889, newspaper headlines read "Gives Up $7 Million." The article told about Katharine Drexel, an heiress from Philadelphia, who had decided to be a Sister of Mercy and use her inheritance of 7 million dollars to help others.

Katharine was born November 26, 1858. Her father was an international banker. Katharine's mother, a Baptist Quaker, died when Katharine was five months old. Her father married a Catholic woman. The Drexels were good Catholics who even had a chapel in their house. Mr. Drexel prayed for a half hour each evening, and Mrs. Drexel opened her home three days a week to those who were poor. Like any wealthy girl, Katharine had received an excellent education, traveled, and made her debut into society. When Katharine's stepmother became ill with cancer, Katharine nursed her for three years until she died. This experience made her think about her values in life and about

becoming a sister. Then, after visiting the West, she became concerned about the Native American population.

One day Katharine had a chance to meet Pope Leo XIII. She asked him to send more missionaries to Wyoming to help her friend Bishop James O'Connor. The pope asked, "Why don't you become a missionary?"

Katharine visited the chief of the Sioux and began helping at the missions. She joined the Sisters of Mercy in Pittsburgh to make a two-year novitiate. Then in 1891, she made her vows as the first sister of the Blessed Sacrament. Her order was dedicated to sharing the Gospel and the life of the Eucharist among Native Americans and African Americans.

After three and a half years of training, Mother Drexel and other sisters opened a boarding school in Santa Fe, New Mexico. She spent her life and her inheritance on her work. During her life, she had established 50 missions for Native Americans in 16 states, a system of Catholic schools for African Americans, 40 mission centers, and 23 rural schools. She had also made the Church and the country more aware of the needs of those who were poor. She spoke out against racial injustices.

Mother Drexel's greatest educational achievement was founding Xavier University in New Orleans, the first university for African Americans in the United States.

A heart attack at the age of 77 forced Katharine to retire. She spent the rest of her days praying in a small room overlooking the sanctuary until she died at 96 on March 3, 1955. She was canonized in 2000.

Suggestions

+ Discuss how the Native American and African American cultures contribute to the richness of the Catholic Church.

+ Encourage the students to pray for an end to prejudice and racism and contribute to an organization that promotes the welfare of both groups.

Mar. 4 Saint Casimir

Saints are seldom found in palaces or castles, but Saint Casimir, prince of Poland, was an exception. Much of Casimir's strength of character can be attributed to the influence of his teacher, John Dlugosz, a Polish historian. Casimir, born in 1458, was highly disciplined and eager to learn. By the time he was 13, his virtue and integrity were so well-known that the nobles in Hungary, dissatisfied with their king, wanted Casimir as ruler. Casimir's father equipped him with an army and sent him to the Hungarian border to take over the country. As Casimir surveyed the situation, he saw that he was outnumbered by the enemy and that the battle would be a waste of lives. Moreover, he learned that Pope Sixtus IV had asked his father not to attack. So Casimir returned home with no kingdom. Casimir's father was angry and felt disgraced. He banished his son to a nearby castle for three months. During this time, he resolved never again to be involved in wars; instead, he would govern by peaceful means. Casimir also decided to remain unmarried. This decision frustrated his parents when he refused to marry the daughter of Emperor Frederick III. Casimir briefly governed the Polish empire while his father was on a tour of Lithuania. But Casimir died at the age of 26 of a lung disease. Casimir loved Our Lady very much and every day repeated the hymn "Daily, Daily, Sing to Mary." He requested that this song be buried with him. Saint Casimir is the patron of Poland and Lithuania.

Suggestions

+ Help the students answer these questions:

   1. How does the Church view war?

   2. What do your families believe about war and peace?

   3. How can you become a more peace-loving person?

+ Pray this prayer for peace:

Lead us from death to life, from falsehood to truth. Lead us from despair to hope, from fear to trust. Lead us from hate to love, from war to peace. Let peace fill our hearts, our world, our universe.

Mar. 9 Saint Frances of Rome

In the 14th century, when Lorenzo Panziano of Rome brought Frances, his beautiful bride, to the altar, his family and the wealthy of the city of Rome were in awe. Not only did he marry one of Rome's most charming maidens, but also one who was virtuous. Frances was 13 when she was married. Her mother had taught her how to pray and love those who were poor as well as how to manage a large household.

Though she had wished to be a nun, Frances married and went obediently to live with Lorenzo and his family. She was young and spirited, and dressed herself in the silks, velvets, and jewels of the family to please her husband, who dearly loved her. She also loved him and willingly took care of her duties at the castle. Frequently, Frances and her sister-in-law Vanozza left the palace in simple dresses and veils to care for those who were sick in the hospitals and to distribute goods to those who were poor. When Lorenzo's relatives found out, they insulted the young women. Frances persuaded Lorenzo to allow her to serve people who were needy.

Frances personally supervised the education of her children. When her mother-in-law died, Frances efficiently took charge of the castle. She treated the servants so well that they did their work more carefully and attended church more often. Though Frances spent long hours in prayer, she always cared for her family first. When floods and famine crippled Rome, Frances opened her house as a hospital and distributed food and clothing. Her father-in-law was outraged at her actions and took away the keys to the supply rooms. But he relented when he saw the corn bin and the wine barrel miraculously replenished after Frances prayed. When Rome was invaded, Frances endured the kidnapping of her husband and the deaths of three of her children. The wars brought plagues and hardships. Again, Frances opened her home as a hospital and drove her wagon to collect wood for fire and herbs for medicine. She was seen everywhere, burying the dead, nursing the sick, serving those who were poor, and taking upon herself the most disagreeable work.

When the wars were over and Frances's husband returned, she founded an order of sisters called the Oblates of Saint Mary. These women lived in their own homes and served those who were poor. Later, the Oblates sisters decided to live a community life, but Frances did not join them until after her husband had died and her children were grown.

Suggestions

✦ The kind of service Frances gave is called pastoral ministry. There are many people involved in pastoral ministry today. Have the students check if the parish has a person involved in this work, and invite him or her to speak to the class. Have the class list the main roles laypersons can take to become involved in the Church today.

✦ Throughout her life Frances, cared for those who were sick. Have the students research the Catholic Church's history of providing health care, especially to those who are poor.

Mar. 17 Saint Patrick

Born in 385, the son of a Roman military officer stationed in Britain, Patrick grew up more interested in a career than in religion. At the age of 16, he was captured by Irish pirates and taken to Ireland. For six years, he worked as a shepherd. All alone among the hills, he turned to God. Eventually, he was able to escape aboard a German vessel. Patrick had changed a great deal and now had a goal to serve God. Patrick studied for the priesthood and zealously fulfilled his duties.

When the Church began to discuss evangelizing Ireland, Patrick struggled to decide whether he should volunteer for this work. When Palladius, the first bishop of Ireland, died, Patrick expressed his desire to become a missionary to that land. He had a dream in which he heard the people calling him, "We beg you come and walk with us again." Now Church officials had to decide whether or not to send Patrick, for he was not well-educated. However, Pope Celestine I saw in him the extraordinary qualities of a missionary. Patrick understood the people of Ireland because he had lived among them, knew their language, and already had spent 15 years in parish ministry. At the age of 42, Patrick was ordained a bishop, and the pope sent him to northern and western Ireland, a place where the Gospel had never been preached.

Bravely, Patrick and several helpers faced the new land. The people of Ireland lived in tribes and clans and worshiped non-Christian gods. Druids, priests of the native religion, kept the people away from any other religion. Patrick knew he would have to convert the chief of a clan before he could win the people. He courageously started with the most powerful clan: Tara. Immediately, the chief respected Patrick, who spoke the chief's language well and who explained his beliefs with sincerity. The chief, Laoghaire, son of Nial of the Nine Hostages, was converted, and Christianity began to take root in Ireland.

Patrick faced danger often, especially from the Druids who plotted to do away with him. But Patrick continued to preach the faith, ready for death at any time. He set up monasteries and convents, established parishes, and adapted Irish celebrations to Christian feasts. His deep prayer kept him calm when British priests criticized his way of ministering or when enemies disgraced his name.

It was in response to his critics that Patrick wrote his *Confessio*, an autobiography in which he writes about his life. Today Patrick is the patron saint of Ireland, but his feast is a worldwide day of celebrations.

Suggestions

✦ Pray or sing the morning prayer of praise called the "Breastplate of Saint Patrick," or the *Lorica*. It was probably written down after Patrick died, but expresses Patrick's love and trust in God. Here is part of it:

Christ be with me, Christ within me,
Christ beside me, Christ to win me,
Christ to comfort and restore me,
Christ behind me, Christ before me,
Christ in quiet, Christ in danger,
Christ in the mouth of friend or stranger,
Christ in the hearts of all who love me,
Christ beneath me, Christ above me.

✦ Have the students research how Saint Patrick's Day is celebrated in various cities and cultures.

Mar. 19 Saint Joseph, Husband of Mary

The Gospels of Matthew and Luke present Joseph as the gentle but strong protector of Mary, the Mother of God. When Matthew traces Jesus' human ancestry, it is Joseph's family that is given, emphasizing his relationship to the House of David. (Matthew 1:16) Saint Luke identifies Mary as the betrothed of a man named Joseph, of the house and family of David. (Luke 1:27) This "just man" is faced with a terrible dilemma when he realizes that the woman he loves and is engaged to is to bear a child (Matthew 1:18–25). Through a dream, Joseph is informed of the tremendous event that had occurred, and his loving protection of Mary is deepened. As the time for Jesus to be born draws near, Mary and Joseph must go to Bethlehem, not only to be enrolled among the members of the house and family of David, but also to have the Messiah born in the city of the Great King, as prophecy has foretold.

At the birth of Jesus, Joseph guards Mary and her child. (Luke 2:4–20) Joseph is present when Jesus is offered to his Father at the Presentation in the Temple. With Mary, Joseph hears the prophetic words of Simeon regarding the sufferings to be endured by Mary and her child. (Luke 2:21–35) When the life of Jesus is in danger because of the hatred of King Herod, Joseph guards and provides for his family in Egypt until he can safely take them back to Nazareth. (Matthew 2:13–23) During one of the difficult sufferings of her life, Mary has Joseph to rely upon. When Jesus is lost in Jerusalem,

Joseph and Mary together seek him and take him back to Nazareth with them. (Luke 2:41–52) After this, Joseph slips out of the Scriptures, except for a few references to Jesus as the "carpenter's son." (Matthew 13:55; Luke 3:23; John 1:45; John 6:42) The word used in Scripture means an artisan or craftsman, a worker in stone, metal, or wood. It is thought that Joseph died before Jesus began his public life. That is why he is the patron of the happy death.

The devotion to Joseph grew and was given worldwide recognition in 1870, when Pope Pius IX proclaimed Saint Joseph the patron of the universal church. Since then, Saint Joseph has been named patron of different groups and countries. In 1955, Pope Pius XII named May 1 as the feast of Saint Joseph the Worker. In 1961, Pope John XXIII proclaimed Joseph the heavenly protector of the Second Vatican Council. In 1962, the same pope included Joseph's name in Eucharistic Prayer I of the Mass.

Suggestions

+ *Abba* is Aramaic for *father*. Have the students think of the influence that a father has on his children. Then let them think of the great love of the Heavenly Father for us and of the influence he has on our lives. Pray the Lord's Prayer with the students.

+ Display famous art pictures of the Holy Family or of Joseph alone. Have the students note how representations of Saint Joseph have changed with the times.

+ Joseph is described as just. The biblical notion of just is very broad and includes such ideas as law-abiding, holy, one transformed by God and open to God's will. Have the students read Matthew 1:18–24 for Joseph's part in Jesus' birth. Have them write a description of the kind of man Joseph was.

April

April 4 Saint Isidore of Seville

As a boy, Isidore of Seville sometimes didn't do his homework and even skipped his studies. After the death of his parents, Isidore was cared for by his older brother Leander, a monk who later became the archbishop of Seville and was venerated as a saint. Leander wanted his younger brother to be educated. One day when he should have been studying, Isidore found an old stone well. He noticed that there were grooves in the stone walls where thin wet ropes had worn the stone away. He realized that just as the rope could wear away the rock by consistently cutting a little bit at a time, so he might become successful at his studies if he tried consistently. Isidore persevered in his studies and became known as one of the most learned men of his time.

Politically, Isidore presided over the council of Toledo in 633. This council helped settle the difference between the reigning king and a usurper to the throne. This council also decreed that Jews be given the freedom to keep their religion rather than be forced to become Christian. Historically, Isidore wrote biographies and a history of the world from Creation to his own time. This work is useful even today as a source book on Spanish history.

Educationally, Isidore worked to establish in each diocese a college to instruct seminarians. His principal work was an encyclopedia that contained all the secular and religious knowledge available at his time. In the area of religion, Isidore worked hard to renew the Church in Spain. He greatly encouraged the reading of Scripture. Some of his theological works helped shape the spiritual outlook of the Middle Ages. For all of this, he was declared a Doctor of the Church in 1722.

Isidore is a saint because he worked hard at being open to God's love and grace. He was also outstanding for helping those who were poor.

Suggestions

+ Have the students think of one goal they have been trying to achieve such as a personal habit that needs changing or a family relationship that needs improving. Encourage them to make a one-week plan, thinking of something they can do each day to achieve their goal.

+ Isidore had difficulty with his homework. Suggest that the students make a resolution to do all their homework this week in honor of Saint Isidore.

April 8 Saint Julie Billiart

Julie Billiart was born into a peasant family in 1751 in Picardy, France. When Julie was in her teens, her father's store was invaded by robbers, who took most of its stock. Later, an enemy shot at her father in the room where Julie was also sitting. No one was hurt, but the shock of the event left her paralyzed.

The French Revolution was over, but the Church was still suppressed. Julie was firm in her faith. She gathered children to her bedside to teach them about God. Soon, however, people reported to the government that she was teaching religion. To avoid arrest, Julie had to be smuggled from house to house. Such moving about was painful for her. Finally, a room was found for her at the home of a wealthy woman, Francoise Blin de Bourdon. It was to Francoise, who became a close friend, that Julie confided her dream of founding a community of women who would teach the faith to children. How could she accomplish such a dream? She was penniless. For more than 20 years, she had been an invalid. Julie and Francoise prayed.

One day, after a novena to the Sacred Heart, the priest who was Julie's confessor commanded her: "If you have any faith in the Sacred Heart of Jesus, walk." And Julie stepped forward! She was cured at the age of 53. Together with Francoise, who gave her money for the project, Julie founded the Sisters of Notre Dame to care for orphans, to educate poor girls, and to train Christian teachers. Julie had learned during her years of pain and sickness that "God is good." Others joined Julie and Francoise in their work to spread the good news of the goodness of God. One day, Julie had a vision of sisters in religious habits, standing around the cross of Christ. A voice said, "Here are the daughters I will give you in the institute marked by the cross." Julie's work was marked by the cross. The government had no use for Catholicism. Some of Julie's own sisters betrayed her, people withdrew financial support from her schools, and bishops were skeptical about her work. But through all of this, Julie's confidence grew. With great hope, she started schools, trained teachers, and performed countless works of charity. Saint Julie is called the "Smiling Saint" because she was cheerful and hopeful even when experiencing great pain or sorrow. She knew that everything God permitted was good.

Suggestions

+ Have the students remember to greet everyone with a smile, even when, and especially when, they are not feeling happy.
+ Saint Julie founded the Sisters of Notre Dame. Have the students research this religious community, reporting on its history and ministry.

April 23 Saint George

George was probably a soldier in the fourth century who courageously defended the faith and encouraged his fellow Christians. For this, he suffered martyrdom under Diocletian and was venerated as a popular saint in the East. By the sixth century, Saint George had become the ideal Christian knight, and the story of his slaying the dragon had become immensely popular. In the seventh and eighth centuries, stained-glass windows in the churches of Europe depicted this sixth-century legend. By this time, Saint George had become a popular saint in the West.

The story of Saint George tells of a dragon that terrorized the land and poisoned with its breath all who approached it. George slew the dragon and was offered anything he'd like. He refused any reward, but made the king promise to build churches, honor priests, and show compassion to those who were poor. George became the personification of all the ideals of Christian chivalry. He was named patron of soldiers, and when the English king Richard I led his soldiers in the Crusades, he placed his army under George's protection. In one famous battle, the Christians were losing. Later, the army leaders insisted that in the midst of the battle, Saint George rode forward and led the troops to victory. From then on, George became the patron saint of England. King Edward III founded an order of knights under his patronage, and his feast was kept as a national festival. Saint George is the patron of soldiers.

Suggestions

+ Have the students write a prayer to Saint George, asking him to protect the men and women in the military.
+ Remind the class to pray for peace and for all who work to keep peace between countries.

April 25 Saint Mark

The pioneer in Gospel writing was Saint Mark whose Gospel appeared about A.D. 65. It is the shortest and the oldest of the Gospels. Little is known of Mark except from the New Testament. He was not one of the twelve apostles, but rather a member of the first Christian community. It was probably Mark's mother who opened her house as a place of prayer for the apostles during Peter's imprisonment. (Acts of the Apostles 12:12) Mark had firsthand experience of the early Church and apostolic life. He was a traveling companion and assistant of Paul's and Barnabas's. Barnabas was Mark's cousin. Mark's Gospel included oral and written tradition concerning the words and deeds of Jesus. He probably secured some of his material from Saint Peter. Mark shows Jesus as the suffering Son of God. Mark knew that it was easy to be a disciple of the risen Jesus and anticipate the assured victory of eternal life. But Mark also knew that to accept the risen Jesus meant to come to terms with the Cross. Mark wrote to proclaim the Good News to a community that had as its members both Jewish and Gentile Christians. His Gospel is direct and simple to read.

Suggestions

+ Have the students select a part of Mark's Gospel to read quietly. Have them write in their reflection notebooks one thought they had while reading this Gospel.

◆ Have the students read and dramatize the parables of the Kingdom of God found in Mark 4:1–32. They might illustrate one of them.

April 28 Saint Peter Chanel

Peter Chanel was born of a French peasant family in 1803. The parish priest noticed Peter's intelligence and prayerful spirit, and he helped the young man enter the seminary. After ordination, Peter was assigned pastor of a parish in a run-down district. Through patience and perseverance in showing kindness to those who were sick and all in need, he revived the parish. But Peter wanted to be a foreign missionary. In 1837, after three years, he joined the new congregation of the Marist Fathers. After teaching for five years in the seminary, he was sent with Bishop Pompallier and other missionaries to islands in the southern Pacific Ocean. The bishop left Peter and a Marist brother on the island of Futuna, promising to return in six months. But it was five years before the bishop could return. Peter and the brother were accepted by some of the natives, and their abilities to heal the sick were respected, but missionary work was difficult. Cannibalism still flourished on these islands, and the language seemed impossible to learn. But Peter continued to work faithfully, even though only a few natives came for instructions and Baptism.

A turning point came, however, when the chief's son asked to be baptized. This conversion made the chief so angry he sent a band of warriors to kill Peter. The warriors entered Peter's hut and clubbed him to death. Peter was the first martyr of Oceania. The chief had thought that the missionary's death would crush Catholicism on the island, but it had the opposite effect. Peter's witness through martyrdom was the seed of faith. Within a year, the whole island was Catholic.

Suggestions

◆ Have each student write on a small slip of paper one action the class can do for missionaries. These papers can be put into a box and the students can draw a slip each day. The students can perform the practice and unite themselves with missionaries throughout the world.

◆ A Marist brother described Peter: "He was often burned by the heat of the sun, and famished with hunger, and he would return home wet with perspiration and completely exhausted. Yet, he always returned in good spirits, courageous and energetic almost every day." Ask the students what they believe was the source of Peter's optimism. Discuss how they deal with times when they feel sad or discouraged.

May

May 3 Saints Philip and James

Philip seems to have been an enthusiastic person. He brought his friend Nathanael to Jesus, insisting to Nathanael that he had found the one about whom Moses had written. Some years later, it was Philip again who, with the help of Andrew, had a group of Greek Gentiles brought to Jesus. Philip the apostle is not to be confused with the Philip of chapter 8 in the Acts of the Apostles, who baptized the Ethiopian, although some writers say that they could be the same person. Philip had a practical mind. He was the apostle who commented that it would take a lot of money to feed more than 5,000 hungry men, women, and children. It was Philip who asked to see the Father when Jesus spoke about him at the Last Supper.

James was the son of Alphaeus and seems to have been born in Caesarea. He is mentioned less frequently in the New Testament than Philip. Sometimes James is called the Less, which might be a hint that he was short, or else that he knew Jesus for less time than the other apostle named James.

After Jesus' Death, James continued to preach the Gospel and is believed to have become the first bishop of Jerusalem. Assuming that James and the first bishop of Jerusalem are the same person, then he met his death as a martyr in Jerusalem about the year A.D. 62. Tradition identifies James as the author of the epistle associated with his name.

Suggestion

Tell the students to read one of the following references, all of which involve Philip: John 1:43–50; John 6:1–15; John 14:1–11. Have them discuss the portrait of Philip these readings give us.

May 14 Saint Matthias

The New Testament mentions Matthias only in the account of how he was chosen to become an apostle. The apostles met to elect someone to replace Judas. Peter presided and reminded the others of the qualifications necessary for being an apostle: first, the candidate had to have been a follower of Jesus Christ from the time of Jesus' baptism until the Ascension; second, the person had to have been a witness to Jesus' Resurrection. Soon the choice was narrowed to two men: Joseph, so good and holy that he was known as Joseph the Just; and Matthias, also a very good and holy man. Matthias was chosen by lots to show that the decision belonged to God. Through the inspiration of the Holy Spirit, the apostles had chosen Matthias rather than Joseph.

After becoming an apostle and a missionary, Matthias quietly dropped out of sight. Tradition links him with the country of Ethiopia, where he is believed to have met his martyrdom.

Suggestion

Have the class say a prayer today for all those persons who must make difficult decisions concerning their vocations or the vocations of others.

May 15 Saint Isidore the Farmer

Isidore was born in Spain more than 900 years ago. As soon as he was old enough, he began to work as a farmer. He worked all his life for a landowner named John de Vergas. While he walked the fields, plowing, planting, and harvesting, he prayed. As a hard-working man, Isidore had three great loves: God, his family, and the soil. He and his wife, Maria, who is also honored as a saint, proved to all their neighbors that poverty, hard work, and sorrow (their only child died as a little boy) cannot destroy human happiness if we accept them with faith and in union with Christ.

During his lifetime, Isidore had the gift of miracles. More than once he fed hungry people with food that seemed to multiply miraculously. He died in 1130 after a peaceful life of hard, manual labor. Today he is honored in Spain as one of her greatest saints, and he is also honored in the rural United States. Saint Isidore is patron of the U.S. National Catholic Rural Life Conference. In New Mexico, his statue is brought into the fields on his feast day and when there is a shortage of rain.

Suggestions

+ Encourage the class to try not to waste food, either at home or at school.

+ Ask the class to make a resolution not to litter today. Suggest that each student resolve to pick up at least one piece of litter today in the school yard and one piece in his or her neighborhood.

+ Have the students pray for all farmers today that they may enjoy good weather, have fine crops, and reap a generous harvest through the intercession of Saint Isidore.

May 20 Saint Bernardine of Siena

Bernardine was born in Italy on September 8, 1380. As a little boy, he lost both parents and was cared for by his aunt. He had a brilliant mind, but when he contracted the plague at age 20, it looked as though he would never have a chance to use his talents. Bernardine did recover, however, and entered the Franciscan order two years later. He was ordained a priest in 1404. In time, he gained fame throughout Italy as a remarkable preacher. Bernardine had the ability to move his listeners to tears and to laughter in the same homily. He had a great devotion to the Holy Name of Jesus and became famous for creating the symbol IHS, which he devised from the first three Greek letters in the name of Jesus.

One thing Father Bernardine preached against was gambling. Once he was approached angrily by a man whose card-making business had suffered as a result of the priest's sermons. The saint suggested that they start making religious cards with the IHS symbol, instead of playing cards. The merchant's first reaction was one of disgust, but he later took Bernardine's advice and became wealthy.

Until his death in 1444, this good priest worked humbly and patiently to spread the Good News of Jesus. He used his power to work miracles to help others. Sometimes Saint Bernardine is pictured with three miters at his feet, because three times he refused to become a bishop. (A miter is the tall head covering that a bishop wears.)

Suggestion

+ Give the students a copy of the Divine Praises or read it aloud to them. Call their attention to the second and fourth invocations. Have them select one of these short prayers and encourage them to say it silently during the day, especially when they meet difficulties or temptations.

May 25 Saint Mary Magdalene de Pazzi

Catherine de Pazzi was born in Florence, Italy, in 1566. Her family was quite wealthy, and it looked as though Catherine would grow up to be a woman of high society, but she surprised everyone by becoming a Carmelite nun at the age of 16. She took the name Mary Magdalene and was soon leading a life of prayer, humility, and penance. After a number of years, she was appointed director of novices and then superior. It was at this time that she was given the ability to read her sisters' thoughts, a gift she used only for the good of her nuns.

Saint Mary Magdalene de Pazzi suffered for three years from a severe illness that finally caused her death in 1607. During this period, she was cheerful and kind to everyone. It was her deep prayer, her humble use of her talents, and the great charity she practiced toward the other nuns that made this quiet nun such a wonderful saint.

Suggestions

✦ Tell the students to say a prayer today for all contemplative nuns and monks, and for men and women who may be considering serving God as a contemplative.

✦ Encourage the students to imitate Saint Mary Magdalene's charity by making a resolution to say nothing mean about anyone and to say something kind instead.

May 26 Saint Philip Neri

The two favorite books of Saint Philip Neri were the New Testament and a book of jokes and riddles. He is remembered for his great sense of humor, his cheerfulness, and his ability to bring out the best in people. He was born in Florence in 1515. The family was poor, but they planned an ambitious future for Philip. When he reached 18, they sent him to the city to be trained as a businessman with his uncle. After working there for several months, Philip sent a thank-you note to his uncle, packed his bags, and headed for Rome. There he tutored and attended the university. During his free time, he would enjoy Rome and pray in the churches and catacombs.

Once, while in prayer at the catacombs, Philip had a mystical experience. He went home, sold his books, and for the next 13 years was a lay minister to the young men of Rome. Soon young men, rich and poor, were coming to work with him. They went to the hospitals, made the beds, cleaned the filth from the floors, and brought food and gifts. Philip was always with them, full of jokes and ready for fun. Philip and the young men would gather in the afternoons for spiritual talks, discussions, prayer, and music. Later he formed these men into a community called the Oratorians.

People persuaded Philip to be ordained. Saint Ignatius Loyola, Saint Francis de Sales, Saint Charles Borromeo, and Saint Camillus de Lellis were saints who had Philip as their spiritual director. Even popes, cardinals, and bishops looked to Philip for guidance.

People enjoyed Philip's good humor and appreciated his humble and simple ways. Philip went about in old clothes, big white shoes, and with his hat cocked to the side. When the pope wanted to make Philip a cardinal, he left a cardinal's hat outside Philip's door. Philip used it to play catch. Another time when people were following him around saying he was a saint, Philip shaved off half his beard.

After hearing about the great conversions of Saint Francis Xavier, Philip wanted to go to the Indies. But a friend persuaded him to continue his good works in Rome. He was to become a "Second Apostle to Rome."

Suggestion

Have the students try to use their natural gifts to give joy and service to others by complimenting others, by readily volunteering to help someone, and by doing what is right despite what others are doing.

May 31 The Visitation

Perhaps the greatest visit ever made was the one Mary made to her relative Elizabeth. This event is called the Visitation. In the Gospel of Luke, after the angel announced to Mary that she was to be the Mother of God, she left at once to visit Elizabeth, who in her old age was to bear a son. As soon as Elizabeth saw Mary, her own child leaped for joy within her. She greeted Mary as the Mother of the Lord. Mary's response was the *Magnificat*. The Church has always praised Mary as the Christ-bearer for two reasons. First, by the power of the Spirit, Mary physically brought Christ to the world. Second, she brings Christ spiritually to everyone by the holiness of her words and example.

Suggestions

✦ Explain to the students that Mary visited the elderly Elizabeth because she was concerned about her relative. Encourage them to visit an elderly neighbor or relative or write to their grandparents on this feast day.

✦ Suggest that the students assist their mothers in some service that evening, as a way of imitating Mary.

June

June 3 Saint Charles Lwanga and His Companions

Uganda lies in central Africa, just west of Kenya. In 1886, a young man named Charles Lwanga was burned to death in Uganda because he would not give up his practice of Christianity.

Charles was probably in his late teens and had begun to live as a page in the king's court. He was

a catechumen at that time. The king learned that Mukasa, master of the court pages, and Charles were helping the Christian boys practice their faith. They encouraged the young men to refuse to take part in the non-Christian customs of the country. This angered the king so much that he ordered Mukasa to be killed. That same night, Charles asked to be baptized. This made the king very angry. He commanded his soldiers to take Charles and 21 of his Christian friends and kill them. Some were burned, and some were beheaded. These brave men, all under 25, prayed and sang as they walked out to their death.

Suggestions

◆ Locate Uganda, Kenya, and Nigeria on a map for the students. Have them pray for missionaries who serve in those countries. Also research the Holy Childhood Association for further mission materials. Contact your diocesan Propagation of the Faith office as well.

◆ These Christian martyrs took their faith seriously and loved the commandments of God. Have the students pray today to be strong in times when they are tempted to sin.

June 6 Saint Norbert

Norbert was born in Germany in the late 11th century, a cousin to the emperor. He had money, popularity, and success. But his carefree life did not make him happy. One day he went horseback riding through the woods. Unexpectedly, a heavy storm began and a sudden bolt of lightning frightened his horse. As the horse reared up, Norbert fell to the ground. When he regained consciousness, he considered the accident a warning from God. Like Saint Paul, he wondered, "Lord, what do you want me to do?" Norbert seemed to hear a voice deep within him say, "Give up the foolish, empty life you are leading. Begin to do good to those around you." Norbert took these words seriously. He sold his property and prepared to be a priest.

Once he was a priest, Norbert preached about the danger of living the way he had lived a few years before. Over the years, so many young men wanted to live the way Norbert did that he started several monasteries. He tried to build these monasteries where people did not hear the Word of God very often. Near each monastery, Norbert usually opened a hospice. Here those who were sick, travelers, and pilgrims could find rest and help. Norbert wrote a rule for his priests to follow. The first sentence begins "Be of one mind and heart in God." When Norbert died in 1134, he was an archbishop. He had worked very hard to stop heresies and to encourage loyalty to the pope.

Suggestions

◆ Have the students get to know the names of their parish priests and how to spell them. They could write letters to the priests telling them how much they appreciate the service the priests give to Christ and his Church.

◆ Respect for the Eucharist meant much to Saint Norbert. Review with the students the importance of being reverent when they receive this sacrament. Remind them not to chew gum or talk when they are at the celebration of the Mass.

◆ Have the students make a checklist of how they use their personal funds. Suggest they add to the list "money to be given to those in need."

June 11 Saint Barnabas

When Joseph left his native island of Cyprus, he may have had no idea what life held for him. Soon he became a Christian, perhaps on the day of Pentecost. The apostles welcomed him and changed his name to Barnabas, which means "son of encouragement." Barnabas sold his property and gave the money to the Jerusalem community. Barnabas, respected by the members of the Jerusalem Church, trusted Paul and took the risk of defending him. He introduced Paul to the apostles and encouraged everyone to accept him.

For a while, Barnabas and Paul were leaders in the Church at Antioch. When they returned to Jerusalem, the Holy Spirit had other plans for them. One day, as a few Church leaders were fasting and praying together, they came to see that Barnabas and Paul were to be set apart by the Holy Spirit for special missionary work. Their mission first took them to Cyprus, where they welcomed many Jewish and Gentile converts into the Church. Then they sailed to the city of Lystra in Asia Minor. There Paul cured a crippled man by telling him to stand up, and the people were astonished. In their native language, they enthusiastically declared Barnabas and Paul to be gods in disguise. Barnabas and Paul tried to explain that they were only men who came to teach about the living God who created the world. But the crowds turned against them.

In every place where they established a Christian community, Barnabas and Paul appointed leaders to guide the local church. Eventually, the two of them separated. Barnabas took the disciple John Mark to Cyprus, while Paul set out on another missionary journey. Tradition tells us that Barnabas was martyred, and a copy of Matthew's Gospel was found clasped to his heart. Pictures of Barnabas often show him carrying the Scriptures.

Suggestions

◆ Barnabas, an important member of the Jerusalem Christian community, took Paul's part when no one else would take the risk. Ask the students to think of someone they know who seems to be lonely. Challenge them to help that person in some way in the coming week.

◆ Barnabas and Paul were once sent to bring relief from Antioch to Christians in Jerusalem who were suffering from famine. Help the students become aware of various Christian organizations that distribute food to starving people in today's world. Then have the class choose one organization and decide on a way of helping that group.

June 13 Saint Anthony of Padua

Anthony was born of noble parents in Lisbon, Portugal, in 1195. For some time, he was in the Order of Saint Augustine. His life changed when he witnessed the burial of Franciscan missionary priests who had been martyred in Morocco, Africa. Anthony obtained permission to become a Franciscan and to sail to Morocco to be a missionary. But the African climate was not good for Anthony, and he became very ill. He decided to return to Portugal, but his boat was driven off course by a strong wind, and he landed in Sicily. He made his way to Italy where the Franciscan priests and brothers were holding an important meeting. Anthony attended that meeting and probably met Francis of Assisi, who was then a frail, old man.

A story is told that at an ordination Mass, the priest who was to give the homily did not arrive on time. At the last minute, Anthony was asked to give the homily. He did, and from that day on, his reputation as preacher spread through Italy and France. Anthony converted so many heretics through his preaching and his works of mercy that he was called the "Wonder Worker."

The fast pace of Anthony's preaching and teaching led to poor health. He died at the age of 36 and was buried in Padua, Italy. According to tradition, Anthony experienced a vision of the child Jesus. That is why many statues of Anthony show him holding a Bible with the child Jesus standing on it.

Suggestion

Many customs and devotions are associated with Anthony of Padua. In Italy, there is a fund that is used for those who are poor, called Saint Anthony's Bread. Have the students research other customs or devotions about Saint Anthony.

June 21 Saint Aloysius Gonzaga

Aloysius Gonzaga was born on March 9, 1568. His mother wanted him to be a priest. His father was determined to have his oldest son become a military leader or famous political figure. At the age of five, Aloysius was sent to a military camp to get started on his career. His mother and his tutor were extremely displeased when he came home using the rough, coarse language of the camp. At the age of seven, Aloysius decided to become a saint. He prayed long hours at night and fasted several times a week.

While on a visit to Spain with his parents, Aloysius read about the lives of Jesuit missionaries and decided to become a Jesuit. His father and other relatives tried to change his mind. Aloysius was not persuaded. He joined the Jesuit order at 17. The novice director told him to cut down on his hours of prayer and to give up some of his penances. Aloysius obeyed. He understood that his obedience was better than "doing his own thing."

In 1591, an epidemic broke out in Rome. Aloysius volunteered to help in the hospital and became very ill. He died at age 23.

Suggestions

◆ Have the students list the actions Aloysius chose in order to become holy like Jesus. (He prayed daily, read the lives of the saints, chose to do difficult things to gain self-control, and asked advice from a priest) Ask the students to make three-point plans for growing in personal holiness.

◆ Direct the students to find three newspaper headlines that reflect needs in our society. Have them cut out the headlines and glue them to a sheet of paper. Then have them write something they can do to respond to these needs with Christian attitudes.

June 24 Birth of Saint John the Baptist

According to Luke's Gospel, Zechariah, John's father, was the first to be prepared for John's birth. While he was offering incense in the Temple, the angel Gabriel came and said that the baby's name would be John, that he would be his father's joy, that he would be filled with the Holy Spirit, and that he would bring people back to God. Zechariah doubted the words of the angel. Because of his momentary lack of faith, Zechariah lost the power to speak until John was born.

The same Gospel also tells of the visit between Mary and Elizabeth, John's mother, before John and Jesus were born. It tells of the joy of relatives and neighbors at John's birth. Eight days later, these people wanted to name the baby Zechariah. However, his father indicated in writing that he wanted his son to be named John. With this, Zechariah recovered his ability to speak, and the people were amazed. They began to ask "What, then, will this child be?" (Luke 1:66) Luke records that John spent his youth in the wilderness, preparing for his mission. What was his mission? His father gave a prophecy on the day that John was named:

"And you, child, will be called prophet of the Most High, for you will go before the Lord to prepare his ways . . . ." (Luke 1:76)

Suggestions

◆ Show the students how *John* is written in Hebrew, which may be the language in which his name was originally written. This name means "Yahweh is gracious."

Then have the students research the name John in different languages. Some forms of the name are given here:

Johannes (Norwegian)	Sean (Gaelic)
Joao (Portuguese)	Evan (Welsh)
Janos (Hungarian)	

◆ Have the students read Luke 1:5–25 and write a news report of the events recounted there. Have them print the report on unlined paper and draw an appropriate illustration to accompany it.

June 29 Saints Peter and Paul

Peter was a fisherman from Bethsaida, a village near the Lake of Galilee. Perhaps he worked with his brother Andrew and friends James and John. Andrew introduced Peter to Jesus. "Jesus looked at him and said, 'You are Simon the son of John; you will be called Kephas' (which is translated Peter)." (John 1:42) *Kephas* in Aramaic means *rock*. Peter showed signs of leadership. He was often the spokesman for the apostles. When Jesus asked, "'But who do you say that I am?' Simon Peter said in reply, 'You are the Messiah, the Son of the living God.'" (Matthew 16:15–16) It was Peter who objected to Jesus' stating that he was on his way to Jerusalem to suffer and die. This time Jesus scolded him. Peter appears to be lovable, impetuous, practical, and sometimes weak under pressure. But Jesus loved him dearly.

Peter became the leader in the early Christian Church. According to the Acts of the Apostles, he was the first to preach on Pentecost Sunday. He arranged for the selection of Matthias to replace Judas. He worked the first public miracle: curing the lame man at the Temple gate. He welcomed the first person who was not Jewish into the Church. People thought just his shadow passing by would cure those who were sick, lame, blind, or deaf.

Peter was put into prison three or four times. As soon as he was released, he began preaching again. Finally, in Rome, he was sentenced to death by crucifixion. Out of respect for his Master, Jesus, he asked the guards to fasten him to the cross upside down. That was how he died in about the year 64 or 65. He was probably buried where the Basilica of St. Peter is today.

Paul was a strict Jew who thought it was his duty to persecute the Christians. One day while traveling to Damascus to drag Christians out of their homes and throw them into prison, he was converted. Once Paul found Jesus, he never lost sight of him. Paul became the greatest missionary. At first, he had great difficulty convincing the Jewish people that the Old Law of Moses did not apply strictly any more. The Jewish people who were part of the early Church were also unwilling to accept anyone for Baptism who was not Jewish. But Paul argued so skillfully that he won, and Gentiles were welcomed as followers of Jesus.

For about 30 years, Paul traveled the Roman Empire, preaching about Christ. From his letters and from the Acts of the Apostles, he seems to have been affectionate, loyal, courageous, and dedicated. He was the right man to build the bridge between the Jewish religion and Christianity. Paul was imprisoned and finally beheaded.

Suggestions

◆ Direct the students to design triptychs showing Jesus, Peter, and Paul. First, have them fold a sheet of construction paper into three equal parts. While the paper is folded, have them cut the top of the paper into an arch. Discuss appropriate symbols for Jesus, Peter, and Paul. On another sheet of paper, have them draw pictures and symbols that represent the three figures. Finally, have them glue their pictures and designs on the background, putting Jesus in the center and Peter and Paul on either side.

◆ Remind the students that the apostles did not lead lives of fame and glory. Have a student read aloud 2 Corinthians 6:3–10. Then discuss these points:

- Christians will meet criticism and mockery from people whose values differ from theirs.

- Their own weakness will sometimes block the good they want to do.

- Christians are not afraid to face suffering for Christ because they rely on God's power.

July

July 3 Saint Thomas

Thomas was a Galilean fisherman like Peter, James, and John. One day, a messenger came to tell Jesus that his friend Lazarus was quite sick. Mary and Martha, the sisters of Lazarus, asked Jesus to come and cure their brother. The apostles knew this would be a dangerous trip for Jesus because he had many enemies living around Jerusalem. Thomas said he would be very glad to go with Jesus, and even to die with him.

On Easter Sunday evening, when the apostles reported that the risen Jesus had appeared to them, Thomas was not present. He refused to believe them. Thomas insisted that he would not believe unless he saw the wounds in Jesus' hands and could put his finger into the wound in his side. A week later, Jesus appeared again to the apostles. This time, Thomas was there. Jesus told him to put his finger into the wounds. Thomas was very ashamed of his unbelief. He fell on his knees and said, "My Lord and my God." Then Jesus said something that should give us great courage and trust. He told Thomas, "Have you come to believe because you have seen me? Blessed are those who have not seen and have believed." (John 20:29)

Tradition says that Thomas went to India and preached there. Perhaps he was martyred there too. The Catholic people of India believe he is their special apostle and patron. He is also the patron of architects.

Suggestions

◆ Encourage the students to pray "My Lord and my God" during the Eucharistic Prayer, when the priest displays the host for everyone to see.

◆ Have the students compose an act of faith and write it on a card.

July 6 Saint Maria Goretti

In 1890, Maria Goretti was born into a poor family living near Anzio, Italy. When she was 10, the family moved to a farm not far from Rome. Her family was so poor that they shared a home and the work on the farm with the Serenelli family. Just two years later, Maria's father died, leaving his wife with several small children.

Maria's mother had to take over the farm work in order to support her family. The managing of the home came to be Maria's job—cooking, cleaning, and mending. Alessandro Serenelli, who was 18, was attracted to Maria. One day, he came in from the fields and tried to persuade Maria to have sexual relations with him. She resisted and told him that what he wanted to do was a serious sin. Because he was terribly angry, he stabbed Maria 14 times.

Maria lived until the next day. Before she died, she forgave Alessandro. She was only 12. Alessandro was sentenced to prison for 30 years. At first, he was angry and resentful. After six years, Alessandro said Maria appeared to him in a dream and gave him a bouquet of lilies. He spent the rest of his prison term trying to make up for his crime. He became a prayerful man.

When he was released from prison, he visited Maria's mother to ask for forgiveness. She did forgive him. Then Alessandro entered a monastery to do penance for his attack on Maria. In 1950, Maria was canonized, and her mother attended the ceremonies with Alessandro Serenelli.

Suggestions

◆ Maria was only 12 when she died for her faith. Have the students pray silently for all young people who are struggling with temptations against chastity or who feel trapped in sinful circumstances. Because the Blessed Virgin wants to help all Christians be chaste, close by having the class pray the Hail Mary.

◆ With the students' help, compile a list of suggestions for living a chaste life.

July 13 Saint Henry

In the 10th century, civil leaders were not elected. They did not have to worry about pleasing their subjects in order to stay in office. Because of this, emperors and kings often did not work for the good of their people. They would ignore or squelch conflict rather than deal with it. Henry, the son of the Duke of Bavaria, however, was a Christlike leader.

Henry was born in 973. By the time he was 34, he had become emperor of Germany. Henry concentrated on the good of his people. He built monasteries, helped those who were in need, fought against unjust seizure of power, and relieved oppression. In 1014, he was crowned emperor of the Holy Roman Empire, making him the ruler of what are now known as Germany, Austria, Switzerland, Belgium, Holland, and northern Italy. Henry was well-known for his missionary spirit and for his protection of the pope. He died in 1024.

Suggestions

◆ Discuss the importance of having Christian leaders in government. Discuss the danger of having leaders who do not value the God-given dignity and rights of each human person.

◆ Have the students write the names of two or three people who look to them for a good example. Then have them write a paragraph explaining how they give a good example to these people.

July 14 Saint Kateri Tekakwitha

Kateri Tekakwitha is called "Lily of the Mohawks." Kateri was a Mohawk born in 1656 in what is now Auriesville, New York. This was 10 years after Isaac Jogues and his companions were martyred there. Her mother was a Christian Algonquin, and her father was a non-Christian Mohawk chief. Her parents and brother died of smallpox when she was only four. Smallpox left Kateri's eyes weak and her face scarred. Anastasia, a friend of Kateri's mother, took care of her and told her stories about the Christian God. When Anastasia left to go to Canada, where there were Christians, Kateri's uncle, a Mohawk chief, took Kateri as his daughter.

When Kateri's uncle and aunts wanted her to marry, she refused. She felt that the Great Spirit was the only one she could love. This angered her uncle.

Kateri learned more about Christianity from a missionary and asked to be baptized. She was baptized on Easter Sunday. It was hard for Kateri to live as a Christian. Children made fun of her and threw stones at her. Kateri endured this for two years.

Finally, a priest advised Kateri to go to Canada where she would be with other Christians. One day, when her uncle was not home, she left. Kateri brought with her a note for a Canadian priest from the missionary priest that said, "I send you a treasure, Katherine Tekakwitha. Guard her well." Kateri went to Mass daily, made frequent visits to the Blessed Sacrament, and prayed the Rosary often. She cared for those who were sick and those who were elderly and taught the children. She did much penance.

Kateri suffered from bad headaches. She was not physically strong and ate very little. Her face was badly scarred from smallpox. On April 17, 1680, when she died at the age of 24, the scars on her face disappeared and she was beautiful. Her last words were "Jesus, I love you." Kateri Tekakwitha was canonized in 2012.

Suggestion

Have the students draw a picture of a scene from Kateri's life.

July 16 Our Lady of Mount Carmel

On one side of Mount Carmel, the many priests of the god Baal stood next to the stone altar dedicated to their false god. They had been praying aloud all day, but no god had answered them. On the other side, the prophet Elijah stood alone next to a stone altar dedicated to Yahweh. That day Yahweh sent fire from heaven onto the altar, proving to be the one true God. The Old Testament records this event on Mount Carmel in northern Palestine in 1 Kings 18:16–39.

Between that event and the year 1156, people who wanted a quiet place to live closely with God came to Mount Carmel. A large monastery was built there to honor the Mother of God. The members of the monastery were called Carmelites. In 1251, according to the tradition of the Carmelites, the Blessed Virgin Mary appeared to Saint Simon, the sixth General of the Carmelite order, and gave him a scapular. The scapular was a long piece of cloth falling from the wearer's shoulders, in front and in back, down to the ankles. All the members of that Carmelite community wore a similar scapular. Today some religious men and women still wear the full scapular. Wearing a shortened scapular or a scapular medal is a way of honoring the Blessed Mother. July 16 is a major feast for all Carmelite priests and sisters.

Suggestions

✦ Show the students the picture of Our Lady of Mount Carmel. Have them recall the times they have previously seen a picture, statue, or stained-glass window of Mary under this title.

✦ Have the students find as many titles of Mary as possible. Post a long sheet of paper on which students can list titles. Let the students make up their own special title for Mary, based on their own experiences.

July 22 Saint Mary Magdalene

Mary, the sister of Martha and Lazarus; Mary the sinner who washed Jesus' feet with her tears; Mary, one of the women who cared for Jesus and his apostles on their journeys; Mary, present on Calvary; and Mary, visiting the tomb very early on Easter morning. It is doubtful that Mary Magdalene can be identified with all these Marys. Matthew, Mark, and John record that Mary Magdalene was present at the crucifixion of Jesus and that she was among the women who visited the tomb on Easter morning. Luke mentions only the Easter incident. The first to proclaim the good news of Jesus' Resurrection, she is called the apostle to the apostles.

What we know for sure is that Mary Magdalene was near Jesus in his darkest hour and again in his most glorious hour. For centuries, Mary has been considered a model of complete generosity and of sincere sorrow for sin.

Suggestions

✦ Ask the students to consider their own friendship with Jesus. Have them write ways that he shows his love for them and ways that they show their love for him.

✦ Have the students listen to the account from John 20:11–18. Then have them write in their reflection notebooks an imaginary letter in which Mary Magdalene recounts the events to her friend.

July 25 Saint James

In Matthew's Gospel (Matthew 20:20–28), the mother of James and John asked Jesus to give her sons a high position in his kingdom. Jesus asked them, "Can you drink the bitter cup of suffering I am going to drink?" They said, "Yes." Then Jesus said that his Father would decide who would sit at his right and his left side.

Jesus called James to follow him early in his public life. He and his brother John were in a boat with their father Zebedee, mending nets. James and John were known as "Boanerges" meaning, "sons of thunder." They seem to have had strong tempers. Along with Peter and John, James was one of the favored three to witness the Transfiguration of Jesus, the raising of Jairus's daughter, and the agony in the garden.

We do not know very much about James's life. Tradition says he may have traveled to Spain. During the Middle Ages, there was a famous shrine to Saint James at Compostela in Spain. Luke records in the Acts of the Apostles: "About that time King Herod laid hands upon some members of the church to harm them. He had James, the brother of John, killed by the sword . . . ." (Acts of the Apostles 12:1–2) James was beheaded.

James is a very popular saint in England. More than 400 churches are dedicated to him in that country.

Suggestions

+ Ask the students to imagine that they are James and have them write an entry for some of the events in Jesus' life as he might have written it.

+ Have the students compose a prayer for missionaries.

July 26 Saints Joachim and Ann

Did you know that your grandparents have a pair of patron saints? They do—Saint Joachim and Saint Ann. They were Mary's parents, and so they were the grandparents of Jesus.

We really do not know very much about these saints. Tradition says that they took their daughter to the Temple in Jerusalem when she was very young. They understood that Mary was a special child, so they dedicated her to God. The name *Ann* means "grace" and has many forms: Annette, Anita, Dina, Hannah, Nancy, Anna. The name *Joachim* means "Yahweh prepares."

Suggestions

+ Encourage those students who have grandparents to contact them through a letter, phone call, e-mail, or text message. Allow students to share with the class any positive results of their experiences.

+ To honor parents, have the students make collages of the gifts, talents, and positive Christian qualities of their parents. Direct them to give the finished pieces to their parents.

July 29 Saint Martha

How good it is to have a home where you can go at any time and find people who accept, love, and understand you. Jesus found such a home in Bethany at the house of a woman named Martha. Martha lived with her sister Mary. Jesus loved both of them and appreciated the gifts that each one had. The Gospel of Luke records that once, when Jesus was visiting, Martha was frustrated by all the work she was doing. Her solution was to get her sister Mary to help. After all, Mary was just sitting at the feet of Jesus listening to his words. Martha wanted Jesus to tell Mary to help. But Jesus showed Martha that because she was worrying so much, she did not have time to enjoy being with him.

Another time, recorded in John's Gospel, the sisters sent a message to Jesus that their brother Lazarus was ill. They knew Jesus would come and cure him because they trusted in his loving care for them. When Jesus did come, Lazarus had already been dead for four days. As soon as she heard that Jesus was nearby, Martha, a woman of action, went out to meet him while Mary stayed in the house. Martha told Jesus honestly what she had expected from him. Jesus asked her to believe that he was the resurrection and that he had power to give eternal life to all who believe in him. Martha trusted Jesus totally and said, "Yes, Lord. I have come to believe that you are the Messiah, the Son of God, the one who is coming into the world." (John 11:27) That day Jesus raised her brother Lazarus from the dead to show that he has the power to give eternal life. Martha is the patron of cooks.

Suggestions

+ Direct the students to write an original, imagined story about a time when Jesus visited their homes.

+ Have the students research why hospitality is considered an important value for organizations such as the Catholic Worker.

August

Aug. 1 Saint Alphonsus Liguori

Alphonsus was born in 1696 to the rich Liguori family of Naples, Italy. He was very intelligent. Alphonsus finished school at 16 and began to practice law. After 11 years, he became so disturbed by the corruption in the courts of Naples that he gave up his career to study for the priesthood.

Alphonsus worked with those who were poor, uneducated, and neglected. Eventually, other young men joined Alphonsus in meeting the spiritual needs of these people. Finally, he began a religious order of priests known as the Redemptorists. Their goal was to preach and to teach, especially in remote rural areas and in slums. His order worked hard to fight Jansenism, a heresy that held the doctrine of predestination and advocated an extremely rigorous code of morals and asceticism. It was responsible for keeping many Catholics from receiving Jesus in the Eucharist. Alphonsus, as a priest and later a bishop, wrote sermons, books, and articles to encourage devotion to Jesus in the Blessed Sacrament. He was also deeply devoted to the Blessed Virgin Mary.

Alphonsus was a friendly, kind man, full of quiet humor. The last years of his life brought him problems of weakening health, misunderstanding, and even a certain amount of failure. But through it all, he kept his awareness of Christ in his life and never lost faith and hope. He died in 1787. He was declared a Doctor of the Church in 1871.

Suggestions

◆ Have the students share any experiences they have had taking a stand for justice, or have them describe incidents when people they knew stood up for justice. Finally, discuss how working for justice is acting as Jesus acted.

◆ Have each student find a quotation on the Christian life from a respected author. Each day, write a quotation on the board.

◆ Have the students research the Redemptorists online to find out about their life and work today. Have the students answer the question: How do the Redemptorists carry on the work of Saint Alphonsus?

Aug. 5 Dedication of St. Mary Major

Today's feast focuses our attention on a church building, a basilica called St. Mary Major. Tradition says that in August 352, the Blessed Virgin Mary appeared to a wealthy nobleman in Rome. She asked that a church be built on the spot where he would find snow. On that summer day, snow mysteriously appeared. A church was built on the spot and dedicated to Our Lady of the Snows.

Apart from the story, however, we know that a church was built on that spot in the fourth century and was rebuilt in 434. The church was rededicated to Mary, the Mother of God. This title of Mary was protected by the ecumenical council of Ephesus. Today, St. Mary Major is the largest church in the world dedicated to Our Lady. This church is called a patriarchal church, one where the pope officiates on certain occasions. There is a special altar in this church used by the Holy Father and by others with special permission. This feast reminds us that Mary has been reverenced throughout the history of the Church as our Mother. "'[F]rom now on will all ages call me blessed.'" (Luke 1:48)

Suggestions

◆ Take the class to the Marian altar in the church or to a local Marian shrine. Sing a hymn to Mary and pray the Magnificat from Luke 1:46–55.

◆ Have the students research shrines dedicated to the Blessed Mother, paying particular attention to the National Shrine of the Immaculate Conception in Washington, D.C.

Aug. 6 Transfiguration

The Synoptic Gospels contain a number of passages that show Jesus' divinity shining through his humanity.

One of these is the passage on the Transfiguration. Jesus took Peter, James, and John up a high mountain. There, while the apostles watched, Jesus' face began to shine much more brightly than the sun. His garments became as white as snow. Moses and Elijah appeared, standing on each side of Jesus. The three of them talked together about Jesus' coming passion and Death. Then Peter, not really knowing what he was saying, exclaimed, "'Lord, it is good that we are here. If you wish, I will make three tents here, one for you, one for Moses, and one for Elijah.'" (Matthew 17:4)

While Peter was still speaking, a bright cloud gathered and covered the apostles with its shadow. Then the apostles heard a voice saying "'This is my beloved Son, with whom I am well pleased; listen to him.'" (Matthew 17:5) Peter, James, and John fell to the ground because they were so frightened. The next moment, Jesus touched them and told them not to fear. When they looked up, there was no one in sight except Jesus, looking like his ordinary self. As they walked down the mountain, Jesus told Peter, James, and John to keep the whole experience a secret. They were not permitted to tell others until after he had risen from the dead.

Suggestion

Write the following letter on stationery and put it in an envelope. Open the letter in class, read it to the students, and ask them to guess who could have written a letter like this.

Dearly Beloved,

As I am here in prison, awaiting execution, I feel the urge to write to you, pleading with you to be faithful to Christ. I am aware that you have shown loyalty to Christ and his teachings, and I thank God for it; but, still, these few words may raise your spirits when you are tempted to give up. Realize that what we have taught you about the coming of Jesus in glory and power are not figments of our imaginations, but actual truths, for we saw Jesus on the mount arrayed in glory and heard the voice from heaven announce "This is my beloved Son." Let me repeat: Jesus will come again, this time in glory and majesty. Keep this truth in mind when the going is rough. It will be a lamp to light your way through the dark night until the morning star appears and the coming of dawn brings light to your heart.

To Jesus be glory.

Adapted from 2 Peter 1:12–19

After the students have guessed, tell them that this is adapted from Second Peter, written while he was in prison. Then guide them to see that Peter used the Transfiguration event to give courage to suffering Christians.

Aug. 11 Saint Clare

Clare was born in 1194 into a wealthy family of Assisi, Italy. As a teenager, she became aware that Francis, the wealthy leader of the young in Assisi, had changed.

He used to spend a great deal of money having a good time and treating others to a good time. Now, he had no money, no possessions, and no family. He dressed in a brown robe, begged for food, and lived on the streets. Yet he seemed to enjoy life more than ever. Clare was puzzled. Gradually, she saw that the real source of his joy and inner peace was his living in poverty with Jesus. In 1211, Clare left home to join Francis. He cut off her long hair, gave her a rough woolen habit to wear, and took her to stay for a while with the Benedictine sisters. Francis found a little house near San Damiano Church. Clare moved into it, and he guided her in beginning a new religious order.

This community wanted to live according to the rule of Francis. They slept on the floor, went barefoot, kept silence much of the day, and spent hours in prayer. They ate only when food was donated because they had no money. Clare became abbess, the head of this community. But she did not spend her time giving orders. She chose the hardest work to do herself. Her example inspired the others to trust in God. In 1240, and again in 1241, the convent and the whole city were threatened by an invasion of the Saracens. Clare told her sisters not to be afraid, but to trust in Jesus. She prayed to Jesus in the Blessed Sacrament to save his people. Both times the convent and city were spared.

Clare died on August 11, 1253, after 27 years of illness. Today her sisters are called the Poor Clares. They continue to radiate the joy and peace that come from living in poverty like Jesus.

Suggestions

+ Have the students research contemplative religious, especially the Poor Clares. They might present what a typical day is like for a nun in the monastery.

+ Have the students reflect on the following questions:

  • Where is there silence in my life?

  • How do I feel when there is silence?

  Discuss why some people love silence and others fill up every moment with music or other sounds.

Aug. 15 Assumption of Mary

God, who created human life, gives it value. Jesus gave his life on the Cross to redeem each individual human person. By doing this, Jesus stated, "Your life is worth my dying to save you." Through his own Resurrection, Jesus showed us the glory of our resurrection. Jesus promised that the body and soul of a person, separated at death, will be joined together again in glory at the Last Judgment. The person will be whole for all eternity. The feast of Mary's Assumption is a preview of what our lives will be. Mary was assumed, or taken up into heaven body and soul. She did not have to wait for the end of the world. God granted her this privilege because she was the Mother of God.

The Church has always believed in Mary's assumption into heaven. But on November 1, 1950, Pope Pius XII focused attention on the Assumption of Mary as a dogma and mystery of our faith. This mystery shows us that God wants every human person, body and soul, to be in glory forever, just as Mary is now. This dogma shows the importance of every human life. Pope Pius XII hoped that by thinking about Mary's Assumption, people all over the world would develop a deeper respect for their own lives and their own bodies. He also hoped that people would grow in that same respect for the lives of others.

Suggestions

+ Review the Glorious Mysteries of the Rosary on page 186 in the student book. [See page T372.]

+ Since the last part of the sixth century, the Eastern Catholic Churches have celebrated the feast of the Dormition of Mary, which led to our feast of the Assumption. The Dormition means the "falling asleep of Mary" at the end of her earthly life. Tell the students that Mary's peaceful crossing over from earthly life to heavenly life is due to Jesus, who died to free her and all of us from the power of death.

Aug. 16 Saint Stephen of Hungary

The people who settled near the Danube River in Europe in the 10th century were a violent and superstitious people. Often one of these tribes would invade a part of western Europe, destroying and stealing. The tribes often fought among themselves.

The national leader of these people was Géza. When Géza's son, Vajk, was born, people expected the boy to take his father's place as leader of this area called Hungary. Then Géza and his son learned about Jesus Christ and were baptized. Vajk received Stephen as his baptismal name. As a young adult, Stephen married a girl named Gisela, whose brother became the future emperor Henry II. When Géza died, Stephen had to lead the country. He wanted all the Hungarian people to become Christians. First, he asked Pope Sylvester II if he could be a king instead of a national leader like his father. The pope agreed and sent a special crown, which can be seen today in Budapest. On Christmas Day, in A.D. 1000, Stephen was crowned the first king of Hungary. Then, as king, he brought the various tribes into one nation.

Stephen invited the Benedictine monks of Germany and Italy to come as missionaries to his people. He built churches and had them decorated with sculptures, mosaics, and murals depicting truths of the Catholic faith. He encouraged the people to come to the churches and to value their local priests.

Stephen was very popular with those who were poor. He often went among them, giving donations. One time the crowd of beggars became so excited that they knocked the king to the ground. But Stephen laughed and assured them that he would continue to share his wealth with them. Stephen's love for those who were poor also kept his officials from getting too powerful and abusing those in need.

Stephen counted on his son Emeric to take his place as king when he died. He is believed to have written *Mirror of Princes* in order to explain to his son how to be a good Christian king. However, young Emeric was killed in a hunting accident, and Stephen faced many family quarrels over who should be the next king. Finally, in 1038, he died and was buried at the Church of Our Lady of Buda in Hungary. Stephen is the patron saint of Hungary.

Suggestions

✦ Read aloud the following selection from the *Mirror of Princes:*

> **Be humble in this life, that God may raise you up in the next. Be truly moderate and do not punish or condemn anyone immoderately. Be gentle so that you may never oppose justice. Be honorable so that you may never voluntarily bring disgrace on anyone. Be chaste so that you may avoid all the foulness of lust like the pangs of death. All these virtues I have noted above make up the royal crown, and without them no one is fit to rule here on Earth or attain to the heavenly kingdom.**

Read the section again and have the students write in their reflection notebooks one idea from it that they think would be good advice for themselves.

✦ Review the names of local and national leaders. Discuss the Christian qualities these leaders need. Lead the students in a litany for these officials, asking God for a special quality that these leaders will need. The response might be "Bless our leaders, Lord."

Aug. 22 Queenship of Mary

In 1954, Pope Pius XII declared a feast day honoring Mary's queenship. The idea of Mary's royalty is already expressed within the feast of the Assumption on August 15. The title of queen is one of the oldest titles given to Mary. When Elizabeth spoke of Mary as "'. . . the mother of my Lord'" (Luke 1:43), she was using the words that mean "queen-mother" in the Old Testament.

Jesus is the Lord and King of heaven and earth. So Mary, who was chosen by the Father, was filled with the Holy Spirit, and was made the Mother of Christ, can be considered a queen. Like a queen, she stood at the Cross on Calvary, supporting her kingly son's sacrifice with her love, faith, and obedience.

Mary's power as queen is manifested in the tenderness of a loving mother who cares for her children. Saint Bernard, who had a great devotion to Mary, wrote:

> In dangers, in doubts, in difficulties, think of Mary, call upon Mary . . . with her for guide, you shall never go astray; while invoking her, you shall never lose heart; so long as she is in your mind, you are safe from deception; while she holds your hand, you cannot fall; under her protection you have nothing to fear . . .

Suggestions

✦ Tell the students about Knute Rockne, one of the greatest college football coaches and a convert to Catholicism. Rockne, who made the forward pass popular, was known for giving University of Notre Dame football teams the ideals of sportsmanship and fortitude. He was killed in a plane accident in 1931. When the rescuers found his body, he had a rosary clutched in his hand. Have interested students learn more about this man and his appreciation for Mary and for the Catholic faith.

✦ Have the students research some of the Marian apparitions such as Fatima and Lourdes. Direct them to learn about what Mary's message was and how it applies to the world today.

Aug. 24 Saint Bartholomew

In the Gospels of Matthew and Luke, Bartholomew is one of the twelve apostles called by Jesus. Mark's Gospel states that Bartholomew is one of the twelve apostles appointed to be Jesus' companions to preach and to cast out devils. In the Acts of the Apostles, Bartholomew is on the list of people who are in the upper room in Jerusalem, waiting for the Holy Spirit. John alone does not mention Bartholomew. John does, however, list a person named Nathanael as an apostle. Some scholars feel that Bartholomew and Nathanael are the same person. If this is so, then John's Gospel gives us an account of Bartholomew's first meeting with Jesus.

According to John, Philip was so excited about meeting Jesus that he asked his friend Nathanael to come to meet him. Nathanael, who was from Cana, was disrespectful when he heard that Jesus was from Nazareth. He thought that Nazareth was unimportant and that nothing good could be produced there. Philip did not argue. Philip told Nathanael to come and see for himself.

On seeing Nathanael, Jesus told him that he was a man without deceit in his heart. "How could Jesus make a snap decision about my personality?" Nathanael must have thought. When Nathanael realized that Jesus knew him in a very deep way, he began to praise Jesus as the real Messiah. After Pentecost, Bartholomew became a missionary going to foreign lands. Armenians honor him as the apostle of their country.

Suggestion

Have the students take up a mission collection and pray this prayer for those who are needy in the missions:

Those who are poor in the missions are not abandoned, Lord. They are just waiting. Waiting for us who know you to know them, too: to see you in them, to love you in them, to call them brother and sister, to share our faith with them. Those who are poor in the missions are not abandoned, Lord. They are just waiting. Help me to do my part so that they need not wait too long.

Aug. 27 Saint Monica

Through her life, Monica shows us how faithfully God answers prayers. She was born in Tagaste, Numidia, in Africa, around 322. She and her sisters were raised by an elderly servant. This wise woman had also raised Monica's father.

Monica was married to a non-Christian official named Patricius. They had at least three children: Navigus, Perpetua, and Augustine, who became a saint. Patricius had a terrible temper. Monica learned to be patient and wait for the right moment to discuss matters with him. By her constant forgiveness and love, she hoped to draw her husband to Christ. Before he died, Patricius was baptized a Christian. Because she and her husband seemed to get along so well, other wives asked Monica for advice.

Because of rumors spread by unhappy servants, Monica's mother-in-law turned against her during the early part of her marriage. Using the same patient forgiveness, Monica was able to win her cooperation. Another source of worry for her was her son, Augustine. He was not yet baptized. Monica tried to penetrate the barrier that seemed to exist between her and her teenage son. She once attempted a dangerous ocean voyage in order to advise him. She prayed and fasted for him. She even tried to convince the local bishop to speak to her son. But the bishop told Monica, "Not yet. He is not ready and would not listen." But he did promise her, "Surely the son of so many tears will not perish."

Clinging to these comforting words, Monica never gave up, but prayed and sacrificed year after year. Slowly, Augustine did change. With the help of the Holy Spirit, he began to realize that God loved him. When he finally gained the courage to be baptized, his mother was the first person he told. In the fall of 387, after his Baptism, Augustine planned to return to Tagaste with his mother, but she died at Ostia where they were waiting to embark to Africa. Their last conversation together was a beautiful sharing of longing for heaven.

Suggestions

✦ Have the students work in groups to design a video entitled "Famous Women in the Church." Have them select at least seven women, including two or three from recent history.

✦ Have the students write letters of appreciation to their mothers on the feast of Saint Monica. Encourage them to offer spontaneous prayers for their mothers and all mothers.

Aug. 29 Martyrdom of Saint John the Baptist

As a youth, John had gone into the desert to fast and pray in order to learn what God wanted him to do. Then one day, he began to walk along the Jordan River, preaching, "Turn from your sins, repent and live for God."

Fearlessly, John jolted people into facing their own behavior. Sometimes he even pointed out their sins. Always he gave them hope and the challenge to live according to God's Law. He told people to be honest and loving, to avoid violence, and to do their jobs well. As a sign of their repentance, the people would confess their sins and John would baptize them in the Jordan River.

When Herod Antipas chose adultery, John publicly told him of the evil of taking another man's wife. Herodias, the brother's wife, wanted to kill John because she was so angry with him. But Herod Antipas admired John for his courageous honesty, but he was too weak to change his life. Instead, he imprisoned John so he could no longer influence people against the king.

As entertainment for a huge banquet Herod gave on his birthday, Salome, Herodias's daughter, danced. Herod was so impressed that he promised to give the girl whatever she wanted. Her mother persuaded her to ask for the head of John the Baptist on a platter. Herod Antipas was too embarrassed to admit before his guests that he had made a foolish promise. He had John executed and his head brought in on a platter.

Suggestions

✦ Have a student read aloud Luke 3:3–18. Then tell the students to write advice John might give to a banker, a doctor, a busy housewife, a factory worker, or a person in another career.

✦ Have volunteers read aloud the Scripture passages that tell what John said about Jesus: Mark 1:7–8; John 1:29–34; John 3:28–30. Then have a volunteer read what Jesus said about John: Luke 7:24–30.

✦ Have the students write a monologue of what John might have thought while he was alone in prison.

The Catechist's Handbook

The Vocation of a Catechist

Jesus said these words to his disciples: "Go, therefore, and make disciples of all nations, baptizing them in the name of the Father, and of the Son, and of the holy Spirit, teaching them to observe all that I have commanded you. And behold, I am with you always, until the end of the age." (Matthew 28:19–20) Jesus' call is the Church's mission and identity. Each one of us—laity, ordained clergy, or religious—responds to Jesus' invitation in his or her own way.

Catechesis (from the Greek word meaning "to echo the teaching") is the Church's ministry of teaching and forming people in faith. Our vocation as catechists opens us to grow in our own faith. Knowing that God is with us always, we freely accept the responsibility of personal conversion and of mentoring others to find a deeper, more personal relationship with God.

As catechists, we assist pastors and bishops in guiding people to a living faith. We follow God's call to be disciples of Jesus and to proclaim his Good News through our words and actions. We grow in a deeper understanding of our faith and explore what it means to live as Catholics. We share in the community of the Church more fully by sharing with others what we know as people of faith. This handbook is your companion on this mission. It will help you to grow in your own faith and to understand the hope that Jesus' message brings to the world. It will be your guide to help you effectively pass on the Catholic faith to others.

Qualities of an Effective Catechist

As catechists, we long to share the truth and beauty of our faith, yet, we worry about our human limitations. As we grow as catechists, we realize that sharing our faith and humanity makes our work personal and authentic. Each catechist shares faith in a unique way. Effective catechists have these qualities in common:

✧ a desire to grow in and share our faith

✧ an awareness of God's grace and the desire to respond to that grace

✧ a commitment to the Church's liturgical and sacramental life and moral teachings

✧ a strength of character built on patience, responsibility, confidence, and creativity

✧ a generosity of spirit, a respect for diversity, and a habit of hospitality and inclusion

Knowledge and Skills of a Catechist

Nothing in life prepares us to be catechists as fully as our life experience as faith-filled adults. As catechists, we yearn for the knowledge and skills that will help us gently nurture students to cultivate a lifelong relationship with God and the Church. We ground our efforts as catechists in these fundamentals:

✧ a basic understanding of Catholic teaching, Scripture, and Catholic Tradition

✧ honest and caring relationships with students

✧ effective teaching techniques and strategies

Christ Our Life offers background and preparation in Church teaching, Scripture and Tradition, prayerful reflection, and chapter presentation support.

As catechists, we share our faith with students and accompany them on their faith journey. We care for and support them as they grow in their own personal relationship with God and with the Catholic Church. We guide them in their faith formation by teaching the truths of the Catholic faith, by being a model of Christian life, by praying with them, by calling them to service of others, and by giving them opportunities to discuss their learning with us and with one another.

Seventh graders

✦ *pursue authenticity.*

✦ *behave inconsistently.*

✦ *challenge authority.*

✦ *seek identity.*

✦ *question faith.*

Cognitive

◇ are capable of logical and abstract thinking based on concrete examples

◇ can reflect on the past; need ideals and goals

◇ begin to be self-directed; seek to be themselves and act on their own convictions

◇ are ready for a more mature approach to life, religion, and redemption

Affective

◇ can be awkward and inconsistent as they formulate their self-image

◇ appear confident, yet question their own judgments

◇ need a holistic, Catholic approach to human sexuality

◇ tend toward hero worship and seek models to imitate

Moral

◇ begin to face choices for which their decisions may have serious moral consequences; are keenly sensitive to right and wrong

◇ notice the gap between moral conduct and Christian faith among adults; may rebel against all authority

◇ because of sexual development, may feel tension in conscience formation

◇ may try to escape rather than endure attempts at self-expression

Social

◇ experience fluctuating moods and strong emotional stress; need support in their struggle to be responsible and adult

◇ withdraw to some degree from family; are critical and challenge adult authority

◇ seek peer approval and are eager to have friends, belong to a group, and be accepted

◇ can give more varied forms of service and need to be challenged to generosity

Faith

◇ seek independence by dissent regarding basic values

◇ begin to discern by doubting, questioning, and challenging faith

◇ need to disagree with adult authority and reject childhood notions of God, faith, Church, and society

◇ seek to understand matters of faith on a deeper level

> *" . . . the catechist must take into consideration all the human factors of a particular age level in order to present the Gospel message in a vital and compelling way."*
>
> *National Directory for Catechesis, 48*

Faith

The seventh-grade program, *Jesus the Way, the Truth, and the Life*, of the *Christ Our Life* series draws students to believe more deeply in Jesus and to commit themselves to him through a study of his life and his loving action in the sacraments today.

Prayer

The seventh-grade program uses a variety of prayer forms to lead young people to open their hearts to the Lord. While the importance of liturgical prayer and daily personal prayer is developed, the students also learn the rich heritage of traditional Catholic prayers. Likewise, they are guided in using the Bible, especially the Gospels, as a source of prayer.Meditation and contemplation are introduced in age-appropriate forms, aiding them toward a reflective, integrated response to life and the presence of God.Communal prayer—within the family, among peers, and with the larger parish community—is developed further through celebrations, suggested activities, and planning sessions. Spontaneous and shared prayer are encouraged during communal prayer time.

Liturgical Life

The catechesis offered in *Jesus the Way, the Truth, and the Life* prepares young adolescents for fuller and more active participation in liturgy. It leads them to a deeper understanding of how they share in the mystery of Christ and his Church and how they can minister to both the community of faith and to the whole world. The program includes catechesis on the liturgical year, the Lectionary, and the liturgical seasons and feasts of the Church year. The Special Seasons and Lessons and the Saints and Feast Days sections provide catechesis on some of the primary celebrations of the Church.

The seventh-grade program helps the students to

- develop a deeper relationship with God and with the community of believers, especially within the parish.
- celebrate the Eucharist in union with Christ and participate actively in this celebration.
- see the value in giving and seeking forgiveness.
- accept sickness, healing, suffering, and death as mysteries demanding Christian care and concern.
- develop the unselfish love that is needed for happy family life and that will lead to more generous concern for the global community.
- become leaders in liturgical prayer by acquainting them with its foundations and structure.
- lead a spiritual life nourished in the sacraments.
- appreciate Christian ritual and symbolism.

Morality

Jesus the Way, the Truth, and the Life helps young adolescents establish a value system based on union with Christ in the Christian community. They are offered guidance and opportunities to choose what will help them live according to the Spirit. The students learn that God has gifted them with freedom to choose good and avoid evil. They see that God respects the creatures he has formed and the gifts he has bestowed on them. Always inviting them to himself, God nonetheless calls them continually to conversion of life and deep union.

The seventh-grade program helps adolescents to

- appreciate God's constant, unconditional, and unfailing love for each person and develop sensitivity and respect for the human rights of all people.
- learn to deal positively with mistakes and failures.
- respect themselves and others and support all that improves the quality of life.
- see the wisdom and value of living the Beatitudes.
- realize that self-discipline and sacrifice are necessary in order for them to remain true to Catholic teaching about the sacredness of each person.
- understand sexuality as a treasured gift for which they have responsibility.
- value their unique capacity for developing meaningful, responsible relationships.
- analyze their motives and determine whether their actions are genuinely Christian.
- learn to make decisions by praying to the Holy Spirit and by reflecting on the principles involved, their Catholic heritage, and their covenantal relationship with God and with others.
- understand the influence their peers have on responsible decision making; cultivate attitudes and habits to help them deal with such influences.
- discover that deep love of God nourishes and supports a moral life and full human development.

Social Justice and Service

Following Christ requires a spirit of loving concern for all people, beginning with family members and then reaching out to others. Catechists have a duty to develop this global awareness in their students.

The plans and activities in the lessons promote care and respect for both friend and stranger, and especially those in need. Students are encouraged not only to become involved in service projects, but also to actively seek out ways to be of service. They are encouraged to live the values of peace, mercy, and love on all levels.

The Catechist's spiritual life enables him or her to know that he or she is God's instrument in the mission "to make disciples of all nations." Catechists water the seed planted by evangelists, but God gives the growth. Their life in the Holy Spirit renews them continually as members of the community of believers in their specific identity as catechists.

National Directory for Catechesis, 56

Growing as a Catechist

Accompanied by the Holy Spirit, catechists strive to accomplish six tasks in their ministry as described in the *National Directory for Catechesis* (#20):

1. To promote knowledge of the faith
2. To promote a knowledge of the meaning of the Liturgy and the sacraments
3. To promote moral formation in Jesus Christ
4. To teach the Christian how to pray with Christ
5. To prepare the Christian to live in community and to participate actively in the life and mission of the Church
6. To promote a missionary spirit that prepares the faithful to be present as Christians in society

Catechists recognize that they need to keep growing, both in spiritual formation and in knowledge and skills, so they are able to pass on the faith to the next generation of Catholics. Catechists strive to

✧ know the teaching of the Magisterium by attending workshops, seminars, courses, and by reading Catholic publications.

✧ become more familiar with the Bible.

✧ nurture their personal prayer and sacramental life.

✧ increase their awareness of the Church's identity as missionary.

✧ educate students in community and global concerns.

✧ seek, implement, and remediate teaching lessons and strategies.

Your Role in Building a Faith Community

Every catechist serves as a vital link between the school or parish and home. Consider the following ideas as you plan for the year.

✧ Establish routine methods of communication with parents and family members.

✧ Invite families to participate in class and at-home activities.

✧ Relay your belief that you value parents as the primary influencers in their child's religious education.

✧ Familiarize yourself with parish and diocesan guidelines for catechetical programs.

✧ Cultivate a warm and cooperative relationship with the school principal, DRE, other teachers and catechists, and students.

✧ Help make the parish a focal point by cooperating in grade-level planning and projects.

✧ Participate in meetings and prayer services for catechists.

✧ Participate in opportunities for spiritual enrichment.

A Catechist's Code of Ethics

Catechists choose to nurture students' faith in words and deed. Catechists strive to display ethical behavior by

✧ speaking respectfully to and about others.

✧ preparing thoroughly for lessons.

✧ observing confidentiality, using information about students or their families prudently.

✧ informing the program director or principal immediately with concerns about students' physical, social, mental, or emotional health.

✧ developing teaching strategies that include students with special needs.

✧ responding to the needs of students of various cultures.

✧ displaying character built on patience, responsibility, creativity, generosity of spirit, respect for diversity, and a habit of hospitality.

✧ affirming and protecting each child with acceptance, humor, and gentle redirection.

Ongoing Self-Improvement

As a catechist, you are a minister of the Word of God. Every student hopes to see and hear the love of Jesus reflected in your facial expressions, your voice, and your very life. If you are receptive to God each day, if you take time to ponder his Word and deepen your relationship with God, if you are convinced of the power of the Gospel message, then the students in your class will hear the Lord reveal the mystery of his love through you. You will discover that as you share your faith, you are personally enriched. Reflect on the following questions periodically to examine your effectiveness as a catechist and to determine areas that need improvement.

✦ Do I present each faith message with the conviction, joy, love, enthusiasm, and hope that comes from commitment to Christ?

✦ Do I pray for inspiration to understand what I am teaching and to know how to present God's Word authentically and persuasively?

✦ Do I reflect on Scripture as part of my preparation for each lesson?

✦ Do I prepare materials before class?

✦ Do I share my heart, my spirit, and my personal faith story as I impart the Christian message?

✦ Do I lead the students in prayer during class? Do I use a variety of prayer forms?

✦ Am I sensitive to the individual needs of the students?

✦ Have I maintained communication with parents?

A catechist is

✦ *confident, but dependent on God.*

✦ *knowledgeable, but open to children's ideas.*

✦ *efficient, but relaxed.*

✦ *spiritual, but practical.*

✦ *businesslike, but caring.*

✦ *enthusiastic, but calm.*

✦ Do I evaluate each lesson and adjust my plans accordingly?

✦ Do I take steps to grow in faith?

✦ Do I show my commitment to the Church's liturgical and sacramental life and moral teachings?

✦ Do I build safe and respectful relationships with students?

✦ Do I participate in training that supports the protection of students?

The catechist is an educator who facilitates maturation of the faith which catechumens and those being catechized obtain with the help of the Holy Spirit . . . . As with any other art the most important factor is that the catechist should acquire his own style of imparting catechesis by adapting the general principles of catechetical pedagogy to his own personality.

General Directory for Catechesis, 244

Prepare the Learning Space

✦ Arrange an attractive prayer center with a Bible, a flameless candle, and other sacred symbols.

✦ Display pictures related to the message of the lesson.

✦ Play reflective music as the students enter.

✦ Display the students' drawings or projects.

✦ Arrange comfortable seating for students.

✦ Note whether light, heat, and ventilation are adequate.

Establish a Climate for Growth

✦ Address the students by name. Learn how to correctly spell and pronounce their names.

✦ Be calm in your manner, reverent in your gestures, and joyful in your presentation.

✦ Express care and interest in students' families, hobbies, sports, interests, and jobs.

✦ Listen to what students are saying verbally and nonverbally. Be eager to understand their fears, worries, plans, stories—even their complaints.

✦ Speak in a well-modulated voice, loud enough for everyone to hear, but soft enough to convey the wonder of the message you share.

✦ Write short, positive notes of encouragement on the students' papers, such as "Sounds good," "I agree," and "I'd like to hear more about your idea," or just "Yes."

✦ See the students as individuals. Try not to generalize, but see each child as gifted by God.

✦ Use frequent eye contact so each child feels you are speaking personally to him or her.

✦ Be sensitive to the students' responses during presentations.

✦ Ask to display or keep the students' work. This is a great form of affirmation.

✦ Ask for the students' help. Everyone likes to be needed.

✦ Love your work. Teaching is hard work, but it is also a privilege. Show students you like teaching because you like them. More importantly, love your work as a person who shares the work of Jesus the Teacher.

✦ Respect and adapt lessons for special needs, multicultural awareness, or learning styles.

✦ Model good manners, respect, and gratitude.

Maintain a Healthy Classroom Discipline

✦ Prepare all materials, such as audiovisuals, before class so you are ready to greet students as they arrive.

✦ Establish procedures and policies on the first day so that the students know exactly what behavior is expected.

✦ Have only a few rules, but enforce them fairly, kindly, and consistently.

✦ Limit discipline problems by thoroughly preparing for lessons.

✦ Speak and act with confidence.

✦ Have the students keep their books closed and materials away until needed.

✦ Phrase directions and corrections positively. For example, instead of saying, "Don't leave a mess," say "Be a good steward. Pick up after yourself."

✦ Vary activities to hold the students' attention and to meet different learning styles.

✦ Involve the students in the lesson. Don't do for them what they can do for themselves.

✦ Be observant and responsive while you are teaching.

✦ Expect, encourage, and acknowledge good behavior.

✦ When a problem arises, use a pleasant but firm tone of voice. Keep calm and avoid becoming angry. This will help you win over rather than antagonize the child.

✦ Encourage self-discipline. Motivate students. Offer incentives and rewards when appropriate.

✦ Address disruptive behavior calmly. Speak with the child after class.

✦ In cooperation with your program director or principal, enlist the help of parents, aides, or other volunteers.

✦ Pray daily with the students.

The Catechist's Reference Book

The *Catechism of the Catholic Church* is a marvelous tool for catechists. It provides information that can be useful in preparing lesson plans, and it also serves as a reference book. Each chapter in the *Christ Our Life* series includes references to paragraphs in the *Catechism* that are related to it.

Note, however, that the *Catechism* is not intended to be used as a student textbook.

A Message for Catechists

In addition to being an authoritative source of our faith, the *Catechism of the Catholic Church* speaks specifically to catechists in paragraphs 426–429. Our mission statement, goal, and job description appear under the heading "At the heart of catechesis: Christ."

Paragraph 426 states, "At the heart of catechesis we find, in essence, a Person, the Person of Jesus of Nazareth, the only Son from the Father . . . who suffered and died for us and who now, after rising, is living with us forever." To catechize is "to reveal in the Person of Christ the whole of God's eternal design reaching fulfillment in that Person. It is to seek to understand the meaning of Christ's actions and words and of the signs worked by him." Only Christ "can lead us to the love of the Father in the Spirit and make us share in the life of the Holy Trinity."

Our call as catechists is to bring people to the Person of Jesus Christ, who lives and who is with us and who loves us. Religion class is not just another class but a community of faith journeying together, sharing faith in Jesus Christ, and growing in faith. Religion class is not just a gathering of information but a forming of disciples—changing lives to be more Christlike.

Seven Essential Messages

Seven essential messages from the *Catechism* are listed here together with their paragraphs for reading and reflection:

131–133	**Teach Scripture.** By reading it, we learn "the surpassing knowledge of Jesus Christ."
282	**Teach creation.** It is of major importance because it concerns the very foundations of both human and Christian life.
426–429	**Teach Christ.** Put people in communion with him.
1072	**Teach liturgy.** In the sacraments, especially in the Eucharist, Christ Jesus works in fullness for our transformation.
1697	**Teach the way of Christ.** Reveal the joy and the demands of the way of Christ.
1917	**Teach hope.** "[T]he future of humanity is in the hands of those who are capable of providing the generations to come with reasons for life and optimism."
2663	**Teach prayer.** Explain its meaning, always in relation to Jesus Christ.

Art

 Throughout history, faith has been expressed in painting and sculpture. Art is a concrete expression of a person's thoughts and feelings. When students see their inner religious thoughts and feelings expressed visually, they can grow spiritually. Art helps them become more aware of religious concepts and relates the messages they have heard to their own lives.

✧ Give clear directions. Provide a sample.

✧ Create a quiet, reflective atmosphere by playing appropriate background music as your students work. Encourage them to think about what they have just experienced or learned.

✧ Give the students who wish to do so an opportunity to talk about their work.

✧ Display the work at the students' eye level so that it can be appreciated.

Celebrations

Celebrations can be powerful learning experiences. Song, prayer, Scripture, ritual, and symbols draw the students more deeply into the message of the lesson. Through the communal prayers and private reflections in the celebrations, the students enter more deeply into the mystery of faith and come to appreciate liturgical elements. The impressions that celebrations make on the students justify the time, preparation, and practice that they entail.

✧ Create an atmosphere of beauty, reverence, peace, and prayer through the use of candles, flowers or plants, cloth, religious art, music, and symbols.

✧ Make sure that the students are prepared for what to do and say during the celebration.

✧ Practice the songs used.

✧ Encourage the students to make the celebration a prayer. Suggest that they offer it for an intention.

✧ Allow the students to choose their roles. Have them take turns.

✧ Use simple props and costumes.

✧ Prepare the performers sufficiently.

✧ Put signs on the participants for identification.

✧ Accept the students' interpretations and affirm their efforts. However, if their interpretations lack insight, guide them to a deeper understanding.

✧ Discuss the activity in the light of Catholic values.

Dramatization

Dramatization effectively reinforces the Christian message, helps students internalize it, and enables them to apply religious truths to daily life.

✧ Maintain an atmosphere of security and seriousness to help give the students self-confidence. Use role-playing only when the students are comfortable with one another.

Games

Playing games is not only fun for the students, but also contributes to their development in many ways. Games provide practice in mental, physical, and social skills, offer opportunities for problem solving and creativity, stimulate imagination, and increase attention spans.

- ✧ Explain the game clearly and simply. Establish ground rules.
- ✧ Have several groups play a game to allow the students to have more turns.
- ✧ Replay the students' favorite games.

Group Discussions

Discussions help the students assimilate, clarify, and understand concepts. Discussions provide the students with opportunities to articulate their faith, to grow in appreciation and understanding of others, and to develop skill in expressing their own opinions.

- ✧ Write the topic on the board.
- ✧ Divide the students into groups. Try to keep the groups small—no more than four or five students in each. Appoint a leader or have the students in each group choose one.
- ✧ Remind the students of the rules for discussion.
  1. Speak quietly.
  2. Speak one at a time.
  3. Stick to the topic.
  4. Contribute to the discussion.
- ✧ Set a time limit. Circulate and give suggestions.
- ✧ Ask leaders to stand and speak slowly, loudly, and clearly when giving reports.
- ✧ Praise the students' efforts.

Group Projects

As the students work together to reach a common goal, qualities needed in community are fostered: consideration, understanding, cooperation, patience, initiative, and responsibility. Small-group activities afford the students an experience of interdependence and provide a welcome change from the classroom routine.

- ✧ Explain the directions clearly. You may wish to write them on the board for the students to reference.
- ✧ Show interest in the groups' work by encouraging them, offering suggestions, and asking questions.
- ✧ Make sure that all the students are participating.

Memorization

Knowledge of certain elements of Catholic belief is best acquired by memorizing them. Pope John Paul II pointed out that "the blossoms . . . of faith and piety do not grow in the desert places of a memoryless catechesis. What is essential is that the texts that are memorized must at the same time be taken in and gradually understood in depth, in order to become a source of Christian life on the personal level and the community level." (*On Catechesis in Our Time*, 55)

- ✧ Students should understand the material they are memorizing.
- ✧ Acknowledge the students' success by charting their progress.
- ✧ Integrate memorized material into the lessons in meaningful ways.
- ✧ Set an example by memorizing the material first.

Prayer

Prayer opens the students' hearts to God's message. It gives them the time and space they need to reflect on God's words and the meaning the words have for their lives. Most important, it provides an avenue for God to touch their lives and change them by love.

✧ Be a person of prayer yourself, and share your own prayer life with the students as appropriate.

✧ Respect each students' needs. Some students will feel comfortable praying aloud and spontaneously. Others will prefer to pray silently. Show respect and appreciation for the various ways to pray.

✧ Prepare the students for prayer experiences by providing time for them to settle down and focus on God. Teach them to adopt a posture that is conducive to prayer.

✧ Give students opportunities to lead the class in prayer.

✧ Create an attractive prayer center. Place in the prayer center a Bible, a crucifix, a banner, a candle, religious statues, or pictures related to the feast, season, or topic of study. Gather the students in the prayer center on a regular basis. Encourage them to use the area for personal prayer. Suggest that they have their families arrange similar prayer centers in their homes.

Questions

Posing questions is an effective technique, used often by Jesus, for guiding students to truth.

✧ Address questions to the entire class before calling on a student to answer.

✧ Be comfortable with the silence during which students are reflecting on a question and how to answer it. Don't rush the students into answering.

✧ Call on every student in the class, not just the same few time and time again.

✧ Vary the type of questions, from simple recall to those that require some thought. Challenge the students to defend their answers.

Storytelling

Through Bible stories and stories from the lives of Christians, we can share the heritage of our faith. Storytelling can also be used to share one's personal faith. Sharing one's faith journey gives witness to the faith. Both forms of storytelling deepen the students' understanding of Jesus and their relationship with him.

❖ Make a story your own by adapting it to your students and to your message.

❖ Practice telling the story using facial expressions, animated gestures, and expression in your voice for effect and emphasis.

❖ Use visuals to enhance the telling, such as pictures, puppets, or a flannel board.

❖ Relate personally to each student when telling a story. Establish eye contact with individuals and be sensitive to how each is responding to the story.

❖ Let the story speak for itself. Its message may be less effective if you moralize.

Audiovisuals/Technology

Audiovisuals (DVDs, videotapes, slides, PowerPoint, CDs, audiotapes, and the Internet) can lead the students to a deeper appreciation of the message in each chapter.

❖ Preview any audiovisual elements and their accompanying guides. Determine whether they are appropriate for your lesson and your class. Decide how you will use them—to introduce a subject or to review it.

❖ Think about how to introduce the audiovisual presentation. Give adequate background information to your students. Tell them what to look for, focusing attention on the main purpose for viewing.

❖ Plan discussion questions and/or activities to follow the presentation.

❖ Introduce new vocabulary and concepts before showing the audiovisual element.

❖ After the presentation, provide time for quiet reflection and/or written response.

❖ Use a slideshow presentation to lead a guided meditation, inviting students to reflect on inspirational images set to reflective music.

❖ Make an outline of a lesson as a visual aid, emphasizing highlights of the lesson. Project the outline on a transparency or slide. Encourage students to copy the outline into their notes to use as study guides.

❖ Project questions or a puzzle for students to discuss and answer.

❖ Use an overhead projector or a slide show presentation to enlarge or display maps and pictures.

Bulletin Boards

An effective bulletin-board display is simple, timely, and catches people's attention. A well-planned bulletin board that has unity, with emphasis on the more important elements, a balanced arrangement, and movement (or flow) can be educational as well as attractive. It is an easily understood teaching aid.

❖ Think of a caption that draws attention, such as a question, a three-dimensional device, a current idiom, or "big" or stylized words.

❖ Create an overall effect to hold interest.

❖ Plan the movement of the board. Displays are usually viewed left to right, top to bottom. Figures of people and animals draw attention. Repeat shapes, textures, and colors—or related variations—for unity.

❖ Achieve balance, which can be symmetrical or asymmetrical. For informal balance, use two or more small shapes with a larger one, a small colorful shape with a larger dull one, a small shape near the bottom with a larger shape near the top, or a small eye-catching shape with a larger common shape.

❖ Make objects touch one another, or connect them with yarn, paper, or colored lines. An odd number of items is better than an even number.

❖ Use wallpaper, wrapping paper, construction paper, shelf paper, velour, felt, or burlap as a background for letters and pictures.

❖ Arrange the students' papers so that they can be easily seen; never place one on top of another.

Literature

Books are one of the most effective tools for shaping attitudes and imparting values. They help the students discover meaning in life. Through stories the students come to understand themselves and others, and they learn to relate to others and to their world in a better way. Good literature presents the readers with basic human problems and helps them understand how to deal with them. It reinforces the Christian message presented in class and helps students apply Christian principles to their lives. Jesus was conscious of the power of stories and used them in his teaching.

◇ Describe a book in class.

◇ Incorporate an incident from a book into a lesson.

◇ Hold up a copy of the book when you talk about it.

◇ Assign books for the students to read and report on.

Music

Music can set the mood for certain lessons and predisposes the students to receive God's message. Besides introducing the lesson, music can be used to review and reinforce the message of a lesson. It can serve as a prayer, before or after class. Music unites the group, provides an enjoyable opportunity for self-expression, and stirs up feelings of love and loyalty to Christ and his Church. Both singing and listening to music have power to open hearts to the Lord.

◇ As you teach a song, consider the following steps:

1. Give a general introduction and ask the students to listen to the song.

2. Have them listen again for specific ideas. Discuss difficult lyrics.

3. Have them sing the song softly or hum along with it as you sing or play it.

◇ Ask the students to sing with enthusiasm and make the song a prayer. Suggest that they think about the meaning of the song and sing with all their hearts.

◇ Invite the students to add gestures or interpretive dance steps.

◇ If you lack musical talent, find ways to compensate. For example, use recorded music or invite the assistance of a member of the community.

◇ Encourage the students to sing spontaneous original songs. Guide them by creating your own.

Pictures and Visuals

The icons of the Eastern Churches are treasured because of their power to sweep us up to God. Stained-glass windows have been a medium of religious instruction for centuries. Similarly, pictures such as art masterpieces and the photos and illustrations in the student book can influence the students' response to the catechesis. They can stimulate learning, awaken an appreciation of the message, and lead to prayer.

◇ Use visuals to arouse interest, to raise questions, and to clarify concepts.

◇ Show visuals that represent a variety of media and different cultural interpretations.

◇ Choose visuals that are artistically good, convey an accurate religious message, and are large enough to be seen by all.

◇ Use questions or comments to guide the students to share insights. Ask them how a picture makes them feel and to explain how it relates to the lesson. Have them create a story based on a picture or role-play the situation depicted.

Puppets

Puppets can be a valuable teaching aid, especially for young or shy students. Because puppets are merely toys, they should not pray or speak the religious message. The faith message should be grounded in reality.

Puppets can be made in the following ways:

- Lunch bags—Draw, paint, or glue on features. The bags may be stuffed and tied or left open so that a hand can be inserted.
- Paper—Mount paper cutouts on pencils, rulers, ice-cream sticks, kitchen utensils (such as spoons and spatulas), or even brooms. Paper plates make good puppet faces.
- Socks and mittens—Fabric scraps can be sewed or glued to them.
- Finger puppets—These can be cut from paper and taped together to fit a finger, or they can be made from old gloves.
- Puppets with arms—In a paper cup or a cardboard tube cut holes on the sides for a thumb or finger.

Social Media and Online Learning

There are many ways you can use social media sites and Web sites in the classroom.

- Share messages from the pope's social media accounts.
- Pray prayers for special seasons and events. Many prayers can be downloaded from the Web site of the U.S. Conference of Catholic Bishops.
- Invite students to follow the parish's youth ministry on social media. Keep youth engaged in parish life!
- Use online retreats and other presentations that facilitate faith sharing.

- Learn from other catechists and share your experiences by following blogs such as The Catechist's Journey (www.catechistsjourney.com).
- Rich online resources, a variety of activities, and support materials for all audiences can be found at www.christourlife.com.

Vocabulary Words

A good vocabulary helps the students better understand and articulate their Catholic faith. By helping them become familiar with the Glossary in the back of their book, you can help them to develop an age-appropriate vocabulary. Give the students words from other grades and ask them to use them in a sentence.

- Invite students to read the definition of a vocabulary word and to use it in a sentence.
- Have the students create an acrostic with a vocabulary word.
- Have the students match words with definitions.
- Create sentences that the students complete by using a vocabulary word.

Drawing and Art

Banners

Book jackets

Booklets (bound with yarn or staples, accordion type)

Bookmarks

Boxes (for art projects or collections)

Bulletin boards

Bumper stickers

Buttons

CD covers

Cartoons

Church seasonal art (Christmas trees, Advent wreaths, Stations of the Cross, Jesse Tree)

Coat of arms

Collages

Comic books

Commemorative stamps

Dioramas

Displays (religious art fair, Church seasons, etc.)

Doorknob hangers

Dot pictures

Finger paintings

Fingerprint pictures from ink pads (details with felt-tipped pens)

Greeting cards

Holy cards

Illustrated Scripture verses

Liturgical calendars

Mobiles

Models (clay or dough)

Mosaics (construction paper, paper punch "holes," Easter egg shells, seeds, beans, noodles, rice)

Murals

Pamphlets

Paper dolls

Paperweights

Pennants

Photo albums with illustrations and captions

Photo essays (magazine pictures or photos)

Place mats

Plaques (coated with shellac)

Portraits

Posters

Pottery

Puppets (finger, sock, balloon, clothespin, mitten, paper bag, lightbulb, paper plate, paper glued on a pencil)

Sacred art

Sculpture (wire, paper, aluminum foil, clay, papier-mâché)

Sewing/Quilting

Sidewalk art with chalk

Silhouettes/cutouts

Sponge paintings

Stained-glass windows

Student-made storybooks

Torn-paper pictures

T-shirts

Yarn-and-cloth pictures

Writing

Acrostics

Blogs

Commercials

E-mails

Interviews

Journals

Letters (creative, letters to the editor, etc.)

Litanies

Logs

Modern parables/stories

Newspaper headlines/stories

Paraphrases of Bible passages

Poems

Prayers

Prayer services

Questions and Answers

Quizzes

Raps

Rebus

Reflections

Reports

Riddles

Skits

Slogans

Song lyrics

Speeches

Stories

Web pages

Audiovisuals

Bulletin boards

CDs, MP3 players, smartphones, tablets

Charts

Colored chalk

Computers

Concrete aids

Diagrams

DVDs

Flannel boards

LCD projectors

Maps

Models

Movies

Multimedia shows

Music

Pictures

Scrapbooks

Slide-show presentation software

Slides

Songs

Transparencies

Videocassettes or audiocassettes

Whiteboards

Role-Playing and Dramatizing

Charades

Choral readings

Dance

Dramatic reading/storytelling

Gestures to songs

Mime

Pageants

Plays

Puppet shows

Role-playing

Shadow plays

Speaking and Singing

Discussions (small group/large group)

Guest speakers

Interviews

Lectures

Panel discussions

Radio play

Questions and Answers

Singing

Storytelling

Playing Games

Bingo

Board games

Card games

Charades

Crossword puzzles

Drawing games

Icebreakers

Quiz shows

Relays

Skill games

Spelling bees

Team games

Tic-tac-toe

Trivia games

Word searches

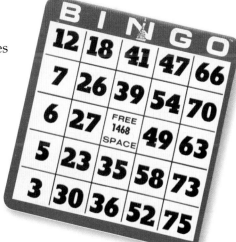

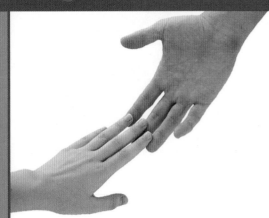

Each person is created in God's image, yet there are variations in individual abilities. Positive recognition of these differences discourages discrimination and enhances the unity of the Body of Christ.

Statement of the U.S. Bishops:
Welcome and Justice for Persons with Disabilities (1998)

General Strategies for Inclusion

Everyone has a right to catechesis. The catechist should choose teaching techniques that meet the needs of students with special needs while emphasizing their strengths. Students with special needs include those with some form of learning challenge, as well as those who are considered gifted.

Use of Scripture Stories

✦ Tell some Bible stories as an eyewitness, using direct address. Be specific.

✦ Use the Bible and pictures during storytelling.

✦ After the story is read, have students dramatize it, perhaps by using pantomime.

Use of Music and Gesture

✦ Provide silent, reflective time to draw students into a sense of the sacred.

✦ Peaceful, calming music may be helpful for centering.

✦ Songs and prayers with echo features are effective.

✦ Songs with direct, simple messages of the faith help retention of basic truths.

✦ Simple gestures for refrains promote participation.

✦ Limit gestures to two or three for each song, selected from those used in American Sign Language.

Use of Questioning Techniques

✦ State questions in their entirety, and then break them down into basic components.

✦ Use leading questions to increase class participation. For example, *How do we help others as Jesus does?*

✦ Ask questions immediately after presenting material.

✦ Use critical-thinking questions when appropriate.

✦ Provide opportunities for students to communicate using the means most comfortable, such as picture exchange, sign language, or other gestures.

Adapting Lessons

Because there are different categories of special needs, you might consider the following suggestions to better serve the students in your care.

Physical Challenges

✦ Consult special education professionals.

✦ Develop strategies, such as buddy systems, to help students with materials and class activities.

✦ Speak confidentially with students who have physical impairments to assess and accommodate their needs. Let students know that you are happy to help them if assistance is needed.

✦ Encourage social interaction through verbal activities and other opportunities.

✦ Adapt work areas to allow safe and easy access.

✦ Keep areas free of obstructions and clean up spills.

Visual Challenges

✦ Consider range of vision and lighting needs. Seat the child away from glaring lights and in the front of the room.

✦ Permit students to move for closer views of charts or demonstrations.

✦ Provide large-print or Braille books, audio materials, and materials with tactile features.

✦ Plan lessons that use senses other than sight.

✦ Allow students to do assignments and tests orally or to record answers.

✦ Assign a partner who does not have visual impairments to help with visual activities.

✦ Keep the learning area clear of hazards, and store materials or supplies in the same place.

✦ Use an auditory or tactile signal instead of a visual sign or cue.

Hearing Impairment

- Face students directly when you talk to them. Remember not to talk when your back is turned or when writing on the board.
- Ask students where they would like to sit to best facilitate communication.
- Gently touch the child on the arm to indicate he/she is being spoken to.
- Speak clearly, using a normal tone and pace.
- Write difficult or unfamiliar words and key words and phrases legibly on the board.
- Make copies of class notes for students.
- Write directions, assignments, schedule changes, special events, etc., on the board.
- Encourage verbal interaction.
- For those students with complete hearing loss, provide an American Sign Language (ASL) translator to communicate what you say.
- Eliminate background noise.

Speech Delay or Impairment

- Speak naturally, distinctly, and in short phrases.
- Use visual and written cues.
- Provide additional assistance before or after class to students whose oral communication needs attention.
- Allow ample time for students to respond to your questions and comments. Do not interrupt or complete sentences for them.

Social and Behavioral Challenges

- Arrange the room to minimize distractions. Carpeting, sound-absorbing materials, and room dividers can help.
- Provide a structured environment, including a schedule.
- Help students develop routines.
- Prepare change-of-pace activities that give students opportunities to move.
- Give students tasks they find interesting.
- Plan stimulating activities for after—not before— periods of concentration.
- Explain the rationale for what students are learning.
- Establish a plan of action for students to complete work.
- Reward students for demonstrating self-control and responsibility and for completing a task in an appropriate length of time.
- Surround the students with others who demonstrate appropriate behavior.
- Provide encouragement; acknowledge good behavior.
- Plan for success but prepare strategies to mitigate difficult behavior.
- Provide clear transitions between activities.

Learning Disabilities

- Provide routine and orderly procedures. Avoid distractions.
- Activate students's prior understanding and experiences to introduce new concepts.
- Keep lessons short and varied. Introduce skills one at a time and review often. Allow extra time and repeated practice opportunities.
- Use books and materials with large print and simple design and graphics.
- Reinforce verbalized concepts with visual and kinesthetic cues.
- Assess content rather than spelling or reading comprehension.
- Provide a rubric so that the students can see expectations before an assignment or project begins.
- Set up situations in which students will experience success. Frequently praise students on their strengths.
- Review and clarify directions.
- Ask questions often to assess students' understanding of the lesson.
- Provide a variety of options for the students to communicate what they know and understand.

Cognitive Differences

◇ Adjust class work to the students' attention span and gross motor and fine motor skill levels.

◇ Individualize learning, and use teacher assistants or volunteers, as necessary.

◇ Simplify concepts, teaching in a concrete manner with a variety of approaches.

◇ Consider writing narrative progress reports rather than using traditional grading scales.

◇ Encourage mentors, such as peers or siblings, to assist in religious education.

Students Identified as Gifted

◇ Challenge students by suggesting independent study, small-group work, enrichment activities, out-of-school activities, and discovery learning that is related to their interests.

◇ Provide supplementary resources and direct students to pursue interesting topics.

◇ Capture students' interest with puzzles, games, and technology.

◇ Ask students to help prepare class materials and demonstrations.

◇ Encourage higher-level thinking by leading conversations with open-ended questions that require research opportunities.

◇ Encourage students to share their analysis of Scripture stories.

◇ Provide opportunities for students to express themselves through creative writing, drawing, or music.

Sacramental Catechesis for Students with Special Needs

Because the sacraments are at the heart of Catholic life, preparing students with special needs for reception is an important part of an adaptive religious education program.

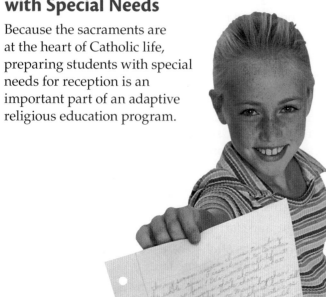

Signs of Readiness for Receiving the Sacraments

◇ desire for the sacrament

◇ development of relationships with people who share faith and prayer

◇ a sense of the sacred manifested in behavior such as eye expression, gesture, or quality of silence

◇ some recognition of symbols as expressive of the sacred

Manner of Catechesis

◇ Use the concrete created world to demonstrate God's goodness and develop appreciation of sacrament as symbol.

◇ Provide visual cues and repeated practices.

◇ Teach catechesis of the sacraments in the place they are celebrated to aid transfer of learning.

Sacrament of the Eucharist

◇ Help students participate actively in the Mass. Encourage reverence.

◇ Practice with students the steps to receive Holy Communion.

◇ Help students distinguish between the Eucharist and ordinary food.

Sacrament of Penance and Reconciliation

◇ Help students express sorrow and forgiveness of others.

◇ Provide opportunities for students to experience loving forgiveness by others.

◇ Practice experiences of the sacrament before actual reception.

Sacrament of Confirmation

◇ Connect the sacrament of Confirmation to students' baptismal promises and beliefs about their Catholic faith.

◇ Help students understand their role as active members of the Church.

Resources from Loyola Press

Visit www.loyolapress.com to obtain resources, including the following:

◇ Adaptive Reconciliation Kit (English and Spanish)

◇ Adaptive First Eucharist Preparation Kit (English and Spanish)

◇ Adaptive Confirmation Preparation Kit (English and Spanish)

From the beginning, this one Church has been marked by a great diversity which comes from both the variety of God's gifts and the diversity of those who receive them. Within the unity of the People of God, a multiplicity of peoples and cultures is gathered together. Among the Church's members, there are different gifts, offices, conditions, and ways of life.

Catechism of the Catholic Church, 814

The Church is enriched by the diversity of its people. Many devotional practices are rooted in different cultures, such as novenas, *posadas, Simbang Gabi,* and *quinceañeras.* To support children from various cultural backgrounds, catechists are encouraged to

- ✦ incorporate the cultures of the people in their catechesis.
- ✦ address the needs of various groups of people.
- ✦ respect and cherish the uniqueness of different groups.
- ✦ lead others to know and respect cultures different from their own.

The following suggestions can help catechists teach more effectively as they promote multicultural awareness and respect.

Responding to the Needs of Various Cultures

- ✦ Understand and be sensitive to both the home and the community to which each student belongs.
- ✦ Learn about the history, traditions, values, and customs of the ethnic groups to which your students belong.
- ✦ Make sure that your teaching takes into account the life experiences of your students.
- ✦ Make the effort to have all written communications to parents or guardians translated into the language spoken at home.
- ✦ Be aware of subgroups within larger groups. For example, Spanish-speaking people come from Mexico, Puerto Rico, Cuba, and other countries. Each of these people has a distinct culture. The same is true of Native Americans, African Americans, Asian Americans, and other ancestries.
- ✦ Consider your class's special needs in relation to justice and peace. Prepare the students to assume responsibility for achievement of their goals.
- ✦ Become familiar with popular devotional practices in different cultures.
- ✦ Point out diversity in culture in saints you study in class, art, and music.
- ✦ Read multicultural books to the children.

Incorporating the Gifts of Various Cultures

- ✦ Encourage students to share their customs and family celebrations with one another.
- ✦ Integrate cultural holidays and feasts, special events, and neighborhood celebrations into the life examples you use in your teaching.
- ✦ In liturgical and social celebrations, especially on important occasions, incorporate the language and the symbols of the groups that make up your learning community.
- ✦ Encourage liturgical and social celebrations that express the spirit, history, and traditions of the different cultural groups.

Educating Students to Know and Respect Various Cultures

- ✦ Watch for unjust or stereotypical treatment of gender, races, and cultures in the materials you use and in your own words as you teach. Raise the consciousness of those around you.
- ✦ Avoid racial, ethnic, or cultural nicknames. Disallow jokes that label or stereotype.
- ✦ Acknowledge contributions made by various cultural groups to the rich traditions of the Catholic Church. Emphasize the universal Church.
- ✦ Share stories about saints from various cultural and social conditions.
- ✦ Be sensitive to the struggle of various cultural groups in finding their place in U.S. society.

Assessment of Faith Formation

Assessment of faith formation differs from assessment done in social studies, math, or science. In academic subject areas, knowledge and skills pertaining to the subject matter are assessed and used as a basis for determining a grade. In faith formation, assessment is used to discern growth into a way of life, namely discipleship. The assessment of knowledge in faith formation is part of the larger assessment of the students' formation into a life of liturgy, morality, prayer, communal life, and missionary activity.

In general, assessment takes three forms:

✧ formal assessment, which includes quizzes, tests, essays, and the Information for Growth/Assessment of Children/Youth Religious Education (IFG/ACRE), a tool that assesses the effectiveness of catechetical/ religious education programs;

✧ informal assessment through observing a student's participation in written work, group work, and group activities; and

✧ authentic assessment through opportunities to put into action what the students have been learning.

Formal Assessment

A formal assessment asks the question *What do you know/understand?* Formal assessment provides you with an opportunity to identify which faith concepts need reinforcement, to affirm for students what they have learned, and to identify where specific assistance is needed. *Christ Our Life* provides several opportunities for formal assessment:

✧ chapter and unit reviews in Student Books

✧ ACRE-style questions on Gather and Go Forth pages

✧ a formal written assessment (Chapter Quiz) at the end of each chapter as a BLM

✧ a unit assessment also provided as a BLM

✧ the for-purchase option of the online Loyola Press Assessment System

Informal Assessment

Informal assessment asks the questions *What can you do with what you know?* and *How do you do it?* Below are a few ways of assessing your students.

✧ Ongoing Assessment—Each chapter offers opportunities to assess the students' grasp of concepts by observing their participation in discussions, group work, and their service to and care for others.

✧ Specific Tasks—Many opportunities to evaluate verbal (oral and written) and nonverbal (drawn, crafted) expressions and responses.

Authentic Assessment

Authentic assessment is genuine and real. It is also performance-based. Learners put into action what they have been learning about by living out the call to discipleship. *Christ Our Life* offers the following forms of authentic assessment.

✧ At the end of each chapter, suggestions are provided (grades 1–4: *Building Family Faith;* grades 5–6: *Things to Do at Home;* grades 7–8: *Reach Out*) for specific ways that the students can put their faith into practice.

✧ Portfolios—One form of authentic assessment that is particularly appropriate for religious education is the use of portfolios. A portfolio is a collection of a student's work. Portfolios can help the students see their growth and progress over time. They also allow catechists to gain insight into the students' effort, progress, achievement, and thought-processes, as well as helping to determine their strengths and needs. File folders or binders can be used as portfolios because it is easy for students to add or take work out of them over time. Students should have easy access to their portfolios and should be encouraged to interact with their portfolios often. While the students are actively engaged in their own ongoing assessment, catechists need to help them identify portfolio-worthy assignments. A portfolio should not just be a scrapbook of every single assignment a student has done. The following are suggestions for portfolio-worthy assignments:

1. written reflections on Scripture passages
2. prayers composed by the student
3. traditional prayers taken to heart (memorized)
4. tear-out pages from the Student Book that show superior work
5. formal assessments (tests, quizzes, etc.)
6. written reflections, such as retreats, service experiences, worship or prayer experiences
7. projects, such as drawings of Scripture stories, designs for a parish bulletin, written versions of contemporary parables, collages showing Catholic social teaching themes in action, or research reports about saints
8. "Faith Surveys," in which the students assess the extent of their participation in Catholic practices, can be done at the beginning and end of a year or at the end of each year a participant is in a catechetical program.

Catechetical Documents

Vatican Documents

Evangelii Gaudium (2013) – Pope Francis's exhortation "The Joy of the Gospel"

YOUCAT (2011) – the Youth Catechism of the Catholic Church

Compendium of the Catechism of the Catholic Church (2005) – a synopsis of the Catechism in a Q & A format

The General Directory for Catechesis (1997) updates and replaces the 1971 GCD

Guide for Catechists (1993) – Document of vocational, formative, and promotional orientation of Catechists, Congregation for the Evangelization of Peoples

The Catechism of the Catholic Church (1992) – a complete summary of the official teachings of the Catholic Church

Adult Catechesis in the Christian Community: Some Principles and Guidelines (1990), International Council for Catechesis

The Rite of Christian Initiation for Adults (1988) – the rites of the catechumenate

The Code of Canon Law (1983) – a codification of laws and regulations by which the Roman Catholic Church is governed

Catechesi Tradendae (1979) – John Paul II's exhortation "On Catechesis in Our Time"

Evangelii Nuntiandi (1975) – Paul VI's exhortation "On Evangelization in the Modern World"

The General Catechetical Directory (1971) – Congregation of the Clergy; a single point of reference for all aspects of catechetical instruction

Vatican II: The Conciliar and Post Conciliar Documents (1963-65) – sixteen documents articulating the vision of the Second Vatican Council.

Documents from the United States Conference of Catholic Bishops and its predecessors

Conformity Listing of Catechetical Texts and Series (Website list updated regularly)

Disciples Called to Witness: The New Evangelization (2012) – resource for creating outreach efforts

Sacramental Catechesis: An Online Resource for Dioceses and Eparchies (2012)

Adaptation of Doctrinal Elements for Use in Parish and Youth Ministry Programs (2010)

Doctrinal Elements for a Curriculum Framework for the Development of Catechetical Materials for Young People of High School Age (2008)

Catechetical Formation in Chaste Living: Guidelines for Curriculum Design and Publication (2008)

The United States Catholic Catechism for Adults (2006) – an adaptation of the *Catechism of the Catholic Church* for the Church in the United States

The National Directory for Catechesis (2003) – an adaptation of the *General Directory for Catechesis* for the Church in the United States

The Real Presence of Jesus Christ in the Sacrament of the Eucharist: Basic Questions and Answers (2001) – fundamental questions and answers about the Eucharist

Our Hearts Were Burning Within Us: A Pastoral Plan for Adult Faith Formation in the United States (1999)

Sharing Catholic Social Teaching: Challenges and Directions (1998) – identifies 7 key themes of Catholic Social teaching

Renewing the Vision: A Framework for Catholic Youth Ministry (1997) – a blueprint for effective youth ministry

Go and Make Disciples: A National Plan and Strategy for Catholic Evangelization in the United States (1992)

Guidelines for Doctrinally Sound Catechetical Materials (1990) – guidelines for producing catechetical materials that are consistent with church teachings

To Teach as Jesus Did (1972) – pastoral letter of the U.S. bishops devoted to the concern of Catholic education.

www.christourlife.com

The *Christ Our Life* Web site is your online partner in faith formation, providing you with program support and regular updates. The resources at **christourlife. com** can be tailored to the needs of students and easily accessed.

Christourlife.com membership is free. Use your access code **COL-2016** to register and explore the wealth of resources, including:

- ✧ **Online Lesson Planning**—The planning feature can be customized to offer increased flexibility, convenience, and support by allowing Christ Our Life users to personalize their lesson plans and save them for future use.
- ✧ **Activity Finder**—This easy-to-use tool offers more than 400 creative learning activities. Search by age, grade, subject, or learning style.
- ✧ **Loyola Press Web sites**—Explore online resources, including **Sunday Connection:** Background information and classroom activities to explore the Sunday readings; **3-Minute Retreat:** Engaging daily reflections help nurture everyday faith; **Arts & Faith:** Celebrate creative expressions of faith; **Daily Inspiration:** Pray and reflect on Scripture; **Special Needs:** Find ways to serve people with special needs; **DRE Connect:** Share with a community of catechists; **Español:** A rich faith resource for Spanish speakers.
- ✧ **Blackline Masters and Assessments**— Downloadable files are available for reference and easy printing.
- ✧ **Interactive Chapter Reviews**—The online chapter reviews allow students the opportunity to test their comprehension and prepare for upcoming assessments.
- ✧ **Comprehensive Search Feature**—This tool helps you navigate the Web site with ease.

Additional online resources for *Christ Our Life* are available:

- ✦ Family resources available in Spanish
- ✦ Study guides for each chapter
- ✦ Interactive games for review
- ✦ Resources for parents
- ✦ Video tutorials

Join Our Online Community

To become part of this free online community:

1. Open your Web browser and go to **www.christourlife.com.**
2. At the bottom of the page under Membership click **Register.**
3. Fill in the necessary information under the E-mail Preferences tab, and click **Submit.**
4. Under the Program Users Access Codes tab, enter your *Christ Our Life* access code: **COL-2016**
5. Click **Submit.**
6. When your registration is complete, choose **Christ Our Life** from the **Educational Programs** menu bar at the top of the page.

It is highly recommended that a parent-youth meeting be held early in the school year to recognize parents as the primary catechists of their child and to help them more effectively guide their adolescents in living the Catholic faith. Students are encouraged to attend this meeting with their parents. The format may vary according to the needs and interests of the parents. In a parochial school, the meeting could be the core of a back-to-school night usually held at the beginning of the year. In a parish religious-education program, the meeting may be held after one of the Sunday Masses. Alternatively, you might have parochial school parents and the religious-education parents and their children at a combined meeting.

As you prepare for the meeting, be aware the variety of family situations. Be careful to respect each student's experience of what family means to him or her.

Planning the Meeting

Reasons for the Meeting

- To encourage parents and their adolescents in their efforts to build a family of love and service in their homes, forming a community that will reach out to others.
- To explain how the catechesis in the Grade 7 *Christ Our Life* program meets the specific needs of the adolescent and provides support for parents who are communicating Gospel values to their children within the family.
- To encourage the process of parents, adolescents, and catechists working together to share the Catholic faith.

Proposed Meeting Outline

1. Welcome (5 minutes)

2. Prayer (5 minutes)

3. Explanation of the seventh-grade program, *Jesus the Way, the Truth, and the Life* (10 minutes)

4. Break for refreshments (15 minutes)

5. Presentation of "Family Communication: What Are We Saying to Each Other?" (45 minutes)

6. Closing prayer (5 minutes)

Meeting Preparation Checklist

1. In my preliminary plan, have I

- ❏ scheduled the meeting for September or early October?
- ❏ notified the parents of the date and time of the meeting?
- ❏ invited a small group of parents and students to come for a planning session?

2. In the small planning session, have I

- ❏ shared my goals and plans for the meeting?
- ❏ allowed the group to decide what adaptations should be made?
- ❏ decided who will give the presentation?
- ❏ discussed how parents and their children might be motivated to attend and how they can be invited and reminded of the meeting?
- ❏ discussed the time schedule for the meeting? (The meeting should not exceed 90 minutes.)
- ❏ discussed the planning of the prayer service for the opening and closing prayer? (Items include assignment of roles such as a prayer leader, several readers, and enthronement of the Bible.)
- ❏ discussed refreshments and other ways of creating a friendly, inviting atmosphere?
- ❏ discussed ways of checking attendance? (Name tags? Clipboard for signing in?)

3. In my immediate preparations, have I

- ❏ made copies of BLM 93A–C to be given out at the meeting?
- ❏ sent an invitation to each parent and student, requesting them to bring a copy of the student book to the meeting? Put out extra copies of the book for those who forget to bring their own?
- ❏ made pencils available for the participants?

> **For more tips and ideas** on supporting parents and families in their role as nurturers of a lived faith, go to www.christourlife.com. Encourage the families in your program to visit this site as well.

Conducting the Meeting

Arrive early enough to welcome the participants informally. A committee of parents and students may assist in creating a warm, friendly atmosphere.

1. Welcome
- Introduce yourself, thank the hospitality committee, and welcome the parents and adolescents who have come. Express your appreciation for their interest in the meeting and for their efforts to attend in spite of possible inconvenience.
- Let parents and adolescents know that you welcome their questions and suggestions throughout the year and express your willingness to meet with them to work for continued spiritual and moral growth.
- Offer a humorous anecdote. You may wish to contrast old styles and new styles or old and new music. You may tell a personal story. (Humor helps ease the tensions associated with self-evaluation. Throughout your presentation, include pertinent, humorous stories and anecdotes. Also use Scripture references and personal experiences.)
- Give a brief outline of the meeting and explain what you hope to accomplish. Be confident and enthusiastic in an effort to raise the expectation level of the group.

2. Prayer
> **BLM 94A** Invite everyone present to join in the opening prayer found on BLM 94A, Parent-Youth Meeting, *Opening Prayer*, which is based on the prayer service for the Unit 3 review. Be sure that those who are taking part in the service are prepared. Pause for 10 to 15 seconds to allow everyone to place themselves in God's presence, and then follow the directions on the BLM.

3. Explanation of the catechesis for the seventh-grade program
- Explain briefly how the catechesis in *Jesus the Way, the Truth, and the Life* is directed toward helping adolescents develop their personal relationship with Jesus. Ideally, parents and adolescents will have copies of the student book in hand as you give your explanation.

- Mention that when seeking directions for travel, the Internet offers many services. Tell the parents and adolescents to imagine that the Internet was down and they needed to provide directions for someone to travel from your present location to another location that you've selected. The location should be fairly local, within about 5 miles.
- Allow a few minutes for the parents and adolescents to work together as a family to come up with a set of directions. Then have each family join with another family to compare their directions. When they are finished, invite volunteers to share their directions with the whole group. Be sure to get a variety of directions from the volunteers.
- Explain that there are many ways of getting from one location to another. Write the word *WAY* on the board, on a poster or on an overhead transparency. Explain that human beings are on a journey, seeking to find God in their lives. Point out that Jesus referred to himself as "the Way, the Truth, and the Life."
- **The title of the seventh-grade book is *Jesus the Way, the Truth, and the Life*. This year, we will be learning about how to follow Jesus more closely as he leads us to his Father through the guidance of the Holy Spirit. I'd like to point out some of the highlights of this book and how it will assist us on our journey.**
- You may wish to refer to BLM 1 **Family Letter** and provide copies for each family if you haven't yet distributed them. Explain the features of the book that make it a family program: textbook examples relating to family life, a Family Feature page at the beginning of each unit, and this meeting.
- Point out the Reach Out activities that accompany each chapter as a way of getting the family involved in reinforcing the concepts presented in the classroom and of keeping lines of communication open. Encourage students to share what happens in school.

4. Break for Refreshments

5. Presentation of "Family Communication: What Are We Saying to Each Other?"

Family Communication: What Are We Saying to Each Other?

Part I: Communicating Love
- Cite an example from your own life or an experience that shows the joy of family support.
- **Just as the outstanding characteristic of every Christian needs to be love, so the outstanding characteristic within every Christian family needs to be love. Let's take a closer look at how we communicate love in our families.**

- **BLM 93A** Distribute the Family Checklist provided on BLM 93A **Communicating Love.** Explain that the checklist need not be shared, but parents and adolescents may want to compare notes at home. Have them also fill out the Discussion Starters. Give them a few minutes to share ideas with people sitting near them. Invite a few volunteers to share their discussion-starter ideas with the large group.

✦ Share some of the following: **Every person here belongs to a family. How important is that family? According to the bishops' pastoral** *To Live in Christ Jesus,* **"Every human being has a need and right to be loved, to have a home where he or she can put down roots and grow. The family is the first and indispensable community in which this need is met. Today, when productivity, prestige or even physical attractiveness is regarded as the gauge of personal worth, the family has a special vocation to be a place where people are loved not for what they do or what they have, but simply because they are."** (*To Live in Christ Jesus: A Pastoral Reflection on the Moral Life,* #33, 1977)

✦ Ask volunteers to describe what we depend upon our families for. Make a list on the board, on a poster, or on an overhead transparency. Be sure to add the following if not mentioned:

  • **our ability to accept ourselves as worthwhile and important**

  • **our ability to develop positive, enriching relationships with others**

  • **our ability to contribute positively to the society in which we live**

  • **our natural ability to develop a personal relationship with God**

  • **our families' dependence on us for the same positive support**

✦ **All of this sounds great, but every family is in the process of becoming, and trying to reach this depth of love. Growth is continually required. Inevitably there will be times of conflict, of crisis, of hurts and disappointments. Some wounds will be easily healed. Others may create barriers difficult to tear down.**

✦ **Nevertheless, my family is** *my* **family, and it is precious to me. I will accept the responsibility to encourage and love each one in my family. I will try to work through difficulties, to look for the good in others, and to find ways of improving my expressions of love and caring. I will especially pray for each member of my family.**

Part II: Communicating Understanding and Respect

✦ Invite the group to play a game of charades. Have a volunteer come forward and provide him or her with the title of a current movie or TV program. Tell the group that they have to guess the name of the movie or TV program based on the signs and gestures communicated by the volunteer. When finished, discuss the following:

✦ **On the surface, communication seems simple. I speak to you, and you hear my message. But in actuality, it is quite complicated. Jesus had to work with his apostles who had problems communicating.** [Cite the apostles arguing and Jesus' teaching in Mark 9:33–37. Cite the apostles misinterpreting Jesus' statement in Mark 8:14–17.]

Let's take a closer look at how we can communicate understanding and respect in our families.

✦ Share some of the following about respect and understanding:

✦ **Communication must be based on respect. I must choose words that will help to build a relationship between myself and my audience—words that describe rather than label or degrade. I also hope the other person will listen respectfully.**

✦ **Communication must also be based on understanding. As a listener, I must give my full attention to the speaker, listening not only for the message, but also for any underlying feelings. I will welcome the other person's sharing, trying to understand his or her unique feelings and way of experiencing life. Communication requires hard work on both the part of the speaker and that of the listener.**

✦ **Let's see how these principles apply. I will read a situation, pause for you to think of a response, and then offer typical responses. We'll be aiming for responses that build up a relationship.**

  • **Situation 1. At the art museum, Jennifer is standing before a painting of abstract art. She says to her dad, "This picture is ugly." How might her dad respond?** *Response 1:* **"What do you know about art? You don't appreciate anything."** *Response 2:* **"You really don't like this type of art, do you? I guess you would prefer paintings that look more like the real objects."**

  • **Situation 2. Stephanie's mother won't let her go on a ski trip with her class because it seems dangerous. How might Stephanie respond?** *Response 1:* **"You treat me like a baby. I can never do anything the other kids do. You just don't care about me. You don't understand."** *Response 2:* **"I'm really disappointed, Mom. I know how afraid you are because skiing looks so dangerous. But the last four times the kids at school went, no one got hurt. Would you be willing to call my teacher and discuss it with him?"**

  • **Situation 3. Jorge is working on a project in the garage with his father. He stands up suddenly and knocks over a box of tacks, scattering them across the floor. How might his father respond?** *Response 1:* **"Let me pick up the tacks for you. You're too clumsy to do it."** *Response 2.* **"If we work together, we'll have the tacks cleaned up in no time and then we can get back to our project."**

✦ **We have many opportunities each day to show respect and understanding through the words we speak, through the messages we try to communicate, and through the interested listening we do for one another.**

✦ `BLM 93B` Distribute BLM 93B **Communicating Understanding and Respect.** Have both parents and adolescents circle the correct number for each statement in the Family Survey. Then have both parents and adolescents fill in the first part of the Parent-Student Quiz to see how well they can match answers. Have the students complete the first three questions. Have the parents complete the first three questions also, trying to answer in the same way their student will answer. Then have both groups share their answers. Now have the parents answer the last three questions. Have the students answer the last three questions also, trying to answer the same way their parents will answer. Then have both groups share their answers.

Part III: Communicating Faith Values

✦ Ask the adolescents to recall the first thing they ever learned about God. Invite a few volunteers to share their thoughts.

✦ **For most of us, our parents were the first people to share stories about God with us and the first to pray with us. These experiences don't have to stop just because our children have moved into adolescence. You can still pray together. You can solve family conflicts guided by Christian principles. You can still share your faith.**

✦ **You can also discover the faith and insights that your own adolescents have to share. Students, your faith in God and your ability to talk openly about religion and about life will encourage your parents and your whole family to share their faith with you.**

✦ **BLM 93C** Distribute copies of BLM 93C **Communicating Faith Values.** Have the parents and students complete their separate sections. Conduct a discussion on ways to encourage faith sharing either in a large group discussion or ask parents and students to share with the people around them.

✦ Share some of the following information.

✦ **One way to find time together as a family is through the keeping of family traditions. These customs may be as simple as having Sunday morning breakfast together or as involved as inviting a family to spend the holidays with your family. Some traditions are family prayer experiences, such as spontaneous meal prayers, the family Rosary, or praying for various family members. Family traditions may include celebrations of birthdays and anniversaries, annual vacations, and customs related to the liturgical seasons of Advent, Christmas, Lent, and Easter.** [Invite examples from the group.]

✦ **Another area of family traditions may include helping as a family with a project sponsored by the parish, taking care of the needs of an elderly neighbor, or regularly bringing food or clothing to those who are poor.** [Invite examples from the group.] **These experiences can bring the members of a family closer together, as well as help them witness strongly to their faith.**

✦ Ask volunteers to summarize the key insights they learned at this meeting about communicating as a family. Ask if there are any questions from the parents or students

✦ **When children move into adolescence, they become involved in more activities away from home. Because of scheduling difficulties, family traditions may suffer. Members begin to wonder, "How important is it for us to do this together or to go there as a family?" Another equally important question to ask is "What are we saying to one another by keeping this tradition?" Keeping family traditions may be a way of saying that we consider being with, listening to, and working with one another a priority.**

6. Closing prayer

BLM 94B Invite everyone present to join in the closing prayer, which can be found on BLM 94B Parent-Youth Meeting, *Closing Prayer,* which is based on the prayer service for the Unit 3 review.

Resources for Parent-Youth Meeting

Raising Faith-Filled Kids, Loyola Press; *Raising Kids Who Will Make a Difference,* Loyola Press; *Good Parents, Tough Times,* Loyola Press; *Some Assembly Required: Youths Talk About Faith* (video, 30 minutes), Loyola Press.

Additional Background Information

Consider including the following information during the meeting as needed:

Jesus Shows Us Selfless Love
In the Gospel, Jesus gave an excellent example of offering this kind of love to others. Cite examples of Jesus' love for those who are sick based on Luke 5:12–16; for those who are hungry based on Mark 6:30–44; for sinners based on Matthew 9:10–13; and for those who are poor based on Luke 21:1–4. Jesus' dying on the Cross for us when we were still helplessly trapped in sin is the best example.

The Foundation of the Family
Why is the family so important in the faith development of children? The family is the place where faith is brought to life. It is the foundation upon which formal catechesis builds. "Within the Christian family, the members first begin to learn the basic prayers of the tradition and to form their consciences in light of the teachings of Christ and the Church. Family members learn more of the Christian life by observing each other's strengths or weaknesses than by formal instruction." (*National Directory for Catechesis,* #29, D)

The Challenge to Be a Loving Family
The Christian family is a community where love, respect, and understanding are shared by the members. Pope Paul VI challenged the family when he wrote that, like the Church, the family needs to be a place where the Gospel is given and lived. (*Evangelization in the Modern World,* #71)

Title / Song	Collection	Publisher	CD*	Track*
Chapter 1: The Impact of Jesus				
All Is Ready	*God Is Here*	GIA	1	8
Gather 'Round This Table	*The Feast of Life*	GIA		
At the Name of Jesus	*Spirit and Song, Vol. 4*	OCP		
Find Us Ready	*Spirit and Song, Vol. 3*	OCP		
Come Just as You Are	*Voices as One, Vol. 2*	WLP		
Chapter 2: Friendship with Jesus				
Joyfully Singing	*Give Your Gifts: The Songs*	GIA	1	2
You Belong to Us	*God Is Here*	GIA	1	7
Lead Us to Your Table	*Spirit and Song, Vol. 2*	OCP		
Lord of the Dance	*Spirit and Song, Vol. 3*	OCP		
Come, Let Us Sing with Joy	*Voices as One, Vol. 2*	WLP		
Chapter 3: Scripture: A Portrait of Jesus				
Open Our Ears	*Give Your Gifts: The Basics*	GIA		
You Alone Are the Word	*With You by My Side: Vol. 1*	GIA		
Open My Eyes	*Spirit and Song, Vol. 1*	OCP		
With One Voice	*Spirit and Song, Vol. 3*	OCP		
Come, Now Enter/Vengan, Vengan	*Voices as One, Vol. 2*	WLP	2	1
Chapter 4: The World Jesus Lived In				
Labyrinth	*Another World*	GIA		
The House of the Lord	*Sacred Land*	GIA		
I Rejoiced	*Spirit and Song, Vol. 2*	OCP		
I Will Lift Up My Eyes	*Spirit and Song, Vol. 4*	OCP		
I Rejoiced (Psalm 122)	*Voices as One, Vol. 2*	WLP	2	9
Chapter 5: The Early Life of Jesus				
He Came Down/Glory To God	*Give Your Gifts: The Basics*	GIA		
Star Child	*Star Child*	GIA	1	15
All the Ends of the Earth	*Spirit and Song, Vol. 1*	OCP		
Lord of the Dance	*Spirit and Song, Vol. 3*	OCP		
Sweet Child Jesus	*Voices as One, Vol. 2*	WLP		
Chapter 6: The Mission of Jesus				
I Will Never Leave You	*With You by My Side: Vol. 2*	GIA		
You Are Mine	*Give Your Gifts: The Songs*	GIA		
Lead Me, Lord	*Spirit and Song, Vol. 3*	OCP		
With All I Am	*Spirit and Song, Vol. 4*	OCP		
Christ the Icon	*Christ the Icon*	WLP	2	8
Chapter 7: The Apostles, Mary, and Others				
Give Your Gifts	*Give Your Gifts: The New Songs*	GIA		
Magnificat	*Blest Are They : The Best of David Haas, Vol. 1*	GIA		
Holy Is His Name (Canticle of Mary)	*Spirit and Song, Vol. 2*	OCP		
The Call	*Spirit and Song, Vol. 3*	OCP		
Blessed One	*Voices as One, Vol. 2*	WLP	2	3

*Two music CDs are available for purchase.

Title / Song	Collection	Publisher	CD*	Track*
Chapter 8: Baptism and Confirmation				
A Child Will Lead Us	Songs from Another Room	GIA	1	10
Who Calls You by Name	With You by My Side, Vol. 2	GIA		
Lead Us to the Water: Dismissal	Spirit and Song, Vol. 1	OCP		
Your Words Are Spirit and Life (Psalm 19)	Spirit and Song, Vol. 1	OCP		
Shine for You	Voices as One, Vol. 2	WLP		
Chapter 9: Unit 1 Review				
Now: Gathering Rite	Give Your Gifts: The Songs	GIA	1	16
You Will Be My Witnesses	With You by My Side, Vol. 2	GIA		
Cry the Gospel	Spirit and Song, Vol. 2	OCP		
My Heart Belongs to You	Spirit and Song, Vol. 1	OCP		
I Send You Out	Voices as One, Vol. 2	WLP	2	17
Chapter 10: Parables: Stories Jesus Told				
Live in the Light	Give Your Gifts: The New Songs	GIA		
Follow the Light	Give Your Gifts: The New Songs	GIA	1	6
I Am the Light of the World	Spirit and Song, Vol. 3	OCP		
We Are the Light	Spirit and Song, Vol. 3	OCP		
In the Light	Voices as One, Vol. 2	WLP		
Chapter 11: Miracles: Signs Jesus Worked				
A Sign	Give Your Gifts: The New Songs	GIA		
You are the Presence	You Are Mine: The Best of David Haas, Vol. 2	GIA		
Awesome God	Spirit and Song, Vol. 1	OCP		
My Life Is in Your Hands	Spirit and Song, Vol. 2	OCP		
Thanks and Praise	Voices as One, Vol. 2	WLP	2	14
I Surrender/St. Theresa's Prayer	Signatures	Troubadour		
Chapter 12: Penance and Anointing of the Sick				
Jesus, Heal Us	With You by My Side, Vol. 2	GIA		
Too Many Walls	Family Resemblance	GIA		
Here I Am	Spirit and Song, Vol. 3	OCP		
There Is a Longing	Spirit and Song, Vol. 1	OCP		
Fountain of Mercy	Voices as One, Vol. 2	WLP	2	11
Chapter 13: The Message of Jesus: Choose Life				
Bambelela/ Never Give Up	Turn My Heart	GIA		
We Choose Life	With You by My Side, Vol. 1	GIA		
Cry the Gospel	Spirit and Song, Vol. 2	OCP		
Go Make a Difference	Spirit and Song, Vol. 2	OCP		
Love One Another	Voices as One, Vol. 2	WLP	2	6
Chapter 14: The Challenge of the Beatitudes				
Beatitudes	The Best of the Dameans, Vol. 1	GIA		
Blest Are They	Blest Are They: The Best of David Haas, Vol. 1	GIA		
We Are the Light of the World	Spirit and Song, Vol. 1	OCP		
With One Voice	Spirit and Song, Vol. 3	OCP		
You Are the Light of the World	Voices as One, Vol. 2	WLP	2	10

*Two music CDs are available for purchase.

Title / Song	Collection	Publisher	CD*	Track*
Chapter 15: Jesus' Kingdom of Justice and Truth				
On Holy Ground	*Give Your Gifts: The Songs*	GIA	1	4
Voices That Challenge	*Blest Are They: The Best of David Haas, Vol. 1*	GIA	1	1
Somos el Cuerpo de Cristo/ We are the Body of Christ	*Spirit and Song, Vol. 1*	OCP		
What Is Our Service to Be	*Spirit and Song, Vol. 1*	OCP		
Your Love, O Lord	*Voices as One, Vol. 2*	WLP		
Chapter 16: Jesus' Kingdom of Love				
Covenant Hymn (Wherever You Go)	*Vision*	GIA		
Gathered in the Love of Christ	*The Song and the Silence*	GIA		
Holy Is His Name: (Canticle of Mary)	*Spirit and Song, Vol. 2*	OCP		
We Are One Body	*Spirit and Song, Vol. 1*	OCP		
Forever	*Voices as One, Vol. 2*	WLP		
Chapter 17: Unit 2 Review				
Hope at the Crossroads	*Give Your Gifts: The New Songs*	GIA	1	12
Remember Your Love	*The Best of the Dameans, Vol. 1*	GIA		
You Are the Way	*Spirit and Song, Vol. 4*	OCP		
Your Words Are Spirit and Life (Psalm 19)	*Spirit and Song, Vol. 1*	OCP		
Shelter Your Name	*Voices as One, Vol. 2*	WLP		
Chapter 18: Living Faith in Jesus				
Follow the Light	*Give Your Gifts: The New Songs*	GIA	1	6
Love Poured Down from Heaven	*Fresh as the Morning*	GIA		
Be Not Afraid	*Spirit and Song, Vol. 4*	OCP		
Mountain of God	*Spirit and Song, Vol. 4*	OCP		
Strong in Faith	*Voices as One, Vol. 2*	WLP		
Chapter 19: Opposition to Jesus				
Pieta: The Silence and the Sorrow	*Ancient Ways, Future Days*	GIA		
The Cloud's Veil	*The Cloud's Veil*	GIA	1	9
Here I Am	*Spirit and Song, Vol. 3*	OCP		
There Is a Longing	*Spirit and Song, Vol. 1*	OCP		
Once Again	*Voices as One, Vol. 2*	WLP		
Chapter 20: The Eucharist				
Come to the Table	*Fresh as the Morning*	GIA		
Jesus, Be with Us Now	*With You by My Side, Vol. 1*	GIA		
Bread for the World	*Spirit and Song, Vol. 3*	OCP		
Lead Us to Your Table	*Spirit and Song, Vol. 2*	OCP		
In This Bread	*Voices as One, Vol. 2*	WLP	2	7
Chapter 21: Jesus' Final Hours				
The Cloud's Veil	*The Cloud's Veil*	GIA	1	9
The Passion	*That You May Have Life*	GIA		
Behold the Cross	*Spirit and Song, Vol. 4*	OCP		
Hope to Carry On	*Spirit and Song, Vol. 2*	OCP		
Hope to Carry On	*Voices as One, Vol. 2*	WLP		

*Two music CDs are available for purchase.

Title / Song	Collection	Publisher	CD*	Track*
Chapter 22: The Victory of Jesus				
Song of the Risen One	*You Are Mine: The Best of David Haas, Vol. 2*	GIA		
We Arise	*As Morning Breaks and Evening Sets*	GIA	1	13
Everybody Sing Alleluia	*Spirit and Song, Vol. 2*	OCP		
Lord of the Dance	*Spirit and Song, Vol. 3*	OCP		
This Is the Day (Psalm 118)	*Voices as One, Vol. 2*	WLP		
Chapter 23: Alive with the Spirit				
Voices That Challenge	*Blest Are They: The Best of David Haas, Vol. 1*	GIA	1	1
Fan the Flame	*Sacred Land*	GIA		
Lead Us to the Water: Dismissal	*Spirit and Song, Vol. 1*	OCP		
One Spirit, One Church	*Spirit and Song, Vol. 2*	OCP		
Spirit of God	*Voices as One, Vol. 2*	WLP		
Chapter 24: Matrimony and Holy Orders				
Give the Lord Your Heart	*How Can We Be Silent?*	GIA		
We Are Called	*Blest Are They : The Best of David Haas, Vol. 1*	GIA	1	17
The Call	*Spirit and Song, Vol. 3*	OCP		
We Are Called to Serve	*Spirit and Song, Vol. 2*	OCP		
I Send You Out	*Voices as One, Vol. 2*	WLP	2	17
Chapter 25: Unit 3 Review				
Sing to the Glory of God	*Give Your Gifts: The New Songs*	GIA		
Joyfully Singing	*Give Your Gifts: The Songs*	GIA	1	2
Lord, I Lift Your Name On High	*Spirit and Song, Vol. 3*	OCP		
Sometimes by Step	*Spirit and Song, Vol. 4*	OCP		
Let Everything That Has Breath	*Voices as One, Vol. 2*	WLP		
SSL 1: Feast of All Saints				
A Litany of Saints	*This Very Morning*	GIA		
City of God	*Spirit and Song, Vol. 4*	OCP		
Come, All You Blessed Ones	*Voices as One, Vol. 2*	WLP	2	12
SSL 2: Advent				
Come, Emmanuel	*Fresh as the Morning*	GIA		
To You, O God, I Lift Up My Soul	*Spirit and Song, Vol. 2*	OCP		
Rise Up, My People	*Voices as One, Vol. 2*	WLP	2	2
SSL 3: Christmas				
Star Child	*Star Child*	GIA	1	15
Go Tell It on the Mountain	*Spirit and Song, Vol. 4*	OCP		
Let Me Be Your Bethlehem	*Voices as One, Vol. 2*	WLP		
SSL 4: Lent				
Now: Gathering Rite	*Give Your Gifts: The Songs*	GIA	1	16
Be Merciful, O Lord	*Spirit and Song, Vol. 3*	OCP		
Homeward Bound	*Voices as One, Vol. 2*	WLP		

*Two music CDs are available for purchase.

Title / Song	Collection	Publisher	CD*	Track*
SSL 5: Holy Week				
God Weeps	*God Is Here*	GIA		
My Heart Belongs to You	*Spirit and Song, Vol. 1*	OCP		
Sing Hosanna to Our King	*Voices as One, Vol. 2*	WLP		
SSL 6: Easter				
We Arise	*As Morning Breaks and Evening Sets*	GIA	1	13
Alleluia! Alleluia! Let the Holy Anthem Rise	*Journey Songs, Vol. 3*	OCP		
He Is Risen	*Voices as One, Vol. 2*	WLP	2	13
SSL 7: Pentecost				
Send Us Your Spirit	*With You by My Side, Vol. 2*	GIA		
Holy Spirit	*Spirit and Song, Vol. 4*	OCP		
Spirit of the Living God	*Voices as One, Vol. 2*	WLP		

*Two music CDs are available for purchase.

Reflective Music

Available from GIA Music (www.giamusic.com)
The Promise Fulfilled by Stephen Petrunak
Coming Home by Jeanne and Richard Cotter
Mystic Vista by Robert Hutmacher and Denise La Giglia
One Bright Star by Marty Haugen and Marc Anderson
Infant Holy by Stephen Petrunak
Catholic Classics Volume 3: Hymn Instrumental by Bobby Fisher
Taizé : Instrumental 2

Available from World Library Publications (www.wlp.jspaluch.com)
For the Beauty of the Earth by Laura Kutscher
In Every Time by Alan Hommerding and Denise La Giglia
Come, Emmanuel by Ron Rendek
Holy Light by Jerry Galipeau and Denise La Giglia

Follow Me

Mary Beth Gray, S.N.D.

1 Will you drink of the cup that I of— fer?
2 Will you fol— low each day the one path— way?
3 Will you speak in my name to all na — tions?

1 Will you suf— fer the things that must be? Will you
2 Will you make of your life one de— sign? Will you
3 Will you wit— ness my word to all peo—ple? Will you

1 clothe your— self for the jour ———— ney? And
2 pattern your life on my dy ———— ing? Will you
3 shine forth to all of cre— a ———— tion, till I

1 come, come fol— low me? Come, fol ——— low me?
2 come, come and be mine? Come, fol ——— low me?
3 come, come once a— gain? Come, fol ——— low me?

Refrain

You are our Way to the Fath ——— er. You are the

Lord of our hearts. Lord, where you go we will fol—low.

Coronet, the Multimedia Company
A Division of Phoenix Learning Group
141 Milwell Drive, Suite A
St. Louis, MO 63043
(800) 221-1274
www.phoenixlearninggroup.com

The Crossroad Publishing Company
16 Penn Plaza, Suite 1550
New York, NY 10001
(800) 707-0670
www.crossroadpublishing.com

Daughters of St. Paul
See Pauline Books & Media

Educational Activities, Inc.
P.O. Box 87
Baldwin, NY 11510
(800) 797-3223
www.edact.com

Franciscan Communications
See St. Anthony Messenger Press

G.I.A. Publications, Inc.
7404 S. Mason Ave.
Chicago, IL 60638
(800) 442-1358
www.giamusic.com

Liguori Publications
1 Liguori Dr.
Liguori, MO 63057-9999
(800) 325-9521
www.liguori.org

The Liturgical Press
2950 Saint John's Road
Collegeville, MN 56321
(800) 858-5450
www.litpress.org

Liturgy Training Publications (LTP)
3949 S. Racine Avenue
Chicago, IL 60609
(800) 933-1800
www.ltp.org

Loyola Press
3441 N. Ashland Ave.
Chicago, IL 60657
(800) 621-1008
www.loyolapress.com

National Catholic Education Association
1005 N. Glebe Rd., Suite 525
Arlington, VA 22201
(800) 711-6232
www.ncea.org

National Conference for Catechetical Leadership
3031 Fourth Street, NE
Washington, DC 20017
(202) 524-4628
www.nccl.org

New City Press
202 Comforter Blvd.
Hyde Park, NY 12538
(800) 462-5980
www.newcitypress.com

North American Liturgy Resources (NALR)
See OCP Publications

Orbis Books
Price Building, Box 302
Maryknoll, NY 10545-0302
(800) 258-5838
www.orbisbooks.com

OCP Publications
P.O. Box 18030
Portland, OR 97218-0030
(800) 548-8749
www.ocp.org

Pauline Books & Media
50 Saint Paul's Ave.
Boston, MA 02130
(800) 876-4463
www.pauline.org

Paulist Press
997 Macarthur Blvd.
Mahwah, NJ 07430
(800) 218-1903
www.paulistpress.com

Paulist Productions
17575 Pacific Coast Hwy.
Pacific Palisades, CA 90272
(310) 454-0688
www.paulistproductions.org

Resource Publications
5369 Camden Ave., #260
San Jose, CA 95124
(408) 286-8505
www.rpinet.com

Sacred Heart Kids' Club
869 South Rimpau Blvd.
Los Angeles, CA 90005
(323) 935-2372
www.sacredheartsisters.com/kidsclub

St. Anthony Messenger Press
Franciscan Media
28 W. Liberty St.
Cincinnati, OH 45202-6498
(800) 488-0488
catalog.americancatholic.org

Sheed & Ward
Rowman & Littlefield Publishers, Inc.
4501 Forbes Blvd., Suite 200
Lanham, MD 20706
(800) 462-6420
www.rowman.com

Sophia Institute Press
P.O. Box 5284
Manchester, NH 03108
(800) 888-9344
www.sophiainstitute.com

Treehaus Communications, Inc.
P.O. Box 249
906 West Loveland Ave.
Loveland, OH 45140
(800) 638-4287
www.treehaus1.com

Twenty-Third Publications
1 Montauk Ave., #200
New London, CT 06320
(800) 321-0411
www.pastoralplanning.com

United States Conference of Catholic Bishops
3211 Fourth St., NE
Washington, DC 20017
(800) 235-8722
www.usccbpublishing.org

Vision Video
P.O. Box 540
Worcester, PA 19490
(800) 523-0226
www.visionvideo.com

Weston Woods Studios
90 Old Sherman Turnpike
Norwalk, CT 06816
800-243-5020
www.westonwoods.scholastic.com

World Library Publications (WLP)
J.S. Paluch Company, Inc.
3708 River Rd., Suite 400
Franklin Park, IL 60131
(800) 566-6150
www.wlp.jspaluch.com

Music Sources

G.I.A. Publications, Inc.
7404 S. Mason Ave.
Chicago, IL 60638
(800) 442-1358
www.giamusic.com

World Library Publications (WLP)
J.S. Paluch Company, Inc.
3708 River Rd., Suite 400
Franklin Park, IL 60131
(800) 566-6150
www.wlp.jspaluch.com

OCP Publications
5536 NE Hassalo St.
Portland, OR 97213-3638
(800) 548-8749
www.ocp.org

Pauline Books & Media
50 Saint Paul's Ave.
Boston, MA 02130
(800) 876-4463
www.pauline.org

Mary Lu Walker Albums & Songbooks (MLW)
www.maryluwalker.com

Visit the Loyola Press Web site at christourlife.com for more resources to help you continue to explore your Catholic faith.

There are many other reliable Catholic Web sites available on the Internet. Here are some helpful navigational hints:

- Start with official Web sites sponsored by your parish or diocese, other dioceses or religious communities, the U.S. Catholic Bishops, and the Vatican.
- Check out the suggested links on those Web sites to see what they recommend.
- When exploring a Web site, read the "About Us" page to see who sponsors it and what they stand for.
- Crosscheck your sources to ensure that the information is accurate or to explore a variety of perspectives.
- Avoid any Web site that contains offensive material.

4 Catholic Educators—portal to information on the Catholic faith and to resources for teachers, catechists, directors of religious education, and pastors

4catholiceducators.com

Catholic Charities of the Archdiocese of St. Paul and Minneapolis—Catholic Social Teaching documents and related information

www.cctwincities.org/CatholicSocialTeaching

Bible Gateway—service for reading and researching Scripture online

www.biblegateway.com

Bible Search: Revised Standard Version—Scripture search engine helps locate words and phrases in the Bible

www.hti.umich.edu/r/rsv

Catechism of the Catholic Church—the *Catechism*, including a search engine, concordance, and glossary

www.vatican.va/archive/ccc/index.htm

Catechist's Journey—Joe Paprocki, author of *The Catechist's Toolbox*, shares reflections on the experience of serving as a catechist for eighth graders

www.catechistsjourney.com

Catholic Campaign for Human Development—assists people to rise out of poverty through empowerment programs that foster self-sufficiency

www.usccb.org/about/
catholic-campaign-for-human-development

Catholic Catechist—comprehensive teaching resources for catechists and teachers

www.catholiccatechist.org

Catholic Charities—helps families and individuals overcome tragedy, poverty, and other life challenges

www.catholiccharitiesusa.org

Catholic Church Extension Society—works to sustain and extend the Catholic faith in poor and remote mission areas of the United States

www.catholic-extension.org

Catholic News Service—reports the news that affects Catholics in their everyday lives

www.catholicnews.com

Catholic Online—information about Catholicism including an online historical and biblical database

www.catholic.org

Catholic Relief Services—the official international relief and development agency of the U.S. Catholic community

www.crs.org

Creighton University Online Ministries—resources in the Catholic prayer tradition and in Ignatian spirituality

http://onlineministries.creighton.edu/
CollaborativeMinistry/online.html

New American Bible—official online version

www.usccb.org/bible

A Nun's Life—a blog about being a Catholic nun in today's world

http://anunslife.org

Patron Saints Index—alphabetical index (including profiles) of patron saints

saints.sqpn.com

Pray-As-You-Go—daily prayer and music for your MP3 player and your soul

www.pray-as-you-go.org

Religious Ministries Online Guide—database of Catholic ministries, religious and lay communities, and a guide to discerning vocations

www.religiousministries.com

Resources for Catholic Educators—resources for Catholic catechists and teachers

www.silk.net/RelEd

Sacred Space—daily prayer online

www.sacredspace.ie

Second Vatican Council Documents—the full text of the 16 major documents of the Second Vatican Council

www.vatican.va/archive/hist_councils/ii_vatican _council

Theology Library at Spring Hill College (The Jesuit College of the South)—links to numerous Church documents and periodicals on a variety of theological topics

www.shc.edu/theolibrary

United States Conference of Catholic Bishops—official Web site of the U.S. Catholic Bishops

www.usccb.org

The Vatican Web Site—official Vatican Web site, which includes the *Catechism,* and other Church documents

www.vatican.va

Vision Vocation Network—includes links to religious communities as well as listings of discernment, service, and educational opportunities

http://vocationnetwork.org

These Web sites are being provided as a convenience and for informational purposes only. Loyola Press neither controls nor endorses such sites, nor have we reviewed or approved any content for subsequent links made from these sites. Loyola Press is not responsible for the legality, accuracy, or inappropriate nature of any content, advertising, products, or other materials on or available from such linked sites. In addition, these sites or services, including their contents and links, may be constantly changing. Loyola Press assumes no responsibility for monitoring the content of these sites.

Glossary

A

Abba an informal word for *father* in Aramaic, the language Jesus spoke. It is like "dad" in English. When Jesus spoke to God the Father, he called him "Abba."

abortion the deliberate ending of a pregnancy that results in the death of the unborn child. The Church teaches that since life begins at conception, abortion is a serious crime against life and is gravely against the moral law.

Abraham the model of faith in God in the Old Testament. Because of his faith, he left his home and traveled to Canaan, where God made a covenant with him that promised him land and many descendants. He became the father of the Chosen People.

absolution the forgiveness we receive from God through the priest in the Sacrament of Penance and Reconciliation

abstain the practice of denying oneself food, drink, or other pleasures. Catholics over age 14 abstain from eating meat on Ash Wednesday and on the Fridays of Lent.

actual grace the gift of God, freely given, that unites us with the life of the Trinity. Actual grace helps us make the choices that conform our lives to God's will.

adore to worship God above all else because he is our Creator. The First Commandment requires us to adore God alone.

adultery an injury to the marriage bond covenant. It occurs when a man or a woman who are married to each other has sexual relations with another person. The Sixth Commandment forbids adultery because it undermines the institution of marriage and is harmful to children, who need the stability of their parents' marriage commitment.

Advocate Jesus' name for the Holy Spirit. The Holy Spirit comforts us, speaks for us in difficult times, and makes Jesus present to us.

Alleluia an acclamation meaning "praise God." Alleluia is sung before the Gospel except during Lent.

altar the table in the church on which the priest celebrates Mass, where the sacrifice of Christ on the Cross is made present in the Sacrament of the Eucharist. The altar represents two aspects of the mystery of the Eucharist. It is the place where Jesus Christ offers himself for our sins and where he gives us himself as our food for eternal life.

ambo a raised stand from which a person reads the Word of God during Mass

Amen a Hebrew word meaning "it is so" or "let it be done." It signifies agreement with what has been said. Prayers in the New Testament, in the Church's liturgies, and the Creed end with *Amen*. In the Gospels, Jesus uses *Amen* to reinforce the seriousness of what he is about to say.

angel a spiritual creature who worships God in heaven. Angels serve God as messengers. They tell us of his plans for our salvation.

Angelus a prayer honoring the Incarnation of Jesus. The *Angelus* is prayed in the morning, at noon, and in the evening.

annulment a finding by a Church tribunal that at least one essential element for a real marriage was not present on the day of the wedding. The Church can declare that the Sacrament of Marriage did not take place if at least one of the parties was not freely choosing to marry, had been married before and that marriage was not annulled, or was not open to having children. An annulment cannot be considered until after a person is divorced. Catholics who receive an annulment are free to marry in the Church and can receive Communion.

Annunciation the announcement to Mary by the angel Gabriel that God had chosen her to be the mother of Jesus. When Mary agreed, the Son of God became human in her. The feast of the Annunciation is celebrated on March 25, nine months before Christmas.

anoint to put oil on things or people to dedicate them to the service of God. The anointing of the kings of Israel was a sign that they were chosen to rule God's people.

Anointing of the Sick one of the seven sacraments. In this sacrament, a sick person has the oil of the sick applied and receives the strength, peace, and courage to overcome the difficulties associated with illness. Through this sacrament, Jesus brings the sick person spiritual healing and forgiveness of sins. If it is God's will, healing of the body is given as well.

apostle one of twelve special men who accompanied Jesus in his ministry and were witnesses to the Resurrection. Apostle means "one sent." These were the people sent to preach the Gospel to the whole world.

Apostles' Creed a statement of Christian belief that developed out of a creed used in Baptism in Rome. The Apostles' Creed lists simple statements of belief in God the Father, Jesus Christ the Son, and the Holy Spirit. The profession of faith used in Baptism today is based on the Apostles' Creed.

(253)

apostolic | catechumenate

apostolic one of the four Marks of the Church. The Church is apostolic because it continues to hand on the teaching of the apostles through their successors, the bishops, in union with the successor of Saint Peter, the pope.

Ark of the Covenant a portable box that held the tablets of the Ten Commandments. The Ark was the most important item in the shrine that was carried through the desert and then placed in the holiest part of the Temple in Jerusalem. Two angels are depicted on the cover of the Ark of the Covenant. The wings of the angels curve upward, representing the place where God came close to Israel and revealed his will.

Ascension the entry of Jesus into God's presence in heaven. In the Acts of the Apostles, it is written that Jesus, after his Resurrection, spent 40 days on earth, instructing his followers. He then returned to his Father in heaven.

Assumption Mary's being taken, body and soul, into heaven. Mary had a special relationship with her Son, Jesus, from the very beginning, when she conceived him. Because of this relationship, she enjoys a special participation in Jesus' Resurrection and has been taken into heaven where she now lives with him. We celebrate this event in the feast of the Assumption on August 15.

B

Baptism the first of the seven sacraments. Baptism frees us from Original Sin and is necessary for salvation. Baptism gives us new life in Jesus Christ through the Holy Spirit. The celebration of Baptism consists of immersing in water or pouring water upon a person while declaring that the person is baptized in the name of the Father, the Son, and the Holy Spirit.

Beatitudes the teachings of Jesus in the Sermon on the Mount in Matthew's Gospel. The Beatitudes are eight ways of living the Christian life. They are the fulfillment of the commandments given to Moses. These teachings present the way to true happiness.

benediction a prayer service in which we honor Jesus in the Blessed Sacrament and receive his blessing

Bible the collection of books containing the truths of God's Revelation to us. These writings were inspired by the Holy Spirit and written by human beings. The Bible is made up of the 46 books in the Old Testament and 27 books in the New Testament.

bishop a man who has received the fullness of Holy Orders. As a successor to the original apostles, he takes care of the Church and is a principal teacher in it.

blasphemy speaking or thinking words of hatred or defiance against God. It extends to language that disrespects the Church, the saints, or holy things. It is also blasphemy to use God's name as an excuse to enslave people, to torture them, or to put them to death. Using God's name to do these things can cause others to reject religion.

Blessed Sacrament the hosts, which are the Body of Christ, that have been consecrated at Mass. They are kept in the tabernacle to adore and to be taken to those who are sick.

blessing a prayer that calls for God's power and care upon some person, place, thing, or special activity

Body and Blood of Christ consecrated by the priest at Mass. In the Sacrament of the Eucharist, all of the risen Lord Jesus Christ—body, blood, soul, and divinity—is present under the appearances of bread and wine.

Buddhism a philosophy based on the teaching of Siddhartha Gautama, who was known as the Buddha, which means "Enlightened One." The Buddha was born to a royal family in northern India about five and a half centuries before Jesus. At age 29 he became disillusioned with life and left his comfortable home to find an answer to the question of why humans suffer.

C

calumny (slander) a false statement about the reputation of someone that makes other people think badly of that person. Calumny, also called *slander,* is a sin against the Eighth Commandment.

canon law the official laws that guide all aspects of Church life. Canon law assists the Church in its task of revealing and communicating God's saving power to the world.

capital sins those sins that can lead us to more serious sin. They are pride, avarice (greed), envy, wrath (anger), gluttony, lust, and sloth.

cardinal virtues the four main virtues that direct right living: prudence, justice, temperance, and fortitude. Cardinal comes from the Latin word *cardo,* which means "hinge."

catechumen a person being formed in the Christian life through instruction and by the example of the parish community. Through conversion and maturity of faith, a catechumen is preparing to be welcomed into the Church at Easter through the Sacraments of Baptism, Confirmation, and the Eucharist.

catechumenate the process of becoming a Christian through the Rite of Christian Initiation for Adults (RCIA). In the early Church, the process took several years.

catholic one of the four Marks of the Church. The Church is catholic because Jesus is fully present in it, because it proclaims the fullness of faith, and because Jesus has given the Church to the whole world. The Church is universal.

Catholic Social Teaching the body of teaching on social justice issues, action on behalf of justice, and work to create a more just world. The Church makes judgments about economic and social matters that relate to the basic rights of individuals and communities. The Church's social teaching is a rich treasure of wisdom about how to build a just society.

charity a virtue given to us by God that helps us love God above all things and love our neighbor as ourselves

chastity the integration of our physical sexuality with our spiritual nature. Chastity helps us be completely human, able to give to others our whole life and love. All people, married or single, are called to practice chastity.

chrism a perfumed oil, consecrated by a bishop, that is used in the Sacraments of Baptism, Confirmation, and Holy Orders. Anointing with chrism signifies the call of the baptized to the threefold ministry of priest, prophet, and king.

Christ a title that means "anointed one." It is from a Greek word that means the same thing as the Hebrew word *Messiah,* or "anointed." It is the name given to Jesus as priest, prophet, and king.

Christian the name given to all those who have been anointed through the gift of the Holy Spirit in Baptism and have become followers of Jesus Christ

Christmas the feast of the birth of Jesus (December 25)

Church the People of God throughout the whole world, or diocese (the local Church), or the assembly of those called together to worship God. The Church is one, holy, catholic, and apostolic.

clergy those men who are set apart as sacred ministers to serve the Church through Holy Orders

collegiality shared decision making between the pope and the bishops

commandment a standard, or rule, for living as God wants us to live. Jesus summarized all of the commandments into two: love God and love your neighbor.

Communion of Saints the unity of all, dead or living, who have been saved in Jesus Christ. The Communion of Saints is based on our one faith, and it is nourished by our participation in the Eucharist.

confession the act of telling our sins to a priest in the Sacrament of Penance and Reconciliation. The sacrament itself is sometimes referred to as "confession."

Confirmation the sacrament that completes the grace we receive in Baptism. It seals, or confirms, this grace through the seven Gifts of the Holy Spirit that we receive as part of Confirmation. This sacrament also makes us better able to participate in the worship and apostolic life of the Church.

conscience the inner voice that helps each of us judge the morality of our own actions. It guides us to follow God's law by doing good and avoiding evil.

consecration the making of a thing or a person to be special to God through a prayer or blessing. At Mass, the words of the priest are a consecration that transforms the bread and wine into the Body and Blood of Jesus Christ. People or objects set apart for God in a special way are also consecrated. For example, churches and altars are consecrated for use in liturgy, and bishops are consecrated as they receive the fullness of the Sacrament of Holy Orders.

contrition the sorrow we feel when we know that we have sinned, followed by the decision not to sin again. Perfect contrition arises from a love that loves God above all else. Imperfect contrition arises from other motives. Contrition is the most important act of the penitent preparing to celebrate the Sacrament of Penance and Reconciliation.

Corporal Works of Mercy kind acts by which we help our neighbors with their everyday material needs. Corporal Works of Mercy include feeding the hungry, giving drink to the thirsty, clothing the naked, sheltering the homeless, visiting the sick and the imprisoned, and burying the dead.

Council of Jerusalem the name of the meeting that happened about A.D. 50 that is described in chapter 15 of the Acts of the Apostles. The meeting was the result of a disagreement between Paul and his followers and the Jewish Christian followers of James, the leader of the Jerusalem Church. James felt that those who became Christians should also observe the rules of traditional Judaism and that the men should be circumcised. Paul said that there should be no such necessity. It was finally agreed that circumcision was not necessary for Gentiles who became Christians.

counsel one of the seven Gifts of the Holy Spirit. Counsel helps us make correct choices in life through reflection, discernment, consulting, and the advising of others.

covenant a solemn agreement between people or between people and God. God made covenants with humanity through agreements with Noah, Abraham, and Moses. These covenants offered salvation. God's new and final covenant was established through Jesus' life, Death, and Resurrection. *Testament* is another word for covenant.

covet to want to take what belongs to someone else. The Ninth and Tenth Commandments tell us it is sinful to covet.

creation God's act of making everything that exists outside himself. Creation is everything that exists. God said that all creation is good.

Creator God, who made everything that is and whom we can come to know through everything he created

creed a brief summary of what people believe. The word *creed* comes from the Latin *credo,* which means "I believe." The Nicene Creed is the most important summary of Christian beliefs.

culture the activity of a group of people that includes their music, art, language, and celebrations. Culture is one of the ways people experience God in their lives.

D

deacon a man ordained through the Sacrament of Holy Orders to the ministry of service in the Church. Deacons help the bishop and priests by serving in the various charitable ministries of the Church. They also help by proclaiming the Gospel, preaching, and assisting at the Liturgy of the Eucharist. Deacons can celebrate Baptisms, witness marriages, and preside at funerals.

detraction the act of talking about the faults and sins of another person to someone who has no reason to hear this and cannot help the person. Detraction damages the reputation of another person without any intent to help that person.

devil a spirit created good by God who became evil through disobedience. The devil tempted Adam and Eve to sin and still tempts us today. But God's grace is stronger than the works of the devil.

dignity of the human person a basic principle at the center of Catholic Social Teaching. It is the starting point of a moral vision for society because human life is sacred and should be treated with great respect. The human person is the clearest reflection of God among us.

dignity of work a basic principle at the center of Catholic Social Teaching. Since work is done by people created in the image of God, it is not only a way to make a living but an important way we participate in God's creation. In work, people fulfill part of their potential given to them by God. All workers have a right to productive work, to decent and fair wages, and to safe working conditions.

diocese the members of the Church in a particular area, united in faith and the sacraments, and gathered under the leadership of a bishop

disciple a person who has accepted Jesus' message and tries to live as he did, sharing his mission, his suffering, and his joys

discrimination the act of mistreating other people because of how they look or act, or just because they are different

Divine Providence the guidance of God over all he has created. Divine Providence exercises care for all creation and guides it toward its final perfection.

Doctor of the Church a man or a woman recognized as a model teacher of the Christian faith

doctrine the revealed teaching of Christ, which the Magisterium of the Church has declared Catholics are obliged to believe. Growth in the understanding of doctrine continues in the Church through the prayer and study of the faithful and theologians and through the teaching of the Magisterium.

E

Easter the celebration of the bodily raising of Jesus Christ from the dead. Easter is the festival of our redemption and the central Christian feast, the one from which other feasts arise.

Eastern Catholic Church a group of churches that developed in the East (in countries such as Lebanon) that are in union with the Roman Catholic Church, but have their own liturgical, theological, and administrative traditions. They show the truly catholic nature of the Church, which takes root in many cultures.

ecumenical council a gathering of Catholic bishops from the entire world, meeting under the leadership of the pope or his delegates. Ecumenical councils discuss pastoral, legal, and doctrinal issues. There have been 21 ecumenical councils recognized by the Catholic Church. The first was the First Council of Nicaea in 325. The most recent was the Second Vatican Council, which took place between 1962 and 1965.

ecumenism the movement for unity among Christians. Christ gave the Church the gift of unity from the beginning, but over the centuries that unity has been broken. All Christians are called by their common Baptism to pray and work to maintain, reinforce, and perfect the unity Christ wants for the Church.

Emmanuel a Hebrew name from the Old Testament that means "God with us." In Matthew's Gospel, Jesus is called Emmanuel.

encyclical a letter written by the pope and sent to the whole Church and sometimes to the whole world. It expresses Church teaching on specific and important issues.

 GLOSSARY

epistle a letter written by Saint Paul or another leader to a group of Christians in the early Church. Of the 27 books of the New Testament, 21 are epistles. The second reading at Mass on Sundays and holy days is always from one of these books.

eternal life the never-ending life after death with God, granted to those who die as God's friends, with the grace of God alive in them

Eucharist the sacrament in which we give thanks to God for giving us Jesus Christ. The Body and Blood of Christ, which we receive at Mass, brings us into union with Jesus' saving Death and Resurrection.

Eucharistic Liturgy the public worship, held by the Church, in which bread and wine are transformed into the Body and Blood of Jesus Christ which we receive in Holy Communion. The Sunday celebration of the Eucharistic Liturgy is at the heart of Church life.

euthanasia an act with the intent to cause the death of a handicapped, sick, or dying person. Euthanasia is considered murder and is gravely contrary to the dignity of the human person and to the respect due to the living God, our Creator.

evangelist anyone engaged in spreading the gospel. Letters in the New Testament, along with the Acts of the Apostles, list evangelists along with apostles and prophets as ministers in the Church. The term is principally used to describe the writers of the four Gospels: Matthew, Mark, Luke, and John.

evangelization the sharing of the good news, by word or example, of the salvation we have received in Jesus Christ. Jesus commissioned his disciples to go forth into the world and tell the good news. Evangelization is the responsibility of every Christian. The New Evangelization calls believers to a deeper faith and invites those who have heard the Gospel but not been transformed by it to have a true encounter with Christ.

examination of conscience the act of prayerfully thinking about what we have said or done in light of what the Gospel asks of us. We also think about how our actions may have hurt our relationship with God or others. An examination of conscience is an important part of our preparing to celebrate the Sacrament of Penance and Reconciliation.

excommunication a severe penalty that is imposed by Church authorities for serious crimes against the Catholic religion. A person who is excommunicated is excluded from participating in the Eucharist and the other sacraments and from ministry in the Church.

Exile the period in the history of Israel between the destruction of Jerusalem in 587 B.C. and the return to Jerusalem in 537 B.C. During this time, many of the Jewish people were forced to live in Babylon, far from home.

Exodus God's liberation of the Hebrew people from slavery in Egypt and his leading them to the Promised Land

F

faith a gift of God that helps us believe in him. We profess our faith in the Creed, celebrate it in the sacraments, live by it through our good conduct of loving God and our neighbor, and express it in prayer. It is a personal adherence of the whole person to God, who has revealed himself to us through words and actions throughout history.

fasting limiting the amount we eat for a period of time to express sorrow for sin and to make ourselves more aware of God's action in our lives. Adults 18 years old and older fast on Ash Wednesday and Good Friday. The practice is also encouraged as a private devotion at other times of penitence.

fear of the Lord one of the seven Gifts of the Holy Spirit. This gift leads us to a sense of wonder and awe in the presence of God because we recognize his greatness.

fortitude the strength to choose to do the right thing, even when it is difficult. Fortitude is one of the four central human virtues, called the cardinal virtues, by which we guide our conduct through faith and the use of reason. It is also one of the Gifts of the Holy Spirit.

free will the ability to choose to do good because God has made us like him. Our free will is what makes us truly human. Our exercise of free will to do good increases our freedom. Using free will to choose sin makes us slaves to sin.

G

Gentiles the name given to foreign people by the Jews after the Exile. They were nonbelievers who worshiped false gods. They stand in contrast to the Jewish people, who received God's law.

Gifts of the Holy Spirit the permanent willingness, given to us by the Holy Spirit that makes it possible for us to do what God asks of us. The Gifts of the Holy Spirit are drawn from Isaiah 11:1–3. They include wisdom, understanding, right judgment, courage, knowledge, and wonder and awe. Church Tradition has added reverence, to make a total of seven.

Gospel | Incarnation

Gospel the good news of God's mercy and love that we experience by hearing the story of Jesus' life, Death, and Resurrection. The story is passed on in the teaching ministry of the Church as the source of all truth and right living. It is presented to us in four books in the New Testament—the Gospels of Matthew, Mark, Luke, and John.

grace the gift of God, given to us without our meriting it. Sanctifying grace fills us with God's life and makes it possible for us always to be his friends. Grace is the Holy Spirit alive in us, helping us live out our Christian vocation. Grace helps us live as God wants us to.

Great Commandment Jesus' commandment that we are to love God and to love our neighbor as we love ourselves. Jesus tells us that this commandment sums up everything taught in the Old Testament.

greed too great a desire for wealth, material possessions, or power. It is also called *avarice* and is one of the seven deadly, or capital, sins.

H

heaven union with God the Father, Son, and Holy Spirit in life and love that never ends. Heaven is a state of complete happiness and the goal of the deepest wishes of the human heart.

Hebrews the descendants of Abraham, Isaac, and Jacob, who were enslaved in Egypt. God helped Moses lead these people out of slavery.

hell a life of total separation from God forever. In his infinite love for us, God can only desire our salvation. Hell is the result of the free choice of a person to reject God's love and forgiveness once and for all.

heresy a religious belief that opposes or denies any divinely revealed truth of the Catholic faith

holiness the fullness of Christian life and love. All people are called to holiness, which is made possible by cooperating with God's grace to do his will. As we do God's will, we are transformed more and more into the image of the Son, Jesus Christ.

holy one of the four Marks of the Church. It is the kind of life we live when we share in the life of God, who is all holiness. The Church is holy because it is united with Jesus Christ.

Holy Communion the reception of the Body and Blood of Christ during holy Mass. It brings us into union with Jesus Christ and his saving death and Resurrection.

holy days of obligation the principal feast days, other than Sundays, of the Church. On holy days of obligation, we celebrate the great things that God has done for us through Jesus and the saints. Catholics are obliged to participate in the Eucharist on these days, just as we are on Sundays.

Holy Family the family of Jesus as he grew up in Nazareth. It included Jesus; his mother, Mary; and his foster father, Joseph.

Holy of Holies the holiest part of the Temple in Jerusalem. The high priest entered this part of the Temple once a year to address God and to ask God's forgiveness for the sins of the people.

Holy Orders the sacrament through which the mission given by Jesus to his apostles continues in the Church. The sacrament has three degrees: deacon, priest, and bishop. Through the laying on of hands in the Sacrament of Holy Orders, men receive a permanent, sacramental mark that calls them to minister to the Church.

Holy Spirit the third Person of the Trinity, who is sent to us as our helper and, through Baptism and Confirmation, fills us with God's life. Together with the Father and the Son, the Holy Spirit brings the divine plan of salvation to completion.

homily the explanation by a bishop, a priest, or a deacon of the Word of God in the liturgy. The homily relates the Word of God to our life as Christians today.

hope the confidence that God will always be with us, make us happy now and forever, and help us live so that we will be with him forever

I

idolatry The worship of false gods, either a person or a thing, in place of worshiping God. Idolatry is worshiping a creature, which could be power, pleasure, or money, in place of the Creator. Idolatry is a sin against the First Commandment.

Immaculate Conception the Church teaching that Mary was free from Original Sin from the first moment of her life. She was preserved through the merits of her Son, Jesus, the Savior of the human race. It was declared a belief of the Catholic Church by Pope Pius IX in 1854 and is celebrated on December 8.

Incarnation the Son of God, Jesus, being born as a full human being in order to save us. The Son of God, the second Person of the Trinity, is both true God and true man.

indulgence a lessening of the punishment due for sins that have been forgiven. Indulgences move us toward our final purification, when we will live with God forever.

inerrancy the teaching of the Church that the Bible teaches the truths of the faith necessary for our salvation without error. Because God inspired the human authors, he is the author of the Sacred Scriptures. This gives us the assurance that they teach his saving truth without error, even though certain historical and scientific information may not be accurate. With the help of the Holy Spirit and the Church, we interpret what God wants to reveal to us about our salvation through the sacred authors.

infallibility the gift the Holy Spirit has given to the Church that assures that the pope and the bishops in union with the pope can proclaim as true the doctrines that involve faith or morals. It is an extension of the fact that the whole body of believers cannot be in error when it comes to questions of faith and morals.

Infancy Narrative accounts of the infancy and childhood of Jesus that appear in the first two chapters of Matthew's and Luke's Gospels. Each Gospel contains a different series of events. They have in common that Jesus was born in Bethlehem through the virginal conception of Mary. The intention of these stories is to proclaim Jesus as Messiah and Savior.

inspired influenced by the Holy Spirit. The human authors of Scripture were inspired by the Holy Spirit. The creative inspiration of the Holy Spirit makes sure that the Scripture is taught according to the truth God wants us to know for our salvation.

intercession prayer or petition on behalf of another or others. Intercession for others in prayer knows no boundaries and includes even those who might wish to do us harm.

interpretation explanation of the words of Scripture, combining human knowledge and the teaching office of the Church, under the guidance of the Holy Spirit

interreligious dialogue the work to build a relationship of openness with the followers of non-Christian religions. The Church's bond with non-Christian religions comes from our common bond as children of God. The purpose of this dialogue is to increase understanding of one another, to work for the common good of humanity, and to establish peace.

Islam the third great religion, along with Judaism and Christianity, professing belief in one God. *Islam* means "submission" to that one God.

Israelites the descendants of Abraham, Isaac, and Jacob. God changed Jacob's name to "Israel," and Jacob's 12 sons and their children became the leaders of the 12 tribes of Israel. (*See* Hebrews.)

J

Jesus the Son of God, who was born of the Virgin Mary and who died and was raised from the dead for our salvation. He returned to God and will come again to judge the living and the dead. His name means "God saves."

Jews the name given to the Hebrew people, from the time of the Exile to the present. The name means "the people who live in the territory of Judah," the area of Palestine surrounding Jerusalem.

Joseph the foster father of Jesus, who was engaged to Mary when the angel announced that Mary would have a child through the power of the Holy Spirit. In the Old Testament, Joseph was the son of Jacob who was sold into slavery in Egypt by his brothers and then saved them from starvation when famine came.

Judaism the name of the religion of Jesus and all the people of Israel after they returned from exile in Babylon and built the second Temple

justice the virtue that guides us to give to God and others what is due them. Justice is one of the four central human virtues, called the cardinal virtues, by which we guide our Christian life.

justification being in a right relationship with God through moral conduct and observance of the Law. We have merit in God's sight and are able to do this because of the work of God's grace in us. Paul speaks of justification in a new way that is no longer dependent on observance of the Law. It comes through faith in Jesus and in his saving Death and Resurrection. To be justified or made righteous in Jesus is to be saved, vindicated, and put right with God through his grace.

K

Kingdom of God God's rule over us, announced in the Gospel and present in the Eucharist. The beginning of the kingdom here on earth is mysteriously present in the Church, and it will come in completeness at the end of time.

knowledge one of the seven Gifts of the Holy Spirit. This gift helps us know what God asks of us and how we should respond.

L

laity those who have been made members of Christ in Baptism and who participate in the priestly, prophetic, and kingly functions of Christ in his mission to the whole world. The laity is distinct from the clergy, whose members are set apart as ministers to serve the Church.

Last Judgment the final judgment of all human beings that will occur when Christ returns in glory and all appear in their own bodies before him to give an account of all their deeds in life. In the presence of Christ, the truth of each person's relationship with God will be laid bare, as will the good each person has done or failed to do during his or her earthly life. At that time God's kingdom will come in its fullness.

Last Supper the last meal Jesus ate with his disciples on the night before he died. At the Last Supper, Jesus took bread and wine, blessed them, and they became his Body and Blood, Soul and Divinity. Jesus' Death and Resurrection, his sacrifice that we celebrate in the Eucharist, were anticipated in this meal.

Law the first five books of the Old Testament. The Hebrew word for *law* is *Torah.* The ancient law is summarized in the Ten Commandments.

Lectionary the official book that contains all the Scripture readings used in the Liturgy of the Word

Lent the 40 days before Easter (not counting Sundays) during which we prepare, through prayer, fasting, and giving aid to the poor, to change our lives and to live the Gospel more completely

liturgical year the celebrations throughout the year of all the mysteries of Jesus' birth, life, Death, and Resurrection. The celebration of Easter is at the heart of the liturgical year. The other feasts celebrated throughout the year make up the basic rhythm of the Christian's life of prayer.

liturgy the public prayer of the Church that celebrates the wonderful things God has done for us in Jesus Christ, our high priest, and the way in which he continues the work of our salvation. The original meaning of *liturgy* was "a public work or service done for the people."

Liturgy of the Eucharist the second half of the Mass, in which the bread and wine are transformed into the Body and Blood of Jesus Christ, which we then receive in Holy Communion

Liturgy of the Hours the public prayer of the Church to praise God and to sanctify the day. It includes an office of readings before sunrise, morning prayer at dawn, evening prayer at sunset, and prayer before going to bed. The

chanting of psalms makes up the major portion of each of these services.

Liturgy of the Word the first half of the Mass, in which we listen to God's Word from the Bible and consider what it means for us today. The Liturgy of the Word can also be a public prayer and proclamation of God's Word that is not followed by the Liturgy of the Eucharist.

Lord the name used for God to replace *Yahweh,* the name he revealed to Moses, which was considered too sacred to pronounce. It indicates the divinity of Israel's God. The New Testament uses the title *Lord* for both the Father and for Jesus, recognizing him as God himself. (*See* Yahweh.)

Lord's Day Sunday is the day Christians set aside for special worship of God. Each Sunday Mass commemorates the Resurrection of Jesus on Easter Sunday. Besides requiring us to offer God the worship owed him, the Third Commandment tells us Sunday is a day to relax the mind and body and to perform works of mercy.

M

Magisterium the living, teaching office of the Church. This office, through the bishops and with the pope, provides an authentic interpretation of the Word of God. It ensures faithfulness to the teaching of the apostles in matters of faith and morals.

Magnificat Mary's song of praise to God for the great things he has done for her and planned for us through Jesus

Marks of the Church the four most important aspects of the Church found in the Nicene Creed. According to the Nicene Creed, the Church is one, holy, catholic, and apostolic.

martyrs those who have given their lives for the faith. *Martyr* comes from the Greek word for "witness." A martyr is the supreme witness to the truth of the faith and to Christ to whom he or she is united. The seventh chapter of the Acts of the Apostles recounts the death of the first martyr, the deacon Stephen.

Mary the mother of Jesus. She is called blessed and "full of grace" because God chose her to be the mother of the Son of God, the second Person of the Trinity.

Mass the most important sacramental celebration of the Church, established by Jesus at the Last Supper as a remembrance of his Death and Resurrection. At Mass, we listen to God's Word from the Bible and receive the Body and Blood of Jesus Christ in Holy Communion.

Matrimony a solemn agreement between a woman and a man to be partners for life, both for their own good and for bringing up children. Marriage is a sacrament when the agreement is properly made between baptized Christians.

meditation a form of prayer using silence and listening that seeks through imagination, emotion, and desire to understand how to adhere and respond to what God is asking. By concentrating on a word or an image, we move beyond thoughts, empty the mind of contents that get in the way of our experience of God, and rest in simple awareness of God. It is one of the three major expressions of the life of prayer.

Mendicant Order a unique variety of religious order that developed in the 13th century. Unlike monks who remain inside a monastery, members of Mendicant Orders have ministries of preaching, teaching, and witnessing within cities. They are called *mendicant* from the Latin word for "begging," which is their main means of supporting themselves. The two main Mendicant Orders are the Dominicans, founded by Saint Dominic de Guzman, and the Franciscans, founded by Saint Francis of Assisi.

Messiah a title that means "anointed one." It is from a Hebrew word that means the same thing as the Greek word *Christ.* Messiah is the title that was given to Jesus as priest, prophet, and king.

miracles signs or acts of wonder that cannot be explained by natural causes but are works of God. In the Gospels, Jesus works miracles as a sign that the Kingdom of God is present in his ministry.

mission the work of Jesus Christ that is continued in the Church through the Holy Spirit. The mission of the Church is to proclaim salvation in Jesus' life, Death, and Resurrection.

missionary one who proclaims the Gospel to others and leads them to know Christ. Missionaries are lay, ordained, and religious people engaged in mission.

monasticism a form of religious life in which men and women live out their vows of poverty, chastity, and obedience in a stable community life in a monastery. The goal of monasticism is to pursue, under the guidance of a rule, a life of public prayer, work, and meditation for the glory of God. Saint Benedict of Nursia, who died around A.D. 550, is considered the father of Western monasticism.

moral choice a choice to do what is right or not do what is wrong. We make moral choices because they are what we believe God wants and because we have the freedom to choose what is right and avoid what is wrong.

moral law a rule for living that has been established by God and people in authority who are concerned about the good of all. Moral laws are based on God's direction to us to do what is right and avoid what is wrong. Some moral laws are "written" in the human heart and can be known through our own reasoning. Other moral laws have been revealed to us by God in the Old Testament and in the new law given by Jesus.

mortal sin a serious decision to turn away from God by doing something that we know is wrong. For a sin to be mortal it must be a very serious offense, and the person must know how serious the sin is and freely choose to do it anyway.

Mother of God the title for Mary proclaimed at the Council of Ephesus in 431. The council declared that Mary was not just the mother of Jesus, the man. She became the Mother of God by the conception of the Son of God in her womb. Because Jesus' humanity is one with his divinity, Mary is the mother of the eternal Son of God made man, who is God himself.

Muslim a follower of the religion of Islam. *Muslim* means "one who submits to God."

mystagogy the last stage of the Rite of Christian Initiation of Adults, in which the newly initiated reflect on the deep meaning of the sacraments they have celebrated and on living the Christian life fully

mystery a religious truth that we can know only through God's Revelation and that we cannot fully understand. Our faith is a mystery that we profess in the Creed and celebrate in the liturgy and sacraments.

Mystical Body of Christ the members of the Church formed into a spiritual body and bound together by the life communicated by Jesus Christ through the sacraments. Christ is the center and source of the life of this body. In it, we are all united. Each member of the body receives from Christ gifts fitting for him or her.

N

natural law the moral law that is "written" in the human heart. We can know natural law through our own reason because the Creator has placed the knowledge of it in our hearts. It can provide the solid foundation on which we can make rules to guide our choices in life. Natural law forms the basis of our fundamental rights and duties and is the foundation for the work of the Holy Spirit in guiding our moral choices.

New Testament the 27 books of the second part of the Bible, which tell of the teaching, ministry, and saving events of the life of Jesus. The four Gospels present Jesus' life, Death, and Resurrection. The Acts of the Apostles tells the story of the message of salvation as it spread through the growth of the Church. Various letters instruct us in how to live as followers of Jesus Christ. The Book of Revelation offers encouragement to Christians living through persecution.

Nicene Creed | Pentecost

Nicene Creed the summary of Christian beliefs developed by the bishops at the first two councils of the Church, held in A.D. 325 and 381. It is the Creed shared by most Christians in the East and in the West.

O

obedience the act of willingly following what God asks us to do for our salvation. The Fourth Commandment requires children to obey their parents, and all people are required to obey civil authority when it acts for the good of all. To imitate the obedience of Jesus, members of religious communities make a special vow of obedience.

Old Testament the first 46 books of the Bible, which tell of God's Covenant with the people of Israel and his plan for the salvation of all people. The first five books are known as the Torah. The Old Testament is fulfilled in the New Testament, but God's covenant presented in the Old Testament has permanent value and has never been revoked.

one one of the four Marks of the Church. The Church is one because of its source in the one God and because of its founder, Jesus Christ. Jesus, through his Death on the Cross, united all to God in one body. Within the unity of the Church, there is great diversity because of the variety of the gifts given to its members.

Ordinary Time the part of the liturgical year outside of the seasons and feasts and the preparation for them. *Ordinary* means not common but counted time, as in ordinal numbers. It is devoted to growth in understanding the mystery of Christ in its fullness. The color of Ordinary Time is green to symbolize growth.

ordination the rite of the Sacrament of Holy Orders, by which a bishop gives to men, through the laying on of hands, the ability to minister to the Church as bishops, priests, and deacons

Original Sin the consequence of the disobedience of the first human beings. They disobeyed God and chose to follow their own will rather than God's will. As a result, human beings lost the original blessing God had intended and became subject to sin and death. In Baptism, we are restored to life with God through Jesus Christ, although we still experience the effects of Original Sin.

P

parable one of the simple stories that Jesus told to show us what the Kingdom of God is like. Parables present images drawn from everyday life. These images show us the radical choice we make when we respond to the invitation to enter the Kingdom of God.

parish a stable community of believers in Jesus Christ, who meet regularly in a specific area to worship God under the leadership of a pastor

particular judgment a judgment made by Christ received by every person at the moment of death that offers either entrance into heaven (after a period of purification, if needed) or immediate and eternal separation from God in hell. At the moment of death, each person is rewarded by Christ in accordance with his or her works and faith.

Paschal Mystery the work of salvation accomplished by Jesus Christ through his passion, Death, Resurrection, and Ascension. The Paschal Mystery is celebrated in the liturgy of the Church, and we experience its saving effects in the sacraments. In every liturgy of the Church, God the Father is blessed and adored as the source of all blessings we have received through his Son in order to make us his children through the Holy Spirit.

Passover the Jewish festival that commemorates the delivery of the Hebrew people from slavery in Egypt. In the Eucharist, we celebrate our passover from death to life through Jesus' Death and Resurrection.

penance the turning away from sin with a desire to change our life and more closely live the way God wants us to live. We express our penance externally by praying, fasting, and helping the poor. This is also the name of the action that the priest asks us to take or the prayers that he asks us to pray after he absolves us in the Sacrament of Penance and Reconciliation. (*See* Sacrament of Penance and Reconciliation.)

Penitential Act that part of the Mass before the Liturgy of the Word in which we ask God's forgiveness for our sins. The Penitential Act prepares us to celebrate the Eucharist.

Pentateuch Greek for "five books." It refers to the first five books of the Bible: Genesis, Exodus, Leviticus, Numbers, and Deuteronomy. The Pentateuch tells of Creation, the beginning of God's special people, and the Covenant. In Hebrew it is called *Torah*, which means "law."

Pentecost the 50th day after Jesus was raised from the dead. On this day, the Holy Spirit was sent from heaven, and the Church was born. It is also the Jewish feast that celebrated the giving of the Ten Commandments on Mount Sinai 50 days after the Exodus.

perjury lying while under oath or making a promise under oath without planning to keep it. Perjury is both a sin and a crime. Perjury is a violation of the Second and Eighth Commandments.

personal sin a sin we choose to commit, whether serious (mortal) or less serious (venial). Although the consequences of Original Sin leave us with a tendency to sin, God's grace, especially through the sacraments, helps us choose good over sin.

Pharisees a party or sect in Judaism that began more than 100 years before Jesus. They saw Judaism as a religion centered on the observance of the Law. The Gospels present a picture of mutual hostility between Jesus and the Pharisees. Pharisees were later found in the Christian community in Jerusalem. (Acts of the Apostles 15:5) Paul was proud to call himself a Pharisee.

piety one of the seven Gifts of the Holy Spirit. It calls us to be faithful in our relationships, both with God and with others. Piety helps us love God and behave responsibly and with generosity and affection toward others.

pope the Bishop of Rome, successor of Saint Peter, and leader of the Roman Catholic Church. Because he has the authority to act in the name of Christ, the pope is called the Vicar of Christ. The pope and all the bishops together make up the living, teaching office of the Church, the Magisterium.

poverty a vow taken by religious men and women to live a simple lifestyle and to give up control of material possessions

prayer the raising of our hearts and minds to God. We are able to speak to and listen to God in prayer because he teaches us how to pray.

prayer of petition a request to God asking him to fulfill a need. When we share in God's saving love, we understand that every need is one that we can ask God to help us with through petition.

precepts of the Church those positive requirements that the pastoral authority of the Church has determined are necessary to provide a minimum effort in prayer and the moral life. The precepts of the Church ensure that all Catholics move beyond the minimum by growing in love of God and love of neighbor.

pride a false image of ourselves that goes beyond what we deserve as God's creation. Pride puts us in competition with God. It is one of the seven capital sins.

priest a man who has accepted God's special call to serve the Church by guiding it and building it up through the ministry of the Word and the celebration of the sacraments

priesthood all the people of God who have been given a share of the one mission of Christ through the Sacraments of Baptism and Confirmation. The ministerial priesthood, which is made up of those men who have been ordained bishops and priests in Holy Orders, is essentially different from the priesthood of the faithful because its work is to build up and to guide the Church in the name of Christ.

prophet one called to speak for God and to call the people to be faithful to the Covenant. A major section of the Old Testament presents the messages and actions of the prophets.

Protestant Reformation a religious, political, and economic movement that swept Europe in the 16th and 17th centuries and separated Protestants from the Catholic Church. The Catholic Reformation, or Counter-Reformation, was an attempt to respond to the major concerns of the Reformers by a sincere reform within the Catholic Church.

prudence the virtue that directs us toward the good and helps us choose the correct means to achieve that good. When we act with prudence, we carefully and thoughtfully consider our actions. Prudence is one of the cardinal moral virtues that guide our conscience and influence us to live according to the law of Christ.

psalm a prayer in the form of a poem, written to be sung in public worship. Each psalm expresses an aspect of the depth of human prayer. Over several centuries, 150 psalms were assembled into the Book of Psalms in the Old Testament. Psalms were used in worship in the Temple in Jerusalem, and they have been used in the public worship of the Church since its beginning.

purgatory a state of final cleansing after death of all our human imperfections to prepare us to enter into the joy of God's presence in heaven

R

racism the opinion that race determines human traits and capacities and that a particular race has an inherent, or inborn, superiority. Discrimination based on a person's race is a violation of human dignity and a sin against justice.

rationalism an approach to philosophy developed by René Descartes. It dominated European thought in the 17th and 18th centuries. The main belief of rationalism was that human reason is the principal source of all knowledge. It stresses confidence in the orderly character of the world and in the mind's ability to make sense of this order. Rationalism recognizes as true only those religious beliefs that can be rationally explained.

real presence the way in which the risen Jesus Christ is present in the Eucharist under the appearances of bread and wine. Jesus Christ's presence is called real because in the Eucharist, his Body and Blood, soul and divinity, are wholly and entirely present.

reconciliation the renewal of friendship after that friendship has been broken by some action or lack of action. In the Sacrament of Penance and Reconciliation, through God's mercy and forgiveness, we are reconciled with God, the Church, and others.

Redeemer Jesus Christ, whose life, sacrificial Death on the Cross, and Resurrection from the dead set us free from the slavery of sin and bring us redemption

redemption our being set free from the slavery of sin through the life, sacrificial Death on the Cross, and Resurrection from the dead of Jesus Christ

religious life a state of life recognized by the Church. In the religious life, men and women freely respond to a call to follow Jesus by living the vows of poverty, chastity, and obedience in community with others.

Resurrection the bodily raising of Jesus Christ from the dead on the third day after his Death on the Cross. The Resurrection is the crowning truth of our faith.

Revelation God's communication of himself to us through the words and deeds he has used throughout history to show us the mystery of his plan for our salvation. This Revelation reaches its completion in his sending of his Son, Jesus Christ.

rite one of the many forms followed in celebrating liturgy in the Church. A rite may differ according to the culture or country where it is celebrated. A *rite* is the special form for celebrating each sacrament.

Rite of Christian Initiation of Adults (RCIA) a series of rituals, accompanied by religious instruction, through which a person is formed in the Christian life through instruction and by the example of the parish community. Through conversion and maturity of faith, a catechumen is preparing to be welcomed into the Church at Easter through the Sacraments of Baptism, Confirmation, and Eucharist. Baptized Christians who are preparing to be received into full communion with the Roman Catholic Church may also take part in the Rite of Christian Initiation of Adults.

Roman Missal the book containing the prayers used for the celebration of the Eucharist. It is placed on the altar for the celebrant to use during Mass.

Rosary a prayer in honor of the Blessed Virgin Mary. When we pray the Rosary, we meditate on the mysteries of Jesus Christ's life while praying the Hail Mary on 5 sets of 10 beads and the Lord's Prayer on the beads in between. In the Latin Church, praying the Rosary became a way for ordinary people to reflect on the mysteries of Christ's life.

S

Sabbath the seventh day, when God rested after finishing the work of creation. The Third Commandment requires us to keep the Sabbath holy. For Christians, Sunday became the Sabbath because it was the day Jesus rose from the dead and the new creation in Jesus Christ began.

sacrament one of seven official rites through which God's life enters our lives in the liturgy through the work of the Holy Spirit. Christ's work in the liturgy is sacramental because his mystery is made present there by the power of the Holy Spirit. Jesus gave us three sacraments that bring us into the Church: Baptism, Confirmation, and the Eucharist. He gave us two sacraments that bring us healing: Penance and Reconciliation and Anointing of the Sick. He also gave us two sacraments that help members serve the community: Matrimony and Holy Orders. (*See also* sacramental.)

Sacrament of Penance and Reconciliation the sacrament in which we celebrate God's forgiveness of sin and our reconciliation with God and the Church. Penance and Reconciliation includes sorrow for the sins we have committed, confession of sins, absolution by the priest, and doing the penance that shows our willingness to amend our ways.

sacramental an object, a prayer, or a blessing given by the Church to help us grow in our spiritual life

Sacraments at the Service of Communion the Sacraments of Holy Orders and Matrimony. These two sacraments contribute to the personal salvation of individuals by giving them a way to serve others.

Sacraments of Healing the Sacraments of Penance and Reconciliation and Anointing of the Sick, by which the Church continues the healing ministry of Jesus for soul and body

Sacraments of Initiation the sacraments that are the foundation of our Christian life. We are born anew in Baptism, strengthened by Confirmation, and receive in the Eucharist the food of eternal life. By means of these sacraments, we receive an increasing measure of divine life and advance toward the perfection of charity.

sacrifice a ritual offering of animals or produce made to God by the priest in the Temple in Jerusalem. Sacrifice was a sign of the people's adoration of God, giving thanks to God, or asking for his forgiveness. Sacrifice also showed union with God. The great high priest, Christ, accomplished our redemption through the perfect sacrifice of his Death on the Cross.

Sacrifice of the Mass the sacrifice of Jesus on the Cross, which is remembered and mysteriously made present in the Eucharist. It is offered in reparation for the sins of the living and of the dead and to obtain spiritual or temporal blessings from God.

sacrilege deliberate damage or harm to a sacred person, place, or thing. A sacrilege can be a mortal or venial sin, depending on the seriousness of the evil done.

saint a holy person who has died united with God. The Church has said that this person is now with God forever in heaven.

salvation the gift, which God alone can give, of forgiveness of sin and the restoration of friendship with him

salvation history the story of God's loving relationship with his people, which tells how God carries out his plan to save all people

sanctify to make holy, to separate from sin, to set aside for sacred use, to consecrate

sanctifying grace the gift of God, given to us without our earning it, that introduces us to the intimacy of the Trinity, unites us with its life, and heals our human nature that has been wounded by sin. Sanctifying grace helps us respond to our vocation as God's adopted children, and it continues the work of making us holy that began at our Baptism.

Satan the enemy of anyone attempting to follow God's will. Satan tempts Jesus in the Gospels and opposes his ministry. In Jewish, Christian, and Muslim thought, Satan is associated with those angels who refused to bow down before human beings and serve them as God commanded. They were thrown out of heaven as a punishment. Satan and the other demons tempt human beings to join them in their revolt against God.

Savior Jesus, the Son of God, who became human to forgive our sins and to restore our friendship with God. *Jesus* means "God saves."

scandal leading another person to sin by bad example

schism a willful split or separation in the Church, stemming from a refusal to obey lawful authority

Scripture the holy writings of Jews and Christians collected in the Old and New Testaments of the Bible

Second Vatican Council the 21st and most recent ecumenical council of the Catholic Church. It met from October 11, 1962 to December 8, 1965. Its purpose, according to Pope Saint John XXIII, was to renew the Church and to help it promote peace and unity among Christians and all humanity.

Sermon on the Mount the words of Jesus, written in chapters 5 through 7 of the Gospel of Matthew, in which Jesus reveals how he has fulfilled God's law given to Moses. The Sermon on the Mount begins with the eight Beatitudes and includes the Lord's Prayer.

sexism a prejudice or discrimination based on sex, especially discrimination against women. Sexism leads to behaviors and attitudes that foster a view of social roles based only on sex.

sin a deliberate thought, word, deed, or failure to act that offends God and hurts our relationships with other people. Some sin is mortal and needs to be confessed in the Sacrament of Penance and Reconciliation. Other sin is venial, or less serious.

social justice the fair and equal treatment of every member of society. It is required by the dignity and freedom of every person. The Catholic Church has developed a body of social principles and moral teachings described in papal and other official documents issued since the late 19th century. This teaching deals with the economic, political, and social order of the world. It is rooted in the Bible as well as in the traditional theological teachings of the Church.

social sin social situations and institutions that are against the will of God. Because of the personal sins of individuals, entire societies can develop structures that are sinful in and of themselves. Social sins include racism, sexism, structures that deny people access to adequate health care, and the destruction of the environment for the benefit of a few.

Son of God the title revealed by Jesus that indicates his unique relationship to God the Father. The revelation of Jesus' divine sonship is the main dramatic development of the story of Jesus of Nazareth as it unfolds in the Gospels.

soul the part of us that makes us human and an image of God. Body and soul together form one unique human nature. The soul is responsible for our consciousness and for our freedom. The soul does not die and is reunited with the body in the final resurrection.

Spiritual Works of Mercy the kind acts through which we help our neighbors meet the needs that are more than material. The Spiritual Works of Mercy include counseling the doubtful, instructing the ignorant, admonishing sinners, comforting the afflicted, forgiving offenses, bearing wrongs patiently, and praying for the living and the dead.

spirituality | Tradition

spirituality our growing, loving relationship with God. Spirituality is our way of expressing our experience of God in both the way we pray and the way we love our neighbor. There are many different schools of spirituality. Some examples of these schools are the monastic, Franciscan, Jesuit, and lay. These are guides for the spiritual life and have enriched the traditions of prayer, worship, and living in Christianity.

suicide the act of deliberately and intentionally taking one's own life. Because we are stewards, not owners, of the life God has given us, suicide is a sin against the Fifth Commandment. But serious psychological disturbances, fears, and suffering can lessen the responsibility of the person committing suicide. By ways known to him alone, God can offer salvation to people who have taken their own life. The Church encourages us to pray for such people.

Summa Theologiae the major work of Saint Thomas Aquinas that organized and clarified thinking on many religious topics in the 13th century. In it Thomas addressed topics such as proof for the existence of God, the nature of the human soul, making moral decisions, the Incarnation, and transubstantiation.

synagogue the Jewish place of assembly for prayer, instruction, and study of the Law. After the destruction of the Temple in 587 B.C., synagogues were organized as places to maintain Jewish faith and worship. Jesus attended the synagogue regularly to pray and to teach. Paul went to the synagogue first in every city he visited. The synagogue played an important role in the development of Christian worship and in the structure of Christian communities.

Synoptic from the Greek word meaning to "see together," it describes the Gospels of Matthew, Mark, and Luke. These are called the Synoptic Gospels because although they are different from one another, there are similarities that can be seen by looking at them together. Most Scripture scholars agree that Mark was the first Gospel written and that Matthew and Luke used Mark as the pattern for their Gospels.

T

tabernacle the container in which the Blessed Sacrament is kept so that Holy Communion can be taken to the sick and the dying. *Tabernacle* is also the name of the tent sanctuary in which the Israelites kept the Ark of the Covenant from the time of the Exodus to the construction of Solomon's Temple.

temperance the cardinal virtue that helps us control our attraction to pleasure so that our natural desires are kept within proper limits. This moral virtue helps us choose to use created goods in moderation.

Temple the house of worship of God, first built by Solomon. The Temple provided a place for the priests to offer sacrifice, to adore and give thanks to God, and to ask for forgiveness. It was destroyed and rebuilt. The second Temple was also destroyed, this time by the Romans in A.D. 70, and was never rebuilt. Part of the outer wall of the Temple mount remains to this day in Jerusalem.

temptation an attraction, from outside us or inside us, that can lead us to disobey God's commands. Everyone is tempted, but the Holy Spirit helps us resist temptation and choose to do good.

Ten Commandments the 10 rules given by God to Moses on Mount Sinai that sum up God's law and show us what is required to love God and our neighbor. By following the Ten Commandments, the Hebrews accepted their Covenant with God.

Theological Virtues those virtues given us by God and not by human effort. They are faith, hope, and charity.

Torah the Hebrew word for "instruction" or "law." It is also the name of the first five books of the Old Testament: Genesis, Exodus, Leviticus, Numbers, and Deuteronomy.

Tradition the beliefs and practices of the Church that are passed down from one generation to the next under the guidance of the Holy Spirit. What Christ entrusted to the apostles was handed on to others both orally and in writing. Tradition and Scripture together make up the single deposit of the Word of God, which remains present and active in the Church.

transubstantiation the unique transformation of the bread and wine in the Eucharist into the Body and Blood of the risen Jesus Christ, while retaining its physical appearance as bread and wine

Trinity the mystery of the existence of God in three Persons—the Father, the Son, and the Holy Spirit. Each Person is God, whole and entire. Each is distinct only in the relationship of each to the others.

U

understanding one of the seven Gifts of the Holy Spirit. This gift helps us make the right choices in life and in our relationships with God and others.

V

venial sin a choice we make that weakens our relationship with God or with other people. Venial sin wounds and lessens the divine life in us. If we make no effort to do better, venial sin can lead to more serious sin. Through our participation in the Eucharist, venial sin is forgiven when we are repentant, strengthening our relationship with God and with others.

viaticum the Eucharist that a dying person receives. It is spiritual food for the last journey we make as Christians, the journey through death to eternal life.

virtue an attitude or way of acting that enables us do good

vocation the call each of us has in life to be the person God wants each to be and the way we each serve the Church and the Kingdom of God. Each of us can live out his or her vocation as a layperson, as a member of a religious community, or as a member of the clergy.

vow a deliberate and free promise made to God by people who want especially to dedicate their lives to God. The vows give witness now to the kingdom that is to come.

W

wisdom one of the seven Gifts of the Holy Spirit. Wisdom helps us understand the purpose and plan of God and live in a way that helps bring about this plan. It begins in wonder and awe at God's greatness.

witness the passing on to others, by our words and by our actions, the faith that we have been given. Every Christian has the duty to give witness to the good news about Jesus Christ that he or she has come to know.

worship the adoration and honor given to God in public prayer

Y

Yahweh the name of God in Hebrew, which God told Moses from the burning bush. *Yahweh* means "I am who am" or "I cause to be all that is."

dove, 326
Easter Vigil, 406
fire, 279, 282
fish, 9
light, 115
sacramental, 91
water, 101

T

Tabernacles (*Sukkot*), 44, 45
Te Deum, 285–86
teaching tools, 498–503
Temperament Indicator, 15
temptation, 69, 70
    weapons against, 71
Ten Commandments. *See*
    Commandments, Ten
thankfulness to God, 414–17
Thanksgiving (poem), 416
Theological virtues, 212, 350, 435
Thérèse of the Child Jesus, Saint,
    359, 453–54
Thomas, Saint, 265, 483–84
Tradition, 318
    definition of, 18, 115
    truths of, 18–19
    vs. tradition, 18
Transfiguration, 222, 223, 224, 487
transubstantiation, 354
    Triduum, 401–3, 405
Trinity, 8, 9, 316
Triumph of the Cross, 450–51
truth, 348
    Jesus', 115, 196
    living in, 179–80

V

Valine, Father, 104–5
venial sin, 69, 71
viaticum, 144
Vincent de Paul, Saint, 333, 452
violence, 157
virgin birth, 56
virtues
    cardinal, 212, 350, 435
    living today, 212, 351
    Theological, 212, 350, 435
Visitation, the, 480
visually-impaired students, 506

W

war, 157
witnessing for Christ, 26, 83, 317

Y

Yom Kippur, 44, 45

Z

Zacchaeus, 177
Zechariah, 67

SCRIPTURE INDEX

Art Credits

Page positions are abbreviated as follows: (t) top, (c) center, (b) bottom, (l) left, (r) right.

FRONT MATTER:
i Lori Lohstoeter. **iii**(t) © iStockphoto.com/sebastianiov; (c) Ryan McVay/Photodisc/Getty Images; (b) The Crosiers/Gene Plaisted, OSC. **iv**(t) Corbis; (c) Phil Martin Photography. **v**(l) Image Source/Getty Images; (r) AgnusImages.com. **vi**(t) Photos.com; (bl) Don Hammond/Design Pics/Corbis; (br) Comstock/PunchStock.

UNIT 1:
1–2 Stockbyte/Getty Images; **2** The Bridgeman Art Library Ltd./Alamy. **4**(c) Design Pics Inc./Alamy; (b) © iStockphoto.com/RonTech2000. **5**(t) Art Directors & TRIP/Alamy; (b) The Crosiers/Gene Plaisted, OSC. **6**(t) © iStockphoto.com/kevinruss; (b) www.colonialarts.com. **9** Warling Studios. **10** The Crosiers/Gene Plaisted, OSC. **11** The Crosiers/Gene Plaisted, OSC. **12** Jose Luis Pelaez/Getty Images. **13**(t) Bill Wittman; (b) The Crosiers/Gene Plaisted, OSC. **14**(bl) Phil Martin Photography; (bc) C Squared Studios/Photodisc/Getty Images. **15** The Crosiers/Gene Plaisted, OSC. **16** The Crosiers/Gene Plaisted, OSC. **17** © iStockphoto.com/VikramRaghuvanshi. **18** The Crosiers/Gene Plaisted, OSC. **19**(b) St. Mark, Michael D. O'Brien, www.studiobrien.com. **20** Franz Waldhaeusl/Alamy. **21** Bill Wood. **22**(t) The Crosiers/Gene Plaisted, OSC; (b) © British Library Board. All Rights Reserved/The Bridgeman Art Library. **23** © iStockphoto.com/JohnArcher. **24** Mary Evans Picture Library/Alamy. **26** Zvonimir Atletic/Shutterstock. **27**(t) © iStockphoto.com/stevenallan; (b) Phil Martin Photography. **28**(b) Erich Lessing/PhotoEdit. **29**(t) Bill Wittman. **30**(t) Richard T. Nowitz/Corbis; (b) Brooklyn Museum/Corbis. **31** Nancy Honey/The Image Bank/Getty Images. **32**(t) Richard T. Nowitz/Corbis; (c) © iStockphoto.com/aviron; (b) © iStockphoto.com/alexsl. **33** Paul Barton/Corbis. **34** The Crosiers/Gene Plaisted, OSC. **35** The Crosiers/Gene Plaisted, OSC. **36**(tcl) Cameraphoto Arte, Venice/Art Resource, NY; (bcl) Cameraphoto Arte, Venice / Art Resource, NY; (b) © iStockphoto.com/Chelnok. **37**(t) James Nedresky; (b) The Crosiers/Gene Plaisted, OSC. **38**(t) Bettmann/Corbis; (b) The Crosiers/Gene Plaisted, OSC. **39** Ocean/Corbis. **41** Radius/SuperStock. **42** Wikimedia PD. **43**(t) Jessie Coates/SuperStock. **44**(t) www.colonialarts.com; (b) Bill Wittman. **45** The Crosiers/Gene Plaisted, OSC. **46** © iStockphoto.com/Graffizone. **47** © iStockphoto.com/ruivalesousa. **49** © iStockphoto.com/emyerson. **50** The Crosiers/Gene Plaisted, OSC. **51**(t) Peter Willi/SuperStock; (c) Jon Hicks/Corbis; (b) Matthias Wassermann/Alamy. **52**(t) The Crosiers/Gene Plaisted, OSC; (b) Bill Wood. **53–54, 55** (tl) Bill Wood. **55**(tr) Sean Gallup/Getty Images News/Getty Images; (b) presidencia.gov.ar [CC-BY-SA-2.0 (http://creativecommons.org/licenses/by-sa/2.0)], via Wikimedia Commons. **56**(t) Loyola Press Photography; (b) eStock Photo/Alamy. **57** Design Pics Inc./Alamy. **59** Fancy Photography/Veer. **60** Zvonimir Atletic/Shutterstock. **61**(t, c, b) Phil Martin Photography. **62** Photofusion Picture Library/Alamy. **63**(b) Stephen Epstein/Ponkawonka.com. **64**(t) The Crosiers/Gene Plaisted, OSC; (b) Phil Martin Photography. **65** Tony Freeman/PhotoEdit. **67** © iStockphoto.com/LindaYolanda. **68** Zvonimir Atletic/Shutterstock. **69** © Isabella Stewart Gardner Museum, Boston, MA, USA/The Bridgeman Art Library. **70** Donald M. Emmerich/The Catholic Church Extension Society. **71** © iStockphoto.com/sebastianiov. **72–73** Neil Emmerson/Media Bakery. **75** © iStockphoto.com/drbimages. **76** The Crosiers/Gene Plaisted, OSC.

UNIT 2:
77–78 Kristy-Anne Glubish/Design Pics/Corbis. **78**(bl) © Office Central de Lisieux; (bc) Bettmann/Corbis; (br) Popperfoto/Alamy. **79** The Crosiers/Gene Plaisted, OSC. **80** All rights reserved, Vie de Jésus MAFA, 24 rue du Maréchal Joffre, F-78000 VERSAILLES; www.jesusmafa.com. **83** The Crosiers/Gene Plaisted, OSC. **84** Photos.com. **85** © iStockphoto.com/jarenwicklund. **86** The Crosiers/Gene Plaisted, OSC. **88**(t) © iStockphoto.com/lilly3; (b) The Bridgeman Art Library Ltd./Alamy. **89** Private Collection/The Bridgeman Art Library. **93** moodboard Photography/Veer. **94** PD Wikimedia. **95** Design Pics/Fotosearch. **98**(t) Greg Kuepfer; (b) Alan Oddie/PhotoEdit. **99** Photo © Boltin Picture Library/The Bridgeman Art Library. **100**(tl) Ruth Palmer/Illustrationweb.com. **101** Darrin Henry/iStock/Thinkstock. **102** The Crosiers/Gene Plaisted, OSC. **103**(t) The Bridgeman Art Library Ltd./Alamy; **104** The Crosiers/Gene Plaisted, OSC. **105** Nancy R. Cohen/Photodisc/Getty Images. **106** SW Productions/Photodisc/Getty Images. **108** © iStockphoto.com/hanita18. **109** The Crosiers/Gene Plaisted, OSC. **110** © iStockphoto.com/lisafx. **111** TongRo Images/Thinkstock. **112** Rafael Lopez. **113**(t) Fine Art Photographic Library/Corbis; **115**(t) allOver photography/Alamy; (b) The Crosiers/Gene Plaisted, OSC. **117** The Crosiers/Gene Plaisted, OSC. **119** © iStockphoto.com/Lietuvis1. **120** The Crosiers/Gene Plaisted, OSC. **121** The Crosiers/Gene Plaisted, OSC. **122**(t) Louvre, Paris, France/Giraudon/The Bridgeman Art Library. **123** David L. Moore—Lifestyle/Alamy. **124** Julia Christe/Getty Images. **127** Nicolette Neish/iStock/Thinkstock. **128** The Crosiers/Gene Plaisted, OSC. **129**(t) The Crosiers/Gene Plaisted, OSC; (b) Loyola Press Photography. **131**(t) © iStockphoto.com/SteveLuker; (b) © iStockphoto.com/duckycards. **132** Amos Morgan/Photodisc/Getty Images. **133** © iStockphoto.com/hitephoto. **134**(b) Digital Vision/Getty Images. **135** Leah-Anne Thompson/iStock/Thinkstock. **138**(t) Visions of America, LLC/Alamy; (b) Phil Martin Photography. **139**(t) The Crosiers/Gene Plaisted, OSC; **140–141** Ted Pink/Alamy. **142** Sister M. Kathleen Glavich, S.N.D. **143** Philippe Lissac/Godong/Corbis. **144** The Crosiers/Gene Plaisted, OSC.

UNIT 3:
146(c) SW Productions/Getty Images. **147**(t) Bill Wittman. **148**(t) The Crosiers/Gene Plaisted, OSC; (b) © iStockphoto.com/joshblake. **149** Noel Hendrickson/Digital Vision/Getty Images. **150**(t) © iStockphoto.com/blackie; (b) Corbis. **151** Iberfoto/SuperStock. **152** © Lviv State Picture Gallery, Ukraine/The Bridgeman Art Library. **153** © iStockphoto.com/aldomurillo. **154** The Crosiers/Gene Plaisted, OSC. **155** Bill Wittman. **156**(tl) © iStockphoto.com/upsidedowndog; (tr) © iStockphoto.com/KameleonMedia; (b) Brooklyn Museum/Corbis. **157**(t) Erich Lessing/Art Resource, NY. **159** The Crosiers/Gene Plaisted, OSC. **160** Mary Evans Picture Library/Alamy. **161** Warling Studios. **162** The Crosiers/Gene Plaisted, OSC. **163**(t) The Crosiers/Gene Plaisted, OSC; (b) © iStockphoto.com/zoom-zoom. **164** Myrleen Pearson/PhotoEdit. **165**(t) Hemera Technologies/Photos.com. **166**(t) JLP/Deimos/Corbis; (b) © iStockphoto.com/philberndt. **167** Ole Graf/Corbis. **169** Warling Studios. **170** The Crosiers/Gene Plaisted, OSC. **171**(t) © Lawrence Steigrad Fine Arts, New York/The Bridgeman Art Library; (c) © iStockphoto.com/barsik. **172**(t) © iStockphoto.com/duckycards; (b) Iberfoto/SuperStock. **173** Photos.com. **174**(t) © iStockphoto.com/Malven; (b) Kieran Scott/Stone/Getty Images. **175** DeAgostini/SuperStock. **176**(tl) © iStockphoto.com/mifaimoltosorridere; (crown) © iStockphoto.com/duckycards; (dice) Loyola Press Photography; (crosses) © iStockphoto.com/Lokibaho; (cross) © iStockphoto.com/Pixlmaker; (pitcher) Medusa Ancient Art, www.medusa-art.com; (bowl) Medusa Ancient Art, www.medusa-art.com; (spikes) © iStockphoto.com/duckycards; (cape) Bonnie's Treasures Vintage Clothing & Costumes, www.bonnies-treasures.com; (lamb) Mary Evans Picture Library/Alamy; (b) Iberfoto/SuperStock. **177** Lucenet Patrice/Oredia Eurl/SuperStock. **178** Julie Lonneman. **179**(t) The Crosiers/Gene Plaisted, OSC; (b) The Crosiers/Gene Plaisted, OSC. **180** Bill Wittman. **181**(l) AgnusImages.com; (r) © iStockphoto.com/michaeldb. **182**(t) The Crosiers/Gene Plaisted, OSC; (b) Robert W. Ginn/PhotoEdit. **183** © iStockphoto.com/innlens. **185** Design Pics/SuperStock. **186** The Crosiers/Gene Plaisted, OSC. **187**(t) The Crosiers/Gene Plaisted, OSC; (b) Associated Press.

275

188(t) AgnusImages.com; (b) © iStockphoto.com/sebastianiov. 189 Phil Martin Photography. 190(bl) The Crosiers/Gene Plaisted, OSC; (br) 191 © iStockphoto.com/EdChambers. 192 Ralph Orlowski/Getty Images News/Getty Images. 194 The Crosiers/Gene Plaisted, OSC. 195 Franco Origlia/Getty Images News/Getty Images. 196(t) © iStockphoto.com/tarinoel; (b) © iStockphoto.com/video1. 197 Con Tanasiuk/Design Pics/Corbis. 198(b) © iStockphoto.com/MsSponge. 199 © marco iacobucci/Alamy. 200 The Crosiers/Gene Plaisted, OSC. 202 Courtesy of the Clerks Regular of the Mother of God. 205(l) © iStockphoto.com/JohnArcher; (r) The Bridgeman Art Library Ltd./Alamy. 207(t) Photos.com; (b) Carsten Koall/StringerGetty Images News/Getty Images. 210 The Crosiers/Gene Plaisted, OSC.

SACRAMENT CHART:
211 The Crosiers/Gene Plaisted, OSC; © iStockphoto.com/dem10; Phil Martin Photography; The Crosiers/Gene Plaisted, OSC; AgnusImages.com. 212 Elio Ciol/Corbis; Greg Kuepfer; Barbara Penoyar/Photodisc/Getty Images; © iStockphoto.com/duncan1890.

SPECIAL SEASONS AND LESSONS:
213(t) Siede Preis/Photodisc/Getty Images; (c) The Crosiers/Gene Plaisted, OSC; (bl) Stockbyte/Getty Images; (br) Photos.com. 214 Julie Lonneman/www.thespiritsource.com. 215(t) Phil Martin Photography; (bc) Leif Skoogfors/Corbis; (br) © Office Central de Lisieux. 216(b) Stockbyte/Getty Images. 217 Thomas Northcut/Photodisc/Getty Images; The Crosiers/Gene Plaisted, OSC. 218 (*Left to right, top to bottom*) Royalty-free image; The Crosiers/Gene Plaisted, OSC; Art Directors & TRIP/Alamy; The Crosiers/Gene Plaisted, OSC; Ablestock.com/Photos.com; C Squared Studios/Photodisc/Getty Images. The Crosiers/Gene Plaisted, OSC; Scala/Art Resource, NY; Royalty-free image; Royalty-free image; © iStockphoto.com/RainforestAustralia; © iStockphoto.com/PixImaker; Royalty-free image; © iStockphoto.com/philberndt; Royalty-free image; Jupiterimages; Photos.com; The Crosiers/Gene Plaisted, OSC. 219(t) Stockbyte/Getty Images; (b) © iStockphoto.com/Hogie. 220(t) Steve Skjold/Alamy; (c) Siede Preis/Photodisc/Getty Images. (b) The Crosiers/Gene Plaisted, OSC. 221(t) © iStockphoto.com/jrsower. 222(t) © iStockphoto.com/morrismedia; (b) Operation Rice Bowl, Catholic Relief Services. 224(t) © iStockphoto.com/akaplummer. 225(t) The

Crosiers/Gene Plaisted, OSC; (b) The Bridgeman Art Library Ltd./Alamy. 226(t) Steven Miric/Alamy; (b) Photos.com. 227(t) The Crosiers/Gene Plaisted, OSC; (b) The Crosiers/Gene Plaisted, OSC. 228(t) The Crosiers/Gene Plaisted, OSC; (b) © iStockphoto.com/mikdam.

WHAT CATHOLICS SHOULD KNOW:
229 © iStockphoto.com/abalcazar. 230(t) © iStockphoto.com/colevineyard; (b) Rob Melnychuk/Digital Vision/Getty Images. 231 Jack Hollingsworth/Photodisc/Getty Images. 235(b) The Crosiers/Gene Plaisted, OSC. 236 AgnusImages.com. 237 Greg Kuepfer. 238 Design Pics/Fotosearch. 240 From Fourteen Mosaic Stations of the Cross © Our Lady of the Angels Monastery Inc., Hanceville, Alabama. All Rights Reserved. 241(b) Digital Vision/Getty Images. 242 Stock Montage, Inc./Alamy. 243 © iStockphoto.com/Lightguard. 244 © iStockphoto.com/TerryHealy. 245 Bob Daemmrich/PhotoEdit. 247(t) © iStockphoto.com/hidesy. 248 Myrleen Pearson/PhotoEdit. 250(t) SuperStock/SuperStock. 251(t) The Crosiers/Gene Plaisted, OSC; (b) Jeff Greenberg/Alamy. 252 © iStockphoto.com/Nnehring.

LESSON PULLOUTS:
277(t) Stockbyte/Getty Images; (c) Design Pics/Fotosearch; (br) Bill Wood.
Map of Palestine: Bill Wood.
Making Sunday Special: (c) © iStockphoto.com/kreci.
Reconciliation Booklet, p. 3: Photos.com.
Reconciliation Booklet, p. 8: The Crosiers/Gene Plaisted, OSC.
Scripture Booklet Cover: Design Pics/Fotosearch.
Scripture Booklet, p. 11: Craft Alan King/Alamy.
Scripture Booklet, p. 2: Stockbyte/Getty Images.
Scripture Booklet, p. 10: © iStockphoto.com/Gordo25.
Scripture Booklet, p. 8: The Crosiers/Gene Plaisted, OSC.
Scripture Booklet, p. 5: (t) © iStockphoto.com/kalistenna.
Scripture Booklet, p. 7: © iStockphoto.com/winterling.

 ART CREDITS